ABOUT THE EDITORS

BERNARD KLEIN is the founder and head of B. Klein and Company, publishers of reference books. He has been the firm's president and chief editor since 1953. He is also the founder and head of a leading direct mail advertising company, and has been the firm's president since 1946.

Mr. Klein is well known in the advertising and publishing fields and is listed in *Who's Who in Commerce and Industry*, in *Contemporary Authors*, and in *Who's Who in the East*.

DANIEL ICOLARI, associate editor of B. Klein and Company, is the editor of several business and educational reference books, among them, *Guide to American Directories* and *Guide to American Educational Directories*.

He is listed in *Contemporary Authors*, and holds membership in the American Montessori Society and the Summerhill Society.

REFERENCE ENCYCLOPEDIA OF THE AMERICAN INDIAN

Bernard Klein and Daniel Icolari

Editors

With an Introduction by
Robert L. Bennett
Commissioner of Indian Affairs
U. S. Department of the Interior

 **B. KLEIN AND COMPANY**   New York, N. Y. 10011

REFERENCE ENCYCLOPEDIA OF THE AMERICAN INDIAN

STAFF:

Research Director: Bernard Klein
Senior Editor: Daniel Icolari
Assistant Editor, Writer: Bernadette Mayer
Writer: Ina Taylor

Jacket by David Houston

Preface

Today, emerging on the contemporary scene, is a new American Indian. . . still too often plagued by the poverty that stems from his physical isolation, but nonetheless a more vocal Indian, with a greater awareness of his place in American history and his role in contemporary society. This new group among the Indian people are newsmakers and trendsetters, as more and more of their number rise in the ranks of teachers and artists, public officials and businessmen.

In assessing the need for this volume, the editors felt that far too little is known -- among Indians and non-Indians alike -- about the history and contemporary life of our nation's "first comers". . . about their diversified cultural and social history, their languages and religious practices, their art forms, and about those individuals whose achievements in all social and cultural realms rank them among the great men and women this nation has produced.

Reference Encyclopedia of the American Indian is an attempt to bridge this knowledge gap by presenting under one cover the most thorough compilation of related source materials ever assembled on this subject.

These information sources are organized by category; the listings are arranged either alphabetically or geographically. At the beginning of each section there is a short explanatory note detailing the type of sources listed and the manner in which they are arranged. The material included in this book has been researched directly from questionnaires or has been gathered from other reliable sources. All listings have been carefully checked to insure their accuracy.

The length of each listing reflects the amount of material received from each source, tailored to meet the criteria established by the editors. For further information on any listed source, it is suggested that the reader write to the source address as given in the listing, or -- concerning a book -- to the address as given in the *Publisher Index*.

The editors have tried to produce as complete and detailed a reference work as is possible. Because of the vast scope of this project, however, some relevant material may unintentionally have been omitted. A continuing research program will be in effect between editions, and we would very much appreciate being advised of information sources which merit inclusion in future volumes.

Bernard Klein and Daniel Icolari
Editors

Contents

Introduction by Robert L. Bennett, Commissioner of Indian Affairs

Introduction

Robert L. Bennett, Commissioner of Indian Affairs

Beneath the strata of various European cultures that underlie the American Civilization there are to be found, coursing through history, certain traces of aboriginal cultures of the many tribes and groups who flourished on the North American continent for centuries before the white man ventured across the Atlantic seas.

To the anthropologist and ethnologist I leave the task of determining the origins of the people we call American Indians -- of whom I am one. There were at one time probably as many as 800 different tribes or bands of "red men" on this continent, and of the nearly 300 distinct groups that are still identifiable, there are so many variations in language, physique, religio-cultural patterns and legend that I venture to say the roots of American Indians are many.

The influence of Indian tribal groups upon the shaping of Europe's colonial settlements in America is recorded in history. The explorers, the traders, the armies of conquest all were confronted by Indians and all have recorded in their annals the influences of these various aboriginal peoples upon the course of history from at least as far back as the 15th century.

The concept of federation which characterizes the American Republic was drawn, in part as least, from the pattern of confederation of the Iroquois Nation, whose leaders were peers of some of the founding fathers of the United States. Among the geographic place names that reveal the United States as a melting pot of civilizations are the hundreds of names taken from American Indian languages. Some of our cities, such as Chicago, began as Indian settlements.

The course of our Government's relations with Indians began in colonial days and underwent several subsequent evolutions. The Continental Congress created the first Indian commissioners -- among whom were Patrick Henry and Benjamin Franklin -- to oversee trade with Indian tribes and cement military alliances. When the period of land purchases began shortly after the United States became an independent nation, there commenced the effort to exchange Indian lands in the East for lands in Indian Territory carved from the Louisiana Purchase. As the American population grew, and western lands also began to be coveted, U.S. Indian policy moved to one of military force. After the Indian wars came the treaty-making period and creation of reservations in the West. Then, later, came the effort to break up tribal Indian land holdings by allotting them to individual tribal members which caused the sale of much of the best Indian lands. Finally, in 1934, we entered a new era under the Indian Reorganization Act, which provided for restoration of tribal governments and launched a policy of Federal financial and technical aid to tribal groups. This is the basis for the trusteeship role played by the Bureau of Indian Affairs today over approximately 50 million acres of Indian lands.

American Indians today number about 550,000. About 380,000 of this small minority group remain reservation- and tribally-oriented. All are citizens of the United States and of their respective states. Those who cling to tribal affiliations also enjoy a third classification of citizenship -- tribal. The relations between the United States Government and many tribal groups still recognize a remnant measure of sovereignty on the part of Indian tribes.

Unintentionally there has evolved a "dependent" society among the tribal groups that emerged after 1934, and, although the situation today can be credited with making possible the survival of some Indian land areas and has slowed down the sale of these lands, it has also deprived the American community of possible contributions that the Indian people might have made to the shaping of contemporary society.

Most American Indians today are people in transition between two worlds. The motorized, mechanized, computerized nature of contemporary life tends to obscure the traditional patterns of Indian culture and custom.

The problem facing Indians now is to adjust to contemporary life and not bury all Indian tradition and philosophy in the dust of history, which would be to deprive the American community of a heritage that is both timeless and timely.

Much has been written about American Indians. Among their ranks are statesmen, scholars and artists. The magnitude of their role can be measured by the mass of material relating to Indians and Indian affairs that has been catalogued in this volume. It should serve the valued purposes of helping the Indian people to know more about themselves and helping their fellow Americans to understand better the contributions Indian people have made to the greatness of America.

Bureau of Indian Affairs
Washington D. C.
May, 1966

Federal, State and Regional Agencies

This section is an alpha-geographical listing of government agencies -- regional and state, mainly -- concerned in various ways with the American Indian and his affairs. The principal Federal agency in this area is the Bureau of Indian Affairs of the United States Department of the Interior. The following is a description of the activities of the Bureau, with a directory of its Central (Washington, D.C.) Office. The geographical listings follow.

BUREAU OF INDIAN AFFAIRS
1951 Constitution Ave., N.W.
WASHINGTON, D.C. 20242

"There are today some 380,000 American Indians served by the Bureau of Indian Affairs. Most Indians still live on reservations or other areas set aside for them by the Federal Government. The Bureau is trustee for more than fifty million acres of such lands and provides various services to the Indian people who own them. The services offered by the Bureau include:

"*Schooling* -- There are approximately 147,000 Indian children of school age, about two-thirds of whom are enrolled in public schools. The Bureau operates 250 schools serving approximately 50,000 Indian students in remote areas where public schooling is often not available.

"*Vocational Training* -- The Bureau conducts an adult vocational training and relocation program whose aim is to equip Indians of working age with occupational skills so they can compete successfully in the job market. Job counseling and placement services are available to all trainees who complete the program.

"*Loans for Indian Enterprises* -- The Bureau has established a revolving load fund which is used in cases where it is not possible for tribes to obtain financing through other sources because of the trust status of their property, low economic status, lack of bankable security, or for other reasons. In the thirty years since the revolving fund's establishment in 1934, over $55 million dollars have been lent to Indian organizations and individuals.

"*Housing* -- The Bureau, in cooperation with the Public Housing Administration, re-cently brought low-cost public housing to the reservations for the first time. Under a special agreement with the P.H.A., tribes are treated as local government units with authority to establish local housing authorities, the instruments through which Indians may obtain low-cost housing loans from the Federal Government. More than sixty tribes have established such housing authorities. A unique feature of the P.H.A. aid to Indians provides an opportunity for families with very low income to contribute labor in lieu of cash for home construction. As of 1964, the P.H.A. had entered into contracts for approximately 3,500 housing units on Indian reservations in eighteen states, about half of which are self-help units. The Bureau assists the tribal housing authorities in the organization, development and operation of the projects; the tribe contributes the land; the participant contributes his labor.

"*General Community Assistance Programs* -- The Bureau of Indian Affairs provides for those Indians living on tax-exempt trust property a number of basic services generally provided by state or county governments to other citizens. These include welfare assistance; road building and maintenance on reservations; schooling for those not served by public schools; community recreation and education programs for youths and adults. In addition, Indians who meet eligibility requirements receive benefits under the Social Security Act. The U.S. Public Health Service operates fifty hospitals and several hundred clinics and provides numerous medical services under a special Indian program."

-- *American Indians and the Federal Government* (United States Government Printing Office, 1965.)

* * *

The following is a directory of the Central (Washington, D.C.) Office of the Bureau of Indian Affairs and its various offices and divisions. Listings of B.I.A. area and field offices and agencies may be found under specific states in the geographical part of this section which follows the Central Office listing below.

Personnel-Office of the Commissioner: Robert L. Bennett, Commissioner; Theodor W. Taylor, Deputy Commissioner; J. Leonard Norwood, Assistant Deputy Commissioner; Frederick M. Haverland, Assistant Deputy Commissioner; James E. Officer, Associate Commissioner; Carl L. Marburger, Assistant Commissioner (Education); William R. Carmack, Assistant Commissioner (Social and Govermental Affairs); E. Reeseman Fryer, Assistant Commissioner (Economic Development); R.H. Riley, Assistant to the Commissioner; F.H. Massey, Assistant Commissioner (Administration); Virginia S. Hart, Information Officer.

Personnel - Office of the Deputy Commissioner: Milton C. Boyd, Chief, Office of Audit; H. M. Joyce, Chief, Office of Inspection; Charles F. Pentz, Chief, Office of Management Analysis; C. McKerahan, Chief, Office of Safety.

Personnel - Office of Associate Commissioner: Chief, Office of Tribal Operations.

Personnel - Division of Administration: Arthur O. Allen, Chief Engineering Adviser (Adm.); Francis M. Wiles, Chief, Budget Branch; Francis E. Briscoe, Chief, Finance Branch; Robert M. Patterson, Chief, Personnel Branch; Ernest H. Page, Chief, Plant Management Branch; Donald J. Prouix, Chief, Property and Supply Branch; Chief, Plant Design and Construction Branch (see state listings under *New Mexico*).

Personnel - Division of Community Services: L. Madison Coombs, Acting Chief, Branch of Education; William B. Benge, Chief, Branch of Law and Order; Walter J. Knodel, Chief, Branch of Employment Assistance; Charles B. Rovin, Chief, Branch of Welfare.

Personnel - Division of Economic Development: Albert Huber, Chief, Branch of Credit and Financing; Perry Skarra, Chief, Branch of Forestry; Chief, Branch of Industrial Development (see state listings under *New Mexico*); Will J. Pitner, Chief, Branch of Land Operations; Chief, Branch of Real Estate Appraisal; Delbert H. Bruce, Chief, Branch of Real Property Management; Paul G. Phillips, Chief, Branch of Projects Development Staff; Robert J. Trier, Chief, Branch of Roads; Mason Barr, Chief, Branch of Housing Development.

Personnel - Arts and Crafts Board: Robert G. Hart, General Manager.

ALASKA

BUREAU OF INDIAN AFFAIRS
Anchorage Area Field Office
528 1/2 - 5th St.   ANCHORAGE 99501
Wallace O. Craig, Area Field Representative

Responsible for six B.I.A. schools, maintenance of plant facilities for additional twenty-one schools; active in numerous other projects and functions related to regional problems. *Tribes served:* Eskimo, Athapascan, Aleut. *Total population served:* 13,360. Under jurisdiction of Juneau Area Office.

BUREAU OF INDIAN AFFAIRS
Bethel Field Office
c/o Area Field Representative
                          BETHEL 99559

Under jurisdiction of Juneau Area Office.

BUREAU OF INDIAN AFFAIRS
Fairbanks Area Field Office
P.O. Box 530   FAIRBANKS 99701
O'Dean L. Williamson, Acting Area Representative

Tribes served: Eskimo, Athapascan. Under jurisdiction of Juneau Area Office.

BUREAU OF INDIAN AFFAIRS
Juneau Area Office
c/o Area Director
P.O. Box 1751   JUNEAU 99801

Area office administers B.I.A. programs for state of Alaska. Responsible for following field offices and schools: Anchorage Area Field Office; Bethel Area Field Office; Fairbanks Area Field Office; Mt. Edgecumbe School; Nome Area Field Office; Wrangell School; Seattle Liaison Office. *Tribes served:* Indian, Eskimo, Aleut. *Total population served:* 43,081.

BUREAU OF INDIAN AFFAIRS
Nome Area Field Office
c/o Area Representative   NOME 99762
    Robert E. McLean, Area Field Representative

Tribe served: Eskimo. Under jurisdiction of Juneau Area Office.

ARIZONA

BUREAU OF INDIAN AFFAIRS
Chinle Subagency   CHINLE 86503
    Paul A. Krause, Superintendent

Under jurisdiction of Navajo Area Office.

BUREAU OF INDIAN AFFAIRS
Fort Defiance Subagency
                FORT DEFIANCE 86504
    Eddie M. Coker, Superintendent

Under jurisdiction of Navajo Area Office.

BUREAU OF INDIAN AFFAIRS
Hopi Agency   KEAMS CANYON 86034
    Clyde W. Pensoneau, Superintendent

Tribes served: Hopi, Paiute. Under jurisdiction of Phoenix Area Office.

BUREAU OF INDIAN AFFAIRS
Colorado River Agency
c/o Superintendent   PARKER 85344
    Homer M. Gilliland, Superintendent

Reservations served by Agency: Colorado River Reservation, Parker, Arizona; Fort Mojave Indian Reservation, Needles, California; Chemehuevi Indian Reservation between Needles and Parker Dam, California; Fort Yuma Indian Reservation, Winterhaven, California; Cocopah Indian Reservation, Somerton, Arizona. *Tribes served by Agency:* Chemehuevi, Cocopah, Mojave, Yuma. *Total population served:* 2,835. Under jurisdiction of Phoenix Area Office.

BUREAU OF INDIAN AFFAIRS
Phoenix Area Office
127 W. Thomas Rd.
P.O. Box 7007   PHOENIX 85013
    W. Wade Head, Area Director

Area office administers B.I.A. programs for regions of Arizona, California, Nevada and Utah. Responsible for following agencies, subagencies and schools: Colorado River Agency; Fort Yuma Subagency; Fort Apache Agency; Hopi Agency; Nevada Agency; Papago Agency; Phoenix Indian School; Pima Agency; Salt River Agency; San Carlos Agency; San Carlos Irrigation Project; Sherman Institute; Truxton Canyon Agency; Uintah and Ouray Agency.

BUREAU OF INDIAN AFFAIRS
Pima Agency   SACATON 85247
    Kendall Cumming, Superintendent

Tribes served: Papago, Pima and Maricopa. Under jurisdiction of Phoenix Area Office.

BUREAU OF INDIAN AFFAIRS
San Carlos Agency
c/o Superintendent   SAN CARLOS 85550
    Charles J. Rives, Superintendent

Tribes served: Apache. Under jurisdiction of Phoenix Area Office.

BUREAU OF INDIAN AFFAIRS
Salt River Agency
Route #1, Box 907   SCOTTSDALE 85257
    William S. King, Superintendent

Tribes served: Pima and Maricopa, Mohave-Apache. Under jurisdiction of Phoenix Area Office.

BUREAU OF INDIAN AFFAIRS
Papago Agency
c/o Superintendent   SELLS 85634
    Homer B. Jenkins, Superintendent

Tribe served: Papago. Under jurisdiction of Phoenix Area Office.

BUREAU OF INDIAN AFFAIRS
Tuba City Subagency   TUBA CITY 86045
    Clinton O. Talley, Superintendent

Under jurisdiction of Navajo Area Office.

BUREAU OF INDIAN AFFAIRS
Truxton Canyon Agency
                                    VALENTINE 86437
    Charles Pitrat, Superintendent

Tribes served: Hualapai, Apache, Havasupai, Yavapai. Under jurisdiction of
Phoenix Area Office.

BUREAU OF INDIAN AFFAIRS
Fort Apache Agency   WHITERIVER 85941
    Robert E. Robinson, Superintendent

Tribe served: Apache. Under jurisdiction
of Phoenix Area Office.

BUREAU OF INDIAN AFFAIRS
Navajo Area Office
                               WINDOW ROCK 86515
    Graham Holmes, Area Director

Tribes served: Navajo (in Arizona, New
Mexico, and Utah). Agency has charge of
five subagencies: Chinle Subagency; Crownpoint Subagency; Fort Defiance Subagency;
Shiprock Subagency; Tuba City Subagency.

BUREAU OF INDIAN AFFAIRS
Fort Yuma Subagency   YUMA 85364
    Asahel A. Perry, Superintendent

Under jurisdiction of Colorado River
Agency

CALIFORNIA

BUREAU OF INDIAN AFFAIRS
Hoopa Area Field Office
c/o Area Field Representative
                                    HOOPA 95546
    Andrew W. Lathem, Area Field Repre-
    sentative

Administration of Indian trust properties,
including monies, lands, timber, minerals,
etc., located in the following counties: Del
Norte County; Humboldt County; Trinity
County; Shasta County; Siskiyou County.
Total population served: 5,000. Under jurisdiction of Sacramento Area Office.

BUREAU OF INDIAN AFFAIRS
Employment Assistance Office
Room 7773
300 N. Los Angeles St.
                               LOS ANGELES 90012
    Donald H. Spaugy, Employment Assist-
    ance Officer

BUREAU OF INDIAN AFFAIRS
Industrial Development Field Office
Room 7122
300 N. Los Angeles St.
                               LOS ANGELES 90012
    John B. Zachry, Officer in Charge

Under jurisdiction of Central Office.

BUREAU OF INDIAN AFFAIRS
Employment Assistance Office
Room 301
Penn Building
354 - 21st St.   OAKLAND 94612
    Daryl L. Mahoney, Employment Assist-
    ance Officer

BUREAU OF INDIAN AFFAIRS
Palm Springs Office
509 Industrial Place
                               PALM SPRINGS 92262
    Paul W. Hand, Director

Under jurisdiction of Sacramento Area
Office.

BUREAU OF INDIAN AFFAIRS
Riverside Area Field Office
6192 Magnolia Ave.   RIVERSIDE 92506
    Arthur N. Arnston, Area Field Repre-
    sentative

Area served: Mission Area in southern
California. *Total population served:* 5,000.
Under jurisdiction of Sacramento Area
Office.

BUREAU OF INDIAN AFFAIRS
California Agency
c/o Area Office
P.O. Box 749   SACRAMENTO 95804

Under direct jurisdiction of Sacramento
Area Office.

BUREAU OF INDIAN AFFAIRS
Sacramento Area Office
2550 Fair Oaks Blvd.
                               SACRAMENTO 95825
    Leonard M. Hill, Area Director

Area Office administers B.I.A. programs
for many regions of California. Responsible
for following agencies, field offices: California Agency; Hoopa Area Field Office;
Palm Springs Office; Riverside Area Field
Office.

BUREAU OF INDIAN AFFAIRS
Employment Assistance Office
Room 205
85 W. Santa Clara St.
SAN JOSE 95113
Marie R. Streeter, Employment Assist-
ance Officer

COLORADO

BUREAU OF INDIAN AFFAIRS

Employment Assistance Office
Room 544
728 - 15th St.   DENVER 80202
Solon G. Ayers, Officer

BUREAU OF INDIAN AFFAIRS
Consolidated Ute Agency
IGNACIO 81137
Jose Zuni, Officer in Charge

Tribe served: Ute. Under jurisdiction of
Gallup Area Office.

BUREAU OF INDIAN AFFAIRS
Plant Management Field Technical Office
P.O. Box 1070
1100 W. Littleton Blvd.
LITTLETON 80121
Arthur B. Colliflower, Officer

Under jurisdiction of Central Office.

CONNECTICUT

STATE DEPARTMENT OF HEALTH AND
WELFARE
c/o Commissioner of Welfare
State Office Bldg.
HARTFORD 06115

Reservations served: Eastern Pequot,
Golden Hill, Schaghticoke, Western Pequot.
Tribe served: Pequot. *Total population
served:* 21.

DISTRICT OF COLUMBIA

BUREAU OF INDIAN AFFAIRS
1951 Constitution Ave., N.W.
WASHINGTON 20242

See *Central Office* listing at the beginning
of this section.

BUREAU OF INDIAN AFFAIRS
Indian Arts and Crafts Board
U.S. Department of the Interior Bldg.
Room 4004   WASHINGTON 20240
Robert G. Hart, General Manager

". . . Serves Indians, Eskimos and the general public as an informational, promotional
and advisory clearing-house for all matters
pertaining to the development of authentic
Indian and Eskimo arts and crafts... pro-
motes the artistic and cultural achievement
of Indian and Eskimo artists and craftsmen
to create a demand and interest in the production of authentic products, and endeavors
to provide the stimulation necessary to
broaden markets and production which results in direct economic benefit to Indians
and Eskimos by providing supplemental income." *Activities:* Sponsors temporary
exhibits; operates Indian arts and crafts
museums. *Publications:* Quarterly, *Smoke
Signals;* fact sheets prepared on various
special subjects.

BUREAU OF INDIAN AFFAIRS
Indian Claims Commission
441 "G" St., N.W.
WASHINGTON 20001

FLORIDA

BUREAU OF INDIAN AFFAIRS
Seminole Agency
6075 Stirling Rd.   HOLLYWOOD 33024
Reginald W. Quinn, Superintendent

Tribe served: Seminole. Under jurisdiction
of Central Office.

BUREAU OF INDIAN AFFAIRS
Miccosukee Agency
P.O. Box # 235   HOMESTEAD 33030
Reginald C. Miller, Superintendent

Tribe served: Miccosukee. Under jurisdiction of Central Office.

IDAHO

BUREAU OF INDIAN AFFAIRS
Fort Hall Agency   FORT HALL 83203
John L. Pappan, Superintendent

Activities: Administration, plant management, land operations, roads, realty, wel-

fare, law and order, projects development, employment assistance, and adult education. *Reservations served:* Fort Hall Indian Reservation, Washakie Indian Reservation. *Tribes served:* Shoshone, Bannock. *Total population served:* 2,983. Under jurisdiction of Portland Area Office.

BUREAU OF INDIAN AFFAIRS
Northern Idaho Agency
                                    LAPWAI 83540
   Thomas H. St. Clair, Superintendent

Tribes served: Coeur d'Alene, Kootenai, Nez Perce, Kalispel (in Washington). Under jurisdiction of Portland Area Office.

ILLINOIS

BUREAU OF INDIAN AFFAIRS
Employment Assistance Office
Room 929
433 W. Van Buren St.
                                    CHICAGO 60607
   Theodore B. White, Officer

BUREAU OF INDIAN AFFAIRS
Industrial Development Field Office
Room 2404
219 S. Dearborn St.
                                    CHICAGO 60604
   G. Gordon Evans, Acting Officer in Charge

Under jurisdiction of Central Office.

IOWA

BOARD OF PUBLIC WELFARE
                              DES MOINES 50309
   Ross Wilbur (Executive Officer)

BUREAU OF INDIAN AFFAIRS
Sac and Fox Area Field Office
                                    TAMA 52339
   Edwin Schlenker, Acting Officer in Charge

Tribes served: Sac and Fox. Under jurisdiction of Minneapolis Area Office.

KANSAS

BUREAU OF INDIAN AFFAIRS
Horton Agency   HORTON 66439
   Buford Morrison, Area Field Representative

Tribes served: Iowa, Kickapoo, Potawatomi, Sac and Fox. *Total population served:* 1,000. Under jurisdiction of Anadarko Area Office.

MAINE

MAINE STATE DEPARTMENT OF INDIAN AFFAIRS
State House   AUGUSTA 04330
   Edward Charles Hinckley, Commissioner

Scope of operations: "Created by an Act of the 102nd Maine Legislature to 'exercise general supervision over the Indian tribes.'" *Reservations served:* Penobscot Reservation, Old Town, Maine; Passamaquoddy Reservation (1.), Princeton, Maine; Passamaquoddy Reservation (2.), Eastport, Maine. *Tribes served:* Passamaquoddy, Penobscot. *Total Indian population served:* 1,000.

MICHIGAN

GOVERNOR'S COMMISSION ON INDIAN AFFAIRS   BRIMLEY 49715
   Herman E. Cameron, Chairman

MINNESOTA

BUREAU OF INDIAN AFFAIRS
Minnesota Agency
P.O. Box #489   BEMIDJI 56601
   Herman P. Mittelholtz, Superintendent

Tribes served: Chippewa, Sioux. Under jurisdiction of Minneapolis Area Office.

U.S. PUBLIC HEALTH SERVICE
Division of Indian Health
203 Federal Bldg.   BEMIDJI 56601
   Robert Gillespie (Executive Officer)

BUREAU OF INDIAN AFFAIRS
Minneapolis Area Office
1312 West Lake St.
                    MINNEAPOLIS 55408
      Paul L. Winsor, Area Director

Area Office administers B.I.A. programs
for regions of Wisconsin, Minnesota, Iowa.
Responsible for the following agencies and
field office: Great Lakes Agency; Minnesota
Agency; Red Lake Agency; Sac and Fox Area
Field Office.

COMMUNITY HEALTH AND WELFARE
   COUNCIL
Citizens Aid Bldg.
                    MINNEAPOLIS 55404
      Omar Schmidt, Executive Director

FAIR EMPLOYMENT PRACTICES COM-
   MISSION
250 South 4th St.
                    MINNEAPOLIS 55401
      Louis H. Ervin, Executive Director

MAYOR'S COMMISSION ON HUMAN RE-
   LATIONS
222 Public Health Bldg.
                    MINNEAPOLIS 55415
      Michael A. Gaines, Executive Director

Administers programs in "all aspects of
human relations" in Minneapolis area. *Total
population served:* Approximately 5,000.

BUREAU OF INDIAN AFFAIRS
Red Lake Agency
                    REDLAKE 56671
      Jerome F. Morlock, Superintendent

Tribe served: Chippewa. Under jurisdiction of Minneapolis Area Office.

DEPARTMENT OF PUBLIC WELFARE
Centennial Office Bldg.
                    ST. PAUL 55101

ECONOMIC OPPORTUNITY OFFICE
State Office Bldg.
                    ST. PAUL
      George Holland (Executive Director)

GOVERNOR'S COMMISSION ON HUMAN
   RIGHTS
Room 72
State Office Bldg.   ST. PAUL
      Larry Borom, Executive Director

MINNESOTA COMMISSION ON INDIAN
   AFFAIRS
Legislative Research Council
State Capitol   ST. PAUL 55101
      Louis Dorweiler (Executive Director)

ST. PAUL COMMISSION ON HUMAN
   AND CIVIL RIGHTS
1745 City Hall and Court House
                    ST. PAUL 55102
      Seth Phillips, Executive Secretary

STATE COMMISSION AGAINST DISCRIMI-
   NATION
State Office Bldg.   ST. PAUL
      Viola Kanatz, Executive Director

STATE INDIAN COMMISSION
Governor's Office - State Capitol
                    ST. PAUL 55101
      Sally Luther (Officer)

MISSISSIPPI

BUREAU OF INDIAN AFFAIRS
Choctaw Agency
P.O. Box #58
                    PHILADELPHIA 39350
      James D. Hale, Superintendent

Administers education, welfare, credit,
employment assistance, forestry, land operations, roads, and resources development
programs. *Tribes served:* Choctaw, Chitimacha (in Louisiana). Under jurisdiction of
Muskogee Area Office.

MISSOURI

U.S. NATIONAL ARCHIVES AND
   RECORDS SERVICE
Federal Records Center - Region #6
2306 East Bannister Rd.
                    KANSAS CITY 64131
      William D. White, Chief Executive

Depository for noncurrent and semicurrent
records, chiefly of recent date, of the U.S.
Government in Iowa, Kansas, North Dakota,
South Dakota, Minnesota, Nebraska and
Missouri.

MONTANA

BUREAU OF INDIAN AFFAIRS
Billings Area Office
316 North 26th St.   BILLINGS 59101
James F. Canan, Area Director

Administers B.I.A. programs for the regions of Montana and Wyoming. Responsible for the following agencies and project: Blackfeet Agency; Crow Agency; Flathead Agency; Flathead Irrigation Project: Fort Belknap Agency; Fort Peck Agency: Northern Cheyenne Agency; Rocky Boy's Agency; Wind River Agency.

BUREAU OF INDIAN AFFAIRS
Missouri River Basin Investigations Project
    Field Office
316 North 26th St.   BILLINGS 59101
Walter U. Fuhriman, Director

Under jurisdiction of Central Office.

BUREAU OF INDIAN AFFAIRS
Rocky Boy's Agency
Rocky Boy's Route
                        BOX ELDER 59521
John R. White, Superintendent

Tribes served by Agency: Chippewa, Cree. *Total population served:* 1,257. Under jurisdiction of Billings Area Office.

BUREAU OF INDIAN AFFAIRS
Blackfeet Agency   BROWNING 59417
William W. Grisson, Superintendent

Tribe served: Blackfeet. Under jurisdiction of Billings Area Office.

BUREAU OF INDIAN AFFAIRS
Crow Agency   CROW AGENCY 59022
Otto K. Weaver, Superintendent

Tribe served: Crow. *Indian population* 4,828. Under jurisdiction of Billings Area Office.

BUREAU OF INDIAN AFFAIRS
Flathead Agency   DIXON 59831
P.T. LaBreche, Superintendent

Tribes served: Salish and Kootenai. *Total population served:* 2,700. Under jurisdiction of Billings Area Office.

BUREAU OF INDIAN AFFAIRS
Fort Belknap Agency   HARLEM 59526
Harold D. Roberson, Superintendent

Tribes served: Gros Ventre, Assiniboine. Under jurisdiction of Billings Area Office.

BUREAU OF INDIAN AFFAIRS
North Cheyenne Agency
                        LAME DEER 59043
John H. Artichoker, Superintendent

Tribe served: Cheyenne. Under jurisdiction of Billings Area Office.

BUREAU OF INDIAN AFFAIRS
Fort Peck Agency   POPLAR 59255
Stanley D. Lyman, Superintendent

Tribes served: Assiniboine, Sioux. Under jurisdiction of Billings Area Office.

NEBRASKA

BUREAU OF INDIAN AFFAIRS
Winnebago Agency   WINNEBAGO 68071
Alfred Dubray, Superintendent

Tribes served: Omaha, Ponca, Santee Sioux, Winnebago. Under jurisdiction of Aberdeen Area Office.

NEVADA

BUREAU OF INDIAN AFFAIRS
Nevada Agency   STEWART 89437
Dale M. Baldwin, Superintendent

Tribes served: Shoshone (in Nevada and Utah), Paiute, Washoe, Goshute. Under jurisdiction of Phoenix Area Office.

NEW MEXICO

BUREAU OF INDIAN AFFAIRS
Albuquerque Area Office
Federal Bldg.
                        ALBUQUERQUE
Walter L. Olson, Area Director

Administers B.I.A. programs for regions of Colorado, New Mexico, Utah, Arizona. Responsible for the following agencies, subagencies, subagencies and schools: Consolidated Ute Agency; Institute of American Indian Arts; Intermountain School; Jicarilla Agency; Mescalero Agency; Navajo Agency; Chinle Subagency; Crownpoint Subagency; Fort Defiance Subagency; Shiprock Subagency; Tuba City Subagency; United Pueblos Agency; Zuni Agency.

BUREAU OF INDIAN AFFAIRS
Division of Economic Development
Branch of Industrial Development
P.O. Box 8327
5301 Central Ave., N.E.
                    ALBUQUERQUE 87108
    G. Gordon Evans, Officer in Charge

Under jurisdiction of Central Office.

BUREAU OF INDIAN AFFAIRS
Division of Administration
Branch of Plant Design and Construction
P.O. Box 8327
5301 Central Ave., N.E.
                    ALBUQUERQUE 87108
    Ralph W. Mize, Officer in Charge

Under jurisdiction of Central Office.

BUREAU OF INDIAN AFFAIRS
United Pueblos Agency
1000 Indian School Rd.
                    ALBUQUERQUE 87104
    Walter O. Olson, General Superintendent

Tribes served: Pueblo, Navajo (off reservation communities). Under jurisdiction of Albuquerque Area Office.

BUREAU OF INDIAN AFFAIRS
Crownpoint Subagency
P.O. Box 328
                    CROWNPOINT 87313
    Kent Fitzgerald, Superintendent

Under jurisdiction of Navajo Area Office.

BUREAU OF INDIAN AFFAIRS
Jicarilla Agency   DULCE 87528
    Ralph B. Armstrong, Superintendent

Tribe served: Apache. Under jurisdiction of Albuquerque Area Office.

BUREAU OF INDIAN AFFAIRS
Mescalero Agency
P.O. Box 175
                    MESCALERO 88340
    Kenneth L. Payton, Superintendent

Tribe served: Apache. *Total population served:* 1,591. Under jurisdiction of Albuquerque Area Office.

NEW MEXICO COMMISSION ON INDIAN
    AFFAIRS
P.O. Box 306   SANTA FE 87501
    Charles E. Minton, Executive Director

"Directs the investigation, study and consideration of the entire subject of Indian conditons and relations within the State of New Mexico, including, but not restricted to, problems of health, economy, education, legislation and government. Directs the presentation and exchange of ideas in respect to Indian affairs of the State by all interested persons." *Total population served:* 60,000.

BUREAU OF INDIAN AFFAIRS
Shiprock Subagency   SHIPROCK 87420
    Elvin G. Jonas, Superintendent

Under jurisdiction of Navajo Area Office.

BUREAU OF INDIAN AFFAIRS
Zuni Agency   ZUNI 87327
    James D. Cornett, Acting Superintendent

Tribes served: Zuni and Ramah Navajo. *Total population served:* 5,929. Under jurisdiction of Albuquerque Area Office.

NEW YORK

STATE INTERDEPARTMENTAL COMMITTEE ON INDIAN AFFAIRS
112 State St.   ALBANY 12207
    John R. Hathorn, Director of Indian Services

Renders all state services to New York State's eight reservations. Services include education, health, public works, social welfare. *Tribes served:* Seneca Nation; Tonawanda Band of Senecas; Cayugas; St. Regis Mohawks; Onondagas; Tuscaroras; Oneidas. *Total population served:* 9,933. The State Interdepartmental Committee on Indian Affairs is a state agency, unrelated to the Bureau of Indian Affairs.

NORTH CAROLINA

BUREAU OF INDIAN AFFAIRS
Cherokee Agency   CHEROKEE 28719
    Don Y. Jensen, Superintendent

Tribe served: Eastern Cherokee. Under
jurisdiction of Central Office.

NORTH DAKOTA

BUREAU OF INDIAN AFFAIRS
Turtle Mountain Agency
            BELCOURT 58316
    William A. Mehojah, Superintendent

Responsible for Fort Totten Subagency.
Tribe served: Chippewa, Sioux. Under
jurisdiction of Aberdeen Area Office.

BUREAU OF INDIAN AFFAIRS
Fort Totten Subagency
            FORT TOTTEN 58335
    Richard R. Bauer, Area Field
        Representative

Under jurisdiction of Turtle Mountain
Agency.

BUREAU OF INDIAN AFFAIRS
Standing Rock Agency
            FORT YATES 58538
    Noralf Nesset, Superintendent

Tribe served: Sioux (in North and South
Dakota). Under jurisdiction of Aberdeen
Area Office.

BUREAU OF INDIAN AFFAIRS
Fort Berthold Agency
            NEW TOWN 58763
    James P. Howell, Superintendent

Tribes served: Gros Ventre, Arikara,
Mandan. Under jurisdiction of Aberdeen
Area Office.

OHIO

BUREAU OF INDIAN AFFAIRS
Employment Assistance Office
Cleveland Transit System Bldg.
1404 East 9th St.   CLEVELAND 44114
    Charles T. Featherstone, Officer
        in Charge

OKLAHOMA

BUREAU OF INDIAN AFFAIRS
Anadarko Agency   ANADARKO 73005
    Robert L. Meshew, Area Field
        Representative

Tribes served: Kiowa, Comanche, Apache,
Caddo, Delaware, Wichita. *Total population
served:* 12,566. Under jurisdiction of Anadarko Area Office.

BUREAU OF INDIAN AFFAIRS
Anadarko Area Office
Federal Bldg.   ANADARKO 73005
    Leslie P. Towle, Area Director

Area Office administers B.I.A. programs
for regions of Oklahoma and Kansas. Responsible for the following agencies and
schools: Anadarko Agency; Chilocco Indian
School; Concho Agency; Haskell Institute;
Horton Agency; Pawnee Agency; Shawnee
Agency.

BUREAU OF INDIAN AFFAIRS
Ardmore Agency
P.O. Box 997   ARDMORE 73401
    Daniel L. McDole, Area Field
        Representative

Tribe served: Chickasaw. Under jurisdiction of Muskogee Area Office.

BUREAU OF INDIAN AFFAIRS
Concho Agency   CONCHO 73022
    Paul Vance, Area Field Representative

Tribes served: Cheyenne, Arapaho. *Total
population served:* 5,000. Under jurisdiction of Anadarko Area Office.

BUREAU OF INDIAN AFFAIRS
Miami Agency
P.O. Box 391   MIAMI 74354
    T.J. Perry, Area Field Representative

Tribes served: Eastern Shawnee, Miami,
Quapaw, Seneca-Cayuga. *Total population
served:* 7,830. Under jurisdiction of Muskogee Area Office.

BUREAU OF INDIAN AFFAIRS
Five Civilized Tribes Agency
Federal Bldg.   MUSKOGEE 74401
    Area Director

Tribes served: Cherokee, Chickasaw,
Choctaw, Creek, Seminole. Under jurisdiction of Muskogee Area Office.

BUREAU OF INDIAN AFFAIRS
Muskogee Area Office
Federal Bldg.   MUSKOGEE 74401
    C. C. Carshall, Acting Area Director

Area Office administers B. I. A. programs
for regions of Oklahoma. Responsible for
the following agencies and school: Ardmore
Agency; Choctaw Agency; Five Civilized
Tribes Agency; Okmulgee Agency; Osage
Agency; Miami Agency; Sequoyah High
School; Tahlequah Agency; Talihina Agency;
Wewoka Agency.

BUREAU OF INDIAN AFFAIRS
Okmulgee Agency   OKMULGEE 74447
    Linus L. Gwinn, Area Field Repre-
    sentative

Tribe served: Creek. Under jurisdiction
of Muskogee Area Office.

BUREAU OF INDIAN AFFAIRS
Osage Agency   PAWHUSKA 74056
    Howard F. Johnson, Superintendent

Tribe served: Osage. Under jurisdiction
of Muskogee Area Office.

BUREAU OF INDIAN AFFAIRS
Pawnee Agency   PAWNEE 74058
    Robert D. Grover, Area Field Repre-
    sentative

Tribes served: Kaw, Otoe, Missouria,
Pawnee, Ponca, Tonkawa. *Total population
served:* 5, 662. Under jurisdiction of Anadarko Area Office.

BUREAU OF INDIAN AFFAIRS
Shawnee Agency   SHAWNEE 74801
    John E. Taylor, Area Field
    Representative

Tribes served: Iowa, Kickapoo, Citizen
Potawatomi, Sac and Fox, absentee Shaw-
nee. *Total population served:* 13, 830.
Under jurisdiction of Anadarko Area Office.

BUREAU OF INDIAN AFFAIRS
Tahlequah Agency
P. O. Box 459   TAHLEQUAH 74464
    John H. Walker, Area Field
    Representative

Tribe served: Cherokee. Under jurisdiction of Muskogee Area Office.

BUREAU OF INDIAN AFFAIRS
Talihina Agency
P. O. Box 187   TALIHINA 74571
    Andrew G. Bidwell, Area Field
    Representative

Tribe served: Choctaw. Under jurisdiction of Muskogee Area Office.

BUREAU OF INDIAN AFFAIRS
Wewoka Agency
P. O. Box 1060   WEWOKA 74884
    Louis H. McGahey, Area Field
    Representative

Tribe served: Seminole. Under jurisdiction of Muskogee Area Office.

OREGON

BUREAU OF INDIAN AFFAIRS
Umatilla Subagency
                      PENDLETON 97801
    Harold A. Duck, Superintendent

Under jurisdiction of Warm Springs Agency.

BUREAU OF INDIAN AFFAIRS
Portland Area Office
1002 N. E. Holladay Pl.
P. O. Box 3785   PORTLAND 97230
    Robert D. Holtz, Area Director

Area Office administers B. I. A. programs
for regions of Oregon, Washington, Idaho.
Responsible for the following agencies, sub-
agencies, school and project: Chemawa
Indian School; Colville Agency; Fort Hall
Agency; Northern Idaho Agency; Wapato
Irrigation Project: Warm Springs Agency;
Umatilla Subagency; Western Washington
Agency; Yakima Agency.

BUREAU OF INDIAN AFFAIRS
Warm Springs Agency
                   WARM SPRINGS 97761
    Doyce L. Waldrip, Superintendent

Responsible for Umatilla Subagency. *Tribes
served:* Paiute, Walla Walla, Chinook, Cayuse, Wasco. Under jurisdiction of Portland
Area Office.

SOUTH DAKOTA

BUREAU OF INDIAN AFFAIRS
Aberdeen Area Office
820 South Main St.   ABERDEEN 57401
    Martin N. B. Holm, Area Director

Area Office administers B. I. A. programs for regions of North Dakota, South Dakota, and Nebraska. Responsible for the follow-ing agencies, subagencies, and schools: Cheyenne River Agency; Flandreau Indian Vocational School; Fort Berthold Agency; Pierre Agency; Pine Ridge Agency; Rose-bud Agency; Yankton Subagency; Sisseton Agency; Standing Rock Agency; Turtle Mountain Agency; Fort Totten Subagency; Wahpeton Indian School; Winnebago Agency.

BUREAU OF INDIAN AFFAIRS
Cheyenne River Agency
                    EAGLE BUTTE 57625
    Howard Dushane, Superintendent

Tribe served: Sioux. Under jurisdiction of Aberdeen Area Office.

BUREAU OF INDIAN AFFAIRS
Pierre Agency   PIERRE 57501
    Edward F. Edwards, Superintendent

Tribe served: Sioux. Under jurisdiction of Aberdeen Area Office.

BUREAU OF INDIAN AFFAIRS
Pine Ridge Agency
                    PINE RIDGE 57770
    Llewellyn Kingsley, Superintendent

Tribe served: Sioux. Under jurisdiction of Aberdeen Area Office.

BUREAU OF INDIAN AFFAIRS
Rosebud Agency   ROSEBUD 57570
    Harold W. Shunk, Superintendent

Responsible for Yankton Subagency. *Tribe served:* Sioux. *Total population served:* 7, 000. Under jurisdiction of Aberdeen Area Office.

BUREAU OF INDIAN AFFAIRS
Sisseton Agency   SISSETON 57262
    Wray P. Hughes, Superintendent

Tribe served: Sioux (South Dakota and North Dakota). Under jurisdiction of Aberdeen Area Office.

BUREAU OF INDIAN AFFAIRS
Yankton Subagency   WAGNER 57380
    George Shubert, Area Field
        Representative

Under jurisdiction of Rosebud Agency.

TEXAS

BUREAU OF INDIAN AFFAIRS
Employment Assistance Office
Room 202
912 Commerce St.   DALLAS 75202
    Ola Beckett, Officer in Charge

UTAH

BUREAU OF INDIAN AFFAIRS
Uintah and Ouray Agency
                    FORT DUCHESNE 84026
    Melvin L. Schwartz, Superintendent

Tribes served: Goshute, Ute. Under juris-diction of Phoenix Area Office.

VIRGINIA

BUREAU OF INDIAN AFFAIRS
Division of Economic Development
6130 Hardin
                    BAILYS CROSSROADS 22041

WASHINGTON

BUREAU OF INDIAN AFFAIRS
Colville Agency   COULEE DAM 99116
    Elmo Miller, Superintendent

Tribes served: Colville, Spokane. *Total population served:* 6, 000. Under jurisdic-tion of Portland Area Office.

BUREAU OF INDIAN AFFAIRS
Western Washington Agency
3006 Colby Ave.   EVERETT 98201
    George M. Felshaw, Superintendent

Tribes served: Chehalis, Hoh, Clallam, Lummi, Makah, Muckleshoot, Nisqually, Suquamish, Puyallup, Quileute, Quinault, Shoalwater, Skokomish, Squaxin Island,

Swinomish, Snohomish. *Total population served:* 14,760. Under jurisdiction of Portland Area Office.

BUREAU OF INDIAN AFFAIRS
Seattle Liaison Office
107 Federal Office Bldg.
909 - 1st Ave.   SEATTLE 98104
    Virgil R. Farrell, Administrative
    Officer

Under jurisdiction of Juneau Area Office.

BUREAU OF INDIAN AFFAIRS
Yakima Agency   TOPPENISH 98948
    Charles S. Spencer, Superintendent

Tribe served: Yakima. Under jurisdiction of Portland Area Office.

WISCONSIN

BUREAU OF INDIAN AFFAIRS
Great Lakes Agency   ASHLAND 54806
    Emmett J. Riley, Superintendent

Tribes served: Chippewa, Oneida, Forest Potawatomi, Stockbridge-Munsee, Winnebago (in Wisconsin and Minnesota). Under jurisdiction of Minneapolis Area Office.

LEGISLATIVE COUNCIL
State Capital   MADISON 53702
    Niki Smith, Executive Officer

WYOMING

BUREAU OF INDIAN AFFAIRS
Wind River Agency
       FORT WASHAKIE 82514

Tribes served: Arapahoe, Shoshone.

Museums

This section presents an alpha-geographical listing of museums maintaining permanent exhibits or collections related to the American Indian. Both large and small holdings are represented so as to provide the reader with as varied a source selection as possible.

ALASKA

COOK INLET HISTORICAL SOCIETY -
  MUSEUM
630 Fifth Ave.   ANCHORAGE 99501
  Melvin B. Ricks, Curator

Museum exhibits Eskimo and Indian relics and artifacts. Library.

UNIVERSITY OF ALASKA MUSEUM
                   COLLEGE 99735
  L. J. Rowinski, Curator

Collections deal with archaeology of western and northern Alaska; ethnographic materials on Alaskan Indians and Eskimos.

SHELDON'S MUSEUM
Lynn Canal Bldg.
P.O. Box 136   HAINES 99827
  Mrs. Felix F. Hakkinen, Owner

Museum contains local Indian artifacts; basketry; carvings.

ALASKA HISTORICAL LIBRARY
  AND MUSEUM
4th between Seward and Main
                   JUNEAU 99801
  Mrs. Susan Barrow, Curator

Displays feature anthropological exhibits of Alaskan Eskimo and Indian objects. Lectures and tours. Publications.

SHELDON JACKSON JUNIOR
  COLLEGE MUSEUM
P.O. Box 479   SITKA 99835
  Rev. R. Rolland Armstrong, President

Features Haida, Eskimo and Tlingit artifacts. Alaskan history collections.

TRAIL OF '98 MUSEUM
McCabe College Bldg.
Spring St.   SKAGWAY 99840
  Paul J. Sincic, Curator

Collection of native Alaskan relics and artifacts.

TRIBAL HOUSE OF THE BEAR
Shakes' Island
P.O. Box 696   WRANGELL 99929

Collection features totem poles, carvings. Historic Tlingit house.

ARIZONA

FORT VERDE MUSEUM
                   CAMP VERDE 96322
  Malcolm S. Stenhouse, Director

Features Indian and pioneer relics.

CANYON DE CHELLY MUSEUM
Visitor Center
Canyon de Chelly National Monument
Post Office Box 8
                   CHINLE 86503
  Meredith M. Guillet, Superintendent

"Exhibit portrays the ecology, archaeology, history and ethnology of Canyon de Chelly from the earliest times to the latest, with representative types of artifacts."

MUSEUM OF NORTHERN ARIZONA
Fort Valley Road
P.O. Box 1389   FLAGSTAFF 86002
  Dr. Edward B. Danson, Director

Indian museum exhibiting arts and artifacts of the Hopi and Navajo Indians.

HISTORICAL MUSEUM
U.S. Army Electronic Proving Ground
Grierson St.
                          FORT HUACHUCA 85613
     Orville A. Cochran, Director
     James Murray, Curator

Contains prehistoric Indian artifacts.

PETE KITCHEN MUSEUM
Pete Kitchen Ranch
U.S. Highway 90
                              NOGALES 85621
     Gil Procter, Director

"The Museum, a replica of Pete Kitchen's
stronghold, is built of sun-dried adobe --
four large rooms and the chapel are filled
with displays of historical items pertinent
to the Southwest. Examples of early Navajo
weaving, ravelled wool, Bayeta, Saxony,
and native wool; old Navajo jewelry, belts
and necklaces, turquoise and silver; Indian
pipes, beadwork and painted skins; Apache
medicine shirt; ceremonial jeweled points;
arrowheads..."

ARIZONA HISTORY ROOM
411 N. Central Ave.
P.O. Box 2551
                              PHOENIX 85004
     Mrs. Lillian Theobald, Acting Curator

Museum exhibits feature local historical
and Indian items.

HEARD MUSEUM OF ANTHROPOLOGY
   AND PRIMITIVE ART
22 E. Monte Vista Rd.
                              PHOENIX 85004
     H. Thomas Cain, Curator of
       Anthropology

Features eighteen exhibition gallaries;
library containing 5,000 volumes. Public
museum and library (anthropology and
Southwestern history) are available for reference purposes only. Collections include
primitive art of North and South America,
with emphasis on the American Indian --
Hohokam, Pima, Papago, Hopi and Apache;
Oceania, Africa, Middle American and
Spanish Colonial (Southwestern U.S.) collections.

PUEBLO GRANDE MUSEUM
4619 E. Washington St.
                              PHOENIX 85034
     Donald H. Hiser, City Archaeologist

Contains 900 to 1,000 books, reports and
pamphlets: Southwestern   archaeology;
limited ethnology and linguistics; general
anthropology. Site museum with exhibits
of prehistoric Hohokam cultural material,
circa A.D. 500 to A.D. 1450; some Maricopa and Pima ethnological material. Library open to students and professionals in
anthropology and related fields. Research
must be conducted on premises.

SHARLOT HALL MUSEUM
Prescott Historical Society
W. Gurley St.
                              PRESCOTT 86301
     Theodore W. Liese, President
     Elsie M. Knight, Custodian

Collection includes Indian artifacts and
woodcarvings.

SMOKI MUSEUM
N. Arizona Ave.
P.O. Box 123
                              PRESCOTT 86301
     Bernice E. Insley, Curator

Indian Museum featuring artifacts of the
Tuzigoot, King and Fitzmaurice ruins.
Paintings. Annual Indian ceremonials.

TONTO NATIONAL MONUMENT
   VISITOR CENTER
                              ROOSEVELT 85545

Collection of items recovered from Monument excavations -- utensils, fabrics, weapons, and other artifacts.

NAVAJO NATIONAL MONUMENT
   MUSEUM
                              TONALEA 86044
     Keith M. Anderson, Archaeologist

Collections consist of material gathered
from Monument excavations -- salvage
archaeology collections, Kayenta Anasazi
PI-early PII. Several collections of PIII
Kayenta Anasazi from the village sites of
Betatakin, Keet Seel, and Inscription House.

ARIZONA PIONEERS' HISTORICAL
SOCIETY MUSEUM
949 E. 2nd St.   TUCSON 85719
Donald E. Phillips, Chief Executive
Officer

Holdings include 30,000 volumes related to
Arizona and the Southwest; Manuscript Division
containing 500 collections of historical
documents. Speaker service to
school groups and organizations. Conducted
tours. Advisory service to other Arizona
museums. Loan exhibits. Programs in
historical archaeology. Research facilities
for study of museum artifacts.

ARIZONA STATE MUSEUM
The University of Arizona
                         TUCSON 85721
Raymond H. Thompson, Director

Contains 92 cases of Southwestern archaeological
and ethnographic material, representing
approximately 570 linear feet of exhibition
space. Includes some Early Man
material, a large collection of Hohokam
items, artifacts representative of the Anasazi
and Mogollon cultures. Ethnographic
collection includes arts and crafts of the
Pueblo, Navajo, Apache, Pima and Papago
Indians.

NAVAJO TRIBAL MUSEUM
P.O. Box 54   WINDOW ROCK 86515
Martin A. Link, Director

Holdings include 1,000 volumes pertaining
to the Navajo and to Southwestern Indians;
other subjects include history, geology,
archaeology, plants and animals of the
Southwest. Permanent exhibits deal with
geology, paleontology, archaeology, life
zones, animals, Navajo history, religion,
arts and crafts. Outside exhibits include a
full-scale, completely furnished *hogan*
(typical Navajo dwelling, built of earth walls,
supported by timber), with adjoining cornfield
and sheep corral, plus a small zoo
housing many of the animals native to the
Navajo Reservation. Collections not on display
but available for research purposes include:
prehistoric pottery, Navajo religious
paraphernalia, contemporary Southwestern
Indian artifacts, Navajo rugs and silverwork,
and most of the manuscripts and associated
material collected in conjunction
with the Navajo Land Claims Case.

ARKANSAS

SAUNDERS MUSEUM
East of Main Square
                    BERRYVILLE 72616
Bernice Hecht, Curator

Small collection of Indian artifacts includes:
Chief Sitting Bull's war bonnet, buckskin
jacket, medicine bags, tobacco pouch, totem
scalps, and moccasins which belonged to his
squaw and daughters. Also on display is a
war belt, with enemy Indian scalps, which
belonged to Chief Geronimo.

UNIVERSITY OF ARKANSAS MUSEUM
University Hall,   FAYETTEVILLE 72703
Charles R. McGimsey, III Director

Exhibits on display: Hall of Man; Hall of
Science; Meneral Room; Pioneer Room.
Indian Exhibits feature materials relative
to Arkansas Indians.

PHILLIPS COUNTY MUSEUM
623 Pecan St.   HELENA 72342
Mrs. Curtis Jeffries, Curator

Collections include pottery, points, axes,
pipes, exhibited with descriptions. Much
of exhibited material derived from local
mound excavations.

ARKANSAS HISTORY COMMISSION
300 W. Markham St.
                    LITTLE ROCK 72201
John L. Ferguson, State Historian

Museum and historic building featuring Indian
and pioneer relics; items of local historical
significance; documents. Library.
Under state jurisdiction.

MUSEUM OF SCIENCE AND NATURAL
HISTORY
MacArthur Park   LITTLE ROCK
Ellis Doyle Herron, Director

Exhibits include material relating to Arkansas
Mound Builders, American Plains
Indians, Southwestern Indians.

ARKANSAS STATE COLLEGE MUSEUM
Drawer HH   STATE COLLEGE 72467
    Eugene B. Wittlake, Director

Collections include 2,200 artifacts, featuring Paleo through Mississippian; 350 historic period artifacts with particular emphasis on Quapaw, Cherokee, and Osage. Special collection of portraits of historic Indian tribes of Arkansas; 150 volumes; files of five periodicals. Collection titles: Paleo-Indian, Archaic Indian and Woodland Indian of Arkansas; Ballard Mound (Early Mississippi); How Temple Mound Indian Made His Pottery; How Archaic Indian Made His Tools and Weapons; Quapaw and Cherokee Exhibit; Osage Exhibit; Southwest Indian Creativity.

CALIFORNIA

KERN COUNTY MUSEUM
3801 Chester Ave.
                 BAKERSFIELD 93301
    Richard C. Bailey, Director

Includes Yokut Indian artifacts.

MALKI MUSEUM, INC.
P.O. Box 614
                 BANNING 92220
    Mrs. Katherine Siva Saubel

The only on-site Indian reservation museum in California. Present exhibits include: basketry; pottery; ceremonial equipage; hunting and gathering materials; trade and commerce items; historical photographs; artifacts related to the Indian cultures of southern California.

UNIVERSITY OF CALIFORNIA
Robert H. Lowie Museum of
    Anthropology
Kroeber Hall
2620 Bancroft Way
                 BERKELEY 94704
    William R. Bascom, Director

An average of forty-eight exhibits installed on separate subjects each year, featuring (1) California Ethnographic: approximately 11,457 catalog entries, majority of which are basketry items representing practically every tribe in California. Larger collections are: Klamath River tribes, especially the Yurok, Modoc, Maidu, Miwok, Pomo, Cahuilla. (2) North American Indian: approximately 8,283 catalog entries for ethnographic collections, of which the Eskimo and Aleut material is the largest and most important single collection, containing a total of 5,115 specimens. The collection consists of skins and furs, ivory carvings, and numerous technological items. Plains Indian artifacts consist chiefly of skin clothing of a wide variety from a number of tribes; large collection of baskets and carvings from Northwest Coast tribes, especially Haida, Tlingit and Tsimshian. Collection of approximately 2,698 wax cylinder recordings containing numerous songs and narratives.

DEL NORTE COUNTY HISTORICAL
    SOCIETY - MUSEUM
910 H St.   CRESCENT CITY 95531
    Ruth Roberts, President

Museum exhibiting Indian artifacts. Publications.

CUYAMACA STATE PARK MUSEUM
                         CUYAMACA

Indian artifacts with emphasis on the Diegueno Indians.

CABOT'S OLD INDIAN PUEBLO
67616 E. Desert View
          DESERT HOT SPRINGS 92240
    Cabot Yerxa, Director

Features Indian and Eskimo artifacts.

CLARKE MEMORIAL MUSEUM
Corner Third and "E" Sts.
                 EUREKA 95501
    Cecile Clarke, Director

Emphasis on Indian artifacts of Humboldt County; reference library.

FRESNO MUSEUM
1944 N. Winery Ave.   FRESNO 93703
    Val Murray, Curator

Furnished reconstruction of a Yokut-type Sierra foothills summer home, with authentic and simulated artifacts and implements used by its inhabitants.

FOREST LAWN MUSEUM
1712 S. Glendale Ave.
                    GLENDALE 91205
   Mary Hunt, Curator

Contains Indian ivory painting, Indian artifacts.

EASTERN CALIFORNIA MUSEUM
County Court House - Edwards St.
                    INDEPENDENCE 93526
   Dorothy C. Cragen, Director

Indian artifacts.

FORT ROSS STATE HISTORIC PARK
   MUSEUM
19005 Coast Highway 1
                    JENNER 95450
   Wayne Colwell, Park Supervisor

Small collection of Pomo Indian material; some Aleut; some Eskimo.

LAKE COUNTY MUSEUM
175 3rd St.   LAKEPORT 95453
   Mrs. Harriette B. Covey, Curator

Features Indian artifacts: basketry, weapons, coins. Geological material from Lake County.

ANTELOPE VALLEY INDIAN RESEARCH
   MUSEUM
15701 East Ave.   LANCASTER 93534
   Mrs. Grace W. Oliver, Director

Museum houses varied Indian material.

SOUTHWEST MUSEUM
10 Highland Park   LOS ANGELES
   Carl S. Dentzel, Director

Indian Art Museum. Publications. Quarterly journal: *The Masterkey.*

MONTEREY STATE HISTORICAL
   MONUMENT
Holman Exhibit of American Indian
   Artifacts
210 Olivier St.   MONTEREY 93940
   Robert W. Reese, State Park Historian

Exhibits cases feature evidence and remains of Early Man -- types of housing; methods of hunting; types of food; articles of war; articles and methods of travel; articles of religion and music; pottery; baby carriers; dress; basketry; arts and crafts.

MORRO BAY MUSEUM OF NATURAL
   HISTORY
Morro Bay State Park
P.O. Box 488   MORRO BAY 93442

Archaeological exhibits featuring Chumash Indian artifacts.

MUSEUM OF MISSION SAN ANTONIO
   DE PALA
Highway 76
P.O. Box 66   PALA 92059
   John B. Cunningham, Curator

Historic Mission Building (Pala Indians). Museum exhibiting Indian artifacts, basketry, stone carvings, pottery, jewelry. Dance festivals.

ADOBE DE PALOMARES
491 E. Cucamonga Ave.
                    POMONA 91766
   Roy Hoover, Host-Curator

Collection of 100 Indian baskets of various tribes; utensils and ceremonial cog wheels.

CALIFORNIA STATE INDIAN MUSEUM
2618 K St.   SACRAMENTO 95816
   Grover C. Allred, State Park Ranger

Collections pertain to the cultures of the Indians of California. Examples of basketry -- Plains, Northwest Coast, Basin and Eskimo; the archaeological collections are of stone, bone and shell work.

THE COTTAGE MUSEUM
P.O. Box 576   SALINAS 93903
   Hilda Hagne, Curator

Exhibit of Indian baskets and stone artifacts of the following areas and tribes: Monterey County, Thompson River, Klamath Lake, Nootka, Pomo, Klamath River, Yuki, Achomawi, Yokut, Miwok, Washo, Paiute, Pima, Papago, and Hopi.

CASA DE ESTUDILLO
400 Mason St.   SAN DIEGO 92110

Historic House featuring Indian relics.

SAN DIEGO MUSEUM OF MAN
Balboa Park   SAN DIEGO

Exhibits on Indians of three Americas --
collections of weapons, Indian habitats;
handicraft shop.

M. H. DE YOUND MEMORIAL MUSEUM
Golden Gate Park
                       SAN FRANCISCO 94100

General art museum, one gallery devoted
to Indian crafts -- basketry, pottery and
textiles of the West and Northwest areas.

JOSEPHINE D. RANDALL JUNIOR
   MUSEUM
Roosevelt Way and 16th St.
                       SAN FRANCISCO 94114

Contains local Indian artifacts.

SAN JACINTO MUSEUM
181 E. Main St.
P.O. Box 835   SAN JACINTO 92383
   Louis B. Ziegler, Curator

Exhibits relate to paleontology and local
Indian history.

SAN LUIS OBISPO COUNTY HISTORICAL
   MUSEUM
696 Monterey St.
                       SAN LUIS OBISPO 93401
   Mrs. Louisiana Clayton Dart

Indian artifacts with emphasis on San Luis
Obispo County.

SANTA CRUZ MUSEUM
1305 E. Cliff Dr.
                       SANTA CRUZ 95062
   Glenn W. Bradt, Curator

Collection of approximately 200 baskets;
many artifacts; modest reference library.

SAN JOAQUIN COUNTY JUNIOR MUSEUM
1305 Occidental Ave.
                       STOCKTON 95203
   Rod C. Rigg, Director

Two small Indian displays.

SAN JOAQUIN PIONEER MUSEUM
   AND HAGGIN ART GALLERIES
Victory Park
1201 N. Pershing Ave.
                       STOCKTON 95203
   Fenton Kastner, Director

Contains Indian and pioneer history and
artifacts.

VENTURA COUNTY PIONEER MUSEUM
Courthouse
77 N. California St.
                       VENTURA 93001
   John H. Morrison, Curator

Indian artifacts and archaeological exhibits.
County historical records.

TULARE COUNTY MUSEUM
27000 Monney Blvd.
                       VISALIA 93277
   Merle F. Harp, Curator

Collection includes large basket exhibit
(primarily of Yokut origin); arrowpoints;
charmstone.

COLORADO

THE GEM VILLAGE MUSEUM
Box 177   BAYFIELD 81112
   Elizabeth X. Gilbert, Director

Collection of Rosa pottery and artifacts;
local plants and minerals; research library.

FOUR CORNERS MUSEUM
Main at Ash St.   CORTEZ 81321
   Ed. F. Roelfs, Curator

Features Indian artifacts and pottery.

DENVER ART MUSEUM
Chappell House Galleries
1300 Logan St.   DENVER 80203
   Norman Feder, Curator

Collection of North American Indian art
(8,500 items) in both an art collection and a
documented ethnographic collection. Included are some fifty complete Indian women's costumes; collection of Navaho and
Pueblo textiles; Pueblo pottery; Hopi Kachina dolls; Blackfoot ceremonial equipment; wood carvings of the Northwest Coast.

DENVER MUSEUM OF NATURAL
   HISTORY
City Park   DENVER 80206
   H. M. Wormington, Curator of
      Archaeology

Hall of the Prehistoric People of the Americas contains exhibits on early man, development of New World agriculture, prehistoric cultures of Peru, Costa Rica, Maya
area, Mexico, Eastern United States, Southwest, California, Northwest Coast. Collection of Paleo-Indian specimens, preceramic sites on the Uncompahgre Plateau,
Colorado, Fremont materials from the
Turner-Look Site, Utah.

JULESBERG HISTORICAL MUSEUM
320 Cedar   JULESBERG 80737
   Mrs. Frank Johnson, Curator

Local Indian artifacts, presumably of the
Brule Sioux, Cheyenne and Arapahoe tribes;
artifacts of a prehistoric tribe of the Platte
River region.

KOSHARE INDIAN KIVA ART MUSEUM
18th and Santa Fe Aves.
                        LA JUNTA 81050
J. F. Burshears, Curator

Collection of Indian and Western art by
Western painters; Indian pottery, baskets,
rugs, dioramas, artifacts.

FRANCISCO FORT MUSEUM
Francisco St.   LA VETA 81055
   Proctor Hayes, Curator

Small collection of Indian artifacts.

KIT CARSON MUSEUM
P.O. Box 44
                        LAS ANIMAS 81054
   Nellie L. Grantham, Curator

Collection of local materials includes blankets, arrowheads, beaded ceremonial items,
grinding stones, arrowhead core, of the
Sioux, Cheyenne, Kiowa and Comanche
tribes.

LOVELAND MUSEUM
503 Lincoln Ave.   LOVELAND 80537
   Mrs. C. J. Minnerly, Director and
      Curator

Indian relics and crafts.

WHITE RIVER MUSEUM
P.O. Box 973   MEEKER 81641

Historic house and museum featuring pioneer and Indian relics.

MESA VERDE NATIONAL PARK MUSEUM
   MESA VERDE NATIONAL PARK 81330
   Chester A. Thomas, Superintendent

Extensive study collections of the Northern
San Juan Anasazi Culture; limited biological
and ethnological collections.

UTE INDIAN MUSEUM
Chipeta Springs   MONTROSE 81401
   Leslie Burton, Curator

Museum depicts history of the Utes through
use of dioramas, objects which the Utes
made and used, photographs and maps.
Life-size figures dressed in Indian clothing
are displayed as are portraits of some Ute
leaders.

SALIDA HISTORICAL MUSEUM
1043 F St.   SALIDA 81201
   Harriet W. Alexander, Curator

Collection includes: rugs and blankets,
paintings, baskets, arrowheads, beaded
ceremonial items; Sioux Indian war bonnet;
blankets; Apache dance crosses, with hoops,
and other artifacts.

TREAD OF PIONEERS HISTORICAL
   COMMISSION - MUSEUM
5th and Oak Sts.
                STEAMBOAT SPRINGS 80477
      Claude Luekens, Chairman

Museum exhibits feature northwestern Colorado and Indian artifacts. Historic house.

OVERLAND TRAIL MUSEUM
Overland Trail
P.O. Box 485   STERLING 80751
      C. H. Williams, Director

Indian artifacts; arrowhead collection.

CONNECTICUT

MANSFIELD HOUSE
22 Jewett Street   ANSONIA 06401
      Mr. and Mrs. Richard Morrison,
         Curators

Historic house featuring Indian artifacts.

P. T. BARNUM MUSEUM
Barnum Institute of Science and History
804 Main St.   BRIDGEPORT 06604
      Elizabeth Sterling Seeley, Curator

Indian exhibits include ten archaeological
models from Arizona and New Mexico;
Eskimo articles; Indian artifacts: pottery,
statues, beads, arrows, mortars, pipes,
war clubs.

CLINTON HISTORICAL SOCIETY -
   MUSEUM
E. Main St.   CLINTON 06413
      Miss Nancy L. Newsom, President

Collections include Indian arrowheads.
Library. Publications.

HENRY WHITTFIELD STATE HISTORICAL
   MUSEUM
Boston St.   GUILFORD 06437

Contains Indian relics.

LITCHFIELD HISTORICAL SOCIETY -
   MUSEUM
South and East Sts.
P.O. Box 384   LITCHFIELD 06759
      Miss Charlotte M. Wiggin, Curator,
         Librarian

Exhibits include local historical documents,
Indian artifacts (Madden Collection), Civil
War relics. Library. Publications.

SLATER MEMORIAL MUSEUM
The Norwich Free Academy
108 Crescent St.   NORWICH 06360
      Joseph P. Gualtieri, Director

Northwest Indian Collection of Captain
Charles Satterlee featuring Eskimo tools,
implements, clothing and artifacts; Northwest Coast boats, fishing tackle, houses,
totems, utensils, trade objects, and basketry of the Tlingit, Haida, Nootka, Klikitat
and Salish Indians. Prehistoric American
Indian collection includes pottery of the
Mound Builders; Pueblo and Hopi basketry.
Publications.

THE STAMFORD MUSEUM AND
   NATURE CENTER
High Ridge at Scofieldtown Rd.
                          STAMFORD 06903
      Ernest T. Luhde, Director

Archaeological and paleontological exhibits;
Indian artifacts.

STRATFORD HISTORICAL SOCIETY -
   MUSEUM
967 Academy Hill   STRATFORD 06497
      Stanley Johnson, President

Museum features Indian relics. Historic
house. Library.

TANTAQUIDGEON INDIAN MUSEUM
Mohegan Hill Place
R.F.D. 4   UNCASVILLE 06382

"To preserve and perpetuate the history and
traditions of the Mohegan and other Indian
tribes." Collections include stone artifacts
from the Mohegan area; ancient and contemporary arts and crafts made by Indians of
New England, the Southwest and Northern
Plains regions.

HISTORICAL MUSEUM OF THE GUNN
  MEMORIAL LIBRARY
Washington Green   WASHINGTON 06793
  Mrs. Newell Withey, Curator

Indian artifacts of the Oglala Sioux; basket
collection; historical documents.

MATTATUCK HISTORICAL SOCIETY -
  MUSEUM
119 W. Main St.   WATERBURY
  Rawson W. Haddon, Director

Collections include historical and archaeological material; Artists of Connecticut,
1740 to date. Junior museum teaching program. Industrial museum.

THE WINDSOR HISTORICAL SOCIETY -
  MUSEUM
96 Palisado Ave.   WINDSOR 06095
  Robert W. Hoskins, President

Collection features Indian relics, genealogies. Library.

DELAWARE

ZWAANENDAEL MUSEUM
Savannah Rd. and Kings Highway
    LEWES 19958
  Mrs. Dorothy L. Collins, Curator

Features local Indian artifacts.

DISTRICT OF COLUMBIA

U. S. DEPARTMENT OF THE
  INTERIOR MUSEUM
19th and C Sts., N.W.
    WASHINGTON 20240
  Theodore H. Drummond, Curator

Collections contain items of handicraft,
tools, utensils, dress, art, etc., of the
American Indians, Eskimos, and natives of
the South Sea Islands. Indian exhibits include: two scale-model dioramas; full-size
brich bark conoe; chief's headdress; three
glass cases of Indian handcraft items; displays illustrating how the U.S. Government
helps American Indians; silhouettes; rugs;
wall maps, etc.

U. S. NATIONAL MUSEUM
Smithsonian Institution
    WASHINGTON 20560

Ten exhibit halls deal with the archaeology
and tehnology of the world, arranged geographically.

FLORIDA

DADE BATTLEFIELD HISTORIC
  MEMORIAL MUSEUM
3180 Dade Battlefield Memorial
P.O. Box 445   BUSHNELL 33513
  N. E. Miller, Director (Florida
    Board of Parks and Historic
    Memorials)

Seminole Indian artifacts. Site of Dade
Massacre.

ST. CLAIR WHITMAN MUSEUM
Cedar Key Historic Memorial
    CEDAR KEY 32625
  N. E. Miller, Director (Florida
    Board of Parks and Historic
    Memorials)

Contains local Indian artifacts.

JOE AND EMILY LOWE ART GALLERY
University of Miami
Miller Drive   CORAL GABLES 33146
  Al. L. Freundlich, Director

Gallery's Barton Wing (Collection) contains
3,500 items -- blankets, Pueblo pottery,
Plains Indian baskets; Kachina dolls, jewelry, costumes and ceramics, largely of
Southwestern origin.

MUSEUM OF ARTS AND SCIENCES
288 White St.   DAYTONA BEACH 32014
  Stanley Howe, Curator

Small collection of local Indian artifacts.

FORT LAUDERDALE MUSEUM OF THE
  ARTS
625 E. Las Olas Blvd.
    FORT LAUDERDALE 33301
  Schubert E. Jonas, Director

Features American Indian art.

JACKSONVILLE CHILDREN'S MUSEUM
1061 Riverside Ave.
                    JACKSONVILLE 32204
     Mrs. Doris L. Whitmore, Director

Ethnology of the Seminole Indian.

SOUTHEAST MUSEUM OF THE NORTH
    AMERICAN INDIAN
P.O. Box 248
U.S. Highway 1
                    MARATHON 33050
     Francis Valentine Crane, Director

Prehistoric and contemporary art and artifacts: stone craving, pottery, metal work,
textiles, weapons, basketry, utensils. Library.

HISTORICAL MUSEUM OF SOUTHERN
    FLORIDA AND THE CARIBBEAN
2010 N. Bayshore Dr.
                    MIAMI 33137
     David T. Alexander, Director

South Florida and Caribbean Indian artifacts.

ST. PETERSBURG HISTORICAL
    MUSEUM
335 Second Ave., N.E.
                    ST. PETERSBURG 33701

Content of collections or exhibits: Indian
artifacts; bones from Indian mounds; early
American documents.

GEORGIA

ALBANY AREA JUNIOR MUSEUM, INC.
516 Flint Ave.   ALBANY
     Mrs. Leonard C. Hirsch, Director

Collection features Indian art and artifacts.

EMORY UNIVERSITY MUSEUM
Bishop's Hall   ATLANTA 30322
     W. B. Baher, Director

Contains a general collection of implements,
beads, arrowheads; special collection from
Etowah Mounds.

GEORGIA STATE MUSEUM OF SCIENCE
    AND INDUSTRY
State Captiol
Washington St.   ATLANTA 30334
     Grey B. Culberson, Director

Collection includes Indian artifacts.

KOLOMOKI MOUNDS MUSEUM
Route 1   BLAKELY 31723

Collection from excavation of Kolomoki
Mounds. Exhibits feature pottery, include
dioramas.

NEW ECHOTA
State Highway 225
                    CALHOUN 30701
     Franklin Fenenga, Director of
        Museums, Georgia Historical
        Commission

Preservation Project (former capitol of
Cherokee Nation). Cherokee Phoenix Print
Shop (replica).

ETOWAH INDIAN MOUNDS MUSEUM
                    CARTERSVILLE 30120
     L. H. Tumlin, Jr., Superintendent

Collections consist of material recovered
from Mound excavations.

COLUMBUS MUSEUM OF ARTS AND
    CRAFTS, INC.
1251 Wynnton Rd.   COLUMBUS 31906
     Edward S. Shorter, Director

Collections include prehistoric and Yuchi
Indian material.

CREEK INDIAN MUSEUM
Indian Springs State Park
                    INDIAN SPRINGS 30231
     Mrs. Jeanelle Robertson, Curator

Indian museum.

LOUISVILLE MUSEUM AND ARCHIVES
Seventh St.   LOUISVILLE 30434

Small collection of local artifacts -- arrowheads, tomahawks, pieces of pottery, etc.

OCMULGEE NATIONAL MONUMENT
   MUSEUM
P.O. Box 4186   MACON 31208
   George R. Fischer, Archaeologist

Extensive collections explain culture of
the Indians who constructed mounds on site
of present Ocmulgee National Monument,
and of five other groups of Indians who have
lived in area during past 10,000 years. Collection from Ocmulgee and immediate vicinity includes approximately two million items
ranging in time from Paleo-Indian through
historic Creek. Included are extensive collections from relief-area archaeology
throughout the Southeast. Ocmulgee serves
as repository for National Park Service
collections in the Southeast and contains
material from the Natchez Trace, Russell
Cave, and several other areas.

SOUTH END HOUSE
          SAPELO ISLAND 31327
   Milton B. Gray, Curator

Relics of prehistoric Indian mound and
shell ring.

IDAHO

COLLEGE OF IDAHO MUSEUM
          CALDWELL 83605
   L. M. Stanford, Curator

Includes anthropological and ethnological
exhibits.

BANNOCK COUNTY HISTORICAL
   MUSEUM
106 S. Garfield St.
P.O. Box 253   POCATELLO 83201
   Homer Davis, Curator

Collection includes local Indian artifacts.

BONNER COUNTY MUSEUM
Community Hall
210 S. First Ave.
P.O. Box 702   SANDPOINT 83864
   Floyd A. Perks, Chairman

Contains Indian artifacts and other local historical material.

CHAMBER OF COMMERCE MUSEUM
715-719 Bank St.
P.O. Box 1167   WALLACE 83873
   Fred R. Levering, Manager and
      Curator

Indian and early American material com-
prise Museum's exhibits.

ILLINOIS

THE AURORA HISTORICAL MUSEUM
304 Oak Ave.
P.O. Box 905   AURORA 60538
   Robert W. Barclay, Curator

Collection of Indian artifacts.

GALE'S PIONEER MUSEUM
R. R. 2   AVA 62907
   Arthur E. Gale, Curator

Contains pioneer and Indian material.

SOUTHERN ILLINOIS UNIVERSITY
   MUSEUM
Altgeld Hall, Campus
          CARBONDALE 62903
   Dr. J. Charles Kelley, Director
   Dr. Melvin L. Fowler, Curator of
      North American Archaeology

Collections related to ethnology, pioneer
and Indian history, Midwest archaeology.

CHICAGO NATURAL HISTORY MUSEUM
Department of Anthropology
Roosevelt Rd. and Lake Shore Dr.
          CHICAGO 60605
   E. Leland Webber, Director

Seven exhibit halls devoted to the American
Indian. Collections and exhibits cover prehistoric and living Indians (and Eskimos)
from Alaska to Cape Horn -- North, Central
and South America. Ethnographic collections of the Northwest Coast, California,
Plains, Southwest, Great Lakes region,
Mexico, and Amazon Basin. Archaeological
collection of the Southwest, Midwest, Mexico and Central America, Columbia, Ecuador, Peru, Chile, and Northwest Argentina.

MADISON COUNTY HISTORICAL MUSEUM
Main St.   EDWARDSVILLE 62025
    Mrs. Louise Ahrans, Curator

Archaeological and historical Indian material.

SCHOOL OF NATIONS MUSEUM
Principia College   ELSAH 62028
    Mrs. Jeralyn P. Hosmer, Curator

Contains more than 650 individual items
(artifacts) -- animal equipment; bags, baskets; clothing; dolls; jewelry; model houses;
models of transportation; pictures; pottery;
textiles; miscellaneous items.

STEPHENSON COUNTY HISTORICAL
    SOCIETY - MUSEUM
1440 S. Carroll Ave.
                        FREEPORT 61032
    Mrs. John Woodhouse, Curator

Collections include historical and industrial
objects, Indian beadwork. Oscar Taylor
home. Farm Museum. Publications.

THE DAVID STRAWN ART GALLERY
331 W. College Ave.
                    JACKSONVILLE 62650
    Clement Allison, Director

Collection of Indian pottery of the Mississippi Valley.

KANKAKEE COUNTY HISTORICAL
    SOCIETY - MUSEUM
8th Ave. at Water St.
                      KANKAKEE 60901
    Mrs. Fannie Still, Curator

Exhibits include Indian and pioneer items.
Library.

NAUVOO STATE PARK MUSEUM
Nauvoo Historical Society
                        NAUVOO 62354
    Mrs. Edna Griffith, President

Collection of Indian artifacts.

ILLINOIS STATE UNIVERSITY
    MUSEUM
                        NORMAL 61761
    Dr. Cecilia Peikert Bunney, Director

Small, general collection of basketry, pottery, stone tools, implements and weapons,
decorative objects and blankets.

ILLINOIS STATE MUSEUM OF NATURAL
    HISTORY AND ART
Spring and Edwards St.
                    SPRINGFIELD 62700
    Milton D. Thompson, Director

Features Indian archaeological material of
Illinois, and anthropological exhibits.

STERLING-ROCK FALLS HISTORICAL
    SOCIETY MUSEUM
Sterling Coliseum
212 Third Ave.   STERLING 61081
    Lloyd R. Casey, President

Features local Indian material.

LAKE COUNTY MUSEUM OF HISTORY
U.S. Highway 41 and Wadsworth Rd.
                      WADSWORTH 60083
    Robert W. Vogel, Director

Indian, pioneer and regional material included.

INDIANA

CHILDREN'S MUSEUM OF INDIANAPOLIS
3010 N. Meridian St.
                    INDIANAPOLIS 46208
    Mrs. Mildred S. Compton, Director

Collections consist of over 2,000 objects
representing the tribes of Woodland, Southeast, Plains, Plateau, Southwest, Northwest
Coast, California and Canadian Indians; predominant are the large collection of artifacts
of a generally prehistoric nature (Indiana
and Midwest), and the collection of leather
and beadwork of the Plains tribes, which includes moccasins, pouches and bags, wearing apparel, and weapons.

INDIANA STATE MUSEUM
Division of State Parks
616 State Office Bldg.
INDIANAPOLIS 46209
Robert D. Starrett, Curator

Exhibits feature Indian relics, costumes, and archaeological material.

MIAMI COUNTY HISTORICAL MUSEUM
11 N. Huntington St.   PERU 46970
Mrs. Horace D. Cook, Curator

Museum's collections include pottery, clothing, weapons, implements, jewelry, ceremonial objects, effigies, hatchets, etc.

JOSEPH MOORE MUSEUM
Earlham College   RICHMOND 47374
J. M. Heilman, Curator of
Anthropology

Collection's emphasis is on Ohio Valley prehistory.

RUSH COUNTY HISTORICAL MUSEUM
619 N. Perkins St.   RUSHVILLE 46173
John Hughes, President

Collection of Indian artifacts.

IOWA

DAVENPORT PUBLIC MUSEUM
704 Brady St.   DAVENPORT 52084
Donald G. Herold, Director

Collection of prehistoric and Indian artifacts from mounds in Arkansas, Illinois, Iowa and Tennessee.

IOWA STATE MUSEUM
State Department of History and Archives
E. 12th and Grand Ave.
DES MOINES 50319
Richard Boyt, Director

Museum's collections include Indian artifacts.

FORT DODGE HISTORICAL MUSEUM
Highway 20 West
FORT DODGE 50501
Mrs. John Amond, Curator

Collection of local Indian material.

MUSEUM OF NATURAL HISTORY
State University of Iowa
MacBride Hall   IOWA CITY 52240
Walter C. Thietje, Curator

Exhibits feature local Indian artifacts, including arrowheads and other weapons.

SAGERS MUSEUM
MAQUOKETA 52060
Paul Sagers, Owner

Features prehistoric artifacts and local material.

EFFIGY MOUNDS NATIONAL MONUMENT
Visitor Center
Box K   McGREGOR 52157
Stuart H. Maule, Superintendent

Fifteen permanent exhibits; Indian burial mounds; archaeology of Upper Mississippi River Valley with emphasis on the Woodland cultures. Library.

SIOUX CITY PUBLIC MUSEUM
2901 Jackson St.   SIOUX CITY 51104
Charles R. DeBush, Director

Artifacts of the Plains and Eastern Woodland Indians on exhibit.

MUSEUM OF HISTORY AND SCIENCE
Park Ave. at South St.
WATERLOO 50701
Genevieve Woodbridge, Director

Six exhibit cases featuring Indian artifacts and beadwork. Rare book collection (53 volumes) of Indian history and lore.

KANSAS

ST. BENEDICT'S COLLEGE MUSEUM
Science Hall   ATCHISON 66002
Rev. Felix Nolte, O.S.B., Director

Anthropological exhibits featuring Plains and Southwest Indian material; local paleontological material.

SOD TOWN PRAIRIE HISTORICAL
  MUSEUM
U.S. Highway 24
P.O. Box 595   COLBY 67701
    V.A. Kear, Owner

Collection of Indian artifacts.

RONIGER MEMORIAL MUSEUM
Union St.   COTTONWOOD FALLS 66845
    Rex Bennet, Manager

Local historical material, including Indian
artifacts.

OLD KAW MISSION
                    COUNCIL GROVE 66846

Historic House and Museum, featuring Kaw
Indian relics.

BEESON MUSEUM
Old Front St.   DODGE CITY 67801

Collection of local Indian relics.

BOOT HILL MUSEUM
500 W. Wyatt Earp
                    DODGE CITY 67801
    George R. Henrichs, Executive
    Director

Two exhibit cases containing Plains Indian
artifacts.

DOUGLASS HISTORICAL MUSEUM
City Bldg.
211 S. Forest   DOUGLASS 67039
    Mrs. Elmer E. Sherar, Curator

Indian and pioneer relics of local origin
exhibited.

FRONTIER HISTORICAL PARK
213 W. 5th St.   HAYS 67601

Exhibits of material relating to local Indian
conflicts.

HIGHLAND IOWA-SAC INDIAN MISSION
  AND MUSEUM
                    HIGHLAND 66035
    Alfred S. Wakefield (Director)

Iowa-Sac artifacts -- tools, housewares,
furniture, Indian heads, local items -- exhibited in original mission building.

STEVENS COUNTY GAS AND HISTORICAL
  MUSEUM
905 S. Adams St.   HUGOTON 67951
    Mrs. Gladys Wilson, President

Contains Indian material related to Stevens
County history.

FORT HARKER MUSEUM
Old Guardhouse   KANOPOLIS 67454

Military Museum featuring Indian relics.

WYANDOTTEE COUNTY MUSEUM
Memorial Bldg.
7th St. and Barnett Ave.
                    KANSAS CITY 66101
    Harry M. Trowbridge, Curator

Displays include Indian beadwork of the
Wyandotte tribe; archival material relating
to the defense of the Huron cemetery; Delaware artifacts.

FORT LARNED NATIONAL SITE MUSEUM
Highway 56   LARNED 67550
    E. E. Newachek, President
    Fort Larned Historical Society
    (temporary operating authority)

Site museum contains small collection of
Indian relics.

RILEY COUNTY HISTORICAL MUSEUM
Memorial Auditorium Building
                    MANHATTAN 66503
    Winifred N. Slagg, Director and
    Curator

Nine hundred Indian relics and artifacts of
northeast Kansas and southwest Nebraska
(The Walter Collection).

EL QUARTELEJO KIVA INDIAN
  MUSEUM
c/o News Chronicle Printing Co., Inc.
P.O. Box 218   SCOTT CITY 67871
    Bill Boyer, Director

Collection features Cheyenne and Pueblo
artifacts, especially Taos; Indian war material.

DON'S HISTORICAL MUSEUM AND
 TRADING POST
U. S. Highway 24   STOCKTON 67669
  Donald E. Grieve, Owner

Collections include pioneer and Indian
articles.

GREAT PLAINS HISTORICAL MUSEUM
Hotel Ames Bldg.   SYRACUSE 67878
  Mrs. Velma E. Daniels, Manager

Collection includes weapons and Indian
relics.

KANSAS STATE HISTORICAL SOCIETY -
 MUSEUM
Memorial Building
120 W. 10th St.   TOPEKA 66612
  Nyle H. Miller, Secretary

Collection features Indian relics, tools,
utensils and clothing related to the history
of Kansas.

MUSEUM AND ARCHIVES - THE MENNIN-
 GER FOUNDATION
5600 W. 6th St.   TOPEKA 66601
  Lewis F. Wheelock, Curator

Archaeological and anthropological display
rooms featuring American Indian history and
prehistory, focusing on "Indian healing ceremonies and artifacts, and emotional expression in handicrafts."

KENTUCKY

KENTUCKY MUSEUM
Western Kentucky State College
              BOWLING GREEN 42102
  Gayle R. Craver, Curator

Indian material on display includes stone,
shell and bone artifacts; skeletal remains.
Library (25-50 volumes related to Kentucky
Indians).

MUSEUM OF ANTHROPOLOGY
University of Kentucky
              LEXINGTON 40506
  Douglas W. Schwartz, Director

Archaeological collections, including Navajo and Eskimo material.

MOUNTAIN LIFE MUSEUM
Levi Jackson Wilderness Road State Park
              LONDON 40741
  Edward McCabbard, Superintendent

Household furnishings, pioneer relics, and
tools of Kentucky housed in farm buildings.

THE FILSON CLUB
118 W. Breckinridge
              LOUISVILLE 40203
  Mrs. Dorothy Thomas Cullen, Curator

Prehistoric Indian relics from Ohio and
Mississippi Valleys; relics of Indian life in
Kentucky. Library. Publications.

THE LOUISVILLE MUSEUM
743 S. 5th St.   LOUISVILLE 40205
  Carlyle D. Chamberlain, Curator

Historical exhibits featuring Indian artifacts.

J. B. SPEED ART MUSEUM
2035 S. 3rd St.   LOUISVILLE 40208
  Addison Franklin Page, Director

Ethnological and archaeological exhibits
illustrating Indian life, costume, arms,
tools, religion and language at the beginning of this century work in flint, stone and
bone, from prehistoric Kentucky and Southern Indiana (Frederick Weygold Collection).

LOUISIANA

MARKSVILLE PREHISTORIC INDIAN
 PARK
Action Rd.   MARKSVILLE 71351

Exhibits illustrate culture of Natchez and
Avoyells Indians who inhabited local area;
restored mound sites.

MAINE

WILSON MUSEUM
Perkins St.   CASTINE 04421
  Mrs. Ellenore W. Doudiet, Curator

Contains Pueblo art and artifacts; Plains
Indian ornamental beadwork; Mississippi-

Ohio area pottery; artifacts of Algonquian origin; local artifacts; tools and implements of Eskimos of Canada and of the Montagnais-Neskapi Indians of Labrador. Museum also features numerous dioramas.

BEACH MUSEUM
1245 Forest Ave.   PORTLAND 04106
    Jessie L. Beach, Owner

Exhibits relate to natural science and include Indian relics.

MARYLAND

MARYLAND HOUSE
Druid Hill Park   BALTIMORE

Natural history exhibits feature Indian artifacts of Maryland.

THE WALTERS ART GALLERY
Charles and Centre Sts.
                               BALTIMORE

Exhibit of two hundred water colors of Alfred Jacob Miller, developed from sketches drawn in Western Indian country in 1837.

FORT FREDERICK STATE PARK
    MUSEUM
State Highway 56   BIG POOL 21711
    Spencer P. Ellis, Head, Maryland
        Department of Parks and Forests
            (operating authority)

Museum houses collection of Indian relics, early firearms, and pioneer household and farm equipment.

OLD STATE HOUSE
                    ST. MARY'S CITY 20686

Local Indian artifacts housed in replica of original Maryland State House.

HISTORICAL SOCIETY OF CARROLL
    COUNTY, INC.
206 E. Main St.   WESTMINSTER 21157
    James M. Shriver, President

Museum features local historical objects and Indian artifacts.

MASSACHUSETTS

THE PEABODY FOUNDATION
Box 71   ANDOVER 01810
    Frederick Johnson, Curator

Exhibits cover archaeology of eastern North America from A. D. 7, 500 to present. Pottery and artifacts of Pecos Pueblo, N. M.

BRONSON MUSEUM
8 N. Main St.   ATTLEBORO 02703

Museum shows four prehistoric New England culture periods through use of sets, dioramas and implement collections. Library.

THE CHILDREN'S MUSEUM
60 Burroughs St.   BOSTON 02130
    Michael Spock, Director

Early American history collections including Indian-related material.

PEABODY MUSEUM OF ARCHAEOLOGY
    AND ETHNOLOGY
Harvard University
11 Divinity Ave.
                         CAMBRIDGE 02138
    J. O. Brew, Director

Large collection of archaeological, ethnological and somatological artifacts; 80, 000 related library items.

CANTON HISTORICAL SOCIETY -
    MUSEUM
1400 Washington St.   CANTON 02021
    Miss Katharine Sullivan, President

Museum houses Colonial, Civil War and Indian items.

CHELMSFORD HISTORICAL SOCIETY -
    MUSEUM
Adams Public Library
Boston Rd.   CHELMSFORD 01824
    Alfred H. Coburn, President

Collections include local and Indian relics.

COHASSET HISTORICAL SOCIETY -
  MUSEUM
Elm St.   COHASSET 02025
    Prescott T. Cummer, President

Exhibits include Colonial and Indian artifacts.

CHILDREN'S MUSEUM, INC.
Russell's Mills Rd.   DARTMOUTH 02714
    Mrs. Arthur G. Wadsworth

Natural science collection includes Indian
objects.

DEDHAM HISTORICAL SOCIETY -
  MUSEUM
612 High St.
P.O. Box 215   DEDHAM 02026
    Miss Marion K. Conant, Librarian

Collections feature local artifacts, Indian
deeds and relics. Library.

INDIAN HOUSE MEMORIAL
Main St.   DEERFIELD 01342

Museum features folk art, including Indian
relics, weaving, pottery. site of French
and Indian attack during 1704 massacre.

FRAMINGHAM HISTORICAL AND
  NATURAL HISTORY SOCIETY -
  MUSEUM
Vernon St.   FRAMINGHAM

Museum houses Indian relics and military
items.

FRUITLANDS MUSEUMS
Prospect Hill   HARVARD 01451
    William Henry Harrison, Director

American Indian Museum contains a selection of North American Indian relics: prehistoric implements, burials, and specimens of Indian arts and industries; dioramas.

HAVERHILL HISTORICAL SOCIETY -
  MUSEUM
240 Water St.   HAVERHILL 01830
    Austin Lewis, President

Collections include Colonial and Indian
exhibits.

HOLYOKE MUSEUM - WISTARIAUHURST
238 Cabot St.   HOLYOKE 01041
    Mrs. William S. Quirk, Director

Collection (largely Northwestern) contains
flint and stone items -- celts axes, ham-
merheads, arrowheads, pestles, game-
stones, Catlinite and carved stone pipes;
shell and stone ornaments; ceremonial objects; Iroquois masks and rattles; pottery
of the Southeast and Southwest. Basketry
from Southwest, Plains and Northwest Coast.
Iroquois quill and beadwork; Plains beadwork.

OLD BRIDGEWATER HISTORICAL
  SOCIETY - MUSEUM
c/o Mrs. Stella J. Snow
20 Forest St.
            WEST BRIDGEWATER 02379

Exhibits feature original deed signed by
Massasoit (Quasamequin) in 1649, in an
agreement with the Pilgrims.

MICHIGAN

EXHIBIT MUSEUM
University of Michigan
                     ANN ARBOR 48103

Six dioramas of Michigan Indian regional
culture types; cases of artifacts of Eskimo,
Northwest Coast, Eastern Woodland, Southwest, and Plains; developing Hall of Anthropology with dioramas and specimen
displays of North and South American Indian
cultures.

MUSEUM OF ANTHROPOLOGY
University of Michigan
University Museum Bldg.
                     ANN ARBOR 48103
    James B. Griffin, Director

American archaeological and ethnological
exhibits.

KINGMAN MUSEUM OF NATURAL
  HISTORY
Leila Arboretum   BATTLE CREEK 49015

Exhibits of Indian arts and crafts from
Southwest, Mexico, Western Canada, South
America.

CRANBROOK INSTITUTE OF SCIENCE
                    BLOOMFIELD HILLS 48013

Collection emphasizes cultures of Great
Lakes area in permanent exhibits; collections from Western and Northern tribes;
special collections in changing exhibits.
Publications.

GREAT LAKES INDIAN MUSEUM
                    CROSS VILLAGE 49723
        Dennis Lessard, Curator

Indian museum featuring historic material
of the Great Lakes region.

DELTA COUNTY HISTORICAL SOCIETY
    MUSEUM
Ludington Park   ESCANABA 49829
        David S. Coon, Director

Items pertaining to local history including
Indian and pioneer relics.

GENESEE COUNTY MUSEUM AND
    HISTORICAL SOCIETY
411 Courthouse   FLINT 48501
        Arthur G. Abraham, Director

Collection includes Indian stone artifacts.

CHIEF BLACKBIRD HOME MUSEUM
268 E. Main St.
                    HARBOR SPRINGS 49740
        A.S. Fuhrman, Curator

Indian museum contains artifacts and relics.

CHARLTON PARK AND BARRY COUNTY
    MEMORIAL MUSEUM
                    HASTINGS 49058
        Irving D. Charlton, Director

Collections include Indian arts and crafts
items, relics.

MICHIGAN HISTORICAL COMMISSION
    MUSEUM
505 N. Washington Ave.
                    LANSING 48933
        Solan R. Weeks, Director
        Dorothy Barnard, Curator

Indian exhibits related to history of Michigan
and old Northwest Territory.

LEELANAU HISTORICAL MUSEUM
Courthouse   LELAND 49654
        Amalia M. Kropp, Director

Includes Chippewa and Navaho beadwork.
Local collection contains arrowheads, axes,
quill and beadwork; basketry; pipestone
head; wood pestle.

MASON COUNTY MUSEUM
Mason County Historical Soceity
305 E. Filer St.   LUDINGTON 49431
        Mrs. Rose D. Hawley, Director

Exhibits feature Indian artifacts of local
historical origin.

SCHOOLCRAFT COUNTY HISTORICAL
    POST HOUSE
Cedar St.
72 Range St.   MANISTIQUE 49854
        Mrs. J. J. Herbert, Curator

Historic house contains Indian artifacts,
arrowheads.

MARQUETTE COUNTY HISTORICAL
    SOCIETY MUSEUM AND J. M.
    LONGYEAR RESEARCH LIBRARY
213 N. Front St.   MARQUETTE 49855
        Ernest H. Rankin, Executive Secretary

Indian archaeological and historical material of the upper peninsula of Michigan.

MIDLAND COUNTY HISTORICAL
    ASSOCIATION - MUSEUM
Midland Room, Grace A. Dow
    Memorial Library
1710 W. St. Andrews Dr.
                    MIDLAND 48640
        Mrs. Glen Cummins, Executive
        Secretary

Museum contains Indian relics. Reading
room.

MILLE LACS STATE INDIAN MUSEUM
                    MILLE LACS LAKE

Contains approximately twenty large displays depicting aboriginal culture of area,
with emphasis on Chippewa and Sioux.

MUSKEGON COUNTY MUSEUM
FOUNDATION
30 W. Muskegon Ave.
MUSKEGON 49440
Florence E. Berggren, Curator

Indian exhibit includes ten dioramas depicting the life of local tribes.

FORT ST. JOSEPH HISTORICAL
MUSEUM
508 E. Main St.   NILES 49120
Mrs. Gertrude B. Johnston, Curator

Plym collection of Sioux Indian artifacts; large collection of Indian artifacts and trade goods from the Fort St. Joseph site; thirteen pictographs drawn by Sitting Bull.

ONTONAGON COUNTY HISTORICAL
SOCIETY MUSEUM
319 River St.   ONTONAGON 49953
Charles William, Curator

Collection includes prehistoric and Indian relics.

THE SAGINAW MUSEUM
1126 N. Michigan Ave.
SAGINAW 48602
Mrs. Julia Roecker, Director

Art museum includes Indian art and artifacts.

FORT ALGONQUIN
U.S. Highway 1   ST. IGNACE 49781
H. Vaughn Norton, Director

Replica of Indian trading post and fort, containing Indian and pioneer artifacts.

TREASURE ISLAND
ST. IGNACE 49781
J. K. Barnhill, Director

Collection includes Indian artifacts -- prehistoric and historic weapons, pottery, basketry.

THE SCHOOLCRAFT INDIAN AGENCY
HOUSE
715 E. Portage Ave.
(800 Cedar St.)
SAULT STE. MARIE
Mrs. Beulah Miller,
Director of Museums

Historic house built by U. S. Indian agent Henry R. Schoolcraft.

LUCKHARD'S MUSEUM - THE INDIAN
MISSION
821 E. Bay St.   SEBEWAING 48759
C. F. Luckhard, Historian
Mr. Gilbert Muller, Curator

Indian artifacts housed in original Indian Mission of the Chippewa Indians (1845).

MINNESOTA

CROW WING COUNTY HISTORICAL
SOCIETY
Court House   BRAINERD 56401

Local Indian materials.

HOLTE MEMORIAL MUSEUM
Community Theatre Bldg.
CROOKSTON 56716
Donald Myrold, President

Museum features Indian artifacts and fur trading items.

BECKER COUNTY HISTORICAL
SOCIETY - MUSEUM
915 Lake Ave.   DETROIT LAKES 56501
Frank J. Long, President

Collections include Indian material related to Becker County history. Library.

A. M. CHISHOLM MUSEUM
1832 E. 2nd St.   DULUTH 55812

Exhibits consist of handicrafts, costumes, depiction of Indian home life and examples of home untensils.

ST. LOUIS COUNTY HISTORICAL
  SOCIETY
2228 East Superior St.
                          DULUTH 55812
  Mrs. Josiah Ensign Greene,
    Executive Secretary

Collections include paintings of Indians who
resided in the St. Louis County region (1856-
1857); Indian artifacts; several volumes
(testaments, dictionaries, hymn books) in
the Chippewa language.

GRANT COUNTY HISTORICAL SOCIETY -
  MUSEUM
                    ELBOW LAKE 56531
  W. M. Goetzinger, President

Museum exhibits archaeological and Indian
artifacts.

GRAND PORTAGE NATIONAL MONUMENT
  MUSEUM
Box 666   GRAND MARAIS 55604

Monument's interim museum houses collection of fur trade and Chippewa handicraft
items, including birchbark containers, canoes and ornaments; cedar bark mats; porcupine quill and beadwork on bark and hide;
embroidery on broadcloth and velveteen;
bone implements; ceremonial objects.

BLUE EARTH COUNTY HISTORICAL
  SOCIETY AND MUSEUM
606 S. Broad St.   MANKATO 56001
  Prof. G. S. Petterson,
    Curator and Director

Exhibits include Indian and pioneer relics;
local historical documents.

REDWOOD COUNTY HISTORICAL
  SOCIETY - MUSEUM
1115 E. Bridge St.
                  REDWOOD FALLS 56283
  M. E. Dirlam, President

Exhibits feature items pertaining to 1862
Sioux uprising. Publications.

MINNESOTA HISTORICAL SOCIETY
  MUSEUM
Cedar St. and Central Ave.
                          ST. PAUL 55101
  Alan R. Woolworth, Curator

Exhibits depicting prehistoric and contemporary Indian life in Minnesota. Archaeological and ethnological collections.

ST. PAUL ART CENTER
30 E. 10th St.   ST. PAUL 55101
  Malcolm E. Lein, Director

Contains approximately 100 Northwest Coast
Indian artifacts, twenty-five Southwest
Indian craft items; twenty-five pre-Colum-
bian artifacts.

THE SCIENCE MUSEUM
St. Paul Institute
51 University Ave.   ST. PAUL 55103

Extensive displays of local Indian material,
including Chippewa and Blackfeet tribes;
dioramas and life-size habitat displays of
Northwest, Southwest and Plains cultures.

DAKOTA COUNTY HISTORICAL MUSEUM
Municipal Bldg.
                  SOUTH ST. PAUL 55075
  Fred E. Lawshe, Curator

Collection of trade goods, clothing, artifacts, skeletal remains.

CARVER COUNTY HISTORICAL
  SOCIETY - MUSEUM
119 Cherry St.   WACONIA 55387
  Edward A. Weinzierl, President

Exhibits include Indian artifacts and implements.

WALKER MUSEUM OF NATURAL HISTORY
  AND INDIAN ARTS AND CRAFTS
Conservation Bldg.   WALKER 56484
  Jake N. Licke, Secretary,
    Walker Museum Board

Collections include Indian arts and crafts
items and relics, mainly of the Chippewa
and Ojibwa tribes.

WINONA COUNTY HISTORICAL SOCIETY
  MUSEUM
Lumbermen's Bldg.
125 W. 5th St.   WINONA 55987
    Dr. Lewis I. Younger, President

Exhibits include Chippewa Indian artifacts
and pioneer items.

MISSISSIPPI

BRICE'S CROSSROADS MUSEUM
P.O. Box 100   BALDWYN 38824
    Claude Gentry, Curator

Collection contains ceremonial pieces, pottery, arrowheads, spearpoints, etc.

LAUREN ROGERS LIBRARY AND
  MUSEUM OF ART
P.O. Box 1108   LAUREL 39441
    Nell Davis, Curator

Primarily a basket collection, but contains
other objects with some weaving detail.
Small collection of Choctaw artifacts --
arrowheads, grinding stones, shards,
scrapers, sticks used in playing stickball;
several Karok items on display. Library
(236 volumes).

OLD SPANISH FORT AND MUSEUM
200 Fort St.   PASCAGOULA 39567
    Mrs. Henry Gautier, President,
    Jackson County Historical Society

Museum features Indian artifacts, tools,
and implements.

OLD COURT HOUSE MUSEUM
Cherry, Jackson, Grove and Monroe Sts.
                  VICKSBURG 39180
    Mrs. Eva W. Davis, Director

Museum features Indian historical items.

MISSOURI

BATES COUNTY HISTORICAL SOCIETY
  MUSEUM
620 W. Harrison   BUTLER 64730
    Wilbur Hasting, President

Collection includes Indian relics, weapons,
books.

CLARKSVILLE MUSEUM
State Highway 79   CLARKSVILLE 63336

Collection features early American historical items, including Indian artifacts.

WASHINGTON STATE PARK MUSEUM
R.R. 2   DE SOTO 63020
    Jasper F. Johnson, Superintendent
    Kenneth G. Middleton, Archaeologist

Collection includes stone petroglyphs of the
Middle Mississippi Indians; Indian artifacts.

DANIEL BOONE HOME
Highway F   DEFIANCE 63341
    Shelby H. Curlee, Director

Museum features Indian artifacts, implements. Historic house designed by Daniel
Boone (1803-1810).

MISSOURI STATE MUSEUM
State Capitol Bldg.
                  JEFFERSON CITY 65101
    Donald M. Johnson, Director

Collections (titled): Musquakie Ceremonial
Material; Stone Artifacts of Missouri; Mis-
souri Pottery; Pottery Making; "Feat of
Clay"; Kemna Cave Artifacts; Indian Burial;
White River Survey; Archaic Indians.

KANSAS CITY MUSEUM OF HISTORY
  AND SCIENCE
3218 Gladstone Blvd.
                  KANSAS CITY 64123
    Wilber E. Phillips, Director

Exhibits include historic and prehistoric
Indian material.

WILLIAM ROCKHILL NELSON GALLERY
  OF ART AND MARY ATKINS MUSEUM
  OF FINE ART
4525 Oak St.   KANSAS CITY

Native arts of the Americas, with particular concentration on the Southwest, Mesoamerica and South America. Publications.

NORTH EAST MISSOURI STATE
  TEACHERS COLLEGE,
  E. M. VIOLETTE MUSEUM
                              KIRKSVILLE 63501

Contains Indian relics, costumes, archives.

LYMAN CENTER FOR ARCHAEOLOGICAL
  RESEARCH
University of Missouri
Van Meter State Park   MIAMI 65344
  Robert T. Bray, Director

Contains twenty-three exhibits, including
extensive research and study collections of
Oneota (protohistoric Missouri Indian tribe);
sizable collections of Woodland and Archaic
artifacts; collections and typescripts of
historic archaeological investigations.

CITY ART MUSEUM
Forest Park   ST. LOUIS 63105
  Charles Buckley, Director

Pottery, artifacts, carvings, basketry,
clothing of the following cultures: Pueblo,
Pueblo Mimbres, Plains, West Coast,
Mound Builder.

MISSOURI HISTORICAL SOCIETY -
  MUSEUM
Jefferson Memorial Bldg.
                          ST. LOUIS 63112
  George R. Brooks, Director

Museum features items of local historical
interest. Library.

OLD JAIL MUSEUM AND OLD FELKER
  HOUSE
                             VIENNA 65582
  Mrs. Carl A. Baldwin, Curator

Museum exhibits Indian and Civil War
relics.

WESTON HISTORICAL MUSEUM
Main at Spring St.   WESTON 64098
  Dr. R. J. Felling, Curator

Collection includes Indian and pioneer
relics.

MONTANA

YELLOWSTONE MUSEUM
P.O. Box 128   BILLINGS
  Mr. and Mrs. H. J. Cook, Curators

Museum contains historical items of Indian
and pioneer culture.

McGILL MUSEUM
Montana State University
                           BOZEMAN 59715
  Merrill G. Burlingame, Curator

Displays include Plains Indian Exhibit;
Blackfeet costume materials; exhibits of
Indian artifacts, dolls, trader-trapper ma-
terials, beadwork, peyote ceremony ma-
terials, cactus buttons, Indian skeleton;
Southwest Indian articles.

MUSEUM OF NATURAL HISTORY
102 1/2 S. Park   BROADUS 59317
  R. D. McCurdy, Curator

Collections of stone artifacts, beadwork,
Sioux arrowheads, Nez Perce baskets,
weapons and tools.

MUSEUM OF THE PLAINS INDIAN
                         BROWNING 59417
  Dr. Claude E. Schaeffer, Curator

Exhibits include collections in Indian anthropology, archaeology, ethnology; native arts
and crafts -- ceremonial costumes, beadwork; Blackfeet Agency records. Publications.

CUSTER BATTLEFIELD NATIONAL
  MONUMENT - MUSEUM
P.O. Box 416   CROW AGENCY 59022
  Andrew M. Loveless, Historian

Collections include historical documents
authored by or associated with George A.
Custer, his wife, Elizabeth B. Custer, the
Battle of the Little Big Horn, and other
events and persons associated with the Indian
Wars on the Northern Plains (1865-1891).
Related military and ethnographic speci-
mens, including items associated with the
Sioux, Crow, and Northern Cheyenne
Tribes.

FRONTIER GATEWAY MUSEUM
    ASSOCIATION
P.O. Box 1181   GLENDIVE 59330
    James L. Carter, President

Indian artifacts, archaeological and historic, of the Montana and North Dakota
region.

BITTER ROOT VALLEY HISTORICAL
    MUSEUM
Chamber of Commerce and Library
                        HAMILTON 59840
    Mrs. Harry Twogood, Director

Exhibits include pictures dealing with Flathead Indian culture. Rare book collection.

MONTANA HISTORICAL SOCIETY -
    MUSEUM
Roberts at 6th Ave.   HELENA 59601
    Michael S. Kennedy, Director

Frontier Museum features chronological
story of Montana's heritage through series
of dioramas. Pioneer Museum contains
Johns Gun Collection and other pioneer and
Indian tools, household items, clothing,
dolls, rare Indian artifacts (Coburn Collection), mounted remains of Big Medicine,
the only white buffalo. Library. Publications.

MONTANA STATE UNIVERSITY MUSEUM
Fine Arts Bldg.   MISSOULA 59801
    Dr. Robert T. Turner, Director

Displays feature Indian art and artifacts
of Montana; American frontier items.

VIRGINIA CITY - MADISON COUNTY
    HISTORICAL MUSEUM
                        VIRGINIA CITY 59755

Collection includes local Indian artifacts.

NEBRASKA

COOK MUSEUM OF NATURAL HISTORY
Agate Springs Ranch
                        AGATE 69330
    Harold J. Cook, Director

Paleontology museum includes Plains Indian collection.

ARTHUR COUNTY HISTORICAL SOCIETY -
    MUSEUM
Court House Square
                        ARTHUR 69121
    Charles Gessford, Chief
        Executive Officer

Museum in original Court House building
houses artifacts of Arthur County. Presentation of pageants reenacting pioneer life,
etc.

MUSEUM OF THE FUR TRADE
Star Route 2
Box 12   CHADRON 69337
    Charles E. Hanson, Jr., Director

Articles of Plains and Woodland cultures -
tools, weapons, bead and quill work, pipes,
games, clothing, horse equipment, rawhide
work, baskets, and utensils. Collection of
Indian trade goods, weapons, beads, blankets, jewelry, ammunition, textiles, tobacco. Outdoor Indian garden of crops obtained from Mandan, Dakota, Assiniboine,
Omaha and Seneca Indians. Restored Indian
trading post and warehouse (1846).

JEFFERSON COUNTY MUSEUM
Box 323
612 4th St.   FAIRBURY 68352
    Floyd Catlin, Director

Local artifacts of the Pawnee, Sioux and
Otoe Indians.

OREGON TRAIL MUSEUM
Scotts Bluff National Monument
Box 427   GERING 69341
    Earl R. Harris, Executive
        Secretary

Exhibits on Sioux Indians, prehistoric Indians of western Nebraska and eastern
Wyoming. Sioux Indian dances in summer.

HASTINGS MUSEUM, HOUSE OF
    YESTERDAY
1330 N. Burlington Ave.
                        HASTINGS 68901
    W. E. Eigsti, Director

Exhibits include Indian artifacts, clothing,
dolls, equipment, war relics, Sioux Indian
habitat group. Indian film. Publications.

FORT KEARNEY MUSEUM
Route 4
Box 84   KEARNEY 68847
    Merl L. Johnson, Curator

Indian art from the Rosebud Indian Reservation.

NEBRASKA STATE HISTORICAL SOCIETY
1500 R. St.   LINCOLN 68508
    Marvin F. Kivett, Museum Director

Museum features collections in art, anthropology, archaeology, costumes, ethnology, artifacts of Indians of Nebraska and the Central Plains.

UNION PACIFIC HISTORICAL MUSEUM
15th and Dodge Sts.   OMAHA 68102
    Mrs. Irene Authier Keeffe, Director

Transportation museum includes Indian artifacts.

CASS COUNTY HISTORICAL MUSEUM
644 Main St.   PLATTSMOUTH 68048
    Mrs. V. W. Perry, President

Exhibits feature Plains Indian material, pioneer relics.

CHERRY COUNTY HISTORICAL SOCIETY,
    INC. - MUSEUM
S. Main St.
P.O. Drawer 152
                               VALENTINE 69201
    Mrs. Minnie Lewis, Secretary

Museum features Indian art and artifacts. Library.

DAUGHTERS OF AMERICAN
    REVOLUTION MUSEUM
222 W. 10th St.   YORK
    Mrs. Anna Bemis Palmer, Director

Displays include historical items and Indian artifacts.

NEVADA

NEVADA STATE MUSEUM
                           CARSON CITY 89701
    J. W. Calhoun, Director

Study collections of Nevada Indian artifacts.

NEVADA HISTORICAL SOCIETY -
    MUSEUM
P.O. Box 1129   RENO 89504
    Clara S. Beatty, President

Collections include primitive art, Indian basketry; natural history exhibits.

NEW HAMPSHIRE

NEW HAMPSHIRE ANTIQUARIAN
    SOCIETY - MUSEUM
c/o Miss Rachel Johnson, Curator
Route 1   CONCORD 03301
    Miss Mildred Raymond, President

Museum features pottery, stone implements, quill and beadwork, pipes, war clubs. Open by appointment.

ANNE E. WOODMAN INSTITUTE
182-192 Central Ave.   DOVER 03820
    Harold G. Merrill, Curator

Collections include Indian artifacts and local historical items.

DARTMOUTH COLLEGE MUSEUM
East Wheelock Street   HANOVER 03755
    Professor Elmer Harp, Jr., Director

General synoptic collections and exhibits covering the major culture areas of the world. Small research collections available for American Southwest, Plains area, New World Arctic.

HISTORICAL SOCIETY OF CHESHIRE
    COUNTY
Keene Public Library
79 West St.   KEENE 03431
    Mrs. Marjorie C. Smith, President
    John C. Perry, Custodian

Museum features historic Indian items from Cheshire County.

THE LIBBY MUSEUM
Route 109   WOLFEBORO 03894
    William B. Carpenter, Director

Collection includes Indian relics.

NEW JERSEY

MORRIS JUNIOR MUSEUM
Normandy Heights and Columbia Rd.
P.O. Box 125   CONVENT 07961
    Chester H. Newkirk, Director

Collection of Indian material of the Southeast, including arrow and spear points.

THE HUNTERDON COUNTY HISTORICAL
    SOCIETY - MUSEUM
1 Maple Ave.   FLEMINGTON 08822
    Mrs. Ray C. Wilson, Librarian

Exhibits include Indian relics, furnishings.
Library. Publications.

MONMOUTH COUNTY HISTORICAL
    ASSOCIATION - MUSEUM
70 Court St.   FREEHOLD 07728
    Edward H. Feltus, III, Director

Museum contains Colonial artifacts. Junior
Museum features Indian relics and war
items. Library. Publications.

CUMBERLAND COUNTY HISTORICAL
    SOCIETY - MUSEUM
Main St.   GREENWICH 08323
    Francis A. Stanger, Jr., President

Exhibits include Indian artifacts, pioneer
implements, war items. Historic house.
Library. Publications.

THE MONTCLAIR ART MUSEUM
3 S. Mountain Ave.
                        MONTCLAIR 07042
    Kathryn E. Gamble, Director

Exhibits feature costumes, jewelry, and
artifacts of Eastern Woodlands, Desert
Pueblo, Navajo, Apache, Plains, California and Northwest Indians, and Eskimos.
Children's program. Library. Gift shop.

THE NEWARK MUSEUM
43-49 Washington St.
                          NEWARK 08901
    Katherine Coffey, Director
    Edward Hunter Ross, Curator of
    Ethnological Collections

Indian art and artifacts representative of
the products of tribes in various parts of
the country. Exhibits include paintings on
skin, totem poles, blankets, Hopi Kachina
dolls, pottery, silverwork, and basketry.
Publications.

VON STEUBEN HOUSE
BERGEN COUNTY HISTORICAL SOCIETY
            NORTH HACKENSACK 07661
    Mrs. Louise Barnett, Director

Indian artifacts of Hackensack, including dugout, wampum, tools, arrowheads,
and baskets.

PASCACK HISTORICAL SOCIETY -
    MUSEUM
19 Ridge Ave.   PARK RIDGE 07656
    Mrs. Jean Massimo and
    Howard I. Durie, Curators

Exhibits feature items of local historical
significance, including wampum making
machine. Historic building. Library. Publications.

PATERSON MUSEUM
268 Summer St.   PATERSON 07501
    Philip J. Del Vecchio, Director

Contains anthropological and archaeological
exhibits; Indian artifacts.

HISTORICAL SOCIETY OF PLAINFIELD
    AND NORTH PLAINFIELD - MUSEUM
602 W. Front St.   PLAINFIELD 07060
    Paul J. Westergard, President

Museum exhibits Indian and military items
and manuscripts. Historic house. Library.

PARAMUS HISTORICAL AND PRESERVA-
TION SOCIETY - MUSEUM
650 E. Glen Ave.   RIDGEWOOD
    Mrs. William M. Murray,
        Museum Director

Exhibits feature Indian and pioneer relics.
Historic house. Publications.

SOMERS MANSION
Shore Rd.   SOMERS POINT 08244
    Mrs. Marjorie Hamell, Caretaker

Atlantic County Historical Society Museum
features Indian artifacts, genealogical records.

SPACE FARMS
Beemerville Rd.   SUSSEX 07461
    Ralph Space (Director)

Indian artifacts of Tennessee, Virginia, and
New Jersey.

NEW JERSEY STATE MUSEUM
W. State St.   TRENTON 08625
    Dr. Kenneth Prescott, Director

Archaeological and ethnological collections.

NEW MEXICO

MUSEUM OF ANTHROPOLOGY
University of New Mexico
University and Roma N.E.
                    ALBUQUERQUE 87106
    Frank C. Hibben, Director

Archaeological and ethnological exhibits.

AZTEC RUINS NATIONAL MONUMENT
    MUSEUM
Route 1
Box 101   AZTEC 87410
    Gerald L. Wood, Park Archaeologist

Contained are archaeological collections
from excavations of area sites and from
sites in the Lower San Juan Basin.

CORONADO STATE MONUMENT MUSEUM
P.O. Box 95   BERNALILLO 87004
    J. P. Blum, Director

Collections consist primarily of material
recovered from site excavations.

CHACO CANYON NATIONAL MONUMENT
    MUSEUM
Box 156   BLOOMFIELD 87413
    Mr. Lynn A. Robbins, Archeologist

Visitor Center Museum features twenty-six
exhibits on prehistoric Pueblo Indians and
Navajo people, early history of Chaco
Canyon, and archaeological research techniques.

CARLSBAD MUNICIPAL MUSEUM
Public Library
Halagueno Park   CARLSBAD 88220
    Mrs. E. E. Jameson, Curator

Natural science exhibits include Indian artifacts.

GALLUP MUSEUM OF INDIAN ARTS AND
    CRAFTS
103 W. 66 Ave.   GALLUP 87301
    Octavia Fellini, Chairman

Contains Indian arts and crafts items.

WOODARD'S INDIAN ARTS
224 W. Coal Ave.   GALLUP 87301
    M. L. Woodard, Manager

Museum houses original Indian paintings,
including work by Beatien Yazz, Andy
Tsinajinnie, etc.; Woodard Collection of
Indian arts and crafts featuring a silver but-
ton display. Kachina dolls, carvings, textiles, silver and ancient objects. Arts and
crafts shop.

BANDELIER NATIONAL MONUMENT
    MUSEUM
                    LOS ALAMOS 87544

Small representative collection of Pueblo
cultural material from the immediate area,
dating from A.D. 1200 to A.D. 1600.

LONGHORN RANCH AND MUSEUM OF
  THE OLD WEST
Highway 66   MORIARTY 87035
  B. B. Hickman, Manager

Collection includes Indian and pioneer relics
and implements.

GRAN QUIVARA NATIONAL MONUMENT
  MUSEUM
Route 1   MOUNTAINAIR 87036

Small museum contains characteristic pottery types, small amounts of bone, stone
and shell artifacts.

PALEO-INDIAN INSTITUTE OF EASTERN
  NEW MEXICO UNIVERSITY
                          PORTALES 88130
  Dr. George A. Agogino, Director

Exhibits illustrating the life of the archaic
and modern Indian. Library.

ROSWELL MUSEUM AND ART CENTER
11th and Main Sts.   ROSWELL 88201
  Eugene A. Smith, Director

Art museum features collection of pre-
Columbian material.

MUSEUM OF NAVAJO CEREMONIAL ART
Camino Lejo, off Old Pecos Rd.
P.O. Box 445   SANTA FE 87501

Collections include graphic reproductions;
Navajo ceremonial recordings; religious
artifacts; Navajo sandpaintings; archives of
unpublished material. Publications.

MUSEUM OF NEW MEXICO, FINE ARTS
  MUSEUM
127 E. Palace Ave.
P.O. Box 1727
                          SANTA FE 87501

Contains Indian Arts Fund collection of pottery, jewelry, costumes; art of the Southwest.

MUSEUM OF NEW MEXICO
P.O. Box 2087   SANTA FE 87501
  Dr. Delmar M. Kolb, Director
  Dr. Alfred E. Dittert, Jr.,
    Curator (Research)
  Mr. Bruce Ellis, Curator
    (Collections)
  Mr. Joseph Haydock, Curator
    (Exhibitions)

Exhibitions housed in Palace of the Governor; Hall of the Modern Indian; Museum of
International Folk Art; Fine Arts Museum.
Archaeology and ethnology collections including Southwestern silverwork, rugs, and
ceramics; folk art; paintings by Southwestern artists; weapons, musical instruments,
representations of Huichol, Naga, and Ji-
varo materials; ethnobotany collections;
Southwest history collections. Library.

THE SCHOOL OF AMERICAN RESEARCH
116 Lincoln Ave.
P.O. Box 1554   SANTA FE 87501
  Edward M. Weyer, Jr., Director
  Eugene McCluney, Staff Archaeologist

Anthropology institution houses archaeology
and ethnology collections related to Southwest, Central and South America; art and
ethnographic material. Anthropological and
archaeological research. Publications.

GRANT COUNTY MUSEUM
                          SILVER CITY 88061
  O. T. Snodgrass, Director

Contains archaeological collections, including pottery.

KIT CARSON HOME AND MUSEUM
P.O. Box 398   TAOS 87571
  Jack K. Boyer, Director

Exhibits and collections pertaining to Indians
of the Taos area, from 3000 B.C. to the
present. Library (1,225 volumes, including
books, pamphlets, periodicals).

THE HARWOOD FOUNDATION
University of New Mexico
Ledoux St.   TAOS 87571
  Toni Tarleton, Director

Indian artifacts, pertaining to the Sioux,
Zuni, Taos, Apache, Cheyenne, Ute, and
Hopi tribes. Library (250 Indian-related
volumes).

NEW YORK

NEW YORK STATE MUSEUM AND SCIENCE SERVICE
31 Washington Ave.   ALBANY 12210
    Charles E. Gillette, Associate
        Curator (Archaeology)

Morgan Collection is mid-19th-century Seneca ethnographic material. The Beauchamp Collection consists of several pieces of Onondaga ethnographic material and approximately seventy-five handwritten notebooks of various sizes on ethnographic and archaeological subjects. The Parker Collection consists primarily of late 19th- and 20th-century Iroquois ethnological and archaeological materials. Also included are materials from field researches and a mask collection.

WALTER ELWOOD MUSEUM
5th Ward School   AMSTERDAM 12010
    Edmund J. Cotter, Director

Exhibits feature pioneer and Indian material.

ATTICA HISTORICAL SOCIETY - MUSEUM
Main St.   ATTICA 14011
    Marian Stevens, Director

Exhibits include Indian and pioneer articles. Reference library.

CAYUGA MUSEUM OF HISTORY AND ART
203 Genesee St.   AUBURN 13021
    Walter K. Long, Director

Collections relate to Civil War and Indian culture.

KATERI MUSEUM (NATIONAL SHRINE OF THE NORTH AMERICAN MARTYRS)
                    AURIESVILLE 12016
    Rev. William J. Schlaerth,
        S. J., Director

Site of martyrdom of Isaac Jogues and his companions by Mohawk Indians in 1642.

HOLLAND LAND OFFICE MUSEUM
131 W. Main St.   BATAVIA 14020
    Charlotte M. Read,
        Genesee County Historian

"Other Fires Were Here Before Ours" exhibit features display cases of artifacts -- implements, pottery, tools, arrowheads, etc.

BROOKLYN CHILDREN'S MUSEUM
185 Brooklyn Ave.   BROOKLYN 11213
    Michael Cohn, Curator of
        Anthropology

Collections include Plains Indian material, New York State archaeology, Southwestern material; teaching collections of Northwest Coast, Mesoamerica, and Eastern Woodland items. Research library contains 300 volumes on the American Indian.

BROOKLYN MUSEUM
188 Eastern Parkway
                    BROOKLYN 11238
    Thomas S. Buechner, Director
    Jane Powell Rosenthal, Curator
        of Primitive Art, New World
        Cultures

Exhibits include Eskimo masks, costumes, implements; Northwest Coast tools, pottery, totem poles, masks; Zuni dolls; Navaho basketry; North American Indian artifacts (Jarvis Collection), with emphasis on Southwest. Art Reference Library (1,000 volumes). Publications.

BUFFALO AND ERIE COUNTY HISTORICAL SOCIETY - MUSEUM
25 Nottingham Court
                    BUFFALO 14216
    Walter S. Dunn, Jr. (Director)

Museum features collections of eastern and western U.S. Indian artifacts. Library.

BUFFALO MUSEUM OF SCIENCE
Humboldt Park   BUFFALO 14211
    Fred T. Hall, Director
    Dr. Virginia L. Cummings,
        Curator of Anthropology

Paleontology and ethnology collections include local Indian relics.

BIG SPRINGS HISTORICAL SOCIETY
  MUSEUM
Main St.   CALEDONIA 14511
  Mrs. Ella K. McGinnis, Curator

Collection consists of arrowheads, pipes,
peacepipes, spoons, skeletal remains.

ONTARIO COUNTY HISTORICAL SOCIETY
  MUSEUM
55 N. Main St.   CANANDAIGUA
  Mrs. Ralph O. Stratton, Curator

Museum contains Indian relics and historic
documents. Library.

MUSEUM OF PIONEER AND INDIAN
  HISTORY
Letchworth State Park
                             CASTILE 14427

Pioneer and Indian exhibits are featured.

HISTORICAL SOCIETY OF THE TOWN OF
  CLARENCE - MUSEUM
6090 Goodrich Rd.
             CLARENCE CENTER 14032
  Mrs. Oneta M. Baker, Curator

Museum features Indian tools and other exhibits depicting Indian history in Clarence.
Local history programs. Child education
classes.

COOPERSTOWN INDIAN MUSEUM
1 Pioneer St.   COOPERSTOWN 13326
  Vivian M. Olson, Curator

Sixteen exhibits include: cultural display of
advance and development of New York State
Indians from 10,000 years ago through historic times; seven dioramas.

DURHAM CENTER MUSEUM, INC.
                  EAST DURHAM 12423
  Vernon Haskins, Curator

Indian and pioneer weapons and implements
are featured.

EAST HAMPTON HISTORICAL SOCIETY -
  MUSEUM
Main St.   EAST HAMPTON, L.I. 11937
  Nelson C. Osborne, President

Museum and historic building house pioneer
and Indian relics and implements. Publications.

NASSAU COUNTY HISTORICAL MUSEUM
Nassau County Park, Salisbury
                   EAST MEADOW 11554
  Edward J. Smits, Curator

Exhibits of Long Island Indian life and prehistoric development. Library (100 Indian-
related volumes).

THE MOHAWK-CAUGHNAWAGA MUSEUM
Route 5
Box 6, RD. 1   FONDA 12068
  Rev. Thomas Grassmann, Director

Contains artifacts of Mohawk Valley Indian
and colonial origin.

FORT ANN MUSEUM OF HISTORY
George St.   FORT ANN 12827
  Paul F. Crumley, Curator

Museum features Indian, colonial, and Revolutionary War artifacts and documents;
reconstructed fort.

MONTGOMERY COUNTY HISTORICAL
  SOCIETY
                      FORT JOHNSON 12070
  Mrs. Richard Evans, Chairman

Museum contains Indian relics and artifacts
especially of Mohawk Valley.   Old Fort
Johnson. Publications.

PROUTY-CHEW MUSEUM
543 S. Main St.   GENEVA 14456
  Miss Laura Merritt, Director

Geneva Historical Society museum features
Indian relics of local origin.

FORT WILLIAM HENRY RESTORATION
  AND MUSEUM
Canada St.   LAKE GEORGE 12845
  Robert Flacke, Director
  James A. Magee, Curator

Reconstruction of 18th century Iroquois village. Museum exhibits include military relics of local origin; original maps and documents pertaining to French and Indian War; archaeological material of northern New York and Lake George-Lake Champlain area.

NIAGARA COUNTY HISTORICAL SOCIETY,
  INC. - MUSEUM
215 Niagara St.
(118 Cottage St.)   LOCKPORT 14094
  Charles Boyer, Curator

Museum features collections pertaining to local area and Iroquois Indian culture. Publications.

OLD MUSEUM VILLAGE OF SMITH'S
  COVE
R.D. 3   MONROE 10950
  Leland A. Smith, President
  Jarold D. Talbot, Director

Collection includes Indian artifacts of the mid-Hudson region. Reconstruction of 19th-century town.

PLUME INDIAN MUSEUM
Route 208   MONROE 10950
  James A. Luongo, President

Ceremonial costumes, artifacts and relics, particularly of the Pueblo, Navaho, Iroquois and Sioux Indians. Indian Trading Post.

AMERICAN MUSEUM OF NATURAL
  HISTORY
Central Park West at 79th St.
                        NEW YORK 10024
  Dr. James A. Oliver, Director
  Dr. Harry L. Shapiro, Chairman,
    Anthropology

Eskimo exhibits depict Central, Western and Greenland Eskimo culture, historic and prehistoric: weaponry, ceremonial artifacts, pottery, basketry, costume, masks, model dwellings, kayak. Indians of the Northwest Coast exhibit features Northwest Coast and Pacific Indian sculpture; totems; Haida canoe, 64' x 8'; art and artifacts of the Coast Salish, Nootka, Haida, Tsimshian, Thompson, Bella Coola, Tlingit, Kwakiutl: shamanistic regalia and ceremonial objects; weaving; basketry; pottery; tools and implements; carvings in wood, stone, and ivory; masks; costume; household items; weapons; pipes; musical instruments. (Southwest and Plains Indian exhibit halls are temporarily closed.) Library and reading room. Natural Science Center. Planetarium. Child and Adult education programs. Audio-visual aids program. *Publications: Natural History Magazine;* Curator.

MUSEUM OF THE AMERICAN INDIAN
Heye Foundation
Broadway at 155th St.
                        NEW YORK 10032
  Dr. Frederick J. Dockstader,
    Director

"To develop a better understanding of the Indian by providing a synopsis of the diverse material cultures of tribes throughout the Western Hemisphere." Eastern and midwestern ethnological collections include costumes, basketry, bead and quill work, wood carving, utensils, weapons, and ritual objects. North American archaeological exhibitions feature specimens from the Spiro Mound, Southeastern pottery, stone artifacts, tools and weapons. Library (50,000 volumes). Photographic archives. Museum Shop. Publications.

MUSEUM OF PRIMITIVE ART
15 W. 54th St.   NEW YORK 10019
  Dr. Robert Goldwater, Chairman

Archaeology and ethnology collections include pre-Columbian American sculpture, weapons, implements, masks, jewelry, pottery.

RIVERSIDE MUSEUM
310 Riverside Drive   NEW YORK 10025
  Peter Farb, Curator of
    American Indian Culture

American Indian watercolors, pottery and baskets.

TRAPHAGEN SCHOOL OF FASHION,
   MUSEUM COLLECTION
1680 Broadway   NEW YORK 10019
   Mrs. Lina P. Manetto, Principal
   Mrs. George Lamplighter,
      Curator

Exhibits include American Indian handicrafts and costumes.

NORTH COLLINS HISTORICAL SOCIETY -
   MUSEUM
North Collins Memorial Library
Center St.   NORTH COLLINS 14111
   Ethelyn Weller, President

Museum features pioneer and Indian items.

SIX NATIONS INDIAN MUSEUM
Roakdale Rd.   ONCHIOTA 12968
   Ray Fadden, Curator

Archaeological and historic collections with emphasis on Six Nations Indians: Iroquois implements, beadwork, costumes; exhibits depicting Indian way of life. Publications.

MADISON COUNTY HISTORICAL
   SOCIETY - MUSEUM
435 Main St.   ONEIDA 13421
   Albert Smoth, President

Exhibits include genealogical records, Indian relics, pioneer and war items. Library. Publications.

UPPER SUSQUEHANNA HISTORICAL
   MUSEUM
11 Ford Ave.   ONEONTA 13820
   Mrs. Lela M. Gibbs, Curator

Indian artifacts. Book collection.

THE YAGER MUSEUM
Hartwick College
19 Ford Ave.   ONEONTA 13820
   Dr. H. Claude Hardy, Curator

Upper Susquehanna Collection of Indian tools and artifacts of the Stone Age Culture -- arrowheads, Knives, mortars, pottery, ornaments. Library (600 volumes).

OYSTERPONDS HISTORICAL
   SOCIETY, INC. - MUSEUM
Village Lane   ORIENT, L.I. 11957
   Mrs. John S. Gilbert,
      Curator-Director

Society maintains Village House (1790) and museum featuring Indian artifacts, war items. Library. Preservation of Indian encampment.

OSSINING HISTORICAL SOCIETY MUSEUM
83 Croton Ave.   OSSINING 10562
   Greta A. Cornell, Director

Collections include local Indian artifacts (projectile points); Plains Indian beadwork (Dr. George J. Fisher Collection). Book collection.

TIOGA COUNTY HISTORICAL SOCIETY
   MUSEUM
110-112 Front St.   OWEGO 13827
   William Lay, Jr., Curator

Collections of local artifacts -- arrowheads, axes, spears, implements, beads, wampum, pipes and tools. Book collection.

SUFFOLK COUNTY HISTORICAL
   SOCIETY - MUSEUM
W. Main St.   RIVERHEAD, L.I. 11901
   Mrs. Marian G. Terry, Custodian

Museum contains Indian artifacts and historic documents. Library.

ROCHESTER MUSEUM OF ARTS AND
   SCIENCES
657 East Ave.   ROCHESTER 14607
   W. Stephen Thomas, Director
   Charles F. Hayes III, Curator of
      Anthropology

Indian material related to archaeology, ethnology and physical anthropology with emphasis on Iroquois and Algonkian cultures. Collections include dioramas; Indian art and artifacts: wood cravings, masks, costumes, utensils, weapons, game equipment; paintings by Ernest Smith. Library. Publications.

FORT STANWIX MUSEUM
117 E. Dominick St.   ROME 13440
    John W. McMonagle, Director

Skeletal and artifact remains of Iroquois
tribe of the 17th century. Some local prehistoric relics.

THE SARATOGA HISTORICAL SOCIETY
    AND THE WALWORTH MEMORIAL
    MUSEUM
11 Clinton St.
Congress Park, Casino
            SARATOGA SPRINGS 12866
    Mrs. Walter A. Britten, Curator

Mohawk and other local artifacts.

SCHENECTADY COUNTY HISTORICAL
    SOCIETY - MUSEUM
32 Washington Ave.
                SCHENECTADY 12305
    H.A. McConville, Curator

Museum contains Algonquian and Mohawk
material.

THE OLD STONE FORT MUSEUM
Main St.   SCHOHARIE 12157
    Myron Vroman, Director

Historic 18th-century building and museum
housing local Indian artifacts and genealogical records.

SENECA FALLS HISTORICAL SOCIETY -
    MUSEUM
55 Cayuga St.   SENECA FALLS 13148
    Mrs. Virginia D. Martin, Director

Museum houses archives; Indian relics;
local items. Library.

SOUTHAMPTON HISTORICAL MUSEUM
Meeting House Lane
P.O. Box 1334
            SOUTHAMPTON, L.I. 11968
    Henry Howell, President
    Mrs. John S. Potter, Curator

Collections include Indian relics of the Montauk and Shinnecock tribes.

CONCORD HISTORICAL SOCIETY
Main St.   SPRINGVILLE 14141
    Mrs. Robert Engel, President

Pop Warner Museum features Indian items.

ONONDAGA HISTORICAL ASSOCIATION -
    MUSEUM
311 Montgomery St.   SYRACUSE 13202
    Richard N. Wright, President

Museum contains Iroquois Indian material
and items of local historical significance.

FORT MOUNT HOPE
Burgoyne Rd.   TICONDEROGA 12883
    Carroll V. Lonergan, Director

Historical items of French and Indian War
origin are featured.

WARWICK VALLEY MUSEUM
Warwick Historical Society
Main St.   WARWICK 10990
    Roy Vail, President and Curator

Indian relics including stone artifacts, bead
and quill work, headdresses, and dolls.

WATERLOO LIBRARY AND HISTORICAL
    SOCIETY - MUSEUM
31 E. Williams St.   WATERLOO 13765
    John S. Genung, Curator

Museum contains Indian and local material.
Library.

JEFFERSON COUNTY HISTORICAL
    SOCIETY - MUSEUM
228 Washington St.   WATERTOWN 13603
    J. Reese Price, Curator

Exhibits feature Indian relics and pioneer
tools and implements. Library.

CHAUTAUQUA COUNTY HISTORICAL
    SOCIETY - MUSEUM
Main St.   WESTFIELD 14787
    R.A. Nixon, Treasurer,
      House Manager
    Marion Baldwin, Librarian

Museum features Indian, Military and archaeological material. Publications.

MIDDLEBURY HISTORICAL SOCIETY -
  MUSEUM
39 Academy St.   WYOMING
  Mark Chamberlain, President

Exhibits include military, pioneer and Indian
artifacts; geological specimens; costumes.
Library.

NORTH CAROLINA

PARK NATURAL HISTORY MUSEUM
Morrow Mountain State Park
Route 2   ALBEMARLE 28001
  Cedric P. Squires,
    Park Superintendent

Displays feature Indian weapons, tools, and
implements of the major civilizations of the
area from prehistoric times to the settlement by the white man.

MUSEUM OF THE AMERICAN INDIAN
Blowing Rock Rd.
P.O. Box 83-B   BOONE 28607
  Ruth Myers Honeycutt, Director and
    Owner

Collections feature Indian handicrafts and
artifacts: bead and quill work; weapons and
ceremonial items.

MUSEUM OF THE CHEROKEE INDIAN
P.O. Box 398   CHEROKEE 28719

Cherokee Indian artifacts and relics.

GASTON MUSEUM OF NATURAL
  HISTORY, INC.
1300 Kendrick Dr.
P.O. Box 953   GASTONIA 28052
  R. N. Schiele, Director

Indian relics included in natural history collection.

GREENSBORO HISTORICAL MUSEUM
220 Church St.   GREENSBORO 27401
  William J. Moore, Director

Exhibits illustrating the life of Indians of
Guilford County through related prehistoric
artifacts: hunting, ceremonial and religious, agricultural.

TOWN CREEK INDIAN MOUND MUSEUM
R.F.D. 3   MOUNT GILEAD 27306

Museum contains archaeological and replica
exhibits depicting ceremonial customs and
everyday life of a Muskogean group, circa
1550-1650.

ROWAN MUSEUM, INC.
114 S. Jackson St.
(202 S. Fulton St.)   SALISBURY 28144
  Mrs. Gettys Guille, Director

Historic house and museum featuring Indian
artifacts of Rowan County.

NORTH DAKOTA

CASS COUNTY HISTORICAL SOCIETY
  MUSEUM
North Dakota State University
Minard Hall   FARGO 58103
  Gertrude E. Hoag, Director

Collection includes Indian artifacts.

FORT LINCOLN STATE PARK MUSEUM
                        MANDAN 58554
  James R. Kittle, Director

Collection of Indian arrowheads, agricultural tools, weapons, models of Indian life
and culture.

INDIAN MUSEUM
Fort Berthold Reservation
                      NEW TOWN 58763

Features Indian artifacts.

GALE MUSEUM
300 Viking Dr.
                    VALLEY CITY 58072
  Vernon T. Gale, Director

Indian relics, tools, implements, weapons
and coins. Library (1,000 volumes).

OHIO

THE AKRON ART INSTITUTE
69 East Market St.   AKRON 44308
    William E. Begger, Director

American Indian art (Dr. Edgar B. Foltz
Collection); Indian artifacts; kachinas, jewelry, musical instruments, blankets, beadwork, basketry, pottery.

MERCER COUNTY HISTORICAL
    SOCIETY, INC. - MUSEUM
126 S. Main St.
P.O. Box 333   CELINA 45822
    Judge Carlton C. Reiser,
        President

Collection includes Indian, local, medical
and military items; archives. Publications.

CINCINNATI ART MUSEUM
Eden Park   CINCINNATI 45202
    Philip R. Adams, Director

Archaeological and ethnological specimens.
Archaeological -- principally Mound Builder. Adena, Hopewell, Fort Ancient cultures from Ohio; stone, bone, metal, shell,
pottery from Tennessee, Arkansas. Casas
Grandes pottery. Ethnological -- principally Plains and Northwest Coast: baskets,
pottery, blankets, clothing and ornaments,
musical instruments, weapons.

JOHNSON-HUMRICK HOUSE MEMORIAL
    MUSEUM
Sycamore St. at 3rd
                    COSHOCTON 43812
    Mrs. Mary M. Shaw,
    Mrs. Beatrice W. Berbyshire,
        Co-Directors

Collections feature pottery, basketry, carving, artifacts and arts and crafts items of
the Eskimo Haida, Rio Grande area, Mound
Builder and Navajo Indians.

FINDLAY COLLEGE MUSEUM
Grose Hall
126 College St.
                    FINDLAY 45840

Contains early American and Indian relics.

FORT RECOVERY HISTORICAL
    SOCIETY, INC. - MUSEUM
Old Fort St.   FORT RECOVERY 45846

Museum features Indian arrowheads, hammerstones, grooved axes, stone and shell
gorget; relics from the Indian Wars (1791-
1794) battleground, in the vicinity.

FOSTORIA MUSEUM
Tiffin and Woods Sts.
                    FOSTORIA 44830
    Lyman Carr, Director

Indian relics of the Plains and Western tribes
and Alaska; carvings, weapons, tools, implements, artifacts.

RUTHERFORD B. HAYES LIBRARY
    AND MUSEUM
1337 Hayes Ave.   FREMONT 43420
    Watt P. Marchman, Director

Collection features approximately 1,500
books and pamphlets; 500 items of exhibition: "study collection includes wide range
of American Indian history; the exhibits and
exhibit material are largely of the Plains
Indians, the Sioux, and some Pueblo; a collection of prehistoric Ohio Indian artifacts."

DARKE COUNTY HISTORICAL SOCIETY
    AND GARST MUSEUM
205 N. Broadway
(223 W. 3rd St.)   GREENVILLE 45331
    J. Lendall Williams, Director and
        President
    Mrs. Gertrude Holzapfel, Curator

Museum contains Indian relics of local historical origin, including Gen. Harmar St.
Clair and Anthony Wayne Collection relating
to Indian wars.

ALLEN COUNTY MUSEUM
Allen County Historical Society
620 West Market St.   LIMA 45801
    Joseph Dunlap, Director

Exhibits pertaining to history of Allen
County, including skeletons and artifacts
from Henry Boose Site (Glacial Kame Culture), Allen County, Ohio.

MEDINA COUNTY HISTORICAL
  SOCIETY - MUSEUM
233 E. Washington St.   MEDINA 44256
  Wade Belden, President

Museum exhibits include Indian and local artifacts.

LICKING COUNTY HISTORICAL
  SOCIETY - MUSEUM
6th St. Park
P.O. Box 535   NEWARK 43055
  Miss Laura Beggs, President

Historic house and museum feature Indian artifacts and 19th-century material. Publications.

OTTAWA COUNTY HISTORICAL MUSEUM
City Hall
2nd and Adams Sts.
              PORT CLINTON 43452
  Marion Cleary, Curator

Indian artifacts, guns, dolls, china, rocks.

PORTAGE COUNTY HISTORICAL
  SOCIETY - MUSEUM
6549 State Route 44
              RAVENNA 44266
  Cyrus Plough, President and
  Curator

Exhibits illustrate Indian life and lore. Publications.

CLARK COUNTY HISTORICAL
  SOCIETY - MUSEUM
Memorial Hall
300 W. Main St.   SPRINGFIELD 45504
  George W. Lohnes, Curator

Museum exhibits contain prehistoric Indian relics, pioneer items. Publications.

WYANDOT COUNTY HISTORICAL
  SOCIETY - MUSEUM
130 S. 7th St.
              UPPER SANDUSKY 43351
  Edward Beard, President

Museum contains local Indian artifacts and pioneer farm implements. Reconstruction of blacksmith shop.

VAN WERT COUNTY HISTORICAL
  SOCIETY MUSEUM
602 N. Washington St.
              VAN WERT 45891
  Jack H. Weaver, President

Collection includes Indian and Civil War items.

RIVER MUSEUM
1607 Buckeye Ave.
P.O. Box 244   WELLSVILLE 43968
  E. V. Pugh, Curator

Wellsville Historical Society Museum features Indian and Civil War items.

BUTLER INSTITUTE OF AMERICAN ART
524 Wick Ave.   YOUNGSTOWN 44502
  J. G. Butler, III, Director

Contains paintings and drawings related to American Indian culture.

OKLAHOMA

EAST CENTRAL STATE COLLEGE
  MUSEUM
College Library
(Station 1)   ADA 74820
  Dr. Robert A. Hasskarl, Director

Exhibits in archaeology and ethnology include Indian material.

ANADARKO CITY MUSEUM
Main and First Sts.   ANADARKO 73005
  Marguerite Carver, Curator

Indian crafts, relics, art, curios, and ceremonial costumes.

INDIAN CITY, U. S. A.
P. O. Box 356   ANADARKO 73005
  Charles F. Goodwin, President

Reconstruction of Plains Indians villages, directed by University of Oklahoma Anthropology Department. Tribal dances.

NATIONAL HALL OF FAME FOR
 FAMOUS AMERICAN INDIANS
P.O. Box 42   ANADARKO 73005
 Mrs. Logan Billingsley, Director

Exhibit features bronze busts of illustrious
American Indians.

SOUTHERN PLAINS INDIAN MUSEUM
 AND CRAFT CENTER
Box 447   ANADARKO 73005

"To create a better understanding of the
technical achievements and aesthetic value
of both the historic and contemporary arts
and crafts of Indian peoples of the area."
Exhibits feature hide painting, metal work,
beadwork, featherwork, carving, and dioramas. Quarterly publication: *Smoke Signals*. Craft Shop. Operated by the Indian
Arts and Crafts Board, U.S. Department of
the Interior.

TUCKER TOWER MUSEUM
Lake Murray State Park
                               ARDMORE 73401

Indian relics included in natural science
exhibits.

WOOLAROC MUSEUM
State Highway 123
                               BARTLESVILLE 74003
 Patrick Patterson, Director

Arts and crafts of the Oklahoma tribes;
Southwest pottery and basketry; Navaho
weaving.

BEAVER MUSEUM
Main St.
P.O. Box 279   BEAVER 73932
 Pearl and Louise Sharp,
   Owners and Curators

Exhibits feature historical artifacts and
documents of local origin.

BLACK KETTLE MUSEUM
                               CHEYENNE 73628
 Mrs. Eli Shotwell, Jr.,
   Manager and Curator

Contains Indian arts and crafts and pioneer
items.

THE LABORATORY OF HISTORY
Central State College
Evans Hall
400 E. Hurd St.
(519 Clegern Dr.)   EDMOND 73034
 L. Jeston Hampton, Director
 Roger Umphers, Curator

Collections include Indian and Civil War records and documents.

FORT SILL MUSEUM (U.S. ARMY
 ARTILLERY AND MISSILE CENTER
 MUSEUM)
346 Randolph Rd.   FORT SILL 73403
 Gillett Griswold, Director

Military exhibits feature relics of Indian
wars. Preserved 19th-century fort.

NO MAN'S LAND HISTORICAL MUSEUM
Sewell St.   GOODWELL 73939
 Nolan McWhirter, Director

Collections in anthropology, archaeology,
paleontology: Indian artifacts (William E.
Baker Collection).

MUSEUM OF THE GREAT PLAINS
Elmer Thomas Park
6th St. and Ferris Ave.
                               LAWTON 73502
 Marvin E. Tong, Jr., Director

Plains Indian history and prehistory. Research Library (6,700 volumes). Archives
(photographs).

BACONE INDIAN MUSEUM
Bacone College   MUSKOGEE 74401

Indian museum features arts and crafts
items.

MUSEUM OF ART
University of Oklahoma
Jacobson Hall   NORMAN 73069
 Sam Olkinetzky, Director

Exhibits include Indian art.

OKLAHOMA HISTORICAL SOCIETY -
MUSEUM
Lincoln Blvd.   NORMAN 73069

Second largest Indian museum in the world
features local historical artifacts. Library.

STOVAL MUSEUM OF SCIENCE AND
HISTORY
University of Oklahoma
Asp St.   NORMAN 73069
Dr. Marion T. Hall, Director

North American archaeological and ethnological specimens, depicting the development of Southern Plains, Southwest and
Northwest Coast Indian culture. Material
from the Spiro Mound excavations, Oklahoma. Museum Shop.

CREEK INDIAN COUNCIL HOUSE AND
MUSEUM
Town Square   OKMULGEE 74447
Theda Wammack, Director

Specimens of Oklahoma archaeology, frontier history, Creek Indian ethnology. Portraits and murals of Indian culture. Library
(books, papers and documents on Creek
culture). Capitol of the old Muskogee Nation.

OSAGE TRIBAL MUSEUM
Osage Agency   PAWHUSKA

Exhibition of artifacts, beadwork, clothing
and pictures related to Osage Indian culture.

PONCA CITY INDIAN MUSEUM
408 S. 7th St.   PONCA CITY 74601
Mrs. Paul T. Powell, Director

Artifacts, books, costume and craftwork of
the Kaw, Otoe-Missouria, Osage, Ponca,
and Tonkawa tribes.

SEQUOYAH MEMORIAL
                        SALLISAW 74955

Historic log cabin, former home of Sequoyah
(noted Cherokee historical figure).

POTTAWATOMIE COUNTY HISTORICAL
ASSOCIATION - MUSEUM
Highway 18
(1111 N. Broadway)   SHAWNEE 74801
Mrs. Clarence Robinson, President

Exhibits feature Indian artifacts, documents, local history. Maintains Shawnee
Mission Church, Shawnee, Okla.

CHEROKEE MUSEUM
Northeastern State College
                        TAHLEQUAH 74464
Gilbert Fites, Director

Cherokee Indian artifacts. Book collection.

YELLOW BULL MUSEUM
Northern Oklahoma Junior College
                        TONKAWA 74653
A.D. Buck, Director

Paleontology exhibits and Indian artifacts
included in collections.

PHILBROOK ART CENTER
2727 S. Rockford Rd.
                        TULSA 74114
Jeanne O. Snodgrass, Curator,
Indian Art

American Indian paintings; ceremonial
costumes and artifacts (Lawson Collection);
basketry and pottery (Clark Field Collection); archaeological material from the Spiro
Mound; murals. American Indian Artists
Annual Competition. Library.

THOMAS GILCREASE INSTITUTE OF
AMERICAN HISTORY AND ART
2401 W. Newton St.
P.O. Box 2419   TULSA 74127
Dean Krakel, Director

Collections include Indian crafts, archaeological material, and contemporary American Indian art.

OREGON

PACIFIC UNIVERSITY MUSEUM
                    FOREST GROVE 97116
    Mrs. Irving C. Story, Curator

Contains historical items of Northwest Indian and pioneer cultures.

HOOD RIVER COUNTY HISTORICAL
    MUSEUM
County Courthouse
State St. between 3rd and 4th
                    HOOD RIVER 97031
    Mrs. Forrest L. Moe, Director

Exhibits include local Indian artifacts: basketry, beadwork, arrowheads.

JACKSONVILLE MUSEUM
P.O. Box 85   JACKSONVILLE 97530
    Mary L. Hanley, Curator

Exhibits feature Takelma, Klamath and Northern California artifacts; Navajo blankets; Southwest pottery, baskets, tools, weapons, and implements. Book collection.

KLAMATH COUNTY MUSEUM
3rd and Klamath Sts.
                    KLAMATH FALLS 97601
    C. William Burk, Curator

Archaeological and historical material relating to the life of Northern Paiute, Klamath, Modoc and Shasta Indians. Historical records of the Modoc Indian War.

OREGON MUSEUM OF SCIENCE AND
    INDUSTRY
4015 S.W. Canyon Rd.
                    PORTLAND 97221
    Loren D. McKinley, Director

Exhibits in paleontology; anthropology, featuring Northwest Indian artifacts.

TILLAMOOK COUNTY PIONEER MUSEUM
2106 2nd St.   TILLAMOOK 97141
    Alexander Walker, Curator

Contains historical Indian relics, pioneer objects.

PENNSYLVANIA

LANE'S MUSEUM
R.F.D. 1
Waterstreet   ALEXANDRIA 16611
    S. Clyde Lane, Director-Owner

Historic mansion and museum featuring Indian relics.

LEHIGH COUNTY HISTORICAL SOCIETY -
    MUSEUM
Trout Hall
414 Walnut St.   ALLENTOWN 18102
    Melville J. Boyer, Executive Officer

Museum contains a fifty-piece Indian pipe collection; pottery; several thousand points, etc. Publications.

TIOGA POINT MUSEUM
724 S. Main St.   ATHENS 18810
    Mrs. Lyle Jackson, Director

Exhibits include Indian artifacts, weapons.

E.M. PARKER INDIAN MUSEUM
R.D. 1   BROOKVILLE 15825
    E.M. Parker, Curator

Indian artifacts of western Pennsylvania.

ERIE PUBLIC MUSEUM
356 W. 6th St.   ERIE 16507
    John V. Alexick, Director

Contains pioneer and Indian crafts, artifacts.

AMERICAN INDIAN MUSEUM
Route 19   HARMONY 16037

Indian clothing, implements, weapons, arts and crafts, of Plains, Desert, Southwest, and Eastern tribes. Indian dances (in summer). Crafts shop.

HISTORICAL SOCIETY OF DAUPHIN
    COUNTY - MUSEUM
219 S. Front St.   HARRISBURG 17104
    Evan J. Miller, Executive Officer

Museum features Indian artifacts.

HERSHEY MUSEUM
Park Ave. and Derry Rd.
HERSHEY 17033
Mrs. Charlotte Light, Manager

Exhibits relate to Indian lore and early American life.

MERCER COUNTY HISTORICAL
SOCIETY - MUSEUM
119 S. Pitt St. MERCER 16137

Museum houses local Indian artifacts. Library.

MUNCY HISTORICAL SOCIETY AND
MUSEUM
42 N. Main St. MUNCY 17756
Mrs. Fred Philips, Director

Features Indian artifacts.

SCHWENKFELDER MUSEUM
Seminary Ave. PENNSBURG 18073
Andrew S. Berky, Director

Indian artifacts -- tools, weapons, implements. Book collection.

READING PUBLIC MUSEUM AND ART
GALLERY
500 Museum Rd. READING 19602
Samuel C. Gundy, Director

Collections include local artifacts; basketry, clothing, pottery; Northwest Indian and Eskimo material.

WESTMORELAND-FAYETTE HISTORICAL
SOCIETY - MUSEUM
West Overton SCOTTDALE 15683
Mrs. Ray Musgrove, Curator

Museum features pioneer and Indian articles, fossils, historic documents and books. Publications.

EVERHART MUSEUM OF NATURAL
HISTORY, SCIENCE AND ART
Nay Aug Park SCRANTON 18510
Donald A. Winer, Director

American Indian artifacts featured in natural history exhibits.

MONROE COUNTY HISTORICAL
SOCIETY - MUSEUM
9th and Main Sts. STROUDSBURG 18360
Mrs. Horrace Walters, Curator

Collection includes Indian relics and pioneer implements. Genealogical and historical library. Publications.

FORT AUGUSTA
1150 N. Front St. SUNBURY 17801
Robert Hoover, Caretaker

Military artifacts including Indian relics of local origin. Model of Fort Augusta.

WYOMING HISTORICAL AND GEOLOGICAL
SOCIETY - MUSEUM
69 S. Franklin St.
WILKES-BARRE 18701
Alan W. Perkins, Executive Officer

Exhibits feature archaeological collection of local artifacts. Library.

LYCOMING HISTORICAL SOCIETY -
MUSEUM
P.O. Box 304 WILLIAMSPORT 17701
Dr. R. Max Gingrich, President

Museum houses Indian material; Civil War and pioneer articles. Publications.

RHODE ISLAND

TOMAQUAG INDIAN MEMORIAL
MUSEUM
Burdickville-Old Hopkinton Rds.
ASHAWAY 02804
Eva L. Butler, Director

Archaeology, ethnology, natural history exhibits related to southern New England Indian cultures.

HAFFENREFFER MUSEUM
Brown University
Mount Hope Grant BRISTOL 02809
Mrs. J.L. Giddings, Curator

Collections of archaic and recent material including Indian weapons, utensils, clothing, baskets, pottery.

MUSEUM OF PRIMITIVE CULTURES
Columbia St. and Kingstown Rd.
                    PEACE DALE 02883

Anthropological artifacts of North America
included in museum collections.

RHOSE ISLAND HISTORICAL SOCIETY -
    MUSEUM
52 Power St.   PROVIDENCE 02906
    Clifford P. Monahan, Director

Museum collections include Indian artifacts
of local origin. Library.

ROGER WILLIAMS PARK MUSEUM
Roger Williams Park
                    PROVIDENCE 02905
    Maribelle Cormack, Director

Exhibits feature Woodland Indian culture --
model village; canoe; model Pueblo; Plains
and Northwest Coast Indian artifacts: Eskimo material; American Indian plants; maps.

SOUTH CAROLINA

THE CHARLESTON MUSEUM
125 Rutledge Ave.
                    CHARLESTON 29401
    E. Milby Burton, Director

Indian relics included in natural history collection. Exhibits related to South Carolina
history.

FLORENCE MUSEUM
Graham and Spruce Sts.
                    FLORENCE 29501
    William S. Dowis, Jr., President

Exhibits include archaeological to contemporary Indian artifacts of Southwest origin.

CHILDREN'S NATURE MUSEUM OF
    YORK COUNTY
Fewell Park   ROCK HILL 29730
    J. Lee Settlemyre, Jr., Director

Collections feature Indian artifacts.

SOUTH DAKOTA

WIEHE'S FRONTIER MUSEUM
25 N. 5th St.
P.O. Box 489   CUSTER 57730
    Carl L. Wiehe, Owner, Curator

Pioneer and Indian material included in historical collection.

LAKE COUNTY HISTORICAL SOCIETY -
    MUSEUM
310 8th St., N.E.   MADISON 57042
    George G. Smith, Executive Officer

Collections feature early maps, local Indian
artifacts.

ZEITNER GEOLOGICAL MUSEUM
                    MISSION 57555
    Mr. and Mrs. C. A. Zeitner,
        Directors

Collection includes Sioux beadwork, local
arrowheads, tools, pottery, peace pipes,
mortars, flutes, effigies.

SOUTH DAKOTA STATE HISTORICAL
    MUSEUM
Soldiers and Sailors Memorial Bldg.
                    PIERRE 57501
    Will G. Robinson, Secretary

Pioneer items, including Dakota Indian artifacts and collections from the prehistoric
earth-lodge peoples. Library (25,000 volumes).

SIOUX INDIAN MUSEUM AND CRAFTS
    CENTER
P.O. Box 1504   RAPID CITY 57701
    Ella C. Lebow, Director

Sioux Indian artifacts including hide painting, metalwork, beadwork, featherwork,
and carving. Publications. Tipi Shop (crafts
shop). Operated by the Indian Arts and
Crafts Board, U.S. Department of the Interior.

PETTIGREW MUSEUM
131 N. Duluth Ave.
                    SIOUX FALLS 57104
    George and Dorothy Rogers, Curators

Sioux Indian ceremonial costumes and artifacts. Collection of George Gatlin lithographs. Rare book (Indian) collection.

DURAND COLLECTION OF ART
Yankton College
Forbes Hall
Douglas Ave.   YANKTON 57078
    Dr. Hans Janssen, Curator

Archaeological Indian artifacts featured in
natural science collection.

TENNESSEE

TRAVELER'S REST
Farrell Parkway   NASHVILLE 37220
    Mrs. Robert D. Herbert, Jr.,
      Chairman
    Mr. and Mrs. M.L. Kieffer, Curators

Historic House with museum featuring Indian
artifacts and costumes.

SHILOH NATIONAL MILITARY PARK
  MUSEUM
P.O. Box 7   SHILOH 38376
    Jerry L. Schober, Chief Historian

Museum exhibits include pre-Columbian
Indian mounds.

FORT LOUDOUN ASSOCIATION -
  MUSEUM
                      VONORE 37885
    Ned Russell, Executive Secretary

Museum exhibits feature local historical and
Cherokee Indian artifacts. Publications.

TEXAS

TEXAS MEMORIAL MUSEUM
University of Texas
24th and Trinity   AUSTIN 78705
    W. W. Newcomb, Director

North American Indian anthropology with
emphasis on Indians of Texas.

FRONTIER TIMES MUSEUM
Two blocks north of Court House
                      BANDERA 78003
    Mrs. E. B. Batto, Manager

Collections include pioneer and Indian artifacts.

BASTROP COUNTY HISTORICAL SOCIETY
  AND MUSEUM
702 Main St.
P.O. Box 83   BASTROP 78602
    Miss Julia Moncure, President

Contains Indian and Civil War relics.

BIGFOOT WALLACE MUSEUM
                      BIGFOOT 78005
    Ralph O. Crawford, Manager
    J. B. Blackwell, President

Pioneer and Indian artifacts included in historical exhibits.

ERNIE WILSON MUSEUM
Box 67 or 267   BUFFALO GAP 79508
2026 1/2 Fulton St.   ABILENE
    Ernie Wilson, Curator

Contains Western and Indian material. Book
collection.

PANHANDLE-PLAINS HISTORICAL
  MUSEUM
2401 4th Ave.   CANYON 79015
    C. Boone McClure, Director

Southwest ethnological collection. Exhibits
relating to history, archaeology, and paleontology of American Indian.

BOSQUE MEMORIAL MUSEUM
Avenue Q   CLIFTON 76634
    Mrs. Ole J. Hoel, President

Contains Indian artifacts.

DE WITT COUNTY HISTORICAL
  MUSEUM
207 E. Main St.   CUERO 77954
    Mrs. A. W. Schaffner, Chairman

Historical Society museum includes Indian
artifacts.

WHITEHEAD MEMORIAL MUSEUM
1400 S. Main St.   DEL RIO 78840
    Mrs. Willie B. Whitehead, Director

Contains Indian relics and Border War
material.

NORTHINGTON-HEARD MEMORIAL
   MUSEUM
                         EGYPT 77436
   George Heard Northington, III,
      Owner

Collection includes Indian relics related to
19th-century Texas; documents.

TREASURE TROVE
Davis and Murphy Sts.
P.O. Box 248   FORT DAVIS 79734
   J. A. Roach, Jr., Director,
      Manager

Indian artifacts included in local historical
collection.

ANNIE RIGGS MEMORIAL MUSEUM
301 S. Main St.
(1101 N. Young St.)
                     FORT STOCKTON 79735
   Mrs. D. S. Beeman, Director

Contains pioneer and Indian material.

MUSEUM OF FINE ARTS OF HOUSTON,
   TEXAS
1001 Bissonet   HOUSTON 77005
   James J. Sweeney, Director

Displays of Indian jewelry and kachinas.

TEXAS TECHNOLOGICAL COLLEGE,
   WEST TEXAS MUSEUM
P.O. Box 4210   LUBBOCK 79409
   William Curry Holden, Director

Yaqui, Comanche and other Indian artifacts.

SOPHIENBURG MEMORIAL MUSEUM
401 W. Coll St.
P.O. Box 398   NEW BRAUNFELS 78130
   Mrs. Martin Faust, Director

Collection includes pioneer tools and implements; Indian artifacts.

ODESSA COLLEGE MUSEUM
2300 Andrews Highway
P.O. Box 3752   ODESSA 79760
   Mrs. Marjorie Morris, Curator

Exhibits include Indian material of local
origin; documents.

CROCKETT COUNTY MUSEUM
11th St. on Highway 290
                         OZONA 76943
   Mrs. E. H. Chandler, Curator

Cave exhibits. Indian artifacts--ornaments,
jewelry, pottery, weapons, utensils, implements and ceremonial costumes.

FORT CONCHO MUSEUM
716 Burges St.   SAN ANGELO 76901
   J. N. Gregory, President
   Corinne Barr, Curator

Indian pottery, idols, weapons, and implements. Contemporary Indian crafts. Preserved Fort Concho buildings.

THE AMERICAN HERITAGE MUSEUM
309 25th St.   SNYDER 79549
   Edgar Schulze, Owner

Texas pioneer and Indian material included
in collection.

GARNER MEMORIAL MUSEUM
333 N. Park St.   UVALDE 78801
   Mrs. Madie A. Davis, Curator

Geological and artifact collections include
Indian arrowheads.

UTAH

OLD STATE HOUSE MUSEUM
City Park   FILLMORE 84631
   Loa B. Hanson, Supervisor

Contains pioneer and Indian material. Site
of former State Capital.

CARBON COLLEGE PREHISTORIC
   MUSEUM
Price City Municipal Bldg.
Geology Department
Carbon College   PRICE 84501
   Don Burge, Curator

Utah archaeological exhibits, including 9th-
century Indian material of the Fremont
Culture. Tours to Indian petroglyphs.

SOUTH-CENTRAL UTAH CULTURAL
  ARTS CENTER
147 W. 2nd, N.   RICHFIELD 84701
  Mr. and Mrs. Lincoln Avery,
    Managers
  MacNeal Magleby, President

Science exhibits feature Indian artifacts.

DAUGHTERS OF UTAH PIONEERS
300 N. Main St.
              SALT LAKE CITY 84116
  Kate B. Carter, President

Indian and pioneer material featured in Historical Society museum.

PIONEER VILLAGE MUSEUM
2998 Connor St.
              SALT LAKE CITY 84109
  Horace A. Sorensen, Director

Preserved frontier buildings house Ute Indian collection; American buffalo herd;
other Western Americana.

VIRGINIA

DANIELS MUSEUM
                            ORWELL
  Mrs. Thomas Daniels, Director,
    Manager

Contains Indian artifacts and military collections.

NORFOLK MUSEUM OF ARTS AND
  SCIENCE
Yarmouth by the Hague
              NORFOLK 23510
  H. B. Caldwell, Director

Local Indian artifacts and relics from paleolithic to pre-colonial times.

THE VALENTINE MUSEUM
1015 E. Clay St.
              RICHMOND 23219
  Major General Leslie D. Carter,
    Director
  Mrs. Jacquelin Willcox,
    Acting Curator

Indian artifacts and local material of historical interest featured in exhibits --
500,000 items, including skeletal remains
from Virginia and North Carolina mounds.

JAMESTOWN FOUNDATION - MUSEUM
Box JF (Jamestown)
              WILLIAMSBURG 23185
  Parke Rouse, Jr., Executive Director

Museum features Virginia Indian artifacts
and pioneer items. Reconstruction of Powhatan's Indian Lodge. Publications.

WASHINGTON

FORT OKANOGAN HISTORICAL MUSEUM
              BREWSTER 98812

Collection of Indian and pioneer material.

WILLIS CAREY HISTORICAL MUSEUM
East Sunset Highway
              CASHMERE 98815
  Robert E. Eddy, President

Exhibits relate to history and prehistory of
central Washington; Indian material.

FORT COLUMBIA STATE PARK
  HISTORICAL MUSEUM
P.O. Box 172   CHINOOK 98614

Contains frontier and Indian artifacts.

ORCAS ISLAND MUSEUM
              EASTSOUND 98245
  Mrs. Walter A. Hall, Museum
    Manager

Exhibits include Indian and pioneer material;
documents.

SKAGIT COUNTY HISTORICAL SOCIETY -
  MUSEUM
Museum Room, Skagit Valley College
2405 College Way
(Route 2, Box 9C)
              MOUNT VERNON 98273
  Glen Stover, Chairman,
    Museum Board

Exhibits feature documents and artifacts of
local origin relating to pioneer and Indian
life; tape recordings with early pioneers.

SNOQUALMIE VALLEY HISTORICAL
  MUSEUM
45 4th Ave. E.   NORTH BEND 98045
  Mrs. Paul Pieper, Curator

Collections include local Indian and pioneer
artifacts; Indian basket collection.

STATE CAPITOL MUSEUM
211 W. 21st Ave.   OLYMPIA 98502
  Kenneth R. Hopkins, Director

Northwest Indian artifacts. Basket collection.

OLYMPIC NATIONAL PARK, PIONEER
  MEMORIAL MUSEUM
600 Park Ave.   PORT ANGELES 98362
  Glenn D. Gallison, Chief Park
    Naturalist

Local historical collection including Northwest Coast Indian artifacts.

KITSAP COUNTY HISTORICAL MUSEUM
County Courthouse - 614 Division St.
P.O. Box 1857, Bremerton
                    PORT ORCHARD 98366
  Mrs. Sigurd Olsen, Director

Contains Indian material; costume collection; photographs.

MUSEUM OF HISTORY AND INDUSTRY
2161 E. Hamlin St.   SEATTLE 98102
  Mrs. Elizabeth Sutton Gustison,
    Director

Contains Indian and Alaskan artifacts.

THE PULLEN KLONDIKE MUSEUM
Food Circus Balcony
Seattle Center   SEATTLE
  Mary P. Kopanski, Director

Northwest Indian artifacts, mainly of the
Tlingit tribes: basketry, totems, implements, ceremonial robes, blankets, beadwork, ivory carvings (Collection of Mrs.
Harriet Pullen).

SEATTLE ART MUSEUM
Volunteer Park   SEATTLE 98102
  Dr. Richard E. Fuller, Director

Collection includes material related to the
Eskimo, Northwest Coast, California, and
Eastern Woodland Indians.

THOMAS BURKE MEMORIAL
  WASHINGTON STATE MUSEUM
University of Washington
                          SEATTLE 98105
  Walter A. Fairservis, Jr., Director

Exhibits relate to Washington prehistory;
Northwest Indian and Pacific Rim tribes
artifacts.

EASTERN WASHINGTON STATE
  HISTORICAL SOCIETY - MUSEUM
W. 2316 1st Ave.   SPOKANE 99202
  Richard G. Conn, Director

Museum features regional collection of Indian arts and crafts items. Library. Publications.

WASHINGTON STATE HISTORICAL
  SOCIETY - MUSEUM
215 N. Stadium Way   TACOMA 98403
  Bruce Le Roy, Director

Museum features local artifacts, Indian and
Alaskan pictures and books. Library. Publications.

CLARK COUNTY HISTORICAL MUSEUM
16th and Main Sts.   VANCOUVER
  J. T. Pagel, Director

Collection includes basketry of the Northwest Coast; artifacts of the Plateau and lower
Columbia River cultures.

U.S. GRANT MUSEUM
Vancouver Barracks
                        VANCOUVER 98660
  Mr. and Mrs. Jerry Shaffer,
    Curators

Indian primitive and historical artifacts included in collections.

WALLA WALLA COUNTY PIONEER AND
HISTORICAL SOCIETY - MUSEUM
City Hall, 3rd and Rose Sts.
(312 S. Division St.)
WALLA WALLA 99362
Margaret Pettyjohn, Curator

Exhibits include pioneer and Indian tools and
implements; Fort Walla Walla relics and
documents. Publications.

WHITMAN COLLEGE MUSEUM OF
NORTHWEST HISTORY
Boyer and College Aves.
WALLA WALLA 99362
Robert L. Whitner, Director

Indian collection relates to Pacific Northwest cultures.

NORTH CENTRAL WASHINGTON
MUSEUM
Chelan and Douglas Sts.
WENATCHEE 99801
Grant Ericson, Director

Collection includes North American Indian
and local material.

YAKIMA VALLEY HISTORICAL
MUSEUM
2105 Tieton Dr.　　　　YAKIMA 98901
Mrs. Claude Smith, Director

Collections include archaeological material;
Yakima Indian artifacts; local history.

WEST VIRGINIA

FAYETTE COUNTY HISTORICAL
SOCIETY - MUSEUM
(Box 17, Oak Hill)
Midland Trail　　　　ANSTED 25812
Rev. Shirley Donnelly, President

Museum features Indian and pioneer mountain artifacts and tools.

WISCONSIN

CHEQAMON HISTORICAL MUSEUM
502 W. 2nd St.　　　ASHLAND 54806
William Sloggy, Director

Indian relics of local origin featured in collection.

DODGE COUNTY HISTORICAL SOCIETY
MUSEUM
127 S. Spring St.　　BEAVER DAM 53916
Mrs. Virgil C. Jackson, Director

Contains Indian material and items of local
origin.

LOGAN MUSEUM OF ANTHROPOLOGY
Beloit College　　　　BELOIT 53512
Dr. Andrew H. Whiteford, Director

Ethnological material from Great Lakes,
Plains and Southwest. Archaeological collections, including skeletal remains from
Mississippi Valley, Plains (Mandan, Arikara), and Southwest.

HOARD HISTORICAL MUSEUM
407 Merchants Ave.
FORT ATKINSON 53538
Zida C. Ivey, Director

Indian artifacts. Book collection (local
history).

NEVILLE PUBLIC MUSEUM
129 S. Jefferson St.
GREEN BAY 54301
James L. Quinn, Director

Collections of Wisconsin archaeological
material representative of Indian cultures
from Paleo-Indian to historic times including Plains, Menominee, Chippewa tribes.

HISTORYLAND
HAYWARD 54843
Anthony Wise, Director

"The museum is geared toward the Indian
people with the hope that they will continue
to identify themselves as Indians and preserve their cultural arts." Ojibwa Indian
crafts and artifacts.

LINCOLN-TALLMAN MUSEUM
Rock County Historical Society
440 N. Jackson St.
JAMESVILLE 53545
Richard Penn Hartung, Director

Local Indian material. Arctic, Wisconsin,
and pre-Columbian artifacts (George K.
Tallman Collection).

KENOSHA PUBLIC MUSEUM
5608 10th Ave., Civic Center
                              KENOSHA 53140
     Kenneth Dearolf, Director

Artifacts of local Chippewa Indians, including stone objects, clothing, weapons, beadwork.

STATE HISTORICAL SOCIETY OF
     WISCONSIN - MUSEUM
816 State St.   MADISON 53706
     Dr. Leslie H. Fishel, Jr.,
        Executive Officer

Museum features 125,000 archaeological
artifacts; 48,000 museum artifacts; 4,500
disc and tape recordings; 100,000 photographs, paintings and graphic representations. Library. Publications.

RAHR CIVIC CENTER AND PUBLIC
     MUSEUM
610 N. 8th St.   MANITOWOC 54220
     Dr. Rajko Lozar, Director

Manitowoc County Indian Artifacts Collection: Indian archaeological material from
Old Copper artifacts to Upper Mississippi
group, including dioramas.

MARINETTE COUNTY HISTORICAL
     SOCIETY - MUSEUM
Stephenson Island   MARINETTE 54143
     Henry E. Hansen, Curator

Museum houses logging and Indian material.

MILTON HOUSE MUSEUM
26th and 59th Sts.   MILTON 53563
     Mrs. Don Gray, Curator

Dean Swift Collection of arrowheads, implements, stone artifacts, tools and weapons.

WISCONSIN GARDENS
Minch Dr. - R. R. 1
                         MINOCOQUA 54548
     Alonzo W. Pond, Manager, Owner

Material related to Indian lore and way of
life housed in aboretum.

DOTY CABIN
Lincoln St.
(637 South Park)   NEENAH 54956
     Harvey Leaman, Curator

Historic house and museum feature frontier
and Indian material.

NEW LONDON PUBLIC MUSEUM
412 S. Pearl St.   NEW LONDON 54961
     Mrs. Harry Macklin, Curator

Contains local, Indian and natural history
items.

OCONTO COUNTY HISTORICAL MUSEUM
917 Park Ave.   OCONTO 54153
     George E. Hall, President

Exhibits feature Copper Culture artifacts;
Menominee Indian relics. Local history
book collection.

OSHKOSH PUBLIC MUSEUM
1331 Algoma Blvd.   OSHKOSH 54901
     John H. Kuony, Director
     Robert J. Hruska, Assistant
        Director and Curator of
        Anthropology

Paleo-Indian to historic anthropological material: Great Lakes lithic and ceramic material; Menominee and Woodland artifacts;
Upper Mississippi collections. Reference
Library (Great Lakes archaeology).

SHEBOYGAN COUNTY HISTORICAL
     SOCIETY - MUSEUM
3110 Erie Ave.   SHEBOYGAN 53081
     Mr. and Mrs. T. Mosch,
        Resident Custodians

Museum collections include Indian relics.
Historic house. Study clubs.

DOUGLAS COUNTY HISTORICAL
     MUSEUM
906 E. 2nd St.   SUPERIOR 54882
     James E. Lundsted, Curator

Exhibits include Indian artifacts; Sioux Indian Portraits (Barry Collection); Catlin
prints; local history archives.

WYOMING

WYOMING STATE MUSEUM
Wyoming State Archives and Historical
  Department
State Office Bldg.   CHEYENNE 82001
    Lola M. Homsher, Director
    Paul M. Edwards, Curator

Sioux, Arapaho, Cheyenne, Blackfeet, Shoshone, and Flathead Indian artifacts.

BUFFALO BILL MUSEUM
Buffalo Bill Historical Center
Box 1262   CODY 82414
    Harold McCracken, Director
    Richard Frost, Curator

Original Western documentary art. Indian
artifacts: beadwork, weapons, tools, implements. Library (600 volumes).

**WYOMING PIONEER MEMORIAL
  MUSEUM**
P.O. Box 561   DOUGLAS 82633
    James W. Vetter, Curator

Pioneer and Indian material of local origin
included in collection.

JACKSON'S HOLE MUSEUM
                         JACKSON 83001
    W. C. Lawrence, Director
    Mrs. Ruth Spicer, Curator

Local Indian artifacts (Shoshone, Arapahoe,
Crow), including pottery, skin paintings,
weapons.

LUSK MUSEUM
4th and Main Sts.   LUSK 82225
    Hans Gautschi, Curator

Indian artifacts; Cheyenne-Deadwood stagecoach; Wyoming relics.

Libraries

These alpha-geographical listings, like those in the Museums section, include libraries with both large and small related holdings.

ARIZONA

COLORADO RIVER TRIBES PUBLIC LIBRARY
c/o Colorado River Tribal Council
Colorado River Agency   PARKER 85344
Denise Florence, Secretary,
Tribal Council

Holdings include books, documents, photographs and magazines related to the history and life of the Mohave and Chemehuevi tribes.

DEPARTMENT OF LIBRARY AND ARCHIVES
State of Arizona
Third Floor Capital   PHOENIX 85007
Marguerite B. Cooley, Director

Contains over 500,000 volumes, including material on Southwest Indians. Numerous exhibits supplement library research and consist primarily of artifacts -- pottery, basketry, paintings, pictures, and odd items.

ARIZONA PIONEERS' HISTORICAL SOCIETY - LIBRARY
949 E. 2nd St.   TUCSON 85719
Donald E. Phillips, Chief
Executive Officer

Holdings include 30,000 volumes related to Arizona and the Southwest; Manuscript Division contains 500 collections of historical documents.

COLORADO

STATE HISTORICAL SOCIETY OF COLORADO - LIBRARY
E. 14th Ave. and Sherman St.
        DENVER 80203
Orian L. Lewis, Deputy Curator

Society's library totals 110,000 items. Holdings include extensive ethnological collections of Plains and Southwest Indians; Mesa Verde, Plains, and Mountain Indian materials; source materials on history of the Indian Wars; materials from the Rosebud Indian Agency, 1885 to 1890. Extensive collection of Indian photographs available to public.

DISTRICT OF COLUMBIA

AMERICAN INDIAN AND ESKIMO CULTURAL FOUNDATION - LIBRARY
919 - 18th St., N.W.
        WASHINGTON 20006
Solomon McCombs, President

Library facilities include related books and language tapes.

LIBRARY OF CONGRESS
General Reference and Bibliography
Division   WASHINGTON 20540
L. Quincy Mumford, Librarian

General collections include 8,000 to 10,000 volumes related to the American Indian; general works, archaeology, prehistory, religion, art, folklore, tribal history. Holdings include popular works, technical monographs, periodicals, government publications, children's books.

LIBRARY OF CONGRESS
Manuscript Division   WASHINGTON 20540
David C. Mearns, Chief

Collection of manuscripts, personal papers, and correspondence, arranged by name of individual.

LIBRARY OF CONGRESS
Music Division
Archive of Folk Song   WASHINGTON 20540
Mrs. Rae Korson, Head

Holdings include over 5,000 items, primarily cylinders of American Indian music; 1,000 books and journals with a 1,800-item bibliography of American Indian music. Reading room and listening facilities available for long-playing records and disc or tape duplications of field recordings. Record series issued.

LIBRARY OF CONGRESS
Prints and Photographs Division
WASHINGTON 20540

Large collection of material dealing with Indians, including artists' conceptions of Indians and their activities during the Colonial period, Indians attacking settlers in the West, conflicts between the U.S. Army and various tribes, portraits of specific Indians (both photographs and drawings), and a variety of photographs relating to the daily life of Indians since the middle of the 19th century.

SMITHSONIAN OFFICE OF ANTHROPOLOGY BRANCH LIBRARY
Smithsonian Institution Libraries
Natural History Bldg.
10th & Constitution Ave., N.W.
WASHINGTON 20560
Miss Mary L. Horgan, Branch Librarian

An amalgamation of the Division of Anthropology and the Bureau of American Ethnology libraries, consisting of 35,000 volumes devoted to the American Indian: Research and source materials on all phases of Indian culture and history, historical study reports and proceedings. Available to scholars and researchers in anthropology.

FLORIDA

FLORIDA HISTORICAL SOCIETY LIBRARY
University of South Florida Library
TAMPA 33620
Margaret L. Chapman, Librarian

Chiefly Seminole Indian material -- books, pictures, clippings, unpublished manuscripts from the Florida Works Progress Administration; material on the Seminole Indian Wars, including maps.

IDAHO

IDAHO STATE HISTORICAL SOCIETY - LIBRARY
610 N. Julia Davis Drive   BOISE 83706
Ronald H. Limbaugh, Historical Librarian

Collections include 200 volumes -- Lapwai Agency records, 1871 to 1883; diaries and private papers; Alice Fletcher-Jane Gay Nez Perce Allotment Photograph Collection, 1888 to 1892; Idaho Superintendency and other Indian records (National Archives microfilm); Indian files in the territorial section of State Archives; Nez Perce and Shoshoni literature.

ILLINOIS

MILNER LIBRARY
Illinois State University   NORMAL 61761

Small collection of Amerindian study and research items.

KANSAS

KANSAS STATE HISTORICAL SOCIETY - LIBRARY
Memorial Bldg.
120 W. 10th St.   TOPEKA 66612
Nyle H. Miller, Secretary

Holdings -- Kansas State public records and documents: 111,201 books, 158,978 pamphlets, 13,366 reels of microfilm, 6,098 maps, atlases and lithographs, 73,553 volumes of newspapers, 1,109 paintings and drawings, 45,616 photographs.

MASSACHUSETTS

BEVERLY HISTORICAL SOCIETY - LIBRARY
Cabot House
117 Cabot St.   BEVERLY 01915
Arthur B. Appleton, President

Collection of 20,000 volumes including Indian-related material.

FALL RIVER HISTORICAL SOCIETY -
    LIBRARY
451 Rock St.   FALL RIVER 02720
    Mrs. Mary B. Gifford, Curator

Book collections include thirty volumes related to local Indian history.

MICHIGAN

WILLIAM L. CLEMENTS LIBRARY
University of Michigan
S. University St.   ANN ARBOR 48104

Holdings include 38,000 books and bound
periodicals on Americana to 1830 -- discovery, exploration, settlement, Indian relations, etc.

MINNESOTA

BECKER COUNTY HISTORICAL SOCIETY -
    LIBRARY
915 Lake Ave.   DETROIT LAKES 56501
    Frank J. Long, President

Holdings include 1,200 volumes pertaining
to the White Earth Indian Reservation,
covering twelve townships of Becker
County, Minn.

MINNESOTA STATE ARCHIVES AND
    RECORDS SERVICE
117 University Ave.   ST. PAUL 55101
    Fred R. Thibodeau, Deputy State
        Archivist

Manuscript material on Indians includes
information on Indian education in the State
Department of Education; listing of Indians
in the State census schedules; correspondence on Indian matters in Governors'
Papers.

MISSOURI

UNIVERSITY OF KANSAS CITY
Snyder Collection of Americana
General Library
5100 Rockhill Rd.   KANSAS CITY 64110
    Helen Bennett, Curator

Holdings include 20,000 volumes featuring
historical and Indian-related works.

MISSOURI HISTORICAL SOCIETY -
    LIBRARY
Jefferson Memorial Bldg.
                        ST. LOUIS 63112
    George R. Brooks, Director

Holdings include more than 10,000 volumes
related to local and Missouri history.

MONTANA

HISTORICAL SOCIETY OF MONTANA
    - LIBRARY
Veterans and Pioneers Bldg.
                        HELENA 59601
    Mary K. Dempsey, Librarian

Holdings include 45,000 volumes on Montana
history, frontier life, Indians and Indian
affairs, Lewis and Clark expedition, and
other related subjects.

NEW MEXICO

MUSEUM OF NAVAJO CEREMONIAL
    ART - MARY CABOT WHEELWRIGHT
    RESEARCH LIBRARY
Museum Hill, off Old Pecos Rd.
(Box 445)   SANTA FE 87502
    Prof. Kenneth E. Foster, Director

Holdings include 10,000 volumes on the religions, history and art of the Navajo and
of other tribes. Library features archives
containing 1,000 examples of Navajo ceremonial art; 3,000 Navajo ceremonial music
recordings; 100 Navajo myth texts; 1,000
Navajo sandpaintings on slides; 100 music
and prayer tapes.

MUSEUM OF NEW MEXICO LIBRARY
Anthropology and Research Division
P.O. Box 2087   SANTA FE 87502
    Carolyn Allers, Librarian

Subject emphasis of collections is on anthropology, archaeology, ethnology, geology,
paleontology, and paleobotany.

NEW MEXICO STATE LIBRARY
123 N. Federal Place   SANTA FE 87501
   Dorothy J. Watkins, State Librarian

Holdings of 144,184 volumes on social sciences, economics, religion, psychology and education, political science, science and technology, fine arts, public administration, philosophy, literature, history, biography. Special collection of Southwest history.

NEW YORK

MUSEUM OF THE AMERICAN INDIAN,
   HEYE FOUNDATION
Huntington Free Reading Room
9 Westchester Square   BRONX 10461
   E.K. Burnett, Librarian

Holdings of 34,000 volumes relate solely to the American Indian.

BUFFALO AND ERIE COUNTY
   HISTORICAL SOCIETY - LIBRARY
25 Nottingham Court   BUFFALO 14216
   Walter S. Dunn, Jr. (Director)

Holdings include books and manuscripts related to the Seneca Indians.

AMERICAN MUSEUM OF NATURAL
   HISTORY - LIBRARY
Central Park West at 79th St.
                    NEW YORK 10024
   George H. Goodwin, Jr., Librarian

Collection includes 7,000 to 8,000 Indian-related volumes, specializing in journals and monographic serials. Reading room.

THE NEW YORK PUBLIC LIBRARY
American History Division
Fifth Ave. at 42nd St.   NEW YORK 10018
   Gerald D. McDonald, Chief

Material on American Indian languages, history, archaeology, anthropology, arts; writings by Indians, runs of related periodicals and serials, pictures (photographs and engravings), works on Indian place names, collection of Indian captivity journals and accounts.

NORTH DAKOTA

STATE HISTORICAL SOCIETY OF NORTH
   DAKOTA - LIBRARY
Liberty Memorial Bldg. BISMARCK 58501
   Margaret Rose, Librarian

Collection of 14,800 books on North Dakota history and the American Indian; Frank Fiske photographs of Standing Rock Indian Reservation.

OKLAHOMA

WILL ROGERS LIBRARY
121 N. Weenonah   CLAREMORE 74017
   Ella Sisler, Librarian

Holdings include 13,896 volumes, many of which concern Will Rogers, noted entertainer of Indian descent, and American Indians.

OKLAHOMA HISTORICAL SOCIETY -
   LIBRARY
Lincoln Blvd.   NORMAN 73069

Holdings of 30,000 volumes; archives contain three million documents of the Five Civilized Tribes; newspaper library of thirty million pages.

UNIVERSITY OF OKLAHOMA LIBRARY
Phillips Collection
Manuscript Division   NORMAN 73069
   Arrell M. Gibson, Curator

Holdings include 18,000 books and pamphlets; 200,000 historic photographs; four million manuscripts. Material is principally regional -- Indian, Oklahoma, and Southwestern history.

CREEK INDIAN MEMORIAL ASSOCIATION
   - LIBRARY
Creek Council House   OKMULGEE 74447
   Theda Wammack, Director,
      Creek Indian Museum

Holdings include 200 volumes related to Oklahoma and Indian history; Creek Indian records and documents.

THOMAS GILCREASE INSTITUTE OF
  AMERICAN HISTORY AND ART -
  LIBRARY
2401 W. Newton   TULSA 74127
  Paul A. Rossi, Director
  Martin A. Wenger, Librarian

Holdings include 22,000 books on the American Indian, discovery and exploration, fur trade, cattle industry, personal pioneer narratives, Mexico.

PENNSYLVANIA

MERCER COUNTY HISTORICAL SOCIETY
  - LIBRARY
119 S. Pitt St.   MERCER 16137

Library's collections include 1,000 volumes, 200 bound periodicals, newspaper collection, maps and surveys -- all pertaining to Mercer County.

AMERICAN PHILOSOPHICAL SOCIETY
  - LIBRARY
104 S. 5th St.   PHILADELPHIA 19106
  Richard H. Shryock, Librarian

Collection of 115,000 volumes of Americana, including early imprints, travels, etc.; American Indian linguistics; Franz Boas collection of 18th- and early 19th-century Indian vocabularies.

UNIVERSITY OF PENNSYLVANIA -
  MUSEUM LIBRARY
33rd & Spruce Sts. PHILADELPHIA 19104

Collection includes 38,124 volumes on the following subjects: Archaeology, anthropology, ethnology; Brinton Collection of aboriginal American linguistics and ethnology.

WYOMING HISTORICAL AND GEOLOGICAL
  SOCIETY - LIBRARY
69 S. Franklin St.
          WILKES-BARRE 18701
  Alan W. Perkins, Executive Officer

Collections include 40,000 volumes; manuscript material.

RHODE ISLAND

JOHN CARTER BROWN LIBRARY
Brown University   PROVIDENCE 02912

Collection's emphasis on history of the Americas to 1801, including history of South and Central America, and the Caribbean.

SOUTH DAKOTA

INSTITUTE OF INDIAN STUDIES LIBRARY
State University of South Dakota
          VERMILLION 57069
  Wesley R. Hurt, Director

Collection of 600 books on ethnology and contemporary affairs of the Northwestern Plains Indians.

TENNESSEE

TENNESSEE STATE LIBRARY AND
  ARCHIVES
State Library Division
Seventh Ave., N.   NASHVILLE 37203
  Isabel Howell, Librarian

Holdings (70,932 books and bound periodicals) strong in material on the Indian Wars, among other subject specialties.

WASHINGTON

OREGON PROVINCE ARCHIVES
Crosby Library
Gonzaga University   SPOKANE 99202
  Wilfred P. Schoenberg, S.J.,
    Archivist

Library's Indian collection contains 1,500 major Indian language items, including original manuscripts, and 1,400 volumes of history and ethnography; periodicals, microfilm, photographs, and approximately 5,000 additional items in pamphlet and clipping form.

WASHINGTON STATE HISTORICAL
  SOCIETY - LIBRARY
215 N. Stadium Way   TACOMA 98403
  Bruce LeRoy, Director

Collection includes books on Indians and Alaskan natives.

WISCONSIN

STATE HISTORICAL SOCIETY OF
  WISCONSIN - LIBRARY
816 State St.   MADISON 53706
    Leslie H. Fishel, Jr., Executive
    Officer

Research library in American history contains 345,206 volumes; 353,705 pamphlets; 40,060 reels of microfilm; 124,519 microprint cards; 8,000,000 pieces of private manuscripts; 15,000 cubic feet of State and local archives; 100,000 sheets of maps and geographical charts.

PIERCE COUNTY HISTORICAL SOCIETY -
  LIBRARY AND ARCHIVES
Wisconsin State College Library
             RIVER FALLS 54022

Holdings of 1,100 books, documents, and manuscripts relate to regional Wisconsin history.

WYOMING

WYOMING STATE ARCHIVES AND
  HISTORICAL DEPARTMENT
State Office Bldg.   CHEYENNE 82001
    Lola M. Homsher, Director

Library's subjects include Western history, particularly Wyoming and adjoining regions; papers and archival records of State, municipalities; pamphlets, pictures, newspapers, microfilm materials.

Associations

This section includes listings of historical societies, Indian affairs organizations, religious, charitable, and philanthropic associations involved in Indian affairs. The listings are arranged alpha-geographically.

ALASKA

COOK INLET HISTORICAL SOCIETY
630 Fifth Ave.   ANCHORAGE 99501
Melvin B. Ricks, Museum Curator

Activities: Society museum features Eskimo and Indian relics and artifacts. Library. Founded 1955.

ARIZONA

THE AMERIND FOUNDATION, INC.
                        DRAGOON 85609
Charles C. Di Peso, Director

Purpose: ". . .promoting, financing and fostering scientific, educational and archaeological study, pursuits, expeditions, excavations, collections, exhibitions and publications, with particular reference to the aboriginal people...and to that end, to acquire, erect, preserve and maintain museums, libraries, exhibitions and collections..." *Activities:*"Sponsors expeditions, carries on research and publishes findings of same; maintains a museum of archaeological and technographic culture, with particular reference to the American Southwest and Mesoamerica; maintains a research library and art and furniture galleries." Publications. Founded 1937.

**ARIZONA PIONEERS' HISTORICAL
  SOCIETY**
949 E. 2nd St.   TUCSON 85719
  Donald E. Phillips, Chief Executive
  Officer

Purpose: "The collection and preservation of the written and narrative historical records, and the antiquities of Arizona and the West, made readily available to the people of Arizona and to research historians." *Activities:* Speaker service to school groups and organizations; conducted tours; advisory service to other Arizona museums; loan exhibits; programs in historical archaeology; research facilities for study of museum artifacts. *Collections:* 30,000 volumes related to Arizona and the Southwest; Manuscript Division contains 500 collections of historical documents. *Publications:* Periodical. *The Journal of Arizona History;* books of regional interest occasionally published. Founded 1884.

NAVAJO ARTS AND CRAFTS GUILD
Box 8   WINDOW ROCK 86515
  Carl Nelson Gorman, Manager

Purpose: ". . . To carry out the purpose and intent of the Act of Congress for the rehabilitation and better utilization of the resources of the Navajo and Hopi Tribes and reservations as (they) relate to the members of the Navajo Tribe; to engage in the promotion, production and sale of Navajo crafts in such a manner as to assist the artists and crafts workers of the Navajo people to make an adequate livelihood at this type of work and to operate on a self-sustaining rather than profit-making basis; to assist Navajo craftsmen to develop and maintain high standards of excellency in workmanship and design in their products which are sold by the Guild; to revive and perpetuate the making of traditional Navajo craft products; to encourage Navajo craftsmen to develop new creations and adaptations to meet modern needs; to assist Navajo artists and artisans (in finding) new outlets for their abilities in other than the traditional crafts, and thus create new opportunities for a livelihood; to develop new markets for fine Navajo arts and crafts among Indian and non-Indian peoples; to maintain a close working relationship with the Arts and Crafts Board of the Department of the Interior in regard to the standards of craftsmanship of products sold through the Navajo Arts and Crafts Guild and in the promotion and sale of handicrafts and in various enterprises to assist in development and appreciation of fine Indian crafts by the general public." *Activities:* "Maintains a headquarters at Window Rock, Arizona, with retail sales outlets at Cameron and Betatakin, and three other stores being built at Chinle, Kayenta and Teec Nos Pos. The Guild operates a mail order business and a large wholesale business from the Window Rock store." *Programs:* "There are craftsmen working in silver at the Window Rock headquarters, and supplies are available for silversmiths, weavers and leather craftsmen who work at home. The crafts exhibit of the Navajo Tribal Fair is handled by the Guild. An annual exhibit is held at the Heard Museum in Phoenix, Arizona, and exhibits are organized at several state fairs." *Grants and awards:* Sponsors an annual Navajo Student Painting Exhibition. Founded 1941.

COLORADO

AMERICAN INDIAN DEVELOPMENT, INC.
205 Devon Pl.   BOULDER 80302
   D'Arcy McNickle, Executive Director

Purpose: Sponsors programs of community development and leadership training among Indian tribes. *Activities:* Workshop on Indian Affairs for Indian college students; community projects; consulting services. *Awards:* Scholarships for students who attend organization's Workshop on Indian Affairs. Founded 1952.

TREAD OF PIONEERS HISTORICAL
  COMMISSION
Fifth and Oak Sts.
          STEAMBOAT SPRINGS 80477
   Claude Luekens, Chairman

Activities: Sponsors museum exhibiting northwestern Colorado and Indian artifacts; maintains historic house. Founded 1959.

CONNECTICUT

CLINTON HISTORICAL SOCIETY
E. Main St.   CLINTON 06413
   Miss Nancy L. Newsom, President

Activities: Museum featuring Indian arrowheads. Library. Publications. Founded 1938.

LITCHFIELD HISTORICAL SOCIETY
South and East Sts.
P.O. Box 384   LITCHFIELD 06759
   Miss Charlotte M. Wiggin, Museum
    Curator and Librarian

Activities: Museum exhibiting local historical documents, Indian artifacts (Madden Collection), and Civil War relics; preservation of historic house. Library. Publications. Founded 1893.

SOCIETY OF THE FOUNDERS OF
  NORWICH, CONNECTICUT, INC.
405 Washington St.   NORWICH 06360
   Philip A. Johnson, President

Purpose: "To perpetuate and preserve the memory of the founders of Norwich." *Activities:* Reconstruction of historic inn, circa 1675. *Collections:* Mohegan Indian arrowheads, stone implements, baskets, succotash bowl with wolf's head handles. Founded 1901.

STRATFORD HISTORICAL SOCIETY
967 Academy Hill   STRATFORD 06497
   Stanley Johnson, President

Activities: Maintains museum featuring Indian relics and historic Judson House (circa 1723). Library. Founded 1925.

MATTATUCK HISTORICAL SOCIETY
119 W. Main St.   WATERBURY
   Rawson W. Haddon, Director

Purpose: "To collect and preserve Connecticut history -- especially Waterbury." *Activities:* Museum houses historical and archaeological collections; collection of work of Artists of Connecticut, 1740 to date; cooperative museum teaching program with local school board, grades five, six and eight; industrial museum. Founded 1877.

THE WINDSOR HISTORICAL SOCIETY
96 Palisado Ave.   WINDSOR 06095
   Robert W. Hoskins, President

Activities: Maintains historic house and museum featuring Indian relics, genealogies. Library. Founded 1921.

DISTRICT OF COLUMBIA

AMERICAN INDIAN AND ESKIMO CULTURAL FOUNDATION
919 - 18th St., N.W.
WASHINGTON 20006
Solomon McCombs, President

Purpose: "To perpetuate and preserve the culture of the Indian and Eskimo through the education of the general public." *Activities:* Monthly meetings with speakers; lectures before civic and other groups (including school children); art exhibits; craft shows; dance pageants and programs. Library of books and language tapes. Founded 1963.

ARROW, INC.
822 Dupont Circle Bldg.
1346 Connecticut Ave., N.W.
WASHINGTON 20036

Purpose: "To help the American Indian achieve for himself a better educational, cultural and economic standard...to promote further public understanding of Indian problems, and to direct the management of programs financed with tax-exempt funds." *Activities:* "...self-help projects in social welfare and economic development..."; annual convention; programs in leadership training, voter education, housing improvement. *Grants sponsored:* Gaylord Philanthropies Scholarship; Willard Beatty Scholarship Fund; supplemental scholarships. *Publication:* Quarterly, *Arrow*. *Membership:* 2,100 members. Founded 1949.

NATIONAL ASSOCIATION OF INTER-GROUP RELATIONS OFFICIALS
2027 Massachusetts Ave., N.W.
WASHINGTON 20036
Frederick B. Routh, Executive Director

Purpose: "To aid professional government and private employees in the fields of civil rights and liberties." *Programs:* Placement service; special committees: Professional Standards, Educational and Professional Training, Interprofessional Relations, International Practice; commissions: Housing and Family Life, Inter-religious Relations, Manpower Utilization, Civil Rights, Research Services, Education,

Nature, Scope and Theory of Intergroup Relations. *Publications:* Quarterly, *Journal of Intergroup Relations;* bimonthly newsletter. *Membership:* 1,000. Founded 1947.

NATIONAL CONGRESS OF AMERICAN INDIANS
1765 "P" St., N.W.
WASHINGTON 20036
Vine Deloria, Jr., Executive Director

Activities: "Information and research program for Indian tribes and the public on topics of Indian interest, including legislation, history, current problems and programs, education, economic resources. Attempts to interpret the current desires and positions of Indian tribes on current movements on the basis of resolution passed during the annual convention of the tribes at which time policies and programs are formulated." *Membership:* 600 (105 tribes represented). Founded 1944.

FLORIDA

ST. PETERSBURG HISTORICAL SOCIETY
335 Second Ave., N.E.
ST. PETERSBURG 33701
Walter P. Fuller, President

Purpose: "To preserve and study historical artifacts and data." *Activities:* Quarterly meeting; sponsors Collectors' Club, St. Petersburg Historical Museum, Haas Museum, Grace S. Turner House. *Publication:* Newsletter, *The Sea Breeze*. *Membership:* 225 members. Founded 1920.

IDAHO

IDAHO STATE HISTORICAL SOCIETY
610 N. Julia Davis Drive
BOISE 83706
Ronald H. Limbaugh, Historical Librarian

Activities: Library. *Collections:* Nez Perce and Shoshoni records, pictures and artifacts.

ILLINOIS

LONE INDIAN FELLOWSHIP
2135 1/4 E. Eldorado St.
                    DECATUR 62521
    Harry G. Deibert, Grand Chief

Activities: Annual convention of twelve
local groups. *Publication:* Periodical,
Lone Indian. Membership: 400 members.
Founded 1926.

AMERICAN ACADEMY OF PEDIATRICS
Committee on Indian Health
1801 Hinman Ave.   EVANSTON 60201
    Harris D. Riley, Jr., M.D.,
        Committee Chairman

Purpose: "To provide leadership in the review and development of methods and procedures that will improve pediatric services to
Indians and Alaskan natives; the direction or
sponsorship of studies of special pediatric
problems; and stimulation of continuing individual and organizational interest in the
Indian health program by pediatricians,
particularly those in Indian country."
Activities: Provides pediatric service to
Indian and Alaskan natives through the Division of Indian Health, U.S. Public Health
Service: forty-seven general hospitals,
three tuberculosis sanatoria, field clinics.
Founded 1965.

STEPHENSON COUNTY HISTORICAL
    SOCIETY
1440 S. Carroll Ave.   FREEPORT 61032
    Mrs. John Woodhouse, Museum
        Curator

Activities: Sponsors museum containing
historical and industrial objects, Indian
beadwork; historic Oscar Taylor Home;
farm museum. Publications. Founded 1944.

KANKAKEE COUNTY HISTORICAL
    SOCIETY
Eighth Ave. at Water St.
                    KANKAKEE 60901
    Mrs. Fannie Still, Museum Curator

Activities: Operates museum exhibiting
Indian and pioneer items. Library. Founded 1908.

GRUNDY COUNTY HISTORICAL SOCIETY
                        MAZON 60444
    Harry L. Hough, Director

Activities: Collections of Lincolniana and
Indian relics displayed in local courthouse.
Founded 1923.

INDIANA

FOUNDATION OF NORTH AMERICAN
    INDIAN CULTURE
Pike and Jackson St.   VERNON 47282
    John Peterson, President

Purpose: "To stimulate the abiding interest
and pride of North American Indian in his
cultural heritage as manifested by his arts,
crafts, achievements, history, philosophy
and way of life." *Activities:* Provision of
retail sales outlets for Indian handicrafts;
work with the Extension Division, University
of North Dakota; annual "Exposition"; Indian
ceremonial dances in nearby communities.
Publications. *Membership:* 357 members.
Founded 1963.

IOWA

HISTORICAL SOCIETY OF MARSHALL
    COUNTY
201 E. State
(911 Turner St.)   MARSHALLTOWN 50158
    Brice W. Springer, President

Activities: Society maintains historic house;
exhibits collection of Indian paintings, implements, and weapons; organizes education
programs for children; preserves and maintains historic schoolhouse and log cabin.
Founded 1908.

KANSAS

BARTON COUNTY HISTORICAL SOCIETY
Cox Bldg.   GREAT BEND 67530
    Ray S. Schulz, President

Activities: Exhibition of Indian relics.
Founded 1960.

KANSAS STATE HISTORICAL SOCIETY
Memorial Bldg.
120 W. 10th St.   TOPEKA 66612
  Nyle H. Miller, Secretary

Purpose: "To collect, preserve and make
available for use materials dealing with the
history of Kansas, the West, Indians, and
genealogy." *Activities:* Museum; library;
official archives of the State of Kansas; exhibits of paintings and drawings.   Founded
1875.

MASSACHUSETTS

BEVERLY HISTORICAL SOCIETY, INC.
Cabot House
117 Cabot St.   BEVERLY 01915
  Arthur B. Appleton, President

Purpose: "To investigate and preserve
local history through the collection of illustrative material." *Activities:* Quarterly
meetings with guest speakers. *Collections:*
20,000 volumes, including Indian-related
material. *Membership:* 340.   Founded
1891.

CANTON HISTORICAL SOCIETY
1400 Washington St.   CANTON 02021
  Miss Katherine Sullivan, President

Activities: Sponsors museum featuring
Colonial, Civil War and Indian items; con-
ducts educational programs for children.
Founded 1893.

CHELMSFORD HISTORICAL SOCIETY
Adams Public Library
Boston Rd.   CHELMSFORD 01824
  Alfred H. Coburn, President

Activities: Maintains museum containing
local Indian relics. Founded 1930.

COHASSET HISTORICAL SOCIETY
Elm St.   COHASSET 02025
  Prescott T. Cummer, President

Activities: Maintains museum exhibiting
Colonial and Indian artifacts; sponsors con-
certs, dance recitals; maintains Maritime
Museum. Founded 1928.

DEDHAM HISTORICAL SOCIETY
612 High St.
P.O. Box 215   DEDHAM 02026
  Miss Marion K. Conant, Librarian

Activities: Museum containing local artifacts, Indian deeds and relics; conducts
historical and genealogical research. Library. Founded 1859.

POCUMTUCK VALLEY MEMORIAL
     ASSOCIATION
                    DEERFIELD 01342
  Miss Mary Wells, Curator

Activities: Maintains historic building
(Memorial Hall, 1799) featuring Indian and
early New England items.

FALL RIVER HISTORICAL
     SOCIETY
451 Rock St.   FALL RIVER 02720
  Mrs. Mary B. Gifford, Curator

Purpose: "To preserve objects of local
historical interest." *Collections:* Library
includes thirty volumes related to local
Indian history. *Membership:* 200. Founded
1921.

FRAMINGHAM HISTORICAL AND
     NATURAL HISTORY SOCIETY
Vernon St.   FRAMINGHAM 01704

Activities: Museum exhibiting Indian relics
and military items.

HAVERHILL HISTORICAL SOCIETY
240 Water St.   HAVERHILL 01830
  Austin Lewis, President

Activities: Maintains museum featuring
Colonial and Indian exhibits; historic house.
Founded 1897.

OLD BRIDGEWATER HISTORICAL
     SOCIETY
c/o Mrs. Stella J. Snow
20 Forest St.
                    WEST BRIDGEWATER 02379

Activities: Museum containing original
deed signed by Massasoit (Quasamequin) in
1649. Founded 1894.

MICHIGAN

MICHIGAN FOLKLORE SOCIETY
1125 Spring St.   ANN ARBOR 48103

Purpose: "To encourage research, papers, publications on Amerindian lore, music, dance." Associated with Society for Ethnomusicology, Dance Research Center.

GENESSEE COUNTY MUSEUM AND HISTORICAL SOCIETY
411 Courthouse   FLINT
   Arthur G. Abraham, Director

Activities: Museum featuring Indian stone artifacts.

MIDLAND COUNTY HISTORICAL ASSOCIATION
Midland Room,
Grace A. Down Memorial Library
1710 W. St. Andrews Dr.
              MIDLAND 48642
   Mrs. Glen Cummins, Executive
   Secretary

Activities: Museum containing Indian relics; reading room; education program for children and adults. Founded 1956.

MINNESOTA

BECKER COUNTY HISTORICAL SOCIETY
915 Lake Ave.   DETROIT LAKES 56501
   Frank J. Long, President

Purpose: "To collect and preserve Becker County history." *Activities:* Society maintains a museum and library in the Court House at Detroit Lakes. *Collections:* Library contains 1,200 volumes pertaining to the White Earth Indian Reservation, covering twelve townships of Becker County, Minn. Founded 1883.

ST. LOUIS COUNTY HISTORICAL SOCIETY
2228 E. Superior St.   DULUTH 55812
   Mrs. Josiah E. Greene, Executive
   Secretary

Activities: Museum exhibits including Eastman Johnson paintings and drawings of

Chippewa Indians, historic documents; programs for children. Publications. Founded 1923.

GRANT COUNTY HISTORICAL SOCIETY
              ELBOW LAKE 56531
   W.M. Goetzinger, President

Activities: Maintains museum exhibiting archaeological and Indian artifacts. Founded 1930.

LAC QUI PARLE COUNTY HISTORICAL SOCIETY
City Hall
404 Sixth Ave.   MADISON 56256
   Arthur Mork, President

Activities: Exhibits Indian and pioneer relics; maintains education programs for children. Publications. Founded 1948.

UNITED CHURCH COMMITTEE ON INDIAN WORK
109 E. Grant St.   MINNEAPOLIS 55426
   Rev. Raymond G. Baines

Purpose: "To assist American Indians in Minnesota (specifically those in Minneapolis and St. Paul) in whatever way possible." *Activities:* Assistance is provided through referrals to existing organizations in housing, employment, medical and legal aid, and education. *Programs:* Short-term assistance program -- distribution of emergency supplies, food, clothing, financial help. Founded 1953.

REDWOOD COUNTY HISTORICAL SOCIETY
1115 E. Bridge St.
            REDWOOD FALLS 56283
   M.E. Dirlam, President

Activities: Museum featuring items pertaining to the 1862 Sioux uprising; historic building. Publications.

CARVER COUNTY HISTORICAL SOCIETY
119 Cherry St.   WACONIA 55387
   Edward A. Weinzierl, President

Activities: Museum containing Indian artifacts and implements. Founded 1940.

MISSOURI

MISSOURI HISTORICAL SOCIETY
Jefferson Memorial Bldg.
ST. LOUIS 63112
George R. Brooks, Director

Purpose: "To provide a museum and library for the collection and preservation of objects and information relating to the history of St. Louis, the State of Missouri, and the Louisiana Purchase territory." *Activities:* Society maintains museum; library containing over 100, 000 books; educational department for school children; lectures for members; repository for Smithsonian Institution, Heye Foundation, and the U.S. Bureau of American Ethnology.

MONTANA

MONTANA HISTORICAL SOCIETY
Roberts at Sixth Ave.
HELENA 59601
Michael S. Kennedy, Director

Purpose: "Dedicated to advancing knowledge, understanding and appreciation of Western history and art." *Activities:* Preservation and marking of historic sites; broad educational-museum program; research library and art exhibits. *Publications; Montana, The Magazine of Western History;* bulletins; *The Montana Post;* leaflets; books (The West Press); *The Montana Heritage Series.*

NEBRASKA

ARTHUR COUNTY HISTORICAL SOCIETY
Court House Square
ARTHUR 69121
Charles Gessford, Chief Executive Officer

Purpose: "To preserve the history of events and articles relating thereto, to be placed in a museum." *Activities:* The operation of a museum in the old, original Court House in Arthur County. Presentation of pageants reenacting pioneer life, etc. Founded 1934.

ASSOCIATED EXECUTIVE COMMITTEE OF FRIENDS ON INDIAN AFFAIRS
1403 - 21st St. CENTRAL CITY 68826
Lindley J. Cook, Executive Secretary

Purpose: "Education...to help local Meetings (churches) understand the needs of the Indians in local centers in Oklahoma." *Activities:* Social service casework, counseling, social groupwork, community development -- with religious emphasis. *Publication:* Periodical, *Indian Progress.* Founded 1869.

NEBRASKA STATE HISTORICAL SOCIETY
1500 "R" St. LINCOLN 68508
Marvin F. Divett, Museum Director

Activities: Museum featuring local items, manuscripts, Indian relics, anthropological and archaeological exhibits; library; education programs for children and adults. Publications. Founded 1867.

CHERRY COUNTY HISTORICAL SOCIETY, INC.
S. Main St.
P.O. Drawer 152 VALENTINE 69201
Mrs. Minnie Lewis, Secretary

Activities: Museum featuring Indian art and artifacts. Library.

NEVADA

NEVADA HISTORICAL SOCIETY
P.O. Box 1129 RENO
Clara S. Beatty, President

Activities: Museum containing primitive art, Indian basketry, natural history exhibits. Founded 1904.

NEW HAMPSHIRE

NEW HAMPSHIRE ANTIQUARIAN SOCIETY
c/o Miss Rachel Johnson, Curator
Route 1 CONCORD 03301
Miss Mildred Raymond, President

Purpose: "The collection of local genealogical and historical material." *Activities:*

Small museum open by appointment containing examples of pottery, stone implements, quill and beadwork, pipes, war clubs, etc. Founded 1859.

NEW JERSEY

THE HUNTERDON COUNTY HISTORICAL
  SOCIETY
1 Maple Ave.   FLEMINGTON 08822
  Mrs. Ray C. Wilson, Librarian

Activities: Museum exhibiting Indian relics, furnishings. Library. Publications. Founded 1885.

MONMOUTH COUNTY HISTORICAL
  ASSOCIATION
70 Court St.   FREEHOLD 07728
  Edward H. Feltus, III, Director

Activities: Museum containing Colonial artifacts; Junior Museum featuring Indian relics and war items. Research library. Publications. Founded 1898.

CUMBERLAND COUNTY HISTORICAL
  SOCIETY
Main St.   GREENWICH 08323
  Francis A. Stanger, Jr., President

Activities: Museum exhibiting Indian artifacts, pioneer implements, war items; maintenance of historic house. Library. Publications. Founded 1905.

PASCACK HISTORICAL SOCIETY
19 Ridge Ave.   PARK RIDGE 07656
  Mrs. Jean Massimo and Mr. Howard
  I. Durie, Curators

Activities: Museum featuring items of local historical significance, including wampum making machine; historic building; education programs for children. Library. Publications. Founded 1942.

HISTORICAL SOCIETY OF PLAINFIELD
  AND NORTH PLAINFIELD
602 W. Front St.
                    PLAINFIELD 07060
  Paul J. Westergard, President

Activities: Museum exhibiting Indian and military items and manuscripts; historic house. Library. Founded 1921.

PARAMUS HISTORICAL AND
  PRESERVATION SOCIETY
650 E. Glen Ave.   RIDGEWOOD 07452
  Frank Moratz, President
  Mrs. William M. Murray,
    Museum Director

Activities: Museum featuring Indian and pioneer relics; historic building; education programs for children. Publications. Founded 1949.

NEW MEXICO

INTER-TRIBAL INDIAN CEREMONIAL
  ASSOCIATION
P.O. Box 1029   GALLUP 87301
  Edward S. Merry, Secretary-Manager

Purpose: "To widen the knowledge and appreciation of traditional American Indian culture and crafts." *Activities:* Four-day annual Indian exposition of dances, sports, crafts; special promotion and protection of genuine Indian arts and crafts; legislative representation; general information services; teacher information services. Publications. *Awards:* Prizes for outstanding dance groups and craftsmen. Founded 1922 -- an official agency of the State of New Mexico since 1939.

HISTORICAL SOCIETY OF NEW MEXICO
Palace of the Governors
Palace Ave.   SANTA FE 87501
  Victor Westphall, President

Activities: Preservation of New Mexico history through anthropological and archaeological archives and exhibits. Publications.

SOUTHWESTERN ASSOCIATION ON
  INDIAN AFFAIRS
P.O. Box 1964   SANTA FE 87501
  Al R. Packard, Presidnet

Purpose: "Dedicated to helping the Indian people safeguard their rights, preserve their culture, and achieve a condition of health, education and economic well-being comparable to the standards for our society as a whole." *Activities:* Association keeps abreast of local and national legislation, regulations and facilities affecting Indian health and welfare, and offers its assistance when problems arise. Sponsors the Annual Indian Market, where authentic arts and crafts items are displayed and judged. *Programs:* Association grants financial aid to deserving Indian students through its education fund.

TAOS COUNTY HISTORICAL
  SOCIETY, INC.
Box 398   TAOS 89571
  Helen G. Blumenschein, President

Purpose: "To mark historic sites in Taos Valley; to select and retain documents or photos of historical interest." *Activities:* Volunteer speaker programs; sponsorship of essay contest in Taos County High Schools. Founded 1961.

NEW YORK

ATTICA HISTORICAL SOCIETY
Main St.   ATTICA 14011
  Marian Stevens, Director
  Lewis Wood, President

Activities: Museum exhibiting Indian and pioneer articles. Reference library. Founded 1937.

BUFFALO AND ERIE COUNTY
  HISTORICAL SOCIETY
25 Nottingham Court   BUFFALO 14216
  Walter S. Dunn, Jr.
    (Executive Officer)

Purpose: "...to discover, procure and preserve whatever may relate to the history of western New York in general and the City of Buffalo in particular." *Activities:* Sponsors museum and library containing, respectively, collections of Eastern and Western U.S. Indian artifacts, and books and manuscripts relating to the Seneca Indians. *Awards:* Sponsors Red Jacket Award, presented annually for distinguished civic accomplishments. Founded 1862.

ONTARIO COUNTY HISTORICAL
  SOCIETY
55 N. Main St.   CANANDAIGUA 14424
  Mrs. Ralph O. Stratton, Curator

Activities: Museum containing Indian relics and historic documents. Library. Founded 1902.

HISTORICAL SOCIETY OF THE TOWN
  OF CLARENCE
6090 Goodrich Rd.
               CLARENCE CENTER 14032
  Mrs. Oneta M. Baker, Curator

Purpose: "The preservation of local history and artifacts." *Activities:* Society sponsors annual programs on local history; classes for seventh-grade children held one week annually, with program on local history and guided tour of Society's Museum. *Collections:* Indian tools, etc., on exhibit, depicting Indian history in Clarence (including photos). Founded 1954.

CORTLAND COUNTY HISTORICAL
  SOCIETY, INC.
Court House, Third Floor
Church St.   CORTLAND 13045
  Dr. Roger C. Heppell, President

Activities: Exhibits local historical and Indian items; genealogies and documents. Library. Publications. Founded 1925.

EAST HAMPTON HISTORICAL SOCIETY
Main St.   EAST HAMPTON, L.I. 11937
  Nelson C. Osborne, President

Activities: Museum and historic building housing pioneer and Indian relics and implements. Publications.

MONTGOMERY COUNTY HISTORICAL
  SOCIETY
               FORT JOHNSON 12070
  Mrs. Richard Evans, Chairman

Activities: Museum containing Indian relics and artifacts, especially of the Mohawk Valley; Society maintains historic Old Fort Johnson (circa 1749). Publications. Founded 1905.

HUNTINGTON HISTORICAL SOCIETY
2 High St.   HUNTINGTON 11743
  Mrs. Sarah Shabaglian, Director

Purpose: "To perpetuate an interest in the history of the Town of Huntington and to collect and preserve colonial and historic relics." *Activities:* Maintains museum and library; presents slide and lecture programs. *Programs:* Exhibits of educational and artistic interest arranged at various times. Meetings include speakers on appropriate topics. *Collections:* Newspaper collection; genealogical records; historical volumes; maps; manuscripts and documents.

NIAGARA COUNTY HISTORICAL
   SOCIETY, INC.
215 Niagara St.
(118 Cottage St.)   LOCKPORT 14094
   Richard Cary, President
   Charles Boyer, Curator

Activities: Museum featuring collections relating to local area and to Iroquois culture; conducts archaeological research. Publications. Founded 1921.

AMERICAN CIVIL LIBERTIES UNION
156 Fifth Ave.   NEW YORK 10010
   John de J. Pemberton, Jr.,
      Executive Director

Purpose: "To attain equality for all regardless of race, color, religion or national origin." *Activities:* Test cases, public protests. *Publication: Civil Liberties. Membership:* 60,000 members. Founded 1920.

AMERICAN INDIAN ETHNOHISTORIC
   CONFERENCE
c/o Eleanor Leacock
Bank Street College of Education
69 Bank Street   NEW YORK 10014
   Eleanor Leacock, Secretary-
      Treasurer

Purpose: "To encourage research in the fields of anthropology, history, and ethnohistory." *Publication:* Quarterly, *Ethnohistory. Membership:* 475. Founded 1955.

ASSOCIATION ON AMERICAN INDIAN
   AFFAIRS, INC.
432 Park Ave. South   NEW YORK 10016
   William Byler, Executive Director

Purpose: "To promote the welfare of the American Indians, Aleuts and Eskimos of the United States by creating an enlightened public opinion; by assisting and protecting Indians against encroachment of their Constitutional rights; by aiding in the improvement of health and education conditions; by preserving and fostering Indian arts and

crafts." *Programs:* Land rights protection and community development programs in Alaska; legal aid program on Pine Ridge Reservation, Pine Ridge, South Dakota; joint sponsorship, with United Sioux Tribes of South Dakota, of a voter participation program; sponsorship of Alaskan native conferences. *Grants:* To combat alcoholism in Southwestern Indian communities; college scholarship program. Founded 1923.

MARQUETTE LEAGUE FOR CATHOLIC
   INDIAN MISSIONS
289 Park Ave. South
               NEW YORK 10016
   Paul G. Reilly, President

Purpose: "To provide financial support for U.S. Catholic Indian missions." Founded 1904.

NATIONAL COUNCIL OF CHURCHES OF
   CHRIST IN THE U.S.A.
475 Riverside Drive   NEW YORK 10027
   Roy G. Ross, General Secretary

Organization is a federation representing thirty-one Protestant and Eastern Orthodox denominations. *Activities:* Administration of schools and colleges; clinical services for foreign missionaries; literacy programs; rehabilitation of war amputees; overseas child care centers and other foreign aid; religious radio and television programs. *Publications: Information Service* (biweekly); *Interchurch News* (monthly); *International Journal of Religious Education* (monthly); *Yearbook of American Churches. Membership:* 31 (denominations). Founded 1950.

NORTH COLLINS HISTORICAL SOCIETY
North Collins Memorial Library
Center St.   NORTH COLLINS 14111
   Ethelyn Weller, President

Activities: Museum featuring pioneer and Indian items; hobby workshops; education programs for children. Founded 1941.

MADISON COUNTY HISTORICAL SOCIETY
435 Main St.   ONEIDA 13421
   Albert Smith, President

Activities: Museum containing genealogical records, Indian relics, pioneer and war items; historic house; conducts genealogical research. Library. Publications. Founded 1900.

OYSTERPONDS HISTORICAL
SOCIETY, INC.
Village Lane ORIENT, L.I. 11957
Dr. Charles H. Campbell, President
Mrs. John S. Gilbert, Curator-
Director

Activities: Maintains historic Village House (1790) and museum featuring Indian artifacts, war items; conducts genealogical research; preserves historic buildings and an Indian encampment. Founded 1944.

SUFFOLK COUNTY HISTORICAL SOCIETY
W. Main St. RIVERHEAD, L.I. 11901
Roy E. Lott, President
Marian G. Terry, Custodian

Activities: Operates museum containing Indian artifacts and historic documents. Library. Founded 1886.

NUNDAWAGA SOCIETY FOR HISTORY
AND FOLKLORE
2155 Portland Ave. RUSHVILLE 14544
(Rochester)
J. Allan Willis, President

Activities: Exhibits Indian costumes of early times, Iroguois pottery (Middlesex Valley Central School), wampum belts; presents pageants. Publications.

SCHENECTADY COUNTY HISTORICAL
SOCIETY
32 Washington Ave. SCHENECTADY 12305
H.A. McConville, Curator

Society operates historical museum containing Algonquian and Mohawk material.

SENECA FALLS HISTORICAL SOCIETY
55 Cayuga St. SENECA FALLS 13148
Mrs. Virginia D. Martin, Director

Activities: Museum containing archives, Indian relics, local items; maintains historic building; conducts education programs for children. Library. Founded 1904.

CONCORD HISTORICAL SOCIETY
Main St. SPRINGVILLE 14141
Mrs. Robert Engel, President

Activities: Maintains Pop Warner Museum, featuring historic Indian items.

ONONDAGA HISTORICAL ASSOCIATION
311 Montgomery St. SYRACUSE 13202
Richard N. Wright, President

Activities: Museum containing Iroquois Indian material and items of local historical significance. Founded 1862.

WATERLOO LIBRARY AND HISTORICAL
SOCIETY
31 E. Williams St. WATERLOO 13165
John S. Genung, Curator

Activities: Sponsors museum containing Indian and local material; maintains historic building. Library and reading room. Founded 1875.

JEFFERSON COUNTY HISTORICAL
SOCIETY
228 Washington St. WATERTOWN 13601
J. Reese Price, Curator

Activities: Museum exhibiting Indian relics, pioneer tools and implements. Library. Founded 1886.

CHAUTAUQUA COUNTY HISTORICAL
SOCIETY
Main St. WESTFIELD 14787
R. A. Nixon, Treasurer, House
Manager
Marion Baldwin, Librarian

Activities: Society operates museum containing Indian, military and archaeological material; maintains historic house; conducts education programs for children. Publications. Founded 1951.

MIDDLEBURY HISTORICAL SOCIETY
39 Academy St. WYOMING 14591
Mark Chamberlain, President

Activities: Sponsors museum containing military, pioneer and Indian artifacts, geological specimens, costumes; maintains historic building. Library. Founded 1916.

OHIO

MERCER COUNTY HISTORICAL
  SOCIETY, INC.
126 S. Main St.
P.O. Box 333   CELINA 45822
    Judge Carlton C. Reiser, President

Activities: Museum containing Indian, local,
medical and military items, archives. Publications. Founded 1957.

FORT RECOVERY HISTORICAL
  SOCIETY, INC.
Old Fort St.   FORT RECOVERY 45846

Purpose: "To create and foster appreciation
of the historical background of Fort Recovery; to acquire and preserve collections
and items of historical significance." *Activities:* Sponsors museum featuring Indian
arrowheads, hammerstones, grooved axes,
stone and shell gorget; relics from the Indian
Wars (1791-1749) battleground. Founded
1946.

MEDINA COUNTY HISTORICAL SOCIETY
233 E. Washington St.   MEDINA 44256
    Wade Belden, President

Activities: Museum exhibiting Indian and
local artifacts. Founded 1922.

LICKING COUNTY HISTORICAL SOCIETY
6th St. Park
P.O. Box 535   NEWARK 43055
    Miss Laura Beggs, President

Activities: Historic house and museum
housing Indian artifacts and 19th century
material. Publications. Founded 1947.

MIAMI COUNTY ARCHAEOLOGICAL
  SOCIETY
Box 137, Route 2   PIQUA 45356
    Harry A. Hopkins, Executive
      Officer

Purpose: "To preserve all archaeological
sites and material within the Miami County,
Ohio, area." *Activities:* Society salvages
archaeological materials; collects Indian
artifacts and lore; engages in surface hunting
for artifacts and mapping of Indian trails,

sites, mounds and fortifications. Conducts
programs of films, slides and professional
speakers. Founded 1961.

PORTAGE COUNTY HISTORICAL
  SOCIETY
State Route 44   RAVENNA 44266
    Cyrus Plough, President and Curator

Activities: Sponsors Indian lore museum
exhibits; maintains historic house. Publications. Founded 1951.

CLARK COUNTY HISTORICAL SOCIETY
Memorial Hall
300 W. Main St.   SPRINGFIELD 45504
    George W. Lohnes, Curator

Activities: Operates museum containing
prehistoric Indian relics, pioneer items.
Publications. Founded 1896.

WYANDOT COUNTY HISTORICAL
  SOCIETY
130 S. 7th St.   UPPER SANDUSKY 43351
    Edward Beard, President

Purpose: "The preservation of local historical sites." *Activities:* Society has developed and maintains a museum containing
local Indian artifacts and pioneer farm implements; reconstruction of blacksmith
shop; operates a three-acre park. Founded
1929.

LOGAN COUNTY HISTORICAL SOCIETY
P.O. Box 45   ZANESFIELD 43360
    Rev. Guy W. Furbay, Executive
      Officer

Purpose: "To preserve and display items
relating to the history of Logan County and
its people." *Activities:* Displays at fairs,
in windows and in the Society-operated
museum; talks with or without slides at
schools, clubs, etc.; articles in local newspaper. *Collections:* Local artifacts. Founded 1945.

OKLAHOMA

OKLAHOMA HISTORICAL SOCIETY
Lincoln Blvd.   NORMAN 73069

Purpose: "To collect, display and restore
the artifacts of Oklahoma history." *Acitiv-*

ties: Society operates second largest Indian museum in the world -- archives contain three million documents of the Five Civilized Tribes; library of 30,000 volumes; newspaper library of thirty million pages. Founded 1893.

OKLAHOMANS FOR INDIAN
    OPPORTUNITY
910 U.S. Post Office Bldg.
                 OKLAHOMA CITY 73102
    Mrs. LaDonna Harris, Chairman

Purpose: "To improve opportunities for Oklahoma Indians and draw them more fully into the Oklahoma economy and culture." Programs to center around Indian education, job opportunity and technical skills, training and retraining, housing, health, business financing. Maintains close working relationship with the Muskogee and Anadarko Area Offices of the Bureau of Indian Affairs. Founded 1965.

POTTAWATOMIE COUNTY HISTORICAL
    ASSOCIATION
Highway 18
1111 N. Broadway   SHAWNEE 74801
    Mrs. Clarence Robinson, President

Activities: Museum containing Indian artifacts, documents, items reflecting local history; maintains Shawnee Mission Church, Shawnee, Okla. Founded 1942.

OREGON

COLUMBIA COUNTY HISTORICAL
    SOCIETY
                    VERNONIA 97064
    Mrs. Pearl Becker, Manager

Activities: Museum housing pioneer and Indian items, manuscripts, geological specimens. Library. Publications. Founded 1962.

PENNSYLVANIA

LEHIGH COUNTY HISTORICAL SOCIETY
Trout Hall
414 Walnut St.   ALLENTOWN 18102
    Melville J. Boyer, Executive Officer

Purpose: "The promotion of local historical study; research, collection, preservation and publication of records, data, artifacts; and the restoration of early homes of Lehigh

County; the acquisition by donation of tools and objects of antiquarian interest." *Activities:* Society maintains a small museum containing a fifty-piece Indian pipe collection; pottery; several thousand points, etc. *Publications: Proceedings.* Founded 1904.

HISTORICAL SOCIETY OF DAUPHIN
    COUNTY
219 S. Front St.   HARRISBURG 17104
    Evan J. Miller, Executive Officer

Purpose: To preserve all historical papers and articles. *Activities:* Tours of Society operated Museum, containing Indian artifacts. Founded 1869.

MERCER COUNTY HISTORICAL SOCIETY
119 S. Pitt St.   MERCER 16137

Purpose: "The collection of data relating to early history of Mercer County; acquisition and preservation of documents, records, relics and memoaabilia dealing with pioneer period of local area." *Activities:* Operates library and museum open to public. *Collections:* (library) 1,000 volumes, 200 bound periodicals, newspaper collection of maps and surveys pertaining to Mercer County; (museum) local Indian artifacts. Founded 1945.

AMERICAN FRIENDS SERVICE
    COMMITTEE
160 N. 15th St.   PHILADELPHIA 19102
    Colin W. Bell, Executive Secretary

Purpose: "The American Friends Service Committee is one of the corporate expressions of Quaker faith and practice. It is rooted in the conviction that each human life is sacred, each man a child of God, and that love, expressed through creative action, is the only power that can overcome hatred, prejudice, and fear. The Committee undertakes programs of relief, service and education, ministering to both the physical and spiritual needs of men." *Activities:* A.F.S.C. projects in progress in following areas: San Carlos Apache Reservation, Arizona; scattered reservations in southern California; Intertribal Friendship House, Oakland, California; volunteer work in Denver, Colorado; Indian Education Program in Washington State; youth project on Northern Cheyenne Reservation, Montana. *Pro-*

grams: Youth services; school desegregation; work with Indian communities. Founded 1917.

INDIAN RIGHTS ASSOCIATION
1505 Race St.
                    PHILADELPHIA 19102
    Lawrence E. Lindley, General
        Secretary

Purpose: "To promote the welfare of Indians and to protect their rights." *Activities:* Maintains close contact with Indians and reservation conditions; follows progress of related legislation in Congress; conducts field studies to gather factual material for presentation to the public, to Congress, and to the Bureau of Indian Affairs. *Publication:* Periodical, *Indian Truth.* Founded 1882.

WESTMORELAND-FAYETTE
    HISTORICAL SOCIETY
West Overton   SCOTTDALE 15683
    William R. Griggin, President
    Mrs. Ray Musgrove, Curator

Activities: Sponsors museum housing pioneer and Indian articles, fossils, historic documents and books; maintains historic houses. Publications. Founded 1948.

MONROE COUNTY HISTORICAL SOCIETY
9th and Main Sts.
                    STROUDSBURG 18360
    Mrs. Horace Walters, Curator

Activities: Operates museum featuring Indian relics and pioneer implements; maintains historic house. Genealogical and historical library. Publications. Founded 1921.

WYOMING HISTORICAL AND
    GEOLOGICAL SOCIETY
69 S. Franklin St.
                    WILKES-BARRE 18701
    Alan W. Perkins, Executive Officer

Purpose: "To further knowledge of and interest in historical and scientific matters pertaining to the northeastern region of Pennsylvania." *Activities:* Exhibits, lectures, publication, library, etc. *Facilities:* Library, exhibit rooms, school tours, operation of historic homestead. *Collections:* (library) 40,000-volumes, over 1,000 cubic

feet of manuscript materials; (museum) archaeological collection of local artifacts. Founded 1858.

LYCOMING HISTORICAL SOCIETY
P.O. Box 304   WILLIAMSPORT 17704
    Dr. R. Max Gingrich, President

Activities: Museum housing Indian material, Civil War and pioneer articles; June pilgrimage to a selected historical spot. Publications.

RHODE ISLAND

THE RHODE ISLAND HISTORICAL
    SOCIETY
52 Power St.   PROVIDENCE 02906
    Clifford P. Monahon, Director

Purpose: The collection of historical materials relating to Rhode Island. *Activities:* The publication of historical works; maintenance of library, historic house and museum; research. *Collections:* Indian artifacts of local origin. Founded 1822.

SOUTH DAKOTA

AMERICAN INDIAN MISSION, INC.
Box 72   CUSTER 57730
    R. L. Gowan, Executive Officer

Purpose: "To supplement the work of individuals and institutions in programs of education, health, religion, social welfare, vocational training, etc., directly benefitting the American Indian." *Activities:* Provides a reliable channel for individuals and organizations to invest in Indian rehabilitation, education and spiritual development through assistance to private Indian schools; hospitals; homes for homeless Indian children; church-related and independent missions; emergency help to individual workers. Mission engages in survey work, hospital visitation, distribution of Bibles, etc., and encourages youth and retired persons to "engage in Peace Corps-like activity on needy Indian reservations and in cities where there is a concentration of Indians." *Grants:* Assistance given to institutions for the construction of classrooms, dormitories, chapels, etc., and for the purchase of necessary equipment. Founded 1951.

LAKE COUNTY HISTORICAL SOCIETY
310 - 8th St., N.E.   MADISON 57042
    George G. Smith, Executive Officer

Purpose: "To preserve the history of the early settlement of local area, and the antique articles used during that period."
Activities: Construction of new museum building. *Collections:* Early maps, local Indian artifacts. Founded 1952.

TENNESSEE

CHATTANOOGA AUDUBON
    SOCIETY, INC.
N. Sanctuary Rd.   CHATTANOOGA 37403
(307 E. 8th St.)
    James B. Cole, President

Activities: Wildlife refuge; maintains historic cabin erected by Cherokee Indians in 1704 containing Indian artifacts. Publications. Founded 1945.

FORT LOUDOUN ASSOCIATION
                        VONORE 37885
    Ned Russell, Executive Secretary

Activities: Operates museum housing local historical and Cherokee Indian artifacts; preservation of Fort Loudoun (circa 1756). Publications. Founded 1933.

VIRGINIA

JAMESTOWN FOUNDATION
Box J F   WILLIAMSBURG 23185
(Jamestown)
    Parke Rouse, Jr., Executive
        Director

Activities: Preservation of English settlement site (1607); reconstruction of James Fort, Powhatan's Indian Lodge, historic ships; museum containing Virginia Indian artifacts and pioneer items. Publications. Founded 1957.

WASHINGTON

SKAGIT COUNTY HISTORICAL SOCIETY
Museum Room, Skagit Valley College
2405 College Way   MOUNT VERNON 98273
(Route 2, Box 9C)
    Glenn Stover, Chairman,
        Museum Board

Activities: Museum housing documents and artifacts of local origin relating to pioneer and Indian life; tape recordings with early pioneers. Founded 1959.

AMERICAN INDIAN WOMEN'S SERVICE
    LEAGUE
Boren Ave. at Stewart St.
                        SEATTLE 98109
    Pearl Warren, Executive Director

Purpose: "To assist reservation Indians arriving in the Seattle area in their adjustment to urban life, and to acquaint the white community with the problems of the Indian."
Programs: Assistance through referrals to educational, social welfare and health agencies. League operates Indian Center for social, educational, cultural and recreational activities; collects and distributes clothing and other supplies during emergency situations. Founded 1960.

EASTERN WASHINGTON STATE
    HISTORICAL SOCIETY
W. 2316 1st Ave.   SPOKANE 99204
    Richard G. Conn, Director

Activities: Society operates a museum containing regional collection of Indian arts and crafts items; maintains historic house; sponsors concert series. Library and reading room. Publications. Founded 1916.

WASHINGTON STATE HISTORICAL
    SOCIETY
215 N. Stadium Way   TACOMA 98403
    Bruce Le Roy, Director

Activities: Operates museum housing local artifacts, Indian and Alaskan pictures and books; conducts educational programs for children. Library and reading room. Publications. Founded 1891.

WALLA WALLA COUNTY PIONEER
  AND HISTORICAL SOCIETY
City Hall, 3rd and Rose Sts.
(312 S. Division St.)
                    WALLA WALLA 99362
Margaret Pettyjohn, Curator

Activities: Museum featuring pioneer and
Indian tools and implements, Fort Walla
Walla relics and documents; educational
programs for children. Publications.
Founded 1886.

WEST VIRGINIA

FAYETTE COUNTY HISTORICAL
  SOCIETY
(Box 17, Oak Hill)
Midland Trail   ANSTED 25812
  Rev. Shirley Donnelly, President

Activities: Museum housing Indian and pioneer mountain artifacts and tools. Founded
1925.

WISCONSIN

JACKSON COUNTY HISTORICAL SOCIETY
              BLACK RIVER FALLS 54615
Mrs. Lois Hurlburt, President

Purpose: "To preserve and make available
materials related to local history." *Activities*: Society sponsors two county parks;
holds work meetings; maintains exchange
programs with other societies. *Collections:*
Pictures, slides and negatives of photo collection spanning period of 1880 to 1930; several hundred negatives and pictures of Winnebago Tribe, from from tintypes to modern
(1850 to 1930); costumes. Founded 1953.

STATE HISTORICAL SOCIETY OF
  WISCONSIN
816 State St.   MADISON 53706
  Dr. Leslie H. Fishel, Jr.,
    Executive Officer

Purpose: "To promote a wider appreciation
of the American heritage, with particular
emphasis on the collection, advancement and
dissemination of knowledge of the history
of Wisconsin and of the West." *Activities:*
Society operates research library in Amer-

ican history; serves as the archival desposi-
tory for the State of Wisconsin and local
units of government; maintains extensive
manuscript and map collections; operates
museum and four historical sites; conducts
historical and archaeological research;
publishes monographs in Wisconsin and
American history; advises affiliated county
and local historical societies; publishes
materials for use in elementary and secondary schools. *Programs:* Highway salvage
archaeology and archaeological digs under
National Park Service grants. *Awards:*
Reuben Gold Thwaites Trophy; Awards of
Merit; Local History Awards of Merit.
Awards bestowed upon individuals, organizations, local historical societies, publishers and others who have made outstanding contributions to historical research,
publication, presentation of resources during the period preceding granting of the
awards. *Collections:* 125,000 archaeological artifacts; 48,000 museum artifacts;
4,500 disc and tape recordings; 100,000
photographs, paintings and graphic representations. *Holdings:* 345,206 volumes;
353,705 pamphlets; 40,060 reels of microfilm; 124,519 microprint cards; 8,000,000
pieces of private manuscripts; 15,000 cubic
feet of state and local archives; 100,000
sheets of maps and geographical charts.
Publications: Quarterly, *Wisconsin Magazine of History.* Founded 1846.

MARINETTE COUNTY HISTORICAL
  SOCIETY
Stephenson Island
                    MARINETTE 54143
  John S. Ramsay, President
  Henry E. Hansen, Curator

Activities: Museum featuring logging and
Indian material. Founded 1962.

SHEBOYGAN COUNTY HISTORICAL
  SOCIETY
3110 Erie Ave.   SHEBOYGAN 53081
  Charles Werner, President
  Mr. and Mrs. T. Mosch,
    Resident Custodians

Activities: Museum collections include
Indian relics. Society maintains historic
house; sponsors study clubs. Founded
1923.

Monuments and State Parks

Included in this section are listings of national and state parks and recreation areas -- often the sites of historic and prehistoric Indian cultures. The listings are alpha-geographically arranged.

ARIZONA

MONTEZUMA CASTLE NATIONAL MONUMENT
P. O. Box 218   CAMP VERDE 86322
   Hugh B. Ebert, Superintendent

Description: Prehistoric Pueblo Indian ruins at the Castle section; smaller ruins, prehistoric irrigation ditch and natural limestone sink at the Well section. *Activities:* Guided trails at both sections with unscheduled tours into the ruins area. *Collections:* Indian artifacts obtained from Monument excavations. Descriptive brochure available.

TUZIGOOT NATIONAL MONUMENT
P. O. Box 36   CLARKDALE 86324

Description: Remnants of a prehistoric town built by Indians who farmed Arizona's Verde Valley between A. D. 1125 and A. D. 1400. *Collections:* Turquoise mosaics; beads and bracelets made of shells, painted pottery. Descriptive brochure available.

CASA GRANDE NATIONAL MONUMENT
P. O. Box 518   COOLIDGE
   Aubrey F. Houston, Superintendent
   David H. Hannah, Park Archaeologist

Archaeology museum contains artifacts of the pre-Columbian Pueblo and Hohokam Indians; skeletal material (cremations and humations); ethnological material of the Pima and Papago Indians -- basketry, ceremonial trappings, pottery. *Activities:* Lectures, guided tours through the Casa Grande Ruins (pre-Columbian, circa A. D. 1300 to A. D. 1450).

WALNUT CANYON NATIONAL MONUMENT
Route 1
Box 790   FLAGSTAFF 86001

Description: Covers an area of approximately three square miles on both sides of Walnut Canyon. There are approximately four hundred single-story cliff dwelling rooms, and an equal number of surface pueblo sites preserved in the Monument. There are remains of the Sinagua farming Indians (A. D. 1200 to A. D. 1300). *Activities:* A guiding trail provides access to twenty-five cliff dwelling rooms. There is a visitor center, with museum. *Collections:* Archaeological specimens -- pottery, woven material, stone and bone material of the 12th and 13th centuries.

WUPATKI NATIONAL MONUMENT
Tuba Star Route   FLAGSTAFF 86003

Description: In an area of fifty-six square miles, Wupatki National Monument contains approximately 800 Indian ruins. The walls of Wupatki Ruin -- the main pueblo -- rise from a sandstone spur at the base of a black lava mesa that overlooks the Painted Desert. A ball court and amphitheater are below the Ruin. Other sites at the Monument are Citadel Ruin, the Lomaki and Wukoki Ruins, and the Crack-in-the-Rock Ruins, which contain reconstructed and unreconstructed fortified apartment houses which are estimated to have contained -- in their original form -- as many as fifty rooms each.

TONTO NATIONAL MONUMENT
ROOSEVELT 85545

Description: Pueblo Indian ruins -- cliff dwellings in three sections, comprising a total of seventy rooms. *Collections:* Items recovered from Monument excavations -- utensils, fabrics, weapons, and other artifacts. Descriptive brochure available.

NAVAJO NATIONAL MONUMENT
TONALEA 86044

Description: The Monument includes three Pueblo III villages of the Kayenta Anasazi Culture, with museum and archaeological laboratory. *Collections:* Material gathered from Monument excavations -- salvage archaeology collections, Kayenta Anasazi PI-early PIII. Several collections of PIII Kayenta Anasazi from the village sites of Betatakin, Keet Seel, and Inscription House.

CHIRICAHUA NATIONAL MONUMENT
Star Route   WILLCOX 85643
    Forrest M. Benson, Jr.,
    Superintendent

Contains natural history museum (anthropology, archaeology, ethnology, Indian artifacts). Information on Indian history of Chiricahua Mountains. Publications.

CALIFORNIA

FORT ROSS STATE HISTORIC PARK
19005 Coast Highway 1   JENNER 95450
    Wayne Colwell, Park Supervisor

Description: Partially restored fort of the Russian-American Fur Company, built and occupied from 1812 to 1841. Small interpretive museum; Russian Orthodox Chapel; two blockhouses; stockade wall. *Collections:* Small exhibit of Pomo Indian material; some Aleut; some Eskimo.

LA PURISIMA MISSION HISTORICAL PARK
R. F. D. Box 102   LOMPOC

History museum contains Chumash Indian artifacts; Spanish Colonial material. *Activities:* Guided tours, lectures. Publications.

WILL ROGERS STATE HISTORIC PARK
14253 Sunset Blvd.
                    PACIFIC PALISADES 90272
    Wendell K. Davis, Park Supervisor

Description: The ranch which belonged to the American humorist, Will Rogers (of Cherokee Indian descent), containing the original buildings and furnishings, including stable, corrals, riding ring and roping arena. *Collections:* Indian rugs and blankets.

SHASTA STATE HISTORICAL MONUMENT
P. O. Box 507   SHASTA

History museum contains Indian artifacts, gun and art collections. *Activities:* Library; reading room.

LAVA BEDS NATIONAL MONUMENT
P. O. Box 867   TULELAKE 96134
    Garrett H. Smathers, Superintendent

Description: Site of prehistoric volcanic eruptions and, centuries later, of the Modoc Indian War (1873-1874). *Collections:* Indian art on rock -- pictographs of red, yellow and green mineral pigments on the walls of caves and the sides of natural bridges; carvings (petroglyphs) found on rocks soft enough to be chiseled. Descriptive brochure available.

COLORADO

MESA VERDE NATIONAL PARK
    MESA VERDE NATIONAL PARK 81330
    Chester A. Thomas, Superintendent

Description: A prehistoric Pueblo Indian community -- pithouses, cliff dwellings, etc. *Collections:* Extensive study materials of the Northern San Juan Anasazi Culture; limited biological and ethnological collections. Descriptive brochure available.

FLORIDA

FORT CAROLINE NATIONAL MONUMENT
Route 1
Box 310   JACKSONVILLE 32211
    Harvey D. Wickware, Management
    Assistant

Description: Sixteenth-century fort, built during French and Spanish colonial period in Florida. *Collections:* Visitor Center Museum exhibits large reproductions of several LeMoyne drawings -- maps, depictions of native life (the first pictorial records of European contact with the American wilderness). Small collection of Timucuan artifacts: pottery, beads, ornaments, balls, arrowheads, tools, and an effigy.

GEORGIA

ETOWAH INDIAN MOUNDS
                    CARTERSVILLE 30120
    L. H. Tumlin, Jr., Superintendent

Description: Large Indian site with seven mounds surrounded by a moat, partially filled. *Activities:* Sponsors annual field dig with student participants from many schools throughout the United States, under the joint direction of Georgia State College and the Georgia Historical Commission. *Collections:* Material recovered from Mound excavations displayed in on-site museum. Descriptive brochure available.

INDIAN CHIEF WILLIAM McINTOSH HOME
U. S. Highway 23   INDIAN SPRINGS
    J. H. Elliott, Jr., Director

Historic house contains Indian artifacts and prehistoric items recovered from local area.

OCMULGEE NATIONAL MONUMENT
P. O. Box 4186   MACON 31208
    George R. Fischer, Archaeologist

Description: Site containing seven mounds constructed by a group of farming Indians who lived in what is now Georgia approximately one thousand years ago; reconstructed ceremonial earthlodge. *Collections:* Extensive museum collections explain culture of the Indians who constructed the mounds and of five other Indian groups who have lived on the site over the past ten thousand years. Collection from Ocmulgee and immediate vicinity includes approximately two million items ranging in time from Paleo-Indian through historic Creek. Included are extensive collections from relief-area archaeology throughout the Southeast. Ocmulgee National Monument serves as repository for National Park Service collections in the Southeast and contains material from the Natchez Trace, Russell Cave, and several other areas.

OKEFENOKEE SWAMP PARK
P. O. Box 117   WAYCROSS
    Liston Atkins, Manager

Park museum contains Indian relics and fossils; photographs and items pertaining to early Swamp residents. *Activities:* Lectures, tours.

ILLINOIS

STEPHEN MACK HOUSE
Macktown Forest Preserve   ROCKTON
    R. Hazel Shotliff, President

Historic house contains Indian artifacts, farm and pioneer tools and implements. *Activities:* Tours.

IOWA

EFFIGY MOUNDS NATIONAL MONUMENT
Box K   McGREGOR 52157
    Stuart H. Maule, Superintendent

Description: Site established to preserve and interpret prehistoric Indian burial mounds of a variety of types, including effigy mounds built in the shape of animals -- bears and birds -- as well as the more common conical forms; linear and compound mounds are also found. Mounds were built for approximately two thousand years, beginning in approximately 500 B. C. *Collections:* Primarily archaeological items of northeastern Iowa.

MARYLAND

GATHLAND STATE PARK
                    BURKITTSVILLE

Historic house contains Indian relics and Civil War mementos.

MINNESOTA

PIPESTONE NATIONAL MONUMENT
                    PIPESTONE 56164
    Ralph K. Shaver, Superintendent

Description: Original pipestone (*catlinite,* named for noted painter of Indians, George Catlin) quarry from which the Dakota Sioux fashioned their ceremonial pipes. *Collections:* Visitor Center contains seventeen panel exhibits and over eight hundred catalogued artifacts and books.

MISSOURI

OLD TAVERN
Arrow Rock State Park   ARROW ROCK
    Mrs. Charles Jones, Hostess

Historic house contains Indian artifacts,
Americana.

MONTANA

CUSTER BATTLEFIELD NATIONAL
    MONUMENT
Box 416   CROW AGENCY 59022
    Andrew M. Loveless, Historian

Description: Historic area commemorating
the Battle of the Little Big Horn, where
Lt. Col. George A. Custer and five troops
of the 7th U. S. Cavalry were annihilated by
Sioux and Cheyenne Indians. *Activities/
Facilities:* Historical museum with thirty
panel and case exhibits, including three
original paintings and two dioramas; tape-
recorded talk concerning the Battle; interpretive talks by uniformed personnel; self-
guiding trail at the Reno-Benteen Defense
Area. Library and historical document and
artifact collections. *Collections:* Historical
documents authored by or associated with
George A. Custer, his wife, Elizabeth B.
Custer, the Battle of the Little Big Horn,
and other events and persons associated with
the Indian Wars on the Northern Plains
(1865-1891). Military and ethnographic
specimens relating to the conflict, including items associated with the Sioux, Crow,
and Northern Cheyenne Tribes.

NEW MEXICO

AZTEC RUINS NATIONAL MONUMENT
Route 1
Box 101   AZTEC 87410
    Gerald L. Wood, Park Archaeologist

Description: Prehistoric Pueblo Indian ruin.
Two- (cultural) phase inhabitation: Chaco
Canyon and Mesa Verde. *Activities:* Self-
guiding tour. Guided tours arranged for
organized groups. *Collections:* Archaeological materials gathered from excavations of area sites and from sites in the
Lower San Juan Basin.

CORONADO STATE MONUMENT
P. O. Box 95   BERNALILLO 87004
    J. P. Blum, Director

Description: Site of a partially reconstructed Pueblo Indian village ruin occupied circa
1300-1600. Includes a completely reconstructed underground ceremonial *kiva*,
which was the first to be discovered bearing ceremonial murals. *Activities:* Tours
and lectures for special groups. *Collections:* Material recovered from Monument
excavations.

CHACO CANYON NATIONAL MONUMENT
Box 156   BLOOMFIELD 87413
    Mr. Lynn A. Robbins, Archaeologist

Description: Eleven large prehistoric
Pueblo Indian ruins which date from A. D.
800 to A.D. 1100; 350 additional sites which
reflect the same cultural traditions. Navajo
and historic Pueblo remains also present.
Activities: Museum tours; slide-illustrated
lectures; limited archaeological research.
Collections: Visitor Center Museum features twenty-six exhibits on prehistoric
Pueblo Indians and Navajo people, early
history of Chaco Canyon, and archaeological research techniques. Library.

CARLSBAD CAVERNS NATIONAL
    MONUMENT
P. O. Box 1598   CARLSBAD
    Henry R. During, Superintendent

Natural science museum contains items on
the geology and archaeology of the Southwest. Park museum.

BANDELIER NATIONAL MONUMENT
                          LOS ALAMOS 87544

Description: Approximately 29,000 acres
in size, Monument preserves ruins of the
Pueblo (Anasazi) Culture, dating from about
A. D. 1200 to A. D. 1600, at the Pueblo III
and IV cultural stages. *Activities:* Self-
guided tours; museum; audio-visual program; conducted tours; evening lectures.
Collections: Small representative collection of Pueblo cultural material from the
immediate area, dating from A. D. 1200 to
A. D. 1600.

GRAN QUIVARA NATIONAL MONUMENT
Route 1   MOUNTAINAIR 87036

Description: Monument preserves the stone ruins of two frontier Spanish Franciscan missions built during the early decades of the 17th century, and the ruins of a large Pueblo Indian village. *Collections:* A small museum contains characteristic pottery types, small amounts of stone, bone and shell artifacts.

NEW YORK

BEAR MOUNTAIN TRAILSIDE MUSEUMS
                BEAR MOUNTAIN 10911
John C. Orth, Curator

Indian Collection relates the man's entry into North America and the cultural history of the Indian in New York State. Exhibits on shelter, food, weapons, tools, pottery, art and mythology; many artifacts recovered from rock shelters and campsites of the area are included.

NORTH CAROLINA

TOWN CREEK INDIAN MOUND
R. F. D. 3   MOUNT GILEAD 27306

Description: Aboriginal ceremonial center, partially restored. *Activities:* Guided tours and lectures for organized groups. *Collections:* Museum contains archaeological and replica exhibits depicting ceremonial customs and everyday life of Muskogean group, circa 1550-1650.

NORTH DAKOTA

FORT LINCOLN STATE PARK
                MANDAN 58501
James R. Kittle, Director

Description: Partially reconstructed Forts McKeen and Abraham Lincoln, and Slant Indian Village. *Collections:* Indian arrowheads, agricultural tools, weapons, models of regional Indian life and culture.

OREGON

CHAMPOEG STATE PARK
Route 1, Box 75   AURORA
    O. J. Shaw, Park Manager

History museum contains early pioneer and Indian artifacts. Publications.

PENNSYLVANIA

BUSHY RUN BATTLEFIELD PARK
                    JEANETTE
    William E. Moog, Superintendent

History museum contains copies of maps and letters relating to the Campaign of 1763, Pontiac's War; Indian artifacts.

SOUTH CAROLINA

ANDREW JACKSON HISTORICAL
STATE PARK
                LANCASTER
    Cecil S. Hayes, Superintendent

History museum contains Indian relics (1750-1850); textile display; art collection; letters and documents. *Activities:* Guided tours; educational programs for children.

SOUTH DAKOTA

WIND CAVE NATIONAL PARK
                HOT SPRINGS
    J. H. Lombard, Superintendent

Natural history museum contains Indian artifacts; historic documents. *Activities:* Guided tours; educational lectures.

WASHINGTON

SACAJAWEA STATE PARK
Route 1   PASCO
    Leonard S. Benton, Ranger

Indian museum contains artifacts, arrowheads and tools.

Reservations

Included in this alpha-geographically arranged section are reservations, bands, communities, and other defined groupings of Indians. Where possible, geographical location and mailing address are given. Where a reservation is served by a Bureau of Indian Affairs agency in another state, listings appear in both states. The existence of tribal councils (representative and policy-making bodies) has also been noted.

ALASKA

AFOGNAK COMMUNITY   AFOGNAK
In residence: 146. *Tribe:* Eskimo.

AKHIOK COMMUNITY   AKHIOK
99615
In residence: 70. *Tribe:* Eskimo.

AKIACHAK COMMUNITY   AKIACHAK
99551
In residence: 175. *Tribe:* Eskimo.

AKIAK COMMUNITY   AKIAK
99552
In residence: 151. *Tribe:* Eskimo.

AKULURAK COMMUNITY   AKULURAK
In residence: 187. *Tribe:* Eskimo.

ALATNA COMMUNITY   ALATNA
In residence: 31. *Tribe:* Eskimo.

ALEKNAGIK COMMUNITY   ALEKNAGIK
99555
In residence: 116. *Tribes:* Athapascan, Indian.

ALLAKAKET COMMUNITY   ALLAKAKET
99720
In residence: 75. *Tribe:* Athapascan, Indian.

ANAKTUVUK PASS COMMUNITY
ANAKTUVUK PASS 99721
In residence: 65. *Tribe:* Eskimo.

ANCHORAGE COMMUNITY   ANCHORAGE
99501
In residence: 140. *Tribes:*   Athapascan, Indian.

ANIAK COMMUNITY   ANIAK
99557
In residence: 90. *Tribe:* Eskimo.

ANVIK COMMUNITY   ANVIK
99558
In residence: 94. *Tribes:*   Athapascan, Indian.

ARCTIC COMMUNITY   ARCTIC
99722
In residence: 53. *Tribe:* Athapascan.

BARROW COMMUNITY   BARROW
99723
In residence: 924. *Tribe:* Eskimo.

BEAVER COMMUNITY   BEAVER
99724
In residence: 86. *Tribes:* Eskimo, Athapascan, Indian.

BELKOFSKI COMMUNITY   BELKOFSKI
In residence: 119. *Tribe:* Aleut.

BETHEL COMMUNITY   BETHEL
99559
In residence: 505. *Tribes:* Eskimo, Indian.

BETTLES COMMUNITY   BETTLES
99726
In residence: 22. *Tribes:* Eskimo, Indian.

CANDLE COMMUNITY   CANDLE
                                                 99728
In residence: 81. *Tribe:* Eskimo.

CANTWELL COMMUNITY   CANTWELL
                                                 99729
In residence: 41. *Tribe:* Athapascan.

CHANELIAK COMMUNITY   CHANELIAK
In residence: 97. *Tribe:* Eskimo.

CHEECHING COMMUNITY   CHEECHING
In residence: 54. *Tribe:* Eskimo.

CHEFORNAK COMMUNITY
                            CHEFORNAK 99561
In residence: 106. *Tribe:* Eskimo.

CHENEGA COMMUNITY   CHENEGA
In residence: 90. *Tribe:* Aleut.

CHEVAK COMMUNITY   CHEVAK
                                                 99563
In residence: 230. *Tribe:* Eskimo.

CHICKEN COMMUNITY   CHICKEN
                                                 99732
In residence: 9. *Tribe:* Athapascan.

CHIFTAK COMMUNITY   CHIFTAK
In residence: 50. *Tribe:* Eskimo.

CHIGNIK COMMUNITY   CHIGNIK
                                                 99564
In residence: 222. *Tribe:* Eskimo.

CHISTOCHINA COMMUNITY
                              CHISTOCHINA
In residence: 13. *Tribe:* Athapascan.

CHITINA COMMUNITY   CHITINA
                                                 99566
In residence: 64. *Tribe:* Athapascan.

CHOWHOCTOLIK COMMUNITY
                            CHOWHOCTOLIK
In residence: 98. *Tribe:* Eskimo.

CHUKFAKTOOLIK COMMUNITY
                            CHUKFAKTOOLIK
In residence: 59.

CIRCLE COMMUNITY   CIRCLE
                                                 99733
In residence: 63. *Tribe:* Athapascan.

CLARKS POINT COMMUNITY
                            CLARKS POINT 99569
In residence: 94. *Tribe:* Athapascan.

COLOVIN COMMUNITY   COLOVIN
In residence: 86. *Tribe:* Eskimo.

COPPER CENTER COMMUNITY
                            COPPER CENTER 99573

In residence: 53. *Tribe:* Athapascan.

CORDOVA COMMUNITY   CORDOVA
                                                 99574
In residence: 218. *Tribes:* Athapascan,
Indian.

COUNCIL COMMUNITY   COUNCIL
In residence: 26. *Tribe:* Eskimo.

CROOKED CREEK COMMUNITY
                            CROOKED CREEK 99575
In residence: 36. *Tribe:* Athapascan.

CURRY COMMUNITY   CURRY
In residence: 13. *Tribe:* Athapascan.

CUTOFF COMMUNITY   CUTOFF

In residence: 62. *Tribe:* Athapascan.

DEERING COMMUNITY   DEERING
                                                 99736
In residence: 150. *Tribe:* Eskimo.

DILLINGHAM COMMUNITY
                            DILLINGHAM 99576
In residence: 293. *Tribes:* Athapascan,
Indian.

DIOMEDE COMMUNITY   DIOMEDE
In residence: 100. *Tribe:* Eskimo.

BESSIE #5, DREDGE CAMP
                          DREDGE CAMP
In residence: 20. *Tribes:* Eskimo, Indian.

EAGLE COMMUNITY   EAGLE
                              99738
In residence: 18. *Tribes:* Eskimo, Indian.

EASTCHESTER COMMUNITY
               EASTCHESTER 99501
In residence: 59. *Tribes:*   Athapascan,
Indian.

EEK COMMUNITY   EEK
                              99578
In residence: 139. *Tribe:* Eskimo.

EGEGIK COMMUNITY   EGEGIK
                              99579
In residence: 82. *Tribes:* Eskimo, Indian.

EKLUTNA COMMUNITY   EKLUTNA
In residence: 24. *Tribe:* Athapascan.

EKWAK COMMUNITY   EKWAK
                              99580
In residence: 113. *Tribe:* Athapascan.

ELEPHANT POINT COMMUNITY
                 ELEPHANT POINT
In residence: 99. *Tribe:* Eskimo.

ELIM COMMUNITY   ELIM
                              99739
In residence: 154. *Tribe:* Eskimo.

ELLAMAR COMMUNITY   ELLAMAR
In residence: 31. *Tribe:* Aleut.

EMANGAK COMMUNITY   EMANGAK
In residence: 67. *Tribe:* Eskimo.

ENGLISH BAY COMMUNITY
                    ENGLISH BAY
In residence: 71. *Tribe:* Eskimo.

ESKIMO COMMUNITY   ESKIMO
In residence: 41. *Tribes:* Eskimo, Indian.

FAIRBANKS COMMUNITY   FAIRBANKS
In residence: 240. *Tribes:*   Athapascan,
Eskimo.

FLAT COMMUNITY   FLAT
                              99584
In residence: 32. *Tribes:*   Athapascan,
Eskimo.

FORT YUKON COMMUNITY
                FORT YUKON 99740
In residence: 396. *Tribes:*   Athapascan,
Indian.

GAKONA COMMUNITY   GAKONA
                              99586
In residence: 25. *Tribe:* Athapascan.

GALENA COMMUNITY   GALENA
                              99741
In residence: 106. *Tribe:* Athapascan.

GAMBELL COMMUNITY   GAMBELL
                              99742
In residence: 294. *Tribes:* Eskimo, Indian.

GLENNALLEN COMMUNITY
               GLENNALLEN 99588
In residence: 41. *Tribes:*   Athapascan,
Indian.

GRAEHL COMMUNITY   GRAEHL
In residence: 43. *Tribes:*   Athapascan,
Indian.

GULKANA COMMUNITY   GULKANA
In residence: 37. *Tribe:* Athapascan.

HAMILTON COMMUNITY   HAMILTON
In residence: 42. *Tribe:* Eskimo.

HOLIKACHUK COMMUNITY
                  HOLIKACHUK
In residence: 96. *Tribe:* Athapascan.

HOLY CROSS COMMUNITY
                    HOLY CROSS 99602
In residence: 154. *Tribes:* Athapascan,
Eskimo.

HOMER COMMUNITY   HOMER
                                    99603
In residence: 27. *Tribes:* Aleut,   Indian.

HOOPER BAY COMMUNITY
                    HOOPER BAY 99604
In residence: 303. *Tribe:* Eskimo.

HOT SPRINGS COMMUNITY
                    HOT SPRINGS 99756
In residence: 7. *Tribe:* Athapascan.

HUGHES COMMUNITY   HUGHES
                                    99745
In residence: 45. *Tribe:* Athapascan.

HUNGRY COMMUNITY   HUNGRY
In residence: 29. *Tribe:* Athapascan.

IGLOO COMMUNITY   IGLOO
In residence: 64. *Tribe:* Eskimo.

ILIAMNA COMMUNITY   ILIAMNA
                                    99606
In residence: 19. *Tribes:*   Athapascan,
Indian.

INDIAN COMMUNITY   INDIAN
In residence: 45. *Tribe:* Athapascan.

KAKHONAK COMMUNITY
                                  KAKHONAK
In residence: 29. *Tribe:* Aleut.

KAKTOVIK COMMUNITY   KAKTOVIK
                                    99747
In residence: 44. *Tribe:* Eskimo, Indian.

KALSKAG COMMUNITY   KALSKAG
                                    99607
In residence: 139. *Tribe:* Eskimo.

KALTAG COMMUNITY   KALTAG
                                    99748
In residence: 119. *Tribe:* Athapascan.

KANAKANAK COMMUNITY
                                  KANAKANAK
In residence: 37. *Tribes:* Eskimo, Indian.

KARLUK COMMUNITY   KARLUK
                                    99608
In residence: 137. *Tribe:* Aleut.

KASIGLOOK COMMUNITY   KASIGLOOK
                                    99609
In residence: 111. *Tribe:* Eskimo.

KENAI COMMUNITY   KENAI
                                    99611
In residence: 102. *Tribes:*   Athapascan,
Indian.

KEYALUVIK COMMUNITY   KEYALUVIK
In residence: 69. *Tribe:* Eskimo.

KIANA COMMUNITY   KIANA
                                    99749
In residence: 168. *Tribe:* Eskimo.

KING COVE COMMUNITY   KING COVE
                                    99612
In residence: 145. *Tribes:* Aleut, Indian.

KIONUK COMMUNITY   KIONUK
In residence: 182. *Tribe:* Eskimo.

KIVALINA COMMUNITY   KIVALINA
                                    99750
In residence: 117. *Tribe:* Eskimo.

KLAKANUK COMMUNITY   KLAKANUK
In residence: 126. *Tribe:* Eskimo.

KOBUK COMMUNITY   KOBUK
                                    99751
In residence: 31. *Tribe:* Eskimo.

KODIAK COMMUNITY   KODIAK
99615
In residence: 238. *Tribes:* Eskimo, Indian.

KOKRINES COMMUNITY   KOKRINES
In residence: 65. *Tribe:* Athapascan.

KOLIGANEK COMMUNITY   KOLIGANEK
In residence: 90. *Tribes:* Athapascan, Indian.

KOTLIK COMMUNITY   KOTLIK
99620
In residence: 44. *Tribe:* Eskimo.

KOTZEBUE COMMUNITY   KOTZEBUE
99752
In residence: 554. *Tribe:* Eskimo.

KOYUK COMMUNITY   KOYUK
99753
In residence: 132. *Tribe:* Eskimo.

KOYUKUK COMMUNITY   KOYUKUK
99754
In residence: 75. *Tribe:* Athapascan.

KOYUKUK RIVER COMMUNITY
KOYUKUK RIVER
In residence: 48. *Tribe:* Athapascan.

KWETHLUK COMMUNITY   KWETHLUK
99621
In residence: 232. *Tribe:* Eskimo.

KWIGILLINGOK COMMUNITY
KWIGILLINGOK 99622
In residence: 239. *Tribe:* Eskimo.

LAKE MINCHUMINA COMMUNITY
LAKE MINCHUMINA 99623
In residence: 26. *Tribes:* Athapascan, Indian.

LARSEN BAY COMMUNITY
LARSEN BAY 99624
In residence: 36. *Tribe:* Eskimo.

LEMETA TRACT COMMUNITY
LEMETA TRACT
In residence: 11. *Tribe:* Athapascan.

LEVELOCK COMMUNITY
LEVELOCK 99625
In residence: 47. *Tribe:* Aleut.

LOWER KALSKAG COMMUNITY
LOWER KALSKAG 99626
In residence: 88. *Tribe:* Eskimo.

McGRATH COMMUNITY   McGRATH
99627
In residence: 64. *Tribes:* Athapascan, Eskimo, Indian.

MANOKOTAK COMMUNITY
MANOKOTAK 99628
In residence: 120. *Tribes:* Eskimo and Indian.

MARSHALL COMMUNITY   MARSHALL
In residence: 78. *Tribe:* Eskimo.

MATANUSKA COMMUNITY
MATANUSKA
In residence: 22. *Tribe:* Athapascan, Indian.

MEAKERVILLE COMMUNITY
MEAKERVILLE
In residence: 10. *Tribe:* Aleut.

MEDFRA COMMUNITY   MEDFRA
99629
In residence: 20. *Tribes:* Athapascan, Indian.

MEKORYOK COMMUNITY   MEKORYOK
99630
In residence: 154. *Tribe:* Eskimo.

MINTO COMMUNITY   MINTO
99758
In residence: 150. *Tribe:* Athapascan, Indian.

MOUNTAIN COMMUNITY   MOUNTAIN
In residence: 209. *Tribe:* Eskimo.

MOUNTAIN VIEW COMMUNITY
                MOUNTAIN VIEW 99504
In residence: 29. *Tribes:* Athapascan,
Eskimo, Indian.

MUMTRAK COMMUNITY   MUMTRAK
In residence: 98. *Tribe:* Eskimo.

NABESNA COMMUNITY   NEBESNA
In residence: 23. *Tribe:* Athapascan.

NAKNEK COMMUNITY   NEKNEK
                                      99633
In residence: 28. *Tribes:* Aleut, Indian.

NANACHUK COMMUNITY   NANACHUK
In residence: 121. *Tribe:* Eskimo.

NANVARNARLUK COMMUNITY
                      NANVARNARLUK
In residence: 116. *Tribe:* Eskimo.

NAPAIMIUT COMMUNITY   NAPAIMIUT
In residence: 42. *Tribe:* Eskimo.

NAPAISKAK COMMUNITY   NAPAISKAK
In residence: 119. *Tribe:* Eskimo.

NAPAKIAK COMMUNITY   NAPAKIAK
In residence: 139. *Tribe:* Eskimo.

NASH HARBOR COMMUNITY
                      NASH HARBOR
In residence: 49. *Tribe:* Eskimo.

NENANA COMMUNITY   NENANA
                                      99760
In residence: 94. *Tribes:*   Athapascan,
Eskimo, Indian.

NEWHALEN COMMUNITY
                      NEWHALEN
In residence: 46. *Tribes:* Aleut, Indian.

NEW HAMILTON COMMUNITY
                      NEW HAMILTON
In residence: 27. *Tribe:* Eskimo.

NEW KNOCK HOCK COMMUNITY
                      NEW KNOCK HOCK
In residence: 122. *Tribe:* Eskimo.

NEW STUYAHOK COMMUNITY
                NEW STUYAHOK 99636
In residence: 88. *Tribe:* Athapascan.

NIGTMUTE COMMUNITY   NIGTMUTE
In residence: 27. *Tribe:* Eskimo.

NIKOLAI COMMUNITY   NIKOLAI
In residence: 86. *Tribes:* Athapascan, Indian.

NILIKLUGUK COMMUNITY
                      NILIKLUGUK
In residence: 40. *Tribe:* Athapascan.

NINILCHIK COMMUNITY   NINILCHIK
                                      99639
In residence: 14. *Tribes:* Athapascan, Indian.

NOATAK COMMUNITY   NOATAK
                                      99761
In residence: 325. *Tribe:* Eskimo, Indian.

NOME COMMUNITY   NOME
                                      99762
In residence: 929. *Tribes:*   Eskimo, Indian.

NONDALTON COMMUNITY
                NONDALTON 99640
In residence: 99. *Tribe:* Athapascan.

NOORVIK COMMUNITY   NOORVIK 99763
In residence: 242. *Tribe:* Eskimo.

NORTHWAY-NABESNA COMMUNITY
                NORTHWAY-NABESNA 99764

In residence: 104. *Tribe:* Athapascan.

NULATO COMMUNITY   NULATO
99765
In residence: 169. *Tribe:* Athapascan.

NUNAPITCHUCK COMMUNITY
NUNAPITCHUCK 99641
In residence: 121. *Tribe:* Eskimo.

NYAC COMMUNITY   NYAC
99642
In residence: 19. *Tribe:* Eskimo.

OHOGAMIUT COMMUNITY
OHOGAMIUT
In residence: 27. *Tribe:* Eskimo.

OLD HARBOR COMMUNITY
OLD HARBOR 99643
In residence: 114. *Tribe:* Eskimo.

OSCARVILLE COMMUNITY
OSCARVILLE
In residence: 26. *Tribes:*   Eskimo, Indian.

PAINGAKMEUT COMMUNITY
PAINGAKMEUT
In residence: 44. *Tribe:* Eskimo.

PAULOFF HARBOR COMMUNITY
PAULOFF HARBOR 99646
In residence: 20. *Tribe:* Aleut.

PEDRO BAY COMMUNITY   PEDRO BAY
99647
In residence: 42. *Tribe:* Athapascan.

PERRYVILLE COMMUNITY
PERRYVILLE 99648
In residence: 92. *Tribe:* Eskimo.

PILE BAY COMMUNITY   PILE BAY
In residence: 23. *Tribes:*   Athapascan, Indian.

PILOT POINT COMMUNITY
PILOT POINT 99649
In residence: 50. *Tribes:* Eskimo, Indian.

PILOT STATION COMMUNITY
PILOT STATION 99650
In residence: 51. *Tribe:* Eskimo.

PITKAS POINT COMMUNITY
PITKAS POINT
In residence: 62. *Tribe:* Eskimo.

PLATINUM COMMUNITY
PLATINUM 99651
In residence: 32. *Tribe:* Eskimo.

POINT HOPE COMMUNITY
POINT HOPE 99766
In residence: 260. *Tribe:* Eskimo.

POINT LAY COMMUNITY
POINT LAY
In residence: 73. *Tribe:* Eskimo.

POINT WHITESHED COMMUNITY
POINT WHITESHED
In residence: 8. *Tribes:*   Aleut, Indian.

PORT GRAHAM COMMUNITY
PORT GRAHAM
In residence: 78. *Tribes:* Eskimo, Indian.

PORT MOLLER COMMUNITY
PORT MOLLER
In residence: 14. *Tribe:* Aleut.

RAMPART COMMUNITY
RAMPART 99767
In residence: 80. *Tribe:* Athapascan.

RUBY COMMUNITY   RUBY
99768
In residence: 92. *Tribe:* Athapascan.

RUSSIAN MISSION COMMUNITY
RUSSIAN MISSION 99657
In residence: 54. *Tribe:* Eskimo.

ST. MICHAEL COMMUNITY
ST. MICHAEL 99659
In residence: 155. *Tribe:* Eskimo.

SAND POINT COMMUNITY
                         SAND POINT 99661
In residence: 54. *Tribe:* Aleut.

SAVOONGA COMMUNITY
                         SAVOONGA 99769
In residence: 246. *Tribe:* Eskimo.

SCAMMON BAY COMMUNITY
                         SCAMMON BAY 99662
In residence: 103. *Tribe:* Eskimo.

SELAWIK COMMUNITY   SELAWIK
                                 99770
In residence: 269. *Tribe:* Eskimo.

SELDOVIA COMMUNITY   SELDOVIA
                                 99663
In residence: 124. *Tribes:* Aleut, Athapascan, Indian.

SEWARD COMMUNITY   SEWARD
                                 99664
In residence: 232. *Tribes:* Athapascan,
Eskimo, Indian.

SHAGELUK COMMUNITY   SHAGELUK
                                 99665
In residence: 97. *Tribe:* Athapascan.

SHAKTOOLIK COMMUNITY SHAKTOOLIK
                                 99771
In residence: 126. *Tribe:* Eskimo.

SHELDON POINT COMMUNITY
                      SHELDON POINT 99666
In residence: 43. *Tribe:* Eskimo.

SHISHMAREF COMMUNITY
                      SHISHMAREF 99772
In residence: 187. *Tribe:* Eskimo.

SHUNGNAK COMMUNITY   SHUNGNAK
                                 99773
In residence: 134. *Tribe:* Eskimo.

SKWENTNA COMMUNITY   SKWENTNA
                                 99667
In residence: 6. *Tribe:* Athapascan.

SLATERVILLE COMMUNITY
                           SLATERVILLE
In residence: 30. *Tribes:* Eskimo, Indian.

SLEETMUTE COMMUNITY
                      SLEETMUTE 99668
In residence: 108. *Tribes:* Athapascan,
Indian.

SOLOMON COMMUNITY   SOLOMON
In residence: 88. *Tribe:* Eskimo.

SPENARD COMMUNITY   SPENARD
                                 99503
In residence: 39. *Tribes:* Athapascan,
Eskimo.

SQUAW HARBOR COMMUNITY
                         SQUAW HARBOR

In residence: 23. *Tribe:* Aleut.

STEBBINS COMMUNITY   STEBBINS
                                 99671
In residence: 113. *Tribe:* Eskimo.

STEVENS VILLAGE COMMUNITY
                   STEVENS VILLAGE 99774
In residence: 80. *Tribe:* Athapascan.

TAKOTNA COMMUNITY   TAKOTNA
                                 99675
In residence: 33. *Tribes:* Eskimo, Indian.

TAKSHAK COMMUNITY   TAKSHAK
In residence: 39. *Tribe:* Eskimo.

TALKEETNA COMMUNITY
                      TALKEETNA 99676
In residence: 23. *Tribes:* Athapascan,
Indian.

TANACROSS COMMUNITY
                           TANACROSS
In residence: 87. *Tribe:* Athapascan.

TANANA COMMUNITY   TANANA
                                 99777
In residence: 144. *Tribes:* Athapascan,
Indian.

TANUNAK COMMUNITY   TANUNAK
In residence: 109. *Tribe:* Eskimo.

TATITLEK COMMUNITY   TATITLEK
                                 99677
In residence: 85. *Tribe:* Aleut.

TELLER COMMUNITY   TELLER
                                 99778
In residence: 125. *Tribe:* Eskimo.

TELLER MISSION COMMUNITY
                       TELLER MISSION
In residence: 102. *Tribe:* Eskimo.

TETLIN COMMUNITY   TETLIN
                                 99779
In residence: 70. *Tribe:* Athapascan.

TIKIKLUK COMMUNITY   TIKIKLUK
In residence: 49. *Tribe:* Eskimo.

TOGIAK COMMUNITY   TOGIAK
                                 99678
In residence: 108. *Tribe:* Eskimo.

TUKLUNG COMMUNITY   TUKLUNG
In residence: 30. *Tribe:* Eskimo.

TULUKSAK COMMUNITY   TULUKSAK
                                 99679
In residence: 111. *Tribe:* Eskimo.

TUNTUTULIAK COMMUNITY
                  TUNTUTULIAK 99680
In residence: 68. *Tribe:* Eskimo.

TYONEK COMMUNITY   TYONEK
                                 99682
In residence: 128. *Tribe:* Athapascan.

UGASHIK COMMUNITY   UGASHIK
                                 99683
In residence: 17. *Tribe:* Eskimo, Indian.

UMKUMUTE COMMUNITY
                           UMKUMUTE
In residence: 99. *Tribe:* Eskimo.

UNALAKLEET COMMUNITY
                  UNALAKLEET 99684
In residence: 411. *Tribes:* Indian, Eskimo.

UNGA COMMUNITY   UNGA
In residence: 16. *Tribe:* Aleut.

UZINKI COMMUNITY   UZINKI
In residence: 171. *Tribe:* Eskimo.

VALDEZ COMMUNITY   VALDEZ
                                 99686
In residence: 96. *Tribes:* Aleut, Athapascan, Indian.

VENETIE COMMUNITY   VENETIE
                                 99781
In residence: 78. *Tribe:* Athapascan.

WAINWRIGHT COMMUNITY
                  WAINWRIGHT 99782
In residence: 221. *Tribe:* Eskimo.

WALES COMMUNITY   WALES
                                 99783
In residence: 139. *Tribe:* Eskimo.

WHITE MOUNTAIN COMMUNITY
                WHITE MOUNTAIN 99784
In residence: 113. *Tribe:* Eskimo, Indian.

WOODY ISLAND COMMUNITY
                      WOODY ISLAND
In residence: 24. *Tribe:* Eskimo.

ARIZONA

HOPI RESERVATION
c/o Hopi Agency   KEAMS CANYON 86034

In residence: 5,176. *Tribe:* Hopi and Tewa. *Area:* 2,472,216 acres. *Local attractions:* Oraibi, oldest continuously inhabited village in U.S.; Awatobi Indian Ruins; Old Franciscan Mission; native Hopi village dwellings; Kit Carson Inscription Rock. *Activities:* Dances and religious ceremonies held throughout the year. *Facilities:* White Bear Lodge at Oraibi. Tribal council. Located seventy miles north of Holbrook, Ariz., within the Navajo Reservation.

KAIBAB RESERVATION
c/o Hopi Agency   KEAMS CANYON 86034

In residence: 95. *Tribe:* Paiute. Tribal council. Located in Arizona and Utah. (See listing under *Utah.*)

CAMP VERDE RESERVATION
c/o Colorado River Agency

PARKER 85344

In residence: 170. *Tribes:* Yavapai-Apache.

COCOPAH RESERVATION
c/o Colorado River Agency

PARKER 85344

In residence: 80. *Tribe:* Cocopah. Tribal council.

COLORADO RIVER RESERVATION
c/o Colorado River Agency

PARKER 85344

In residence: 1,431. *Tribes:* Mohave and Chemehuevi. *Area:* 225,836 acres in Arizona. *Local attractions:* Lakes Moovalya and Havasu; ruins of the townsite of LaPaz, a former mining town. *Activities:* Annual Parker Rodeo. *Facilities:* Lodging and other tourist accommodations. Tribal council. Located along the Colorado River in southwest Arizona and southeast California. (See listing under *California.*)

FORT MOJAVE RESERVATION
c/o Colorado River Agency

PARKER 85344

In residence: 277 (in California). *Tribe:* Mojave. (See listing under *California.*)

FORT YUMA RESERVATION
c/o Colorado River Agency

PARKER 85344

In residence: 890 (in California). *Tribe:* Quechan. (See listing under *California.*)

HAVASUPAI RESERVATION
c/o Colorado River Agency

PARKER 85344

In residence: 186. *Tribe:* Havasupai. *Area:* 3,058 acres. *Activities:* Dances on Memorial Day and during August; Peach Festival held annually in August. *Facilities:* Tribal lodge. Tribal council. Located in Cataract Canyon, within Grand Canyon National Park.

HUALAPAI AND BIG SANDY RESERVATION
c/o Colorado River Agency

PARKER 85344

In residence: 422. *Tribe:* Haulapai.

QUECHAN COMMUNITY
c/o Colorado River Agency

PARKER 85344

Tribal council. Located in California. (See listing under *California*).

YAVAPAI RESERVATION
c/o Colorado River Agency

PARKER 85344

In residence: 73. *Tribe:* Yavapai. Tribal council. Located in Prescott, Ariz.

GILA RIVER RESERVATION
c/o Pima Agency   SACATON 85247

In residence: 6,000. *Tribes:* Pima, Maricopa. Tribal council.

MARICOPA (AK CHIN) RESERVATION
c/o Pima Agency   SACATON 85247

In residence: 140. *Tribe:* Papago. Tribal council.

MOHAVE APACHE COMMUNITY
c/o Pima Agency   SACATON 85247

Tribal council.

SAN CARLOS RESERVATION
c/o San Carlos Agency

SAN CARLOS 85550

In residence: 4,115. *Tribe:* Apache. *Area:* 1,877,216 acres. *Local attractions*: Coolidge Dam; San Carlos Reservoir; Tonto

National Forest, northwest of the Reservation; abandoned Dominion Copper Mine and Smelter near Globe; Gila County Museum, Globe. *Activities:* Annual San Carlos Apache Tribal Fair in October at San Carlos; Pioneer Day Celebration in July at Stafford; San Carlos Indian Round-up in May and November; annual Javelina Archery Hunt in January. *Facilities:* Lodging at Globe and Miami. Tribal council. Located four miles east of Globe, Ariz.

FORT McDOWELL RESERVATION
c/o Salt River Agency
Route 1
Box 907   SCOTTSDALE 85251

In residence: 315. *Tribe:* Mohave-Apache. *Area:* 24,680 acres. *Local attractions:* Roosevelt Dam and Reservoir; Bartlett Reservoir; fishing and waterfowl hunting in area. Tribal council. Located twenty miles northeast of Phoenix, Ariz., on the Verde River.

SALT RIVER RESERVATION
c/o Salt River Agency
Route 1
Box 907   SCOTTSDALE 85251

In residence: 1,936. *Tribes:* Pima and Maricopa. *Area:* 46,619 acres. Tribal council. Located in Salt River Valley, adjacent to Phoenix, Ariz.

GILA BEND RESERVATION
c/o Papago Agency   SELLS 85634

Tribal membership: 5,500 (125 in residence). *Tribe:* Papago. *Area:* 10,000 acres. *Local attractions:* Kitt Peak National Observatory on San Xavier Reservation. *Activities:* Annual All-Indian Rodeo in October. *Tribal enterprise:* Papago Tribal Herd Enterprise. Tribal council. Located four miles north of Gila Bend.

SELLS RESERVATION
c/o Papago Agency   SELLS 85634

Tribal membership: 5,500 (4,400 in residence). *Tribe:* Papago. *Area:* 2,774,000 acres. *Local attractions:* Kitt Peak National Observatory on San Xavier Reservation. *Activities:* Annual All-Indian Rodeo in October. *Tribal enterprise:* Papago Tribal Herd Enterprise. Tribal council. Located twenty-five miles west of Tucson, Ariz.

FORT APACHE RESERVATION
c/o Fort Apache Agency
                    WHITERIVER 85941

In residence: 4,250. *Tribe:* Apache. *Area:* 1,664,872 acres. *Local attractions:* Hawley Lake; the Kinishba Ruins, site of an ancient Indian village. *Activities:* Annual White Mountain Apache Tribal Fair; autumn rodeo at Whiteriver. *Facilities:* White Mountain Tourist Enterprise (tribe-operated), including 750 camp and picnic sites; Hon-Dah Motel; lease lots for summer homes (Hawley Lake Tribal Enterprise). Tribal council. Located eighty-five miles south of Holbrook, Ariz., along the Salt and Black Rivers.

WHITE MOUNTAIN APACHE
  RESERVATION
c/o Fort Apache Agency
                    WHITERIVER 85941
Tribal council.

NAVAJO RESERVATION
c/o Navajo Agency
                    WINDOW ROCK 86515

In residence: 52,300. *Tribe:* Navajo. *Area:* 8,969,284 acres. *Local attractions:* Forked stick *hogans* (a type of native dwelling); Indian ruins; Navajo Arts and Crafts Guild Shop at Window Rock; Monument Valley; the Pillars of Hercules. *Activities:* Annual Inter-Tribal Ceremonial at Gallup in mid-August; annual Navajo Tribal Fair at Window Rock in September. *Facilities:* Tribe-operated motels and resturants in Shiprock, N.M., and Window Rock, Ariz. Tribal council. Located thirty miles west of Gallup, N.M., extending into Utah and Arizona. (See listings under *New Mexico* and *Utah.*

CALIFORNIA

COLORADO RIVER RESERVATION
c/o Colorado River Agency
                    PARKER 85344
                    (Arizona)

In residence: 1,431. *Tribes:* Mohave and Chemehuevi. *Area:* 225,836 acres. *Local attractions:* Lakes Moovalya and Havasu; ruins of the townsite of LaPaz, a former

mining town. *Activities:* Annual Parker
Rodeo. *Facilities:* Lodging and other tourist
accommodations. Tribal council. Located
along the Colorado River in southwest California. (See listing under *Arizona.*)

FORT MOJAVE RESERVATION
c/o Colorado River Agency
                                    PARKER 85344
                                        (Arizona)

In residence: 277. *Tribe:* Mojave. (See
listing under *Arizona.*)

FORT YUMA RESERVATION
c/o Colorado River Agency
                                    PARKER 85344
                                        (Arizona)

In residence: 890. *Tribe:* Quechan. (See
listing under *Arizona.*)

QUECHAN COMMUNITY
c/o Colorado River Agency
                                    PARKER 85344
                                        (Arizona)

Tribal council. (See listing under *Arizona.*)

WASHOE RESERVATION
c/o Nevada Agency   STEWART 89437
                                        (Nevada)

In residence: 132. *Tribe:* Washoe. Tribal council. (See listing under *Nevada.*)

BARONA RESERVATION   ALPINE
                                        92001
In residence: 123.

ALTURAS RANCHERIA   ALTURAS
                                        96101
In residence: 9.

XL INDIAN RESERVATION   ALTURAS
Box 763   96101
        Norman Forrest, President,
        Board of Directors

In residence: 50. *Tribe:* Pit River. *Area:*
8,700 acres. *Activities:* Pit River Home
and Agricultural Cooperative Association
(beef ranching tribal project).

RAMONA RESERVATION   ANZA
                                        92306
Unoccupied.

MORONGO RESERVATION   BANNING
                                        92220
In residence: 257.

BERRY CREEK RANCHERIA
                        BERRY CREEK 95916
Unoccupied.

BIG BEND RANCHERIA   BIG BEND
                                        96011
In residence: 5.

BIG PINE RESERVATION   BIG PINE
                                        93513
In residence: 56.

BISHOP RESERVATION   BISHOP
                                        93514
In residence: 570.

LA POSTA RESERVATION   BOULEVARD
                                        92005
Unoccupied.

CAMPO RESERVATION   CAMPO
                                        92006
In residence: 53.

CEDARVILLE RANCHERIA
                        CEDARVILLE 96104
In residence: 13.

SULPHUR BAND RANCHERIA
                    CLEARLAKE OAKS 95423
In residence: 35.

COLFAX RANCHERIA   COLFAX
                                        95713
Unoccupied.

COLUSA RANCHERIA   COLUSA
                                        95932
In residence: 40. Tribal council.

ROUND VALLEY RESERVATION
COVELO 95428
In residence: 1, 115. Tribal council.

SYCUAN RESERVATION   EL CAJON
92020
In residence: 12.

SHINGLE SPRINGS RANCHERIA
EL DORADO 95623
In residence: 5.

FORT BIDWELL RESERVATION
FORT BIDWELL 96112
In residence: 104. Tribal council.

DRY CREEK RANCHERIA
GEYSERVILLE 95441
In residence: 20.

SANTA ROSA RESERVATION   HEMET
92343
In residence: 15.

HOOPA RESERVATION
c/o Hoopa Area Field Office
HOOPA 95546

In residence: 992. *Tribe:* Hoopa. *Area:*
86, 042 acres. Site of former military post
at which General Ulysses S. Grant was sta-
tioned prior to the Civil War. Tribal council. Located along Trinity River, thirty-
five miles northeast of Eureka, Calif.

QUARTZ VALLEY COMMUNITY
c/o Hoopa Area Field Office
HOOPA 95546
Tribal council.

FORT INDEPENDENCE RESERVATION
INDEPENDENCE 93526
In residence: 32.

CABAZON RESERVATION   INDIO
99201
In residence: 11.

CAHUILLA RESERVATION   INDIO
92201
In residence: 62. *Tribe:* Cahuilla.

JACKSON RANCHERIA   JACKSON
95642
In residence: 6.

RESIGHINI RANCHERIA   KLAMATH
95548
In residence: 57.

BARON LONG RESERVATION -
VIEJAS RESERVATION
ALPINE 92001
In residence: 102.

CAPITAN GRANDE RESERVATION
LAKESIDE 92040
Unoccupied.

LAYTONVILLE RANCHERIA
LAYTONVILLE 95454
In residence: 50.

SANTA ROSA RANCHERIA   LEMOORE
93245
In residence: 96.

LIKELY RANCHERIA   LIKELY
96116
Unoccupied.

LONE PINE RESERVATION
LONG PINE 93545
In residence: 82.

LOOKOUT RANCHERIA
LOOKOUT 96054
In residence: 4.

MIDDLETOWN RANCHERIA
MIDDLETOWN 95461
In residence: 40.

MONTGOMERY CREEK RANCHERIA
MONTGOMERY CREEK 96065
Unoccupied.

ROARING CREEK RANCHERIA
MONTGOMERY CREEK 96065
In residence: 4.

BIG LAGOON RANCHERIA   ORICK
                                    95555
In residence: 6.

GRINDSTONE CREEK RANCHERIA
                            ORLAND 95963
In residence: 28.

ENTERPRISE RANCHERIA
                            OROVILLE 95965
In residence: 8.

PALA RESERVATION   PALA
                                    92059
In residence: 215. Tribal council.

AGUA CALIENTE RESERVATION
                        PALM SPRINGS 92262
In residence: 78. Tribal council.

COSMIT-INAJA RESERVATION
                        PINE VALLEY 92062
In residence: 20.

CUYAPAIPE RESERVATION
                        PINE VALLEY 92062
In residence: 1.

MANZANITA RESERVATION
                        BOULEVARD 92062
In residence: 19.

MANCHESTER-POINT ARENA
   RESERVATION
                        POINT ARENA 95468
In residence: 92.

TULE RIVER RESERVATION
                        PORTERVILLE 93257
In residence: 325.

MISSION CREEK BAND
c/o Riverside Area Field Office
6848 Magnolia Ave.   RIVERSIDE 92506
Tribal council.

RINCON SAN LUISINO COMMUNITY
c/o Riverside Area Field Office
6848 Magnolia Ave.   RIVERSIDE 92506
Tribal council.

RUMSEY RANCHERIA   RUMSEY
                                95679
In residence: 17. Tribal council.

BIG VALLEY RANCHERIA COMMUNITY
c/o Sacramento Area Office
2550 Fair Oaks Blvd.
                        SACRAMENTO 95825
Tribal council.

HOPLAND RANCHERIA
c/o Sacramento Area Office
2550 Fair Oaks Blvd.
                        SACRAMENTO 95825
Tribal council.

MANCHESTER COMMUNITY
c/o Sacramento Area Office
2550 Fair Oaks Blvd.
                        SACRAMENTO 95825
Tribal council.

OWENS VALLEY COMMUNITY
c/o Sacramento Area Office
2550 Fair Oaks Blvd.
                        SACRAMENTO 95825
Tribal council.

PINOLEVILLE COMMUNITY
c/o Sacramento Area Office
2550 Fair Oaks Blvd.
                        SACRAMENTO 95825
Tribal council.

SANTA ROSA COMMUNITY
c/o Sacramento Area Office
2550 Fair Oaks Blvd.
                        SACRAMENTO 95825
Tribal council.

TULE RIVER COMMUNITY
c/o Sacramento Area Office
2550 Fair Oaks Blvd.
                        SACRAMENTO 95825
In residence: 205. Tribal council.

UPPER BAND OF POMO INDIANS
c/o Sacramento Area Office
2550 Fair Oaks Blvd.
                        SACRAMENTO 95825
Tribal council.

WILTON RANCHERIA
c/o Sacramento Area Office
2550 Fair Oaks Blvd.
SACRAMENTO 95825
Tribal council.

SAN MANUEL RESERVATION
SAN BERNARDINO
In residence: 37.

SOBOBA RESERVATION
SAN JACINTO 92383
In residence: 213.

SANTA YNEZ RESERVATION
SANTA YNEZ 93460
In residence: 50. Tribal council.

MESA GRANDE RESERVATION
SANTA YSABEL 92070
In residence: 49.

SANTA YSABEL RESERVATION
SANTA YSABEL 92070
In residence: 136.

SHEEP RANCH RESERVATION
SHEEP RANCH 95250
In residence: 3.

STEWARTS POINT RANCHERIA
STEWARTS POINT 95480
In residence: 66. Tribal council.

STRATHMORE RANCHERIA
STRATHMORE 93267
Unoccupied.

SUSANVILLE RANCHERIA
SUSANVILLE 96130
In residence: 32.

TAYLORSVILLE RANCHERIA
TAYLORSVILLE 95983
Unoccupied.

PECHANGA RESERVATION
TEMECULA 92390
In residence: 17.

AUGUSTINE RESERVATION
THERMAL 92274
In residence: 2.

TORRES-MARTINEZ RESERVATION
THERMAL 92274
In residence: 75.

TRINIDAD RANCHERIA   TRINIDAD
95570
In residence: 27. Tribal council.

TUOLUMNE RANCHERIA
TUOLUMNE 95379
In residence: 46. Tribal council.

TWENTY-NINE PALMS RESERVATION
TWENTY-NINE PALMS 92277
Unoccupied.

LA JOLLA RESERVATION
VALLEY CENTER 92082
In residence: 76.

PAUMA-YUIMA RESERVATION
VALLEY CENTER 92082
In residence: 55.

RINCON RESERVATION
VALLEY CENTER 92082
In residence: 165. Tribal council.

SAN PASQUAL RESERVATION
VALLEY CENTER 92082
In residence: 57. Tribal council.

RAMONA RESERVATION
VALLEY VISTA
Unoccupied.

LOS COYOTES RESERVATION
WARNER SPRINGS 92086
In residence: 29.

HOOPA EXTENSION RESERVATION
WEITCHPEC
In residence: 360.

MISSION CREEK RESERVATION
                    WHITE WATER 92282
In residence: 16. Tribal council.

CORTINA RANCHERIA
                    WILLIAMS 95987
In residence: 14.

SHERWOOD VALLEY RANCHERIA
Sherwood Valley   WILLITS 95490
In residence: 12.

COLORADO

SOUTHERN UTE RESERVATION
c/o Consolidated Ute Agency
                    IGNACIO 81137

In residence: 679. *Tribe:* Ute. *Area:* 304,655 acres. Tribal council. Located forty-three miles south of Durango, along the New Mexico State line.

UTE MOUNTAIN RESERVATION
c/o Consolidated Ute Agency
                    IGNACIO 81137
Tribal council.

CONNECTICUT

EASTERN PEQUOT RESERVATION
c/o State Commissioner of Welfare
State Office Bldg.   HARTFORD 06115

In residence: 9. *Tribe:* Pequot. *Area:* 220 acres. Located in North Stonington, Conn.

GOLDEN HILL RESERVATION
c/o State Commissioner of Welfare
State Office Bldg.   HARTFORD 06115

In residence: 2. *Tribe:* Pequot. Located in Trumbull, Conn.

SCHAGHTICOKE INDIAN RESERVATION
c/o State Commissioner of Welfare
State Office Bldg.   HARTFORD 06115

In residence: 5. *Area:* 400 acres. Located in Kent, Conn.

WESTERN PEQUOT RESERVATION
c/o State Commissioner of Welfare
State Office Bldg.   HARTFORD 06115

In residence: 5. *Tribe:* Pequot. *Area:* 184 acres. Located in Ledyard, Conn.

MOHEGAN INDIAN VILLAGE
Fort Hill Area   MONTVILLE 06353

Tribe: Mohegan.

FLORIDA

DANIA (SEMINOLE) RESERVATION
c/o Seminole Agency
6075 Stirling Rd.   HOLLYWOOD 33024

In residence: 272. *Tribe:* Seminole. *Area:* 480 acres. *Local attractions:* Seminole Indian Village featuring typical village life and customs, native arts and crafts, native animal exhibits. *Activities:* Indian ceremonials held annually in mid-July. *Facilities:* Lodging near Reservation. Tribal council. Located on U. S. 441, four miles west of Dania in the Fort Lauderdale - Miami area.

MICCOSUKEE TRIBAL ENTERPRISE
  AND COMMUNITY
c/o Miccosukee Agency
P.O. Box 1369   HOMESTEAD 33030

In residence: 128. *Tribe:* Miccosukee. *Activities:* Tribe-operated restaurant and filling station, part of a projected complex to include native dwellings of the Everglades Indians and a motel. Tribal council. Located on Tamiami Trail, forty miles west of Miami, Fla.

BIG CYPRESS RESERVATION

In residence: 131. *Tribe*: Mikasuki Seminole. Located in southern Florida.

BRIGHTON RESERVATION

In residence: 125. *Tribe*: Cow Creek Seminole. Located in south central Florida.

GEORGIA

INDIAN VILLAGE
Shellbluff Landing   BURKE COUNTY

Tribes: Cherokee and Creek.

WACCANAW COMMUNITY

In residence: 468. *Tribe:* Waccanaw. Located in southeast Georgia.

IDAHO

DUCK VALLEY RESERVATION
c/o Nevada Agency   STEWART 89437
(Nevada)

In residence: 750 in Nevada, 250 in Idaho. *Tribes:* Shoshone, Paiute. Tribal council. Located near Owylee, Nev. (See listing under *Nevada.*)

FORT HALL RESERVATION
c/o Fort Hall Agency
FORT HALL 83201

In residence: 2,100. *Tribes:* Shoshone, Bannock. *Area:* 523,917 acres. *Local attractions:* American Falls. Tribal council. Located near Pocatello, Idaho, east and south of the Shake River.

COEUR D'ALENE RESERVATION
c/o Northern Idaho Agency
LAPWAI 83540

Tribal membership: 711. *Tribe:* Coeur D' Alene (Skitswish). *Area:* 69,435 acres. *Activities:* Annual event, "Tepee Town," held near Tensed in August. Tribal council. Located thirty-five miles south of Coeur D'Alene, Idaho.

KOOTENAI RESERVATION
c/o Northern Idaho Agency
LAPWAI 83540

Tribal membership: 107 (40 in residence). *Tribe:* Kootenai. Tribal council. Located in Boundary County, near Mirror Lake and the Canadian border.

NEZ PERCE RESERVATION
c/o Northern Idaho Agency
LAPWAI 83540

Tribal membership: 1,524 (737 in residence). *Tribe:* Nez Perce. *Area:* 92,685 acres. *Activities:* Nez Perce Tribal Indian Encampment near Lapwai open in summer, featuring Indian Village, pageant and tribal dance. *Facilities:* Recreational areas along Clearwater River. Tribal council. Located in Nez Perce, Lewis, Clearwater and Idaho Counties.

IOWA

THE SAC AND FOX TRIBE OF THE
MISSISSIPPI IN IOWA (RESERVATION)
c/o Horton Agency   HORTON 66439
(Kansas)

In residence: 625. *Tribe:* Sac and Fox. Tribal council. *Address:* Tama, Iowa 52339.

KANSAS

KICKAPOO RESERVATION
c/o Horton Agency   HORTON 66439

In residence: 343. *Tribe:* Kickapoo. Tribal council.

POTAWATOMI RESERVATION
(PRAIRIE BAND)
c/o Horton Agency   HORTON 66439

Tribal council.

LOUISIANA

CHITIMACHA RESERVATION
c/o Choctaw Agency
PHILADELPHIA 39350
(Mississippi)

In residence: 120. *Tribe:* Chitimacha. Tribal council. (See listing under *Mississippi.*)

HOUMA INDIAN COMMUNITIES

In residence: 2,291 (six communities). *Tribe:* Houma. Located in southeast Louisiana.

MAINE

MALECITE COMMUNITIES
                                    AROOSTOOK COUNTY

In residence: 353. *Tribe:* Malecite.

PENOBSCOT RESERVATION
c/o Maine State Department of Indian Affairs
State House   AUGUSTA 04330

In residence: 500. *Tribe:* Penobscot. Located in Indian Island, Oldtown, Me.

PLEASANT POINT RESERVATION
                                         PERRY 04667

Tribal membership: 1,200 (800 in residence). *Tribe:* Passamaquoddy. *Area:* 100 acres. Tribal council.

INDIAN TOWNSHIP RESERVATION
                                    PRINCETON 04668

Tribe: Passamaquoddy. Indian communities at Peter Dana Point and "The Strip." Tribal council.

MASSACHUSETTS

**CAPE COD (MASHPEE) INDIAN SETTLE-
    MENTS   BARNSTABLE COUNTY**

Located in Mashpee, Yarmouth and Waquoit.

CAPE COD INDIAN VILLAGE
                                      BRISTOL COUNTY
Near Fall River, Mass.

INDIAN VILLAGE
Norfolk County   CANTON 02021

WAMPANOAG INDIAN VILLAGE
Martha's Vineyard Island
                                        DUKES COUNTY

Tribe: Wampanoag.

INDIAN VILLAGE
Assawompset Pond
                                    PLYMOUTH COUNTY

MICHIGAN

BAY MILLS INDIAN COMMUNITY
                                       BRIMLEY 49715

In residence: 289. *Tribe:* Chippewa. Tribal council.

KEWEENAW BAY INDIAN COMMUNITY
                                         L'ANSE 49946
    William E. Jondreau, President,
    Tribal Council

In residence: 542. *Tribe:* Chippewa. *Area:* 10,000 acres. *Local attractions:* Keweenaw Bay; Lake Superior; Virgin Forests. *Activities:* Tribe owns and operates Ojibwa Trailer Park and holds powwows during tourist season. Tribal council.

ISABELLA RESERVATION
                            MOUNT PLEASANT 48858

In residence: 264. *Tribe:* Saginaw Chippewa.

ONTONOGAN RESERVATION
                                    ONTONOGAN 49946

In residence: 1,323. *Tribe:* Chippewa.

THE HANNAHVILLE INDIAN COMMUNITY
                                        WILSON 49896

In residence: 169. Tribal council.

MINNESOTA

LEECH LAKE RESERVATION
                                    BALL CLUB 56622

In residence: 2,400. *Tribe:* Chippewa. Tribal council.

**GRAND PORTAGE (PIGEON RIVER)
    RESERVATION**
c/o Minnesota Agency
P.O. Box 489   BEMIDJI 56601

In residence: 335. *Tribe:* Chippewa. *Area:* 43,836 acres. *Local attractions:* Grand

Portage National Historic Stie and Monument; Isle Royal National Park. *Facilities:* Restaurant and lodging at Pigeon River. Tribal council. Located near Lake Superior, adjacent to Canadian border.

RED LAKE RESERVATION
c/o Minnesota Agency
P.O. Box 489   BEMIDJI 56601

In residence: 2,801. *Tribe:* Chippewa. *Area:* 564,364 acres. *Local attractions:* St. Mary's Mission at Red Lake; Indian saw mill and fisheries at Redby; Indian handicrafts. *Activities:* Annual fair in August; Fourth of July Indian celebration. *Facilities:* Lodging in Bemidji. Tribal council. Located along lower Red Lake, thirty miles north of Bemidji, Minn.

WHITE EARTH RESERVATION
                    CALLAWAY 56521

In residence: 2,300. *Tribe:* Chippewa. Tribal council.

FOND DU LAC RESERVATION
                    CLOQUET 55720

In residence: 785. *Tribe:* Chippewa. Tribal council.

THE UPPER SIOUX INDIAN COMMUNITY
                    GRANITE FALLS 56241

In residence: 85. *Tribe:* Sioux. Tribal council.

MILLE LACS RESERVATION
                    McGREGOR 55760

In residence: 780. *Tribe:* Chippewa. Tribal council.

LOWER SIOUX INDIAN COMMUNITY
                    MORTON 56270

In residence: 160. *Tribe:* Sioux. Tribal council.

NETT LAKE RESERVATION
                    TOWER 55790

In residence: 625. *Tribe:* Chippewa (Deer Creek). Tribal council.

PIPESTONE SIOUX INDIAN
COMMUNITY   PIPESTONE 56165

Tribe: Sioux.

PRAIRIE ISLAND INDIAN COMMUNITY
                    WELCH 55089

In residence: 86. *Tribe:* Sioux. Tribal council.

MISSISSIPPI

CHOCTAW RESERVATION
                    CONEHATTA 39057

In residence: 2,622. *Tribe:* Choctaw. Located in central Mississippi.

CHITIMACHA RESERVATION
c/o Choctaw Agency
                    PHILADELPHIA

In residence: 120. *Tribe:* Chitimacha. Tribal council. Reservation located in Louisiana. (See listing under *Louisiana*.)

MONTANA

ROCKY BOY'S RESERVATION
c/o Rocky Boy's Agency
                    BOX ELDER 59521

Tribal membership: 1,480 (450 in residence). *Tribes:* Chippewa, Cree. *Area:* 107,532 acres. Tribal council. Located in Bear Paw Mountains, north-central Montana.

BLACKFEET RESERVATION
c/o Blackfeet Agency
                    BORWNING 59417

Tribal membership: 12,000 (6,000 in residence). *Tribe:* Blackfeet. *Area:* 955,241 acres. *Local attractions:* Museum of the Plains Indian, Browning Glacier National Park. *Activities:* Annual Blackfeet Medicine Lodge Ceremonial and Sun Dance at Browning in July. *Facilities:* Restaurant and lodging at Browning. *Tribal enterprises:* Tribal cattle enterprise; Blackfeet Crafts Organization operating the Northern Plains Craft Shop at Museum of the Plains

Indian and a retail store at St. Mary's in Glacier Park; forest products enterprise. Tribal council. Located west of Glacier National Park, south of the Canadian border.

CROW INDIAN RESERVATION
c/o Crow Agency   CROW AGENCY 59022

In residence: 3,526. *Tribe:* Crow. *Area:* 1,575,326 acres. *Local attractions:* Custer Battlefield National Monument and Museum; ruins of Fort C.F. Smith at Hardin; Custer National Forest; the Bear Tooth Wilderness area. *Activities:* Crow Indian Fair at Crow Agency; All-American Indian Days Pageant at Sheridan, Wyo., in August; Crow Sun Dance on Reservation in June. *Facilities:* Lodging at Custer Battlefield. Tribal council. Located fifteen miles southeast of Hardin, Mont.

FLATHEAD RESERVATION
Flathead Agency   DIXON 59831
    Walter W. McDonald, Chairman,
       Tribal Council

In residence: 5,000. *Tribes:* Salish (Flathead) and Kootenai. *Area:* 140,000 acres. *Facilities:* Camas Hot Springs Resort (tribe-operated) near Hot Springs, Mont.; overnight lodging; restaurants in nearby towns. Tribal council.

FORT BELKNAP RESERVATION
c/o Fort Belknap Consolidated Agency
                         HARLEM 59526

Tribal membership: 3,557 (1,636 in residence). *Tribes:* Gros Ventre, Assiniboine. *Area:* 622,644 acres. *Local attractions:* St. Paul Jesuit Mission; Monument Peak in Little Rocky Mountains; Limestone Natural Bridge; old gold-mining towns of Landusky and Zortman. *Activities:* Annual dances on Reservation in summer and at Christmas at Lodge Pole. *Facilities:* Lodging at Harlem. Tribal council. Located fifty miles east of Havre, Mont.

NORTHERN CHEYENNE RESERVATION
c/o Northern Cheyenne Agency
                     LAME DEER 59043

Tribal membership: 2,900 (800 in residence). *Tribe:* Cheyenne. *Area:* 236,637 acres.

FORT PECK RESERVATION
c/o Fort Peck Agency
P.O. Box 637   POPLAR 59255

Tribal membership: 6,728 (3,071 in residence). *Tribes:* Assiniboine, Sioux. *Area:* 981,144 acres. *Local attractions:* Fort Peck Dam and Reservoir. *Activities:* Wolf Point Wild Horse Stampede in July; Oil Discovery Day celebration in August. *Facilities:* Lodging in Culbertson, Poplar, Wolf Point, and Glasgow. Tribal council. Located twenty miles south of the Canadian border.

NEBRASKA

OMAHA RESERVATION
c/o Winnebago Agency
                      WINNEBAGO 68071

In residence: 1,169. *Tribe:* Omaha. *Area:* 27,701 acres. *Activities:* Annual ceremonial dances in August. *Facilities:* Lodging in Reservation towns. Tribal council. Located twenty miles south of Sioux City, Iowa.

PONCA RESERVATION
c/o Winnebago Agency
                      WINNEBAGO 68071

In residence: 441. *Tribe:* Ponca. Tribal council.

SANTEE-SIOUX RESERVATION
c/o Winnebago Agency
                      WINNEBAGO 68071

In residence: 1,372. *Tribe:* Santee-Sioux. Tribal council.

WINNEBAGO RESERVATION
                      WINNEBAGO 68071

In residence: 2,006. *Tribe:* Omaha. Tribal council.

SAC AND FOX COMMUNITY

In residence: 129. *Tribe:* Sac and Fox. Located in the south- and northeast corners of Kansas and Nebraska.

NEVADA

BATTLE MOUNTAIN COLONY
c/o Nevada Agency   STEWART 89437

In residence: 62. *Tribes:* Paiute, Shoshone.

CARSON COLONY
c/o Nevada Agency   STEWART 89437

In residence: 108. *Tribes:* Washoe, Paiute.

DRESSLERVILLE RESERVATION
c/o Nevada Agency   STEWART 89437

In residence: 131. *Tribe:* Washoe. Tribal council.

DUCK VALLEY RESERVATION
c/o Nevada Agency   STEWART 89437

In residence: 750 in Nevada, 250 in Idaho. *Tribes:* Shoshone, Paiute. Tribal council. (See listing under *Idaho.*)

DUCKWATER RESERVATION
c/o Nevada Agency   STEWART 89437

In residence: 50. *Tribe:* Paiute. Tribal council.

ELKO COLONY
c/o Nevada Agency   STEWART 89437

In residence: 110. *Tribe:* Shoshone.

ELY COLONY
c/o Nevada Agency   STEWART 89437

In residence: 25. *Tribes:* Paiute, Shoshone.

FALLON COLONY
c/o Nevada Agency   STEWART 89437

In residence: 59. *Tribes:* Shoshone, Paiute. Tribal council.

FALLON RESERVATION
c/o Nevada Agency   STEWART 89437

In residence: 119. *Tribes:* Shoshone, Paiute. Tribal council.

FORT McDERMITT RESERVATION
c/o Nevada Agency   STEWART 89437

In residence: 428. *Tribe:* Paiute. Tribal council.

GOSHUTE RESERVATION
c/o Nevada Agency   STEWART 89437

In residence: 37 in Nevada, 37 in Utah. *Tribe:* Goshute. Tribal council. Reservation located in Nevada and Utah. (See listing under *Utah.*)

LAS VEGAS COLONY
c/o Nevada Agency   STEWART 89437

In residence: 43. *Tribe:* Paiute. Tribsl council.

LOVELOCK COLONY
c/o Nevada Agency   STEWART 89437

In residence: 94. *Tribe:* Paiute.

MOAPA RIVER RESERVATION
c/o Nevada Agency   STEWART 89437

In residence: 105. *Tribe:* Paiute. Tribal council.

ODGERS RANCH RESERVATION
c/o Nevada Agency   STEWART 89437

In residence: 3. *Tribe:* Paiute.

PYRAMID LAKE RESERVATION
c/o Nevada Agency   STEWART 89437

In residence: 338. *Tribe:* Paiute. Tribal council.

RENO-SPARKS RESERVATION
c/o Nevada Agency   STEWART 89437

In residence: 418. *Tribes:* Washoe, Paiute. Tribal council.

RENO-SPARKS RESERVATION
c/o Nevada Agency   STEWART 89437

In residence: 273. *Tribe:* Paiute. Tribal council.

RUBY VALLEY RESERVATION
c/o Nevada Agency   STEWART 89437

In residence: 15. *Tribe:* Shoshone.

SOUTH FORK (TE-MOAK) RESERVATION
c/o Nevada Agency   STEWART 89437

In residence: 70. *Tribe:* Shoshone.

SUMMIT LAKE RESERVATION
c/o Nevada Agency   STEWART 89437

In residence: 6. *Tribe:* Paiute. Tribal council.

WALKER RIVER RESERVATION
c/o Nevada Agency   STEWART 89437

In residence: 344. *Tribes:* Paiute, Shoshone. Tribal council.

WASHOE RESERVATION
c/o Nevada Agency   STEWART 89437

Tribe: Washoe. Tribal council.

WINNEMUCCA COLONY
c/o Nevada Agency   STEWART 89437

In residence: 42. *Tribe:* Paiute.

YERINGTON COLONY
c/o Nevada Agency   STEWART 89437

In residence: 127. *Tribe:* Paiute. Tribal council.

YERINGTON (CAMPBELL RANCH) RESERVATION
c/o Nevada Agency   STEWART 89437

In residence: 52. *Tribe:* Paiute. Tribal council.

YOMBA RESERVATION
c/o Nevada Agency   STEWART 89437

In residence: 134. *Tribe:* Shoshone. Tribal council.

AUSTIN COLONY

In residence: 139. *Tribe:* Paiute. Located in central Nevada.

BEOWAWE COMMUNITY

In residence: 61. *Tribe:* Shoshone. Located in north central Nevada.

CAMPBELL RANCH

In residence: 50. *Tribe:* Paiute. Located in north central Nevada.

CARLIN COMMUNITY

In residence: 13. *Tribe:* Shoshone. Located in north central Nevada.

EUREKA COMMUNITY

In residence: 23. *Tribe:* Shoshone. Located in central Nevada.

NEW MEXICO

NAVAJO RESERVATION
c/o Navajo Agency   WINDOW ROCK 86515
(Arizona)

In residence: 52,300. *Tribe:* Navajo. *Area:* 8,969,284 acres. *Local attractions:* Forked stick hogans (a type of native dwelling); Indian ruins; Navajo Arts and Crafts Guild Shop at Window Rock; Monument Valley; the Pillars of Hercules. *Activities:* Annual Inter-Tribal Ceremonial at Gallup in mid-August; annual Navajo Tribal Fair at Window Rock in September. *Facilities:*   Tribe-operated motels and restaurants in Shiprock, N.M., and Window Rock, Ariz. Tribal council. Located thirty miles west of Gallup, N.M., extending into Utah and Arizona. (See listings under *Utah* and *Arizona*.)

ACOMA PUEBLO
c/o United Pueblos Agency
1000 Indian School Rd.
ALBUQUERQUE 87104

In residence: 2,013. Tribal council. Located fifty miles west of Albuquerque, N.M.

COCHITI PUEBLO
c/o United Pueblos Agency
1000 Indian School Rd.
ALBUQUERQUE 87104

In residence: 500. Tribal council. Located in Sandoral County near U.S. 85 on the west bank of the Rio Grande River.

ISLETA PUEBLO
c/o United Pueblos Agency
1000 Indian School Rd.
ALBUQUERQUE 87104

In residence: 1,863. Tribal council. Located thirteen miles south of Albuquerque, N.M., on U.S. 85.

JEMEZ PUEBLO
c/o United Pueblos Agency
1000 Indian School Rd.
ALBUQUERQUE 87104

In residence: 1,076. *Tribe:* Jemez. *Area:* 88,387 acres. Tribal council. Located forty-four miles north of Albuquerque, N.M.

LAGUNA PUEBLO
c/o United Pueblos Agency
1000 Indian School Rd.
ALBUQUERQUE 87104

In residence: 3,654. Tribal council. Located forty miles west of Albuquerque, N.M., on U.S. 66.

NAMBE PUEBLO
c/o United Pueblos Agency
1000 Indian School Rd.
ALBUQUERQUE 87104

In residence: 190. Tribal council. Located five miles east of Pojoaque, N.M., on Highway 285.

PICURIS (SAN LORENZO) PUEBLO
c/o United Pueblos Agency
1000 Indian School Rd.
ALBUQUERQUE 87104

In residence: 158. Tribal council. Located east of the Rio Grande River, twenty miles south of Taos, N.M.

SANDIA PUEBLO
c/o United Pueblos Agency
1000 Indian School Rd.
ALBUQUERQUE 87104

In residence: 187. Tribal council. Located fourteen miles north of Albuquerque, N.M., on U.S. 85.

SAN FELIPE PUEBLO
c/o United Pueblos Agency
1000 Indian School Rd.
ALBUQUERQUE 87104

In residence: 1,031. Tribal council. Located ten miles north of Bernalillo, N.M., off U.S. 85.

SAN ILDEFONSO PUEBLO
c/o United Pueblos Agency
1000 Indian School Rd.
ALBUQUERQUE 87104

In residence: 239. Tribal council. Located twenty miles northwest of Santa Fe, N.M., off U.S. Highway 285.

SAN JUAN PUEBLO
c/o United Pueblos Agency
1000 Indian School Rd.
ALBUQUERQUE 87104

In residence: 975. Tribal council. Located five miles north of Espanola, N.M., near U.S. Highway 64.

SANTA ANA PUEBLO
c/o United Pueblos Agency
1000 Indian School Rd.
ALBUQUERQUE 87104

In residence: 368. Tribal council. Located near Jemez Creek, eight miles from Bernalillo, N.M.

SANTA CLARA PUEBLO
c/o United Pueblos Agency
1000 Indian School Rd.
ALBUQUERQUE 87104

In residence: 535. *Tribe:* Santa Clara. *Area:* 45,744 acres. Tribal council. Located twenty-five miles northwest of Santa Fe, N.M.

SANTO DOMINGO PUEBLO
c/o United Pueblos Agency
1000 Indian School Rd.
ALBUQUERQUE 87104

In residence: 1,210. Tribal council. Located in Taos County, ten miles east of the Rio Grande River.

TESUQUE PUEBLO
c/o United Pueblos Agency
1000 Indian School Rd.
ALBUQUERQUE 87104

In residence: 193. Tribal council. Located ten miles north of Santa Fe, N.M.

ZIA PUEBLO
c/o United Pueblos Agency
1000 Indian School Rd.
ALBUQUERQUE 87104

In residence: 347. Tribal council. Located sixteen miles northwest of Bernallilo, N.M.

JICARILLA APACHE RESERVATION
c/o Jicarilla Agency   DULCE 87528

In residence: 1,394. *Tribe:* Apache. *Area:* 742,303 acres. *Local attractions:* Wild Horse and Honolulu Mesas; prehistoric Indian ruins. *Activities:* Dances and ceremonies; annual Tribal Celebration at Stone Lake in September. *Facilities:* Lodgings at Chama. Tribal council. Located approximately two hundred miles northwest of Albuquerque, N.M.

MESCALERO APACHE RESERVATION
c/o Mescalero Agency
MESCALERO AGENCY 88340

In residence: 1,317. *Tribe:* Apache. *Area:* 460,173 acres. *Local attractions:* Old Lincoln Town, hiding place of Billy the Kid. *Activities:* Annual ceremonial dances; feast and rodeo in July. *Facilities:* Apache Summit Lodge (tribe-operated). Tribal council. Located thirty miles northeast of Alamagordo, N.M.

ZUNI RESERVATION
c/o Zuni Agency   ZUNI 87327

In residence: 4,000. *Tribe:* Zuni. *Area:* 406,967 acres. *Activities:* Shalako dances held in November. Tribal council. Located twenty-one miles south of Gallup, N.M., on the Arizona border.

ALAMO NAVAJO COMMUNITY

In residence: 322. *Tribe:* Navajo. Located in west central New Mexico.

CANONCITA NAVAJO COMMUNITY

In residence: 390. *Tribe:* Navajo. Located in west central New Mexico.

RAMAH NAVAJO COMMUNITY

In residence: 578. *Tribe:* Navajo. Located in west central New Mexico, near the Zuni Reservation.

NEW YORK

ALLEGHENY RESERVATION
c/o Mr. John Hathorn, Director of Indian
  Services, Interdepartmental Committee
  on Indian Affairs
112 State St.   ALBANY 12207
  Martin Seneca, President

Tribe: Seneca Nation. *Area:* 30,469 acres. Located along the Allegheny River on route 17.

CATTARAUGUS RESERVATION
c/o Mr. John Hathorn, Director of Indian
  Services, Interdepartmental Committee
  on Indian Affairs
112 State St.   ALBANY 12207

Tribal membership (enrolled): 4,297. *Tribes:* Cayuga, Seneca. *Area:* 21,680 acres. Located along Route 438.

OIL SPRING RESERVATION
c/o Mr. John Hathorn, Director of Indian
  Services, Interdepartmental Committee
  on Indian Affairs
112 State St.   ALBANY 12207

Tribe: Seneca Nation. *Area:* 640 Acres. Unoccupied. Located near Cuba Lake in Allegheny County.

ONEIDA TERRITORY
c/o Mr. John Hathorn, Director of Indian
    Services, Interdepartmental Committee
    on Indian Affairs
112 State St.   ALBANY 12207

Tribe: Oneida. *Area:* 350 acres. Not a
reservation.

ONONDAGA RESERVATION
c/o Mr. John Hathorn, Director of Indian
    Services, Interdepartmental Committee
    on Indian Affairs
112 State St.   ALBANY 12207
    Irving Powless, Chief

Tribal membership: (enrolled): 1,132.
Tribe: Onondaga. Located in Nedrow, six
miles south of Syracuse, N.Y.

POOSEPATUCK RESERVATION
c/o Mr. John Hathorn, Director of Indian
    Services, Interdepartmental Committee
    on Indian Affairs
112 State St.   ALBANY 12207

In residence: 75. *Tribe:* Poosepatuck.
Area: 60 acres. Located on Mastic River
near Brookhaven, L.I., N.Y.

ST. REGIS RESERVATION
c/o Mr. John Hathorn, Director of Indian
    Services, Interdepartmental Committee
    on Indian Affairs
112 State St.   ALBANY 12207
    John Cook, Chief

Tribal membership: (enrolled): 2,150.
Tribe: Mohawk. *Area:* 28,390 acres.
Located in Franklin County on Route 37.

SHINNECOCK INDIAN VILLAGE
c/o Mr. John Hathorn, Director of Indian
    Services, Interdepartmental Committee
    on Indian Affairs
112 State St.   ALBANY 12207

Located in Suffolk County, near Southhamp-
ton, L.I., N.Y.

TONAWANDA RESERVATION
c/o Mr. John Hathorn, Director of Indian
    Services, Interdepartmental Committee
    on Indian Affairs
112 State St.   ALBANY 12207
    Corbett Sundown, Chief;
    Beeman Logan, Chief

Tribal membership(enrolled): 324. *In residence:* 189. *Tribe:* Tonawanda Seneca.
Area: 7,549 acres. Located on Route 267,
near Batavia, N.Y.

TUSCARORA RESERVATION
c/o Mr. John Hathorn, Director of Indian
    Services, Interdepartmental Committee
    on Indian Affairs
112 State St.   ALBANY 12207

Tribe: Tuscarora. *Area:* 5,700 acres.
Located in Niagara County near Sanborn
and Lewiston on Upper Mountain Rd.

ABENAKI INDIAN VILLAGE
                LAKE GEORGE 12845

MATINECOCK INDIAN VILLAGE

Located near Cold Spring Harbor, L.I.,
N.Y.

MONTAUK INDIAN VILLAGE

Located near Montauk Point, L.I., N.Y.

SETAUKET INDIAN VILLAGE

Located between Stony Brook and Waking
River in Suffolk County, N.Y.

NORTH CAROLINA

CHEROKEE RESERVATION
c/o Cherokee Agency   CHEROKEE 28719

In residence: 3,200. *Area:* 56,572 acres.
Local attractions: Replica of an Oconaluftee
Indian village; Museum of the Cherokee;
Qualla Arts and Crafts Cooperative. *Acti-
vities:* "Unto These Hills," an outdoor
drama, presented during summer; annual
Indian Fair held in autumn. *Facilities:*

Lodging and other tourist accommodations available on and near Reservation. Tribal council. Located fifty miles west of Asherville, N.C.

CROATAN INDIAN VILLAGE
c/o State Superintendent of Public
   Instruction   RALEIGH 27551

Located in Macon County.

INDIAN VILLAGE
c/o State Superintendent of Public
   Instruction   RALEIGH 27551

Located in Hash County.

LUMBEE INDIAN TERRITORY
c/o State Superintendent of Public
   Instruction   RALEIGH 27551

In residence: 26,243. *Tribe:* Lumbee (Croatan). Located on Lumbee River in Robeson County.

NORTH DAKOTA

TURTLE MOUNTAIN RESERVATION
c/o Turtle Mountain Agency
                   BELCOURT 58316

In residence: 5,530. *Tribe:* Chippewa. Area: 34,528 acres. *Local attractions:* Bulova Watch jewel-bearing plants, staffed by Indian workers; International Peace Garden on the Canadian border near Dunseith; Lake Metigoshe State Park and Museum north of Bottineau. *Activities:* Annual Indian sun dance in June; annual Indian Fair in October. *Facilities:* Lodging and other accommodations available at Rolla and Dunseith. Tribal council. Located west of the Canadian border.

FORT TOTTEN RESERVATION
                 FORT TOTTEN

In residence: 1,300. *Tribe:* Sioux. Tribal council.

FORT BERTHOLD RESERVATION
c/o Fort Berthold Agency
                 NEW TOWN 58763

In residence: 2,254. *Tribes:* Gros Ventre, Arikara, Mandan. *Area:* 421,964 acres. *Local attractions:* "Missouri Breaks" along the Garrison Reservoir; Scout Cemetery, burial ground of Army Indian Scouts; Four Bears Bridge west of New Bears Bridge; Garrison Dam; Fort Mandan, Site of Lewis and Clark campground; Theodore Roosevelt National Memorial Park near Medora. Tribal council. Located above Garrison Dam on the Missouri River, southwest of Minot, N.D.

STANDING ROCK RESERVATION
c/o Standing Rock Agency
                 FORT YATES 58538

In residence: 2,050 in North Dakota, 2,300 in South Dakota. *Tribe:* Sioux. *Area:* 306,333 acres in North Dakota. *Local attractions:* Old Fort Manuel, built in 1812; grave of Sitting Bull on the Missouri River bluffs, west of Mobridge; Lake Oahe recreational area. Tribal council. Located sixty miles south of Bismarck, N.D., in North and South Dakota. (See listing under South Dakota.)

OJIBWA OF THE RED RIVER

In residence: 800. *Tribe:* Ojibwa (Chippewa). Located in Northeast North Dakota.

OKLAHOMA

NOTE: There are no "reservations" in Oklahoma. Rather, they are land holdings of the various Oklahoma tribes. The word *reservation* is used where an official term such as *band, group* or *land* has not been supplied.

CADDO, DELAWARE, WICHITA
   (RESERVATION)
c/o Anadarko Agency   ANDARKO 73005

In residence: 1,809. *Tribe:* Caddo, Delaware, Wichita. Tribal council.

KIOWA, COMANCHE, APACHE
(RESERVATION)
c/o Anadarko Agency   ANADARKO 73005

Tribal council.

CHICKASAW NATION (RESERVATION)
c/o Ardmore Agency   ARDMORE 73401

In residence: 9,000.   *Tribe:* Chickasaw.
Tribal council.

CHEYENNE-ARAPAHO (RESERVATION)
c/o Concho Agency   CONCHO 73022

In residence: 3,102.   *Tribe:* Cheyenne,
Arapaho. Tribal council.

EASTERN SHAWNEE (RESERVATION)
c/o Miami Agency
P.O. Box 391   MIAMI 74354

In residence: 440. *Tribe*: Eastern Shawnee.
Tribal council.

MIAMI (RESERVATION)
c/o Miami Agency
P.O. Box 391   MIAMI 74354

In residence: 323. *Tribe:* Miami. Tribal
council.

QUAPAW TRIBE (RESERVATION)
c/o Miami Agency
P.O. Box 391   MIAMI 74354

In residence: 720. *Tribe:* Quapaw. Tribal
council.

SENECA-CAYUGA TRIBE (RESERVATION)
c/o Miami Agency
P.O. Box 391   MIAMI 74354

In residence: 930. *Tribe:* Seneca-Cayuga.
Tribal council.

CHEROKEE LAND
c/o Five Civilized Tribes Agency
Federal Bldg.   MUSKOGEE 74401

In residence: 13,215. *Tribe:* Oklahoma
Cherokee. *Local attractions:* Tahlequah,
former Cherokee capital, and Five Civilized Tribes Museum. Located northeast
of Tulsa, Okla.

CHICKASAW LAND
c/o Five Civilized Tribes Agency
Federal Bldg.   MUSKOGEE 74401

In residence: 3,491. *Tribe:* Chickasaw.
Local attractions: Tishomingo, former
Chickasaw capital. Located south of Okla-
homa City, Okla.

CHOCTAW LAND
c/o Five Civilized Tribes Agency
Federal Bldg.   MUSKOGEE 74401

In residence: 7,729.   *Tribe:* Choctaw.
Local attractions: Tuskahoma, former
Choctaw capital (Council House and burial
ground). Located in southeast Oklahoma,
between the Red and Canadian rivers.

WYANDOTTE TRIBE (RESERVATION)
c/o Muskogee Area Office
MUSKOGEE 74401

In residence: 894. *Tribe:* Wyandotte. Tribal council.

ALABAMA-QUASSARTE CREEK TRIBAL
TOWN
c/o Okmulgee Agency
P.O. Box 671   OKMULGEE 74447

Tribal council.

CREEK NATION
c/o Okmulgee Agency
P.O. Box 671   OKMULGEE 74447

In residence: 20,000. *Tribe:* Creek. Tribal council.

KIALEGEE CREEK (RESERVATION)
c/o Okmulgee Agency
P.O. Box 671   OKMULGEE 74447

Tribal council.

THLOPTHLOCCO CREEK (RESERVATION)
c/o Okmulgee Agency
P.O. Box 671   OKMULGEE 74447

Tribal council.

OSAGE (RESERVATION)
c/o Osage Agency   PAWHUSKA 74056

In residence: 4,923. *Tribe:* Creek. Tribal council.

KAW (RESERVATION)
c/o Pawnee Agency   PAWNEE 74058

In residence: 544. *Tribe:* Kaw. Tribal council.

OTOE-MISSOURIA (RESERVATION)
c/o Pawnee Agency   PAWNEE 74058

In residence: 866. *Tribe:* Otoe and Missouria. Tribal council.

PONCA (RESERVATION)
c/o Pawnee Agency   PAWNEE 74058

In residence: 926. *Tribe*: Ponca. Tribal council.

TONKAWA TRIBE (RESERVATION)
c/o Pawnee Agency   PAWNEE 74058

In residence: 57. *Tribe:* Tonkawa. Tribal council.

BAND OF POTAWATOMI
c/o Shawnee Agency   SHAWNEE 74801

In residence: 2,976. Tribe: Potawatomi. Tribal council.

KICKAPOO (RESERVATION)
c/o Shawnee Agency   SHAWNEE 74801

In residence: 283. Tribe: Kickapoo. Tribal council.

SAC AND FOX TRIBE
c/o Shawnee Agency   SHAWNEE 74801

In residence: 996. Tribal council.

CHEROKEE NATION
c/o Tahlequah Agency
P.O. Box 459   TAHLEQUAH 74464

In residence: 75,000. *Tribe:* Cherokee. Tribal council.

UNITED KEETOOWAH (RESERVATION)
c/o Tahlequah Agency
P.O. Box 459   TAHLEQUAH 74464

Tribal council.

CHOCTAW NATION
c/o Talihina Agency
P.O. Box 187   TALIHINA 74571

Tribal council.

SEMINOLE TRIBE
c/o Wewoka Agency   WEWOKA 74884

Tribal council.

OREGON

BURNS PAIUTE INDIAN COLONY
                    BURNS 97720
    James Stanley, Chairman,
    Tribal council

Tribal membership: 225. *Tribe*: Paiute (97 per cent full blood). Area: 11,944 acres. Located in Harney Basin, Harney County.

ALL TRIBES RESERVATION
                    LA GRANDE

UMATILLA RESERVATION
                    PENDLETON

Tribal membership: 1,251 (541 residence). *Tribes:* Umatilla, Cayuse, Walla Walla. *Area:* 95,273 acres. Local attractions: Umatilla National Forest. Activities: Pendleton Round-Up held annually in September. Tribal council. Located in Umatilla County, adjacent to Pendleton and west of Umatilla National Forest.

WARM SPRINGS RESERVATION
c/o Warm Springs Agency
                    WARM SPRINGS 97761

In residence: 1,200. *Tribes:* Warm Springs, Wasco, Paiute, Walla Walla, Waco. *Area:* 563,916 acres. Activities: Annual Root Festival in April at Warm Springs; Annual Huckleberry Festival in August at He He

Butte Camp on the Reservation; amateur Indian rodeo on Labor Day; Indian ceremonial dances. Tribal council. Located in Jefferson and Wasco Counties, east of the Cascade Mountains.

KLAMATH (RESERVATION)

In residence: 450. *Area:* 860,936 acres. Reservation status officially terminated in 1962; one settlement remains. Located in southern Oregon.

EMPIRE AND SOUTH OREGON COAST

In residence: 803. *Tribes:* Coos Bay, Lower Umpqua, Suyskwim, Chetco, and others -- scattered communities located on southwest Oregon coast.

GRANDE RONDE RESERVATION

In residence: 502. Located in northwest Oregon.

SILETZ RESERVATION

In residence: 685. Located on northwest Oregon coast.

PENNSYLVANIA

CORNPLANTER RESERVATION
WARREN COUNTY 16365

SOUTH CAROLINA

CATAWBA RESERVATION
ROCK HILL 29730

In residence: 138. *Tribe:* Catawba. *Area:* 630 acres.

SOUTH DAKOTA

STANDING ROCK RESERVATION
c/o Standing Rock Agency
FORT YATES 58538
(North Dakota)

In residence: 2,050 in North Dakota, 2,300 in South Dakota. *Tribe:* Sioux. *Area:* 306,333 acres in North Dakota. *Local at-*

tractions: Old Fort Manuel, built in 1812; grave of Sitting Bull on the Missouri River bluffs, west of Mobridge; Lake Oahe recreational area. Tribal council. Located sixth miles south of Bismark, N.D., in North and South Dakota. (See listing under *North Dakota.*)

CHEYENNE RIVER RESERVATION
c/o Cheyenne River Agency
EAGLE BUTTE 56725

In residence: 4,307. *Tribe:* Sioux. Tribal council.

CROW CREEK RESERVATION
FORT THOMPSON 57339

In residence: 1,132. *Tribe:* Sioux. Tribal council.

FLANDREAU SANTEE-SIOUX (RESERVATION)
c/o Flandreau School   FLANDREAU 57028

Tribe: Santee Sioux. Tribal Council.

LOWER BRULE SIOUX TRIBE (RESERVATION)
c/o Pierre Agency   PIEREE 57501

In residence: 705. *Tribe:* Sioux. Tribal council.

PINE RIDGE RESERVATION
c/o Pine Ridge Agency
PINE RIDGE 57770

In residence: 8,780. *Tribe:* Sioux. *Area:* 1,560,196 acres in South Dakota. *Local attractions:* Wounded Knee Battlefield fifteen miles northeast of Pine Ridge; Holy Rosary Jesuit Mission and School near Oglala; Mount Rushmore National Memorial; Badlands National Monument; Black Hills of South Dakota; Indian Museum and Dinosaur Park at Rapid City. *Activities:* Annual Oglala Sioux Sun Dance in August; district Indian Fairs held during September. Tribal council. Located sixty miles east of the Black Hills, extending into Nebraska. (See listing under *Nebraska*.)

ROSEBUD RESERVATION
c/o Rosebud Agency   ROSEBUD 57570

In residence: 7,201. *Tribe:* Sioux. *Area:* 964,778 acres. *Local attractions:* Crazy Horse Canyon Park on the reservation (tribe operated); St. Francis Mission near Rosebud; Sioux Indian Museum; Geological Museum. *Activities:* Indian Pageant during the summer; Indian Village depicting Indian life, arts and crafts. *Facilities:* Lodging and other at Mission. Tribal council. Located in south central South Dakota, adjoining the Nebraska state line.

SISSETON RESERVATION
c/o Sisseton Agency   SISSETON 57262

In residence: 3,542. *Tribe:* Sisseton Wahpeton Sioux. Tribal council.

YANKTON SIOUX TRIBE
c/o Yankton Subagency   WAGNER 57380

In residence: 2,391. *Tribe:* Yankton Sioux. Tribal council. Located in North and South Dakota.

TEXAS

ALABAMA-COUSHATTA RESERVATION
c/o Indian Agent   LIVINGSTON 77351

In residence: 394. *Area:* 14,300 acres. *Tribe:* Alabama-Coushatta. Located near Big Sandy Creek in Rube, Texas (Livingston County), eighty miles north of Houston.

UTAH

KAIBAB RESERVATION
c/o Hopi Agency
              KEAMS CANYON 86034
                   (Arizona)

In residence: 95. *Tribe:* Paiute. Tribal council.

NAVAJO RESERVATION
c/o Navajo Agency
              WINDOW ROCK 86515
                   (Arizona)

In residence: 52,300. *Tribe:* Navajo. *Area:* 8,969,284 acres. *Local attractions:* Forded sticked *hogans* (a type of native dwelling); Indian ruins; Navajo Arts and Crafts Guild Shop at Window Rock; Monument Valley; the Pillars of Hercules. *Activities:* Annual Inter-Tribal Ceremonial at Gallup in mid-August; annual Navajo Tribal Fair at Window Rock in September. *Facilities:* Tribe-operated motels and restaurants in Shiprock, N.M., and Window Rock, Ariz. Tribal council. Located thirty miles west of Gallup, N.M., extending into Utah and Arizona. (See listings under *New Mexico* and *Arizona*.)

GOSHUTE RESERVATION
c/o Nevada Agency   STEWART 89437
                   (Nevada)

In residence: 37 in Nevada, 37 in Utah. *Tribe:* Goshute. Tribal council. Reservation located in Nevada and Utah. (See listing under *Nevada*.)

SKULL VALLEY RESERVATION
c/o Uintah and Ouray Agency
              FORT DUCHESNE 84926

In residence: 15. *Tribe:* Goshute.

UINTAH AND OURAY RESERVATION
c/o Uintah and Ouray Agency
              FORT DUCHESNE 84026

In residence: 1,565. *Tribe:* Ute. *Area:* 852,411 acres. *Local attractions:* Fort Duchesne, old U.S. Army post, now the site of the Uintah and Ouray Agency and tribal headquarters; Utah Field House of Natural History at Vernal; Dinosaur National Monument, thirty miles east of the Reservation. *Activities:* Annual Bear Dance of the Ute Tribe; annual Sun Dance in July; Indian Pageant at annual Uintah Basin Industrial Convention in Roosevelt; rodeos. *Facilities:* Lodging in Vernal, Roosevelt, and Duchesne. Tribal council. Located in the Uintah Basin in northeast Utah.

CEDAR CITY

In residence: 28. *Tribe*: Paiute. Located in southwest Utah.

INDIAN PEAK COMMUNITY

In residence: 12. *Tribe*: Paiute. Located in southwest Utah.

KANOSH RESERVATION

In residence: 28. *Tribe:* Ute. Located in southwest central Utah.

KOOSHAREN COMMUNITY

In residence: 27. *Tribe:* Ute. Located in south central Utah.

SANFORD COMMUNITY

In residence: 80. *Tribe:* Catawba. Located in southwest Utah.

SHIVWITTS RESERVATION

In residence: 108. *Tribe:* Paiute. Located in the southwest corner of Utah.

VIRGINIA

MATTAPONY RESERVATION
KING WILLIAM COUNTY

PAMUNKEY RESERVATION
KING WILLIAM COUNTY

WASHINGTON

COLVILLE RESERVATION
c/o Colville Agency
COULEE DAM 99116

Tribal membership: 4,338 (2,727 in residence). Tribes: Colville, Okanogan, Lakes, San Poil, Nespelem, Methow, Entiat, Wenatchee, Moses, Nez Perce, Palouse. *Area:* 1,087,271 **acres**. *Local attractions:* Grand Coulee Dam; Old Fort Okanogan; burial place of Nez Perce Chief, Joseph; Moses Mountain. *Activities:* Annual celebrations. Tribal council. Located in Okanogan and Ferry counties.

SPOKANE RESERVATION
c/o Colville Agency
COULEE DAM 99116

Tribal membership: 1,421 (597 in residence). *Tribe:* Colville. *Area:* 138,750 acres. *Local attraction:* Old Fort Spokane; Tshimakain Mission (1838). Tribal council. Located in the southwest corner of Stevens county.

CHEHALIS RESERVATION
c/o Western Washington Agency
EVERETT 98201

Tribal membership: 115. *Area:* 1,949 acres. Tribal council. Located near Olympia and Oakville, Wash.

CELILO VILLAGE
c/o Western Washington Agency
EVERETT 98201

Tribe: Yakima.

DUWAMISH COMMUNITY
c/o Western Washington Agency
EVERETT 98201

Tribal council.

LOWER ELWHA RESERVATION
c/o Western Washington Agency
EVERETT 98201

In residence: 134. *Tribe:* Elwha Band of Clallam Indians. *Area:* 372 acres. Tribal council.

LOWER SKAGIT TRIBE
c/o Western Washington Agency
EVERETT 98201

Tribal representatives.

LUMMI RESERVATION
c/o Western Washington Agency
EVERETT 98201

Tribal membership: 600. *Tribe:* Lummi. *Area:* 8,338 acres. *Activities:* Lummi *stomish,* a two-day race of war canoes off Lummi Island, held annually in the summer. Tribal council.

MAKAH RESERVATION
c/o Western Washington Agency
                    EVERETT 98201

In residence: 558. *Tribe:* Makah. *Area:* 27,012 acres. *Local attractions:* Olympic National Park and Forest; Vancouver Island. *Activities:* Annual Indian celebration at Neah Bay in August. Tribal council. Located at the conjunction of Juan de Fuca Straits and the Pacific Ocean.

CHINOOK INDIAN COMMUNITY
c/o Western Washington Agency
                    EVERETT 98201

Tribal membership: 900. Tribal council.

COWLITZ INDIAN COMMUNITY
c/o Western Washington Agency
                    EVERETT 98201

Tribal council.

KIKIALLUS INDIAN COMMUNITY
c/o Western Washington Agency
                    EVERETT 98201

Tribal representatives.

MUCKLESHOOT RESERVATION
c/o Western Washington Agency
                    EVERETT 98201

In residence: 270. *Tribe:* Muckleshoot. *Area:* 1,959 acres. Tribal council.

NISQUALLY RESERVATION
c/o Western Washington Agency
                    EVERETT 98201

In residence: 90. *Tribe:* Nisqually. *Area:* 941 acres. Tribal council.

NOOKSACK COMMUNITY
c/o Western Washington Agency
                    EVERETT 98201

In residence: 303. *Tribe:* Nooksack (Salish). *Area:* 2,906 acres. Tribal council.

PORT GAMBLE COMMUNITY
c/o Western Washington Agency
                    EVERETT 98201

In residence: 120. *Area:* 1,301 acres. Tribal council.

OZETTE RESERVATION
c/o Western Washington Agency
                    EVERETT 98201

Unoccupied. Located in Clallam County.

PORT MADISON RESERVATION
c/o Western Washington Agency
                    EVERETT 98201

In residence: 181. *Tribes:* Swamish, Etakmur, Lummi, Snohomish, Suquamish. *Area:* 3,561 acres. Suquamish Tribal Council.

PUYALLUP RESERVATION
c/o Western Washington Agency
                    EVERETT 98201

In residence: 479. *Tribes:* Nisqually, Puyallup, Muckleshoot, Skwawksnamish, Steilacoom. *Area:* 33 acres. Tribal Council.

QUILEUTE RESERVATION
c/o Western Washington Agency
                    EVERETT 98201

In residence: 154. *Tribe:* Quileute. *Area:* 594 acres. Tribal council. Located on the Pacific Ocean.

QUINAULT RESERVATION
c/o Western Washington Agency
                    EVERETT 98201

In residence: 594. *Tribe:* Quinault. *Area:* 136,456 acres. *Local attractions:* Indian village at Taholah. *Activities:* Annual celebration in July at Taholah; Lake Quinaielt Trout Derby held in May. Tribal council. Located forty miles north of Hoguiam, on the Pacific Ocean.

SAMISH TRIBE OF INDIANS
c/o Western Washington Agency
                    EVERETT 98201

Tribal council.

SAN JUAN INDIAN TRIBE
c/o Western Washington Agency
EVERETT 98201

Tribal representatives.

SHOALWATER RESERVATION
c/o Western Washington Agency
EVERETT 98201

In residence: 28. *Tribes:* Quinault, Chehalis. *Area:* 335 acres. Reservation representative. Located in Pacific County, near Tokeland, Wash.

SNOHOMISH INDIAN TRIBE
c/o Western Washington Agency
EVERETT 98201

Tribal council.

SNOQUALMIE TRIBE
c/o Western Washington Agency
EVERETT 98201

Tribal membership: 630. Tribal council.

SQUAXIN ISLAND RESERVATION
c/o Western Washington Agency
EVERETT 98201

In residence: 29. *Tribes:* Squaxin Island, Nisqually, Steilacoom, and others. Tribal council.

STEILACOOM INDIAN TRIBE
c/o Western Washington Agency
EVERETT 98201

Tribal representatives.

STILLAGUAMISH INDIAN TRIBE
c/o Western Washington Agency
EVERETT 98201

Tribal council.

SUIATTLE TRIBE
c/o Western Washington Agency
EVERETT 98201

Tribe: Sauk-Suiattle. Tribal council.

SWINOMISH RESERVATION
c/o Western Washington Agency
EVERETT 98201

In residence: 216. *Tribes:* Suiattle, Skagit, Kikiallus, Swinomish. *Area:* 973 acres. *Activities:* Traditional Indian dances at annual Treaty Day Celebration. Swinomish Indian Senate (tribal council).

TULALIP RESERVATION
c/o Western Washington Agency
EVERETT 98201

In residence: 327. *Tribes:* Snohomish, Snoqualmie, Skagit, Suiattle, Samish, and allied bands. *Area:* 13,829 acres. Tulalip Board of Directors (tribal council).

UPPER SKAGIT INDIANS
c/o Western Washington Agency
EVERETT 98201

Tribal membership: 215. Tribal council.

HOH RESERVATION
c/o Mr. Theodore Hudson, Sr.
Lower Hoh   FORKS 98331

In residence: 26. *Tribe:* Quileute-Hoh. *Area:* 443 acres. *Activities:* Annual celebration at Neah Bay -- canoe races, dances. Tribal council. Located at Cape Flattery in northwest Clallam County.

JAMESTOWN BAND OF CLALLAM
INDIANS   SEQUIM 98382

Tribal membership: 50. Tribal council.

SKOKOMISH INDIAN RESERVATION
Star Route 1   SHELTON 98584
Thomas Pulsifer, Chairman,
Tribal Council

In residence: 500. *Tribe:* Mixed. *Area:*
3,500 acres. *Local attractions:* Fishing in
nearby Skokomish River, regulated by Reservation members through a five per cent
fishing tax during the commercial season;
Reservation also sells steelhead fishing per-
mits to non-members.

YAKIMA RESERVATION
                    SUNNYSIDE DAM 98944

In residence: 4,844. *Tribes:* Yakima,
Palouse, Pisquoise, and others. *Area:*
1,134,830 acres. *Activities:* All-Indian
rodeo in June at White Swan; July Pow Wow
at Toppenish; Huckleberry feasts in August.
Tribal enterprise: Wapato Indian Irrigation
Project. Tribal council.

KALISPEL RESERVATION   USK

In residence: 145. *Tribe:* Kalispel. *Area:*
4,629 acres. Tribal council.

WISCONSIN

BAD RIVER RESERVATION
c/o Great Lakes Agency   ASHLAND 54806

In residence: 509. *Tribe:* Chippewa. *Area:*
54,720 acres. *Facilities:* Lodging in Ashland. Tribal council. Located on Lake Superior, southeast of Duluth, Minn.

RED CLIFF RESERVATION
c/o Great Lakes Agency   ASHLAND 54806

In residence: 380. *Tribe:* Chippewa. *Area:*
7,311 acres. Tribal council. Extends over
Lake Superior approximately twenty-five
miles northwest of Ashland, Wis.

THE WINNEBAGO TRIBE OF WISCONSIN
                  BLACK RIVER FALLS 54616

In residence: 1,384. Tribal council.

STOCKBRIDGE RESERVATION
R.R. 1   BOWLER 54416

Tribal membership: 954 (369 in residence).
Tribe: Stockbridge-Munsee (Mohican).
Area: 16,000 acres. *Activities:* Arts and
crafts enterprise. *Facilities:* Campsites;
fishing and hunting. Tribal council.

LAC COURTE OREILLES RESERVATION
c/o New Post   COUDERAY 54828

In residence: 846. *Tribe*: Chippewa. Tribal council.

FOREST COUNTY POTAWATOMI
      COMMUNITY   CRANDON 54520

Tribal membership: 400 (200 in residence).
Tribe: Forest County (Wisconsin Band of)
Potawatomi. *Area:* 10,000 acres. Tribal
council.

SOKAOGON CHIPPEWA COMMUNITY
      (MOLE LAKE)   CRANDON 54520

In residence: 106. *Tribe:* Chippewa. Tribal council.

LAC DU FLAMBEAU BAND OF LAKE
    SUPERIOR CHIPPEWA INDIANS
    RESERVATION
              LAC DU FLAMBEAU 54538

In residence: 893. *Tribe:* Chippewa. Tribal council.

ONEIDA RESERVATION   ONEIDA 54155

In residence: 388. *Tribe:* Oneida. Tribal
council.

ST. CROIX CHIPPEWA RESERVATION
                      WEBSTER 54893

In residence: 303. *Tribe*: St. Croix Chippewa. Tribal council.

WYOMING

WIND RIVER RESERVATION
c/o Wind River Agency
                  FORT WASHAKIE 82514

Tribal membership: 4,400 (3,500 in residence). *Tribes:* Arapaho, Shoshoni. *Area:*
1,887,372 acres. *Local attractions:* Fort
Washakie; hot springs east of Fort. Tribal
council. Located in west central Wyoming.

Tribal Councils

Listed in this section are reservation tribal councils, which handle tribal and/or reservation affairs and which represent the tribes and create policy on land, enrollment, etc.

ARIZONA

HOPI TRIBAL COUNCIL
c/o Hopi Agency   KEAMS CANYON 86034

KAIBAB TRIBAL COUNCIL
c/o Hopi Agency   KEAMS CANYON 86034

Tribe served: Paiute (in Utah).

COLORADO RIVER TRIBAL COUNCIL
c/o Colorado River Agency
                    PARKER 85344
    Denise Florence, Secretary

Tribes served: Mohave and Chemehuevi.
Activities: Colorado River Tribes Public Library containing Indian-related books, magazines, and photographs; Mohave archives.

FORT MOHAVE TRIBAL COUNCIL
c/o Colorado River Agency
                    PARKER 85344

Serves Mojave Tribe in California and Arizona.

HAVASUPAI TRIBAL COUNCIL
c/o Colorado River Agency
                    PARKER 85344

Tribe served: Havasupai.

HUALAPAI TRIBAL COUNCIL
c/o Colorado River Agency
                    PARKER 85344

Tribe served: Hualapai.

YAVAPAI APACHE COMMUNITY COUNCIL
c/o Colorado River Agency
                    PARKER 85344

Tribe served: Yavapai.

YAVAPAI BOARD OF DIRECTORS
c/o Colorado River Agency
                    PARKER 85344

Tribe served: Yavapai.

AK CHIN INDIAN COMMUNITY COUNCIL
c/o Pima Agency   SACATON 85247

Tribe served: Papago.

GILA RIVER INDIAN COMMUNITY
    COUNCIL
c/o Pima Agency   SACATON 85247

Tribe served: Papago.

MOHAVE APACHE COMMUNITY COUNCIL
c/o Pima Agency   SACATON 85247

SAN CARLOS COUNCIL
c/o San Carlos Agency
                    SAN CARLOS 85550

Tribe served: Apache.

SALT RIVER PIMA-MARICOPA
    COMMUNITY COUNCIL
c/o Salt River Agency Route #1
Box 907   SCOTTSDALE 85251

Tribes served: Pima and Maricopa.

PAPAGO COUNCIL
c/o Papago Agency   SELLS 85634
    Robert Mackett, Chairman

Tribal membership: 5,500. *Tribe served:* Papago. *Reservations served:* Sells, San Xavier, Gila Bend. *Activities:* Papago Tribal Herd Enterprise. Four members.

COCOPAH TRIBAL COUNCIL
P. O. Box 26   SOMERTON 85350
    Mrs. Clara Brown, Chairman

Tribal membership: 85. *Tribe served:* Cocopah.

WHITE MOUNTAIN APACHE TRIBAL
  COUNCIL
c/o Fort Apache Agency
                      WHITERIVER 85941

NAVAJO TRIBAL COUNCIL
c/o Navajo Agency   WINDOW ROCK 86515

Serves Arizona and New Mexico Navajo
Tribe.

CALIFORNIA

FORT MOHAVE TRIBAL COUNCIL
c/o Colorado River Agency
                      PARKER 85344
                      (Arizona)

Serves Mojave Tribe in California and
Arizona.

QUECHAN TRIBAL COUNCIL
c/o Colorado River Agency
                      PARKER 85344
                      (Arizona)

Serves Quechan Community in California.

WASHOE TRIBAL COUNCIL
c/o Nevada Agency   STEWART 89437
                        (Nevada)

Serves Washoe Tribe in Nevada and California.

HOOPA VALLEY BUSINESS COUNCIL
c/o Hoopa Area Field Office
                      HOOPA 95546

Tribe served: Hoopa.

QUARTZ VALLEY GENERAL
  COMMUNITY COUNCIL
c/o Hoopa Area Field Office
                      HOOPA 95546

LA JOLLA GENERAL COUNCIL
c/o Riverside Area Field Office
6848 Magnolia Ave.   RIVERSIDE 92506

MISSION CREEK BAND COUNCIL
c/o Riverside Area Field Office
6848 Magnolia Ave.   RIVERSIDE 92506

PALA GENERAL COUNCIL
c/o Riverside Area Field Office
6848 Magnolia Ave.   RIVERSIDE 92506

RINCON SAN LUISINO BUSINESS
  COMMITTEE
c/o Riverside Area Field Office
6848 Magnolia Ave.   RIVERSIDE 92506

SAN PASQUAL BAND OF MISSION INDIANS
c/o Riverside Area Field Office
6848 Magnolia Ave.   RIVERSIDE 92506

SANTA YNEZ BUSINESS COUNCIL
c/o Riverside Area Field Office
6848 Magnolia Ave.   RIVERSIDE 92506

BIG VALLEY RANCHERIA COMMUNITY
  COUNCIL
c/o Sacramento Area Office
2550 Fair Oaks Blvd.
                      SACRAMENTO 95825

COLUSA INDIAN COMMUNITY COUNCIL
c/o Sacramento Area Office
2550 Fair Oaks Blvd.
                      SACRAMENTO 95825

COVELO INDIAN COMMUNITY COUNCIL
c/o Sacramento Area Office
2550 Fair Oaks Blvd.
                      SACRAMENTO 95825

FORT BIDWELL GENERAL
  COMMUNITY COUNCIL
c/o Sacramento Area Office
2550 Fair Oaks Blvd.
                      SACRAMENTO 95825

HOPLAND RANCHERIA
c/o Sacramento Area Office
2550 Fair Oaks Blvd.
                      SACRAMENTO 95825

MANCHESTER COMMUNITY COUNCIL
c/o Sacramento Area Office
2550 Fair Oaks Blvd.
SACRAMENTO 95825

OWENS VALLEY COUNCIL
c/o Sacramento Area Office
2550 Fair Oaks Blvd.
SACRAMENTO 95825

PALM SPRINGS (AGUA CALIENTE)
TRIBAL COUNCIL
c/o Sacramento Area Office
2550 Fair Oaks Blvd.
SACRAMENTO 95825

PINOLEVILLE COMMUNITY COUNCIL
c/o Sacramento Area Office
2550 Fair Oaks Blvd.
SACRAMENTO 95825

RUMSEY FARMING ASSOCIATION
c/o Sacramento Area Office
2550 Fair Oaks Blvd.
SACRAMENTO 95825

SANTA ROSA BUSINESS COMMITTEE
c/o Sacramento Area Office
2550 Fair Oaks Blvd.
SACRAMENTO 95825

STEWARTS POINT RANCHERIA
COMMUNITY COUNCIL
c/o Sacramento Area Office
2550 Fair Oaks Blvd.
SACRAMENTO 95825

TRINIDAD RANCHERIA COMMUNITY
COUNCIL
c/o Sacramento Area Office
2550 Fair Oaks Blvd.
SACRAMENTO 95825

TULE RIVER TRIBAL COUNCIL
c/o Sacramento Area Office
2550 Fair Oaks Blvd.
SACRAMENTO 95825

TOULUMNE RANCHERIA COMMUNITY
COUNCIL
c/o Sacramento Area Office
2550 Fair Oaks Blvd.
SACRAMENTO 95825

UPPER BAND OF POMO INDIANS
COMMUNITY COUNCIL
c/o Sacramento Area Office
2550 Fair Oaks Blvd.
SACRAMENTO 95825

WILTON RANCHERIA
c/o Sacramento Area Office
2550 Fair Oaks Blvd.
SACRAMENTO 95825

COLORADO

SOUTHERN UTE TRIBAL COUNCIL
c/o Consolidated Ute Agency
IGNACIO 81137

Tribe served: Ute.

UTE MOUNTAIN TRIBAL COUNCIL
c/o Consolidated Ute Agency
IGNACIO 81137

FLORIDA

SEMINOLE TRIBAL COUNCIL
c/o Seminole Agency
6075 Stirling Rd.   HOLLYWOOD 33024

Tribe served: Seminole.

MICCOSUKEE BUSINESS COUNCIL
c/o Miccosukee Agency
P. O. Box 1369   HOMESTEAD 33030

Tribe served: Miccosukee. *Activities:*
Tribally-operated restaurant and filling station, part of a projected complex to include
native dwellings of the Everglades Indians
and a motel.

IDAHO

KOOTENAI TRIBAL COUNCIL
                 BONNERS FERRY 83805
Baptiste Cutsack, Chairman

Tribal membership: 67. *Tribe served:*
Kootenai. Five members.

FORT HALL BUSINESS COUNCIL
c/o Fort Hall Agency   FORT HALL 83201
     Herbert Le Claire, Chairman

Tribal membership: 2,500. *Tribes served:*
Shoshone, Bannock. Seven members.

NEZ PERCE TRIBAL EXECUTIVE
     COMMITTEE
                 LAPWAI 83540
     Richard A. Halfmoon, Chairman

Tribal membership: 2,232. *Tribe served:*
Nez Perce. Nine executive members and a
general council.

COEUR D'ALENE TRIBAL COUNCIL
                 PLUMMER 83851
     Joseph R. Garry, Chairman

Tribal membership: 851. *Activities:* Quarterly meetings. Six members.

IOWA

SAC AND FOX TRIBE OF THE
     MISSISSIPPI IN IOWA (TRIBAL
     COUNCIL)
Route 2, Box 121   TAMA 52339
     George Youngbear, Sr., Chairman

Tribe served: Sac and Fox.

KANSAS

IOWA GENERAL TRIBAL COUNCIL
     (Kansas and Nebraska)
c/o Horton Agency   HORTON 66439

KICKAPOO TRIBAL COUNCIL
c/o Horton Agency   HORTON 66439

POTAWATOMI BUSINESS COMMITTEE
     (PRAIRIE BAND)
c/o Horton Agency   HORTON 66439

LOUISIANA

CHITIMACHA TRIBAL COUNCIL
c/o Choctaw Agency
               PHILADELPHIA 39350
               (Mississippi)

MAINE

PASSAMAQUODDY TRIBAL COUNCIL
c/o Indian Township Reservation
               PRINCETON 04668
     Chief John Stevens (Chairman)

Tribal membership: 1,200. *Tribe served:*
Passamaquoddy. *Reservations served:* Indian Township and Pleasant Point. Six
members from each reservation.

MICHIGAN

BAY MILLS INDIAN COMMUNITY
     EXECUTIVE COUNCIL
               BRIMLEY 49715
     Herman E. Cameron, President

KEWEENAW BAY INDIAN COMMUNITY
     TRIBAL COUNCIL
               L'ANSE 49946
     William Jondreau, President

SAGINAW CHIPPEWA INDIAN TRIBE OF
     MICHIGAN TRIBAL COUNCIL
Route 4   MOUNT PLEASANT 48858
     Willis Jackson, Sr., Chief

HANNAHVILLE INDIAN COMMUNITY
     COUNCIL
Route 1   WILSON 49896
     O. Joe Sagataw, Chairman

MINNESOTA

LEECH LAKE RESERVATION BUSINESS
COMMITTEE
BALL CLUB 56622
Allen Wilson, Chairman

WHITE EARTH RESERVATION BUSINESS
COMMITTEE
CALLAWAY 56521
Bernard Martin, Chairman

FOND DU LAC RESERVATION BUSINESS
COMMITTEE
1390 David Rd.   CLOQUET 55720
Sherman Smith, Chairman

THE MINNESOTA CHIPPEWA TRIBE
Tribal Executive Committee
c/o Peter Du Fault, President
709 Larch St.   CLOQUET 55720

GRAND PORTAGE RESERVATION
BUSINESS COMMITTEE
GRAND PORTAGE 55605
William Bushman, Chairman

Tribe served: Chippewa.

THE UPPER SIOUX INDIAN COMMUNITY
Board of Trustees
GRANITE FALLS 56241
Dean F. Blue, Chairman

MILLE LACS RESERVATION BUSINESS
COMMITTEE
McGREGOR 57760
Sam Yankee, Chairman,

THE LOWER SIOUX INDIAN COMMUNITY
Community Council   MORTON 56270
Albert Prescot, President

THE RED LAKE BAND OF CHIPPEWA
INDIANS
Tribal Council   REDLAKE 56671
Roger A. Jourdain, Chairman

Tribe served: Chippewa.

TWIN CITIES CHIPPEWA COUNCIL
1592 E. Hoyt   ST. PAUL 55106
Donald Glass, President

Tribe served: Chippewa.

NETT LAKE RESERVATION BUSINESS
COMMITTEE
TOWER 57790
Vincent J. Chosa, Chairman

THE PRAIRIE ISLAND INDIAN
COMMUNITY
Community Council   WELCH 55089
Amos Owen, President

MONTANA

CHIPPEWA-CREE BUSINESS COMMITTEE
BOX ELDER 59521
Peter Sutherland, Chairman

Tribes served: Chippewa, Cree. Nine
members.

BLACKFEET TRIBAL BUSINESS COUNCIL
c/o Blackfeet Agency   BROWNING 59417
Earl Old Person, Chairman

Tribal membership: 12,000. *Tribe served:*
Blackfeet. Thirteen members.

CROW TRIBAL COUNCIL
c/o Crow Agency   CROW AGENCY 59022
John Wilson, Sr., Chairman

Tribe served: Crow. Four members.

CONFEDERATED SALISH AND KOOTENAI
TRIBAL COUNCIL
c/o Flathead Agency   DIXON 59831
Walter W. McDonald, Chairman

Tribal membership: 5,000. *Tribes served:*
Salish (Flathead) and Kootenai. Ten members.

FORT BELKNAP COMMUNITY COUNCIL
c/o Fort Belknap Consolidated Agency
                              HARLEM 59526
    Tom Bell, President

Tribal membership: 3,557. *Tribes served:*
Gros Ventre, Assiniboine. Twelve members.

THE TRIBAL COUNCIL OF THE
    NORTHERN CHEYENNE
c/o Northern Cheyenne Agency
                         LAME DEER 59043
    John Woodenlegs, President

Tribal membership: 2,900. *Tribe served:*
Cheyenne.

FORT PECK TRIBAL EXECUTIVE BOARD
c/o Fort Peck Agency
P. O. Box 637   POPLAR 59255
    William Youpee, Chairman

Tribal membership: 6,728. *Tribes served:*
Assiniboine, Sioux.

NEBRASKA

OMAHA TRIBAL COUNCIL
c/o Winnebago Agency
                         WINNEBAGO 68071

Tribe served: Omaha.

PONCA BOARD OF GOVERNORS
c/o Winnebago Agency
                         WINNEBAGO 68071

Tribe served: Ponca.

SANTEE-SIOUX TRIBAL COUNCIL
c/o Winnebago Agency
                         WINNEBAGO 68071

Tribe served: Santee-Sioux.

WINNEBAGO TRIBAL COUNCIL
c/o Winnebago Agency
                         WINNEBAGO 68071

Tribe served: Winnebago.

NEVADA

MOAPA BUSINESS COUNCIL
c/o Colorado River Agency
                            PARKER 85344
                            (Arizona)

Tribes served: Paiute, Shoshone (in Nevada).

INTER-TRIBAL COUNCIL OF NEVADA,
    INC.
877 Aitken St.   RENO 89502
    John Dressler, Chairman
    Ralph F. Keen, Executive Secretary

Membership: 10,000. *Activities:* Head
Start program; Neighborhood Youth Corps
program; Community Development project;
technical assistance in law enforcement,
water and sewer systems, street lights,
tribal organization. Serves fourteen out of
twenty-three Nevada Indian communities
regardless of tribal membership. Four
members.

WALKER RIVER PAIUTE TRIBAL
    COUNCIL
                            SHURZ 89427
    Melvin D. Thom, Chairman

Tribal membership: 600. *Tribe served:*
Northern Paiute. *Activities:* Agriculture,
livestock, Indian arts and crafts.

CARSON COLONY COUNCIL
c/o Nevada Agency   STEWART 89437

Tribes served: Washoe, Paiute.

DUCK VALLEY COUNCIL
c/o Nevada Agency   STEWART 89437

Tribes served: Shoshone, Paiute.

DUCKWATER SHOSHONE TRIBAL
    COUNCIL
c/o Nevada Agency   STEWART 89437

Tribe served: Shoshone.

FALLON BUSINESS COUNCIL
c/o Nevada Agency   STEWART 89437

Tribes served: Shoshone, Paiute. Council represents Fallon Reservation and Fallon Colony.

FORT McDERMITT TRIBAL COUNCIL
c/o Nevada Agency   STEWART 89437

Tribe served: Paiute.

GOSHUTE BUSINESS COUNCIL
c/o Nevada Agency   STEWART 89437

Tribe served: Goshute (in Utah).

LAS VEGAS COLONY COUNCIL
c/o Nevada Agency   STEWART 89437

Tribe served: Paiute.

PYRAMID LAKE PAIUTE TRIBAL
  COUNCIL
c/o Nevada Agency   STEWART 89437

Tribe served: Paiute.

RENO-SPARKS INDIAN COUNCIL
c/o Nevada Agency   STEWART 89437

Tribes served: Washoe, Paiute.

SUMMIT LAKE PAIUTE COUNCIL
c/o Nevada Agency   STEWART 89437

Tribe served: Paiute.

TE-MOAK WESTERN SHOSHONE COUNCIL
c/o Nevada Agency   STEWART 89437

WASHOE TRIBAL COUNCIL
c/o Nevada Agency   STEWART 89437

Serves Washoe Tribe in California and Nevada.

YERINGTON PAIUTE TRIBAL COUNCIL
c/o Nevada Agency   STEWART 89437

Tribe served: Paiute.

YOMBA TRIBAL COUNCIL
c/o Nevada Agency   STEWART 89437

Tribe served: Shoshone.

NEW MEXICO

UNITED PUEBLOS ALL PUEBLO
  COUNCIL
c/o United Pueblos Agency
1000 Indian School Rd.
                ALBUQUERQUE 87103

Serves all of the following pueblos whose individual governors may be contacted through the United Pueblos Agency:

ACOMA PUEBLO

COCHITI PUEBLO

ISLETA PUEBLO

JEMEZ PUEBLO

LAGUNA PUEBLO

NAMBE PUEBLO

POJOAQUE PUEBLO

SAN FELIPE PUEBLO

SAN ILDEFONSO PUEBLO

SAN JUAN PUEBLO

PICURIS (SAN LORENZO) PUEBLO

SANDIA PUEBLO

SANTA ANA PUEBLO

SANTA CLARA PUEBLO

SANTO DOMINGO PUEBLO

TAOS PUEBLO

TESUQUE PUEBLO

ZIA PUEBLO

JICARILLA APACHE REPRESENTATIVE
  TRIBAL COUNCIL
c/o Jicarilla Agency   DULCE 87528

Tribe served: Apache.

MESCALERO APACHE TRIBAL COUNCIL
c/o Mescalero Agency
                    MESCALERO 88340

Tribe served: Apache. *Activities:* Tribally operated Apache Summit Lodge.

ZUNI TRIBAL COUNCIL
c/o Zuni Agency   ZUNI 87327

Tribe served: Zuni.

NORTH CAROLINA

CHEROKEE TRIBAL COUNCIL
c/o Cherokee Agency   CHEROKEE 28719

Tribe served: Cherokee.

NORTH DAKOTA

TURTLE MOUNTAIN TRIBAL COUNCIL
c/o Turtle Mountain Agency
                    BELCOURT 58316

Tribe served: Chippewa.

DEVIL'S LAKE TRIBAL COUNCIL
  (FORT TOTTEN)
c/o Fort Totten Subagency
                    FORT TOTTEN 58335
Lewis Goodhouse, Chairman

Tribal membership: 1,400. *Tribe served:*
Devil's Lake Sioux.

STANDING ROCK SIOUX TRIBAL COUNCIL
c/o Standing Rock Agency
                    FORT YATES 58538

Tribe served: Sioux.

FORT BERTHOLD TRIBAL BUSINESS
  COUNCIL
c/o Fort Berthold Agency
                    NEW TOWN 58763

Tribes served: Gros Ventre, Arikara, Mandan.

OKLAHOMA

CADDO BUSINESS COMMITTEE
c/o Anadarko Agency   ANADARKO 73005

DELAWARE TRIBAL COUNCIL
c/o Anadarko Agency   ANADARKO 73005

FORT SILL APACHE TRIBAL COUNCIL
c/o Anadarko Agency   ANADARKO 73005

KIOWA, COMANCHE, APACHE TRIBAL
  BUSINESS COMMITTEE
c/o Anadarko Agency   ANADARKO 73005

WICHITA COUNCIL
c/o Anadarko Agency   ANADARKO 73005

CHICKASAW NATION, GOVERNOR
c/o Ardmore Agency   ARDMORE 73401

CHEYENNE-ARAPAHO BUSINESS
  COMMITTEE
c/o Concho Agency   CONCHO 73022

EASTERN SHAWNEE COUNCIL
c/o Miami Agency
P.O. Box 391   MIAMI 74354

MIAMI BUSINESS COMMITTEE
c/o Miami Agency
P.O. Box 391   MIAMI 74354

QUAPAW TRIBAL BUSINESS COMMITTEE
c/o Miami Agency
P.O. Box 391   MIAMI 74354

SENECA-CAYUGA TRIBAL BUSINESS
  COMMITTEE
c/o Miami Agency
P.O. Box 391   MIAMI 74354

WYANDOTTE TRIBAL BUSINESS
  COMMITTEE
c/o Muskogee Area Office
                    MUSKOGEE 74401

ALABAMA-QUASSARTE CREEK TRIBAL
   TOWN COUNCIL
c/o Okmulgee Agency
P.O. Box 671   OKMULGEE 74447

CREEK NATION (TRIBAL COUNCIL)
c/o Okmulgee Agency
P.O. Box 671   OKMULGEE 74447

KIALEGEE CREEK BUSINESS
   COMMITTEE
c/o Okmulgee Agency
P.O. Box 671   OKMULGEE 74447

THLOPTHLOCCO CREEK BUSINESS
   COUNCIL
c/o Okmulgee Agency
P.O. Box 671   OKMULGEE 74447

OSAGE TRIBAL COUNCIL
c/o Osage Agency   PAWHUSKA 74056

KAW TRIBAL COUNCIL
c/o Pawnee Agency   PAWNEE 74058

OTOE-MISSOURIA TRIBAL COUNCIL
c/o Pawnee Agency   PAWNEE 74058

PAWNEE BUSINESS COUNCIL
c/o Pawnee Agency   PAWNEE 74058

PONCA BUSINESS COMMITTEE
c/o Pawnee Agency   PAWNEE 74058

TONKAWA TRIBAL COUNCIL
c/o Pawnee Agency   PAWNEE 74058

ABSENTEE-SHAWNEE BUSINESS
   COMMITTEE
c/o Shawnee Agency   SHAWNEE 74801

CITIZEN BAND OF POTAWATOMI
   COUNCIL
c/o Shawnee Agency   SHAWNEE 74801

IOWA BUSINESS COMMITTEE
c/o Shawnee Agency   SHAWNEE 74801

KICKAPOO BUSINESS COMMITTEE
c/o Shawnee Agency   SHAWNEE 74801

SAC AND FOX BUSINESS COMMITTEE
Route 1   STROUD 74079
   Elmer Manatowa, Jr., Principal Chief

Tribal membership: 1,800. *Tribe served:*
Sac and Fox. Five members.

CHEROKEE NATION
c/o Tahlequah Agency
P.O. Box 459   TAHLEQUAH 74464
   William Wheeler, Principal Chief

UNITED KEETOOWAH COUNCIL
c/o Tahlequah Agency
P.O. Box 459   TAHLEQUAH 74464

CHOCTAW NATION, PRINCIPAL CHIEF
c/o Talihina Agency
P.O. Box 187   TALIHINA 74571

SEMINOLE TRIBE, PRINCIPAL CHIEF
c/o Wewoka Agency   WEWOKA 74884

OREGON

BURNS PAIUTE COLONY BUSINESS
   COMMITTEE
                  BURNS 97720
   James Stanley, Chairman

Tribal membership: 225. *Tribe served:*
Paiute (97 per cent full blood). Five members.

CONFEDERATED TRIBES OF THE
   UMATILLA RESERVATION
             PENDLETON 97801
   David S. Hall, Chairman

Tribal membership: 1,245. *Tribes served:*
Umatilla, Cayuse, Walla Walla. *Activities:*
Committees dealing with scholarships,
credit, fish, approval and enrollment. Eight
members.

TRIBAL COUNCIL, CONFEDERATED
  TRIBES OF THE WARM SPRINGS
  RESERVATION
                       WARM SPRINGS 97761
  Olney Pratt, Chairman

Tribal membership: 1,690. *Tribes served:*
Warm Springs, Wasco, Paiute. Eleven
members.

SOUTH DAKOTA

CHEYENNE RIVER SIOUX TRIBAL
  COUNCIL
c/o Cheyenne River Agency
                     EAGLE BUTTE 57625
  Frank D. Ducheneaux, Chairman

Tribal membership: 6,204. *Tribes served:*
Cheyenne River Sioux. *Activities:* Farming and stock raising. *Tribe-operated enterprises:* Two cattle programs, Super-
Valu Store, Sales Pavilion, filling station,
laundromat, tribe-owned beef herd. Tribe
operates the only Indian telephone company
in the United States. Four members.

FLANDREAU SANTEE-SIOUX GENERAL
  BUSINESS COUNCIL
c/o Flandreau School   FLANDREAU 57028
  Richard K. Wakeman, President

Five members.

CROW CREEK TRIBAL COUNCIL
c/o Pierre Agency   PIERRE 57501

LOWER BRULE SIOUX TRIBAL COUNCIL
c/o Pierre Agency   PIERRE 57501

OGLALA SIOUX TRIBAL COUNCIL
c/o Pine Ridge Agency
                       PINE RIDGE 57770

Tribe served: Sioux.

ROSEBUD SIOUX TRIBAL COUNCIL
c/o Rosebud Agency   ROSEBUD 57570

Tribe served: Sioux. *Activities:* Tribe-
operated Crazy Horse Canyon Park on
Rosebud Reservation.

SISSETON-WAHPETON SIOUX TRIBAL
  COUNCIL
c/o Sisseton Agency   SISSETON 57262

Tribe served: Sioux.

YANKTON SIOUX TRIBAL BUSINESS AND
  CLAIMS COMMITTEE
c/o Yankton Subagency   WAGNER 57380

Tribe served: Sioux.

UTAH

UINTAH AND OURAY TRIBAL
  BUSINESS COMMITTEE
c/o Uintah and Ouray Agency
                      FORT DUCHESNE 84026

Tribe served: Ute.

WASHINGTON

CHINOOK INDIANS - GENERAL COUNCIL
c/o Western Washington Agency
                          EVERETT 98201
  Kent Elliott, Chairman

Tribal membership: 900. *Tribe served:*
Chinook. Four members.

COWLITZ INDIANS (GOVERNING BODY)
c/o Western Washington Agency
                          EVERETT 98201
  Clifford Wilson, Chairman

Tribe served: Cowlitz.

DUWAMISH TRIBAL COUNCIL
c/o Western Washington Agency
                          EVERETT 98201
  Mrs. Ruth Eley Scranton, Chairman

Tribal membership: 390. *Tribe served:*
Duwamish. Ten members.

KIKIALLUS INDIANS (GOVERNING BODY)
c/o Western Washington Agency
                          EVERETT 98201
  Alfonso Sampson, Representative

Tribe served: Kikiallus.

LOWER ELWHA, ELWHA BAND OF
  CLALLAM INDIANS
c/o Western Washington Agency
                    EVERETT 98201
    Martin Hopie, Chairman

Tribal membership: 134. *Tribe served:*
Elwha Band of Clallam Indians.

LOWER SKAGIT TRIBE
c/o Western Washington Agency
                    EVERETT 98201
    Tandy Wilbur, Tribal Representative

MUCKLESHOOT INDIAN TRIBAL COUNCIL
c/o Western Washington Agency
                    EVERETT 98201
    Mrs. Bertha McJoe, Chairman

Tribal membership: 271. *Tribe served:*
Muckleshoot. Six members.

NISQUALLY COMMUNITY COUNCIL
c/o Western Washington Agency
                    EVERETT 98201
    Reuben Wells, Chairman

Tribal membership: 49. *Tribe served:*
Nisqually. Four members.

NOOKSACK TRIBAL COUNCIL
c/o Western Washington Agency
                    EVERETT 98201
    Ray George, President

Tribal membership: 370. *Tribe served:*
Nooksack (Salish). Eight members.

PUYALLUP TRIBAL COUNCIL
c/o Western Washington Agency
                    EVERETT 98201
    Frank Wright, Chairman

Tribal membership: 450. *Tribes served:*
Puyallup, Muckleshoot, Skwawksnamish,
Steilacoom. Five members.

QUILEUTE TRIBAL COUNCIL
c/o Western Washington Agency
                    EVERETT 98201
    Fred Woodruff, Chairman

Tribal membership: 250. *Tribe served:*
Quileute. Five members.

SAMISH TRIBE OF INDIANS
  (GOVERNING BODY)
c/o Western Washington Agency
                    EVERETT 98201
    Harold C. Hatch, Chairman

Ten members.

SAN JUAN INDIAN TRIBE
  (GOVERNING BODY)
c/o Western Washington Agency
                    EVERETT 98201
    Mrs. Maybelle Little,
      Tribal Representative

SAUK-SUIATTLE INDIAN TRIBE
  (GOVERNING BODY)
c/o Western Washington Agency
                    EVERETT 98201
    Paul Harvey, Chairman

Tribal membership: 150. *Tribe served:*
Sauk-Suiattle. Two members.

SHOALWATER RESERVATION
  (GOVERNING BODY)
c/o Western Washington Agency
                    EVERETT 98201
    Mr. Earl Davis,
      Reservation Representative

Tribal membership: 12. *Tribes served:*
Quinault, Chehalis. Two representatives.

SNOHOMISH INDIAN TRIBE
  (GOVERNING BODY)
c/o Western Washington Agency
                    EVERETT 98201
    H. T. Hawkins, Chairman

Eleven members.

SNOQUALMIE INDIAN TRIBE
  (GOVERNING BODY)
c/o Western Washington Agency
                    EVERETT 98201
    Emil Williams, Chairman

Tribal membership: 630. *Tribe served:*
Snoqualmie. Four members.

STEILACOOM INDIAN TRIBE
  (GOVERNING BODY)
c/o Western Washington Agency
                    EVERETT 98201
    Lewis Layton, Tribal Representative

STILLAGUAMISH INDIAN TRIBE
  (GOVERNING BODY)
c/o Western Washington Agency
                                    EVERETT 98201
    John Silva, Chairman

Three members.

SUQUAMISH TRIBAL COUNCIL
Port Madison Reservation
c/o Western Washington Agency
                                    EVERETT 98201
    Ed Sigo, Chairman

Tribal membership: 200. Five members.

UPPER SKAGIT TRIBAL COUNCIL
c/o Western Washington Agency
                                    EVERETT 98201
    Charles Boome, Chairman

Tribal membership: 215. *Tribe served:*
Upper Skagit. Eight members.

HOH TRIBAL COUNCIL
c/o Mr. Theodore Hudson, Sr.
Lower Hoh   FORKS 98331

Tribes served: Quileute, Hoh. *Activities:*
Committees dealing with timber leasing,
enrollment, law and order. Five members.

SWINOMISH INDIAN SENATE
                                    LA CONNER 98257
    Dewey Mitchell, Chairman

Tribal membership: 320. *Tribes served:*
Suiattle, Swinomish, Skagit, Kikiallus. *Activities:* Committees dealing with fisheries,
oysters, and sawmills. Eleven members.

LUMMI BUSINESS COUNCIL
Lummi Reservation   MARIETTA 98268
    Forrest Kinley, Chairman

Tribal membership: 600. *Tribe served:*
Lummi. Eleven members.

TULALIP BOARD OF DIRECTORS
                                    MARYSVILLE 98270
    George Williams, Chairman

Tribal membership: 700. *Tribes served:*
Snohomish, Snoqualmie, Skagit, Suiattle,

Samish and allied bands. *Activities:* Committees dealing with land, lease and loan;
education; enrollment; water and roads;
hunting and fishing; recreation. Seven
members.

MAKAH TRIBAL COUNCIL
                                    NEAH BAY 98357
    Quentin Markishtum, Chairman

Tribal membership: 700. *Tribe served:*
Makah. Five members.

COLVILLE BUSINESS COUNCIL
Confederated Tribes of the Colville
  Reservation
P. O. Box 158   NESPELEM 99155
    Narcisse Nicholson, Jr., Chairman

Tribal membership: 4,338. *Activities:*
Quarterly meetings; regulation of tribal af-
fairs through the following committees:
Finance; Health, Education and Welfare;
Planning; Employment; Realty; Legis-
lative; Land and Forestry; Enrollment;
Fish and Wildlife; Law and Order; Election.
Tribes served: Colville; Okanogan; Lakes;
San Poil; Nespelem; Methow; Entiat; Wen-
atchee; Moses; Nez Perce; Palouse. Four-
teen members.

CHEHALIS COMMUNITY COUNCIL
                                    OAKVILLE 98568
    Percy Youckton, Chairman

Tribal membership: 115. *Activities:* Community service program. Twenty-five
members.

PORT GAMBLE BAND OF CLALLAM
  INDIANS
                                    PORT GAMBLE 98364
    Aaron Purser, Chairman

Tribal membership: 120. *Tribe served:*
Port Gamble Band of Clallam Indians. Five
members.

JAMESTOWN TRIBAL COUNCIL
                                    SEQUIM 98382
    Jacob Hall, Chairman

Tribal membership: 550. *Tribe served:*
Jamestown Band of Clallam Indians. Five
members.

SKOKOMISH TRIBAL COUNCIL
Star Route 1   SHELTON 98584
    Thomas Pulsifer, Chairman

Tribal membership: 500. *Tribe served:*
Mixed. *Activities:* Children's summer
recreation program, Autumn commercial
fishing (Sept. 15 through Dec. 31). Five
members.

SQUAXIN ISLAND TRIBAL COUNCIL
                    SHELTON 98584
    Florence Sigo, Chairman

Tribal membership: 100. *Tribes served:*
Squaxin Island, Nisqually, Steilacoom, and
others. Five members.

QUINAULT TRIBAL COUNCIL
                         TAHOLAH
    James Jackson, President

Tribal membership: 574. *Tribe served:*
Quinault. *Activities:* Business committee.
Nine members.

YAKIMA TRIBAL COUNCIL AND
    YAKIMA GENERAL COUNCIL
c/o Yakima Agency   TOPPENISH 98948
    Eagle Seelatsee, Chairman

Tribal membership: 5,235. *Tribes served:*
Yakima, Palouse, Pisquouse, and others.
Activities: Tribe-operated Wapato Indian
Irrigation Project. Five members (Tribal
council). Four members (General council).

KALISPEL BUSINESS COUNCIL
                      CUSICK 99119
    Ray Pierre, Chairman

Tribal membership: 154. *Tribe served:*
Kalispel. Three members.

SPOKANE BUSINESS COUNCIL
                    WELLPINIT 99040
    Alex Sherwood, Chairman

Tribal membership: 1,400. *Tribe served:*
Colville. Three members.

WISCONSIN

WINNEBAGO TRIBE OF WISCONSIN -
    BUSINESS COMMITTEE
Route 4   BLACK RIVER FALLS 54615
    Rev. Mitchell Whiterabbit, Chairman

RED CLIFF BAND OF LAKE SUPERIOR
    CHIPPEWA INDIANS (GOVERNING
    BODY)
Route 1   BAYFIELD 54893
    Henry G. Daley, Chairman

STOCKBRIDGE-MUNSEE TRIBAL
    COUNCIL
RR #1   BOWLER 54416
    Arvid E. Miller, President

Tribal membership: 954. *Tribe served:*
Stockbridge-Munsee (Mohican). *Activities:*
Housing project; forest industries; Arts
and Crafts Enterprise. Seven members.

LAC COURTE OREILLES BAND OF LAKE
    SUPERIOR CHIPPEWA INDIANS -
    TRIBAL BUSINESS COMMITTEE
c/o New Post   COUDERAY 54828
    John A. Anderson, Chairman

FOREST COUNTY POTAWATOMI
    EXECUTIVE COUNCIL
                    CRANDON 54520
    Art Crawford, Chairman

Tribal membership: 400. *Tribe served:*
Forest County (Wisconsin Band of) Potawatomi. *Activities:* Community action programs. Six members.

SOKAOGON CHIPPEWA TRIBAL COUNCIL
Route 1
Box 325   CRANDON 54520
    Charles W. Fox, Sr., Chairman

LAC DU FLAMBEAU BAND OF LAKE
    SUPERIOR CHIPPEWA INDIANS
    TRIBAL COUNCIL
            LAC DU FLAMBEAU 54538
    Alex M. Bobidosh, President

BAD RIVER TRIBAL COUNCIL
                              ODANAH 54861
        Albert Whitebird, Chairman

Tribe served: Bad River Band of Lake
Superior Tribe of Chippewas.

ONIEDA TRIBE OF INDIANS -
    EXECUTIVE COMMITTEE
Route 11   ONEIDA 54155
        Norbert S. Hill, Chairman

ST. CROIX CHIPPEWA INDIANS COUNCIL
Route 2   WEBSTER 54893
        Ollie Taylor, President

WYOMING

ARAPAHOE BUSINESS COUNCIL
c/o Wind River Agency
                          FORT WASHAKIE 82514
        Scott Dewey, Chairman

Serves Arapahoe population of Wind River
Reservation. Six members.

SHOSHONE BUSINESS COUNCIL
c/o Wind River Agency
                          FORT WASHAKIE 82514
        Robert N. Harris, Sr., Chairman

Serves Shoshone population of Wind River
Reservation. Six members.

Schools

Listed here are elementary and high schools operated by the Bureau of Indian Affairs, state education departments, schools operated by missions and religious orders. The listings of the Bureau of Indian Affairs schools are arranged by type of school (i. e., day and instructional aid schools, boarding schools), and by geographical location.

ALASKA

BUREAU OF INDIAN AFFAIRS
Akiachak Day School   AKIACHAK 99551

BUREAU OF INDIAN AFFAIRS
Akiak Day School   AKIAK 99552

BUREAU OF INDIAN AFFAIRS
Alakanuk Day School   ALAKANUK 99554

BUREAU OF INDIAN AFFAIRS
Arctic Village Day School
    ARCTIC VILLAGE 99554

BUREAU OF INDIAN AFFAIRS
Atka Day School
c/o U.S. Navy #230
Box 99   Seattle, Washington
    ATKA
    Adrian J. Robinson, Principal

Enrollment: 36 (Aleut). Full curriculum from first through eighth grades.

BUREAU OF INDIAN AFFAIRS
Barrow Day School   BARROW 99723
    Lawrence B. Welch, Principal

Enrollment: 476 (Eskimo). Full curriculum from first through eighth grades. Adult education and directed study programs conducted for adults.

BUREAU OF INDIAN AFFAIRS
Barter Island Instructional Aid School
    BARTER ISLAND

BUREAU OF INDIAN AFFAIRS
Beaver Day School   BEAVER 99724

BUREAU OF INDIAN AFFAIRS
Birch Creek Day School   BIRCH CREEK

BUREAU OF INDIAN AFFAIRS
Brevig Mission Day School
    BREVIG MISSION 99785

BUREAU OF INDIAN AFFAIRS
Buckland Day School   BUCKLAND 99727

BUREAU OF INDIAN AFFAIRS
Canyon Village Instructional Aid School
(via Fort Yukon)
    CANYON VILLAGE 99740
    Donald Shelton, Principal

Enrollment: 14.

BUREAU OF INDIAN AFFAIRS
Chalkyitsik Instructional Aid School
    CHALKYITSIK 99788
    Marian L. Nickelson, Principal

Enrollment: 33. Full elementary school curriculum.

BUREAU OF INDIAN AFFAIRS
Chevak Day School   CHEVAK 99563

BUREAU OF INDIAN AFFAIRS
Chifornak Day School   CHIFORNAK 99561

BUREAU OF INDIAN AFFAIRS
Deering Day School   DEERING 99736
    Walter D. Allen, Principal

Enrollment: 23. Full curriculum from first through eighth grades, with emphasis on academic and social guidance; Bureau special summer educational program (recreational, academic and/or work projects).

BUREAU OF INDIAN AFFAIRS
Diomede Day School   DIOMEDE

BUREAU OF INDIAN AFFAIRS
Eagle Day School   EAGLE 99738

BUREAU OF INDIAN AFFAIRS
Eek Day School   EEK 99578

BUREAU OF INDIAN AFFAIRS
Elim Day School   ELIM 99739

BUREAU OF INDIAN AFFAIRS
Emmonak Day School   EMMONAK 99581

BUREAU OF INDIAN AFFAIRS
English Bay Day School   ENGLISH BAY

BUREAU OF INDIAN AFFAIRS
Galena Day School   GALENA 99741

BUREAU OF INDIAN AFFAIRS
Gambell Day School   GAMBELL 99742

BUREAU OF INDIAN AFFAIRS
Golovin Day School   GOLOVIN 99762

BUREAU OF INDIAN AFFAIRS
Goodnews Bay Day School
                    GOODNEWS BAY 99589
          Marshall L. Lind, Principal-Teacher

BUREAU OF INDIAN AFFAIRS
Hooper Bay Day School
                    HOOPER BAY 99604
          Laurence B. Matson, Administrator

Enrollment: 182 (Eskimo); 1 (White). Curriculum meets elementary through junior high school requirements.

BUREAU OF INDIAN AFFAIRS
Kalskag Day School   KALSKAG 99607

BUREAU OF INDIAN AFFAIRS
Kaltag Day School   KALTAG 99748

BUREAU OF INDIAN AFFAIRS
Kasigluk Day School   KASIGLUK 99609

BUREAU OF INDIAN AFFAIRS
Kiana Day School   KIANA 99749

BUREAU OF INDIAN AFFAIRS
Kipnuk Day School   KIPNUK 99614
          Ray F. Steward, Principal Teacher

Enrollment: 89.   Full elementary school curriculum.

BUREAU OF INDIAN AFFAIRS
Kivalina Day School   KIVALINA 99750

BUREAU OF INDIAN AFFAIRS
Klukwan Day School   KLUKWAN 99831

BUREAU OF INDIAN AFFAIRS
Koliganek Instructional Aid School
                    KOLIGANEK

BUREAU OF INDIAN AFFAIRS
Kotlik Day School   KOTLIK 99620

BUREAU OF INDIAN AFFAIRS
Kotzebue Day School   KOTZEBUE 99752

BUREAU OF INDIAN AFFAIRS
Koyuk Day School   KOYUK 99753

BUREAU OF INDIAN AFFAIRS
Kwethluk Day School   KWETHLUK 99621

BUREAU OF INDIAN AFFAIRS
Kwigillingok Day School
                    KWIGILLINGOK 99622

BUREAU OF INDIAN AFFAIRS
Kwinhagak Day School
                    KWINHAGAK 99655

BUREAU OF INDIAN AFFAIRS
Lower Kalskag Day School
                    LOWER KALSKAG 99626

BUREAU OF INDIAN AFFAIRS
Manakotak Day School
                    MANAKOTAK 99628

BUREAU OF INDIAN AFFAIRS
Mekoryuk Day School
                    MEKORYUK 99630

BUREAU OF INDIAN AFFAIRS
Minto Day School   MINTO 99758

BUREAU OF INDIAN AFFAIRS
Mountain Village Day School
              MOUNTAIN VILLAGE 99632
Gordon R. Slate, Principal-Teacher

Enrollment: 92.   Full elementary school
curriculum.

BUREAU OF INDIAN AFFAIRS
Napaskiak Day School
                    NAPASKIAK 99559
Charlie P. Ercolin, Principal-Teacher

Enrollment: 52 (Eskimo).   Standard elementary school program with emphasis on
the language arts.

BUREAU OF INDIAN AFFAIRS
New Stuyahok Day School
               NEW STUYAHOK 99636
A. B. Kracher, Principal

Enrollment: 53 (52 Eskimo).   Standard elementary curriculum.

BUREAU OF INDIAN AFFAIRS
Newktok Day School   NEWKTOK 99636

BUREAU OF INDIAN AFFAIRS
Nightmute Day School
                    NIGHTMUTE 99637

BUREAU OF INDIAN AFFAIRS
Noatak Day School   NOATAK 99761

BUREAU OF INDIAN AFFAIRS
Noorvik Day School   NOORVIK 99763

BUREAU OF INDIAN AFFAIRS
Northway Day School
                    NORTHWAY 99764

BUREAU OF INDIAN AFFAIRS
Nunapitchuk Day School
                  NUNAPITCHUK 99641
Delbert J. Smith, Principal

Enrollment: 135.   Elementary school curriculum.

BUREAU OF INDIAN AFFAIRS
Pilot Station Day School
                    PILOT STATION 99650

BUREAU OF INDIAN AFFAIRS
Point Hope Day School
                    POINT HOPE 99766

BUREAU OF INDIAN AFFAIRS
St. Michael Day School
                    ST. MICHAEL 99659

BUREAU OF INDIAN AFFAIRS
Savoonga Day School   SAVOONGA 99769

BUREAU OF INDIAN AFFAIRS
Scammon Bay Day School
                    SCAMMON BAY 99662

BUREAU OF INDIAN AFFAIRS
Selawik Day School   SELAWIK 99770
M. Lester Richesin, Principal

Enrollment: 101 (Eskimo).   Curriculum
features English for beginners.

BUREAU OF INDIAN AFFAIRS
Shageluk Day School   SHAGELUK 99665

BUREAU OF INDIAN AFFAIRS
Shaktoolik Day School
                    SHAKTOOLIK 99771
Sarah Christensen, Principal-Teacher

Enrollment: 60.   Pre-school preparation
program.

BUREAU OF INDIAN AFFAIRS
Shishmaref Day School
SHISHMAREF 99772

BUREAU OF INDIAN AFFAIRS
Shungnak Day School   SHUNGNAK 99773

BUREAU OF INDIAN AFFAIRS
Sleetmute Day School
SLEETMUTE 99668
Monroe Rougeau, Principal-Teacher

Enrollment: 29. Elementary school curriculum featuring special reading programs.

BUREAU OF INDIAN AFFAIRS
Stebbins Day School   STEBBINS 99671

BUREAU OF INDIAN AFFAIRS
Stevens Village Day School
STEVENS VILLAGE 99774

BUREAU OF INDIAN AFFAIRS
Tanacross Day School
TANACROSS 99776

BUREAU OF INDIAN AFFAIRS
Tanunak Day School   TANUNAK 99681

BUREAU OF INDIAN AFFAIRS
Tetlin Day School   TETLIN 99779

BUREAU OF INDIAN AFFAIRS
Togiak Day School   TOGIAK 99678

BUREAU OF INDIAN AFFAIRS
Tuluksak Day School   TULUKSAK 99679

BUREAU OF INDIAN AFFAIRS
Tuntutuliak Day School
TUNTUTULIAK 99680
Ernest E. Rush, Sr., Principal-
Teacher

Enrollment: 41 (Eskimo). Elementary
school curriculum.

BUREAU OF INDIAN AFFAIRS
Unalakleet Day School
UNALAKLEET 99684

BUREAU OF INDIAN AFFAIRS
Venetie Day School   VENETIE 99781
William J. Henderson, Principal-
Teacher

Enrollment: 33. Elementary school curriculum.

BUREAU OF INDIAN AFFAIRS
Wainwright Day School
WAINWRIGHT 99782

BUREAU OF INDIAN AFFAIRS
Wales Day School   WALES 99783

BUREAU OF INDIAN AFFAIRS
White Mountain Day School
WHITE MOUNTAIN 99784

ARIZONA

BUREAU OF INDIAN AFFAIRS
Blue Gap Day School   CHINLE 86503

BUREAU OF INDIAN AFFAIRS
Round Rock Day School
Box 313   CHINLE 86503
David L. Rouen, Principal

Enrollment: 330. Basic elementary school program.

BUREAU OF INDIAN AFFAIRS
Salina Springs Day School
CHINLE 86503

BUREAU OF INDIAN AFFAIRS
Smoke Signal Day School
CHINLE 86503

BUREAU OF INDIAN AFFAIRS
White Cone Day School
INDIAN WELLS 86031

BUREAU OF INDIAN AFFAIRS
Red Lake Day School   TONALEA 86044

FLORIDA

BUREAU OF INDIAN AFFAIRS
Miccosukee Instructional Aid School
Box 237   HOMESTEAD 33030

IOWA

BUREAU OF INDIAN AFFAIRS
South Tama County School District
c/o Sac and Fox Area Field Office
R. R. 2   TAMA 52339
  Raymond R. Wolf, Administrator

Provides education facilities for local Indian children, grades one through six; consultation services for adults. *Tribe served:* Sac and Fox. *Total population served:* 750.

MONTANA

BUREAU OF INDIAN AFFAIRS
Birney Day School   BIRNEY 59012

NEW MEXICO

BUREAU OF INDIAN AFFAIRS
San Felipe Day School
               ALGODONES 87001

BUREAU OF INDIAN AFFAIRS
Paraje Day School
               CASA BLANCA 87007

BUREAU OF INDIAN AFFAIRS
Seama Day School   CUBERO 87014

BUREAU OF INDIAN AFFAIRS
Santa Clara Day School
               ESPANOLA 87532

BUREAU OF INDIAN AFFAIRS
Bread Springs Day School
               GALLUP 87301

BUREAU OF INDIAN AFFAIRS
Iyanbito Day School   GALLUP 87301

BUREAU OF INDIAN AFFAIRS
Jones Ranch Day School
               GALLUP 87301

BUREAU OF INDIAN AFFAIRS
Isleta Day School   ISLETA 87022
  Jim Kirkham, Principal

Enrollment: 245. Elementary education -- grades one through six; year of pre-first grade education to older five-year-olds.

BUREAU OF INDIAN AFFAIRS
Jemez Day School   JEMEZ PUEBLO

BUREAU OF INDIAN AFFAIRS
Laguna Day School
P. O. Box 191   LAGUNA 86026
  Roy L. Jameson, Principal

Enrollment: 344. Academic program.

BUREAU OF INDIAN AFFAIRS
Mesita Day School   LAGUNA 86026

BUREAU OF INDIAN AFFAIRS
Paguate Day School   PAGUATE 87040

BUREAU OF INDIAN AFFAIRS
Cochiti Day School
               PENA BLANCA 87041

BUREAU OF INDIAN AFFAIRS
Borrego Pass Day School
               PREWITT 87045

BUREAU OF INDIAN AFFAIRS
Acomita Day School   SAN FIDEL 87049

BUREAU OF INDIAN AFFAIRS
McCarty Day School   SAN FIDEL 87049

BUREAU OF INDIAN AFFAIRS
San Juan Day School   SAN JUAN 87566

BUREAU OF INDIAN AFFAIRS
Zia Day School   SAN YSIDRO 87053

BUREAU OF INDIAN AFFAIRS
San Ildefonso Day School
Route 1, Box 308   SANTA FE 87501
    Mrs. Iradell M. Andrews, Principal-
    Teacher

Enrollment: 60.

BUREAU OF INDIAN AFFAIRS
Tesuque Day School   SANTA FE 87501

BUREAU OF INDIAN AFFAIRS
Beclabito Day School   SHIPROCK 87420

BUREAU OF INDIAN AFFAIRS
Cove Day School   SHIPROCK 87420

BUREAU OF INDIAN AFFAIRS
Taos Pueblo Day School   TAOS 87571

NORTH CAROLINA

BUREAU OF INDIAN AFFAIRS
Cherokee Central Day School
                    CHEROKEE 28719

BUREAU OF INDIAN AFFAIRS
Snowbird Day School
                    ROBBINSVILLE 28771

NORTH DAKOTA

BUREAU OF INDIAN AFFAIRS
Houle Day School   BELCOURT 58316
    Erling E. Anderson, Principal-
    Teacher

Enrollment: 65. Curriculum follows North
Dakota State Course of Study, grades one
through six.

BUREAU OF INDIAN AFFAIRS
Roussin Day School
                    BELCOURT 58316

BUREAU OF INDIAN AFFAIRS
Turtle Mountain Community Day School
                    BELCOURT 58316

BUREAU OF INDIAN AFFAIRS
Dunseith Day School   DUNSEITH 58329

BUREAU OF INDIAN AFFAIRS
White Shield Day School   EMMET 58534

BUREAU OF INDIAN AFFAIRS
Fort Totten Day School
                    FORT TOTTEN 58335

BUREAU OF INDIAN AFFAIRS
Twin Buttes Day School
                    HALLIDAY 58636
    John W. Steffen, Principal

Enrollment: 86. Summer Program featuring pre-school training and special reading classes.

SOUTH DAKOTA

BUREAU OF INDIAN AFFAIRS
Allen Day School   ALLEN 57714

BUREAU OF INDIAN AFFAIRS
Cherry Creek Day School
                    CHERRY CREEK 57622

BUREAU OF INDIAN AFFAIRS
Thunder Butte Day School
                    DUPREE 57623

BUREAU OF INDIAN AFFAIRS
Red Scaffold Day School
R. F. D.   FAITH 57626
    Benjamin P. Ward, Principal

Enrollment: 33. Elementary school curriculum.

BUREAU OF INDIAN AFFAIRS
Fort Thompson Community Day School
                    FORT THOMPSON 57339

BUREAU OF INDIAN AFFAIRS
Swift Bird Day School
GETTYSBURG 57442

BUREAU OF INDIAN AFFAIRS
Bridger Day School   HOWES 57748

BUREAU OF INDIAN AFFAIRS
Little Wound Day School   KYLE 57752

BUREAU OF INDIAN AFFAIRS
Lower Brule Day School
LOWER BRULE 57548
Donald C. Peters, Principal-Teacher

Enrollment: 83. Elementary school curriculum.

BUREAU OF INDIAN AFFAIRS
Manderson Day School
MANDERSON 57756

BUREAU OF INDIAN AFFAIRS
Promise Day School   MOBRIDGE 57601

BUREAU OF INDIAN AFFAIRS
Loneman Day School   OGLALA 57764

BUREAU OF INDIAN AFFAIRS
Big Coolee Day School   PEEVER 57257

BUREAU OF INDIAN AFFAIRS
Porcupine Day School
PORCUPINE 57772
John K. Ballard, Principal, Director

Enrollment: 216. Elementary school curriculum.

BUREAU OF INDIAN AFFAIRS
Iron Lightning Day School
RED ELM 57258

BUREAU OF INDIAN AFFAIRS
Old Agency Day School   SISSETON 57262

BUREAU OF INDIAN AFFAIRS
Wanblee Day School   WANBLEE 57577

BUREAU OF INDIAN AFFAIRS
Enemy Swim Day School
WAUBAY 57273

BUREAU OF INDIAN AFFAIRS
White Horse Day School
WHITE HORSE 57661

BOARDING SCHOOLS

ALASKA

BUREAU OF INDIAN AFFAIRS
Mt. Edgecumbe School
MT. EDGECUMBE 99835

BUREAU OF INDIAN AFFAIRS
Wrangell Institute School
WRANGELL 99929

ARIZONA

BUREAU OF INDIAN AFFAIRS
Wide Ruins School   CHAMBERS 86502

BUREAU OF INDIAN AFFAIRS
Chinle School   CHINLE 86503

BUREAU OF INDIAN AFFAIRS
Low Mountain School   CHINLE 86503

BUREAU OF INDIAN AFFAIRS
Rock Point School   CHINLE 86503

BUREAU OF INDIAN AFFAIRS
Rough Rock School   CHINLE 86503

BUREAU OF INDIAN AFFAIRS
Theodore Roosevelt School
FORT APACHE 85926

BUREAU OF INDIAN AFFAIRS
Crystal School
FORT DEFIANCE 86504

BUREAU OF INDIAN AFFAIRS
Greasewood School   GANADO 86505

BUREAU OF INDIAN AFFAIRS
Klageton School   GANADO 86505

BUREAU OF INDIAN AFFAIRS
Nazlini School   GANADO 86505

BUREAU OF INDIAN AFFAIRS
Steamboat School   GANADO 86505

BUREAU OF INDIAN AFFAIRS
Pine Springs School   HOUCK 86506

BUREAU OF INDIAN AFFAIRS
Denehotso School   KAYENTA 86033

BUREAU OF INDIAN AFFAIRS
Kayenta School   KAYENTA 86033

BUREAU OF INDIAN AFFAIRS
Keams Canyon School
                 KEAMS CANYON 86034

BUREAU OF INDIAN AFFAIRS
Leupp School   LEUPP 86035

BUREAU OF INDIAN AFFAIRS
Lukachukai School
                 LUKACHUKAI 86507
     Miss Jean Combs, Principal

Enrollment: 600.

BUREAU OF INDIAN AFFAIRS
Phoenix Indian School   PHOENIX 85000
     James D. Wallace, Superintendent

Enrollment: 1,050. Course offerings include (1) college preparatory - courses
meeting college entrance requirements; (2)
business education -- preparing students
for business schools; (3) vocational program -- courses preparing students for
entrance into trade and technical schools,
with a decreasing number applying for direct employment upon graduation.

BUREAU OF INDIAN AFFAIRS
Pinon School   PINON 86510

BUREAU OF INDIAN AFFAIRS
Hunters Point School
                 ST. MICHAELS 86511

BUREAU OF INDIAN AFFAIRS
Kinlichee School   GANADO 86505
     Leroy Falling, Principal

Enrollment: 256. State-required elementary program, plus basic goals for Indian
students. Emphasis on Navajo culture in
presenting materials.

BUREAU OF INDIAN AFFAIRS
Santa Rosa School   SELLS 85634

BUREAU OF INDIAN AFFAIRS
Kaibeto School   TONALEA 86044

BUREAU OF INDIAN AFFAIRS
Shonto School   TONALEA 86044

BUREAU OF INDIAN AFFAIRS
Navajo Mountain School
                 TUBA CITY 86045

BUREAU OF INDIAN AFFAIRS
Rocky Ridge School   TUBA CITY 86045
     John C. Jones, Principal

Enrollment: 126. Elementary (beginner)
program -- emphasis on English as a second language.

BUREAU OF INDIAN AFFAIRS
Tuba City School   TUBA CITY 86045

BUREAU OF INDIAN AFFAIRS
Dilcon School
Star Route   WINSLOW 86047
     J. Royce Brunk, Principal

Enrollment: 234. Elementary program --
general course of study with emphasis on
oral language activities.

BUREAU OF INDIAN AFFAIRS
Seba Dalkai School   WINSLOW 86047

CALIFORNIA

BUREAU OF INDIAN AFFAIRS
Sherman Institute   RIVERSIDE 92502

KANSAS

BUREAU OF INDIAN AFFAIRS
Haskell Institute   LAWRENCE 66044
W. E. Galluzzi, Principal

Offers trade, technical and business courses
of study; two-year program.

MISSISSIPPI

BUREAU OF INDIAN AFFAIRS
Conehatta School   CONEHATTA 39057

BUREAU OF INDIAN AFFAIRS
Bogue Chitto School
Route 2   PHILADELPHIA 39350

BUREAU OF INDIAN AFFAIRS
Pearl River School
     PHILADELPHIA 39350

MONTANA

BUREAU OF INDIAN AFFAIRS
Busby School   BUSBY 59016

NEVADA

BUREAU OF INDIAN AFFAIRS
Stewart Indian School   STEWART 89437

NEW MEXICO

BUREAU OF INDIAN AFFAIRS
Albuquerque School
     ALBUQUERQUE 87100

BUREAU OF INDIAN AFFAIRS
Coyote Canyon School   BRIMHALL 87310

BUREAU OF INDIAN AFFAIRS
Crownpoint School   CROWNPOINT 87313

BUREAU OF INDIAN AFFAIRS
Lake Valley School   CROWNPOINT 87313

BUREAU OF INDIAN AFFAIRS
Pueblo Pintado School
     CROWNPOINT 87313
     Roy T. Ussrey, Principal

Enrollment: 185. Elementary program,
first through fourth grades. Emphasis on
spoken English.

BUREAU OF INDIAN AFFAIRS
Standing Rock School
     CROWNPOINT 87313

BUREAU OF INDIAN AFFAIRS
White Horse School   CROWNPOINT 87313

BUREAU OF INDIAN AFFAIRS
Torreon School   CUBA 87013

BUREAU OF INDIAN AFFAIRS
Wingate Vocational School
     FORT WINGATE 87316

BUREAU OF INDIAN AFFAIRS
Nenahnezad School   FRUITLAND 87416
     Clarence Eugene Pegues, Principal

BUREAU OF INDIAN AFFAIRS
Cheechilgeetho School   GALLUP 87301

BUREAU OF INDIAN AFFAIRS
Mariano Lake School   GALLUP 87301

BUREAU OF INDIAN AFFAIRS
Pinedale School   GALLUP 87301

BUREAU OF INDIAN AFFAIRS
Twin Lakes School   GALLUP 87301

BUREAU OF INDIAN AFFAIRS
Cononcito School   LAGUNA 87026

BUREAU OF INDIAN AFFAIRS
Baca School   PREWITT 87045

BUREAU OF INDIAN AFFAIRS
Institute of American Indian Arts
Cerrillos Rd.   SANTA FE 87502
    George A. Boyce, Superintendent

Enrollment: 300. The Institute of American
Indian Arts for Indian youth offers an accredited high school program with arts
electives and post-high school vocational
arts program as preparation for college and
technical schools, and employment in arts
vocations. High school program -- grades
ten through twelve, plus two-year post-high
school program -- grades thirteen and fourteen. Academic and arts programs for
Indians of all tribes. Arts electives include
four fields: (1) performing arts and creative writing; (2) textile and fabrics; (3)
three-dimensional (ceramics, metals and
sculpture); (4) fine arts (painting, graphic
arts, commercial arts).

BUREAU OF INDIAN AFFAIRS
Red Rock School   SHIPROCK 87420

BUREAU OF INDIAN AFFAIRS
San Juan School   SHIPROCK 87420

BUREAU OF INDIAN AFFAIRS
Teecnospos School   SHIPROCK 87420

BUREAU OF INDIAN AFFAIRS
Thoreau School   THOREAU 84323

BUREAU OF INDIAN AFFAIRS
Toadlena School   TOADLENA 87324
    Frederick Arnold Goranson, Education
    Specialist

BUREAU OF INDIAN AFFAIRS
Tohatchi Public School
                            TOHATCHI 87325
    Robert Carlton Brown, Principal

Enrollment: 590. Curriculum features
reading programs and Language Arts for
non-English speaking students.

NORTH DAKOTA

BUREAU OF INDIAN AFFAIRS
Standing Rock Community School
                       FORT YATES 58538

BUREAU OF INDIAN AFFAIRS
Wahpeton School   WAHPETON 58075

OKLAHOMA

BUREAU OF INDIAN AFFAIRS
Riverside Indian School
                            ANADARKO 73005

BUREAU OF INDIAN AFFAIRS
Chilocco Indian School   CHILOCCO 74635

BUREAU OF INDIAN AFFAIRS
Cheyenne-Arapaho School
                             CONCHO 73022

BUREAU OF INDIAN AFFAIRS
Concho Demonstration School
                             CONCHO 73022

BUREAU OF INDIAN AFFAIRS
Fort Sill School   LAWTON 73503

BUREAU OF INDIAN AFFAIRS
Sequoyah High School
                       TAHLEQUAH 74464
    Diamond Roach, Superintendent
    Edwin S. Moore, Principal

Enrollment: 380. High school curriculum.

BUREAU OF INDIAN AFFAIRS
Seneca Indian School
                       WYANDOTTE 74370
    Richard E. Fitzgerald, Superintendent

Enrollment: 200. Elementary school curriculum.

OREGON

BUREAU OF INDIAN AFFAIRS
Chemawa Indian School
CHEMAWA 97822

Enrollment: Navajo and Alaskan. Curriculum features Special Five Year Navajo Program; Comprehensive Accelerated Program. Health center.

SOUTH DAKOTA

BUREAU OF INDIAN AFFAIRS
Cheyenne-Eagle Butte School
EAGLE BUTTE 57623

Enrollment: 950. High school curriculum.

BUREAU OF INDIAN AFFAIRS
Flandreau School   FLANDREAU 57028

BUREAU OF INDIAN AFFAIRS
Rosebud Boarding School
MISSION 57555

BUREAU OF INDIAN AFFAIRS
Pierre Indian School   PIERRE 57501

BUREAU OF INDIAN AFFAIRS
Oglala Community High School
PINE RIDGE 57770

UTAH

BUREAU OF INDIAN AFFAIRS
Aneth Boarding School   ANETH 84510

BUREAU OF INDIAN AFFAIRS
Intermountain School
BRIGHAM CITY 84302

SCHOOLS — MISCELLANEOUS

INDEPENDENT SCHOOL DISTRICT NO. 38
REDLAKE, MINN. 56671
Leonard J. Olson, Superintendent

Follows Minnesota curriculum with emphasis on Indian culture as it relates to course work. *Total population served:* 816 (enrolled Indian students).

ST. LABRE INDIAN SCHOOL
ASHLAND, MONT. 59003
Rev. Emmett Hoffmann, Director and Superintendent

Enrollment: 362. Elementary and high school curriculum, featuring remedial reading, vocational and commercial training, home economics. *Publications: The Race of Sorrows.*

STATE DEPARTMENT OF EDUCATION - INDIAN DIVISION
State Superintendent's Office
OKLAHOMA CITY, OKLA.
Overton James, Staff Member

ST. FRANCIS INDIAN MISSION
ST. FRANCIS, S.D. 57572
Rev. Joseph C. Gill, S.J., Principal

Enrollment: 526. College preparatory and pre-vocational training. *Publication:* Bimonthly, *Little Sioux.*

STATE DEPARTMENT OF PUBLIC INSTRUCTION
148 State Capital   MADISON, WIS.
Angus B. Rothwell, State Superintendent

Supervises Indian education in public elementary and high schools of Wisconsin; oversees Federal aid, college scholarship grant program for Indian students. *Total population served:* 15,000. Affiliated with Great Lakes Agency (Bureau of Indian Affairs).

Indian-Related Course Offerings

This section lists departments and personnel of various institutions of higher learning which offer courses on the American Indian. The section is arranged geographically.

ALABAMA

UNIVERSITY OF ALABAMA
UNIVERSITY 35486

Name of Department: Sociology and Anthropology
Course instructors: Prof. David L. DeJarnette, Dr. Paul H. Nesbitt, Dr. Ansael T. Hansen

ALASKA

UNIVERSITY OF ALASKA
COLLEGE 99735

Name of Department: Anthropology and Geography
Course instructors: Dr. Erna Gunther, Dr. William Loyens

ARIZONA

ARIZONA STATE UNIVERSITY
TEMPE 85281

Name of Department: Anthropology
Course instructors: R. J. Ruppe, J. A. Jones, K. M. Stewart, J. F. Martin

Indian Education Division
Dr. Robert A. Roessel, Principal

Indian education courses include *Methods and Materials for Teaching Indian Children; Curriculum and Practices for Indian Education; Educational Applications in Anthropology; Problems of Teachers of Indian Children; School-Community Relations in Indian Education; Education of Indian Adults; Guidance for the Indian Student; Community Development in Indian Education.*

UNIVERSITY OF ARIZONA
TUCSON 85721

Name of Department: Anthropology
Course instructors: T. Patrick Culbert, James F. Downs, Edward P. Dozier, Harry T. Getty, Kenneth L. Hale, William A. Longacre, Edward H. Spicer, Clara Lee Tanner, Bernard L. Fontana, Frederick R. Pleasants

CALIFORNIA

CHICO STATE COLLEGE
CHICO

Name of Department: Sociology-Anthropology
Course instructors: Albyn K. Mark, Asst. Prof. Keith Johnson, Asst. Prof. James Myers

COLORADO

UNIVERSITY OF COLORADO
BOULDER 80302

Name of Department: Anthropology
Course instructor: Omer C. Stewart

COLORADO COLLEGE
COLORADO SPRINGS 80903

Name of Department: Anthropology
Course instructors: Kutsche, Nowak

WESTERN STATE COLLEGE
GUNNISON 81230

Name of Department: Savage Library
Course instructor: Pat T. Julio

IDAHO

UNIVERSITY OF IDAHO
MOSCOW 83843

Name of Department: Social Sciences
Course instructor: Dr. Alfred W. Bowers

INDIANA

INDIANA UNIVERSITY
BLOOMINGTON 47401

Name of Department: Anthropology (Social
Science #108)
Course instructors: C. F. Voegelin, Alan
Merriam, Harold Driver, James Kellar,
Paul Gebhard, Paul Doughty, Wesley
Hunt, Georg Neumann

BALL STATE UNIVERSITY
2000 University Ave.   MUNCIE 47306

Name of Department: Sociology and
Anthropology
Course instructors: Dr. Bert Anson, Dr.
David L. Scruton, Prof. Jack M. White-
head, Dr. B. K. Swartz, Jr.

KANSAS

KANSAS STATE TEACHERS COLLEGE
EMPORIA 66801

Name of Department: Division of Social
Sciences

KANSAS STATE UNIVERSITY
MANHATTAN 66502

Name of Department: Sociology and
Anthropology
Course instructors: Robert B. Taylor
(Indians of North America), Michael B.
Stanislawski (Archaeology of North
America)

WICHITA STATE COLLEGE
WICHITA 67208

Names of Departments: History, Anthro-
pology
Course instructors: Dr. Schlesier, Dr.
Unrou

MASSACHUSETTS

HARVARD UNIVERSITY
CAMBRIDGE

Name of Department: Anthropology
Course instructors: G. R. Willey, Evon
Z. Vogt, Thomas Patterson, David
Maybury-Lewis, Stephen Williams,
Philip Phillips

SMITH COLLEGE
NORTHAMPTON 01060

Name of Department: Sociology and
Anthropology
Course instructor: Elizabeth Hopkins

MICHIGAN

MICHIGAN STATE UNIVERSITY
EAST LANSING 48823

Name of Department: Anthropology
Course instructor: Seymour Parker

MISSOURI

ST. LOUIS UNIVERSITY
221 N. Grand Blvd.
ST. LOUIS 63103

Name of Department: Sociology and
Anthropology
Course instructor: Dr. Allen Spitzer

NEW MEXICO

UNIVERSITY OF NEW MEXICO
ALBUQUERQUE 87106

Name of Department: Anthropology
Course instructors: Dr. John M. Camp-
bell, Dr. Florence H. Ellis, Dr. Frank
C. Hibben, Dr. W. W. Hill, J. J. Brody,
Dr. Stanley S. Newman, Dr. Karl H.
Schwerin

OHIO

KENT STATE UNIVERSITY
KENT 44240

Names of Departments: History, Sociology and Anthropology

MIAMI UNIVERSITY
OXFORD 45056

Course instructors: Edward Kurjack (Anthropology), Dwight Smith (American History)

OKLAHOMA

THE UNIVERSITY OF TULSA
600 South College
TULSA 74104

Name of Department: Sociology
Course offering: "People of the Southwest"

PENNSYLVANIA

HAVERFORD COLLEGE
HAVERFORD 19041

Name of Department: Sociology and Anthropology
Course instructors: Alexander, deLaguna, Hare, Hetzel

UNIVERSITY OF PENNSYLVANIA
University Museum
PHILADELPHIA 19104

Name of Department: Anthropology
Course instructors: Dr. Alfred Kidder, II; Dr. William Loe; Dr. Linton Satterthwaite; Dr. Ruben Reina

TENNESSEE

GEORGE PEABODY COLLEGE
NASHVILLE 37203

Name of Department: Division of Social Science
Course instructor: Dr. Norman G. Greenberg

TEXAS

BAYLOR UNIVERSITY
WACO 76703

Name of Department: Sociology and Anthropology
Course instructors: Charles W. McNett, Charles M. Tolbert

UTAH

BRIGHAM YOUNG UNIVERSITY
PROVO

Name of Department: Indian Education
Course instructors: Dr. Merlin Moyers, Dr. Roy Mathery, Dr. William Hofen, Dr. Lymon Tyler, Dr. Ted Warner, Prof. Paul E. Felt

WASHINGTON

WASHINGTON STATE UNIVERSITY
PULLMAN 99163

Name of Department: Anthropology
Course instructors: R. D. Daugherty, D. E. Walker, H. R. Bernard, R. E. Ackerman, J. A. Goss, A. H. Smith

Arts and Crafts Shops

The following is an alpha-geographical list of suppliers of Indian arts and crafts, noting address, personnel, and types of merchandise carried by each; the availability of catalogs has also been noted. No claim is made regarding the authenticity of the materials offered by these firms and organizations, and no recommendation should be construed because of their inclusion in this volume.

ALASKA

ALASKA NATIVE ARTS & CRAFTS COOPERATIVE ASSOCIATION, INC.
Box 889   JUNEAU 99801
    Don Burrus, Manager
Alaskan Eskimo and Indian carved ivory; baskets, skin sewing, sketches, wood carvings. Catalog available.

ARIZONA

GAP TRADING POST
North Highway 89   CAMERON 86020
    Troy Washburn, Manager
Navajo rugs; Navajo, Hopi and Zuni jewelry; Hopi pottery; Paiute, Hopi and Navajo baskets and plaques; Navajo and Hopi woven belts and sashes; Navajo moccasins; Hopi, Zuni and Laguna dolls; Navajo weaving looms.

HANK'S TRADING POST
Tuba City Star Route   FLAGSTAFF
    Hank Young, Manager
"General merchandise."

THE WIGWAM
8 E. Santa Fe
(Box 519)   FLAGSTAFF 86001
    Mr. Mastin, Manager
Navajo, Hopi and Zuni jewelry; Hopi and Papago basketry; Hopi and Santa Clara pottery; Navajo rugs; original paintings; handmade Kaibab moccasins; Hopi kachina dolls.

THE BROOKES
1914 E. Avalon Drive   PHOENIX 85016
    Frank H. Brookes, Manager
Navajo and Hopi Indian handmade jewelry; Zuni fetishes; artifacts; Bureau of American

Ethnology publications and out-of-print books. Collectors' item search service.

D'ARCY'S INDIAN & SOUTHWESTERN GIFTS
Thomas Mall   PHOENIX
    D'Arcy Smith, Jr., Manager
Reservation Indian handmade jewelry, pottery, wool woven neckties, rugs and blankets; moccasins, Indian-design wind bells; hand-carved Indian figures; Indian prints and stationery.

GODBER'S GIFT SHOP
1639 W. Betany Home Rd.   PHOENIX

Handmade Navajo, Zuni and Hopi jewelry; baskets and pottery; moccasins; kachina dolls; Navajo rugs and dolls.

PANCHO'S OF ARIZONA
56 Park Central Mall   PHOENIX 85013
    T. E. Coxwell, Manager
Indian arts and crafts from all Southwestern tribes -- jewelry, pottery, art and art reproductions, baskets, beadwork, carvings, kachina dolls.

TANDY LEATHER CO.
230 E. Roosevelt
P.O. Box 13273   PHOENIX 85002
    Eldon G. Wilkins, Manager
Indian beads and beadwork for costumes; feathers and fluffy plumes; bells; leather kits for many costumes; how-to books, etc. Catalog available.

HOLIDAY SHOP
136 S. Montezuma   PRESCOTT 86301
    Howard Hinson, Manager
Jewelry, basketry and pottery, rugs and beadwork.

STEVENS FINE APACHE ARTS
P.O. Box 47   SAN CARLOS 85550
      George J. Stevens, Manager
Burden baskets, shallow and bowl baskets,
water jugs, dolls, moccasins, handmade jewelry, Navajo rugs, Apache Crown Dance
figurines and headdresses, miniature and
various sized cradle boards, bolo ties and
beaded necklaces, etc.

AZTEC STUDIO SHOP
22 E. Main St.   SCOTTSDALE
      Mr. Dolny, Manager
Hand-crafted silver and turquoise jewelry
of the Navajo, Zuni and Hopi.

D'ARCY'S INDIAN & SOUTHWESTERN
   GIFTS
22 W. 5th Ave.   SCOTTSDALE
      D'Arcy R. Smith, Sr., Manager
Reservation Indian handmade jewelry, pottery, wool woven neckties, rugs and baskets, moccasins, Indian-design wind bells,
hand-carved Indian figures, Indian prints
and stationery.

HOUSE OF THE SIX DIRECTIONS
101 W. 5th Ave.   SCOTTSDALE 85251
      Paul F. Huldermann, Owner
Representations of all Southwestern Indian
handcrafted contemporary items; contemporary items by Central and South American
Indians; historic and prehistoric, pre-
Columbian material.

AMERICAN INDIAN CRAFTS
P.O. Box Z   TEMPE 85281
      Byron F. Hunter, Manager
Indian handicrafts and artifacts; antiques.

DESERT HOUSE CRAFTS, INC.
2841 N. Campbell Ave.   TUCSON 85719
      J. Tanner, Manager
Weaving (rugs, clothing, ceremonial costumes), jewelry and pottery, basketry, kachina dolls, fetishes, drums, paintings,
etc.

THUNDERBIRD SHOP
199 N. Stone   TUCSON 85701
      Frank Patania, Jr., Manager
Hopi, Zuni and Navajo jewelry.

VAUGHN'S INDIAN CRAFTS
121 E. Bill Williams Ave.   WILLIAMS
      Wallace E. Hiatt, Manager
Only authentic Indian jewelry, rugs, pottery, baskets, and other handicrafts.

VANG'S JEWELRY & GIFT SHOP
2544 - 4th Ave.   YUMA 85364
      Urban S. Johns, Owner-Manager
Beadwork, baskets and jewelry, rugs and
pottery, sandpaintings, curios.

CALIFORNIA

INDIAN STORE AT HOBBY CITY
1240 Beach Blvd.   ANAHEIM 92804
      Robert Taylor, Manager
All Indian-made items: rugs, jewelry, baskets, pottery, novelties, etc. Complete line
of crafts and kits pertaining to Indians.

RAKU GALLERY
367 N. Camden Drive   BEVERLY HILLS
      Jerry Martin, Manager
Baskets and pottery, blankets and jewelry,
kachinas, toys and ceremonial pieces.

INDIAN LIFE CRAFTS & SUPPLIES
1220 W. Burbank Blvd.   BURBANK 91502
      Mr. Jay Olin, Manager
Beads, feathers, bells, leathers, costumes,
moccasins, books, records, etc.; authentic reservation-made items; collectors'
items. Catalog available.

BUFFALO ROBE INDIAN TRADING POST
7244 Remmet Ave.   CANOGA PARK
      Pat Tearney, Owner-Manager
Custom-made moccasins and vests, leather-
style shirts and jackets, Indian craft kits of
all types, beads, bells, feathers, leathers,
furs, etc. Catalog available.

JUANITA'S INDIAN HERBS CO.
846 W. Sacramento Ave.   CHICO 95926
      Juanita Stryker, Manager
Firm deals in Indian herbs to be used for
medicinal purposes.

RAKU GALLERY
305 W. Foothill   CLAREMONT

Jerry Martin, Manager
Baskets and pottery, blankets and jewelry, kachinas, toys and ceremonial pieces.

FOUR WINDS TRADING POST
577 Fifth St.   OAKLAND 94607
    G.H. Anderson, Manager
Hopi, Papago and Alaskan basketry, Southwest pottery, Navajo rugs, Zuni and Navajo jewelry and beadwork, Alaskan and Canadian Eskimo carvings, desert foods and stationery.

YA-A-T'EH GIFT SHOP
2220 Mountain Blvd.   OAKLAND 94611
    Arthur W. Hiscock, Owner-Manager
Authentic silver jewelry, basketry, pottery, moccasins, Navajo rugs, kachina dolls. Catalog available.

B'TZALEL
1839 Divisadero St.
                    SAN FRANCISCO 94115
    Hyla Strauch, Manager
Indian jewelry, baskets, rugs, toys, etc.; Indian information books. Catalog available.

BEST'S STUDIO
P.O. Box 455
        YOSEMITE NATIONAL PARK 95389
    Ernest Johanson, Manager
Navajo rugs, Indian jewelry, pottery, paintings, kachinas, Indian crafts books.

COLORADO

KIVA CORP.
1708 - 15th St.   BOULDER
    C. Katona, Manager
Arts and crafts of one hundred and ten tribes.

NOTAH DINEH TRADING CO.
309 N. Broadway   CORTEZ
    Bob Leighton, Manager
Ute beadwork and artifacts, Navajo and Zuni jewelry; Navajo rugs and baskets, new and old.

KOHLBERG'S
429 - 17th St.   DENVER 80202
    Erich Kohlberg, Manager
Complete stock of new and old authentic Indian articles. Catalog available.

TEPEE TRADING POST
7600 E. Colfax   DENVER 80220
    Helen Munson, Manager
Jewelry, pottery, basketry, rugs, etc.

WESTERN TRADING POST
31 Broadway   DENVER 80203
    C.M. Eberhart, Manager
"Craft supply items (beads, bells, feathers, beads etc.), books on all tribes, pottery and silver, bead and basket work, fine art." Catalog available.

FLORIDA

SEMINOLE ARTS AND CRAFTS SHOP
6037 Stirling Rd.   HOLLYWOOD 33020

Seminole dolls, clothing, woodcarving, basketry; crafts from other North American and Alaskan tribes.

IDAHO

AMERICA HOUSE
                    SUN VALLEY 83353
    Luther A. Douglas, Manager
Navajo ceremonial sandpaintings, pottery, rugs, baskets, jewelry. Catalog available.

MICHIGAN

ARTS AND CRAFTS GIFT SHOP
Red Arrow Court
P.O. Box 2   MARQUETTE 49855
    Mrs. Ellen Salminen, Manager
Craft items.

ARROWHEAD TRADING POST
433 N. Washington Ave.
                    ROYAL OAK 48067
    William Poland, Manager
"Complete line of Indian craft supplies -- raw materials, beads, bells, feathers, costume kits, drums, recordings, books, leather, furs." Catalog available.

MINNESOTA

PIPESTONE INDIAN SHRINE
    ASSOCIATION
Pipestone National Monument
P.O. Box 727   PIPESTONE 56164
    Ralph K. Shaver, Executive
        Secretary
Catlinite (pipestone) ceremonial pipes and other articles. Catalog available.

MISSOURI

BROADSTREET'S, INC.
315 E. McDaniel   SPRINGFIELD 65806
     Lydia Broadstreet, Manager
Furniture, arts and crafts, household articles, including Indian material.

MONTANA

NORTHERN PLAINS INDIAN CRAFTS
  ASSOCIATION
Federal Bldg.
316 N. 26th St.
Room 1017   BILLINGS 59101

Reservation-made Indian arts and crafts. Catalog available.

NORTHERN PLAINS INDIAN CRAFTS
  ASSOCIATION
c/o Museum of the Plains Indian
                        BROWNING 59417
     Mrs. Mueller, Manager
Authentic Indian arts and crafts. Catalog available.

NEVADA

DESERT INDIAN SHOP
108 N. 3rd St.   LAS VEGAS 89101
     L. Carlton, Manager
Rugs, baskets, pottery and jewelry; small selection of artifacts.

WADSWORTH ANTIQUES
P.O. Box 90   WADSWORTH 89442
     Mrs. Carl Kubler, Manager
"We buy and sell anything old or new in Indian goods."

NEW JERSEY

A.G. HANAK
Box 23   HIBERNIA 07842
     A.G. Hanak, Manager
Hand-carved wooden Indians, 6' to 7' tall.

NEW MEXICO

BOWLIN'S RUNNING INDIAN
Box 1212   ALAMAGORDO 88310
     C.R. Major, Manager
Navajo rugs, beaded items, arrowheads and artifacts, Chimayo blankets, Hopi and Papago baskets, jewelry and pottery.

BAURES JEWELRY CO.
438 Morningside, N.E.
                        ALBUQUERQUE 87108
     W.L. Tarter, Manager
Navajo rugs, Zuni, Hopi and Navajo handmade jewelry, all types of pottery, Hopi and Papago baskets, beadwork of the Zuni and Navajo.

ENCHANTED MESA INDIAN ARTS
9612 Central Ave., S.E.
                        ALBUQUERQUE 87108
     Fred Chase, Manager
"Authentic Indian arts and crafts of the Southwest: Navajo rugs, Navajo and Zuni handmade jewelry, Kaibab Navajo moccasins and squaw moccasins, Pueblo pottery, paintings, kachina dolls, basketry."

EUKABI PUBLISHERS
P.O. Box 7481   ALBUQUERQUE 87104
     Charles V. White, Manager
"Indian-design notepaper, books, novelties, Zuni, Navajo, Santo Domingo handmade jewelry, beaded novelties, Jemez and Santa Clara pottery." Catalog available.

THE FREED CO.
107 - 1st St., N.W.
                        ALBUQUERQUE 87104
     Philip Freed, Manager
Navajo rugs, Indian goods of all kinds, wampum necklaces, etc. Catalog available.

INDIAN SILVER CRAFTS, INC.
1701 Central Ave., N.W.
                        ALBUQUERQUE
     J. Chakerian, Manager
Handmade Indian jewelry.

SILVER SANDS TRADING POST
2043 South Plaza, N.W.
                        ALBUQUERQUE
     A. Thorwaldsen, Manager
Handmade Indian jewelry. Catalog available.

WRIGHT'S TRADING POST
518 Central, S.W.
                                    ALBUQUERQUE
Sam Chernoff, Manager
Handmade Indian jewelry, pottery and rugs,
collectors' items.

VILLAGE SCHOOL OF INDIAN ARTS
P.O. Box 8036
c/o Seama Village   CUBERO 87014
   C.F. Chavez, Manager
Portraits on commission, kachina wall
plaques.

SANTO DOMINGO INDIAN TRADING POST
Santo Domingo Reservation
                                    DOMINGO 87001
   Fred Thompson, Manager
Handmade jewelry, rugs, pottery and
general Indian crafts.

HATCH BROS. TRADING POST
P.O. Box 8   FRUITLAND 87416
   R.S. Hatch, Manager
Navajo rugs, Indian arts and crafts.

ALL TRIBES TRADING CO.
911 W. Coal Ave.
Box 1435   GALLUP 87301
   W.P. Davis, Manager
Navajo and Zuni jewelry, basketry and pottery, rugs and original paintings by Indian
artists.

GALLUP INDIAN TRADING CO.
1000 W. Highway 66
P.O. Box 1358   GALLUP 87301
   J.W. Kennedy, Manager
Handmade Indian arts and crafts -- Navajo,
Zuni and Hopi jewelry, Navajo rugs, pottery
from all the producing pueblos.

TOBE TURPEN'S INDIAN TRADING POST
South Zuni Highway and Nizhoni Rd.
                                    GALLUP 87301
   Tobe Turpen, Manager
Handmade Indian crafts and arts only, raw
materials for Indian jewelry-making.

WOODARD'S INDIAN ARTS
224 W. Coal Ave.   GALLUP 87301
   M.L. Woodard, Manager

General Indian merchandise -- jewelry,
rugs, pottery, paintings, baskets, fans,
lapidary tools and supplies, silversmith
tools and implements, cradles, etc.

LA GALERIA DE LOS ARTESANOS
On the Plaza   LAS VEGAS 87702
   Mrs. J.W. Stein, Owner
Indian paintings, reproductions, jewelry,
pottery, basketry, bookshop featuring
Western Americana.

SHALAKO SHOP
1210 - 17th St.
P.O. Box 970   LOS ALAMOS 87544
   T.J. White, Manager
Indian arts and crafts -- handmade jewelry,
Navajo rugs, sandpaintings, pottery, books
on the Southwest.

LA TIENDA
P.O. Box 127   MESILLA 88046
   Dorothy Dalton, Manager
Handmade turquoise and sterling silver
jewelry, Papago baskets, books pertaining
to Indian culture, handmade pottery.

ARROWSMITH'S
402 College   SANTA FE 87501
   Rex Arrowsmith, Manager
"We are suppliers to museums and collectors throughout the world and operate a
working Indian trading post dealing in prehistoric, historic and contemporary Indian
arts and crafts. We have a large stock of
prehistoric artifacts, historic costumes,
pottery, jewelry, textiles, basketry, and
paintings -- Indian items from South
America to the Arctic Circle."

ORIGINAL CURIO STORE
201 W. San Francisco St.
                                    SANTA FE 87501
   W.H. Wright, Manager
Old and new baskets, pottery, blankets,
paintings, dolls, kachinas, beadwork,
fetishes, etc.

POPOVI DA - STUDIO OF INDIAN ARTS
Route 1
Box 309   SANTA FE 87501
   Popovi Da, Manager
Jewelry, rugs, pottery and baskets.

JIM RILEY, TRADER
P.O. Box 192   SANTA FE 87501
    James K. Riley, Manager
Pueblo and Southwest Indian crafts, prehistoric and contemporary pottery, baskets,
jewelry, artifacts, and other crafts.

THE TREASURE CHEST
119 E. Palace Ave.   SANTA FE 87501
    O.T. Branson, Manager
"Indian goods, old and new, kachinas,
jewelry, etc."

INDIAN HOUSE
P.O. Box 472   TAOS 87571
    David A. Isaacs, Manager
"Selected works of American Indian art,
specializing in Southwest pottery, Plains
beadwork, original paintings, phonograph
recordings of Indian music, and baskets
old and new." Polaroid photos sent upon
request.

VANDER WAGEN, INC.
Hawikuh Trading Post
Box 485   ZUNI
    Mike Vander Wagen, Manager
Authentic handmade Zuni, Navajo and Hopi
jewelry, rugs, pottery, old pawn, kachinas,
fetishes, etc.

NEW YORK

GREY OWL INDIAN CRAFT MANU -
    FACTURING CO., INC.
150-02 Beaver Rd.   JAMAICA 11433
    D.W. Miller, Manager
Complete line of Indian craft costume kits,
books, recordings, photos, beadwork, war
bonnet headdresses, moccasins. Catalog
available.

WANDA'S ANTIQUES
525 Winsor St.   JAMESTOWN 14701
    Gus Chili, Manager
Replicas of wood-carver's art: cigar store
Indian, Indian princess, etc. Catalog
available.

PLUME TRADING AND SALES CO., INC.
P.O. Box 585   MONROE 10950
    James M. Luongo, Manager
Indian craft supplies; curios. Catalog
available.

THE AMERICAN INDIAN ARTS CENTER
1051 Third Ave.   NEW YORK 10021
    Norma Reinke, Manager
Contemporary North American Indian,
Eskimo and Aleut arts and crafts. Paintings,
sculpture, basketry, weavings and carvings,
silver and turquoise jewelry, pottery and
barkware. Inquiries personally answered.

GETTINGER FEATHER CO.
19 W. 38th St.   NEW YORK 10018

Raw and dyed feathers.

MUSEUM SHOP
Museum of the American Indian
Broadway at 155th St.   NEW YORK 10032
    Mary W. Williams, Manager
Contemporary and ancient Indian material,
including pre-Columbian pottery, sculpture,
basketry, dolls, masks, textiles, beadwork.

PLUME TRADING AND SALES CO., INC.
155 Lexington Ave.   NEW YORK 10016
    James M. Luongo, Manager
All types of supplies for American Indian
crafts -- beads, feathers, buckskin, porcupine quills, sinew, shells, rawhide,
bonebeads, trade cloth, etc. Catalog
available.

NORTH CAROLINA

THE CHEROKEES
Qualla Indian Reservation
                        CHEROKEE 28719
    P.K. Ferree, Manager
Indian moccasins and crafts. Catalog
available.

OHIO

TANDY LEATHER CO.
911 Main St.   CINCINNATI 45202
    Mike Rusin, Manager

"Leather and Indian craft." Catalog
available.

OKLAHOMA

OKLAHOMA INDIAN ARTS AND CRAFTS COOPERATIVE
Box 447   ANADARKO 73005
    Mrs. Nettie Standing, Manager
Indian costumes, leather work, records, jewelry, drums, dolls, books, maps and pamphlets related to the American Indian. Pricelist available.

LYON'S INDIAN STORE
700 S. Main   TULSA 74119
    Frank C. Lyon, Manager
"Anything available in Indian handicraft: beadwork, costumes, rugs, blankets, baskets, jewelry, stone-age relics, arrowheads, etc.; raw materials used by the Indians of Oklahoma -- beads, feathers, plumes, sinew, fur, hides, etc."

SOUTH DAKOTA

TIPI SHOP, INC.
P.O. Box 1504   RAPID CITY 57701
    Mrs. Emma Amiotte, Manager
Indian arts and crafts: dolls, costumes, jewelry, beadwork and ceramics, carvings, books, basketry. Pricelist available.

TENNESSEE

LOG CABIN CRAFT SHOP
Route 8   GREENEVILLE 37743
    Mrs. Marion Edens, Manager
Items made by members of the Southern Highland Handicraft Guild, including work of the Cherokees.

TEXAS

ANTIQUE HOUSE
3903 Lemmon Ave.   DALLAS 75219
    Frank L. Williams, Manager
Indian artifacts.

TANDY LEATHER CO.
1001 Foch St.   FORT WORTH 76107
    Harlan Swain, President

Kits of leather and suede crafts, beadwork and feathers, belts and miscellaneous items. Catalog available.

UTAH

WARDLES INDIAN CURIO SHOP
P.O. Box 82   ROOSEVELT

Ute Indian beadwork, beading supplies.

VIRGINIA

MEXICAN CRAFT SHOP
Two miles north of Roanoke
Routes 11 and 220   HOLLINS 24019
    Robert Preston, Manager
Indian jewelry, cards, pictures, Cherokee toys, headdresses and arrowheads, Mexican crafts.

WASHINGTON

THE COLLECTORS GALLERY
Crossroads   BELLEVUE 98004
    Robert Carpenter, Owner
"Quality" contemporary Indian arts and crafts from the United States and Canada, including sculpture, paintings, graphics, and crafts such as rugs, jewelry, carvings, baskets, etc. Annual invitational Contemporary Indian Arts and Crafts Show held in September.

MUSEUM SHOP
Cheney Cowles Memorial Museum
W. 2316 1st Ave.   SPOKANE 99204
    Delbert J. McBride, Manager
Beaded gloves, moccasins, ornaments, jewelry (Spokane and Coeur d'Alene craftsmen), basketry of the Makah and Yakima tribes, woodcarvings of the Northwest tribes, Indian-design notepaper.

WYOMING

TURQUOISE BLUE
Box 601   DUBOIS 82513
    Peter W. Nichols, Manager

Navajo jewelry and rugs, Zuni jewelry, Hopi jewelry and kachinas, Papago baskets, Shoshoni, Arapaho and Bannock beadwork.

INDIAN GIFT SHOP
Box 428   FORT WASHAKIE 82514

Richard and Jeri Greeves, Managers

Handmade beadwork and other Shoshoni and Arapaho arts and crafts from the Wind River Reservation.

Visual and Instructional Aids

Included here are listings of sources for related recordings, picture sets and maps, etc. Entries are arranged by name or title of item. Source address is listed directly below.

FILMS

ARTS AND CRAFTS OF THE SOUTHWEST INDIANS
Santa Fe Film Bureau
Santa Fe General Office Bldg.
Amarillo, Texas 79101

Part I deals with the nomadic Navajos and the production of jewelry and rugs; Part II describes the arts and crafts of the Pueblo tribes, specifically Zuni silverwork, basketry and pottery. 1953. 16 mm. Sound. 22 minutes.

BIG POW-WOW AT GALLUP
Inter-Tribal Indian Ceremonial Association, Inc.
P.O. Box 1029
Gallup, N.M. 87301

Highlights of annual Ceremonial, including street parades, afternoon sports, evening dances, Exhibit Hall scenes. 16 mm. Sound and color. 19 minutes. Produced by Humble Oil Co.

THE CIBECUE WATERSHED
Information Office
Bureau of Indian Affairs
Room 138
1951 Constitution Ave., N.W.
Washington, D.C. 20242

Shows the steps taken to improve methods in watershed management on the Fort Apache Reservation, Ariz., including water use, livestock, irrigation, forest and recreation. 16 mm. Sound and color. 22 minutes. Available for loan to schools, churches, civic and other organizations in the Washington, D.C., Metropolitan area.

DESERT PEOPLE
Branch of Education
Bureau of Indian Affairs
Washington, D.C. 20242

Describes Papago Indian life in the Sonoran Desert. 16 mm. Sound and color. 25 minutes. Available for purchase ($63.06).

DOWN NORTH
Consulate General of Canada
Film Library
310 S. Michigan Ave.
Chicago, Ill. 60604

Records the progress of recent subarctic developments in the Mackenzie District in mining, lumber and other industries, and the effect of these developments on Eskimo and Indian populations. (Distribution restricted to Illinois, Indiana, Iowa, Kansas, Kentucky, Minnesota, Missouri, Nebraska, North Dakota, South Dakota, and Wisconsin.) 16 mm. Sound and color. 30 minutes.

ENEMY OF YOUR EYES
Branch of Education
Bureau of Indian Affairs
Washington, D.C. 20242

A documentary concerning blindness produced by trachoma, a disease of the eye formerly prevalent among Indians. 16 mm. Sound and color. 13 minutes. Available for purchase ($32.78).

ESKIMO FAMILY
Information Office
Bureau of Indian Affairs
Room 138
1951 Constitution Ave., N.W.
Washington, D.C. 20242

Presents a picture of Eskimo family life, during the journey to spring hunting grounds, at the camp site, trading post, and town -- in view of the Eskimo's increasing contact with the world. 16 mm. Sound. 17 minutes. Available for loan to schools, churches, civic and other organizations in the Washington, D.C., metropolitan area.

THE FIRST AMERICANS
Information Office
Bureau of Indian Affairs
Room 138
1951 Constitution Ave., N.W.
Washington, D.C. 20242

Describes cultural changes and current programs for today's Indians, with narration by Johnny Batchelder. Color and sound. 17 minutes. Available for loan to schools, churches, civic and other organizations in the Washington, D.C., metropolitan area.

GLOOSCAP COUNTRY
Consulate General of Canada
Film Library
310 S. Michigan Ave.
Chicago, Ill. 60604

Presents an ancient legend of the Micmac Indians of Nova Scotia. (Distribution is restricted to Illinois, Indiana, Iowa, Kansas, Kentucky, Minnesota, Missouri, Nebraska, North Dakota, South Dakota, and Wisconsin.) 16 mm. Sound and color. 13 minutes.

GRASS IS GOLD
Branch of Education
Bureau of Indian Affairs
Washington, D.C. 20242

Indicates the relationship of grass to the cattle industry. 16 mm. Sound and color. 17 minutes. Available for purchase ($75.32).

HOW DO YOU DO BOYS
Branch of Education
Bureau of Indian Affairs
Washington, D.C. 20242

Repetitive impact social skills series: introductions for boys. 16 mm. Sound. Five minutes. For Bureau use only ($5.89).

HOW DO YOU DO GIRLS
Branch of Education
Bureau of Indian Affairs
Washington, D.C. 20242

Repetitive impact social skills series: introductions for girls. 16 mm. Sound. Five minutes. For Bureau use only ($5.46).

INDIAN ARTS AND CRAFTS
Information Office
Bureau of Indian Affairs
Room 138
1951 Constitution Ave., N.W.
Washington, D.C. 20242

Exhibits products of the Navajo and Pueblo Indians: silver, rugs, baskets, and pottery. 16 mm. Sound and color. 20 minutes. Available for loan to schools, churches, civic and other organizations in the Washington, D.C., metropolitan area.

INDIAN CEREMONIALS
Information Office
Bureau of Indian Affairs
Room 138
1951 Constitution Ave., N.W.
Washington, D.C. 20242

Covers the Ceremonial parade at Gallup, N.M., including rodeos and dances. 16 mm. Sound and color. 20 minutes. Available for loan to schools, churches, civic and other organizations in the Washington, D.C., metropolitan area.

INDIAN CEREMONIALS
Santa Fe Film Bureau
Santa Fe General Office Bldg.
Amarillo, Texas 79101

Scenes from the annual Indian Ceremonials at Gallup, N.M., including parades, rodeos and dances. 16 mm. Sound. 18 minutes.

INDIAN DAYS
Canadian Travel Film Library
Suite 2320
230 N. Michigan Ave.
Chicago, Ill. 60601

Features the summer festival in British Columbia, near the town of Kamloops, including parades, a rodeo, and Indian dances. 16 mm. Sound and color. 12 1/2 minutes.

THE INDIAN SANITARIAN
Branch of Education
Bureau of Indian Affairs
Washington, D.C. 20242

Depicts the importance of environmental sanitation to health. 16 mm. Sound. Nine minutes. Available for purchase ($11.21).

INDIANS OF EARLY AMERICA
Information Office
Bureau of Indian Affairs
1951 Constitution Ave., N.W.
Washington, D.C. 20242

Identifies and describes four major regions
of the United States, the Eastern Woodlands,
the Midwestern Plains, the Southwest, and
the Northwest, as they were before the settlement of the white man. 16 mm. Sound
and color. 25 minutes. Available for loan
to schools, churches, civic and other organizations in the Washington, D.C., metropolitan area.

INDIANS ON PARADE
New Mexico Department of Development
Tourist Division
State Capital
Santa Fe, N.M. 87501

Presents a picture of the Inter-Tribal Indian
Ceremonial at Gallup, N.M., in which Indians from over thirty tribes participate
each year. Includes the Hoop Dance performed by Tony Whitecloud, and various
dance and arts and crafts exhibitions. 16
mm. Sound and color. 11 minutes.

THE LONGHOUSE PEOPLE
Consulate General of Canada
Film Library
310 S. Michigan Ave.
Chicago, Ill. 60604

Records the life and religious ceremonies
of the Iroquois Indians at the present time.
(Distribution is restricted to Illinois, Indiana, Iowa, Kansas, Kentucky, Minnesota,
Missouri, Nebraska, North Dakota, South
Dakota, and Wisconsin.) 16 mm. Sound.
20 minutes.

NAVAJOS LOOK AHEAD
Modern Talking Picture Service
10 Rockefeller Plaza
New York, N.Y. 10020

A story of the present-day life of Navajo
Indians on their reservation in Paradox
Basin, Utah, including rodeos, tribal fairs,
and housing projects. Recommended for
ninth grade and above. Produced by Humble
Oil Co. 16 mm. Sound and color. 13 minutes.

NO LONGER VANISHING
Consulate General of Canada
Film Library
310 S. Michigan Ave.
Chicago, Ill. 60604

Portrays the present status of Canada's
Indian population and its role in Canadian
affairs. (Distribution restricted to Illinois,
Indiana, Iowa, Kansas, Kentucky, Minne-
sota, Missouri, Nebraska, North Dakota,
South Dakota, and Wisconsin.) 16 mm.
Sound and color. 28 minutes.

PEOPLE OF THE PUEBLOS
Branch of Education
Bureau of Indian Affairs
Washington, D.C. 20242

A presentation of Pueblo life in the Southwest, past and present. 16 mm. Sound
and color. 20 minutes. Available for purchase ($90.12).

PEOPLE OF THE SKEENA
Consulate General of Canada
Film Library
310 S. Michigan Ave.
Chicago, Ill. 60604

Deals with the history and customs of the
Getikshan and Tsimshian Indians of north-
ern British Columbia and their way of life.
(Distribution is restricted to Illinois, In-
diana, Iowa, Kansas, Kentucky, Minnesota,
Missouri, Nebraska, North Dakota, South
Dakota, and Wisconsin.) 16 mm. Sound.
15 minutes.

PUEBLO BOY
Ford Motor Co.
Educational Affairs Department
The American Road
Dearborn, Mich. 48121

Tells the story of a young Indian boy being
instructed in the ancient and modern ways
and traditions of his people, the Pueblos of
the Southwest. 16 mm. Sound and color.
20 minutes.

RICH MAN! POOR MAN!
Information Office
Bureau of Indian Affairs
1951 Constitution Ave., N.W.
Washington, D.C. 20242

Points out misconceptions about Indians and depicts their lives on and off reservations. 16 mm. Sound. 25 minutes. Available for loan to schools, churches, civic and other organizations in the Washington, D. C., metropolitan area.

RIVER PEOPLE
Branch of Education
Bureau of Indian Affairs
Washington, D.C. 20242

Relates the story of the Pima Tribe. 16 mm. Sound and color. 25 minutes. Available for purchase ($60.48).

THE SILENT ONES
Canadian Travel Film Library
Suite 2320
230 N. Michigan Ave.
Chicago, Ill. 60601

Record of an expedition to an island in the Queen Charlotte group off the coast of British Columbia to recover totem poles and other relics of the Haida Indian culture. 16 mm. Sound and color. 25 minutes.

TIMBER TODAY AND TOMORROW
Branch of Education
Bureau of Indian Affairs
Washington, D.C. 20242

Teaches the scientific method used to perpetuate Indian forests. 16 mm. Sound and color. 17 minutes. Available for purchase ($80.28).

TRAIL TO HEALTH
Branch of Education
Bureau of Indian Affairs
Washington, D.C. 20242

A documentary on the discovery and cure of tuberculosis. 16 mm. Sound and color. 20 minutes. Available for purchase ($89.56).

WHITE MOUNTAIN APACHE
Information Office
Bureau of Indian Affairs
Room 138
1951 Constitution Ave., N.W.
Washington, D.C. 20242

Progress of the White River Apache Indians in developing resources and in managing tribal affairs. 16 mm. Sound and color. 15 minutes. Available for loan to schools, churches, civic and other organizations in the Washington, D.C., metropolitan area.

MAPS AND CHARTS

DISTRIBUTION OF INDIAN TRIBES OF
  NORTH AMERICA
Southwest Museum
Highland Park
Los Angeles, Calif. 90042

Shows location of tribes at the time of the first contact with the white settlers. Prepared by A. L. Kroeber. 21 x 28". 35¢.

THE GABRILENO INDIANS AT THE TIME
  OF THE PORTOLA EXPEDITION
Southwest Museum
Highland Park
Los Angeles, Calif. 90042

Map showing locations of ancient Indian villages in southern California. 22 x 15". 50¢.

INDIAN LAND AREAS
Superintendent of Documents
U.S. Government Printing Office
Washington, D.C. 20402

Three-color map shows Indian lands under Federal responsibility. Listed are field offices of the Bureau of Indian Affairs, and the tribes within their jurisdiction. 1965. 4 x 8" (folded). 30¢.

INDIAN MAP OF THE SOUTHWEST
Butler Art Service
P.O. Box 88
Orange, Calif. 92669

Map shows major tribes, languages, culture groups and customs of the Southwest, with all important reservations. Illustrated in color. $1.00.

INDIAN SYMBOLIC DESIGNS
Southwest Museum
Highland Park
Los Angeles, Calif. 90042

Chart illustrating approximately one hundred symbols, compiled by Velma Adams. 16 x 18''. 35¢.

INDIANS OF THE U. S. A.
Friendship Press
475 Riverside Drive
New York, N. Y. 10027

A multicolored map illustrating the original tribal territories of the American Indians (including Alaskan Eskimos). Also notes famous events in history, and the names of those persons -- Indian and white -- involved in the events. 1944.

THE NORTH AMERICAN INDIANS
Department of Anthropology
University of Chicago
Chicago, Ill. 60601

Map illustrates the distribution of descendants of the aboriginal population of Alaska, Canada, and the United States, as of the 1950 census. Prepared by Samuel Stanley, Robert K. Thomas, Bruce MacLachlan, and Myron Rosenberg, under the direction of Sol Tax.

PICTURE MAP OF ALASKA
Friendship Press
475 Riverside Drive
New York, N. Y. 10027

A decorative map, which may be colored, together with an insert sheet containing informative notes and twenty-one pictures to be cut out and pasted on the map. 1948. 9 1/2 x 12 1/2'' (folded).

PICTURE MAP OF INDIAN AMERICANS
Friendship Press
475 Riverside Drive
New York, N. Y. 10027

A decorative map, which may be colored, together with an insert sheet containing informative notes and pictures to be cut out and pasted on the map. 1955. 9 1/2 x 12 1/2'' (folded).

SCHOOL PACKET ON UTAH
Utah Tourist and Publicity Council
State Capital
Salt Lake City, Utah 84114

Consists of the following maps, leaflets and pamphlets: Utah Highway Map, Climate of Utah, Great Salt Lake, Utah Indians, and The Utah Story. Available only to teachers.

TYPICAL INDIAN DWELLINGS OF THE
UNITED STATES
Southwest Museum
Highland Park
Los Angeles, Calif. 90042

Chart illustrating twenty-two types of aboriginal dwellings. 16 x 19''. 35¢.

PICTURE SETS

DIGEST OF SOUTHWESTERN TRIBES
Inter-Tribal Indian Ceremonial Association
P. O. Box 1029
Gallup, N. M. 87301

Contains information on the Indians of the Southwestern United States, including the Pueblo, Apache, Navajo and Ute Tribes. Single copies available to teachers and librarians only.

FAMOUS INDIAN CHIEFS
M. A. Donohue & Co.
711 S. Dearborn St.
Chicago, Ill. 60605

Intended for classroom use, set consists of eleven pictures of famous Indian chiefs. $1.00.

INDIAN ART REPRODUCTIONS
James Ladd Delkin
205 S. 6th St.
Las Vegas, Nev. 89101

Ten full-color art reproductions on cards of American Indians, taken from original oil paintings by E. A. Burbank. $1.00.

INDIANS OF MINNESOTA
Minnesota Historical Society
Central and Cedar Aves.
St. Paul, Minn. 55101

Sixteen pictures show how Minnesota's two major tribes, the Sioux and the Chippewa, lived, and how their customs differ. Text included.

INDIANS OF YESTERDAY
M. A. Donohue & Co.
711 S. Dearborn St.
Chicago, Ill. 60605

Intended for classroom use, set consists of
six pictures. $1.00.

MASTERPIECES OF PRIMITIVE ART
Museum of Fine Arts
469 Huntington Ave.
Boston, Mass. 02115

Silkscreen reproductions by Louie Ewing of
eight examples of primitive art, suitable
for framing. 10 x 13". Set, $5.00.

PICTURE SET
Associated Executive Committee of Friends
  on Indian Affairs
1403 - 21st St.
Central City, Neb. 68826

Available for rental from Miss Corona Cook,
Chairman of Education and Publicity, at the
above address.

SANDPAINTING REPRODUCTIONS
Museum of Navajo Ceremonial Art
Box 445
Santa Fe, N.M. 87501

Reproduced in silkscreen -- Blessing Chant,
showing coyote stealing fire from Fire God
to give to First Man and First Woman (23"
square, five colors, $20.00); Dontso print
from Hail Chant (9 1/4 x 12 1/4", $2.00).

SILKSCREEN REPRODUCTIONS OF THE
  KUAHA MURALS
School of American Research
Box 1554
Santa Fe, N.M. 87501

Five-color screenings, approximately 13 x
40". Seventeen sheets per set. $3.00.

SLIDES
Associated Executive Committee of Friends
  on Indian Affairs
1403 - 21st St.
Central City, Neb. 68826

Available for rental from Miss Corona Cook,
Chairman of Education and Publicity, at the
above address. Script included.

SLIDES
Museum of the American Indian
Heye Foundation
Broadway at 155th St.
New York, N.Y. 10032

A selection of 35 mm. color transparencies
on cardboard mounts, chosen from the Museum's collection. 50¢ per slide.

TEACHER PACKAGE
Inter-Tribal Indian Ceremonial Association
P.O. Box 1029
Gallup, N.M. 87301

Contains Indian-related magazines, pamphlets and book list.

WORLD FRIENDS: *Indian Americans*
Friendship Press
475 Riverside Drive
New York, N.Y. 10027

Picture album by Loretta Ingalls contains
fifteen photographs in black and white, with
a descriptive text depicting Indian life and
customs.

RECORDINGS

AMERICAN INDIAN DANCES
Folkways Records
165 W. 46th St.
New York, N.Y. 10036

Rabbit Dance (Sioux), Sun Dance (Sioux),
Omaha Dance (Sioux), Devil Dance (Apache),
Eagle Dance (San Ildefonso), Harvest Dance
(Zuni), Rain Dance (Zuni), Squaw Dance
(Navajo), War Dance (Plains), Snake Dance,
Pow-Wow Dance (Flathead), Dog Dance
(Plains). 12". 33 1/3 rpm. $5.95.

APACHE
Library of Congress Music Division
c/o Superintendent of Documents
U.S. Government Printing Office
Washington, D.C. 20402

Selections include Crown Dance Songs, Sun-
rise Dance Songs, Love Songs, Fire Dance
Song. Recorded and edited by Willard
Rhodes. 33 1/3 rpm. $5.40.

AS LONG AS THE GRASS SHALL GROW
Folkways Records
165 W. 46th St.
New York, N. Y. 10036

Songs written and sung by Peter La Farge
with notes from John Collier, Sr., John La
Farge, War of 1812 Documentary, and
Moses Asch. Text included. 12". 33 1/3
rpm.

DELAWARE, CHEROKEE, CHOCTAW,
  CREEK
Library of Congress Music Division
c/o Superintendent of Documents
U. S. Government Printing Office
Washington, D. C. 20402

Delaware Peyote and war dance songs;
Cherokee lullaby, stamp dance songs, horse
dance song, quail dance song, pumpkin
dance song; Choctaw hymn; Creek ball
game songs, lullaby, etc. Recorded and
edited by Willard Rhodes. 33 1/3 rpm.
$5. 40.

ESKIMO MUSIC OF ALASKA AND THE
  HUDSON BAY
Folkways Records
165 W. 46th St.
New York, N. Y. 10036

Johnnie Bull Song, Before We Came to this
Region, Girls' Game, Children's Game,
Bird Imitations, Animal Stories, Hunting
Song, Dance Songs, Story Songs. Record
and notes by Laura Boulton. 12". 33 1/3
rpm. $6. 95.

FLATHEAD INDIAN MUSIC
Folkways Records
165 W. 46th St.
New York, N. Y. 10036

A complete musical culture of the Salish
people: musical accompaniment to the various dances, stick games; drum music included. Illustrated notes supplied. 12".
33 1/3 rpm. $6. 95.

GREAT BASIN: *Paiute, Washo, Ute, Ban-*
  nock, Shoshone
Library of Congress Music Division
c/o Superintendent of Documents
U. S. Government Printing Office
Washington, D. C. 20402

Northwest tribes' dances, games, parade
songs and lullabies, sung by Logan Brown,
Charles Washakie, Judy Pete, and others.
Recorded and edited by Willard Rhodes.
33 1/3 rpm. $5. 40.

HEALING SONGS OF THE AMERICAN
  INDIANS
Folkways Records
165 W. 46th St.
New York, N. Y. 10036

Healing songs of the Chippewa, Sioux, Yuman, Northern Ute, Papago, Makah and
Menominee Indians. Text included. 12".
33 1/3 rpm. $6. 95.

HOPI KATCHINA SONGS
Folkways Records
165 W. 46th St.
New York, N. Y. 10036

Recorded in Arizona in 1924. Text included. 12". 33 1/3 rpm. $6. 95.

HOPI KATCHINA SONGS
Rio Grande Press
1734 E. 71st Pl.
Chicago, Ill. 60649

Hopi chanters, recorded in 1924 under the
direction of Dr. Jesse Fewkes. $5. 98.

INDIAN MUSIC OF THE CANADIAN
  PLAINS
Folkways Records
165 W. 46th St.
New York, N. Y. 10036

Recordings of the Blood, Cree, Blackfoot
and Assiniboine Indians made on the reservations, including war songs, greeting
songs, stick games, Chicken Dance, Grass
Dance, Owl Dance, Sun Dance, Crazy Dog
Dance, and others. Recorded by Ken Peo-
cock for the National Museum of Canada.
Notes included. 12". 33 1/3 rpm. $6. 95.

INDIAN MUSIC OF THE SOUTHWEST
Folkways Records
165 W. 46th St.
New York, N. Y. 10036

A reissue of Hopi, Zuni, Navajo, Taos,
San Ildefonso, Santa Ana, Mohave, Papago,

Pima and Apache music, including harvest songs, squaw dances, night chant, corn dance, horse song, bird songs, medicine songs, social dances. Recorded by Laura Boulton with descriptive notes. 12". 33 1/3 rpm. $5.95.

INDIAN SONGS OF TODAY
Library of Congress Music Division
c/o Superintendent of Documents
U.S. Government Printing Office
Washington, D.C. 20402

Seminole, Creek, Potawatomi, Sioux, Navajo, Tlingit and Kiowa songs sung by Indian youths. Recorded and edited by Willard Rhodes. 33 1/3 rpm. $5.40.

KIOWA
Folkways Records
165 W. 46th St.
New York, N.Y. 10036

Dance and war songs of the Kiowa Indians, including Kiowa Flag Song, Trot, Gourd, Buffalo, War Mother's Songs, and others. Text included. 33 1/3 rpm. $6.95.

KIOWA OHOMA SOCIETY DANCE SONGS
American Indian Soundchief
1415 Carlson Drive
Klamath Falls, Ore. 97601

Recorded by tribal singers. 33 1/3 rpm. $4.00.

MUSIC OF THE AMERICAN INDIANS OF
  THE SOUTHWEST
Folkways Records
165 W. 46th St.
New York, N.Y. 10036

Includes the Navajo, Zuni, Hopi, San Ildefonso, Taos, Apache, Yuma, Papago, Walapai and Havasupai tribal music. Recorded by Willard Rhodes in cooperation with the Bureau of Indian Affairs. Notes by Harry Tschopik, Jr., and Willard Rhodes. 12". 33 1/3 rpm. $6.95.

MUSIC OF THE PAWNEE
Folkways Records
165 W. 46th St.
New York, N.Y. 10036

Documentary recording of forty-five Pawnee Indian songs sung by Mark Evarts. Recorded by Dr. Gene Weltfish. Text included. 12". 33 1/3 rpm.

MUSIC OF THE PUEBLOS, APACHE, AND
  NAVAJO
Taylor Museum
Colorado Springs Fine Arts Center
Colorado Springs, Colo. 80901

Recording of American Indian music containing selections from the Pueblo, Taos, Santa Clara and Zuni; Apache instrumental and vocal music; several Navajo selections. Included with the record is a book and a set of notes with translations of the song texts, with information about each selection. Recorded by David P. McAllester and Donald N. Brown; edited by Donald N. Brown. 1961. $4.50.

MUSIC OF THE SIOUX AND NAVAJO
Folkways Records
165 W. 46th St.
New York, N.Y. 10036

Sioux recordings include Rabbit Dance, Sun Dance, Omaha Dance, love songs, cult songs, honoring song; Navajo recordings include Squaw Dance, Night Chant, riding song, corn-grinding song, silversmith's song, spinning dance, song of happiness. Notes included. Recorded in Indian communities by Willard Rhodes in cooperation with the Bureau of Indian Affairs. 12". 33 1/3 rpm. $6.95.

PUEBLO: *Taos, San Ildefonso, Zuni, Hopi*
Library of Congress Music Division
c/o Superintendent of Documents
U.S. Government Printing Office
Washington, D.C. 20402

Songs, dances, lullabies and chants recorded and edited by Willard Rhodes. 33 1/3 rpm. $5.40.

NAVAHO
Library of Congress Music Division
c/o Superintendent of Documents
U.S. Government Printing Office
Washington, D.C. 20402

Navaho chants; game, love and peyote songs. Recorded and edited by Willard Rhodes. 33 1/3 rpm. $5.40.

NORTHERN CHEYENNE WARRIORS
  DANCES AND SUN DANCE SONGS
American Indian Soundchief
1415 Carlson Drive
Klamath Falls, Ore. 97601

Recorded by tribal singers.   33 1/3 rpm.
$4. 50.

NORTHERN AND SOUTHERN PLAINS
  TRIBES OWL AND CIRCLE DANCE
  SONGS
American Indian Soundchief
1415 Carlson Drive
Klamath Falls, Ore. 97601

Recorded by tribal singers.   33 1/3 rpm.
$4. 50.

NORTHWEST (PUGET SOUND)
Library of Congress Music Division
c/o Superintendent of Documents
U. S. Government Printing Office
Washington, D. C. 20402

Skagit, Lummi, Chinook, Klallam, Quinault
and Tsaiyak songs. Recorded and edited by
Willard Rhodes. 33 1/3 rpm. $5. 40.

ON THE WARPATH
Folkways Records
165 W. 46th St.
New York, N. Y. 10036

Songs written and sung by Peter La Farge;
drum accompaniment by Nick Navarro.
Notes by Skip Weshner. 12". 33 1/3 rpm.

PLAINS: *Comanche, Cheyenne, Kiowa,
  Caddo, Wichita, Pawnee*
Library of Congress Music Division
c/o Superintendent of Documents
U. S. Government Printing Office
Washington, D. C. 20402

Selections include raid, war, love, rain, flag
and hunting songs. Recorded and edited by
Willard Rhodes. 33 1/3 rpm. $5. 40.

SENECA SONGS FROM COLDSPRING
  LONGHOUSE
Library of Congress Music Division
c/o Superintendent of Documents
U. S. Government Printing Office
Washington, D. C. 20402

Songs include Drum Dance, Quavering Song,
Bear Society Dance, and others. Recorded
and edited by William N. Fenton in cooperation with the Smithsonian Institution. 33 1/3
rpm. $5. 40.

SIOUX
Library of Congress Music Division
c/o Superintendent of Documents
U. S. Government Printing Office
Washington, D. C. 20402

Sioux love, death, dance and peyote songs
recorded and edited by Willard Rhodes.
33 1/3 rpm. $5. 40.

SIOUX AND CROW GRASS DANCES-SONGS
American Indian Soundchief
1415 Carlson Drive
Klamath Falls, Ore. 97601

Recorded by tribal singers.   33 1/3 rpm.
$4. 50.

SONGS OF THE CHIPPEWA
Library of Congress Music Division
c/o Superintendent of Documents
U. S. Government Printing Office
Washington, D. C. 20402

Chippewa dream songs, war songs, songs
for the treatment of the sick, and dancing
songs. Recorded and edited by Frances
Densmore. Five 78 rpm records, $9. 50;
one 33 1/3 rpm longplay record, $5. 40.

SONGS AND DANCES OF GREAT LAKES
  INDIANS
Folkways Records
165 W. 46th St.
New York, N. Y. 10036

Music of the Algonquins and Iroquois, including animal, medicine, pow wow, peace
and hunting songs and dances; eagle, bear
and deer songs and dances; flute melodies.
Recorded on location in Iowa, Wisconsin,
Michigan and New York State by Gertrude
P. Kurath. Text included. 12". 33 1/3
rpm. $6. 95.

SONGS FROM THE IROQUOIS LONGHOUSE
Library of Congress Music Division
c/o Superintendent of Documents
U.S. Government Printing Office
Washington, D.C. 20402

Selections include Creator's Songs, Mid-
winter Festival Chants, Medicine Men's
Celebration (Onondaga). Recorded and
edited by William N. Fenton in cooperation
with the Smithsonian Institution. Five 78
rpm. records, $9.50; one 33 1/3 rpm. long-
play record, $5.40.

SONGS OF THE MENOMINEE, MANDAN
  AND HIDATSA
Library of Congress Music Division
c/o Superintendent of Documents
U.S. Government Printing Office
Washington, D.C. 20402

Hunting, war, dream and legendary songs
and chants, recorded and edited by Frances
Densmore. 33 1/3 rpm. $5.40.

SONGS OF THE NOOTKA AND QUILEUTE
Library of Congress Music Division
c/o Superintendent of Documents
U.S. Government Printing Office
Washington, D.C. 20402

Potlatch, dancing and game songs, recorded
and edited by Frances Densmore. 33 1/3
rpm. $5.40.

SONGS OF THE PAPAGO
Library of Congress Music Division
c/o Superintendent of Documents
U.S. Government Printing Office
Washington, D.C. 20402

Songs related to legends, ceremonies, expeditions, and treatment of the sick; dream
songs, war songs, etc. Recorded and edited by Frances Densmore. 33 1/3 rpm.
$5.40.

SONGS OF THE PAWNEE AND NORTHERN
  UTE
Library of Congress Music Division
c/o Superintendent of Documents
U.S. Government Printing Office
Washington, D.C. 20402

Selections include Ghost Dance Songs, Buffalo and Lance Dance Songs, Hand Game

Songs, War Songs, and others. Recorded
and edited by Frances Densmore. 33 1/3
rpm. $5.40.

SONGS OF THE SIOUX
Library of Congress Music Division
c/o Superintendent of Documents
U.S. Government Printing Office
Washington, D.C. 20402

Sioux Sun Dance, War Dance, Grass Dance,
and other songs, recorded and edited by
Frances Densmore. 33 1/3 rpm. $5.40.

SONGS OF THE YUMA, COCOPA, AND
  YAQUI
Library of Congress Music Division
c/o Superintendent of Documents
U.S. Government Printing Office
Washington, D.C. 20402

Selections include Yuma and Yaqui Deer
Dance Songs; Cocopa Bird Dance Songs;
Yuma Lightning Songs; songs used in treatment of the sick, etc. Recorded and edited
by Frances Densmore. 33 1/3 rpm. $5.40.

SOUTHERN AND NORTHERN PLAINS
  TRIBES HONOR AND VICTORY DANCE
  SONGS
American Indian Soundchief
1415 Carlson Drive
Klamath Falls, Ore. 97601

Recorded by tribal singers. 33 1/3 rpm.
$4.50.

WAR WHOOPS AND MEDICINE SONGS
Folkways Records
165 W. 46th St.
New York, N.Y. 10036

Music of the American Indian, including
songs of the Winnebago, Chippewa, Sioux,
Zuni and Acoma, collected and edited by
Charles Hoffman. 12". 33 1/3 rpm. $6.95.

SONGBOOKS

SONGS OF THE WIGWAM
Cooperative Recreation Service
Delaware, Ohio 43015

Songbook (with written sheet music) of the
Ottawa and Chippewa Indians, "chosen for
their tunefulness and reflection of native
life and thought in the forests around the
Great Lakes." 1955. 22 pp. Illus. 25¢.

Government Publications

The following is a list of publications (primarily in paperback or pamphlet form) issued by various agencies of the Federal Government. The list is arranged by source, then alphabetically by publication title.

The following titles are available from: Publications Service, Haskell Institute, Lawrence, Kan. 66044.

AMERICAN INDIANS AND THE AMERICAN SOCIETY

Pamphlet containing remarks by Philleo Nash, former Commissioner of Indian Affairs. 1965. 6 pp.

AWAY TO SCHOOL
Cecil S. King

First in the series, *Navajo New World Readers,* intended to present a picture of off-reservation life to Indian adolescents. Paper. 15¢.

BLACKFEET CRAFTS
John C. Ewers

A description of the crafts of the Blackfoot Indians of Montana and Alberta (Can.), including painting, beadwork, quillwork, featherwork, pipemaking, and others. Illus. Paper. 50¢.

BRAVE AGAINST THE ENEMY
Ann (Nolan) Clark; illustrated with photographs by Helen Post

A tale of three generations of Indians. (English and Teton-Lakota text.) Junior and senior high school level. Cloth, $1.50; paper (English only), 75¢.

BRINGER OF THE MYSTERY DOG
Ann (Nolan) Clark; illustrated by Oscar Howe

How the horse (*mystery dog,* in the Dakota tongue) first came to the Sioux Indians of the Great Plains. Junior high school level. Paper. 35¢.

COYOTE TALES
William Morgan, Robert Young and Hildegard Thompson

Old Navajo children's tales collected and translated. Reader for the *Navajo Life Series.* Paper. 30¢.

A DIGEST OF INFORMATION ON THE EDUCATION OF INDIANS

Information related to the mission schools, Federal schools, and public accommodations which provide education for the American Indian. 1965.

DOORWAY TOWARD THE LIGHT
L. Madison Coombs

The story of the Special Navajo Education Program undertaken by the Bureau of Indian Affairs. Paper. $1.80.

DORMITORY LIFE: *Is It Living?*

An inservice training pamphlet which emphasizes the need for each child to have a varied program of dormitory living. Paper. 20¢.

DORMITORY RECREATION EQUIPMENT

A booklet to assist dormitory personnel in developing a recreational and leisure program for Indian boys and girls. Paper. 15¢.

EDUCATION FOR ACTION
Willard W. Beatty *and associates*

Reprints of selected articles which appeared between 1936 and 1943 in *Indian Education,* a semimonthly periodical for B. I. A. personnel, setting forth the philosophies, policies and practices of the Bureau of Indian Affairs as related to Indian education. $2.00.

EDUCATION FOR CROSS-CULTURAL
ENRICHMENT
     Hildegard Thompson *and associates*

Reprints of selected articles which appeared in *Indian Education* during the years
1952 through 1964. $1.30.

EDUCATION FOR CULTURAL ADJUST-
MENT: *A Special Five-Year Program for
Adolescent Indians*

The Special Navajo Education Program described in this pamphlet is designed to help
Navajo children, aged twelve to eighteen,
who have not previously attended school.
Paper. 15¢.

EDUCATION FOR CULTURAL CHANGE
     Willard W. Beatty *and associates*

Reprints of selected articles which appeared in *Indian Education* during the years
1944 through 1951. $2.75.

EDUCATIONAL ACHIEVEMENT OF
INDIAN CHILDREN
     Kenneth E. Anderson, E. Gordon Col-
     lister, and Carl E. Ladd

Re-examination of the question, How well
are Indian children educated? Cloth, $1.25;
paper, 80¢.

FIELD MOUSE GOES TO WAR
     Edward Kennard; illustrated by Fred
     Kabotie

A picture of Hopi ceremonial life, in English
and Hopi. Paper. 50¢.

THE FLAG OF MY COUNTRY
     Cecil S. King

Second in the series, *Navajo New World
Readers,* intended to present a picture of
off-reservation life to Indian adolescents.
Paper. 20¢.

FUNDAMENTAL EDUCATION IN AN
AMERINDIAN COMMUNITY
     Pedro T. Orata

A description of a community school program on the Pine Ridge Reservation, 1937
to 1938, and an evaluation of its effect on
the community. Cloth, $2.00; paper, $1.50.

THE GRASS MOUNTAIN MOUSE
     Ann (Nolan) Clark; illustrated by
     Andrew Standing Soldier

A story of Sioux life, in English and Teton-
Lakota text. Paper. 50¢.

HARNESSING THE BIG MUDDY
     Frances Cushman and Gordon Mac-
     Gregor

A text for junior and senior high school
levels about the Missouri Basin. Prepared
by the Missouri Basin Development Staff of
the Bureau of Indian Affairs. Illus. Cloth,
$1.75; paper, $1.25.

THE HEN OF WAHPETON
     Ann (Nolan) Clark; illustrated by
     Andrew Standing Soldier

Four stories of Indian life, in which a group
of animals personify Indian customs. Elementary school level. Paper. 50¢.

HERE COME THE NAVAHO!
     Ruth M. Underhill

A history of the Navaho people and their
adaptation to changing conditions since their
appearance in the Southwest. Junior and
senior high school level. Paper. Illus.
$1.00.

THE INDIAN CHILD GOES TO SCHOOL
     L. Madison Coombs, Ralph E. Kron,
     E. Gordon Collister, and Kenneth E.
     Anderson

A report of the testing program conducted
by the Bureau of Indian Affairs with the aid
of the University of Kansas. Paper. $1.20.

INDIAN LAND AND ITS CARE
     Edgar L. Wight, David P. Weston, and
     Clyde W. Hobbs

Booklet designed to inform Indian school-children and their parents about the condition of Indian land in the United States and to outline the methods used to maintain and improve the productive capacity of these lands. Junior and senior high school levels. Paper. 40¢.

THE INDIANS OF SOUTHERN CALIFORNIA
Ruth M. Underhill

A story of the Indians first encountered by Fra Junipero Serra in his journey along the Pacific Coast. Paper. 50¢.

INDIANS OF THE PACIFIC NORTHWEST
Ruth M. Underhill

A story of the Indians of the Northwest Coast and their relationship with the white man. Paper. $1.25.

IROQUOIS CRAFTS
Carrie A. Lyford

The crafts of the Six Nations of New York State, including a portfolio of Iroquois designs. Paper. 40¢.

LITTLE BOY WITH THREE NAMES
Ann (Nolan) Clark; illustrated by Tonita Lujan

A story of Taos Pueblo -- two little Indian boys spend their summer vacation learning things Indians should know, culminating in their participation in the Gallup Indian Ceremonial. Paper. 50¢.

LITTLE HERDER SERIES
Ann (Nolan) Clark; illustrated by Hoke Denetsosie

Prose stories telling of the life of a Navajo girl through the four seasons of the year. Third to fifth grade level. Series consists of *Little Herder in Spring, Little Herder in Summer, Little Herder in Autumn, Little Herder in Winter*. Paper. 50¢ each. *Four Seasons Series* (complete), $1.75.

LITTLE HOPI
Edward Kennard; illustrated by Charles Loloma

A series of short stories of Hopi child life. Paper. 40¢.

LITTLE MAN'S FAMILY (preprimer)
J. B. Enochs

Contents pertain to the family life of the Navajo. Illus. Paper. 20¢.

LITTLE MAN'S FAMILY (primer)
J. B. Enochs

Contents based on the family life of the Navajo. Illus. Paper. 20¢.

LITTLE MAN'S FAMILY (reader)
J. B. Enochs

Contents based on the family life of the Navajo. Illus. Paper. 50¢.

NAVAJO-ENGLISH DICTIONARY
Leon Wall and William Morgan

A Navajo vocabulary with English definitions. Paper. $1.00.

NAVAJO HISTORICAL SELECTIONS
Robert W. Young and William Morgan

Deals with the Navajo Tribe's involvement in events of historical significance. For older students and adults. Paper. $1.00.

NAVAJO LIFE SERIES (preprimer)
Hildegard Thompson; illustrated by Van Tsinnahjinnie

Contents based on Navajo life. Paper. 10¢.

NAVAJO LIFE SERIES (primer)
Hildegard Thompson; illustrated by Van Tsinnahjinnie

Contents based on Navajo life. 10¢.

NAVAJO NATIVE DYES
Nonabah G. Bryan and Stella Young

Relates the formulae for making Navajo dyes from plants, minerals, and other environmental elements. Paper. 50¢.

THE NEW TRAIL

A volume of creative writing by students of the Phoenix Indian School -- a presentation of contemporary life of eight Southwestern tribes. Paper. $1.45.

THE NORTHERN PAIUTE INDIANS
    Ruth M. Underhill

The story of the first inhabitants of the great basin of eastern California and Nevada. Paper. 60¢.

OJIBWA CRAFTS
    Carrie A. Lyford

Description of the crafts of this Great Lakes tribe, with a portfolio of Ojibwa (Chippewa) designs. Paper. 80¢.

ORIENTING NEW EMPLOYEES

A manual treating briefly the philosophy, policies and operations of the Bureau of Indian Affairs -- its responsibilities and relations concerning the Indian, and regulations pertaining to employees' rights. Paper. 50¢.

THE PAPAGO INDIANS OF ARIZONA AND THEIR RELATIVES THE PIMA
    Ruth M. Underhill

Story of the dwellers in the southern desert area of the United States. Paper. 50¢.

PEOPLE OF THE CRIMSON EVENING
    Ruth M. Underhill

A story of Papago life before the coming of the white man. Paper. $1.00.

THE PINE RIDGE PORCUPINE
    Ann (Nolan) Clark; illustrated by Andrew Standing Soldier

A story of Sioux life, in which animals personify Indian customs. Elementary level. Paper. 35¢.

PROTECT AND IMPROVE PRECIOUS INDIAN SOIL
    Evan L. Flory; cartoons by Robyn A. Toney

A photographic account of erosion on Indian land, with soil and moisture conservation practices for protecting and improving the soil. Upper elementary and high school levels. Paper. 30¢.

PUBLICATIONS PRICELIST

Lists publications available from Haskell Institute, with prices and descriptive material. Available free of charge.

PUEBLO CRAFTS
    Ruth M. Underhill

A collection of known facts about the crafts of the Pueblo Indians, including a definition of pottery and weaving types. Paper. 50¢.

QUILL AND BEADWORK OF THE WESTERN SIOUX
    Carrie A. Lyford

Describes the use of porcupine quills on buckskin, later replaced by trade beads imported by white traders. Contains a portfolio of design plates. Paper. 50¢.

THE RAMAH NAVAJOS
    Son of Former Many Beads; translated by Robert W. Young and William Morgan

Brochure deals with matters of historical significance relating to the Navajo Tribe. Paper. 10¢.

SCHOLARSHIPS FOR AMERICAN INDIAN YOUTH
    Amanda H. Finley

Booklet listing college, university and nursing school scholarships and fellowships; tribal grants, aids and loans; Federal grants, loans, scholarships and special training programs. Biblio. 46 pp. Paper. 1963. Single copies available free of charge.

SINGING SIOUX COWBOY
Ann (Nolan) Clark; illustrated by Andrew Standing Soldier

A reader depicting the life of a young Sioux in the prairie country. English and Teton-Lakota text. Elementary grade level. Paper. 50¢.

SLIM BUTTE RACCOON
Ann (Nolan) Clark; illustrated by Andrew Standing Soldier

A story of Sioux Indian life for elementary schoolchildren. Paper. 35¢.

SPRUCE ROOT BASKETRY OF THE ALASKA TLINGIT
Frances Paul

A portfolio of designs of the Tlingit Indians of southwest Alaska and the Pacific Northwest. Paper. 45¢.

STATISTICS CONCERNING INDIAN EDUCATION, *Fiscal Year 1964*

A compilation of current statistics related to Indian education. 1964. 37 pp.

THE STORY OF THE BLACKFEET
John C. Ewers

The story of the Montana and Canadian tribes who dominated the Northern Plains. Illus. Paper. 50¢.

THE STORY OF THE MISSISSIPPI CHOCTAWS
Thelma V. Bounds; illustrated by students of Conehatta School, Miss.

A history of the Choctaw Tribe for elementary level schoolchildren. Paper. 35¢.

SUGGESTED BOOKS FOR INDIAN SCHOOLS

An annotated list of textbooks, library books, maps, globes and charts chosen for their suitability for Indian schools. 1965. 50¢.

SUN JOURNEY
Ann (Nolan) Clark; illustrated by Percy Sandy

A story of Grandfather, the Zuni Sun Priest, and his ceremonial duties. Paper. 60¢.

THERE STILL ARE BUFFALO
Ann (Nolan) Clark; illustrated by Andrew Standing Soldier

The biography of a buffalo bull calf and his development. Junior high school level. Paper. 35¢.

THE TROUBLE AT ROUND ROCK
Left-Handed Mexican Clansman and others; translated by Robert W. Young and William Morgan

Deals with the Navajo Tribe's involvement in events of historical significance. Paper. 45¢.

WHO WANTS TO BE A PRARIE DOG?
Ann (Nolan) Clark; illustrated by Van Tsinnahjinnie

A story of Navajo life. Third grade level. Paper. 30¢.

WORKADAY LIFE OF THE PUEBLOS
Ruth M. Underhill

The story of the Indians who lived in villages of stone and adobe before the coming of the Spanish. Paper. $1.00.

YOUNG HUNTER OF PICURIS
Ann (Nolan) Clark; illustrated by Velino Herrera

The story of a turkey hunt. Paper. 30¢.

The following titles are available from various state agencies and area offices of the Bureau of Indian Affairs. The address of the source has been noted in the listing.

DIRECTORY OF TRIBAL OFFICIALS
Bureau of Indian Affairs
Portland Area Office
10002 N.E. Holladay
P.O. Box 3785
Portland, Ore. 97208

Lists by reservation or community name the tribal governments over which the Portland Area Office has jurisdiction, including names and addresses of tribal officials. 1964. 48 pp.

INDIAN RESERVATIONS OF THE
  NORTHWEST
Bureau of Indian Affairs
Portland Area Office
10002 N. E. Holladay
P. O. Box 3785
Portland, Ore. 97208
  Compiled and edited by W. L. Wight, Mary Mitchell and Marie Schmidt; illustrated by Lester Beal

Provides comprehensive information on Indian reservations in Idaho, Oregon and all areas of Washington, emphasizing the Indians' relationships with the Federal Government. 1960. 97 pp.

THE INDIAN TODAY IN NEW YORK STATE
State Interdepartmental Committee on
  Indian Affairs
New York State Department of Social
  Welfare
112 State St.
Albany, N. Y. 12201

Pamphlet provides information on all aspects of Indian life in New York State and the public services available to Indian citizens through various units of government. 1964. 16 pp. Biblio.

MINNESOTA'S INDIAN CITIZENS
Governor's Human Rights Commission
72 State Office Bldg.
St. Paul, Minn. 55101

Presents the historical background and a critical discussion of Indians in Minnesota today, including the history of the Minnesota Indian, particularly the Chippewa Tribe. Discusses the Revised Constitution and Bylaws of the Red Lake Band of Chippewa Indians; the five-year study of the Governor's Human Rights commission; the Van Loon Report; and the Attorney General's Opinion on Public Law 280. 1965. $1.00.

THE MONTANA-WYOMING INDIAN
Bureau of Indian Affairs
Billings Area Office
Billings, Mont.

Describes the economy, social and political status and way of life of the Montana and Wyoming Indian, with special emphasis on Federal policies and Indian education. 1965. 58 pp.

The following titles are available from the Smithsonian Institution, Washington, D. C.

ARCHAEOLOGY OF YAKUTAT BAY AREA,
  ALASKA

245 pp. Illus. (24 pls. , 4 maps). 1965. $3. 25.

ETHNOGRAPHY - HURON INDIANS,
  1615-49

183 pp. 1964. $1. 00.

GEORGE CATLIN, *Painter of Indians and*
  the West
  John C. Ewers

An account of George Catlin's experiences in painting American Indians, 1828 through 1838, with a critical appraisal of the value of his contribution to history, science, and art. Separate reprint of an article in the *Annual Report* of the Smithsonian Institution (pp. 483-528 and pl. 1-20). 1960. 55¢.

GUSTAVUS SOHON'S PORTRAITS OF
  FLATHEAD AND PEND D'OREILLE
  INDIANS, 1854
  John C. Ewers

An account of Sohon's experiences in picturing Indians of the Northwest, with a biographical sketch of the artist, and accounts of the Indians who were the subjects of his sketches, including historical descriptions of the tribes and biographies of the famous Indians pictured in portraits. Smithsonian Miscellaneous Collections, Vol. 110, No. 7, 1948. Illus. (20 pls.). $2. 00.

THE HORSE IN BLACKFOOT INDIAN CULTURE
John C. Ewers

A consideration of the acquisition of the horse by the Blackfoot Indians and of the roles played by the horse in historic Blackfoot culture, including detailed data on the use of the horse in hunting, moving camp, warfare, the role of the horse in trade, recreation, religion, etc., and comparative material from other Western tribes. Bureau of American Ethnology Bulletin 159, 1955. 374 pp. Illus. (17 pls., 33 figs.). $2.75.

IROQUOIS MUSIC AND DANCE, *Ceremonial Arts of Two Seneca Longhouses*

1964. 268 pp. Illus. $1.50.

ISLETA SANDPAINTINGS
Esther S. Goldfrank, Editor; Introduction and Commentary by Elsie C. Parsons

Depicts the ceremonies of a small pueblo culture south of Albuquerque, illustrated by a member of the community, including explanations of the ceremonies and descriptions of the objects used in them. 1962. 299 pp. Illus. $10.00.

THE PONCA TRIBE

Presents a delineation of Ponca history, culture, economy, costume, art, and other related subjects. A Bureau of American Ethnology Bulletin, 1965. 191 pp. Illus. (26 pls.). $2.25.

SEMINOLE MUSIC

1956. 233 pp. Illus. (18 pls.). $1.00.

SENECA THANKSGIVING RITUALS

1961. 302 pp. Illus. $2.25.

The following publications are available from the Superintendent of Documents, U.S. Government Printing Office, Washington, D.C. 20402.

AMERICAN INDIAN CALENDAR

Lists outstanding events that take place on Indian reservations during the year, including ceremonials, rodeos, fairs, feasts and celebrations; exhibitions of Indian art and handicrafts also noted. 1965. 51 pp. Illus. 20¢.

AMERICAN INDIANS AND THE FEDERAL GOVERNMENT

Pamphlet outlines in brief the historic relationships between American Indians and the Federal Government, and describes current programs of the Bureau of Indian Affairs. 1965. 26 pp. Illus. Biblio. 20¢.

ANSWERS TO QUESTIONS ABOUT AMERICAN INDIANS

Subjects covered include the Indian and his economy, resources, education, health, law, and government. Suggested supplementary reading lists are included. 1964. 36 pp. 20¢.

THE ARCHAEOLOGICAL SURVEY OF WETHERILL MESA, MESA VERDE NATIONAL PARK, COLORADO

One of series of research studies devoted to specialized topics which have been explored in connection with the National Park System, this report contains information on the results of excavations at Wetherill Mesa. 1964. 200 pp. Illus. $3.75.

AZTEC RUINS NATIONAL MONUMENT

Historical handbook tells the story of the men in San Juan Valley -- early hunters and gatherers, the basketmakers, the Pueblos, and the Aztec Pueblo. It describes the explorations and excavations of these well-preserved ruins, as well as the Ruins as they are today. 1963. 66 pp. Illus. 30¢.

BANDELIER NATIONAL MONUMENT, NEW MEXICO

Gives a brief history of the ancient Pueblo Indians who lived in the area, and describes the prehistoric ruins of the region. 1964. 14 pp. Illus. 15¢.

THE BARK CANOES AND SKIN BOATS OF
NORTH AMERICA

Contains descriptions of materials and tools
employed by Indian and Eskimo craftsmen
to build watercraft, including explanations
of procedures used. 1964. 242 pp. Appendix. Illus. $3.25.

BIG HOLE NATIONAL BATTLEFIELD,
MONTANA

Folder describing the Battle of Big Hole,
August 9-10, 1877. 5¢.

CANYON DE CHELLY NATIONAL
MONUMENT, ARIZONA

Pamphlet presents the story of Canyon de
Chelly, where prehistoric Indians lived and
modern Navajos build their summer *hogans*.
10¢.

CASA GRANDE RUINS NATIONAL
MONUMENT, ARIZONA

Pamphlet describes the Casa Grande, ancient watchtower-apartment house, and
portrays the lives of the former Indian inhabitants of Arizona's desert valleys. 5¢.

CHACO CANYON NATIONAL MONUMENT,
NEW MEXICO

Pamphlet describes the ruins of Chaco Canyon National Monument, site of archaeological excavations. 10¢.

CODE OF FEDERAL REGULATIONS

Publication contains codification of documents of general applicability and future
effect as of January 1, 1958, relating to
Indians. Ancillaries, index and supple-
ments (issued annually). 1958. 375 pp.
$4.50.

COLONIALS AND PATRIOTS

Part I presents the historical background
of the American Colonial period; Part II
consists of classified, evaluated descriptions of historic sites and structures. 1964.
320 pp. Illus. $2.75.

DIGEST OF DECISIONS OF THE
DEPARTMENT OF THE INTERIOR IN
CASES RELATING TO THE PUBLIC
LANDS

Includes material related to Indian land holdings, etc.

THE ECONOMIC OPPORTUNITY ACT
OF 1964

Implications of the Economic Opportunity
Act for American Indians. 1964. Single
copies available free of charge.

EDUCATION - *The Chance to Choose*

Remarks by Philleo Nash, former Commissioner of Indian Affairs, June, 1965. Single
copies available free of charge.

EXCAVATIONS AT CLAY BANK, IN
GLOUCESTER COUNTY, VA., 1962-63

Contains a description and analysis of late
17th- and early 18th-century artifacts ranging from crude earthenwares to the stem
and foot of an elaborate drinking glass or
candlestick now in the collections of the
Smithsonian Institution. Contributions from
the Museum of History and Technology, Paper 52. 28 pp. Illus. 1964.

EXCAVATIONS IN A 17th-CENTURY
JUMANO PUEBLO GRAN QUIVARA

1964. 168 pp. Illus. $1.25.

GOVERNING BODIES OF INDIAN GROUPS
UNDER FEDERAL SUPERVISION

A list of Indian tribal groups, listing address and name and title of presiding officer. 1965. 13 pp.

IMPLEMENTATION OF THE ECONOMIC
OPPORTUNITY ACT OF 1964

Excerpts from an address of Philleo Nash,
former Commissioner of Indian Affairs,
October, 1964.

INDIAN AFFAIRS

In this progress report from former Commissioner of Indian Affairs Nash are facts about current Bureau of Indian Affairs programs to benefit American Indians -- programs for education and other community services, and for economic development of reservations. 1964. 28 pp. Illus. 15¢.

THE INDIAN BUREAU AND THE WAR ON POVERTY

Remarks by Philleo Nash, former Commissioner of Indian Affairs, June 18, 1964. 7 pp. Single copies available free of charge.

INDIANS - AS CITIZENS

A sheet on the civil and other rights of the American Indian. 1963. Single copies available free of charge.

INDIANS - AS YOUR HOSTS

Booklet listing Indian celebrations and festivities open to the public. Single copies available free of charge.

INDIANS - LANGUAGES

A note on Indian languages, including a bibliography. 1965. Single copies available free of charge.

INDIANS OF . . .

A series of twelve pamphlets dealing with the history and contemporary life of various Indian tribes, including: *Indians of Oklahoma; Indians of North Carolina; Indians, Eskimos and Aleuts of Alaska; Indians of Arizona; Indians of New Mexico; Indians of Montana and Wyoming; Indians of the Pacific Northwest; Indians of California; Indians of the Dakotas; Indians of the Great Lakes Region; Indians of Florida and the Gulf Coast; Indians of Kansas-Nebraska.* 15¢ each.

INDIANS ON FEDERAL RESERVATIONS

A series of seven booklets, starting in 1958, giving a summary of location, land, tribes, population, education, economic characteristics, health, and special problems.

INDIANS - RELIGIONS AND CEREMONIALS

A note on Indian ceremonials, including a bibliography. 1964. Single copies available free of charge.

INDIANS - SURVIVING GROUPS IN EASTERN AND SOUTHERN STATES

A listing by state of the remaining Indian groups and scattered communities in the Eastern and Southern United States, including tribe, approximate location, and supervising agency, if any. 1963. Single copies available free of charge.

INDIANS - WARS AND LOCAL DISTURBANCES

A list of Indian-related wars and uprisings from 1782 to 1898, with an extensive bibliography. 1963. Single copies available free of charge.

LAW AND ORDER ON INDIAN RESERVATIONS

A leaflet which answers recurring questions related to the maintenance of police and other means of protection on Indian reservations. 1965.

MESA VERDE NATIONAL PARK, COLORADO

Describes the preservation of the ruins of prehistoric Indian dwellings on the mesa tops and in the caves of nearby canyons and relates the story of the life and culture of the inhabitants. 15¢.

MINERAL RESOURCES OF SAN CARLOS INDIAN RESERVATION, ARIZONA

1956. Illus. (3 maps). $1.25.

MONTEZUMA CASTLE NATIONAL MONUMENT, ARIZONA

Relates the story of Montezuma Castle, a cliff dwelling, and of its inhabitants. 1958. 40 pp. Illus. 25¢.

MOUND CITY GROUP NATIONAL
MONUMENT, OHIO

Presents the story of the life and culture
of the Hopewell people and the prehistoric
Indian burial mounds in southern Ohio. 10¢.

NAVAJO NATIONAL MONUMENT,
ARIZONA

Describes three Indian cliff dwellings, the
remains of ancient occupancy of northeastern Arizona's canyon country. Being revised.

OCMULGEE NATIONAL MONUMENT,
GEORGIA

Pamphlet tells the story of each of the six
successive occupations by different Indian
groups of the surrounding area, from prehistoric times to the 18th century.   5¢.

PIPESTONE NATIONAL MONUMENT,
MINNESOTA

Presents the story of the Minnesota quar-
ries from which the Plains and other Indians obtained the red stone (*catlinite*, named
for the noted Indian painter, George Catlin)
for making tobacco pipes.   10¢.

PUEBLO OF SIA, NEW MEXICO

1962. 358 pp. Illus. (12 pls., map). $2.75.

POVERTY IN THE UNITED STATES

Basic information relative to problems of
poverty in the U. S. , formulated by the Committee on Education and Labor, House of
Representatives (88th Congress, 2nd Session), including material relevant to the
income and health problems of Indians.
Biblio. 1964. 304 pp.

QUESTIONS AND ANSWERS ABOUT INDIAN
ALLOTMENTS ON PUBLIC LANDS

Booklet prepared by the U. S. Department
of the Interior and the Department of Agriculture providing information on the allotment of public lands to qualified Indian applicants. 10 pp.

RUSSELL CAVE NATIONAL
MONUMENT, ALABAMA

Folder depicts the life and culture of the
prehistoric inhabitants of Russell Cave.
10¢.

TONTO NATIONAL MONUMENT,
ARIZONA

Folder presents the story of the 14th-cen-
tury cliff dwellings of the Arizona Salado
Tribe, noted as craftsmen of the prehistoric
Pueblo Indian grouping.   10¢.

TUZIGOOT NATIONAL MONUMENT,
ARIZONA

Describes the excavated ruins of the prehistoric pueblo that flourished between the
12th and 15th centuries, A. D.   5¢.

VACATIONING WITH INDIANS

A guide to tourist campgrounds and attractions on Indian reservations. 1965. 74 pp.
Illus. 30¢.

WALNUT CANYON NATIONAL
MONUMENT, ARIZONA

Folder discusses the inhabitants of more
than three hundred small, prehistoric cliff
dwellings. 5¢.

Newspapers, Magazines and Periodicals

Arranged alphabetically by publication name, this section lists the related publications of historical societies, archaeological and anthropological societies, etc. Listings detail nature of publication, special related features, personnel (editor), publication frequency. An asterisk (*) indicates publisher failed to complete and return questionnaire.

AMERICAN HERITAGE
551 Fifth Ave.
New York, N. Y. 10017
    Bruce Catton, Editor

Covers all aspects and periods of American history, with frequent articles on Indian personalities, events associated with the Indian, and interaction between the Indian and white communities and their individual members. Extensive use of illustrations and photographs -- many in color. Hardbound. Published every two months with an annual index appearing in February. Single copies, $2.95. Year's subscription, $12.50 (U.S.); $13.50 (foreign).

AMERICAN JOURNAL OF ARCHAEOLOGY
Archaeological Institute of America
100 Washington Square East
New York, N. Y. 10003

Professional archaeological journal; carries book reviews on New World archaeology. Quarterly. $10.00.

THE AMERINDIAN
1263 W. Pratt Blvd.
Chicago, Ill. 60626
    Marian E. Gridley, Editor and
    Publisher

National in scope, bimonthly presents news of personalities and developments in Indian affairs. Book review column. $3.00 per year.

*ANNALS OF WYOMING
Wyoming State Archives
    and Historical Department
State Office Building
Cheyenne, Wyo.

ANTHROPOLOGICAL PAPERS
The American Museum of Natural History
Central Park West at 79th St.
New York, N.Y. 10024

Contains the current reports of the Museum's Department of Anthropology. Publication established in 1906 and devoted exclusively to anthropology.

ARCHAEOLOGICAL NEWSLETTER
Section of Man
Carnegie Museum
Pittsburgh, Penna. 15213

Mimeographed newsletter issued "as a service to local archaeologists." Contains local related news and periodic reports on findings of expeditions conducted by the Carnegie Museum. Published three times annually.

ARCHAEOLOGY
Archaeological Institute of America
100 Washington Square East
New York, N.Y. 10003

A popular illustrated magazine written by archaeologists for intelligent laymen. Consistent treatment of the archaeology of North or South American Indians; book reviews on the art and archaeology of the Americas. Quarterly. $5.00 per year.

*ARKANSAS HISTORICAL QUARTERLY
University of Arkansas
Fayetteville, Ark.

THE BEAVER
Hudson's Bay Co.
79 Main St.
Winnipeg 1, Man., Can.
    Malvina Bolus, Editor

Magazine devoted to the history and present-day life and culture of the Hudson's Bay

(Canada) area. Includes numerous articles on Canadian Indians and Eskimos. Book review section, *Northern Books,* included. Quarterly. $2.00 per year.

BULLETIN
The Archaeological Society of New Jersey
New Jersey State Museum
McCrullish and Quigley (Sts.)
Trenton, N. J.
J. Alden Mason, Editor

Contains articles on the archaeology of New Jersey and the surrounding region. Published semiannually and sent free with membership in the Archaeological Society of New Jersey. Individual issues, $1.00 each.

BULLETIN
The Archaeological Society of Virginia
1946 Lansing Ave.
Richmond, Va. 23225

Contains articles on Virginia Indians, archaeology, and colonial history. Quarterly. Library subscription, $3.00 per year.

BULLETIN OF THE BUREAU OF
   AMERICAN ETHNOLOGY
Smithsonian Institution
Washington, D.C. 20560

Publishes numerous articles relating to American Indian life and culture. "Applicants for publications are requested to state the grounds for their requests as the Institution is able to supply papers only as an aid to the researches or studies in which applicants are especially interested. Publications are available in most large libraries in the U.S. and abroad. Requests for publications should be addressed to the Publications Distribution Section, Editorial and Publications Division, Smithsonian Institution, Washington, D.C. 20560."

THE CHRONICLES OF OKLAHOMA
Oklahoma Historical Society
Oklahoma City, Okla. 73105
   Muriel H. Wright, Editor

Publication treats events, places and personalities in Oklahoma history, often touching upon events related to the American Indian. Footnotes and information sources

given. Book review section included. Quarterly. Publication free with membership in The Oklahoma Historical Society ($5.00 per year).

*COLORADO INFORMATION
   PUBLICATIONS
100 W. 13th Ave.
Denver, Colo.

*CORVALLIS
P.O. Box 122
Corvallis, Ore.

*EL PALACIO
Archaeological Society of New Mexico
124 E. Lupita Rd.
Santa Fe, N. M.

*ETHNOHISTORY
I.U. Press Building
Indiana University
10th & Morton Sts.
Bloomington, Ind.

THE FLORIDA HISTORICAL QUARTERLY
Florida Historical Society
P.O. Box 3645
University Station
Gainesville, Fla. 32601

"The offical publication of the Florida Historical Society, *The Florida Historical Quarterly* has numerous articles on Florida Indians, including an entire special issue on Osceola."

*FOCUS
American Geographical Society
Broadway at 156th St.
New York, N.Y. 10032

FRONTIER TIMES (MAGAZINE)
Western Publications, Inc.
P.O. Box 3668
Austin, Texas 78704
   Pat Wagner, Editor

Accounts of Western history dealing with events, places, personalities, legends, etc., some of which relate to the Indian and notable Indian historical figures. Many illustrations and photographs. Book review section, *Western Book Roundup*, included. Issued bimonthly. $4.00 per year.

*GEOGRAPHY JOURNAL
National Council for Geographic
Education
Box 303
Faculty Exchange
University of Oklahoma
Norman, Okla. 73069

INDIAN AFFAIRS
Association on American Indian Affairs, Inc.
432 Park Ave., S.
New York, N.Y. 10016
William Byler, Executive Editor

Covers current news about and of interest to American Indians, and to those interested in Indian affairs. Published five times yearly (minimum), with occasional special issues. $3.00 per year.

INDIAN LIFE
Inter-Tribal Indian Ceremonial Association
P.O. Box 1029
Gallup, N.M. 87301
Edward S. Merry, Editor

Publication treats Indian history, current events, present-day and historical personalities; Indian religion, cooking, arts and crafts; listings of exhibits of Indian artifacts and art; sidelights. Published once yearly. $1.00 per copy.

INDIAN PROGRESS
Associated Executive Committee
of Friends on Indian Affairs
1403 - 21st St.
Central City, Neb. 68826
Lindley J. Cook, Educational Secretary

Newsletter of the Associated Executive Committee of Friends on Indian Affairs (a Quaker organization). Reports Committee news and general information about and/or of interest to the Indian community, and to those interested in Indian affairs. $2.00 per year.

INDIAN RECORD
Canadian Publishers, Ltd.
207-276 Main St.
Winnipeg, Man., Can.
Rev. G. Laviolette, O.M.I.,
Editor and Manager

A national publication for the Indians of Canada. Highlights local news, present-day and historical personalities, Indian culture. Published ten times yearly. Single issues, 10¢ each; year's subscription.

*INDIAN SENTINEL
Bureau of Catholic Indian Missions
2021 "H" St., N.W.
Washington 6, D.C.

INDIAN TRUTH
Indian Rights Association, Inc.
1505 Race St.
Philadelphia, Penn. 19102
Lawrence E. Lindley, Editor

National in scope, publication reports current developments in Indian affairs. $2.00 per year.

*JOURNAL OF AMERICAN INDIAN
EDUCATION
College of Education
Arizona State University
Tempe, Ariz.
Robert A. Roessel, Editor

THE JOURNAL OF ARIZONA HISTORY
Arizona Pioneers' Historical Society
949 E. 2nd St.
Tucson, Ariz. 85719
Andrew Wallace, Editor

Publication treats events, places and personalities in Arizona history, often touching upon events related to the American Indian. Many photographs and illustrations; footnotes and information sources given. Book review section, *Books in the Saddlebag*, included.

*THE KIVA
Arizona Archaeological and
Historical Society
Tucson, Ariz.

*LONE INDIAN
Lone Indian Fellowship
2135 1/4 E. Eldorado St.
Decatur, Ill.

*LORE
Friends of the Museum
Milwaukee Public Museum
818 W. Wisconsin Ave.
Milwaukee 3, Wis.

THE MASTERKEY
Southwest Museum
Highland Park
Los Angeles, Calif. 90042
     Bruce Bryan, Editor

Publication devoted to the "Indian lore and
history" of the Southwest. Photographs and
illustrations, information sources given.
Book reviews included. Published quarterly. Available at $3.50 per year; sent
free to Southwest Museum members.

MINNESOTA HISTORY
The Minnesota Historical Society
690 Cedar St.
St. Paul, Minn. 55101
     Russell W. Fridley,
       Editor-in-Chief

Magazine deals with events, places and personalities in Minnesota history, often touching upon events related to Minnesota's Indian
tribes. Published quarterly. Sent free with
membership in The Minnesota Historical
Society; individual issues, $1.00.

MONTANA, *The Magazine of Western
     History*
Montana Historical Society
Roberts and Sixth Ave.
Helena, Mont. 59601

Deals with Western history, often touching
upon the Indian's involvement. Published
quarterly at $1.00 per issue.

N.C.A.I. SENTINEL
National Congress of American Indians
1346 Connecticut Ave., N.W.
Washington, D.C. 20036

Publication covers current news about and
of interest to American Indians, and to those
interested in Indian affairs.

THE NEW MEXICO HISTORICAL REVIEW
The University of New Mexico
Albuquerque, N.M. 87106
     Eleanor B. Adams, Editor

Concerned with events, places and personalities in New Mexico history, often touching upon events related to the American Indian. Published quarterly. Sent free with
membership in the Historical Society of New
Mexico ($6.00 per year).

*NEW MEXICO MAGAZINE
Department of Development
State of New Mexico
Santa Fe, N.M.

*NEWSLETTER
Oklahoma Anthropological Society, Inc.
University of Oklahoma
Norman, Okla. 73069

*NORTH DAKOTA QUARTERLY
University of North Dakota Press
Grand Forks, N.D.

OLD WEST (MAGAZINE)
Western Publications, Inc.
P.O. Box 3668
Austin, Texas 78704
     Pat Wagner, Editor

Accounts of Western history, dealing with
events, places, personalities, legends,
etc., many related to the American Indian.
Most articles signed. Book review section,
Western Book Roundup, included. Issued
quarterly. 50¢ per copy.

*OREGON HISTORICAL QUARTERLY
Oregon Historical Society
235 S.W. Market St.
Portland 1, Ore.

THE PALIMPSEST
State Historical Society of Iowa
Centennial Bldg.
Iowa City, Iowa 52240
     William J. Petersen, Editor

Articles deal with the history of the Indian in
Iowa. Generous use of photographs, illustrations and maps. Published monthly.

Sent free with membership in the State
Historical Society of Iowa ($3.00 per year);
individual issues available at 25¢ (regular
issues) or 50¢ (special issues).

*PLAINS ANTHROPOLOGIST
Plains Conference
Research Institute
North Campus
University of Oklahoma
Norman, Okla. 73069

POWWOW TRAILS
Box 268
Somerset, N.J. 08873
    William K. Powers, Editor and
    Publisher

A bimonthly newsletter for American Indian
buffs and hobbyists, with information on
Indian celebrations, current events, arts
and crafts, dancing and music, costume
making; reports on powwows; scholarly and
lay articles. Also contains material about
activities in England, France, Germany,
Holland, Switzerland and Canada which relate to the American Indian. $3.00 per
year; two-year subscription, $5.00.

REAL WEST
Charlton Publications, Inc.
Division St.
Derby, Conn. 06418
    Philip R. Rand, Editor

Accounts of Western history, dealing with
events, places, personalities, legends, etc.,
some related to the American Indian. Many
illustrations and photographs; some reprints. Most articles signed; information
sources and bibliography either listed or
available from each author upon request.
Continuing department, *The American Indian*, written by Nono Minor, Curator of
Plains Indians, Kansas City Museum of
History. Book review section, *Bunkhouse
Bookshelf*, included.

SCIENCE OF MAN
10421 Lampson Ave.
Garden Grove, Calif. 92640
    Joseph E. Vincent, Editor

"A magazine devoted to the story of Man,
his works and his past, and to the popular

presentation of the . . . story of archaeology, ethnology, and the other sciences of
man." Published bimonthly. $4.00 per
year.

SOUTHERN INDIAN STUDIES
The Archaeological Society of North
  Carolina
Box 561
Chapel Hill, N.C. 27514

"Established . . . as a medium of publication and discussion of information pertaining to the life and customs of the Indians in
the Southern states, both prehistoric and
historic." Sent free with membership in
The Archaeological Society of North Carolina ($3.00 per year). Non-member sub-
scriptions, $1.00.

*SOUTHWESTERN HISTORICAL
  QUARTERLY
8059 University Station
Austin 12, Texas

SOUTHWESTERN LORE
The Colorado Archaeological Society
University of Colorado
Boulder, Colo. 80304
    David A. Breternitz, Editor

An archaeological quarterly of the Southwest. Sent free with membership in The
Colorado Archaeological Society ($2.50 per
year).

*SOUTHWESTERNER
Saddlebag Press
Box 217
Columbus, N.M.

*THE TOTEM POLE
Aboriginal Research Club
6584 Balfour St.
Allen Park, Mich.

TRUE WEST (MAGAZINE)
Western Publications, Inc.
P.O. Box 3668
Austin, Texas 78704
    Pat Wagner, Editor

Accounts of Western history, dealing with
events, places, personalities, legends, etc.,

some of which relate to the American Indian. Most articles signed. Book review section, *Western Book Roundup,* included. Issued bimonthly. $4.00 per year.

TUNDRA TIMES
Box 1287
Fairbanks, Alaska 99701
    Howard Rock, Editor

Published twice monthly, newspaper reports news about and of interest to Alaskan natives, and to those interested in native affairs. Year's subscription (Alaska), $6.00 per year; other states, $7.00 per year.

VILTIS (HOPE) MAGAZINE
P.O. Box 1226
Denver, Colo. 80201
    V. F. Beliajus, Editor and Publisher

While primarily a magazine of dance and folklore, *Viltis* treats periodically various aspects of Indian culture -- medicine, tribal history, dances, etc. Published six times annually. $3.50 per year.

WALAM-A-WAGAN
Box 5
Perry, Me. 04667

Mimeographed weekly reports news about and of interest to the Passamaquoddy Tribe (Maine), and to those interested in Tribal affairs.

THE WISCONSIN ARCHAEOLOGIST
Wisconsin Archaeological Society
2243 S. Woodward
Milwaukee, Wis. 53207

Published quarterly "for the purpose of advancing the study and preservation of Wisconsin Indian antiquities." Figures, photographs, charts; information sources given. Book review section, *The Bookshelf,* included. Sent free with membership in the Wisconsin Archaeological Society (Annual, $3.00; Institutional, $3.00; Sustaining, $5.00; Life, $50.00; Endowment, $500.00).

*WRITINGS ON AMERICAN HISTORY
American Historical Association
400 "A" St., S.E.
Washington 3, D.C.

Bibliography

This section contains an alphabetical listing of approximately 2,000 in-print books about or relating to Indians of North America. In each listing, the reader will find -- where sufficient material has been provided -- the title, author or editor, a short description of content, information on pagination, whether illustrated, indexed, etc., name of publisher, the year of publication, and price. The addresses of the publishers are contained in the *Publisher Index*. Length of listings reflects the amount of material received. An asterisk (*) preceding a title indicates it is of primarily juvenile or young adult interest; the specific age group for which such titles are intended has been noted, if available. If you require material on a particular subject or interest area, refer to the subject listings in the *Subject Classifications* section. For additional titles, see *Government Publications*.

A

ABORIGINAL AMERICAN ORATORY: *The Tradition of Eloquence Among the Indians of the United States*
Louis Thomas Jones
A study of American Indian oratory, with extended quotations from Red Jacket, Pontiac, Black Hawk, Red Cloud, Chief Joseph, and many others. 160 pp. 23 pls. Southwest Museum, 1964. $5.00.

ABORIGINAL CALIFORNIA: *Three Studies in Culture History*
Edited by Robert F. Heizer and Albert B. Elsasser
University of California Press, $3.50.

AN ABORIGINAL QUARTZITE QUARRY IN EASTERN WYOMING
G. A. Dorsey
13 pp. 12 halftones. Fieldiana: Anthropology Vol. II, No. 4, Chicago Natural History Museum. 50¢.

ABORIGINAL RELATIONSHIPS BETWEEN CULTURE AND PLANT LIFE IN THE UPPER GREAT LAKES REGION
Richard Asa Yarnell
218 pp. 4 maps. Fig. Anthropological Papers No. 23, Museum of Anthropology, University of Michigan Press, 1964. $2.50.

ACCULTURATION AND MATERIAL CULTURE - I
George I. Quimby and Alexander Spoehr
41 pp. 29 illus. Fieldiana: Anthropology Vol. 36, No. 6, Chicago Natural History Museum, 1951. $1.00.

ACCULTURATION IN SEVEN AMERICAN INDIAN TRIBES
R. Linton
Peter Smith, $7.50.

ACOMA, THE SKY CITY
Mrs. W. T. Sedgwick
Reprint of the 1927 edition. A study in Pueblo Indian history and civilization, describing how the Spanish conquistadors besieged and reduced Acoma, an ancient city built high on an inaccessible mesa in New Mexico. The Rio Grande Press, Inc., 1964. $7.50.

*ACROSS FROM INDIAN SHORE
Barbara Robinson; illustrated by Evaline Ness
"Young Luke's fondest wish was to meet the real Indian princess who lived across the lake. Luke gathered the courage to row across only when his mother desperately needed help." Grades 4 to 6. Lothrop, Lee & Shepard Co., 1962. $3.70.

ADVENTURES IN THE UNKNOWN INTERI-
OR OF AMERICA
    Cabeza de Vaca; edited and translated
    by Cyclone Covey
Peter Smith, $3.00.

ADVENTURES IN THE WILDERNESS
    Clark Wissler and others
Illus. United States Publishers' Association, Inc., $10.75.

THE ADVENTURES OF CAPTAIN BONNE-
VILLE
    Washington Irving; illustrated by Robert
    Reynolds
An account of three years of travel and ex-
ploration in the northern Rocky Mountain
country from 1832 to 1835, by the author of
The Legend of Sleepy Hollow, Astoria, and
others. 375 pp. Illus. Maps. Appendices.
Biblio. Index. Binfords & Mort, $6.00.

THE ADVENTURES OF CAPTAIN BONNE-
VILLE, U.S.A., *in the Rocky Mountains
and the Far West*
    Washington Irving; edited by Edgeley
    W. Todd
As above. 424 pp. Illus. Maps. Appendices. Editor's biblio. Annotations. Index. University of Oklahoma Press, 1961.
$7.95.

THE ADVENTURES OF DAVY CROCKETT
    David Crockett
Selected narrative from the journal of Davy
Crockett, written in 1834. Included also is
"Colonel Crockett's Texas Exploits," which
ends with the defense of the Alamo. 246 pp.
Illus. Charles Scribner's Sons, 1955.
$3.95.

*THE ADVENTURES OF LEWIS AND
CLARK
    John Bakeless; illustrated by B. Holmes
Describes the expedition of Meriwether
Lewis and William Clark (with their Indian
guide, Sacajawea) which led them, in 1803,
across the newly acquired Western lands.
Grades 7 to 11. Houghton Mifflin Co., 1962.
$1.95.

THE ADVENTURES OF ZENAS LEONARD
    John C. Ewers, Editor
Includes extensive first-hand accounts of
the Crow and other Indians of the Rocky
Mountain-Great Basin region, by a mountain man who knew these Indians in the early
1830's. University of Oklahoma Press,
1959. $4.00.

ADVENTURES ON THE COLUMBIA RIVER
    Ross Cox; edited by Alfred Powers
Condensed from the 1831 edition. A sourcebook of adventures on the Columbia, written
by an Astor party man, later of the Hudson's
Bay Company. Records encounters with
native Indians, describes their customs and
ways of life, tells about hardships of hunger
and cold and of being lost in the wilderness.
124 pp. Photos. Binfords & Mort, 1957.
$2.50.

AGRICULTURAL AND HUNTING METHODS
OF THE NAVAHO INDIANS
    Hill
Human Relations Area Files Press, 1964.
$5.00.

*AGUK OF ALASKA
    Nancy M. Webb
"Aguk is a twelve-year-old boy living in the
Arctic Circle. The outer world of the wilds
is cold, mysterious, and full of the experiences of growing and of eternal dangers, but
the inner world of (his) igloo and family life
is warm and full of tradition and content-
ment." 64 pp. Illus. Prentice-Hall, Inc.,
1963. $3.50.

AL SIEBER, CHIEF OF SCOUTS
    Dan L. Thrapp
432 pp. Map. Illus. Biblio. Index. University of Oklahoma Press, 1964. $6.95.

ALASKA IN TRANSITION: *The Southeast
Region*
    George W. Rogers
The author examines the resource economics and politics of southeast Alaska and
contends that creation of the proper attitudes
and atmosphere to assist in the Indian's
adaptation to a rapidly changing economic
and social environment is of crucial importance to the Indian and also to the future of
the region, for it will determine the role he
will play in the future and will set limits
upon it. Also discussed are the Indian Reorganization Act, the Johnson-O'Malley
Act, and the General Allotment Act, among
other pertinent legislation. 384 pp. The
Johns Hopkins Press, 1960. $7.00.

ALASKA INDIAN BASKETRY
    L. W. MacDowell
A facsimile of the 1904 edition. Discussion
of types of baskets, how they are made, and
how to start a collection. 14 pp. Illus.
Paper. Shorey Publications, 1966. $1.00.

ALASKA INDIAN DICTIONARY: *Common Words in the Dialects of the Aleutian Indian Language*
Compiled by Charles A. Lee
A facsimile of the 1896 edition. 23 pp. Appendix. Shorey Publications, 1965. $1.00.

*ALASKA, THE FORTY-NINTH STATE
Willis Lindquist; Foreword by Ernest Gruening
An illustrated introduction to Alaska -- as it was, and as it is today. Grades 4 to 6. McGraw-Hill Book Co., 1959. $3.00.

*ALASKA: *The Land and the People*
Evelyn I. Butler and George A. Dale
Illus. Grades 6 to 9. Viking Press, 1957. $3.75

ALASKAN ESKIMO CEREMONIALISM
Margaret Lantis
The ceremonies studied include those marking life crises; hunting festivals; memorial feasts; secret society performances; and fishing, hunting, building, and war rituals. Maps. An American Ethnological Society Monograph reissued by the University of Washington Press. $5.00.

ALEUT DIALECTS OF ATKA AND ATTU
Knut Bergsland
Presents ethnolinguistic material from the western dialects of Aleut. Part I deals with proper names: the names of the nation and the ancient Aleut tribes, with a historical and demographic survey; personal names; approximately 1,000 place names, with maps and photographs and an introductory formal and semantic analysis. Part II contains modern and older texts and translations; the bulk of the modern texts are tape recordings of historical tradition dealing with former intertribal fights, with life of the Aleuts under the Russian regime, and with the coming of the Americans after the purchase of Alaska in 1867. 128 pp. 23 figs. 26 maps. American Philosophical Society, 1959. $3.00

THE ALEUT LANGUAGE
R. H. Geoghegan
Paper. Shorey Publications, 1944. $5.00.

ALLUVIAL AND PALYNOLOGICAL RECONSTRUCTION OF ENVIRONMENTS, NAVAJO RESERVOIR DISTRICT
James Schoenwetter and Frank W. Eddy, with sections by Eleanor Jane Nettle

Discusses two thousand years of environmental change in northwestern New Mexico and its effect on prehistoric cultures by integrating geological, palynological, faunal and archaeological research approaches. Illus. Biblio. 156 pp. Papers in Anthropology No. 13, Museum of New Mexico Press, 1964. $3.00

ALMOST WHITE
Brewton Berry
The story of a little-known minority racial group of Americans -- part white, part Negro, part Indian -- who are rebuffed by whites, unwilling to identify themselves with Negroes, and only partially accepted by Indians. Illus. The Macmillan Co., 1963. $5.95.

THE AMAZING RED MAN
Mack Parker
Describes the manner in which the Indian has survived despite many hardships, and recounts his contributions to American culture. Covers over 150 tribes. 76 pp. The Naylor Co., 1960. $1.95.

*AMERICA AND ITS INDIANS
Jerome Leavitt
As below. Grades 3 to 6. Children's Press, Inc., $5.50.

*AMERICA AND ITS INDIANS
Jerome E. Leavitt; illustrated by Robert Glaubke
A review of the distinctive facets of American Indian culture, from coast to coast -- food, housing, clothes, crafts, customs, forms of government, social life, and religion, from the ancient period to the present day. 220 pp. Grades 3 to 6. Grosset & Dunlap, Inc., 1962. $4.95.

THE AMERICAN HERITAGE BOOK OF INDIANS
By the editors of *American Heritage*; Introduction by President John F. Kennedy
Account follows the thread of history, century by century, of all the Indians, as they affected each other and the white man, and as the white man affected them. The narrative touches upon times as early as 20,000 B.C., tells about the first peoples who came to America from Asia, and carries the story of these different peoples, and the places where they lived and roamed, to the present day. 424 pp. Illus. American Heritage Publishing Co., 1961; distributed

by Simon and Schuster, Inc. Regular edition, $15.00; deluxe edition, $17.50.

THE AMERICAN HERITAGE HISTORY OF
THE GREAT AMERICAN WEST
By the editors of *American Heritage*
The story of the opening of the West -- the mountain men, the trappers, the Indians of forest and plain, the prospectors, outlaws, cowboys, etc., who lived the saga of America's epic push westward. 416 pp. Illus. American Heritage Publishing Co., 1965; distributed by Simon and Schuster, Inc. Regular edition, $16.50; deluxe edition, $19.00.

*THE AMERICAN INDIAN
William Brandon and Anne Terry White
For ages 10 to 14. Random House, 1963. $5.95.

*THE AMERICAN INDIAN
Oliver LaFarge; illustrated by Andre
Durenceau
A complete history. Illus. Photos. Golden Press, 1960. $4.95.

THE AMERICAN INDIAN
Sue Northey
Describes the life, habits and environment of the Indian tribes, and the contributions each has made. Tells their earliest known origins and divides them into their original four groupings: Woodlands, Plains, Southwest, and Northwest. Glossary. Illus. Index. Biblio. The Naylor Co., 1962. $4.95.

AMERICAN INDIAN ARTS, A WAY OF LIFE
Julia M. Seton
Captures the vanishing arts and handicrafts of the Indians of North America through a presentation of the distinctive skills of each tribe in creating the necessities of daily life as well as artistic accomplishments in painting, music, and other art forms. Full instructions on how to make decorative and utilitarian objects through the processes employed by the Iroquois, Chippewa, Hopi, Navajo, and other tribes. Observations on tribal life and customs, historic and present-day. Bibliography and suggested readings for each chapter. 244 pp. Illus. The Ronald Press Co., 1962. $6.00.

AMERICAN INDIAN ARTS, A WAY OF LIFE
Julia M. Seton
As above. 250 pp. Illus. Seton Village, $6.00.

AMERICAN INDIAN AND WHITE RELATIONS TO 1830
William Nelson Fenton
A survey of the common ground between history and ethnology. 150 pp. Biblio. Published for the Institute of Early American History and Culture by the University of North Carolina Press, 1957. $3.50.

*THE AMERICAN INDIAN AS FARMER
Loverne Morris; illustrated by Henry
Luhrs
Nine separate stories showing how the Indians in different parts of the country raised their crops before the coming of the white man. 48 pp. Reading level, 4; interest level, 3 to 6. Melmont Publishers, Inc., 1963. $2.50.

AMERICAN INDIAN DANCES: *Steps, Rhythms, Costumes, and Interpretation*
John L. Squires and Robert E. McLean
Gives instructions for executing Indian dances and making authentic and inexpensive costumes and accessories. Describes the steps and rhythms of representative dances, and provides insight into the meaning and interpretation of dances for a variety of occasions. Presents the dances as closely to the true Indian style as possible, and explains the significance and importance of each dance, as well as footwork and body positions, rhythms, and traditional apparel. 132 pp. Illus. The Ronald Press Co., 1964. $4.50.

THE AMERICAN INDIAN IN GRADUATE
STUDIES: *A Bibliography of Theses and Dissertations*
Frederick J. Dockstader, Compiler
A bibliography listing 3,684 theses and dissertations from 203 colleges and universities in the United States, Canada and Mexico on the Indians of North, Central and South America, and the Eskimo. Related not only to anthropology, but also to history, sociology, education, literature, the arts, and other non-ethnological subjects. 399 pp. Annotations. Tribe and subject index. Paper. Contributions of the Museum of the American Indian, Heye Foundation, 1957. $5.00.

THE AMERICAN INDIAN IN NORTH
CAROLINA
Douglas L. Rights
A history of the American Indian in North Carolina, drawing on the accounts of early Spanish and English explorers, the work of

ethnologists and archaeologists, giving a picture of the life and customs of the North Carolina Indians of today. 298 pp. Illus. John F. Blair, Publisher, 1957. $6.00.

AMERICAN INDIAN PROSE AND POETRY
     Margot Astrov, Editor
An anthology of the prose and poetry of many American tribes. 384 pp. Paper. A Capricorn Book, G. P. Putnam's Sons, 1962. $1.85.

AMERICAN INDIAN PROSE AND POETRY
     Margot Astrov, Editor
As above. Peter Smith, $3.50.

THE AMERICAN INDIAN: *Our Relations and Responsibilities*
     Theodore Heline
A mystical approach to the plight of the American Indian. Discussed: Removing misconceptions through education; early territorial aggrandizement; the three hundred years' war; a century of treaty-making; the guardian and ward theory; military service; present conditions; racial character and capacities; Indian leaders; religion; psychism; spiritual philosophy; Indian festivals; healing. 45 pp. Paper. New Age Press, Inc., 1964. $1.00.

AMERICAN INDIAN POLICY IN THE FORMATIVE YEARS: *The Indian Trade and Intercourse Acts, 1790-1834*
     Francis Paul Prucha
A study of developing legislation (The Indian Trade and Intercourse Acts) showing, through Congressional documents and records, how existing conditions governed and modified the enactments of Congress. 292 pp. Index. Harvard University Press, 1962. $6.75.

*THE AMERICAN INDIAN STORY
     May McNeer; illustrated by Lynd Ward
A study of the Indians of the United States from coast to coast. The story of *The First to Come* through *The Great Indian Heroes, The Powerful Tribes, The Fierce Wars;* information on *Indians of the Forest, Indians of the Great Plains,* and those of the mountains and the deserts; facts on origins, ways of life, and arts. 96 pp. Illus. Grades 7 to 10. Farrar, Straus & Giroux, Inc., 1963. $4.25.

THE AMERICAN INDIAN: *Then and Now*
     Gertrude M. Golden

Traces the history of the American Indian -- from the Incas, Aztecs and Mayas -- on the two American continents. 284 pp. The Naylor Co., 1957. $2.50.

AMERICAN INDIAN TOMAHAWKS
     Harold L. Peterson; Appendix by Milford G. Chandler
Traces the development of Indian cutting implements and reviews the evolution of the trade axe and pipe tomahawk. The appendix comments on manufacturing techniques and the role of the blacksmith in Indian life. Illus. 142 pp. 113 pls. 18 text figs. Contributions of the Museum of the American Indian, Heye Foundation, 1965. $8.50.

THE AMERICAN INDIAN WARS
     John W. Tebbel and Keith Jennison
Illus. Harper & Row, Publishers, 1960. $6.50.

THE AMERICAN INDIAN: *Who is He?*
     George Whitfield Ray
Forum Publishing Co., 1951. $3.00.

AMERICAN INDIANS
     Walter M. Daniels, Compiler
Compilation of articles reprinted with some abridgment from general and scholarly magazines, with introductory comments by the compiler. 219 pp. H. W. Wilson Co., 1957. $3.00.

*AMERICAN INDIANS
     Sydney E. Fletcher
Illus. Grades 7 to 9. True Books, Grosset and Dunlap, Inc., 1954, $2.95; Silver Dollar Library, Grosset and Dunlap, Inc., $1.00.

AMERICAN INDIANS
     William T. Hagan
"A history of the relationship between the white man and the Indian, showing how this relationship was doomed at the start by the conflict of cultures and attitudes. Author shows that while there were instances of conscientious guardianship and corresponding loyalty, the story was more frequently one of callous disregard of Indian rights." 190 pp. Illus. University of Chicago Press, 1961. Cloth, $4.50; paper, $1.95.

AMERICAN INDIANS IN THE PACIFIC
     Thor Heyerdahl
An investigation of the relationships between Polynesian natives and the Northwest American tribes is conducted in Part II of this

volume. 821 pp. Biblio. Index. Rand
McNally & Co., $15.00.

*AMERICAN INDIANS: *Yesterday and Today*
    Bruce Grant; illustrated by L. F.
    Bjorklund
An alphabetically arranged encyclopedia designed as a reference work as well as a history of the American Indian, from the time
of the discovery of America to the present
day. Each entry is a compact description
of the lore, the legends, the beliefs, the
customs, the food, and the characteristics
of all known tribes. There are biographies
of great Indian chiefs and leaders, and entries pertaining to the influence of the Indian
language on that of the white man, and to the
hundreds of places in America that bear Indian names. 352 pp. Grades 6 to 9. E. P.
Dutton & Co., Inc., 1958. $4.95.

AMERICAN KNIVES
    Harold Peterson
Charles Scribners' Sons, $4.95.

*AMERICANS BEFORE COLUMBUS
    Elizabeth Chesley Baity; illustrated by
    C. B. Falls
The story of life on the American continents
from ice-age animals to the civilization of
the Incas. 224 pp. Illus. Grades 9 to 12.
The Viking Press, 1961. $5.00.

*AMERICA'S BURIED PAST
    Gordon C. Baldwin; Introduction by
    Frank H. H. Roberts, Jr.
Story of North American Indian cultures
from the Asiatic migrations to the arrival
of Columbus. Utilizing archaeological findings, the author reconstructs the hunting,
food gathering and farming communities of
prehistoric people -- what they ate and how
they fulfilled their family and community
obligations. 192 pp. G. P. Putnam's Sons,
Inc., 1962. $3.50.

AMERICA'S CONCENTRATION CAMPS:
    *The Facts About Our Indian Reservations
    Today*
    Carlos B. Embry
An indictment of America's solution to the
"Indian problem" -- the reservation. Included is a proposition for a practical program to make Indians true Americans.
David McKay Co., Inc., 1965. Distributed
by the Embry Newspapers, $5.00.

AMERICA'S INDIAN BACKGROUND
    Edwin F. Walker
Southwest Museum, 25¢.

THE AMERICAS ON THE EVE OF
DISCOVERY
    Edited by Harold E. Driver
Portraits of Indian cultures in the Americas
at the time of their first contact with Europeans, including seven eyewitness accounts
by European explorers, and four by 20th-
century specialists, recording initial impressions of the varied ways of life of eleven
different tribes and nations -- from the advanced civilizations of the Incas and Aztecs
to the primitive Eskimos and Tierra del
Fuegians. Illus. Prentice-Hall, Inc., 1964.
Hardcover, $4.50; paper, $1.95.

ANCIENT ART OF THE AMERICAS
    Jane P. Rosenthal
Map. 38 pls. 68 pp. The Brooklyn Museum, 1959. $1.25.

ANCIENT ARTS OF THE AMERICAS
    G. H. S. Bushnell
An introduction to pre-Columbian art of the
Americas. Material is arranged chronologically (from approximately 2,500 B.C.
to the Spanish conquest in the 16th century)
and is subdivided by country and region.
Major attention is given to Peru and Mexico,
but the many varieties and permutations of
the art of North America, the West Indies,
and Central America are also discussed in
a historical framework, with attention given
to the cultural or religious patterns that
shaped and changed them. 288 pp. 45 pls.
Illus. Frederick A. Praeger, Inc., 1965.
Cloth, $7.50; paper, $3.95.

THE ANCIENT BASKETMAKERS
    Charles A. Amsden
Southwest Museum, 25¢.

ANCIENT CULTURE OF THE BERING SEA
AND THE ESKIMO PROBLEM
    Sergi I. Rudenko; translated by Paul
    Tolstoy
Illus. University of Toronto Press, 1961.
$3.00.

ANCIENT LIFE AMONG THE SOUTHERN
CALIFORNIA INDIANS
    M. R. Harrington
Southwest Museum, 50¢.

ANCIENT MAN IN NORTH AMERICA
    H. M. Wormington
An explanation for the layman of the archaeological clues and conclusions about early
life in America based on findings of stone
implements and skeletal remains. 322 pp.

Glossary. Biblio. Index. Denver Museum of Natural History, 1957. Cloth, $5.20; paper, $3.65.

*THE ANCIENT ONES: *Basketmakers and Cliff Dwellers of the Southwest*
   Gordon C. Baldwin
The story of the *Anasazi* (Navajo term meaning "ancient ones") who lived in the Southwest approximately 2,000 years ago. W.W. Norton & Co., Inc., $3.50.

ANCIENT RELIGIONS
   Vergilius Ture Anselm Ferm, Editor
Originally published as *Forgotten Religions*, book describes extinct creeds as well as living primitive forms of worship. 392 pp. Illus. Biblio. Paper. Citadel Press, 1965. $2.25.

AN ANCIENT SITE AT BORAX LAKE, CALIFORNIA
   M. R. Harrington
Southwest Museum, 25¢.

ANCIENT TRIBES OF THE BOULDER DAM COUNTRY
   M. R. Harrington
Southwest Museum, 25¢.

ANGEL OF HUDSON BAY
   William Ashley Anderson
The story of Maud Watt, her life in Canada's far north, and her work among the Indians of Hudson Bay. 217 pp. Illus. Map. E. P. Dutton & Co., Inc., 1961. $4.50.

ANGEL TO THE PAPAGOS
   Charlsie Poe
A story of the Papago Indians, living on their original land in a remote area of Arizona desert and their association with a white woman who has given them much needed assistance. 178 pp. Illus. The Naylor Co., 1964. $4.95.

ANTELOPE BILL
   Parker I. Pierce; chapter head drawings by Mary Mitchell
Facsimile of the 1898 edition. A participant's account of the Sioux Uprising of 1862. Ross & Haines, Inc. $12.50.

*ANTELOPE SINGER
   Ruth M. Underhill; illustrated by Ursula Koering
The story of the Hunt family's adventures as they travel by covered wagon to California, and their friendship with the Paiute

Indians. Ages 9 to 13; grades 3 to 7. Coward-McCann, Inc., 1961. $3.50.

AN ANTHROPOLOGICAL BIBLIOGRAPHY OF THE EASTERN SEABOARD, Vol. II
Section on archaeological techniques, and items from Alabama, Michigan and Ontario. vi + 82 pp. Maps. New Jersey State Museum, $1.50.

ANTIQUITIES OF LONG ISLAND
   Gabriel Furman
Two vols. Ira J. Friedman, Inc.

AN APACHE CAMPAIGN IN THE SIERRA MADRE
   John G. Bourke; Introduction by J. Frank Dobie
A reprint of the 1886 edition. An eyewitness chronicle of the United States Army's 1883 campaign against the Apache Indians in the Sierra Madre. Charles Scribner's Sons, $3.00.

*THE APACHE INDIANS, *Raiders of the Southwest*
   Sonia Bleeker; illustrated by Althea Karr
Information about the Apache tribe. 160 pp. Index. Ages 8 through 12; grades 4 to 6. William Morrow & Co., Inc., 1951. $2.95.

AN APACHE LIFE-WAY: *The Economic, Social, and Religious Institutions of the Chiricahua Indians*
   Morris Edward Opler
An account of the economic, social and religious institutions of the Chiricahua Apaches of the Southwest, based on the author's two years of field work. Events are introduced in the order in which they are experienced during the course of normal Chiricahua life. Through infancy, childhood, adolescence, marriage, adulthood, to death -- the life-cycle of the average Chiricahua is gradually unfolded in natural context. xviii + 500 pp. Illus. Map. Cooper Square Publishers, Inc., 1966. $10.00.

AN APACHE LIFE-WAY: *The Economic, Social, and Religious Institutions of the Chiricahua Indians*
   Morris Edward Opler
As above. xiii + 500 pp. University of Chicago Press, 1941. $8.50.

APACHE, NAVAHO, AND SPANIARD
   Jack D. Forbes
304 pp. Illus. Maps. Biblio. Index. University of Oklahoma Press, 1960. $5.95.

APACHE PLAYING CARDS
 Virginia Wayland
Southwest Museum, 25¢.

*APACHE WARRIOR
 David C. Cooke
The story of the Apaches and their history
of betrayal by the white man. 203 pp. Pho-
tos. Grades 7 to 10. W. W. Norton & Co.,
Inc., 1963. $3.50.

*APACHES
 Marion Israel; illustrated by Harry L.
 Timmins
A picture of the way of life of the Apache
Indians before the coming of the frontiers-
man. Reading level, 3; interest level, 1
through 6. Melmont Publishers, Inc., 1959.
$2.50.

APOLOGIES TO THE IROQUOIS
 Edmund Wilson
Concerns the present situation of the Indians
of the Six Nations Confederacy in the United
States and Canada. Relates the author's
adventures in exploring the Iroquois world
-- its politics, ceremonies and personalities. 310 pp. Empire State Historical Publications, 1960. $3.75.

APOLOGIES TO THE IROQUOIS
 Edmund Wilson
As above. 310 pp. Farrar, Straus & Gir-
oux, Inc., 1960. $4.95.

APOLOGIES TO THE IROQUOIS
 Edmund Wilson
As above. 310 pp. Paper. Vintage Books,
1966. $1.95.

THE ARAPAHO SUN DANCE: *The Ceremony of the Offerings Lodge*
 G. A. Dorsey
228 pp. 127 halftones. 10 pls. Fieldiana:
Anthropology Vol. IV, Chicago Natural History Museum, 1903. $5.00.

THE ARAPAHO WAY
 Althea Bass
Memoirs of the life of Carl Sweezy, one of
the last full-blooded Arapaho Indians. A
narrative and Sweezy's own full-color illustrations create a portrait of his early years
on a reservation, and the way of life he
knew. 136 pp. Illus. Clarkson N. Potter,
Inc., $5.00.

ARCHAEOLOGICAL EXCAVATIONS AT
 WILLOW BEACH, ARIZONA, 1950
 Albert H. Schroeder
University of Utah Press, 1961. $3.25.

ARCHAELOGICAL INVESTIGATIONS OF
 THE UNCOMPAHGRE PLATEAU
 H. M. Wormington and Robert H. Lister; Appendix by Charles D. Hunt
This report describes the excavation of a
number of sites in west central Colorado.
129 pp. 3 maps. 66 illus. Denver Museum
of Natural History, $2.50.

AN ARCHAEOLOGICAL SITE NEAR
 GLEESON, ARIZONA
 William Shirley Fulton and Carr Tuthill
The Amerind Foundation, 1940. $3.00.

ARCHAEOLOGICAL SURVEY OF THE
 CHUSKA VALLEY AND THE CHACO
 PLATEAU
 Stewart Peckham, John P. Wilson,
 Arthur H. Harris, James Schoenwetter
 and Helene Warren
An ecological investigation of Pueblo and
Navajo remains in northwestern New Mexi-
co with emphasis on a new Pueblo mani-
festation. Discusses the blending of Chaco,
Mesa Verde and Kayenta cultural traits.
Describes architecture, pottery and arti-
facts and includes geological analysis of
stone artifact material. Analyzes modern
and prehistoric pollen, and summarizes the
ethnohistory of the Navajo in the Chuska
Valley. 300 pp. Museum of New Mexico
Papers in Anthropology, No. 15, 1965.
Museum of New Mexico Press, $6.00.

AN ARCHAEOLOGICAL SURVEY OF THE
 TRENT WATERWAY IN ONTARIO, CAN-
 ADA, AND ITS SIGNIFICANCE FOR NEW
 YORK STATE PREHISTORY
 William A. Ritchie
In the summer of 1948, the Rochester Mu-
seum of Arts and Sciences conducted a sur-
vey along the Trent Waterway in Ontario,
Canada, for the purpose of determining po-
tential Canadian relationships to the New
York State Point Peninsula, Hopewell and
Owasco Cultures. The main body of the
report concerns the excavations of East
Sugar Island and the Picton Site. 52 pp. 12
figs. Biblio. Research Records of the
Rochester Museum of Arts and Sciences
No. 9, 1949. $1.50. Available from the
Rochester Museum Association.

ARCHAEOLOGICAL SURVEY OF THE
TWENTY-NINE PALMS REGION
Elizabeth W. Crozer Campbell
93 pp. 48 pl. Maps. Southwest Museum,
$3.50.

ARCHAEOLOGICAL WORK IN THE ACK-
MEN-LOWRY AREA, SOUTHWESTERN
COLORADO, 1937
Paul S. Martin
88 pp. 67 pl., 4 text figs., 4 maps. Fieldiana: Archaeological Vol. XXIII, No. 2. Chicago Natural History Museum, 1938. $3.00.

THE ARCHAEOLOGY OF CARACAJOU
POINT: *With an Interpretation of Oneota
Culture in Wisconsin* (2 Vols.)
Robert L. Hall
An examination of an archaeological excavation in Jefferson County, Wisconsin, and an
evaluation and comparison of the find as related to similar discoveries and the Indian
history of the central United States, presenting a new interpretation of the Oneota
cultural tradition and the consequent re-
alignment of current views on Wisconsin
prehistory. Vol. 1, 208 pp.; Vol. 2, 160
pp. 83 pl. University of Wisconsin Press,
1962. Set, $8.00.

*THE ARCHAEOLOGY OF NEW YORK
Robert C. Suggs; illustrated by Leonard
Everett Fisher
An account of the prehistoric Indian world
of this area. 156 pp. Ages 12 and up.
Thomas Y. Crowell Co., 1966. $3.50.

THE ARCHAEOLOGY OF NEW YORK
STATE
William A. Ritchie
A complete account of ancient man in the
New York State area, describing the various
Indian cultures that existed and succeeded
one another in the State and neighboring
areas until the advent of Europeans early
in the 17th century. 357 pp. Illus. Maps.
Photos. The Natural History Press, 1965.
$12.50.

THE ARCHAEOLOGY OF SAN FRANCISCO
Robert C. Suggs
Illus. Thomas Y. Crowell Co., 1965. $3.50.

ARCHAEOLOGY OF THE EASTERN
UNITED STATES
James B. Griffin, Editor
Twenty-eight archaeologists present an
archaeological survey of the area east of
the Rocky Mountains. The succession of

prehistoric cultures, research methods,
and problems in this area are described as
are specific culture areas. Among con-
tributors are Carl E. Guthe, Fred R. Eggan, George I. Quimby, Kenneth G. Orr,
and Merceau S. Maxwell. 598 pp. 204 pls.
and figs. University of Chicago Press,
1952. $17.50.

THE ARCHAEOLOGY OF THE HISTORIC
PERIOD IN THE WESTERN GREAT LAKES
REGION, A. D. 1600-1820
George Irving Quimby
A chronologically oriented history and ar-
chaeology of material culture of Indian
tribes and cultures of the western Great
Lakes region, aimed at bridging the exist-
ing gaps between history and prehistory.
Book synthesizes existing information in
scattered and obscure sources, presents
new data, and provides interpretations.
University of Wisconsin Press, 1966.

ARCHAEOLOGY OF THE UPPER COLUM-
BIA REGION
D. Collier, *et al*
Presents the results of field work carried
on by the Columbia Basin Archaeological
Survey in eastern Washington from 1939
through 1940, along both banks of the river
from Grand Coulee Dam to the Canadian
boundary above Northport. In this region
extensive excavations were made at thirty-
five Indian sites. An analysis of the finds
from these sites comprises the greater
part of the report. 177 pp. Paper. University of Washington Press, 1942. $4.00.

ARCHAEOLOGY OF THE UTE DAM AND
RESERVOIR, NORTHEASTERN NEW
MEXICO
Laurens C. Hammack
The results of a cooperative effort involving the Museum of New Mexico and the New
Mexico Interstate Stream Commission.
Presents historical and archaeological data
from the little known Canadian River area
in northeastern New Mexico. Discusses the
Apache and Comanche occupation of the area
and describes the four types of sites -- open
lithic, tipi ring, rock shelter, and historic
-- found along the Canadian and its tribu-
taries in the Ute Dam Reservoir. Includes
extensive artifact analysis. Museum of New
Mexico Papers in Anthropology, No. 14,
1965. 75 pp. Illus. Biblio. University of
New Mexico Press, $2.50.

ARCHEOLOGY AND ETHNOLOGY PA-
PERS, *Nos. 1-9, Museum of Anthropology,
University of Utah*
One-volume edition, $3.25; Nos. 17 to 19
in one-volume edition, $1.00.

ARCHEOLOGY OF CAPE DENBIGH
James L. Giddings
Illus. Brown University Press, 1963.
$12.50.

ARCHEOLOGY OF COASTAL NORTH
CAROLINA
William G. Haag
Illus. Paper. Louisiana State University
Press, 1958. $3.00.

THE ARCHEOLOGY OF PLEISTOCENE
LAKE MOHAVE
Elizabeth W. C. and William H. Campbell, *et al*
118 pp. 57 pl. 3 figs. Southwest Museum,
1937. $4.00.

ARIZONA IN THE 50's
James H. Tevis
Illus. University of New Mexico Press,
1954. $2.00.

THE ARIZONA STORY
Joseph Miller, Editor; illustrations by
Ross Santee
Taken from stories written by frontier re-
porters of the white man and the Indian in
the 19th century. 345 pp. Hastings House,
Publishers, Inc., 1952. $5.50.

ARK OF EMPIRE: *The American Frontier,
1784-1803*
Dale Van Every; Foreword by Henry
Steele Commager
"The . . . story of an earlier cold war in
(American) history." 288 pp. Maps. Wil-
liam Morrow & Co., Inc., 1963.

ARK OF EMPIRE: . *The American Frontier,
1784-1803*
Dale Van Every
As above. New American Library, 75¢.

ARMS AND ARMOR IN COLONIAL
AMERICA, 1526-1783
Harold L. Peterson
A two-hundred-year history of firearms,
ammunition, equipment and edged weapons
from the Age of Colonization and Exploration through the French and Indian Wars and
the Revolution. 350 pp. Illus. Bramhall
House, 1965. $3.95.

ARMS AND ARMOR IN COLONIAL
AMERICA, 1526-1783
Harold L. Peterson
As above. The Stackpole Co., $12.50.

*ARROWS AND SNAKESKIN
Sidney N. Riggs
J. B. Lippincott Co., 1962. $3.25.

ARROWS OVER TEXAS
Robert S. Reading
Presents information on early Indian cultures. 286 pp. Illus. The Naylor Co.,
1960. $4.95.

ART AND ARCHITECTURE OF ANCIENT
AMERICA
George Kubler
Illus. Penguin Books, Inc., 1961. $16.50.

ART BEFORE COLUMBUS
Andre Emmerich
Simon and Schuster, $10.00.

THE ART OF AMERICAN INDIAN COOKING
Yefee Kimball and Jean Anderson; line
drawings by Yefee Kimball
A sampling of the wide gastronomical range
of the first Americans, presenting nearly
two hundred historic recipes. 216 pp.
Doubleday & Co., Inc., 1965. $4.50.

ART OF THE EASTERN PLAINS INDIAN
Norman Feder
Background material and catalog of the Nathan Sturgis Jarvis Collection, assembled
in Minnesota between 1833 and 1836. Contains fifty-five black-and-white plates of
objects and paintings of the period. 67 pp.
1964. The Brooklyn Museum, $2.00.

*THE ART OF THE ESKIMO
Shirley Glubok
Selection spans more than a thousand years
of Eskimo art, providing a fresh impression
of these people; the text presents an intro-
duction to their life and customs. 48 pp.
Photos. Grades 2 to 5. Harper & Row,
Publishers, 1964. $3.95.

*THE ART OF THE NORTH AMERICAN
INDIAN
Shirley Glubok
A treatment of the full range of American
Indian art -- from the Plains warrior, show-
ing off his exploits on a painted buffalo hide,
to the elaborate double-masks of the North-
west Coast Indians; from the lively kachina

dolls of the Southwest to the historic wampum belts of eastern Indians. Photos. Harper & Row, Publishers, 1964. $3.95.

ART OF THE NORTHWEST COAST INDIANS
    R. Bruce Inverarity
Illustrated document of the art of the Northwest Coast Indians. 244 pp. Illus. Pls. University of California Press, 1950. $7.50.

ART ON STONE BY THE AMERICAN
    INDIAN IN NEW JERSEY
    Anthony Comunale
Illus. Vantage Press, 1963. $2.75.

ARTISTS OF THE OLD WEST
    John C. Ewers
An illustrated study of the top ranking artists, American and European, who captured on canvas the sights, scenes and spirit of the American West. The text details the artists' lives, tells of their experiences painting in the field, and describes the stories behind the paintings. Some of the artists included are: Charles Willson Peale, Titian Ramsay Peale, Charles Bird King, George Catlin, Karl Bodner, Frederic Remington, and Charles M. Russell. 208 pp. Doubleday & Co., Inc., 1965. $12.95.

ARTISTS OF THE TUNDRA AND THE SEA
    Dorothy Jean Ray
A synthesis of the author's field work with Alaskan carvers and her study of principal museum collections of Eskimo ivory carving; book describes and analyzes archaeological and historical art styles as well as the attitudes, products, and cultural significance of the contemporary carvers. Includes photographs showing the techniques used by the carvers. 184 pp. Map. Illus. Biblio. University of Washington Press, 1961. $5.75.

THE ASSINIBOINES: *From the Accounts of the Old Ones Told to First Boy (James Larpenteur Long)*
    Edited and with an Introduction by
    Michael Steven Kennedy; drawings by
    William Standing
209 pp. Illus. Maps. Appendix. Biblio. Index. University of Oklahoma Press, 1961. $5.00.

ATLANTIC JOURNAL AND FRIEND OF
    KNOWLEDGE
    C. S. Rafinesque
Stechert-Hafner Service Agency, Inc., 1923-33. Eight parts (unbound), $4.50.

AUTOBIOGRAPHY OF A WINNEBAGO
INDIAN
    Paul Radin
A reissue of the 1920 edition. Originally recorded in the Winnebago language from the Indian known (in the book) as S. B., the text relates S. B.'s life as he looked back upon it with all the emphases, interpretations and values he considered important. Translated into English with annotations. Includes a chapter on folkways based upon the instructions of the tribal elders. 91 pp. Paper. Dover Publications, Inc., 1963. $1.00.

AUTOBIOGRAPHY OF A WINNEBAGO
INDIAN
    Paul Radin
As above. Peter Smith, $3.00.

AYORAMA
    Raymond de Coccola and Paul King
Oxford University Press, 1956. $4.50.

B

BAD MEDICINE AND GOOD
    Wilbur Nye; illustrated by Nick Eggenhofer
291 pp. Illus. Index. Maps. University of Oklahoma Press, 1962. $5.00.

*BADGER, THE MISCHIEF MAKER
    Kay Hill; illustrated by John Hamberger
Indian legends about the youth Badger's escapades. Illus. Ages 9 and up. Dodd, Mead and Co., 1965. $3.25.

THE BALTASAR BACA "GRANT": *History of an Encroachment*
    Myra Ellen Jenkins
Discusses Spanish land policy and Indian rights. Recounts the struggle of Laguna Pueblo to preserve its lands from encroachment over a period of one hundred and seventy years. 37 pp. A reprint from *El Palacio,* Vol. 68, Nos. 1 and 2. Museum of New Mexico Press, 1961. $1.00.

BASIS OF AMERICAN HISTORY, 1500-1900
    Livingston Farrand
Frederick Ungar Publishing Co., Inc., $5.00.

BASKET MAKER III SITES NEAR
    DURANGO, COLORADO
    Roy L. Carlson

82 pp. Series in Anthropology No. 8, June,
1963. University of Colorado Press, 1963.
$3.50.

BASKET WEAVERS OF ARIZONA
Alambert E. Robinson

A survey of the craft among the various
Arizona tribes, discussing methods, designs
and uses of basketry in ancient and modern
times. 64 pp. Illus. University of New
Mexico Press, 1965. $7.50.

THE BATTLE OF PLATTE BRIDGE
Jesse W. Vaughn

132 pp. Illus. Index. Biblio. Maps. University of Oklahoma Press, 1964. $3.95.

THE BATTLE OF SAND CREEK
Morse H. Coffin; edited with Introduction and Notes by Alan W. Farley

The eyewitness description of a famous battle. 40 pp. Illus. W. M. Morrison Books,
1965. $6.00.

THE BATTLE OF THE LITTLE BIGHORN
Mari Sandoz

J. B. Lippincott Co., 1966. $4.50.

BATTLEFIELD AND CLASSROOM: *Four Decades with the American Indians*
Richard Henry Pratt; edited by Robert
Utley

The story of General Pratt's support of education for Indians and of Federal Indian policy. 358 pp. Illus. Yale University Press,
1964. $8.50.

THE BAYOU GOULA SITE, IBERVILLE PARISH, LOUISIANA
George I. Quimby

84 pp. Illus. Maps. Vol. 47, No. 2., Chicago Natural History Museum, 1957. $1.75.

BEADS AND BEADWORK OF THE AMERICAN INDIAN
William C. Orchard

This study discusses trade beads, wampum
and beads of metal, stone, pearl, glass,
and other materials from South, Central,
and North America, with special emphasis
on the technique of beadwork. 140 pp. Illus.
Museum of the American Indian, $5.00.

BEAUTYWAY: *A Navajo Ceremonial*
Texts recorded or translated by Fr.
Berard Haile and Maud Oakes; Com-
mentaries by Leland C. Wyman

A Navajo Indian myth is given in the translation of Father Berard, Franciscan missionary and lifetime student of the Navajo.

Sandpaintings from the ceremonial are giv-
en in color or line, after paintings by Maud
Oakes and others. Navajo text in separate
booklet. xii + 218 pp. Illus. Index. Bollingen Series, 1957. $8.50.

*BEAR TEETH FOR COURAGE
Florence Scull; illustrated by Blair
Lent

Young Circling Hawk of the Delaware Tribe
learns the language of the Quakers and how
to be useful to his people. 176 pp. D. Van
Nostrand Co., Inc., 1964. $3.75.

*BEARS, PIRATES AND SILVER LACE
Anne B. Fisher

Historic tales of early California, including
the story of the building of the Spanish missions. 146 pp. Illus. Grades 5 to 6. Binfords and Mort, 1960. $2.50.

*THE BEAVER MEN
Mari Sandoz

Book deals with the spearheads of empire
who probed the interior mysteries of the
North American Continent, and tells of the
Indians they met. 360 pp. Index. Illus.
Biblio. Notes. Hastings House Publishers,
Inc., 1964. $5.95.

*BEAVERBIRD
Ruth M. Underhill

Beaverbird is captured by outlaw Indians
and must prove his worth in a strange land.
Illus. Ages 8 to 12. Coward-McCann, Inc.,
1959. $3.00.

*BEFORE THE WHITE MAN CAME
Meldred Jenkins

Through the eyes and ears of two young
Northwest Coast Indians we learn how the
Pacific Coast Indians really lived before
the white man came. 182 pp. Illus. Line
drawings. Grades 5 to 6. Binfords and
Mort, 1951. $3.00.

BEHIND MUD WALLS
William H. Wiser and Charlotte Viall

A study of a northern Indian village; included are the author's findings upon his return,
several years later. 249 pp. Illus. University of California Press, 1963. $1.95.

*BEHIND THE ZUNI MASKS
Val Gendron

A true story of the Koshares and their conflict with the Zuni Indians who unjustly ac-
cused them of making a mockery of the Zuni
religion. Illus. Grades 7 to 9. David Mc-
Kay Co., Inc., 1958. $3.25.

BENJAMIN HAWKINS: *Indian Agent*
     Merritt B. Pond
This book gives a comprehensive view of the social and diplomatic work Hawkins performed on behalf of the American Indian. 279 pp. Index. Illus. Biblio. University of Georgia Press, 1951. $4.00.

BEOTHUK AND MICMAC
     Frank C. Speck
Comments on the now extinct Beothuk and the Micmacs of Newfoundland, and the contacts that once may have occurred between them. Includes information on Micmac housing, crafts, dress, and hunting territories. 187 pp. Illus. Paper. Museum of the American Indian, Heye Foundation, $3.50.

BIBLIOGRAPHICAL CHECKLIST OF NORTH AND MIDDLE AMERICAN INDIAN LINGUISTICS IN THE EDWARD E. AYER COLLECTION, Two Vols.
     Ruth Lapman Butler, Editor
Newberry Library, 1941. $5.00.

BIBLIOGRAPHY OF NORTH AMERICAN FOLKLORE AND FOLKSONG
     Charles Haywood
Reissue of the 1951 edition. This two-volume work is the only bibliography of records, books, articles and folk song covering the different categories of American folklore. Volume Two lists all available information on the myths and rituals of more than 250 tribes of American and Canadian Indians, and Eskimos. 1,301 pp. Illus. Index. Biblio. Dover Publications, Inc., 1961. Two-volume set, $15.00.

√ BIBLIOGRAPHY OF THE CONSTITUTIONS AND LAWS OF THE AMERICAN INDIANS
     Lester Hargrett
A descriptive list of the printed constitutions, the statutes, session acts and resolutions passed by properly authorized bodies, of once semi-independent and self-governing Indian tribes and nations within the present United States. Illus. Harvard University Press, 1947. $4.00.

BIOGRAPHICAL AND HISTORICAL INDEX OF AMERICAN INDIANS AND PERSONS INVOLVED IN INDIAN AFFAIRS
     U.S. Department of the Interior, Office of Indian Affairs
This index lists the biography, history and social conditions of American Indians from the latter half of the 19th century to about 1920. There are listings of names of Indian agents, other personnel of the Bureau of Indian Affairs, Indian chiefs, historically prominent Indians, and additional information related to tribal affairs. 6,600 pp. Index. Appendices. Biblio. G. K. Hall & Co., 1966. $640.00.

A BIOGRAPHY OF OLIVER LA FARGE
     D'Arcy McNickle
A biography of Oliver La Farge, who pursued his interest in the archaeology, linguistics and ethnology of the American Indian, and guided the Association on American Indian Affairs to become one of the most effective organizations working in behalf of the Indian people. 224 pp. Indiana University Press (in preparation). $5.75.

BIRD STONES OF THE AMERICAN INDIAN
     E. D. Townsend
Illus. Heinman Imported Books, 1959. $30.00.

A BIRD'S-EYE VIEW OF THE PUEBLOS
     Stanley A. Stubbs
Illus. University of Oklahoma Press, 1950. $3.00.

THE BIRTH OF THE GODS
     Guy E. Swanson
A study of the origin of primitive beliefs. 256 pp. University of Michigan Press, 1960. Paper, $1.95; cloth, $4.95.

THE BLACK DOG TRAIL
     Tillie Karns Newman
The story of the Osage Indians and the efforts of two great chiefs on behalf of their people. 221 pp. Christopher Publishing House, 1957. $3.00.

THE BISHOP OF ALL BEYOND: *Sheldon Jackson*
     Winifried Hulbert
The story of a missionary among the Indians. 24 pp. Friendship Press, 25¢.

BLACK ELK SPEAKS, BEING THE LIFE STORY OF A HOLY MAN OF THE OGLALA SIOUX
     John G. Neihardt
As below. Peter Smith, $3.50.

BLACK ELK SPEAKS, BEING THE LIFE STORY OF A HOLY MAN OF THE OGLALA SIOUX
     John G. Neihardt

A description of the Oglala Sioux religious ceremonies as told to the author by Black Elk, an Oglala *wichasha wakon* (holy man, priest). Contains an account of the Messiah Movement (Ghost Dance craze). 282 pp. Illus. Paper. University of Nebraska Press, 1961. $1.50.

BLACK HAWK
    Arthur J. Beckhard
A biography of the leader of the Sauk and Fox Indians who attempted to protect his people from pioneer expansion in the West. Includes material on the Black Hawk War of 1832. 192 pp. Julian Messner, 1957. $3.25.

BLACK HAWK: *An Autobiography*
    Donald Jackson, Editor
177 pp. Maps. Paper. The University of Illinois Press, 1964. $1.75.

*BLACK ROBE PEACEMAKER: *Pierre de Smet*
    Joseph G. E. Hopkins
Illus. Grades 5 to 8. P. J. Kenedy & Sons, 1958. $2.50.

BLACK SAND: *Prehistory in Northern Arizona*
    Harold S. Colton
132 pp. Illus. Maps. Index. Biblio. University of New Mexico Press, 1960. $4.00.

*THE BLACK STONE KNIFE
    Alice Marriott; illustrated by Harvey Weiss
An account of the trek of some young Kiowas to "find the summer." The journey of over two years started in 1825 and took them from Oklahoma through Mexico. It is based on a true story told by the Tribe. 192 pp. Illus. Thomas Y. Crowell Co., 1957. $3.95.

BLACKFEET AND BUFFALO
    James Willard Schultz; edited by K. C. Seale
384 pp. Illus. Index. Glossary. Map. University of Oklahoma Press, 1962. $5.95.

THE BLACKFEET: *Raiders on the Northwestern Plains*
    John C. Ewers
A detailed history of the Blackfeet Indians. 348 pp. Illus. Maps. University of Oklahoma Press, 1958. $5.75.

THE BLACKFOOT BEAVER BUNDLE, I
    Walter McClintock
Southwest Museum, 25¢.

THE BLACKFOOT BEAVER BUNDLE, II
    Walter McClintock
Southwest Museum, 25¢.

BLACKFOOT LODGE TALES, *The Story of a Prairie People*
    George B. Grinnell
As below. Peter Smith, $3.50.

BLACKFOOT LODGE TALES, *The Story of a Prairie People*
    George B. Grinnell
Folktales of the Blackfeet Indians. 312 pp. Paper. University of Nebraska Press, 1962. $1.50.

BLACKFOOT MEDICINE-PIPE CEREMONY
    Walter McClintock
Southwest Museum, 25¢.

THE BLACKFOOT TIPI
    Walter McClintock
Southwest Museum, 25¢.

BLACKFOOT WARRIOR SOCIETIES
    Walter McClintock
Southwest Museum, 25¢.

*BLUE WAMPUM
    Constance Conrader
Grades 6 to 10. Duell, Sloan and Pearce, 1958. $3.00.

THE BONANZA TRAIL
    Muriel S. Wolle
The story of the men who prospected for gold from California to the eastern rim of the Rocky Mountains -- a guidebook to the West as well as a narrative. 510 pp. Indiana University Press, 1953. $10.00.

*BOW FOR TURTLE
    Dorothy Heiderstadt
Illus. Grades 2 to 4. David McKay Co., Inc., 1960. $2.50.

THE BOOK OF AMERICAN INDIAN GAMES
    Allan A. Macfarlan
Contains 150 authentic North American Indian games, to be played in the home and outdoors. 284 pp. Illus. The Association Press, 1958. $3.95.

THE BOOK OF AMERICAN INDIANS
    Ralph B. Raphael
Describes the Indians of prehistory; routes from Asia; language; characteristics and cultural areas; great chiefs and their battles; ceremonials and legends; arts and

crafts; the Indian today, and his reservations. 144 pp. Illus. Index. Biblio. Arco Publishing Co., 1960. $2.50.

THE BOOK OF INDIAN CRAFTS AND
COSTUMES
    Barnard S. Mason; drawings by Frederic H. Koch
Describes the crafts and customs of the Indians of the Woodlands and the Plains, the wigwam Indians, the canoe Indians, the riders of the prairies, the tipi Indians, the buffalo hunters and the Indians who rode horses. 118 pp. Illus. The Ronald Press Co., 1946. $5.50.

*THE BOOK OF INDIAN CRAFTS AND
INDIAN LORE
    Julian H. Salmon
A general discussion of the Indians of the United States -- tipis and wigwams, fire making and cooking, costumes, dances and ceremonies, producing an Indian pageant, weapons and war paint, are some of the subjects described. 418 pp. Biblio. Index. Grades 5 to 9. Harper & Row, Publishers, 1928. $4.95.

BOOK OF INDIAN LIFE CRAFTS
    Oscar E. Norbeck; illustrated by John B. Eves
Contains full instructions for projects that reflect the personal, home and village activities of many tribes. 253 pp. Illus. Index. The Association Press, 1958. $5.95.

*BOOK OF INDIANS
    Holling C. Holling
A presentation of the North American Indian's legends, traditions, and daily life. 128 pp. Illus. Grades 3 to 6. The Platt & Munk Company, Inc., 1962. $2.95.

BOOK OF THE ESKIMOS
    Peter Freuchen
An introduction to the Eskimos of Greenland, northern Canada, and Alaska. Fawcett Publications, 1965. Paper, 95¢.

BOOK OF THE ESKIMOS
    Peter Freuchen
As above. 464 pp. Illus. World Publishing Co., 1965. $7.50.

√ THE BOOK OF THE HOPI
    Frank Waters
This book reveals the Hopi view of life, the meaning of which the Tribe kept secret for uncounted generations. Some thirty elders

of the Hopi Indian Tribe in northern Arizona are the spokesmen who provided the material for this book. 448 pp. Illus. The Viking Press, Inc., 1963. $10.00.

*THE BRAVE RIDERS
    Glenn Balch; illustrated by Ezra Jack Keats
A Pawnee Indian comes to manhood in a story depicting life within the Indian societies during the time of Pike's explorations. 208 pp. Illus. Thomas Y. Crowell Co., 1959. $3.95.

BRAVE WARRIORS
    Norman B. Wiltsey
Short histories of seven western Indian tribes -- Nez Perce, Cheyenne, Crow, Modoc, Apache, Comanche, and Sioux. Illus. Caxton Printers, Ltd., 1963. $6.50.

BREEDS AND HALFBREEDS: *The Vagabond Heroes of the American Frontier*
    Gordon Speck
This book discusses the voyagers, trappers, fugitives, Indians and mountain men who lived in America's frontier country. The Devin-Adair Co., 1966. $6.50.

A BRIEF HISTORY OF NAVAJO
SILVERSMITHING
    Arthur Woodward
84 pp. Northern Arizona Society of Science and Art, $2.00.

BRIEF MISCELLANEOUS HOPI PAPERS
    H. R. Voth
61 pp. Illus. Volume XI, No. 2. Chicago Natural History Museum, 1912. $1.00.

*BROKEN ARROW
    Elliott Arnold
The story of Cochise, an Apache Chief, and an American scout, Tom Jeffords, who developed a friendship which led them to become blood brothers. Grades 7 to 8. Duell, Sloan & Pearce, 1954. $3.50.

BROKEN PEACE PIPES
    Irvin M. Peithmann
The true story of the American Indian's loss of the land which was his birthright and of the decline of our natural resources since the Indian was banished to his reservation. 320 pp. Charles C. Thomas, Publisher, 1964. $7.50.

*BUFFALO GRASS
    C. Steven Laury, illustrated by Carl
    Kidwell
A fourteen-year-old boy from Boston is
saved from being captured by the Indians
when a buffalo hunter rescues him. He lives
the life of the hunters until he is reunited
with his family. 164 pp. Illus. Ages 10 to
14. The Dial Press, 1966. $3.25.

*BUFFALO HORSE
    Gardell Dano Christensen
A young warrior brings the first horses to
the Nez Perce Indians. Thomas Nelson &
Sons, 1961. $2.00.

*BUFFALO KILL
    Gardell Dano Christensen
A recreation of a great hunt in which the
prehistoric Indians of the Great Plains must
kill enough buffalo to provide meat and hides,
and to make clothing and tipis for all members of the tribe. 97 pp. Illus. Thomas
Nelson & Sons, 1959. $3.25.

*THE BUFFALO ROBE
    Gardell Dano Christensen
When a boy of the Great Plains Indians became a warrior, he was expected to record
his deeds on his own robe of buffalo hide,
captured in an act of bravery. After a long
hunt during which he learns much of nature,
White Calf wins his robe of history. 96 pp.
Thomas Nelson & Sons, 1961. $3.25.

BY CHEYENNE CAMPFIRES
    George B. Grinnell; Foreword by Omer
    C. Stewart
Historical events, ethical values and oral
history are revealed as the Cheyenne tell of
their wars, their heroes, and of their relationships with supernatural powers. Yale
University Press, 1962. Paper, $1.95;
cloth, $7.50.

C

CABOT TO CARTIER
    Bernard G. Hoffman
An analysis of the early history and first
contacts with Indians of North American explorers. 287 pp. Biblio. Index. University of Toronto Press, 1961. $8.00.

THE CAHUILLA INDIANS
    Harry C. James

A study of the Cahuilla Indians of southern
California, their history and legends. 185
pp. Westernlore Press, 1960. $7.50.

THE CALENDAR STICK OF TSHI-ZUN-
HAU-KAU
    Robert H. Merrill
An analysis of the only known Indian calendar extant north of Mexico, that of a Winnebago warrier of the early 19th century. 12
pp. Illus. Cranbrook Institute of Science,
1945. 25¢.

*CALICO CAPTIVE
    Elizabeth George Speare; illustrated
    by W. T. Mars
Based on an actual narrative, this book tells
the story of a young girl and her family who
were captured by Indians in 1754, and then
sold to the French in Montreal and held for
ransom. Grades 7 to 8. Houghton Mifflin
Co., 1957. $3.50.

*CALIFORNIA INDIAN DAYS
    Helen Bauer
Doubleday & Co., Inc., 1963. $3.50.

THE CALIFORNIA INDIANS: *A Source Book*
    R. F. Heizer and M. A. Whipple,
    Editors
"A balanced collection of writings, some in
print for the first time." Illus. University
of California Press. 1957. $6.50.

THE CALIFORNIA INDIANS VERSUS THE
UNITED STATES
    Kenneth M. Johnson
History of claims of California Indians re-
sulting from non-ratification of 1852 treaties. 100 pp. Illus. Dawson's Book Shop,
1965. $9.00.

*CALIFORNIA'S FATHER SERRA
    Sally Duque
The story of the great Father Serra, who
founded many missions and helped colonize
early California. His religious traditions,
way of life and missions are now a part of
California's heritage. 40 pp. Illus. Grades
3 to 4. Binfords and Mort, 1957. $2.50.

CALIFORNIA'S GABRILENO INDIANS
    Bernice Eastman Johnson
198 pp. Illus. Maps. Southwest Museum,
1962. Paper, $3.75; cloth, $5.00.

CAMPAIGNING WITH CROOK
    Charles King; Introduction by Don
    Russell
166 pp. Illus. Map. University of Oklahoma Press, 1964. $2.00.

CANNIBAL COAST
    Ed Kilman
The life and history of the Karankawa Indians of Texas. 310 pp. Illus. Mapped end
sheets. The Naylor Co., 1959. $5.00.

CANOE AND SADDLE
    Theodore Winthrop; Introduction by
    Alfred Powers
Travelogue of the Far West in the 1850's by
a Yale man. 210 pp. Illus. Chinook vocabulary. Binfords and Mort, 1955. $3.75.

CAPTAIN JACK, MODOC RENEGADE
    Doris Payne
Account of the Modoc War of 1872, with a
portrayal of the Modoc Chief and his unique
place in the winning of the West. 271 pp.
Illus. Binfords and Mort, 1958. $3.95.

*CAPTAIN WAYMOUTH'S INDIANS
    Anne Molloy; illustrated by Douglas
    Gorsline
An account of five Indians kidnapped and
taken to England in 1605. 189 pp. Illus.
Ages 10 to 14. Hastings House, Publishers,
Inc., 1956. $2.95.

*CAPTIVES OF THE SENECAS
    John Brick
Duell, Sloan and Pearce, 1964. $3.50.

*THE CAPTURE OF WEST WIND
    Rutherford Montgomery
"There had to be a first Indian to catch and
ride a horse; this book is the author's idea
of how Gray Eagle, a fifteen-year-old Sioux,
might have done it." Grades 4 to 6. Duell,
Sloan and Pearce, 1962. $3.27.

CARBINE AND LANCE: *The Story of Old
    Fort Sill*
    W. S. Nye
Illus. University of Oklahoma Press, 1957.
$5.00.

CATAWBA HUNTING, TRAPPING AND
    FISHING
    Frank G. Speck
University Museum Press, 1946. 75¢.

*CATHERINE TEKAKWITHA
    Frances Taylor Patterson

An account of an Indian girl who "survived
the cruelty of the Iroquois." Grades 7 to 8.
Sheed & Ward, 1958. $3.00.

CATHLAMET ON THE COLUMBIA
    Thomas Nelson Strong
A Northwest epic of early pioneers and Indians of the lower Columbia River, written
by a man who spent his boyhood among them.
135 pp. Binfords and Mort, 1954. $3.00.

CAVES OF THE RESERVE AREA
    Paul S. Martin, *et al*
227 pp. Illus. Chicago Natural History
Museum, 1954. $5.00.

THE CENTRAL ESKIMO
    Franz Boas
As below. Illus. Peter Smith, $3.75.

THE CENTRAL ESKIMO
    Franz Boas
Covers all aspects of native tribal life --
subsistence, social and religious patterns,
etc. 266 pp. Illus. Paper. University of
Nebraska Press, 1964. $1.75.

THE CENTURIES OF SANTA FE
    Paul Horgan
The Spanish-Indian history of one of Ameri-
ca's most colorful cities. 165 pp. Illus.
Map. E. P. Dutton & Co., Inc., 1965.
Hardcover, $6.50; paper, $1.75.

A CENTURY OF DISHONOR
    Helen Hunt Jackson
A description of the early crusade for Indian
reform. Paper. Harper & Row, Publishers,
$1.75.

A CENTURY OF DISHONOR
    Helen Hunt Jackson
As above. 530 pp. Index. Ross & Haines,
$8.75.

A CENTURY OF DISHONOR: *The Early
    Crusade for Indian Reform*
    Helen Hunt Jackson
As above. Peter Smith, $4.00.

CEREMONIAL COSTUMES OF THE
    PUEBLO INDIANS
    Virginia More Roediger
Detailed descriptions of the dance dramas
of the Pueblos, with information about the
costumes and how to make them. Includes
a history of the Pueblo tribes and remarks
on contemporary Pueblo life. Illus. Peter
Smith, $4.00.

CEREMONIAL COSTUMES OF THE
PUEBLO INDIANS
Virginia More Roediger
As above. 251 pp. Illus. University of
California Press, 1961. $1.95.

CEREMONIAL PATTERNS IN THE GREAT-
ER SOUTHWEST
Ruth M. Underhill
Describes a variety of ceremonial patterns
associated with vision, agriculture, communal hunting, shamanism, and curing, as
practiced over a wide area of the southwestern United States and Mexico. An American
Ethnological Society Monograph reissued by
the University of Washington Press. Bound
with *Factionalism in Isleta Pueblo,* an A.E.S.
Monograph published by the University of
Washington Press.

CEREMONIAL SONGS OF THE CREEK AND
YUCHI INDIANS
Frank G. Speck
University Museum Press, 1911.   Paper,
$1.75.

CERTAIN RECENTLY EXPLORED
MOUNDS AND THEIR PROBABLE
RELATION TO THE HOPEWELL
CULTURE
William Ritchie
A summary description of a group of Hope-
wellian-inspired mounds at Squawkie Hill,
Livingston County, N. Y., and of one located at Geneseo, in the same county. The
author describes in detail the features and
artifacts most characteristic of the Mound
Builder Culture in New York State, specifically in the region of the Genessee Valley.
42 pp. 19 pls. 3 figs. Biblio. Research
Records of the Rochester Museum of Arts
and Sciences No. 4, Anthropology 4, 1938.
$1.00. Available from the Rochester Mu-
seum of Arts and Sciences.

CHACO: *America's First Metropolis*
J. Marshall Miller
The story of the redevelopment of the met-
tropolis located in Chaco Canyon, N. M.,
the only pre-Columbian metropolis in the
Western Hemisphere. Books International
(in preparation).

CHANGING CONFIGURATIONS IN THE
SOCIAL ORGANIZATION OF A BLACK-
FOOT TRIBE DURING THE RESERVE
PERIOD
Esther S. Goldfrank

Making use of documentary sources, the
author analyzes the shifts in social institutions from 1877 to 1940, with particular
attention given to the effects of new patterns
of life on interpersonal relations. An American Ethnological Society Monograph reissued by the University of Washington
Press. Bound with *Observations on Northern Blackfoot Kinship,* an A. E. S. Monograph published by the University of Washington Press.

CHANGING WASHO KINSHIP
Stanley A. Freed
Paper. University of California Press,
1960. $1.50.

CHAPTERS IN THE PREHISTORY OF
EASTERN ARIZONA, I
Paul S. Martin
244 pp. Illus. Index. Chicago Natural
History Museum, 1962. $6.00.

CHEROKEE DANCE AND DRAMA
Frank G. Speck *et al*
106 pp. Illus. Paper. University of California Press, 1951. $2.50.

THE CHEROKEE FRONTIER, *Conflict and
Survival, 1740-62*
David H. Corkran
302 pp. Index. Biblio. Illus. Maps. University of Oklahoma Press, 1962. $5.00.

*THE CHEROKEE: *Indians of the Mountains*
Sonia Bleeker; illustrated by Althea
Karr
The story of the powerful Cherokees and of
their life before and after the white man's
coming. 160 pp. Ages 8 to 12. William
Morrow & Co., Inc., 1952. $2.75.

*CHEROKEES
Marion Israel; illustrated by Harry L.
Timmins
Depicts the way of life of the Cherokees be-
fore their contact with the white man's ci-
vilization. 32 pp. Reading level, 3; interest
level, 2 to 6. Illus. Melmont Publishers,
Inc., 1961. $2.50.

THE CHEROKEES
Grade Steele Woodward
359 pp. Index. Biblio. Maps. Illus. University of Oklahoma Press, 1963. $5.95.

CHEROKEES OF THE OLD SOUTH
    Henry T. Malone
Emphasis on the social development of the Cherokees under the influence of white civilization prior to their ejection from their Appalachian homeland. 251 pp. Index. Illus. Biblio. Maps. University of Georgia Press, 1956. $4.50.

CHEYENNE AND ARAPAHO MUSIC
    Frances Densmore
111 pp. Illus. Songs. Southwest Museum, 1936. $2.50.

CHEYENNE AUTUMN
    Mari Sandoz
An account of the flight of the Cheyennes from Indian Territory. Paper. Avon Books, 1964. 95¢.

CHEYENNE AUTUMN
    Mari Sandoz
As above. 282 pp. Index. Illus. Maps. Hastings House Publishers, Inc., 1953. $5.95.

THE CHEYENNE IN PLAINS INDIAN
    TRADE RELATIONS, 1795-1840
    Joseph Jablow
A study of the effects of the fur trade and diffusion of the horse upon the Cheyenne. 110 pp. Index. Illus. Biblio. Maps. University of Washington Press, 1951. $2.50.

THE CHEYENNE INDIANS: *Their History and Ways of Life* (Two Vols.)
    George Bird Grinnell; Introduction by Mari Sandoz
A study of the Cheyennes' history as a warrior people; the organization of tribal life; ceremonials and religions. Illus. Vol. 1, xix + 358 pp; Vol. 2, vii + 430 pp. Cooper Square Publishers, Inc. Two-volume set, $20.00.

THE CHEYENNE, I: *Ceremonial Organization*
    G. A. Dorsey
55 pp. Illus. Chicago Natural History Museum, 1905. $2.50.

A CHEYENNE SKETCHBOOK
    William Cohoe; Commentary by E. Adamson Hoebel
96 pp. Illus. Catalogue of art. Index. University of Oklahoma Press, 1964. $5.95.

CHEYENNE TRAILS
    Lois R. Habegger
Paper. Faith and Life Press, 1949. $2.00.

THE CHEYENNE, II: *The Sun Dance*
    G. A. Dorsey
132 pp. Illus. Chicago Natural History Museum, 1905. $4.00.

THE CHEYENNE WAY: *Conflict and Case Law in Primitive Jurisprudence*
    Karl N. Llewellyn and E. Adamson Hoebel
360 pp. Illus. Index. University of Oklahoma Press, 1961. $5.00.

THE CHEYENNES: *Indians of the Great Plains*
    E. Adamson Hoebel
A portrait of the Cheyenne Indians "who represent much of the Plains Indian way of life." 110 pp. Illus. Paper. Holt, Rinehart & Winston, Inc., 1960. $1.75.

*CHI-WEE
    Grace Moon
Illus. Grades 3 to 7. Doubleday & Co., Inc., 1925. $3.50.

*CHIEF JOSEPH: *War Chief of the Nez Perce*
    Russell Davis and Brant Ashabranner
The true story of one of the greatest fighting chiefs of the Western Indian Wars. 192 pp. McGraw-Hill Book Co., 1962. $3.00.

CHIEF PUSHMATAHA: *American Patriot*
    Anna Lewis
Biography of a Choctaw Indian leader whose people fought for the U. S. Government in two wars -- the Creek War and the War of 1812 -- and subsequently lost land to the Government. The book also surveys the history of the Choctaws. 204 pp. Illus. Biblio. Exposition Press, 1959. $3.50.

CHIEF SEATTLE
    Eva Greenslit Anderson
The life story of Chief Seattle and of early Puget Sound life in Washington State among the Indians. 390 pp. Caxton Printers, Ltd., 1950. $5.00.

*CHIEF SEATTLE
    Elizabeth Rider Montgomery
The story of Chief Seattle's boyhood and of his aid to the white settlers in the Puget Sound area. Garrard Publishing Co., 1966.

CHIEF SPOKEN GARRY
Thomas Jessett
T. S. Denison & Co., Inc., $3.95.

CHILDHOOD AND YOUTH IN JICARILLA
APACHE SOCIETY
Morris E. Opler
170 pp. Illus. Map. Southwest Museum,
1946. $3.00.

CHILDREN OF NANIH WAIYA
Thelma V. Bounds
The history of the Choctaw Indians from the
days of DeSoto to our own. 74 pp. The
Naylor Co., 1964. $3.95.

*CHILDREN OF THE NORTH POLE
Ralph Harrimanns; translated by Anna-
belle Macmillan
Illus. Harcourt, Brace & World, Inc., 1964.
$2.50.

CHILDREN OF THE PEOPLE: *The Navaho
Individual and His Development*
Dorothea C. Leighton and Clyde Kluckhohn
The study of the Navaho as an individual,
including a report of a many-sided testing
program performed upon several hundred
Navaho children. Illus. Harvard University Press. $4.50.

*CHILDREN OF THE SEED GATHERERS
Mary Worthylake
A story of the "seed gatherers" who lived
in the central valleys of California and Oregon. 48 pp. Illus. Grades 2 to 4. Melmont Publishers, Inc., 1964. $2.50.

CHINOOK: *A History and Dictionary*
Edward Harper Thomas
Complete description of the Chinook jargon,
with dictionaries, a history of the language
and details of Indian customs. 186 pp. Binfords and Mort, 1954. $3.50.

CHIPPEWA INDIANS OF YESTERDAY AND
TODAY
Sister M. Carolissa Levi, F.S.P.A.
Historical record of the Chippewas from
their earliest beginnings to the present day.
385 pp. Illus. Index. Marycliff Convent,
$5.00.

*THE CHIPPEWA INDIANS: *Rice Gatherers
of the Great Lakes*
Sonia Bleeker; illustrated by Patricia
Boodell

The tribal way of life as shown through the
activities of one Chippewa family. 160 pp.
Ages 8 to 12. Illus. William Morrow &
Co., Inc., 1955. $2.75.

*THE CHOCTAW CODE
Russell G. Davis and Brent K. Ashabranner
The story of a white boy and his friendship
with a Choctaw Indian condemned to death
by tribal law. 160 pp. Ages 10 and up.
McGraw-Hill Book Co., 1961. $3.00.

CHRONOLOGICAL HISTORY OF THE
CONTINENT OF FLORIDA
Jean B. Bossu
University of Florida Press, 1962. $15.00.

*CHUKCHI HUNTER
Dorothy Stall
Illus. Grades 3 to 7. William Morrow and
Co., Inc., 1946. $2.75.

THE CHUMASH INDIANS OF SOUTHERN
CALIFORNIA
Leif C. W. Landberg
Fourteen chapters. 158 pp. Illus. Maps.
Charts. Southwest Museum, 1965. Paper,
$4.50; cloth, $6.50.

CIVIL WAR IN THE NORTHWEST: *Nebraska, Wisconsin, Minnesota and the Dakotas*
Robert Huhn Jones
216 pp. Illus. Appendices. Index. Biblio.
Maps. University of Oklahoma Press, 1961.
$4.00.

THE CIVIL WAR IN THE WESTERN TER-
RITORIES: *Arizona, Colorado, New Mexico and Utah*
Ray C. Colton
230 pp. Illus. Index. Biblio. Maps. University of Oklahoma Press, 1959. $5.00.

CIVILIZATION IN DESERT LANDS
Richard B. Woodbury, Editor
Collection of five papers on the adaptation
of primitive civilizations to the desert and
how they developed. 94 pp. University of
Utah Press, 1962. $1.50.

THE CLAN SYSTEM OF THE FORT
MOJAVE INDIANS
Lorraine Sherer
Provides a roster of the tribe by clan names
to parallel the English names under which
they are registered with the Department of
the Interior. 85 pp. Illus. Maps. Historical Society of Southern California, 1965.
$7.50.

*CLIFF DWELLERS OF WALNUT CANYON
  Carroll Lane Fenton and Alice Epstein;
    drawings by Albert Orbaan
The story of a tribe that lived in Arizona
approximately 800 years ago. 64 pp. Draw-
ings. Map. Grades 3 to 6. The John Day
Co., 1960. $2.25.

*CLIFF DWELLINGS
  Carroll B. Colby
Photographs and discussion of the ruins and
artifacts of the Pueblo Indians of the South-
west. Illus. Maps. Grades 3 to 7. Coward-
McCann, Inc., 1965. $2.50.

CLIFF DWELLINGS OF THE MESA VERDE
  Don Watson
History and description of major dwellings
and ruins. Illus. Paper. Mesa Verde
Museum Association, $1.00.

THE COAST SALISH OF BRITISH
  COLUMBIA
  Homer G. Barnett
A detailed account of the native culture of
twelve Salish ethnic groups, natives of the
Georgian Strait area that separates Victoria
Island from the British Columbia mainland.
xii + 320 pp. Illus. University of Oregon
Press, 1955. $5.00.

COCHISE AND MOGOLLON SITES, PINE
LAWN VALLEY, WESTERN NEW MEXICO
  Paul S. Martin, John B. Rinaldo and
    Ernst Antevs
232 pp. Illus. Vol. 38, No. 1, Chicago
Natural History Museum, 1949. $3.50.

*COCHISE, *Apache Warrior and Statesman*
  Edgar Wyatt; illustrated by Allan Hou-
    ser
A biography of the Apache warrior Cochise.
192 pp. Illus. Ages 9 to 13. McGraw-Hill
Book Co., 1953. $3.00.

COCHITI: *A New Mexico Pueblo, Past and
  Present*
  Charles H. Lange
An observation of an American Indian tribe
in transition from past to present. 618 pp.
Illus. University of Texas Press, 1959.
$10.00.

COFFEE IN THE GOURD
  Frank J. Dobie
Southern Methodist University Press, 1923.
$3.75.

COLONIAL VIRGINIA
  Richard L. Morton
The story of America's beginnings and of
our growth as a nation. 910 pp. Illus.
Index. University of North Carolina Press,
1960. $15.00.

THE COLUMBIA RIVER
  Ross Cox; Introduction by Edgar I.
    Stewart and J. R. Stewart
398 pp. Illus. Index. Biblio. Maps. University of Oklahoma Press, 1957. $5.75.

COLUMBUS IN THE NEW WORLD
  Bradley Smith
A photographic retracing of Columbus' route
describing what he saw. 192 pp. Illus.
Maps. Doubleday & Co., Inc., 1962. $15.00.

COMANCHE BONDAGE
  Carl C. Rister
Arthur H. Clark Co., 1955. $10.00.

COMANCHE LAND
  J. Emmor Harston
Little-known facts about the Comanches in
Texas. 236 pp. Illus. Index. Appendices.
The Naylor Co., 1963. $5.95.

COMANCHE, *Last Custer Survivor*
  Anthony A. Amarel
Illus. Westernlore Press, 1961. $5.50.

*COMANCHE OF THE SEVENTH
  Margaret Leighton
The life story of the only survivor of Custer's Last Stand, Captain Miles Keogh's
horse, Comanche. Describes the Indians'
reaction to their unfair treatment at the
hands of the white man. 216 pp. Illus.
Grades 10 to 12. Farrar, Straus & Giroux,
Inc., $3.00.

COMANCHES, *Lords of the South Plains*
  Ernest Wallace and E. Adamson Hoebel
382 pp. Illus. Index. Biblio. University
of Oklahoma Press, 1964. $5.95.

*COME TO OUR SALMON FEAST
  Martha Ferguson McKeown
The story of the last great salmon feast of
the Wyam Indians at Celilo Falls on the Col-
umbia River. 80 pp. Illus. Grades 5 to 6.
Binfords and Mort, 1959. $2.50.

COMMENTS ON CERTAIN IROQUOIS
  MASKS
  Joseph Keppler

A monograph on the False Face Society of the Iroquois. 65 pp. Illus. Color plates. Paper. Museum of the American Indian, Heye Foundation, $1.50.

COMMERCE OF THE PRAIRIES
    Josiah Gregg; edited by A. Hanna
A detailed source history of Santa Fe trade and life on the Southern Plains in the 1830's. J. B. Lippincott, 1962. Two-volume set (paper), $1.75, two-volume set (cloth), $7.95.

COMMERCE OF THE PRAIRIES
    Josiah Gregg; edited by M. Moorhead
As above. xxxvii + 469 pp. Illus. Maps. Biblio. Glossary. Index. University of Oklahoma Press, 1954. $7.50.

COMMON EDIBLE AND USEFUL PLANTS OF THE WEST
    Muriel Sweet
Describes how Indians and settlers used plants for food, clothing, medicine and other needs. 64 pp. Illus. Naturegraph Co., 1962. Paper, $1.00; cloth, $3.00.

√ THE COMPACT HISTORY OF THE AMERICAN INDIAN WARS
    John Tebbel
Illus. Hawthorn Books, Inc., 1966. $6.50.

COMPANION OF ADVENTURE
    Joseph T. Hazard
The life of Isaac I. Stevens, famous Indian arbitrator and first governor of Washington Territory. 251 pp. Illus. Binfords and Mort, $3.50.

A COMPANY OF HEROES: *The American Frontier*
    Dale Van Every
An account of life on the American frontier from 1775 to 1783. 312 pp. Index. Biblio. Maps. William Morrow and Co., Inc., 1962. $6.00.

A COMPANY OF HEROES: *The American Frontier*
    Dale Van Every
As above. Paper. New American Library, 75¢.

COMPARATIVE STUDIES OF NORTH AMERICAN INDIANS
    Harold E. Driver and William C. Massey
Deals with various aspects of subsistence, material culture, economics, and social

organization. Detailed geographical distributions of hundreds of culture elements are given on the maps within the text which depict separate territories for all the major tribes. 292 pp. 164 maps. 31 figs. American Philosophical Society, 1957. $5.00.

COMPLETE GUIDE TO THE SOUTHWEST
    Andrew Hepburn
A comprehensive tourist guide. Devotes special attention to the Pueblo ruins. 199 pp. Photo. Maps. Paper. Doubleday & Co., Inc., 1963. $1.95.

CONCISE NATURAL HISTORY OF EAST AND WEST FLORIDA
    Bernard Romans; edited by Rembert W. Patrick
Written in 1775, one of the first books to describe Florida and its inhabitants. 431 pp. Illus. University of Florida Press, 1962. $8.50.

√ CONFEDERATE INDIANS
    Frank Cunningham
Factual documentation of the war record of General Stand Waite, the only Indian general in the Confederate Army. 280 pp. Illus. The Naylor Co., 1959. $5.00.

THE CONNECTICUT STORY
    Joseph B. Hoyt
Illus. Readers Press, Inc., 1962. $8.95.

CONSPIRACY OF PONTIAC
    Francis Parkman
Paper. Collier, $1.50.

CONSPIRACY OF PONTIAC
    Francis Parkman
Peter Smith, $3.50.

CONTEMPORARY PUEBLO INDIAN POTTERY
    Francis H. Harlow and John V. Young
Describes and illustrates the types of pottery currently available from the Pueblo Indians. 50 pp. Illus. Paper. Museum of New Mexico Press, 1965. $1.00.

CONTENT AND STYLE OF AN ORAL LITERATURE: *Clackamas Chinook Myths and Tales*
    Melville Jacobs
The results of the first scientific analysis of an oral literature. Part I presents Clackamas folktales; Part II analyzes content,

forms and styles in terms of social relationships, value ideal and worldwide culture. viii + 285 pp. University of Chicago Press, 1959. $5.00.

A CONTINENT LOST - A CIVILIZATION WON: *Indian Land Tenure in America*
  Jay P. Kinney
A chronological presentation of the process through which the American Indian lost the greater part of his patrimony. 366 pp. The Johns Hopkins Press, 1937. $5.00.

CONTRIBUTIONS TO MESA VERDE ARCHAEOLOGY, I: *Site 499, Mesa Verde National Park, Colorado*
  Robert H. Lister
91 pp. Paper. University of Colorado Press, 1964. $3.00.

CONTRIBUTIONS TO MESA VERDE ARCHAEOLOGY, II: *Site 875, Mesa Verde National Park, Colorado*
  Robert H. Lister
University of Colorado Press (in press).

CONTRIBUTIONS TO THE ETHNOLOGY OF THE KUTCHIN
  Cornelius Osgood
Human Relations Area Files Press, 1964. $5.50.

THE CONQUEST OF CALIFORNIA AND NEW MEXICO
  James Madison Cutts
A story of conflict at the time the United States took over the territory which now comprises the states of New Mexico, Arizona and California. 276 pp. Horn and Wallace, 1965. $7.50.

CONQUEST OF NEW MEXICO AND CALIFORNIA IN 1846
  Phillip St. George Cooke
An account of the war with New Mexico in the Southwest. 307 pp. Horn and Wallace, 1965. $8.00.

COOMBS SITE
  Robert H. Lister *et al*
University of Utah Press. In three volumes: Part I (1959), $1.50; Part II (1960), $3.50; Part III (1961), $2.25. In one volume, $6.00.

COOPERATION AND COMPETITION AMONG PRIMITIVE PEOPLES
  Margaret Mead

A collection of essays examining the cultural character and social structure of primitive peoples. 544 pp. Index. Biblio. Paper. Beacon Press, 1961. $2.95.

COOPERATION AND COMPETITION AMONG PRIMITIVE PEOPLES
  Margaret Mead
As above. Peter Smith, $5.00.

COOS MYTH TEXTS
  Melville Jacobs
133 pp. Paper. University of Washington Press, 1940. $2.00.

COOS NARRATIVE AND ETHNOLOGIC TEXTS
  Melville Jacobs
125 pp. Paper. University of Washington Press, 1939. $2.00.

COPPERMINE JOURNEY
  Farley Mowatt, Editor
An account of Samuel Hearne's exploration of Canada's barren lands from 1769 to 1772. 144 pp. Little, Brown and Co., 1958. $3.75.

CORN AMONG THE INDIANS OF THE UPPER MISSOURI
  George F. Will and George E. Hyde
Describes corn varieties and corn growing among the Indians of the upper Missouri. 324 pp. Paper. University of Nebraska Press, 1964. $1.60.

CORN AMONG THE INDIANS OF THE UPPER MISSOURI
  George F. Will and George E. Hyde
As above. Illus. Peter Smith, $3.75.

THE CORN GODDESS AND OTHER TALES FROM INDIAN CANADA
  Diamond Jenness, Editor
Twenty-five tales illustrating the Canadian Indian's conception of the universe. 111 pp. Illus. Paper. National Museum of Canada, $2.00.

THE CORONADO EXPEDITION
  George Parker Winship
Republication of part of fourteenth annual Bureau of American Ethnology report, with related documents on the Spanish entrada into what is now New Mexico. 283 pp. Pls. Maps. The Rio Grande Press, Inc., $15.00.

*COUNCIL FIRE AND CANNON
    John H. Vrooman
Contains true stories of New York State --
from its discovery to Revolutionary times,
including the founding of the great League
as told by the Iroquois. 185 pp. Illus.
Follett Publishing Co., 1962. $3.50.

*THE COUNTRY OF THE HAWK
    August Derleth
An account of the settling of Sac Prairie and
of the Black Hawk War. Duell, Sloan and
Pearce, 1952; also available from Arkham
House: Publishers, Sauk City, Wis.

*THE COURAGE OF SARAH NOBLE
    Alice Dalgliesh; illustrated by Leonard
    Weisgard
The story of an eight-year-old girl in Colonial days who stays with Indians in Connecticut while her father is away. Illus. Grades
1 to 3.   Charles Scribner's Sons, 1954.
$3.80.

COURSE OF EMPIRE
    Bernard DeVoto
Houghton Mifflin Co., 1952. Cloth, $6.50;
paper, $2.65.

COWBOYS AND COLONELS
    Edmond Mandat-Grancey
Originally published in French in 1884. A
Frenchman views the American West, its
people and their culture. J. B. Lippincott
Co., 1963. Paper, $1.60; cloth, $5.50.

COYOTE WISDOM
    Frank J. Dobie, Editor
The theme and hero of this volume, Old Man
Coyote, a folk character, is discussed -- the
Aztec meanings of his name, the many nick-
names attached to him, his clever tricks,
his preeminent place in Indian folklore as a
creative power. Indian legends are well
represented, as are folk customs. 300 pp.
Illus. Southern Methodist University Press,
1965. $6.95.

CRAZY HORSE
    Mari Sandoz
The biography of Crazy Horse, Chief of the
Oglala Sioux, touching upon the hunting and
slaughter of the buffalo, from 1867 to 1883.
428 pp. Illus. Hastings House, Publishers,
Inc., 1955. $4.95.

CRAZY HORSE
    Mari Sandoz
As above. Paper. University of Nebraska
Press, 1961. $1.65.

*CRAZY HORSE: *Sioux Warrior*
    Enid LaMonte Meadowcroft
The story of Crazy Horse, Chief of the Oglala Tribe of Sioux Indians and of his fight
to retain his people's lands. 80 pp. Garrard Publishing Co., 1965. $1.98.

THE CREEK FRONTIER, 1540-1783
    David H. Corkran
A history of the Creek Tribe during the colonial period. 360 pp. Illus. Biblio. In-
dix. University of Oklahoma Press, 1967.
$5.95.

CROOKED RIDGE VILLAGE
    Joe Ben Wheat
Illus. Paper. University of Arizona Press,
1954. $1.00.

CROW INDIAN BEADWORK
    William Wildschut and John C. Ewers
A descriptive and historical study of the
beadwork of the Crow Indians of Montana.
52 pp. Illus. Color Plates. Volume XVI,
Contributions from the Museum of the American Indian, Heye Foundation, 1959. $3.00.

CROW INDIAN MEDICINE BUNDLES
    William Wildschut and John C. Ewers
Comprehensive report on Crow bundles and
medicine shields, including examples of
Plains Indian art. 178 pp. Illus. Color
Plates. Contributions from the Museum of
the American Indian, Heye Foundation, 1960.
$6.50.

√ THE CROW INDIANS
    R. H. Lowie
Discusses the tribal organization, kinship
system, literature, club life, war and religion, and ceremonialism of the Crow Indians. vii + 350 pp. Illus. Appendices.
Paper. Glossary. Index. Holt, Rinehart
and Winston, Inc., 1956. $4.75.

*THE CROW INDIANS: *Hunters of the
    Northern Plains*
    Sonia Bleeker; illustrated by Althea
    Karr
Habits, history and adventures of the Crow
Indian buffalo hunters. 160 pp. Ages 8 to
12. Illus. Index. William Morrow & Co.,
Inc., 1953. $2.95.

CROW TEXTS
    Robert H. Lowie, Editor
A picture of the Crow Indians, their history,
legends and culture. University of California Press, 1960. $8.50.

CROW WORD LISTS
Robert H. Lowie
A bilingual dictionary including legends, songs, prayers, and other material. 424 pp. Appendices. University of California Press, 1960. $8.50.

THE CULTIVATION AND WEAVING OF
COTTON IN THE PREHISTORIC SOUTH-
WESTERN UNITED STATES
(Kate Peck Kent)
Describes the part cotton has played in the lives of the Southwestern Indians, from its introduction until the present, through an analysis of woven cotton from prehistoric sites in Arizona, New Mexico, southern Utah, and southern Colorado. 276 pp. Illus. Photo. Maps. American Philosophical Society, 1957. $4.00.

CULTURAL AND NATURAL AREAS OF
NATIVE NORTH AMERICA
Alfred L. Kroeber
Illus. University of California Press, 1940. $6.50.

CULTURAL RELATIONS IN THE PLATEAU
REGION OF NORTHWESTERN AMERICA
Verne F. Ray
154 pp. Maps. Southwest Museum, 1939. $3.50.

CULTURAL SEQUENCES AT THE DALLES
OREGON: *A Contribution to Pacific North-
west Prehistory*
Luther S. Cressman *et al*
A monograph describing the continuity and change of culture at The Dalles of the Columbia River, Oregon. 108 pp. Maps. Paper. American Philosophical Society, 1960. $3.00.

CULTURE AND EXPERIENCE
A. Irving Hallowell
University of Pennsylvania Press, 1957. $8.50.

CURTIS' WESTERN INDIANS
Ralph W. Andrews
Story of historian Edward S. Curtis, a living chronicle of more than eighty tribes. 176 pp. Photo. Superior Publishing Co., 1962. $12.50.

CUSTER AND THE GREAT CONTROVERSY
Robert M. Utley

Discussion of the Battle of Little Big Horn including a history of the origins and developments of the legends that have grown from that historic battle. 184 pp. Illus. Westernlore Press, $6.75.

CUSTER BATTLE BOOK
Herbert H. Coffeen
Carlton Press, Inc., $2.00.

*CUSTER COUNTRY
Ralph E. Scudder
The story of the Custer Massacre at the Little Big Horn, showing the country, the line of march, and the battlefield. 64 pp. Aerial photographs. Line drawings. Charts. Grades 7 to 9. Binfords & Mort, 1963. $3.00.

THE CUSTER MYTH
Colonel W. A. Graham
Part I is a group of Indian accounts of various battles. Part II and III contain Benteen's account of the Battle of the Little Big Horn. Part IV is a series of articles by Fred Dustin. 435 pp. Illus. The Stackpole Co., 1954. $10.00.

CUSTER'S FALL
David Humphreys Miller
Duell, Sloan and Pearce, 1957. $4.50.

CUSTER'S LAST BATTLE: *By One of His
Troop Commanders*
A facsimile of the 1892 edition. 37 pp. Illus. Paper. Shorey Publications, 1964. $2.00.

*CUSTER'S LAST STAND
Quentin Reynolds
The story of The Battle of the Little Big Horn, including a running biography of General Custer. 185 pp. Illus. Grades 4 to 6. Random House, Inc., 1951. $1.95.

CUSTER'S LUCK
Edgar I. Stewart
522 pp. Illus. Index. Biblio. University of Oklahoma Press, 1955. $6.95.

CYCLES OF CONQUEST: *The Impact of
Spain, Mexico and the United States on In-
dians of the Southwest, 1543-1960*
Edward H. Spicer
Illus. University of Arizona Press, 1962. $12.50.

D

DAHCOTAH: *Life and Legend of the Sioux*
Mary Eastman
Facsimile of the 1847 edition. The author,
wife of Captain Seth Eastman, accompanied
her husband to his various military stations
among the Indians. This is an account of
her researches into the customs and mythology of the Sioux. Ross & Haines, Inc.,
$6.75.

*DAKOTAS
Marion Israel; illustrated by Paul M.
Souza
A picture of the Dakota Indians of long ago,
showing the importance of each person in
the community and the excitement of a buffalo hunt. 32 pp. Illus. Reading level, 3;
interest level, 1 to 6. Melmont Publishers,
Inc., 1959. $2.50.

DANCES AND STORIES OF THE AMERICAN
INDIAN
Bernard S. Mason; photographs by Paul
Boris and others; drawings by Frederic H. Koch
Tells the story behind sixty-eight Indian
dances; describes the properties and cos-
tuming for the conduct of the dances; shows
the basic steps and body movements essen-
tial to recapturing the Indian ritual and routine. 269 pp. 112 illustrations. 28 plates
in sepia. 3 maps. The Ronald Press Co.,
1944. $5.50.

DANCES OF THE BLACKFOOT INDIANS
Southwest Museum, 25¢.

*DANCING CLOUD
Mary and Conrad Buff
Illus. Grades 2 to 5. The Viking Press,
Inc., 1957. $3.00.

DANCING GODS: *Indian Ceremonials of
New Mexico and Arizona*
Erna Fergusson
Dances and ceremonials of Pueblo, Apache
and Navajo Indians. Sixteen paintings by
eminent Southwestern artists. 328 pp.
University of New Mexico Press, 1959.
$5.00.

*THE DANCING HORSES OF ACOMA *and
Other Indian Stories*
Helen Rushmore, with Wolf Robe Hunt
The first publication of twelve traditional

stories of the Acoma Indians, a Southwestern Pueblo tribe still inhabiting the oldest
continuously inhabited pueblo dwelling in the
United States. 160 pp. Illus. Grades 5 to
9. The World Publishing Co., 1963. $4.50.

DANGER CAVE
Jesse D. Jennings
Illus. University of Utah Press, 1957.
$6.00.

*DANIEL BOONE
Shannon Garst; illustrated by Bill Barss
A biography of the most famous of American
pioneers and backwoodsmen who, through
his exploration, opened the wilderness to
settlers. This is his story, his involvement
in Indian wars, and his part in preparing
Kentucky for statehood. Follett Publishing
Co., $1.95.

*DARK ARROW
Lucille Mulcahy
Illus. Grades 5 to 9. Coward-McCann,
Inc., 1953. $2.75.

*DARK PILGRIM, *The Story of Squanto*
Feenie Ziner
The story of the Patuxet Indian, Squanto,
who made his mark on American history
when he became friend and counselor to the
Pilgrims who had settled on the shores of
Massachusetts Bay. 158 pp. Biblio. Notes.
Chilton Books, 1965. $3.98.

*DAUGHTER OF THE TEJAS
Ophelia Ray
Tiwana, a twelve-year-old child, stubborn-
ly vowed that she would somehow bring her
mother, who had been captured by the Apaches, back to safety. 126 pp. Grades 5
through 8. New York Graphic Society Publishers, Ltd., 1965. $2.95.

DAWN IN ARCTIC ALASKA
Diamond Jenness; illustrated by Gia-
como Raimondi
An appreciation of the Alaskan Eskimo by
a scientist who has lived closely among
them. 222 pp. Illus. University of Minnesota Press, 1957. $4.75.

*A DAY IN ORAIBI - A HOPI INDIAN
VILLAGE
Harry C. James; illustrated by Don
Perceval
Depicts life in a Hopi Indian village, *kiva*,
and typical home. 36 pp. Reading level,
3; interest level, 2 to 5. Melmont Pub-
lishers, Inc., 1959. $2.50.

*A DAY WITH HONAU - *A Hopi Indian Boy*
    Harry C. James, illustrated by Don
    Perceval
A simple story of a Hopi boy's life. 32 pp.
Reading level, 3; interest level, 2 to 5.
Melmont Publishers, Inc., 1957. $2.50.

*A DAY WITH POLI - *A Hopi Indian Girl*
    Harry C. James; illustrated by Don
    Perceval
The way of life of the Hopi Indians is revealed in the work and play of Poli, sister
of the main character in *A Day with Honau -
A Hopi Indian Boy*. 32 pp. Reading level,
3; interest level, 2 to 5. Melmont Publishers, Inc., 1957. $2.50.

DECORATIVE ART OF THE SOUTHWEST
  INDIANS
    Dorothy S. Sides
A reissue of the 1936 edition. Book gathers
nearly three hundred examples of the finest
authentic Southwestern Indian decorations.
These have been redrawn in black and white
by the author and the selections range from
the 13th-century geometric art of the Pueblos to the handcrafts carried on by the nomadic and Pueblo peoples of the present.
The main emphasis is on ceramic decoration, and the author includes pieces from
the archaeological sites of Pecos, Sikyatki,
the Mimbres, and modern Pueblo pottery
from Acoma, Zuni, Cochiti and the Hopi.
She also includes designs and motifs from
the basketry of the Apache, Pima and Papago; beadwork from the Mojave; authentic
Zuni masks; Hopi kachina dolls; sandpaintings and blanket designs from the Navajo.
101 pp. Paper. Dover Publications, Inc.,
1961. $1.00.

DECORATIVE ART OF THE SOUTHWEST-
  ERN INDIANS
    Dorothy S. Sides
As above. Illus. Peter Smith, $3.00.

DECORATIVE ART OF THE TETES DE
  BOULE OF QUEBEC
    D. S. Davidson
Comments on the decorative motifs used on
birchbark containers and moccasins by the
Tetes De Boule of Quebec, a seminomadic
tribe, and the deteriorating effects of acculturation on its artistry. 38 pp. Paper. Illus. Museum of the American Indian, Heye
Foundation, $1.25.

*THE DELAWARE INDIANS: *Eastern Fish-
  ermen and Farmers*
    Sonia Bleeker; illustrated by Patricia
    Boodell
Story of the tribe whose former territory is
now Pennsylvania, Maryland, Delaware,
New Jersey, and southern New York State.
160 pp. Index. Ages 8 to 12. William Morrow & Co., Inc., 1953. $2.95.

*THE DELAWARES
    Norma Dobrin; illustrated by Arnold
    Dobrin
Shows how Delawares hunt, farm, dance and
tell the stories of "the old ones." 32 pp.
Reading level, 3; interest level, 2 to 5.
Melmont Publishers, Inc., 1963. $2.50.

DELIGHT MAKERS
    A. F. Bandelier
Illus. Dodd, Mead and Co., $4.00.

DESCRIPTION OF LOUISIANA NEWLY DIS-
  COVERED TO THE SOUTHWEST OF NEW
  FRANCE BY THE ORDER OF THE KING
    Fr. Louis Hennepin; translated by Ma-
    rion E. Cross
Originally published in Paris in 1683. The
story of Father Louis Hennepin's explorations (1679 to 1680) of territory which now
comprises the states of Michigan, Wisconsin, Indiana, Illinois, Iowa, and Minnesota.
xxi + 190 pp. Illus. University of Minnesota Press, 1938. $3.50.

*THE DESERT PEOPLE
    Ann Nolan Clark; illustrated by Allan
    Houser
Poetic prose tells of the life of the Papago
Indians through the year's seasonal changes.
56 pp. The Viking Press, Inc., 1962. $3.00.

DESIGN MOTIFS OF THE PUEBLO INDIANS
    Beula Wadsworth
An analysis and demonstration of Pueblo
styles and patterns, their intricacies and
nuances. Includes a discussion of methods
by which modern students may apply these
styles, and how they can serve as the basis
for novel design and creation. 112 pp. Illustrated by the author. The Naylor Co.,
1957. $5.00.

DESIGNS ON PREHISTORIC POTTERY OF
  ARIZONA
    Eleanor P. Clarke
Illus. Paper. University of Arizona Press,
1933. $1.00.

THE DESPERATE PEOPLE
Farley Mowat
Includes a short history of the Eskimo peoples from their first appearance in Canada to the 20th century -- the growth of contact between white man and Eskimo; the disease, diminishing caribou herds, starvation, and neglect, and how, despite all this, the Ihalmiut have managed to survive. 293 pp. Illus. Appendix. Atlantic Monthly Press, 1959. $4.95.

DIARIES OF H. H. SPALDING AND ASA B. SMITH
H. H. Spalding; edited by Clifford M. Drury
Arthur H. Clark Co., 1958. $12.50.

DIARIES AND ACCOUNTS OF THE ROMERO EXPEDITIONS IN ARIZONA AND CALIFORNIA
Lowell Bean and William M. Mason
The Ward Ritchie Press, 1963. $10.00.

DICTIONARY CATALOG OF THE EDWARD E. AYER COLLECTION OF AMERICANA AND AMERICAN INDIANS, THE NEWBERRY LIBRARY
Represents some 90,000 volumes whose main fields relate to North and South American Indians, from prehistory and archaeology to modern studies in ethnology and anthropology; contact of the white man with native tribes, including 18th- and 19th-century books of travel and descriptions which mention Indians; voyages and travels during the period of exploration and early settlement; cartography, especially from the 15th through the 18th century; and Hawaii, the Philippines, and Oceania. Catalog reproduces 160,300 cards. 8,062 pp. G. K. Hall & Co., 1961. Sixteen-volume set, $650.00 (U.S.); $715.00 (foreign).

DID CUSTER DISOBEY ORDERS AT THE BATTLE OF THE LITTLE BIG HORN?
Charles Kuhlman
Illus. Paper. William C. Brown Co., Publishers, $1.00.

DIEGO RAMIREZ VISITA
Walter V. Scholes
99 pp. Paper. University of Missouri Press, 1964. $1.25.

DIGGING INTO HISTORY
Paul S. Martin
157 pp. Illus. Map. Chicago Natural History Museum, 1959. $1.50.

DIGGING INTO HISTORY
Paul S. Martin
Oceana Publications, Inc., 1960. $3.25.

DIGGING UP AMERICA
Frank C. Hibben
Illus. Hill & Wang, Inc., 1960. $5.00.

THE DISCOVERY, SETTLEMENT AND PRESENT STATE OF KENTUCKE
John Filson; Introduction by William H. Masterson
One of the earliest histories of Kentucky. Contains a reproduction of the state's first published map and introduces Daniel Boone. 118 pp. Map. Table. Paper. Corinth Books, 1962. $1.25.

THE DISCOVERY, SETTLEMENT AND PRESENT STATE OF KENTUCKY
John Filson
As above. Peter Smith, $3.25.

DISINHERITED: *The Lost Birthright of the American Indian*
Dale Van Every
The story of the events preceding the Removal Act, its shattering effect on the eastern Indians, and the significance it had (and still has) for all Americans. Maps. Index. Biblio. William Morrow & Co., Inc., 1966. $6.00.

*DOG SOLDIERS: *The Famous Warrior Society of the Cheyenne Indians*
Glen Dines and Raymond Price; illustrated by Peter Burchard
42 pp. Glossary. Biblio. The Macmillan Co., 1962. $1.95.

*A DOG TEAM FOR ONGLUK
Terry Shannon; illustrated by Charles Payzant
In this book, a little Eskimo boy's dearest wish comes true. Ongluk, his family, and their life in the Northland are an integral part of the story. 32 pp. Illus. Reading level, 2; interest level, kindergarten to 3. Melmont Publishers, Inc., 1962. $2.50.

DONIPHAN'S EXPEDITION
John T. Hughes
A reprint of the 1848 edition. An eyewitness narrative of the American conquest of the Southwest. 408 pp. Illus. The Rio Grande Press, Inc., $8.00.

DOORS OF PERCEPTION
    Aldous Huxley
Paper. Harper & Row, Publishers, 1954.
Hardcover, $3.95; paper, $1.35.

DOWN FROM THE LONELY MOUNTAIN
    Jane L. Curry
Illus. Harcourt, Brace & World, Inc., 1965.
$3.00.

DOWN THE COLORADO
    Robert B. Stanton; edited and with an
        Introduction by Dwight L. Smith
A record of the 1889 exploration to build a
railroad along the Colorado River. 237 pp.
Illus. Map. Index. University of Oklahoma
Press, 1965. $5.95.

DOWN THE SANTA FE TRAIL AND INTO
    MEXICO: *The Diary of Susan Shelby Mag-*
    offin, 1846-1847
        Susan Shelby Magoffin; edited by Stella
            Drumm, with an Introduction by How-
            ard R. Lamar
The diary of a young bride journeying to
Mexico, including accounts of life on the
trail, people met, miles traveled, and general information about the countryside. xxxv
+ 294 pp. Illus. Map. Frontispiece. Yale
University Press, 1962. Cloth, $7.50; pa-
per, $1.95.

DU BAY: *Son-in-Law of Oshkosh*
    Merton E. Krug
382 pp. Brown Book Co., 1946. $5.00.

DUTCH HOLLOW, AN EARLY HISTORIC
    PERIOD SENECA SITE IN LIVINGSTON
    COUNTY, NEW YORK
        William A. Ritchie
In September, 1934, the author excavated a
total of sixty-seven graves at the Dutch Hollow site in Avon, Livingston County, N. Y.
This report is a description of this early
17th-century Seneca burial ground and of
the objects which he uncovered. 98 pp. 30
pls. 6 tables. Biblio. Research Records
of the Rochester Museum of Arts and Sciences No. 10, 1954. $2.25. Available from
The Rochester Museum Association.

THE DYNAMICS OF STYLISTIC CHANGE
    IN ARIKARA CERAMICS
        James Deetz
111 pp. 3 maps. 27 figs. Paper. Illinois
Studies in Anthropology, No. 4, 1965. University of Illinois Press, $2.50.

E

*EAGLE FEATHER
    Clyde Robert Bulla
The story of a Navajo Indian boy of today,
his love for his family and *hogan,* and his
experiences in the white man's school for
Indian children. 87 pp. Illus. Grades 2 to
5. Thomas Y. Crowell Co., 1953. $3.50.

THE EAGLE, THE JAGUAR, AND THE
SERPENT
    Miguel Covarrubias
Illus. Alfred A. Knopf, Inc., 1954. $15.00.

*EAGLE WING
    Sister Bernard Coleman
A story of the Chippewas before their culture was destroyed, as told in the adventures of a young tribesman.   Greenwich
Book Publishers, Inc., $2.00.

*THE EARLIEST AMERICANS
    William E. Scheele
An introduction to prehistoric man in America, particularly the Folsom people, based
on recent archaeological findings. 64 pp.
Illus. Grades 5 to 8. The World Publishing Co., 1963. $2.75.

EARLY DAKOTA DAYS
    Winnifred Reutter, Editor
A collection of many eyewitness accounts of
the early days in South Dakota, including
descriptions of local Indian life.   Illus.
Winifred Reutter, 1966. $10.00.

EARLY DAYS AMONG THE CHEYENNE
AND ARAPAHOE INDIANS
    John Seger; edited by Stanley Vestal
146 pp. Appendix. Illus. University of
Oklahoma Press, 1956. $3.50.

EARLY DAYS AND INDIAN WAYS
    Madge Hardin Walters
An autobiography of Madge Hardin Walters,
her association with the Sioux, the Bloods,
and the Navajos. 254 pp. Westernlore
Press, 1956. $5.50.

EARLY INDIANS OF TEMECULA
    Horace Parker
Illus. Paper. Paisano Press Inc., 1965.
$1.00.

EARLY KLICKITAT VALLEY DAYS
Robert Ballou
A collection of Klickitat country tales of Indians and settlers. 496 pp. Illus. Photographs. Binfords and Mort, 1960. $10.00.

EARLY MAN IN THE NEW WORLD
Kenneth MacGowan and Joseph A. Hester, Jr.; Foreword by Gordon Elkholm
Examines and assesses the prevailing theories on the appearance of man in America during the late Ice Age, and his relationship to the American Indian. Line drawings. Paper. Doubleday & Co., Inc., 1962. $1.45.

EARLY MAN IN THE NEW WORLD
Kenneth MacGowan and Joseph A. Hester, Jr.
As above. Peter Smith, $3.50.

EARLY MAN PROJECTILE POINTS IN THE SOUTHWEST
Kenneth Honea
Illus. Museum of New Mexico Press, 1965. 25¢.

EARLY NAVAJO MIGRATIONS AND ACCULTURATION IN THE SOUTHWEST
James J. Hester
An ethnological and historic treatise based on salvage archaeology in the Navajo Reservoir District and on historical documents pertaining to Navajo contacts with Europeans. 130 pp. Illus. Biblio. Museum of New Mexico Press, 1962. $3.00.

EARLY PIT HOUSE VILLAGE OF THE MOGOLLON CULTURE: *Forestdale Valley, Arizona*
Emil W. Haury and E. B. Sayles
Illus. Paper. University of Arizona Press, 1947. $1.25.

AN EARLY SITE IN CAYUGA COUNTY, NEW YORK
William A. Ritchie
The author's field work in 1939 and 1940 at the Frontenac Island site in Cayuga Lake prepared the way for a clearer understanding of the intermediary stages between Lamoka Lake and the Laurentian sites of Brewerton. Although possessing traits of each tradition, Frontenac Island was, by itself, a "third hitherto unknown Archaic complex." 158 pp. 27 pls. Fig. Map. 8 tables. Biblio. Research Records of the Rochester Museum of Arts and Sciences No. 7, 1945. $1.50. Available from the Rochester Museum Association.

EASTER AT PASCUA VILLAGE
Muriel T. Painter
Illus. Paper. University of Arizona Press, 1960. $1.00.

*EASTER FIRES
Wilma Pitchford Hayes; illustrated by Peter Burchard
The story of Little Bow, who saved his sister from sacrifice; includes material on the origin of the Indian custom of lighting bonfires on Easter eve. Illus. Grades 8 to 12. Coward McCann, Inc., 1960. $2.75.

EASTER OJIBWA
Leonard Bloomfield
An extended study of the Central Algonquin syntax. 284 pp. University of Michigan Press, 1957. $10.00.

*THE EASTERN WOODLAND INDIANS
A description of the New York State Indians prior to the arrival of the white man. Third-grade reading level. Frank E. Richards, $2.00.

*EDGE OF MANHOOD
Thomas Fall; illustrated by Henry C. Pitz
A portrayal of a Shawnee boy who must learn that his maturity rests in his ability to accept certain relations with other people, as well as in his own physical prowess. 96 pp. Illus. Ages 9 to 12. The Dial Press, 1964. $3.00.

THE EFFECT OF SMALLPOX ON THE DESTINY OF THE AMERINDIAN
Allen E. Stearn and E. W. Stearn
153 pp. Brown Book Co., 1945. $2.50.

THE EFFECTS OF WHITE CONTACT UPON BLACKFOOT CULTURE
Oscar Lewis
A developmental study of Blackfoot institutions showing the changes that occurred in the economy, social organization, marriage and warfare following contact with Western civilization. An American Ethnological Society Monograph reissued by the University of Washington Press. $5.00.

EIGHTEENTH CENTURY NAVAJO FORTRESSES OF THE GOBERNADOR DISTRICT
Roy Carlson
University of Colorado Press, 1965. $3.50.

EIGHTEENTH-CENTURY TRAVELS IN PENNSYLVANIA AND NEW YORK
St. John de Crevecoeur; translated and edited by P. G. Adams
Illus. University of Kentucky Press, 1961; $5.00.

EL GRINGO: *or, New Mexico and Her People*
William W. H. Davis
Deals with old Spain in New Mexico after the American conquest in 1848. 432 pp. Illus. The Rio Grande Press, Inc., $7.50.

ELIAS BOUDINOT, CHEROKEE, AND HIS AMERICA
Ralph Henry Gabriel
190 pp. Illus. Appendix. Map. University of Oklahoma Press, 1941. $3.75.

*ELIZA AND THE INDIAN WAR PONY
Beryl and Paul Scott; illustrated by Donald Bolognese
The story of the first white child born in Idaho and her life among the Indians. Ages 8 to 12. Illus. Lothrop, Lee and Shepard Co., 1961. $3.00.

EMERGENCE MYTH (According to the Upward-Reaching Rite)
Rewritten by Mary C. Wheelwright; illustrated by Louie Ewing
Myth recounted by various medicine men, with commentary by the author. 186 pp. Illus. Index. Appendix. Glossary. Navajo Religion Series, Vol. iii, 1949. Museum of Navajo Ceremonial Art, $12.00.

*ESCAPE FROM THE SHAWNEES
Herbert Witten
Tells how Whit Martin escaped from the Shawnees, survived, and helped to save Gabe Stoner, a friend of Daniel Boone. 197 pp. Illus. Ages 10 to 14. Follett Publishing Co., 1958. $2.95.

ESKIMO ADVENTURE
Edward L. Keithahn
A personal account of life with primitive Eskimos. Illus. Superior Publishing Co., 1963. $5.95.

*THE ESKIMO: *Arctic Hunters and Trappers*
Sonia Bleeker; illustrated by Patricia Boodell
Describes the customs and occupations of the Eskimos. 160 pp. Illus. Ages 8 to 12. William Morrow & Co., Inc., 1959. $2.75.

*ESKIMO BOY
Pipaluk Freuchen; illustrated by Ingrid Vang Nyman
After seeing a walrus kill his father, young Ivik must hunt, trap, and fish as a man, to provide for his family on Greenland Island. Illus. Grades 4 to 6. Lothrop, Lee and Shepard Co., 1951. $2.95.

ESKIMO CHILDHOOD AND INTERPERSONAL RELATIONSHIPS: *Nunivak Biographies and Genealogies*
Margaret Lantis
This collection of life stories of eighteen Eskimos contributes to understanding of one facet of human behavior: the reciprocation between longitudinal personality processes and a changing cultural milieu. An American Ethnological Society Monograph reissued by the University of Washington Press. $5.50.

*ESKIMO ISLAND
Phillip Viereck
Illus. Grades 6 to 10. Prentice-Hall, Inc., 1962. $3.37.

ESKIMO MASKS AND CEREMONIALISM
Dorothy Jean Ray; photographs by Alfred A. Blaker
Study examines the functional aspects of masks in ceremonialism and social organization as well as the aesthetic components of the masks themselves. It also contains a consideration of the archaeological and historical backgrounds. Map. An American Ethnological Society Monograph reissued by the University of Washington Press.

ESKIMO SCULPTURE
Jorgen Mildgaard
An examination of art from prehistoric to contemporary times. Illus. Clarkson N. Potter, 1962. $3.95.

AN ESKIMO VILLAGE IN THE MODERN WORLD
Charles C. and Jane M. Hughes
In this study, the author records some of the changes which have occurred in the lives of the Eskimos who inhabit St. Lawrence Island and views these transformations in the light of geographical, historical, ethnographic and conceptual backgrounds, including quotations from the Eskimos themselves, taken from field notes. xiv + 419 pp. Photos. Cornell University Press, 1960. $8.50.

ESKIMOS
    Edward Carpenter *et al*
66 pp. Illus. Color plates. Photographs.
Line drawings. Paper. University of Toronto Press, 1959. $3.95.

THE ESKIMOS: *Their Environment and Folkways*
    Edward M. Weyer
xvii + 491 pp. Yale University Press, 1962.
$12.50.

*THE ESKIMOS KNEW
    Tillie S. Pine; illustrated by Ezra Jack Keats
Describes the ingenuity of the Eskimos in adapting to their surroundings. 32 pp. Illus. Grades kindergarten to 3. McGraw-Hill Book Co., 1962. $2.95.

ESSAYS IN PRE-COLUMBIAN ART AND ARCHAEOLOGY
    Samuel K. Lothrop *et al*
A compilation of the work of experts on multiple facets of the achievement of pre-Columbian Indians of the Americas. Illus. Index. Harvard University Press, 1961. $12.50.

ETHNOBOTANY OF WESTERN WASHINGTON
    Erna Gunther
Deals with plants, their uses and preparation by the Indians, with notes on the rapidly disappearing nature lore of the tribes of the Washington region. 61 pp. Index. Biblio. Map. University of Washington Press, 1945. $1.75.

ETHNOGRAPHIC BIBLIOGRAPHY OF NORTH AMERICA
    George P. Murdock
A bibliography of all native Indian tribes in North America, including those of northern Mexico. 395 pp. Illus. Index. Biblio. Maps. Human Relations Area Files Press, 1960. $6.75.

ETHNOGRAPHY OF THE TANAINA
    Cornelius Osgood
A description of the manifest culture of the Tanaina of Cook Inlet, Alaska, as it would have appeared just previous to historic contact. 228 pp. Tables. 14 pls. 32 figs. Biblio. Human Relations Area Files Press, 1966. $5.00.

EVA: *An Archaic Site*
    Thomas M. N. Lewis and Madeline Kneberg Lewis
The 7,000-year-old site of Eva, which was inhabited by some of the earliest Indians in the South, is the subject of this archaeological report. Four distinct layers offered an opportunity to separate the information into successive periods, and to determine the different cultural changes that took place during the 5,000 years of the Site's occupation. 188 pp. Illus. Index. Tables. Photographs. Paper. University of Tennessee Press, 1962. $3.00.

EXCAVATIONS AT HAWIKUH
    Frederick Webb Hodge
Report on the Hendericks-Hodge expedition to Zuni to excavate the ancient Pueblo of Hawikuh. 250 pp. Illus. Index. Biblio. Museum of the American Indian, Heye Foundation, 1964. $8.00.

EXCAVATIONS AT KOLOMOKI: *Final Report*
    William H. Sears
Summary report on excavation techniques and findings at eight Indian mounds near Blakely, Georgia. 121 pp. Index. Appendix. Biblio. Paper. University of Georgia Press, 1956. $3.00.

EXCAVATIONS AT LOS PINOS PHASE SITES IN THE NAVAJO RESERVATION DISTRICT
    Frank W. Eddy
Describes salvage operations conducted by the Museum of New Mexico at sites of the Los Pinos Phase (A.D. 1,400), considered to be a local variant of the San Juan Basket Maker II Culture. 107 pp. Illus. Index. Biblio. Museum of New Mexico Press, 1961. $3.00.

EXCAVATIONS AT NANTACK VILLAGE, POINT OF PINES, ARIZONA
    David A. Breternitz
Illus. Paper. University of Arizona Press, 1959. $1.75.

EXCAVATIONS AT PUEBLO PARDO
    Joseph H. Toulouse, Jr., and Robert L. Stephenson
Describes the excavation at Pueblo Pardo on the Chupadero Mesa, in central New Mexico. 44 pp. Index. Paper. 1960 Papers in Anthropology, No. 3, Museum of New Mexico Press.

EXCAVATIONS AT SNAKETOWN
Harold Gladwin and others
University of Arizona Press, 1937. $7.00.

EXCAVATIONS AT THE LODAISKA SITE
H. J. Irwin and C. C. Irwin
Report on the first stratified site excavated in Denver, Colorado, with records covering a period of 1,000 years. Illus. Index. Denver Museum of Natural History, $2.50.

EXCAVATIONS IN MANCOS CANYON, COLORADO
Erik K. Reed
Describes excavations (conducted in 1942) of small sites damaged or threatened by road construction in the Mancos Canyon, southwestern Colorado, on the Ute Reservation below Mesa Verde. 224 pp. Illus. University of Utah Press, 1958. $4.00.

EXCAVATIONS IN THE UPPER LITTLE COLORADO DRAINAGE
Paul S. Martin and John B. Rinaldo
129 pp. Illus. Index. Tables. Map. Chicago Natural History Museum, 1960. $4.00.

EXCAVATIONS, 1940, AT UNIVERSITY RUIN
Julian Hayden
Contains a detailed report of the excavations, and comparisons with other well known archaeological sites. xii + 234 pp. Illus. Appendix. Photographs. Maps. Southwestern Monuments Association, 1958. $4.00.

EXILES OF FLORIDA
Joshua R. Giddings; edited by A. W. Thompson
A historical, military, and sociological account of the changes wrought by the forced migration of slaves from their native areas of Florida to South Carolina and Georgia. Included is coverage of the Seminole Wars. University of Florida Press, 1964. $8.00.

EXPANSION AND AMERICAN INDIAN POLICY
Reginald Horsman
From the Contents: *Introduction; Establishing a Policy, 1783-1784; The Policy in Practice, 1784-1786; A New Start, 1786-1789; The Old Northwest, 1789-1795; The Ambivalence of Thomas Jefferson; The South, 1799-1809; The Old Northwest, 1795-1809; The Coming of War; Conclusion.*
Michigan State University Press, 1966.

EXPEDITION DOWN THE ZUNI AND COLORADO RIVERS IN 1851
Captain Lorenzo Sitgreaves
Source material on that part of the Southwest drained by the Zuni and Colorado Rivers. 198 pp. Illus. Index. Maps. The Rio Grande Press, Inc., $8.00.

EXPERIENCES AS AN INDIAN AGENT
E. E. White; Introduction by Edward Everett Dale
The true account of Eugene Elliott White, who was appointed special Indian agent to the large Indian reservations in the West and Southwest. His responsibilities were the inspection of Indian agencies and reporting to the Indian Bureau in Washington on efficiency, accounting practices, and other matters. 256 pp. Illus. Appendix. University of Oklahoma Press, 1965. $2.00.

EXPLORATION OF ALASKA
Morgan B. Sherwood
An account of the government exploration of Alaska between 1865 and 1900. 207 pp. Illus. Yale University Press, 1965. $6.50.

EXPLORATIONS OF PIERRE ESPRIT RADISSON
Pierre E. Radisson; edited by Arthur T. Adams
Illus. Ross and Haines, Inc., 1961. $8.75.

EXPLORING OUR PREHISTORIC INDIAN RUINS
Deveux Butcher
Describes the many ancient Indian structures and the cultures they reflect. 64 pp. Illus. Paper. National Parks Association, $1.35.

EXPLORING THE GREAT BASIN
Gloria Griffen Cline
The story of the Great Basin of the West, last large area of the United States to be explored. 268 pp. Illus. Index. Biblio. Maps. University of Oklahoma Press, 1963. $4.95.

EXPLORING WITH FREMONT: *The Private Diaries of Charles Preuss, Cartographer for the First, Second, and Fourth Expeditions to the Far West*
Edited and translated by Erwin and Elisabeth Gudde
162 pp. Illus. Index. Maps. University of Oklahoma Press, 1958. $3.95.

F

FACTIONALISM IN ISLETA PUEBLO
David H. French
Traces the history and political organization of Isleta Pueblo since 1870, with a lengthy discussion of the causal relationships in Isleta factionalism. An American Ethnological Society Monograph reissued by the University of Washington Press. Bound with *Ceremonial Patterns on the Greater Southwest*, an A. E. S. Monograph published by the University of Washington Press.

FAIR GODS AND STONE FACES
Constance Irwin
346 pp. Illus. St. Martin's Press, Inc., 1963. $7.50.

FAITH, FLOWERS AND FIESTAS
Muriel Painter
Illus. Paper. University of Arizona Press, 1962. $1.00.

*FAMOUS INDIAN CHIEFS
John W. Moyer; illustrated by Joseph L. Vlasaty
Authentic descriptions of the lives of eleven famous Indian chiefs and their importance in American history. 92 pp. Illus. Ages 8 to 11. M. A. Donohue & Co., 1957. $3.50.

*FAMOUS INDIAN TRIBES
David C. Cooke and William Moyers
Illus. Ages 5 to 8. Random House, Inc., 1954. $1.95; library edition, $2.49.

*FAMOUS PIONEERS
Franklin Folsom; illustrated by Joseph Papin
A story of the early Americans who pushed West, and the Indians they met along the way. 251 pp. Illus. Harvey House, Inc., Publishers, 1963. $3.95.

√ **THE FAR WESTERN FRONTIER (1830-1860)**
Ray A. Billington
Illus. Harper & Row, Publishers, $6.00.

*FATHER KINO, PRIEST TO THE PIMAS
Ann Nolan Clark; illustrated by H. Lawrence Hoffman
The story of the Italian Jesuit priest who set up twenty-nine missions and mapped areas of Mexico and Arizona in the 1600's. Ages 9 to 12. Farrar, Straus and Giroux, Inc., 1963. $2.25.

THE FIELD NOTES OF CAPT. WILLIAM CLARK, 1803-1805
Ernest S. Osgood, Editor
Collection of notes taken by Captain William Clark between 1803 and 1805. Brings into focus new descriptions of the Lewis and Clark expedition. 335 pp. Yale University Press, 1964. $20.00.

FIFTY YEARS BELOW ZERO
Charles D. Brower
Illus. Dodd, Mead & Co., 1942. $5.00.

FIFTY YEARS ON THE TRAIL
John Young Nelson and Harrison O'Reilly; Foreword by Donald E. Worcester
A true story of Western life. 291 pp. Drawings. University of Oklahoma Press, 1963. $2.00.

THE FIGHTING CHEYENNES
George Bird Grinnell; Introduction by Stanley Vestal
453 pp. Illus. Index. Maps. University of Oklahoma Press, 1964. $5.95.

√ **FIGHTING INDIANS OF THE WEST**
Martin F. Schmitt
Story of the struggle between the United States Government and the Western Indian tribes who chose to fight rather than be removed to reservations. 384 pp. Illus. Charles Scribner's Sons, 1955. $15.00.

THE FIGHTING PARSON
Reginald S. Craig
A documented study of Col. John M. Chivington, hero of the Battle of Glorietta Pass, who reputedly directed the Sand Creek Massacre against the Cheyennes. 285 pp. Westernlore Press, 1959. $7.50.

FIGHTING WITH PROPERTY: *A Study of Kwakiutl Potlatching and Warfare, 1792-1930*
Helen Codere
A study tracing the history and psychology of the famous potlatch of the Kwakiutl Indians of the Northwest Coast. Illus. An American Ethnological Society Monograph reissued by the University of Washington Press. $5.00.

√ **THE FINAL CHALLENGE:** *The American Frontier, 1804-1845*
Dale Van Every; Foreword by Allan Nevins

A history of the frontier people who thrust westward across the Mississippi to the Pacific. Illus. Maps. William Morrow and Co., Inc., 1964. $6.00.

*THE FIRST BOOK OF ALASKA
Edith Stull

The story of the largest American state: its modern cities, Arctic wilderness, Indian tribes, Eskimos and homesteaders. 88 pp. Illus. Photo. Grades 4 to 6. Franklin Watts, Inc., 1965. $2.65.

*THE FIRST BOOK OF ESKIMOS
Benjamin Brewster; illustrated by Ursula Koering

Describes how the Eskimos build houses, make clothes, fish and hunt, establish family life, devise a code of ethics, and entertain themselves. 48 pp. Illus. Ages 8 to 10. Franklin Watts, Inc., 1952. $2.65.

*THE FIRST BOOK OF INDIANS
Benjamin Brewster; illustrated by Ursula Koering

Describes the way in which American Indians once lived, and how they created their own culture, as contrasted with how they live today. 72 pp. Illus. Grades 4 to 6. Franklin Watts, Inc., 1963. $2.65.

*FIRST BOOK OF THE INDIAN WARS
Richard B. Morris

Grades 2 to 6. Illus. Franklin Watts, Inc., 1950. $2.65.

*THE FIRST BOW AND ARROW
Chester G. Osborne; illustrations by Richard N. Osborne

In this adventure story of prehistoric times, the boy Chica makes the first bow and arrow, with which he saves his people from a giant cave bear. 89 pp. Illus. Follett Publishing Co., 1951. $3.95.

*THE FIRST CALIFORNIAN: *The Story of Fray Junipero Serra*
Donald Demarest; illustrated by Joseph Romer

176 pp. Illus. Ages 10 to 14. Guild Press, 1965. $2.95.

THE FIRST COMERS: *Indians of America's Dawn*
Alice Marriott

A book about the archaeological investigations of the earliest American Indians, including cultural patterns, descriptions of techniques, and data interpretation. 246 pp. Illus. David McKay Co., Inc., 1960. $3.79.

*THE FIRST LAKE DWELLERS
Chester G. Osborne; illustrated by Richard N. Osborne

Enemies destroy the lake people's village and capture Arvi's father, the chief. Arvi finds a way to build a shelter on his father's raft, and from his idea a whole village of lake dwellings develops. 128 pp. Illus. Follett Publishing Co., 1956. $2.90.

FIRST LOOK AT STRANGERS
Robert Bunker and John Adair

This book tells the story of a training course and a system which was established to equip American and foreign administrators and technologists with methods of working with people of backward countries. 151 pp. Rutgers University Press, 1959. $5.00.

FIRST MAN WEST
Walter Sheppe

Illus. University of California Press, 1962. $7.50.

FIRST MARTYRS OF NORTH AMERICA
J. A. O'Brien

University of Notre Dame Press, 1960. $3.50.

FIRST SOCIAL EXPERIMENTS IN AMERICA
Lewis Hanke

Peter Smith, 1964. $3.00.

*THE FIRST WHEEL
Chester G. Osborne; illustrated by Richard N. Osborne

The story of the first economic revolution, in which man learned to grow his food instead of gathering it. 128 pp. Illus. Follett Publishing Co., 1959. $2.90.

FISHING AMONG THE INDIANS OF NORTHWESTERN CALIFORNIA
Alfred L. Kroeber

Illus. Paper. University of California Press, 1960. $4.50.

FIVE FUR TRADERS OF THE NORTHWEST
Charles M. Gates, Editor; Foreword by Theodore C. Blegen

The authentic journals of five fur traders, telling of their experiences with the Indians. The Minnesota Historical Society, 1965. $7.25.

FIVE INDIAN TRIBES OF THE UPPER
MISSOURI: *Sioux, Arikaras, Assiniboines,
Crees, Crows*
   Edwin T. Denig; edited and with an Introduction by John C. Ewers
217 pp. Illus. Index. Biblio. Map. University of Oklahoma Press, 1961. $4.00.

FIVE PREHISTORIC ARCHAEOLOGICAL
SITES IN LOS ANGELES COUNTY, CALI-
FORNIA
   E. F. Walker
116 pp. Pls. Figs. Southwest Museum,
1951. $3.50.

FLAGELLANT ON HORSEBACK: *The Life
Story of David Brainerd*
   Richard E. Day
Judson Press, $3.00.

*FLAMING ARROWS
   William O. Steele; illustrated by Paul
   Galdone
This story demonstrates the fallacy in blam-
ing a son for his father's evil. 178 pp. Har-
court, Brace & World, Inc., 1957. $2.75.

FLINTLOCKS OF THE IROQUOIS
   1620-1687
   Joseph R. Mayer
Author describes in detail many archaeological examples of flintrocks which were used
by the Iroquois Indians during the 17th century in western New York State, and notes
their historical significance. 59 pp. Illus.
17 figs. Map. Biblio. Research Records
of the Rochester Museum of Arts and Sciences No. 6, History, 1943. $1.00. Avail-
able from the Rochester Museum of Arts
and Sciences.

THE FLORIDA OF THE INCA
   Garcilaso de la Vega; translated by
   John and Jennette Varner
The first American historian's account of
the DeSoto expedition. 670 pp. Illus. Uni-
versity of Texas Press, $7.50.

FLORIDA'S SEMINOLE INDIANS
   Wilfred T. Neill
"History and experiences in the Ever-
glades." 90 pp. Illus. Paper. Great
Outdoors Association, $1.00.

FLORIDA'S SEMINOLE INDIANS
   Wilfred T. Neill
As above. Ross Allen's Reptile Institute,
$1.00.

FOLLOWING THE INDIAN WARS
   Oliver Knight
The adventures of newspaper correspond-
ents covering the Indian campaigns. 348
pp. Illus. Index. Biblio. Maps. University of Oklahoma Press, 1960. $5.95.

FOOTE CANYON PUEBLO, EASTERN
ARIZONA
   John B. Rinaldo
154 pp. Illus. Tables. Vol. 49, No. 2,
Chicago Natural History Museum, 1959.
$4.00.

FORMAL EDUCATION IN AN AMERICAN
INDIAN COMMUNITY
   Murray L. Wax and Rosalie H. Wax
An account of findings of a research project conducted on the Pine Ridge Reservation to study the problems and existing policies of Indian education in relation to cultural disharmony, lack of motive, and
preservation of Indian identity. Supplement
to *Social Problems,* Spring, 1964, a Society
for the Study of Social Problems Monograph.
$2.00.

FORT HALL: *Gateway to the Oregon
Country*
   Frank C. Robertson
A history of Fort Hall, from its founding in
1834 to its present use as a Bureau of Indi-
an Affairs agency. 320 pp. Illus. Index.
Notes. Hastings House Publishers, Inc.,
$5.95.

FORT McPHERSON, NEBRASKA TERRI-
TORY
   Louis A. Holmes
Johnsen Publishing Co., 1963. $7.50.

FORTH TO THE WILDERNESS
   Dale Van Every
The story of the early years of our country,
when the frontiersman became aware of his
identity. Illus. 367 pp. Index. Biblio.
Maps. William Morrow & Co., Inc., 1961.
$6.00.

FORTH TO THE WILDERNESS
   Dale Van Every
As above. Illus. Paper. New American
Library, Inc., 75¢.

FORTS ON THE PENNSYLVANIA FRON-
TIER, 1753-1758
   William A. Hunter
This book describes the breakdown of Penn-
sylvania's peaceful Indian relations in the

French and Indian wars. 596 pp. Illus. Pennsylvania Historical and Museum Commission, 1960. $5.00.

FORTY MILES A DAY ON BEANS AND HAY
Don Rickey, Jr.
An account of the enlisted soldier fighting the Indian Wars in the post-Civil War days. 382 pp. Illus. Index. Biblio. Maps. University of Oklahoma Press, 1963. $5.95.

FORTY YEARS AMONG THE INDIANS
Daniel W. Jones
A reprint of the 1880 edition. Westernlore Press, 1960. $8.50.

FOUR AGES OF TSURAI: *A Documentary History of the Indian Village of Trinidad Bay*
Robert F. Heizer and John E. Mills
Illus. University of California Press, 1952. $3.75.

THE FOUR DIRECTIONS OF TIME
C. A. Burland
Discusses the similarities between the Mexican and Navajo conceptions of religion. 16 pp. Illus. Museum of Navajo Ceremonial Art.

***FOUR WAYS OF BEING HUMAN**
Gene Lisitzky; illustrated by C. B. Falls
An introduction to anthropology -- description of four primitive tribes living in different lands and climates, demonstrating the way mankind develops cultures to utilize environment. 304 pp. Grades 10 to 12. Illus. The Viking Press, Inc., 1956. Hardcover, $5.00; paper, $1.45.

FREDERICK REMINGTON'S OWN WEST
Frederick Remington; edited with an Introduction by Harold McCracken
The Western artist's accounts of his expeditions and adventures on the frontier. Illus. The Dial Press, 1960. $7.50.

THE FRENCH AND INDIAN WARS
Edward P. Hamilton
A description of wilderness, forts and weapons, and the role of the American Indian during the French and Indian Wars. 318 pp. Illus. Index. Doubleday & Co., Inc., $5.95.

***THE FRENCH AND INDIAN WARS**
By the editors of *American Heritage*
Describes the seventy-year struggle between Britain and France for the control of

the New World. 154 pp. Grades 7 to 8. American Heritage Publishing Co., 1962. $3.95.

***THE FRENCH AND INDIAN WARS**
As above. Paper. Harper & Row, Publishers, 75¢.

FRIENDLY PEOPLE: *The Zuni Indians*
Bertha O. Dutton
A short introduction to the history, social organization and religious ceremonies of the Zuni. Describes the architectural arrangement of their dwellings, and discusses their crafts. 28 pp. Illus. Paper. Museum of New Mexico Press, 1963. $1.00.

***FRIENDS OF THE WOLF**
Robert Carse
Grades 5 to 8. G. P. Putnam's Sons, 1961. $2.95.

FRIENDS OF THUNDER: *Folktales of the Oklahoma Cherokees*
Jack Frederick and Anna Gritts Kilpatrick, Editors and Translators
Translation, from Cherokee tongue, of stories, anecdotes, jokes and legends, comprehensively reflecting inner workings of an American Indian social organism, linguistically and ethnologically authentic, but easily accessible to the general reader. 183 pp. Southern Methodist University Press, 1964. $5.00.

FROM EVERY ZENITH: *A Memoir*
John Collier
The autobiography of John Collier, former Commissioner of Indian Affairs, covering his entire career in and out of government, and describing his efforts on behalf of the Indian and other dependent peoples. 477 pp. Illus. Sage Books, 1963. $6.50.

FROM FEATHER, BLANKET AND TEPEE, *The Indian's Fight for Equality*
George A. Trotter
196 pp. Brown Book Co., 1955. $3.50.

***FROM UNGSKAH, 1, TO OYAYLEE, 10:** *A Counting Book for All Little Indians*
Lucille Corcos
Grades 1 to 3. Illus. Pantheon Books, Inc., 1965. $3.50.

FRONTIER LIFE IN OKLAHOMA
Allie B. Wallace
136 pp. Public Affairs Press, 1964. $4.50.

FRUITLAND, NEW MEXICO
   Tom Taketo Sasaki
A clinical study in several dimensions of
the changes made in a traditional Navajo
community life, after the coming of the
pipeline in 1950.   234 pp.   Illus.   Map.
Cornell University Press, 1960. $4.75.

*FUN AND FESTIVAL FROM THE UNITED
   STATES AND CANADA
   Larry Eisenberg
Paper.   Friendship Press, 75¢.

*FUN BOOK OF INDIANS
   R. S. Plattner
McGraw-Hill Book Co., $1.00.

√ FUNK & WAGNALLS STANDARD DICTION-
   ARY OF FOLKLORE, MYTHOLOGY, AND
   LEGEND
   Maria Leach, Editor; Jerome Fried,
   Associate Editor
Over 8,000 entries and dozens of survey
articles by folklorists and specialists cover
the entire range of world folklore.   In two
volumes.   531 pp.; 665 pp.   Funk & Wagnalls, 1949, 1950.   Individual volumes,
$10.00 each; boxed set, $20.00.

FUR HUNTERS OF THE FAR WEST
   Alexander Ross; edited by Kenneth A.
   Spaulding
304 pp.   Illus.   Index.   University of Oklahoma Press, 1960. $5.00.

THE FUR TRADE IN CANADA
   Harold A. Innis
A study of the significance of the fur trade
in the expansion of the Dominion of Canada.
446 pp.   Index.   Appendix.   Maps.   Paper.
Yale University Press, 1962. $2.45.

√ THE FUR TRADER AND THE INDIAN
   Lewis O. Saun
A history of beliefs, myths, and attitudes of
traders and Indians who helped to shape his-
tory.   375 pp.   University of Washington
Press, 1965. $7.50.

                                   G

THE GALVANIZED YANKEES
   D. Alexander Brown
243 pp.   Illus.   Photographs.   University
of Illinois Press, 1963. $5.50.

GENERAL CROOK AND THE APACHE
   WARS
   Charles F. Lummis; illustrated by Don
   Perceval
On-the-scene newspaper reports filed by
the journalist, Charles Lummis, in his cam-
paign against Geronimo and the Apaches.
224 pp.   Illus.   Northland Press, 1965.
$6.50.

GENERAL GEORGE CROOK, HIS
   AUTOBIOGRAPHY
   George Crook; edited and annotated by
   Martin F. Schmit
326 pp.   Illus.   Index.   Appendix.   Biblio.
Maps.   University of Oklahoma Press, 1960.
$5.00.

GEORGE CATLIN: *Episodes from "Life
   Among the Indians" and "Last Rambles"*
   George Catlin; edited by Marvin C. Ross
357 pp.   Illus.   Index.   Biblio.   University
of Oklahoma Press, $12.50.

GEORGE CATLIN AND THE OLD
   FRONTIER
   Harold McCracken
This book is a comprehensive picture gal-
lery and biography of George Catlin, one of
America's leading artists.   Illus.   Index.
Biblio.   The Dial Press, 1959. $18.50.

GEORGE CROGHAN: *Wilderness Diplomat*
   Nicholas B. Wainwright
A study of George Washington's Indian agent
during the French and English wars -- the
most successful Indian trader in colonial
Pennsylvania.   336 pp.   Illus.   University
of North Carolina Press, 1959. $6.00.

*GERONIMO, THE LAST APACHE WAR
   CHIEF
   Edgar Wyatt; illustrated by Allan
   Houser
192 pp.   Illus.   Ages 6 to 12.   McGraw-Hill
Book Co., 1952. $2.95; library edition,
$2.96.

*GETTING TO KNOW ALASKA
   Jim Breetveld
Illus.   Grades 2 to 6.   Coward-McCann,
Inc., 1958. $2.52.

*GETTING TO KNOW AMERICAN INDIANS
   TODAY
   Hildegard Thompson
Grades 2 to 6.   Coward-McCann, Inc., 1965.

GHOST DANCE
David Humphrey Miller
Duell, Sloan and Pearce, 1959. $4.95.

GHOST-DANCE RELIGION AND THE SIOUX
OUTBREAK OF 1890
James Mooney; edited by Anthony F.
Wallace
This is a firsthand account of the ghost
dance doctrine which aroused new fears of
a Sioux uprising, due to its revolutionary
message. xvi + 205 pp. University of Chicago Press, 1965. Paper, $2.95; cloth,
$6.95.

THE GHOST DANCE RELIGION: *Smohalla
and His Doctrine*
James Mooney
Deals with the religious practices of the
Columbia River Indians of the Northwest
Coast, and the high priest of the Wa'napum
Tribe, Smohalla. 29 pp. Illus. Paper,
Shorey Publications, $1.50.

THE GHOST DANCE RELIGION: *The Shak-
ers of Puget Sound*
James Mooney
Describes a Northwest Coast religious
movement. 17 pp. Illus. Paper. Shorey
Publications, $1.50.

THE GIFT IS RICH
E. Russell Carter
An account of the contributions the American Indian has made to our culture in medicine, art, music, crafts, and "spiritual
perception." 128 pp. Illus. Paper. Friendship Press, 1955. $1.25.

THE GILA, RIVER OF THE SOUTHWEST
Edwin Corle
As below. Illus. Peter Smith, $3.75.

THE GILA, RIVER OF THE SOUTHWEST
Edwin Corle
This book includes material on the Indian
tribes of southern Arizona and southwestern
New Mexico, and contains an account of their
relations with the whites. 402 pp. Paper.
University of Nebraska Press, 1951. $1.60.

THE GILDED MAN
Adolph F. A. Bandelier
A study of Coronado's search for New World
gold. 302 pp. Illus. The Rio Grande Press,
Inc., $7.00.

*GLOOSCAP AND HIS MAGIC
Kay Hill

Illus. Grades 4 to 7. Dodd, Mead & Co.,
1963. $3.50.

*GLOOSKAP'S COUNTRY
Cyrus MacMillan
A collection of Indian folktales and legends
from Canada. 280 pp. Henry Z. Walck,
Inc., 1956. $4.00.

THE GOLDEN AGE OF AMERICAN
ANTHROPOLOGY
Margaret Mead and Ruth Bunzel,
Editors
George Braziller, Inc., $10.00.

*THE GOLDEN BOOK OF INDIAN CRAFTS
AND LORE
W. Ben Hunt
This book shows, by use of patterns and
diagrams, how to make many Indian craft
items. Directions for performing ritual
dances and information about other lore is
included. 112 pp. Illus. Grades 5 to 7.
Golden Press, Inc., 1954. $1.95.

*GOOD HUNTING, LITTLE INDIAN
Peggy Parish, illustrated by Leonard
Weisgard
A little Indian boy sets out bravely in the
forest, with his new bow and arrows. He
has many experiences before he brings the
meat home for dinner. Illus. Grades 1 to
3. W. R. Scott, Inc., 1962. $3.00.

GOODBYE TO A RIVER
John Graves
Narrative of a canoe trip down the Texas
Brazos River, with a history of its people,
including the Comanches and Kiowas. 301
pp. Biblio. Alfred A. Knopf, Inc., $4.50.

GOSPEL OF THE REDMAN
Ernest T. Seton
Seton Village, $2.00.

GRAMMATICAL NOTES ON THE LANG-
UAGE OF THE TLINGIT INDIANS
Franz Boas
Paper. University Museum, 1917. $2.00.

GRANDMA GOES TO THE ARCTIC
By Alberta Weed, as related by Lola
Kirkland
The true story of Lola Kirkland, a woman
past sixty, who pursued her way to a point
far beyond the Arctic Circle in Alaska --
her experiences with Eskimos, wolves,
whales and seals. 279 pp. Dorrance & Co.,
1961. $3.50.

GREAT DAY IN THE WEST
    Kent Ruth
Material on the historical significance of
more than one hundred frontier forts, posts,
and rendezvous. 324 pp. Illus. Index. University of Oklahoma Press, 1963. $12.50.

*THE GREAT HERITAGE
    Katherine B. Shippen
Illus. Grades 8 to 12. The Viking Press,
Inc., 1963. $4.50.

THE GREAT NORTH TRAIL
    Dan Cushman
This book tells the story of the Great North
Trail which runs from Alaska to Mexico.
320 pp. Maps. McGraw-Hill Book Co.,
1966. $7.95.

THE GREAT SIOUX NATION
    Frederick M. Hans
A history and study of the Sioux, including
a fifty-page dictionary of the Sioux language. Ross & Haines, Inc., 1964. $8.75.

GREAT STAR CHART AND PRAYERS, AND
    COYOTE CHANT (Navajo)
    Mary C. Wheelwright; illustrated by
        Louie Ewing
Illus. Glossary. Index. Museum of Navajo Ceremonial Art, $20.00.

GREAT TRAIL OF NEW ENGLAND
    Harral Ayres
Forum Publishing Co., 1940. $5.00.

*GREAT WHITE BUFFALO
    Harold McCracken
Illus. J. B. Lippincott Co., 1946. $3.75.

THE GROS VENTRES OF MONTANA: *Part
II, Religion and Ritual*
Catholic University of America Press, 1957.
$5.00.

*GROWING UP IN ALASKA
    Iola F. Bunn
Tells the story of an uneducated, non-Chris-
tian Eskimo family befriended by a white
man in Alaska. 126 pp. Illus. Exposition
Press, 1965. $4.00.

A GUIDE TO THE INDIAN TRIBES OF
    OKLAHOMA
    Muriel H. Wright
300 pp. Illus. Index. Biblio. University
of Oklahoma Press, 1965. $5.95.

GUIDE TO MATERIALS BEARING ON
    CULTURAL RELATIONS IN NEW MEXICO
    Lyle Saunders
University of New Mexico Press, 1944.
$3.00.

*GUNPOWDER FOR BOONESBOROUGH
    John Clagett
A sixteen-year-old Philadelphia boy meets
a group of men smuggling gunpowder to Kentucky settlements for defense against Indians and Tories. For young adults. The
Bobbs-Merrill Co., Inc., 1965. $3.95.

GYPSUM CAVE, NEVADA
    M. R. Harrington
206 pp. Illus. Southwest Museum, 1933.
$5.00.

                    H

THE HAIDAH INDIANS OF QUEEN
    CHARLOTTE'S SOUND, B.C.
    James G. Swan
A facsimile of the 1874 edition. Description of carvings, tatoo designs, etc. 18 pp.
Index. Illus. Paper. Shorey Publications,
1966. $5.00.

HALF-SUN ON THE COLUMBIA
    Robert H. Ruby and John A. Brown
A biography of Chief Moses of the Colum-
bia Indians. 352 pp. Illus. Index. Biblio.
Maps. University of Oklahoma Press, 1965.
$5.95.

HANDBOOK OF AMERICAN INDIANS
NORTH OF MEXICO
    Frederick W. Hodge
Originally published in 1912, this history
contains basic information about North
American Indian tribes. 193 pp. Two vol-
umes. Rowman & Littlefield, Inc., 1959.
Two-volume set, $27.50.

HANDBOOK OF MIDDLE AMERICAN INDI-
ANS, VOLUME I: *Natural Environment
and Early Cultures*
    Edited by Robert Wauchope and R. C.
        West
University of Texas Press, $15.00.

HANDBOOK OF MIDDLE AMERICAN INDI-
ANS, VOLUMES 2 and 3: *Archaeology of
Southern Mesoamerica*
    Edited by Robert Wauchope and Gordon
        R. Willey
University of Texas Press, $15.00 each.

HANDBOOK OF THE INDIANS OF CALI-
FORNIA
A. L. Kroeber
Detailed descriptions of all the known tribes
of California. 995 pp. Maps. Illus. Cali-
fornia Book Co., 1953. $15.00.

*HAPPY HUNTING GROUNDS
Stanley Vestal
Grades 5 to 9. Lyons & Carnahan, $3.50.

HAPPY PEOPLE: *The Huichol Indians*
Bertha P. Dutton
Discusses the history, habitat, religion,
social and political organization and econo-
my of the Huichol Indians. 56 pp. Illus.
Reference list. Museum of New Mexico
Press, 1962. $1.00.

HARDIN VILLAGE SITE
Lee H. Hanson, Jr.
A description of the features, burials and
material culture of the Fort Ancient Indian.
The author postulates that the site was occupied from A. D. 1500 to A. D. 1675 by
Shawnee Indians who abandoned it because
of Iroquois pressure. From his stratigraphic analysis of the materials recovered
from the Hardin Village Site, Mr. Hanson
delineates traits that distinguish four periods of occupation. University of Kentucky
Press, $5.00.

HAVASUPAI RELIGION AND MYTHOLOGY
Carma Lee Smithson and Robert C.
Euler
An ethnographic study of the Havasupai
tribe. 120 pp. Biblio. University of Utah
Press, 1964. $2.00.

HAVASUPAI WOMAN
Carma L. Smithson
Describes studies of the Havasupai, particularly the woman, and is concerned with
such topics as geographical and cultural
setting, infancy and childhood, puberty and
adolescence, marriage, motherhood, economic status and role, leadership and public participation, ceremonies, and other
public activities. 178 pp. Illus. University of Utah Press, 1959. $3.00.

HE WALKED THE AMERICAS
L. Taylor Hansen
A collection of authentic Indian legends telling of a white man who "walked the Americas." Illus. Amherst Press, 1963. $6.95.

HEAP MANY TEXAS CHIEFS
Roy D. Holt
Profiles of numerous Indian chiefs, portray-
ing the entire scope of Indian government
and military relationships in Texas from
the days of the Republic to the Indian Resettlement in Indian territory. 400 pp. Illus. Biblio. The Naylor Co., 1966. $7.95.

*HENRY STARR: *Last of the Real Badmen*
Glenn Shirley
The biography of Henry Starr, part Cherokee, part white, "the most unusual train and
bank robbing outlaw in America." 208 pp.
Grades 7 to 8. David McKay Co., Inc.,
1965. $4.50.

*HERE IS ALASKA
Evelyn Stefansson
Illus. Grades 4 to 8. Charles Scribner's
Sons, 1959. $3.65.

HERE IS YESTERDAY
Don Buchan
An account of the Spirit Lake Massacre of
1857. J. D. Buchan, 1965. $5.00.

HIGGINS FLAT PUEBLO, WESTERN NEW
MEXICO
Paul S. Martin, John B. Rinaldo, Elaine
A. Bluhm, and Hugh C. Cutler
218 pp. Illus. Chicago Natural History
Museum, 1956. $4.50.

HILLS OF YESTERDAY
Martha McKelvie
"Stories from the Black Hills of South Dakota -- the last hunting ground of the Indians
-- have been collected by the author in a
series of vignettes of the land where the
Great Spirit supposedly made his home."
117 pp. Dorrance & Co., Inc., 1960. $3.50.

*THE HIPPITY HOPPER
Lucille Wallower
A legend of the war between Indian tribes in
Pennsylvania. Provides regional lore and
a moral. Grades 2 to 4. Illus. 32 pp. Da-
vid McKay Co., Inc., 1957. $2.50.

*HIS INDIAN BROTHER
Hazel Wilson
Alone in the Maine wilderness, Brad Porter would have starved without the help of
the Indian boy, Sabattis, who showed him
how to survive in nature the way the American Indians did. Illus. Grades 4 to 6. Abingdon Press, 1955. $3.31.

HISTORICAL ATLAS OF OKLAHOMA
John Morris and Edwin McReynolds
A history of original Indian territory. 143 pp. Index. References. University of Oklahoma Press, 1965. Paper, $1.95; cloth, $3.95.

HISTORICAL SKETCH OF THE FLATHEAD NATION
Peter Ronan; Introduction by Michael Kennedy
Index. Ross & Haines, Inc., $4.75.

HISTORY AND PRESENT STATE OF VIRGINIA
Hugh Jones; edited with an Introduction and notes by Richard L. Morton
A history of Virginia and its people, in the early 18th century. University Press of Virginia, 1956. $5.00.

HISTORY OF ARIZONA AND NEW MEXICO
Hubert H. Bancroft
The story of Arizona and New Mexico from the earliest Spanish explorations through the first forty-two years of territorial struggle. 829 pp. Illus. Horn and Wallace, $15.00.

HISTORY OF CAROLINA
John Lawson; edited by Frances L. Harris
Illus. Garrett & Massie, Inc., $4.00.

HISTORY OF CHOCTAW, CHICKASAW AND NATCHEZ INDIANS
Horatio B. Cushman; edited by Angie Debo
A reprint of the 1899 edition. 493 pp. Index. Redlands Press, 1961. $12.50.

A HISTORY OF MINNESOTA, Vols. 1 and 2
William W. Folwell
The history of the state from the French exploration to the close of the Civil War. 533 pp., 477 pp. Illus. Index. Maps. The Minnesota Historical Society, 1956, $6.50. 1961, $7.75.

HISTORY OF PIKE AND DUBOIS COUNTIES
Includes a history of the Northwest, the Indian territory, and the State of Indiana. viii + 786 pp. Index. Illus. Sketches. Notes. Unigraphic, Inc., 1965. $10.00

HISTORY OF THE ANCIENT SOUTHWEST
Harold S. Gladwin
The history of the Southwest, from its earliest settlements through the 1800's. 400 pp. Illus. Maps. The Bond Wheelwright Co., 1965. $10.00.

HISTORY OF THE CALUMET AND OF THE DANCE
Jacques LeSueur
A reprint of an account written in 1744 by a Jesuit missionary concerning the Calumet dance of the Abenakis. 22 pp. Illus. Museum of the American Indian, Heye Foundation, $2.00.

THE HISTORY OF THE FIVE INDIAN NATIONS
Cadwallader Colden
The observations of a colonial scholar and political leader of the Iroquois Nation. 205 pp. Paper. Cornell University Press, 1958. $1.95.

HISTORY OF THE GIRTYS
C. W. Butterfield
Long's College Book Co., 1950. $7.50.

HISTORY OF THE INDIANS OF CONNECTICUT FROM THE EARLIEST KNOWN PERIOD TO 1850
John W. DeForest
Illus. The Shoe String Press, Inc., 1964. $10.00.

THE HISTORY OF THE LEWIS AND CLARK EXPEDITION
Elliott Coues, Editor
The history of the Lewis and Clark expedition, with descriptions of Indian tribes. Illus. Index. Biblio. Tables. Four vols. Dover Publications, Inc. Individual volumes, $2.25 each; set, $6.75.

HISTORY OF THE NEW YORK IROQUOIS
William Beauchamp
A history of the Iroquois tribe by an archeologist and historian. 337 pp. Empire State Historical Publications, $6.95.

HISTORY OF THE OJIBWAY NATION
William W. Warren
Facsimile of 1885 edition. A history of the Ojibwa Indians, their migrations, conflicts with the Sioux, and eventual settlement. Map. Ross & Haines, Inc., $8.75.

HISTORY OF THE OLD CHERAWS
Alexander Gregg
Contains an account of the aborigines of the Pee Dee -- the first white settlements, their

subsequent progress, civil changes, the struggle of the Revolution and the growth of the country afterwards extending from about 1730 to 1810, with notices of families and sketches of individuals. 546 pp. Reprint Co., 1965. $15.00.

A HISTORY OF THE PACIFIC NORTHWEST
George W. Fuller
Illus. Alfred A. Knopf, Inc., 1931. $5.00.

HISTORY OF THE SECOND
SEMINOLE WAR
John K. Mahon
University of Florida Press, 1964. $9.50.

HISTORY OF THE SIERRA NEVADA
Francis P. Farquhar
The book follows the discovery, exploration and development of the Sierra Nevada from November, 1542, when Juan Rodriguez Cabrillo and his men first saw the range. University of California Press, 1965.

A HISTORY OF THE UNITED STATES
INDIAN FACTORY SYSTEM, 1795-1822
Ora Brooks Peake
A study of the United States Indian factory system: one of the earliest efforts on the part of the United States Government to conduct a business in competition with private industry. 340 pp. Illus. Index. Appendix. Biblio. Sage Books, 1954. $5.00.

HISTORY OF THE UPPER COUNTRY OF
SOUTH CAROLINA
John H. Logan
A natural history of South Carolina, including material on the Indians and early trade routes. 521 pp. Reprint Co., 1965. $15.00.

HIWASSEE ISLAND
Thomas M. N. Lewis and Madeline Klineberg Lewis
A technical study of four prehistoric peoples who inhabited one of the largest islands in the Tennessee River. 316 pp. Illus. Paper. Tables. Maps. University of Tennessee Press, 1946. $5.50.

*HOKAHEY! *American Indians Then and Now*
Edith Dorian
A complete book on American Indians, with information on their origin, number of tribes, languages, adaptation to environment, cultures, and arts. 96 pp. Illus. Grades 5 to 9. McGraw-Hill Book Co., 1957. $3.50.

*HOME OF THE RED MAN: *Indian North America Before Columbus*
Robert Silverberg; illustrated by Judith Ann Lawrence
Discusses the American Indian's origins, his way of life, manner of dress, and languages, and traces his development to the present. 272 pp. Illus. Ages 12 to 16. Maps. New York Graphic Society, Publishers, Ltd., 1966. $3.95.

THE HOPEWELL MOUND GROUP OF OHIO
W. K. Moorehead
126 pp. Illus. Etchings. Fieldiana: Anthropology. Vol. VI, No. 5. Chicago Natural History Museum, 1922. Paper, $3.00; cloth, $4.00.

HOPEWELL VILLAGE: *A Social and Economic History of an Ironmaking Community*
Joseph E. Walker
University of Pennsylvania Press, 1965. $8.00.

HOPI CHILD
Wayne Dennis
Paper. Science Editions, $1.95.

*HOPI INDIAN BUTTERFLY DANCE
Harry C. James; illustrated by Don Perceval
The book opens with the participants in the ceremonial dance practicing in the *kiva* (a Pueblo Indian dwelling -- a large room used for religious or other purposes). Then Honau and Poli (the main characters of two other books about Hopi Indians by the author), don their costumes for the dance. This is followed by a description of the dance and a feast. 36 pp. Reading level, 3; interest level, 2 to 5. Illus. Melmont Publishers, Inc., 1959. $2.50.

THE HOPI INDIANS
Ruth DeEtte Simpson
Southwest Museum, $1.00.

HOPI KACHINA DOLLS
Harold Colton
Illus. University of New Mexico Press, 1959. $6.00.

HOPI KATCINAS DRAWN BY NATIVE
ARTISTS
Jesse W. Fewkes
A collection of primitive and aboriginal American Indian art, including a full color gallery of the dancing gods of the Hopi Indians. 160 pp. Illus. The Rio Grande Press, Inc., $15.00.

HOPI PROPER NAMES
　　H. R. Voth
52 pp. Fieldiana: Anthropology. Vol. vi,
No. 3, Chicago Natural History Museum,
1905. 75¢.

THE HOPI WAY
　　Laura Thompson and Alice Joseph:
　　Foreword by John Collier
Russell & Russell, Publishers, 1965. $7.50.

*THE HORSECATCHER
　　Mari Sandoz
Young Elk does not wish to become a warrior; instead he wishes to catch and tame
the wild horses. He learns that in order to
attain this freedom from tribal tradition, he
must assume basic responsibilities to family and village. 186 pp. Illus. Westminster Press, 1959. $3.25.

*HORSEMEN OF THE WESTERN
　　PLATEAUS: *The Nez Perce Indians*
　　　Sonia Bleeker; illustrated by Patricia
　　　Boodell
The work and play, hunting, fishing and
horsemanship, legends and history of the
Nez Perce Indians. 160 pp. Ages 8 to 12.
Illus. William Morrow & Co., Inc., 1957.
$2.75.

HOSTEEN KLAH: *Navaho Medicine Man
and Sand Painter*
　　Franc Johnson Newcomb
227 pp. Illus. Index. Biblio. Map. University of Oklahoma Press, 1964. $5.95.

HOUSES AND HOUSELIFE OF THE
　　AMERICAN ABORIGINES
　　　Lewis H. Morgan; edited and with an
　　　Introduction by Paul Bohannan
University of Chicago Press, 1965.

*HOW AND WHY WONDER BOOK OF
　　NORTH AMERICAN INDIANS
　　　Felix Sutton
Grades 2 to 6. Paper. Grossett and Dun-
lap, Inc. (Wonder Books), 1965. Hardcover,
$1.00; library binding, $2.08; paper, 50¢.

HOWL OF THE MALEMUTE
　　Sara Machetanz
Illus. William Sloane Associates, 1961.
$5.00.

THE HUNTING OF THE BUFFALO
　　E. Douglas Branch
The story of the decimation of the buffalo
herds, drawing on Indian legends, travelers' tales, old letters and diaries. 240 pp.

Illus. Paper. University of Nebraska
Press, $1.40.

HUPA WARFARE
　　William J. Wallace
Southwest Museum, 25¢.

I

I WILL FIGHT NO MORE FOREVER
　　Merrill D. Beal
An Indian tribe's heroic fight against relocation is recounted on the basis of documents and travel over the entire area where
the Nez Perce War was fought. 384 pp.
Illus. University of Washington Press,
1963. Paper, $1.95; cloth, $6.00.

IGLOO FOR THE NIGHT
　　Mrs. T. Manning
234 pp. Illus. Map. University of Toronto Press, $3.00.

*IN MY MOTHER'S HOUSE
　　Ann N. Clark; illustrated by Velino
　　Herrera
A description, taken from Indian children's
notebooks, of their homes, crops, work
horses, and their festivals. 56 pp. Grades
kindergarten to 3. Illus. The Viking Press,
Inc., 1941. $3.00.

IN NAVAHO LAND
　　Laura Adams Armer
Author's description of the Navajos, their
hogans, tribal dances, and symbolic sandpaintings taken from personal experiences
while living on the Navajo reservation. 96
pp. Illus. David McKay & Co., Inc., 1962.
$3.95.

IN QUEST OF THE WHITE GOD
　　Pierre Honore
G. P. Putnam's Sons, 1964. $5.95.

IN THE COMPANY OF MAN
　　Joseph B. Casagrande, Editor
Seven anthropological studies of the Ameri-
can Indian and Eskimo. Harper & Row,
Publishers, 1960. Paper, $2.75; cloth,
$6.50.

IN THE LAND OF THE GRASSHOPPER
SONG
　　Mary Ellicott Arnold and Mabel Reed
Illus. Vantage Press, Inc., $4.25.

THE INCREDIBLE WILLIAM BOWLES
   Joseph Millard
The life story of a white man who became a
renegade war chief of the Creek Indians.
Chilton Books, $3.95.

INDIAN AFFAIRS IN COLONIAL NEW YORK
   Allan W. Trelease
A history of the political, military and economic developments which affected the Indians, with emphasis on the Algonquian
tribes. xv + 379 pp. Illus. Index. Biblio.
Cornell University Press, 1960. $6.75.

THE INDIAN: *America's Unfinished Business*
   William A. Brophy and Sophie D. Aberle
A report on the present social and economic
status of the American Indian. 302 pp. Illus. Index. Map. University of Oklahoma
Press, 1966. $5.95.

INDIAN AND CAMP HANDICRAFTS
   W. Ben Hunt
A book of thirty crafts projects of Indian
origin that can be made using a pocket knife
as the major tool. Illus. Bruce Publishing
Co., 1945. $3.00.

INDIAN AND ESKIMO ARTIFACTS OF
   NORTH AMERICA
   Charles Miles
A panorama of 1,400 photographs showing
over 2,000 separate artifacts made by the
native races of North America. 244 pp.
Illus. Henry Regnery Co., 1963. $25.00.

*THE INDIAN AND HIS HORSE
   Robert Hofsinde
Relates how the Indians caught and trained
their horses for trading, buffalo hunts, war
and rituals. 96 pp. Illus. Ages 8 to 12.
William Morrow & Co., Inc., 1960. $2.95.

*THE INDIAN AND HIS PUEBLO
   Louise Floethe
A study of the life of the Indians whose
pueblos are near the Rio Grande. 32 pp.
Grades kindergarten to 3. Illus. Charles
Scribner's Sons, 1963. $3.50.

INDIAN AND SPANISH SELECTED
   WRITINGS
      John Goggin; edited by C. Fairbanks
      and others
University of Miami Press, 1964. $5.50.

*THE INDIAN AND THE BUFFALO
   Robert Hofsinde

A description of how the Indians hunted for
buffalo and how these animals were sources
of food, clothing, shelter and other needs.
96 pp. Illus. Ages 8 to 12. William Morrow & Co., Inc., 1961. $2.95.

THE INDIAN AND THE HORSE
   Frank Gilbert Roe
434 pp. Illus. Index. Biblio. Map. University of Oklahoma Press, 1962. $5.95.

THE INDIAN AND THE WHITE MAN
   Wilcomb E. Washburn, Editor
As below. Paper. Doubleday & Co., Inc.,
1965. $1.95.

THE INDIAN AND THE WHITE MAN
   Wilcomb E. Washburn, Editor
A documentary history of the most important aspects of Indian-white relationships,
highlighting the Indian as a part of the American experience. xxiii + 480 pp. Illus.
Photographs. New York University Press,
1964. $7.50.

*INDIAN ANNIE: *Kiowa Captive*
   Alice Marriott; illustrated by Allan
   Thomas
Story of a pioneer girl who is captured by
the Kiowa Indians, grows up among them,
and becomes a translator and teacher. 192
pp. Grades 7 to 11. Illus. David McKay
Co., Inc., 1965. $3.75.

INDIAN ART IN AMERICA
   Frederick J. Dockstader
The arts and crafts of the North American
Indian from prehistoric times to the pres-
ent. 224 pp. Illus. Index. Biblio. New
York Graphic Society, Publishers, Ltd.,
1966. $25.00.

INDIAN ART OF THE AMERICAS
   Donald Collier
64 pp. Illus. Chicago Natural History Museum, 1959. $1.00.

INDIAN ARTIFACTS
   Virgil Y. Russell
A presentation of methods of hunting for,
classifying, identifying, and preserving
Indian artifacts. 172 pp. Illus. Index.
Mrs. Virgil Y. Russell, 1962. $4.00.

*INDIAN BEADWORK
   Robert Hofsinde
History of Indian beadwork, with detailed
instructions and diagrams for making and
decorating many items. 128 pp. Illus.

Ages 10 to 14. William Morrow & Co., Inc., 1961. $2.75.

*INDIAN CAMPFIRE TALES
    W. S. Phillips; Foreword by Alan Mac-
      farlan
An adaptation of ten favorite Indian legends. 64 pp. Illus. Grades preschool to 3. Platt & Munk, Inc., 1963. $2.50.

*INDIAN CANOE-MAKER
    Patricia Beatty
Illus. Grades 5 to 8. Caxton Printers, Ltd., 1960. $4.00.

*INDIAN CAPTIVE: *The Story of Mary Jemison*
    Lois Lenski
An account of Mary Jemison's capture by the Seneca Indians and her years spent among them. 270 pp. Illus. Grades 7 to 8. J. B. Lippincott Co., 1941. $5.50.

*INDIAN CHILDREN OF AMERICA
    Margaret C. Farquhart
Illus. Grades 1 to 2. Holt, Rinehart & Winston, Inc., 1964. $2.75.

INDIAN CIVILIZATIONS
    Robert S. Reading
An account of Indian civilizations, artifacts and culture in North and South America. 212 pp. Illus. The Naylor Co., 1961. $4.95.

INDIAN CRADLES
    Robert E. Ritzenthaler
A study of several kinds of cradles and baby carriers used among North American tribes. 5 pp. Illus. Paper. Milwaukee Public Museum, 25¢.

INDIAN CREATION STORIES
    Julia M. Seton
Seton Village, 1952. $3.95.

*INDIAN ENCOUNTERS
    Elizabeth Coatsworth; illustrated by
      Frederick T. Chapman
An anthology of Indian stories and poems. Illus. Ages 10 to 14. Macmillan Co., 1960. $3.50.

*INDIAN FIGHTER: *The Story of Nelson A. Miles*
    Ralph E. Bailey
A biography of a general who fought in many battles against the Indians of the West. 224 pp. Ages 12 and up. Maps. William Morrow & Co., Inc., 1965. $3.50.

*INDIAN FIGHTERS
    William Kendrick
Illus. Follett Publishing Co., 1961. $2.08.

INDIAN FIGHTS: *New Facts on Seven Encounters*
    J. W. Vaughn
Accounts of Indian battles with notes on the officers and soldiers of the U. S. Army serving in the West during and after the Civil War. 192 pp. Illus. Index. Appendix. Biblio. University of Oklahoma Press, 1966. $4.95.

*INDIAN FISHING AND CAMPING
    Robert Hofsinde
A presentation of Indian fishing methods, with instructions and diagrams for making one's own "gear." 96 pp. Illus. Ages 8 to 12. William Morrow & Co., Inc., 1963. $2.95.

*INDIAN FOLK AND FAIRY TALES
    Joseph Jacobs
Illus. Grades 4 to 6. G. P. Putnam's Sons, $3.50.

*INDIAN FRIENDS AND FOES
    Dorothy Heiderstadt
A study of the personalities of thirteen famous Indians. 144 pp. Grades 5 to 9. Illus. David McKay Co., Inc., 1958. $3.75.

*INDIAN GAMES AND CRAFTS
    Robert Hofsinde
A book of instructions, pictures and diagrams showing how to make the equipment for twelve Indian games and describing how they are played. 128 pp. Illus. Ages 10 to 14. William Morrow & Co., Inc., 1957. $2.95.

*INDIAN HILL
    Clyde R. Bulla; illustrated by James
      J. Spanfeller
The problems a child faces when he moves from one community to another are portrayed in this story of present-day Navajo Indians who must leave their reservation. 74 pp. Illus. Thomas Y. Crowell Co., 1963. $3.00.

*INDIAN HUNTING
    Robert Hofsinde
A description of Indian weapons, hunting methods and the ceremonials connected with the hunt. 96 pp. Illus. Ages 8 to 12. William Morrow & Co., Inc., 1962. $2.95.

THE INDIAN IN AMERICAN HISTORY
  William T. Hagan
Written for teachers of history, pamphlet describes the role of the Indian in American history from the founding of Jamestown to the present, with emphasis on the Indian's cultural diversity. Contains a description and listing of related historical and anthropological sources. 26 pp. Paper. Service Center for Teachers of History, 1963. 50¢.

✓ THE INDIAN IN MODERN AMERICA
  David A. Baerreis, Editor
A collection of essays on Indian affairs in contemporary America, including education, and problems arising from the Indians' changing social status. xx + 70 pp. Wisconsin State Historical Society, 1956. $2.00.

*INDIAN ISLAND MYSTERY
  Mary C. Jane; illustrated by Raymond Abel
The story of the two young Wymans, who join with the Indians to solve the mystery of the missing bear's tooth necklace. 136 pp. Illus. J. B. Lippincott Co., 1965. $2.95.

THE INDIAN JOURNALS, 1859 to 1862
  L. Morgan; edited and with an Introduction by Leslie A. White; illustrations selected and edited by Clyde Walton
A first-hand account of life on the American frontier, with material on the white man's methods of dealing with the Indian. 246 pp. Illus. University of Michigan Press, 1959. $17.50.

INDIAN LAND: *New Mexico and Arizona*
  Inter-Tribal Indian Ceremonial Association
Contents: *The Ceremonial; Indian Arts and Crafts; Gallup, The Indian Capital; The Indians of Indianland; Side Trips and Circle Tours of Indianland; Calendar of Indian Events; Tourist Business Directory.* 43 pp. Illus. Maps. Inter-Tribal Indian Ceremonial Association, 1965. 50¢.

INDIAN LEGENDS FROM THE NORTHERN ROCKIES
  Ella E. Clark
A collection of myths, legends, personal narratives and historical traditions of the Indians of Idaho, Montana and Wyoming. 378 pp. Illus. Index. Biblio. University of Oklahoma Press, $6.95.

*INDIAN LEGENDS OF AMERICAN SCENES
  Marian E. Gridley

A collection of forty-seven Indian legends. 158 pp. Illus. Ages 8 to 14. M. A. Donohue & Co., 1939. $3.00.

INDIAN LEGENDS OF EASTERN AMERICA
  Johanna Lyback
Illus. The Meredith Publishing Co., 1963. $3.95.

INDIAN LEGENDS OF THE GREAT WEST
  Johanna Lyback
Illus. The Meredith Publishing Co., 1963. $3.95.

INDIAN LEGENDS OF THE PACIFIC NORTHWEST
  Ella Clark
Illus. Paper. University of California Press, 1953. $1.95.

INDIAN LIFE IN THE UPPER GREAT LAKES 11,000 B.C. To A.D. 1800
  George I. Quimby
A survey of the Indians of the Upper Great Lakes region, including material on their differing cultures and changing environment from the end of the Ice Age to the coming of the Europeans. xv + 182 pp. University of Chicago Press, 1960. $6.50.

*INDIAN LIFE ON LONG ISLAND
  Jacqueline Overton
A historical account and description of the Indians of Long Island, N. Y. 150 pp. Empire State Historical Publications, 1963. $4.95.

INDIAN LORE
  E. W. Lamb and L. W. Shultz
Information about Indiana history before the white man came. Series of maps of Indiana, locating Indian tribal areas, villages and sections ceded to the United States by numerous dated treaties. Poems, stories, legends. Glossaries of Miami Indian words and general Indian names. 192 pp. Illus. Index. Lawrence W. Shultz, 1964. $3.00.

INDIAN MASKS BOOKLET
  Museum of the American Indian
Full-color reproductions of ten outstanding masks from North, Central, and South America. 10 pp. Museum of the American Indian, 25¢.

*THE INDIAN MEDICINE MAN
  Robert Hofsinde
Book describes the work of medicine men from six tribal groups, with examples of

each. Ages 8 to 12. William Morrow & Co., Inc., 1966. $2.95.

INDIAN MUSIC IN THE SOUTHWEST
David P. McAllester

An introduction to the music of the Pueblo, Apache and Navajo Indians, including material on the role of music in each of these cultures. 15 pp. Illus. Paper. The Taylor Museum, Colorado Springs Fine Arts Center, 1961. 50¢.

INDIAN MYTHS OR LEGENDS AND TRA-DITIONS OF THE ABORIGINES OF AMERICA
Ellen R. Emerson

A study of the Indian in the United States, with comparisons of the beliefs of the Indians and those held by other ancient peoples. 720 pp. Ross & Haines, Inc., 1965. $8.75.

INDIAN OUTBREAKS
Daniel Buck

Reprint of the 1904 edition. A history of the Sioux uprising of 1862 written by a witness of many of the incidents. Ross & Haines, Inc., 1965. $6.75.

*INDIAN PAINT
Glenn Balch

Grades 4 to 6. Grosset & Dunlap, Inc., $1.95.

INDIAN PATHS OF PENNSYLVANIA
Paul A. W. Wallace

A discussion of Indian paths and of Indian pathfinding in general, including maps by which the motorist can trace most of these paths. 228 pp. Maps. Pennsylvania Historical and Museum Commission, 1965.

*INDIAN PICTURE WRITING
Robert Hofsinde

An explanation of Indian picture-writing methods, including instructions for "secret" letter-writing. 96 pp. Illus. Ages 10 to 14. William Morrow & Co., Inc., 1959. $3.25.

INDIAN PLACE NAMES IN NEW JERSEY
Donald W. Becker

Contains two hundred Indian geographical designations currently found in New Jersey; fifty place names not currently in use. Main section lists cities, counties, municipalities, rivers, lakes, streams, mountains and areas having Indian names. Approximately fifty per cent of the names are of Lenni-Lenape or Delaware derivation. The

balance represent other Indian nations, and are imports. Geographical location, interpretation or translation of names, and variations in spelling, are included. Thirty-five works have been cited in the bibliography. 111 pp. Phillips-Campbell Publishing Co., Inc., 1964. $4.25.

INDIAN PLACE NAMES OF NEW ENGLAND
John C. Huden, Compiler

Contains approximately 5,366 terms, their geographical location, linguistic origin and translation; historical comments appear throughout the text. 408 pp. Index. Glossary. Appendix. Museum of the American Indian, Heye Foundation, $7.50.

THE INDIAN PLACE NAMES ON LONG ISLAND AND ISLANDS ADJACENT
William Wallace Tooker

320 pp. Empire State Historical Publications, $7.50.

INDIAN POLICE AND JUDGES: *Experiments in Acculturation and Control*
William T. Hagan

A study of the Indian's acculturation to the legal systems inaugurated by the Office of Indian Affairs and enforced on most reservations west of the Mississippi. 200 pp. Illus. Yale University Press, $6.50.

*INDIAN PONY
Glen Dines

A discussion of the importance of horses in Indian culture. 48 pp. Illus. Grades 2 to 6. Glossary. Biblio. Map. The Macmillan Co., 1963. $3.50.

INDIAN PORTRAITS OF THE PACIFIC NORTHWEST
George M. Cochran

Contains thirty Northwest Indian portraits, showing tribal cast of feature and dress, with a brief tribal history and a regional map. Illus. 64 pp. Grades 8 to 9. Binfords and Mort, 1959. $2.50.

AN INDIAN PREACHER IN ENGLAND
Leon Burr Richardson, Editor

A collection of letters and diaries of Samson Occom and Nathaniel Whitaker who went to England in 1765 to collect funds for an Indian school, which eventually became Dartmouth College. Dartmouth Publications, $4.00.

INDIAN PREHISTORY OF PENNSYLVANIA
John Witthoft

Summarizes the life of the Indian in North America, particularly those who lived in the East and in what is now Pennsylvania. 34 pp. Pennsylvania Historical and Museum Commission, 1965. 50¢.

INDIAN PRIMITIVE
　　Ralph W. Andrews
Discusses how the Northwest Coast Indians lived at the time the white man arrived on the North American continent. 175 pp. Illus. Photo. Superior Publishing Co., 1960. $12.50.

INDIAN RELICS OF THE PACIFIC
　NORTHWEST
　　N. G. Seaman
A first-hand observation and study of Indian relics found in Oregon, Washington and northern California. 164 pp. Index. Illus. Binfords and Mort, 1956. $3.50.

INDIAN REMOVAL - *The Emigration of the Five Civilized Tribes of Indians*
　　G. Foreman
Illus. University of Oklahoma Press, 1956. $6.00.

INDIAN ROCK PAINTINGS OF THE GREAT
　LAKES
　　Selwyn Dewdney and Kenneth E. Kidd
A study of an important group of rock paintings of the Ojibwa Indians in the Lake Superior district. 136 pp. Illus. University of Toronto Press, 1965. $4.75.

INDIAN SANDPAINTING OF THE GREATER
　SOUTHWEST
　　David Villasenor
Contains sixteen sandpainting reproductions, with brief descriptions of their meanings. 32 pp. Illus. Naturegraph Co., 1963. $1.00.

INDIAN SHAKERS: *A Messianic Cult of the Pacific Northwest*
　　H. G. Barnett
An anthropological study of a distinct religious cult of the Indian tribes of the Pacific Northwest. Traces the Shaker cult's development, its ceremonies, ritual elements, faith, and doctrine. 384 pp. Southern Illinois University Press, 1957. $5.75.

*INDIAN SIGN-LANGUAGE
　　Robert Hofsinde
A description of how to form more than five hundred words in Indian sign language. 96 pp. Illus. Ages 10 and up. William Morrow & Co., Inc., 1956. $2.95.

INDIAN SILVERSMITHING
　　W. Ben Hunt
A description of Indian silversmithing, the tools required and how to make them. Illus. Bruce Publishing Co., 1960. $3.95.

INDIAN SILVERWORK OF THE
　SOUTHWEST
　　Harry P. Mera
A history of the development of Southwestern Indian jewelry from the mid-1800's to 1940. 128 pp. Illus. Dale S. King Publishers, 1960. Paper, $1.50; cloth, $3.00.

INDIAN SITES AND CHIPPED STONE
　MATERIALS IN THE NORTHERN LAKE
　MICHIGAN AREA
　　George I. Quimby and Lewis R. Binford
31 pp. Illus. Tables. Vol. 36, No. 12. Chicago Natural History Museum, 1963. 75¢.

INDIAN SKETCHES: *Taken During an Expedition to the Pawnee Tribes (1833)*
　　J. Irving, Jr.; edited and annotated by John Travis McDermott
275 pp. Illus. Index. Biblio. Map. University of Oklahoma Press, 1955. $5.00.

INDIAN TALES
　　Jaime de Angulo
A collection of folklore, legends and songs of the Pit River Indians of California. 246 pp. Illus. Paper. Hill & Wang, Inc., 1962. $1.65.

*INDIAN TALES OF THE DESERT PEOPLE
　　William D. Hayes
A collection of stories related by the ancestors of Arizona's Pima Indians. 128 pp. Illus. Grades 5 to 9. David McKay Co., Inc., 1957. $3.00.

INDIAN TERRITORY: *A Frontier Photographic Record*
　　W. S. Prettyman, edited by Robert E. Cunningham
174 pp. Illus. Index. University of Oklahoma Press, 1958. $5.95.

THE INDIAN TIPI - ITS HISTORY,
　CONSTRUCTION AND USE, etc.
　　Reginald and Gladys Laubin, Stanley Vestal
208 pp. Illus. Figures. Index. Biblio. University of Oklahoma Press, 1964. $4.95.

INDIAN TRADE GOODS
Arthur Woodward
Describes the trade goods used in exchange with Indians of the Pacific Northwest and the way natives adapted these to their own use. 40 pp. Illus. Paper. Binfords and Mort, 1965. $1.00.

THE INDIAN TRADERS
Frank McNitt
393 pp. Illus. Index. Biblio. Map. University of Oklahoma Press, 1963. $5.95.

INDIAN TRIBES OF ALASKA AND CANADA
John R. Swanton
A reprint of the 1952 edition. Handbook details the physical location of each tribe, its subdivisions, history, and population. 79 pp. Map. Paper. Shorey Publications, 1965. $4.00.

✓ INDIAN TRIBES OF THE AMERICAN SOUTHWEST
John R. Swanton
An extract from Bureau of American Ethnology Bulletin 145, *The Indian Tribes of North America*, 1952. Describes Indians of Arizona, California, Colorado, Nevada, New Mexico and Utah. 202 pp. Paper. Shorey Publications, 1965. $6.00.

INDIAN TRIBES OF THE PACIFIC NORTHWEST
John R. Swanton
Shorey Publications, 1952. $6.00.

INDIAN TRIBES OF THE SOUTHWEST
Tom Bahti
64 pp. Illus. K. C. Publications, 1966. $1.00.

✓ INDIAN TRIBES OF THE UNITED STATES:
Ethnic and Cultural Survival
D'Arcy McNickle
Explains the ethnological and historical reasons for the American Indian's frequent inability to adjust to certain aspects of our national life. Describes the present situation and speculates upon the future. Appendix. Maps. Paper. Oxford University Press, 1962. $1.20.

THE INDIAN WAR OF 1864
Capt. Eugene F. Ware; edited by C. C. Walton
An archaeological study of the origin of Mexican, Central and South American civilizations. 483 pp. St. Martin's Press, Inc., 1961. $7.50.

THE INDIAN WAR OF 1864
Capt. Eugene F. Ware
As above. 484 pp. Illus. Index. Appendix. Notes. Paper. University of Nebraska Press, 1965. $1.65.

*INDIAN WARRIORS AND THEIR WEAPONS
Robert Hofsinde
Briefly describes the weapons, war dress, charms, and fighting methods of seven representative North American Indian tribes. 96 pp. Illus. Ages 8 to 12. William Morrow & Co., Inc., 1965. $2.75.

*INDIAN WARS AND WARRIORS, Vols. I and II
Paul I. Wellman
An account of the Indian wars east and west of the Mississippi, from the Jamestown massacres of 1662 to the treaty that ended the Seminole War in 1842, and dealing with the white man's struggle with the Apaches, the Woodland and Teton Sioux, the Cheyennes, the Comanches, and other tribes west of the Mississippi. Grades 7 to 11. Illus. Houghton Mifflin Co., 1959. Vol. I (East), $1.95; Vol. II (West), $2.20.

INDIAN WARS OF TEXAS
Mildred P. Mayhall
A study of the Indian wars of Texas from 1871 to 1874. 296 pp. Texian Press, 1965. $7.50.

INDIAN WARS OF THE UNITED STATES ARMY, 1776-1865
Fairfax D. Downey
Doubleday & Co., Inc., 1963. $4.75.

THE INDIAN WARS OF THE WEST
Potomac Corral of the Westerners; introductory chapter by John C. Ewers
A description of Indian fighting methods, including a discussion of the Indian Wars. Doubleday & Co., Inc., 1960. $4.95.

INDIAN WARS OF THE WEST
Paul Wellman
Illus. Doubleday & Co., Inc., 1954. $6.50.

*INDIAN WOMEN
Lela and Rufus Waltrip
A collection of biographies of thirteen American Indian women who have made cultural contributions to American life, from the 16th century to the present. 192 pp. David McKay Co., Inc., 1964. $3.75.

INDIANCRAFT
   W. Ben Hunt
A book of projects on Indian lore and camp
handicrafts. Bruce Publishing Co., 1942.
$3.95.

*INDIANS
   Claude Appell; translated by Matt Chisholm
A documented history of the American Indian and his culture, from the earliest days
to the present. 72 pp. Illus. Follett Publishing Co., 1966. $4.95.

*INDIANS
   Alice Marriott and Carol K. Rachlin
A collection of individual biographies of Indians and their roles in pioneer times. 80
pp. Illus. Grades 2 to 5. Garrard Publishing Co. Three-volume set, $5.94; in-
dividual volumes, $1.98 each.

*INDIANS
   Edwin Tunis
A description of Indian life before the arrival of the white man. 160 pp. Grades 7
to 9. Illus. The World Publishing Co.,
1959. $5.95.

INDIANS AND ARCHAEOLOGY OF
   MISSOURI
   Carl H. and Eleanor Chapman
Illus. Paper. University of Missouri Press,
1964. $1.00.

INDIANS AND OTHER AMERICANS
   Harold E. Fey and D'Arcy McNickle
An account of the history of official relations with the Indians -- administration of
their affairs, their present situation and
potential future. 220 pp. Index. Appendix.
Notes. Map. Harper & Row, Publishers,
1959. $3.95.

THE INDIANS AND THE NURSE
   Elinor D. Gregg
An account of the author's experiences as a
nurse for the Indian Bureau from 1922 to
1937. 160 pp. University of Oklahoma
Press, $2.00.

INDIANS AS THE WESTERNER SAW THEM
   Ralph Andrews
Old manuscripts and photos reveal experiences of pioneers, settlers, traders and
Army wives with Indians of the Great Plains.
176 pp. Illus. Superior Publishing Co.,
1962. $12.50.

*INDIANS AT HOME
   Robert Hofsinde
A survey of typical Indian homes in North
America, their construction and the life led
inside them. 96 pp. Illus. Ages 8 to 12.
William Morrow & Co., Inc., 1964. $2.95.

INDIANS BEFORE COLUMBUS: *Twenty
Thousand Years of North American History
Revealed by Archaeology*
   Paul S. Martin, George I. Quimby and
   Donald Collier
A study of the nature and purpose of archae-
ology and the trends of cultural development
among the pre-Columbian Indians of North
America. xxiv + 582 pp. Illus. Charts.
Glossary. University of Chicago Press,
1947. $8.50.

INDIANS IN MINNESOTA
   Minnesota League of Women Voters
Contents: *The Federal Government and
Minnesota Indians; Minnesota Indians; Special problems of Indians in Minnesota; Conclusion.* 66 pp. Biblio. Minnesota League
of Women Voters, 1962. 50¢.

INDIANS IN PENNSYLVANIA
   Paul A. W. Wallace
An account of the Indian groups who have
lived in Pennsylvania from the time of the
first exploration by Europeans to the present, with emphasis on the Delawares. 194
pp. Pennsylvania Historical and Museum
Commission, 1964. Paper, $1.50; cloth,
$2.50.

INDIANS IN SEVENTEENTH CENTURY
VIRGINIA
   Ben C. McCary
As below. Garrett and Massie, Inc., $1.00.

INDIANS IN SEVENTEENTH CENTURY
VIRGINIA
   Ben C. McCary
An account of the locations of Indian tribes,
their way of life, and their relations with
the settlers. 93 pp. Illus. Map. Paper.
University Press of Virginia, 1957. 75¢.

*INDIANS IN WINTER CAMP
   Therese O. Deming
Illus. Grades 2 to 4. Albert Whitman &
Co., 1957. $2.50.

*INDIANS, INDIANS, INDIANS
   Phyllis Fenner, Editor; illustrated by
   Manning deV. Lee

Fifteen stories about American Indians including those by Jim Kjelgaard, Lois Maloy, Carl Lane and LeGrand. 256 pp. Grades 5 to 8. Illus. Franklin Watts, Inc., 1962. $3.95.

*THE INDIANS KNEW
Tillie S. Pine; illustrated by Ezra Jack Keats

Describes how the American Indian employed numerous basic concepts which underlie many of man's recent scientific and technological accomplishments. Includes a simple experiment for children. 32 pp. Illus. Ages 5 to 9. McGraw-Hill Book Co., 1957. $2.95.

INDIANS OF CAPE FLATTERY: *At the Entrance to the Strait of Fuca, Washington Territory*
James G. Swan

A facsimile of the 1868 edition. Discusses tribal name, its geographical position, character of the reservation, tribal census, etc. ix + 108 pp. Index. Illus. Paper. Shorey Publications, 1966. $7.50.

*THE INDIANS OF CARLISLE
William Heuman

The story of the Carlisle Industrial School, created to prepare American Indians to survive in a white man's world by teaching them trades as well as reading and writing. 128 pp. Illus. Ages 10 to 14. G. P. Putnam's Sons, 1965. $3.50.

*INDIANS OF EARLY CHICAGO

A brief summary of the food, clothing, ceremonies and culture of the early inhabitants of the Chicago, Illinois, area. 18 pp. Illus. Ages 8 to 14. Paper. Chicago Museum of Natural History, 25¢.

*INDIANS OF EARLY MARYLAND
Harold R. Manakee

A study in the ways of life of the Indian tribes who lived in Maryland from 1634 to 1700. 47 pp. Grades 4 to 8. Illus. Maryland Historical Society, 1959. $1.80.

INDIANS OF LASSEN
Paul E. Schulz

A study of the Indians who once inhabited Lassen, California, and vicinity. 176 pp. Illus. Biblio. Maps. Loomis Museum Association, 1954. 85¢.

*THE INDIANS OF NEW JERSEY: *Dickon Among the Lenapes*
Mark R. Harrington

An account of Lenape Indian culture, crafts, language and customs, told through the adventures of Dickon, an English cabinboy. 352 pp. Illus. Rutgers University Press, 1963. Paper, $1.95; cloth, $4.95.

INDIANS OF NORTH AMERICA
Harold E. Driver

A presentation of the variation of culture patterns among North American Indians at the high points of their histories. xviii + 668 pp. Illus. University of Chicago Press, 1961. Paper, $5.00; cloth, $10.95.

*INDIANS OF PENNSYLVANIA
Lucille Wallower, assisted by Martha Trullinger White

Tells where the Pennsylvania Indians lived, how they lived, and why they lived as they did. 93 pp. Illus. Grades 3 to 4. Map. Pennsylvania Valley Publishers, 1956. $2.96.

INDIANS OF PUGET SOUND
Hermann Haeberlin and Erna Gunther

A study of the culture of the Snohomish and Snuqualin tribes now living on the Tulalip Reservation in Washington State. 87 pp. Illus. Biblio. Map. Paper. University of Washington Press, 1930. $1.50.

THE INDIANS OF QUETICO
Emerson S. Coatsworth and Robert C. Dailey

The industrious life of the Ojibwas before the arrival of the white man. 58 pp. Illus. Photographs. Maps. University of Toronto Press, $1.75.

INDIANS OF SOUTHERN CALIFORNIA
Edwin F. Walker

Southwest Museum, 25¢.

INDIANS OF SOUTHERN ILLINOIS
Irvin M. Peithmann

Traces 10,000 years of prehistoric Indian occupation by examining four cultures. 172 pp. Illus. Charles C. Thomas, Publisher, 1964. $6.50.

INDIANS OF TEXAS: *From Prehistoric to Modern Times*
W. W. Newcomb, Jr.

Covers all aspects of Indian life within the present borders of Texas. xviii + 404 pp. Illus. University of Texas Press, 1961. $5.75.

INDIANS OF THE AMERICAS
John Collier
Deals with the American Indian from the Paleolithic Age to the present; includes a prediction for the future. 187 pp. Paper. New American Library, 1960. 60¢.

INDIANS OF THE AMERICAS
John Collier
As above. Illus. W. W. Norton & Co., Inc., 1947. $6.95.

INDIANS OF THE AMERICAS
Edwin R. Embree
A presentation of the way of life of prehistoric Indians through the reconstruction of life among the various culture areas of the Western Hemisphere. Illus. Index. Biblio. Houghton Mifflin Co., $4.50.

INDIANS OF THE AMERICAS
Matthew W. Stirling, Editor
A collection of articles on Indians from the Arctic to the Amazon. 423 pp. Illus. National Geographic Society, 1965. $7.50.

INDIANS OF THE HIGH PLAINS: *From the Prehistoric Period to the Coming of the Europeans*
George E. Hyde
231 pp. Illus. Index. Biblio. Maps. University of Oklahoma Press, 1959. $4.00.

*INDIANS OF THE LONGHOUSE
Sonia Bleeker; illustrated by Althea Karr
An account of the Iroquois and their way of life in pre-Colonial days. 160 pp. Illus. Ages 8 to 12. William Morrow & Co., Inc., 1950. $2.95.

INDIANS OF THE MESA VERDE
Donald Watson
A history of the Mesa Verde area and a reconstruction of the life of prehistoric Indians who occupied it. Illus. Paper. Mesa Verde Museum Association, $1.25.

INDIANS OF THE NORTHWEST COAST
Philip Drucker
A study of the Indians who lived in the area from Yakutat Bay (Alaska) to the northern coast of California. Illus. Doubleday & Co., Inc., 1963.

INDIANS OF THE PASSAIC VALLEY
Edward Hunter Ross
An archaeological and ethnological study of the Lenni Lenape or Delaware Indians of New Jersey. 20 pp. Illus. Biblio. Map. Paper. The Newark Museum, 1963.

INDIANS OF THE PLAINS
M. R. Harrington
Southwest Museum, 30¢.

INDIANS OF THE PLAINS
Robert H. Lowie
A comprehensive study of the prehistory and culture of the tribes who inhabited the Plains from the Mississippi to the Rockies. Illus. Paper. The Natural History Press, $1.95.

*INDIANS OF THE PLAINS
Eugene Rachlis; Introduction by John C. Ewers
A history of the Plains Indians, their traditional customs, and their relations with the white men. 153 pp. Illus. Index. Biblio. Maps. Grades 4 to 8. American Heritage Publishing Co., 1960. $3.95.

*INDIANS OF THE PLAINS
Eugene Rachlis; Introduction by John C. Ewers
As above. 128 pp. Biblio. Paper. Harper & Row, Publishers, Inc., 75¢.

INDIANS OF THE SOUTHWEST
M. Jourdon Atkinson
A study of the Indian's arts, sciences and the laws by which he lived before the colonization of America. 364 pp. Illus. Biblio. Index. Maps. The Naylor Co., 1963. $5.95.

INDIANS OF THE SOUTHWEST
Bertha P. Dutton
160 pp. Illus. Southwestern Association on Indian Affairs, $1.50.

INDIANS OF THE UNITED STATES: *Four Centuries of Their History and Culture*
Clark Wissler
Illus. Doubleday & Co., Inc., 1939. $4.95.

INDIANS OF THE WESTERN FRONTIER: *Paintings of George Catlin*
George I. Quimby
78 pp. Illus. Chicago Natural History Museum, 1958. 60¢.

INDIANS OF THE WESTERN GREAT LAKES, 1615-1760
W. Vernon Kinietz
440 pp. Paper. University of Michigan Press, 1965. Paper, $2.95; cloth, $4.40.

INDIANS OF THE WOODLANDS, FROM
PREHISTORIC TIMES TO 1725
  George E. Hyde
Discusses the Mound Builder Woodland Indians of the Hudson and Mississippi valleys.
295 pp. Illus. Index. Biblio. University
of Oklahoma Press, 1962. $5.00.

INDIANS OF TODAY
  Marian Gridley; Foreword by Ethel
  Frazier Walker
A collection of short biographical sketches
of prominent living American Indians active
in the arts, the business world, and the
professions. Photographs included in majority of listings. 234 pp. Illus. Index.
Indian Council Fire, 1960. $6.00.

INDIANS OF WASHTENAW COUNTY,
  MICHIGAN
  W. B. Hinsdale
68 pp. George Wahr Publishing Co., 1927.
60¢.

*INDIANS OF YESTERDAY
  Marian Gridley; illustrated by Lone
  Wolf
80 pp. Illus. Ages 10 to 14. M. A. Donohue & Co., 1940. $3.50.

*INDIANS ON THE WARPATH
  David C. Cooke
Biographies of ten Indian leaders who fought
to preserve their lands. Illus. Grades 7
through 11. Dodd, Mead & Co., 1957.
$3.50.

*THE INDIAN'S SECRET WORLD
  Robert Hofsinde
A presentation of Indian symbols and ceremonies. 96 pp. Illus. Grades 4 to 6. William Morrow & Co., Inc., 1955. $4.44.

*INDIANS, SETTLERS, AND PIONEERS
  IN NEW YORK STATE
  Catherine Urell and Jennifer Chatfield
An elementary social studies textbook. Part
I presents the life of a Woodland Indian boy.
224 pp. Illus. Index. Glossary. Map.
Follett Publishing Co., 1955.

INGALIK MATERIAL CULTURE
  Cornelius Osgood
Human Relations Area Files Press, 1964.
$8.25.

INKLE AND YARIKO ALBUM
  Lawrence M. Price
Illus. University of California Press, 1937.
$1.00.

INLAND WHALE, *Nine Stories Retold from
California Indian Legends*
  Theodora Kroeber; illustrations by
  Joseph Crivy
A collection of California Indian folklore.
201 pp. Illus. Paper. Peter Smith, $1.50.

INLAND WHALE, *Nine Stories Retold from
California Indian Legends*
  Theodora Kroeber
As above. Illus. Paper. University of
California Press, 1959. $1.50.

INTRODUCTION TO THE STUDY OF
SOUTHWESTERN ARCHAEOLOGY
  Alfred Vincent Kidder; Introduction by
  Irving Rouse
A summary of Pueblo archaeology, showing
historic development and interrelationships.
ix + 377 pp. Illus. Yale University Press,
1962. Paper, $2.45; cloth, $10.00.

INTRODUCTION TO ZUNI FETISHISM
  Ruth Kirk
A discussion of the general forms of Zuni
religion with explanation of various fetishes
and their specific uses. 65 pp. Illus. Biblio. Paper. School of American Research,
$3.00.

THE INVASION
  Janet Lewis
A study of the Indian-white relations in the
Old Northwest territory. Sage Books. Pa-
per, $1.95; cloth, $4.00.

*IROQUOIS
  Irene Estep; illustrations by Robert D.
  Smith
A brief account of the home and communal
life of the people of the longhouses, with
emphasis on the League of Five Nations.
32 pp. Illus. Reading level, 3; interest
level, 2 to 6. Melmont Publishers, Inc.,
1961. $2.50.

THE IROQUOIS
  Richard L. McCarthy and Harrison
  Newman
Contents: *The People of the Long House;
A Matriarchy; The League of Six Nations;
Daily Life; Village Organization; Religious
Beliefs; Crafts (Pottery, Beadwork, Wood
Carving, Basket Making); Games*. Photo.
16 pp. Buffalo and Erie County Historical
Society, 1960. 50¢.

THE IROQUOIS
Frank G. Speck
An interpretation of Iroquois culture. 95 pp. Illus. Cranbrook Institute of Science, 1965. $1.00.

THE IROQUOIS BOOK OF RITES
Horatio Hale, Editor
Ethnological study of the political and social life, as well as the individual character and capacity of the Iroquois Indian. 222 pp. Annotated. University of Toronto Press, 1963. $7.50.

IROQUOIS FOLK LORE GATHERED FROM THE SIX NATIONS OF NEW YORK
William M. Beauchamp
Ira J. Friedman, Inc., $6.50.

*THE IROQUOIS TRAIL
M. R. Harrington
The story of Dickon, an English boy rescued and adopted by Lenape Indians, and what he learns about the tribes of the five Iroquois nations. 215 pp. Grades 4 to 8. Rutgers University Press, 1965. Cloth, $5.00; paper, $1.95.

ISHI IN TWO WORLDS: *A Biography of the Last Wild Indian in North America*
Theodora Kroeber
A biography of the lone survivor of a California Yahi tribe, the last "wild" Indian in America. 255 pp. Illus. Biblio. University of California, 1961. Cloth, $5.95; paper, $1.95.

*ISHI, LAST OF HIS TRIBE
Theodora Kroeber; illustrated by Ruth Robbins
A biography of Ishi, the lone survivor of the Yahi Californian Indians. 209 pp. Grades 4 to 8. Illus. Maps. Parnassus Press, 1964. Cloth, $3.95; paper, $1.95.

ISLAND OF THE LOST
Paul F. Cooper
G. P. Putnam's Sons, 1961. $4.00.

J

JACK SQUIRES - A SCOUT WITH KIT CARSON
Ernest Jack Sharp
A true historical narrative of the early West, as it was lived by scouts, Indians and pioneers. Illus. Newt Publications, $1.50.

*JAMESTOWN: *First English Colony*
Marshall William Fishwick
Traces the history of the first permanent English settlement in this country, which eventually became a prosperous plantation society. 151 pp. Illus. American Heritage Publishing Co., 1965. $3.95.

JEDEDIAH SMITH AND THE OPENING OF THE WEST
Dale Morgan
As below. Peter Smith, $4.00.

JEDEDIAH SMITH AND THE OPENING OF THE WEST
Dale Morgan
Biography of a mountain man and fur trader, including accounts of his associations with all the major Plains tribes. Describes the Arikara defeat of 1823, the Mojave massacre of 1827, and the Umpqua massacre of 1828. 460 pp. University of Nebraska Press, 1953. $1.85.

JESUIT RELATIONS
Edna Kenton, Editor
Vanguard Press, Inc., $6.00.

JESUIT RELATIONS AND ALLIED DOCUMENTS
R. G. Thwaites, Editor
Illus. Loyola University Press, 1959. Seventy-three original volumes bound in thirty-six-volume set, $175.00.

JESUIT RELATIONS AND OTHER AMERICANA IN THE LIBRARY OF JAMES F. BELL: *A Catalogue*
Frank K. Walter and Virginia Doneghy, Editors
xiv + 434 pp. Illus. University of Minnesota Press, 1950. $12.50.

THE JESUITS IN NORTH AMERICA
Francis Parkman
586 pp. Biblio. Peter Smith, 1965. $4.50.

THE JESUITS AND THE INDIAN WARS OF THE NORTHWEST
Robert Ignatius Burns, S. J.
An examination and illumination of the world of the upper interior of Oregon, including the 1855 treaty troubles, the war against the Northern Indians of 1858 to 1859, and the Nez Perce War of 1877. 472 pp. Yale University Press, 1965. $10.00.

THE JESUITS IN NORTH AMERICA
Francis Parkman

An account of the Jesuits' efforts to "Christianize" the Algonquin, Huron and Iroquois tribes of Canada and northern United States, during the years 1634 to 1670. xvii + 586 pp. Paper. Little, Brown and Co., 1963. $2.45.

JIM SAVAGE AND THE TULARENO
INDIANS
    Annie R. Mitchell
A biographical study of the legendary Jim Savage, the blond King of the Tulares, and discoverer of Yosemite. 181 pp. Westernlore Press, 1957. $5.50.

*JIM THORPE, INDIAN ATHLETE
    Guernsey Van Riper, Jr.; illustrated
    by William Riley
Illus. Grades 3 to 6. The Bobbs-Merrill Co., Inc., 1956. $2.25.

*THE JIM THORPE STORY: *America's
Greatest Athlete*
    Gene Schoor
The life story of an all-American Sauk-Fox sports star, who was a descendant of the famed Indian chief, Black Hawk. 186 pp. For teen-agers. Julian Messner, $3.25.

*JOHN BILLINGTON, FRIEND OF
SQUANTO
    Clyde R. Bulla; illustrated by Peter
    Burchard
A biography of Squanto, including historical facts of the first year at Plymouth. 96 pp. Illus. Thomas Y. Crowell Co., 1956. Cloth, $3.50.

JOHN HOWARD PAYNE TO HIS
COUNTRYMEN
    Clements De Baillou, Editor
This is a reprint of Payne's version of his arrest at the home of the Cherokee chief, and his address on behalf of the Cherokees prior to their removal across the Mississippi. 66 pp. University of Georgia Press, 1961. $2.00.

JOHN McLOUGHLIN: *"Father of Oregon"*
    Robert C. Johnson
A story of the Oregon country, from 1824 to McLoughlin's final days in Oregon City. Traces McLoughlin's involvement with Indians, his stint in the fur trade, etc. 330 pp. Illus. Index. Biblio. Binfords and Mort, $3.75.

*JOHN RATTLING-GOURD OF BIG COVE
    Corydon Bell

A collection of Cherokee legends as told by Mr. Gan-se-ti to Cherokee boys and girls of the present day. Illus. Ages 8 to 12. Macmillan Co.

JOHN ROSS, CHIEF OF AN EAGLE RACE
    Gertrude McDaris Ruskin
The life story of a Cherokee chief, and the restoration of his home in 1963, in Rossville, Georgia. 85 pp. Illus. Gertrude McDaris Ruskin, $2.00.

JOSEPH BRANDT: *Mohawk*
    Harvey Chalmers and Ethel Brandt
    Monture
The story of the Mohawks' and the white man's culture, and how Joseph Brandt strove to help the white man understand the merits of the Indians' culture. Michigan State University Press, $5.00.

*JOSEPH, THE CHIEF OF THE NEZ
PERCE
    Dean Pollock
The deeds of Chief Joseph, last of the great Indian chieftains. 64 pp. Illus. Grades 7 to 9. Binfords and Mort, 1957. $2.50.

JOURNAL
    Jonathan Dickinson; revised and edited
    by Evangeline and Charles M. Andrews
Paper. Yale University Press, 1961. $1.25.

JOURNAL
    Jose L. Martinez; edited and translated by Lesley B. Simpson
John Howell, Books, 1961. $12.50.

A JOURNAL OF LA SALLE'S LAST
VOYAGE
    Henri Joutel; Introduction by Barrett
    B. Rutman
187 pp. Paper. Corinth Books, 1962. $1.50.

JOURNAL OF THE ADVENTURES OF
MATTHEW BUNN
    Matthew Bunn
Paper. Newberry Library, $1.75.

A JOURNAL OF THE PILGRIMS AT
PLYMOUTH
    Introduction by Dwight B. Heath
96 pp. Illus. Corinth Books, 1963. $1.45.

JOURNALS, 1762-1769
    Charles Beatty; edited by Guy S. Klett
Pennsylvania State University Press, 1962. $6.00.

THE JOURNALS OF MAJOR ROBERT
ROGERS
    Robert Rogers; Introduction by Howard
    H. Peckham
Paper. 171 pp. Corinth Books, 1961.
$1.50.

JOURNEY INTO NORTHERN PENNSYL-
VANIA AND THE STATE OF NEW YORK
    Michel-Guillaume St. Jean de Creve-
    coeur; translated by C. S. Bostelmann
The first complete translation of the memoirs of a Frenchman traveling in America
during the early 18th century. 700 pp. Illus. University of Michigan Press, $15.00.

JOURNEY INTO WILDERNESS
    Jacob Rhett Motte; edited by James F.
    Sunderman
The journal of an army surgeon during the
Creek and Seminole Wars, 1836 to 1838.
361 pp. Illus. University of Florida Press,
1953. $7.50.

JOURNEY OF CABEZA DE VACA IN 1528-
1536
    Fanny Bendelier
The story of four men who walked across
the Continent when it was a savage wilderness. 232 pp. The Rio Grande Press, Inc.,
$7.50.

K

THE KACHINA AND THE WHITE MAN
    Frederick J. Dockstader
A study of the influences of the white culture on the Hopi kachina cult, with a Hopi-
English glossary and a historical summary
of Hopi-white contacts during the period of
1540 to 1850. 204 pp. Illus. Index. Biblio. Cranbrook Institute of Science, 1954.
$5.00.

KAIBAH: *Recollection of a Navajo Girlhood*
    Kay Bennett
The true story of a Navajo girl and her fam-
ily, as lived by the author. 253 pp. Illus.
Westernlore Press, 1964. $7.50.

KALAPUYA TEXTS
    Melville Jacobs
Ethnography and tales of the Kalapuya of
Willamette Valley in western Oregon. Three
parts. 396 pp. Index. Map. Paper. University of Washington Press, $6.50.

*KARANKAWA BOY
    Audrey Adams; illustrated by Dick
    Gooch
Story of the nomadic Karankawas -- how
they lived, why they were hated, and what
became of them -- depicted through the experiences of Kwash, son of the chief. 84
pp. Illus. Grades 4 to 8. The Naylor Co.,
1965. $2.95.

THE KASKA INDIANS: *An Ethnographic
Reconstruction*
    Honigmann
Human Relations Area Files Press, 1964.
$4.00.

KICKAPOOS: *Lords of the Middle Border*
    Arrell M. Gibson
391 pp. Illus. Index. Biblio. Map. University of Oklahoma Press, 1963. $6.95.

*KIDLIK'S KAYAK
    Terry Shannon
Illus. Grades 3 to 5. Albert Whitman &
Co., 1959. $2.75.

*KILLER-OF-DEATH
    Betty Baker
Grades 6 to 10. Harper & Row, Publishers, 1963. $2.95.

*KING PHILIP, LOYAL INDIAN
    Cecile P. Edwards
The biography of a Wampanoag chief who
attempted to unite the New England tribes
against the injustice and invasions of the
white man. 192 pp. Illus. Ages 8 to 12.
Houghton Mifflin Co., 1962. $1.95.

*KING PHILIP, THE INDIAN CHIEF
    Esther Averill
The story of the proud chief of the Wampanoag Indians of Massachusetts, who led
his people in war against the colonists in
1675. Illus. Ages 12 and up. Harper &
Row, Publishers, 1950. $3.50.

KINGDOM OF THE SEAL
    Francis M. Menager
Illus. Loyola University Press, 1962.
$3.00.

THE KIOWAS
    Mildred P. Mayhall
315 pp. Illus. Index. Biblio. Appendix.
University of Oklahoma Press, 1962. $5.95.

KITCHI-GAMI: *Wanderings Around Lake Superior*
>   Johann G. Kohl; Introduction by Russell W. Fridley

A study of the customs and lore of the Ojibwa Indians. Ross & Haines, Inc., $8.75.

THE KLAMATH TRIBE: *A People and their Reservation*
>   Theodore Stern

An ethnohistorical account that documents the changing response by American Indian society to the Euro-American world -- from subtle shifts in diet and clothing to sweeping changes in religion, economy, and education. Illus. An American Ethnological Society Monograph reissued by the University of Washington Press, 1965. $6.95.

KLAMATH PREHISTORY: *The Prehistory of Klamath Lake Area, Oregon*
>   L. S. Cressman

This book describes Klamath Indian cultural development and adaptation to the ecological situation, from the time of its earliest manifestations. 139 pp. Illus. Volume 46, Part 4 of the *Transactions* of the American Philosophical Society, 1956. $2.00.

KNOW THE NAVAJO
>   Sandy Hassell; illustrated by Paul Bringle

A discussion of Navajo customs, traditions and superstitions. 40 pp. Illus. Paper. Victor H. Walker, 1965. 50¢.

*KOMANTCIA
>   Harold Keith

Two Spanish brothers are captured in a raid by Comanche Indians, and forced to serve as Comanche slaves until they are absorbed into the tribe. 304 pp. Ages 12 and up. Thomas Y. Crowell Co., 1965. $3.95.

KWAKIUTL CEREMONIAL ART
>   Audrey Hawthorn

A description of Kwakiutl society, religion, mythology, technology, and iconography that views the art of these Northwest Coast Indians as both a distinctive aesthetic achievement and an integral element of tribal life. Presents a study collection of Kwakiutl ceremonial paraphernalia. Maps. Illus. An American Ethnological Society Publication. University of Washington Press.

KWAKIUTL GRAMMAR, WITH A GLOSSARY OF THE SUFFIXES
>   Franz Boas; edited by Helene Boas Yampolsky with the collaboration of Zellig S. Harris

A complete grammar of the Kwakiutl Indian language of the Pacific Northwest, prepared by Professor Franz Boas over a period of many years and nearly completed at the time of his death. 177 pp. Paper. American Philosophical Society, 1947. $2.50.

L

LAKE OF THE SKY
>   George Wharton James

The early history of Lake Tahoe, extending from its discovery through the pioneer days of the old West, including material on the Indians of the region and their folklore. xlvi + 464 pp. Illus. Maps. Charles T. Powner, 1956. $4.95.

*LAND OF PROMISE
>   John L. Field; illustrated by Allistair Maitland

The story of early Canada from its beginnings to the year 1800, describing native Indian tribes, explorers, conquerors, fur-traders, missionaries, and French colonists. 288 pp. Illus. Ages 12 and up. Abelard-Schuman Ltd., 1962. $4.50.

LAND OF THE DACOTAHS
>   Bruce Nelson

Peter Smith, $3.75.

LAND OF THE DACOTAHS
>   Bruce Nelson

Illus. Paper. University of Nebraska Press, 1964. $1.60.

LAND OF THE MIDNIGHT SUN
>   William C. Emerson

The story, in words and pictures, of Alaska: the Alaska Highway, the Alaska Indians and the Eskimos. 179 pp. Illus. Dorrance and Co., Inc., 1956. $3.00.

LANDMARKS OF NEW MEXICO
>   Edgar L. Hewett and Wayne L. Mauzy

A travel guide to the state of New Mexico that provides information on archaeology, ethnology, and culture backgrounds. 194 pp. Illus. School of American Research, $4.50.

LANGUAGE, CULTURE AND
  PERSONALITY
    Edited by Leslie Spier, A. Irving Hal-
    lowell, and Stanley S. Newman
A group of essays dealing with such topics
as problems of linguistic classification,
linguistic behavior and thought, the development of culture patterns, and culture norms
and the individual. 298 pp. University of
Utah Press, 1960. $3.75.

*LARRY
    Edith J. Agnew
Adventures of Larry and his Indian friend
Chesty in Oklahoma. 128 pp. Illus.
Friendship Press, 1960. Cloth, $2.95; pa-
per, $1.50.

*THE LAST CHIEF
    Hanns Radau; illustrated by Heiner
    Rothfuchs
An adventure story of an Alaskan boy who
struggles to make something of himself.
Illus. Abelard-Schuman, Ltd., 1962. $3.00.

√ THE LAST DAYS OF THE SIOUX NATION
    Robert M. Utley
Describes the Sioux as they were when they
first came to the reservation, and tells how
the life that the whites had prepared for
them was unsuited to their needs, and how
their reaction to the new system led to the
last confrontation of the Army and the Sioux.
xiv + 314 pp. Illus. Index. Biblio. Maps.
Yale University Press, 1963. Paper, $1.95;
cloth, $7.50.

LAST GRASS FRONTIER
    Bob Lee and Dick Williams
The history of the development of the cattle
industry in the Dakotas, describing the
opening of the Indian reservation grass-
lands; the settlement of the Sioux on separate reservations; the relations between
cattlemen and Indians; the treaties with the
Sioux; the Wounded Knee engagement on the
Pine Ridge Indian Reservation, and a history of the South Dakota Stock Growers Association from the 1880's to 1964. 453 pp.
Black Hills Publishers, Inc., 1964. $6.50.

LAST OF THE FEW
    Kaare Rodahl
Illus. Harper & Row, Publishers, 1963.
$4.95.

*THE LAST OF THE GREAT WAMPANOAG
  INDIAN SACHEMS
    Milton A. Travers

A story of King Philip's war and of New
England history during this period. 93 pp.
Christopher Publishing House, 1963. $2.75.

LAST OF THE INDIAN WARS
    Forbes Parkhill
Collier Publishing Co., 1962. 95¢.

LAST OF THE MIAMIS, *Little Turtle*
    Otho Winger
"The history of Meshingomesia and Little
Turtle." Illus. Lawrence W. Shultz, 1935.
$2.00.

LAST PORTAGE
    Walter O'Meara
Houghton Mifflin Co., 1962. $5.00.

THE LAST STAND OF THE NEZ PERCE
    Harry Chalmers
An account of the unhappy fate of an Indian
tribe that fell victim to western expansion.
288 pp. Twayne Publishers, Inc., 1962.
$6.00.

LAST TREK OF THE INDIANS
    Grant Foreman
Illus. University of Chicago Press, 1946.
$5.00.

THE LAST WAR TRAIL: *The Utes and the
Settlement of Colorado*
    Robert Emmitt; drawings by Bettina
    Steinke
333 pp. Index. Biblio. University of Oklahoma Press, 1954. $4.50.

LATE MOGOLLON COMMUNITIES
    Paul S. Martin, John B. Rinaldo, and
    Eloise R. Barter
144 pp. Illus. Tables. Volume 49, No. 1.
Chicago Natural History Museum, 1957.
$4.00.

LATE MOGOLLON POTTERY TYPES OF
THE RESERVE AREA
    John B. Rinaldo, Elaine A. Bluhm
39 pp. Illus. Map. Volume 36, No. 7.
Chicago Natural History Museum, 1956.
$1.25.

LATE PALEO-INDIAN
    Martha Ann Rolingsen and Douglas W.
    Schwartz
The authors report the detailed analysis of
basic data from the four sites of Paleo-
Indian habitation in Kentucky. University
of Kentucky Press. $5.00.

THE LATE PREHISTORIC OCCUPATION IN SOUTHWESTERN NEW YORK: *An Interpretive Analysis*
 Alfred K. Guthe
This report represents an expanded research project, discussing the "cultural relationships of the Westfield site" in Chautauqua County and seven other major sites in the region, and a cultural and temporal analysis of the entire region. 100 pp. 32 pls. 2 figs. Table. Biblio. Research Records of the Rochester Museum of Arts and Sciences No. 11, 1958. $2.00. Available from the Rochester Museum Association.

LATEST AZTEC DISCOVERIES
 Guy E. Powell
"New digs in Texas have uncovered artifacts which appear to belong to an ancient Indian civilization and which suggest this area is the possible birthplace of the Aztecs and the site where they returned to hide their treasure." 106 pp. The Naylor Co., 1966. $3.95.

*LAUGHING BOY
 Oliver LaFarge
Houghton Mifflin Co. Paper, $1.95; cloth, $4.00.

LAW AND GOVERNMENT OF THE GRAND RIVER IROQUOIS
 John A. Noon
A study of case histories and decisions, rendered by the chiefs, which show the social control of the Iroquois, and the positive function of the law in patterning their behavior. 186 pp. Johnson Reprint Corp., 1964. $10.00.

LAW AND STATUS AMONG THE KIOWA INDIANS
 Jane Richardson
Despite a homogeneous society with no economic specialization, the Kiowa are shown to have had a surprisingly articulate procedure with a wide range of choices in criminal and dispute situations. An American Ethnological Society Monograph reissued by the University of Washington Press. $5.00.

LAWS OF THE CREEK NATION
 Antonio J. Waring, Editor
Printed from the original handwritten manuscript (1825) by the son of a half-Scot Creek chief, William McIntosh. 32 pp. University of Georgia Press, 1960. $1.00.

LAWSON'S HISTORY OF CAROLINA
 Frances Latham Harriss, Editor
This book describes early travels in America, through the eyes of John Lawson, who recorded everything he saw and heard on his journeys through Virginia and the Carolinas. 275 pp. Illus. Garrett & Massie, Inc., $4.00.

THE LEADING FACTS OF NEW MEXICAN HISTORY
 Ralph H. Twitchell
A record of events from the time the Spaniards came to New Mexico until the time of statehood. Two vols. 1,137 pp. Illus. Index. Maps. Horn and Wallace, $25.00.

LEAGUE OF THE HO-DE-NO-SAU-NEE OR IROQUOIS
 Lewis Henry Morgan
Two vols. Burt Franklin Publications, 1966. $37.50.

LEAGUE OF THE IROQUOIS
 Lewis Henry Morgan; Introduction by William N. Teuton
477 pp. Corinth Books, 1962. $2.95.

LEGAL CONSCIENCE: *Selected Papers of Felix S. Cohen*
 Felix S. Cohen; edited by Lucy Kramer Cohen, with a Foreword by Supreme Court Justice Felix Frankfurter, and an Introduction by Eugene Rostow
The selections are divided into three parts: 1. *Logic, Law, and Ethics;* 2. *The Indians' Quest for Justice;* and 3. *The Philosophy of American Democracy.* xvii + 505 pp. Index. Biblio. Yale University Press, 1960. $12.50.

LEGEND INTO HISTORY: *The Custer Mystery*
 Charles Kuhlman
A reconstruction of the Little Big Horn battle. The Stackpole Co., 1951. $5.00.

THE LEGEND OF GRIZZLY ADAMS: *California's Greatest Mountain Man*
 Richard Dillon
The exploits of John Grizzly Adams, a man who went west in 1849 and became known as a great hunter and animal collector, a great practical joker, and a good friend of the Indians. G. P. Putnam's Sons, $5.00.

*LEGENDS OF GREEN SKY HILL
 Louise Jean Walker; illustrated by Grace Hoyt

A book of Chippewa Indian legends. 204 pp. Illus. Wm. B. Eerdmans Publishing Co., 1961. $3.25.

LEGENDS OF THE LONGHOUSE
        Jesse J. Cornplanter; Introduction by Carl Carmer
A book of folklore, philosophy, customs and anthropology of primitive peoples. 217 pp. Empire State Historical Publications, 1938. $5.00.

LEGENDS OF THE SHAWANGUNK (SHON-GUM) AND ITS ENVIRONS
        Philip H. Smith
A book of legends, historical sketches, biographical notes, border incidents and adventures. 212 pp. Syracuse University Press, 1965. $5.50.

LEGENDS OF VANCOUVER
        E. Pauline Johnson
176 pp. McClelland & Stewart, Ltd. Paper, $1.50; cloth, $2.50.

*LET'S BE INDIANS
        Peggy Parish; illustrated by Arnold Lobel
A book illustrating simple methods by which children can create Indian lore items such as headdresses and tipis; included is a section of basic facts about Indians. Illus. Grades 1 to 4. Harper & Row, Publishers, 1962. $2.75.

LET'S EXPLORE INDIAN VILLAGES: *Past and Present*
        Bertha P. Dutton
Outlines four exploratory trips to Indian villages. Includes background material, descriptive data, and a general discussion of prehistoric and historic Indian life in New Mexico. 56 pp. Maps. Museum of New Mexico Press, 1962. $1.00.

LET'S FIND OUT ABOUT INDIANS
        Martha and Charles Shapp
Illus. Grades Kindergarten to 3. Franklin Watts, Inc., $2.50.

*LET'S GO TO AN INDIAN CLIFF DWELLING
        Barbara Williams
Illus. G. P. Putnam's Sons, 1965. $1.97.

LETTERS AND NOTES ON THE NORTH AMERICAN INDIANS
        George Catlin

A noted painter's experiences in the West, including material on the customs and manners of the American Indian. Ross & Haines, Inc., $17.50.

LETTERS OF ELEAZAR WHEELOCK'S INDIANS
        James Dow McCallum, Editor
A collection of letters written by Indian students. Dartmouth College Publications, $4.00.

LETTERS OF THE LEWIS AND CLARK EXPEDITION: *With Related Documents, 1783-1854*
        Donald Jackson, Editor
728 pp. Illus. University of Illinois Press, $10.00.

√ **THE LEWIS AND CLARK EXPEDITION**
        Meriwether Lewis
Lewis's day-by-day account of the exploration, including the anthropological and topographical reports. J. B. Lippincott Co., 1962. Three vols. Individual paper volumes, $1.25 each; three-volume set, $2.25. Three-volume cloth set, $12.50.

LEWIS WETZEL, INDIAN FIGHTER
        Clarence B. Allman
Illus. The Devin-Adair Co., 1961. $5.00.

LIFE AND ADVENTURES OF FRANK GROUARD
        Joe DeBarthe; edited and with an Introduction by Edgar I. Stewart
268 pp. Illus. Index. Maps. University of Oklahoma Press, 1958. $5.00.

LIFE AND DIARY
        Jonathan Brainerd; edited by J. Edwards
Paper. Moody Press, 89¢.

LIFE IN THE FAR WEST
        George Frederick Ruxton; edited by Leroy R. Hafen
An authentic tale of the mountain men in the West of the 1840's. 252 pp. Illus. Index. Appendix. University of Oklahoma Press, 1964. $5.00.

*LIFE OF AN INDIAN CAPTIVE
        Lillie M. Ross
A fourteen-year-old boy's experiences as an Indian captive during the 1860's in Texas. 94 pp. Dorrance & Co., 1965. $3.00.

*THE LIFE OF POCAHONTAS
  Doris Faber; illustrated by Elinor Jaeger
The life of Pocahontas from age twelve to adulthood. Illus. Ages 8 to 11. Prentice-Hall, Inc., 1963. $3.50.

LIFE OF TOM HORN, *Government Scout and Interpreter*
  Tom Horn; Introduction by Dean Krakel
The story of a man who served as a scout in capturing Geronimo, with letters and statements by his friends. Appendix. 326 pp. University of Oklahoma Press, 1964. $2.00.

*LIGHTFOOT
  Katherine B. Shippen
Illus. Grades 4 to 7. The Viking Press, Inc., 1950. $3.00.

LINCOLN'S SECRETARY GOES WEST
  John G. Nicolay; edited and with an Introduction by Theodore C. Blegen
Two reports on frontier Indian troubles prepared by President Abraham Lincoln's private secretary, John G. Nicolay. 69 pp. Photo. Map. Sumac Press, 1965. $3.00.

*LINDA'S INDIAN HOME
  Martha Ferguson McKeown; photographs by Archie McKeown
The picture story of an Indian girl who lives with her family in the fishing village of Celilo Falls, on the Columbia River. 80 pp. Illus. Binfords and Mort, 1957. $2.50.

LINGUISTIC STRUCTURES OF NATIVE AMERICA
  Harry Hoijer *et al;* Cornelius Osgood, Editor
423 pp. Viking Fund Publications in Anthropology, No. 6. Johnson Reprint Co., 1965. $10.00.

THE LITERARY VOYAGER
  Henry Schoolcraft; Philip P. Mason, Editor
Contains the thirteen issues of the *Literary Voyager (Muzzeniegun),* the first magazine published in Michigan, with articles, poems and announcements on all aspects of Indian life and customs. 200 pp. Michigan State University Press, 1962. $5.00.

*LITTLE ANTELOPE
  Berta and Elmer Hader
A youngster stays out of school to visit the Hall of Indians at the Museum of Natural History. Picture Book. Illus. Grades 1 to 3. The Macmillan Co., 1962. $3.00.

*LITTLE EAGLE
  Therese O. Deming and Thelma Shaw
Illus. Grades 1 to 3. Albert Whitman & Co., 1957. $2.50.

*LITTLE ELK HUNTS BUFFALO
  Jessie Brewer McGraw
The story of a Cheyenne boy's first buffalo hunt is told in Indian pictographs and simple text. 96 pp. Illus. Ages 6 to 10. Thomas Nelson & Sons, 1961. $3.25.

*LITTLE FOX, ALASKAN TRAPPER
  Hanns Radau; illustrated by Heiner Rothfuchs
Tells the story of Little Fox, who became a trapping partner with Trapper Fred, and describes their fight for survival in Alaska. 160 pp. Illus. Ages 10 to 14. Abelard-Schuman, Ltd., 1963. $3.00.

*LITTLE HAWK AND THE FREE HORSES
  Glenn Balch; illustrated by Ezra Keats
In this story of the Comanche tribe, Little Hawk, with the help of Shy Girl, goes out to stalk and eventually capture a stallion, then frees his father from the Apaches. 181 pp. Illus. Thomas Y. Crowell Co., 1957. $3.00.

*THE LITTLE INDIAN BASKET MAKER
  Ann Nolan Clark; illustrated by Harrison Begay
A little Papago Indian girl learns to plait a mat, the first step in becoming a basket maker. 32 pp. Illus. Reading level, 3; interest level, 1 to 5. Melmont Publishers, Inc., 1957. $2.50.

*THE LITTLE INDIAN POTTERY MAKER
  Ann N. Clark; illustrated by Don Perceval
A Pueblo mother helps her daughter fashion a bowl of clay. 32 pp. Illus. Reading level, 3; interest level, 1 to 5. Melmont Publishers, Inc., 1955. $2.50.

*LITTLE LEO
  Leo Politi
The story of a small boy who took his treasured Indian suit along on a visit to an Indian village. Grades 1 to 3. Charles Scribner's Sons, 1951. $4.00.

*LITTLE NAVAHO BLUEBIRD
  Ann Nolan Clark
Illus. Grades 2 to 5. The Viking Press, Inc., 1943. $3.25.

*LITTLE OWL INDIAN
    Hetty B. Beatty
A picture book about Little Owl, his pony, and his forest friends. Illus. Houghton Mifflin Co., 1951. $3.25.

*LITTLE RUNNER OF THE LONGHOUSE
    Betty Baker; illustrations by Arnold Lobel
The story of an Iroquois boy's desire to participate in his people's New Year celebration. 64 pp. Illus. Grades 1 to 3. Harper & Row, Publishers, 1962. $2.25.

*LITTLE SIOUX GIRL
    Lois Lenski
The story of a little Sioux girl's lost doll and of her people's struggles against hunger, blizzards, floods and poverty. 128 pp. J. B. Lippincott Co., 1958. $2.95.

*LITTLE TURTLE, MIAMI CHIEF
    Jean Carper and Grace Dickerson
Illus. Grades 4 to 7. Albert Whitman & Co., 1959. $2.75.

LIVING LIKE INDIANS
    Allan MacFarlan
A book containing more than 1,000 indoor and outdoor ideas and projects from authentic American Indian lore. The Association Press, $6.95.

*LODGE STORIES
    Edward W. Dolch
Tales told by the Cherokee, the Natchez, and the Seminole Indians. 176 pp. Garrard Publishing Co., 1959. $2.19.

*LOKOSHI LEARNS TO HUNT SEALS
    Raymond Creekmore
Illus. Grades 2 to 3. The Macmillan Co., 1946. $3.50.

LONE EAGLE: *The White Sioux*
    Floyd S. Maine
Describes Indian lore and camp life among the Plains tribes; covers Custer's death and gives accounts of the Ghost Dance. 220 pp. Illus. Photo. University of New Mexico Press, $3.00.

THE LONG DEATH
    Ralph K. Andrist
A history of the conquest of the Plains, with an account of Federal treachery toward the Plains Indian patriots. The Macmillan Co., 1964. $8.95.

*LONG KNIFE
    Glen Dines
The story of the fighting U. S. Cavalry of the 1860 frontier and their encounters with the Indians of the various Plains tribes. 44 pp. Illus. Biblio. Glossary. Diagrams. Songs. Map. The Macmillan Co., 1961. $1.95.

*LONG ROPE
    Elizabeth Lambert Wood; illustrated by Mary Wilhelm
Two teen-age boys and their Indian friend decide to set up and run their own cattle ranch. They join a cattle drive at Jacksonville and head for the Dalles on the Columbia River. 176 pp. Grades 7 to 9. Binfords and Mort, 1955. $2.50.

*THE LONG-TAILED BEAR AND OTHER INDIAN LEGENDS
    Natalia Belting; illustrated by Louis F. Cary
Contains American Indian legends explaining animal characteristics. 95 pp. Illus. The Bobbs-Merrill Co., Inc., $2.85.

THE LONG WALK
    L. R. Bailey
A history of the Navajo wars, 1846 to 1868, which resulted in the destruction of the Navajo nation, and its imprisonment at Bosque Redondo. 252 pp. Westernlore Press, 1964. $7.95.

LONGHORNS BRING CULTURE
    A. H. Schatz
The story of the settling of the Black Hills of South Dakota by cattle ranchers. 240 pp. Christopher Publishing House, 1961. $4.75.

*THE LOON FEATHER
    Iola Fuller
During the fur trading days at Mackinac Island, Ontario, Tecumseh's daughter, adopted by a French couple, struggles to maintain the best of her Indian heritage, while absorbing the best of the white man's world. Grades 7 to 8. Harcourt, Brace & World, Inc., 1940. $4.47.

LORD OF ALASKA
    Hector Chevigny
A biography of Alexander Baranox, the czar of Russian Alaska, and his relations with the Eskimo. 320 pp. Binfords and Mort, $3.75.

LORETTO ON THE OLD FRONTIER
    1823-1864
        Sister M. L. Owens
This is a history of the pioneering Sisters
of Loretto in Missouri and Kentucky. 150
pp. Illus. Index. Biblio. Loretto Literary and Benevolent Institution, 1965, $5.00.

THE LOST AMERICANS
    Frank C. Hibben
Paper.   Apollo Editions, 1961. $1.25.

THE LOST AMERICANS
    Frank C. Hibben
Illus. Peter Smith, $3.25.

LOST SISTER AMONG THE MIAMIS
    Otho Winger
The story of Frances Slocum, held captive
among the Miami Indians. 150 pp. Illus.
Lawrence W. Shultz, 1936. $2.00.

LOST TRIBES AND SUNKEN CONTINENTS
    Robert Wauchope
A report on the long feud over the ancestry
and movements of American Indians that
has raged between anthropologists and the
"crackpots." x + 156 pp. University of Chicago Press, 1962. $3.95.

THE LOST UNIVERSE
    Gene Weltfish
A study of the Pawnee Indians, describing
their way of life and the world view of Pawnee culture. 506 pp. Basic Books, Inc.,
1965. $12.50.

LURE OF THE FRONTIER
    Ralph H. Gabriel
Illus. United States Publishers' Association, Inc., $10.75.

M

McGILLIVRAY OF THE CREEKS
    John Walton Caughey
385 pp. Illus. Index. Biblio. University
of Oklahoma Press, 1959. $5.95.

*MADE IN CANADA
    Mary G. Bonner
Illus. Grades 4 to 9. Alfred A. Knopf, Inc.,
1943. $3.00.

THE MAKAH INDIANS
    Elizabeth Colson

An anthropological study of an Indian tribe
in American society today. xvi + 336 pp.
University of Minnesota Press, 1953. $4.75.

MAN OF THE PLAINS: *Recollections of*
    Luther North
        Luther North; edited by Donald F. Dan-
        ker
A firsthand account of the activities of the
Pawnee scouts, 1864 to 1877, including a
description of the Powder River campaign
of 1876. xx + 352 pp. University of Nebraska Press, 1961. $4.75.

MANKIND IN THE MAKING
    William Howells
382 pp. Doubleday & Co., Inc., 1959. $5.95.

MANNERS AND CUSTOMS OF SEVERAL
    INDIAN TRIBES WEST OF THE MISSIS-
    SIPPI
        John D. Hunter
The personal narrative of a white man who
was captured by the Indians as an infant,
and grew into manhood among them. Ross
& Haines, Inc., $8.75.

MANSFIELD ON THE CONDITION OF THE
    WESTERN FORTS, 1853-1854
        Robert W. Frazer, Editor
"The official reports of Colonel Joseph K.
F. Mansfield, whose perceptive eye and
broad curiosity saw more than the Army
sent him to inspect." 240 pp. Illus. Index. Appendix. Biblio. Tables. University of Oklahoma Press, 1963. $4.95.

MANUEL LISA AND THE OPENING OF THE
    MISSOURI FUR TRADE
        Richard E. Oglesby
The story of the forgotten man of the fur
traders, Manuel Lisa, who pioneered the
business that others exploited. 256 pp. Illus. Index. Biblio. University of Oklahoma Press, 1963. $5.95.

THE MARCH OF THE MONTANA COLUMN
    James H. Bradley
The story of the prelude to the Custer disaster. 182 pp. Illus. Index. Map. University of Oklahoma Press, 1961. $4.00.

MARCHING WITH CUSTER
    Elwood L. Nye and C. Friswold
Arthur H. Clark Co., 1964. $8.50.

MARIA: THE POTTER OF SAN
ILDEFONSO
Alice Marriott; illustrated by Margaret
Lefranc
The story of Maria Martinez, an Indian pot-
ter, honored in her own country and abroad.
294 pp. Illus. Decorative end paper. Uni-
versity of Oklahoma Press, 1963. $4.95.

THE MARICOPAS
Paul H. Ezell
An ethnohistory of the Maricopa people. 30
pp. Illus. Biblio. University of Arizona
Press, $2.25.

*MARIE TANGLEHAIR
Dorothy Heiderstadt; illustrated by
Ursula Koering
A young Huron girl finds it difficult to settle
into the sedate routine of a convent school
in 17th-century Quebec. 128 pp. Illus.
Ages 8 to 12. David McKay Co., Inc., 1965.
$3.25.

MARIN INDIANS
Mary Hill, Ann Rice, and Lee Raymond
A sketch of the daily life of the Miwok In-
dians of Marin County, with emphasis on
material culture. 16 pp. Illus. Paper.
Pages of History, 1956. 50¢.

THE MARIPOSA INDIAN WAR
C. Gregory Crampton, Editor
University of Utah Press, 1957. $6.00.

*MARK OF THE TURTLE
Thomas V. O'Leary
Chilton Books, 1961. $3.50.

THE MASCOUTEN OR PRARIE POTAWA-
TOMIE: *Mythology and Folklore*
Alanson Skinner
A collection of the religious myths, with in-
formation of historical interest pertaining
to the Potawatomi tribe. 70 pp. Paper.
Milwaukee Public Museum, 75¢.

MASKED GODS
Frank Waters
A history and discussion of Navajo and Pueb-
lo ceremonialism. Sage Books, 1962. $5.75.

MASKS, MANTAS, AND MOCCASINS: *Dance
Costumes of the Pueblo Indians*
Donald N. Brown
A discussion of Pueblo Indian dance and
dance costumes, with special sections on

Hopi katchina dances, society dances, animal dances, corn dances, and foreign dances. 16 pp. Illus. Photo. Drawings. Taylor Museum, 1962. 75¢.

MASKS OF THE NORTH AMERICAN
INDIANS
Robert E. Ritzenthaler
A brief description of face coverings made
and used among several Indian tribes, with
information on their ceremonial signifi-
cance. 10 pp. Illus. Paper. Milwaukee
Public Museum, 25¢.

*MASSACRE AT SAND CREEK
Irving Werstein
Illus. Grades 7 to 10. Charles Scribner's
Sons, 1963. $3.25.

MASSACRE: *The Tragedy at White River*
Marshall Sprague
Illus. Little, Brown and Co., 1957. $6.00.

MASTERPIECES IN THE MUSEUM OF
PRIMITIVE ART: *Africa, Oceania, North
America, Mexico, Central to South America, Peru*
134 pp. Illus. Maps. Museum of Primitive Art, 1965. $4.95.

MATERIAL CULTURE OF THE MENOMINI
Alanson Skinner
A monograph presenting details on the culture, housing, dress, foods, and crafts of
an Algonquian tribe, the Menomini Indians,
residing in Wisconsin. 478 pp. Illus. Museum of the American Indian, Heye Foundation, $7.50.

MATTHEW ELLIOT, *British Indian Agent*
Reginald Horsman
Wayne State University Press, 1964. $9.95.

*MATUK, *The Eskimo Boy*
Vee Cawston
Grades kindergarten to 2. Lantern Press,
Inc., 1965. $2.95.

MEDICINE AMONG THE AMERICAN
INDIANS
Eric Stone
An analysis of the practice of medicine
among the American Indians, with material
on their spiritual and religious life in relation to their medical practices. 139 pp.
Illus. Biblio. Map. Paper. Hafner Publishing Co., 1962. $2.45.

*MEDICINE MAN'S DAUGHTER
Ann N. Clark; illustrated by Donald
Bolognese
The story of a Navajo girl -- about to become a medicine woman -- who is sent to
a mission school where she receives medical training. Illus. Grades 7 to 8. Farrar, Straus & Giroux, Inc., 1963. $2.95.

*MEDICINE MEN OF HOOPER BAY
Charles E. Gillham
Contains eighteen stories which provide an
accurate picture of Eskimo life. Ages 8 to
12. The Macmillan Co., Inc., 1966. $2.95.

THE MEDORA SITE, WEST BATON ROUGE
PARISH, LOUISIANA
George L. Quimby
59 pp. Illus. Vol. xxiv, No. 2, Fieldiana:
Anthropology, Chicago Natural History Mu-
seum, 1951. $1.25.

*MEET OUR CHOCTAW FRIENDS
Thelma V. Bounds
Book acquaints young people with the Choctaw Indians of Mississippi, one of the few
tribes who never fought against the United
States. Illus. Exposition Press, Inc.,
1961. $2.50.

*MEET THE NORTH AMERICAN INDIANS
Elizabeth Payne; illustrated by Jack
Davis
A description of the life of the North Amer-
ican Indian as he lived at the time of the
discovery of America. Illus. Ages 7 to 11.
Random House, Inc., 1965. $1.95.

MELLETTE COUNTY MEMORIES
Winifred Reutter, Editor
A collection of stories and pictures of early
pioneers, cowboys and Indians of Dakota
country. 95 pp. Illus. Argus Printers,
1961. $2.50.

MEMOIRS OF LIEUTENANT HENRY
TIMBERLAKE, 1756-1765
Henry Timberlake; Introduction and
notes by Samuel Cole Williams
A book of Cherokee history and customs,
with material on the Southern colonists in
the French and Indian War. 197 pp. Americana Publishers, 1948. $4.95.

MEMOIRS: Or, Quick Glance at My Various
Travels and My Sojourn in the Creek Nation
General LeClerc Milfort; translated
and edited by B. C. McCary

A graphic portrayal of Creek manners and
customs, including customs of the Caddo,
Choctaw and Chickasaw Indians. 250 pp.
Americana Publications, 1959. $7.50.

THE MEMORIAL OF FRAY ALONSO DE
BENAVIDES, 1630
Alonso de Benavides; annotated by
Frederick Webb Hodge and Charles
Fletcher
A report on conditions in the Southwest as
Benavides, the first religious superior of
the Catholic Church in this territory, found
them in the late 1620's. 309 pp. Illus. In-
dex. Biblio. Map. Horn and Wallace,
1965. $7.00.

THE MEN AND THE MOUNTAIN
William Brandon
A reconstruction of an expedition made by
John Charles Fremont. Maps. William
Morrow & Co., Inc., 1955. $5.00.

MEN OF ANCIENT IOWA: As Revealed by
Archaeological Discoveries
Marshall McKusick
Describes and integrates the discoveries of
archaeologists concerning the ancient Indians who once lived within the borders of
Iowa. It includes the growth and decline of
their various cultures, aspects of ways of
life, and their place in the pattern of Western civilization. 260 pp. Iowa State University Press, 1964. $6.50.

THE MENOMINI INDIANS OF WISCONSIN
Felix M. Keesing
Author traces the process of cultural change
of the Menomini Indians of northern Wisconsin through use of historical records, a
critical approach to ethnographic materials,
and by personal observation of their daily
life. xi + 261 pp. Illus. Paper. American Philosophical Society, 1939. $1.25.

THE MENOMINI LANGUAGE
Leonard Bloomfield; Preface by
Charles F. Hockett
A study of the Algonquian family of Indian
languages, and the distillation of the auth-
or's personal experience with the Menomini
tribe. 515 pp. Yale University Press,
1962. $10.00.

MENOMINI PEYOTISM
J. S. Slotkin
This is a study made of the American Indian
Peyote Cult, based upon knowledge of its

inner workings by an anthropologist who participated in the Cult as a member. The overt aspects of the Cult are described, but emphasis is placed upon what the Cult and its details mean to the members. Attention is focused on a tribe in which the Cult members form a primary group with a relatively homogenous culture. Within this group, individual differences in overt and covert usages are analyzed in order to study the range of variability. The data presented are derived from observations and interviews, and include a representative sample of autobiographical accounts. A representative sample of musical transcriptions is also included. 136 pp. American Philosophical Society, 1952. $2.00.

THE MESCALERO APACHES
 C. L. Sonnichsen
303 pp. Illus. Index. Biblio. Maps. University of Oklahoma Press, 1958. $5.75.

*MIAMI INDIAN STORIES
 Clarence Godfroy; edited by Una McClurg
A book of Indian tales and legends intended for teachers and children. Illus. Lawrence W. Shultz, 1961. $3.00.

THE MICMAC INDIANS OF EASTERN CANADA
 Wilson Dallam Wallis and Ruth Sawtell Wallis
An anthropological study of the Micmac tribe from the 17th century to the present, including a collection of folklore. xvi + 515 pp. Illus. University of Minnesota Press, 1955. $7.50.

THE MIDDLE FIVE: *Indian Schoolboys of the Omaha Tribe*
 Frances LaFlesche; Foreword by David A. Baerreis
The informal account by an Omaha Indian, of his experiences in a mission school of the mid-19th century. 152 pp. Illus. The University of Wisconsin Press, 1963. Paper, $1.65; cloth, $5.00.

*THE MIGHTY MIAMIS
 Marvin Baker
A description of the life of the Miami Indian tribe in the midwest United States. 24 pp. Grades 4 to 8. E. C. Seale & Co., Inc., 1963. Cloth, $1.25; paper, 49¢.

*THE MIGHTY SOO: *Five Hundred Years at Sault Ste. Marie*
 Clara Ingram Judson; illustrated by Robert Frankenberg
An epic of five hundred years at the rapids, the place which has come to be known as the "Miracle Mile" to the upper lake country, and to all America. 192 pp. Illus. Grades 5 to 8. Follett Publishing Co., 1955. $3.50.

THE MILITARY CONQUEST OF THE SOUTHERN PLAINS
 William H. Leckie
269 pp. Illus. Index. Biblio. Maps. University of Oklahoma Press, 1963. $5.95.

MINERAL CREEK SITE AND HOOPER RANCH PUEBLO, EASTERN ARIZONA
 Paul S. Martin, John B. Rinaldo, and William A. Longacre
181 pp. Illus. Volume 52. Chicago Natural History Museum, 1961. $5.50.

MINNESOTA IN THE CIVIL AND INDIAN WARS, 1861-1865
This volume contains official reports and correspondence related to the two wars. 652 pp. Volume 2, 1899. Minnesota Historical Society, $5.00.

MINNESOTA'S MAJOR HISTORIC SITES: *A Guide*
 June D. Holmquist and Jean A. Brookins, Editors
This book includes information on major Indian sites in Minnesota. xii + 182 pp. Illus. Index. Maps. Minnesota Historical Society, 1963. $3.50.

MIRACLE OF THE MOHAWKS
 Marion B. Stephenson
96 pp. Pageant Press, 1964. $2.75.

MISCELLANEOUS COLLECTED PAPERS
 James H. Gunnerson and others
This report is a collection of archaeological findings from seven sites in central and southern Utah -- Nine Mile Canyon, Hammond Canyon, St. George, Castle Valley, Fish Springs National Wildlife Refuge (two papers), Frei Site. 170 pp. Illus. University of Utah Press, 1962. $2.75.

*MISSION INDIANS OF CALIFORNIA
 Sonia Bleeker; illustrated by Althea Karr
The life and history of southern California Indians, before and after the arrival of the

Spaniards, is seen through the viewpoint of a ceremonial singer. 160 pp. Illus. Ages 8 to 12. William Morrow & Co., Inc., 1956. $2.95.

MISSION OF CHANGE IN ALASKA: *Eskimos and Moravians on the Kuskokwim*
 Wendell H. Oswalt
Henry E. Huntington Library and Art Gallery, 1963. $6.00.

MISSIONARY TO OREGON: *Jason Lee*
 Gilbert Q. LeSourd
An account of the work of early pioneer missionaries to Oregon. 23 pp. Friendship Press, 1946. 25¢.

MISSIONS AND PUEBLOS OF THE OLD SOUTHWEST
 Earle R. Forrest
A description of myths, legends, fiestas and ceremonials of Pueblo Indians of the 1920's. 386 pp. Illus. The Rio Grande Press, Inc., $7.00.

*MOCCASIN TRAIL
 Eloise Jarvis
Runaway Jim Keath, trapping for beaver, is left to die after a grizzly's attack. He is found and adopted by Crow Indians, and knows no other life until a letter comes from his brother. Grades 7 to 8. Coward-McCann, Inc., 1952. $3.89.

THE MODE IN HATS AND HEADDRESS
 R. Turner Wilcox
A survey of the styles of headgear, hair styles, jewelry, and cosmetics, from Egyptian times to the present. 348 pp. Illus. Charles Scribner's Sons, 1959. $7.95.

MODERN INDIAN PAINTING
 Dorothy D. Kramer
Illus. University of New Mexico Press (in preparation).

MODIFIED BASKET MAKER SITES, WESTERN COLORADO, 1938
 Paul S. Martin
196 pp. Illus. Maps. Vol. xxiii, No. 3. Chicago Natural History Museum, 1939. $4.00.

THE MODOCS AND THEIR WAR
 Keith A. Murray
346 pp. Illus. Index. Appendix. Biblio. Map. University of Oklahoma Press, 1965. $5.95.

MOHAVE CULTURE ITEMS
 Leslie Spier
35 pp. Paper. Northern Arizona Society of Science and Art, $1.00.

MOHAVE ETIQUETTE
 George Devereux
Southwest Museum, 25¢.

MOHAVE TATOOING AND FACE-PAINTING
 Edith S. Taylor and William J. Wallace
Southwest Museum, 25¢.

MOHAWK BARONET
 James Thomas Flexner
The biography of William Johnson, the most influential white man among the Indians of colonial times. 400 pp. Illus. Index. Harper & Row, Publishers, $6.00.

A MOHAWK FORM OF RITUAL
 John Deserontyon
This manuscript is an attempt by a Mohawk Indian to preserve the customary forms of sacred rituals and chants for future generations. It includes both a literal and interlinear translation. 23 pp. Illus. Paper. Museum of the American Indian, Heye Foundation, 75¢.

*MOHAWK GAMBLE
 Julia Brown Ridle
The story of a 17th-century explorer and trader held captive by Indians. 256 pp. Illus. Ages 12 and up. Map. Harper & Row, Publishers, 1963. $3.50.

MOHEGAN CHIEF: *The Story of Harold Tantaquidgeon*
 Virginia Frances Voight; illustrated by
 Stan Campbell
A true story recounting Chief Tantaquidgeon's boyhood schooling in Indian lore, his bravery while in our country's military service, and his efforts to preserve his tribal heritage. 192 pp. Illus. Funk & Wagnalls, 1965. $3.95.

MOJAVE OF THE COLORADO
 Mary Hill
An account of the Mojave tribe at the time of their first contact with the white man (1776 to 1853). 24 pp. Pages of History, 1960. 50¢.

MONTAGNAIS ART IN BIRCH-BARK, A CIRCUMPOLAR TRAIT
 Frank G. Speck

Discusses the making and ornamentation of birchbark containers in the lower St. Lawrence region, largely those of the Montagnais bands at Lake St. John. 175 pp. Illus. Paper. Museum of the American Indian, Heye Foundation, $2.50.

MONUMENTS IN CEDAR
  Edward L. Keithahn
An explanation of the totem pole and its place in the culture of the Northwest Coast Indian. Superior Publishing Co., $12.50.

*MOOLACK: *Young Salmon Fisherman*
  Mary M. Worthylake; illustrated by
  Roy Schroeder
An Indian boy of the Tsimshian tribe in southeastern Alaska helps his father and grandfather build a canoe. Given a canoe of his own, he goes out and catches the first salmon of the season, which means he has a part in the salmon ceremony. 48 pp. Illus. Grades 3 to 6. Melmont Publishers, Inc., 1963. $2.50.

MOONLIGHT AT MIDDAY
  Sally Carrighar
Alfred A. Knopf, Inc., 1958. $6.50.

*MORE INDIAN FRIENDS AND FOES
  Dorothy Heiderstadt; illustrated by
  David Humphrey
Illus. Ages 8 to 12. David McKay Co., Inc., 1963. $3.75.

*MORNING STAR
  Lucille Wallower
Illus. Grades 3 to 7. David McKay Co., Inc., 1957. $2.95.

MOTHERS OF THE MIXED BLOODS: *The Marginal Woman in the History of the Upper Missouri*
A presentation of the roles played by Indian women who married fur traders, from the time of Sacajawea. One chapter by John C. Ewers of the Smithsonian Institution. 70 pp. Museum of New Mexico Press, 1962. $5.00.

*THE MOUND BUILDERS
  William E. Scheele
An account of the Hopewells and their Adena ancestors, whose culture flourished in the Ohio Valley for 1,500 years. 65 pp. Illus. Grades 5 to 8. World Publishing Co., 1960. $2.75.

THE MOUNTAIN MEADOWS MASSACRE
  Juanita Brooks
316 pp. Illus. Index. Biblio. Appendix. Maps. University of Oklahoma Press, 1964. $5.95.

MOUNTAIN WOLF WOMAN, SISTER OF CRASHING THUNDER: *The Autobiography of a Winnebago Indian*
  Edited by Nancy Oestreich Lurie; Foreword by Ruth Underhill
The life story of a Winnebago woman, told in her own words, revealing seventy-five years of her life. 156 pp. University of Michigan Press, 1961. $4.95.

THE MOVEMENT FOR INDIAN ASSIMILATION, 1860-1890
  Henry L. Fritz
Illus. University of Pennsylvania Press, 1963. $6.00.

*THE MUD PONIES
  Lace Kendall
Based on a Pawnee Indian myth, this is the story of Running Star, who was treated as a stranger among his own people. Illus. Ages 7 to 10. Coward-McCann, Inc., 1963. $2.75.

MURDER AND ROBBERY OF THE INDIANS
  Elvin Wagner
A protest regarding the crimes committed against the Indians. Candor Press, 1964. $3.00.

MUSIC OF THE MAIDU INDIANS OF CALIFORNIA
  Frances Densmore
67 pp. 7 figs. 53 songs. Southwest Museum Publications, 1958. Paper, $3.75; cloth, $5.00.

MUSIC OF SANTO DOMINGO PUEBLO, NEW MEXICO
  Frances Densmore
Contains 103 songs and music. 186 pp. 16 plates. 18 figures. Southwest Museum, $3.50.

MY CAPTIVITY AMONG THE SIOUX INDIANS
  Fanny Kelly; Introduction by Jules Zanger
The story of a frontier woman's experiences during the opening of the West and of her brief captivity among the Sioux. 285 pp. Illus. Paper. Corinth Books, 1962. $1.75.

*MY ESKIMOS: *A Priest in the Arctic.*
    Roger Buliard, O. M. I.
A Catholic missionary tells of his life among
the Eskimo. Illus. Grades 4 to 7. Farrar,
Straus & Giroux, Inc., 1956. $1.95.

*MY INDIAN TALE LIBRARY
Tales about Indian life. Illus. Platt &
Munk, Inc., 1965. Boxed set of eight books,
$1.50.

*MY LIFE AS AN INDIAN
    James. W. Schultz
As below. Paper. Fawcett Publications,
60¢.

*MY LIFE AS AN INDIAN
    James W. Schultz; edited by Robert E.
    Gard
Illus. Grades 7 to 10. The Meredith Publishing Co., 1957. $3.00.

MY LIFE IN THE MOUNTAINS AND ON
THE PLAINS
    David Meriwether; edited and with an
    Introduction by Robert A. Griffin
The memoirs of a frontiersman and moun-
tainman, who became governor of New Mexico. 320 pp. Illus. Index. Appendix. University of Oklahoma Press, 1965. $5.95.

MY LIFE ON THE PLAINS
    George A. Custer
As below. Peter Smith, $4.00.

MY LIFE ON THE PLAINS
    George A. Custer; edited by Milo Mil-
    ton Quaife
An autobiographical account of Custer's
service on the Great Plains from 1867 to
the Black Hills expedition of 1874, including
his experiences with the Sioux, the Cheyennes, the Kiowas, the Apaches, and the
Arapahoes. xiii + 626 pp. University of
Nebraska Press, 1952. $1.85.

MY LIFE WITH THE ESKIMO
    Vilhjalmur Stefansson
Paper. Collier Publishing Co., $1.50.

MY SIXTY YEARS ON THE PLAINS: *Trapping, Trading, and Indian Fighting*
    W. T. Hamilton; Introduction by Donald
    J. Berthrong
184 pp. Illus. University of Oklahoma
Press, 1960. $2.00.

MYSTERIOUS HORSES OF WESTERN
NORTH AMERICA
    E. A. Berg
Pageant Press, Inc., 1960. $3.50.

*MYSTERY OF THE TALKING TOTEM
    POLE
    Gladys Hall Murray
A teen-ager finds adventure, mystery and
friendship while visiting her great aunt in
Sitka, Alaska. viii + 208 pp. For teen-
agers. Dodd, Mead & Co., 1965. $3.50.

MYTH AND CULT AMONG PRIMITIVE
PEOPLES
    A. E. Jensen; translated by Marianna
    Tax Choldin and Wolfgang Weissleder
This study of comparative religion examines the beliefs of early man through the use
of anthropological data, and indicates an
intellect as lively as that of modern man.
x + 349 pp. Index. University of Chicago
Press, 1963. $8.75.

MYTHS OF NAVAJO CHANTS
Abbreviated in bulletin form. Includes
Night Chant, Big Star and Coyote, Eagle
and Bead, Wind and Feather, Mountain
Chant, Beauty Chant, Creation, Red Ant
and Shooting Chant. Museum of Navajo
Ceremonial Art. 50¢ each.

MYTHOLOGY OF SOUTHERN PUGET
SOUND
    A. C. Ballard
119 pp. Paper. University of Washington
Press, 1929. $2.50.

N

NALAKIHU: *Excavations at a Pueblo III
Site on Wupatki National Monument*
    Dale S. King
A report of the 1933 C. W. A. excavations
of a small masonry pueblo, which revealed
a mixture of traits of several Indian groups,
such as a cremation burial and jar-shaped
pits. 183 pp. Plates. Tables. Southwestern Monuments Association, 1949. $4.00.

NARRATIVE OF THE CAPTIVITY AND AD-
VENTURES OF JOHN TANNER DURING
THIRTY YEARS OF RESIDENCE AMONG
THE CHIPPEWA, OTTAWA AND OJIBWA
TRIBES
    Edwin James; Introduction by Noel
    Loomis
Facsimile of 1825 edition. Indian captivity
narrative. Ross & Haines, Inc., $8.75.

NARRATIVE OF AN EXPEDITION TO THE SOURCE OF ST. PETER'S RIVER
William H. Keating; Introduction by Roy P. Johnson
A facsimile of the 1825 edition. Illus. Map. Ross & Haines, Inc., $8.75.

NARRATIVE OF THE LIFE OF MRS. MARY JEMISON
James E. Seaver; Introduction by Allen W. Trelease
An account of the life of Mrs. Mary Jemison who, taken by Indians at age twelve, lived among them and eventually married into the tribe. 191 pp. Appendix. Paper. Corinth Books, 1961. $1.50.

NARRATIVE OF THE LIFE OF MRS. MARY JEMISON
James E. Seaver
As above. Peter Smith, $3.50.

NARRATIVES OF CAPTIVITY AMONG THE INDIANS OF NORTH AMERICA: *A List of Books and Manuscripts in the E. E. Ayer Collection*
Paper. Newberry Library, 1912. $4.00; supplement, 1928. $1.00.

NARRATIVE OF THE INDIAN WARS (1675-1699)
Charles H. Lincoln, Editor
Partial contents: *A Relacion of the Indyan Warre,* by John Easton, 1675; *The Present State of New England,* by N. S., 1675; *A New and Further Account of the State of New England,* by N. S., 1676; *The War in New England Visibly Ended,* by R. H., 1677. 316 pp. Barnes and Noble, 1959. $5.75.

NASKAPI LAW (LAKE ST. JOHN AND LAKE MISTASSINI BANDS): *Law and Order in a Hunting Society*
Julius E. Lips
A story dealing with the law of a primitive people, the Montagnais-Naskapi Indians of the Labrador Peninsula, whose economy is based solely on hunting and trapping. 114 pp. 19 figs. Paper. American Philosophical Society, 1947. $1.75.

THE NATION OF THE WILLOWS
Frank Cushing
The first eyewitness account of the Havasupais and their Grand Canyon homeland, as originally published in 1882. 80 pp. Illus. Northland Press, 1965. $4.00.

THE NATIVE AMERICANS
Robert F. Spencer
Nine studies of the prehistory and ethnology of the pre-Columbian Indian, ranging from the Arctic to Middle America. Harper & Row, Publishers, 1965. $10.90.

NATIVE ARTS OF THE PACIFIC NORTHWEST
Robert Tyler Davis, Editor
Stanford University Press, 1949. $10.00.

THE NATURAL HISTORY OF THE LEWIS AND CLARK EXPEDITION
Raymond D. Burroughs, Editor
Detailed highlights of the expedition, concentrating on Lewis's and Clark's observations and descriptions of wildlife populations, interspersed with reports of Indian encounters and customs. xii + 340 pp. Michigan State University Press, 1961. $7.50.

THE NAVAHO
Frances E. Watkins
Southwest Museum, 30¢.

THE NAVAHO
Clyde Kluckhohn and Dorothea C. Leighton
Describes the various aspects of Navaho life today, with a discussion of an interesting experiment in government administration of the problems of a dependent people. Illus. Harvard University Press, 1946. $4.50.

THE NAVAHO
Clyde Kluckhohn and Dorothea C. Leighton; Foreword by Stanley A. Freed; revised by Lucy H. Wales and Richard Kluckhohn
As above. 355 pp. Paper. Natural History Press, 1962. $1.45.

NAVAHO ART AND CULTURE
George Mills; Introduction by Clyde Kluckhohn
221 pp. Illus. Biblio. Tables. Taylor Museum, 1959. $4.50.

NAVAHO AUTOBIOGRAPHY
Walter Dyk; Cornelius Osgood, Editor
A study of Navaho adult problems and tasks, related through anecdotal material to illustrate the functioning of clan and kin. 218 pp. Illus. Notes. Paper. Johnson Reprint Corp., 1964. $10.00.

THE NAVAHO DOOR: *An Introduction to Navaho Life*
    Alexander H. Leighton and Dorothea C. Leighton
A pattern for medical and administrative service among people whose cultures differ widely from our own. Harvard University Press. $4.00.

NAVAHO EXPEDITION
    James H. Simpson; edited by Frank McNitt
A journal of a military reconnaissance from Santa Fe, New Mexico, to the Navaho country, made in 1849. 296 pp. Illus. Appendix. Index. Epilogue. Sources. University of Oklahoma Press, 1964. $5.95.

*NAVAHO LAND, YESTERDAY AND TODAY
    Solveig Paulson Russell; illustrated by Baida Whitebead
This book deals with the early life of the Navahos and their life on the reservation today. 32 pp. Illus. Reading level, 3; interest level, 2 to 5. Melmont Publishers, Inc., 1961. $2.50.

NAVAHO MEANS PEOPLE
    Evon Z. Vogt and Clyde Kluckhohn
Illus. Harvard University Press, 1951. $5.00.

THE NAVAHO RECONNAISSANCE
    Captain J. G. Walker and Captain O. L. Shepherd
A report on Navajo country made during a military exploration in 1859, with insights into the political atmosphere of the times. Illus. Westernlore Press, $6.50.

NAVAHO SANDPAINTING: *The Huckel Collection*
    Leland C. Wyman
An introduction to Navajo life and ceremonial practices, particularly sandpainting, in which aesthetic, medical, and metaphysical preoccupations are blended. 88 pp. Illus. Biblio. Paper. Taylor Museum, 1960. $1.75.

NAVAHO SILVER
    Elizabeth Compton Hegemann
Southwest Museum, 50¢.

*NAVAHO STORIES
    Edward W. Dolch
Folktales of the largest tribe of Indians in the United States. 179 pp. Grades 2 to 3. Garrard Publishing Co., 1959. $2.19.

NAVAHO TRADING DAYS
    Elizabeth Hegemann
University of New Mexico Press, $7.50.

NAVAHO WEAVING, *Its Technic and History*
    Charles Avery Amsden
A study of the history, materials, design and techniques of primitive textile and rug weaving. 262 pp. Illus. The Rio Grande Press, Inc. $12.00.

NAVAHO WEAVING, *Its Technic and History*
    Charles Avery Amsden
As above. 261 pp. Illus. Plates. Figs. Southwest Museum, $12.00.

NAVAHO WEAVING TODAY
    Bertha P. Dutton
A guide to the purchase of Navajo rugs and blankets, including a discussion of the historical development and present status of Navajo weaving. Paper. 39 pp. Illus. Museum of New Mexico Press, 1962. $1.00.

NAVAHO WITCHCRAFT
    Clyde Kluckhohn
Beacon Press, 1962. $4.95.

NAVAHOS HAVE FIVE FINGERS
    T. D. Allen
The author's recollection of a spring and summer spent at a remote outstation of the Ganado Mission of the United Presbyterian Church, in the heart of a Navajo reservation. 249 pp. Illus. Index. Biblio. Map. University of Oklahoma Press, 1965. $4.95.

THE NAVAJO AND PUEBLO SILVERSMITHS
    John Adair
220 pp. 24 halftone plates. Figures. Chart. Illus. Index. Map. University of Oklahoma Press, 1962. $5.95.

NAVAJO GRAMMAR
    Gladys A. Reichard
Museum of the American Indian, 1950.

*THE NAVAJO: *Herders, Weavers, and Silversmiths*
    Sonia Bleeker; illustrated by Patricia Boodell
Description of the arts and crafts, customs and history of the Navajo tribe. 160 pp. Illus. Ages 8 to 12. William Morrow & Co., Inc., 1958. $2.75.

NAVAJO INDIANS TODAY
    Dorothy F. Robinson
Describes life on a modern Navajo reservation in northeastern Arizona -- age-old tribal customs and ceremonies and a new interest in education and in the development of natural resources are projected against the background of Navajo history. 112 pp. The Naylor Co., 1966. $3.95.

NAVAJO NEIGHBORS
    Franc Johnson Newcomb
The author reminisces about the Navaho neighbors and friends made during the twenty-five years she and her husband operated the Blue Mesa Trading Post on the Navajo reservation; includes material on Navajo customs and traditions. 256 pp. Illus. Index. University of Oklahoma Press, $5.95.

NAVAJO RELIGION: *A Study of Symbolism* (Two vols.)
        Gladys Reichard; Introduction by Oliver La Farge
The dogma, ritual, and symbolism in religion of the Navaho. xlviii + 805 pp. Illus. 31 text figures. 23 charts. Index. Bollingen Series, 1964. $5.00.

NAVAJO RUGS, *Past, Present and Future*
    Gilbert S. Maxwell
The history of rug weaving, its techniques and types, including a buyer's guide. Illus. Biblio. Paper. Desert-Southwest Publishing Co., $2.00.

*NAVAJO SISTER
    Evelyn Sibley Lampman; illustrated by Paul Lantz
A story about Indians learning the language and customs of the white man, and of a Navajo girl who finds a family for herself and her grandmother when she goes to the Chemawa Indian School. 189 pp. Illus. Doubleday & Co., Inc., 1956. $3.25.

NAVAJO SKETCHBOOK
    Don Perceval and Clay Lockett
Illus. Northland Press, 1962. $14.50.

NAVAJOLAND PUBLICATIONS
A series of five pamphlets: *Catalogue of Plants from Window Rock, Arizona; Navajo Pottery and Ethnohistory; Navajo Sandpaintings; The Mammals of Navajoland;* and *Navajo Sacred Places.* Approx. 30 pp. each. Illus. Navajo Tribal Museum, 25¢ each.

THE NAVAJOS
    Ruth M. Underhill
299 pp. Illus. Index. Biblio. Maps. University of Oklahoma Press, 1963. $5.00.

NEHALEM TILLAMOOK TALES
    Recorded by Elizabeth Derr Jacobs; edited by Melville Jacobs
This collection of sixty tales dictated by a full-blooded Nehalem, Mrs. Clara Pearson, is classified into three periods, the Myth Age, the Era of Transformation, and the Period of True Happiness. ix + 175 pp. Paper. University of Oregon Press, 1959. $3.00.

NEVER THE GOLDEN CITY
    Sr. Mary Jean Dorcy
Sheed & Ward, 1962. $3.95.

THE NEW ENGLAND COMPANY
    William Kellaway
A history of the New England Company, an English Protestant missionary society founded in 1649, dedicated to the religious conversion of the Indians. 303 pp. Barnes and Noble, 1962. $8.50.

THE NEW ENGLAND FRONTIER: *Puritans and Indians, 1620-1675*
    Alden T. Vaughan
An account of the relations between the white colonists and the New England tribes from 1620 to 1675. xvii + 430 pp. Little, Brown and Co., 1965. $7.50.

NEW MEXICO
    Erna Fergusson
Illus. Alfred A. Knopf, 1964. $6.95.

THE NEW PEOPLE: *The Eskimo's Journey into our Time*
    Edith Iglauer
Discusses the Eskimos' entry into the modern world, without the loss of their culture. 216 pp. Doubleday & Co., Inc., 1966. $4.50.

NEW TRACTS IN NORTH AMERICA
    William Bell
An account of a surveying expedition conducted in 1867, organized by the Kansas Pacific Railroad to find the best route to the Pacific. Includes a detailed botanical report of the area. 570 pp. Horn and Wallace, $9.00.

THE NEW WORLD: *The First Pictures of America*
    Stefan Lorant, Editor
A collection of the earliest known pictures of the Indians and of the flora and fauna of the New World. Illus. Duell, Sloan & Pearce, 1965. $20.00.

THE NEZ PERCE INDIANS AND THE OPENING OF THE NORTHWEST
    Alvin M. Josephy, Jr.
The story of the Nez Perce Indians' conquest and dispossession by the white men, from the time of the Lewis and Clark expedition to the great fighting retreat of the bands associated with Chief Joseph and others in 1877. 480 pp. Illus. Yale University Press, 1965. $12.50.

*NIKI ILLAHEE *(My Homeland)*
    Mary M. Worthlake; illustrated by Henry Luhrs
A sensitive Indian girl living on a reservation in the Pacific Northwest talks about her homeland as she knows it, and as her grandmother has told her it was. 32 pp. Illus. Reading level, 3; interest level, 2 to 5. Melmont Publishers, Inc., 1962. $2.50.

*NINE TALES OF COYOTE
    Fran Martin; illustrated by Dorothy McEntee
"A book of once upon a time, when animals ruled the earth and lived in tepees like their Indian brothers." 60 pp. Illus. Harper & Row, Publishers, 1952. $3.25.

*NINE TALES OF RAVEN
    Fran Martin; illustrated by Dorothy McEntee
A collection of Northwest Indian council fire tales -- tales of their animal ancestors, and of the miracles accomplished by means of their knowledge of magic. 60 pp. Illus. Grades 3 to 7. Harper & Row, Publishers, 1951. $3.25.

*NKWALA
    Edith L. Sharp
The story of a Salish Indian boy growing up in the Pacific Northwest hundreds of years ago. 125 pp. Ages 9 to 11. Illus. Little, Brown and Co., 1958. $3.50.

NO STONE UNTURNED
    Louis A. Brennan; illustrated by Ingrid Fetz
An almanac of North American archaeology, synthesizing the story of life in North America as it was lived 40,000 years ago. Random House, 1959. $5.00.

NO TURNING BACK
    Polingaysi Qoyawayma, as told to Vada F. Carlson
The autobiography of a Hopi girl who chose the white man's way and spent her life as a teacher to bridge the gap between the two worlds. 180 pp. University of New Mexico Press, $5.00.

NOBLE SAVAGE
    Hoxie N. Fairchild
Russell and Russell Inc., 1961. $8.50.

*THE NORTH AMERICAN INDIANS
    Ernest Berke
A panorama of American Indian life and legend from New England to the far West. Illus. Grades 1 to 4. Doubleday & Co., Inc., 1964. $3.75.

NORTH AMERICAN MYTHOLOGY
    Hartley B. Alexander
Illus. Copper Square Publishers, 1964. $13.00.

THE NORTH CAROLINA INDIANS
    James Hall Rand
Contents: *Distribution of Tribes; Characteristics and Mode of Life; Relation of Indians with the Settlers; Permanent Settlements; Winning of North Carolina from the Indians;* and *Conclusion.* 42 pp. Paper. University of North Carolina Press, 1926. $1.25.

NORTH CAROLINA LANDS
    Kenneth B. Pomeroy and J. G. Yoho
Study of the ownership, use and management of forest and related lands in North Carolina; evolution of land ownership and the origins of various public policies are examined. The transfer of land from Indian to white ownership during colonial and subsequent periods is traced, and all known Indian cessions, treaties and subsequent acquisitions in North Carolina are cited. 372 pp. The American Forestry Association, 1964. $6.00.

NORTH TO ALASKA'S SHINING RIVER
    Hazel D. Berto
The Bobbs-Merrill Co., Inc., 1959. $3.50.

NORTHWEST COAST INDIAN ART: *An Analysis of Form*
    Bill Holm

A study of the common characteristics of organization and form of Pacific Coast Indian arts and crafts. 144 pp. Illus. University of Washington Press, 1965. $7.50.

NORTHWEST SAHAPTIN TEXTS
   Melville Jacobs
Myths, stories and tales of the Klikitat of Oregon and Washington are given in Sahaptin and English languages. 78 pp. Paper. University of Washington Press, 1929. $1.50.

NORTHWEST TRAIL BLAZERS
   Helen Addison Howard
A book about seventeen Indian and non-Indian personalities significant in Northwest history. 418 pp. Illus. The Caxton Printers, Ltd., 1963. $6.00.

NOTES ON CHASTA COSTA PHONOLOGY AND MORPHOLOGY
   Edward Sapir
Paper. University Museum Press, 1914. $1.00.

NOTES ON MAHIKAN ETHNOLOGY
   Alanson Skinner
Brief observations of Algonquian Indians taken from archaeological research and historical accounts. 27 pp. Illus. Paper. Milwaukee Public Museum, 75¢.

NOTES ON SKIDI PAWNEE SOCIETY
   George A. Dorsey and James R. Murie
56 pp. 1 text fig. Vol. 27, No. 2. Chicago Natural History Museum, 1940. 75¢.

NOTICES OF FLORIDA AND THE CAMPAIGNS
   M.M. Cohen; O.Z. Tyler, Editor
An on-the-scene account of the operations of Major Winfield Scott's army against the Florida Indians. 300 pp. University of Florida Press, 1964. $8.50.

NUN-MIP-NI-SHEEK (We Remember)
A collection of remembrances of early Northwest days to commemorate the 1959 National Indian Encampment at Pendleton, Oregon. 64 pp. Illus. Paper. Indian Festival of Art, 1959. $1.25.

THE NUNAMIUT ESKIMOS, Hunters of Caribou
   Nicholas J. Gubser
An ethnographic study of the Nunamiut Eskimos and their social institutions. 384 pp. Biblio. Maps. Yale University Press, 1965. $8.50.

O

OBSERVATIONS ON NORTHERN BLACKFOOT KINSHIP
   L. M. Hanks, Jr., and Jane Richardson
A kinship study that establishes an "orientation group," including those relatives who serve as points of orientation toward the larger circle of kinsmen. An American Ethnological Society Monograph reissued by the University of Washington Press. Bound with Changing Configurations in the Social Organization of a Blackfoot Tribe During the Reserve Period, an A.E.S. Monograph published by the University of Washington Press.

OBSERVATIONS ON THE ETHNOLOGY OF THE SAUK INDIANS
   Alanson Skinner
A brief history of the tribe, with notes on its customs, social structure, games, dances and ceremonies. 57 pp. Paper. Milwaukee Public Museum, 80¢.

OJIBWA MYTHS AND LEGENDS
   Sr. Bernard Coleman, Estelle Eich and Ellen Frogner; illustrated by Ruth Maney
The myths and legends of the Ojibwa Indians. Illus. Ross & Haines, Inc., $4.50.

*OJIBWAY
   Marion Israel; illustrated by Harry L. Timmins
A description of the life of the Ojibwa and Chippewa Indians before the coming of the white man. 32 pp. Illus. Reading level, 3; interest level, 2 to 6. Melmont Publishers, Inc., 1962. $2.50.

OKLAHOMA DELAWARE CEREMONIES, FEASTS AND DANCES
   Frank G. Speck
A study of twenty rites and ceremonies of the Delaware or Lenape Indians, now residing in Oklahoma, two thousand miles from their homeland of two hundred years ago in Pennsylvania and New Jersey. viii + 161 pp. Illus. Paper. American Philosophical Society, 1937. $1.00.

OKLAHOMA PLACE NAMES
   George H. Shirk
Contains an alphabetical listing of approximately 3,500 names of Oklahoma counties,

cities, rivers, mountains, and lakes. 248 pp. Biblio. University of Oklahoma Press, $4.95.

THE OLD COPPER CULTURE AND THE KEWEENAW WATERWAY

George I. Quimby and Albert Spaulding 13 pp. Illus. Vol. 36, No. 8. Chicago Natural History Museum, 1957. 40¢.

OLD FATHER, THE STORY TELLER

Pablita Velarde

A book of Santa Clara Pueblo legends. 68 pp. Illus. Index. Dale S. King Publishers, 1960. $7.95.

THE OLD NORTHWEST

R. Carlyle Buley

The history of the pioneer period of 1815 to 1840. Two-volume set. xxi + 1,318 pp. Illus. Index. Sketches. Maps. Indiana University Press, 1963. $17.50.

THE OLD ONES: *Indians of the American Southwest*

Robert Silverberg

The story of Pueblo Indian life from prehistoric times to the present day, with a directory of historic sites. 225 pp. Illus. Drawings. Photographs. Maps. New York Graphic Society Publishers, Ltd., 1965. $4.95.

ON THE BORDER WITH CROOK

John G. Bourke

An eyewitness account of the territorial army's efforts to capture the Apache, Geronimo, and subdue the Southwestern Indians. 492 pp. Illus. The Rio Grande Press, Inc., 7.50.

ON THE GLEAMING WAY

John Collier

Deals with the Navajo, the Eastern Pueblo, the Zuni, the Hopi, and the Apache Indians -- their land and their meaning to the world. 163 pp. Illus. Sage Books, 1962. $3.50.

ON THE INDIANS: *And on the Law of War*

Francisco de Vitoria

Oceana Publications, $7.50.

ON THE OREGON TRAIL: *Robert Stuart's Journey of Discovery (1812-1813)*

Robert Stuart; edited by Kenneth A. Spaulding

192 pp. Illus. Index. Appendix. Biblio. Map. University of Oklahoma Press, $3.75.

*ONCE UPON A TOTEM

Christie Harris; illustrated by John Frazer Mills

Five legends illustrating courage, nobility of character, strength of purpose, and gentleness of spirit. 160 pp. Grades 4 to 7. Illus. Atheneum Publishers, 1965. $3.50.

*ONE AMONG THE INDIANS

Martha Bennett Stiles

Describes Indian life and the grueling tests young Indian boys approaching manhood must face. 192 pp. Ages 10 to 14. The Dial Press, 1962. $3.50.

*ONE LITTLE INDIAN

Grace Moon

Illus. Preschool through grade 2. Albert Whitman & Co., 1950. $2.00.

1,000 YEARS ON MOUND KEY

Rolfe F. Schell

The story of the Caloosa Indians on the west coast of Florida, near Fort Myers Beach and its surrounding bay waters. 40 pp. Paper. The Island Press, 1962. 75¢.

*OOTOOK, YOUNG ESKIMO GIRL

Lyn Harrington; photographs by Richard Harrington

A book about how Eskimos live, illustrated with photographs of real people in everyday life situations. 127 pp. E. M. Hale and Co., 1964. $1.98.

THE ORAIBI MARAU CEREMONY

H. R. Voth

88 pp. Illus. Volume xi, No. 1. Chicago Museum of Natural History, 1912. $1.50.

ORAIBI NATAL CUSTOMS AND CEREMONIES

H. R. Voth

17 pp. Illus. Etching. Fieldiana: Anthropology. Vol. vi, No. 2. Chicago Natural History Museum, 1905. 25¢.

THE ORAIBI OAQOL CEREMONY

H. R. Voth

46 pp. Illus. Fieldiana: Anthropology. Vol. vi, No. 1. Chicago Natural History Museum, 1903. $1.50.

THE ORAIBI SUMMER SNAKE CEREMONY

H. R. Voth

97 pp. Illus. Fieldiana: Anthropology. Vol. iii, No. 4. Chicago Natural History Museum, 1903. $2.50.

*THE ORDEAL OF THE YOUNG HUNTER
  Jonreed Lauritzen; illustrated by Hoke
  Denetsosie
The story of a Navajo boy's adventure with
a cougar, and how the boy avenges the death
of his father's sheep. Illus. Grades 7 to 8.
Little, Brown and Co., 1954.

THE OREGON STORY
  Vivian Corbett Atterbury
Sketches of early Oregon, her history, her
Indians, and her first inhabitants. 112 pp.
Illus. Binfords and Mort, $2.50.

THE OREGON TRAIL
  Francis Parkman
Paper. Airmont Publishing Co., Inc., 1964.
50¢.

ORIGIN AND MEANING OF THE INDIAN
PLACE NAMES OF MARYLAND
  Hamill Kenny
Includes a list of Indian place names and
abbreviations in Maryland. xix + 186 pp.
Index. Biblio. Maps. Appendix. Waverly
Press, 1961. $7.00.

ORIGIN LEGEND OF THE NAVAHO
ENEMY WAY
  Pennington Haile
Human Relations Area Files Press, 1964.
$6.50.

ORIGIN, PROGRESS, AND CONCLUSION
OF THE FLORIDA WAR
  John T. Sprague; edited by John K.
  Mahon
An account of the second Seminole War,
1835 to 1842. 608 pp. University of Flori-
da Press, 1964. $12.50.

*ORIMHA OF THE MOHAWKS
  Charles Norman; illustrated by Johan-
  nes Troyer
An adventure story and biography of Pierre
Radisson's experiences among the Indians.
The Macmillan Co., 1961. $2.95.

THE ORRINGH STONE TAVERN AND
THREE SENECA SITES OF THE LATE
HISTORIC PERIOD
  Charles F. Hayes, III
Introduces the subject of both Indian and
non-Indian historic site archaeology of the
period 1770 to 1830 in the Genesee Country
of New York. It is a compilation of already
existing data on scattered Seneca sites in
the files of the Rochester Museum as well
as recent data obtained in the excavation at

a non-Indian tavern site. Acculturation in
Indian and white artifact categories is dis-
cussed. vi + 82 pp. 22 pls. 4 figs. Table.
Biblio. Research Records of the Rochester
Museum of Arts and Sciences No. 12, 1965.
$2.00. Available from the Rochester Mu-
seum Association.

THE OSAGES, *Children of the Middle Waters*
  John Joseph Mathews
826 pp. Illus. Biblio. Index. Maps. University of Oklahoma Press, 1961. $7.95.

*OSCEOLA: *Young Seminole Indian*
  Electa Clark; illustrated by Robert
  Doremus
The story of Osceola and of his fight to pro-
tect his people's Florida settlement. 200
pp. Grades 4 to 8. Illus. Biblio. The
Bobbs-Merrill Co., Inc., 1965. $2.25.

OUR AMERICAN INDIANS AT A GLANCE
  Monroe Heath
A general discussion of the American Indians, their history, leaders, customs, status, and some principal tribes. Illus. Pacific Coast Publishers, 1961. Paper, $1.95;
cloth, $2.50.

OUR INDIAN HERITAGE
  Richard Kirk and Clara Lee Turner
How American Indian handicrafts were de-
veloped from the simplest skills. Follett
Publishing Co.

OUR INDIAN HERITAGE: *Profiles of 12
Great Leaders*
  C. Fayne Porter
Profiles of twelve American Indians span-
ning over four centuries of Indian history.
228 pp. Illus. Index. Chilton Books, 1964.
$4.95.

*OUR LANGUAGE: *The Story of the Words
We Use*
  Eloise Lambert
Grades 7 to 11. Lothrop, Lee & Shepard
Co., 1955. $3.00.

*OUR LITTLE INDIANS
  Harry Klepper
45 pp. Carlton Press, Inc., 1965. $2.00.

OUR PRIMITIVE CONTEMPORARIES
  George Peter Murdock
Brief descriptions of eighteen different primitive peoples representative of all the great
regions and races of the world, and of all

the major types and levels of culture. 614 pp. Illus. Index. Biblio. The Macmillan Co., 1964. $6.95.

√ THE OXFORD HISTORY OF THE AMERICAN PEOPLE
Samuel Eliot Morison
A social and political history of America. 1,177 pp. Illus. Musical examples. Maps. Index. Biblio. Oxford University Press, 1965. $12.50.

THE OZARK BLUFF-DWELLERS
M. R. Harrington
A monograph on the rock shelter culture of Arkansas, based on archaeological excavations in Benton and Carroll counties. 185 pp. Illus. Museum of the American Indian, Heye Foundation, $4.50.

P

PACIFIC NORTHWEST INDIAN WARS
Ray H. Glassley
The story of the Northwest Indian wars. 274 pp. Illus. Index. Biblio. Binfords and Mort, 1953. $3.95.

*PACO'S MIRACLE
Ann N. Clark
"Only Old Pierre and young Paco remain from a tiny French settlement in New Mexico. Paco repays the generous Spanish people who care for him when the Old One becomes ill." Illus. Grades 4 to 6. Farrar, Straus & Giroux, Inc., 1962. $2.95.

PADRE KINO
Illustrated by Ted De Grazia
The events and times of Padre Kino, the priest colonizer of the Southwest. 55 pp. Illus. Map. Southwest Museum, $2.50.

PAGANS, CONQUISTADORES, HEROES AND MARTYRS
Merle Armitage and Peter R. Ortega Academy Guild Press, 1960. Paper, $2.75; cloth, $7.50.

PAINT THE WIND
Alberta Hannum; paintings by Beatien Yazz
A continuation of the story of the young Navajo artist of *Spin a Silver Dollar,* with examples of his later work. 192 pp. Illus. The Viking Press, Inc., 1958. $4.50.

*PAINTED PONY RUNS AWAY
Jessie Brewer McGaw
A Cheyenne boy's runaway pony leads him into the camp of the hostile Sioux, where he is taken prisoner. In authentic Indian picture-writing, Little Elk tells the story of his escape and the rescue of a Sioux boy. 96 pp. Illus. Grades 1 to 4. Thomas Nelson & Sons, 1958. $3.25.

PAINTED TIPIS AND PICTURE-WRITING OF THE BLACKFOOT INDIANS
Walter McClintock
Southwest Museum, 25¢.

PAIUTE
Sessions S. Wheeler
A history dealing with a period of Indian wars and gold and silver discoveries in Nevada, 1859 to 1860, when the area was still a part of the Utah Territory. The Caxton Printers, Ltd., $5.95.

PAIUTE SORCERY
Beatrice B. Whiting
Paper. Johnson Reprint Corp., 1950. $10.00.

PAJARITO PLATEAU AND ITS ANCIENT PEOPLE
Edgar L. Hewett
A summary of sixty years' research into the life of the vanished peoples of New Mexico's Jemez mountain country. Illus. University of New Mexico Press, $4.50.

PALEO-INDIAN CULTURE IN KENTUCKY
Martha A. Rolingson
An analysis of the Kentucky Paleo-Indian and his characteristic artifact, the projectile point, deriving subtypes from the five accepted types and correlating these with other prehistoric cultures at known sites throughout the state. Paper. 112 pp. University of Kentucky Press, 1964. $2.00.

PALETTE AND TOMAHAWK
Robert Plate
An account of George Catlin whose paintings of Indians helped 19th-century Americans to understand them. 244 pp. Illus. Biblio. David McKay Co., Inc., $4.50.

PAPAGO INDIAN POTTERY
Bernard L. Fontana
Changing traditions caused by exposure of this Arizona tribe to a non-Indian culture and economy are shown in new perspective as the author considers origins, evolution,

use, and discontinuation of various pottery forms. 185 pp. University of Washington Press, 1962. $5.75.

PAPERS FROM A TRAINING PROGRAM IN SALVAGE ARCHAEOLOGY
Henry C. Greminger
Illus. Paper. Museum of New Mexico Press, 1961. $2.00.

THE PATHFINDERS
Gerald Rawling
The narrative of the mountain men who opened the West, and the Indians they subdued in the process. 326 pp. Illus. Biblio. Map. The Macmillan Co., 1964. $6.95.

THE PATRIOT CHIEFS: *A Chronicle of American Indian Leadership*
Alvin M. Josephy
A historical account of the Indian's struggle with the white man, based on the lives of representative chiefs. 384 pp. The Viking Press, Inc., 1961. $6.50.

PATTERAN
K. S. Johnson
The story of Reverend Leeds, who ministered to the Koasati Indians of Louisiana and who was instrumental in organizing more than twenty other missions and churches. 162 pp. Illus. The Naylor Co., 1964. $4.95.

PATTERNS OF CULTURE
Ruth Benedict
Houghton Mifflin Co. Paper, $1.95; hardcover, $4.00.

PAWNEE BILL
Glenn Shirley
A brief history of the Pawnee Indians, with emphasis on their reservation and post-reservation periods. 256 pp. Illus. Paper. University of Nebraska Press, 1958. $1.50.

PAWNEE BILL
Glenn Shirley
As above. Illus. University of New Mexico Press, $5.00.

PAWNEE, BLACKFOOT AND CHEYENNE
George Bird Grinnell; with an Introduction by Dee Brown
A selection from the writings of one of the great experts on tribal history and folklore of the Plains Indians. 320 pp. Charles Scribner's Sons, 1961. $4.95.

PAWNEE HERO STORIES AND FOLK TALES
George Bird Grinnell
Peter Smith, $3.75.

PAWNEE HERO STORIES AND FOLK TALES
George Bird Grinnell
xiv + 418 pp. University of Nebraska Press, 1961. $1.65.

*PEETIE THE PACK RAT AND OTHER DESERT STORIES
Van Clark; illustrated by Andy Tsina-jinnie
A collection of animal stories illustrated by a Navajo Indian authentically depicting life in the Southwest. 108 pp. The Caxton Printers, Ltd., 1961. $5.00.

THE PEOPLE ARE COMING SOON
Melville Jacobs
Analyses of Clackamas Chinook myths and tales. 359 pp. Paper. University of Washington Press, 1960. $4.50.

PEOPLE OF THE DEER
Farley Mowat
The story of a tribe of Eskimos called the Ihalmiut, who lived in the great barrens northwest of Hudson's Bay. Fifty years ago these inland Eskimos numbered a prosperous two thousand; in 1948 there were a mere forty survivors. This book tells how the intrusion of the white man has driven these people to the verge of extinction. It also tells how the white man was responsible for the decimation of the great herds of caribou upon which these people lived. 344 pp. Illus. Atlantic Monthly Press, 1952. $5.95.

PEOPLE OF THE MIDDLE PLACE
Dorothea C. Leighton and John J. Adair
A study reporting the results of the Indian Education Research Project, whose aim was to investigate, analyze and compare the development of five Indian tribes in the context of their total environment. 175 pp. Illus. Biblio. Tables. Paper. Human Relations Area Files Press, 1965. $4.50.

PEOPLE OF THE PUEBLO
Celeste C. Murphy
"The story of Sonoma, California." 303 pp. Illus. Binfords and Mort, $3.75.

*PEOPLE OF THE SNOW
Wanda N. Tolboom
Illus. Grades 6 to 10. Coward-McCann, Inc., 1957. $3.25.

PEOPLE OF THE TWILIGHT
 Diamond Jenness
viii + 251 pp. Illus. Paper. University of
Chicago Press, 1959. $1.50.

THE PEOPLE WE CALL INDIANS
 Loretto Douglas
63 pp. Brown Book Co., 1954. $2.00.

THE PERSONAL NARRATIVE OF JAMES
 O. PATTIE
 James O. Pattie; Introduction by Wil-
 liam H. Goetzmann
A tale of exploits among the Indians and
Spaniards throughout the West between 1825
and 1830. J. B. Lippincott Co., 1962. Pa-
per, $1.45; cloth, $4.50.

PERSPECTIVES IN AMERICAN INDIAN
 CULTURE CHANGE
 Edward H. Spicer, Editor
A social and anthropological study of the
changes in the Indian way of life from the
earliest contacts with Europeans to the
present. x + 549 pp. University of Chicago
Press, 1961. $10.00.

PETER FREUCHEN'S MEN OF THE FRO-
 ZEN NORTH
 Peter Freuchen
A book of fact and fiction about the people
of Greenland, northern Canada, Siberia,
Lapland, Scandinavia, and Alaska, told
through tales and narratives. 320 pp. The
World Publishing Co., 1962. $6.00.

*PETER JUMPING HORSE
 Gordon Langley Hall
Holt, Rinehart & Winston, Inc., $2.75.

THE PEYOTE CULT
 Weston LaBarre
188 pp. Illus. The Shoe String Press, Inc.,
1964. $7.50.

PEYOTE MUSIC
 David P. McAllester
Paper. Johnson Reprint Corp., 1949.
$10.00.

PEYOTISM AND NEW MEXICO
 Charles B. Dustin
This book gives the historical background
and psychological functions of Peyotism;
discusses Taos peyotism and Navajo peyotism in perspective of their social and legal
struggle with state and tribal governments.
51 pp. Illus. Dustin Publications, 1962.
$2.00.

PHONOLOGY OF ARIZONA YAQUI WITH
 TEXTS
 Lynne S. Crumrine
Paper. University of Arizona Press, 1961.
$2.00.

PHOTOGRAPHER OF THE SOUTHWEST
 Adam Clark Vroman
Photographs of Indian life and customs from
1895 to 1906. The Ward Ritchie Press,
$12.00.

PHOTOGRAPHERS OF THE FRONTIER
 WEST
 Ralph Warren Andrews
A book about frontier photographers' lives
and work. 182 pp. Illus. Superior Pub-
lishing Co., 1965. $12.95.

A PICTORIAL HISTORY OF THE AMERI-
 CAN INDIAN
 Oliver LaFarge
"The story of the Indians of North America
from the time the first white men landed to
the present." Illus. Crown Publishers,
Inc., 1956. $3.25.

*PICTURE-SKIN STORY
 Alex W. Bealer, III
An old Sioux Indian tells, by means of pic-
tures drawn on a buffalo hide, the story of
his first hunt. 32 pp. Illus. Holiday House,
Inc., 1957. $3.00.

PIMA AND PAPAGO INDIAN
 AGRICULTURE
 Edward Castetter and Willis Bell
Illus. University of New Mexico Press,
1942. $3.50.

A PIMA REMEMBERS
 George Webb
A description of traditional Pima life as recounted by an aging tribesman. 126 pp. Illus. University of Arizona Press, $3.00.

THE PINTO BASIN SITE
 Elizabeth W. C. and William H. Campbell
51 pp. Illus. Southwest Museum, 1935.
$3.00.

A PINTO SITE NEAR LITTLE LAKE,
 CALIFORNIA
 M. R. Harrington
91 pp. Illus. Southwest Museum, 1957.
Paper, $3.75; cloth, $5.00.

*PINTO'S JOURNEY
  Wilfred S. Bronson
Grades 5 to 8. Julian Messner, 1948. $2.95.

PIONEER AMERICA
  John R. Alden
The story of American society, from prehistoric times to the end of the Civil War, concentrating on social and political developments rather than on dates and figures. Author emphasizes our European heritage in education, religion, and politics; the class structures and economies of the various colonies; the influences of such institutions as slavery; the frontier; and regional differences. 309 pp. Alfred A. Knopf, Inc., 1966. $6.95.

*PIONEER HORSE
  George C. Franklin
Illus. Grades 2 to 5. Houghton Mifflin Co., 1960. $2.50.

PIONEERS OF THE POTOWMACK
  H. P. Hobbs, Jr.
A narrative history of the discovery and exploration of the Potomac River, with encounters and battles with the Indians of this region. 155 pp. Illus. Paper. Horace P. Hobbs, Jr., 1964. $4.00.

PIPELINE ARCHAEOLOGY: *A Report of the Salvage Operations in the Southwest*
  Fred Wendorf, Nancy Fox and Orian A. Lewis
410 pp. Paper. Northern Arizona Society of Science and Art, $4.00.

PIRATES, INDIANS AND SPANIARDS
  James W. Covington and A. F. Falcones
A book of the writings of Spanish missionaries to Florida in the late 16th century, with much on life of the early Indians. 175 pp. Illus. Great Outdoors Association, $5.00.

PLAINS INDIAN PARFLECHE DESIGNS
  Leslie Spier
30 pp. Paper. University of Washington Press, 1931. 75¢.

THE PLAINSMEN OF THE YELLOWSTONE
  Mark H. Brown
A history of the Crow, Cheyenne, Gros Ventres, Teton Sioux, and others, 480 pp. Index. Illus. G. P. Putnam's Sons, 1961. $7.50.

PLANT GEOGRAPHY AND CULTURE HISTORY IN THE AMERICAN SOUTHWEST
  George F. Carter
Illus. Paper. Johnson Reprint Corp., 1945. $10.00.

PLENTY-COUPS, CHIEF OF THE CROWS
  Frank B. Linderman
As below. Paper. Peter Smith, 1962. $3.50.

PLENTY-COUPS, CHIEF OF THE CROWS
  Frank B. Linderman
A biography of the Crow chieftain. x + 326 pp. University of Nebraska Press, 1962. $1.50.

*POCAHONTAS
  Patricia Miles Martin
The story of an Indian maiden who brought peace to Jamestown. 64 pp. Grades 1 to 3. G. P. Putnam's Sons, 1965. $2.95.

*POCAHONTAS AND HER WORLD
  Frances Carpenter
Illus. Ages 10 to 14. Alfred A. Knopf, Inc., 1957. $3.00.

*POCAHONTAS: *Brave Girl*
  Flora Warren Seymour; illustrated by William Moyer
A biography of Pocahontas. 200 pp. Illus. Grades 3 to 6. The Bobbs-Merrill Co., Inc., $2.25.

POINT HOPE, *An Eskimo Village in Transition*
  James W. Van Stone
A study of the group and interpersonal relationships of one of the oldest Eskimo communities, and the degree to which European and American values have affected the villages. 192 pp. Illus. University of Washington Press, 1962. $5.25.

POLLEN PATH: *A Collection of Navajo Myths*
  Margaret Schevill
Stanford University Press, $6.00.

POMO INDIAN MYTHS
  Cora Clark and T. B. Williams
148 pp. Brown Book Co., 1954. $3.00.

THE PONCA SUN DANCE
  G. A. Dorsey
21 pp. Illus. Fieldiana: Anthropology, Vol. vii, No. 2. Chicago Natural History Museum, 1905. $2.00.

PONTIAC AND THE INDIAN UPRISING
Howard H. Peckham
346 pp. Index. Paper. University of Chicago Press, 1947. $1.95.

*PONTIAC, *Lion in the Forest*
Wilma P. Hays
Illus. Houghton Mifflin Co., 1965. $2.20.

*PONTIAC: *Young Ottawa Leader*
Howard H. Peckham; illustrated by Robert Doremus
A biography of one of the chiefs of the Ottawa tribe. 200 pp. Illus. Grades 2 to 5. The Bobbs-Merrill Co., Inc., 1963. $2.25.

*PONY SOLDIER
Lee McGriffin
E. P. Dutton & Co., Inc., 1961. $3.00.

PONY TRACKS
Frederick Remington
Long's College Book Co., 1951. $5.00.

PONY TRACKS
Frederick Remington
Illus. University of Oklahoma, 1961. $2.00.

POPULAR ACCOUNTS OF THE KIOWA LANGUAGE
McKenzie Parker and John P. Harrington
A report on phonematics, morphomatics and lexics of the Kiowa language. 21 pp. Glossary. Paper. School of American Research, $2.00.

THE POOL AND IRVING VILLAGES
John C. McGregor
A study of Hopewell occupations in the Illinois River valley. 236 pp. Illus. Paper. University of Illinois Press, 1958. $3.50.

PORTAGE INTO THE PAST
J. Arnold Bolz
An Indian history woven into a description of the author's canoe journey over the route of the early voyagers. viii + 181 pp. Illus. Index. University of Minnesota Press, 1960. $5.00.

POTAWATOMI INDIANS
Otho Winger
History and biography of the Potawatomis. 159 pp. Illus. Lawrence W. Shultz, 1939. $2.00.

POTSHERDS: *An Introduction to the Study of Prehistoric Southwestern Ceramics and Their Use in Historic Reconstruction*
Harold S. Colton
86 pp. Northern Arizona Society of Science and Art, $3.00.

THE POTTERY OF SANTO DOMINGO
K. M. Chapman
A detailed study of ceramic decoration. 192 pp. Illus. School of American Research, $6.50.

*POWHATAN AND CAPTAIN JOHN SMITH
Olga W. Hall-Quest; illustrated by Douglas Gorshine
Illus. Grades 4 to 7. Farrar, Straus & Giroux, Inc., 1957. $2.75.

PRAYER: The Compulsive Word
Gladys A. Reichard
A discussion of Navajo prayers and their place in Navajo ritual. Illus. An American Ethnological Society Monograph reissued by the University of Washington Press. $5.00.

PRE-COLUMBIAN ARCHITECTURE
Donald Robertson
George Braziller, Inc. Paper, $2.95; cloth, $4.95.

PRE-SPANISH JEWELRY AND ORNAMENT IN THE SOUTHWEST
Alfred E. Dittert, Jr.
Illus. Paper. Museum of New Mexico Press, 1965. 25¢.

A PREHISTORIC FORTIFIED VILLAGE SITE AT CANADAIGUA, ONTARIO COUNTY, N. Y.
William A. Ritchie
A summary of the 1934 excavations of an Owasco village and cemetaries situated on the Charles Sackett farm at Canandaigua, Ontario County, N. Y. 75 pp. 26 pls. 24 diagrams. 2 figs. 4 tables. Research Records of the Rochester Museum of Arts and Sciences No. 3, Anthropology 3, 1936. $1.50. Available from the Rochester Museum of Arts and Sciences.

PREHISTORIC INDIAN SETTLEMENTS OF THE CHANGING MISSISSIPPI RIVER DELTA
William G. McIntire
Illus. Paper. Louisiana State University Press, 1958. $3.00.

PREHISTORIC INDIANS OF THE SOUTH-
WEST
H. M. Wormington
The story of the cliff dwellers of Mesa
Verde and various other groups. 192 pp.
Illus. Appendix. Index. Biblio. Denver
Museum of Natural History, 1964. Paper,
$2.20; cloth, $3.20.

*PREHISTORIC INDIANS OF WISCONSIN
Robert E. Ritzenthaler
A portrayal of the life of the early inhabitants of this area as deduced from archaeological explorations. 43 pp. Illus. Ages
8 to 14. Paper. Milwaukee Public Museum, 75¢.

PREHISTORIC MAN ON THE GREAT
PLAINS
Waldo J. Wedel
355 pp. Illus. Index. Biblio. University
of Oklahoma Press, 1964. $5.95.

PREHISTORIC MAN IN THE NEW WORLD
Jesse D. Jennings and Edward Norbeck,
Editors
The principal findings of the most recent
research in American archaeology as well
as the accumulated results of many years'
study in non-technical language are brought
together in this book. x + 633 pp. University of Chicago Press, 1964. $10.00.

PREHISTORIC MEN
Robert J. Braidwood
A study of the techniques of toolmaking by
Paleolithic man. Primary consideration is
given to European methods, but material is
also presented on American Indian flint-
flaking. 188 pp. Illus. Paper. Oceana
Publications, Inc., $1.50.

PREHISTORIC PEOPLE
Joe Ben Wheat
An account of prehistoric inhabitants of the
Four Corners area. 39 pp. Illus. Paper.
Navajo Tribal Museum, 70¢.

PREHISTORIC PEOPLE OF NEW YORK
STATE
Richard L. McCarthy and Harrison
Newman
From the Contents: *Archaic Period; La-
moka Culture; Laurentian Culture; Early
Woodland; Middlesex and Hopewellian Cul-
tures; Middle Woodland; Late Woodland
Culture; Prehistoric Culture; Prehistoric*

Indians; Weapons; and photographs of exhibits and artifacts. 16 pp. Paper. Buffalo and Erie County Historical Society,
1961. 50

PREHISTORIC SETTLEMENT AND
PHYSICAL ENVIRONMENT IN THE
MESA VERDE AREA
Joyce Herold
A synthesis of published knowledge about
basketmaking and Pueblo remains of the
Mesa Verde area, with analysis of sites.
218 pp. Illus. Biblio. Maps. University
of Utah Press, 1961. $3.00.

PREHISTORIC SETTLEMENT PATTERNS
IN THE NEW WORLD
Gordon R. Wiley
Illus. Paper. Johnson Reprint Corp.,1956.
$10.00.

PREHISTORIC SOUTHWESTERNERS,
FROM BASKETMAKER TO PUEBLO
Charles Avery Amsden; with an Intro-
duction by Alfred Kidder
xiv + 163 pp. 39 plates. 46 figures. 2 maps.
Southwest Museum, $3.50.

PREHISTORIC WEAPONS IN THE
SOUTHWEST
Stewart Peckham
Illus. Paper. Museum of New Mexico
Press, 1965. 25¢.

PRELIMINARY ARCHAEOLOGICAL
INVESTIGATIONS IN THE NAVAJO
PROJECT AREA
Alfred E. Dittert, Jr.
An introduction to the salvage archaeology
of the Navajo Reservoir District, describing the project area and defining cultural
phases, including an analysis of artifacts
collected during the preliminary survey.
26 pp. Museum of New Mexico Press, $1.00.

PRIMITIVE ART
Franz Boas
Discusses theories in primitive art; historical depth in art history; technical vir-
tuosity; unconscious levels of patterning
symbolism; styles; literature; music and
dance. 376 pp. Illus. Paper. Dover Publications, Inc., $2.00.

PRIMITIVE ART
Douglas Fraser
A study of the primitive art of four conti-
nents (including North America), and the
relationship between them. 320 pp. Illus.
Doubleday & Co., Inc., 1962. $7.50.

PRIMITIVE MAN AS A PHILOSOPHER
Paul Radin

An anthropological work covering primitive thought on such topics as the purpose of life, marital relations, freedom of thought, symbolism, death, resignation, the nature of reality, personality, gods, and many others. xviii + 402 pp. Index. Biblio. Paper. Dover Publications, Inc., $2.25.

PRIMITIVE MAN AND HIS WAYS
Kaj Birket-Smith

Author examines six societies that have adapted their ways of life to the primitive forces of nature. The societies are: the Lapps, the aborigines of Australia, the Maori, the Tuareg, and two groups of North American Indians. 215 pp. Paper. New American Library, 1957. 75¢.

PRIMITIVE PRAGMATISTS: *The Modoc Indians of Northern California*
Verne F. Ray

A study of the highly individualistic and unified culture of the Modoc Indians. 256 pp. Published for the American Ethnological Society by the University of Washington Press, 1963. $5.00.

PRIMITIVE RELIGION
Robert H. Lowie

A description of the beliefs, codes and practices of a variety of primitive religions with a survey of their beliefs, including psychological and historical aspects. 405 pp. Paper. Liveright Publishing Corp., $2.45.

PRIMITIVE RELIGION
Paul Radin

A treatment of the nature and origin of man's belief in the supernatural and the influences that have shaped religious expression in primitive societies. x + 322 pp. Index. Biblio. Paper. Dover Publications, Inc., 1957. $2.00.

PROGRAM OF THE HISTORY OF AMERICAN INDIANS
Pedro Armillas

142 pp. Paper. Pan American Union. English edition, $1.25; Spanish edition, $1.50.

PUEBLO GODS AND MYTHS
Hamilton A. Tyler

313 pp. Index. Biblio. Table. Map. University of Oklahoma Press, 1964. $5.95.

*THE PUEBLO INDIANS: *Farmers of the Rio Grande*
Sonia Bleeker; illustrated by Patricia Boodell

The culture and history of the Pueblo Indians. 160 pp. Illus. Index. Ages 8 to 12. William Morrow & Co., Inc., 1955. $2.75.

*PUEBLO STORIES
Edward W. Dolch

Stories of the strange customs of the Pueblo, and about the drama of life in a Pueblo village. 176 pp. Grades 1 to 6. Garrard Publishing Co., 1959. $2.95.

PUEBLO PERIOD SITES IN THE PIEDRA RIVER SECTION, NAVAJO RESERVOIR DISTRICT
Alfred E. Dittert and Frank W. Eddy

The archaeology of several important Pueblo sites of the period from A.D. 850 to A.D. 975 in the Four Corners area. 122 pp. Illus. Biblio. University of New Mexico Press, 1963. $3.00.

PUEBLO WARRIORS AND SPANISH CONQUEST
Oakah L. Jones, Jr.

An examination of the procedures, organization, contributions and significance of the Pueblo auxiliaries from 1692 to 1794 in the vital central sector of New Spain's northern frontier in North America. 232 pp. Illus. Index. Biblio. Maps. University of Oklahoma Press, 1966. $5.00.

PULSE OF THE PUEBLO
Julia Seton

A collection of experiences and glimpses of Indian life. Seton Village, $3.95.

Q

QUANAH PARKER
Clyde and Grace Jackson

A biography of Quanah Parker, a Comanche chieftain, with detailed information about the civilization, mores and psychology of the era. 184 pp. Illus. Exposition Press, 1963. $4.00.

*THE QUEST OF THE FISH-DOG SKIN
James Willard Schultz

Life among the Western Indians, describing the adventures of Tom Fox, who leaves his home in St. Louis to live at the American

Fur Company on the Missouri River. Illus. Ages 10 and up. Houghton Mifflin Co., 1960. $2.50.

QUOTH THE RAVEN: *A Little Journey into the Primitive*
Oliver Maxson Salisbury
The story of a couple's experiences with the Thlinget Indians of Alaska during the 1920's. 275 pp. Illus. Superior Publishing Co., 1962. $6.95.

R

RANGERS AND REGULARS
George E. Hyde
Long's College Book Co., 1933. $5.00.

RANK AND WARFARE AMONG THE PLAINS INDIANS
Bernard Mishkin
Examines the economic implications and the historical interrelationships of horse culture, rank, and warfare, and their roles in the framework of Plains society. An American Ethnological Society Monograph reissued by the University of Washington Press. $5.00.

RAPPAHANNOCK TAKING DEVICES: *Traps, Hunting and Fishing*
Edmund Carpenter
University Museum, 1946. 50¢.

REAL BOOK ABOUT INDIANS
Michael Gorham
Illus. Grades 3 to 7. Doubleday & Co., Inc., 1953. $1.95.

A REAPPRAISAL OF THE FREMONT CULTURE
H. M. Wormington
An analysis of the culture of the Fremont people who lived in portions of Utah, Nevada and California from the Christian era until A.D. 1050. 200 pp. Illus. Denver Museum of Natural History, $3.00.

RECENT GEOMORPHIC HISTORY OF THE PONTCHARTRAIN BASIN
Roger T. Saucier
Paper. Louisiana State University Press, 1964. $3.00.

THE RECOLLECTIONS OF PHILANDER PRESCOTT: *Frontiersman of the Old Northwest, 1819 to 1862*
Donald D. Parker, Editor
Reminiscences of a fur trader, interpreter, and government farmer among the Sioux of the upper Mississippi from 1819 to 1862, including a description of the relations between the Sioux, the Chippewas, the Winnebagos, the Menominees, the Sauks, the Foxes, and their relations with the U. S. Government. xiv + 272 pp. University of Nebraska Press, 1966. $5.95.

A RECORD OF TRAVELS IN ARIZONA, AND CALIFORNIA, 1775 to 1776
Francisco Tomas Hermenegildo Garces; edited by John Galvin
Concerns the Indian tribes with whom the author, a Franciscan missionary, worked. 113 pp. Illus. Biblio. Maps. John Howell, Books, 1965. $7.50.

THE RED ANTWAY OF THE NAVAHO
Leland C. Wyman
A documented study of the Antway ceremony, with descriptions of its preparations, chants, mythological meanings, and sandpaintings. Illus. References. Paper. Museum of Navajo Ceremonial Art, $3.25.

RED, BLACK, BLOND AND OLIVE
Edmund Wilson
A description of the social and economic conditions, religious practices and culture of the Zuni Indians. Oxford University Press, 1956. $6.95.

*RED BROTHER
R. Baker
George Wahr Publishing Co., 1927. 75¢.

*RED CLOUD
Shannon Garst; illustrated by Art Seiden
The story of a Sioux chief who united the Plains tribes and led them into battle in an effort to preserve their way of life against the encroachment of white settlers. Illus. Ages 10 and up. Follett Publishing Co., 1965. $1.95.

RED CLOUD AND THE SIOUX PROBLEM
James C. Olson
A detailed study of the relations between the Sioux and the U. S. Government in the decades after the Civil War. xvi + 376 pp. Illus. Biblio. Maps. University of Nebraska Press, 1965. $5.95.

RED CLOUD'S FOLK: *A History of the Oglala Sioux Indians*
George E. Hyde
331 pp. Illus. Appendix. Biblio. University of Oklahoma Press, 1957. $5.00.

*RED EAGLE AND THE ABSAROKA
    Francis Haines
Illus. The Caxton Printers, Ltd., 1960.
$3.50.

*RED FOX AND HIS CANOE
    Nathaniel Benchley; illustrated by Arnold Lobel
Red Fox discovers that having one of the
world's largest canoes has its disadvantages
when half the forest animals feel obliged to
ride along. 64 pp. Illus. Ages 1 to 3.
Harper & Row, Publishers, 1964. $3.25.

*RED INDIAN FOLK AND FAIRY TALES
    Ruth Manning Sanders; illustrated by
    C. Walter Hodges
Sorcerers, animals and Indian braves all
play a part in this collection of tales from
the plains and forests of North America.
222 pp. Grades 6 to 10. Illus. Roy Publishers, 1962. $3.75.

RED MAN'S CONTINENT
    Ellsworth Huntington
United States Publishers Association, Inc.,
$3.95.

RED MAN'S RELIGION
    Ruth M. Underhill
This book discusses in non-technical terms
the religious beliefs and rituals of Indians
throughout history, giving special attention
to the effect of religious practices on the
kind of lives they lived. 350 pp. Illus.
University of Chicago Press, 1965. $7.95.

THE RED MAN'S WEST
    Michael Kennedy, Editor
A collection of articles about the Indians of
the High Plains and the Rockies and their
relationships with the white man, extracted
from *Montana, The Magazine of Western
History.* 384 pp. Illus. Hastings House,
Publishers, Inc., 1965. $10.00.

**RED MEN CALLING ON THE GREAT
WHITE FATHER**
    Katherine C. Turner
236 pp. Illus. Biblio. Index. University
of Oklahoma Press, 1951. $3.75.

RED MEN OF FIRE: *A History of the Cherokee Indians*
    Irvin M. Peithmann; Foreword by N. B.
    Johnson
Relates true stories gleaned from historical
accounts of the Cherokee nation from the
time of deSoto. 184 pp. Illus. Charles C.
Thomas, Publisher, 1964. $6.50.

RED MEN'S AMERICA
    Ruth M. Underhill
A complete survey written for the lay reader of Indian societies from the first Stone
Age hunters to the American citizens of today. x + 400 pp. Illus. University of Chicago Press, 1953. $7.50.

**THE RED OCHER CULTURE OF THE UPPER GREAT LAKES AND ADJACENT
AREAS**
    Robert E. Ritzenthaler and George I.
    Quimby
33 pp. Illus. Tables. Vol. 36, No. 11.
Chicago Natural History Museum, 1962.
$1.00.

*THE RED WAR POLE
    Louis Capron; illustrated by David
    Stone
This is the story of a white boy who becomes an adopted member of a tribe of
Seminole Indians and his attempts to alleviate problems between the Indians and white
men. 186 pp. Illus. The Bobbs-Merrill
Co., Inc., 1963. $3.75.

REDSKINS, RUFFLESHIRTS AND REDNECKS
    Mary Elizabeth Young
A book concerning Indian allotments in Alabama and Mississippi, 1830 to 1860. 217
pp. Illus. Index. Graphs. Biblio. Tables.
Maps. University of Oklahoma Press, 1961.
$5.00.

**THE REEVE RUIN OF SOUTHEASTERN
ARIZONA**
    Charles C. DiPeso
The Amerind Foundation, 1958. $7.50.

**RELATIONS WITH THE PLAINS INDIANS
1857-1861**
    LeRoy Hafen
Arthur H. Clark Co., 1959. $12.00.

REMEMBER THE WIND: *A Prairie Memoir*
    William M. Chapman
Contains the author's account of his three
years at St. Elizabeth's School on Standing
Rock Reservation in South Dakota with sixty
young Sioux Indians. 240 pp. J. B. Lippincott Co., 1965. $5.95.

REMINISCENCES OF A RANCHMAN
    Edgar Beecher Bronson
Book concerns the author's experiences with
the Sioux at the Pine Ridge (Indian) Agency,
his relationship with an Indian agent, and

includes a description of the Cheyenne Outbreak of 1878. xvi + 370 pp. Illus. Paper. University of Nebraska Press, 1962. $1.50.

REMINISCENCES OF A RANCHMAN
    Edgar Beecher Bronson
As above. Illus. Paper. Peter Smith, 1962. $1.50.

REMINISCENCES OF THE SECOND SEMINOLE WAR, 1835 to 1842
    John Bemrose; edited by John K. Mahon
University of Florida Press, 1964. $6.50.

REMOVAL OF THE CHEROKEE NATION: *Manifest Destiny or National Dishonor?*
    Louis Filler and Allen Guttmann, Editors
A collection of readings providing a historical framework for the Indian removal policy of the 1820's and 1830's, written by participants in the conflict. vii + 113 pp. Paper. D. C. Heath & Co., 1962. $1.60.

RENO COURT OF INQUIRY
    William A. Graham, Editor
A condensed version of the substance of the hearings of the Court of Inquiry into the Battle of the Little Big Horn, centering around the supposed cowardice of two officers in Custer's regiment. xxx + 305 pp. Photos. Maps. Index. The Stackpole Co., 1954. $5.00.

REPORT ON INDIAN EARTHWORKS IN OGEMAW COUNTY, MICHIGAN
    Fred Dustin
An account of the surveying, mapping, and study of four pre-Columbian Indian earthworks of Algonquin origin. 33 pp. Illus. Paper. Cranbrook Institute of Science, 1932. 10¢.

REPORT ON THE EXCAVATIONS OF A SMALL RUIN NEAR POINT OF PINES, EAST CENTRAL ARIZONA
    Fred Wendorf
Illus. University of Arizona Press, 1965. Paper, $4.00; cloth, $6.50.

THE REYNOLDS CAMPAIGN ON POWDER RIVER
    J. W. Vaughn
238 pp. Illus. Index. Biblio. Maps. University of Oklahoma Press, 1961. $5.00.

RHYTHM OF THE REDMAN
    Julia M. Buttree; Introduction, art section and illustrations by Ernest Thompson Seton

A collection of North American Indian songs, dances, ceremonies, lore, and art. 280 pp. Illus. Music scores and songs. Index. The Ronald Press Co., 1930. $5.00.

RICHARD WETHERILL: *Anasazi*
    Frank McNitt
The story of a pioneer explorer of ancient ruins of the Mesa Verde, Chaco Canyon, and Basket Maker cultures. 376 pp. Photos. Maps. University of New Mexico Press, $10.00.

*THE RIDDLE OF THE PAST
    Gordon C. Baldwin
A book for young readers describing how archaeologists solve prehistoric puzzles. 149 pp. Illus. Ages 10 to 14. W. W. Norton & Co., Inc., 1965. $3.50.

*RIDE LIKE AN INDIAN
    Henry Larom; illustrated by Wesley Dennis
A quiet boy suddenly finds himself spending a summer on a dude ranch and learns from an Indian boy how to train his pony to run with the swiftest horses. 140 pp. Illus. McGraw-Hill Book Co., $3.00.

RIDERS FROM THE WEST
    George Charles Kastner
An epic poem about the four Indians who went from the Nez Perce country in 1831 to St. Louis in search of the white man's "Book of Heaven." 155 pp. Binfords and Mort, 1932. $2.00.

*RIFLES FOR WATIE
    Harold Keith
A young farm boy joins the Union forces to become a scout and is thus a member of Stand Watie's Cherokee Rebels. 322 pp. Illus. Thomas Y. Crowell Co., 1957. $3.75.

RIO GRANDE
    Harvey Fergusson; illustrated by Colden Whitman
A portrait of the Rio Grande Valley of New Mexico and the men whose ideas shaped it. 296 pp. Illus. William Morrow & Co., Inc., 1955. $5.00.

THE RISE AND FALL OF THE CHOCTAW REPUBLIC
    Angie Debo
317 pp. Illus. Index. Biblio. Maps. University of Oklahoma Press, 1961. $5.00.

THE RISE OF THE WEST
    Francis S. Philbrick
A re-examination of the West's development
as it affected or was affected by the rest of
the country during the years 1754 to 1830.
xviii + 398 pp. Illus. Biblio. Index. Maps.
Harper & Row, Publishers, 1965. $6.00.

*THE RIVER SPIRIT AND THE MOUNTAIN
DEMONS
    Evelyn C. Nevin; woodcuts by Anita
    Bernarde
In 1811, a captive Indian girl joins the first
party of white fur traders to make a trip up
the Columbia River. 160 pp. Illus. Ages
12 and up. D. Van Nostrand Co., Inc.,
1965. $3.50.

ROAD OF LIFE AND DEATH
    Paul Radin; Foreword by Mark Van
    Doren
A presentation of the most sacred ritual of
the Winnebago Indians of Wisconsin. xiv +
345 pp. Pantheon Books, Inc., $4.50.

ROCK ART IN THE NAVAJO RESERVOIR
DISTRICT
    Polly Schaafsma
An illustrated study of the Navajo and Pueblo Reservoir District. 74 pp. Illus. Biblio. Paper. Museum of New Mexico Press,
$3.00.

THE ROCK PAINTINGS OF THE CHUMASH:
A Study of a California Indian Culture
    Campbell Grant; Foreword by Robert
    F. Heizer
An examination of cave art north of Santa
Barbara, including a history of the extinct
California tribe that produced it. xviii +
163 pp. Illus. Biblio. Maps. University
of California Press, 1965. $10.00.

*A ROMANCE OF OLD FORT HALL
    Minerva Teichert
The history of Fort Hall in pioneer days --
located near what is now Pocatello, Idaho
-- is presented in this Indian romance. 180
pp. Illus. Grades 7 to 9. Binfords and
Mort, $2.00.

S

THE SAC AND FOX INDIANS
    William T. Hagan
Illus. University of Oklahoma Press, 1958.
$5.00.

*SACAGAWEA: *Bird Girl*
    Flora Warren Seymour; illustrated by
    Robert Doremus
The story of Shoshoni tribal life told through
the experiences of an Indian girl named Sacagawea. 200 pp. Illus. Grades 3 to 6.
The Bobbs-Merrill Co., Inc., $2.25.

*SACAGAWEA: *Indian Guide*
    Wyatt Blassingame
The story of the kidnapping of a Shoshoni
Indian girl and her trip to the Pacific Northwest with the Lewis and Clark expedition.
80 pp. Garrard Publishing Co., 1965.
$1.98.

*SACAJAWEA: *Guide to Lewis and Clark*
    Jerry Seibert
The story of the life of a Shoshoni Indian
girl and the important part she played in
the success of the overland expedition. 192
pp. For teen-agers. Illus. Houghton Mifflin Co., 1960. $1.95.

SACAJAWEA OF THE SHOSHONES
    Della Emmons
A behind-the-scenes narrative of the Lewis
and Clark expedition as it revolved around
an Indian girl guide, Sacajawea, who traveled
for a year and a half with thirty-one frontier soldiers. Binfords and Mort, 1955.
$3.75.

SACRED BUNDLES OF THE SAC AND FOX
INDIANS
    Mark R. Harrington
Paper. University Museum, 1914. $3.50.

SAGA OF CHIEF JOSEPH
    Helen Addison Howard and Dan McGrath
A biography of the Nez Perce chief of the
Northwest whose military exploits ranked
him high among America's Indian leaders.
395 pp. The Caxton Printers, Ltd., 1965.
$4.95.

SAGEBRUSH SURGEON
    Florence Crannell Means
The story of a mission doctor's service to
the Navajos in the 1920's. 166 pp. Paper.
Friendship Press, $1.50.

SALVAGE ARCHAEOLOGY IN PAINTED
ROCKS RESERVOIR, WESTERN ARIZONA
    William W. Wasley and A. Johnson
The record of the salvage operation in Ho-
hokam sites of the Colonial, Sedentary and
Classic periods. xi + 123 pp. Illus. Bib-
lio. Map. Appendix. Paper. University

of Arizona Anthropology Papers, No. 9. University of Arizona Press, 1965. $5.00.

SALVATION AND THE SAVAGE
Robert F. Berkhofer, Jr.

A historical account of the outlook of the whites and the cultural values of the Indian tribes during the 1800's, including a discussion of the role of missionaries during this period. 256 pp. University of Kentucky Press, 1965. $6.00.

SAM HOUSTON'S INDIANS - *The Alabama-Coushatti*
P. V. Malone

A history of the Alabama-Coushatti and their adoption of the language, religion and laws of the white man, while retaining many of their own cultural traits. 78 pp. The Naylor Co., 1960. $3.50.

SAMSON OCCOM
Harold Blodgett

A biography of the Mohegan Indian who collected thousands of dollars in England for the founding of Dartmouth College and returned to find that it would be a school for whites only. Illus. Dartmouth Manuscript Series, No. 3, Dartmouth College Publications, 1935. $3.50.

THE SAN CARLOS INDIAN CATTLE INDUSTRY
Harold T. Getty

Paper. Illus. Anthropological Papers No. 7, University of Arizona Press, $3.25.

THE SAND CREEK MASSACRE
Stan Hoig

217 pp. Illus. Index. Appendix. Biblio. Maps. University of Oklahoma Press, $4.00.

THE SANILAC PETROGLYPHS
Robert T. Hatt, Darrel J. Richards and Mark L. Papworth

A record and analysis of ancient Indian inscriptions on bedrock in southern Michigan. 48 pp. Illus. Maps. Cranbrook Institute of Science, 1958. $1.50.

*SANTE FE
Elizabeth L. Crandall; illustrated by Lili Cassel Wronker

A description of the city under Spanish, Mexican and American rule. 143 pp. Illus. Maps. Rand McNally and Co., 1965. $2.95.

THE SAVAGE YEARS
Brian Connell

A history of the French and Indian Wars. Illus. Harper & Row, Publishers, 1959. $5.50.

THE SAWMILL SITE
Elaine A. Bluhm

A study of a reserve phase village in Pine Lawn Valley, western New Mexico. 88 pp. Illus. Maps. Vol. 47, No. 1, Chicago Natural History Museum, 1957. $2.25.

THE SAVAGES OF AMERICA: *A Study of the Indian and the Idea of Civilization*
Roy H. Pearce

A study of writings on the Indian which have appeared in political pamphlets, missionaries' reports, drama, poetry, novels, and anthropologists' accounts. 260 pp. Illus. The Johns Hopkins Press, 1965. $6.00.

SAYNDAY'S PEOPLE: *The Kiowa Indians and the Stories They Told*
Alice Marriott

A collection of Kiowa folk tales. xx + 226 pp. Illus. University of Nebraska Press, 1963. $1.75.

SCALPS AND TOMAHAWKS
Frederick Dimmer, Editor

Coward-McCann, Inc., 1961. $6.00.

SCHOOLCRAFT'S EXPEDITION TO LAKE ITASCA
Henry R. Schoolcraft; edited by Philip P. Mason

An account of Schoolcraft's expedition to the upper Mississippi region to quell the feud between the Chippewa and the Sioux. xxvi + 390 pp. Illus. Appendix. Michigan State University Press, 1958. $7.50.

SCHOOLCRAFT'S INDIAN LEGENDS
Henry Schoolcraft; edited by Mentor L. Williams

A collection of Indian legends as originally published in Schoolcraft's two volumes of *Algic Researches*. Appendices include Indian tales and legends collected from other Schoolcraft works. 322 pp. Michigan State University Press, 1956. $7.50.

A SCHOOLMASTER WITH THE BLACK-FEET INDIANS
Douglas Gold

A study of the social adaptation of the Blackfeet Indians to American culture since 1914. 287 pp. The Caxton Printers, Ltd., 1964. $5.00.

SEA BEARS
    Fredericka I. Martin
Illus. Chilton Books, 1960. $3.50.

*SEA OF GRASS
    Louise Floethe
Little Billy Panther, Seminole Indian boy,
goes fishing in the Everglades, where he
hopes to catch bass for his grandmother.
As he poles his dugout canoe through the
water paths he sees the fascinating sights
and sounds of the glades. 32 pp. Grades
kindergarten to 3. Illus. Charles Scribner's Sons, 1963. $3.50.

*SEA HUNTERS: *Indians of the Northwest
    Coast*
    Sonia Bleeker; illustrated by Althea
        Karr
A book of facts about the land and sea activities of the Northwest Coast Indians. 160
pp. Grades 4 to 6. Illus. Index. William
Morrow & Co., Inc., 1951. $2.75.

*THE SECRET STORY OF THE PUEBLO
    BONITO
    Mary Elting and Michael Folsom; il-
        lustrated by Kathleen Elgin
The true story of the archaeological dis-
coveries in diggings at Pueblo Bonito, New
Mexico, over a period of fifty years. 48 pp.
Illus. Grades 2 to 5. Harvey House, Inc.,
Publishers, $2.50.

SELECTED PAPERS FROM *THE AMERI-
    CAN ANTHROPOLOGIST,* 1888-1920
    Frederica DeLaguna, Editor
Harper & Row, Publishers, 1960. $8.95.

*THE SEED IS BLOWN
    Alice Wright; illustrated by Joan Berg
A music box and a Shawnee Indian help unite
a family separated on their westward journey after the Revolution. Illus. Grades 4
to 7. Rand McNally and Co., $3.95.

SELECTED WRITINGS OF EDWARD SAPIR
    IN LANGUAGE, CULTURE, AND PER-
    SONALITY
    Edward Sapir; edited by David G. Man-
        delbaum
University of California Press, 1951. $6.50;
text edition, $5.00.

*THE SEMINOLE INDIANS
    Sonia Bleeker; illustrated by Althea
        Karr
A fictional presentation of the past and
present life of the Seminole Indians of

Florida. 160 pp. Ages 8 to 12. William Morrow & Co., Inc., 1954.
$2.75.

*SEMINOLE WARS
    H. Buckmaster
Grades 8 to 12. Macmillan Co., 1965.
$2.50.

*SEMINOLES
    Irene Estep; illustrated by Henry Luhrs
Depicts the way of life of the Indians in the
Florida Everglades. 32 pp. Illus. Reading
level, 4; interest level, 3 to 6. Melmont
Publishers, Inc., 1963. $2.50.

THE SEMINOLES
    Edwin C. McReynolds
397 pp. Illus. Biblio. Index. Maps. University of Oklahoma Press, 1957. $5.75.

THE SEMINOLES OF FLORIDA
    Wyatt Blassingame
A history of the Seminole Indians, their culture, and their way of life in present-day
Florida. 50 pp. Illus. Biblio. Map. Paper. Peninsular Publishing Co. 1963.
$1.50.

SEPASS POEMS
    Eloise Street
A translation of the Songs of *Y-Ail-Mihth,*
the famed creation myth of the Lenape. Illus. Vantage Press, Inc., $2.75.

SEQUOYAH CONSTITUTIONAL CONVEN-
    TION
    Amos D. Maxwell
Illus. Forum Publishing Co., 1953. $2.50.

*SEQUOYAH: *Leader of the Cherokees*
    Alice Lee Marriott; illustrations by
        Bob Riger
The biography of a half-breed Cherokee who
invented the syllabary which enabled thousands of Indians to read and write the Cherokee language. Illus. Grade 5 to 8. Random
House, Inc., 1956. $1.95.

*SEQUOYAH: *Young Cherokee Guide*
    Dorothea Snow; illustrated by Frank
        Giacoia
The life of Sequoyah and his devotion to the
single purpose of teaching his people to
read and write their own language. 200 pp.
Illus. The Bobbs-Merrill Co., $2.25.

THE SERI
 A. L. Kroeber
60 pp. Illus. Southwest Museum, 1931.
$1.50.

SETH EASTMAN: *Pictorial Historian of the Indian*
 John Francis McDermott
270 pp. Illus. Index. Biblio. University of Oklahoma Press, 1961. $10.00.

SEVEN AND NINE YEARS AMONG THE APACHES AND COMANCHES: *An Autobiography*
 Edwin Eastman
Reprint of 1874 edition. 304 pp. Frontier Book Co., 1964. $4.50.

THE SHADOW OF SEQUOYAH: *Social Documents of the Cherokees*
 Jack Frederick and Anna Gritts Kilpatrick, Translators and Editors
A presentation of social documents of the Cherokee Indians. 144 pp. Illus. Biblio. University of Oklahoma, 1965. $4.50.

*THE SHAMAN'S LAST RAID
 Betty Baker; illustrated by Leonard Shortall
The story of a pair of twins' adventures during their Apache greatgrandfather's visit to their town while a television company is filming a motion picture about Indians. 192 pp. Illus. Grades 3 to 7. Harper & Row, Publishers, $2.95.

THE SHOSHONIS: *Sentinels of the Rockies*
 Virginia Cole Trenholm and Maurine Carley
367 pp. Illus. Index. Biblio. Maps. University of Oklahoma Press, 1964. $5.95.

*SHOWDOWN AT LITTLE BIG HORN
 Dee Brown
Illus. G. P. Putnam's Sons, 1964. $3.50.

A SIOUX CHRONICLE
 George E. Hyde
334 pp. Illus. Index. University of Oklahoma Press, 1956. $5.00.

*THE SIOUX INDIANS: *Hunters and Warriors of the Plains*
 Sonia Bleeker; illustrated by Kisa Sasaki
A study of the life of the Sioux Indians. 160 pp. Illus. Ages 8 to 12. William Morrow & Co., 1962. $2.75.

THE SIOUX: *Life and Customs of a Warrior Society*
 Royal B. Hassrick
337 pp. Illus. Appendix. Index. Biblio. Maps. University of Oklahoma Press, 1964. $5.95.

THE SIOUX, 1798-1922
 Alexis Praus
A book interpreting a winter count record that originated with the Hunkpapa band of the Dakotas. These counts consist of pictographs symbolizing an event which marks a particular winter or year. 35 pp. Illus. Cranbrook Institute of Science, 1962. $1.75.

THE SIOUX UPRISING OF 1862
 Kenneth Carley
A pictorial history of the Sioux uprising covering the thirty-eight-day conflict of 1862. 524 pp. Illus. Minnesota Historical Society, 1953. $5.00.

*SISTER BEATRICE GOES WEST
 Catherine Corely Anderson
The story of a nun teaching on a Navajo reservation who has a talent for sports and a way with the most difficult students. Ages 11 to 15. Bruce Publishing Co., 1961. $2.75.

SITES OF THE RESERVE PHASE, PINE LAWN VALLEY, WESTERN NEW MEXICO
 E. Martin and J. Rinaldo
177 pp. Illus. Vol. 38, No. 3, Chicago Museum of Natural History, 1950. $3.00.

SITTING BULL: *Champion of the Sioux, A Biography*
 Stanley Vestal
349 pp. Illus. Index. Biblio. University of Oklahoma Press, 1965. $5.00.

*SITTING BULL: *Dakota Boy*
 Augusta Stevenson; illustrated by Robert Jenney
Jumping Badger felt that living was an adventure, and that each day he learned something new that he would be able to use in later life. 200 pp. Illus. The Bobbs-Merrill Co., Inc., $2.25.

THE SKELETON FROM MESA HOUSE
 Bruno Oetteking
44 pp. Illus. Southwest Museum, 1930. $1.00.

A SKETCH OF NORTHERN SAHAPTIN
GRAMMAR
    Melville Jacobs
Paper. 292 pp. Index of *Morphologic Elements and Compounded Verb Roots*. Tables.
Map. Vol. 4, No. 2, University of Washington Publications in Anthropology, University of Washington Press, 1931. $2.00.

SKETCHES OF A TOUR TO THE LAKES
    Thomas L. McKenney
A sourcebook of early Indian life among the
Chippewa and the Sioux, with a detailed
study of the Treaty of Fond du Lac. Illus.
Ross & Haines, Inc., $8.75.

SKETCHES OF SOME OF THE FIRST SET-
TLERS OF UPPER GEORGIA
    George R. Gilmer
463 pp. Index. Map. Genealogical Publishing Co., 1965. $12.50.

SLAVE WIVES OF NEHALEM
    Claire Warner Churchill
A collection of stories of the North Oregon
Coast Indians with descriptions of their
marriage, death, birth, religion, and pride
of race. 112 pp. Biblio. Binfords and
Mort, 1933. $1.00.

SMOKE UPON THE WINDS
    Willoughby F. Senior
An account of the author's experiences
among the Hopi Indians and of the tribe's
basic philosophy and traditions. Illus.
Sage Books, 1961. $3.50.

SNAKE DANCE OF THE HOPI INDIANS
    Earle R. Forrest
A study of the Snake Dance rituals of the
Hopis. 172 pp. Illus. Westernlore Press,
1961. $5.75.

SNAKE DANCE OF THE MOQUI INDIANS
(HOPI) OF ARIZONA
    John G. Bourke
372 pp. Illus. The Rio Grande Press, Inc.,
$8.00.

THE SNOQUALMIE-DUWAMISH DIALECTS
OF PUGET SOUND COAST SALISH: *An
Outline of Phonemics and Morphology*
    Colin Ellidge Tweddell; edited by Mel-
    ville Jacobs
A formal analysis of the Snoqualmie-Du-
wamish dialect of the Puget Sound Coast.
78 pp. Paper. Volume 12, University of
Washington Publications in Anthropology,
University of Washington Press, 1950.
$2.00.

SO YOU WANT TO BUY A NAVAJO RUG?
    Edward S. Merry
A brief explanation of the factors to be considered when buying a Navajo rug, with a
glossary of relevant terms. Contains instructions for cleaning a Navajo rug. 16
pp. Illus. Biblio. Map. Paper. Inter-
Tribal Ceremonial Association, 1965. 50¢.

THE SOBAIPURI INDIANS OF THE UPPER
SAN PEDRO RIVER VALLEY, SOUTH-
EASTERN ARIZONA
    Charles C. DiPeso
The Amerind Foundation, 1953. $7.50.

SOCIAL AND ECONOMIC CHANGE AMONG
THE NORTHERN OJIBWA
    R. W. Dunning
Illus. University of Toronto Press, 1959.
$5.50.

SOCIAL ANTHROPOLOGY OF NORTH
AMERICAN INDIAN TRIBES
    Fred Eggan, Editor
An analysis of the social organization and
kinship systems of the North American In-
dian tribes. xv + 574 pp. University of
Chicago Press, 1955. $8.00.

SOCIAL ANTHROPOLOGY OF THE WEST-
ERN PUEBLOS
    Fred Eggan
A study of the Pueblo Indians of New Mexico and Arizona. xviii + 373 pp. University
of Chicago Press, 1950. $6.00.

THE SOCIAL CULTURE OF THE NUNIVAK
ESKIMO
    Margaret Lantis
This book is the product of one year's research (1939-40) on the island of Nunivak,
located in the Bering Sea off the coast of
Alaska, where the author observed the daily
routine of the Eskimos and learned about
their traditions and customs handed down
from previous generations. 171 pp. 84
figs. 2 maps. Paper. American Philosophical Society, 1940. $2.50.

SOCIAL ORGANIZATION OF THE CENT-
TRAL ALGONKIAN INDIANS
    Charles Callender
140 pp. Illus. Biblio. Appendix. Maps.
Milwaukee Public Museum, 1962. $4.00.

THE SOCIAL ORGANIZATION OF THE
WESTERN APACHE
    Grenville Goodwin
721 pp. Brown Book Co., 1942. $6.00.

SOCIO-ECONOMIC IMPACT OF THE LEAS-
ING, SALE, AND IMPROVEMENT OF IN-
DIAN LAND IN CALIFORNIA
    Robert E. Ahrens
26 pp. Bureau of Business and Economic
Research, School of Business Administra-
tion, San Diego State College, 1965.

SOLDIER AND BRAVE
    National Park Service
A narrative of relations in the 19th century
between the white men and the Indians and
a complete listing of historical sites. Illus. Maps. Harper & Row, Publishers,
$6.95.

SOME PLANTS USED BY THE YUKI INDI-
ANS OF ROUND VALLEY, NORTHERN
CALIFORNIA
    L. S. Curtin
Southwest Museum, 25¢.

*SOMETHING FOR THE MEDICINE MAN
    Flora Mae Hood; illustrated by Robert
    Dranko
A present-day Cherokee girl must decide
what her contribution will be when she and
her classmates are asked to bring a gift
for an ailing medicine man. 48 pp. Illus.
Reading level, 3; interest level, 2 to 6.
Melmont Publishers, Inc., 1962. $2.50.

SONGS AND STORIES OF THE AMERICAN
INDIANS
    Beatrice Krone and others
Illus. Paper. Neil A. Kjos Music Co.,
Publisher, 1949. $1.00.

SONGS OF THE NOOTKA INDIANS OF
WESTERN VANCOUVER ISLAND
    Helen H. Roberts and Morris Swadesh
A study of ninety-five songs collected on
phonograph records in 1910 during a reconnaissance trip among Canadian Indians for
the Geological Survey of Canada, intended
to be not only a presentation of song types
in primitive music, but an exposition of
methods of study. The songs are tran-
scribed into notation and analyzed for me-
lodic form and content. Included is a brief
section on the linguistics and poetry of the
texts, as well as ethnological data on the
songs. 129 pp. The American Philosophical Society, 1955. $2.00.

SONGS OF THE YOKUTS AND PAIUTES
    Alfred Pietroforte
A book of Yokut and Paiute songs, with
notes on their meanings, and methods for

use in schools to teach understanding of
California Indian culture. 64 pp. Naturegraph Publishers, 1965. $1.50.

SONS OF THE SHAKING EARTH
    Eric Wolf
303 pp. Illus. University of Chicago Press,
1959. Paper, $1.50; cloth, $5.00.

SOUTHEASTERN INDIANS, LIFE PORT-
RAITS
    Emma Lila Fundaburk and Mary Doug-
    las Foreman, Editors
Illus. Emma Lila Fundaburk, $7.50.

THE SOUTHERN CHEYENNES
    Donald J. Berthrong
A study of the Cheyennes' life on the Plains,
including the beginning of life on the reservation and the role of the Friends (Quakers)
under the presidency of Ulysses S. Grant
in 1869. 446 pp. Illus. Biblio. Index.
Maps. University of Oklahoma Press, 1963.
$5.95.

THE SOUTHERN FRONTIER - 1670-1732
    Verner W. Crane
370 pp. Paper. University of Michigan
Press, 1956. $2.25.

THE SOUTHERN INDIANS: *The Story of
the Civilized Tribes Before Removal*
    R. S. Cotterill
255 pp. Illus. Index. Biblio. Maps. University of Oklahoma Press, 1963. $4.95.

SOUTHERN PAIUTE ETHNOLOGY
    Isabel T. Kelly
An in-depth study of the Karbab band of the
Ute-Chemehuevi Indians based on material
gathered in the field in 1932. 214 pp. Illus. Biblio. University of Utah Press,
1932. $2.85.

SOUTHWEST INDIAN PICTOGRAPHS AND
PETROGLYPHS
    Polly Schaafsma
A description of the methods by which pictographs and petroglyphs are made and recorded, including an explanation of their
meaning. Paper. 12 pp. Illus. Museum
of New Mexico Press, 1965. 50¢.

THE SOUTHWEST: *Old and New*
    W. Eugene Hollon
A social, political and cultural history of
the Southwest, from the age of the Cliff
Dwellers to the present day. 486 pp. Il-
lus. Index. Biblio. Maps. Alfred A.
Knopf, Inc., $7.50.

SOUTHWESTERN ARCHAEOLOGY
John C. McGregor
511 pp. Illus. University of Illinois Press, 1965. $9.50.

SOUTHWESTERN INDIAN ARTS AND CRAFTS
Tom Bahti
Covers all phases of Indian artistry, with examples of some of their finest work. 32 pp. Illus. Biblio. Paper. KC Publications, 1964. $1.00.

SOUTHWESTERN LORE
James F. Dobie
As below. Folklore Associates, 1965. $5.50.

SOUTHWESTERN LORE
James F. Dobie
A sampling of the legends and lore of four Southwestern groups -- Cowboys, Mexicans, Negroes and Indians. 198 pp. Southern Methodist University Press, 1931. $5.00.

SPANISH EXPLORERS IN THE SOUTHERN U. S., 1528-1543
Edited by Frederick W. Hodge and T. H. Lewis
The Narrative of Alvar Nunez Cabeca de Vaca; The Narrative of the Expedition of Hernando de Soto, by the Gentlemen of Elvas; The Narrative of the Expedition of Coronado, by Pedro de Castaneda. 413 pp. Barnes and Noble, Inc., 1959. $5.75.

SPANISH SETTLEMENTS WITHIN THE PRESENT LIMITS OF THE UNITED STATES
Woodbury Lowery
Illus. Russell and Russell, Inc. Vol. 1, 1513-1561; Vol. 2, Florida, 1562-1574. Two-volume set, $15.00.

SPANISH STRUGGLE FOR JUSTICE IN THE CONQUEST OF AMERICA
Lewis Hanke
University of Pennsylvania Press, 1959. $5.00.

SPARKMAN GRAMMAR OF LUISENO
Alfred L. Kroeber and George W. Grace
Paper. University of California Press, 1960. $4.00.

SPIN A SILVER DOLLAR
Alberta Hannum; illustrated by Beatien Yazz

A personal narrative about an Indian trading post and the talented Navajo boy discovered there. 190 pp. Illus. The Viking Press, Inc., 1945. $5.00.

*SPIRIT ROCKS AND SILVER MAGIC
Phyllis A. Manning; illustrated by Andy Tsinajinie
This narrative portrays the daily problems and beliefs of a Navajo family group. 202 pp. Grades 10 to 12. Illus. The Caxton Printers, Ltd., 1962. $5.00.

THE SPIRITUAL LEGACY OF THE AMERICAN INDIAN
Joseph Epes Brown
A discussion of the necessity for the understanding and preservation of the traditions and religious values of the American Indian. Paper. 32 pp. Illus. Pendle Hill Publications, 1964. 45¢.

THE SPIRO MOUND COLLECTION
E. K. Burnett
A catalog of specimens from Spiro Mound, Leflore County, Oklahoma, and a history of the site. 68 pp. Illus. Index. Museum of the American Indian, Heye Foundation, $5.00.

*SPOTTED HORSE
Glenn Balch; illustrated by Lorence F. Bjorklund
A tale of a young boy who leaves his tribe for the love of a horse. 176 pp. Illus. Grades 4 to 8. Thomas Y. Crowell Co., 1961. $3.50.

SPOTTED TAIL'S FOLK: *A History of the Brule Sioux*
George E. Hyde
329 pp. Illus. Index. Biblio. Maps. University of Oklahoma Press, 1961. $5.00.

*SQUANTO: *Friend of the White Men*
Clyde R. Bulla; illustrated by Peter Burchard
The history of a Patuxet Indian destined to learn the white man's ways by living with them. 120 pp. Illus. Grades 2 to 5. Thomas Y. Crowell Co., 1954. $3.50.

*SQUANTO: *Indian Adventurer*
Stewart and Polly Anne Graff
The story of Squanto and of the aid he rendered to the first white settlers in America. 80 pp. Garrard Publishing Co., 1965. $1.98.

*SQUANTO: *Young Indian Hunter*
    Augusta Stevenson; illustrated by Nathan Goldstein
The early years of Squanto, an Indian who taught the Pilgrims how to cope with the rigors of New England life. 200 pp. Illus. Grades 3 to 7. The Bobbs-Merrill Co., Inc., 1962. $2.25.

*SQUAW DOG
    Patricia Beatty; illustrated by Franz Altschuler
The story of a Northwest Indian boy and his faithful dog. 192 pp. Illus. Ages 8 to 12. William Morrow & Co., Inc., 1965. $3.25.

STAR LORE AMONG THE NAVAJOS
    Berard Haile
44 pp. Illus. Museum of the Navajo Ceremonial Art, $6.00.

*STAR: *The Story of an Indian Pony*
    Forrestine Hooker
Illus. Grades 1 to 4. Doubleday & Co., Inc., 1964. $3.25.

STATES' RIGHTS AND INDIAN REMOVAL: *The Cherokee Nation vs. the State of Georgia*
    Allen Guttman
xi + 94 pp. Biblio. Map. Paper. D. C. Heath and Co., 1965. $1.12.

STATUS TERMINOLOGY AND SOCIAL STRUCTURE OF THE NORTH AMERICAN INDIANS
    Munro S. Edmonson
An analysis of ten North American Indian (Eskimo, Chippewa, Shoshone, Kwakiutl, Yokut, Zuni, Sioux, Algonquin, Choctaw) societies. 92 pp. Biblio. Appendix. Published for the American Ethnological Society by the University of Washington Press, 1958. $3.00.

STONE AGE ON THE COLUMBIA RIVER
    Emory Strong
An account of prehistoric Indian culture along the Columbia River. 256 pp. Illus. Maps. Binfords and Mort, 1960. $4.50.

*STONE AGE PEOPLES TODAY
    Gordon C. Baldwin
A book describing the race, language and culture of the eleven Stone Age tribes of today. 183 pp. Illus. Ages 10 and up. W. W. Norton & Co., Inc., 1964. $3.50.

STONE ARTIFACTS OF THE NORTHWESTERN PLAINS
    Louis G. Steege and Warren W. Welch
A book of photographs and sketches of prehistoric artifacts to exact proportion and shape, and approximate dating. 160 pp. Northwestern Plains Publisher, $4.10.

*STONES, BONES AND ARROWHEADS
    Terry Shannon; illustrated by Charles Payzant
Illus. Grades 4 to 8. Albert Whitman & Co., $3.00.

*STORIES CALIFORNIA INDIANS TOLD
    Anne B. Fisher; illustrated by Ruth Robbins
A collection of campfire stories told by California Indians. 110 pp. Illus. Ages 8 to 12. Parnassus Press, 1957. $3.25.

*THE STORY CATCHER
    Mari Sandoz; illustrated by E. J. McCorkell
A young Sioux Indian endures hardship and sorrow in his effort to record the story of his people. The Westminster Press, 1963. $3.25.

*THE STORY OF ARCHAEOLOGY IN THE AMERICAS
    Mary Elting and Franklin Folsom; illustrated by Kathleen Elgin
Stories of recent archaeological discoveries in North and South America and how youthful "archaeologists" may participate in digs near their homes. 160 pp. Illus. Index. Biblio. Glossary. Maps. Ages 9 and up; grades 4 to 7. Harvey House, Inc., Publishers, 1960. $3.50.

STORY OF INYO
    W. A. Chalfant
A history of the Paiutes and their neighbors and of the exploration of Death Valley in 1849. vii + 430 pp. Pinon Book Store, 1964. $5.95.

THE STORY OF NAVAHO WEAVING
    Kate Peck Kent
A brief history of the ancient craft of weaving, tracing the development of the most important types of textiles. 47 pp. Illus. The Heard Museum of Anthropology and Primitive Art, $1.75.

THE STORY OF PUEBLO POTTERY
    H. M. Wormington and A. Neal
64 pp. Illus. Denver Museum of Natural History, 1965. $1.00.

THE STORY OF THE AMERICAN INDIAN
Paul Radin
A history of the Indians of North and South America. 410 pp. Illus. Liveright Publishing Corp., 1957. $4.95.

THE STORY OF THE LITTLE BIG HORN
Colonel W. A. Graham
An account of the battle of the Little Big Horn, Custer's last fight. Illus. The Stackpole Co., $5.00.

*THE STORY OF THE SOUTHWEST
May McNeer; lithographs by Cornelius DeWitt
The history of the people of the Southwest. Illus. Grades 3 to 7. Harper & Row, Publishers, 1948. $3.50.

*THE STORY OF THE TOTEM POLE
Ruth Brindze; illustrated by Yeffe Kimball
The story of the totem pole's origin, its uses, and how to read its strange and colorful decorations. 64 pp. Grades 4 to 7. Illus. The Vanguard Press, Inc., $3.95.

THE STORY TELLING STONE: *Myths and Tales of the American Indian*
Edited and with an Introduction by Susan Feldman
A collection of fifty-two myths and tales handed down by American Indian tribes. Introduction by the author explains the mythic bases for these tales, which are divided into three sections: *In the Days of Creation; Trickster; Tales of Heroes, Supernatural Journeys, and Other Folktales*. 271 pp. Biblio. Paper. Dell Publishing Co., Inc., 1965. 60¢.

STRANGE EMPIRE: *A Narrative of the Northwest*
Joseph Kinsey Howard; Introduction by Bernard DeVoto
The tragic destiny of a half-breed group of American primitives, the Metis. 608 pp. Illus. William Morrow & Co., Inc., 1952. $6.95.

STRANGE JOURNEY
Louise Lone Dog
The autobiography of a psychic Mohawk-Delaware woman. 64 pp. Illus. Naturegraph Co., 1964. Paper, $1.00; cloth, $3.00.

A STRATIFIED PREHISTORIC SITE AT BREWERTON, N. Y.
William A. Ritchie
A description of a multi-component site excavated in 1943 and 1945 on the property of Harry and Frank Wickham in Oswego County, N. Y. The stratigraphic sequence of Point Peninsula and later Owasco cultures is illustrated with both text and photographs. 53 pp. 14 pls. 6 figs. 7 tables. Biblio. Research Records of the Rochester Museum of Arts and Sciences No. 8, 1946. $1.50. Available from the Rochester Museum of Arts and Sciences.

STRATIGRAPHY AND ARCHAEOLOGY OF VENTANA CAVE, ARIZONA
Emil Haury
Illus. University of New Mexico Press, 1950. $15.00.

STRATIGRAPHY AND ARCHAEOLOGY OF VENTANA CAVE, ARIZONA
Emil Haury
Illus. Paper. University of Arizona Press, 1947. $1.25.

THE STRUCTURE OF A MORAL CODE: *A Philosophical Analysis of Ethical Discourse Applied to Ethics of the Navaho Indians*
John Ladd; Foreword by Clyde Kluckhohn
A philosophical analysis of the nature and structure of a moral code, based on the ethics of the Navaho Indians, and related to the codes of other societies. Harvard University Press, 1957. $9.00.

THE STRUGGLE FOR SURVIVAL, *Indian Cultures and the Protestant Ethic in British Columbia*
F. E. LaViolette
A study of the cultural adjustment of the coastal Indian of British Columbia to white society and the development of leadership among the Indians in response to the changes they have experienced in Canada. xii + 202 pp. University of Toronto Press, 1961. $5.50.

STUDIES AT NAVAJO PERIOD SITES IN THE NAVAJO RESERVOIR DISTRICT
James J. Hester and Joel Shiner
A study of archaeology of selected hogan, pueblito and rock shelter sites of 1550 to 1775 and the initial Navajo-Pueblo contact. 79 pp. Illus. Biblio. 1964 Papers in Anthropology No. 9, Museum of New Mexico Press, $2.00.

STUDIES OF CALIFORNIA INDIANS
C. Hart Merriam
A collection of twenty-one articles based on material gathered on field trips from 1910 to 1942. 252 pp. Illus. University of California Press, $5.00.

SUN CHIEF: *The Autobiography of a Hopi Indian*
Leo W. Simmons, Editor; Foreword by Robert V. Hine
The autobiography of Don C. Talayesva of Oraibi, who was raised as a Hopi until he was ten years old, at which time he came to live in and as part of the white world, eventually renouncing Christianity and returning to his people. xviii + 460 pp. Illus. Index. Appendix. Tables. Graphs. Published for the Institute of Human Relations by Yale University Press, 1963. Paper, $2.95; cloth, $8.50.

SUN CIRCLES AND HUMAN HANDS: *The Southeastern Indians, Art and Industries*
Emma Fundaburk and Mary Foreman, Editors
A pictorial history of four major southeastern Indian culture periods told through artifacts, early paintings, and description. 232 pp. Illus. Biblio. Emma Lila Fundaburk, $7.50.

SUN FATHER'S WAY: *The Kiva Murals of Kuana*
Bertha P. Dutton
Illus. University of New Mexico Press, $15.00.

SUN IN THE SKY
Walter Collins O'Kane
267 pp. Illus. Index. Appendix. Maps. University of Oklahoma Press, 1958. $5.50.

SUSQUEHANNOCK MISCELLANY
John Witthoft and W. Fred Kinsey
A collection of essays examining the progress of archaeology in the Northeast, the role of the Susquehannocks, their ancestry and culture, and an analysis of pottery types. 167 pp. Pennsylvania Historical and Museum Commission, 1959. $1.50.

*SWAMP CHIEF
Zachary Ball
Joe Panther is now a first mate and in line to become the leader of his tribe, but he is caught between conflicting loyalties. 212 pp. Holiday House, Inc., 1952. $3.50.

SWEAT OF THE SUN AND TEARS OF THE MOON: *Gold and Silver in Pre-Columbian Art*
Andre Emmerich
Gives an overall view of the use of precious metals in pre-Columbian times. Illus. Map. University of Washington Press, 1965. $15.00.

T

TABLE ROCK PUEBLO, ARIZONA
Paul S. Martin and John B. Rinaldo
172 pp. Illus. Maps. Vol. 51, No. 2. Chicago Natural History Museum, 1960. $5.50.

TAKELMA TEXTS
Edward Sapir
Paper. University Museum Press, 1909. $1.75.

*TALE OF AN ALASKA WHALE
Alva W. Blackerby
An Indian legend from Alaska of a cedar killer whale and his tilt with the Thlinget braves; includes material on the customs of the Alaskan Indians. 32 pp. Grades 5 to 6. Binfords and Mort, $1.50.

TALES OF NANABOZHO
Dorothy N. Reid
A collection of twenty-one Indian legends told by the Ojibwa tribe of Canada. The tales center around Nanabozho, born of a human mother, whose father is the west wind. 128 pp. Grades 3 to 7. Henry Z. Walck, 1963. $3.50.

TALES OF THE CHEYENNES
Grace Penney
Grades 5 to 8. Illus. Houghton Mifflin Co., 1953. $3.00.

*THE TALKING LEAF
Weyman Jones; illustrated by E. Harper Johnson
Atsee's dream is to become a scout like his father, but he decides to put aside his dream and to take up reading and writing for the future of the Cherokee nation. 96 pp. Grades 8 to 12. Illus. The Dial Press, Inc., 1965. $3.25.

*TALKING TOTEM POLE
   Lurline Mayol
A book of legends and stories of the North
Pacific Indians. Includes explanations of
the meanings of the various totems on the
totem pole. 140 pp. Ages 9 and up. Illus.
Binfords and Mort, 1963. $2.50.

*TALL AS GREAT STANDING ROCK
   T. D. Allen
"The story of an Indian boy standing at the
base of his own reed of emergence from defiance to creative acceptance of a new world
where Navajo and white are one." 160 pp.
Ages 7 to 10. The Westminster Press, 1963.
$3.25.

TAOS ADOBES
   Jean Lee Booth and William R. Sims, Jr.
A book of ground plans, photographs and
numerous architectural details from twelve
old adobe buildings in the Taos area, including the merging of Spanish colonial and
Anglo architectural traditions in New Mexico. 80 pp. Illus. Museum of New Mexico
Press, 1964. $4.95.

TAOS PUEBLO
   Phillip Reno; Introduction by John Col-
      lier
Contains information on Taos Pueblo his-
tory, customs and rights. 36 pp. Illus.
Paper. Sage Books, 1963. $1.00.

TAPESTRIES IN SAND
   David Villasenor
A book of interpretations of meanings of
several sandpaintings and the philosophy
that underlies them. 112 pp. Illus. Paper. Naturegraph Co., 1963. Paper, $2.95;
cloth, $4.50.

TECUMSEH: *Destiny's Warrior*
   David C. Cooke
Grades 8 to 12. Julian Messner, 1959.
$3.25.

*TECUMSEH: *Shawnee Boy*
   Augusta Stevenson
The biography of Tecumseh, an adopted son
of Chief Black Fish of the Shawnee Indians.
200 pp. Illustrated by the author. Grades
3 to 6. The Bobbs-Merrill Co., Inc., 1955.
$2.25.

THE TEN GRANDMOTHERS
   Alice Marriott
306 pp. Biblio. Illus. Map. University
of Oklahoma Press, 1963. $5.00.

TEPEE IN HIS FRONT YARD
   Clifford Merrill Drury
The biography of H. T. Cowley, describing
his role in the transformation of the wilderness of Spokane, Washington, into a great
city. 215 pp. Illus. Binfords and Mort,
1949. $3.50.

*TEPEE STORIES
   Edward Dolch
Tales depicting the rugged life of the Plains
Indians in their struggle for existence. 176
pp. Grades 1 to 6. Garrard Publishing Co.,
1959. $2.25.

TERRITORY OF FLORIDA
   John Lee Williams; edited by Herbert
      J. Doherty, Jr.
A description of territorial Florida, includ-
ing climate, geography, history, animal
and plant life, and Indian lore. 319 pp.
University of Florida Press, 1962. $7.50.

TEXTILES
   Kate Peck Kent
(Montezuma Castle Archaeology, Part 2).
Illus. Southwestern Monuments Associa-
tion, 1955. $2.00.

TEXTS OF THE NAVAJO CREATION
   CHANTS
      Harry Hoijer, Translator
A book of songs, with notes and a musical
analysis. 36 pp. Illus. Museum of the
Navajo Ceremonial Art, $2.25.

TE-YOK-KEEN (HEAR YE)
Contributed articles, poems, legends, history by Indians of the Yakima, Nez Perce,
Umatilla, Klamath, and Quapaw tribes. Illus. Paper. Indian Festival of Art, $1.25.

*THERE REALLY WAS A HIAWATHA
   Alida Sims Malkus; illustrated by Jon
      Nielson
The life of the 16th-century American Indian
whose ideals influenced the United States
Constitution and earned him semi-deifica-
tion among his Indian brothers. Grades 5
to 8. Grosset and Dunlap, 1963. $3.50.

THESE ARE THE PEOPLE
   Alice Marriott
A tourist's guide, with backgrounds, cul-
ture, tips for buying crafts, and a schedule
of Indian events. 82 pp. Illus. Biblio.
School of American Research, $1.95.

THESE WERE THE SIOUX
Mari Sandoz
The philosophy and practical wisdom of the Sioux Indians, including their beliefs and customs. 108 pp. Illus. Hastings House, Publishers, Inc., 1961. $3.50.

THEY SANG FOR HORSES
LaVerne Harrell Clark; illustrated by Ted de Grazia
An examination of the impact of the horse upon traditional forms of Navajo and Apache folklore during more than three centuries of influence and the horse's symbolic significance in ceremonies, song, prayer and custom. 240 pp. Illus. University of Arizona Press, $12.00.

THIRTY THOUSAND MILES WITH JOHN HECKEWELDER
Paul A. W. Wallace, Editor
Journals of an 18th-century American traveler. 448 pp. Illus. Index. Glossaries. Maps. University of Pittsburgh Press, $7.50.

THIRTY YEARS OF ARMY LIFE ON THE BORDER
Randolph B. Marcey; Introduction by Edward S. Wallace
A description of the Indian wars in the West before the Civil War and of the hardships endured by American soldiers. 402 pp. J. B. Lippincott Co., 1963. Paper, $1.75; cloth, $5.95.

*THIS FOR THAT
Ann Nolan Clark; illustrated by Don Freeman
A little Indian boy must learn that when he is sent on an errand those who send him want what is asked for rather than something in its place. 62 pp. Ages 5 to 8. Illus. Golden Gate Junior Books, 1965. $3.50.

THIS IS A HOPI KACHINA
Barton Wright and Evelyn Roat
An explanation of kachinas as spirits, kachina dances, kachina dolls and an impersonation of kachinas. 28 pp. Photos. Paper. Northern Arizona Society of Art and Science, $1.00.

THIS IS THE INDIAN AMERICAN
Louisa Rossiter Shotwell
A discussion of American Indian culture, contributions to the American way of life, and the missionary work in all fields done for and by the Indian people. 33 pp. Illus. Paper. Friendship Press, 1955. 60¢.

THREE YEARS AMONG THE COMANCHES: *The Narrative of Nelson Lee, the Texas Ranger*
Nelson Lee; Introduction by Walter Prescott Webb
179 pp. Illus. University of Oklahoma Press, 1957. $2.00.

THREE YEARS AMONG THE INDIANS AND MEXICANS
Thomas James
The story of a pioneer New Mexican trading among the Spaniards and Comanches. Illus. Paper. J. B. Lippincott Co., 1962. $1.25.

THREE YEARS AMONG THE INDIANS AND THE MEXICANS IN 1821-1824
Thomas James
As above. 316 pp. Illus. The Rio Grande Press, Inc., $7.50.

THUNDER IN THE MOUNTAINS
Hilda M. Hooke
A collection of Canadian legends. Index. Biblio. Illus. Oxford University Press, 1947. $3.00.

TIKTA'LIKTAK: *An Eskimo Legend*
James Houston
James Houston, a Canadian artist who lived and worked with the Eskimos for twelve years, retells and illustrates the legend of a young Eskimo hunter who was carried to sea one day on a drifting ice floe. Harcourt, Brace & World, Inc., $2.95.

*TIME OF THE TOMAHAWK
Robert E. Alter
Illus. G. P. Putnam's Sons, 1964. $3.50.

THE TLINGIT INDIANS: *Results of a Trip to the Northwest Coast of America and the Bering Straits*
Aurel Krause; translated by Erna Gunther
A report of the early culture of the Tlingit Indians of Southeastern Alaska. 320 pp. Illus. University of Washington Press, 1956. $4.50.

*TOHI - A CHUMASH INDIAN BOY
Elsa Falk
Tohi learns a man's work by making a sandstone bowl, fashioning beads from shells, mending a hole in a thatched hut, and helping his father build a canoe. 36 pp. Illus. Reading level, 3; interest level, 2 to 5. Melmont Publishers, Inc., 1959. $2.50.

*THE TOMAHAWK FAMILY
  Natalie Savage Carlson; illustrated by
  Stephen Cook
In this book Alice and Frank Tomahawk discover what it is like to lead both the traditional Indian life and the modern American one. Illus. Ages 7 to 11. Harper & Row, Publishers, 1960. $2.75.

*TOMAHAWK TRAIL
  John Brick
Grades 7 to 10. Duell, Sloan and Pearce, 1962. $3.50.

*THE TOTEM CASTS A SHADOW
  Margaret E. Bell
In this book both brother and sister are torn between their respect for the Haida Indians of Alaska and their father's prejudice against them, when the brother marries an Indian girl. 224 pp. Grades 7 to 8. William Morrow & Co., Inc., 1949. $3.50.

THE TOTEM POLE INDIANS
  Joseph H. Wherry
A description of the seven Indian nations of the Pacific Northwest -- their myths, their daily lives, potlatches and totem poles. 152 pp. Illus. Index. Appendix. Map. Funk and Wagnalls, $6.50.

A TOUR ON THE PRAIRIES
  Washington Irving; edited with an introductory essay by John Francis McDermott
xxxii + 214 pp. Map. University of Oklahoma Press, $2.00.

*TOYANUKI'S RABBIT
  Lois Harvey
A story of a Paiute boy in the mountain valleys of the West, growing to manhood and killing his first rabbit. 64 pp. Illus. Reading level, 3; interest level, 2 to 4. Melmont Publishers, Inc., 1964. $2.50.

TRADE TOMAHAWKS
  Cyril B. Courville
Southwest Museum, 25¢.

TRADERS TO THE NAVAJOS
  Frances Gillmore and L. W. Wetherill
The story of John Wetherill, who discovered the ruins of Mesa Verde, Betatakin, Keet Seel, and others. 265 pp. Biblio. Paper. University of New Mexico Press, $2.00.

TRADITIONS OF THE ARAPAHO
  G. A. Dorsey and A. L. Kroeber
476 pp. Fieldiana: Anthropology Vol. v, 1903, Chicago Natural History Museum, $5.00.

TRADITIONS OF THE CROWS
  S. C. Simms
44 pp. Fieldiana: Anthropology Vol. ii, No. 6, Chicago Natural History Museum, 1903. 50¢.

TRADITIONS OF THE HOPI
  H. R. Voth
320 pp. Fieldiana: Anthropology, Vol. viii, Chicago Natural History Museum, 1905. $3.50.

TRADITIONS OF THE OSAGE
  G. A. Dorsey
60 pp. Fieldiana: Anthropology Vol. vii, No. 1, Chicago Natural History Museum, 1904. $1.00.

*THE TRAIL OF THE SPANISH HORSE
  James W. Schultz
A description of the life of the Western Indians. Illus. Ages 10 and up. Houghton Mifflin Co., 1960. $2.75.

*TRAIL TO OKLAHOMA
  Jim Booker
Grades 4 to 7. Broadman Press, 1959. $2.95.

TRAVELS IN THE INTERIOR OF NORTH AMERICA, 1751-1762
  Jean B. Bossu; translated and edited by Seymour Feller
xviii + 342 pp. Illus. Map. Index. University of Oklahoma Press, 1962. $4.50.

TRAVELS OF WILLIAM BARTRAM
  Mark Van Doren, Editor
This book contains descriptions of the Cherokee, Creek and Seminole Indians in Florida, Georgia and the Carolinas, from 1773 to 1778. 414 pp. Illus. Maps. Paper. Dover Publications, Inc., 1947. $2.00.

TRAVELS THROUGH THE INTERIOR PARTS OF NORTH AMERICA
  Jonathan Carver
Ross & Haines, Inc., $8.75.

TREASURE OF THE SANGRE DE CRISTOS:
Tales and Traditions of the Spanish Southwest
> Arthur L. Campa; paintings by Joe Beeler

xvi + 223 pp. Illus. Index. Biblio. Map. University of Oklahoma Press, 1963. $5.95.

TREASURES OF ANCIENT AMERICA
> Samuel K. Lothrop

Illus. Skira International Corp., 1964. $29.50.

*TREASURY OF AMERICAN INDIAN TALES
> Theodore Ressler

Forty-four short stories pertaining to twenty-seven different Indian tribes, describing their customs and character. 310 pp. Grades 3 to 6. The Association Press, 1957. $3.95.

TREASURY OF MEMORY-MAKING CAMP-FIRES
> Allan A. Macfarlan

A collection of campfire games, ceremonies, stories and stunts for scouts or Indian lore groups. 285 pp. Illus. Index. The Association Press, $9.95.

THE TREATY OF MEDICINE LODGE
> Douglas C. Jones

The story of the last great council of hostile Indians and government officials, held at Medicine Lodge, Kansas, in the fall of 1867, involving all the hostile tribes south of the Platte River. 304 pp. Illus. Biblio. Index. University of Oklahoma Press, 1966. $5.95.

*TREE IN THE TRAIL
> Holling Clancy Holling

A history of the Santa Fe Trail told through the life of a cottonwood tree. Illus. Grades 4 to 6. Houghton Mifflin Co., 1942. $4.50.

TREE RING DATES AND SOUTHWESTERN POTTERY
> David A. Breternitz

Paper. University of Arizona Press, 1965. $5.00.

TRIBES THAT SLUMBER: *Indians of the Tennessee Region*
> Thomas M. N. Lewis and Madeline Kneberg

A history of the Indians of the Tennessee region by a University of Tennessee archaeologist, based on twenty-five years of research in the area. 208 pp. Illus. University of Tennessee Press, 1958. Paper, $3.25; cloth, $4.75.

TROOPERS WITH CUSTER
> E. A. Brininstool

A report on disputed questions, such as: Was there a Custer survivor?; Were Custer's remains ever positively identified? The famous letter from Major Brisbin to Colonel Godfrey is included. 343 pp. The Stackpole Co., 1952. $5.00.

TROPHIES OF GRACE
> H. C. Nitz

Contains ten stories depicting the evangelization of the Apache Indians. 65 pp. Paper. Northwestern Publishing House, 1962. 40¢.

*THE TRUE BOOK OF INDIANS
> Teri Martini; illustrated by Charles Heston

Illus. Reading level, 1 to 2; interest level, kindergarten to 4. Children's Press, Inc., 1954. $2.00.

*TRUE BOOK OF LITTLE ESKIMOS
> Donalda Copeland; illustrated by Mary Gehr

Grades kindergarten to 3. Children's Press, Inc., 1953. $2.50.

TRUE INDIAN STORIES
> Jacob P. Dunn

Stories of the Miamis and Potawatomis. 320 pp. Illus. Glossary. Lawrence W. Shultz, 1908. $4.00.

THE TRUTH ABOUT GERONIMO
> Britton Davis; Foreword by Robert M. Utley; edited by Milo M. Quaife

A historical account of the Geronimo campaign of 1885 to 1886, including a description of Indians as beings. xvii + 253 pp. Illus. Index. Maps. Yale University Press, 1963. Paper, $1.95; cloth, $7.50.

TRUTHFUL HATCHET
> M. Sullivan and R. Shanks

The true account of William Smalley, who was abducted as a child by the Iroquois, grew up among them, and was educated as a chief's son. As an adult he was sent as an emissary to George Washington to make peace between white man and Indian. 176 pp. The Naylor Co., 1966. $4.95.

TULE SPRINGS, NEVADA: *With Other Evidences of Pleistocene Man in North America*
> M. R. Harrington and R. D. Simpson

146 pp. Illus. Maps. Southwest Museum, $3.75.

TURKEY FOOT RIDGE SITE, A MOGOLLON VILLAGE, PINE LAWN VALLEY, WESTERN NEW MEXICO
    Paul S. Martin and John B. Rinaldo
162 pp. Illus. Vol. 38, No. 2, Chicago Natural History Museum, $2.75.

THE TWANA, CHEMAKUM AND KLALLAM INDIANS OF WASHINGTON TERRITORY, 1887
    Myron Eells
Facsimile of the 1887 edition. 76 pp. Paper. Shorey Publications, 1965. $3.00.

TWENTY TEPEE TALES
    M. Marvin Lotz and Douglas Monohan
The Association Press, 75¢.

TWO FREMONT SITES AND THEIR POSITION IN SOUTHWESTERN PREHISTORY
    Dee C. Taylor
This paper discusses in detail the archaeological findings of two Fremont sites, then relates these findings to Anasazi and Puebloid traits, theorizing on their common ancestry, a Great Basin ancient desert culture. 196 pp. Illus. University of Utah Press, 1957. $3.50.

TWO PREHISTORIC VILLAGE SITES AT BREWERTON, NEW YORK
    William A. Ritchie
The author describes the excavations of the Robinson and Oberlander I sites in Onondago and Oswego Counties. 107 pp. 32 pls. Table. 2 maps. Biblio. Research Records of the Rochester Museum of Arts and Sciences No. 5, Anthropology 5, 1940. $1.50. Available from the Rochester Museum of Arts and Sciences.

TWO PUEBLO RUINS IN WEST CENTRAL ARIZONA
    Edward H. Spicer and Louis H. Caywood
Paper. University of Arizona Press, 1936. 50¢.

*TYEE'S TOTEM POLE
    Terry Shannon; illustrated by Charles Payzant
When Tyee catches his first salmon he earns the right to carve his first totem pole. Illus. Grades 3 to 4. Albert Whitman & Co., 1956. $2.75.

U

UNCAS: *Sachem of the Wolf People*
    Virginia Frances Voight
The biography of a living Mohegan Indian chief who tells the story of his initiation into tribal customs. 209 pp. Biblio. Funk and Wagnalls, 1963. $3.50.

THE UNCONQUERED SEMINOLES
    Irvin M. Peithmann
A history of the Seminole Indians. 95 pp. Illus. Paper. Great Outdoors Association, $1.25.

THE UNREGIMENTED GENERAL
    Virginia W. Johnson
An account of the white man's subjugation of the Indians told through the exploits of an Army Indian fighter, Nelson A. Miles. 416 pp. Photos. Biblio. Maps. Houghton Mifflin Co., $6.00.

UP THE COLUMBIA FOR FURS
    Cycil Dryden
Illus. The Caxton Printers, Ltd., 1949. $4.00.

THE UPPER PIMA OF THE SAN CAYETANO DEL TUMACACORI
    Charles C. Di Peso
The Amerind Foundation, 1956. $15.00.

UTE MASSACRE
    Josephine Meeker
Set in Colorado in the 1870's, this book tells the story of Nathan Meeker and the Ute Massacre. Vic Press, 1966.

UTE RORSCHACH PERFORMANCES AND SOME NOTES ON FIELD PROBLEMS AND METHODS
    Paul A. Hauck
Describes the reactions of Ute Indians of various ages to a field researcher and a Rorschach (psychological) examination, noting the general tendency of the subjects to attempt to fit all new experiences into broad existing frameworks, and discusses the Indian's aggressiveness, passivity, or indifference in relation to his age. 18 pp. University of Utah Press, 1955. 50¢.

V

VALLEJO, SON OF CALIFORNIA
Myrtle M. McKittrick
A biography of the Spaniard who developed an empire for himself while he sought to hold together the structure of government under Mexican rule with the aid of his Indian allies. 400 pp. Illus. Binfords and Mort, $4.50.

VALLEY OF THE SIX NATIONS
Charles M. Johnson, Editor
A collection of documents on the Indian lands of the Grand River. xcvi + 344 pp. Illus. University of Toronto Press, 1965. $5.00.

VANCOUVER'S DISCOVERY OF PUGET SOUND
Edmond S. Meany
The discovery, exploration and history of Puget Sound, including a section of Vancouver's original journals. 410 pp. Illus. Index. Map. Binfords and Mort, $5.00.

VARIATION IN VALUE ORIENTATIONS
Florence R. Kluckhohn and Fred L. Strodtbeck
A report of the nature of value systems and the influences which values have upon behavior. 437 pp. Diagrams. Index. Tables. Appendix. Harper & Row, Publishers, 1961. $8.50.

VERTEBRATE REMAINS AND PAST ENVIRONMENTAL RECONSTRUCTION IN THE NAVAJO RESERVOIR DISTRICT
Arthur H. Harris and Frank W. Eddy
An analysis of bones recovered from archaeological operations in the Navajo Reservoir District. 71 pp. Illus. Biblio. Museum of New Mexico Press, $2.00.

VOYAGES OF SAMUEL DE CHAMPLAIN, 1604-1618
W. L. Grant, Editor
From the Contents: The Voyages of 1604-1607; The Voyages to the Great River St. Lawrence, 1608-1612; The Second Voyage to New France in the Year 1610; Third Voyage of Sieur de Champlain in the Year 1611; Fourth Voyage of Sieur de Champlain, Made in the Year 1613; Voyages and Discoveries in New France from 1615 to 1618; Voyages of 1615 and Voyages and Discoveries in the Year 1618. 374 pp. Barnes and Noble, Inc., 1959. $5.75.

W

*WAKAPOO AND THE FLYING ARROWS
Terry Shannon
Illus. Grades 3 to 5. Albert Whitman & Co., 1963. $2.75.

WAKEMAP MOUND
Arthur Woodward
A report of the excavations at Wakemap Mound and nearby stratified sites, revealing the extent and diversity of the great Indian culture that once existed at the Long Narrows of the Columbia River. 40 pp. Illus. Paper. Binfords and Mort, $1.00.

WALAPAI ETHNOGRAPHY
A. L. Kroeber, Editor
A report on the life and customs of the Walapai. 293 pp. Illus. Appendix. School of American Research, 1935. $3.25.

WALK IN YOUR SOUL: *Love Incantations of the Oklahoma Cherokees*
Jack Frederick Kilpatrick and Anna Gritts Kilpatrick; illustrated by William D. Wittliff
An annotated rendering in English of erotic charms from manuscripts collected by the authors. This little-known magic is used for attracting, abasing, to break up friendships, love affairs and marriage, to remake oneself, and for other purposes. 159 pp. Illus. Southern Methodist University Press, 1965. $5.00.

WALKARA, HAWK OF THE MOUNTAINS
Paul Bailey
A biographical study of the great Ute war chief, Walkara. 185 pp. Westernlore Press, 1954. $4.00.

THE WAMPANOAG INDIAN FEDERATION
Milton Travers
A story of the early dwellers of Cape Cod and southeastern Massachusetts. 450 pp. Illus. Christopher Publishing House, 1961. $4.50.

WAR CHIEF JOSEPH
Helen Addison Howard and Dan L. McGrath
Book contains a biography of Chief Joseph of the Nez Perce, and a tribal history of his people. 368 pp. University of Nebraska Press, 1964. $1.65.

WAR EAGLE: *A Life of General Eugene A. Carr*
>James T. King

Illus. University of Nebraska Press, 1963. $6.00.

*WARPATH
>Bruce Grant

Illus. Grades 6 to 8. The World Publishing Co., 1954. $2.95.

WAR-PATH AND BIVOUAC: *Or, the Conquest of the Sioux*
>John F. Finerty; Introduction by Oliver Knight

357 pp. Illus. Appendix. Map. University of Oklahoma Press, 1962. $2.00.

THE WARRIOR APACHES
>Gordon C. Baldwin; illustrated by Harold A. Wolfinberger, Jr.

A description of ancient tribal life and customs and the war history of the Chiricahua and western Apaches. 144 pp. Illus. Dale S. King Publishers, 1965. Paper, $1.95; cloth, $3.50.

WARRIORS OF THE COLORADO: *The Yumas of the Quechan Nation and Their Neighbors*
>Jack D. Forbes

University of Oklahoma Press, 1965. $5.95.

WARRIORS OF THE RAINBOW
>William Willoya and Vinson Brown

A discussion of the prophetic visions of the Indian peoples of both America and Asia, including the departure of the Indian spirit after the conquest by the white men, and its subsequent return. 96 pp. Illus. Naturegraph Co., 1962. $1.95.

*THE WARRIORS' PATH
>Herbert Witten

Kiah Bowen and his half-Indian friend, Brown Hawk, enter the wilderness to find the Shawnee town where Bowen's parents are being held captive. Ages 10 to 14. Follett Publishing Co.

WARS OF THE AMERICAN INDIAN
>Pat Musilli, Editor

In four parts (Books One, Two, Three and Four), covering the periods 1500 to 1850, 1862 to 1873, 1876 to 1879, and 1891 to 1923. Events and personalities covered include: Invasion -- Exploration and Conquest by the Spaniards; El Pope -- The Pueblo Revolt; Battle Creek Massacre; The

Mad Dream of Chief Kanim -- Puget Sound Northwest Indians on the Warpath; The Revenge of Little Crow; Death of Roman Nose -- The Bloody Battle of Beecher's Island; Apache Vengeance -- Chief Eskiminzin Strikes Back; Satanta's Red Raiders -- The Texas Massacre that Changed History; Death Cry of the Pawnees -- Indian Against Indian; Curley, Custer's Scout; The Utes Revert to Savagery -- Blood at White River; Casey's Cheyenne Scouts -- Death in the Black Hills; Indian Armor; The Last Warrior. Illus. A special issue of *Real West* magazine. Paper. Charlton Publications, Inc., 50¢.

WARS OF THE IROQUOIS: *A Study of Intertribal Trade Relations*
>George T. Hunt

218 pp. Illus. University of Wisconsin Press, 1960. Paper, $1.65; cloth, $6.00.

THE WASHO INDIANS OF CALIFORNIA AND NEVADA
>Warren L. d'Azevedo, Editor

A study of the cultural history of the Washo Indians. 201 pp. Biblio. Notes. Anthropological Papers, No. 67, University of Utah Press, 1964. $2.75.

WASHOE RAMBLES
>Dan DeQuille; edited and with an Introduction by Richard E. Lingenfelter

A narrative of a journey through western Nevada in 1861 with many observations on the Paiutes. 169 pp. Westernlore Press, 1963. $7.50.

*WATERLESS MOUNTAIN
>L. A. Armer

David McKay Co., Inc., 1931. $4.95.

WATER AND HALL CHANTS (NAVAJO)
>Mary C. Wheelwright; illustrated by Louie Ewing

237 pp. Index. Appendix. Glossary. Museum of Navajo Ceremonial Art, $20.00.

*WAYAH OF THE REAL PEOPLE
>William O. Steele; illustrated by Isa Barnett

As a service to his tribe, a young Cherokee attends a white man's school where -- according to his grandfather -- he must strive to remain true to his heritage. xii + 128 pp. Colonial Williamsburg, 1964; distributed by Holt, Rinehart & Winston, Inc., $3.50.

WEST TO THE SETTING SUN
Harvey Chalmers
The story of the involvement of Joseph Brandt, a Mohawk chief, in events which led to the Revolutionary War. 384 pp. Twayne Publishers, Inc., 1965. $6.00.

WESTERN COUNTRY IN THE 17th CENTURY
Antoine Lamouthe Cadillac and Pierre Liette
Deals with the tribes in the Great Lakes region and Upper Mississippi Valley and gives a detailed account of the Illinois Indians of the 1690's. 171 pp. Peter Smith, $3.50.

WESTERN JOURNALS OF 1849-1850
John W. Audubon
An account of a trip from New York to Texas and an overland journey through Mexico to the California gold fields. 250 pp. Illus. Map. The Rio Grande Press, Inc., 1966. $7.50.

WESTERN WORDS: *A Dictionary of the American West*
Ramon F. Adams
A dictionary of words used by the cowman, the sheepman, the freighter, the packer, the boatman, the logger, the Indian, the Western gambler and the miner. 272 pp. University of Oklahoma Press, $5.95.

*WESTWARD ADVENTURE
William O. Steele
Illus. Harcourt, Brace & World, Inc., 1962. $3.25.

WESTWARD VISION
David Lavender
A story of the Indians along the Oregon Trail and of the white men who invaded their land. 320 pp. Illus. McGraw-Hill Book Co., 1963. $8.95.

*THE WHALE PEOPLE
Roderick Haig-Brown; illustrated by Mary Weiler
A narrative of a Nootka Indian boy's growth into strength and manhood, including descriptions of the whale hunt for which these pre-Columbian people are known. 256 pp. Illus. Grades 7 to 8. William Morrow & Co., Inc., 1963. $3.25.

*WHAT INDIAN IS IT?
Anna Pistorius
A "review" of the many tribes of American Indians. Illus. Grades 1 to 5. Follett Publishing Co., $1.00.

WHEN BUFFALO RAN
George Bird Grinnell
This narrative recounts the true incidents and experiences of the Indian boy Wikas with his family, his tribe, and describes his growth to manhood. 128 pp. Illus. University of Oklahoma Press, $2.00.

WHEN OLD TRAILS WERE NEW
Blanche C. Grant
The story of the village of Taos, where history was made by Kit Carson, the mountain men, and by the traders on the Santa Fe Trail from 1800 to the American conquest. 344 pp. The Rio Grande Press, Inc., $7.50.

*WHEN THE MOON IS NEW
Laura Bannon
Illus. Grades 3 to 5. Albert Whitman & Co., $2.75.

WHIPPLE REPORT, 1849
Amiel W. Whipple
Westernlore Press, $5.50.

A WHITE BIRD FLYING
R. C. Field
41 pp. Pageant Press, Inc., 1963. $2.50.

*THE WHITE BUFFALO
John D. Nicholoson
An Indian legend of a Crow boy who finds a rare white buffalo. He cares for it and protects it from the hunters who seek to kill it. The relationship of the boy and buffalo becomes almost mystical, and ultimately involves the survival of the whole tribe. 48 pp. The Platt & Munk Co., Inc., 1965. $1.50.

*THE WHITE CALF
Cliff Faulknor
A story of the Blackfoot Indians of Montana during the 1850's, and of one boy who adopted a rare white buffalo calf. 180 pp. Ages 10 and up. Little, Brown and Co., 1965. $3.75.

*WHITE CAP FOR RECHINDA
Carroll Voss
Tells how Rechinda Iron Wing solves the problem of her two worlds -- life at the hospital where she works as a student nurse,

and the Indian reservation where she was
born. Ages 11 to 14. Ives Washburn, Inc.,
1966. $3.75.

*WHITE CAPTIVE OF THE SIOUX
   Mark Miller
The story of a young boy held captive by the
Sioux -- his life among the Indians, his
blood brother, and his eventual escape. Illus. Grades 6 to 9. Holt, Rinehart & Winston, Inc., 1953. 210 pp. $2.50.

WHITE MOUNTAIN REDWARE
   Roy Carlson
Paper. University of Arizona Press, 1965.
$5.00.

THE WHITE PATH
   W. E. S. Folsom-Dickerson
A study of the Alabama-Koasati Indians, including a chapter on medicines used in ancient tribal rituals that are still employed
by modern-day physicians. 162 pp. Illus.
Biblio. The Naylor Co., 1965. $3.95.

WHITEHALL AND THE WILDERNESS: *The
Middle West in British Colonial Policy,
1760 to 1775*
   Jack M. Sosin
A description of British colonial policy regarding the Indian tribes of North America.
xvi + 308 pp. University of Nebraska Press,
1961. $6.50.

WHITTLING WITH BEN HUNT
   W. Ben Hunt
A book presenting the fundamentals of whittling, with forty projects from various
sources -- Indian and African cultures, and
nature. Bruce Publishing Co., $3.95.

*WHY THE NORTH STAR STANDS STILL:
And Other Indian Legends
   William R. Palmer; illustrated by Urs-
   ula Koering
The Paiute legends of the origin of all living
things. Illus. Grades 3 to 6. Prentice-
Hall, Inc., 1957. $3.95.

*WIGWAM STORIES
   Edward W. Dolch
Customs of the Indians who lived in the East
and Middle West are told in these stories.
176 pp. Illus. Grades 1 to 6. Garrard
Publishing Co., 1959. $2.19.

THE WILD HORSE OF THE WEST
   Walker D. Wayman

The story of the origin of the wild horse
and its place in both the Indians' and white
men's lives. University of Nebraska Press.

*WILD LIKE THE FOXES
   Anauta Blackmore
The true story of an Eskimo girl whose
mother died when she was ten and who grew
up hunting and fishing like her brothers.
Grades 7 to 8. The John Day Co., Inc.,
1956. $3.31.

WILDERNESS MESSIAH
   Thomas R. Henry
An interpretation of the culture and genius
of the Iroquois symbolized by Hiawatha, who
united them in the Great Peace of the 15th
century. William Sloane Associates, 1955.
$4.00.

WILLIAM TECUMSEH SHERMAN AND THE
SETTLEMENT OF THE WEST
   Robert G. Athearn
371 pp. Illus. Biblio. Index. Maps. University of Oklahoma Press, 1956. $5.00.

WINDIGO PSYCHOSIS: *A Study of a Rela-
tionship Between Belief and Behavior
Among the Indians of Northeastern Canada*
   Morton L. Teicher
135 pp. Paper. University of Washington
Press, $3.50.

THE WINDWAYS OF THE NAVAHO
   Leland C. Wyman
A study of two related Navaho chants with
reproductions of the appropriate sandpaintings and an analysis of Navaho mythology.
328 pp. Illus. Biblio. Tables. Taylor
Museum, 1962. $3.00.

*WINGED MOCCASINS
   Frances J. Farnsworth; illustrated by
   Lorence F. Bjorklund
The story of a Shoshone Indian girl, Saca-
jawea, who guided the Lewis and Clark ex-
pedition. Ages 13 and up. Julian Messner,
$3.25.

THE WINNING OF THE WEST, 1796-1807
   Theodore Roosevelt
Fawcett Publications, Inc. Paper, 75¢.

THE WINNING OF THE WEST
   Theodore Roosevelt
Hastings House, Publishers, Inc., 1963.
$5.95.

THE WINNING OF THE WEST, 1796-1807
Theodore Roosevelt
256 pp. Abridged. Index. Maps. Paper.
G. P. Putnam's Sons, 1962. $1.45.

THE WINNING OF THE WEST
Theodore Roosevelt
Selections from *The Winning of The West.*
Peter Smith, $3.50.

*WINTER WITHOUT SALT
Georgiana Dorcas Ceder; illustrated
by Charles Walker
Young Peter develops a hatred of the Indians
which almost causes tragedy in this story of
pioneer days in Kentucky. 128 pp. Illus.
Grades 4 to 6. William Morrow & Co., Inc.,
1962. $2.75.

WITH CROOK AT THE ROSEBUD
J. W. Vaughn
The story of the Battle and the situations
instrumental in bringing about the tragedy
at the Little Big Horn. 245 pp. Index. Biblio. Photos. The Stackpole Co., 1956.
$5.00.

WITH HEARTS COURAGEOUS
Edna Kenton
The story of the French missionaries who
opened up the St. Lawrence, the Canadian
wilderness, and the Mississippi. 320 pp.
Illus. Liveright Publishing Corp., 1965.
$4.95.

*WITH THE INDIAN IN THE ROCKIES
J.W. Schultz; illustrated by Lorence
Bjorklund
A description of life among the Western
Indians. Illus. Ages 10 and up. Houghton
Mifflin Co., 1960. $2.95.

WITHIN TWO WORLDS
David M. Cory
Shows how past mistakes and present prob-
lems have grown out of the meeting of white
and Indian cultures. 92 pp. Friendship
Press, 1955. $1.25.

THE WOLF AND THE RAVEN: *Totem Poles
of Southeastern Alaska*
Viola E. Garfield and Linn A. Forrest
A description of the social structure, hardships and general philosophy of the Haida
and Tlingit Indians of Alaska. 161 pp. Illus. University of Washington Press, 1961.
$2.95.

*WOLF BROTHER
Jim Kjelgaard
The story of the old West is told from "the
other side," as a young Apache flees from
his people to become part of an outlaw band
of Indians. 189 pp. Grades 7 to 8. Holiday House, Inc., 1957. $3.25.

THE WOLF RITUAL OF THE NORTHWEST
COAST
Alice Henson Ernst
A description in four versions of the masked
Indian ceremonial practiced by the Indians
in coastal Washington and British Columbia.
ix + 107 pp. Illus. Photos. Paper. Uni-
versity of Oregon Press, 1952. $1.75.

*THE WONDERFUL YEARS
Nancy Barnes
Grades 5 to 8. Julian Messner, $2.95.

WOODEN LEG: *A Warrior Who Fought
Custer*
Thomas B. Marquis
An eyewitness account of the Battle of the
Little Big Horn by a Cheyenne warrior. xii
+ 390 pp. Paper. University of Nebraska
Press, 1957. $1.90.

WORLD CROPS DERIVED FROM THE
INDIANS
Edwin F. Walker
Southwest Museum, 25¢.

*WORLD FRIENDS: *Indian Americans*
Illus. Grades 2 to 6. Paper. Friendship
Press, 1955. $1.50.

*THE WORLD OF MANABOZHO: *Tales of
the Chippewa Indians*
Thomas B. Leekley; illustrations by
Yeffe Kimball
A collection of stories about Manabozho, the
great wonder worker of the Algonquian family, describing the countless shapes in which
he can appear. Illus. Vanguard Press,
Inc., 1964. $3.50.

WORLD OF WAKARA
Conway B. Sonne; illustrated by Tom
Jones and George Hughey
The story of the early settlement of the
West and Southwest, and of Wakara, chief
of the Utes, and his fight against the white
men. 250 pp. Illus. The Naylor Co.,
1962. $4.95.

THE WORLD'S RIM: *Great Mysteries of the North American Indians*
Hartley Burr Alexander
The great mysteries of the North American Indian -- conveying Indian conceptions of the essence of men's lives -- are discussed in this book, lending insights into a common humanity. xx + 260 pp. University of Nebraska Press, 1953. $4.75.

WOVOKA, THE INDIAN MESSIAH
Paul Bailey
A biographical study of the Paiute messiah Wovoka, whose Ghost Dance religion swept the American tribes as one of the greatest mystical movements of all time. 223 pp. Westernlore Press, 1957. $5.50.

Y

*YAKIMA BOY
Grace W. McGavran
A tale of two Indian boys and their friendship. 128 pp. Grades 4 to 6. Paper. Friendship Press, 1952. $1.25.

*YOUNG BRAVE ALGONQUIN
Priscilla Garden
A story of the Algonquin tribes during the 1650's and of one boy's friendship with the white settlers. 147 pp. Ages 9 to 11. Little, Brown and Co., 1956. $2.75.

*YOUNG READERS INDIAN STORIES
A. L. Furman, Editor
Grades 4 to 6. Grosset & Dunlap, Inc. $1.50.

YUMAN INDIAN AGRICULTURE: *Primitive Subsistence on the Lower Colorado and Gila Rivers*
Edward F. Castetter and Willis H. Bell
A report on the Mohave, Yuma, Cocopah, Maricopa and Pima Indians. 288 pp. Photographs. Maps. University of New Mexico Press, $4.00.

Z

ZUNI DAILY LIFE - ZUNI KIN TERMS
David M. Schneider and John M. Roberts
A report of ethnographic observations made of Zuni life during 1951, including Zuni kin terminology and the import of these findings for an understanding of the Zuni kinship system. 160 pp. Illus. Paper. Human Relations Area Files Press, 1965. $3.50.

ZUNI GRAMMAR
Stanley Stewart Newman
77 pp. Biblio. Publications in Anthropology, No. 14, University of New Mexico Press, 1965.

Subject Classifications

The following is a list of books contained in the *Bibliography*, classified by subject. The reader will note that individual tribes have been grouped into geographical regions -- under "Apache Indians," the reader is referred to "Indians of North America -- Southwest." Indian leaders or others prominent in history have been assigned individual headings, however.

The annotation for any book listed in this section may be found in the main section, the *Bibliography,*

As in the *Bibliography*, an asterisk (*) indicates a title of primarily juvenile or young adult interest. Such titles are listed not only in the "Indians of North America -- Juvenile Literature" and "Indians of North America -- Fiction, Juvenile" sections, but are included in other sections where pertinent.

AGRICULTURE

Agricultural and Hunting Methods of the Navaho Indians

Common Edible and Useful Plants of the West

Corn Among the Indians of the Upper Missouri

Pima and Papago Indian Agriculture

Some Plants Used by the Yuki Indians of Round Valley, Northern California

World Crops Derived from the Indians

Yuman Indian Agriculture: *Primitive Subsistence on the Lower Colorado and Gila Rivers*

ALASKA

Alaska in Transition: *The Southeast Region*

*Alaska, the Forty-ninth State

Exploration of Alaska

*The First Book of Alaska

ANTIQUITIES

An Aboriginal Quartzite Quarry in Eastern Wyoming

Alluvial and Palynological Reconstruction of Environments, Navajo Reservoir District

*The Ancient Ones: *Basketmakers and Cliff Dwellers of the Southwest*

An Ancient Site at Borax Lake, California

Archaeological Investigations of the Uncompahgre Plateau

An Archaeological Site near Gleeson, Arizona

Archaeological Survey of the Chuska Valley and the Chaco Plateau

An Archaeological Survey of the Trent Waterway in Ontario, Canada, and Its Significance for New York State Prehistory

Archaeological Survey of the Twenty-nine Palms Region

Archaeological Work in the Ackmen-Lowry Area, Southwestern Colorado

The Archaeology of New York (Suggs)

The Archaeology of New York State (Ritchie)

Archaeology of the Eastern U.S.

Archaeology of the Historic Period in the Western Great Lakes Region, A.D. 1600-1820

Archaeology of the Ute Dam and Reservoir, Northeastern New Mexico

The Archeology of Pleistocene Lake Mohave

Basket Maker III Sites Near Durango, Colorado

The Bayou Goula Site, Iberville Parish, Louisiana

Bird Stones of the American Indian

The Orringh Stone Tavern and Three Seneca Sites of the Late Historic Period

The Ozark Bluff-Dwellers

Paleo-Indian Culture in Kentucky

The Pinto Basin Site

A Pinto Site Near Little Lake, California

Pipeline Archaeology: *A Report of the Salvage Operations in the Southwest*

Potsherds: An Introduction to the Study of Prehistoric Southwestern Ceramics and Their Use in Historic Reconstruction

The Pottery of Santo Domingo

A Prehistoric Fortified Village Site at Canandaigua, Ontario County, N.Y.

Prehistoric Man in the New World

Prehistoric Man on the Great Plains

Prehistoric Men

Prehistoric Settlement Patterns in the New World

Prehistoric Southwesterners, from Basketmaker to Pueblo

Prehistoric Weapons in the Southwest

Preliminary Archaeological Investigations in the Navajo Project Area

Recent Geomorphic History of the Pontchartrain Basin

The Reeve Ruin of Southeastern Arizona

Report on Indian Earthworks in Ogemaw County, Michigan

*The Riddle of the Past

The Rock Paintings of the Chumash

The Skeleton from Mesa House

Southwestern Archaeology

The Spiro Mound Collection

*Stone Age Peoples Today

Stone Artifacts of the Northwestern Plains

A Stratified Prehistoric Site at Brewerton, New York

Stratigraphy and Archaeology of Ventana Cave, Arizona

Studies at Navajo Period Sites in the Navajo Reservoir District

Susquehannock Miscellany

Table Rock Pueblo, Arizona

Tule Springs, Nevada: *With Other Evidences of Pleistocene Man in North America*

Turkey Foot Ridge Site, a Mogollon Village, Pine Lawn Valley, Western New Mexico

Two Fremont Sites and their Position in Southwestern Prehistory

Two Prehistoric Village Sites at Brewerton, New York

Two Pueblo Ruins in West Central Arizona

Vertebrate Remains and Past Environmental Reconstruction in the Navajo Reservoir District

Wakemap Mound

*The Whale People

ANTIQUITIES — ESKIMOS

Archeology of Cape Denbigh

Indian and Eskimo Artifacts of North America

APACHE INDIANS — See INDIANS OF NORTH AMERICA — SOUTHWEST

ARCHITECTURE

Eighteenth Century Navajo Fortresses of the Gobernador District

Taos Adobes

ARMS AND ARMOR

*Indian Warriors and their Weapons

ART

Alaska Indian Basketry

American Indian Arts, a Way of Life

American Indian Dances: *Steps, Rhythms, Costumes and Interpretation*

Ancient Art of the Americas (Rosenthal)

Ancient Arts of the Americas (Bushnell)

Art and Architecture of Ancient America

Art Before Columbus

Art of the Eastern Plains Indian

*The Art of the North American Indian

Art of the Northwest Coast Indians

Art on Stone by the American Indian in New Jersey

Basket Weavers of Arizona

A Brief History of Navajo Silversmithing

Ceremonial Costumes of the Pueblo Indians

Decorative Art of the Southwest Indians

Decorative Art of the Tetes de Boule of Quebec

Design Motifs of the Pueblo Indians

The Eagle, the Jaguar, and the Serpent

Essays in Pre-Columbian Art and Archaeology

*The Golden Book of Indian Crafts and Lore

Hopi Katcinas Drawn by Native Artists

Indian and Camp Handicrafts

Indian Art in America

Indian Art of the Americas

Indian Rock Paintings of the Great Lakes

Indiancraft

Kwakiutl Ceremonial Art

*Made in Canada

Masterpieces in the Museum of Primitive Art: *Africa, Oceania, North America, Mexico, Central to South America, Peru*

Modern Indian Painting

Montagnais Art in Birch-bark, a Circumpolar Trait

Native Arts of the Pacific Northwest

Navaho Art and Culture

Navaho Sandpainting: *The Huckel Colletion*

Northwest Coast Indian Art: *An Analysis of Form*

Plains Indian Parfleche Designs

Pre-Columbian Architecture

Pre-Spanish Jewelry and Ornament in the Southwest

Primitive Art (Boas)

Primitive Art (Fraser)

Rock Art in the Navajo Reservoir District

Southwest Indian Pictographs and Petroglyphs

Southwestern Indian Arts and Crafts

Sun Father's Way: *The Kiva Murals of Kuana*

Sweat of the Sun and Tears of the Moon: *Gold and Silver in Pre-Columbian Art*

Treasures of Ancient America

The Windways of the Navajo

ART — ESKIMOS

*The Art of the Eskimo

Artists of the Tundra and the Sea

Eskimo Sculpture

Eskimos

Native Arts of the Pacific Northwest

ASSINIBOINE INDIANS — See INDIANS OF NORTH AMERICA — THE WEST

BABY CARRIERS AND CRADLES

Indian Cradles

BASKET MAKING

The Ancient Basketmakers

BEADWORK

Beads and Beadwork of the American Indian

Crow Indian Beadwork

BIBLIOGRAPHY

The American Indian in Graduate Studies: *A Bibliography of Theses and Dissertations*

Bibliographical Checklist of North and Middle American Indian Linguistics in the Edward E. Ayer Collection

Bibliography of North American Folklore and Folksong

Bibliography of the Constitutions and Laws of the American Indians

Dictionary Catalog of the Edward E. Ayer Collection of Americana and American Indians, The Newberry Library

Ethnographic Bibliography of North America

Guide to Materials Bearing on Cultural Relations in New Mexico

Narratives of Captivity Among the Indians of North America: *A List of Books and Manuscripts in the Edward E. Ayer Collection*

BIOGRAPHY

Biographical and Historical Index of American Indians and Persons Involved in Indian Affairs

A Biography of Oliver La Farge

Black Elk Speaks, Being the Life Story of a Holy Man of the Oglala Sioux

Black Hawk (Beckhard)

Black Hawk: *An Autobiography*

Chief Pushmataha: *American Patriot*

Chief Seattle (Anderson)

*Chief Seattle (Montgomery)

Confederate Indians

*Crazy Horse: *Sioux Warrior*

Du Bay: *Son-in-Law of Oshkosh*

*Famous Indian Chiefs

Heap Many Texas Chiefs

*Indian Friends and Foes

Indians of Today

*Indians on the Warpath

Ishi in Two Worlds: *A Biography of the Last Wild Indian in North America*

*Ishi, Last of his Tribe

*Jim Thorpe, Indian Athlete

*The Jim Thorpe Story: *America's Greatest Athlete*

John Billington, Friend of Squanto

John Ross, Chief of an Eagle Race

Joseph Brandt: *Mohawk*

Joseph, the Chief of the Nez Perce

*King Philip, Loyal Indian

*King Philip, the Indian Chief

*The Life of Pocahontas

*Little Turtle, Miami Chief

Mohegan Chief: *The Story of Harold Tantaquidgeon*

No Turning Back

Northwest Trail Blazers

*Osceola: *Young Seminole Indian*

Our Indian Heritage: *Profiles of 12 Great Leaders* (Porter)

The Patriot Chiefs: *A Chronicle of American Indian Leadership*

*Pocahontas

*Pocahontas and her World

*Pocahontas: *Brave Girl*

Quanah Parker

*Sacagawea: *Bird Girl*

*Sacagawea: *Indian Guide*

*Sacajawea: *Guide to Lewis and Clark*

Sacajawea of the Shoshones

Saga of Chief Joseph

Samson Occum

*Sequoyah: *Leader of the Cherokees*

*Sequoyah: *Young Cherokee Guide*

Sitting Bull: Champion of the Sioux, *A Biography*

*Sitting Bull: *Dakota Boy*

*Squanto: *Friend of the White Men*

*Squanto: *Indian Adventurer*

*Squanto: *Young Indian Hunter*

Sun Chief: *The Autobiography of a Hopi Indian*

Tecumseh: *Destiny's Warrior*

*Tecumseh: *Shawnee Boy*

Uncas: *Sachem of the Wolf People*

Walkara, Hawk of the Mountains

War Chief Joseph

*Winged Moccasins

Wovoka, the Indian Messiah

BLACKFEET INDIANS — See INDIANS OF NORTH AMERICA — THE WEST

CAPTIVITIES, INDIAN

Comanche Bondage

*Indian Captive: *The Story of Mary Jemison*

Journal of the Adventures of Matthew Bunn

Last Portage

*Life of an Indian Captive

Lost Sister Among the Miamis

Manners and Customs of Several Indian Tribes West of the Mississippi

*Moccasin Trail

*Mohawk Gamble

My Captivity Among the Sioux Indians

Narrative of the Captivity and Adventures of John Tanner During Thirty Years of Residence Among the Chippewa, Ottawa and Ojibwa Tribes

Narrative of the Life of Mrs. Mary Jemison

Narratives of Captivity Among the Indians of North America: *A List of Books and Manuscripts in the E. E. Ayer Collection*

Scalps and Tomahawks

Three Years Among the Comanches: *The Narrative of Nelson Lee, the Texas Ranger*

Truthful Hatchet

A White Bird Flying

*White Captive of the Sioux

CATLIN, GEORGE (painter of Indians), d. 1872

Artists of the Old West

George Catlin and the Old Frontier

Palette and Tomahawk

CHEROKEE INDIANS — See INDIANS OF NORTH AMERICA — EASTERN STATES

CHEYENNE INDIANS — See INDIANS OF NORTH AMERICA — THE WEST

CHIPPEWA INDIANS — See INDIANS OF NORTH AMERICA — MIDWEST

CLALLAM (OR KLALLAM) INDIANS — See INDIANS OF NORTH AMERICA — NORTHWEST, PACIFIC

CLIFF DWELLINGS

*Let's Go to an Indian Cliff Dwelling

COLLIER, JOHN (former Commissioner of Indian Affairs), 1884-

From Every Zenith: *A Memoir*

COLUMBIA RIVER AND VALLEY

Adventures on the Columbia River

The Columbia River

Stone Age on the Columbia River

COMANCHE INDIANS — See INDIANS OF NORTH AMERICA — THE WEST

COMMERCE

The Cheyenne in Plains Indian Trade Relations, 1795-1840

A History of the United States Indian Factory System, 1795-1822

Indian Trade Goods

The Indian Traders

The Southern Frontier - 1670-1732

Traders to the Navajos

Wars of the Iroquois: *A Study in Intertribal Trade Relations*

COSTUMES

The Book of Indian Crafts and Costumes

The Mode in Hats and Headdress

CRAFTS

Living Like Indians

CROCKETT, DAVID, d. 1836

The Adventures of Davy Crockett

CROW INDIANS — See INDIANS OF NORTH AMERICA — THE WEST

CULTURE

Aboriginal California: *Three Studies in Culture History*

Aboriginal Relationships Between Culture and Plant Life in the Upper Great Lakes Region

Acculturation and Material Culture - I

Acculturation in Seven American Indian Tribes

The Amazing Red Man

An Apache Life-way: *The Economic, Social, and Religious Institutions of the Chiricahua Indians*

The Arapaho Way

Archaeological Survey of the Chuska Valley and the Chaco Plateau

The Archaeology of New York State (Ritchie)

Blackfoot Warrior Societies

Changing Configurations in the Social Organization of a Blackfoot Tribe During the Reserve Period

Changing Washo Kinship

Childhood and Youth in Jicarilla Apache Society

Children of the People: *The Navaho Individual and his Development*

Cooperation and Competition Among Primitive Peoples

Cultural and Natural Areas of Native North America

Cultural Relations in the Plateau Region of Northwestern America

Cultural Sequences at the Dalles, Oregon: *A Contribution to Pacific Northwest Prehistory*

Culture and Experience

Cycles of Conquest: *The Impact of Spain, Mexico and the United States on Indians of the Southwest, 1543-1960*

The Effects of White Contact Upon Blackfoot Culture

The Gift is Rich

Handbook of Middle American Indians, Volume 1: *Natural Environment and Early Cultures*

The Indian and the Horse

Ingalik Material Culture

The Klamath Tribe: *A People and Their Reservation*

Klamath Prehistory: *The Prehistory of Klamath Lake Area, Oregon*

Law and Status Among the Kiowa Indians

Material Culture of the Menomini

Myth and Cult Among Primitive Peoples

Navaho Trading Days

Observations on Northern Blackfoot Kinship

The Old Copper Culture and the Keweenaw Waterway

Our Primitive Contemporaries

Patterns of Culture

Primitive Man as a Philosopher

A Reappraisal of the Fremont Culture

A Schoolmaster with the Blackfeet Indians

Smoke Upon the Winds

Stratigraphy and Archaeology of Ventana Cave, Arizona

Status Terminology and Social Structure of the North American Indians

The Structure of a Moral Code: *A Philosophical Analysis of Ethical Discourse Applied to the Ethics of the Navaho Indians*

Susquehannock Miscellany

Walapai Ethnography

The World's Rim: *Great Mysteries of the North American Indians*

Zuni Daily Life - Zuni Kin Terms

CULTURE — BIBLIOGRAPHY

An Anthropological Bibliography of the Eastern Seaboard, Vol. II

CULTURE — ESKIMOS

Eskimo Childhood and Interpersonal Relationships: *Nunivak Biographies and Genealogies*

DANCES

American Indian Dances: *Steps, Rhythms, Costumes, and Interpretation*

Ceremonial Costumes of the Pueblo Indians

Cherokee Dance and Drama

The Cheyenne, II: *The Sun Dance*

Dances and Stories of the American Indian

Dances of the Blackfoot Indians

Dancing Gods: *Indian Ceremonials of New Mexico and Arizona*

*The Golden Book of Indian Crafts and Lore

History of the Calumet and of the Dance

*Hopi Indian Butterfly Dance

Masks, Mantas, and Moccasins: *Dance Costumes of the Pueblo Indians*

Oklahoma Delaware Ceremonies, Feasts and Dances

The Ponca Sun Dance

Snake Dance of the Hopi Indians

Snake Dance of the Moqui Indians (Hopi) of Arizona

This is a Hopi Kachina

*The Whale People

The Wolf Ritual of the Northwest Coast

DWELLINGS

The Blackfoot Tipi

The Indian Tipi - Its History, Construction, and Use

Taos Adobes

EDUCATION

Formal Education in an American Indian Community

An Indian Preacher in England

Letters of Eleazar Wheelock's Indians

*The Middle Five: *Indian Schoolboys of the Omaha Tribe*

ESKIMOS — ALASKA

*Alaska: *The Land and the People*

Dawn in Arctic Alaska

Eskimo Adventure

An Eskimo Village in the Modern World

Fifty Years Below Zero

Grandma Goes to the Arctic

Howl of the Malemute

Kingdom of the Seal

Land of the Midnight Sun

Last of the Few

Lord of Alaska

*Medicine Men of Hooper Bay

Mission of Change in Alaska: *Eskimos and Moravians on the Kuskokwim*

Moonlight at Midday

North to Alaska's Shining River

Point Hope, An Eskimo Village in Transition

ESKIMOS — ALASKA — FICTION, JUVENILE

*Mystery of the Talking Totem Pole

*Wild Like the Foxes

ESKIMOS — CANADA

Ayorama

The Central Eskimo

The Desperate People

Eskimos

Igloo for the Night

Island of the Lost

People of the Deer

People of the Twilight

Tikta'liktak: *An Eskimo Legend*

ESKIMO — GENERAL

*Aguk of Alaska

Ancient Culture of the Bering Sea and the Eskimo Problems

*The Art of the Eskimo

Book of the Eskimos

*Children of the North Pole

*A Dog Team for Ongluk

*The Eskimo: *Arctic Hunters and Trappers*

*Eskimo Boy

*Eskimo Island

*The Eskimos Knew

The Eskimos: *Their Environment and Folkways*

*The First Book of Eskimos

*Getting to Know Alaska

*Here is Alaska

In the Company of Man

*Kidlik's Kayak

*Lokoshi Learns to Hunt Seals

*Matuk, the Eskimo Boy

*My Eskimos: *A Priest in the Arctic*

My Life with the Eskimo

The New People: *The Eskimo's Journey into Our Time*

*Ootook, Young Eskimo Girl

*People of the Snow

People of the Twilight

*True Book of Little Eskimos

ETHNOLOGY

Cabot to Cartier

Houses and Houselife of the American Aborigines

The Native Americans

FIVE CIVILIZED TRIBES

Indian Removal - *The Emigration of the Five Civilized Tribes of Indians*

The Southern Indians: *The Story of the Civilized Tribes Before Removal*

FOLKLORE, ESKIMO

The Eskimos: *Their Environment and Folkways*

FOLKLORE, INDIAN

Bibliography of North American Folklore and Folksong

Blackfoot Lodge Tales, *The Story of a Prairie People*

Content and Style of an Oral Literature: *Clackamas Chinook Myths and Tales*

Coyote Wisdom

Dahcotah: *Life and Legend of the Sioux*

Funk & Wagnalls Standard Dictionary of Folklore, Mythology, and Legend

Hopi Katcinas Drawn by Native Artists

*Indian Folk and Fairy Tales

Indian Tales

Iroquois Folk Lore Gathered from the Six Nations of New York

John Rattling-Gourd of Big Cove

The Mascouten or Prairie Potawatomie: *Mythology and Folklore*

Northwest Sahaptin Tales

Pawnee Hero Stories and Folk Tales

Schoolcraft's Indian Legends

Southwestern Lore

Star Lore Among the Navajos

Takelma Texts

FOLSOM POINTS

Early Man Projectile Points in the Southwest

FOOD

The Art of American Indian Cooking

Common Edible and Useful Plants of the West

FUR TRADE — CANADA

The Fur Trade in Canada

FUR TRADE — U. S.

Five Fur Traders of the Northwest

The Fur Trader and the Indian

Manuel Lisa and the Opening of the Missouri Fur Trade

GAMES

Apache Playing Cards

The Book of American Indian Games

GHOST DANCE

Ghost Dance (Miller)

Ghost-Dance Religion and the Sioux Outbreak of 1890

The Ghost Dance Religion: *Smohalla and his Doctrine*

The Ghost Dance Religion: *The Shakers of Puget Sound*

The Last Days of the Sioux Nation

GOVERNMENT RELATIONS

American Indian and White Relations to 1830

American Indian Policy in the Formative Years: *The Indian Trade and Intercourse Acts, 1790-1834*

American Indians (Hagan)

The Baltasar Baca "Grant": *History of an Encroachment*

Benjamin Hawkins: Indian Agent

Broken Peace Pipes

The California Indians Versus the United States

Carbine and Lance: *The Story of Old Fort Sill*

A Century of Dishonor

Companion of Adventure

A Continent Lost - A Civilization Won: *Indian Land Tenure in America*

Disinherited: *The Lost Birthright of the American Indian*

Expansion and American Indian Policy

Experiences as an Indian Agent

First Look at Strangers

From Feather, Blanket and Tepee, *The Indian's Fight for Equality*

Heap Many Texas Chiefs

A History of the United States Indian Factory System, 1795-1822

The Indian in Modern America

Indian Police and Judges

Indians and Other Americans

John Howard Payne to his Countrymen

The Last Days of the Sioux Nation

Legal Conscience: *Selected Papers of Felix S. Cohen*

The Long Death

Mansfield on the Condition of the Western Forts, 1853-1854

Matthew Elliot, *British Indian Agent*

The Movement for Indian Assimilation

Murder and Robbery of the Indians

Red Cloud and the Sioux Problem

Red Men Calling on the Great White Father

Redskins, Ruffleshirts, and Rednecks

Removal of the Cherokee Nation

The Rise and Fall of the Choctaw Republic

Schoolcraft's Expedition to Lake Itasca

Socio-Economic Impact of the Leasing, Sale, and Improvement of Indian Land in California

States' Rights and Indian Removal: *The Cherokee Nation v. the State of Georgia*

The Struggle for Survival, *Indian Cultures and the Protestant Ethic in British Columbia*

The Treaty of Medicine Lodge

Whitehall and the Wilderness: *The Middle West in British Colonial Policy, 1760 to 1775*

GREAT NORTH TRAIL

The Great North Trail

HEALTH AND HYGIENE

The Indians and the Nurse

HISTORY

Broken Peace Pipes

The Civil War in the Western Territories: *Arizona, Colorado, New Mexico and Utah*

Course of Empire

Elias Boudinot, Cherokee, and his America

The History of the Five Indian Nations

History of the New York Iroquois

History of the Ojibway Nation

The Indian in American History

Indian Tribes of the United States: *Ethnic and Cultural Survival*

Indians of the High Plains: *From the Pre-historic Period to the Coming of the White Man*

Indians of the United States: *Four Centuries of Their History and Culture*

Indians of the Woodlands, from Prehistoric Times to 1725

Red Cloud's Folk

Red Men's America

The Sac and Fox Indians

A Sioux Chronicle

HOPEWELL CULTURE

*The Mound Builders

*The Pool and Irving Villages

HOPEWELL VILLAGE

Hopewell Village: *A Social and Economic History of an Ironmaking Community*

HOPI INDIANS — See INDIANS OF NORTH AMERICA — SOUTHWEST

HUNTING AND FISHING

Agricultural and Hunting Methods of the Navaho Indians

Catawba Hunting, Trapping and Fishing

Fishing Among the Indians of Northwestern California

The Hunting of the Buffalo

*Indian Fishing and Camping

*Indian Hunting

Naskapi Law (Lake St. John and Lake Mis-tassini Bands): *Law and Order in a Hunting Society*

Rappahannock Taking Devices: *Traps, Hunting and Fishing*

IMPLEMENTS

American Knives

Arms and Armor in Colonial America, 1526-1783

Trade Tomahawks

INDIAN REMOVAL ACT, THE, 1830

Disinherited: *The Lost Birthright of the American Indian*

INDIANS, ORIGIN OF

The American Indian: *Who is He?*

Ancient Man in North America

Early Man in the New World

Fair Gods and Stone Faces

Lost Tribes and Sunken Continents

INDIANS, TREATMENT OF

American Indians (Hagan)

Broken Peace Pipes

Diego Ramirez Visita

Disinherited: *The Lost Birthright of the American Indian*

Expansion and American Indian Policy

First Social Experiments in America

The Indian: *America's Unfinished Business*

The Invasion

Last Trek of the Indians

The Movement for Indian Assimilation, 1860-1890

Murder and Robbery of the Indians

On the Indians: *And on the Law of War*

Spanish Struggle for Justice in the Conquest of America

The Unregimented General

Within Two Worlds

INDIANS — GENERAL

The American Heritage Book of Indians

The American Indian (Brandon and White)

The American Indian: *Then and Now*

*Americans Before Columbus

The Americas on the Eve of Discovery

In Quest of the White God

Indian Civilizations

Indians of the Americas (Collier)

Indians of the Americas (Embree)

Indians of the Americas (Stirling)

Noble Savage

Program of the History of American Indians

Selected Papers from *The American Anthro-pologist,* 1888-1920

*The Story Catcher

The Story of the American Indian

INDIANS IN LITERATURE

Inkle and Yariko Album

INDIANS OF NORTH AMERICA — ALASKA

Alaska in Transition: *The Southeast Region*

Alaska Indian Basketry

Indian Tribes of Alaska and Canada

Indians of the Northwest Coast

Land of the Midnight Sun

*The Last Chief

Peter Freuchen's Men of the Frozen North

Sea Bears

INDIANS OF NORTH AMERICA — CANADA

Angel of Hudson Bay

Contributions to the Ethnology of the Kutchin

Explorations of Pierre Esprit Radisson

First Man West

Glooskap's Country

Indian Tribes of Alaska and Canada

The Indians of Quetico

Jesuit Relations

*Land of Promise

The Micmac Indians of Eastern Canada

Mountain Wolf Woman, Sister of Crashing Thunder: *The Autobiography of a Winne-bago Indian*

Peter Freuchen's Men of the Frozen North

Social and Economic Change Among the Northern Ojibwa

The Struggle for Survival: *Indian Cultures and the Protestant Ethic in British Colum-bia*

Thunder in the Mountains

Voyages of Samuel de Champlain, 1604-1618

With Hearts Courageous

INDIANS OF NORTH AMERICA — EASTERN STATES

The American Indian in North Carolina

Antiquities of Long Island

Apologies to the Iroquois

Archeology of Coastal North Carolina

Art on Stone by the American Indian in New Jersey

Benjamin Hawkins: *Indian Agent*

The Cherokee Frontier, *Conflict and Sur-vival, 1740-63*

The Cherokees

Cherokees of the Old South

Chief Pushmataha: *American Patriot*

Children of Nanih Waiya

Chronological History of the Continent of Florida

The Connecticut Story

*Council Fire and Cannon

The Creek Frontier, 1540-1783

*The Eastern Woodland Indians

Eva: *An Archaic Site*

The Florida of the Inca

Florida's Seminole Indians

Forts on the Pennsylvania Frontier, 1753-1758

Frontier Life in Oklahoma

George Croghan: *Wilderness Diplomat*

The Gilded Man

Great Trail of New England

History and Present State of Virginia

History of Carolina

History of Choctaw, Chickasaw and Natchez Indians

History of Pike and Dubois Counties

INDIANS OF NORTH AMERICA — FICTION, JUVENILE

*Beaverbird

*The Black Stone Knife

*Blue Wampum

*Bow for Turtle

*The Brave Riders

*Broken Arrow

*Buffalo Grass

*Buffalo Horse

*Buffalo Kill

*The Buffalo Robe

*Calico Captive

*California Indian Days

*Captain Waymouth's Indians

*Captives of the Senecas

*The Capture of the West Wind

*Chi-Wee

*The Choctaw Code

*The Courage of Sarah Noble

*Dancing Cloud

*Daughter of the Tejas

*A Day with Honau - *A Hopi Indian Boy*

*A Day with Poli - *A Hopi Indian Girl*

*Escape from the Shawnees

*Easter Fires

*Edge of Manhood

*The First Bow and Arrow

*The First Lake Dwellers

*Flaming Arrows

*Friends of the Wolf

*Good Hunting, Little Indian

*Great White Buffalo

*Happy Hunting Grounds

*His Indian Brother

*The Horsecatcher

*Indian Annie, Kiowa Captive

*Indian Canoe-Maker

*Indian Encounters

*Indian Hill

*Indian Island Mystery

*Indian Paint

*Indians in Winter Camp

*Indians, Indians, Indians

*Karankawa Boy

*Killer-of-Death

*Komantcia

*Lightfoot

*Little Antelope

*Little Eagle

*Little Fox, Alaskan Trapper

*Little Hawk and the Free Horses

*Little Leo

*Little Owl Indian

*Little Runner of the Longhouse

*Little Sioux Girl

*Long Rope

*The Loon Feather

*Mark of the Turtle

*Moccasin Trail

*The Mud Ponies

*Navajo Sister

*Nkwala

*One Little Indian

*Painted Pony Runs Away

*Pinto's Journey

*Pioneer Horse

*Pony Soldier

*Ride Like an Indian

*A Romance of Old Fort Hall

*The Seed is Blown

*The Shaman's Last Raid

*Sister Beatrice Goes West

*Something for the Medicine Man

*Spirit Rocks and Silver Magic

*Spotted Horse

*Squaw Dog

*Star: *The Story of an Indian Pony*

*Swamp Chief

*Tale of an Alaska Whale

*Tall as Great Standing Rock

*This for That

*The Tomahawk Family

*The Totem Casts a Shadow

*Toyanuki's Rabbit

*The Trail of the Spanish Horse

*Trail to Oklahoma

*Treasury of American Indian Tales

*Tree in the Trail

*Tyee's Totem Pole

*Wakapoo and the Flying Arrows

*Warpath

*The Warriors' Path

*Waterless Mountain

*When the Moon is New

*The White Buffalo

*The White Calf

*White Cap for Rechinda

*Winter Without Salt

*Young Brave Algonquin

INDIANS OF NORTH AMERICA — GENERAL

Adventures in the Unknown Interior of America

Adventures in the Wilderness

The American Heritage Book of Indians

The American Indian (Northey)

The American Indian: Our Relations and Responsibilities

American Indians (Daniels)

America's Indian Background

Basis of American History

The Book of American Indians

Breeds and Halfbreeds: The Vagabond Heroes of the American Frontier

Cheyenne Autumn

Comparative Studies of North American Indians

The Discovery, Settlement and Present State of Kentucke

Early Days and Indian Ways

The Effect of Smallpox on the Destiny of the Amerindian

Ethnography of Tanaina

Experiences as an Indian Agent

Forty Years Among the Indians

Indians Before Columbus: Twenty-thousand Years of North American History Revealed by Archaeology

The Golden Age of American Anthropology

Handbook of American Indians North of Mexico

The Indian and the White Man

Indians of North America

*Indians of Yesterday

Journal (Dickinson)

*Laughing Boy

Letters and Notes on the North American Indians

Lure of the Frontier

Mankind in the Making

Narrative of the Captivity and Adventures of John Tanner During Thirty Years of Residence Among the Chippewa, Ottawa and Ojibwa Tribes

The New World: The First Pictures of America

Our American Indians at a Glance

Our Indian Heritage (Kirk and Tanner)

The Oxford History of the American People

The People We Call Indians

A Pictorial History of the American Indian

Pueblo Gods and Myths

Red Man's Continent

Selected Writings of Edward Sapir in Language, Culture, and Personality

Sons of the Shaking Earth

Spanish Explorers in the Southern U.S., 1528-1543

Spanish Settlements Within the Present Limits of the United States

*The Story Catcher

This is the American Indian

Within Two Worlds

INDIANS OF NORTH AMERICA —
JUVENILE LITERATURE

*America and Its Indians

*The American Indian (Brandon and White)

*The American Indian (LaFarge)

*The American Indian as Farmer

*The American Indian Story

*American Indians (Fletcher)

*American Indians: *Yesterday and Today*

*America's Buried Past

*The Ancient Ones: *Basketmakers and Cliff
   Dwellers of the Southwest*

*Antelope Singer

*The Apache Indians, *Raiders of the South-
   west*

*Apache Warrior

*Apaches

*Arrows and Snakeskin

*The Art of the North American Indian

*Badger, the Mischief Maker

*Before the White Man Came

*Behind the Zuni Masks

*The Book of Indian Crafts and Indian Lore

*Book of Indians

*California's Father Serra

*Catherine Tekakwitha

*The Cherokee: *Indians of the Mountains*

*Cherokees (Israel)

*Chief Joseph: *War Chief of the Nez Perce*

*Children of the Seed Gatherers

*The Chippewa Indians: *Rice Gatherers of
   the Great Lakes*

*Chukchi Hunter

*Cliff Dwellers of Walnut Canyon

*Cliff Dwellings

*Cochise, Apache Warrior and Statesman

*Comanche of the Seventh

*Come to Our Salmon Feast

*Council Fire and Cannon

*The Crow Indians: *Hunters of the Northern
   Plains*

*Dakotas

*The Dancing Horses of Acoma *and Other
   Indian Stories*

*Daniel Boone

*Dark Arrow

*Dark Pilgrim

*A Day in Oraibi - *A Hopi Indian Village*

*The Delaware Indians: *Eastern Fishermen
   and Farmers*

*The Delawares

*The Desert People

*Dog Soldiers: *The Famous Warrior Society
   of the Cheyenne Indians*

*Eagle Feather

*Eagle Wing

*Eliza and the Indian War Pony

*Famous Indian Tribes

*Famous Pioneers

*The First Book of Indians

*First Book of the Indian Wars

*The First Wheel

*Four Ways of Being Human

*From Ungskah, 1, to Oyaylee, 10: *A Count-
   ing Book for All Little Indians*

*Fun Book of Indians

*Geronimo, the Last Apache War Chief

*Getting to Know American Indians Today

*The Golden Book of Indian Crafts and Lore

*The Great Heritage

*Gunpowder for Boonesborough

*Henry Starr, Last of the Real Badmen

*The Hippity Hopper

*Hokahey! *American Indians Then and Now*

*Home of the Red Man: *Indian North America
   Before Columbus*

*Hopi Indian Butterfly Dance

*Horsemen of the Western Plateaus: *The Nez
   Perce Indians*

*How and Why Wonder Book of North Ameri-
   can Indians

*In My Mother's House

*The Indian and His Horse

*The Indian and His Pueblo

*The Indian and the Buffalo

*Indian Beadwork

*Indian Children of America

*Indian Fishing and Camping

*Indian Folk and Fairy Tales

*Indian Friends and Foes

*Indian Games and Crafts

*Indian Life on Long Island

*Indian Pony

*Indian Women

*Indians (Appell)

*Indians (Marriott and Rachlin)

*Indians (Tunis)

*Indians at Home

*The Indians Knew

*The Indians of Carlisle

*Indians of Early Chicago

*Indians of Early Maryland

*The Indians of New Jersey: *Dickon Among the Lenapes*

*Indians of Pennsylvania

*Indians of the Longhouse

*Indians of the Plains (Rachlis)

*Indians on the Warpath

*The Indian's Secret World

*Iroquois

*The Iroquois Trail

*Jim Thorpe, Indian Athlete

*John Rattling-Gourd of Big Cove

*The Last Chief

*Laughing Boy

*Let's Be Indians

*Let's Find Out About Indians

*Linda's Indian Home

*Little Elk Hunts Buffalo

*The Little Indian Basket Maker

*The Little Indian Pottery Maker

*Long Knife

*Marie Tanglehair

*Medicine Man's Daughter

*Meet Our Choctaw Friends

*Meet the North American Indians

*The Mighty Soo: *Five Hundred Years at Sault Ste. Marie*

*Mission Indians of California

*Mohawk Gamble

*Moolack: *Young Salmon Fisherman*

*More Indian Friends and Foes

*My Indian Tale Library

*Navaho Land, Yesterday and Today

*The Navajo: *Herders, Weavers, and Silversmiths*

*Nika Illahee *(My Homeland)*

*Nine Tales of Coyote

*Nine Tales of Raven

*The North American Indians

*Ojibway

*Once Upon a Totem

*One Among the Indians

*The Ordeal of the Young Hunter

*Orimha of the Mohawks

*Our Little Indians

*Paco's Miracle

*Peetie the Pack Rat and Other Desert Stories

*Peter Jumping Horse

*Pocahontas

*Pocahontas and Her World

*Pocahontas: *Brave Girl*

*Powhatan and Captain John Smith

*The Pueblo Indians: *Farmers of the Rio Grande*

*Pueblo Stories

*The Quest of the Fish-Dog Skin

*Real Book About Indians

*Red Brother

*Red Eagle and the Absaroka

*Red Fox and His Canoe

*The Red War Pole

*Rifles for Watie

*The River Spirit and the Mountain Demons

*Sacagawea: *Bird Girl*

*Sacagawea: *Indian Guide*

*Sacajawea: *Guide to Lewis and Clark*

*Sea of Grass

*Sea Hunters: *Indians of the Northwest Coast*

*The Secret Story of Pueblo Bonito

*The Seminole Indians

*Seminoles

*Sequoyah: *Leader of the Cherokees*

*Sequoyah: *Young Cherokee Guide*

*The Sioux Indians: *Hunters and Warriors of the Plains*

*Sitting Bull: *Dakota Boy*

*Squanto: *Friend of the White Men*

*Squanto: *Indian Adventurer*

*Squanto: *Young Indian Hunter*

*Stone Age Peoples Today

*Stones, Bones and Arrowheads

*The Story of Archaeology in the Americas

*The Talking Leaf

*Tecumseh: *Shawnee Boy*

*There Really Was a Hiawatha

*Time of the Tomahawk

*Tohi - A Chumash Indian Boy

*The True Book of Indians

*Wayah of the Real People

*Westward Adventure

*The Whale People

*What Indian is It?

*Winged Moccasins

*With the Indian in the Rockies

*Wolf Brother

*The Wonderful Years

*World Friends: *Indian Americans*

*Young Readers' Indian Stories

INDIANS OF NORTH AMERICA — MIDWEST

Chippewa Indians of Yesterday and Today

*The Chippewa Indians: *Rice Gatherers of the Great Lakes*

Early Dakota Days

A History of Minnesota, Vols. 1 and 2

Indian Life in the Upper Great Lakes, 11,000 B.C. to A.D. 1800

Indians in Minnesota

Indians of the Western Great Lakes, 1615-1760

Indians of Washtenaw County, Michigan

The Menomini Indians of Wisconsin

The Red Ocher Culture of the Upper Great Lakes and Adjacent Areas

Western Country in the 17th Century

INDIANS OF NORTH AMERICA — NEWFOUNDLAND

Beothuk and Micmac

INDIANS OF NORTH AMERICA — NORTHWEST

The Adventures of Captain Bonneville

The Archaeology of Carcajou Point

The Autobiography of a Winnebago Indian

Behind Mud Walls

*The Country of the Hawk

Five Fur Traders of the Northwest

Fort Hall: *Gateway to the Oregon Country*

Last Grass Frontier

Longhorns Bring Culture

Mellette County Memories

The Old Northwest

On the Oregon Trail: *Robert Stuart's Journey of Discovery* (1812-1813)

The Oregon Story

The Plainsmen of the Yellowstone

*Prehistoric Indians of Wisconsin

The Recollections of Philander Prescott: 1819 to 1862

Road of Life and Death

Sketches of a Tour to the Lakes

True Indian Stories

INDIANS OF NORTH AMERICA — NORTHWEST, PACIFIC

Adventures on the Columbia River

American Indians in the Pacific

Archaeology of the Upper Columbia Region

Art of the Northwest Coast Indians

*Before the White Man Came

Cathlamet on the Columbia

Chief Spoken Garry

The Coast Salish of British Columbia

The Columbia River

Coppermine Journey

Cultural Sequences at the Dalles, Oregon: *A Contribution to Pacific Northwest Prehistory*

Early Klickitat Valley Days

Ethnobotany of Western Washington

Fur Hunters of the Far West

The Haidah Indians of Queen Charlotte's Sound, B.C.

Half-Sun on the Columbia

A History of the Pacific Northwest

Indian Portraits of the Pacific Northwest

Indian Primitive

Indian Shakers: *A Messianic Cult of the Pacific Northwest*

Indian Tribes of the Pacific Northwest

Indians of Cape Flattery: *At the Entrance to the Strait of Fuca, Washington Territory*

Indians of Puget Sound

Indians of the Northwest Coast

John McLoughlin: *"Father of Oregon"*

The Kaska Indians: *An Ethnographic Reconstruction*

The Makah Indians

Monuments in Cedar

Narrative of an Expedition to the Source of St. Peter's River

Native Arts of the Pacific Northwest

The Nez Perce Indians and the Opening of the Northwest

Northwest Coast Indian Art: *An Analysis of Form*

Nun-mip-ni-sheek *(We Remember)*

*Once Upon a Totem

Pacific Northwest Indian Wars

Primitive Pragmatists

Quoth the Raven

Slave Wives of Nehalem

Stone Age on the Columbia River

The Story of the Totem Pole

The Tlingit Indians: *Results of a Trip to the Northwest Coast of America and the Bering Straits*

The Totem Pole Indians

Travels Through the Interior Parts of North America

The Twana, Chemakum and Klallam Indians of Washington Territory, 1887

Up to the Columbia for Furs

Vancouver's Discovery of Puget Sound

Westward Vision

*The Whale People

The Wolf and the Raven: *Totem Poles of Southeastern Alaska*

INDIANS OF NORTH AMERICA — SOUTHWEST

Aboriginal California: *Three Studies in Culture History*

Acoma, the Sky City

Agricultural and Hunting Methods of the Navaho Indians

Ancient Life Among the Southern California Indians

Ancient Tribes of the Boulder Dam Country

Angel to the Papagos

Apache, Navaho, and Spaniard

Archaeological Excavations at Willow Beach, Arizona, 1950

Archaeology of San Francisco

Kaibah: *Recollection of a Navajo Girlhood*

Know the Navajo

Lake of the Sky

Landmarks of New Mexico

The Leading Facts of New Mexican History

Let's Explore Indian Villages: *Past and Present*

The Lost Universe

The Maricopas

Marin Indians

Masked Gods

The Mescalero Apaches

Miscellaneous Collected Papers

Mojave of the Colorado

My Life in the Mountains and on the Plains

The Nation of the Willows

The Navaho (Kluckhohn and Leighton)

The Navaho (Watkins)

Navaho Autobiography

The Navaho Door: *An Introduction to Navaho Life*

Navaho Expedition

Navaho Means People

The Navaho Reconnaissance

Navaho Trading Days

Navaho Witchcraft

Navahos Have Five Fingers

Navajo Indians Today

Navajo Neighbors

Navajo Sketchbook

The Navajos (Underhill)

New Mexico

New Tracts in North America

The Old Ones: *Indians of the American Southwest*

On the Gleaming Way

Origin Legend of the Navaho Enemy Way

Padre Kino

Paint the Wind

Pajarito Plateau and Its Ancient People

Papers from a Training Program in Salvage Archaeology

People of the Middle Place

People of the Pueblo

A Pima Remembers

Plant Geography and Culture History of the American Southwest

Prehistoric Indians of the Southwest

Prehistoric People

Prehistoric Settlement and Physical Environment in the Mesa Verde Area

Pueblo Gods and Myths

Pueblo Period Sites in the Piedra River Section, Navajo Reservoir District

Rangers and Regulars

Red, Black, Blond and Olive

Red Man's Religion

Report on the Excavations of a Small Ruin Near Point of Pines, East Central Arizona

Richard Wetherill

Rio Grande

Rock Art in the Navajo Reservoir District

The Rock Paintings of the Chumash

Sites of the Reserve Phase, Pine Lawn Valley, Western New Mexico

The Sobaipuri Indians of the Upper San Pedro River Valley, Southeastern Arizona

Southern Paiute Ethnology

The Southwest: *Old and New*

Spin a Silver Dollar

Story of Inyo

The Story of the Southwest

Stratigraphy and Archaeology of Ventana Cave, Arizona

Studies of California Indians

Sun in the Sky

Taos Pueblo

Tapestries in Sand

These Are the People

They Sang for Horses

Three Years Among the Indians and Mexicans

Two Fremont Sites and Their Position in Southwestern Prehistory

The Upper Pima of the San Cayetano Del Tumacacori

Ute Rorschach Performances and Some Notes on Field Problems and Methods

Vallejo, Son of California

Variations in Value Orientations

Warriors of the Colorado: *The Yumas of the Quechan Nation and Their Neighbors*

The Washo Indians of California and Nevada

Washoe Rambles

Western Journals of 1849-1850

When Old Trails were New

Whipple Report, 1849

INDIANS OF NORTH AMERICA — THE WEST

The Adventures of Zenas Leonard

The American Heritage History of the Great American West

An Apache Life-way: *The Economic, Social, and Religious Institutions of the Chiricahua Indians*

The Assiniboines: *From the Accounts of the Old Ones Told to First Boy*

Bad Medicine and Good

The Black Dog Trail

Black Elk Speaks, Being the Life Story of a Holy Man of the Oglala Sioux

Blackfeet and Buffalo

The Blackfeet: *Raiders on the Northwestern Plains*

Blackfoot Lodge Tales, *The Story of a Prairie People*

The Bonanza Trail

Brave Warriors

The Cheyenne Indians: *Their History and Ways of Life*

A Cheyenne Sketchbook

The Cheyenne Way: *Conflict and Case Law in Primitive Jurisprudence*

The Cheyennes: *Indians of the Great Plains*

Comanche Land

Comanches, *Lords of the South Plains*

Corn Among the Indians of the Upper Missouri

Cowboys and Colonels

Curtis' Western Indians

Crazy Horse

The Crow Indians

Dahcotah: *Life and Legend of the Sioux*

Description of Louisiana Newly Discovered to the Southwest of New France by the Order of the King

Down the Colorado

Early Days Among the Cheyenne and Arapahoe Indians

Exploring the Great Basin

Exploring with Fremont: *The Private Diaries of Charles Preuss, Cartographer for the First, Second, and Fourth Expeditions to the Far West*

The Far Western Frontier (1830-1860)

Fifty Years on the Trail

The Final Challenge: *The American Frontier, 1804-1845*

Five Indian Tribes of the Upper Missouri: *Sioux, Arikaras, Assiniboines, Crees, Crows*

From Feather, Blanket and Tepee, *The Indian's Fight for Equality*

George Catlin: *Episodes from "Life Among the Indians" and "Last Rambles"*

George Catlin and the Old Frontier

Great Day in the West

The Great Sioux Nation

Hills of Yesterday

Historical Sketch of the Flathead Nation

History of the Old Cheraws

The Indian Journals, 1859 to 1862

Indian Sketches: *Taken During an Expedition to the Pawnee Tribes (1833)*

Indians as the Westerner Saw Them

Indians of the High Plains: *From the Prehistoric Period to the Coming of the Europeans*

Jack Squires - *A Scout with Kit Carson*

Jedediah Smith and the Opening of the West

Jim Savage and the Tulareno Indians

The Kiowas

Land of the Dacotahs

The Legend of Grizzly Adams: *California's Greatest Mountain Man*

Letters and Notes on the North American Indians

Life in the Far West

Life of Tom Horn, *Government Scout and Interpreter*

Lone Eagle: *The White Sioux*

The Long Death

The Men and the Mountain

Men of Ancient Iowa: *As Revealed by Archaeological Discoveries*

The Middle Five: *Indian Schoolboys of the Omaha Tribe*

The Military Conquest of the Southern Plains

My Captivity Among the Sioux Indians

*My Life as an Indian

My Sixty Years on the Plains: *Trapping, Trading, and Indian Fighting*

Mysterious Horses of Western North America

The Oregon Trail

The Osages: *Children of the Middle Waters*

The Pathfinders

Pawnee Bill

The Personal Narrative of James O. Pattie

Perspectives in American Indian Culture Change

Pioneer America

Plenty-Coups, Chief of the Crows

Prehistoric Man on the Great Plains

Rangers and Regulars

Red Cloud and the Sioux Problem

The Red Man's West

Relations with the Plains Indians, 1857-1861

Remember the Wind: *A Prairie Memoir*

Reminiscences of a Ranchman

The Reynolds Campaign on Powder River

The Rise of the West

Sacred Bundles of the Sac and Fox Indians

Saynday's People: *The Kiowa Indians and the Stories They Told*

A Schoolmaster with the Blackfeet Indians

Seven and Nine Years Among the Apaches and Comanches: *An Autobiography*

The Shoshonis: *Sentinels of the Rockies*

The Sioux: *Life and Customs of a Warrier Society*

The Southern Cheyennes

Spotted Tail's Folk: *A History of the Brule Sioux*

Thirty Years of Army Life on the Border

Three Years Among the Comanches: *The Narrative of Nelson Lee, the Texas Ranger*

A Tour on the Prairies

When Buffalo Ran

The Wild Horse of the West

William Tecumseh Sherman and the Settlement of the West

The Winning of the West, 1796-1807

Wooden Leg: *A Warrior Who Fought Custer*

INDUSTRIES

*The Book of Indian Crafts and Indian Lore

Indian Art in America

IROQUOIS INDIANS — See INDIANS OF NORTH AMERICA — EASTERN STATES

JOSEPH (Nez Perce chief)

*Chief Joseph: *War Chief of the Nez Perce*

*Joseph, the Chief of the Nez Perce

The Nez Perce Indians and the Opening of the Northwest

The Patriot Chiefs: *A Chronicle of American Indian Leadership*

Saga of Chief Joseph

War Chief Joseph

JUSTICE, ADMINISTRATION OF

Indian Police and Judges: *Experiments in Acculturation and Control*

Naskapi Law (Lake St. John and Lake Mistassini Bands): *Law and Order in a Hunting Society*

LANGUAGES

Alaskan Indian Dictionary: *Common Words in the Dialect of the Aleutian Indian Language*

Aleut Dialects of Atka and Attu

The Aleut Language

American Indian Prose and Poetry

Atlantic Journal and Friend of Knowledge

Beautyway: *A Navajo Ceremonial*

Bibliographical Checklist of North and Middle American Indian Linguistics in the Edward E. Ayer Collection

Canoe and Saddle

Chinook: *A History and Dictionary*

Crow Texts

Crow Word Lists

Eastern Ojibwa

Grammatical Notes on the Language of the Tlingit Indians

Hopi Proper Names

Kalapuya Texts

Kwakiutl Grammar, with a Glossary of the Suffixes

Language, Culture and Personality

League of the Iroquois

Linguistic Structures of Native America

The Menomini Language

Narrative of the Captivity and Adventures of John Tanner During Thirty Years of Residence Among the Chippewa, Ottawa and Ojibwa Tribes

Navajo Grammar

Northwest Sahaptin Texts

Notes on Chasta Costa Phonology and Morphology

Our Language: *The Story of the Words We Use*

Phonology of Arizona Yaqui with Texts

Popular Accounts of the Kiowa Language

A Sketch of Northern Sahaptin Grammar

The Snoqualmie-Duwamish Dialects of Puget Sound Coast Salish: *An Outline of Phonetics and Morphology*

Sparkman Grammar of Luiseno

Takelma Texts

Western Words: *A Dictionary of the American West*

Zuni Grammar

LEGENDS

Blackfeet and Buffalo

Blackfoot Lodge Tales, *The Story of a Prairie People*

By Cheyenne Campfires

Content and Style of an Oral Literature: *Clackamas Chinook Myths and Tales*

Coos Myth Texts

Coos Narrative and Ethnologic Texts

The Corn Goddess and Other Tales from Indian Canada

Coyote Wisdom

*The Dancing Horses of Acoma *and* Other Indian Stories*

Down from the Lonely Mountain

Eighteenth-Century Travels in Pennsylvania and New York

Emergence Myth *(According to the Upward-Reaching Rite)*

Friends of Thunder: *Folktales of the Oklahoma Cherokees*

*Glooscap and His Magic

*Glooskap's Country

He Walked the Americas

*The Hippity Hopper

*Indian Campfire Tales

Indian Creation Stories

Indian Legends from the Northern Rockies

*Indian Legends of American Scenes

Indian Legends of Eastern America

Indian Legends of the Great West

Indian Legends of the Pacific Northwest

Indian Myths or Legends and Traditions of the Aborigines of America

Indian Tales

*Indian Tales of the Desert People

Inland Whale, *Nine Stories Retold from California Indian Legends*

Iroquois Folk Lore Gathered from the Six Nations of New York

Journey into Northern Pennsylvania and the State of New York

Kalapuya Texts

*Legends of Green Sky Hill

Legends of the Longhouse

Legends of the Shawangunk *(Shon-Gum) and Its Environs*

Legends of Vancouver

*Lodge Stories

*The Long-Tailed Bear *and Other Indian Legends*

*Miami Indian Stories

*Navajo Stories

Nehalem Tillamook Tales

Never the Golden City

*Nine Tales of Raven

Ojibwa Myths and Legends

Old Father, the Story Teller

Pawnee, Blackfoot and Cheyenne

Pawnee Hero Stories and Folk Tales

The People are Coming Soon

*Picture-Skin Story

*Red Indian Folk and Fairy Tales

Saynday's People: *The Kiowa Indians and the Stories They Told*

Schoolcraft's Indian Legends

Songs and Stories of the American Indians

Stories California Indians Told

The Story Telling Stone: *Myths and Tales of the American Indian*

Takelma Texts

*Tales of the Cheyennes

*Tales of Nanabozho

*Talking Totem Pole

The Ten Grandmothers

*Tepee Stories

Te-yok-keen *(Hear Ye)*

Thunder in the Mountains

Tikta'liktat: *An Eskimo Legend*

Treasure of the Sangre de Cristos: *Tales and Traditions of the Spanish Southwest*

Treasury of Memory-Making Campfires

*Twenty Tepee Tales

Why the North Star Stands Still: *And Other Indian Legends*

*Wigwam Stories

Windigo Psychosis: *A Study of a Relationship Between Belief and Behavior Among the Indians of Northeastern Canada*

*The World of Manabozho: *Tales of the Chippewa Indians*

LEWIS AND CLARK EXPEDITION

*The Adventures of Lewis and Clark

The Field Notes of Capt. William Clark, 1803-1805

The History of the Lewis and Clark Expedition

Letters of the Lewis and Clark Expedition: *With Related Documents, 1783-1854*

The Lewis and Clark Expedition

The Natural History of the Lewis and Clark Expedition

LITTLE BIG HORN, BATTLE OF THE, 1876

The Battle of the Little Big Horn

Comanche, *Last Custer Survivor*

Custer and the Great Controversy

Custer Battle Book

Custer Country

The Custer Myth

Custer's Fall

Custer's Last Battle

*Custer's Last Stand

Did Custer Disobey Orders at the Battle of
   the Little Big Horn?

Legend into History: *The Custer Mystery*

Marching with Custer

The Reno Court of Inquiry

*Showdown at Little Big Horn

The Story of the Little Big Horn

Troopers with Custer

With Crook at the Rosebud

Wooden Leg: *A Warrior Who Fought Custer*

LITTLE WOLF, CHEYENNE CHIEF,
d. 1904

Cheyenne Autumn

MAN, PREHISTORIC — AMERICA

Ancient Life Among the Southern California
   Indians

Ancient Man in North America

Early Man in the New World

The Lost Americans

No Stone Unturned

Prehistoric Man in the New World

MARICOPA INDIANS — See INDIANS
OF NORTH AMERICA —
SOUTHWEST

MASKS

Comments on Certain Iroquois Masks

Indian Masks Booklet

Masks of the North American Indians

MEDICINE

Crow Indian Medicine Bundles

*The Indian Medicine Man

Medicine Among the American Indians

MENOMINI INDIANS — See INDIANS OF
NORTH AMERICA — EASTERN
STATES

MIAMI INDIANS — See INDIANS
OF NORTH AMERICA — EASTERN
STATES

MICMAC INDIANS — See INDIANS OF
NORTH AMERICA — CANADA and
INDIANS OF NORTH AMERICA —
NEWFOUNDLAND

MISSIONS

The Bishop of All Beyond: *Sheldon Jackson*

*Black Robe Peacemaker: *Pierre de Smet*

Cheyenne Trails

Diaries of H.H. Spalding and Asa B. Smith

*Father Kino, Priest to the Pimas

Flagellant on Horseback: *The Life Story of
   David Brainerd*

Jesuit Relations

Jesuit Relations and Allied Documents

Jesuit Relations and Other Americana in the
   Library of James F. Bell: *A Catalogue*

The Jesuits and the Indian Wars of the Northwest

The Jesuits in North America

Letters of Eleazar Wheelock's Indians

Life and Diary (Brainerd)

Loretto on the Old Frontier

The Memorial of Fray Alonso de Benavides,
   1630

Missionary to Oregon: *Jason Lee*

The New England Company

Padre Kino

Patteran

Pirates, Indians and Spaniards

A Record of Travels in Arizona and California, 1775 to 1776

The Southern Cheyennes

Strange Empire: *A Narrative of the Northwest*

Tepee in His Front Yard

Trophies of Grace

With Hearts Courageous

MISSIONS — ESKIMOS

My Eskimos: *A Priest in the Arctic*

MIXED BLOODS

Almost White

Mothers of the Mixed Bloods: *The Marginal Woman in the History of the Upper Missouri*

MOHAWK INDIANS — See INDIANS OF NORTH AMERICA — EASTERN STATES

MOJAVE INDIANS — See INDIANS OF NORTH AMERICA — SOUTHWEST

MOUND BUILDERS

*The Mound Builders

MOUNDS

Excavations at Kolomoki: *Final Report*

Prehistoric Indian Settlements of the Changing Mississippi River Delta

MUSIC

Bibliography of North American Folklore and Folksong

*The Book of Indian Crafts and Indian Lore

Cheyenne and Arapaho Music

Indian Music in the Southwest

Music of the Maidu Indians of California

Music of Santo Domingo Pueblo, New Mexico

Peyote Music

Rhythm of the Redman

Songs and Stories of the American Indians

Songs of the Nootka Indians of Western Vancouver Island

Songs of the Yokuts and Paiutes

Texts of the Navajo Creation Chants

Walk in Your Soul: *Love Incantations of the Oklahoma Cherokees*

Water and Hail Chants (Navajo)

NAMES, GEOGRAPHICAL — INDIAN

Indian Place Names in New Jersey

Indian Place Names of New England

The Indian Place Names on Long Island and Islands Adjacent

Oklahoma Place Names

Origin and Meaning of the Indian Place Names of Maryland

NAVAJO INDIANS — See INDIANS OF NORTH AMERICA — SOUTHWEST

OJIBWA INDIANS — See INDIANS OF NORTH AMERICA — CANADA

ORATORY

Aboriginal American Oratory: *The Tradition of Eloquence Among the Indians of the United States*

PAIUTE INDIANS — See INDIANS OF NORTH AMERICA — SOUTHWEST

PAPAGO INDIANS — See INDIANS OF NORTH AMERICA — SOUTHWEST

PERIODICALS

The Literary Voyager

PEYOTE

Doors of Perception

Menomini Peyotism

The Peyote Cult

Peyote Music

Peyotism and New Mexico

PICTURES, ILLUSTRATIONS, etc.

*The American Indian (LaFarge)

Curtis' Western Indians

*Famous Indian Chiefs

Frederick Remington's Own West

George Catlin and the Old Frontier

Indian and Eskimo Artifacts of North America

Indian Primitive

Indians of the Americas (Stirling)

Indians of the Western Frontier: *Paintings of George Catlin*

*Indians of Yesterday

Navajo Sketchbook

Photographer of the Southwest

A Pictorial History of the American Indian

Seth Eastman: *Pictorial Historian of the Indian*

Southeastern Indians, Life Portraits

PICTURE-WRITING, INDIAN

Coffee in the Gourd

*Indian Picture Writing

*Little Elk Hunts Buffalo

*Painted Pony Runs Away

Painted Tipis and Picture-Writing of the Blackfoot Indians

*Picture-Skin Story

PIMA INDIANS — See INDIANS OF NORTH AMERICA — SOUTHWEST

POETRY

*Indian Encounters

Riders from the West

PONTIAC, OTTAWA CHIEF, d. 1769

Conspiracy of Pontiac

Pontiac and the Indian Uprising

*Pontiac, *Lion in the Forest*

*Pontiac: *Young Ottawa Leader*

*Time of the Tomahawk

POTAWATOMI(E) INDIANS — See INDIANS OF NORTH AMERICA — EASTERN STATES

POTTERY

Contemporary Pueblo Indian Pottery

Designs on Prehistoric Pottery of Arizona

The Dynamics of Stylistic Change in Arikara Ceramics

Late Mogollon Pottery Types of the Reserve Area

Maria: *The Potter of San Ildefonso*

Papago Indian Pottery

The Story of Pueblo Pottery

Tree-Ring Dates and Southwestern Pottery

White Mountain Redware

PSYCHOLOGY

Culture and Experience

PUEBLO INDIANS — See INDIANS OF NORTH AMERICA — SOUTHWEST

PUEBLOS

A Bird's-eye View of the Pueblos

Complete Guide to the Southwest

Excavations at Pueblo Pardo

Social Anthropology of the Western Pueblos

Two Pueblo Ruins in West Central Arizona

RAPPAHANNOCK INDIANS — See INDIANS OF NORTH AMERICA — EASTERN STATES

READERS — INDIANS

*Indian Fighters

*Larry

*Lodge Stories

*Navaho Stories

*Tepee Stories

*Wigwam Stories

*Yakima Boy

RELIGION AND MYTHOLOGY

Ancient Religions

The Birth of the Gods

The Four Directions of Time

Ghost-Dance Religion and the Sioux Outbreak of 1890

Gospel of the Redman

Great Star Chant and Prayers, and Coyote Chant (Navajo)

The Gros Ventres of Montana: *Part II, Religion and Ritual*

Havasupai Religion and Mythology

He Walked the Americas

Hopi Kachina Dolls

Indian Myths or Legends and Traditions of the Aborigines of America

Indian Shakers: *A Messianic Cult of the Pacific Northwest*

Introduction to Zuni Fetishism

The Mascouten or Prairie Potawatomie: *Mythology and Folklore*

Menomini Peyotism

Myths of Navajo Chants

Mythology of Southern Puget Sound

Navajo Religion: *A Study of Symbolism*

North American Mythology

The Peyote Cult

Pollen Path: *A Collection of Navajo Myths*

Pomo Indian Myths

Prayer: The Compulsive Word

Primitive Religion (Lowie)

Primitive Religion (Radin)

Red Man's Religion

Sepass Poems

Snake Dance of the Hopi Indians

The Spiritual Legacy of the American Indian

Strange Journey

Tapestries in Sand

Warriors of the Rainbow

The Windways of the Navaho

Wovoka, the Indian Messiah

RESERVATIONS

America's Concentration Camps: *The Facts About Our Indian Reservations Today*

RITES AND CEREMONIES

The Arapaho Sun Dance: *The Ceremony of the Offerings Lodge*

Beautyway: *A Navajo Ceremonial*

Blackfoot Medicine-Pipe Ceremony

Ceremonial Patterns in the Greater Southwest

Ceremonial Songs of the Creek and Yuchi Indians

Ghost Dance (Miller)

The Kachina and the White Man

Kwakiutl Ceremonial Art

Masked Gods

A Mohawk Form of Ritual

Navajo Witchcraft

On the Gleming Way

The Oraibi Marau Ceremony

Oraibi Natal Customs and Ceremonies

The Oraibi Oaqol Ceremony

The Oraibi Summer Snake Ceremony

The Peyote Cult

Prayer: The Compulsive Word

The Red Antway of the Navaho

Road of Life and Death

This is a Hopi Kachina

The Windways of the Navaho

The World's Rim: *Great Mysteries of the North American Indians*

RITES AND CEREMONIES — ESKIMOS

Alaskan Eskimo Ceremonialism

Eskimo Masks and Ceremonialism

SACAJAWEA (or SACAGAWEA), interpreter and guide to Lewis and Clark expedition, d. 1812

ᵏSacagawea: *Bird Girl*

*Sacagawea: *Indian Guide*

*Sacajawea: *Guide to Lewis and Clark*

Sacajawea of the Shoshones

*Winged Moccasins

ST. CLAIR'S CAMPAIGN, 1791

Journal of the Adventures of Matthew Bunn

SAND CREEK, BATTLE OF, 1864

The Battle of Sand Creek

*Massacre at Sand Creek

SANDPAINTINGS

Beautyway: *A Navajo Ceremonial*

Indian Sandpainting of the Greater Southwest

Tapestries in Sand

SANTA FE, N. M.

The Centuries of Santa Fe

Commerce of the Prairies

SEMINOLE INDIANS — See INDIANS OF NORTH AMERICA — EASTERN STATES

SEQUOYAH (inventor of a system of writing the Cherokee language) d. 1843

*Sequoyah: *Leader of the Cherokees*

*Sequoyah: *Young Cherokee Guide*

SHAKERS, INDIAN

Indian Shakers: *A Messianic Cult of the Pacific Northwest*

SIEBER, ALBERT, d. 1907

Al Sieber, Chief of Scouts

SIGN LANGUAGE

*Indian Sign-Language

SILVERSMITHING

A Brief History of Navajo Silversmithing

Indian Silversmithing

Indian Silverwork of the Southwest

Navaho Silver

The Navajo and Pueblo Silversmiths

SIOUX INDIANS — See INDIANS OF NORTH AMERICA — THE WEST

SITTING BULL (Sioux leader and medicine man), d. 1890

Sitting Bull: Champion of the Sioux, *A Biography*

*Sitting Bull: *Dakota Boy*

SOCIAL DOCUMENTS

The Shadow of Sequoyah: *Social Documents of the Cherokees*

SOCIAL LIFE AND CUSTOMS

Autobiography of a Winnebago Indian

The Book of American Indian Games

The Book of Indian Crafts and Costumes

*The Book of Indian Crafts and Indian Lore

Book of Indian Life Crafts

The Cheyenne, I: *Ceremonial Organization*

The Clan System of the Fort Mojave Indians

*Come to Our Salmon Feast

Cooperation and Competition Among Primitive peoples

Factionalism in Isleta Pueblo

Fighting with Property: *A Study of Kwakiutl Potlatching and Warfare, 1792-1930*

*Fun and Festival from the United States and Canada

In the Company of Man

The Indian Journals, 1859 to 1862

Indians of the Southwest

Indian of the United States: *Four Centuries of Their History and Culture*

*Indians of Yesterday

Kitchi-Gami: *Wanderings Around Lake Superior*

Law and Status Among the Kiowa Indians

Manners and Customs of Several Indian Tribes West of the Mississippi

Material Culture of the Menomini

Missions and Pueblos of the Old Southwest

Mohave Etiquette

Mohave Tatooing and Face-Painting

A Mohawk Form of Ritual

*My Life as an Indian

Narrative of the Captivity and Adventures of John Tanner During Thirty Years of Residence Among the Chippewa, Ottawa and Ojibwa Tribe

Notes on Skidi Pawnee Society

Observations on Northern Blackfoot Kinship

Observations on the Ethnology of the Sauk Indians

Oklahoma Delaware Ceremonies, Feasts and Dances

Paiute Sorcery

Primitive Man and His Ways

Pulse of the Pueblo

Rank and Warfare Among the Plains Indians

A Reappraisal of the Fremont Culture

Social Anthropology of North American Indian Tribes

The Social Culture of the Nunivak Eskimo

Social Organization of the Central Algonkian Indians

The Social Organization of the Western Apache

These Were the Sioux

Traditions of the Arapaho

Traditions of the Crows

Traditions of the Hopi

Traditions of the Osage

The Warrior Apaches

SOCIAL LIFE AND CUSTOMS — ESKIMOS

The Nunamiut Eskimos, *Hunters of Caribou*

SOCIETIES

Comments on Certain Iroquois Masks

SQUANTO (a friend to the Pilgrims), d. 1622

*Squanto: *Friend of the White Men*

*Squanto: *Indian Adventurer*

*Squanto: *Young Indian Hunter*

STONE IMPLEMENTS

American Indian Tomahawks

TERRITORY, INDIAN

Indian Territory: *A Frontier Photographic Record*

Sequoyah Constitutional Convention

Socio-Economic Impact of the Leasing, Sale, and Improvement of Indian Land in California

TEXTILE INDUSTRY AND FABRICS

The Cultivation and Weaving of Cotton in the Prehistoric Southwestern United States

Navaho Weaving, *Its Technic and History*

Navaho Weaving Today

Navajo Rugs, *Past, Present and Future*

So You Want to Buy a Navajo Rug?

The Story of Navaho Weaving

Textiles

TLINGIT INDIANS — See INDIANS OF NORTH AMERICA — NORTHWEST, PACIFIC

TRAILS, INDIAN

Great Trail of New England

UTE INDIANS — See INDIANS OF NORTH AMERICA — SOUTHWEST

WAMPANOAG INDIANS — See INDIANS OF NORTH AMERICA — EASTERN STATES

WARS — GENERAL

The American Indian Wars

Brave Warriors

Carbine and Lance: *The Story of Old Fort Sill*

The Compact History of the American Indian Wars

Fort McPherson, Nebraska Territory

*Indians on the Warpath

The Last War Trail: *The Utes and the Settlement of Colorado*

The Long Death

Soldier and Brave

Wars of the American Indian

WARS — 1600 — 1815

The Adventures of Davy Crockett

Ark of Empire: *The American Frontier, 1784-1803*

The Cherokee Frontier: *Conflict and Survival, 1740-62*

A Company of Heroes: *The American Frontier*

The Discovery, Settlement and Present State of Kentucke

The French and Indian Wars (Hamilton)

*The French and Indian Wars (Editors of *American Heritage*)

Forth to the Wilderness

History of the Girtys

*Indian Wars and Warriors

Indian Wars of the United States Army, 1776-1865

The Journals of Major Robert Rogers

*The Last of the Great Wampanoag Indian Sachems

Lewis Wetzel, Indian Fighter

Memoirs of Lieutenant Henry Timberlake, 1756-1765

Narrative of the Indian Wars (1675-1699)

Pontiac and the Indian Uprising

Pueblo Warriors and Spanish Conquest

*Tomahawk Trail

Wars of the American Indian

Wars of the Iroquois: *A Study in Intertribal Trade Relations*

WARS — 1815 — 1895

Al Sieber, Chief of Scouts

Antelope Bill

An Apache Campaign in the Sierra Madre

The Assiniboines: *From the Accounts of the Old Ones Told to First Boy*

The Battle of Platte Bridge

Battlefield and Classroom: *Four Decades with the American Indian*

Campaigning with Crook

Captain Jack, Modoc Renegade

Civil War in the Northwest: *Nebraska, Wisconsin, Minnesota and the Dakotas*

The Conquest of California and New Mexico

Conquest of New Mexico and California in 1846

Custer's Luck

Exiles of Florida

The Fighting Cheyennes

Fighting Indians of the West

The Fighting Parson

Following the Indian Wars

Forty Miles a Day on Beans and Hay

The Galvanized Yankees

General George Crook, his Autobiography

Ghost Dance (Miller)

Ghost Dance Religion and the Sioux Outbreak of 1890

Here is Yesterday

History of the Second Seminole War

Hupa Warfare

I Will Fight No More Forever

*Indian Fighter: *The Story of Nelson A. Miles*

Indian Fights: *New Facts on Seven Encounters*

Indian Outbreaks

The Indian War of 1864

*Indian Wars and Warriors

Indian Wars of Texas

Indian Wars of the United States Army, 1776-1865

Indian Wars of the West (Potomac Corral of The Westerners)

Indian Wars of the West (Wellman)

The Jesuits and the Indian Wars of the Northwest

Journey into Wilderness

The Last Days of the Sioux Nation

Last of the Indian Wars

The Last Stand of the Nez Perce

Life and Adventures of Frank Grouard

Life of Tom Horn, *Government Scout and Interpreter*

Lincoln's Secretary Goes West

The Long Walk

Man of the Plains: *Recollections of Luther North*

The March of the Montana Column

The Mariposa Indian War

Massacre: *The Tragedy at White River*

The Military Conquest of the Southern Plains

Minnesota in the Civil and Indian Wars, 1861-1865

The Modocs and their War

The Mountain Meadows Massacre

My Captivity Among the Sioux Indians

My Life on the Plains

Notices of Florida and the Campaigns

On the Border with Crook

Origin, Progress, and Conclusion of the Florida War

*Osceola: Young Seminole Indian

Pacific Northwest Indian Wars

Paiute

Pony Tracks

*The Red War Pole

Relations with the Plains Indians, 1857-1861

*Seminole Wars

The Sioux Uprising of 1862

The Truth About Geronimo

Ute Massacre

War Eagle: *A Life of General Eugene A. Carr*

War-Path and Bivouac: *Or, the Conquest of the Sioux*

Wars of the American Indian

Wooden Leg: *A Warrior Who Fought Custer*

World of Wakara

WASHO INDIANS — See INDIANS OF NORTH AMERICA — SOUTHWEST

WINNEBAGO INDIANS — See INDIANS OF NORTH AMERICA — NORTHWEST and INDIANS OF NORTH AMERICA — CANADA

WOOD-CARVING

Whittling with Ben Hunt

Brief Miscellaneous Hopi Papers

Indian and Spanish Selected Writings

ZUNI INDIANS — See INDIANS OF NORTH AMERICA — SOUTHWEST

Publisher Index

The following is a list of publishers -- publishing companies, organizations, museums, libraries, etc. -- whose books are listed in the *Bibliography*.

The listings are arranged alphabetically, with complete addresses.

A

Abelard-Schuman, Ltd., 6 W. 57th St., New York, N.Y. 10019

Abingdon Press, 201 - 8th Ave., S., Nashville, Tenn. 37203

Academy Guild Press, 2430 E. McKinley St., Fresno, Calif. 93621

Airmont Publishing Co., Inc., 22 E. 60th St., New York, N.Y. 10022

American Catholic Historical Association, Mullen Memorial Library, Room 305, Catholic University of America, Washington, D.C. 20017

The American Forestry Association, 919 - 17th St., N.W., Washington, D.C. 20006

American Heritage Publishing Co., Inc., 551 Fifth Ave., New York, N.Y. 10017

American Philosophical Society, 104 S. 5th St., Philadelphia, Penna. 19106

The Amerind Foundation, Dragoon, Ariz. 85609

Amherst Press, Amherst, Wis. 54406

Apollo Editions, Inc., 425 Park Ave., S., New York, N.Y. 10016

Appleton-Century, c/o The Meredith Publishing Co., 1716 Locust St., Des Moines, Iowa 50303

Arco Publishing Co., Inc., 219 Park Ave., S., New York, N.Y. 10003

Association Press, Inc., 291 Broadway, New York, N.Y. 10007

Atheneum Publishers, Inc., 162 E. 38th St., New York, N.Y. 10016

The Atlantic Monthly Press, 8 Arlington St., Boston, Mass. 02116

Avon Books, 959 Eighth Ave., New York, N.Y. 10019

B

Barnes and Noble, 105 Fifth Ave., New York, N.Y. 10003

Basic Books, Inc., Publishers, 404 Park Ave., S., New York, N.Y. 10016

Beacon Press, 25 Beacon St., Boston, Mass. 02108

Binfords and Mort, 2505 S.E. 11th Ave., Portland, Ore.

Bismarck Tribune Co., Bismarck, N.D. 58501

Black Hills Publishers, Inc., 1022 Main St., Sturgis, S.D. 57785

John F. Blair, Publisher, 404 North Carolina National Bank Bldg., Winston-Salem, N.C. 27101

The Bobbs-Merrill Co., Inc., 4300 W. 62nd St., Indianapolis, Ind. 46206

Bollingen Series, c/o Pantheon Books, Inc., 22 E. 51st St., New York, N.Y. 10022

Books International, 134 Stockbridge Ave., Alhambra, Calif.

Bramhall House, 419 Park Ave., S., New York, N.Y. 10016

George Braziller, Inc., 1 Park Ave., New York, N.Y. 10016

Broadman Press, 127 - 9th Ave., N., Nashville, Tenn.

The Brooklyn Museum, 188 Eastern Pkwy., Brooklyn, N.Y. 11238

William C. Brown Co., Publishers, 135 S. Locust St., Dubuque, Iowa 52003

Brown Book Co., 239 Park Ave., S., New York, N.Y. 10016

The Bruce Publishing Co., 400 N. Broadway, Milwaukee, Wis. 53201

J.D. Buchan, 919 E. 7th St., Spencer, Iowa 51301

Buffalo and Erie County Historical Society, 25 Nottingham Court, Buffalo, N.Y. 14216

C

California Book Co., 2310 Telegraph Ave., Berkeley, Calif. 94704

Candor Press, 103 Clements Ave., Dexter, Mo. 63841

Carlton Press, Inc., 84 Fifth Ave., New York, N.Y. 10011

The Catholic University of America Press, 620 Michigan Ave., N.E., Washington, D.C. 20017

The Caxton Printers, Ltd., Caldwell, Idaho

Charlton Publications, Inc., Division St., Derby, Conn.

Chicago Natural History Museum, Roosevelt Rd. and Lake Shore Drive, Chicago, Ill. 60605

Children's Press, Inc., 1224 W. Van Buren St., Chicago, Ill. 60607

Chilton Books, 525 Locust St., Philadelphia, Penna. 19106

Christopher Publishing House, 1140 Columbus Ave., Boston, Mass. 02120

Citadel Press, 222 Park Ave., S., New York, N.Y. 10003

Arthur H. Clark Co., 1264 S. Central Ave., Glendale, Calif. 91204

Collier Publishing Co., c/o Crowell, Collier & Macmillan, Inc., 866 Third Ave., New York, N.Y. 10022

Cooper Square Publishers, Inc., 59 Fourth Ave., New York, N.Y. 10003

Corinth Books, c/o Citadel Press, 222 Park Ave., S., New York, N.Y. 10003

Cornell University Press, 124 Roberts Pl., Ithaca, N.Y. 14851

Coward-McCann, Inc., 200 Madison Ave., New York, N.Y. 10016

Cranbrook Institute of Science, Bloomfield Hills, Mich. 48013

Thomas Y. Crowell Co., 201 Park Ave., S., New York, N.Y. 10003

Crowell, Collier & Macmillan, Inc., 866 Third Ave., New York, N.Y. 10022

Crown Publishers, Inc., 419 Park Ave., S., New York, N.Y. 10003

D

Dartmouth College Publications, Hanover, N.H. 03755

Dawson's Book Shop, 550 S. Figueroa St., Los Angeles, Calif. 90017

The John Day Co., Inc., 200 Madison Ave., New York, N.Y. 10016

Dell Publishing Co., Inc., 750 Third Ave., New York, N.Y. 10017

T.S. Denison & Co., Inc., 315 Fifth Ave., S., Minneapolis, Minn. 55415

Denver Museum of Natural History, City Park, Denver, Colo. 80206

Desert-Southwest Publishing Co., Palm Desert, Calif. 92260

The Devin-Adair Co., 23 E. 26th St., New York, N.Y. 10010

The Dial Press, Inc., 750 Third Ave., New York, N.Y. 10017

Dodd, Mead & Co., 432 Park Ave., S., New York, N.Y. 10016

M.A. Donohue & Co., 711 S. Dearborn St., Chicago, Ill. 60605

Donohue & Henneberry, c/o M.A. Donohue & Co., 711 S. Dearborn St., Chicago, Ill. 60605

Dorrance & Co., 1809 Callowhill St., Philadelphia, Penna. 19130

Doubleday & Co., Inc., Garden City, N.Y. 11530

Dover Publications, Inc., 184 Varick St., New York, N.Y. 10014

Duell, Sloan & Pearce, c/o The Meredith Publishing Co., 1716 Locust St., Des Moines, Iowa 50303

Dustin Publications, Box 1661, Albuquerque, N.M. 87103

E.P. Dutton & Co., Inc., 201 Park Ave., S., New York, N.Y. 10003

E

Wm. B. Eerdmans Publishing Co., 255 Jefferson Ave., S.E., Grand Rapids, Mich. 49502

The Embry Newspapers, 220 N. Main St., Beaver Dam, Ky. 42302

Empire State Historical Publications, c/o Ira J. Friedman, Inc., Port Washington, N.Y. 11050

Exposition Press, 386 Park Ave., S., New York, N.Y. 11016

F

Faith and Life Press, 724 Main St., Newton, Kan. 67114

Farrar, Straus & Giroux, Inc., 19 Union Square West, New York, N.Y. 10003

Fawcett Publications, Inc., Fawcett Place, Greenwich, Conn. 06830

Folklore Associates, 12 Meetinghouse Road, Hatboro, Penna. 19040

Follett Publishing Co., 1010 W. Washington Blvd., Chicago, Ill. 60607

Forum Publishing Co., 324 Newbury St., Boston, Mass. 02115

Burt Franklin, 235 E. 44th St., New York, N.Y. 10017

The Free Press, c/o Crowell, Collier & Macmillan, Inc., 866 Third Ave., New York, N.Y. 10022

Ira J. Friedman, Inc., Port Washington, N.Y. 11050

Friendship Press, 475 Riverside Drive, New York, N.Y. 10027

Frontier Book Co., Box 31, Toyahvale, Texas 79786

Emma Lila Fundaburk, Luverne, Ala. 36049

Funk & Wagnalls, 360 Lexington Ave., New York, N.Y. 10017

G

Garrard Publishing Co., 1607 N. Market St., Champaign, Ill. 61821

Garrett & Massie, Inc., Box 1837, Richmond, Va. 23215

Genealogical Publishing Co., 521-23 St. Paul Place, Baltimore, Md. 21202

Golden Gate Junior Books, Box 398, 543 Old Country Rd., San Carlos, Calif. 94071

Great Outdoors Association, 4747 - 28th St., N., St. Petersburg, Fla. 33714

Greenwich Book Publishers, Inc., 282 Seventh Ave., New York, N.Y. 10001

Grosset & Dunlap, Inc., 51 Madison Ave., New York, N.Y. 10010

Guild Press, Box 7410, Benjamin Franklin Station, Washington, D.C. 20044

H

Hafner Publishing Co., Inc., 31 E. 10th St., New York, N.Y. 10003

G.K. Hall & Co., 70 Lincoln St., Boston, Mass. 02111

E.M. Hale and Co., 1201 S. Hastings Way, Eau Claire, Wis. 54702

Harcourt, Brace & World, Inc., 757 Third Ave., New York, N.Y. 10017

Harper & Row, Publishers, 49 E. 33rd St., New York, N.Y. 10016

Harvard University Press, 79 Garden St., Cambridge, Mass. 02138

Harvey House, Inc., Publishers, Irvington-on-Hudson, N.Y. 10533

Hastings House, Publishers, Inc., 151 E. 50th St., New York, N.Y. 10022

Hawthorn Books, Inc., 70 Fifth Ave., New York, N.Y. 10011

The Heard Museum of Anthropology and Primitive Art, 22 E. Monte Vista Rd., Phoenix, Ariz. 85004

D.C. Heath & Co., 285 Columbus Ave., Boston, Mass. 02116

Heinman Imported Books, 400 E. 72nd St., New York, N.Y. 10021

Hill & Wang, Inc., 141 Fifth Ave., New York, N.Y. 10010

Historical Society of Southern California, 815 S. Hill St., Los Angeles, Calif. 90014

Horace B. Hobbs, Jr., 2719 - 36th Place, N.W., Washington, D.C. 20007

Holiday House, Inc., 8 W. 13th St., New York, N.Y. 10011

Holt, Rinehart & Winston, Inc., 383 Madison Ave., New York, N.Y. 10017

Horn and Wallace, Box 4204, Albuquerque, N.M. 87106

Houghton Mifflin Co., 2 Park St., Boston, Mass. 02107

John Howell, Books, 434 Post St., San Francisco, Calif. 94102

Human Relations Area Files Press, c/o Taplinger Publishing Co., Inc., 29 E. 10th St., New York, N.Y. 10003

Henry E. Huntington Library & Art Gallery, 1151 Oxford Rd., San Marino, Calif. 91108

I

Indian Council Fire, 1263 W. Pratt Blvd., Chicago, Ill. 60626

Indian Festival of Art, Box 193, La Grande, Ore. 97850

Indiana University Press, 10th & Morton Sts., Bloomington, Ind. 47401

Indiana University Research Center in Anthropology, Folklore and Linguistics, Patton House, 516 E. 6th St., Bloomington, Ind. 47401

Inter-Tribal Indian Ceremonial Association, P.O. Box 1029, Gallup, N.M. 87301

Iowa State University Press, Press Bldg., Ames, Iowa 50012

Ives Washburn, Inc., 750 Third Ave., New York, N.Y. 10017

J

The Johns Hopkins Press, Homewood, Baltimore, Md. 21218

Johnsen Publishing Co., 1135 R St., Lincoln, Neb. 68508

Johnson Reprint Corp., 111 Fifth Ave., New York, N.Y. 10003

Judson Press, Valley Forge, Penna. 19481

K

K.C. Publications, 2115 N. Talkington Drive, Flagstaff, Ariz. 86001

P.J. Kenedy & Sons, 12 Barclay St., New York, N.Y. 10008

Dale S. King Publishers, Six Shooter Gulch, Route 4, Box 865, Tucson, Ariz. 85704

Neil A. Kjos Music Co., Publisher, 525 Busse, Park Ridge, Ill. 60068

Alfred A. Knopf, Inc., 501 Madison Ave., New York, N.Y. 10022

L

Lane Magazine & Book Co., Menlo Park, Calif. 94025

Lantern Press, Inc., 257 Park Ave., S., New York, N.Y. 10010

J.B. Lippincott Co., East Washington Square, Philadelphia, Penna. 19105

Little, Brown and Co., 34 Beacon St., Boston, Mass. 02106

Liveright Publishing Corp., 386 Park Ave., S., New York, N.Y. 10016

Long's College Book Co., Columbus, Ohio 43201

Loomis Museum Association, Lassen Volcanic National Park, Mineral, Calif. 96043

Loretto Literary and Benevolent Institution, Nerinx, Ky. 40049

Lothrop, Lee & Shepard Co., 419 Park Ave., S., New York, N.Y. 10016

Louisiana State University Press, Baton Rouge, La. 70803

Loyola University Press, 3441 N. Ashland Ave., Chicago, Ill. 60657

Lyons & Carnahan, 407 E. 25th St., Chicago, Ill. 60616

M

McClelland & Stewart, Ltd., 25 Hollinger Rd., Toronto 16, Ont., Can.

McGraw-Hill Book Co., 330 W. 42nd St., New York, N.Y. 10036

David McKay Co., Inc., 750 Third Ave., New York, N.Y. 10017

The Macmillan Co., c/o Crowell, Collier & Macmillan, Inc., 866 Third Ave., New York, N.Y. 10022

Marycliff Convent, W. 815 - 7th St., Spokane, Wash. 92204

Maryland Historical Society, 201 W. Monument St., Baltimore, Md. 21201

Melmont Publishers, Inc., c/o Children's Press, Inc., 1224 W. Van Buren St., Chicago, Ill. 60607

The Meredith Publishing Co., 1716 Locust St., Des Moines, Iowa 50303

Mesa Verde Museum Association, Mesa Verde National Park, Colo. 81330

Julian Messner, 1 W. 39th St., New York, N.Y. 10018

Michigan State University Press, Box 550, East Lansing, Mich. 48824

Milwaukee Public Museum, 800 W. Wells St., Milwaukee, Wis. 53233

Minnesota Historical Society, Cedar and Central, St. Paul, Minn. 55101

Moody Press, 820 W. LaSalle St., Chicago, Ill. 60610

W. M. Morrison Books, Box 3277, Waco, Texas 76707

William Morrow & Co., Inc., 425 Park Ave., S., New York, N.Y. 10016

Museum of the American Indian, Heye Foundation, Broadway at 155th St., New York, N.Y. 10032

Museum of Anthropology, University of Michigan, University Museum Bldg., Ann Arbor, Mich.

Museum of Navajo Ceremonial Art, Box 445, Santa Fe, N.M. 87501

Museum of New Mexico Press, Box 2087, Santa Fe, N.M. 87501

Museum of the Plains Indian, Browning, Mont. 59417

Museum of Primitive Art, 15 W. 54th St., New York, N.Y. 10019

N

National Geographic Society, 17th & M Sts., N.W., Washington, D.C. 20036

National Museum of Canada, Metcalfe & McLeod Sts., Ottawa, Ont., Can.

National Parks Association, 1500 New Hampshire Ave., N.W., Washington, D.C. 20036

Natural History Press, Garden City, N.Y. 11531

Naturegraph Co., 8339 W. Dry Creek Rd., Healdsburg, Calif. 95448

Navajo Tribal Museum, Window Rock, Ariz. 86515

The Naylor Co., 1015 Culebra Ave., San Antonio, Texas 78201

Thomas Nelson & Sons, Capewood & Davis Sts., Camden, N.J. 08103

New Age Press, Inc., 1544 Cerro Gordo St., Los Angeles, Calif. 90026

The New American Library, Inc., 1301 Avenue of the Americas, New York, N.Y. 10019

New Jersey State Museum, State Cultural Center, P.O. Box 1868, Trenton, N.J. 08625

New Mexico School of Mines, Socorro, N.M. 87801

New York Graphic Society, Publishers, Ltd., 140 Greenwich Ave., Greenwich, Conn. 06830

New York University Press, Washington Square, New York, N.Y. 10003

The Newark Museum, 43-49 Washington St., Newark, N.J. 07102

Newberry Library, 60 W. Walton St., Chicago, Ill. 60610

Newt Publications, 1155 S. Woodland Drive, White Cloud, Mich. 49349

Northern Arizona Society for Science and Art, P.O. Box 402, Flagstaff, Ariz. 86002

Northland Press, Box N, Flagstaff, Ariz. 86002

Northwestern Plains Publisher, Box 72, Colorado Springs, Colo. 80901

Northwestern Publishing House, 3616-32 W. North Ave., Milwaukee, Wis. 53208

W. W. Norton & Co., Inc., 55 Fifth Ave., New York, N.Y. 10003

O

Oceana Publications, Inc., Dobbs Ferry, N.Y. 10522

Oxford University Press, 417 Fifth Ave., New York, N.Y. 10016

P

Pacific Coast Publishers, Campbell Ave., at Scott Drive, Menlo Park, Calif. 94026

Pageant Press, Inc., 101 Fifth Ave., New York, N.Y. 10003

Pages of History, Box 6, Sausalito, Calif. 94165

Paisano Press, Inc., Box 85, Balboa Island, Calif. 92662

Pan American Union, Sales and Promotion Division, Washington, D.C. 20006

Pantheon Books, Inc., 22 E. 51st St., New York, N.Y. 10022

Parnassus Press, 2422 Ashby Ave., Berkeley, Calif. 94705

Peacock Press, P.O. Box 875, Berkeley, Calif. 94701

Pendle Hill Publications, Pendle Hill, Wallingford, Penna. 19086

Penguin Books, 3300 Clipper Mill Road, Baltimore, Md. 21211

Peninsular Publishing Co., Jackson Bluff Rd., Tallahassee, Fla. 32304

Pennsylvania Historical and Museum Commission, State Museum Bldg., Harrisburg, Penna.

Pennsylvania State University Press, University Press Bldg., University Park, Penna. 16802

Pennsylvania Valley Publishers, State College, Penna.

Pinon Book Store, 206 N. Main St., Bishop, Calif. 93514

The Platt & Munk Co., Inc., 200 Fifth Ave., New York, N.Y. 10010

Clarkson N. Potter, Inc., c/o Crown Publishers, Inc., 419 Park Ave., S., New York, N.Y. 10016

Charles T. Powner, 407 S. Dearborn St., Chicago, Ill. 60605

Frederick A. Praeger, Inc., 111 Fourth Ave., New York, N.Y. 10003

Prentice-Hall, Inc., Englewood Cliffs, N.J. 07632

Public Affairs Press, 419 New Jersey Ave., S.E., Washington, D.C. 20003

G.P. Putnam's Sons, 200 Madison Ave., New York, N.Y. 10016

R

Rand McNally & Co., Box 7600, Chicago, Ill. 60680

Random House, Inc., 457 Madison Ave., New York, N.Y. 10022

Readers Press, Inc., 130 Bristol St., New Haven, Conn. 06511

Redlands Press, 620 S. Main St., Stillwater, Okla. 74074

Henry Regnery Co., 114 W. Illinois St., Chicago, Ill.

Reprint Co., 154 W. Cleveland Pk. Drive, Spartanburg, S.C. 29303

Winifred Reutter, White River, S.D. 57579

Frank E. Richards, Publisher, 215 Church St., Phoenix, N.Y. 13135

The Rio Grande Press, Inc., 1734 E. 71st Place, Chicago, Ill. 60649

The Ward Ritchie Press, 3044 Riverside Drive, Los Angeles, Calif. 90039

Rochester Museum of Arts and Sciences, 657 East Ave., Rochester, N.Y. 14607

Rochester Museum Associates, Book Shop, 657 East Ave., Rochester, N.Y. 14607

The Ronald Press Co., 15 E. 26th St., New York, N.Y. 10010

Ross & Haines, Inc., 413 S. 4th St., Minneapolis, Minn. 55415

Rowman & Littlefield, Inc., 84 Fifth Ave., New York, N.Y. 10011

Roy Publishers, Inc., 30 E. 74th St., New York, N.Y. 10021

Gertrude McDaris Ruskin, 2663 Fair Oaks Rd., Decatur, Ga. 30033

Mrs. Virgil Y. Russell, 1342 S. Poplar, Casper, Wyo. 82601

Russell & Russell Publishers, 156 Fifth Ave., New York, N.Y. 10010

Rutgers University Press, 30 College Ave., New Brunswick, N.J. 08903

Rydal Press, Inc., Box 250, Santa Fe, N.M. 87501

S

Sage Books, 2679 S. York St., Denver, Colo. 80210

St. Martin's Press, Inc., 175 Fifth Ave., New York, N.Y. 10010

School of American Research, Box 1554, Santa Fe, N.M. 87501

Science Editions, John Wiley & Sons, Inc., 605 Third Ave., New York, N.Y. 10016

Charles Scribner's Sons, 597 Fifth Ave., New York, N.Y. 10017

E.C. Seale & Co., Inc., 1053 E. 54th St., Indianapolis, Ind. 46220

Service Center for Teachers of History, 400 A St., S.E., Washington, D.C. 20003

Seton Village, Santa Fe, N.M. 87501

Sheed & Ward, 64 University Place, New York, N.Y. 10003

The Shoe String Press, Inc., 60 Connolly Pkwy., Hamden, Conn. 06514

Shorey Publications, 815 Third Ave., Seattle, Wash. 98104

Lawrence W. Shultz, Box 25, North Manchester, Ind. 46962

Simon and Schuster, Inc., 630 Fifth Ave., New York, N.Y. 10020

Skira International Corp., c/o The World Publishing Co., 2231 W. 110th St., Cleveland, Ohio 44102

William Sloane Associates, c/o William Morrow & Co., Inc., 425 Park Ave., S., New York, N.Y. 10016

Peter Smith, 6 Lexington Ave., Magnolia, Mass. 01930

Society for the Study of Social Problems, Oakland University, Rochester, Minn. 55901

Southern Illinois University Press, Carbondale, Ill. 62901

Southern Methodist University Press, Dallas, Texas 75222

Southwest Museum, Highland Park, Los Angeles, Calif. 90042

Southwestern Association on Indian Affairs, P.O. Box 1964, Santa Fe, N.M. 87501

Southwestern Monuments Association, Box 1562BA, Gila Pueblo, Globe, Ariz. 85501

The Stackpole Co., Cameron and Kelker Sts., Harrisburg, Penna. 17105

Stanford University Press, Stanford, Calif. 94305

Stechert-Hafner Service Agency, Inc., 31 E. 10th St., New York, N.Y. 10003

Sumac Press, 613 N. 22nd St., LaCrosse, Wis. 54601

Superior Publishing Co., Box 1710, Seattle, Wash. 98111

Syracuse University Press, Box 8, University Station, Syracuse, N.Y. 13210

T

Taplinger Publishing Co., Inc., 31 E. 10th St., New York, N.Y. 10003

Taylor Museum, Colorado Springs Fine Arts Center, 30 W. Dale St., Colorado Springs, Colo. 80903

Texian Press, 1301 Jefferson St., Waco, Texas 76702

Charles C. Thomas, Publisher, 301-27 E. Lawrence Ave., Springfield, Ill. 62703

Twayne Publishers, Inc., 31 Union Square West, New York, N.Y. 10003

U

Frederick Ungar Publishing Co., Inc., 131 E. 23rd St., New York, N.Y. 10010

Unigraphic, Inc., 4400 Jackson Ave., Evansville, Ind. 47715

United States Publishers' Association, Inc., 386 Park Ave., S., New York, N.Y. 10016

University Museum, Third and Spruce Sts., Philadelphia, Penna. 19104

University of Arizona Press, Box 3398, College Station, Tucson, Ariz. 85700

University of California Press, Berkeley, Calif. 94720

University of Chicago Press, 5750 Ellis Ave., Chicago, Ill. 60637

University of Colorado Press, Regent Hall, University of Colorado, Boulder, Colo. 80304

University of Florida Press, 15 N.W. 15th St., Gainesville, Fla. 32601

University of Georgia Press, Lustrat House, Athens, Ga. 30601

University of Illinois Press, Urbana, Ill. 61801

University of Kentucky Press, McVey Hall, University of Kentucky, Lexington, Ky. 40506

The University of Michigan Press, Ann Arbor, Mich. 48106

University of Minnesota Press, 2037 University Ave., S.E., Minneapolis, Minn. 55455

University of Missouri Press, Columbia, Mo. 65201

University of Nebraska Press, Lincoln, Neb. 68508

University of New Mexico Press, Albuquerque, N.M. 87106

University of North Carolina Press, Bynum Bldg., Chapel Hill, N.C. 27515

University of Notre Dame Press, Notre Dame, Ind. 46556

University of Oklahoma Press, Norman, Okla. 73069

University of Oregon Press, Eugene, Ore. 97403

University of Pennsylvania Press, 3729 Spruce St., Philadelphia, Penna. 19104

University of Pittsburgh Press, 3309 Cathedral of Learning, Pittsburgh, Penna. 15213

University of Tennessee Press, Publications Bldg., University Station, Knoxville, Tenn. 37916

University of Texas Press, Box 7819, University Station, Austin, Texas 78712

University of Toronto Press, Front Campus, University of Toronto, Toronto 5, Can.

University of Utah Press, Bldg. 301, Salt Lake City, Utah 84112

University of Washington Press, Seattle, Wash. 98105

University of Wisconsin Press, Box 1379, Madison, Wis. 53701

University Press of Virginia, The Rotunda, Charlottesville, Va. 22903

V

D. Van Nostrand Co., Inc., 120 Alexander St., Princeton, N.J. 08540

Vanguard Press, Inc., 424 Madison Ave., New York, N.Y. 10017

Vantage Press, 120 W. 31st St., New York, N.Y. 10001

Vic Press, Box 1611, Grand Junction, Colo. 80402

The Viking Press, Inc., 625 Madison Ave., New York, N.Y. 10022

Vintage Books, 457 Madison Ave., New York, N.Y. 10022

W

George Wahr Publishing Co., 316 S. State St., Ann Arbor, Mich. 48108

Henry Z. Walck, Inc., 19 Union Square West, New York, N.Y. 10003

Victor H. Walker, Estes Park, Colo. 80517

Winifred F. Walters, Estell Munn Letter Service, Farmington, N.M. 87401

Washington University Press, St. Louis, Mo. 63130

Franklin Watts, Inc., 575 Lexington Ave., New York, N.Y. 10022

Waverly Press, 428 E. Preston St., Baltimore, Md. 21202

Wayne State University Press, 5980 Cass, Detroit, Mich. 48202

Westernlore Press, Box 41073, E.R. Station, Los Angeles, Calif. 90041

The Westminster Press, Witherspoon Bldg., Philadelphia, Penna. 19107

The Bond Wheelwright Co., Porter's Landing, Freeport, Me. 04032

Albert Whitman & Co., 560 W. Lake St., Chicago, Ill. 60606

H. W. Wilson Co., 950 University Ave., Bronx, N.Y. 10452

Wisconsin State Historical Society, 816 State St., Madison, Wis. 53706

The World Publishing Co., 2231 W. 110th St., Cleveland, Ohio 44102

Y

Yale University Press, 149 York St., New Haven, Conn. 06511

Who's Who

The following is an alphabetically arranged listing of American Indians prominent in Indian affairs, business, the arts and professions as well as non-Indians active in Indian affairs, history, art, anthropology, archaeology, etc., and the many varied fields to which the subject of the American Indian is related.

Here are included the biographical sketches of individuals named in other sections -- authors of books listed in the *Bibliography*, curators listed in the *Museums* section, officials of government agencies listed in the *Federal, State and Regional Agencies* section, etc.

FORMAT AND STYLE

The reader will note that these biographical sketches concentrate primarily on professional achievement; therefore, the usual personal data -- name of spouse, date of marriage, birthdates and names of children, etc. -- have not been included. The greater bulk of the information has been culled from research questionnaires completed by the individuals themselves; however, in the case of a hastily written or otherwise incomplete questionnaire, the editors have composed more complete listings by consulting other reliable published sources. Whenever possible, direct quotations have been employed to give the reader greater insight into the life and work of each person listed than mere facts can supply. While a definite format has been followed, occasional variations have become necessary in keeping with the varied occupations and activities of those listed. The length of each listing is merely a reflection of the quantity of material received; no judgment is intended nor should be construed. Home and/or business addresses have been included, when available.

CRITERIA

As stated earlier, selection has been made on the basis of professional achievement -- through our research, and through consultation and assistance received from several individuals long active in Indian affairs and related fields, for whose help we are most grateful. They are: Robert L. Bennett, Commissioner of Indian Affairs; Virginia S. Hart, Chief of Information and Reports of the Central Office of the Bureau of Indian Affairs; Robert G. Hart, General Manager of the Indian Arts and Crafts Board of the United States Department of the Interior; Charles E. Minton, Executive Director of the New Mexico Commission on Indian Affairs; Miss Yeffe Kimball and Mrs. Edna H. Massey, noted Indian artists.

A

ABERLE, DAVID FRIEND, 1918-
(anthropologist, educator)

Born November 23, 1918, St. Paul, Minn. *Education:* Harvard University, B.A., 1940; University of New Mexico, 1938-40; Columbia University, Ph.D., 1950. *Principal occupation:* Professor of anthropology. *Home address:* 3325 Storey Blvd., Eugene, Ore. 97405. *Affiliations:* Instructor, Harvard University, 1947-50; visiting associate professor, Johns Hopkins University, 1950-52; associate professor and professor, University of Michigan, 1952-60; visiting professor and honorable research associate, Manchester University, 1960-61; professor, Brandeis University, 1961-63; professor of anthropology, University of Oregon, 1963-. *Military service:* U.S. Army, 1942-46 (Army Commendation Ribbon). *Community activities:* Faculty-Student Committee to Stop the War in Vietnam, University of Oregon (chairman, 1965).

339

Memberships: American Anthropological Association (Fellow); American Sociological Association; Royal Anthropological Institute of Great Britain and Ireland; American Ethnological Society; Society of Applied Anthropology. *Awards, honors:* Sohier Prize for B. A. thesis, Harvard University; Phi Beta Kappa; Fellow, Center for Advanced Study in the Behavioral Sciences, 1955-56. *Interests:* Navajo Indians; Native American Church and other religious movements; Mongol culture. *Published works: Psychological Analysis of a Hopi Life-History* (Comp. Psych. Monog. Series, 1951); *Kinship System of the Kalmuk Mongols* (University of New Mexico Publications in Anthropology, 1953); *Navaho and Ute Peyotism: A Chronological and Distributional Study,* with Omer C. Stewart (University of Colorado Series in Anthropology, 1957); *The Peyote Religion Among the Navaho* (Aldine Press, 1966).

ABERLE, SOPHIE D.   (consultant in education)

Born Schenectady, N. Y. *Education:* Stanford University, B. A., 1923, M. A. 1925, Ph. D., 1927; Yale University School of Medicine, M. D., 1930. *Principal occupation:* Consultant in education. *Home address:* Route 3, Box 3030, Albuquerque, N. M. 87105. *Affiliations:* Teacher, Stanford University, 1925-26 (Research Fellow); instructor in anthropology, Yale University, Institute of Human Relations, 1927-30; instructor, Yale University School of Medicine, 1930-34; general superintendent, United Pueblos Agency, Bureau of Indian Affairs, 1935-44; Division Medical Sciences, National Research Council, 1944-49; chief of nutrition, Bernalillo County Indian Hospital, 1953-; director, Survey Indian Education, Bureau of Indian Affairs, 1963-; staff member, Bernalillo County Indian Hospital, Planned Parenthood, 1963-. *Other professional posts:* Chairman, board of directors, Southwest Field Training School for Federal Service, 1937-41; administrator of management and protocol of certain medical advisory committees, Division of Medical Science of the National Research Council, 1942-48; special research director, University of New Mexico, 1947-57; executive committee, National Science Board, 1952-54; acting executive director, Committee on Rights, Liberties and Responsibilities of the American Indian, Fund for

the Republic, 1957-59 (executive director, 1959-); staff member, Department of Psychiatry, University of New Mexico Medical School. *Community activities:* Southwest Superintendent Council of U. S. Indian Service (secretary, 1935-44); Upper Rio Grande Drainage Basin Committee, National Resources Planning Board (member, 1936-44); planner and administrator, Inter-American Indian Council, Mexico City, 1940; State of New Mexico Nutrition Committee (member, 1940-); Defense Savings Committee, State of New Mexico (member, 1940-44); Emergency Medical Service, State of New Mexico, Office of Civilian Defense (chief, 1942-44); Bernalillo County Hospital Committee (chairman, 1949-50); Committee on Maternal and Infant Mortality, New Mexico Medical Society, 1950-54; National Science Board, National Science Foundation (member, 1950-58); Museum Committee, Albuquerque Chamber of Commerce (member, 1950-56); Health Committee, All Pueblo Council (consultant, 1953); Y. W. C. A., Albuquerque, N.M. (board of directors, 1963-); Governors' Interstate Indian Council (board of directors, 1966-); New Mexico Commission on Indian Affairs (member, 1966-). *Memberships:* Albuquerque Academy of Medicine; American Association for the Advancement of Science; American Medical Association; American Association of Anatomists; Bernalillo County Heart Association; American Anthropological Association; New Mexico Academy of Science; New Mexico Medical Society (Committee on Maternal and Infant Mortality). *Awards, honors:* Alpha Omega Alpha (Medicine); Iota Sigma Pi (Chemistry); Sigma Xi (Scientific). *Interests:* Engaged in part-time field work among Pueblo Indians under grant from Committee for Research in Problems of Sex, National Research Council, and from the Carnegie Corporation of New York, 1927-35. *Published works: Primate Malaria* (National Research Council, 1945); *Twenty-five Years of Sex Research* (W. B. Saunders Co., 1953); *The Indian: America's Unfinished Business* (University of Oklahoma Press, 1966); numerous articles in scientific journals.

ABEYTA, NARCISO *(Ha-Sodeh)* (Navajo) 1918-   (interpreter)

Born December 18, 1918, Canyoncito, N. M. *Education:* Santa Fe Indian School, 1939;

University of New Mexico, B. A. (Fine Arts
and Economics). *Principal occupation:* In-
terviewer-interpreter, New Mexico State
Employment Commission, 1952-. *Home
address:* 102 Viro Eirile, Galley, N. M.
Military service: U. S. Army, 1941-45.
Community activities: American Legion.
Memberships: International Association of
Personnel in Employment Security, 1953-
65; Trek Expedition, Community Schools,
St. Louis, Mo. *Awards, honors:* Second
Prize, Advertising Poster, San Francisco
Exposition, 1939. *Published works:* Illus-
trator, *Aychee, Son of the Desert* (Hoffman
Birney Penn Publishing Co. , 1935).

ADAMS, AUDREY 1925- (teacher)

Born May 2, 1925, Lovelady, Texas. *Education:* Sam Houston State Teachers College, B. S. , 1942; University of Houston,
M. S. , 1948; now doing graduate work at
University of Texas. *Principal occupation:*
Teacher. *Affiliations:* Teacher, Lovelady
Independent Schools, Lovelady, Texas;
teacher, Goose Creek Independent Schools,
Baytown, Texas; teacher, Austin Independent Schools, Austin, Texas. *Community
activities:* Highlands Elementary School
P. T. A., Baytown, Texas (treasurer, 1952-
53); Highlands Book Club, Highlands, Texas
(president, 1954-55); Harris Elementary
School P. T. A., Austin, Texas (program
chairman, 1962-63). *Memberships:* American Business Women's Association, 1964-
65; Texas State Teachers' Association,
1942-; Baytown Education Association (secretary, 1950-51); Austin Teachers' Association, 1959-. *Awards, honors:* Citation of
Commendation, Austin Public Schools Committee, Austin, Texas, 1963-64. *Interests:*
Remedial reading techniques; psychology;
"attending the University of Texas for professional improvement"; writing historical
fiction for children, short stories for magazines, religious literature for Bible schools.
Published works: The Moabite Boy (Firm
Foundation Publishing House, 1962); series,
We Learn to Live (Firm Foundation Publishing House, 1961-65); *Karankawa Boy* (Naylor, 1965); has written ten teacher manuals
and two pupil books, and has edited eight
pupil books.

AGNEW, EDITH J. 1897- (teacher,
    writer, editor)

Born October 13, 1897, Denver, Colo. *Edu-
cation:* Park College, B. A. , 1921. *Prin-
cipal occupation:* Teacher, writer, editor.
Home address: 532 Columbia St. , Delta,
Colo. 81416. *Affiliations:* Teacher, Delta,
Colo. , public schools, 1921-24; teacher,
Presbyterian mission schools in Logan,
Utah, Ganado, Ariz. , and Holman, N. M. ,
1924-45; publicity writer, Presbyterian
Board of National Missions, 1945-50; edi-
tor, Presbyterian Board of Christian Edu-
cation, 1950-57. *Community activities:*
United Presbyterian Women (historian);
Western Colorado Presbyterial Society;
Chapter B. K. , P. E. O. (chaplain); Delta
County Migrant Committee (chairman).
Award, honors: Membership in Omega
State Chapter, Delta Kappa Gamma (hon.).
Interests: Miss Agnew writes, "My experi-
ence at Ganado Mission, Ariz. , was among
Navajo and Hopi Indians. (I) have traveled
in Mexico and through Arizona, (the latter)
to pick up data for *Larry.* (I have) con-
tributed to numerous church publications on
the subject of Indians. " *Published works:
Songs of Marcelino,* verse (privately print-
ed, 1936); *My Alaska Picture Story Book*
(Friendship Press, 1948); *Sandy and Mr.
Jalopy* (Friendship Press, 1949); *The Three
Henrys and Mrs. Hornicle* (Friendship
Press, 1950); *The Gray Eyes Family*
(Friendship Press, 1952); *Beyond Good Fri-
day,* a play (Friendship Press, 1953); *Hand
on My Shoulder,* with Gabino Rendon (Pres-
byterian Board of National Missions, 1954);
Nezbah's Lamb (Friendship Press, 1954);
Leo of Alaska (Friendship Press, 1958);
People of the Way (Westminster Press,
1959); *Edge of the Village,* with Margaret
Jump, a play (Friendship Press, 1959);
Larry (Friendship Press, 1960); *Treasures
for Tomas* (Friendship Press, 1964).

AGOGINO, GEORGE A. 1920-
    (anthropologist)

Born November 18, 1920, West Palm Beach,
Fla. *Education:* University of New Mexico,
B. A. (Anthropology), 1949, M. A. (Socio-
logy), 1951; Syracuse University, D. S. S.
(Anthropology), 1958; Harvard University,
postdoctoral (Anthropology), 1961-62.
Principal occupation: Associate professor
of anthropology. *Home address:* 1701
W. 17th St. , Portales, N. M. *Affiliations:*
Associate professor of anthropology, East-
ern New Mexico University; director, Paleo-
Indian Institute. *Other professional posts:*

Former editor, *W. H. Over News;* advisory editor (Early Man), *Science of Man;* advisory editor (Early Man), *La Conquista* (Italy). *Memberships:* Accademia Romana de Scienze ed Arti (honorary doctor); American Association for the Advancement of Science (Fellow); Royal Anthropological Institute of Great Britain and Ireland (Fellow); Instituto-InterAmericano (Fellow); Current Anthropology (associate); Wyoming Archaeological Society (honorary life member); Senato Accademico, Accademia Romana de Scienze ed Arti (Regent); American Society of Clinical Hypnosis. *Research grants:* American Philosophical Society, 1959, 1961, 1962; American Academy of Arts and Sciences, 1959, 1960; Wenner-Gren Foundation in Anthropology, 1958, 1959, 1960, 1961, 1962, 1963, 1964; Western Foundation, Inc., 1954; National Geographic Society, 1959, 1960, 1961, 1962, 1963, 1964; Sigma Xi, 1962, 1964; Milton Fund, 1961. *Published works:* Over one hundred articles published in American and foreign journals.

AGUILAR, JOSE V. *(Suwa-Peen)* (Tewa Pueblo) 1924- (artist)

Born January 8, 1924, San Ildefonso, N. M. *Education:* Otis Art Institute, Certificate, 1949; Hill and Canyon School of Art, 1950. *Principal occupation:* Technical artist. *Home address:* 9682 Mt. Darnard Dr., Buena Park, Calif. 90620. *Affiliation:* Technical artist, Space and Information System Division, North American Aviation, Downey, Calif., 1954-. *Military service:* U. S. Army, 1944-46 (European Theatre Medal; Purple Heart). *Memberships:* National Congress of American Indians, 1954-. *Awards, honors:* Certificate of Merit, Inter-Tribal Indian Ceremonial Association, 1949; First Purchase Award, Philbrook Art Center, 1953; Denver Art Museum Purchase Award; Mary Day Wartrous Award, 1954; Honorable Mention, Philbrook Art Center, 1959; Lippencott and Wellington Award; Museum of New Mexico Award for Collection of Museum of Contemporary Art; paintings in permanent collections of Philbrook Art Center, Museum of New Mexico, Museum of the American Indian.

ALDEN, JOHN R. 1908- (professor of history)

Born 1908, Mich. *Education:* University of Michigan, B. A., M. A., Ph. D. *Principal occupation:* Professor of history. *Home address:* 2736 Dogwood Rd., Durham, N. C. *Affiliations:* Professor of history, University of Nebraska, 1945-55; summer sessions, University of Chicago, University of Michigan, Columbia University; professor of history, Duke University, 1955- (chairman, History Department, 1957-60; James B. Duke professor of history, 1963-). *Awards, honors:* Postdoctoral fellowship, University of Michigan; Johnson Faculty Fellowship, University of Nebraska; Albert J. Beveridge Prize, American Historical Association, 1945; Commonwealth Fund Lecturer, University College, London, 1960; Donald Fleming Lecturer, Louisiana State University, 1961; Guggenheim Fellow, 1955-56. *Published works: John Stuart and the Southern Colonial Frontier* (University of Michigan Press, 1944); *General Gage in America* (Louisiana State University Press, 1948); *General Charles Lee* (Louisiana State University Press, 1951); editor, *War of the Revolution,* by Christopher Ward, (Macmillan, 1952); *The American Revolution, 1775-1783* (Harper's, 1954); *The South in the Revolution, 1769-1789* (Louisiana State University Press, 1957); *A History of the United States,* with Alice Maginis (American Book Co., 1960); *The First South* (Louisiana State University Press, 1961); *Rise of the American Republic* (Harper's 1963).

ALEXANDER, HARRIET W. 1881 (museum director)

Born September 27, 1881, Newport, Ky. *Education:* Oxford College. *Principal occupation:* Museum director. *Home address:* 1043 F St., Salida, Colo. 81201. *Affiliations:* Director, Salida Museum, Salida, Colo. *Community activities:* City councilman, 1955-65; American Red Cross (home service chairman, 1917-). *Memberships:* Chamber of Commerce; Salida Golf Club; Salida Women's Republican Club (past president); Episcopal Guild; Salida Women's Club (president and secretary, 1941). *Awards:* Honorary membership, Delta Kappa Gamma; honorary member, American Association of University Women; Salida Airfield named Harriet Alexander Airport, 1963; Good Citizen Award, Salida Chamber of Commerce.

ALLEN, DON B.   1889-   (professor, researcher, writer)

Born September 27, 1889, Kansas City, Mo. *Education:* Westminster College, B. A., 1920; Princeton Theological Seminary, B.D., 1917, Th. M. , 1922; University of Texas, M. A. , 1924; Columbia University; University of Pennsylvania; University of Oklahoma. *Principal occupation:* Free-lance writer. *Home addresses:* "Words and Music," Carmel-by-the-Sea, Calif. 93921, and P. O. Box 425, Santa Fe, N. M. 87501. *Memberships:* Delta Tau Delta; Phi Delta Kappa; Kappa Delta Pi; American Academy of Political and Social Science. *Awards:* General Education Board Fellowship, 1927-28. *Published works: Doctor in Buckskin* (Harper and Row, 1951; Perennial Paperback, 1965); *Troubled Border* (Harper and Row, 1954); *Ambush at Buffalo Wallow* (Fawcett, 1956); *Miss Alice and the Cunning Comanche,* a play (Friendship Press, 1958); *Prisoners of the Polar Ice* (Westminster Press, 1962); *Tall as Great Standing Rock* (Westminster Press, 1963); *Navahos Have Five Fingers* (University of Oklahoma Press, 1963); *Doctor, Lawyer, Merchant, Chief* (Westminster Press, 1965). All works co-authored with T. Diener Allen.

ALLEN, T. DIENER   1908-   (writer)

Born August 13, 1908, Douglas, Okla. *Education:* Phillips University, B. A. , 1929; Yale University, B. D. , 1935; University of Oklahoma; Columbia University; New York University; U. C. L. A. *Principal occupation:* Free-lance writer. *Home addresses:* "Words and Music," Carmel-by-the-Sea, Calif. 93921, and P. O. Box 425, Santa Fe, N. M. 87501. *Other occupations:* Teacher, creative writing, Institute of American Indian Arts. *Memberships:* Authors' League. *Published works: Doctor in Buckskin* (Harper and Row, 1951; Perennial Paperback, 1965); *Troubled Border* (Harper and Row, 1954); *Ambush at Buffalo Wallow* (Fawcett, 1956); *Miss Alice and the Cunning Comanche,* a play (Friendship Press, 1958); *Prisoners of the Polar Ice* (Westminster Press, 1962); *Tall as Great Standing Rock* (Westminster Press, 1963); *Navahos Have Five Fingers* (University of Oklahoma Press, 1963); *Doctor, Lawyer, Merchant, Chief* (Westminster Press, 1965). All works co-authored with Don B. Allen.

ALLEN, WALTER D.   1933-   (teacher, administrator)

Born November 9, 1933, Morgan County, Ohio. *Education:* Bob Jones University, B. A. , 1957; Ohio University. *Principal occupation:* Teacher and administrator. *Home address:* Deering, Alaska 99736. *Affiliation:* Teacher and administrator, Deering (B. I. A.) Day School, Deering, Alaska 99736. *Memberships:* Bob Jones Alumni Association.

ALLERS, CAROLYN   1909-   (sociologist)

Born July 1, 1909, Evanston, Ill. *Education:* New School for Social Research, M. A., 1962. *Principal occupation:* Librarian and associate editor, Museum of New Mexico. *Home address:* San Sebastian Ranch, Santa Fe, N. M. *Memberships:* Eastern Sociological Association; American Sociological Association. *Awards:* William A. Davis Award for B. A. thesis.

ALLRED, GROVER C.   1927-   (park ranger)

Born February 9, 1927, Como, Texas. *Education:* Stockton College, A. A. , 1949; University of the Pacific, B. A., 1951; University of Alaska; University of Washington, M. A. , 1956. *Principal occupation:* State park ranger. *Home address:* 1815 Venus Drive, Sacramento, Calif. 95825. *Affiliations:* State park ranger, Shasta Historic Monument. *Military service:* U. S. Army, 1945-46; U. S. Naval Reserve, 1951-53. *Memberships:* American Anthropological Association; American Ethnological Society; Washington State Historical Society; American Association for State and Local History; Kroeber Anthropological Society; Linguistic Society of America; Sierra Club. *Interests:* California and North Pacific Coast ethnology and history; natural science.

AMIOTTE, ARTHUR DOUGLAS (Oglala-, Teton-Sioux)   1942-   (artist, teacher)

Born March 25, 1942, Pine Ridge, S. D. *Education:* Northern State College, B. S.

(Art Education), 1964. *Principal occupation:* Artist, teacher. *Home address:* 504 38th St. Pl. , Sioux City, Iowa 51104. *Affiliations:* Iowa State Education Association, 1964-; Sioux City Education Association, 1964-. *Community activities:* Community speakers panel on promoting minority and ethnic group awareness; lecturer on American Indians. *Memberships:* Student National Art Education Association, 1962-64; Sigma Tau Delta; Phi Delta Kappa, 1964-66; Kappa Delta Pi, 1964-66; Northern Art Education Association, 1963-66. *Awards, honors:* South Dakota Indian Scholarship, 1960-64; inclusion in *Who's Who in American Universities and Colleges,* 1964; C. A. Schwarz Art Education Award Scholarship, 1963; Award for Outstanding Achievement and Accomplishment in Art Education, 1964; Honorable Mention in Sculpture, 18th Annual National Exhibition of American Indian Art, Philbrook Art Center, 1963; Honorable Mention for Painting, Foundation of North American Indian Culture, 1963; First Place Award for Painting, Foundation of North American Indian Culture, 1964; exhibitions at Department of Interior, Gallery of American Indian Art, 1964, Philbrook Art Center, 1963-66, Institute of American Indian Art, 1966; nominated for Outstanding Teacher of Year, Sioux City, 1966. *Interests:* Art education; Plains Indian culture.

ANDERSON, CATHERINE CORLEY   1909- (teacher, writer)

Born March 21, 1909, Chicago, Ill. *Education:* Art Institute of Chicago, 1929-32; Chicago University, 1931-32; St. Xavier College, 1932-33. *Principal occupation:* Teacher in art crafts. *Home address:* 2347 N. Moody Ave. , Chicago, Ill. 60639. *Other professional posts:* Art teacher, Mercy High School; editorial assistant, Scott, Foresman Co. ; *Junior Magazine*; teacher in art crafts, Chicago Park District. *Memberships:* Children's Reading Round Table (president, vice president, program director), 1946-. *Interests:* Writing and illustrating of children's books; Indian lore and history. *Published works: Officer O'Malley on the Job* (Albert Whitman, 1954); *Sister Beatrice Goes to Bat* (Bruce, 1958); *Sister Beatrice Goes West* (Bruce, 1961); *Sister Beatrice and the Mission Mystery* (Bruce, 1963).

ANDERSON, ERLING E.   1904- (teacher, administrator)

Born November 30, 1904, Buffalo, N. D. *Education:* Concordia College, B. A., 1929; North Dakota University, M. A. (Education), 1960. *Principal occupation:* Principal, teacher, and administrator, Houle Day School. *Home address:* Houle (B. I. A.) Day School, Belcourt, N. D. 58316. *Community activities:* Boy Scouts; Kiwanis Club; Sportsmen's Club. *Memberships:* Phi Delta Kappa, 1955-; National Federation of Federal Employees.

ANDERSON, EVA   1889-   (writer)

Born May 20, 1889, Surprise, Neb. *Education:* Nebraska Wesleyan University, B. A. , 1910; University of Washington, M. A. , 1926, Ph. D. , 1937; Columbia University. *Principal occupation:* Writer, teacher, state legislator, historian. *Home address:* Cascadian Hotel, Suite 808, Wenatchee, Wash. *Affiliations:* State legislator, State of Washington; teacher in Nebraska and Washington; *Wenatchee Daily World. Community activities:* Chamber of Commerce committees (chairman, Roads Committee, 1963-65); board of curators, Washington State Historical Society; other civic, fraternal, and public service groups. *Memberships:* American Pen Women; Pi Lambda Theta; Phi Delta Nu; Soroptimist Club; Gamma Delta Kappa; American Association of University Women; Methodist Church; Grange; Washington State Press Women; Chamber of Commerce. *Awards, honors:* Pioneer Award, Washington State Press Women, 1965; American Association for State and Local History, 1954; Outstanding Alumnae, Nebraska Wesleyan, 1959; Outstanding Woman of Achievement, State of Washington, 1949; National Phi Delta Nu for "authorship, " 1962. *Published works: Child's Story of Washington* (University Publishing Co. , 1938); *Dog Team Doctor* (Caxton, 1942); *Oregon Stories* (University Publishing Co. , 1942); *Chief Seattle* (Caxton, 1943); pioneer biographies *(Wenatchee World,* 1945-65); *Rails Over the Cascades (Wenatchee World,* 1954); *The Wenatchee Kid (Wenatchee World,* 1955); *Touring Ten Countries of Europe* (1957); *Behind the Iron Curtain and Beyond* (1958); *Africa and Beyond* (1960); *Round the World* (1962); *Down Mexico Way* (1963); *Inside-Outside South America* (1965).

ANDERSON, HELEN JEAN   1930-
(editor)

Born October 12, 1930, Raleigh, N. C. *Education:* Cornell University, B.S. , 1951; Columbia University, M.S. , 1957. *Principal occupation:* Senior editor, *Venture. Home address:* 11 Bank St. , New York, N. Y. 10014. *Memberships:* Phi Kappa Phi; Omicron Nu; Gamma Phi Beta. *Awards, honors:* Pulitzer Traveling Scholar, 1958. *Interests:* Travel throughout western Europe, Greece, United States, Canada, the Caribbean. *Published works: The Art of American Indian Cooking,* with Yefee Kimball (Doubleday, 1965); *Who Says You Can't Cook* (Westminster, 1966).

ANDERSON, KEITH M.   1933-
(archaeologist)

Born August 17, 1933, Wellsville, N. Y. *Education:* University of Washington; Washington State University, B. A. , 1957; University of Utah, M.A. , 1960. *Principal occupation:* Archaeologist. *Home address:* Navajo National Monument, Tonalea, Ariz. 86044. *Affiliation:* Archaeologist, National Park Service, Navajo National Monument. *Military service:* U. S. Air Force, 1953-54. *Memberships:* Society for American Archaeology; American Anthropological Association; Sigma Xi. *Interests:* Southwestern archaeology; culture change; cultural evolution; ethnohistory. *Awards:* Laura A. Meier Award; Phi Beta Kappa. *Published works: 1960, 1959 Glen Canyon Archaeology* (University of Utah Anthropological Papers, 1960, 1961); *The Creeping Dune Site* (*American Antiquity,* 1962); *Ceramic Clues to Pueblo-Puebloid Relationships* (*American Antiquity,* 1963); *Survey of Fish Springs Wildlife Refuge* (University of Utah Anthropological Papers, 1963).

ANDERSON, WILLIAM ASHLEY   1890-
(writer)

Born April 13, 1890, Red Bank, N. J. *Education:* Staff College, Langres, France, 1918. *Principal occupation:* Writer. *Home address:* "Hill Billet," R.D. 3, East Stroudsburg, Pa. 18301. *Affiliations:* Editorial staff member, *Asia, Literary Digest,* Butterick Publications; associate director of copy, N. W. Ayer and Son. *Military service:* Company commander, King's African

Rifles, German East Africa; captain of infantry, A. E. F. Staff College, Langres, France. *Awards:* Harvard Book Award for the most outstanding campaign of national advertising. *Interests:* Work in China, Manchuria and Mongolia during last days of Imperial regime, 1911-12; travel throughout Asia, Arabia, Zanzibar, Abbyssinia, Africa. *Published works: Yellow Flood* (McBride); *Witch of Gondar* (Butterick); *South of Suez; Angel of Hudson Bay* (Dutton, 1961); short stories in *Cosmopolitan, Harper's, Red Book, Argosy, Saturday Evening Post,* etc.

ANDREWS, IRADELL M.   1896-
(teacher)

Born May 8, 1896, Marwood, Butler County, Penna. *Education:* Slippery Rock State Teachers College, B.S. , 1934; University of Pittsburgh, M.E. , 1953. *Principal occupation:* Teacher. *Home address:* Route 1, Box 308, Santa Fe, N. M. 87501. *Affiliations:* San Ildefonso (B. I. A.) Day School, Tesuque (B. I. A.) Day School, and others. *Military service:* Women's Army Corps (Good Conduct Medal, American Theater). *Community activities:* American Legion; Disabled American Veterans. *Memberships:* New Mexico Education Association; American Association of University Women; American Association of Retired Persons; National Retired Teachers Association. *Awards:* Second Place, National History, Rocky Boy's Post, American Legion.

ANDREWS, RALPH WARREN   1897-
(writer, salesman)

Born January 12, 1897, Denver, Colo. *Education:* University of Minnesota. *Principal occupation:* Writer, salesman. *Home address:* 2405 S. 122nd St. , Seattle, Wash. *Affiliations:* Salesman and advertising agency copywriter, 1925-52; writer of "pulp" paper fiction, 1927-40. *Memberships:* Friends of the Seattle Public Library; various historical societies. *Awards:* Certificate of Merit for *This Was Logging,* Seattle Historical Society, 1955. *Interests:* History, particularly of western America; related travels. *Published works: This Was Logging* (Superior Publishing Co. , 1954); *Glory Days of Logging* (Superior, 1955); *This Was Seafaring,* with Harry A. Kirwin (Superior, 1956); *Redwood Classic* (Superior,

1958); *This Was Sawmilling* (Superior, 1957); *Fish and Ships*, with A. K. Larssen (Superior, 1959); *Heroes of the Western Woods* (Dutton, 1959); *Indian Primitive* (Superior, 1960); *Curtis' Western Indians* (Superior, 1962); *Indians as the Westerners Saw Them* (Superior, 1963); *Picture Gallery Pioneers* (Superior, 1964); *Photographers of the Frontier West* (Superior, 1965).

ANDRIST, RALPH K.   1914- (editor, writer)

Born January 11, 1914, Crookston, Minn. *Education:* University of Minnesota, B. A., 1937. *Principal occupation:*   Editor, writer. *Home address:* Chichester Rd., New Canaan, Conn. 06840. *Affiliations:* Editor, American Heritage Publishing Co.; free-lance writer; associate director, Episcopal Church Foundation, New York, N. Y. *Military service:*   U. S. Navy, 1942-45, Bronze Star. *Community activities:* Democratic Party; member, Democratic Town Committee of New Canaan. *Memberships:* Sigma Delta Chi (professional journalism). *Interests:* Writing American history, especially about the Frontier period, the westward movement, and the American Indian. *Published works: California Gold Rush* (American Heritage Publishing Co., 1961); *Heroes of Polar Exploration* (American Heritage Publishing Co., 1962); *Steamboats on the Mississippi* (American Heritage Publishing Co., 1962); *Andrew Jackson, Soldier and Statesman* (American Heritage Publishing Co., 1963); *The Erie Canal* (American Heritage Publishing Co., 1964); *The Long Death* (Macmillan, 1964); writer of pictorial commentary text and captions, *American Heritage Book of the Great West* (American Heritage Publishing Co., 1965).

ANNESS, MILFORD E.   1918- (attorney)

Born February 14, 1918, Metamora, Ind. *Education:* Ball State University, 1936-37; Indiana University, B. A., 1940; Indiana University School of Law, LL. B., 1954. *Principal occupation:* Attorney. *Home address:* R. R. 7, Columbus, Ind. 47201. *Affiliations:* State senator, Indiana, 1947-55; judge, Fayette County (Ind.) Circuit Court, 1955-62; practicing attorney, Columbus, Ind., 1962-. *Military service:* U. S. Army, 1943-45. *Community activities:*

Cincinnati Bible Seminary, Cincinnati, Ohio (trustee); Central African Churches of Christ Mission (director, legal advisor); Indiana Judicial Council, 1960-64; Governor's Council on Children and Youth (Fayette County representative), 1958-62; Indiana Sesquicentennial Advisory Committee, 1964-; First Christian Church, Columbus, Ind. (teacher, men's bible class); Indiana Chapter, Sons of the American Revolution (state treasurer); Indiana Chapter, Bible Study League of America (president); Alexander Christian Foundation, Indianapolis, Ind. (vice president); Church of Christ; American Legion; Kiwanis; Odd Fellows; Veterans of Foreign Wars. *Memberships:* Lambda Chi Alpha; Sigma Delta Kappa; Indiana Historical Society; Indiana State Bar Association; Bartholomew County Bar Association. *Awards, honors:* Honorary member, Creek Indian Council, 1964-; Sagamore of the Wabash Award, 1954; Good Citizenship Medal, Sons of the American Revolution, Indiana Chapter, 1966. *Interests:* "Active in Indiana Republican politics -- possible candidate for U. S. senator; writer, speaker and lecturer on fields of church, Indiana and Indian history; write articles for *The Christian Standard* (Cincinnati, Ohio) and for *Restoration Herald* (Cincinnati, Ohio); write songs and compose music for songs. " Is now writing a sequel to *Song of Metamoris*, to be entitled *Forever the Song*, and a book on current political thought entitled *To This Cause. Published works: Song of Metamoris* (Caxton Printers, Ltd., 1964).

ARTICHOKER, JOHN HOBART, Jr. (Sioux) 1930- (B. I. A. agency superintendent)

Born January 17, 1930, Pine Ridge, S. D. *Education:* State University of South Dakota, B. S. (Education), 1951, M. A. (Education), 1957. *Principal occupation:* B. I. A. agency superintendent. *Home address:* Box 306, Lame Deer, Mont. *Affiliations:* Director of Indian education, State of South Dakota, 1951-61; tribal operations officer, B. I. A., Billings, Mont., 1961-62; superintendent, Northern Cheyenne Indian Reservation, 1963-. *Community activities:* Division of Indian Services, University of Montana (advisory council); Tongue River Jaycees (board of directors); National Advisory Committee on Indian Work, National Council of the Episcopal Church. *Awards:* Ten

Outstanding Young Men Award, U. S. J. C. 's, 1965; Indian Achievement Award, 1965. *Published works: Indians of South Dakota* (South Dakota Department of Public Instruction, 1956); *The Sioux Indian Goes to College*, with Neil Palmer (master's thesis), Institute of Indian Studies, Vermillion, S. D.

ASHABRANNER, BRENT 1921- (Peace Corps director)

Born November 3, 1921, Stillwater, Okla. *Education:* Oklahoma State University, B.S., 1948, M. A. , 1951. *Principal occupation:* Peace Corps director. *Home address:* 3140 Elmwood, Oklahoma City, Okla. *Affiliations:* Instructor, Oklahoma State University, 1952-55; free lance writer; educational materials advisor, Point Four, Ethiopia, 1955-57; I. C. A. , Libya, 1957-59; A. I. D. , Nigeria, 1960-61; deputy Peace Corps representative, Nigeria, 1961-62; deputy Peace Corps director, India, 1962-64; peace corps director, India, 1965-. *Military service:* U. S. Navy, 1942-45. *Interests:* Overseas development; American Indian and African folklore; primitive art; travels in Ethiopia, Libya, and several West African countries. *Published works: The Choctaw Code* (McGraw-Hill, 1961); *Chief Joseph* (McGraw-Hill, 1962).

ATHERTON, LEWIS E. 1905- (professor of history)

Born March 1, 1905, Bosworth, Mo. *Education:* University of Missouri, B. A., 1927, M. A. , 1930, Ph. D. , 1937. *Principal occupation:* Professor of history. *Affiliations:* Professor of history, University of Missouri, 1936-. *Other professional posts:* Past president, Agricultural History Society; past member, boards of editors, *Agricultural History, Mississippi Valley Historical Review,* and *Journal of Southern History. Memberships:* Mississippi Valley Historical Association; Southern Historical Association; American Historical Association; Western History Association. *Awards, honors:* Guggenheim Fellow, 1940; Newberry Library Fellow, 1950; University of Missouri Distinguished Faculty Award, 1960. *Interests:* American West and South. *Published works: Pioneer Merchant in Mid-America* (University of Missouri Press, 1939); *The Southern Country Store* (Louisiana State University Press, 1949); *Main*

Street on the Middle Border (Indiana University Press, 1954); *The Cattle Kings* (Indiana University Press, 1961).

ATKINSON, M. JOURDAN 1898- (researcher, teacher)

Born April 3, 1898. *Education:* University of Texas, B.A. , 1926; Oklahoma A & M, M. A. and Ed. D. , 1955; University of Mexico. *Principal occupation:* Researcher, teacher. *Home address:* Box 33, Texas Southern University, Houston, Texas 77004. *Affiliations:* Associate professor, Texas Southern University, 1956-. *Other professional posts:* Private research on acculturation of the Southwest, 1926-49. *Memberships:* Texas Association of College Teachers; Current Anthropology (associate); International Congress de Americanistas; Western Historical Association. *Awards, honors:* French Poetry Prize, University of Texas, 1921, 1923. *Published works: The Texas Indians as Indians of the Southwest* (Naylor, 1935); *When the World Was Young* (Naylor, 1957); editor, *Student's Guide to Research* (Wm. C. Brown).

AUSTIN, FRANK *(Bahah-Zhonie)* (Navajo) 1938- (artist)

Born April 10, 1938, Tsegi Canyon, Tonalea, Ariz. *Education:* Phoenix Indian School; University of Arizona; Tempe College, 1959. *Principal occupation:* Textile artist and painter. *Home address:* 1707 E. 2nd St. , Santa Fe, N. M. 87502. *Memberships:* American Craftsmen's Council, 1961; American Institute of Interior Designers; Arizona Arts and Crafts. *Awards, honors:* American Institute of Interior Design Award; Walter Bimson Grand Award; Catharine J. McWhirter Grand Award, Scottsdale National Art Exhibit.

B

BAERREIS, DAVID A. 1916- (professor of anthropology)

Born November 2, 1916, New York, N. Y. *Education:* University of Oklahoma, B. A., 1941, M. A. , 1943; Columbia University,

Ph. D. , 1948. *Principal occupation:* Professor of anthropology. *Home address:* 1233 Sweet Briar Rd., Madison, Wis. 53705. *Affiliations:* Professor of anthropology, University of Wisconsin, 1947-. *Military service:* U. S. Army. *Memberships:* Society for American Archaeology (secretary, 1959-65; president, 1962); American Association for the Advancement of Science (chairman, secretary, vice-president, 1963); American Anthropological Association (Fellow); Royal Anthropological Institute. *Awards, honors:* Lapham Research Medal, Wisconsin Archaeological Society. *Interests:* Prehistory and ethnohistory of North and South American Indians; field trips to Wisconsin, Oklahoma, New Mexico, South Dakota, Iowa, Brazil. *Published works: The Preceramic Horizons of Northeastern Oklahoma* (Anthropological Papers, Museum of Michigan, No. 6, 1951); editor, *The Indian in Modern America* (State Historical Society of Wisconsin, 1956); articles in various journals.

BAILEY, RALPH EDGAR 1893-
(newspaperman, writer)

Born September 24, 1893, East Greenwich, R. I. *Education:* East Greenwich Academy. *Principal occupation:* Newspaperman, writer. *Home address:* 25 Sargent Park, Newton, Mass. 02158. *Affiliations:* Reporter, political editor, public affairs writer, managing editor, editor, *News, News Tribune, Star Tribune,* Providence, R. I. , 1914-38; rewrite man, desk editor, copy desk chief, wire editor, *Boston Traveler,* 1941-62. *Military service:* First Separate Squadron, Cavalry, R. I. N. G. , 1916-17. *Community activities:* Republic State Committee, Rhode Island (assistant to chairman, 1938-40). *Memberships:* Boston Authors Club. *Interests:* History and biography; trade history; travel in United States. *Published works: Argosies of Empire* (Dutton, 1947); *Sea Hawks of Empire* (Dutton, 1948); *Tim's Fight for the Valley* (Dutton, 1951); *Tony Sees it Through* (Dutton, 1953); *Indian Fighter, The Story of Nelson A. Miles* (Morrow, 1965); articles in various magazines.

BAINES, RAYMOND GEORGE (Tlingit-Tsimpshean) 1926- (pastor)

Born September 26, 1926, Ketchikan, Alaska. *Education:* Phillips University, B. A. , 1959; Pacific School of Religion, B.D., 1963. *Principal occupation:* Pastor. *Home address:* 1426 Hillsboro Ave., St. Louis Park, Minn. 55426. *Affiliations:* Executive director, United Church Committee on Indian Work; pastor of churches, El Cerrito and Berkeley, Calif., Gardiner, Ore., and Metlakatta and Sitka, Alaska. *Military service:* U. S. Army Infantry, 1944-45. *Community activities:* School Board; P. T. A. , Metlakatta, Alaska (vice president); Central Council, Tlingit and Haida Indians of Alaska (executive treasurer). *Memberships:* Minnesota, Minneapolis, St. Paul councils of churches; Governor's Advisory Committee on Children and Young; Minnesota Fair Employment Practices Commission; Minnesota Council on Religion and Race.

BAITY, ELIZABETH CHESLEY 1907-
(writer)

Born March 5, 1907, Hamilton, Texas. *Education:* Texas State University for Women, B. A. , B. S. , 1924-28; University of North Carolina, M. A. , 1929, M. A. , 1952, M. S. (Anthropology), 1962. *Principal occupation:* Writer in ethnoprehistory and of literacy readers for emerging countries. *Home address:* 1503 Mason Farm Rd. , Chapel Hill, N. C. 27514. *Affiliations:* Writer, World Team, Committee for World Literacy and Christian Literature, Pakistan, 1953, South Sudan, 1954, East Africa, 1956. *Awards, honors: Herald Tribune* Award for *Americans Before Columbus;* North Carolina Mayflower Club Annual Award for *America Before Man. Interests:* Protohistory; literacy books for new literates in Africa and Asia; archaeology. *Published works: Man is a Weaver* (Viking, Macmillan, Junior Literacy Guild, George Harrap, 1942); *Americans Before Columbus* (Viking, Junior Literacy Guild, Macmillan, 1951); *America Before Man* (Viking, Macmillan); series of Library Extension booklets, "The Modern Woman"; *The Forgotten World of the Steppes* (in progress).

BAKER, BETTY 1928- (writer)

Born June 20, 1928, Bloomsburg, Penna. *Principal occupation:* Writer. *Home address:* 6917 Bonnie Brae, Tuscon, Ariz. 85710. *Other occupation:* Editor, *The*

Roundup, monthly house organ of the Western Writers of America (association). *Memberships:* Western Writers of America, 1963-; American Press Women, 1964-. *Awards:* Western Heritage Awards for *Killer-of-Death,* 1963. *Interests:* The American Indian. Author proposes the non-Indian recognize the differing cultural traits of the many American tribes, instead of lumping them together in one mass. Miss Baker writes, "I detest authors who portray Indians as one's next-door neighbors in costume. Tribes differed as much as Indian and white-eye. The tribal beliefs, codes, and even the geography of their lands, formed thought, action and reaction. Apaches didn't think like Papagos, nor did Hopi react like Iroquois, but few authors take the trouble of slipping inside the Indian's mind. The view is entirely different from back of the eyes." *Published works: Little Runner of the Longhouse* (Harper, 1962); *The Shaman's Last Raid* (Harper, 1963); *Killer-of-Death* (Harper, 1963); *The Treasure of the Padres* (Harper, 1964); *Walk the World's Rim* (Harper, 1965); *Blood of the Brave* (Harper, 1966).

BALCH, GLENN 1902- (writer)

Born December 11, 1902, Venus, Texas. *Education:* Baylor University, B. A., 1925; graduate work, Columbia University, 1935. *Principal occupation:* Writer. *Home address:* 1114 Houston Rd., Boise, Idaho 83704. *Military service:* U. S. Army Air Force, 1942-46 (Air Medal); reserve and active duty service during the Korean War, U. S. Army. *Awards:* Three George Washington Memorial Awards for essays written as a member of the Armed Forces. *Interests:* Western history, particularly as it pertains to Indian tribes; research pertaining to the Nez Perce, Bannocks, Shoshone, Loupe Pawnees. *Published works: Little Hawk and the Free Horses, Squaw Boy, Indian Saddle-up, Indian Fur, Brave Riders, Spotted Horse,* all published by Thomas Y. Crowell Co.

BALDWIN, GORDON C. 1908- (archaeologist, writer)

Born June 5, 1908, Portland, Ore. *Education:* University of Arizona, B.A., 1933, M.A., 1934; University of Southern California, Ph. D., 1941. *Principal occupation:* Archaeologist, writer. *Home address:* 2920 E. Mabel St., Tucson, Ariz. 85716. *Affiliations:* Museum curator and instructor, Arizona State Museum and University of Arizona, 1934-40; archaeologist, National Park Service, 1940-53; instructor in archaeology, University of Omaha, 1953-54. *Memberships:* Society for American Archaeology, 1935-55, 1964-; Arizona Archaeological and Historical Society, 1934-42, 1964-; Western Writers of America (board of directors; editor, *The Roundup*), 1958-. *Interests:* Archaeology and American Indians; expeditions throughout Arizona, New Mexico, Nevada, Utah and Colorado. *Published works: America's Buried Past* (Putnam, 1962); *The Ancient Ones* (W. W. Norton, 1963); *The World of Prehistory* (Putnam, 1963); *Stone Age Peoples Today* (W.W. Norton, 1964); *The Riddle of the Past* (W. W. Norton, 1965); *The Warrior Apaches* (Dale Stuart King, 1965); *Race Against Time* (Putnam, 1966); eight Western novels published by Arcadia and Avalon, 1957-61.

BALL, ZACHARY (Kelly Masters) 1897- (writer)

Born June 16, 1897, Millgrove, Mo. *Education:* Elementary school. *Principal occupation:* Writer. *Home address:* P.O. Box 665, N. W. Branch, Miami, Fla. *Awards, honors:* Honor Book Award, New York *Herald Tribune* Book Festival for *Bristle Face,* 1962; Junior Literary Guild Award for *Bristle Face;* Dorothy Canfield Fisher Award, Scholastic Book Club, for *Bristle Face; Bristle Face* selected as one of the *Notable Books of 1962,* American Library Association; William Allen White Children's Book Award, William Allen White Memorial Library, Kansas State Teachers College, 1965. *Travels:* "Anywhere in America." *Interests:* Mr. Ball writes, "I have been writing fiction for twenty-five years. The first ten years of my writing career were devoted to magazine short stories. During that time my writings were published in *Saturday Evening Post, Collier's, Esquire, Country Gentleman* and others... about thirty in all. Fifteen years ago I began writing novels. I am now at work on my eighteenth book. All but two of these are juvenile fiction. My juvenile books (have been) published throughout Europe as well as in the United States, (its) possessions, and Canada." *Published works: Joe Panther* (Holiday House); *Swamp Chief* (Holiday House); *Skin Diver* (Holiday

House); *Salvage Diver* (Holiday House); *Piney* (Little, Brown); *Kep* (Holiday House); *Young Mike Fink* (Holiday House); *Bar Pilot* (Holiday House); *North to Abilene* (Holiday House); *Wilderness Teacher* (Rand McNally); *Keelboat Journey* (E. P. Dutton); *Bristle Face* (Holiday House); *Sputters* (Holiday House); *Tent Show* (Holiday House); *Sky Divers* (Holiday House).

BALLARD, JOHN K.   (Cherokee)   1920-
    (principal)

Born September 20, 1920, Bernice, Okla. *Education:* Arizona State College, B. S., 1949; Northern State College, M. S., 1957. *Principal occupation:* Elementary school principal. *Home address:* Porcupine, S. D. 57772. *Affiliations:* Teacher, Santa Fe, Indian School, 1949-53; teacher, Mt. Edgecumbe Indian School, 1953-56; teacher, Cheyenne River Boarding School, 1956-60; Chemawa Indian School, 1960-65; principal, Porcupine Day School, Porcupine, S. D. *Military service:* U. S. Navy, 1941-45 (Purple Heart). *Community activities:* Explorer Scouts (advisor); 4-H Clubs (leader). *Memberships:* Toastmasters International, S. D. E. A. *Interests:* Woodworking, metals, welding, mechanics, machine operations, agriculture.

BALLARD, LOUIS WAYNE   (Quapaw-
    Cherokee)   1931-   (composer,
    educator)

Born July 8, 1931, Miami, Okla. *Education:* Northeast Oklahoma A & M, A.A., 1951; Tulsa University, B. A., B. Mus., 1953, M. Mus, 1962. *Principal occupation:* Composer, educator. *Home address:* Box 4552, Santa Fe, N. M. *Affiliations:* Head of music and drama, Institute of American Indian Arts. *Other professional posts:* President, Santa Fe Symphony. *Memberships:* National Music Educators Association; New Mexico Music Teachers Association. *Awards, honors:* F. B. Parriott Graduate Fellowship, 1961. *Interests:* Composition of ballet music. *Published works: Koshare, an American Indian Ballet* (Harkness Ballet Co., 1966).

BARNES, NANCY (Helene Loudon)   1897-
    (writer)

Born June 10, 1897, Goodlawn, Kan. *Education:* Washburn College, 1914. *Principal occupation:* Writer. *Home address:* 441 S. Main St., Geneva, N. Y. *Awards:* Julia Ellsworth Ford Foundation Award for *The Wonderful Year. Published works: Carlota, American Empress* (Julian Messner, 1943); *The Wonderful Year* (Julian Messner, 1945); short stories in national magazines.

BARNETT, HOMER G.   1906-
    (professor)

Born April 25, 1906, Bisbee, Ariz. *Education:* Stanford University, B. A., 1927; University of California, Berkeley, Ph. D., 1938. *Principal occupation:* Professor. *Home address:* 2327 Jefferson St., Eugene, Ore. 97405. *Affiliations:* Professor, University of Oregon, 1939-. *Other professional posts:* Smithsonian Institution, 1944-46. *Community activities:* Staff anthropologist for U. S. Trust Territory of the Pacific Islands. *Memberships:* American Anthropological Association; American Association for the Advancement of Science; Society for Applied Anthropology (president, 1961-62). *Awards, honors:* National Science Foundation Fellow. 1956-57; Center for Advanced Study of the Behavioral Sciences (Fellow, 1964-65). *Interests:* Field trips to Indian reservations on Pacific Coast from Alaska to California; research trips to Micronesia and Melanesia. *Published works: Innovation: The Basis of Cultural Change* (McGraw-Hill, 1953); *Anthropology in Administration* (Row, Peterson and Co., 1956); *Indian Shakers: A Messianic Cult of the Pacific Northwest* (Southern Illinois University Press, 1957).

BASCOM, WILLIAM RUSSEL   1912-
    (professor of anthropology, museum
    director)

Born May 23, 1912. *Education:* University of Wisconsin, B. A., 1933, M. A., 1936; Northwestern University, Ph. D., 1939. *Principal occupation:* Professor of anthropology, museum director. *Affiliations:* Professor of anthropology, Northwestern University, 1939-57; professor of anthropology, University of California, and director, Robert H. Lowie Museum of Anthropology, 1957-. *Other professional posts:* Office of Strategic Services, 1942; Foreign

Economic Administration, 1942-45; U.S. Commercial Company Economic Survey of Micronesia, 1946. *Community activities:* California League for American Indians (board of directors), 1954-; Oakland Museums Association (board of directors), 1963-64, 1965-. *Memberships:* American Folklore Society (president, 1952-54); Central States Anthropological Association (president, 1950-51); American Association of Museums (council), 1962-; California Folklore Society (vice president), 1962-. *Awards, honors:* Predoctoral fellowship, Social Science Research Council, 1937-38; Fulbright Grant, 1950-51; senior postdoctoral fellowship, National Science Foundation, 1958. *Field research:* Among the Kiowas of Oklahoma, 1935; the Yoruba of Nigeria, 1937-38, 1950-51, 1960, 1965; the Gullah Negroes of Georgia and South Carolina, 1939; the people of Ponape in the Caroline Islands, 1946; the Negroes of Cuba, 1948. *Published works: The Sociological Role of the Yoruba Cult-Group* (American Anthropological Association, 1944); *Handbook of West African Art* (Milwaukee Public Museum, 1953, 1965); *Continuity and Change in African Cultures* (University of Chicago Press, 1959, 1962); *A Pacific Economy in Transition* (Anthropological Records, University of California, 1965).

BEALER, ALEX W., III   1921-
(advertising agency executive)

Born March 6, 1921, Valdosta, Ga. *Education:* Emory University, B.A., 1942; Northwestern University, 1946. *Principal occupation:* Advertising agency executive. *Home address:* 5180 Riverview Rd., N.W., Atlanta, Ga. *Affiliations:* Vice president, McRae and Bealer, Inc., Advertising, Atlanta, Ga. *Military service:* United States Marine Corps Reserves, 1942-61. *Community activities:* Georgia Republican Party (state, district, and county executive committees; press secretary); Pocket Theatre, Atlanta, Ga. (president, board of directors). *Memberships:* Commerce Club, Atlanta, Ga., 1960-; Atlanta Press Club, 1965-. *Awards:* Eagle Scout, B.S.A. *Interests:* Advertising; writing (published articles since 1936 in *Outdoor Life, Atlanta Journal* magazine, Emory University *Quarterly,* Atlanta *Journal, Progressive Farmer, House Beautiful*); wrote and helped produce a half-hour television documentary on the Cherokee Removal, shown on W.S.B.-TV, Atlanta,

in December, 1965); painting; furniture design and hand manufacture; historical research; study of the American Indian; camping and woodcraft; politics; the theatre; and others. *Published works: The Picture-Skin Story* (Holiday House, 1957).

BEATTY, PATRICIA   1922-   (novelist)

Born August 26, 1922, United States. *Education:* Reed College, B.A., 1944. *Principal occupation:* Novelist. *Home address:* 3113 Wendell Way, Riverside, Calif. 92507. *Affiliations (author-publisher):* The Macmillan Co., McGraw-Hill Book Co., William Morrow & Co., Inc. *Community activities:* Former high school teacher; librarian. *Memberships:* Authors' Guild; International Platform Association. *Awards, honors:* Honorary member, Quileute Tribe of Washington. *Interests:* English history of the 16th to 18th centuries; the Pacific Northwest; rose growing. *Published works: Indian Canoemaker* (Caxton, 1960); *Bonanza Girl* (Morrow, 1962); *At the Seven Stars,* with J.L. Beatty (Macmillan, 1963); *The Nickel Plated Beauty* (Morrow, 1964); *Squaw Dog* (Morrow, 1965); *Campion Towers,* with J.L. Beatty (Macmillan, 1965); *The Royal Dirk* (Morrow, 1966); *A Donkey for the King,* with J.L. Beatty (Macmillan, 1966); *The Queen's Own Grove* (Morrow, 1966); *The Lady from Black Hawk* (McGraw-Hill, 1967); *The Queen's Wizard,* with J.L. Beatty (Macmillan, 1967).

BEAVER, FRED   (Creek)   1911-   (artist)

Born July 2, 1911, Eufala, Okla. *Education:* Haskell Institute, 1935; Bacone College, 1931-32. *Principal occupation:* Artist. *Home address:* 437 Locust St., N.W., Ardmore, Okla. 73401. *Affiliations:* Former clerk, Indian Service Field Offices, Okmulgee, Okla., Ardmore, Okla. *Military service:* U.S. Army Air Force, 1942-45. *Community activities:* Federal Employees Union, Ardmore (president); Credit Union, Ardmore (supervisor); Boy Scouts of America, Ardmore (counselor on art and music). *Awards:* Eighteen awards, Philbrook Art Center; Waite-Phillips Indian Artist Award, 1963. Numerous other awards, prizes, and joint and one-man exhibits.

BECKER, DONALD WILLIAM   1921-
   (elementary school principal)

Born April 14, 1921, Jersey City, N.J. *Education:* New Jersey State Teachers College, B.S. (Elementary Education), 1950; Rutgers University, Ed. M. , 1951; Harvard University. *Principal occupation:* Elementary school principal. *Home address:* 37 Charlotte Drive, M. R. 12, Somerville, N. J. 08876. *Military service:* U. S. Army Air Force, 1942-46. *Memberships:* American Association of School Administrators; Department of Elementary School Principals, National Education Association; Phi Delta Kappa; Archaeological Society of New Jersey; American Name Society. *Interests:* Philology, mythology, archaeology, anthropology, semantics and orthography. Travels throughout the United States and Canada. *Published works: Indian Place Names in New Jersey* (Phillips-Campbell Publishing Co. , 1964).

BELINDO, DENNIS WAYNE *(Aun-So-Te)*
   (Kiowa-Navajo)   1938-   (artist)

Born December 12, 1938, Phoenix, Ariz. *Education:* Bacone College, Diploma, 1958; University of Oklahoma, B. F. A. , 1962. *Principal occupation:* Art teacher. *Home address:* 1403 N. McKinley, Oklahoma City, Okla. *Affiliations:* Indian dancer and artist at Disneyland, 1957; art teacher, Central High, Oklahoma City, Okla. , 1963-. *Other professional posts:* Free lance commercial artist. *Military service:* U. S. National Guard, 1955-57. *Memberships:* Delta Phi Delta, 1962-63; Artists of Oklahoma. *Awards, honors:* Honorable Mention, Philbrook Art Center Indian Annual, 1956, 1961; First Award, Poster Division, Gallup Inter-Tribal Ceremonials, 1965; First Award, Plains Division, Gallup Inter-Tribal Ceremonials, 1960.

BELL, CORYDON WHITTEN   1894-
   (illustrator and writer)

Born July 16, 1894, Tiffin, Ohio. *Education:* University of Michigan; Western Reserve University; Army Medical School. *Principal occupation:* Illustrator and writer. *Home address:* Cashiers, North Carolina. *Military service:* Army Medical Corps, 1917-19. *Interests:* Natural and physical sciences, folklore; history of costume; artifacts and invention; music and musicology, especially relating to the interval encompassing the 14th through 18th century; small-scale reconstruction of stages and sets of theatres, 18th and early 19th centuries. *Published works: Come Snow for Christmas* (Tower Press, 1947); *Like the Down of a Thistle* (Tower Press, 1948); *John Rattling-Gourd of Big Cove* (Macmillan Co. , 1955); *The Wonder of Snow* (Hill and Wang, Inc. , 1957); *Thunderstorm,* with Thelma Harrington Bell (Viking Press, 1960); *A History of Champion Papers* (Champion Papers Inc. , 1963); *The Riddle of Time,* with Thelma Harrington Bell (Viking Press, 1963).

BELL, MARGARET E.   (Mrs. Samuel R.
   Wiks)   1898-   (writer)

Born December 29, 1898, Thorne Bay, Alaska. *Education:* Annie Wright Seminary; University of Alaska. *Principal occupation:* Writing. *Home address:* Loring via Ketchikan, Ketchikan, Alaska. *Military service:* Red Cross hospital recreation worker, 1942-46. *Awards, honors:* Thomas Edison National Award (mass media) for biography of George Stiller, *Touched with Fire. Interests:* "Wood sculpture; literature (novels for young people based on experiences of my grandfather's families.)" *Published works: Pirates of Icy Straits* (1943); *Danger on Old Baldy* (1944), *Enemies on Icy Straits* (1945), *Watch for a Tall White Sail* (1948), *The Totem Casts a Shadow* (1949), *Ride Out the Storm* (1951), *Kit Carson: Mountain Man* (1952), *Love is Forever* (1954), *Daughter of Wolf House* (1957), *Touched with Fire* (1960), all published by William Morrow & Co. , Inc.

BELVIN, HARRY J. W.   (Choctaw)
   (teacher, rancher)

Born Choctaw County, Okla. *Education:* Southeastern State College, B. S. ; University of Oklahoma, M. A. *Principal occupation:* Teacher, rancher. *Affiliations:* Classroom teacher, Bryan and Choctaw County schools, Okla., 1923-39; county superintendent of public instruction, Bryan County, Okla., 1941-52. *Other professional posts:* Principal chief, Choctaw Nation, 1948-65; Bryan County representative to Oklahoma Legislature, 1954-60; state senator (Bryan and Choctaw Counties), 1960-64. *Memberships:* First Presbyterian

Church of Durant, Okla. (bench of elders);
Phi Delta Kappa; Kappa Delta Pi; Boule
Scholarship Fraternity; Durant Chapter,
Independent Order of Odd Fellows; Choctaw-
Chickasaw Confederation of Oklahoma (past
president); National Congress of American
Indians; Association on American Indian Af-
fairs; ten Choctaw councils throughout the
Old Choctaw Nation; Itanaha Indian Club
(secretary); Inter-tribal Council of the In-
dians of Oklahoma. *Awards, honors:*
Award, "Outstanding Indian of Oklahoma, "
Tulsa Indian Democratic Club, 1957; "Out-
standing American Indian," Anadarko Indian
Exposition, 1959. *Biographical sources:*
Indians of Today (Indian Council Fire, 1960).

BENCHLEY, NATHANIEL G.   1915-
  (writer)

Born November 13, 1915, Newton, Mass.
Education: Harvard College, B.S., 1938.
Principal occupation: Writer. *Home address:* 103 E. 86th St., New York, N.Y.
Affiliations: Reporter, New York *Herald
Tribune,* 1939-41; assistant entertainment
editor, *Newsweek* magazine, 1947. *Military
service:* U.S. Naval Reserve, 1941-45.
Memberships: The Century Association;
The Coffee House; Pacific Club. *Interests:*
Part-time landscape painting. *Published
works: Side Street* (Harcourt, Brace, 1950);
editor, *The Benchley Roundup* (Harper,
1954); *Robert Benchley* (McGraw-Hill,
1955); *One to Grow On* (McGraw-Hill, 1958);
Sail a Crooked Ship (McGraw-Hill, 1960);
The Off-Islanders (McGraw-Hill, 1961);
Catch a Falling Spy (McGraw-Hill, 1963);
Red Fox and His Canoe (Harper and Row,
1964); *A Winter's Tale* (McGraw-Hill,
1964); *The Visitors* (McGraw-Hill, 1965);
A Word or Two (McGraw-Hill, 1965).

BENN, ROBERT C. (Choctaw) 1934-
  (printer)

Born September 10, 1934, Philadelphia,
Miss. *Education:* Clarke Memorial College;
Mississippi College, B.A., 1956. *Principal occupation:* Printer. *Home address:*
R.F.D. 7, Box 9-A, Carthage, Miss. *Military service:* U.S. Navy, 1957-62. *Interests:* "Promoting and encouraging younger
Choctaws to prepare themselves and become better citizens of America. "

BENNETT, KAY C. (Navajo) 1922-
  (writer, doll maker)

Born July 15, 1922, Sheepsprings Trading
Post, N.M. *Education:* "Acquired, for the
most part, as a teacher-interpreter at the
Phoenix, Arizona Indian Boarding School
over a six year period of employment. "
Principal occupation: Writer, doll maker.
Home address: 6 Aida Ct., Gallup, N.M.
Memberships: Inter-Tribal Indian Ceremo-
nial Association, 1960-65. *Awards, honors:*
First prize for Navajo and character dolls
at the Inter-Tribal Ceremonial, Northern
Navajo Fair, Navajo Tribal Fair, New Mexico State Fair, Arizona State Fair; First
Prize for Navajo dress designs at the Inter-
Tribal Ceremonial, New Mexico State Fair,
Navajo Tribal Fair. *Interests:* Doll making;
dress designing; introducing Navajo designs
and adaptations; entertaining; has published
an album of Navajo songs. *Travel:* Has
traveled through the Middle East and Mexico; lecture tours in New England. *Published
works: Kaibah: Recollections of a Navajo
Girlhood* (Westernlore Press, 1965).

BENNETT, ROBERT L. (Oneida) 1912-
  (Commissioner of Indian Affairs)

Born November 16, 1912, Oneida, Wis.
Education: Haskell Institute; Southeastern
University, LL.B., 1941. *Principal occupation:* Commissioner of Indian Affairs,
Bureau of Indian Affairs, U.S. Department
of the Interior. *Addresses:* 6015 Landon
Lane, Bethesda, Md. 20024 (home); Bureau
of Indian Affairs, 1951 Constitution Ave.,
Washington, D.C. 20242 (office). *Affiliations:* Former area director, Bureau of Indian Affairs; Commissioner of Indian Affairs, Bureau of Indian Affairs, 1966-. *Military service:* U.S. Marine Corps, 1944-45.
Community activities: Durango Chamber of
Commerce, Durango, Colo. (board of directors); Ignacio Lions Club, Ignacio, Colo.
(charter president); American Legion Post,
Window Rock, Ariz. (charter commander);
Juneau Rotary Club, Juneau, Alaska (variety
show director); Arrow, Inc. (board of directors). *Memberships:* American Society
for Public Administration; Society for Applied Anthropology; American Academy of
Political and Social Science, 1960-. *Awards,
honors:* Indian Achievement Award, Indian
Council Fire, 1962. *Biographical source:*

Indians of Today (Indian Council Fire, 1960). *Published works:* Introduction, Klein, Bernard and Daniel Icolari, *Reference Encyclopedia of the American Indian* (B. Klein and Co., 1967).

BERGAN, K. W.   1895-   (educational administrator)

Born February 22, 1895, Sacred Heart, Minn. *Education:* Luther College, B. A., 1915; University of Minnesota, M. A., 1929; University of Montana. *Principal occupation:* Educational administrator. *Home address:* Rimini Gulch Route, Helena, Mont. *Affiliations:* Superintendent of public schools; state supervisor, Indian Education, Montana; coordinator, State of Montana Indian Affairs (Committee), 1960-. *Other professional posts:* Secretary, Governor's Interstate Indian Council; president, Montana Educational Association, 1930. *Community activities:* Boy Scouts of America; Red Cross (chairman); Blackfeet Reservation (district governor); Lions International, 1937-38. *Memberships:* Phi Delta Kappa Education Honor Fraternity; National Education Association; American Association of School Administrators. *Awards:* Beaver Scout, Boy Scouts of America. *Published works: History of Montana Indian Tribes,* 1965; *Termination of Federal Supervision over Indian Reservations,* 1961; *State Jurisdiction on Indian Reservations,* 1961 (all privately printed).

BERGGREN, FLORENCE E.   1909-   (museum director)

Born March 11, 1909, Chicago, Ill. *Education:* Metropolitan Business College, 1926. *Principal occupation:* Museum director. *Home address:* 2122 Harrison Ave., Muskegon, Mich. 49441. *Affiliation:* Director, Muskegon County Museum Foundation, 1965. *Community activities:* Muskegon County P. T. A. Council (board member). *Memberships:* State and county historical societies; Philathea Club (Sunshine chairman).

BERKHOFER, ROBERT F., Jr.   1931-   (educator)

Born November 20, 1931, Teaneck, N. J. *Education:* Albany State Teachers College, B. A., 1953; Cornell University, M. A., 1955, Ph. D., 1960. *Principal occupation:*

Associate professor. *Home address:* 3506 Edmund Blvd., Minneapolis, Minn. 55406. *Affiliations:* Instructor, Ohio State University, 1959-60; research analyst, U. S. Department of Justice; associate professor, University of Minnesota, 1960-. *Other professional posts:* Member, Project Social Studies Curriculum Center, University of Minnesota. *Memberships:* American Historical Association, 1953-; Organization of American Historians; American Studies Association; American Indian Ethnohistorical Conference, 1965. *Awards, honors:* McKnight Prize in American History, 1963. *Interests:* History of American frontier and American Indian; ethnohistory; methodology and synthesis in historical analysis. *Published works: Salvation and the Savage: An Analysis of Protestant Missions and American Indian Response, 1787-1862* (University of Kentucky Press, 1965).

BERRIGAN, TED (Choctaw)   1934-   (poet)

Born November 15, 1934, Providence, R. I. *Education:* La Salle Academy, Classical Diploma; University of Tulsa, B. A., M. A. (English Literature). *Principal occupation:* Poet. *Home address:* 411 E. 6th St., New York, N. Y. *Affiliations:* Editor, *"C,"* A *Journal of Poetry,* 1963-; New York editor, *Long Hair* magazine, London; editorial assistant, *Art News* magazine. *Military service:* U. S. Army, 1954-57 (Good Conduct Medal; United Nations Service Medal; Korean Service Medal; Sharpshooter's Medal). *Published works: The Sonnets* (C Press, 1964).

BERRY, BREWTON   1901-   (professor)

Born August 9, 1901, Orangeburg, S. C. *Education:* Wofford College, B. A., 1922; Yale University, B. D., 1925; University of Edinburgh, Ph. D. *Principal occupation:* Professor of sociology and anthropology. *Home address:* 2221 Brixton Rd., Columbus, Ohio 43221. *Affiliations:* Professor of sociology and anthropology, University of Missouri, 1931-35; professor and head, Department of Sociology and Anthropology, University of Rhode Island, 1945-46; professor of sociology and anthropology, Ohio State University, 1946-. *Other professional posts:* Director, Anthropological Museum, University of Missouri, 1932-45; director, Archaeological Survey of Missouri, 1933-45; editor, *The Missouri Archaeologist,* 1934-45; editor, *The Ohio Valley Sociologist,*

1947-50; associate editor, *American Socio-logical Review,* 1950-53. *Community activities:* Governor's Committee on Refugee Resettlement (member); Episcopal Church (senior warden, junior warden, vestryman, delegate to triennial convention). *Memberships:* American Anthropological Association (Fellow); American Sociological Association (Fellow); Ohio Valley Sociological Society (president, 1954-55). *Awards, honors:* Anisfield-Wolf Award, 1952, for *Race Relations.* *Interests:* Archaeological expeditions in Missouri, 1937-41; travels to Europe, Africa, Asia, Yucatan, Caribbean, Mexico; study of American Indian groups in eastern United States. *Published works: Archaeology of Boone County* (Missouri Archaeological Society, 1938); *You and Your Superstitions* (Lucas Brothers, 1940); *Archaeology of Wayne County* (Missouri Archaeological Society, 1940); *Fundamentals of Sociology* (Thomas Y. Crowell, 1950); *Race Relations* (Houghton Mifflin, 1951, 1958, 1965); *Almost White* (Macmillan, 1963); articles in various journals.

BERTHRONG, DONALD J.   1922-
(professor of history)

Born October 2, 1922, La Crosse, Wis. *Education:* LaCrosse State; University of Wisconsin, B.S., 1947, M.S., 1948, Ph.D., 1952. *Principal occupation:* Professor of history. *Address:* Department of History, University of Oklahoma, Norman, Okla. 73069. *Affiliations:* Instructor, University of Kansas City; assistant professor, associate professor, professor of history, University of Oklahoma, Norman, Okla. *Military service:* U.S. Army, 1943-46. *Memberships:* American Historical Association; Association of American History; Oklahoma Historical Society; Western Historical Society. *Awards, honors:* Fellowship, Social Science Research Council; Fellowship, American Philosophical Society; Award of Merit, Society for State and Local History for *The Southern Cheyennes. Interests:* Western U.S. history, with special emphasis on Indian history; expert witness before the Indian Claims Commission; currently a Fulbright lecturer in American history at the University of Hong Kong and Chinese University (Hong Kong, B.C.C.). *Published works:* Co-editor, *Joseph Redford Walker and the Arizona Adventure* (University of Oklahoma Press, 1956); *The Southern Cheyennes* (University of Oklahoma Press, 1963).

BERTO, HAZEL MAY (DIMAWAY) 1906-
(writer)

Born October 21, 1906, Kosmos, Wash. *Education:* Central College of Education, Teachers Certificate, 1925, Teachers Life Diploma, 1929; University of Washington. *Principal occupation:* Writer. *Home address:* 6211 Lake Wash. Blvd., N.E., Kirkland, Wash. 98033. *Community activities:* Parent-Teachers' Association (secretary); Service League; Houghton Community Club; Friends of the Library; Kirkland Congregational Church (clerk). *Memberships:* Washington Education Association; National League of American Pen Women, 1960-; Free-Lance Writers (secretary-treasurer, 1959-66); Pacific Northwest Writers Conference (past panelist), 1960-. *Awards, honors:* Invited to Matrix Table for Women of Achievement for writing, Seattle, Wash., 1960-66. *Interests:* Mrs. Berto writes, "Traveling with my husband, the cameras, and notepads, for article and book ideas. Our travels have taken us across the U.S., into Cuba (1959), Alaska, Canada, Mexico, and, this summer, across Europe. In our travels, we use trailerhouses, planes, buses, trains -- even camping. While my husband and I taught in Alaska for the Bureau of Indian Affairs (1925-28), we sent various artifacts to the Smithsonian Institution. During those three years, we worked closely with the Eskimos, not only in school work, but also in their daily lives. We supervised their reindeer herds -- butchering, corraling, and marking -- helped them in giving birth, in sickness, in dying, and in burying their dead. In fact, we were responsible for the entire village. Our interests range from serious subjects to rocks, dinosaurs and beekeeping, thence into history and music. Particularly interested in old cultures, histories of ancient peoples, and prehistoric times. Reading!" *Published works: North to Alaska's Shining River* (Bobbs-Merrill, 1959).

BIGSPRING, WILLIAM F., Sr. (Blackfeet)
1919-   (rancher, artist)

Born January 3, 1919, East Glacier Park, Mont. *Education:* Elementary school. *Principal occupation:* Rancher, artist. *Home address:* Bigspring Ranch, Box 531, East Glacier Park, Mont. *Military service:* U.S. Army Infantry, 1944-45. *Community activities:* Art Exhibition, Glacier Park,

Mont. (chairman). *Memberships:* Black-feet Artists Group (president, 1964); Montana Institute of Arts, 1962-.

BIRKET-SMITH, KAJ (anthropologist)

Education: University of Copenhagen, Ph.D.; University of Pennsylvania, D.Sc. (Hon.); University of Oslo, Ph.D. (hon.). *Principal occupation:* Keeper, Ethnographical Department, National Museum, Copenhagen, Denmark. *Memberships:* Royal Danish Academy of Letters and Sciences; Academies of Oslo, Helsinki, and Gothernburg; Royal Institute of Great Britain (hon. Fellow); others. *Published works: Primitive Man and his Ways* (New American Library, 1957); and others, mainly on Eskimos and North American Indians.

BLASSINGAME, WYATT 1909- (writer)

Born February 6, 1909, Demopolis, Ala. *Education:* Howard College; University of Alabama, B.A., 1930; University of Alabama, 1931-33; New York University, 1951-52. *Principal occupation:* Writer. *Home address:* 102 Maple St., Anna Maria, Fla. *Affiliation:* Teacher of creative writing, Florida history, and the modern novel, Manatee Junior College. *Military service:* U.S. Naval Reserve, 1942-45 (Bronze Star; Presidential Unit Citation). *Awards:* Benjamin Franklin Award, University of Illinois, for best short story of 1956. *Published works: For Better, for Worse* (Crowell, 1951); *Great Trains of the World* (Random House, 1953); *French Foreign Legion* (Random House, 1955); *His Kingdom for a Horse* (Franklin Watts, 1957); *Live from the Devil* (Doubleday, 1959); *They Rode the Frontier* (Franklin Watts, 1959); *The Golden Geyser* (Doubleday, 1961); *The Mountain Men,* with Richard Glendinning (Franklin Watts, 1962); *First Book of Florida* (Franklin Watts, 1963); *The Frontier Doctors,* with Richard Glendinning (Franklin Watts, 1963); *Halo of Spears* (Doubleday, 1963); *Out Island Doctor,* with Evans Cottman (E.P. Dutton, 1963); *U.S. Frogmen in World War II* (Random House, 1964); *Naturalist Explorers* (Franklin Watts, 1964); *Stephen Decatur* (Garrard Publishing Co., 1964); *First Book of the Seashore* (Franklin Watts, 1964); *First Book of American Expansion* (Franklin Watts, 1965); *Ponce de Leon* (Garrard Publishing Co., 1965); *Sacagawea* (Garrard Publishing Co., 1965).

BLUM, J.P. 1930- (museum curator)

Born April 2, 1930. *Education:* University of New Mexico, B.A., 1957; University of California, M.S., 1961. *Principal occupation:* Museum curator, monument director. *Home address:* P.O. Box 95, Bernalillo, N.M. 87004. *Affiliation:* Superintendent, Coronado State Monument. *Memberships:* American Anthropological Association, 1954-; Western History Association, 1963-. *Interests:* Southwestern prehistory and history, specifically, the history of the contact between Indian and Spanish cultures from about 1500 through 1700.

BLUMENSCHEIN, HELEN G. 1909- (artist)

Born November 21, 1909, New York, N.Y. *Education:* Packer Collegiate Institute; art school. *Principal occupation:* Artist. *Home address:* Box 256, Taos, N.M. 87571. *Military service:* WACS, 1943-45. *Memberships:* New Mexico Archaeology Society (board member), 1960-65, 1965-; Taos County Historical Society (president, 1965). *Exhibits:* Print exhibits nationally and abroad, 1936-45; one-man show of charcoal heads, Oklahoma City Art Center, 1951; Terre Haute, Ind., 1958; New Mexico Museum of Art, Santa Fe; Los Alamos, N.M., 1964. *Awards:* First Prize Oil, Studio Club, New York, N.Y., 1938; First Prize Watercolor, Pen and Brush Club, New York, N.Y., 1946; First Prize, Oil Expressionist Group, New Mexico State Fair, 1951; prizes and prints in New Mexico and Arizona state fairs in 1930's. *Interests:* Hunting, local history, and archaeology. *Published works:* Several articles published in *El Palacio* (periodical).

BOLZ, J. ARNOLD 1918- (physician)

Born May 3, 1918, Elgin, Ill. *Education:* University of Chicago, B.S., 1940; University of Chicago School of Medicine, M.D., 1943. *Principal occupation:* Physician. *Home address:* Lake Jaques, Grand Rapids, Minn. *Affiliations:* American Medical Association. *Military service:* U.S. Army Medical Corps, 1953-55. *Community activities:* Isaac Walton League (wilderness committee). *Memberships:* Range Medical Society, 1960-65; Minnesota Medical Society, 1945-; American Medical Association, 1945-. *Awards, honors:* Phi Beta Kappa,

University of Chicago, 1941. *Interests:* "Psychiatry; philosophy and psychology of religion, especially the basic religious experience as related to wilderness and the experience of primitive peoples." *Published works: Portage into the Past* (University of Minnesota Press, 1960).

BOSIN, F. BLACKBEAR (Comanche, Kiowa) 1921- (artist)

Born June 5, 1921, Anadarko, Okla. *Principal occupation:* Artist; owner, Great Plains Studios. *Home address:* 1032 W. 13th St., Wichita, Kan. 67202. *Military service:* U.S. Marines, 1943-45. *Community activities:* Lions International. *Memberships:* Wichita Artist Guild (past vice president, board of directors), 1948-; International Arts and Letters (Fellow), 1956-.

BOUNDS, THELMA V. 1903- (teacher, writer)

Born November 16, 1903, Baileu, Miss. *Education:* University of Southern Mississippi, B. A., 1934; graduate work, Arizona State Teachers College, Mississippi State University, Mississippi College. *Principal occupation:* Teacher, writer. *Home address:* Conehatta Indian School, Conehatta, Miss. 39057. *Affiliations:* Teacher, Navajo Indian Agency, Conehatta Indian School. *Community activities:* Order of the Eastern Star (member); Conehatta Community Club (advisor, religion committee); Conehatta Baptist Church. *Memberships:* Xi Chapter, Delta Kappa Gamma, 1957-; Mississippi Education Association, 1950-. *Published works: The Story of the Mississippi Choctaws* (Haskell Institute, 1958); *Meet Our Choctaw Friends* (Exposition Press, 1960); *Children of Nanih Waiya* (Naylor, 1964).

BOURGEAU, DEAN (Colville) 1928- (musician)

Born July 14, 1928, Inchelium, Wash. *Principal occupation:* Musician. *Home address:* Inchelium, Wash. *Affiliations:* Colville Business Council; Indian police. *Military service:* U.S. Army, 1950-52, 1956-57. (U.N. Service Medal, Combat Medal). *Community activities:* American Legion; Eagles.

BOY, CALVIN J. (Warring Shield) (Blackfoot) 1923- (artist)

Born September 18, 1923, Browning, Mont. *Education:* Browning High School. *Principal occupation:* Artist. *Home address:* Browning, Mont.

BOYCE, GEORGE A. 1898- (teacher, administrator)

Born January 20, 1898, Scranton, Penna. *Education:* Trinity College, B. S., 1920; Cornell University, M. A., 1926; Teachers College, Columbia University, Ed. D., 1941. *Principal occupation:* Teacher of science and mathematics; curriculum specialist; school administrator. *Affiliation:* Teacher, administrator, Institute of American Indian Arts, Santa Fe, N. M. 87501. *Military service:* U.S. Naval Reserve Force, 1918. *Community activities:* National Council, Boy Scouts of America (member at large). *Awards, honors:* Distinguished Service Medal and Citation, Secretary of the Interior, for developing socio-economic material and long-range plan for Navajo Reservation and organizing Intermountain School, Brigham City, Utah, as nation's largest boarding school. *Interests:* Community social and economic problems; education; textbook writing. *Published works: Mathematics of Everyday Life,* five vols. (Inor Publishing Co., 1936); various magazine articles on education; pamphlets published by Bureau of Indian Affairs.

BOYER, JACK K. 1911- (museum curator)

Born September 2, 1911, Van Houton, N. M. *Principal occupation:* Museum curator. *Home address:* P. O. Box 398, Taos, N. M. 87571. *Affiliations:* Curator, Kit Carson Home and Museum, 1953-. *Military service:* U.S. Army, 1940-48 (American Defense, Philippine Defense, Asiatic-Pacific Theater, U.S. President Unit Award with three clusters, Purple Heart, Philippine Unit Award). *Community activities:* Selective Service Board (chairman); Taos Volunteer Fire Department (president); Civil Defense (assistant director); councilman; Boy Scouts of America. *Memberships:* New Mexico Historical Society; New Mexico Archaeological Society; Taos County Historical

Society; New Mexico Folklore Society; Historical Society of Colorado; Western History Association; El Corral de Santa Fe Westerners (deputy sheriff); American Association of Museums; New Mexico Spanish-Colonial Arts Society; Denver Western's Posse; American Association for State and Local History. *Interests:* Western history, particularly during the fur trade period; Taos (N. M.) history and archaeology; life of Kit Carson.

BOYER, MELVILLE J.   1895-   (teacher, historian)

Born April 4, 1895, Lehigh County, Penna. *Education:* Muhlenberg College, B. A., 1916; University of Pennsylvania, M. A., 1921. *Principal occupation:* Teacher, historian. *Home address:* 2933 Liberty St., Allentown, Penna. 18104. *Affiliations:* Instructor, Carthage College, 1916-17; professor, Taylor University, 1917-18; head of social studies, Allentown School District, 1921-60. *Other professional posts:* Author and editor, *Proceedings,* Lehigh County Historical Society. *Community activities:* Tire Panel, WW II, Allentown and Lehigh County, Penna., Office of Price Administration (chairman). *Memberships:* Pennsylvania Historical Association (vice president); Pennsylvania German Society; Sons of the American Revolution; Schoolmen's Club of Allentown, Penna. *Awards:* Junior Chamber of Commerce Award for teaching American citizenship. *Published works:* Editor, *American Boyers* (1940; supplement, 1962).

BRADT, GLENN W.   1889-   (museum director)

Born July 2, 1889, Marcellus, Mich. *Education:* Michigan State University, B. S., M. S., 1921-26; University of Michigan, Ph. D., 1937. *Principal occupation:* Museum director. *Home address:* 2880 Chesterfield Dr., Santa Cruz, Calif. 48962. *Affiliations:* Instructor of zoology, Michigan State University; field biologist and director, Wildlife Experiment Station, Michigan Department of Conservation; chairman, City Museum Commission, and director, City Museum, Santa Cruz, Calif. *Military service:* U. S. Navy, 1910-12; U. S. Army, 1917-20. *Community activities:* Western Museums League (vice president, 1965);

Ground Observer Corps, Aptos, Calif. (supervisor, 1954-59). *Expeditions:* British Guiana (University of Pittsburgh), 1925; White Sands and Lava Beds of New Mexico (Carnegie Institution), 1928, 1929, 1930; Lava Beds of Arizona (Carnegie Institution and University of Michigan), 1932. *Published works: Michigan Wildlife Sketches* (Michigan Department of Conservation, 1947); *Michigan Beaver Management* (Michigan Department of Conservation, 1947).

BRANDON, WILLIAM   1914-   (writer)

Born September 21, 1914, Kokomo, Ind. *Principal occupation:* Writer. *Home address:* Box 1289, Monterey, Calif. *Military service:* U. S. Air Force, 1944-45. *Awards, honors:* Western Heritage Award, 1961, for *The American Heritage Book of Indians. Interests:* American and American Indian history. *Published works: The Men and the Mountain* (William Morrow, 1955); *The American Heritage Book of Indians* (American Heritage Publishing Co., 1961; Dell, 1964).

BRAY, ROBERT TAYLOR   1925- (assistant professor)

Born January 23, 1925, Sparta, Mo. *Education:* Southwest Missouri State College, B. S., 1953; University of Missouri, M. A., 1955. *Principal occupation:* Assistant professor of anthropology. *Address:* University of Missouri Archaeological Research Center, Miami, Mo. 65344. *Affiliations:* Assistant professor of anthropology, University of Missouri. *Other professional post:* Editor, *The Missouri Archaeologist,* journal of the Missouri Archaeological Society. *Military service:* U. S. Army, 1944-46 (Philippine Campaign Ribbon; Occupation Medal). *Interests:* Missouri archaeology, especially Oneonta and historic remains; microscopy; paleontology. *Published works: Archaeology of the Rice Site* (Missouri Archaeological Society, 1956); *Exploring the Past at Van Meter* (*National Parks* Magazine, 1961); *The Flynn Site* (Iowa Archaeological Society, 1961).

BRENNAN, LOUIS ARTHUR   1911- (writer)

Born February 5, 1911. *Education:* University of Notre Dame, B. A., 1932. *Principal occupation:* Writer. *Home address:*

39 Hamilton Ave., Ossining, N. Y. 10562. *Affiliations:* Associate editor, *Croton-Cortlandt News;* director, Briarcliff College Center for Hudson Valley Archaeology and Prehistory. *Military service:* U. S. Naval Reserve, 1943-45 (Bronze Star for gallantry in action). *Memberships:* Society for American Archaeology; New York State Archaeological Association (editor, *Bulletin*). *Awards, honors:* New York State Archaeological Association Achievement Award for *No Stone Unturned. Interests:* North American archaeological and historical developments, particularly as related to the Hudson Valley area. *Published works: The Long Knife* (Dell, 1957); *No Stone Unturned* (Random House, 1959); *The Buried Treasure of Archaeology* (Random House, 1964); *Tree of Arrows* (Macmillan Co., 1964).

BRINDZE, RUTH   1903-   (author)

Born July 18, 1903, U. S. A. *Education:* Columbia University, B. Lit., 1924. *Principal occupation:* Writer. *Home address:* 299 E. Grand St., Mount Vernon, N. Y. *Published works: The Story of the Totem Pole* (Vanguard Press, 1951), among others.

BRITTEN, EVELYN B.   (museum curator)

Education: State College, Albany, N. Y. *Principal occupation:* City historian, Saratoga Springs, N. Y., 1932-. *Home address:* 11 Clinton St., Saratoga Springs, N. Y. 12866. *Affiliations:* Former society editor, *The Saratogian,* Saratoga Historical Society; curator, Walworth Memorial Museum. *Community activities:* Katrina Trask Garden Club and Civic League, Inc. (president); Saratoga Chapter, Daughters of the American Revolution (regent); World War I Memorial (chairman); American Legion Auxiliary of Saratoga Springs, N. Y. (founder and president). *Memberships:* Saratoga Historical Society; Business and Professional Women's Club. *Published works: Chronicles of Saratoga* (*The Saratogian,* 1942, 1948; Gerald J. Rickard, 1959).

BROADFOOT, L. L. (Cherokee)   (artist)

Born Eminence, Shannon County, Mo. *Education:* Federal Schools of Art. *Principal occupation:* Artist. *Home address:* 306 S. McArthur St., Salem, Mo. *Affiliations:*

Director, Wildwood Art Gallery. *Memberships:* Modern Woodman Lodge; American Association of Museums (associate); Eugene Field Society (honorary member); Shannon County Historical Society. Work exhibited in numerous shows and exhibitions.

BRONSON, WILFRID S.   1894-   (author, illustrator)

Born October 24, 1894, Chicago, Ill. *Education:* Chicago Art Institute, 1913-14, 1914-15. *Principal occupation:* Author, illustrator. *Home address:* Warwick, N. Y. 10990. *Affiliations:* Assistant to Ezra Winters, mural painter, New York City; expeditionary limner on three voyages in tropical waters for the Bingham Oceanographic Collection, Peabody Museum, Yale University, and on one voyage to the Galapagos Islands with Vincent Astor. *Military service:* U. S. Air Service, 1917-18. *Interests:* "Art and nature, especially *critters;* people and animals of Africa, south of the Sahara." Has traveled to Europe several times. *Published works: Fingerfins* (Macmillan, 1930); *Paddlewings* (Macmillan, 1931); *Pollwiggle* (Macmillan, 1932); illustrator, *The Sea for Sam,* by Max Reed (Harcourt, Brace and World, 1935); *The Wonder World of Ants* (Harcourt, Brace and World, 1937); numerous other titles on natural history subjects published by Harcourt, Brace and World, 1937-; *Pinto's Journey* (Julian Messner, 1948); co-author and illustrator, *Peter Freuchen's Story of Life in the Seven Seas* (Julian Messner, 1957).

BROWN, DONALD NELSON   1937-   (anthropologist)

Born February 1, 1937, Colorado Springs, Colo. *Education:* Harvard College, B. A., 1959; University of Arizona, 1963-. *Principal occupation:* Anthropologist. *Home address:* 2147 E. Juanita, Tucson, Ariz. 85719. *Affiliation:* Assistant curator, Taylor Museum, Colorado Springs Fine Arts Center, 1960-63. *Memberships:* American Anthropological Association; Society for Ethnomusicology; Dance Research Center. *Awards:* Honorarium (for dance research), Laboratory of Anthropology, Museum of New Mexico, 1959. *Interests:* Music and dance (Southwestern Indian); culture change among the American Indians; alcohol and American

Indians; social and ceremonial organization among the Rio Grande Pueblos; recording of Indian music. *Published works: Masks, Mantas, and Moccasins* (Taylor Museum, 1962); *Music of the Pueblos, Apache, and Navaho* (Taylor Museum, 1961); articles on dance in *Ethnomusicology* and *El Palacio*.

BROWN, JOHN (Seminole) 1914- (tribal official)

Born February 20, 1914, Sasakwa, Okla. *Education:* Elementary school. *Principal occupation:* Tribal official. *Home address:* P.O. Box 24, Sasakwa, Okla. *Affiliation:* Chairman, General Council, Seminole Nation of Oklahoma. *Memberships:* Five Civilized Tribes Inter-Tribal Council; S.E.E., Inc. (board of directors); Five Civilized Tribes Foundation, Inc.; Inter-Tribal Council (secretary and treasurer); Five Tribes Museum (board of directors).

BROWN, JOHN A. 1914- (teacher)

Born August 28, 1914, Burlington, Wash. *Education:* Seattle Pacific College; University of Washington, B.A., 1938, M.A., 1941. *Principal occupation:* Teacher. *Home address:* 1325 South Hills Drive, Wenatchee, Wash. *Affiliations:* Instructor, Wenatchee Valley College, 1945-65; dean of men, Wenatchee Valley College, 1948-52. *Community activities:* Apollo Club (men's choir); U.G.N., Wenatchee Valley College (chairman). *Memberships:* Washington Education Association; National Education Association; Western Historical Association. *Interests:* History, particularly the American West; anthropology; studies on Indian reservations of the Pacific Northwest; archaeology; the Columbia River Basin. *Published works: Half-Sun on the Columbia* (University of Oklahoma Press, 1965).

BROWN, JOSEPH EPES 1920- (teacher)

Born September 9, 1920, Ridgefield, Conn. *Education*: Bowdoin College, 1940-42; Haverford College, B.A., 1947; University of New Mexico, 1954-56; Stanford University. *Principal occupation:* Teacher. *Home address:* 630 La Mesa Drive, Menlo Park (Ladera), Calif. 94026. *Affiliations:* Teacher, Verde Valley School, Sedona, Ariz.,

1955-65; teaching assistant, Stanford University, 1965-66. *Memberships:* American Anthropological Association; Museum of Northern Arizona; Foundation of North American Indian Culture (advisory board). *Awards, honors:* Smith-Mundt Grant to teach in Morocco, 1960-61; The Joseph E. Brown American Indian Scholarship Fund established in Mr. Brown's honor at Verde Valley School, Sedona, Ariz. *Interests:* Research among the Plains Indians; has traveled extensively and has done research in Morocco, North Africa; has organized foreign travel study tours for students. Major interest within anthropology is the study of values and the religions of diverse cultures. *Published works: The Sacred Pipe* (University of Oklahoma Press, 1953); *The Spiritual Legacy of the American Indian* (Pendle Hill Publications, 1964); several works in translations; numerous articles in journals; two works, *The Plains Indian and the World of Nature* and *The American Indian in the Modern World,* in progress.

BROWN, ROBERT CARLTON 1921- (school administrator)

Born January 7, 1921, Gallup, N.M. *Education:* New Mexico Highlands University, M.A., 1951. *Principal occupation:* School administrator. *Home address:* Tohatchi Public School, Teachorage, Tohatchi, N.M. 87325. *Affiliations:* Principal, Gallup, McKinley County schools; principal, Tohatchi School. *Military service:* U.S. Army, 1942-46. *Community activities:* Las Vegas City Schools Association (past president); McKinley County Education Association (past president). *Memberships:* New Mexico Administrators' Association; National Administrators' Association.

BROWN, VINSON 1912- (writer, naturalist)

Born December 7, 1912, Reno, Nev. *Education:* University of California, B.A., 1939; Stanford University, M.A., 1947. *Principal occupations:* Writer, naturalist, publisher. *Home address:* 8339 W. Dry Creek Rd., Healdsburg, Calif. 95488. *Affiliations:* Owner, Naturegraph Publishers, Healdsburg, Calif., 1945-. *Military service:* U.S. Army, 1945-46. *Memberships:* American Association of Icthyologists and Herpitologists. *Travels:* Three expeditions of about nine months' duration each to Panama and Costa Rica, collecting animals and plants for museums and private collectors; four months as a seaman on O & O freighter, *Golden Wall,* to China, Indo-China and the Philippines, 1930; one-and-a-half years' lecturing on Panama for National Schools Assemblies throughout the West; yearly collecting, natural history and Indian reservation trips during summers of 1937 to 1965. *Published works (as author or co-author): The Amateur Naturalist's Handbook* (Little, Brown, 1948); *It All Happened Right Here* (Stanford University Press, 1949); *John Paul Jones* (Harper & Row, 1949); *Black Treasure* (Little, Brown, 1950); *The California Wildlife Region* (Naturegraph, 1953, 1961, 1965); *How to Make a Home Nature Museum* (Little, Brown, 1954); *The Sierra Nevadan Wildlife Region* (Naturegraph, 1954, 1962); *How to Make a Miniature Zoo* (Little, Brown, 1956, 1957); *How to Understand Animal Talk* (Little, Brown, 1957); *Rocks and Minerals of California* (Naturegraph, 1957, 1965); *Wildlife of the Intermountain West* (Naturegraph, 1960); *Exploring Ancient Life* (Science Mat. Center, 1961); *Handbook of California Birds* (Naturegraph, 1962, 1965); *How to Explore the Secret Worlds of Nature* (Little, Brown, 1962); *Warriors of the Rainbow* (Naturegraph, 1962); *Backyard Wild Birds of California and the Pacific Northwest* (T. F. H. Publications, 1965).

BRUNER, EDWARD M.   1924-
   (professor of anthropology)

Born September 28, 1924, New York, N. Y. *Education:* Ohio State University, M. A., 1950; University of Chicago, Ph. D., 1950. *Principal occupation:* Professor of anthropology. *Home address:* 2022 Cureton Dr., Urbana, Ill. *Affiliations:* Professor, University of Illinois. *Memberships:* American Anthropological Association; American Ethnological Society; Central States Anthropological Society. *Awards, honors:* Fellowship, Center for Advanced Study in the Behavioral Sciences; senior scholarship, East-West Center, University of Hawaii. *Interests:* Anthropological field studies among Navajo Indians, 1948; among Fort Berthold Indians, 1951, 1952-53; among Batah of Sumatra, Indonesia, 1957-58; processes of cultural and social change; urbanization. *Published works:* Perspectives in American Indian Culture Change, with E. H. Spear (University of Chicago Press, 1962).

BUDD, EDNA J.   1890-   (historian)

Born November 24, 1890, New York, N. Y. *Education:* Trenton State College. *Principal occupation:* Historian. *Home address:* 28 Elmwood Ave., Chatham, N. J. 07928. *Community activities:* Parent-Teachers' Association (president); Woman's Society (church-affiliated), president; North Jersey Alumni Association (president); Planned Parenthood Association of Morris County (vice president). *Memberships:* Archaeological Society of New Jersey (third vice president); Chatham Historical Society (honorary member); Morris County Historical Society; New Jersey Historical Society. *Interests:* Local and state history; archaeology; planned parenthood; travel throughout United States and to Europe, the Aegean Islands, and Egypt.

BULEY, R. CARLYLE   1893-
   (teacher-writer)

Born July 8, 1893, Georgetown, Ind. *Education:* Indiana University, B. A., 1914; University of Wisconsin, Ph.D., 1958. *Principal occupation:* Teacher, writer. *Affiliations:* Professor of history, Indiana University. *Military service:* U. S. Army. *Memberships:* Indiana Historical Society; Ohio Historical Society; Mississippi Valley Historical Association; American Historical Association. *Awards, honors:* Pulitzer Prize in history, 1951; Elizur Wright Award, 1953. *Interests:* Midwestern history prior to 1860; recent U. S. history; business and economic history. *Published works: The Political Balance in the Old Northwest* (Indiana University Press, 1926); *The Midwest Pioneer, His Ills, Cures and Doctors,* with Madge E. Pickard (Henry Shuman, 1946); *The Old Northwest Pioneer Period, 1815-1840,* two vols. (Indiana Historical Society and Indiana University Press, 1951, 1962); *The Equitable Life Assurance Society of the U. S., 1859-1959* (Appleton-Century-Crofts, 1959).

BULLA, CLYDE ROBERT   1914-
   (writer)

Born January 9, 1914, King City, Mo. *Education:* "Largely self-educated." *Principal occupation:* Writer. *Home address:* 2953 Denby Ave., Los Angeles, Calif. 90039. *Affiliations:* Columnist, *Tri-County News,* King City, Mo. *Memberships:* Authors'

Guild, 1965-; Southern California Council on Literature for Children and Young People, 1960-; International P. E. N. Clubs, 1958-. *Awards:* Gold Medal Award, Boys' Clubs of America, for *Squanto, Friend of the White Men,* 1955; Rupert Hughes Award, Hollywood Authors Club, for *Benito,* 1961; Award, Southern California Council on Literature for Children and Young People, 1962. *Interests:* Composing music for children; painting. *Published works: These Bright Young Dreams* (Penn, 1941); *The Donkey Cart,* 1946, *Riding the Pony Express,* 1948, *The Secret Valley,* 1949, *Surprise for a Cowboy,* 1950, *A Ranch for Danny,* 1951, *Song of St. Francis,* 1952, *Johnny Hong of Chinatown,* 1952, *Eagle Feather,* 1953, *Star of Wild Horse Canyon,* 1953, *Down the Mississippi,* 1954, *Squanto, Friend of the White Men,* 1954, *White Sails to China,* 1955, *The Poppy Seeds,* 1955, all published by Thomas Y. Crowell Co. ; *A Dog Named Penny* (Ginn and Co. , 1955); *John Billington, Friend of Squanto,* 1956, *The Sword in the Tree,* 1956, *Old Charlie,* 1957, *Ghost Town Treasure,* 1957, *Pirate's Promise,* 1958, *The Valentine Cat,* 1959, *Stories of Favorite Operas,* 1959, *Three-Dollar Mule,* 1960, *A Tree is a Plant,* 1960, *The Sugar Pear Tree,* 1960, *Benito,* 1961, *The Ring and the Fire,* 1962, *What Makes a Shadow?,* 1962, all published by Thomas Y. Crowell Co.

BUNKER, ROBERT   1918-   (teacher)

Born June 4, 1918, Boston, Mass. *Education:* Harvard College, B. A. , 1939; University of New Mexico, Ph. D., 1955. *Principal occupation:* Teacher. *Affiliations:* Professor, New Mexico Highlands University, 1956-65; tutor, St. John's College, 1965. *Military service:* U. S. Navy, 1942-46. *Published works: Amanda Said the Grass Was Green* (Swallow-Morrow, 1948); *Other Men's Skies* (Indiana University Press, 1956); *Crow Killer,* with R. W. Thorp (Indiana University Press, 1958); *The First Look at Strangers,* with John Adair (Rutgers University Press, 1961).

BUNN, IOLA FINCH   1896-   (teacher)

Born January 26, 1896, Louisburg, N. C. *Education:* East Carolina Teachers College, 1915-19; Cornell University, 1922; North Carolina University, 1924-28. *Principal occupation:* Teacher. *Home address:* 208

N. Lee St., Whiteville, N. C. 28472. *Community activities:* American Legion Auxiliary (president); Parent-Teachers' Association (president); Women's Missionary Society (president); Woman's Club (program chairman); First Baptist Church (Sunday school adult women's teacher). *Memberships:* Delta Kappa Gamma, 1942-; National Retired Teachers Association (library representative). *Awards, honors:* Gold Pin Award, American Legion. *Interests:* "Teaching, public and private; church and community activities; library work. Avocational interest is homemaking, gardening, and being mother to two daughters, their husbands, four grandsons and two granddaughters. Travels include Alaska, Hawaii, and three tours of areas of Canada and the United States. " *Published works: Woolly, the Unclaimed Lamb* (Exposition Press, 1964); *Growing Up in Alaska* (Exposition Press, 1965).

BUNNEY, CECILIA H.   (PEIKERT)
(museum director)

Born Saginaw, Michigan. *Education:* Central Michigan University, B. A., 1934; University of Michigan, M. S., 1944; University of Iowa, Ph. D. , 1956. *Address:* Illinois State University Museum, Normal, Ill. 61761. *Principal occupation:* Director of museums, Illinois State University. *Other professional post:* Curator of science, Detroit Children's Museum. *Community activities:* Altrusa Club; McLean County Historical Association. *Memberships:* American Association of Museums; Midwest Museums Conference; Illinois Academy of Science; American Association of University Professors; Illinois Education Association; National Education Association; Delta Kappa Gamma. *Interests:* Archaeology, botany, Illinois pioneer life. *Travels:* Yucatan, Mexico (Maya ruins).

BUNTING, BAINBRIDGE   1913-
(professor)

Born November 23, 1913, Kansas City, Mo. *Education:* University of Illinois, B.S., 1937; Harvard University, Ph. D., 1952. *Principal occupation:* Professor. *Home address:* 5021 Guadalupe Trail, Albuquerque, N. M. 87017. *Affiliation:* Professor, University of New Mexico, 1948-. *Other professional posts:* Survey director, survey of historical architecture in Cambridge, Mass. , Cambridge Historical Commission; co-editor, *New Mexico Architecture. Memberships:* Society of Architectural Historians. *Published works: Taos Adobes* (Museum of New Mexico Press, 1964); *Historical Architecture in Cambridge: East Cambridge* (Cambridge Historical Commission, 1966); *Architectural Development of the Basle Bay Area in Boston* (Harvard University Press, 1966).

BURK, C. WILLIAM (museum curator)

Born Ashland, Ore. *Education:* University of Oregon, B. S. , 1965. *Principal occupation:* Museum curator. *Home address:* 850 Riverside, Klamath Falls, Ore. *Affiliation:* Curator, Klamath Museum. *Military service:* Army information specialist, 1962-64. *Community activities:* Klamath Art Association. *Memberships:* Klamath County Museum Associates (secretary-treasurer). *Interests:* Art, museum direction.

BURNS, ROBERT IGNATIUS 1921-
(associate professor)

Born August 16, 1921, San Francisco, Calif. *Education:* Johns Hopkins University, Ph.D., 1958; Universite de Fribourg (Switzerland), Doc. es Sc. Hist. , 1961. *Principal occupation:* Associate professor of history. *Home address:* Faculty Residences, University of San Francisco, Golden Gate Ave. at Parker, San Francisco, Calif. 94117. *Affiliations:* Assistant archivist, Jesuit Historical Archives, Spokane, Wash. , 1945-47; associate professor of history, University of San Francisco. *Memberships:* American Association of University Professors; American Historical Association; Pacific Historical Association; American Society of Church History; Catholic Historical Association; Medieval Academy of America (these are principal memberships.) *Awards, honors:* Guggenheim Fellow, 1963-64. *Interests:* "I have two fields, allied but distinct, in which I publish regularly. The medieval field is the moving frontier of the 13th-century Catalonia, particularly the absorption by the Catalan peoples of the Valencian Kingdom of the Moslems. The American field is the Pacific Northwest, particularly, Indian-white relations and troubles, 1840 to 1880, as illumined especially by Jesuit documentation here and in Europe. Ethnohistory and the Pacific Northwest frontier is thus seen not in isolation but as illumined by other frontier experiences. " *Published works:* Co-author, *I Lift My Lamp: Jesuits in America* (1955); *Indians and Whites in the Pacific Northwest: Jesuit Contributions to Peace* (1961); *The Jesuits and the Indian Wars of the Northwest* (Yale University Press, 1965); articles in *American Historical Review, Pacific Historical Review, Oregon Historical Quarterly, Pacific Northwest Quarterly, Mid-America, Church History, Records of the American Catholic Historical Society,* etc. , including editions of ethnohistorical documents; book dealing with medieval frontier in press.

BURROUGHS, RAYMOND DARWIN 1899-
(biologist and conservation educator)

Born August 20, 1899, Rolfe, Iowa. *Education:* Nebraska Wesleyan University, B. A. , 1924; Princeton University, M. A., 1925. *Principal occupation:* Biologist and conservation educator. *Home address:* 318 Hunt Dr. , Fayetteville, N. Y. 13066. *Affiliations:* Assistant professor of biology, Willamette University, 1925-27; assistant professor of biology, Oklahoma City University, 1927-29; associate professor of biology, Macalester College, 1930-37; wildlife biologist and conservation education supervisor, Michigan Department of Conservation, Lansing, Mich. , 1937-65; visiting professor of biology, Willamette University, 1965-66. *Memberships:* Wildlife Society; Conservation Education Association; American Institute of Biological Sciences; Michigan Academy of Science, Arts, and Letters; Historical Society of Greater Lansing (president, 1961-62). *Awards, honors:* Delivered annual invitational Lewis Cass Lecture, Detroit Historical Society, 1952. *Interests:* History of exploration of Louisiana Territory and Pacific Northwest, with emphasis on primitive populations and geographic range of plants and animals; conservation of natural resources and conservation education; photography; ethnology of American Indians. *Published works: Natural History of the Lewis and Clark Expedition* (Michigan State University Press, 1961); *Peninsular Country* (Wm. B. Eerdmans Publishing Co., 1965).

BURTON, JIMALEE *(Ho-Chee-Nee)* (Cherokee) 1910- (artist, writer, musician)

Born January 23, 1910, Elreno, Okla. *Education:* Tulsa University, 1940-43; Oklahoma State Teachers College; other art

schools. *Home address:* Plymouth Harbor,
Inc., Sarasota, Fla. 33581. *Principal occupation:* Artist, writer, musician, lecturer. *Affiliations:* U. S. associate editor,
Native Voice (Vancouver, B. C.); radio continuity for Smiling Dan; poetry program and
advertising; Burton Laundry and Dry Clean-
ers. *Community activities:* Tulsa Federated Choir; art associations, Tulsa and Sarasota; Woman's Auxiliary, Kiwanis Club.
Memberships: National League of American Pen Women, Inc.; Oklahoma Poets; Artists Guild of Tulsa; Philbrook Art Center;
Ringling Museum; Sarasota Art Center;
Friends of the Arts, Sarasota. *Awards,
honors:* First Prize, Indian Legend, American Pen Women, 1963; thirty-two ribbons on
paintings, Oklahoma state fairs; Purchase
Awards, Philbrook Art Center. *Interests:*
Travel in Peru, Panama, Virgin Islands,
Canada and Alaska, studying native cultures
and civilizations.

BURTON, LESLIE   1904-   (museum
   curator)

Born August 25, 1904, Jamestown, Kan.
Education: University of Idaho, B. S., 1930.
Principal occupation: Museum curator.
Home address: 735 N. 3rd St., Montrose,
Colo. 81401. *Affiliations:* Curator, Ute
Indian Museum. *Other occupation:* For-
ester. *Interests:* Hunting, fishing, West-
ern history.

BUSHNELL, GEOFFREY HEXT SUTHER-
   LAND   1903-   (museum curator)

Born May 31, 1903, England. *Education:*
Cambridge University, B. A., 1925, M. A.,
1929, Ph. D., 1947. *Principal occupation:*
Museum curator. *Home address:* 4 Words-
worth Grove, Cambridge, England. *Affiliations:* Curator, University Museum, Cambridge. *Military service:* Army, 1940-46.
Memberships: Society of Antiquaries of
London (vice president, 1961-65); Society
for American Archaeology; Royal Anthropological Institute; American Anthropological Association. *Interests:* American
archaeology; medieval art and architecture
of Europe. *Published works: Archaeology
of Santa Elena Peninsula, Ecuador* (Cambridge University Press, 1951); *Ancient
American Pottery,* with A. Digby (Faber
and Faber, 1955); *Peru* (Thames and Hudson, 1963); *Arts of Ancient America* (Thames
and Hudson, 1965; Praeger).

BYLER, WILLIAM   1931-   (organization
   executive)

Born August 24, 1931, Chicago, Ill. *Education:* Yale University, B. A., 1955. *Principal occupation:* Organization executive.
Affiliations: Executive director, Association on American Indian Affairs. *Other professional posts:* Administrative assistant,
U. S. House of Representatives. *Memberships:* Lakota Tuberculosis and Health Association.

C

CAIN, H. THOMAS   1913-   (museum
   curator, anthropologist)

Born May 18, 1913, Seattle, Wash. *Education:* University of Washington, B. A.,
1938; University of Arizona, M. A. (Anthropology), 1946. *Principal occupation:* Museum curator. *Addresses:* 1824 E. Oco-
tillo Rd., Phoenix, Ariz. (home); Heard
Museum of Anthropology and Primitive Art,
22 E. Monte Vista Rd., Phoenix, Ariz.
85704 (business). *Affiliations:* Curator of
anthropology, San Diego Museum of Man,
1946-50; director/curator, Heard Museum
of Anthropology and Primitive Art, 1952-.
Other professional posts: Instructor of museum methods course, Arizona State University. *Military service:* U. S. Marine
Corps, 1944. *Memberships:* American Anthropological Association (Fellow); American Association of Museums. *Awards:*
Thaw Fellow, Harvard University, 1950;
University Fellow, University of Arizona,
1945-46; American Museum Scandinavian
Seminar, 1965. *Expeditions:* Field work
in Canadian Arctic, Alaska, Georgia, New
Mexico, North Dakota. Museum travel to
Canada, Mexico, Guatemala, Norway, Sweden, Finland, Denmark, Great Britain,
Wales, Ireland and Scotland. *Published
works: Petroglyphs of Central Washington*
(University of Washington Press); *Pima
Indian Basketry* (Heard Museum Publica-
tions in Anthropology).

CALKIN, LAURIE ARCHER   (Cherokee)
   1935-   (designer)

Born February 17, 1935, Corbin, Ky. *Education:* Colorado College, B. A., 1959; City
College. *Principal occupation:* Designer.

Home address: Route 1, Box 267, Santa Fe, N. M. 87501. *Other professional posts:* Former professional dancer, New York City. *Memberships:* Don Juan Little Theatre; Los Alamos Light Opera Association. *Awards, honors:* John Hay Whitney Fellow in theatre; Fulbright Scholar to Peru in dance and the arts.

CAMPA, ARTHUR L.   1905-   (professor)

Born February 20, 1905, Guaymas, Mexico. *Education:* University of New Mexico, B. A., 1928, M. A., 1930; Columbia University, Ph. D., 1940. *Principal occupation:* Professor. *Address:* University of Denver, Denver, Colo. *Affiliations:* Professor, University of New Mexico, sixteen years; professor, University of Denver, nineteen years; cultural attache, U. S. Embassy, Lima, Peru; lecturer, U. S. Department of State, Spain. *Military service:* U. S. Army (Bronze Star, ten campaign ribbons, two Presidential Group Citations). *Community activities:*Editor,Denver Westerners' *Roundup* magazine; president, Pan American Club; president, Colorado Folklore Society. *Memberships:* American Folklore Society (councillor, 1936-); Modern Language Association; American Association of Teachers of Spanish. *Awards:* One Guggenheim fellowship; two Rockefeller fellowships; three Cutting fellowships; two Authors League prizes for book and articles. *Interests:* Southwestern culture, area of acculturation and folklore; has traveled extensively gathering data throughout the Southwest over the past thirty years; has lived among the Laguna Pueblo Indians of New Mexico. *Published works: Spanish Folkpoetry in New Mexico* (University of New Mexico Press, 1934); *Spanish Religious Folktheatre in the Spanish Southwest* (University of New Mexico Bulletin, 1934); *Treasure of the Sangre de Christos* (University of Oklahoma Press, 1962); several articles in periodicals and journals.

CANNON, T. C.   (Caddo-Kiowa)   1946-
(artist)

Born September 27, 1946, Lawton, Okla. *Education:* Institute of American Indian Arts. *Principal occupation:* Artist. *Home address:* Box 143, Gracemont, Okla. *Awards:* Second Prize, American Indian

Exposition; First Prize, Southwestern Interscholastic Exhibit, 1962, 1964.

CARD, B. Y.   1914-   (sociologist)

Born 1914, Cardston, Alberta, Can. *Education:* Brigham Young University, 1932-33; University of Utah, 1936-37; University of Alberta, 1940-42, 1946-47; Stanford University, Ph.D., 1950. *Principal occupation:* Sociologist. *Affiliations:* Research physicist, Army Experimental Station, Suffield, Alberta, 1942-45; research director, Delta Chapter, Phi Delta Kappa, Stanford University, 1949; research director, University of Alberta Committee for Social Research, 1960, 1963; research fellow, Department of Sociology, University of California at Berkeley, 1960-61; assistant to professor of education (sociology of education), University of Alberta, 1950- (sessional lecturer in physics, 1945-46; special lecturer on the faculty of arts and sciences in social science and social psychology, 1952-57). *Military service:* Canadian Army, 1942-45. *Memberships:* American Sociological Association; Sociology and Anthropology Chapter, Canadian Political Science Association; Canadian Education Association; Phi Delta Kappa; Community Planning Association of Canada (national councillor, 1952-55). *Published works: The Canadian Prairie Provinces from 1870 to 1950: A Sociological Introduction* (J. M. Dent and Sons, 1960); *The Metis in Alberta Society,* with Hirabayashi and French, in collaboration with Greenhill, Reuther and MacArthur (University of Alberta Committee for Social Research Report, 1963); articles and papers for various professional journals and societies.

CARLEY, KENNETH A(LLEN)   1915-
(newspaperman, writer)

Born May 20, 1915, Rochester, Minn. *Education:* University of Minnesota, B. A., 1939. *Principal occupation:* Newspaperman, writer. *Home address:* 3442 Ulysses St., N. E., Minneapolis, Minn. 55418. *Affiliations:* Newspaper writer, Sunday supplement, Minneapolis *Tribune. Other professional posts.* Tenor soloist for various churches; writer, Ortonville, Minn., *Independent,* 1939-41. *Community activities:* Twin Cities Civil War Round Table (past president and co-founder); Minnesota Civil

War and Sioux Uprising Centennial Commission (citizens advisory committee). *Memberships:* Sigma Delta Chi, 1939- ; Twin Cities Newspaper Guild; Minnesota Press Club (charter member). *Awards, honors:* Page One Award, Twin Cities Newspaper Guild, 1961; Certificate of Appreciation, State of Minnesota Department of Military Affairs for books and articles on military history, 1963. *Interests:* Pictorial journalism; Minnesota and U. S. history; Civil War and Indian historical sites. *Published works: The Sioux Uprising of 1862* (Minnesota Historical Society, 1961); *Minnesota in the Civil War* (Ross and Haines, 1961); articles in *Minnesota History,* publication of the Minnesota Historical Society.

CARLEY, MAURINE 1893- (teacher)

Born September 5, 1893, Chadron, Neb. *Education:* Colorado College, B. A. , 1915; Columbia University, M. A. , 1934. *Principal occupation:* Teacher. *Home address:* 2517 Capitol Ave. , Cheyenne, Wyo. *Community activities:* Junior Red Cross (county chairman); Y. W. C. A. (board of directors); Cheyenne Centennial Celebration Committee; Wyoming 75th Anniversary Committee, 1965. *Memberships:* Cheyenne, Wyoming, Classroom Teachers (president); Wyoming Classroom Teachers (state president); Wyoming Pioneers (state president); National Education Association; Wyoming Education Association; Wyoming State Historical Society (state secretary, 1953-). *Awards, honors:* Award for *The Shoshonis: Sentinels of the Rockies,* Wyoming State Historical Society, 1965. *Interests:* Travels to Europe, China, Mexico, Japan, the Philippines, Canada, Guatemala, the Caribbean. *Published works: Wyoming Pageant* (Prairie Publishing Co. , 1946); *History of Congregational Church* (Pioneer Printing Co. , 1958); *Early Cheyenne Homes* (Pioneer Printing Co. , 1962); *The Shoshonis: Sentinels of the Rockies* (University of Oklahoma Press, 1964).

CARR, LYMAN 1895- (museum director)

Born May 30, 1895. *Education:* Chicago Academy of Fine Art; Chicago Art Institute; Cincinnati University. *Principal occupation:* Museum director. *Addresses:* 301 S. Union, Fostoria, Ohio (home); 146 W. Tiffin,

Fostoria, Ohio (business). *Affiliations:* Owner, Carr Furniture Co., 1924-52; owner-director, Fostoria Museum, 1952-. *Military service:* U. S. Army (W. W. I), French Ambulance Service. *Community activities:* American Legion; Chamber of Commerce; Masonic Order; Elks. *Memberships:* Phi Delta Theta. *Awards, honors:* Croix de Guerre.

CARTER, EDWARD RUSSELL 1910- (minister)

Born December 8, 1910, Bloomingdale, Ind. *Education:* Earlham College, B. A. , 1932; Kansas State University, M.A., 1947. *Principal occupation:* Minister. *Home address:* 66 Linwood St. , Bergenfield, N. J. 07621. *Affiliations:* Director, Special Ministries, Division of Christian Life and Mission, National Council of Churches, 1937-. *Memberships:* National Social Welfare Assembly; Council on Indian Affairs; National Fellowship of Indian Workers. *Interests:* "Extensive involvement in Indian life and affairs as well as with seasonal farm workers, Spanish Americans, and natives of Alaska. (I) frequently travel to Alaska and Mexico as well as (to) Indian reservation areas in the United States." *Published works: The Gift is Rich* (Friendship Press, 1954).

CATLIN, FLOYD 1886- (museum director)

Born October 23, 1886, Lenora, Kan. *Education:* High school. *Principal occupation:* Museum curator. *Home address:* 1416 "C," Fairbury, Neb. 68352. *Affiliations:* Curator, Jefferson County Museum, Fairbury, Neb. *Community activities:* Y. M. C. A. (board member); Bible school superintendent and teacher. *Memberships:* Mayflower Society; Nebraska Police (honorary member); Y. M. C. A.; Kiwanis Club; Boy Scouts of America. *Interests:* The family of George Catlin, noted painter of Indians and the West.

CEDER, GEORGIANA DORCAS (author)

Born Chicago, Ill. *Education:* Columbia Business College. *Principal occupation:* Author of juvenile fiction. *Home address:* 6342 N. Sheridan Rd. , Chicago, Ill. 60626. *Memberships:* Children's Reading Round

Table; Women's National Book Association; Women's Overseas Service League; Society of Midland Authors. *Interests:* Middle Eastern countries; travel to Middle East, England, New Zealand. *Published works:* Ya-Ya (Abingdon Press, 1947); *Ethan, the Shepherd Boy* (Abingdon Press, 1948); *Ann of Bethany* (Abingdon Press, 1951); *Joel, the Potter's Son* (Abingdon Press, 1953); *Winter Without Salt* (William Morrow, 1952); *Little Thunder* (Abingdon Press, 1966); *Reluctant Jane* (Funk and Wagnalls, 1966).

CHALEE, POP   (Taos Pueblo)   1905-
(artist)

Born March 20, 1905, Castle Gate, Utah. *Education:* U. S. Indian School, Santa Fe, 1937. *Principal occupation:* Artist. *Home address:* c/o V. L. Belle, 3835 East 1st St., Apt. 3, Long Beach, Calif. *Affiliations:* Former art teacher, U. S. Indian School, Santa Fe. *Awards, honors:* Awards, Inter-Tribal Indian Ceremonials, Gallup, N. M. Works exhibited in museums in England, France, Germany, Hawaii and India. Murals commissioned by Marshall Field; Santa Fe Railway; T. W. A. Airport, Albuquerque; Arkansas Valley Bank, Pueblo, Colo.; Santa Fe Airport.

CHALMERS, HARVEY, II   1889-
(writer)

Born September 11, 1899, Amsterdam, N. Y. *Education:* Yale University, B. A., 1913. *Principal occupation:* Writer. *Home address:* 439 Guy Park Ave., Amsterdam, N. Y. *Affiliations:* Salesman, Boston, Mass., 1914-19; manufacturer of pearl and plastic buttons; 1920-64; factory owner, 1945-. *Military service:* U. S. Army, 1916-17. *Interests:* Creative writing; radio and television lecturing. *Published works:* West to the Setting Sun (Macmillan, 1942); *Drums Against Frontenac* (Richard Smith, 1949); *Joseph Brant, Mohawk* (Michigan State University Press, 1955); *Birth of the Erie Canal* (Bookman Associates, 1960); *Last Stand of the Nez Perce* (Twayne, 1963); *How the Irish Built the Erie* (Bookman Associates, 1964).

CHAPMAN, WILLIAM McK.   1905-
(public relations director)

Born August 9, 1905, Brooklyn, N. Y. *Education:* Public Schools. *Principal occupation:* Public relations director. *Home address:* 30 King St., Charleston, S. C. 29401. *Affiliations:* "Since 1942 have worked for *Time, Life, Sports Illustrated, House and Garden* as editor and for *Time* and *Life* as correspondent in Paris." Director, St. Elizabeth's School for Indian Children, Wakpala, S. D., 1958-61; founding director, Colorado Outward Bound School, 1961-63. *Memberships:* The Century Association. *Published works:* Films on Art (American Federation of Arts, 1952); *Remember the Wind: A Prairie Memoir* (J. B. Lippincott, 1965).

CHAVEZ, CALVIN FENLEY (Laguna and San Felipe Pueblo) 1924- (artist)

Born December 27, 1924, Winslow, Ariz. *Education:* Arizona State College. *Principal occupation:* Commercial artist. *Home address:* P. O. Box 8036, c/o Seama Village, Cubero, N. M. 87014.

CHIKOYAK, JOSEPH LEO   (Eskimo)
1942-   (artist)

Born February 1, 1942, Tununak, Alaska. *Education:* Institute of American Indian Arts. *Home address:* Nelson Island, Tununak, Alaska, 99681. *Military service:* Army National Guard of Alaska, 1959-62. *Community activities:* Tununak Native Teen Club. *Awards:* Second Prize, Native Talent Contest, Fairbanks, Alaska, 1963; certificates, Institute of American Indian Arts. *Interests:* Sculpture, engineering, hunting, trapping.

CHILTOSKEY, GOINGBACK   (Cherokee)
1907-   (arts and crafts specialist)

Born April 20, 1907, Cherokee, N. C. *Education:* Chicago Art Institute; Purdue University. *Principal occupation:* Arts and crafts specialist. *Home address:* Cherokee, N. C. 28719. *Affiliations:* Instructor, Cherokee Indian School, Cherokee, N. C., 1937-42, 1947-53; modelmaker, Engineer Board, Ft. Belvoir, Va., 1942-46; partner, Imagineering Associates, Hollywood, Calif., 1946-47; modelmaker, E. R. D. L., Ft. Belvoir, Va., 1954-66; self-employed as craftsman, Cherokee, N. C., 1966-. *Memberships:* Southern Highlands Handicraft Guild,

1948- ; Qualla Arts and Crafts Mutual, 1947- ; Washington Society of Artists, 1960-63; Federal Artists and Designers, 1962-64. *Awards, honors:* Purchase Award, North Carolina Art Society, 1953; First Prize, Blowing Rock, N. C., Exhibit; Second Prize, Philbrook Art Center, Tulsa, Okla.; prizes at North Carolina State Fair and Cherokee Indian Fair. Work chosen for exhibit at Smithsonian Institution. *Interests:* Mr. Chiltoskey writes, "(My) instructional career included teaching high school students and adults to do wood carving, sculpture, and furniture-making. Modelmaking at Ft. Belvoir (Va.) included making instructional aid models of a variety of military equipment. During spare time and since retirement (I) design and make wood carvings and sculpture. Lapidary and jewelry making are other interests. Summer camp counseling and personal interests have taken me into most states in the U. S." *Published works: To Make My Bread: Cherokee Cooklore* (Stephens Press, 1951).

CHRISTENSEN, GARDELL DANO

Education: Art Students League. *Principal occupation:* Museum curator, writer. *Home address:* Spencer Town, N. Y. *Affiliations:* Former staff member, American Museum of Natural History, New York, N. Y.; curator of exhibits, Schenectady Museum, Schenectady, N. Y. *Published works: Buffalo Horse* (T. Nelson); *Buffalo Kill* (T. Nelson); *Buffalo Robe* (T. Nelson); *Mrs. Mouse Needs a House; Fearless Family; Mr. Hare; Chuck Woodchuck's Secret.*

CLARK, ANN NOLAN   1896-   (teacher, writer)

Born December 5, 1896, Las Vegas, N. M. *Education:* Highlands University. *Principal occupation:* Teacher, writer. *Home address:* R. R. 4, Box 49A, Santa Fe, N. M. *Affiliation:* Teacher, supervisor, educational consultant, Bureau of Indian Affairs, Washington, D. C. *Memberships:* Authors League of America; National Council of Women. *Awards:* Newberry Award; Regina Medal Award; Distinguished Service Award. *Travel:* Latin America; Brazil and France (UNESCO). *Published works: Who Wants to Be a Prairie Dog?* (U. S. Office of Indian Affairs, 1940); *Little Herder in Spring* (U. S.

Office of Indian Affairs, 1940); *Little Herder in Autumn* (U. S. Office of Indian Affairs, 1940); *Little Boy with Three Names* (U. S. Office of Indian Affairs, 1940); *The Pine Ridge Porcupine* (U. S. Office of Indian Affairs, 1941); *In My Mother's House* (Viking, 1941); *A Child's Story of New Mexico,* with Frances Carey (University Publishing, 1941); *The Slim Butte Racoon* (U. S. Department of the Interior, Bureau of Indian Affairs, 1942); *Little Herder in Winter* (U. S. Office of Indian Affairs, 1942); *Little Herder in Summer* (U. S. Office of Indian Affairs, 1942); *Buffalo Caller* (Row, Peterson & Co., 1942); *About the Slim Butte Racoon* (U. S. Office of Indian Affairs, 1943); *Little Navajo Bluebird* (Viking, 1943); *Bringer of the Mystery Dog* (Department of the Interior, Bureau of Indian Affairs, 1943); *Singing Sioux Cowboy Reader* (U. S. Indian Service, 1947); *Magic Money* (Viking, 1950); *Little Herder in Spring, in Summer,* an incorporation of two earlier books (U. S. Indian Service, 1950); *Little Herder in Autumn, in Winter,* an incorporation of two earlier books (U. S. Indian Service, 1950); *Little Navajo Herder,* an incorporation of four earlier books (U. S. Indian Service, 1951); *Secret of the Andes* (Viking, 1952); *Looking-for-Something* (Viking, 1952); *Blue Canyon Horse* (Viking, 1954); *Santiago* (Viking, 1955); *The Little Indian Pottery Maker* (Melmont, 1955); *Third Monkey* (Viking, 1956); *The Little Indian Basket Maker* (Melmont, 1957); *There Still Are Buffalo* (Haskell Institute, 1958); *A Santo for Pasqualita* (Viking, 1959); *World Song* (Viking, 1960); *Paco's Miracle* (Farrar, Straus, 1962); *The Desert People* (Viking, 1962); *Tia Maria's Gardens* (Viking, 1963); *Medicine Man's Daughter* (Farrar, Straus, 1963); *Father Kino* (Farrar, Straus, 1963).

CLARK, ELECTA (Mrs. James E. Clark)   1910-   (writer)

Born May 17, 1910, Chicago, Ill. *Education:* Purdue University, B. S., 1933. *Principal occupation:* Writer. *Home address:* 3254 W. 39th Place, Indianapolis, Ind. 46208. *Affiliations:* Children's Museum, Indianapolis, Indiana, docent, 1957-63. *Memberships:* American Association of University Women, 1962-65. *Awards:* Junior Literary Guild Award for *The Dagger, the Fish, and Casey McKee.* *Interests:* Family trips; non-academic study of history; reading. *Published works: The Pennywinks* (Bobbs-

Merrill, 1949); *Robert Peary, Boy of the North* (Bobbs-Merrill, 1951); *Pennywink Carnival* (Bobbs-Merrill, 1951); *The Seven Q's* (Bobbs-Merrill, 1952); *Tony for Keeps* (Winston, 1953); *The Dagger, the Fish, and Casey McKee* (David McKay, 1954); *Spanish Gold and Casey McKee* (David McKay, 1955); *Wildcat the Seminole* (American Books, 1956); *River Show Folks* (David McKay, 1957); *Osceola: Seminole Indian Boy* (Bobbs-Merrill, 1965).

CLARK, THOMAS D. 1903- (professor)

Born July 14, 1903. *Education:* University of Mississippi, B. A. , 1929; University of Kentucky, M. A. , 1929; Duke University, Ph. D. , 1932. *Principal occupation:* Professor of American history. *Affiliations:* Assistant professor, professor, University of Kentucky, 1931-. *Other professional posts:* Editor, *Journal of Southern History,* 1948-52; professor, University of Vienna; special professor, Oxford University, University of Athens, University of Thessalonica. *Community activities:* Lexington (Ky.) Kiwanis Club (president, 1952). *Memberships:* Southern Historical Association (president); Organization of American Historians (president, 1957; chairman, executive committee, 1957-63); Bradford Historical Society; American Historical Association. *Awards, honors:* Tom Wallace Forestry Award, 1962. *Interests:* American history (specifically, the history of the westward movement); history of the South; forestry. *Published works: Beginning of the L. & N.* (Standard Publishing Co. , 1933); *Pioneer Southern Railroad* (University of North Carolina Press, 1936); *History of Kentucky* (Prentice-Hall, 1937); *The Rampaging Frontier* (Bobbs-Merrill, 1939; Indiana University Press, 1964); *The Kentucky Rivers of America* (Farrar & Rinehart, 1942); *Pills, Petticoats and Plows* (Bobbs-Merrill, 1945); *Southern Country Editor* (Bobbs-Merrill, 1948); *The Rural Editor and the New South* (Louisiana State University Press, 1948); *The Bluegrass Cavalcade* (University of Kentucky Press, 1950); *Frontier America* (Scribners, 1958); editor, *Southern Travels* (University of Oklahoma Press, 1948, 1962); *Three Paths to the Modern South* (University of Georgia Press, 1965); six elementary history textbooks; approximately one hundred articles and special contributions to collaborative books.

CLARK, VAN DEUSEN 1909- (secondary school counselor)

Born December 26, 1909, Deming, N. M. *Education:* University of New Mexico, B. A. , 1932; M. A. , 1938; Arizona State University, Ph. D. , 1966. *Principal occupation:* Secondary school counselor. *Home address:* 2326 E. Clarendon, Phoenix, Ariz. 85016. *Military service:* U. S. Army Air Force. *Memberships:* Phi Delta Kappa; Kappa Delta Phi; National Education Association; Arizona Education Association; Classroom Teachers' Association; American Personnel and Guidance Association; Arizona Personnel and Guidance Association. *Interests:* Counseling; children's literature; Indian art. *Published works: Peetie the Pack Rat* (Caxton Printers, Ltd. , 1960).

CLOUD, RED THUNDER (Catawba) 1919- (Indian dance troupe director)

Born May 30, 1919, Usquepaug, R. I. *Education:* University of Pennsylvania. *Principal occupation:* Director, Accabonac Indian Dancers. *Home address:* Abrahams (Abrahams Path), Three Mile Harbor, East Hampton, L. I. , N. Y. *Affiliations:* Collaborator in south- and northeastern ethnology, Department of Anthropology, University of Pennsylvania, 1938-50; dictator of texts in Catawba language to junior and senior anthropology classes, University of Pennsylvania; field collector, Museum of the American Indian, Heye Foundation, 1942; field collector, American Museum of Natural History, 1943; field collector (South Carolina), University of Pennsylvania, 1944, 1945; technical assistant to Prof. G. Hubert Matthews in recording grammar and syntax of Catawba language, Modern Language Department, Massachusetts Institute of Technology. *Other posts:* Editor, *The Indian War Drum,* 1945-46; writer of Indian feature stories for *Indian Chief, Roy Rogers, Lone Ranger* and *Tonto* comic books (Dell Publishing Co.); editor, *The Federated Eastern Indian League Bulletin* (Federated Eastern Indian League); director, Accabonac Indian Dancers, a troupe presenting Indian dance programs at schools, camps, civic organizations and children's theaters in the East; recording artist, Prestige International Records. *Community activities:* Federated Eastern Indian League, Inc. (field chief, 1962). *Interests:* Mr.

Cloud writes, "(I am) interested in the organization of the tribes from Maine to Florida (and) in closer ties between Indians of the U.S., Canada and Latin America. (I have a) deep interest in anthropology, archaeology, ethnohistory and linguistics as they relate to the American Indian. (I am) interested in photography (and) have a wide variety of photos of Eastern Indian types, tribal occupations, etc." *Published works:* Numerous articles in scholarly journals and magazines.

COATSWORTH, ELIZABETH (Mrs. Henry Beston) 1893- (writer)

Born May 31, 1893, Buffalo, N.Y. *Education:* Vassar College, B.A., 1915; Columbia University, M.A., 1916. *Principal occupation:* Writer *Home address:* Chimney Farm, Nobleboro, Me. 04555. *Awards, honors:* Newberry Medal for *The Cat Who Went to Heaven*, 1930; Phi Beta Kappa, 1914; honorary Litt.D., University of Maine, 1955; L.H.D., New England College, 1958. *Interests:* Travel to Mexico, Egypt, Far East, North Africa, Europe. *Published works:* (Poetry) *Fox Footprints* (Knopf, 1923); *Atlas and Beyond* (Harper, 1924); *Compass Rose* (Coward, 1929); *Country Poems* (Macmillan, 1942); *Summer Green* (Macmillan, 1948); *Night and the Cat* (Macmillan, 1950); *Mouse Chorus* (Pantheon, 1955); *Poems* (Macmillan, 1957); *The Peaceful Kingdom, and Other Poems* (Pantheon, 1958); *The Children Come Running* (Golden Press, 1960); (Novels and New England sketches) *Here I Stay* (Coward, 1938); *The Trunk* (Macmillan, 1941); *Country Neighborhood* (Macmillan, 1944); *Maine Ways* (Macmillan, 1947); *South Shore Town* (Macmillan, 1948); *The Enchanted, an Incredible Tale* (Pantheon, 1951); *Silky, an Incredible Tale* (Pantheon, 1953); *Mountain Bride, an Incredible Tale* (Pantheon, 1954); *The White Room* (Pantheon, 1958). (Books for children) *The Cat and the Captain* (Macmillan, 1927); *Toutou in Bondage* (Macmillan, 1929); *The Sun's Diary* (Macmillan, 1929); *The Boy With the Parrot* (Macmillan, 1930); *The Cat Who Went to Heaven* (Macmillan, 1930); *Knock at the Door* (Macmillan, 1931); *Cricket and the Emperor's Son* (Macmillan, 1932); *Away Goes Sally* (Macmillan, 1934); *The Golden Horseshoe* (Macmillan, 1935); *Sword of the Wilderness* (Macmillan, 1936); *Alice-All-By-Herself* (Macmillan, 1937); *Dancing Tom* (Macmillan,

1938); *Five Bushel Farm* (Macmillan, 1939); *The Fair American* (Macmillan, 1940); *The Littlest House* (Macmillan, 1940); *A Toast to the King* (Coward, 1940); (Mabel O'Donnel, Editor) "Runaway Home," "Alice and Jerry Books," sixth grade reader (Row Peterson & Co., 1940-42); *Tonio and the Stranger, a Mexican Adventure* (Grosset, 1941); *You Shall Have a Carriage* (Macmillan, 1941); *Forgotten Island* (Grosset, 1942); *Houseboat Summer* (Macmillan, 1942); *The White Horse* (Macmillan, 1942); *Thief Island* (Macmillan, 1943); *Twelve Months Make a Year* (Macmillan, 1943); *The Big Green Umbrella* (Grosset, 1944); *Trudy and the Tree House* (Macmillan, 1944); *The Kitten Stand* (Grosset, 1945); *The Wonderful Day* (Macmillan, 1946); *Plum Daffy Adventure* (Macmillan, 1947); *Up Hill and Down* (Knopf, 1947); *The House of the Swan* (Macmillan, 1948); *The Little Haymakers* (Macmillan, 1949); *The Captain's Daughter* (Macmillan, 1950); *First Adventure* (Macmillan, 1950); *Door to the North* (Winston, 1950); *Dollar for Luck* (Macmillan, 1951); *The Wishing Pear* (Macmillan, 1951); *The Last Fort* (Winston, 1952); *Boston Bells* (Macmillan, 1952); *The Giant Golden Book of Cat Stories* (Simon and Schuster, 1953); *The Giant Golden Book of Dog Stories* (Simon and Schuster, 1953); *Old Whirlwind, the Story of Davy Crockett* (Macmillan, 1953); *Aunt Flora* (Macmillan, 1953); *Horse Stories,* with Kate Barnes (Simon and Schuster, 1954); *The Sod House* (Macmillan, 1954); *Cherry Ann and the Dragon Horse* (Macmillan, 1955); *Hide and Seek* (Pantheon, 1956); *The Peddler's Cart* (Macmillan, 1956); *The Giant Golden Book of Dogs, Cats and Horses,* with Kate Barnes, a compilation of three earlier works (Simon and Schuster, 1957); *The Dog from Nowhere* (Row, Peterson & Co., 1958); *Down Tumbledown Mountain* (Row, Peterson & Co., 1958); *The Cave* (Viking, 1958); *You Say You Saw a Camel!* (Row, Peterson & Co., 1958); *Pika and the Roses* (Pantheon, 1959); *Desert Dan* (Viking, 1960); *Lonely Maria* (Pantheon, 1960); *The Noble Doll* (Viking, 1961); *Ronnie and the Chief's Son* (Macmillan, 1962); *The Princess and the Lion* (Pantheon, 1963); *Jock's Island* (Viking, 1963); *Jon the Unlucky* (Holt, 1963).

COCHRAN, GEORGE McKEE (Cherokee) 1908- (artist, barber)

Born October 5, 1908, Stilwell, Okla. *Education:* Haskell Institute, 1927. *Principal occupation:* Artist, barber. *Home address:* 681 Chase St., Eugene, Ore. 97402. *Community activities:* Kiwanis Club. *Memberships:* Cherokee Foundation, Inc. ; Indian Festival of Arts, Inc. (board member); Maude I. Kerns Art Center; National Congress of American Indians; Oregon Archaeological Society (life member), 1964-; Red Dirt or War Paint Clan of the North American Indian; Mormon Church; Journeymen Barbers, Hairdressers, Cosmetologists and Proprietors' International Union of America, Eugene, Ore. *Awards, honors:* American Eagle Feather Award for outstanding work among the Indian people, American Indian Council, 1960; Grand Award, American Indian Festival of Arts, Inc. , 1960-61; Grand Award, All American Indian Art Exhibit, 1961-62; several others. Mr. Cochran's work has been exhibited in many one-man shows over the country, including the Seattle Public Library; Haskell Institute; Philbrook Art Center; Barnsdall Art Gallery; Truman Library; University of Oregon; Hotel Utah Art Gallery; Lloyd's Center Art Gallery; Wilshire Federal and Loan Art Gallery. *Published works: Indian Portraits of the Pacific Northwest* (Binfords and Mort, 1959).

CODERE, HELEN   1917-   (teacher, anthropologist)

Born September 10, 1917, Winnipeg, Manitoba, Can. *Education:* University of Minnesota, B. A. , 1939; Columbia University, Ph. D. , 1950. *Principal occupation:* Professor of anthropology. *Home address:* 44 York St., Lexington, Mass. 02173. *Affiliations:* Professor of anthropology, Vassar College, 1958-62; professor of anthropology, Brandeis University, 1963-. *Memberships:* American Anthropological Association (Fellow); African Studies Association; American Association for the Advancement of Science; American Ethnological Society; Society for Applied Anthropology; American Folklore Society; Society for Ethnomusicology. *Awards, honors:* Phi Beta Kappa; Guggenheim Fellow, 1959-60. *Field work:* Iceland, summer, 1950; British Columbia (Kwakiutl), 1951, 1954-55; Africa, 1959-60. *Published works: Fighting with Property* (Monograph 18, American Ethnological Society, 1950); editor, Franz Boas, *Kwakiutl Ethnography* (University of Chicago Press, 1966).

COE, PAM   1934-   (organization executive)

Born September 17, 1934, Memphis, Tenn. *Education:* Columbia University, B.S., 1956, M. A., 1961. *Principal occupation:* Organization executive. *Home address:* 1908 Pine St. , Philadelphia, Penna. 19103. *Affiliations:* Research assistant, Southern Regional Council, 1960; assistant to community relations secretary, American Friends Service Committee, 1960-62; VISTA field worker, 1962-64; national representative, American Friends Service Committee, 1964-. *Community activities:* Council on Indian Affairs (secretary). *Memberships:* National Association of Intergroup Relations Officials, 1960-62, 1964-65; National Congress of American Indians, 1965; National Committee for Support of the Public Schools, 1965. *Interests:* Community development in American Indian communities. *Field work:* Philadelphia, Miss. , 1959, in preparation for M.A. thesis, *The Social Organization of the Mississippi Choctaw;* San Carlos Apache Reservation, 1962-64.

COLLIER, JOHN   1884-   (former Commissioner of Indian Affairs)

Born May 4, 1884, Atlanta, Ga. *Education:* Columbia and Woods Hole, 1902-05; College de France, 1906-07. *Principal occupation:* Indian affairs (former commissioner, Bureau of Indian Affairs). *Home address:* Box 89, Rancos de Taos, N. M. *Affiliations:* Editor, *American Indian Life,* 1926-33; professor, City College of New York, 1947-54; executive secretary, American Indian Defense Association, 1923-33. *Other professional posts:* Director, National Indian Institute, 1945-50. *Memberships:* Institute of Ethnic Affairs, Washington, D. C. (president). *Awards, honors:* Anisfield-Wolf Award for "best works on race published during the previous year" *(Indians of the Americas),* 1948. *Published works: The Indwelling Splendor,* poetry (The Stonehouse Press, 1911); *The City Where Crime is Play,* with E. J. Barrows, 1913; *Harp of the Human,* poetry (The Stonehouse Press, 1913); *Shadows Which Haunt the Sun-Rain,* poetry (The Stonehouse Press, 1917); *Door Succeeds Door,* poetry (The Stonehouse Press, 1919); *Entry to the Desert,* poetry (The Stonehouse Press, 1922); *America's Colonial Record,* 1946; *Indians of the Americas* (Mentor, New American Library, 1947,

1948; amplified version published as *Los Indios de las Americas,* 1960); *Patterns and Ceremonials of the Indians of the Southwest,* 1949; *On the Gleaming Way: Navajos, Eastern Pueblos, Zunis, Hopis, Apaches, and their Land; and their Meaning in the World* (Sage Books, 1962); *From Every Zenith: A Memoir* (Sage Books, 1963).

COLLINS, ADELE VICTOR (Chickasaw)
1908- (artist)

Born January 24, 1908, Blanchard, Okla. *Education:* St. Elizabeth Academy; Mount St. Mary's Academy; private study of art and painting. *Home address:* 1631 Curtis Dr., Las Vegas, Nev. 89104. *Principal occupation:* Artist. *Community activities:* Las Vegas Art League (workshop chairman); American Pen Women. *Awards, honors:* First Prize in oils, Gallup Ceremonials, 1963; R. J. Erickson Award, New Mexico Contemporary Indian Exhibit, 1963; one-man show at Heard Museum, 1966.

COLLINS, HENRY B. 1899-
(anthropologist)

Born April 9, 1899, Geneva, Ala. *Education:* Millsaps College, B. A., 1922, D. Sc., 1940; George Washington University, M. A., 1925. *Principal occupation:* Anthropologist. *Home address:* 2557 - 36th St., N. W., Washington, D. C. 20007. *Affiliations:* Anthropologist, Smithsonian Institution, Washington, D. C., 1924-. *Military service:* U. S. Army, 1918. *Memberships:* Society for American Archaeology; Anthropological Society of Washington (president, 1938-39); Washington Academy of Sciences; American Association of Physical Anthropologists; Sigma Xi; American Anthropological Association (Fellow); American Association for the Advancement of Science; Arctic Institute of North America (board of directors). *Awards:* Gold Medal, Royal Academy of Sciences and Letters of Denmark, 1936. *Interests:* Anthropology, especially archaeology and physical anthropology of Arctic and Southeastern United States. *Expeditions:* Southeast United States, Alaska, Arctic Canada, 1925-30, 1936, 1948-50, 1953-55; study of museum collections in Denmark, Norway, Sweden, Finland, England, France, Switzerland, Germany, Austria, U. S. S. R.; Second International Congress of Anthropology and Ethnology, Copenhagen, 1938 (vice president, chairman

of American delegation); 32nd International Congress of Americanists, Copenhagen, 1956 (honorary vice president); Seventh International Congress of Anthropology and Ethnology, Moscow, 1964 (vice president); Ethnogeographic Board (assistant director and director, 1943-46); *Arctic Bibliography* (chairman, directing committee, 1947); *Anthropology of the North: Translations from Russian Sources* (chairman, advisory committee). *Published works: Prehistoric Art of the Alaskan Eskimo* (Smithsonian Institution, 1929); *Archaeology of St. Lawrence Island, Alaska* (Smithsonian Institution, 1945); editor, *Science in Alaska* (Arctic Institute of North America, 1952); *Arctic Area, Program of the History of America* (Comision de Historia, Mexico, 1954).

COMUNALE, ANTHONY R. 1899-
(physician and surgeon)

Born December 2, 1899, Iselin, N. J. *Education:* Rutgers University, B. S., 1923; Medical College of Virginia, 1928; St. Francis Hospital. *Principal occupation:* Physician and surgeon. *Home address:* 1709 Irving St., Rahway, N. J. 07065. *Affiliations:* Physician and surgeon, Rahway Hospital, Rahway, N. J., 1933-. *Other professional posts:* City physician, Rahway; police surgeon, Rahway Police Department; surgeon, Pennsylvania Railroad Company. *Military service:* Blood Bank Service, American Red Cross. *Memberships:* American Medical Association; New Jersey State Medical Society; Union County Medical Society; American Physicians Art Association; Northern Nut Growers Association. *Awards, honors:* Merit Award in Art, American P. A. A., 1953; Author Award, New Jersey Association of Teachers of English in the category of art, for *Art on Stone by the American Indian in New Jersey. Interests:* Indian artifacts; art on stone and its transcription; minerology and geology; fruit tree grafting and honey bees; propagation of the chestnut tree; oil painting; masonry. *Published works: Art on Stone by the American Indian in New Jersey* (Vantage Press, 1962).

COOK, JOHN A. (St. Regis Mohawk)
1922- (tribal chief)

Born April 22, 1922, Syracuse, N. Y. *Education:* University of Idaho; Loyola University; National Radio Institute; Franklyn Tech. *Principal occupation:* Tribal chief, iron welder. *Home address:* R. F. D. , Hogansburg, N. Y. *Affiliations:* Chief, St. Regis Mohawk Tribe. *Military service:* U.S. Air Force, 1942-45 (Air Medal). *Community activities:* Economic Opportunity Council of Franklyn County (director); Masons; American Legion.

COOK, LINDLEY J. 1900- (minister)

Born March 25, 1900, New Castle, Ind. *Education:* Earlham College, B. A. , 1923. *Principal occupation:* Minister. *Home address:* 1403 21st St. , Central City, Neb. 68826. *Affiliations:* Pastor, Central City Friends Church. *Memberships:* Associated Executive Committee of Friends on Indian Affairs (executive secretary).

COOK, VESPER 1917- (museum curator)

Born June 21, 1917, Peru, Ind. *Principal occupation:* Curator, Miami County Historical Museum. *Address:* 11 N. Huntington St. , Peru, Ind. 46970. *Other professional posts:* Research, Indiana Historical Society, Indianapolis, 1952-53. *Memberships:* Miami County Historical Society, 1960-; Indiana Historical Society, 1962-; Midwest Museums Conference of the American Association of Museums, 1962-; American Numismatics Association, 1963-; Circus Historical Society, 1964-; Circus Fans Association of America, 1964-; Monday Night Literary Club, 1959-; Methodist Church, 1965. *Awards:* Four First Awards, one Second and one Third, Photographic Competition, Miami Lens Club, Peru, Ind. *Interests:* Journalism; museum direction; historical research; archaeology; genealogy; architecture and architectural drafting; photography; numismatics; Indian history; history of the circus and railroads prior to 1945. Articles on local history published in Peru *Daily Tribune*.

COOKE, DAVID C. 1917- (writer)

Born June 7, 1917, Wilmington, Del. *Education:* New York University, 1946-47. *Principal occupation:* Writer. *Home address:* 57 E. Carpenter St., Valley Stream, N. Y. *Affiliations:* Publications officer, U. S. Information Service, New Delhi, India. *Awards, honors:* Edgar Award, for *Best*

Detective Stories of the Year, 1960. *Interests:* Writing; aviation; the American Indian; travel in United States, Europe, and China. *Published works: Famous Indian Tribes* (Random House, 1953); *Fighting Indians of the West* (Dodd, Mead, 1954); *Indians on the Warpath* (Dodd, Mead, 1957); *Tecumseh: Destiny's Warrior* (Julian Messner, 1959); *Indian Wars and Warriors* (Dodd, Mead, 1966).

COOMBS, L. MADISON 1907- (educator)

Born November 19, 1907, St. Joseph, Mo. *Education:* Westminster College, B. A. , 1930; University of Kansas, M. A. , 1942. *Principal occupation:* Educator. *Home address:* 4501 Arlington Blvd. , Arlington, Va. 22203. *Affiliations:* Superintendent of schools, Republic County, Kan. , 1937-41; instructor in education, University of Kansas, 1942-44; acting director of education, Bureau of Indian Affairs, Washington, D. C. *Memberships:* National Education Association; American Association of School Administrators; Phi Delta Kappa. *Interests:* Educational measurement; guidance; adult education. *Published works: The Indian Child Goes to School* (Haskell Press, Bureau of Indian Affairs, 1958); *Doorway Toward the Light* (Haskell Press, Bureau of Indian Affairs, 1962).

CORKRAN, DAVID H. 1902- (teacher, writer)

Born May 11, 1902, Westport, N. Y. *Education:* Wesleyan University, B. A. , 1923; Harvard University, M. A. , 1926. *Principal occupation:* Teacher, writer. *Home address:* 2349 N. Cleveland Ave., Chicago, Ill. 60614. *Affiliations:* Teacher, North Shore Country Day School, 1926-34; assistant headmaster, North Shore Country Day School, 1934-43; teacher, Black Mountain College, 1944-50; assistant professor, Roosevelt University, 1956-60. *Community activities:* Winnetka Public Library Board, 1941-43. *Memberships:* North Carolina Archaeological Society. *Awards, honors:* Newberry Fellowship, Newberry Library, 1962. *Interests:* American Indian history in the Colonial period; mountain hiking. *Published works: The Cherokee Frontier, 1740-1762* (University of Oklahoma, 1962); *The Creek Frontier, 1540-1783* (in press).

CORMACK, MARIBELLE 1902-
(museum director, writer)

Born January 11, 1902, Buffalo, N. Y. *Education:* Cornell University, B. A. , 1923; University of Geneva, summer, 1925; University of Vienna, 1924-25; Brown University, M. A. , 1928. *Principal occupation:* Museum director, writer. *Home address:* 233 Warrington St., Providence, R. I. 12907. *Affiliations:* Science teacher, Buffalo Museum of Science, 1923-24, 1925-26; assistant director, director, Park Museum, 1926-47, 1947-. *Community activities:* Rhode Island Astronomical Society (charter member and past president); Daughters of the American Revolution; A. X. D.; Knights of Cortereal. *Memberships:* American Association for the Advancement of Science, 1965; American Association of Museums; Bishop Museum Association (Honolulu). *Awards, honors:* Ford Foundation Prize for juvenile literature; several Junior Literary Guild selections. *Published works: Horns of Gur* (American Book Co.), and nineteen other juvenile and adult titles; several books in braille; translations into Polish, German, and Swedish.

CORNELL, GRETA A. (museum director)

Born Ossining, N. Y. *Education:* Mount Holyoke College, B. A. , 1932; New York University, M. A. , 1937. *Principal occupation:* Museum director. *Home address:* 68 Croton Ave. , Ossining, N. Y. 10562. *Affiliations:* Director, Ossining Historical Society Museum. *Other professional posts:* Town and village historian of Ossining, 1955-. *Community activities:* Ossining Women's Club. *Memberships:* American Association of Museums; Historical Society of Derby, Conn. ; Westchester County Historical Society.

CORNETT, JAMES D. 1923-
(conservationist)

Born January 1, 1923, Moorewood, Okla. *Education:* Sayre Junior College, 1949-50; Oklahoma State University, B. A. , 1952. *Principal occupation:* Conservationist. *Address:* Zuni Indian Agency, Zuni, N. M. 87327. *Affiliations:* Soil scientist, Fort Peck Agency, Bureau of Indian Affairs, 1952-56; soil conservationist, Blackfeet Agency, Bureau of Indian Affairs, 1956-62;

land operations officer, Zuni Agency, Bureau of Indian Affairs, 1962-. *Military service:* U. S. Navy, 1942-48 (Campaign Medal, Good Conduct Medal). *Community activities:* Cub Scouts; Boy Scouts; Lions Club; Zuni T. V. Association (past president); Sayre College Student Council (past president). *Awards, honors:* Outstanding Student Award, Sayre Junior College; Alpha Zeta, Phi Kappa Phi, 1949, 1952; Commendation for outstanding and accurate radio communications, U. S. S. Loeser, 1946. *Interests:* Administration of government facilities concerning social and economic betterment of the Indian people; conservation of Indian land, water, and resources; civic betterment; photography; sports.

CORY, DAVID MUNROE 1903-
(clergyman, chaplain, social worker)

Born February 10, 1903, New York, N. Y. *Education:* Columbia University, B. A. , 1923; New College (Edinburgh, Scotland); Union Theological Seminary, S. T. M., Th. D. *Principal occupation:* Clergyman, chaplain, social worker. *Home address:* 2048 E. 14th St. , Brooklyn, N. Y. 11229. *Affiliations:* Pastor, Cuyter Presbyterian Church, Brooklyn, N. Y., 1926-55; executive secretary, Brooklyn Division of Protestant Council, New York, N. Y. , 1955-60; pastor, Homecrest Presbyterian Church, Brooklyn, N. Y. , 1960-. *Community activities:* Sheepshead Bay Civic and Community Council (president). *Memberships:* Indian Rights Association; National Fellowship of Indian Workers; Long Island Historical Society (president); Presbyterian Historical Society. *Awards, honors:* Brown-Downie Award (church history), Scotland. *Interests:* Civil War (contributed series of articles to *Journal of Long Island History,* 1962-65); Boy Scouts of America; Girl Scouts of America; Iceberg Athletic Club (president, 1955-). *Published works: Faustus Socinus* (Beacon Press, 1932); revisor and editor, *Rok* (Luke), American Bible Society, 1941; *Teieriwakwata* (Caughnawaga hymnal), 1939, 1957; *Within Two Worlds* (Friendship Press, 1955).

COSGROVE, STEPHEN FRANCIS (Sioux) 1943- (professional baseball player)

Born March 8, 1943, Marysville, Kansas. *Education:* Haskell Institute. *Principal occupation:* Professional baseball player. *Home address:* 7836 Rue Carre 35, Houston, Texas. *Affiliation:* Baltimore Orioles (baseball team).

COTTER, LEONARD N. (Wyandotte) 1906-
(chief, Wyandotte Tribe)

Born July 3, 1906, Wyandotte, Indian Territory, Okla. *Education:* High school. *Principal occupation:* Chief, Wyandotte Tribe; diesel mechanic. *Home address:* Box 15, Wyandotte, Okla. 74370. *Affiliations:* Garage and service station attendant and owner, 1926-37; staff member, Indian Roads Department, Okla., 1938-40; Dunning, James & Patterson Construction Co., Oklahoma City, Okla., 1942-43; E. A. Martin Machinery Co., Joplin, Mo., 1943-44; S. E. Evans Construction Co., Ft. Smith, Ark., 1944-45; diesel mechanic, Oklahoma State Highway Department, 1946-. *Other professional posts:* Second chief, Wyandotte Tribe, 1932-36; chief, 1936-42; chief, 1948-54; chief, 1963-. *Military service:* U. S. Marines, 1943. *Community activities:* Masons (past master); Wyandotte Lions Club (past president); Wyandotte Methodist Church (past lay leader); American Legion. *Published works: Constitution and By-laws of the Wyandotte Tribe of Oklahoma* (Department of the Interior, 1937); *Corporate Charter of the Wyandotte Tribe of Oklahoma* (Department of the Interior, 1937).

COTTERILL, R. S. 1884-
(professor of history)

Born August 12, 1884, Battle Run, Ky. *Education:* Kentucky Wesleyan, B. A., 1904; University of Virginia, M. A., 1907; University of Wisconsin, Ph. D., 1918. *Home address:* 1507 Marion Ave., Tallahassee, Fla. 32303. *Principal occupation:* Professor of history. *Affiliations:* Kentucky Wesleyan, 1910-14; Western Maryland College, 1915-20; University of Louisville, 1920-28; Florida State University, 1928-55. *Memberships:* Southern Historical Association (past president). *Published works: History of Pioneer Kentucky* (Johnson and Hardin, 1917); *The Old South* (Arthur H. Clark & Co., 1935); *A Short History of the Americas* (Prentice-Hall, 1939); *The Southern Indians* (University of Oklahoma Press, 1954).

CRAGUN, JOHN W. 1906- (attorney)

Born December 8, 1906, Ogden, Utah. *Education:* George Washington University, B. A., 1932, LL. B., 1934. *Principal occupation:* Partner, Wilkinson, Cragun and Barker, General Practice of Law. *Home address:* 1026 16th St., N. W., Washington, D. C. 20036. *Affiliations:* General counsel, Confederated Salish and Kootenai Tribes, Flathead Reservation, Montana, Quinault Tribe of the Quinault Reservation, Washington. *Other professional posts:* Member, American Bar Association House of Delegates, 1956-60; chairman, American Bar Association Section of Administrative Law, 1952-54; many committee chairmanships and memberships. *Memberships:* Bar Associations: American, District of Columbia, Virginia State; American Judicature Society; Torch Club of Washington; University Club of Washington. *Interests:* Representation of American Indian tribes as tribal attorney, claims counsel, or both.

CRAMPTON, C. GREGORY 1911-
(professor of history)

Born March 22, 1911, Kankakee, Ill. *Education:* Modesto Junior College, 1933; University of California (Berkeley), B.A., 1935; M. A., 1936; Ph. D., 1941. *Principal occupation:* Professor of history. *Home address:* 327 S. 12th, E., Salt Lake City, Utah 84102. *Affiliations:* Teaching assistant in history, University of California (Berkeley) 1937-40; special agent, Federal Bureau of Investigation, U. S. Department of Justice, 1943-45; depot historian, California Quartermaster Depot, U. S. War Department, 1944-45; professor of history, University of Utah, 1945-; visiting assistant professor of history, Northwestern University, 1946; visiting professor of history, University of Panama, 1955; professor, Overseas Program, University of Maryland, 1956-57; visiting lecturer, Eastern Montana College of Education, 1961. *Awards:* Rockefeller Foundation, traveling Fellowship, 1941-42; postwar Fellowship, Humanities, 1948-49; University of Panama. *Memberships:* Phi Alpha Theta (vice president, 1941-48; president, 1949-50). *Published works: The Gold Rushes in the United States, 1800-1900* (University of California Press, 1936); *The Opening of the Mariposa Mining Region, 1849-59* (University of California Press, 1941); editor, *Greater America, Essays in*

Honor of Herbert E. Bolton (University of California Press, 1945); *Outline History of the Glen Canyon Region, 1776-1922* (University of Utah Press, 1959); *Historical Sites in Glen Canyon, Mouth of the San Juan River to Lee's Ferry* (University of Utah Press, 1960); editor with Dwight L. Smight, *The Hoskaninni Papers of Robert B. Stanton, Mining in Glen Canyon, 1897-1902* (University of Utah Press, 1961); *Historical Sites in Glen Canyon, Mouth of Hansen Creek to Mouth of San Juan River* (University of Utah Press, 1962); *The San Juan Canyon Historical Sites* (University of Utah Press, 1964); *Historical Sites in Cataract and Narrow Canyons, and in Glen Canyon to California Bar* (University of Utah Press, 1964); *Standing Up Country, the Canyon Lands of Utah and Arizona* (Alfred A. Knopf; University of Utah Press in association with the Amon Carter Museum of Western Art); numerous articles in journals.

CRANE, FRANCIS VALENTINE 1903-
(museum curator)

Born November 28, 1903, Westwood, Mass. *Education:* Harvard University, B.A., 1925. *Principal occupation:* Museum curator. *Home address:* P.O. Box 248, Marathon, Fla. 33050. *Affiliations:* Curator, Southeast Museum of the North American Indian.

CRANE, VERNER W. 1889- (professor of history)

Born August 28, 1889, Tecumseh, Mich. *Education:* University of Michigan, B.A., 1911; Harvard University, M.A., 1912; University of Pennsylvania, Ph.D., 1915. *Principal occupation:* Professor of history. *Home address:* 2360 Earhart Rd., Ann Arbor, Mich. 48105. *Affiliations:* Research fellow, University of Pennsylvania, 1915-16; instructor, University of Michigan, 1916-20; assistant and associate professor, Brown University, 1920-30; professor, University of Michigan, 1930-59; professor of history emeritus, University of Michigan, 1959-. *Other professional posts:* Visiting lecturer, Harvard University, 1925-26, 1928-29; University of Chicago, 1930; University of Michigan, 1965; Colver Lecturer, Brown University, 1935; Commonwealth Fund Lecturer, University of London, 1957; editorial board, *American Historical Review;* editorial board, *Mississippi Valley*

Historical Review; council, Institute of Early American History. *Awards, honors:* Phi Beta Kappa, Russel Lecturer, University of Michigan. *Interests:* American colonial history; history of the American Revolution; Anglo-French conflict on the Southern frontier, involving Indian affairs. *Published works: Southern Frontier, 1670-1732* (Duke University Press, 1929); *Benjamin Franklin, Englishman and American* (Brown University Press, 1936); *Benjamin Franklin's Letters to the Press, 1758-1775* (University of North Carolina Press, 1950); *Benjamin Franklin and a Rising People* (Little, Brown, 1954).

CRESSMAN, LUTHER S. 1897-
(anthropologist)

Born October 24, 1897, Pottstown, Penna. *Education:* Pennsylvania State College, B.Sc., 1941; New York University, M.Sc., 1942; University of Chicago, Ph.D., 1949. *Home address:* 7309 Hansford St., Washington, D.C. 20028. *Affiliations:* Research and teaching, University of Chicago, 1946-49; consultant, U.S. Air Force Weather Service, 1949-54; director, Joint Weather Bureau, Navy-Air Force Numerical Weather Prediction Unit, 1954-; National Meteorological Center, 1958-. *Military service:* A.U.S., 1942-45. *Awards, honors:* Exceptional Service Award, U.S. Air Force, 1956; Exceptional Service Award, Department of Commerce, 1961. *Memberships:* American Meteorological Society (councilor, 1956-59; associate editor, *Journal,* 1954-); Association of Computing Machines; Washington Academy of Sciences. *Published works: Cultural Sequences at the Dalles, Oregon: A Contribution to Pacific Northwest Prehistory* (American Philosophical Society, 1960).

CROSS, MARION E. 1903- (writer)

Born September 17, 1903, Minneapolis, Minn. *Education:* Smith College, B.A., 1926; University of Minnesota, M.A., 1933. *Principal occupation:* Writer. *Home address:* 1944 Penn Ave., S., Minneapolis, Minn. 55405. *Published works:* Translator, Hennepin, L., *Description of Louisiana* (University of Minnesota Press, 1938); *Pioneer Harvest* (Farmers and Mechanics Savings Bank of Minneapolis, 1949); *From*

Land, Sea, and Test Tube (Archer Daniels Midland Co. , 1954, 1957); *Orally Speaking* (Webb Publishing Co. , 1957).

CROUSE, CARL (editor)

Home address: Arthur, Nebraska 69121. *Affiliation:* Editor, *Arthur Enterprise.* *Other professional posts:* Minister. *Community activities:* Arthur County Historical Society, Arthur, Nebraska (president); county historian.

CROW, JOHN O. (Cherokee) 1912-
(B. I. A. official)

Born September 7, 1912, Salem, Mo. *Education:* Haskell Institute. *Home address:* 2386 N. Edgewood St., Arlington, Va. 22207. *Principal occupation:* Associate director, Bureau of Land Management, Bureau of Indian Affairs. *Other professional posts:* Former Bureau of Indian Affairs superintendent at Truxton Canyon Agency, Mescalero Agency, Fort Apache Agency, Uintah and Ouray Agency; chief of realty, 1960-61; acting commissioner, 1961; deputy commissioner, 1961-65. *Awards, honors:* Career Service Award, 1964, National Civil Service League.

CUNNINGHAM, FRANK HARRISON 1911-
(author, editor)

Born March 13, 1911, Roanoke, Va. *Education:* Loyola University, 1929-30; Washington and Lee, B. A. , 1932; Sequoia University, M. A. , Litt. D. ; Fremont College, HH. D. ; Burton College, D. Journalism, Ed. D.; Evergreen University, Lit.D., Trinity Southern, D. South Lit.; Phoenix University (Italy), D. Eng. Lit. ; St. Andrews College, Ph. D.; University of West, Ph. D. ; College of Seminarians, LL. D. ; Andhra Research University (Fellow). *Principal occupation:* Author, editor. *Home address:* The Embassy, 1001 3rd St. , Santa Monica, Calif. 90403. *Affiliations:* Correspondent, United Press, Washington Herald, WRBX, Transradio Press, 1932-36; "journalistic work," Santa Monica, Calif. , 1936-. *Other professional posts:* Assistant to president, Sequoia University, 1955-58; vice president, Sequoia University and Fremont College,

1955-58; director, Sequoia University Press, 1955-58; contributor to national magazines. *Military service:* California National Guard, 1940-41; Illinois National Guard. *Community activities:* California commander, Sons of Confederate Veterans; Order of the Stars and Bars; Armies of the West, Confederate High Command; honorable California chairman, Gettysburg Battlefield Preservation Association; Civil War Press Corps. *Memberships:* Manuscripters Club (past president); Society of Pan American Culture (board of directors, 1963-); Santa Monica Chapter, National Society of Arts and Letters (vice president, 1958-); Santa Monica Writers Club; Artists of the West; Santa Monica Opera; Pacific Coast Opera; California Pan Americans; English Speaking Union; International Platform Association; New York Southern Society; Delta Upsilon; Sigma Delta Chi; Mark Twain and Eugene Field Societies. *Awards, honors:* Freedoms Foundation Award, Valley Forge, 1951, 1952, 1955-57; Fight Communism Committee, 1958; Liberty Award, Congress of Freedom, 1959; knight commander, Order of the Crown of Thorns; Cross of Lorraine (France); Cross of Honor, International Institute of American Ideals; military service crosses, Sons of Confederate Veterans and Order of the Stars and Bars; Fellow, Sequoia Research Institute; Fellow, International Institute of Arts and Letters (Switzerland); Confederate Caucus (England); six awards, Manuscripters Club; Americanism in Journalism Award, Pan American Press Syndicate; California Division Award, United Daughters of Confederacy; Best Book Award, Confederate High Command; Best Book Award, National Railroad Association; Best Book Award, *Leash and Collar* magazine; Best Essay Award, California Citizens Committee on Government Affairs. *Published works: Sky Master* (Dorrance, 1943); *Big Dan* (Deseret News Press, 1947); *Red Rock II,* with Gen. W.R. White (Olivier, Maney and Klein, 1950); *Operation Nightmare,* with Pat Barham (Sequoia University Press, 1953); *Gen. Stand Waite's Confederate Indians* (Naylor, 1959); *Knight of the Confederacy* (Naylor, 1960); radio plays and serials (Greenberg, 1941).

CURRIE, DAVID 1938- (Indian relic collector)

Born December 10, 1938, Youngstown, Ohio. *Education*: Bethany College; Lehigh

University. *Home address:* 23 Lincoln St., Roseland, N. J. *Principal occupation:* Owner, Colonial America, Inc., Route 46 and Hook Mountain Rd., Pine Brook, N. J. *Memberships:* New Jersey State Archaeological Society; Lenni Lenape Indian Relic Collection Association; Shongum Chapter, Genuine Indian Relic Society. *Interests:* American Indian prehistoric and historic artifacts. *In preparation:* A work on American Indian relic fakes.

CUSHMAN, DAN   1909-   (author)

Born June 9, 1909, Marion, Mich. *Education:* University of Montana, B.S., 1934. *Principal occupation:* Author. *Home address:* 1500 Fourth Ave., N., Great Falls, Mont. 59401. *Affiliations:* Mr. Cushman writes, "(I have been) a writer (for) newspapers and magazines (and) for radio, a geologist, prospector (and) assayer, but without regular employment except as a free lance writer, chiefly a novelist, since 1946, although now I do some consulting and special geological work." *Awards, honors:* Spur Award for *The Silver Mountain* as best historical novel of the year, Western Writers of America, 1957; award for *The Grand and the Glorious* as one of the ten best books of the year for pre-college readers, National Association of Independent Schools, 1963. *Interests:* "As far as Indian lore is concerned, the only thing of mine that has received much recognition is my novel, *Stay Away, Joe,* a modern story of Indians on and near a northern Montana reservation; was basis for the Broadway musical–comedy *Whoop-Up* and is still selling briskly in hardcover after twelve years here in the Northwest. It was with no little surprise and collateral pride to me when *Stay Away, Joe*'s publishers were asked for fifty copies of the book, one for each person enrolling in the 1965 Summer Institute for Advanced Study on Disadvantaged Youth, American Indians, at Western Montana College, Dillon, Mont." *Published works: Stay Away, Joe* (Viking, 1953); *The Silver Mountain* (Appleton, 1955); *The Old Copper Collar* (Ballantine, 1955); *Goodbye, Old Dry* (Doubleday, 1959); *Brothers in Kickapoo* (McGraw-Hill, 1962); *The Grand and the Glorious* (McGraw-Hill, 1963); *The Great North Trail* (McGraw-Hill, 1966); numerous paperback titles.

D

DANKER, DONALD F.

Born October 7, 1922, Riverton, Neb. *Education:* University of Nebraska, B.S., 1948, M.A., 1949, Ph.D., 1955. *Principal occupation:* Historian. *Home address:* 3178 Puritan Ave., Lincoln, Neb. 68502. *Affiliations:* Professor of history, York College, 1949-52; archivist, Nebraska State Historical Society, 1952-63; instructor, University of Nebraska, 1955-63; historian, Nebraska State Historical Society, 1964-; assistant professor of history, Washburn University, 1963-64. *Military service:* U.S. Army, 1941-45. *Memberships:* Kansas State Historical Society, 1958-; Mississippi Valley Historical Association, 1958-; Western History Association, 1960-; Nebraska Writers Guild (vice president, 1961-62, president, 1963). *Interests:* History of the American West. *Published works: Mollie: The Journal of Mollie Dorsey Sanford* (University of Nebraska Press, 1959); *Man of the Plains: Recollections of Luther North, 1856-82* (University of Nebraska Press, 1961).

DAVIS, RUSSELL G.   (Naragansett)   1922-   (professor)

Born October 29, 1922, Boston, Mass. *Education:* Holy Cross College, B.A., 1943; Harvard University, Ed.M., M.A., Ed.D., 1955. *Principal occupation:* Professor, Harvard University. *Home address:* 15 Rogers St., Newton Highlands, Mass. *Military service:* U.S. Marine Corps, 1943-46. *Memberships:* American Association for the Advancement of Science (Fellow); American Academy of Political and Social Science; Society for International Development; Linguistic Society of America. *Awards: Herald Tribune* Spring Award; Elliot scholarship; various literary prizes. *Interests:* Latin American specialists' statistics applied to educational planning. *Travels:* "Have lived and worked in Africa, Latin America, and the Far East." *Published works: The Lion's Whiskers* (Little, Brown, 1959); *Point Four Assignment* (Little, Brown, 1959); *Ten Thousand Desert Swords* (Little, Brown, 1960); *The Choctaw Code* (McGraw-Hill, 1961); *Marine at War* (Little, Brown, 1961); *Chief Joseph* (McGraw-Hill, 1962); *West Africa: Land in the Sun* (Little, Brown, 1963); *Strangers in Africa* (McGraw-Hill, 1963); thirty articles published in various journals.

D'AZEVEDO, WARREN L.   1920-
(anthropologist, sociologist)

Born August 19, 1920, Oakland, Calif. *Education:* University of California, Berkeley, B. A., 1942, 1949-53; Northwestern University, Ph. D., 1962. *Principal occupation:* Associate professor of anthropology. *Home address:* 1815 Windsor Way, Reno, Nev. *Affiliations:* Lecturer, Northwestern University, 1958; assistant professor, University of California, 1958-59; consultant to Liberian Peace Corps Training Project; chairman, Department of Sociology and Anthropology, University of Nevada (assistant and associate professor, 1960-). *Memberships:* American Anthropological Association; African Studies Association; American Association of University Professors; Sigma Xi; Great Basin Anthropological Conference (chairman, 1964-66). *Awards, honors:* Carnegie Research Assistantship, 1954-55; Ford Foundation and S. S. R. C. fellowship for field work in Africa; research fellowship, Program of African Studies, Northwestern University; Bollingen Foundation Fellowship. *Interests:* African and North American ethnology, social organization; sociocultural change and integration; religion and esthetics. *Published works:* Editor, *The Washo of California and Nevada* (University of Utah Press, 1963); *Current Status of Anthropological Research in the Great Basin, 1964* (Desert Research Institute, University of Nevada, 1966); *The West African Artist* (in preparation).

DE BAILLOU, CLEMENT   1903-
(museum director, writer)

Born December 30, 1903, Vienna, Austria. *Education:* University of Salzburg, B. A., 1922. *Principal occupation:* Museum director, writer. *Home address:* 1121 Monte Sano Ave., Augusta, Ga. *Affiliations:* Austrian Foreign Service, 1937-38; assistant professor, Language Department, Clark University, Worcester, Mass., 1942-47; University of Massachusetts, 1947-49; University of Georgia, 1949-52; University of Georgia, 1952-63. *Military Service:* Austrian Cavalry. *Memberships:* Southeastern Archaeological Association; South Atlantic Modern Language Association. *Interests:* Archaeology; has traveled extensively through Europe, the Near and Middle East,

and Brazil. *Published works: John Howard Payne to his Countryman* (University of Georgia Press); numerous articles in journals in English and German.

DEBO, ANGIE   1890-   (writer)

Born January 30, 1890, Beattie, Kan. *Education:* University of Oklahoma, B. A., 1918; University of Chicago, M. A., 1924; University of Oklahoma, Ph. D., 1933. *Principal occupation:* Writer. *Home address:* P. O. Box 133, Marshall, Okla. 73056. *Affiliations:* Teacher of history, Enid High School, Enid, Okla., 1919-23; assistant professor of history, West Texas State University, 1924-34; state supervisor, Federal Writers Project, Oklahoma City, Okla., 1940-42; member, library staff, Oklahoma State University, 1947-55. *Community activities:* Association on American Indian Affairs (board of directors); Indian Rights Association; Oklahoma Civil Liberties Union; Marshall (Okla.) Women's Club; Committee on Christian Social Action, United Church of Christ; Kansas-Oklahoma Conference. *Memberships:* Phi Beta Kappa; Phi Gamma Mu; Delta Kappa Gamma (state honorary member); Theta Sigma Phi (honorary member); Stillwater (Okla.) Writer's Club (lifetime honorary member); Oklahoma Historical Society (lifetime honorary member). *Awards, honors:* John H. Dunning Prize, American Historical Association, for *The Rise and Fall of the Choctaw Republic,* 1935; Alfred A. Knopf Historical Fellowship, 1942, for *Prairie City. Interests:* Indian and Oklahoma history, Western Americana; Indian welfare; outdoor life; photography; contacts with international college students; social studies seminars to Western Europe, Poland, U. S. S. R., Finland, Mexico; travels to England and Canada. *Published works: Historical Background of the American Policy of Isolation,* with Fred Rippy (Smith College Studies, Vol. 9, 1924); *The Rise and Fall of the Choctaw Republic* (University of Oklahoma Press, 1934, 1961); *And Still the Waters Run* (Princeton University Press; Gordion Press, 1940); *The Road to Disappearance* (University of Oklahoma Press, 1941); editor, *Oklahoma: A Guide to the Sooner State* (University of Oklahoma Press, 1941); *Tulsa: From Creek Town to Oil Capital* (University of Oklahoma Press, 1943); *Prairie City: The Story of an American Community*

(Alfred A. Knopf, 1944); *Oklahoma: Footloose and Fancy Free* (University of Oklahoma Press, 1949); editor, *The Cowman's Southwest* (Arthur H. Clark & Co. , 1953).

DELORIA, VINE, Jr. (Standing Rock Sioux) 1933- (organization executive)

Born March 26, 1933, Martin, S. D. *Education:* Iowa State University, B. S. , 1958; Lutheran School of Theology, B. D. , 1963. *Principal occupation:* Organization executive. *Home address:* 2440 S. Monroe, Denver, Colo. 80210. *Affiliations:* Executive director, National Congress of American Indians. *Military service:* U. S. Marine Corps, 1954-56.

DENTON, COYE (Cherokee) 1914-
(artist)

Born October 14, 1914, Romulus, Okla. *Education:* East Central State College, B.S. , 1941. *Principal occupation*: Artist. *Home address:* Box 444, Ada, Okla. 74820. *Affiliations:* Secretary, Denco Bus Lines, Ada, Okla. *Community activities:* Fortnightly Tanti (past president); Tantettes; Wednesday Morning Music, Salvation Army Auxiliary; Great Books Organization; Salvation Army (advisory board). *Memberships:* Ada Artists Association (charter member and president, 1956-); Roloes (artists), 1947-55.

DERLETH, AUGUST 1909- (writer,
editor, teacher, lecturer, publisher)

Born February 24, 1909, Sauk City, Wis. *Education:* University of Wisconsin, B. A. , 1930. *Principal occupation:* Writer, editor, lecturer, teacher, publisher. *Home address:* Place of Hawks, Sauk City, Wis. 53583. *Community activities:* Board of Education; Men's Club of Sauk City (president). *Memberships:* Authors' Guild; American Society of Historians; The Cliff Dwellers; State Historical Society of Wisconsin; Midland Authors. *Awards, honors:* Guggenheim Fellowship, 1938; Midland Authors' Poetry Award, 1964. *Published works: Murder Stalks the Wakely Family* (Loring and Mussey, 1943); *The Man on All Fours* (Loring and Mussey, 1934); *Place of Hawks* (Loring and Mussey, 1935); *Sign of Fear* (Loring and Mussey, 1935); *Three*

Who Died (Loring and Mussey, 1935); *Consider your Verdict* (Stackpole, 1937); *Still is the Summer Night* (Scribners, 1937); *Any Day Now* (Normandie, 1938); *Hawk on the Wind* (Ritten House, 1938); *Wind Over Wisconsin* (Scribners, 1938); *Atmosphere of Houses* (Prairie Press, 1939); *Man Track Here* (Ritten House, 1939); *Restless is the River* (Scribners, 1939); *Biography of Zona Gale* (Appleton, 1940); *Bright Journey* (Scribners, 1940); *Country Growth* (Scribners, 1940); *Here on a Darkling Plain* (Ritten House, 1940); *Narracong Riddle* (Scribners, 1940); *Sentence Deferred* (Scribners, 1940); *Evening with Spring* (Scribners, 1941); *Someone in the Dark* (Arkham, 1941); *Village Year: A Sac Prairie Journal* (Coward, 1941); *Wind in the Elms* (Ritten House, 1941); *Rind of Earth* (Decker, 1942); *Sweet Genevieve* (Scribners, 1942); *The Wisconsin: River of a Thousand Isles* (Farrar and Rinehart, 1942); *Seven Who Waited* (Scribners, 1943); *Shadow of Night* (Scribners, 1943); *And You, Thoreau* (New Directions, 1944); *Mischief in the Lane* (Scribners, 1944); *Selected Poems* (Decker, 1944); editor, *Sleep No More* (Farrar and Rinehart, 1944); *The Edge of Night* (Decker, 1945); *H. P. L. : A Memoir* (Ben Abramson, 1945); *In Re: Sherlock Holmes, The Adventure of Solar Pons* (Mycroft and Moran, 1945); *Lurker at the Threshold* (Arkham, 1945); *No Future for Luana* (Scribners, 1945); *Oliver, The Wayward Owl,* with Clare Victor Dwiggins (Stanton and Lee, 1945); *Shield of the Valiant* (Scribners, 1945); *Something Near* (Arkham, 1945); *Habitant of Dusk* (Walden, 1946); editor, *Who Knocks* (Rinehart, 1946); *Writing Fiction* (Writer Publications, 1946); *A Boys Way* (Stanton and Lee, 1947); editor, *The Night Side* (Rinehart, 1947); editor, *The Sleeping and the Dead* (Pellegrini and Cudahy, 1947); *Village Daybook: A Sac Prairie Journal* (Pellegrini and Cudahy, 1947); *Its a Boy's World* (Stanton and Lee, 1948); *The Milwaukee Road: Its First 100 Years* (Creative Age, 1948); *Not Long for this World* (Arkham, 1948); *Sac Prairie People* (Stanton and Lee, 1948); *Sauk County: A Centennial History* (Sauk County Centennial Committee, 1948); editor, *Strange Ports of Call* (Pellegrini and Cudahy, 1948); editor, *The Other Side of the Moon* (Pellegrini and Cudahy, 1949); editor, *Beyond Time and Space* (Pellegrini and Cudahy, 1950); editor, *Far Boundaries* (Pellegrini and Cudahy, 1951); *Memoirs of Solar Pons* (Mycroft and Moran, 1951); editor, *The Outer Reaches* (Pellegrini and Cudahy,

1951); editor, *Beachheads in Space* (Pellegrini and Cudahy, 1952); *The Captive Island* (Alladin, 1952); *Country of the Hawk* (Aladdin, 1952); editor, *Night's Yawning Peal* (Pellegrini and Cudahy, 1952); *Rendezvous in a Landscape* (Fine Editions, 1952); *Three Problems of Solar Pons* (Mycroft and Moran, 1952); editor, *Worlds of Tomorrow* (Pellegrini and Cudahy, 1952); *Death by Design* (Arcadia, 1953); *Empire of Fur* (Aladdin, 1953); *Fell Purpose* (Arcadia, 1953); *House of Moonlight* (Prairie Press, 1953); *Psyche* (Prairie Press, 1953); *Land of Grey Gold* (Aladdin, 1954); editor, *Portals of Tomorrow* (Rinehart, 1954); editor, *Time to Come* (Farrar, Straus, 1954); *Fr. Marquette and the Great Rivers* (Farrar, Straus, 1955); *Land of Sky Blue Water* (Aladdin, 1955); *Country Poems* (Prairie Press, 1956); *St. Ignatius and the Company of Jesus* (Farrar, Straus, 1956); *Columbus and the New World* (Farrar, Straus, 1957); *The Survivors and Others*, with H. P. Lovecraft (Arkham, 1957); *The House on the Mound* (Duell, 1958); *The Mask of Cthulhu* (Arkham, 1958); *The Moon Tenders* (Duell, 1958); *The Return of Solar Pons* (Mycroft and Moran, 1958); *Arkham House: The First Twenty Years, 1939-1959* (Arkham, 1959); *The Mill Creek Irregulars* (Duell, 1959); *Some Notes on H. P. Lovecraft* (Arkham, 1959); *Wilbur, the Trusting Whippoorwill* (Stanton and Lee, 1959); *The Hills Stand Watch* (Duell, 1960); *The Pinkertons Ride Again* (Duell, 1960); *West of the Morning* (Golden Quill, 1960); *Fire and Sleet and Candlelight* (Arkham, 1961); *Ghost of Black Hawk Island* (Duell, 1961); *The Reminiscences of Solar Pons* (Mycroft and Moran, 1961); *Concord Rebel: A Life of Henry D. Thoreau* (Chilton, 1962); editor, *Dark Mind, Dark Heart* (Arkham, 1962); *Lonesome Places* (Arkham, 1962); *Sweet Land of Michigan* (Aladdin, 1962); *This Wound* (Prairie Press, 1962); *The Trial of Cthulhu* (Arkham, 1962); *The Shadow in the Glass* (Duell, 1963); and others.

DESJARLAIT, PATRICK ROBERT (Chippewa) 1921- (commercial artist)

Born March 1, 1921, Red Lake, Minn. *Principal occupation:* Commercial artist. *Home address:* 7641 - 62nd Ave., N., New Hope, Minn. 55428. *Military service:* U. S. Navy, 1941-45 -- visual education training, slide films, animation, training films. *Memberships:* Minneapolis Art Directors Club. *Award, honors:* First Prize, Philbrook Art Center, Tulsa, Okla., 1946; First Prize, Elkus Memorial Award, Inter-Tribal Indian Ceremonial, Gallup, N. M., 1964; Second Award, Scottsdale National Indian Arts Exhibition, 1964. *One-man shows and exhibitions:* Fine Arts Gallery, San Diego, Calif., 1945; St. Paul Art Gallery, St. Paul, Minn., 1946; Gallery of American Indian Art, U. S. Department of the Interior, Washington, D. C., 1965.

DINES, GLEN 1925- (writer, illustrator)

Born November 19, 1925, Casper, Wyo. *Education:* Los Angeles Art Center School; University of Washington; Sacramento State College, B. A., M. A. *Principal occupation:* Writer, illustrator. *Home address:* 30 Rockridge Rd., Fairfax, Calif. *Military service:* WW II, U. S. Army. *Published works:* (as writer and illustrator) *The Useful Dragon of Sam Long Toy* (Macmillan, 1956); *The Mysterious Machine* (Macmillan, 1957); *Pitiode the Color Maker* (Macmillan, 1958); *Tiger in the Cherry Tree* (Macmillan, 1959); *The Fabulous Flying Bicycle* (Macmillan, 1959); *Overland Stage* (Macmillan, 1961); *Long Knife* (Macmillan, 1962); *Bull Wagon* (Macmillan, 1963); *Indian Pony* (Macmillan, 1963); (as writer) *Dog Soldier* (Macmillan, 1962); *End o' Steel* (Macmillan, 1964); (illustrated) *Millikan's Ark* (Nelson, 1955); *Daniel Boone* (Putnam's, 1964); *Bony Pony* (Putnam's, 1965); editor, *Clipper Ship* (Putnam's, 1963); *Silver and Lead* (Putnam's, 1962).

DI PESO, CHARLES C. 1920- (foundation director)

Born October 20, 1920, St. Louis, Mo. *Education:* Beloit College, B. S., B. A., 1942; American Institute of Foreign Trade, B. F. T., 1947; University of Arizona, Ph.D., 1953. *Principal affiliation:* Foundation director. *Address:* The Amerind Foundation, Inc., Dragoon, Ariz. 85609. *Affiliations:* Member, board of directors, The Amerind Foundation, Inc. *Other professional posts:* Member, board of directors, Cochise College, Douglas, Ariz. *Military service:* U. S. Army Air Force, 1942-46. *Memberships:* Society for American Archaeology (Fellow); American Association for the Advancement of Science (Fellow); Arizona Academy of

Science (Fellow). *Awards:* Alfred Vincent
Kidder Award for Achievement in American
Archaeology, 1959. *Interests:* Archaeology
and archaeohistory of the American Southwest and Mexico. *Expeditions:* Principal
director, Joint Casas Grandes Expedition,
Northwestern Chihuahua, Mexico, sponsored
by The Amerind Foundation, Inc. and the
Republic of Mexico. *Published works: The
Babocomari Village Site on the San Pedro
River, Southeastern Arizona* (The Amerind
Foundation, 1951); *The Sobaipuri Indians of
the Upper San Pedro River Valley, Southeastern Arizona* (The Amerind Foundation,
1953); *The Upper Pima of the San Cayetano
del Tumacacori* (The Amerind Foundation,
1956); *The Reeve Ruin of Southeastern Arizona* (The Amerind Foundation, 1958).

DITTERT, ALFRED E., Jr.   1922-
   (archaeologist)

Born February 24, 1922, Dallas, Texas.
Education: University of New Mexico, B. A.,
1947, M.A., 1949; University of Arizona,
Ph. D., 1959; U. S. A. F. I., 1945-46. *Home
address:* 415 W. Buena Vista, Santa Fe,
N. M. 87501. *Principal occupation:* Cura-
tor-in-charge, Research Division, Museum
of New Mexico; visiting professor, College
of Santa Fe, 1965-. *Affiliations:* Graduate
assistant, Department of Anthropology, University of New Mexico, 1948-49; assistant
instructor, University of New Mexico Field
School, 1949; co-director, Peabody Museum
of Harvard University Expedition and Excavations at Cebolleta Mesa and Acoma Pueblo, 1951; archaeologist, Acoma Land
Claim, 1951-54; assistant curator, Museum
of New Mexico, 1955-56; research assistant,
Museum of New Mexico Navajo Dam Project,
1956-57; research assistant, Museum of
New Mexico and School of American Research Navajo Dam Project, 1957-59; research associate, Museum of New Mexico,
Navajo Dam Project, 1959-61; curator of
salvage archaeology, Museum of New Mexico, 1961-62; curator of archaeological research, Museum of New Mexico, 1962-64.
Military service: U.S. Air Force, 1943-
46 (Battle Star; Good Conduct Medal; American Theater Ribbon; European-African-
Middle Eastern Ribbon). *Memberships:*
Archaeological Society of New Mexico, 1956-
(board of trustees, 1963-); Society for
American Archaeology, 1955-; Current
Anthropology (Associate, 1959); Sigma Xi,

1951-; American Anthropological Association (Fellow, 1965-); *El Palacio* (advisory
board, 1965); ex-officio member, Governor's Historic Sites Committee, 1965; Museum of New Mexico representative, Steering Committee, Northern Rio Grande Resources Conservation and Development,
1964; Task Force on Research Planning for
Comprehensive Mental Health Services,
1964. *Awards, honors:* National Science
Foundation Grant for archaeological excavations; fellowship, University of Arizona,
1950. *Excavations:* Galisteo Basin, New
Mexico, 1938; Gallina Phase ruin, New Mexico, 1941; Isleta Cave, University of New
Mexico Field School, 1946; Cebolleta Mesa,
1947-48; Pa-ako, 1949; Acoma Pueblo,
1952. *Published works: The Prehistoric
Population and Architecture of the Cebolleta
Mesa Region, Central Western New Mexico,*
M.A. thesis (University of New Mexico
Press, 1949); *Preliminary Archaeological
Investigations in the Navajo Project Area of
Northwestern New Mexico* (Museum of New
Mexico Papers in Anthropology No. 1, 1958);
*Culture Change in the Cebolleta Mesa Re-
gion, Central Western New Mexico* Ph. D.
dissertation (University of Arizona Press,
1959); *Pueblo Period Sites in the Piedra
River Section, Navajo Reservoir District,*
with Frank W. Eddy (Museum of New Mexico Papers in Anthropology, No. 10, 1963);
numerous papers, reports, reviews and
articles published in various scholarly
journals.

DOCKSTADER, FREDERICK J.   1919-
   (museum director)

Born February 3, 1919, Los Angeles, Calif.
Education: Arizona State College, B. A.,
M.A.; Western Reserve University, Ph. D.,
1951. *Principal occupation:* Museum director. *Home address:* 165 W. 66th St.,
New York, N. Y. 10023. *Affiliations:*
Teacher, Flagstaff, Ariz., schools, 1936-
41; teacher, Cranbrook, Mich., schools,
1942-50; staff ethnologist, Cranbrook Institute of Sciences, 1950-52; faculty member
and curator of anthropology, Dartmouth
Coll., 1952-55; ass't. director, director,
Museum of the American Indian, Heye Foundation, 1955-60, 1960-. *Other professional
posts:* Advisory editor, *Encyclopedia
Americana,* 1957-; commissioner, Indian
Arts and Crafts Board, U. S. Department of
the Interior, 1955-; visiting professor of
art and archaeology, Columbia University,

1961-; member, New York State Museum Advisory Council. *Memberships:* American Association for the Advancement of Science (Fellow); Cranbrook Institute of Sciences (Fellow); American Anthropological Association (Fellow); Society for American Archaeology; Cosmos Club. *Awards, honors:* First Prize (silversmithing), Cleveland Museum of Art, 1950; Fellow, Rochester Museum of Arts and Sciences. *Published works: The Kachina and the White Man* (Cranbrook Institute of Sciences, 1954); *The American Indian in Graduate Studies* (Museum of the American Indian, Heye Foundation, 1957); *Indian Art in America* (New York Graphic Society, 1960); *Indian Art in Middle America* (New York Graphic Society, 1964); *Kunst in Amerika: I* (Stuttgart, 1965); *Kunst in Amerika: II* (Stuttgart, 1966); *Indian Art in South America* (New York Graphic Society, 1966).

DOONKEEN, EULAMAE N(ARCOMEY)
(Crying Wind) (Seminole) 1931-
(artist)

Born December 12, 1931, Oklahoma City, Okla. *Education:* Central State College, B.A. (Education), 1965; Hills Business University, 1955-56. *Principal occupation:* Portrait painter. *Home address:* 1608 N.W. 35th, Oklahoma City, Okla. *Memberships:* Oklahomans for Indian Opportunity; Seminole Inter-tribal Association; Congress of American Indians; American Association of University Women; Amateur Fencers League of America; Oklahoma City Y.M.C.A.; P.T.A.; Kappa Pi Honorary Art Fraternity; Central State College Alumni Association; Bacone College Alumni Association. *Awards:* Oklahoma Collegiate Novice State Fencing Champion, 1965; Third Place, Oklahoma Open Fencing Champion, 1965; Seminole Tribal Princess, 1946-56; Gallup Ceremonial Women's Singing Award; Second Place, Fencing, Oklahoma Collegiate Women's Advanced Section, 1965.

DORIAN, EDITH McEWER 1900-
(writer, teacher)

Born May 5, 1900. *Education:* Smith College, B.A., 1921; Harvard University, 1922; Columbia University, M.A., 1927. *Principal occupation:* Writer, teacher. *Home address:* 39 Elm St., Topsham, Me. 04086.

Affiliations: Instructor, assistant professor of English, Douglass College, Rutgers State University, 1922-32; advisor, The Macmillan Co., 1940-48; instructor in English, Douglass College, 1959-60. *Community activities:* Middlesex County Tuberculosis and Health League (board of directors, 1941-50); Child and Family Service Bureau (board of directors, 1948-62); New Jersey Child Care Committee (chairman of board, 1950-52; personnel committee, 1955-62); Highland Park Free Public Library (trustee, 1945-55); New Jersey Library Trustees Association (executive committee, 1952-54); New Brunswick Community Chest (director, 1948-50); United Fund of New Brunswick (film committee, 1955-62); Cub Scouts, Brownies, Girl Scouts, 1941-50; Topsham Public Library (trustee, 1964-); Topsham Museum Committee (member); Topsham School Library (chairman, 1963-). *Memberships:* O.B.K., 1921-; Authors Guild, 1955-. *Awards, honors:* First Lady Award, Beta Sigma Phi, 1949, Junior Book Award for *Hokahey!*, Boys Club of America, 1957; Illuminated Scroll, Family Counseling Service, New Brunswick, 1962, for service on the Board of Child and Family Service as president, chairman of the personnel committee, and for service on the national personnel committee, Family Service Association of America. *Interests:* Writing fiction and non-fiction (American history); libraries; "swimming in the chilly waters of Casco Bay"; poe carpentry. *Published works: High Water Cargo* (McGraw-Hill, 1950); *Ask Dr. Christmas* (McGraw-Hill, 1951); *No Moon on Graveyard Head* (McGraw-Hill, 1953; paperback, Berkeley, 1958); *Trails West and Men Who Made Them* (McGraw-Hill, 1955; also published in Sweden); *The Twisted Shadow* (McGraw-Hill, 1956; paperback, Berkeley, 1963); *Hokahey! American Indians Then and Now* (McGraw-Hill, 1957; Swedish edition, 1962); *Animals that Made U.S. History* (McGraw-Hill, 1964; published in Sweden as *Djuren Giorde Historia,* 1965).

DOUDIET, ELLENORE W. (museum director)

Born Binghamton, New York. *Education:* New York University. *Home address:* Nautilus Island, Castine, Me. 04421. *Principal occupation:* Director, Wilson Museum, Castine, Me. *Community activities:* Maine Archaeological Society (vice president,

1964-66); Castine Scientific Society (treasurer, 1950-66); Girl Scouts; St. Croix Region Garden Clubs; Castine Woman's Club. *Published works: Castine* (Castine Scientific Society); *Wilson Museum and Museum Bulletin* (Castine Scientific Society).

DOWNING, ERNEST V. (Cherokee and Caddo) 1910- (government official)

Born November 26, 1910, Verden, Okla. *Education:* Oklahoma City University, 1929-30; University of Kansas, 1931-32. *Principal occupation:* Government official. *Home address:* 4713 N. W. 29th, Oklahoma City, Okla. 73127. *Affiliations:* Employed in various capacities by the Bureau of Indian Affairs in Arizona, Illinois, New Mexico and Oklahoma, 1933-55; executive officer, U. S. Public Health Service, Oklahoma City, Okla., 1955-. *Community activities:* Interstate Council on Indian Affairs (governor's representative, 1952-54). *Interests:* Mr. Downing writes, "(I am) interested in fine arts. Presently and for the past six years (I) have participated in Oklahoma county libraries' sponsoring of adult discussion groups by moderating discussion groups in the liberal arts and great books programs. (I) moderated a television series of eight programs on public-interest subjects sponsored by the Oklahoma Better Business Bureau, 1965."

DREW, ROBERT (Creek) 1922-
(government official)

Born June 12, 1922, Eufala, Okla. *Education:* Bacone Junior College, Certificate, 1947, B. S. (Education), 1949; Southeastern State College, M. S. (Education), 1957; University of Minnesota, graduate work, 1962-63. *Principal occupation:* Government official. *Home address:* 12229 Fox Hill Lane, Bowie, Md. *Affiliations:* Teacher-coach, Bureau of Indian Affairs, Parmelee, S. D., 1949-50; principal-teacher, Bureau of Indian Affairs, Mission, S.D., 1950-52; principal-teacher, Bureau of Indian Affairs, Cherry Creek, S. D., 1952-55; principal-teacher, Bureau of Indian Affairs, Eagle Butte, S. D., 1955-57, community health worker, Public Health Service, Division of Indian Health, Pine Ridge, S. D., 1957-59; education specialist (health), Public Health Service, Division of Indian Health, Bemidji, Minn., 1959-62; area tribal affairs officer,

Public Health Service, Division of Indian Health, Oklahoma City, Okla., 1963-65; acting chief, Office of Tribal Affairs, Public Health Service, Division of Indian Health, Silver Spring, Md., 1966-. *Military service:* U. S. Army, 45th Infantry Division, 1940-41, 1942-45 (Purple Heart and Silver Star). *Community activities:* American Legion Posts, Eufala, Okla., Mission, S. D., Dupree, S. D., Pine Ridge, S. D. (athletic and Americanism officer), Bemidji, Minn.; Black Hills Council, Boy Scouts of America, S.D. (area Boy Scout council member), 1957-59. *Memberships:* South Dakota Education Association, 1950-57; Minnesota Public Health Association, 1959-63; Oklahoma Indian Council, 1965; National Congress of American Indians, 1965-; Oklahoma Health and Welfare Association, 1965-. *Interests:* Mr. Drew writes, "(I was an) athletic official in high school football and basketball, 1951-58, (and) organized and managed independent football teams in Indian communities, 1949-57, in South Dakota."

DRIVER, HAROLD E. 1907-
(professor of anthropology)

Born November 17, 1907, Berkeley, Calif. *Education:* University of California, Berkeley, B. A., 1930; M. A., 1934; Ph. D., 1936. *Principal occupation:* Professor of anthropology. *Home address:* 1824 E. Hunter Ave., Bloomington, Ind. 47403. *Affiliations:* Professor of anthropology, Indiana University, 1958- (assistant professor, 1949-53; associate professor, 1953-58). *Other professional posts:* Research fellow, University of California, Berkeley, 1936-37; research associate, University of California, Berkeley, 1948-49. *Memberships:* American Anthropological Association, 1949-; American Ethnological Society, 1949-; Central States Anthropological Society, 1949-; Indian Academy of Science, 1949-; American Association for the Advancement of Science, 1949-. *Awards, honors:* Fellow, Social Science Research Council, 1937-38. *Interests:* Anthropological field work in California, 1932-35; Mexico, 1955-56; Africa and Europe, 1963. *Published works: Comparative Studies of North American Indians* (American Philosophical Society, 1957); *Indians of North America* (University of Chicago Press, 1961); *The Americas on the Eve of Discovery* (Prentice-Hall, 1964); *Ethnography* and *Acculturation of the Chichimeca-Jonaz of Northeast Mexico* (Indiana University Press, 1963); *American Indian Farmers* (Rand McNally, 1966).

DRUMMOND, THEODORE H.   1908-
(museum curator and administrator)

Born June 17, 1908, Salt Lake City, Utah. *Education:* University of Utah, B. S., 1931; University of Southern California, 1942-44. *Principal occupation:* Museum curator and administrator. *Home address:* 1212 Tanley Rd. , Silver Spring, Md. , 20904. *Affiliations:* Curator and administrator, U. S. Department of the Interior Museum, Washington, D.C. *Memberships:* International Platform Association, 1965; American Association of Museums, 1958; American Museum of Natural History, 1964-. *Awards:* Superior Performance Awards: Bureau of Land Management, 1956; U. S. Department of the Interior, 1962. *Interests:* Museum work of all types; photography; painting; sculpture; woodcarving; teaching of art; illustration; illumination; heraldry; music; writing; travel. *Published works: A Syllabus of Measurement* (Maddox and Hopkins, 1954); *The Public Land Records, Footnotes to American History* (Bureau of Land Management, 1959).

DRURY, CLIFFORD MERRILL   1897-
(Presbyterian minister, professor of church history)

Born November 7, 1897, Early, Iowa. *Education:* Buena Vista College, B. A. , 1918; San Francisco Theological Seminary, B. D., 1922; University of Edinburgh, Ph. D., 1933. *Principal occupation:* Presbyterian minister, professor of church history. *Home address:* 2889 San Pasqual St. , Pasadena, Calif. 91107. *Affiliations:* Pastor, Community Church (American), Shanghai, China, 1923-27; pastor, First Presbyterian Church, Moscow, Idaho, 1928-38; professor of church history, San Francisco Theological Seminary, San Anselmo, Calif. 1938-63; chaplain, U. S. Naval Reserve, 1933-57; active duty, 1941-46, with special duty during twelve summers as historian of Chaplain Corps. *Military service:* U. S. Army, World War I; chaplain, U. S. Navy, World War II. *Memberships:* Masons; Kiwanis Club; several historical societies. *Interests:* Missionary history of the Pacific Northwest; missionaries to the Cayuse,

Nez Perce and Spokane Indians. *Published works:* A five-volume history of the Chaplain Corps, U. S. Navy, U. S. Government Printing Office, 1949-57; *Marcus Whitman, M. D.* (1936), *Henry Harmon Spalding* (1937), *Elkanah and Mary Walker* (1940), all published by The Caxton Printers, Ltd. ; *A Tepee in his Front Yard* (Binfords and Mort, 1949); *Diaries and Letters of Henry A. Spaulding and Asa B. Smith* (Arthur H. Clark & Co. , 1958); *First White Woman Over the Rockies,* Vols. I and II, Vol. III in press (Arthur H. Clark & Co. , 1962, 1966).

DU BRAY, ALFRED WILLIAM (Rosebud Sioux)   1913-   (B. I. A. agency superintendent)

Born April 1, 1913, Tripp County, S. D. *Education:* Mitchell Business College, 1937. *Principal occupation:* Bureau of Indian Affairs agency superintendent. *Address:* c/o Bureau of Indian Affairs, Winnebago Agency, Winnebago, Neb. 68071. *Affiliations:* Mr. DuBray has held various positions with the Bureau of Indian Affairs since 1938; superintendent, Winnebago Agency, 1963-. *Military service:* U. S. Army, 1945-46. *Interests:* Mr. DuBray writes, "My entire career in the federal service has been with the Bureau of Indian Affairs. I am keenly interested in the affairs of the American Indians and the policies and programs that have been developed for the improvement of conditions on the Indian reservations. My position as superintendent of an Indian agency has provided the opportunity to be associated with various tribal groups and with individual members of the tribes involved. Such experience provides a real opportunity to observe first hand the problems faced by the American Indian people in their struggle to advance socially and economically and to become part of the mainstream of American life. "

DUCHENEAUX, FRANK DOUGLAS (Cheyenne River Sioux)   1903-   (rancher)

Born February 28, 1903, Promise Community, Cheyenne River Reservation, S. D. *Principal occupation:* Rancher; raiser of Hereford cattle and horses. *Home address:* Star Route 2, Gettysburg, S. D. 57742. *Affiliations:* Charter member, council member, chairman, Cheyenne River Sioux Tribal Council, 1935-. *Community activities:*

United Sioux Tribes (treasurer); Surgeon General of Public Health Service (advisor); South Dakota State Indian Commission (member); South Dakota Great Lakes Association (member); Special Legal Committee to Consider Public Law 776 (member); Oahe Project (member); Lakota Tuberculosis and Health Association of South Dakota (member); Action Group (member); Agency/Tribe Advisory Committee (member). *Memberships:* National Congress of American Indians, 1946-. *Interests:* Economic and social betterment, and legal aid for the American Indian.

DUNLOP, RICHARD 1921- (writer)

Born June 20, 1921, Chicago, Ill. *Education:* Northwestern University, B.S., 1945. *Principal occupation:* Writer. *Home address:* 1115 Mayfair Rd., Arlington Heights, Ill. 60004. *Affiliations:* Associate editor, *Home and Highway* magazine, 1954-56; assistant to the president, National College of Education, 1950-52; president, Richard B. Dunlop, Inc. (foreign trade), 1948-50. *Other professional posts:* Contributing editor, *Chicago* magazine, 1954-57; editorial consultant to Rand McNally. *Military service:* Office of Strategic Services, 1943-45 (four campaign ribbons; Presidential Distinguished Unit Citation). *Community activities:* Arlington Heights United Fund (board member); Presbyterian Men's Club (president); Boy Scouts of America (scoutmaster). *Memberships:* Authors Guild of Authors League of America; Society of American Travel Writers; The Cliff Dwellers. *Awards:* Spur Award (co-winner) for best Western non-fiction, 1958. *Interests:* Frontier and Indian medicine; archaeology; Indian culture. *Travels:* Mexico, western United States, Canada, Southeast Asia. *Published works: Doctors of the American Frontier* (Doubleday, 1965); *Rand McNally Vacation Guide* (Rand McNally and Co., 1964, 1965, 1966); *Texaco Touring Atlas* (Rand McNally and Co., 1965, 1966).

DUSHANE, HOWARD S. (Eastern Shawnee) 1911- (B.I.A. officer)

Born July 10, 1911, Seneca, Mo. *Education:* Oklahoma Baptist University, 1931-32.

Principal occupation: B.I.A. officer. *Home address:* 9415 Arvada, N.E., Albuquerque, N.M. 87112. *Affiliations:* Truxton Canyon Agency, Bureau of Indian Affairs, 1934-50; district agent, Hoopa, Calif., 1950-52; program officer, Hoopa, Calif., 1952-55; area program officer, Portland, Ore., 1955-57; superintendent, Fort Belknap Agency, Mont., Bureau of Indian Affairs, 1957-60; superintendent, Cheyenne Agency, S.D., Bureau of Indian Affairs, 1960-66; area credit officer, Albuquerque Area Office, Bureau of Indian Affairs, 1966-. *Military service:* U.S. Army, 1945-46. *Community activities:* Lions International; Eagle Butte Mens Club; Eagle Butte Community Club. *Interests:* "Vocational interests have, of course, been in the development and progress of the Indian people with whom assigned in both cultural and economic fields. Being of Indian extraction, have been involved and intensely interested in the progress of the American Indian, and my entire adult life has been devoted to this cause." *Biographical sources: Indians of Today* (Indian Council Fire).

DUSTIN, CHARLES BURTON 1935- (stock broker)

Born November 13, 1935, Salt Lake City, Utah. *Education:* University of Denver, B.S., 1957; University of New Mexico, 1958-59. *Principal occupation:* Stock broker. *Home address:* 2814 Quincy, N.E., Albuquerque, N.M. 87110. *Affiliations:* Sales representative, Sandoz Pharmaceuticals, Hanover, N.J., 1961-64; account executive, Merrill, Lynch, Pierce, Fenner and Smith, Albuquerque, N.M., 1964-. *Interests:* "Alteration of consciousness through neuro-psycho-pharmacology and orgonomy as well as the institutional approach to human behavior." *Published works: Peyotism and New Mexico* (C.B. Dustin, 1960).

DUTTON, BERTHA P. 1903- (anthropologist)

Born March 29, 1903, Algona, Iowa. *Education:* University of Nebraska, 1929-31; University of New Mexico, B.A., 1935, M.A., 1937; Columbia University, Ph.D.,

1952. *Principal occupation:* Anthropologist. *Home address:* Box 2087, Santa Fe, N. M. 87501. *Affiliations:* Secretary, University of New Mexico, Department of Anthropology, 1933-36; director's assistant and curator, Museum of New Mexico, 1936-. *Community activities:* Southwestern Association on Indian Affairs (board member); League of Women Voters of Santa Fe (past board member); Community Concerts Association of Santa Fe (past board member); Inter-Tribal Indian Ceremonial Association (judge of arts and crafts); New Mexico State Fair (judge of arts and crafts). *Memberships:* American Association for the Advancement of Science (chairman, social sciences section, 1951; local chairman, 1955); Archaeological Society of New Mexico; Arizona Society of Science and Art; New Mexico Historical Society; Arizona Archaeological and Historical Society; Southwestern Anthropological Association; International Congress of Americanists; Sociedad de Antropologia (Mexico); National Platform Association. *Awards, honors:* Thank You Badge, Girl Scouts of America; Alice Fletcher Traveling Fellowship, 1935; School of American Research Scholarship, 1936; School of American Research Grant-in-Aid, 1950; American Association of University Women Scholarship, 1953-54; Wenner-Gren Foundation Grant-in-Aid, 1962; Columbus Explorations Fund Grant, 1964, 1965. *Interests:* Archaeology and ethnology of Mesoamerica; expeditions to Bolivia, Ecuador, Panama, Peru, Guatemala, Mexico; archaeology and ethnology of the American Southwest; expeditions at Abo, Chaco Canyon, Galisteo Basin, Jemez region, Puaray (at Bandelier National Monument); travels in France, Germany, Spain, Sweden, Russia. *Published works: Excavations at Tajumulco, Guatemala,* with H. R. Hobbs (University of New Mexico Press, 1943); *The Pueblo Indian World,* with E. L. Hewett (University of New Mexico Press, 1945); *Pajarito Plateau and Its Ancient People,* with E. L. Hewett (University of New Mexico Press, 1953); *Navajo Weaving Today* (Museum of New Mexico Press, 1961, 1962); *Happy People: The Huichol Indians* (Museum of New Mexico Press, 1962); *Let's Explore! Indian Villages, Past and Present* (Museum of New Mexico Press, 1962); *Friendly People: The Zuni Indians* (Museum of New Mexico Press, 1963); *Sun Father's Way* (University of New Mexico Press, 1963); *Indians of the Southwest* (Southwestern Association on Indian Affairs, 1965).

E

EAGLE FEATHER, ELIJAH MELVIN (Rosebud Sioux) 1926- (artist, carpenter)

Born June 15, 1926, Hamill, S. D. *Education:* Rosebud Boarding School. *Principal occupation:* Artist, carpenter. *Home address:* Parmelee, S. D. 57566. *Military service:* Army Paratroops, 1944-46 (Asiatic Pacific Campaign Ribbon, Good Conduct Ribbon, Victory Medal). *Awards:* Midwest Art Association Award, 1951.

ECHOHAWK, BRUMMETT (Pawnee) 1922- (artist, writer, cartoonist)

Born March 3, 1922, Pawnee, Okla. *Education:* Detroit School of Arts and Crafts, 1945; Art Institute of Chicago, 1945-48. *Addresses:* 2525 W. Easton St., Tulsa, Okla. (home); P. O. Box 1922, Tulsa, Okla. 74101 (business). *Professional posts:* Staff artist, *Chicago Times,* 1947; staff artist, Mid-Continent Petroleum Corp., Tulsa; cover artist, *Western Horseman* magazine. *Military service:* U. S. Army, 1940-45 (Purple Heart with oak leaf cluster; Combat Infantry Badge; European Theater Ribbon with Battle Stars; Army Commendation Citation; Pre-Pearl Harbor Ribbon). *Community activities:* Tulsa Junior Chamber of Commerce, 1957. *Memberships:* Chicago Westerners; National Congress of American Indians; Council of American Indians of Tulsa (president, 1960); Southwestern District of the American Indian College Foundation (vice president, 1965). *Awards:* Third Place and Museum Purchase prize in First Representational Show, Gilcrease Institute of American History and Art, 1958.

EDDY, FRANK W. 1930- (archaeologist)

Born May 7, 1930, Roanoke, Va. *Education:* University of New Mexico, B. A., 1952; University of Arizona, M. A., 1958; graduate work, University of Colorado, 1965-66. *Principal occupation:* Archaeologist. *Address:* c/o Department of Anthropology, University of Colorado, Boulder, Colo. *Affiliations:* Salvage archaeologist, Museum of New Mexico, 1958-65. *Military service:* U. S. Army, 1952-54. *Memberships:*

Society for American Archaeology. *Interests:* Cultural ecology; prehistoric settlement studies; cultural change as revealed by archaeology; technology of primitive societies. *Expeditions:* Navajo Reservoir Project, 1958-65; Museum of New Mexico Expedition to Egyptian Nubia, 1963-64. *Published works: An Archaeological Survey of the Navajo Reservoir District, Northwestern New Mexico,* with Alfred E. Dittert, Jr., and James J. Hester (Monograph of the School of American Research and the Museum of New Mexico, No. 23, 1961); *Excavations at Los Pinos Phase Sites in the Navajo Reservoir District* (Museum of New Mexico Papers in Anthropology, No. 4, 1961); *Alluvial and Palynological Reconstruction of Environments, Navajo Reservoir District,* with J. Schoenwetter (Museum of New Mexico Papers in Anthropology, No. 13, 1964); *Prehistory in the Navajo Reservoir District, Northwestern New Mexico* (Museum of New Mexico Papers in Anthropology, 1966); several articles in journals.

EDMONSON, ED 1919- (congressman)

Born April 7, 1919, Muskogee, Okla. *Education:* University of Oklahoma, B.A., 1940; Georgetown University, LL.B., 1947. *Principal occupation:* Member of Congress, 2nd Dist., Okla. *Home address:* 219 N. 14th St., Muskogee, Okla. *Military service:* U.S. Navy, World War II; U.S. Naval Reserve. *Memberships:* American Bar Association; Oklahoma Bar Association. *Awards, honors:* Honorary memberships in several Oklahoma Indian tribes. *Interests:* Committee on Interior and Insular Affairs (member); Subcommittee on Indian Affairs (second-ranking Democrat); Committee on Public Works, U.S. House of Representatives (member).

EDWARDS, BRONSON W. (Ottawa Tribe of Oklahoma) 1910- (artist)

Born May 22, 1910, Miami, Okla. *Education:* High school; Art Instruction, Inc., Minneapolis, Minn. *Principal occupation:* Artist, sign painter. *Home address:* 1022 A St., N.W., Miami, Okla. 74354. *Affiliations:* Lobby display and stage set designer, Video Theatres, Inc.; employed at various Army, Navy and Marine bases as interior decorator; free lance artist. *Community activities:* First Christian Church

(deacon); Painters and Decorators Local Union #1546 (past president). *Awards, honors:* Third Award, Philbrook Art Center, 1958; Second Award, Inter-Tribal Indian Ceremonial, Gallup, N.M., 1958; First Award, Philbrook Art Center, Tulsa, Okla., 1960; Honor Mention, Philbrook Art Center, 1965. *Biographical sources: Dictionary of American Indian Artists,* by Jeanne Snodgrass (in press).

EDWARDS, PAUL M. 1933- (museum director)

Born February 26, 1933, Independence, Mo. *Education:* Washburn University, B.A., 1959; University of South Dakota, M.A., 1960; Western Reserve University, 1962; Institute on History of Science, University of Oklahoma, 1963. *Principal occupation:* Museum director. *Home address:* 6825 Bonneville Pl., Cheyenne, Wyo. 82001. *Affiliations:* Assistant professor of history, Graceland College, 1960-64; museum assistant, Kansas State Historical Society, 1956-59; assistant manager, Limerick Finance, 1955-56; chief, Museum Division, Wyoming State Archives and Historical Department. *Military service:* U.S. Army, 1953-55. *Memberships:* Phi Alpha Theta; Pi Alpha Sigma; American Association for State and Local History; Mississippi Valley Historical Society; American Association of Museums; Wyoming, Kansas, Iowa and Missouri Historical Societies; American Philosophical Association. *Awards, honors:* Whiting Scholar; National Science Foundation (Fellow, History and Philosophy of Science); McVicar Award. *Published works: Fort Wadsworth and the Santee Sioux* (South Dakota Historical Society, 1962); co-author, *Quest for Meaning* (Herald House Press, 1965).

EGGAN, FRED 1906- (anthropologist)

Born September 12, 1906, Seattle, Wash. *Education:* University of Chicago, Ph.B., 1927; M.A., 1928, Ph.D., 1933. *Principal occupation:* Professor of anthropology. *Home address:* 1321 E. 56th St., Chicago, Ill. 60637. *Affiliations:* Professor of anthropology, University of Chicago, 1935. *Other professional posts:* Director, Civil Affairs Training School, 1943-45. *Military service:* U.S. Army, 1943. *Memberships:* American Anthropological Association (president, 1953). *Awards, honors:* Viking Fund Award and Medal, 1956; Award, American Anthropological Association, for contributions to anthropology. *Interests:* American Indian and Philippines; expeditions to Choctaw, Cheyenne, Arapaho, Hopi country; northern Luzon. *Published works: Social Organization of the Western Pueblos* (University of Chicago Press, 1950); *Social Anthropology of North American Tribes* (editor, second edition, University of Chicago Press, 1955); *The American Indians* (Aldine Press, 1966).

ELLIS, SPENCER P. (administrator)

Education: Texas A & M, B.S., 1943, B. S. (Landscape Architecture), 1948; Infantry School, Fort Benning, Georgia; Command and General Staff College; National War College. *Home address:* Eastport, Annapolis, Maryland. *Principal occupation:* Director, Maryland Department of Forests and Parks, 1963-. *Affiliations:* Superintendent of parks, City of Corpus Christi, Texas, 1948-54; director of parks and recreation, Wichita Falls, Texas, 1954-63. *Military service:* U. S. Army, World War II (Distinguished Service Medal; Silver Star; Army Commendation Medal; Bronze Star; Purple Heart with Cluster); National Guard; U. S. Army Reserve. *Memberships:* Southwest Chapter, American Society of Landscape Architects (former president); Texas Recreation Society; American Institute of Park Executives; American Recreation Society; National Board for Registration of Professional Recreators; Maryland Board of Natural Resources; Maryland Scenic Beauty Commission; Master Planning Committee. *Published works:* Articles in *Recreation; Landscape Architecture; Parks and Recreation; The American Recreation Journal.*

ELTING, MARY 1906- (writer)

Born June 21, 1906, Creede, Colo. *Education:* University of Colorado, B. A. , 1927. *Principal occupation:* Writer of childrens' books. *Home address:* Roosevelt, N. J. *Memberships:* Archaeological Society of New Jersey; Authors' League of America. *Interests:* American Indians; Western travel. *Published works: The Answer Book* and *Answers and More Answers* (Grosset and Dunlap, 1959, 1962); *The Story of*

Archaeology in the Americas with Franklin Folsom (Harvey House, 1960); *The Secret Story of Pueblo Bonito,* with Michael Folsom (Harvey House, 1963).

EMBRY, CARLOS B. 1906-
(newspaper publisher)

Born January 21, 1906, Baizetown, Ky. *Education:* Western Kentucky State College, B. A. , 1929; University of Arizona, 1949-50. *Principal occupation:* Newspaper publisher. *Addresses:* 211 N. Main St., Beaver Dam, Ky. (home); 220 N. Main St., Beaver Dam, Ky. (business). *Affiliations:* Principal, junior high school, Bulloch County, 1926-27; principal, Lynnvale High School, 1928-29; owner-publisher, *Ohio County Messenger,* 1930-; owner, The Embry Newspapers, Inc. ; builder-owner, Embry's Valley Shopping Center. *Other professional posts:* Member, Kentucky Senate, 10th Dist. , 1945-49. *Community activities:* Kentucky Republican Committee (director, 1944). *Awards, honors:* Kentucky Statesman Award, 1964. *Memberships:* Beaver Dam Board of Trade; Baptist Church; Lions Club. *Published works: America's Concentration Camps: The Facts About Our Indian Reservations Today* (David McKay, 1956).

EMERSON, ROBERTA J. (Sioux and Assiniboine) 1932- (artist)

Born June 18, 1932, Brockton, Mont. *Education:* Montana State College. *Home address:* Box 6, New Cuysma, Calif. 93254.

EMERSON, WILLIAM C. 1893-
(physician, surgeon, writer)

Born September 8, 1893, Council Grove, Kan. *Education:* Stetson University, 1913-16; University of Chicago, B.S. , 1917; Medical Department, University of Georgia, 1921-23; Columbia University, M.D., 1925. *Principal occupation:* Physician, surgeon, writer. *Home address:* 316 N. Washington St. , Rome, N. Y. 13440. *Military service:* U.S. Army, 1941-44. *Memberships:* Oneida County Medical Society; Rome Academy of Medicine. *Interests:* "Florida and the Florida Everglades, where I spend several months each year. I have spent considerable time in Alaska, where I visited with and photographed the Alaskan Indians and Eskimos." *Published works: Stories and Spirituals of the Negro Slave* (Gorham Press, 1930);   *The Seminoles: Dwellers of the Everglades* (Exposition Press, 1954);   *The Land of the Midnight Sun* (Dorrance and Co., 1956);   *Belle of the Everglades* (Pageant Press, 1958);   *The Hunted* (Vantage Press, 1961);   *Land of Beauty and Enchantment* (Dorrance and Co., 1966); currently working on a story about the (Seminole) Green Corn Dance.

EMMERICH, ANDRE   1924-   (writer, art dealer)

Born October 11, 1924, Frankfurt, Germany. *Education:* Oberlin College, B.A., 1944. *Principal occupation:* Writer, art dealer. *Affiliation:* Owner, Andre Emmerich Gallery, 1956-. *Community activities:* Art Dealers Association of America (board of directors). *Published works: Art Before Columbus* (Simon and Schuster, 1963); *Sweat of the Sun and Tears of the Moon* (University of Washington Press, 1965).

EMMITT, ROBERT   1925-   (editor, writer)

Born February 8, 1925, Akron, Ohio. *Education:* University of Colorado. *Principal occupation:* Editor, writer. *Home address:* Route 5, Franklin, Tenn. *Affiliations:* New York *Herald Tribune,* 1953-58; associate editor, Vanderbilt University Press, Nashville, Tenn., 1958-. *Awards:* First John Day Award for novel manuscript, 1954. *Interests:* Writing, presently on Ute War of 1879; travel through Ute country, living on the present Ute Reservation at Whiterocks, Utah. *Published works: The Last War Trail* (University of Oklahoma Press, 1954).

ERNST, ALICE HENSON   (free lance writer)

Born Washburne, Me. *Education:* University of Washington, B.A. (magna cum laude), 1912, M.A., 1913; graduate work, Radcliffe College, 1919-20; Yale School of Drama, 1928. *Principal occupation:* Free lance writer. *Home address:* Treetops, 194 Sunset Drive, Eugene, Ore. 97403. *Affiliations:* Associate in English, University of Washington, 1920-23; industrial correspondent, New York Evening *Post,* 1920-23; assistant professor of English, associate professor, University of Oregon, 1924-52; free lance writer -- books, magazine articles (*Theatre Arts,* and others); special newspaper features, Portland *Oregonian.* "As writing has been always my principal vocation, it has continued, taking progressively more time. Am just now writing magazine articles, book reviews and working on a book." *Community activities:* Very Little Theatre, Eugene, Ore.; Civic Music Association; Friends of Library; American National Theatre and Academy (A.N.T.A.); various charitable organizations. *Memberships:* Phi Beta Kappa, 1914-; Theta Sigma Pi, 1914-; League of American Penwomen, 1924; Pacific Northwest Writers' Conference; National Press Women of America. *Awards, honors:* Denny Fellowship (English), University of Washington, 1912; research grants for study of northwest masked ritual dances), University of Oregon; two-year grant (for research of book on early northwest theatres, *Trouping in the Oregon Country,* Graduate School, University of Oregon; award for *Trouping in the Oregon Country,* University Theatre, 1962. *Interests:* "Filling in gaps, small or large, in human knowledge is rewarding, mentally, as I discovered while working on *The Wolf Ritual of the Northwest Coast,* read by Dr. Franz Boas of Columbia University and published by the University of Oregon Press. It so happened that I was able to set down records of vanishing beliefs and customs before they faded -- which of course was the reason for the research grants and for Dr. Boas' interest. I had something of a head start by growing up in the Olympic Peninsula (Washington), and by having excellent help from William Newcombe, of the Provincial Museum, Victoria, B.C., whose father, Dr. C. F. Newcombe, aided in the collection of masks at the Field Museum and elsewhere. I was pushed into completion of the years of study and work needed by Dr. Heye, of the Museum of the American Indian, New York City, and by Mrs. Isaacs, editor of *Theatre Arts,* who had become interested in some of my plays. The series of articles for *Theatre Arts* on native northwest ritual dances (primitive theatre, of course) have also been extensively listed and quoted, both for anthropology and dance. Though I later returned to the more conventional field of theatre with the book on early northwest theatre (*Trouping in the*

Oregon Country) -- again a record of vanishing material -- I have recently been
snared (last fall) by the primitive, and
sources in the Yale Library's Coe Collection of Western Americana, during a session of reading there and a month's visit to
New York. At the moment am working out
some smaller studies from earlier notes
made during journeys up and down the West
Coast. Am finding a good deal of unused
detail, including sketches. That's what it is
to have an inquiring mind -- and an itching
heel! At any rate, the days never seem
quite long enough." *Published works: High
Country: Four Plays from the Pacific Northwest* (Metropolitan Press, 1935); *Back-
stage at Xanadu: A Book of Plays* (Binfords
and Mort, 1938); *The Wold Ritual of the
Northwest Coast* (University of Oregon
Press, 1952); *Trouping in the Oregon Country: A History of Frontier Theatre* (Oregon Historical Society, 1961).

ESCHERICH, ELSA ANTOINE (Elsa Falk)
  1888- (writer)

Born March 20, 1888, Davenport, Iowa.
Education: Chicago Art Institute; Davenport
Teachers Training School; University of
California, Los Angeles, B. Ed., 1932; Uni-
versity of Southern California, M.S. (Edu-
cation), 1948. *Principal occupation:* Writer.
Home address: 2180 N. Altadena Drive,
Pasadena, Calif. 91107. *Affiliations:* For-
mer teacher, public schools of Iowa and
California, and University of California Ex-
tension Division. *Memberships:* National
League of American Pen Women, 1954-;
Southern California Women's Press Club,
1944. *Interests:* Travels to Europe, Alas-
ka, South America, South Africa, India,
Malaya, Cambodia, Philippine Islands,
China, Japan, Thailand, Singapore, Hawaii,
North Africa, Canary Islands, Turkey,
Egypt. *Published works:* (under the name
Elsa Falk): *Fog Island* (Follett, 1953); *Win-
ter Journey* (Follett, 1955); *Fire Canoe*
(Follett, 1956); *Fence Across the Trail*
(Follett, 1957); *Tohi, A Chumash Indian
Boy* (Melmont, 1959); *Shoes for Matt* (Fol-
lett, 1960); *Akio and the Moon Goddess*
(Follett, 1961).

ESTEP, IRENE 1905- (writer)

Born January 28, 1905, Hall County, Neb.
Education: Whittier College, 1924-26; Whit-

tier Business College, 1933-34. *Principal
occupation:* Writer. *Home address:* 5291
Bennett Rd., Paradise, Calif. 95969. *Affiliations:* Office manager, Montgomery
Ward; columnist, Granada Hills *Outlook;*
free lance writer. *Memberships:* Ventura
County Writers Association, 1943-45; Valley Writers' Council, 1961-64; Word-
crafters, 1963-64; Armed Forces Writers
League, 1963-65. *Interests:* Research and
writing related to American history; travel
to western United States, including Indian
schools and reservations. *Published works:*
Pioneer Tenderfoot (Benefic Press, 1957);
Pioneer Buckaree (Benefic Press, 1958);
Pioneer Sodbuster (Benefic Press, 1958);
Pioneer Pilgrim (Benefic Press, 1959); *Pioneer Engineer* (Benefic Press, 1959); *Iroquois* (Melmont Publishers, 1961); *Good
Times with Maps* (Melmont Publishers,
1962); *Seminoles* (Melmont Publishers,
1963); poetry, articles and juvenile stories
published in periodicals.

EULER, ROBERT C. 1924-
  (anthropologist)

Born August 8, 1924, New York, N. Y.
Education: Arizona State College, B.A.
(Economics), 1947, M.A. (Economics),
1948; University of New Mexico, Ph.D.
(Anthropology), 1958. *Principal occupation:* Professor of anthropology. *Affiliations:* Ranger, National Park Service,
Wupatki National Monument, 1948-49; anthropological consultant, Albuquerque Area
Office, Bureau of Indian Affairs, 1950-51;
instructor, associate professor, Arizona
State College, 1952-64; curator of anthropology, Museum of Northern Arizona, 1952-
56; research associate, Museum of Northern
Arizona, 1956-; visiting assistant professor
of anthropology, Wesleyan University, 1958;
staff anthropologist, National Science Foundation Institute in Anthropology, 1963; associate professor and chairman, Department
of Anthropology, University of Utah, 1964-;
professor of anthropology, Prescott College,
1966. *Other professional posts:* Anthropological consultant, Hualapai Tribe, land
claim litigation, 1953-57; member, board
of trustees, Museum of Navajo Ceremonial
Art, 1954-64; anthropological consultant,
United States Department of Justice, Southern Paiute land claim litigation, 1956; consultant in cross-cultural education, Phoenix,
Arizona, public school system, 1961, 1964;
ethnohistorian, Upper Colorado River Basin

Archaeological Salvage Project, University of Utah, 1962; Arizona Governor's Historical Advisory Committee, 1961-64; ethnohistorical consultant, Arizona Commission on Indian Affairs, 1962-64; anthropological consultant, Operation Headstart, U. S. Office of Economic Opportunity, involving Navajo, Paiute, Mojave and Chemehuevi participation, 1965. *Memberships:* American Anthropological Association; American Ethnological Society; Society for Applied Anthropology (Fellow); Society for American Archaeology; Current Anthropology; American Association for the Advancement of Science (Fellow); American Indian Ethnohistoric Conference; The Society of the Sigma Xi; The Western History Association (member, editorial board, *The American West*); Arizona Academy of Science (charter member; president, 1962-63); Museum of Northern Arizona (research associate); Arizona Archaeological and Historical Society; Arizona Pioneers' Historical Society; New Mexico Historical Society; New Mexico Archaeological Society; Utah Historical Society. *Interests:* Ethnographic field work involving historical ethnography, ethnohistory and applied anthropology among Navajo, Hopi, Walapai, Havasupai, Yavapai, Chemehuevi, Southern Paiute, Southern Ute, Isleta Pueblo, and Sia Pueblo; historic archaeological research in Walapai, Havasupai, Yavapai, and Southern Paiute sites; prehistoric archaeological survey and excavations in northern Arizona; salvage projects on highways, pipelines and in reservoir basins. *Published works:* Editor, *Woodchuck Cave, A Basketmaker II Site in Tsegi Canyon, Arizona,* with H. S. Colton (Museum of Northern Arizona Bulletin 26, 1953); *Walapai Culture History* (University of New Mexico doctoral dissertation, University Microfilms, 1958); *Southern Paiute Archaeology in the Glen Canyon Drainage: A Preliminary Report* (Nevada State Museum Anthropological Papers, No. 9, 1963); *An Archaeological Survey of the South Rim of Walnut Canyon National Monument, Arizona* (Arizona State College Anthropological Papers, No. 1, 1964); *Havasupai Religion and Mythology* (Anthropological Papers of the University of Utah, No. 68, 1964); numerous articles, reviews and monographs.

EWERS, JOHN CANFIELD   1909-
(ethnologist)

Born July 21, 1909, Cleveland, Ohio. *Education:* Dartmouth College, B. A., 1931;

Yale University, M.A. (Anthropology), 1934. *Principal occupation:* Ethnologist. *Home address:* 4432 - 26th Rd., N., Arlington, Va. 22207. *Affiliations:* Field curator, Museum Division, National Park Service, 1935-40; curator, Museum of the Plains Indian, 1941-44; associate curator of ethnology, administrative officer, assistant director and director, Museum of History and Technology, Smithsonian Institution, 1946-. *Other professional posts:* Editor, *Journal of the Washington Academy of Sciences,* 1955; member, editorial board, *The American West. Military service:* U. S. Naval Reserve, 1944-46. *Memberships:* American Indian Ethnohistoric Conference (president, 1961); American Anthropological Association (Fellow); American Association of Museums (Fellow); Washington Academy of Sciences (Fellow); Sigma Xi (president, D. C. Chapter). *Awards, honors:* Exceptional Service Award, Smithsonian Institution, for contributions to American history and ethnology, 1965. *Interests:* Field research in ethnology and ethnohistory conducted among the Blackfeet tribes of Montana and Alberta (Canada), the Assiniboine of Montana, the Flathead of Montana, the Sioux of South Dakota, and the Kiowa of Oklahoma; studies of Indian art since 1932; reviewer of books in anthropology and Western history for The New York *Times, Saturday Review, American Anthropologist,* etc. *Published works:* Mr. Ewers writes, "I have published more than a dozen books and monographs, and (over) 100 articles on the American Indian, the fur trade of the American West, artists who interpreted Indians, etc. Among the books -- *Plains Indian Painting* (Stanford University Press, 1939); *The Horse in Blackfeet Indian Culture* (Smithsonian Institution, 1955); *The Blackfeet: Raiders on the Northwestern Plains* (University of Oklahoma Press, 1958); *Artists of the Old West* (Doubleday, 1965). Others include: Editor, Denig, Edwin T., *Five Indian Tribes of the Upper Missouri* (University of Oklahoma Press, 1961); editor, Leonard, Zenas, *Adventures of Zenas Leonard, Fur Trader* (University of Oklahoma Press, 1961)."

F

FALLING, LEROY (Cherokee)   1926-
(administrator)

Born June 15, 1926, Estella, Okla. *Education:* Warner Pacific College, Diploma, 1948; Anderson College, B. S., 1950; Oregon College of Education, Diploma, 1951; Arizona State University, M.S., 1966. *Principal occupation:* Administrator. *Address:* c/o Kinlichee Boarding School, Ganado, Ariz. 86505. *Affiliations:* Teacher, Lapwai Public School, York Public School, educational specialist, Window Rock, Arizona. *Military service:* U. S. Navy, 1944-46 (WW II Victory Medal). *Community activities:* Window Rock-Fort Defiance Lions Club (vice president, 1963-64); Bonita Canyon Sportsman Club (vice president, 1960-61); vice-chairman, Leadership Training, Kit Carson Council; Boy Scouts of America; president, Indian Workers Conference, 1965-66; member, National-International Social Concerns Committee, 1964-66. *Memberships:* Lions Club International; National Board Association; National Rifle Association; National Federation of Federal Employees; National Archery Association. *Awards:* Woodbadge Beads, Boy Scouts of America.

FAULKNOR, CLIFFORD VERNON 1913- (journalist)

Born March 3, 1913, Vancouver, B.C., Canada. *Education:* University of British Columbia, B.S.A., 1949. *Principal occupation:* Journalist. *Home address:* 2919 - 14th Ave., N.W., Calgary, Alberta, Can. *Affiliations:* Associate editor, *Country Guide* magazine, Winnipeg, Manitoba; land inspector, B. C. Department of Lands and Forests, 1949-54. *Military service:* Canadian Army, 1939-45. *Memberships:* B. C. Institute of Agrologists, 1950-54; Agricultural Institute of Canada, 1949-; Canadian Farm Writers Federation (past president). *Awards:* CFWF Press Editorial Award for 1961; Little, Brown Canada Children's Book Award, 1964. *Interests:* Traveled over most of Canada and the U. S. A. into northern Mexico; sport fishing; photography. *Published works: The White Calf* (Little, Brown and Co., 1965).

FELTS, JACK LEON (Choctaw) 1921- (publisher, writer)

Born January 7, 1921, Blanchard, Okla. *Principal occupation* Publisher, writer. *Home address:* Route 2, Tahlequah, Okla.

74464. *Affiliations:* Founder, Pan Press, Hollywood, Calif. ; associate, Beth Kramer Literary Agency, 1953-; scenarist, 1953-56. *Military service:* U. S. Coast Guard, 1943-46. *Memberships:* International director, Individualist Society (editor, I. S. *Tablet*); member, Descendant of the Choctaws. *Interests:* Established Tahlequah Writers' Conferences, 1961-65; exploration and excavation in Mexico and Central America, 1963-65, directing historical acquisition and study.

FENNER, PHYLLIS 1899- (writer, librarian)

Born October 24, 1899, Almond, N.Y. *Education:* Mount Holyoke, B. A.,1921; School of Library Science, Columbia University, B. L. S., 1935. *Principal occupation:* Librarian (retired), writer, speaker, anthologist, storyteller, book reviewer. *Home address:* Box 653, Manchester, Vt. 05254. *Affiliations:* Advisory board, *Children's Digest;* editorial board, Cadmus Books, Eau Claire, Wis. ; editorial board, Weekly Reader Book Club. Middletown, Conn. *Memberships:* Women's National Book Association; Pen and Brush Club; American Library Association. *Interests:* Traveled throughout Yugoslavia, Greece, Italy, Portugal, Spain, Japan, England, and Mexico; reading; writing; gardening. *Published works: The Proof of the Pudding: What Children Read* (John Day Co.); *Our Library* (John Day Co.); *Something Shared: Children and Books* (John Day Co.); thirty-two anthologies in print published by Franklin Watts, Alfred Knopf, William Morrow, John Day, D. C. Heath.

FENTON, WILLIAM NELSON 1908- (anthropologist, museum administrator)

Born December 15, 1908, New Rochelle, N.Y. *Education:* Dartmouth College, B.A., 1931; Yale University, Ph. D., 1937. *Principal occupation:* Anthropologist, museum administrator. *Home address:* 7 N. Helderberg Pkwy., Slingerlands, N.Y. 12159. *Affiliations:* Community worker, U. S. Indian Service, 1935-37; instructor, assistant professor, St. Lawrence University, 1937-39; ethnologist, Smithsonian Institution, Bureau of American Ethnology, 1939-51; executive secretary for anthropology and psychology, National Academy of Sciences, National Research Council, 1952-54; associate commissioner, State Museum and Science Service, New York State Education Department, 1954-. *Military service:* Research associate, Ethnogeographic Board, 1942-45. *Memberships:* American Anthropological Association (executive board); American Folklore Society (Fellow; past president); American Ethnological Society (past president); American Indian Ethnohistorical Society (past president); American Association for Advancement of Science (Fellow). *Awards, honors:* Adopted Seneca (Iroquois); Peter Doctor Award, Seneca Nation of Indians, 1958, for outstanding services to the Iroquoian people; Cornplanter Medal for Iroquois Research, 1965, Cayuga County Historical Society. *Published works: The Iroquois Eagle Dance* (Bureau of American Ethnology, 1953); editor, *Symposium on Local Diversity in Iroquois Culture* (Bureau of American Ethnology, 1955); editor, *Symposium on Cherokee and Iroquois Culture* (Bureau of American Ethnology, 1961); *American Indian and White Relations to 1830* (Institute of Early American History and Culture; University of North Carolina, 1957).

FERGUSSON, HARVEY   1890-   (writer)

Born January 28, 1890, Albuquerque, New Mexico. *Education:* Washington and Lee, B. A., 1911. *Home address:* 1404 Glendale Ave., Berkeley, Calif.

FEY, HAROLD E.   1898-   (professor, journalist)

Born October 12, 1898, Elwood, Ind. *Education:* Cotner College, B. A., 1922; Yale Divinity School, B. D., 1927. *Home address:* 332 W. 44th St., Indianapolis, Ind. 46208. *Principal occupation:* Professor, Christian social ethics; journalist. *Affiliations:* Professor of sociology, Union Theological Seminary, Philippine Islands, 1929-32; editor, *World Call,* 1932-35; editor, *Fellowship* magazine, 1935-40; member, editorial staff, *Christian Century,* 1940-; editor, *Christian Century* 1956-64; visiting professor, Christian social ethics, Christian Theological Seminary, 1964-. *Military service:* U.S. Army, 1918. *Community activities:* Associated Church Press (past president); Christian Century Foundation

(past president). *Memberships:* Honorary member, Sigma Delta Chi; honorary life member, Associated Church Press; American Civil Liberties Union. *Awards, honors:* Distinguished Service Citation, National Congress of American Indians, for writing on Indian affairs; American Civil Liberties Union Award; Sixth Annual Award, National Christian Writers Center, 1964. *Interests:* "... Issues in which religion and politics meet with a bearing on the welfare of disadvantaged people, including racial and cultural minorities." *Published works: The Lord's Supper* (Harper, 1948); *Indians and Other Americans,* with D'Arcy McNickle (Harper, 1959); co-editor, *Christian Century Reader* (Association Press, 1962); *Co-operation in Compassion* (Friendship Press, 1966).

FIELD, RUFUS CHESTER   1890-   (dentist)

Born April 5, 1890, Lowell, Mass. *Education:* University of Michigan Dental School, D. D. S. , 1914. *Principal occupation:* Dentist. *Home address:* 13130 Elgin Ave., Huntington Woods, Mich. *Memberships:* American Dental Association; Michigan State Dental Association; Detroit District Dental Society. *Interests:* Writing poems and genealogical stories of the Field family. *Published works: The Persistent Fool* (privately printed); *Life and Trials of Cyrus West Field, Layer of the Atlantic Cable* (1962); *A White Bird Flying* (Pageant Press, 1963).

FISCHER, GEORGE R.   1937-   (archaeologist)

Born May 4, 1937. *Education:* B.A., Stanford University. *Principal occupation:* Archaeologist. *Address:* c/o Ocmulgee National Monument, Macon, Ga. *Affiliations:* Archaeologist, U. S. National Park Service, Ocmulgee National Monument, 1964-.

FISHEL, LESLIE H. , Jr.   1921-   (historian)

Born November 14, 1921, New York, N. Y. *Education:* Oberlin College, B. A. , 1943; Harvard University, M. A. , 1947, Ph. D., 1954. *Principal occupation:* Historian.

Affiliations: Director, State Historical Society of Wisconsin. *Military service:* U. S. Naval Reserve, 1943-46. *Community activities:* Madison Friends of Urban League (co-president, 1963-65; second vice president, 1965-); University Y. M. C. A. (director, 1963-); First Congregational Church (trustee and moderator, 1964-); Wisconsin Executive Residence Foundation (director, 1964-); Historic Sites Foundation (executive vice president, 1960-); Wisconsin History Foundation (secretary, 1959-); Veterans' Memorial Commission, 1962-; Wisconsin Civil War Centennial Commission (secretary, 1959-). *Memberships:* Madison Literary Society; Lincoln Fellowship of Wisconsin (secretary, 1962); Governor's Committee on Portage Canal (chairman, 1964-); Society of American History, 1955-; American Historical Association, 1957-; American Association for State and Local History (council member, 1963-); Wisconsin Academy of Arts, Sciences and Letters (vice president, 1965-). *Awards:* Emerton Traveling Fellowship, Harvard University, 1948. *Interest:* American Negro history. *Published work: The American Negro, A Documentary Story* (Scott, Foresman and Co., 1966).

FITES, GILBERT G.   1921-   (librarian)

Born June 30, 1921, Springfield, South Dakota. *Education:* Kent State University, B. S., 1947; Denver University, M. A., 1948. *Principal occupation:* Librarian. *Home address:* 603 W. Delaware, Tahlequah, Okla. 74464. *Affiliations:* Librarian, Arizona State College, 1960-; Cherokee Museum, Tahlequah, Okla. *Memberships:* American Library Association; Circus Historical Society.

FITZGERALD, RICHARD EDWARD   1910(educator)

Born November 1, 1910, Sardis, Okla. *Education:* Murray Junior College, 1929-32; Southeastern State College, B. S., 1942; Oklahoma University, M. A., 1947. *Principal occupation:* Educator. *Affiliations:* Rural school teacher, Pushmataha County, 193242; defense work, 1943-45; high school principal, Soper, Okla., 1945; high school principal and coach, Goodland High School, Okla., 1946-50; teacher, Seneca Indian

School, 1951-53; principal, Sequoyah Vocational Indian School, 1953-56; superintendent, Seneca Indian School, 1956-. *Military service:* Field Artillery, 1943. *Community activities:* Boy Scouts of America; Lions Club (neighborhood commissioner). *Memberships:* Federation of Federal Employees. *Published works:* Developed draft, *Basic Goals for Elementary Children* (Bureau of Indian Affairs, 1964).

FLEMING, DARRELL (Cherokee)   1911(government administrator)

Born June 22, 1911, Bernice, Okla. *Education:* Haskell Institute, 1927-33. *Principal occupation:* Government administrator. *Home address:* 8906 Knox Ave., S., Minneapolis, Minn. 55431. *Affiliations:* Assistant area director, Minneapolis, Minn., Bureau of Indian Affairs. *Military service:* U. S. Navy, 1944-46. *Community activities:* Lions International; Rotary Club; Masons; York Rite; Scottish Rite; Shriners. *Awards, honors:* Presidential Citation in recognition of outstanding contribution to greater economy and improvement in government operations, 1964.

FLOETHE, LOUISE LEE   1913-   (writer)

Born March 13, 1913, New York, N.Y. *Education:* Columbia University, 1931-33. *Principal occupation:* Writer. *Home address:* 1391 Harbor Dr., Sarasota, Fla. *Community activities:* Biracial group for City of Sarasota; Friends of Libraries of Sarasota (vice president). *Memberships:* Authors Guild. *Interests:* Tennis, sailing, gardening; active in Unitarian Church work; travels around the world. *Published works: If I Were Captain, The Farmer and His Cows, The Indian and His Pueblo, Sea of Grass, Blueberry Pie, The Story of Lumber, The Islands of Hawaii, The New Roof, Fountain of the Friendly Lion, The Cowboy on the Ranch,* all published by Charles Scribners' Sons; *The Winning Colt* (Sterling, 1957); *Terry Sets Sail* (Harper, 1958); *Triangle X* (Harper, 1960); *A Year to Remember* (Lothrop, 1958); *Sara* (Farrar, Straus, 1961); *Bittersweet Summer* (Farrar, Straus, 1964).

FLORES, WILLIAM VANN (Cherokee-
Papago)   1927-   (medical illustrator)

Born October 2, 1927, Appleton, Wis. *Education:* Chilocco Indian School, 1947; Kansas City Art Institute, 1949-51; Art Center School, Los Angeles, 1955-57; Oklahoma City University, 1958-59; El Reno Junior College, 1965-. *Principal occupation:* Medical illustrator. *Home address:* P.O. Box 84, Concho, Okla. 73022. *Affiliations:* Medical illustrator, Federal Aviation Agency, Will Rogers Field, Oklahoma City, Okla., 1961-. *Military service:* U.S. Army, 1952-54 (Korean Service Medal with two Bronze Service Stars; Presidential Unit Citation; Meritorious Unit Commendation; Good Conduct Medal; National Defense Service Medal; United Nations Service Medal). *Memberships:* Kappa Pi Art Society; Oklahoma City Art Directors Club; Oklahoma City Art Guild; Artists of Oklahoma, Yukon, Okla.; Society of Art Center Alumni, Los Angeles, Calif.; Veterans of Foreign Wars.

FOLSOM, FRANKLIN (pseudonyms: Benjamin Brewster, Franklin Brewster, Samuel Cutler, Sidney E. Fletcher, Michael Gorham, Lyman Hopkins, Troy Nesbit) 1907- (writer)

Born July 21, 1907, Boulder, Colorado. *Education:* University of Colorado, B. A., 1928; Dartmouth College, 1924-25; Oxford University, B. A., 1932, M. A., 1963. *Home address:* Roosevelt, N. J. *Principal occupation:* Writer. *Military service:* U. S. Merchant Marine, 1944-46. *Memberships:* Archaeological Society of New Jersey (vice president); Association on American Indian Affairs; National Speleological Society. *Awards, honors:* Rhodes Scholarship, 1930. *Published works: It's a Secret* by Benjamin Brewster (Wonder Books, 1950); *The First Book of Baseball* by Benjamin Brewster (Watts, 1950); *The First Book of Cowboys* by Benjamin Brewster (Watts, 1950); *The First Book of Indians* by Benjamin Brewster (Watts, 1950); *The Big Book of Real Boats and Ships* by Benjamin Brewster (Grosset and Dunlap, 1951); *Columbus the Exploring Burro* by Benjamin Brewster (Whitman, 1951); *The First Book of Firemen* by Benjamin Brewster (Watts, 1951); *The Real Book About Abraham Lincoln* by Michael Gorham (Garden City, 1951); *72 Sure-Fire Ways of Having Fun,* with Fred Menaker (Sentinel, 1951); *The Cowboy and his Horse* by Sydney E. Fletcher (Grosset and Dunlap, 1951); *The Real Book of*

American Tall Tales by Michael Gorham (Garden City, 1952); *Sand Dune Pony* by Troy Nesbit (Whitman, 1952); *The Real Book About Cowboys* by Michael Gorham (Garden City, 1952); *The Big Book of the Real Circus* by Benjamin Brewster, with Felix Sutton (Grosset and Dunlap, 1953); *The Indian Mummy Mystery* by Troy Nesbit (Whitman, 1953); *The Real Book of Great American Journeys* by Michael Gorham (Garden City, 1953); *The Real Book about Indians* by Michael Gorham (Garden City, 1953); *The Jinx of Payrock Canyon* by Troy Nesbit (Whitman, 1954); *The American Indian* by Sydney E. Fletcher (Grosset and Dunlap, 1954); *Famous Pioneers* by Samuel Cutler (Gabriel and Son, 1955); *The First Book of Eskimos* by Benjamin Brewster (Watts, 1953); *The Diamond Cave Mystery* by Troy Nesbit (Whitman, 1956); *Exploring American Caves* (Crown, 1956); *The Hidden Ruin* (Funk and Wagnalls, 1957); *The Mystery at Rustlers' Fort* by Troy Nesbit (Whitman, 1957); *The Real Book About Baseball* by Lyman Hopkins (Garden City, 1958, 1962); *The Explorations of America* (Grosset and Dunlap, 1958); *Beyond the Frontier* (Funk and Wagnalls, 1959); *Fury and the Mystery at Trappers Hole* by Troy Nesbit (Whitman, 1959); *Wagon Train* by Troy Nesbit (Whitman, 1959); *The Mystery at Ruslers' Fort* (Harvey House, 1960); *Sand Dune Pony Mystery* (Harvey House, 1960); *The Story of Archaeology in the Americas,* with Mary Elting (Harvey House, 1960); *The Diamond Cave Mystery* (Harvey House, 1962); *The Forest Fire Mystery* by Troy Nesbit (Whitman, 1962); *The Indian Mummy Mystery* (Whitman, 1962); *The Language Book* (Grosset and Dunlap, 1963); *Famous Pioneers* (Harvey House, 1963); *Men Who Won the West* (Scholastic Book Services, 1963); *The Forest Fire Mystery* (Harvey House, 1963); *Soviet Union: A View from Within* (Thomas Nelson, 1965); *The Answer Book of Geography,* with Mary Etling (Grosset and Dunlap, 1966).

FOLSOM, MICHAEL BREWSTER 1938- (teaching assistant)

Born November 22, 1938, New York, N. Y. *Education:* Antioch College, B. A., 1961; Leeds University, 1960-61; Rutgers University, M. A., 1963. *Principal occupation:* Graduate student and teaching assistant. *Home address:* 1416 Grant, Berkeley,

Calif. *Interests:* Literary history; travel in United States and Europe. *Published works: The Secret Story of Pueblo Bonito,* with Mary Elting (Harvey House, 1963); *Keep Your Eyes Open* (Grosset and Dunlap, 1965). *Work in progress: The Story of Maize.*

FOLSOM-DICKERSON, W. E. S. (Choctaw)
   1898- (teacher, author)

Born December 26, 1898, Durant, Indian Territory (now Oklahoma). *Education:* University of Texas, B. A., 1939, M. A., 1952. *Principal occupation:* Teacher, author. *Home address:* 1601 Elmhurst, Austin, Texas 78741. *Affiliations:* Teacher in Texas public schools for thirty years. *Military service:* U. S. Infantry, 1918. *Memberships:* Texas State Teachers Association, 1965-66. *Awards:* Phi Beta Kappa, University of Texas, 1939. *Interests:* Research on the American Indian, which includes visiting every major tribe in the U. S. *Published works: The White Path* (Naylor Co., 1965); *The Handbook of Texas,* two vols. (Texas State Historical Association, 1952).

FORBES, JACK D. 1934- (associate professor of history)

Born January 7, 1934, Long Beach, Calif. *Education:* Glendale College, A. A., 1953; University of Southern California, B. A., 1955, M. A., 1956, Ph. D., 1959. *Principal occupation:* Associate professor of history. *Home address:* 870 Ruby Ave., Reno, Nev. 89503. *Affiliations:* Teaching assistant, University of Southern California, 1956; substitute teacher, Los Angeles City Schools, 1956-59; lecturer in history, University of Southern California, 1958-59; instructor, Citrus College, 1959-60; assistant professor, San Fernando Valley State College, 1960-64; associate professor of history and director, Center for Western North American Studies, University of Nevada, 1964-. *Other professional posts:* Editor, *El Tlatolo,* newsletter of Southwest Branch, American Indian Ethnohistoric Conference, 1961-62; reader of manuscripts, University of Oklahoma Press, 1961-; board of editors, *Journal of the West,* 1962-. *Community activities:* Ventura County Junior College District (board of directors, 1962-64); Simi Valley Democratic Club

(charter president, 1960-61); American Indian College Committee (chairman, 1961-62); Ventura County Democratic Council, 1960-61; Mayor's Committee, History of Los Angeles, 1962-64; Nevada Inter-tribal Council Advisory Committee, 1965-. *Memberships:* American Indian Ethnohistoric Conference, 1960-; Western History Association, 1961-; American Historical Association, 1963-; Pacific Coast Council on Latin American Studies, 1963-. *Awards, honors:* Social Science Research Council Research Training Fellow, 1957-58; Social Science Research Council Grant in Aid, 1961-62; Guggenheim Memorial Foundation Fellow, 1963-64; Phi Beta Kappa; Phi Alpha Theta. *Interests:* Tribal or folk groups and their interactions with supra-tribal populations; ethnohistory; American Indian history; Southwestern United States-North Mexican history; race mixture and frontier history; travel to Spain, Mexico, England, Scotland, France, Italy, Switzerland, and Morocco. *Published works: Apache, Navaho and Spaniard* (University of Oklahoma Press, 1960); *The Indian in America's Past* (Prentice-Hall, 1964); *Warriors of the Colorado* (University of Oklahoma Press, 1965); articles in various journals and magazines.

FORREST, ERIM (Modoc-Pit River)
   1920- (rancher)

Born January 12, 1920, Alturas, Calif. *Education:* Riverside Junior College. *Principal occupation:* Rancher. *Home address:* Box 763, XL Indian Reservation, Alturas, Calif. 96101. *Affiliations:* Self-employed rancher; California Inheritance Tax Appraisers Association; manager, Pit River Home and Agricultural Cooperative Association. *Military service:* U. S. Army, 1942-45. *Community activities:* Kiwanis Club; Northeastern California Sportsmens Council (president); Modoc County Economic Development Commission; Modoc County Democratic Central Committee; State Democratic Central Committee; Governor's Interstate Indian Council; California-Oregon Interstate Deer Herd Committee; Modoc County Economic Opportunity Committee; California Advisory Committee on Indian Affairs; Northern Counties Wildlife Conservation Association; California Intertribal Council (president). *Awards:* Outstanding Indian from the West,

American Indian Chicago Conference. *Interests:* Cattle ranching; anthropology; wildlife. *Published work: Declaration of Indian Purpose,* with D'Arcy McNickle (University of Chicago).

FRAKER, ELMER L.   1896-
    (administrator)

Born November 18, 1896. *Education:* University of Oklahoma, B.A., M.A. *Principal occupation:* Administrator. *Affiliations:* Former president, Mangum Junior College; administrative secretary, Oklahoma Historical Society. *Military service:* U.S. Infantry, World War I. *Community activities:* Rotary Club. *Memberships:* American Association for State and Local History; American Historical Association; Southern Historical Association; Western Historical Association; Mississippi Valley Historical Association. *Published works: United States History and Tests; World History and Tests.*

FRASER, DOUGLAS FERRAR   1929-
    (professor)

Born September 3, 1929, Hornell, N.Y. *Education:* Columbia College, B.A., 1951; Columbia University, M.A., 1955, Ph.D., 1959. *Principal occupation:* Associate professor of art history and archaeology. *Home address:* 39 Claremont Ave., New York, N.Y. 10027. *Affiliations:* Associate professor of art history and archaeology, 1959-. *Military service:* U.S. Navy, 1951-54. *Memberships:* College Art Association; Society of Architectural Historians; Current Anthropology (associate); Royal Anthropological Institute (Fellow); African Studies Association. *Interests:* Primitive art; trans-Pacific contacts; pre-Columbian art. *Published works: Primitive Art* (Doubleday-Chanticleer, 1962); *The Many Faces of Primitive Art: A Critical Anthology* (Prentice-Hall, Inc., 1966).

FREDERICKS, OSWALD WHITE BEAR
    (Hopi) 1905- (artist)

Born February 6, 1905, Old Oraibi, Ariz. (Hopi Reservation). *Education:* Haskell Institute; Bacone College, B.S. *Principal occupation:* Artist, wood carver. *Home address:* Box 127, Hopi Reservation, Oraibi,

Ariz. *Affiliations:* Art instructor, Boys' Club of America, Phoenix, Ariz.; instructor, Y.M.C.A., N.J. *Community activities:* Glee Club, Bacone College; church organizations. *Memberships:* Boys' Club of America; Indian Guide Club of New Jersey. *Awards:* Golf award, for two "hole in one" shots, Shawnee on Delaware Golf Club; other sports awards. *Interests:* Travel; teaching and lecturing; working in vocational instruction for young people; the history of the Hopi people, their crafts and ceremonials. *Published works: Book of the Hopi* with Frank Waters (Viking Press, 1962).

FREEMAN, ROBERT LEE (Crow-Creek-
    Sioux) 1939- (artist)

Born January 1, 1939, Rincon Indian Reservation, Calif. *Education:* Elementary school. *Principal occupation:* Artist. *Home address:* Box 235, Valley Center, Calif. *Military service:* Army, 1957-60. *Awards:* Scottsdale National Art Award, First Prize, pen and ink, 1963; Second Prize, oil paintings, 1964, wood sculpture, 1965. *Interests:* All art media.

FROST, RICHARD I.   1917- (museum
    curator)

Born May 18, 1917, Cody, Wyo. *Education:* University of Wyoming, B.S., 1939. *Principal occupation:* Museum curator. *Home address:* 901 10th St., Cody, Wyo. 84214. *Affiliation:* Owner, Frost Curio Shops; curator, Buffalo Bill Museum, Cody, Wyo. *Military service:* U.S. Army, 1941-46. *Community activities:* Cody Chamber of Commerce (vice president); Cody Lions Club; American Legion (commander); Wyoming Travel Commission (chairman); Wyoming State Library and Archives Historical Board; Wyoming State Land and Water Conservation Commission; Buffalo Bill Memorial Association (vice president). *Memberships:* American Association of Museums; Wyoming Historical Society. *Interests:* Plains Indians; Western culture; life of Buffalo Bill.

FULLER, IOLA   (professor of English)

Born Marcellus, Mich. *Education:* University of Michigan, B.A., 1935, M.A., 1940, M.A., 1960. *Principal occupation:*

Professor of English, writer. *Home address:* Route 1, Box 356A, Big Rapids, Mich. 49307. *Affiliations:* Associate professor of English, Ferris State College; librarian, U. S. Indian School, Santa Fe, N. M., 1954-57; fiction leader, Kansas Writer's Conference, 1962 and 1963; teacher of library science, University of Michigan. *Memberships:* American Institute of University Professors; National Association of Press Women. *Awards:* Phi Beta Kappa; Avery Award for Creative Writing. *Interests:* Travel for pleasure and research in U. S., Canada, Mexico and Europe; research at the British Museum. *Published works: The Loon Feather* (Harcourt, Brace, 1940); *The Shining Trail* (Duell, Sloan, and Pearce, 1943); *The Guiled Torch* (G. P. Putnam's, 1957).

FULLER, RICHARD E. 1897- (museum director)

Born June 1, 1897, New York, N. Y. *Education:* Yale University, Ph. B., 1918; University of Washington, B. S., 1924, M. S., 1925, Ph. D., 1930; Washington State College, LL. D., 1944. *Principal occupation:* Museum director. *Home address:* 3801 E. Prospect, Seattle, Wash. 98102. *Affiliations:* Assistant professor, University of Washington, 1930-34 (research appointment, associate professor, 1934-40; research professor, 1940-); director, Barkon Tube Lighting Corp., 1933-35 (chairman, 1935-37; president, 1937-39); director, Cornucopia Gold Mines, 1935-36 (vice president and treasurer, 1936-38; president, 1938-41); director, Northwestern Glass Co., 1940-48 (chairman, 1948); director, National Bank of Commerce of Seattle; president and director, Seattle Art Museum, 1933-. *Other professional posts:* President, Art Institute of Seattle, 1930-33; trustee, Seattle Chamber of Commerce (chairman, arts and education committee, 1946-48); president, Seattle Foundation, 1946-50; chairman, Northwest Division, Institute of Pacific Relations, 1950-51; co-chairman, Northwest Regional Auditions Board, Metropolitan Opera, 1957-61 (regional chairman, national council, 1962); incorporator, Pacific Science Center, 1962. *Military service:* American Field Service, France, 1917; A. E. F., 1918-19; Army Specialist Corps, 1942-43. *Community activities:* Seattle War Chest (director, 1942-44); British-American War Relief, 1941-44;

Russian War Relief, 1941-45; U. S. Committee for Study of Particutin, Division of Geology of the National Research Council (chairman, 1944-50). *Memberships:* Geological Society of America (Fellow); Mineralogical Society of America (Fellow); American Association for the Advancement of Science; American Geophysical Union (president, colvanology section, 1944-47); American Association of Museums (council, 1954-61); International Council of Museums (U. S. national committee, 1958-62); Japan Society of Seattle (president, 1957-58); A. I. D.; Association of Art Museum Directors (vice president, 1956-57); honorary member, A. I. A.; Phi Beta Kappa; Sigma Xi; Rainier Club; University Club; Rotary Club of Seattle; Yale Club. *Awards, honors:* Award for Outstanding Civic Service, Seattle Real Estate Board, 1940; King's Medal (Great Britain) for Service in the Cause of Freedom, 1946; Raymond W. Huff Award, Seattle World Affairs Council, 1960. *Published works:* Geological articles in various scientific journals.

G

GABRIEL, RALPH HENRY 1890- (professor, writer)

Born April 29, 1890, Reading, N. Y. *Education:* Yale University, B.A., 1913, M.A., 1915, Ph. D., 1919. *Principal occupation:* Professor of history, writer. *Home address:* 3440 - 38th St., N. W., Washington, D. C. 20016. *Affiliations:* Professor of history, Yale University, 1915-58; visiting professor, New York University, 1933; Stanford University, 1934, 1949; University of Colorado, 1941, 1942; University of Sydney (Australia), 1946; Cambridge University, 1951-52; University of Wyoming, 1954; professor of American civilizations, School of International Service, American University, 1958-63; Phi Beta Kappa visiting scholar, 1963-64; Pitt professor of American history and institutions. *Military service:* U.S. Army. *Other professional posts:* Alternate delegate, U.S. Delegation, 10th Conference, UNESCO, 1958; member, consulting committee on historic sites, National Park Service, 1963; member, U. S. National Commission for UNESCO, 1958-64; lecturer, War Department School for Military Government, Charlottesbille, Va., 1943-46; member, board of trustees, Yale-in-China,

1922-1964. *Memberships:* American Historical Association; Massachusetts Historical Association; Colonial Society; New Haven Colony Historical Society; American Studies Association (president, 1963, 1964). *Awards:* Phi Beta Kappa, Sigma Xi; Litt. D. (hon.), Bucknel University, 1952; Litt. D. (hon.), Williams College, 1958; D.H.L., (hon.), Colgate University, 1963. *Interests:* American intellectual history; photography; hiking and canoeing; travel. *Published works: Evolution of Long Island* (Yale, 1921; Ira J. Friedman, 1960); editor, *Christianity and Modern Thought* (Yale, 1924); editor, with Henri L. Bourdin and Stanley T. Williams, *Sketches of Eighteenth Century America, More "Letters from an American Farmer"* (Yale, 1925); *Toilers of Land and Sea* (Yale, 1926); editor, *The Pageant of America,* fifteen vols. (Yale, 1926-29); *The Winning of Freedom,* with William Wood (Yale, 1927); *In Defense of Liberty,* with William Wood (Yale, 1928); *The Lure of the Frontier* (Yale, 1929); *The Story of the American Nation,* with Mabel B. Casner (Harcourt, Brace and World, 1931, 1965); editor, *A Frontier Lady* (Yale, 1932); editor, with Stanley T. Williams and Harry R. Warfel, *The American Mind, An Anthology* (American Book Co., 1937; revised 1963); contributing author, *The Constitution Reconsidered* (Columbia University Press, 1938); *Course of American Democratic Thought* (Ronald, 1940; revised and enlarged, 1956); *Elias Boudinot, Cherokee, and His America* (University of Oklahoma Press, 1941); *Main Currents in American History* (D. Appleton-Century Co., 1942); contributing author, *Education and the Faith of America* (Packer Collegiate Institute, 1945); contributing author, *Wellsprings of the American Spirit* (Institute for Religious and Social Studies, 1948); editor, *Hamilton, Madison and Jay on the Constitution, Selections from the Federalist Papers* (Liberal Arts Press, 1954); contributing author, *National Policies for Education, Health and Social Services* (Doubleday and Co., 1955); *Religion and Learning at Yale* (Yale, 1958); contributing author, *American Perspectives* (Harvard University Press, 1961); *Traditional Values in American Life,* a pamphlet (Harcourt, Brace and World, 1963); contributing author, *American Studies in Transition* (University of Pennsylvania Press, 1964); contributing author, *Interpreting and Teaching American History* (National Council for the Social Studies).

GAINES, MICHAEL A. 1937- (human relations executive)

Born April 13, 1937, Detroit, Mich. *Education:* Wayne State University, B. A. (Sociology and Social Psychology), 1958; graduate study in sociology and social psychology, 1958-64. *Principal occupation:* Human relations executive. *Home address:* 2559 Xenwood Ave., Minneapolis, Minn. *Affiliations:* Research assistant, Detroit City Planning Commission, 1957-58; assistant director, Michigan Regional Anti-Defamation League, 1958-62; regional director, Minnesota-Dakotas Regional Anti-Defamation League, 1962-64; staff seminar leader, B'nai B'rith Youth Organization District Convention, 1961-64; Workshop in Human Relations, Wayne State University; Workshop in Inter-Group Education, University of Michigan; Workshop in Human Relations, Eastern Michigan University; lecturer in social psychology and race relations, Detroit Institute of Technology; instructor in Jewish history, ethics, modern Jewish problems, Temple Israel; instructor in contemporary Jewish problems and world Jewry, Minneapolis Talmud Torah. *Memberships:* Alpha Kappa Delta; American Civil Liberties Union; executive committee and regional advisory board, Anti-Defamation League of B'nai B'rith; Catholic Interracial Council; Goldenberg Lodge of B'nai B'rith; Joint Committee on Equal Opportunity; Minneapolis Urban League; Minnesota Council on Civil and Human Rights; National Association for the Advancement of Colored People; National Association of Inter-Group Relations Officials; St. Louis Park Human Relations Council; St. Paul Council on Human Relations; Temple Israel, Minneapolis, Minn. *Published work:* Article in *Anti Defamation League Bulletin*

GALE, VERNON T. 1886- (museum curator)

Born December 2, 1886, Stillman Valley, Ill. *Education:* Valley City High School. *Principal occupation:* Museum curator. *Home address:* 300 Viking Dr., Valley City, N. D. 58072. *Affiliations:* Curator, Gale Museum; superintendent, Valley City Post Office, 1908-1952; secretary, Federal Civil Service Board, 1911-12. *Military service:* National Guard; U.S. Army, 1908-11. *Community activities:* Valley City Fire Department; Boy Scouts; Masonic Order; state representative, National Federation of Post Office Clerks. *Memberships:* North Dakota Historical Society; treasurer, Barnes County Historical Society (defunct). *Awards, honors:* National Guard Marksman; Red River Valley Boy Scouts' Scoutmaster Key. *Published work:* Map of Indian sites along Cheyenne River.

GARCIA, MARCELINO (Tewa Pueblo) 1932- (instructional aid worker, B.I.A.)

Born June 2, 1932, San Juan Pueblo, N. M. *Education:* U.S. Indian School, Santa Fe, N.M. *Principal occupation:* Instructional aid worker, B.I.A. *Home address:* San Juan Pueblo, P.O. Box 854, N.M. *Community activities:* San Juan Pueblo Church (chairman). *Awards:* Prize for Indian ceremonial sash belt, New Mexico State Fair.

GARREAUX, HAZEL (Cheyenne River Sioux) 1916- (tribal official)

Born June 23, 1916, LaPlant, S. D. *Education:* Normal Training School; commercial diploma, Haskell Institute, 1940. *Principal occupation:* Tribal official. *Home address:* Box 44, Eagle Butte, S.D. 57625. *Affiliations:* Secretary, Cheyenne River Sioux Tribal Council, Eagle Butte, S.D., 1946-49, 1959-.

GATES, PAUL W. 1901- (teacher, writer)

Born December 4, 1901, Nashua, N.H. *Education:* Colby College, B.S., 1924; Clark University, M.A., 1925; Harvard University, Ph.D., 1930. *Principal occupation:* Teacher, Cornell University, 1936-. *Home address:* Ellis Hollow Rd., Ithaca, N.Y. *Community activities:* Consultant on land values, Department of Justice; consultant, Second Hoover Commission on Organization of Executive Branches of Government. *Memberships:* Mississippi Valley Historical Association (president, 1962). *Published works: The Illinois Central Railroad* (1934); *The Wisconsin Pine Lands of Cornell University* (1944, 1965); *Fifty Million Acres* (1954); *The Farmer's Age* (1960); *Agriculture and the Civil War* (1965).

GAYTON, ANNA H. 1899- (associate professor)

Born September 20, 1899, Santa Cruz, Calif. *Education:* University of California, B.A., 1923, M.A., 1924, Ph.D., 1928. *Principal occupation:* Associate professor. *Home address:* P.O. Box 880, Santa Cruz, Calif. 95061. *Affiliations:* Associate professor of decorative art, associate curator of textiles, Lowie Museum of Anthropology, University of California, Berkeley, 1948-54; professor and curator, Lowie Museum of Anthropology, 1955-. *Memberships:* American Anthropological Association; Society for American Archaeology (Fellow); American Folklore Society (Fellow; president, 1950); Institute for Andean Studies (vice president, director, 1965). *Awards, honors:* National Research Council Fellow, 1928-30; Guggenheim Fellow, 1947. *Interests:* Western American Indian ethnology and folklore; Peruvian archaeology; archaeological and ethnic textile research. *Published works: Yokuts and Western Mono Myths,* with Stanley S. Newman (*Anthropological Records,* University of California, Vol. 5, 1940); *Yokuts and Western Mono Ethnography* (*Anthropological Records,* University of California, Vol. 10, 1948).

GELLERS, DON COTESWORTH 1936- (attorney)

Born May 2, 1936, United States. *Education:* Arizona State College, B.A., 1956; Columbia University School of Law and School of International Affairs, LL.B.-M.I.A., 1962. *Principal occupation:* Attorney for Passamaquoddy Tribe of Indians, 1964-. *Home address:* 9 Key St., Eastport, Me. *Other professional posts:* United States Representative, United Nations Interne Programme, 1959.

GENTRY, CLAUDE 1902- (museum curator)

Born July 25, 1902, Baldwyn, Miss. *Principal occupation:* Curator, Brice's Crossroads Museum, Baldwyn, Miss. *Home address:* Highway 45 N., Baldwyn, Miss. 38824. *Affiliations:* Owner (retired), Gentry Insurance Agency. *Community activities:* Northeast Mississippi Historical

Society (president). *Memberships:* Mississippi Historical Society (board of directors; president, 1963-64). *Awards:* "Outdoor Writer of 1960," Mississippi Wildlife Federation. *Interests:* Historical writing; research expeditions. *Published works: Private John Allen* (Magnolia Publishers, 1951); *Crossroads* (Magnolia Publishers, 1954); *Kit Carson* (Magnolia Publishers, 1956); *The Battle of Brice's Crossroads* (Magnolia Publishers, 1963).

GIBSON, ARRELL M.   1921-
  (professor)

Born December 1, 1921, Pleasanton, Kan. *Education* University of Oklahoma, Ph.D., 1964. *Principal occupation:* Professor of history. *Address (home and business):* Norman, Okla. 73069. *Affiliations:* Chairman, Department of History, University of Oklahoma; associate professor of history, University of Oklahoma. *Military service:* U.S. Navy, 1942-1946. *Memberships:* Oklahoma Civil War Centennial Commission; Western Historical Association; Oklahoma Historical Society; Mississippi Valley Historical Association. *Awards, honors:* Rockefeller Grant (research); American Philosophical Society Grant (research). *Interests:* Teaching, research, and writing on the American West. *Published works: The Kickapoos: Lords of the Middle Border* (University of Oklahoma Press, 1963); *Life and Death of Colonel Fountain* (University of Oklahoma Press, 1965); *Oklahoma: A History of Five Centuries* (Harlow Press, 1965).

GIDDINGS, RUTH W.   1919-   (museum curator)

Born June 17, 1919, Yonkers, N.Y. *Education:* University of Mexico, 1939; University of Arizona, B.A., 1943, M.A., 1945. *Principal occupation:* Museum curator. *Home address:* Mount Hope Grant, Bristol, R.I. 02809. *Affiliations:* Curator, Haffenreffer Museum, Brown University. *Memberships:* Sigma Xi; American Association for the Advancement of Science, 1944-50; American Anthropological Association, 1965. *Interests:* Ethnography, archaeology and museum work; related travel to Mexico, western Arctic, Denmark, Spain. *Published works: Yaquis of Mexico and Their Folk Literature* (Arizona Archaeological

and Historical Society, Vol. 8, No. 1, 1943); *Yaqui Myths and Legends* (University of Arizona Anthropological Papers, No. 2, 1959).

GILBERT, WILLIAM HARLEN   1904-
  (writer, teacher)

Born July 28, 1904, Covington, Ky. *Education:* University of Cincinnati, B.A., 1927; University of Chicago, M.A., 1930, Ph.D., 1934. *Principal occupation:* Writing reports, drafting speeches and furnishing counsel on Indian affairs. *Home address:* 9015 - 1st Ave., Silver Spring, Md. *Affiliations:* Teacher of social sciences, anthropology, sociology and economics, University of Cincinnati, 1935-36; Alabama Polytechnic University, 1936-37; New York State University for Teachers, 1938-39; American University, 1939-41; North Texas State Teachers University, summer, 1936; Emory University, summer, 1937; C.W.A. research and tutoring, University of Chicago, 1933-35; ethnohistory research, University of Tennessee, summer, 1938; researcher, Library of Congress, 1941-. *Community activities:* P.T.A. Awards Committee, Montgomery Blair Senior High; American Association of University Women; study group leader, comparative religions. *Memberships:* Anthropological Society of Washington (secretary; vice president; representative on board of Washington Academy of Sciences); American Anthropological Association (Fellow); Anthropological Society of Washington (Fellow). *Interests:* American Indians; ethnic groups; world travel; archaeological survey and excavation; ethnological field studies, Umatilla Reservation, Oregon, summer, 1930, and Cherokee Reservation, North Carolina, fall, 1932; mixed blood groups (Wesorts and Guineas), Maryland and West Virginia, summer, 1945; field visits to Indian reservations. *Published works:* Co-author, *Social Anthropology of North American Tribes* (University of Chicago, 1937, 1956); co-author, *Peoples of India* (Smithsonian Institution, War Background Series, 1943); co-editor, *U.S. Congress House Report 2503,* 1952.

GILL, JOSEPH C., S.J.   1926-
  (educator)

Born July 15, 1926, Madison, Wis. *Education:* Marquette University, 1944-46; St.

Louis University, B. A., 1950, M. A., 1953, S. T. L., 1961. *Principal occupation*: Principal and superintendent, St. Francis Indian Mission School.

GILLILAND, HOMER M.   1912-
  (B. I. A. agency superintendent)

Born March 8, 1912, Tremont, Miss. *Education*: Mississippi State University, B. S., 1934; graduate study, Mississippi State University. *Principal occupation*: B. I. A. agency superintendent. *Home address*: Parker, Ariz. 85344. *Affiliations*: Superintendent, Colorado River Indian Agency, Parker, Ariz. 85344. *Community activities*: Rotary Club; Elks Lodge; Masonic Lodge; Colorado River Development Association. *Awards, honors*: Distinguished Service Award, Department of the Interior; Superior Performance Award, Bureau of Indian Affairs.

GLADWIN, HAROLD S.   1883- (writer)

Born December 21, 1883, New York, N. Y. *Education*: Wellington College. *Principal occupation*: Writer. *Home address*: 1555 E. Valley Rd. , Santa Barbara, Calif. *Interests*: Southwestern United States. *Published works*: *Medallion Papers* (privately printed); *Men Out of Asia* (Whittlesley House); *A History of the Ancient Southwest* (Bond Wheelwright).

GLUBOK, SHIRLEY (writer, lecturer)

Born St. Louis, Mo. *Education*: Washington University, B. A. (Art and Archaeology); Columbia University, M. A. (Childhood Education). *Principal occupation*: Author; lecturer on art for children, Metropolitan Museum of Art, 1958-. *Home address*: 59 E. 80th St., New York, N. Y. 10021. *Other professional posts*: Elementary teacher, private schools, New York. *Memberships*: American Archaeological Society; American Association of Museums; Washington University Archaeological Society; Association of Teachers of Independent Schools; Authors League of America. *Awards, honors*: Lewis Carroll Shelf Award for *The Art of Ancient Egypt*. *Published works*: *The Art of Ancient Egypt* (Atheneum, 1962); *The Art of Lands in the Bible* (Atheneum, 1963); *The Art of Ancient Greece* (Atheneum, 1963);

The Art of the North American Indian (Harper and Row, 1964); *The Art of the Eskimo* (Harper and Row, 1964); *The Art of Ancient Rome* (Harper and Row, 1965); *The Art of Africa* (Harper and Row, 1965); *The Fall of the Aztecs* (St. Martin's Press, 1965).

GOLD, DOUGLAS 1894- (psychologist)

Born March 24, 1894, Newburgh, Ind. *Education*: Waynesburg College, B. A. , 1914; U. S. Naval Academy, 1917; University of Montana, M.A., 1934; Columbia University, Ed. D. *Principal occupation*: Psychologist. *Home address*: Box 505, RR #3, Heatherville, Va. *Affiliations*: Counselor, U. S. Veterans Administration, 1943-48; Central Office, U.S. Veterans Administration, 1951-62; chief clinical psychologist, U. S. Veterans Administration Hospital, 1962-64; director of testing bureau and visiting professor of psychology, Hampton Institute, 1964-65; visiting professor of psychology, Richmond Professional Institute, 1965-66. *Military service*: U. S. Navy, 1917-19. *Memberships*: American Psychological Association (Fellow); American Personnel and Guidance Association. *Awards*: Award, U. S. Veterans Association, for suggestion on improvement techniques for counseling; honorary adoption by Blackfeet Tribe. *Interests*: Teaching; psychotherapy and counseling; American Indian lore; the Lewis and Clark expedition. *Published works*: *Primer for Adult Illiterates* (U. S. Department of the Interior, 1933); *Americanization Manual* (Montana American Legion, 1935); *Manual for Course of Study for Montana Elementary Schools* (1942); *A Schoolmaster with the Blackfeet Indians* (Caxton Printers, Ltd. , 1963).

GORANSON, FREDERICK ARNOLD 1926-
  (educator)

Born January 11, 1926, Waltham, Mass. *Education*: University of Wyoming, B. S. , 1951; University of Oregon, M. S. , 1958. *Principal occupation*: Education of Indians, Eskimos, and Aleuts. *Address*: Toadlena, N. M. *Affiliations*: Head teacher, Alaskan Territorial Schools at Pilot Point, Karluk and Teller, Alaska, 1954-57, 1959-60; principal teacher, Bureau of Indian Affairs schools at Savoonga and Arctic Village, Alaska, 1960-64; education specialist, Adult Education, Toadlena, New Mexico, 1964-.

Military service: U. S. Army, 1943-45 (Purple Heart). *Memberships:* Adult Education Association of the U. S. A. *Interests:* Education of the American Indian and Eskimo.

GORMAN, CARL NELSON   *(Kin-ya-onny beyeh)* (Navajo) 1907-   (artist)

Born October 5, 1907, Chinle, Ariz. *Education:* Otis Art Institute, Los Angeles, Calif. , Graduate, 1951, extension courses, 1952, 1953. *Principal occupation:* Artist. *Address*: c/o Navajo Arts & Crafts Guild, Window Rock, Ariz. 86515. *Affiliations:* Illustrator and technical illustrator, Douglas Aircraft Co. , Santa Monica, Lawndale, Torrance, Calif. , 1951-63; manager, Navajo Arts & Crafts Guild, 1964-. *Other posts:* Partner, Desert Designs Silk Screening, Window Rock, Ariz., 1963-64; *Kin-ya-onny beyeh* Originals, professional arts and crafts, 1951-. *Military service:* U. S. Marine Corps, 1942-45, "with group that developed Navajo Code. " *Community activities:* Navajo Club of Los Angeles (board director, chairman, vice chairman, treasurer) 1955-64; Veterans of Foreign Wars; Inter-Tribal Indian Ceremonial (exhibit committee); Navajo Tribal Fair (arts and crafts exhibit chairman); American Indian Artists, San Francisco, Calif. (advisory board); 2nd Marine Division Association. *Memberships:* Otis Institute Alumni Association, 1952-; American Craftsmen's Council, 1965-. Mr. Gorman's work has appeared in numerous one-man and group shows and is part of public and private collections. *Interests:* All phases of art -- subjects chiefly Navajo and horses, but including non-Indian subjects, realistic, semiabstract, some impressionistic; works in varied art media. "Interested in improving quality of crafts, expanding markets, and new and adaptive crafts. I am also interested in other phases of Navajo and Indian culture, and worked up the now well known 'Gourd Rattle Dance' for the Youth Group of the Navajo Club of Los Angeles, utilizing an old Yei-bi-chai song as sung by the Hopis in 1917. I like to record Navajo songs, have taken many photos and have gathered material of historical and cultural interest which I plan to put into book form. "

GORMAN, R. C.   (Navajo) 1934- (artist)

Born July 26, 1934, Chinle, Ariz. *Education:* Arizona State College; Mexico City College; San Francisco State College. *Principal occupation:* Student of English; artist. *Home address:* 4135 Army St. #10, San Francisco, Calif. *Military service:* U. S. Navy, 1952-56. *Memberships:* American Indian Artists of San Francisco (painting chairman, 1966). *Awards:* First, Second and Third Prizes, Scottsdale National Indian Arts Exhibition and Annual American Indian Artists Exhibition; First Prize, Wayne State University Exhibit (American Indian Art Exposition); First and Second Prizes, Window Rock Navajo Inter-Tribal Fair; Honorable Mention, Museum of New Mexico Contemporary Indian Artists Annual Exhibition. *Interests:* Mexican art and artists; lithography.

GOWAN, R. L.   1914-   (minister)

Born August 19, 1914, Custer, S. D. *Principal occupation:* Minister, Wesleyan Methodist Church of America. *Affiliations:* Minister, Garden City, S. D. , Page, Neb. , Glendale, Ariz. ; field man, foreign missions, Tabor, Iowa; business manager and treasurer, Hot Springs, S. D. ; founder and director, American Indian Mission, Custer, S. D. *Awards, honors:* Wesleyan Methodist Church, for twenty-five years' service; Bronze Plaque, Little White Church, for continuous service. *Interests:* Building; plumbing; contracting; printing; photography; travel in United States, Canada, Cuba, Haiti, and Mexico; American Indian film in progress.

GRAFF, POLLY ANNE   1908-   (writer)

Born June 20, 1908, Cleveland, Ohio. *Education:* Whitman College, B. A. , 1931. *Home address:* 157 W. Clinton Ave. , Irvington-on-Hudson, N. Y. 10533. *Principal occupation:* Writer. *Community activities:* Westchester County Society for Prevention of Cruelty to Children (member of board, 1959-); Irvington Public Library (member of board, 1962-). *Published works:* Secret Castle (Alfred A. Knopf, 1961); *Theodosia* (Holt, Rinehart & Winston, 1963); *Mr. Lincoln's Wife* (Holt, Rinehart & Winston, 1964); *Squanto*, with Stewart Graff (Garrard Publishing Co., 1965); other titles -- a total of twenty-four books.

GRAFF, STEWART 1908- (trade association executive)

Born May 8, 1908, Worthington, Penna. *Education:* Harvard College, B. A., 1930; Harvard Law School, LL. B., 1936. *Principal occupation:* Trade association executive. *Home address:* 157 W. Clinton Ave., Irvington-on-Hudson, N. Y. 10533. *Affiliations:* Associate attorney, Brown, Cross & Hamilton, 1936-42, 1946-48; executive secretary, Synthetic Organic Chemical Manufacturers Association, 1948-. *Military service:* U. S. Army Air Force, 1942-46. *Community activities:* Parent-Teachers Association (chairman, scholarship committee); Citizens Committee to Evaluate School Needs. *Memberships:* New York County Lawyers Association, 1937-. *Interests:* "Continuing interest in historical studies, biography; travels in U. S., Europe, and South America." *Published works: John Paul Jones* (Garrard Publishing Co., 1961); *George Washington* (Garrard Publishing Co., 1964); *Squanto,* with Polly Anne Graff (Garrard Publishing Co., 1965); *Helen Keller,* with Polly Anne Graff (Garrard Publishing Co., 1965).

GRANT, BRUCE 1893- (writer)

Born April 17, 1893, Wichita Falls, Texas. *Education:* Kentucky Military Institute Training School; University of Kentucky. *Principal occupation:* Writer. *Affiliations:* Editor, Chicago *Times,* Louisville *Courier-Journal, The Standard* (Buenos Aires); World War II correspondent. *Military service:* U. S. Army, World War I. *Memberships:* National Professional Swimmers Association (co-founder). *Published works: Tong War! A History of the Chinese Tongs* (Nicholas Brown, 1930); *Isaac Hill, Captain of Old Ironsides* (Pellegrini-Cudahy, 1947); *Eagle of the Sea* (Rand McNally, 1948); *Leather Braiding* (Cornell Maritime Press, 1950); *Cowboy Encyclopedia* (Rand McNally, 1951); *Boy Scout Encyclopedia* (Rand McNally, 1952); *How to Make Cowboy Horse Gear* (Cornell Maritime Press, 1953); *War Path* (World, 1954); *Fight for a City* (Rand McNally, 1955); *Six Gun* (World, 1955); *Longhorn* (World, 1956); *Leopard Horse Canyon* (World, 1957); *Pancho* (World, 1958); *American Indians: Yesterday and Today* (Dutton, 1960); *American Forts: Yesterday and Today* (Dutton, 1965).

GRAY, CAROLINE 1911- (museum curator)

Born August 22, 1911, Little Genesee, N.Y. *Education:* Milton College, B. A. *Home address:* 233 Janesville St., Milton, Wis. 53563. *Affiliation:* Curator, Milton House Museum, Milton, Wis. *Community activities:* Seventh Day Baptist Women's Society.

GREGG, ELINOR D. 1886- (nurse)

Born May 31, 1886, Colorado Springs, Colo. *Education:* Colorado College; Simmons College; Waltham Training School for Nurses, Certificate, 1909. *Principal occupation:* Nurse. *Home address:* P. O. Box 1924, Santa Fe, N. M. *Affiliations:* Superintendent, Boston Infants Hospital, 1915-17; assistant supervisor of nurses, Cleveland City Hospital, 1917. *Military service:* U. S. Army Nurse Corps, Base Hospital #5, 1917-19. *Interests:* "Institutional, public health, visiting and industrial nursing. Travels to England, France, Norway and Sweden -- usually as a nurse or companion." *Published works: The Indian and the Nurse* (University of Oklahoma Press, 1965).

GRIDLEY, MARION E. 1906- (writer, publicist)

Born November 16, 1906, White Plains, N. Y. *Education:* Northwestern University. *Principal occupation:* Writer and publicist. *Home address:* 1263 W. Pratt Blvd., Chicago, Ill. 60626. *Affiliations:* Director of public relations or publicity, Children's Memorial Hospital, Illinois Heart Association; Chicago Medical School, Francis W. Parker School; and others. *Other professional posts:* Lecturer. *Memberships:* National Federation of Press Women; Illinois Hospital Association; Chicago Publicity Club; Midland Authors; Children's Reading Round Table; Indian Council Fire (executive secretary). *Awards:* American Hospital Association; Illinois Hospital Association; National Federation of Press Women; Illinois Women's Press Association; Chicago Publicity Club; Woman of the Year, Illinois Women's Press Association, 1965. *Published works: Indians of Today* (Indian Council Fire); *Indians of Yesterday* (M. A. Donohue); *Indian Legends of American Scenes* (M.A. Donohue); *Hiawatha* (Rand McNally); *Pocahontas* (Rand McNally);

Jamie's Dog (Encyclopedia Britannica); *Indian Statues of America* (in press).

GRIFFITH, GLADYS GIBSON   1925-
   (artist)

Born March 15, 1925, Piqua, Ohio. *Education:* High school. *Home address:* 263 E. Main St., Piqua, Ohio 45356. *Memberships:* Miami County Archaeological Society; Ohio State Archaeological Society; Ohio Historical Society. *Awards:* Grand Prize, Art Contest, WHIO-TV, 1951; First Award, Professional Piqua Hobby Show, 1954; art scholarship.

GRISSOM, WILLIAM W.   1920-
   (B. I. A. agency superintendent)

Born January 24, 1920, Noble, Okla. *Education:* Oklahoma A & M, B. S. , 1949. *Principal occupation:* B. I. A. agency superintendent. *Home address:* P. O. Box 343, Browning, Mont. *Affiliations:* Superintendent, Blackfeet Agency, B. I. A. ; former soil conservationist and land operations officer for B. I. A. agencies. *Military service:* U. S. Coast Guard, 1941-46. *Community activities:* Junior Chamber of Commerce; Lions Club; American Legion.

GUALTIERI, JOSEPH P.   1916-
   (museum director, art instructor)

Born December 25, 1916, Royalton, Ill. *Education:* Chicago Art Institute, Diploma, 1939. *Principal occupation:* Museum director. *Affiliations:* Director, Slater Memorial Museum. *Memberships:* Essex Art Association; Mystic Art Association; Connecticut Watercolor Society. *Awards, honors:* Logan Medal, Chicago Art Institute; two Purchase Awards, Pennsylvania Academy; Second Prize, Springfield Fair; three First Prizes, Connecticut Watercolor Society. *Interests:* Art, architecture.

GUBSER, NICHOLAS J.   1938-
   (anthropologist)

Born September 14, 1938, Tulsa, Okla. *Education:* Yale College, B. A., 1962; Oxford University, B. Lit. , 1964. *Principal occupation:* Student. *Home address:* 3941

S. Florence Pl. , Tulsa, Okla. *Memberships:* Yale Anthropology Club (president, 1961-62); Sigma Xi, 1962-. *Awards, honors:* Phi Beta Kappa; grants, Arctic Institute of North America, for field research among the Nunamiut Eskimos; dean's prize for senior thesis, 1962; Foreign Area Training Fellowship; Rhodes Scholar, Oxford University, 1962-64. *Interests:* Ethnographic investigation of Nunamiut Eskimos at Anaktuvak Pass, Alaska, 1960-61; archaeological field assistant, University of New Mexico, in central Brooks range, Alaska; travel in Europe, Pakistan, India, Japan, Mexico, Ethiopia, and Middle East. *Published works: The Nunamiut Eskimos: Hunters of Caribou* (Yale University Press, 1965).

GUNTHER, ERNA   1896-
   (professor, museum director)

Born November 9, 1896, Brooklyn, N. Y. *Education:* Barnard College, B. A. , 1919; Columbia University, M. A. , 1920, Ph. D. , 1925. *Principal occupation:* Professor. *Address:* c/o Department of Anthropology, University of Alaska, College, Alaska 99735. *Affiliations:* Professor, University of Washington, 1929-66; professor of anthropology, University of Alaska. *Other professional posts:* Director, Washington State Museum, 1929-62. *Memberships:* American Anthropological Association; American Folklore Society; American Ethnological Society. *Interests:* Primitive art; ethnohistory.

GUTHE, ALFRED K.   1920-   (museum director)

Born April 30, 1920, Detroit, Mich. *Education:* University of North Carolina, 1937-39; University of Michigan, B. A. , 1941; University of Chicago, M. A. , 1948; University of Michigan, Ph. D. , 1956. *Principal occupation:* Museum director. *Home address:* 8008 Chesterfield Dr., Knoxville, Tenn. *Affiliations:* Director and head, Department of Anthropology, McClung Museum. *Military service:* U. S. Naval Reserve, 1942-45. *Community activities:* Kiwanis International; Fort Loudoun Association (board of directors). *Memberships:* Sigma Xi; American Anthropological Association; Society for American Archaeology.

Interests: Eastern United States archaeology; museum administration. *Biographical sources: Who's Who in America; American Men of Science. Published works: The Late Prehistoric Occupation in Southwestern New York: An Interpretive Analysis* (Rochester Museum of Arts and Sciences, 1958).

H

HAGAN, WILLIAM T.   1918-
(professor)

Born December 19, 1918, Huntington, W.Va. *Education:* Marshall University, B.A., 1941; University of Wisconsin, Ph.D., 1950. *Principal occupation:* Professor of history. *Affiliations:* Professor of history, North Texas State University, 1950-65; professor of history, chairman of department, State University College, Fredonia, N.Y., 1965-. *Military service:* U. S. Army, 1942-45. *Memberships:* American Historical Association; American Indian Ethnohistoric Conference; Organization of American Historians. *Published works: The Sac and Fox Indians* (University of Oklahoma Press, 1958); *American Indians* (University of Chicago Press, 1961).

HAIG-BROWN, RODERICK L.   1908-
(writer)

Born February 21, 1908, Lancing, Sussex, England. *Education:* Charterhouse School, 1921-25. *Principal occupation:* Writer. *Home address:* R.R. 2, Campbell River, British Columbia, Canada. *Other professional posts:* Provincial magistrate; judge, Family and Childrens Court of British Columbia. *Military service:* Canadian Army, World War II. *Memberships:* Authors' Guild; Canadian Authors' Association; Society of Authors. *Awards, honors:* Canadian Library Association Medal, 1947, 1963; Governor General's Citation, 1948; hon. LL.D., University of British Columbia, 1952; Crandall Conservation Trophy, 1955; University of Alberta National Award in Letters, 1956. *Published works: Silver* (Black); *Pool and Rapid* (Collins); *Panther* (Collins); *Western Angler* (Collins); *Return to the River* (Collins); *Timber* (Collins); *Starbuck Valley Winter* (Collins); *River Never Sleeps* (Collins); *Saltwater Summer*

(Collins); *Measure of the Year* (Collins); *On the Highest Hill* (Collins); *Mounted Police Patrol* (Collins); *Fisherman's Spring* (Collins); *Fisherman's Winter* (Collins); *Captain of the Discovery* (Macmillan); *Fisherman's Summer* (Collins); *The Farthest Shores* (Longman); *The Living Land* (Macmillan); *Fur and Gold* (Longman); *The Whale People* (Collins); *A Primer of Fly Fishing* (Collins); *Fisherman's Fall* (Collins).

HAINES, FRANCIS   1899-   (professor)

Born June 3, 1899, Buckhannon, W. Va. *Education:* Montana State College, B.A., 1923; University of Montana, M.A., 1932; University of California, Ph.D., 1938. *Home address:* 415 S. Broad St., Monmouth, Ore. 97361. *Affiliations:* Professor of history, Oregon College of Education, 1951-64. *Military service:* U.S. Army, 1917-19 (Purple Heart). *Community activities:* Planning Commission, Monmouth, Ore. *Awards, honors:* Best Western Documentary Film, *Appaloosa*, 1962, National Cowboy Hall of Fame and Western Heritage Center, Oklahoma City. *Interests:* Nez Perce Indians; Northwestern Indians; Western horses, especially Appaloosa. *Published works: Red Eagles of the Northwest* (Scholastic Press, 1939); *Story of Idaho* (Syms-York, 1942); *Nez Perces* (University of Oklahoma Press, 1955); *Appaloosa: The Spotted Horse in Art and History* (University of Texas Press, 1963); *Red Eagle and the Absaroka* (Caxton, 1960).

HALL, CLIFFORD GLENN   1897-
(funeral director, farmer)

Born December 15, 1897, Watertown, N.Y. *Education:* Central City Business Institute; Simmons School of Mortuary Science. *Principal occupation:* Funeral director; owner, Red Wing Valley Farms. *Home address:* 6031 Cherry Valley Rd., LaFayette, N.Y. 13084. *Affiliations:* Agent, Onondaga Tribe of Indians, Onondaga Reservation, under Department of Social Welfare, State of New York. *Community activities:* LaFayette Community Council (former director); Boy Scouts; Red Cross; Town of LaFayette (former supervisor -- fourteen years); New York State and Onondaga County Funeral Directors' Associations (former president and director); LaFayette Rural Cemetary

Association (president, 1954-); New York State Pinto Horse Association (director). *Memberships:* New York State Hereford Association; New York State Beef Cattle Association; Scottish Rite; national, state and local Grange. *Interests:* Health (preventive infection and disease measures; nutrition); breeding and training of saddle horses and Hereford cattle; study and service to low-income groups; travel in western United States, including visits to Indian reservations; South American Indians.

HALLOWELL, A. IRVING 1892-
(professor of anthropology)

Born December 28, 1892, Philadelphia, Penna. *Education:* University of Pennsylvania, B. S., 1914, M. A., 1920, Ph. D., 1924. *Principal occupation:* Professor of anthropology. *Home address:* 401 Woodland Ave., Wayne, Penna. *Affiliations:* Professor of anthropology, University of Pennsylvania, 1923-63. *Memberships:* American Anthropological Association; American Folklore Society (president); Society for Projective Techniques (president); National Academy of Sciences. *Awards, honors:* Guggenheim Fellowship, 1940; Wenner-Gren Foundation, Viking Medal and Award, 1955. *Interests:* Northern Ojibwa Indians of Canada and other Algonkian peoples; kinship and social organization; folklore; culture; personality; history of anthropology; psychological dimensions of human evolution. *Published works: Bear Ceremonialsim in the Northern Hemisphere* (American Anthropologist, 1926); *The Role of Conjuring in Saulteaux Society* (University of Pennsylvania, 1942); *Culture and Experience* (University of Pennsylvania, 1955).

HAMMACK, LAURENS CARY 1936-
(archaeologist)

Born July 11, 1936, Chicago, Ill. *Education:* University of New Mexico, B. A., 1959, M. A., 1964. *Principal occupation:* Archaeologist. *Home address:* 924 Canyon Rd., Santa Fe, N. M. *Affiliation:* Curator, Research Division, Museum of New Mexico, Santa Fe, N. M., 1964-. *Military service:* U. S. Army, 1959-61. *Memberships:* Society for American Archaeology, 1964-. *Interests:* Southwest and northern Mexico archaeology and ethnology; collecting of

antique guns and Southwest Indian materials; archaeological excavations throughout New Mexico. *Published works: Archaeology of the Ute Dam and Reservoir* (Museum of New Mexico, 1965); article in *New Mexico Magazine.*

HANNUM, ALBERTA PIERSON 1906-
(writer)

Born August 3, 1906, Condit, Ohio. *Education:* Ohio State University, B. A., 1927; graduate work in English, Columbia University, 1928. *Principal occupation:* Writer. *Home address:* Waynesburg Pike, Moundsville, W. Va. *Published works: Thursday April* (Harper, 1931); *The Hills Step Lightly* (Morrow, 1934); *The Gods and One* (Duell, Sloan and Pearce, 1941); *The Mountain People* (Vanguard Press, 1943); *Spin a Silver Dollar* (Viking Press, 1945; Michael Joseph, 1946); *Roseanna McCoy* (Henry Holt, 1948; translated into seven languages; filmed by Samuel Goldwyn, 1949); *Paint the Wind* (Viking Press, 1958; Michael Joseph, 1959; Russian translation, 1960).

HANSEN, JOAN LOUISE (Cherokee) 1945- (reporter, photographer)

Born February 2, 1945, New Orleans, La. *Education:* Bacone College. *Principal occupation:* Reporter, photographer. *Home address:* 2310 E. Broadway, Muskogee, Okla. *Affiliations:* Reporter, photographer, *Muskogee Daily Phoenix* and *Times Democrat.* *Awards:* Paintings shown at Philbrook Indian Annual, Tulsa, Okla.; paintings shown at Department of the Interior, Washington, D. C.; numerous awards at local fair. *Interests:* Reading of Plains Indian traditions and legends; automotive machinery; swimming; art; riding and training horses.

HANSON, CHARLES E., Jr. 1917-
(engineer)

Born April 4, 1917, Holdrege, Neb. *Education:* Nebraska State Teachers College, 1934-35; University of Colorado, 1948-50. *Principal occupation:* Administrative engineer (twenty-five years' professional experience). *Home address:* 6108 42nd Ave., Hyattsville, Md. 20781. *Affiliations:* Director, Museum of the Fur Trade, Chadron,

Neb. *Memberships:* Potomac Corral, The Westerners, 1960-; Company of Military Historians, 1961-; Potomac Arms Collectors, 1959-; Maryland Arms Collectors, 1959-; National Muzzle-Loading Rifle Association, 1945-; American Society of Arms Collectors. *Awards, honors:* Alexander Culbertson Memorial Commission (honorary chairman); Company of Military Historians (Fellow); First Prize for article in *Gun Report* magazine, 1964. *Interests:* U. S. and foreign travel; antique arms; Indian crafts. *Published works: The Northwest Gun* (Nebraska State Historical Society, 1955); *The Plains Rifle* (Stackpole Company, 1960); contributor, *Encyclopedia of Firearms* (Dutton and Co., 1964); contributor to *Nebraska History, Missouri Archaeologist, American Rifleman; Muzzle Blasts, Gun Digest, Canadian Journal of Arms Collecting, Museum of the Fur Trade Quarterly.*

HARDY, H. CLAUDE 1887-
  (curator, professor, lecturer)

Born February 27, 1887, Glenwood, Penna. *Education:* Wesleyan University, B. A., 1911; University of Rochester, M. A., 1921; Syracuse University, M.A., 1923; New York University, Ph. D., 1931. *Principal occupation:* Museum curator, professor of sociology. *Home address:* 89 Elm St., Oneonta, N. Y. 13820. *Affiliations:* Curator, Yager Museum; professor of sociology, Hartwick College. *Military service:* World War II. *Memberships:* New York State Teachers Association (president, 1942-44); White Plains Salvation Army (former chairman, advisory board); New York Schoolmaster's Club (president, 1946); White Plains Rotary Club (president, 1934-35); White Plains Hospital (board of governors); White Plains Y.M.C.A. (board of directors); Fifteenth Yearbook Commission, Department of Superintendence, National Education Association, 1937; Save the Children Federation (executive vice president, 1948-49); Otsego County Committee on Historic Observances (chairman, 1959). *Published works: Evolution of Office of Superintendent of Schools* (New York University doctoral dissertation, 1931); *His Honor, the Mayor* (The Norwich Publishing Co., 1953); *Hardy and Hardie, Past and Present* (Syracuse Typesetting Co., 1935); various articles and pamphlets, including *The History of Willard Yager* (Walton Reporter).

HARLOW, FRANCIS H. 1928-
  (physicist)

Born January 22, 1928, Seattle, Wash. *Education:* University of Washington, B. S., 1949; Ph. D., 1953. *Principal occupation:* Theoretical physicist. *Home address:* 1407 11th St., Los Alamos, N. M. 87544. *Affiliations:* Group leader, Los Alamos Scientific Laboratory, 1953-; research associate, Museum of New Mexico, 1965-. *Military service:* U. S. Army, 1946-47. *Memberships:* Indian Arts Fund; School of American Research (trustee). *Interests:* Theoretical fluid dynamics and numerical analysis; Pueblo Indian pottery, history, technology, and artistry. *Published works: Contemporary Pueblo Indian Pottery* (Museum of New Mexico, 1965) *Northern Pueblo Matte Paint Pottery of the Historic Period* (Museum of New Mexico, 1966); various publications related to physics.

HARRINGTON, MARK RAYMOND 1882-
  (archaeologist, ethnologist, museum curator)

Born July 6, 1882, Ann Arbor, Mich. *Education:* University of Michigan; Columbia University, B. S., 1907, M. A., 1908. *Principal occupation:* Archaeologist, ethnologist, museum curator. *Home address:* 11039 Memory Park Ave., Mission Hills, Calif. 91340. *Affiliations:* American Museum of Natural History, New York City, 1899-1903; Museum of the American Indian, Heye Foundation, New York City, 1915-18, 1919-28; University of Pennsylvania Museum, 1911-14; Southwest Museum, 1928-64. *Other professional posts:* Advisor on restoration of La Purisima and San Fernando Missions, California. *Military service:* Field artillery, Officer Training Corps, 1918-19; Reserve, ten years. *Memberships:* Society for American Archaeology; American Association for the Advancement of Science; National Speleological Society; San Fernando Valley Historical Society; Santa Inez Historical Society. *Awards, honors:* Honorary doctorate, Occidental College, Los Angeles, 1956. *Interests:* Ethnographic field work among forty-two American Indian tribes; archaeological work in New Jersey, New York, Tennessee, Texas, Arkansas, Nevada, California, Oklahoma. *Published works: Certain Caddo Sites in Arkansas* (Museum of the American Indian, 1920); *Religion and Ceremonies of the Lenape* (Museum of the American Indian, 1921); *Cherokee and Earlier Remains on Upper Tennessee River* (Museum of the American Indian, 1922); *Lovelock Cave,* with L. L. Loud (University of California Press, 1929); *Gypsum Cave, Nevada* (Southwest Museum, 1933); *Dickon Among the Lenape Indians* (John C. Winston Co., 1938; reprinted in England as *Dickon Among the Indians,* 1949); *An Ancient Site at Borax Lake, California* (Southwest Museum, 1948); *How to Build a California Adobe* (Ward Ritchie Press, 1948); *Ancient Life Among the Southern California Indians* (Southwest Museum, 1955); *A Pinto Site at Little Lake* (Southwest Museum, 1957); *The Ozark Bluff-Dwellers* (Museum of the American Indian, 1960); *Tule Springs, Nevada* with Ruth D. Simpson (Southwest Museum, 1961); *The Indians of New Jersey* (reprint of *Dickon Among the Lenape Indians,* Rutgers University Press, 1963); *The Iroquois Trail* (Rutgers University Press, 1965).

HARRINGTON, VIRGIL N.   (Choctaw)
  1919-   (B. I. A. area director)

Born 1919, Kiowa, Okla. *Education:* Oklahoma A & M College, B. A. (Agriculture), 1942. *Principal occupation:* B. I. A. area director. *Address:* 221 S. 12th, Muskogee, Okla. 74401. *Affiliations:* Civilian supervisor, U. S. Navy Department, 1943-48; soil conservationist, Pawnee Indian Agency, 1948-55; land operations officer, Consolidated Ute Agency, 1955-58; superintendent; Seminole Indian Agency, 1958-63; area director, Muskogee Area Office, 1963-. *Military service:* U. S. Army Signal Corps, 1942-43. *Community activities:* Lions Club (past president); Rotary Club (past president); American Legion (past commander of two posts); Cub Scouts (past cub master); Elks Club; Masons; Oklahoma State Fair (board of directors); Five Civilized Tribes (board of directors, child welfare advisory board). *Interests:* "Improvement and development of human resources from educational, sociological and economic viewpoints."

HARRIS, LA DONNA (Mrs. Fred R.
  Harris) (Comanche) 1931-
  (organization official, housewife)

Born February 15, 1931, Temple, Okla. *Education:* High school. *Principal occupation:* Organization official, housewife.

Home address: 1104 Waverly Way, McLean, Va. 22102. *Community activities:* Oklahomans for Indian Opportunity, Inc. (president); Oklahoma Mental Health Association (board member); Oklahoma Health and Welfare Association (board member). *Awards, honors:* Award, "Outstanding American Citizen of 1965," Anadarko (Okla.) American Indian Exposition and the Tulsa Indian Council, 1965. *Interests:* "Traveled through Argentina, Brazil, Chile and Peru in November, 1965, with (my) husband, Senator Harris, and Senator and Mrs. Birch Bayh of Indiana."

HART, ROBERT G.   1921-   (B. I. A.
  agency official)

Born December 28, 1921, San Francisco, Calif. *Principal occupation:* B. I. A. agency official. *Home address:* 916 25th St., N.W., Washington, D. C. *Affiliations:* General manager, Indian Arts and Crafts Board, Bureau of Indian Affairs, U. S. Department of the Interior. *Military service:* U. S. Army, 1943-45. *Interests:* Folk art. *Published works: How to Sell Your Handicrafts* (David McKay, 1953); *Guide to Alaska* (David McKay, 1959); editor, *Egyptian Sculpture of the Late Period* (Brooklyn Museum Press, 1959); editor, *Masters of Contemporary American Crafts* (Brooklyn Museum Press, 1960); editor, *Japanese Ceramics* (Brooklyn Museum Press, 1960); editor, *The Nude in American Painting* (Brooklyn Museum Press, 1961).

HART, VIRGINIA S.   (B. I. A. official)

Born Worcester, Mass. *Education:* Clark University, B. A., 1945; American University, M. A., 1959. *Principal occupation:* B. I. A. official. *Home address:* 4107 27th Rd., N., Arlington, Va. 22207. *Business affiliations:* Feature writer, Voice of America; information officer, U. S. Office of Education; editor, U. S. Department of State; director of public information, Bureau of Indian Affairs. *Other professional posts:* Free-lance writing; lecturing, American University; radio and television productions with Ed Hart Associates; public relations director, Korean Affairs Institute. *Memberships:* American Newspaper Women's Club. *Travel:* North Africa, Europe (survey of employment conditions in western Europe).

HARTUNG, RICHARD PENN (museum director)

Born Columbus, Ohio. *Education:* University of Chicago, B.A., 1958. *Principal occupation:* Museum director. *Home address:* 255 S. Jackson, Janesville, Wis. 53545. *Affiliations:* Director, Lincoln-Tallman Museum, Rock County Historical Society, Janesville, Wis., 1964-. *Memberships:* National Trust for Historic Preservation; Society of Architectural Historians; American Historical Association; local and state historical societies. *Interests:* Architectural history; local history. *Published works: Joseph Russell Jones* (1965).

HARVEY, LOIS F. 1905- (school principal)

Born July 4, 1905, Newark, N.J. *Education:* Rutgers University, B.S., 1940; University of California, Berkeley, M.A., 1952. *Principal occupation:* Principal, San Diego City Schools. *Home address:* 1430 E. Lexington Ave., El Cajon, Calif. 92021. *Other professional posts:* Teacher; director of education. *Memberships:* National Education Association; National Council of Teachers of Mathematics; National Council of Teachers of Social Studies; Sierra Club; state and local organizations. *Interests:* Travel in United States, Mexico, Central America. *Published works: Cotton Growing* (Melmont, 1958); *Toyanuki's Rabbit* (Melmont, 1965).

HASSRICK, ROYAL H. 1917- (anthropologist)

Born July 10, 1917, Ocean City, N.J. *Education:* Dartmouth College, B.A., 1935. *Principal occupation:* Anthropologist. *Home address:* Lone Star Ranch, Elizabeth, Colo. *Affiliations:* Assistant director, Denver Art Museum. *Military service:* U.S. Army, 1944. *Biographical source: Who's Who in the West. Published works: The Sioux* (University of Oklahoma Press, 1964); and others.

HATHORN, JOHN R. 1913- (Indian affairs agency officer)

Born June 30, 1913, Ballston Spa, N.Y. *Education:* Duke University, B.A., 1936.

Principal occupation: Indian affairs agency officer. *Home address:* 16 Columbia Ave., Ballston Spa, N.Y. *Affiliations:* Administrative assistant, Saratoga County Department of Welfare, 1936-59; director of Indian services, New York State Interdepartmental Committee on Indian Affairs, 1959-. *Military service:* U.S. Marine Corps Reserve, 1936-42. *Community activities:* Lions Club; Ballston Golf Club.

HATT, ROBERT T. 1902- (museum director, zoologist)

Born July 17, 1902, Lafayette, Ind. *Education:* University of Michigan, B.Sc., 1923; Columbia University, Ph.D., 1932. *Principal occupation:* Museum director, zoologist. *Home address:* Bloomfield Hills, Mich. 48013. *Affiliations:* Instructor, New York University, 1923-28; assistant curator, American Museum of Natural History, 1928-35; director, Cranbrook Institute of Science, Bloomington Hills, Mich., 1935-. *Awards, honors:* Founders Medal, The Cranbrook Foundation. *Interests:* Travel in North America, Africa, Middle East. *Published works: Island Life in Lake Michigan* (1948); *Mammals of Iraq* (1959); contributor to various professional journals.

HAURY, EMIL W. 1904- (professor)

Born May 2, 1904, Newton, Kan. *Education:* Bethel College, 1923-25; University of Arizona, B.A., 1927, M.A., 1928; Harvard University, Ph.D., 1934. *Principal occupation:* Professor. *Home address:* 2749 E. 4th St., Tucson, Ariz. 85717. *Affiliations:* Professor and head, Department of Anthropology, University of Arizona, 1937-64; director, Arizona State Museum, 1938-64; professor of anthropology, University of Arizona, 1964-; advisor, Arizona State Museum, 1964-. *Other professional posts:* Instructor, University of Arizona, 1928-29; research assistant in dendrochronology, University of Arizona, 1929-30; assistant director, Gila Pueblo, Globe, Ariz., 1930-37. *Community activities:* Advisory Board on National Parks, Historic Sites, Buildings and Monuments. *Memberships:* American Academy of Arts and Sciences; National Speleological Society (honorary life member); Society for American Archaeology (vice president,

1941-42; president, 1943-44); American Anthropological Association (president, 1956); National Academy of Sciences (chairman, Division of Anthropology and Psychology, National Research Council, 1960-62; chairman, Anthropology Section, 1960-63); Tree Ring Society; American Association for the Advancement of Science; Phi Kappa Phi; Sigma Xi. *Awards, honors:* Guggenheim Fellow, 1949-50; Viking Fund Medalist for Anthropology, 1950; University of Arizona Alumni Achievement Award, 1957; University of Arizona Faculty Achievement Award, 1962; LL. D. , University of New Mexico, 1959. *Interests:* "Archaeological theory and method; early man in western America; the later Southwestern prehistoric societies. " *Travels and expeditions:* National Geographic Society Archaeological Expedition, Mexico City, Mexico, 1925; archaeological excavation, Bogota, Colombia, 1949-50; International Congress of Americanists, Copenhagen, Denmark, 1956; Symposium at Burg Wartenstein near Gloggnitz, Austria, and International Congress of Americanists, Vienna, Austria, 1960; International Congress of Anthropological and Ethnological Sciences, Paris, France, 1960; has also visited as a tourist cities in Germany, Norway, France, England, Peru, Ecuador. *Published works: The Stratigraphy and Archaeology of Ventana Cave, Arizona* (University of Arizona Press, 1950; University of New Mexico Press); several articles in professional journals.

HAYES, CHARLES F. , III   1932-
  (anthropologist)

Born March 6, 1932, Boston, Mass. *Education:* Harvard University, B. A. , 1954; University of Colorado, M. A. , 1958. *Principal occupation:* Anthropologist. *Home address:* 333 Barrington St. , Rochester, N. Y. 14607. *Affiliations:* Laboratory assistant, Peabody Museum, Harvard. University, 1953-54; junior anthropologist, Rochester Museum of Arts and Sciences, 1959-61; associate curator of anthropology, Rochester Museum of Arts and Sciences, 1961-. *Military service:* U. S. Air Force, 1954-56; currently in U. S. Air Force Reserve. *Memberships:* New York State Archaeological Association (vice president, 1963-65; secretary); Lewis Henry Morgan Chapter, New York State Archaeological Association (president, 1964-; secretary);

American Anthropological Association; American Association of Museums; Society for American Archaeology; New York State Archaeological Association. *Interests:* Archaeology of northeast North America; general museology; participant in Glen Canyon Archaeological Survey, Utah, 1957, and University of Colorado Archaeological Field School, 1953. *Published works:* Articles on archaeology and museology in *Museum Service* and the *Pennsylvania Archaeologist; Orringh Stone Tavern and Three Seneca Sites of the Late Historic Period* (*Research Records,* No. 12, Rochester Museum of Arts and Sciences, 1965).

HAYMAN, BERTRAM   (Modoc)   1899-
  (hydraulic engineer)

Born May 10, 1899, Ottawa County, Okla. *Education:* Oklahoma A and M College, B. S. , 1928. *Principal occupation:* Hydraulic engineer. *Home address:* 832 N. Belview, Springfield, Mo. *Affiliations:* Hydraulic engineer, Tulsa Fire Department, Tulsa, Okla. , 1928-50; fire prevention engineer, U. S. Corps of Engineers, Fort Crowder, Mo. , 1951-1960. *Military service:* U. S. Marines, 1917-1919, (Purple Heart, Croix de Guerre, Battalion Decoration). *Community activities:* Junior Chamber of Commerce, Tulsa, Okla. ; Governors State Sugar Rationing Board of Oklahoma; representative from Oklahoma, President's first Fire Prevention Conference, 1948. *Memberships:* Alpha Lambda Chi, 1926-28; "O" Club, 1926-28; Scottish Rite Mason, 32nd Degree, 1934-; International Association of Fire Fighters, Washington, D. C. , 1941-1950 (Eleventh District vice president); First Methodist Church, Miami, Okla. *Interests:* Played professional baseball in minor leagues, 1921-28.

HEIDERSTADT, DOROTHY   1907-
  (writer, librarian)

Born October 8, 1907, Geneva, Neb. *Education:* Kansas City Junior College, A. A. , 1926; University of California, B. A. , 1936; Simmons College, B. S. (Library Science), 1937. *Principal occupation:* Writer, librarian. *Home address:* 3028 Shelby Rd. , Independence, Mo. 64052. *Affiliations:* Director of work with children, Bethlehem Public Library, 1937-42; branch librarian,

1943-65; children's and young adult librarian, Kansas City Public Library, 1965-. *Memberships:* Oklahoma Historical Society; American Library Association. *Awards, honors:* Phi Beta Kappa. *Interests:* Travel in Europe, Canada, Mexico, United States; photography. *Published works: A Book of Heroes* (Bobbs-Merrill, 1954); *Indian Friends and Foes* (David McKay, 1959); *To All Nations* (Nelson, 1959); *Knights and Champions* (Nelson, 1960); *A Bow for Turtle* (David McKay, 1961); *Ten Torch Bearers* (Nelson, 1961); *Frontier Leaders and Pioneers* (David McKay, 1962); *More Indian Friends and Foes* (David McKay, 1963); *Lois Says Aloha* (Nelson, 1963); *Marie Tanglehair* (David McKay, 1965).

HEILMAN, J.M., III 1944- (museum curator)

Born June 29, 1944, Charleston, W. Va. *Education:* Earlham College, B. S. , 1966. *Principal occupation:* Museum curator. *Home address:* 2828 Heritage St. , N. W. , Canton, Ohio 44718. *Affiliations:* Curator of archaeology, Joseph Moore Museum, Earlham College, Richmond, Ind. *Memberships:* Ohio Archaeological Society; Miami County Archaeological Society; Central States Archaeological Society. *Award:* Best Junior Collection in Miami County Archaeological Society. *Field trips:* Excavation of an Adena mound near Columbus, Ohio; early Hopewell mound.

HEIZER, ROBERT F. 1915- (professor of anthropology)

Born July 13, 1915, Denver, Colo. *Education:* University of California, Ph. D., 1940. *Principal occupation:* Professor of anthropology. *Home address:* 85 Menlo Place, Berkeley, Calif. 94707. *Memberships:* Society for American Archaeology; American Anthropological Association; Societe des Americanistes de Paris; Institute for Andean Research. *Interests:* Archaeology and ethnology of American Indians. *Published works: Francis Drake and the California Indians, 1579* (University of California Press, 1947); *A Manual of Archaeological Field Methods* (The National Press, 1949, 1950, 1953, and 1958, under title *A Guide to Archaeological Field Methods);* editor, *The California Indians*, with M. A. Whipple (University of California Press,

1951); *The Four Ages of Tsurai*, with John E. Mills (University of California Press, 1952); *The Archaeologist at Work* (Harper and Bros. , 1959); *Prehistoric Rock Art of Nevada and Eastern California*, with M. A. Baumhoff (University of California Press, 1962); *Man's Discovery of His Past* (Spectrum Books, Prentice-Hall, Inc., 1962); *An Introduction to Prehistoric Archaeology*, with F. Hole (Holt, Rinehart & Winston, Inc., 1965); numerous papers in professional journals.

HELINE, THEODORE 1883- (teacher, lecturer, writer)

Born August 14, 1883, Los Angeles, Calif. *Education:* Augustana College, B. A., 1909; Royal Academy of Dramatic Art, London, England, 1911-12. *Principal occupation:* Teacher, lecturer, writer. *Affiliations:* Executive director, New Age Press, Inc. Los Angeles and Santa Monica, Calif. *Published works:* Series of pamphlets, *Studies of This Changing World* (New Age Press); *The New Age Interpreter* (quarterly magazine); *The Spiritual Legacy of the American Indian* (New Age Press).

HENDERSON, WILLIAM JAMES 1908- (educator)

Born August 4, 1908, Keldron, S. D. *Education:* State Teachers College, Diploma, 1932; University of Montana, B. A. (Education), 1952, M. A. (Education), 1956. *Principal occupation:* Educator. *Home address:* Box 452, Wallowa, Ore. 97885. *Affiliations:* Elementary principal, Gardiner Public Schools, Mont. , 1949-51; acting principal, Superior Public Schools, Mont. , 1952-53; elementary principal, Crow Agency Public School, Mont., 1953-57; instructor in Latin and history, Chestertown High School, Md. , 1957-59; elementary principal, Sagle Public School, Idaho, 1959-60; elementary principal, Wallow Public School, Ore. ; principal-teacher, Bureau of Indian Affairs School, Stevens Village, Alaska, 1962-64; principal-teacher, Venetie Day School, Bureau of Indian Affairs, Venetie, Alaska, 1964-. *Military service:* U. S. Army, 1941-48 (American Defense Service Ribbon; American Theater of Operations Service Ribbon; Good Conduct Medal; Army of Occupation Medal; Victory Medal; Meritorious Service Badge). *Community activities:* Golden Heart Post, Veterans of Foreign Wars, Fairbanks, Alaska. *Memberships:* National Education Association (life member, 1954-); Gamma Zeta Chapter, Phi Delta Kappa, University of Montana (charter member, 1953-); Big Horn County Unit, Montana Education Association (vice president, 1955-56); Wallowa County Unit, Oregon Education Association (vice president, 1961-62). *Awards, honors:* Honorary member, Sioux Tribe (honorary name, *Little Crow*); attended N. D. E. A. Institute on Disadvantaged Youth, 1965. *Interests:* Classical languages and antiquities; anthropology of the American Indian; travel; coin collecting; photography. *Published works: The Cultural, Social and Religious Backgrounds of the Education of the Crow Indians, 1885-1955*, master's thesis (University of Montana, 1956).

HESSING, VALJEAN McCARTY
(Choctaw) 1934- (artist)

Born August 30, 1934, Tulsa, Okla. *Education:* Mary Hardin-Baylor College, 1952-54; Tulsa University, 1954-55. *Principal occupation:* Artist. *Home address:* Box 169 RC, Route 1, Owasso, Okla. 74055. *Awards, honors:* "Sixteen awards and a scholarship to Mary Hardin-Baylor College (received) while in elementary, junior and senior high schools; Honorary Paint and Palette Award, Mary Hardin-Baylor College, 1954; Third Place, Art Unlimited Exhibit, Tulsa Art Organization, 1964; Second and Third Place, Art Unlimited Exhibit, Tulsa Art Organization, 1964; Honorable Mention, Scottsdale (Ariz.) Arts and Crafts Center, 1966; Second Award in Special Category, Twenty-first Indian Annual, Philbrook Art Center, 1966." *Interests:* Mrs. Hessing writes, "(I am) interested in illustrating books; (am) interested in aiding children and adults in art, especially those who have little or no opportunity to have instruction of any kind. "

HESTER, JAMES J. 1931-
(anthropologist)

Born September 21, 1931, Anthony, Kan. *Education:* University of New Mexico, B.A., 1953; University of Arizona, Ph. D., 1961. *Principal occupation:* Anthropologist. *Home address:* 108 Southbrook, Bethesda, Md. 20014. *Affiliations:* Assistant curator, Museum of New Mexico, 1959-64; adjunct professor, Southern Methodist University, 1964-65; scientist administrator, National Institute of Health, 1965-. *Military service:* U. S. Air Force, 1954-56. *Memberships:* American Anthropological Association (Fellow); Society for American Archaeology; Sigma Xi; American Society of Naturalists; Current Anthropology. *Interests:* Archaeology of Navajo Indians; prehistory of Sahara desert; directed culture change; relationship of man to his environment. *Published works: An Archaeological Survey of the Navajo Reservoir District, Northwestern New Mexico*, with A. E. Dittert, Jr. and Frank W. Eddy (Museum of New Mexico, 1961); *Early Navajo Migrations and Acculturation in the Southwest* (Museum of New Mexico, 1962); *Studies at Navajo Period Sites in the Navajo Reservoir District*, with Joel Shiner (Museum of New Mexico, 1963).

HETZEL, THEODORE BRINTON 1906-
(professor)

Born September 28, 1906, Philadelphia, Penna. *Education:* Haverford College, B.S., 1928; University of Pennsylvania, B. S., 1929; Technische Hochschule, 1931-33; Pennsylvania State University, Ph. D., 1936. *Principal occupation:* Professor. *Home address:* 768 College Ave. , Haverford, Penna. 19041. *Affiliations:* Teacher and chairman of Engineering Department, Haverford College. *Community activities:* William Penn Charter School (overseer); Emlen Institution (board member); Indian Rights Association (board of directors, 1955-); National Indian Program, American Friends Service Committee, 1955-. *Memberships:* Franklin Institute, American Society of Mechanical Engineers; Society of Automotive Engineers (chairman, 1945-46); American Society for Engineer Education; American Association of University Professors. *Awards, honors:* Honorary adoption by the Senecas of New York

State. *Interests:* Engineering education; secondary education; contemporary affairs of American Indians; photography; lecturing on American Indians; travel to Indian communities, especially in Alaska; travel in Europe. *Published works:* Articles in *Indian Truth,* publication of the Indian Rights Association.

HEYERDAHL, THOR 1914- (writer, archaeologist)

Born October 6, 1914, Larvik, Norway. *Education:* College, 1933; graduate study, University of Oslo. *Principal occupation:* Writer, archaeologist. *Affiliation:* Board member, Kon-Tiki Museum, Oslo, Norway. *Military service:* Norwegian Air Force, Canada, 1941-45. *Expeditions:* Marquesas Islands, University of Oslo, 1937-38; Kon-Tiki expedition, 1947; Norwegian Archaeological Expedition to Galapagos Islands, 1952; Norwegian Archaeological Expedition to Easter Island and the East Pacific, 1955, 1956. *Awards, honors:* Commander of the Order of St. Olav; Officer of Distinguished Merits, Government of Peru; medalist, geographical and anthropological societies in Sweden, Scotland, France, and United States; Vega Medal, awarded by King Gustaf Adolf, 1962; Academy Award for best documentary feature. *Memberships:* Norwegian Academy of Sciences; New York Academy of Sciences (Fellow); Ph. D. honoris causa, University of Oslo; honorary member of geographical societies in Norway, Sweden, Belgium, Brazil and Peru. *Published works: Pa Jakt efter Paradiset* (Oslo, 1938); *The Kon-Tiki Expedition* (Oslo, 1948; translated into fifty-seven languages); *American Indians in the Pacific, the Theory Behind the Kon-Tiki Expedition* (Stockholm, London, Chicago, 1952); *Archaeological Evidence of Pre-Spanish Visits to the Galapagos Islands,* with A. Skjolsvold (Society for American Archaeology Memoir, No. 12, 1956); *Aku-Aku, The Secret of Easter Island* (Oslo, 1957; translated into twenty-seven languages); *Archaeology of Easter Island* with E.N. Ferdon, W. Mulloy, A. Skjolsvold, and C.S. Smith, Reports of the Norwegian Archaeological Expedition to Easter Island and the East Pacific (Monograph No. 24, School of American Research and Museum of New Mexico, 1961); numerous papers read and published.

HIBBEN, FRANK C. 1910- (professor)

Born December 5, 1910, Lakewood, Ohio. *Education:* Princeton University, B.A., 1933; University of New Mexico, M.S., 1935; Harvard University, Ph.D., 1940. *Home address:* 3005 Campus Blvd., N.E., Albuquerque, N.M. *Principal occupation:* Professor of anthropology, director, Museum of Anthropology, University of New Mexico. *Military service:* U.S. Army Air Force, 1943; U.S. Navy, 1943-46; U.S. Naval Reserve. *Community activities:* Albuquerque Park Board (chairman); New Mexico Game Commission (chairman). *Memberships:* American Anthropological Association (Fellow); Society for American Archaeology; American Association for the Advancement of Science. *Interests:* Archaeology, hunting. *Published works: The Lost Americans* (Thomas Y. Crowell); *Prehistoric Man in Europe* (University of Oklahoma Press); *Digging Up America* (Hill and Wang).

HILL, ARLEIGH (Seneca) 1909- (associate in Indian arts and crafts)

Born June 5, 1909, Grand River Reservation, Ont., Can. *Education:* Rochester Museum of Arts and Sciences. *Principal occupation:* Associate in Indian arts and crafts. *Home address:* 463 Mt. Read Blvd., Rochester, N.Y. 14606. *Affiliations:* Associate, Education Division, Rochester Museum of Arts and Sciences, 1934-44; associate in Indian arts and crafts, Rochester Museum of Arts and Sciences, 1944-; consultant on Indian programs for radio and television. *Community activities:* National Youth Administration (Indian camp counselor); Civilian Defense (educational instructor); Neighborhood Indian Society of Rochester (president); Indian Day Programs (chairman). *Memberships:* Imperial Order of Red Men, 1934-63; Stadium Club of Rochester, 1960-. *Awards, honors:* State Championship in Lacrosse, 1936-37, 1938; Lacrosse Silver Trophy, 1936, 1937, 1938; Citation, Police Athletic League of Rochester, 1956; Civil Defense Citation, 1945; Citation of Merit, Rochester Museum of Arts and Sciences, 1959; *John-sqwah-geh,* honorary name bestowed by Turtle Clan of the Seneca Indians, 1951. *Interests:* Local and national Indian affairs; research and writing on the American Indian. *Published works:* Articles for various sports magazines and for the Rochester Museum of Arts and Sciences *Bulletin.*

HILL, JOAN (Cherokee, Creek) 1930-
   (artist)

Born December 19, 1930, Muskogee, Okla. *Education:* Muskogee Junior College, A. A., 1950; Northeastern State College, B. A. (Education), 1952. *Principal occupation:* Artist. *Home address:* Route 3, Box 151, Harris Rd., Muskogee, Okla. 74401. *Affiliations:* Art instructor, Tulsa Public Schools, 1952-56. *Community activities:* Sunday school teacher, Harris Sunday School and Church, 1946-48 (member, 1930-50); First Baptist Church, 1948-66; National Democratic Party; Tulsa County Democratic Indian Club, 1955-56; American Association of University Women consultant for art careers, Career Day, Muskogee Central High School, 1962-63; Young Women's Christian Association, 1957, 1965-; Muskogee Annual Art Show (board member, planning and organization, 1961-63); publicity director, 1st and 2nd Annual Muskogee Art Show, 1961, 1962; co-chairman, 3rd Annual Muskogee Art Show, 1963; teacher, adult education night classes. *Memberships:* National Education Association; Oklahoma Education Association; Tulsa Classroom Teachers Association; National Congress, Parent-Teachers Association; Tulsa Secondary Art Teachers (treasurer, 1954-55); Muskogee Art Guild (telephone chairman, 1958-60; art director, 1960-62; publicity director, 1962-64); Phi Theta Kappa, 1950-. *Awards, honors:* Forty-one awards, 1959-66 (twenty-four of these from national competitions); seven awards -- guild critiques, art authorities, 1957-63; awards from ten Oklahoma state fairs (Tulsa and Muskogee); eighty-five prizes and three grand awards, 1957-65.

Interests: Miss Hill writes, "For the present, my major vocational interest is painting -- all media -- but especially experimentation with new concepts in oil, gouache and polymer sand collage (some traditional painting for the self-discipline it fosters), but always exploration, searching for an original and more creative approach in the expression not only of Indian art, but of other subject matter as well. I work in most painting media as well as in graphics (ink and serigraphy). In the last few years, I have done some woodcarving, clay and wax sculpture for reproduction in bronze, and am eager to try welded sculpture. The styles I work in range from representational realism through abstract expressionism with subject matter drawn from portraiture, traditional Indian painting, landscape, still-life, and combinations of these.

"I do some writing, and am in the process of trying to perfect my college French and to learn Spanish, as well as a smattering of the languages of all the countries I will visit so that I can at least greet (the natives) and thank them in their own language(s). This has led to some delightful experiences in the past.

"In addition to these art-related interests, I swim at our local 'Y' and make use of isometric and yoga exercises as often as I can manage. My family and I attend as many ballet, opera and theatre performances in Tulsa and Oklahoma City as we can. We try to combine our vocations with trips for my one-woman shows, as we did for my show at the Heard Museum in Phoenix (February, 1965)."

Published works: Miss Hill's illustrations appear in the following publications -- *The Five Civilized Tribes Museum Brochure* (Five Civilized Tribes Museum, 1957); *A History of the Baird-Scales Family* (Go-Ye Mission, Inc., 1960); *Corning Glass Works in the Sooner State* (Corning Glass Co., 1960).

HINCKLEY, EDWARD C. 1934-
   (educator)

Born December 16, 1934, Bridgewater, Mass. *Education:* Harvard College, B. A. (Cultural Anthropology), 1955; Harvard University, M. Ed. (Elementary Education), 1959. *Home address:* P. O. Box 86, Readfield, Me. 04355. *Principal occupation:* Education and community development work, Maine State Department of Indian Affairs. *Affiliations:* Elementary school teacher, Bureau of Indian Affairs, Utah and Arizona, 1959-61; education specialist (Papago, Paiute, Washoe, Shoshone), U. S. Public Health Service, Arizona and Nevada, 1961-65; education and community development, Maine State Department of Indian Affairs, 1965-. *Military service:* U. S. Army, 1956-58. *Memberhips:* National Association for

Community Development. *Interests:* Indian affairs on a national current level; Indian culture and history; education and community development.

HINDS, PATRICK SWAZO (Tewa Pueblo) 1929- (artist)

Born March 25, 1929, Tesuque Pueblo, N. M. *Education:* Hill and Canyon School of Art (summers), 1947, 1948; California College of Arts and Crafts, B. A., 1952; Mexico City College, 1952-53; Chicago Art Institute, 1953, 1955. *Principal occupation:* Artist. *Home address:* 1912 McGee Ave., Berkeley, Calif. 94703. *Military service:* U. S. Marine Corps, 1945-46, 1950-51 (two Purple Hearts). *Memberships:* Oakland Art Association; Society of Western Artists; American Indian Artists Association (painting chairman); Berkeley Art Festival Guild; Arts and Crafts Co-op, Berkeley (chairman, Fine Arts Guild; teacher of sketch class and oil painting class). *Awards, honors:* First Award, San Marin Art Festival, 1964; Purchase Award, Oakland Jewish Community Center, 1965; Walter Simson Grand Award, First Award, Honor Mention, Scottsdale National Indian Art Exhibition, 1966. *Exhibitions:* Legion of Honor; Richmond Art Center; College of Arts and Crafts Alumni Show; Kaiser Bldg., Oakland, Calif.; Gallery Nine; Harwood Anderson Gallery; Brick Wall Gallery; Walnut Creek Annual; Jack London Square Annual; Berkeley Art Festival; El Cerrito Festival of Arts; and others.

HISER, DONALD (HOWARD) 1923- (archaeologist, museum director)

Born November 20, 1923, Columbiana, Ohio. *Education:* University of Arizona, B. A., 1953; Arizona State University, 1957-1958. *Principal occupation:* Archaeologist, museum director. *Business address:* 4619 E. Washington St., Phoenix, Arizona 85034. *Affiliations:* Director, Pueblo Grande Museum, 1953-. *Other professional posts:* Lecturer in anthropology, Phoenix Evening College; lecturer, Traveling Science Institute of Arizona Academy of Science (sponsored by the National Science Foundation). *Military service:* U. S. Naval Reserve, 1943-45; 1946-50. *Community activities:* Balsz School Parent-Teachers' Association (president, Indian affairs committee, 1960-61).

Memberships: Arizona Academy of Science (past secretary, anthropology section); American Anthropological Association (institutional member); Society for American Archaeology; Archaeological Institute of America. *Interests:* Southwestern (U. S.) archaeology -- Hohokam; avo-physical anthropology, ceramic research, teaching and lecturing on Southwestern archaeology. *Published works: Pueblo Grande Museum Popular Series* (Pueblo Grande Museum).

HLADY, WALTER M. 1924- (anthropologist)

Born November 20, 1924, Winnipeg, Manitoba, Canada. *Education:* University of Manitoba; University of North Dakota, B. A., 1951; University of Manitoba, M. A., 1966. *Principal occupation:* Anthropologist. *Home address:* 907 Autumnwood Dr., St. Boniface 6, Manitoba, Canada. *Affiliations:* Regional liaison officer, Canadian Citizenship Branch, Canadian Government, Winnipeg, Manitoba. *Other professional posts:* Lecturer, University of Manitoba. *Military service:* Canadian Army, 1943-45. *Community activities:* Manitoba Archaeological Society (president). *Interests:* Action anthropology; ethnology and archaeology, particularly of Great Plains and northern Canada. *Published works: People of Indian Ancestry in Rural Manitoba,* with B. R. Poston (Queen's Printer, 1959); *A Social and Economic Study of Sandy Bay* (Saskatchewan Government Regina, 1960); *A Community Development Project Among the Churchill Band at Churchill, Manitoba* (Center for Community Studies, 1960); editor, *Northern Training* (Center for Community Studies, 1961).

HOBBS, CLYDE W. 1917- (B. I. A. agency superintendent)

Born February 23, 1917, Winslow, Ark. *Education:* Oklahoma State University, B.S., 1942, M. S., 1951. *Principal occupation:* B. I. A. agency superintendent. *Home address:* P. O. Box 248, Fort Washakie, Wyo. 82514. *Affiliations:* Soil conservationist, Oklahoma and Montana, 1946-57; superintendent, Crow Indian Reservation, Montana, 1957-61; superintendent, Wind River Reservation, Fort Washakie, Wyo. *Military service:* U. S. Army, 1942-46 (Theater Ribbon, Philippine Islands). *Community activities:*

American Legion; Lions Club. *Awards, honors:* Alpha Zeta; Phi Kappa Phi, Oklahoma State University. *Interests:* Rural American Indian society. *Published works: Effect of Chemical Seed Treatment on Germination and Emergence* (master's thesis, 1951); *Indian Land and Its Care* (Haskell Press, 1953).

HOEBEL, (EDWARD) ADAMSON 1906-
(professor of anthropology)

Born November 16, 1906, Madison, Wis. *Education:* University of Wisconsin, B.A., 1928; University of Cologne, 1928-29; New York University, M.A., 1930; Columbia University, Ph.D., 1934. *Principal occupation:* Professor of anthropology. *Home address:* 2273 Folwell St., St. Paul, Minn. 55108. *Affiliations:* Professor, New York University, 1929-47; professor and dean, University of Utah, 1948-53; professor of anthropology, University of Minnesota, 1954-. *Other professional posts:* Visiting professor, University of Wisconsin, University of Washington, Harvard University, University of Chicago, Oxford University; senior specialist, East-West Center, Honolulu, 1964-65; Fellow, Center for Advanced Study in Behavioral Sciences. *Community activities:* Association on American Indian Affairs (director, 1936-55). *Memberships:* American Anthropological Association, 1932 (president, 1956-57); American Ethnological Society, 1932-; American Philosophical Society, 1964-. *Interests:* Field research among Comanche Indians, 1933; Shoshone, 1934; Northern Cheyenne, 1935-36; New Mexico Pueblos, 1945-49; West Pakistan, 1961; comparative law, tribal ethnologies, and general anthropology. *Published works: The Cheyenne Way,* with K.N. Llewellyn (University of Oklahoma, 1941); *Man in the Primitive World* (McGraw-Hill, 1948, 1959); *The Comanches: Lords of the South Plains,* with E. Wallace (University of Oklahoma, 1953); *The Law of Primitive Man* (Harvard University, 1954); *The Cheyennes: Indians of the Great Plains* (Holt, Rinehart and Winston, 1961); editor, *A Cheyenne Sketchbook* by Cohoe, with K. Peterson (University of Oklahoma, 1964).

HOFFMANN, EMMETT 1926- (educator)

Born July 27, 1926, Marathon, Wis. *Education:* St. Mary's Seminary, B.A. (Philosophy), 1950; St. Anthony's Seminary,

degree in Theology, 1954. *Principal occupation:* Educator. *Home address:* c/o St. Labre Indian School, Ashland, Mont. 59003. *Affiliations:* Director and superintendent, St. Labre Indian School, 1954-; originating novelty and costume jewelry industry, Cheyenne River Reservation. *Community activities:* Jaycees; Mission Arts Employees Credit Union (director and president). *Memberships:* Montana Pilot Association. *Awards, honors:* Outstanding Boss of the Year, Tongue River Jaycees and United States Junior Chamber of Commerce, 1965. *Published works:* Editor, *Race of Sorrows* (quarterly); editor, *The Morning Star People* (quarterly).

HOIG, STANLEY W. 1924- (educator)

Born June 24, 1924, Duncan, Okla. *Education:* Oklahoma State University, B.A., 1949; University of Oklahoma, M.A., 1964. *Principal occupation:* Educator. *Affiliations:* Superintendent of publications, Central State College, Edmund, Okla. *Military service:* U.S. Air Force, 1943-45. *Memberships:* Oklahoma Press Association. *Published works: The Humor of the American Cowboy* (Caxton Printers, Ltd., 1959; Signet Books, 1961); *The Sand Creek Massacre* (University of Oklahoma Press, 1963).

HOIJER, HARRY 1904- (professor of anthropology)

Born September 6, 1904, Chicago, Ill. *Education:* University of Chicago, A.B., 1927, A.M., 1929, Ph.D., 1931. *Principal occupation:* Professor of anthropology. *Home address:* 191 Beloit Ave., Los Angeles, Calif. 90049. *Affiliations:* Instructor, University of Chicago, 1931-40; professor of anthropology, University of California, Los Angeles, 1940-. *Other professional posts:* Center for Advanced Study in the Behavioral Sciences (Fellow, 1959-60); editor, *Notes and Reviews, International Journal of American Linguistics,* 1952-63; chairman and American Council of Learned Societies representative, Committee on Research in Native American Languages, 1950-. *Memberships:* Sigma Xi, 1931- (vice-president, University of California, 1958-59); American Anthropological Association, 1933- (Fellow, vice-president, 1949; executive board, 1953-56; president-elect, 1957;

president, 1958); Linguistic Society of America, 1933- (vice-president, 1951; president, 1959). *Published works: Tonkawa, An Indian Language of Texas* (Handbook of American Indian Languages, Part 3, ed. by Franz Boas, Columbia University Press, 1933); *Chiricahua and Mescalero Apache Texts* (University of Chicago Press, 1938); *Navaho Texts* with Edward Sapir (Yale University Press, 1942); *Navaho Phonology* (University of New Mexico Publications in Anthropology, No. 1, 1945); *Linguistic Structures of Native America*, with others (Viking Fund Publications in Anthropology, No. 6, 1946); *An Introduction to Anthropology*, with R. L. Beals (Macmillan, 1953, 1959); *Language in Culture: Proceedings of a Conference on the Interrelations of Language and Other Aspects of Culture* (Memoir 79, American Anthropological Association and the University of Chicago Press, 1954); articles in various linguistic and anthropological journals.

HOLLING, HOLLING CLANCY   1900-
   (writer, illustrator)

Born August 2, 1900, Holling Corners, Henrietta Co. (Jackson), Mich. *Education:* Albion College, 1918; Chicago Art Institute, 1919-23. *Principal occupation:* "Writer of informational books for young people and illustrator of same." *Home address:* 1445 Edgecliff Lane, Pasadena, Calif. 91107. *Affiliations:* Staff member, Chicago Natural History Museum, 1923-25; National Advertising Art, Chicago, 1924-37. *Other posts:* Professor of art, Pioneer University World Cruise, 1926-27; produced health films for Mexico and Central America (Rockefeller Foundation Fund); produced aviation training films during World War II. *Military service:* S. A. T. C., Albion College. *Memberships:* P. E. N. International, 1946-; Southern California Writers Guild, 1940- (board member, 1952-); Los Angeles Corral of Westerners (contributor to annual historical publication); Southwest Museum; historical societies. *Awards, honors:* Body of Work of Lasting Value, Southern California Council on Literature for Young People; Boys' Club of America Award for *Minn of the Mississippi;* Award, Commonwealth Club of California; Lewis Carroll Bookshelf, University of Wisconsin. *Interests:* Mr. Holling writes, "Informational books and educational films for young people. Anthropology, especially ethnology of

our American Indian, has long been a major avocational interest. History, especially of the Americas and of the Old West. Geography and world travel are also of great interest and value in my work. In my earlier years, zoology and museum techniques, including hunting expeditions for display groups, started my career. Experimentation, using primitive man's (especially Amerindian) techniques of manufacturing his artifacts and living as he did (off the land) while in wilderness expeditions. " *Published works: Little Big-Bye-and-Bye* (Volland, 1926); *Claws of the Thunderbird* (Volland, 1927); *Rum-Tum-Tummy* (Volland, 1927); *Choo-Me-Shoo the Eskimo* (Volland, 1928); *Roll Away Twins* (Volland, 1928); *Rocky Billy; The Twins Who Flew Around the World* (Platt and Munk, 1931); *Book of Indians* (Platt and Munk, 1935); *Book of Cowboys* (Platt and Munk, 1936); *Little Buffalo Boy* (Garden City, 1939); *Paddle to the Sea* (Houghton, 1941); *Tree in the Trail* (Houghton, 1942); *Pagoo* (Houghton, 1947); *Seabird* (Houghton, 1948); *Minn of the Mississippi* (Houghton, 1951).

HOLLOWBREAST, DONALD   (Northern
   Cheyenne) 1917- (editor)

Born May 17, 1917, Birney, Mont. *Education:* Chemawa Indian School; Busby School. *Principal occupation:* Editor. *Home address:* Box 145, Birney, Mont. 59012. *Affiliations:* Editor, *The Birney Arrow* (newsletter).

HOLT, ROY D.   1897- (teacher, school
   administrator)

Born August 25, 1897, Santa Anna, Texas. *Education:* Trinity University, B. A., 1920; University of Texas, M. A., 1926, University of Texas, 1926-27. *Principal occupation:* Teacher, school administrator. *Home address:* 203 Oak St., Copperas Cove, Texas 76522. *Affiliations:* Superintendent of schools, Eldorado, Texas, 1927-35; superintendent of schools, Sanderson, Texas 1935-42. Has "spent thirty-nine years in Texas public schools as teacher, athletic coach, and administrator. " *Other professional posts:* Since 1958, has held various teaching posts at Hardin-Simmons University, Sul Ross State College, Mary Hardin-Baylor College. *Military service:* World War I. *Community activities:* Lions Club;

Rotary Club; Chamber of Commerce. *Memberships:* Texas State Historical Association, 1935- ; West Texas Historical Society. *Awards, honors:* High School History Teachers Award, University of Texas, 1925. *Interests:* "Collect books and stories from oldtimers concerning the Southwest; have written many articles on the Southwest in *The Cattleman, The Sheep and Goat Raiser, The Western Horseman, West Texas Historical Yearbooks,* etc." *Published works: History of Schleicher County, Texas* (privately printed, 1930); *So You Don't Like Texas* (privately printed, 1965); *Heap Many Texas Chiefs* (The Naylor Co., 1966).

HOLTZ, ROBERT DEAN 1903- (B. I. A. area director)

Born August 10, 1903, Newton, Iowa. *Education:* Nebraska Central Academy and Iowa State College, B. S., 1930; Oregon State College, 1931. *Principal occupation:* B. I. A. area director. *Home address:* 9951 Concord Ave., Sun City, Ariz. 85351. *Affiliations:* Area director, Portland Area Office, Bureau of Indian Affairs. *Other professional posts:* President, director, Nava-Apache Electric Cooperative, Pacific Northwest Field Committee, 1961-65; Portland Federal Council, 1961-65; Society of American Foresters (past chairman, Southwestern section). *Community activities:* Boy Scouts, 1948-53; Lutheran Family Service, 1962- ; Portland City Club; Oregon Chapter, Iowa State University Alumni, (president, 1965).

HOMSHER, LOLA M. (museum director)

Education: Colorado State University, B. S., 1936; University of Wyoming, M. A. (History), 1949; American University, certificate in archives administration, 1948. *Principal occupation:* Museum director. *Business affiliations:* Teacher, city schools, Lovell, Wyoming, Roswell, New Mexico, Laramie, Wyo. ; executive director, Girl Scouts of America, Great Falls, Montana and Cheyenne, Wyo. ; assistant historian, Wyoming, 1941-43; assistant archivist, 1943; research fellow, Rockefeller Project, Western Range Cattle Industry Study, 1943-45; university archivist and curator of manuscripts, University of Wyoming, 1945-51; director, Wyoming State Archives and Historical Department and State Museum,

1951-. *Memberships:* Wyoming State Historical Society (executive secretary); Fort Laramie Historical Association (honorary member); Grand Teton Natural History Association (member, advisory council); Bureau of Public Records Collection and Research (honorary member, advisory board); National Pony Express Centennial Association (vice president); Wyoming Pony Express Centennial Commission and Civil War Centennial (president); American Association for State and Local History (council member; chairman, Region 10 Awards Committee; member, National Awards Committee). *Awards, honors:* Phi Kappa Phi; Pi Gamma Mu; Alpha Chi Alpha; Pacemaker, 1936; Mortar Board; Fellow, Society of American Archivists, 1959; three Awards of Merit, American Association for State and Local History. *Published works: Ghost Towns of Wyoming* (Hastings House, 1956); *South Pass, 1868* (University of Nebraska Press, 1960); articles in professional magazines: *Mississippi Valley Historical Review; American Archivist;* Wyoming section, World Book Encyclopaedia Britannica, Jr., and others; editor, *Annals of Wyoming* and *History News;* column, "Wyoming -- From the State Archives," appearing in fifteen Wyoming daily and weekly newspapers.

HOPKINS, HARRY A. 1920- (machinist)

Born February 9, 1920, Bradford, Ohio. *Education:* Training in electronics, anthropology. *Home address:* Route 3, Box 322, Piqua, Ohio 45356. *Principal occupation:* Machinist. *Military service* U. S. Army, World War II (Marksman's Medal, Carbine and Rifle). *Community activities:* 4H Club (advisor). *Memberships:* Ohio Archaeological Society, 1956- ; Ohio Historical Society, 1964- ; West Central States Archaeological Society, 1964-. *Awards, honors:* Miami County Fair Awards for Indian artifact collection. *Interests:* Salvaging of archaeological sites. *Published works:* Articles in *Ohio Archaeologist.*

HOPKINS, KENNETH R. 1922- (museum director)

Born August 24, 1922, Springfield, Mass. *Education:* Pratt Institute, 1941-43; University of Vermont, 1943-44; Parsons

School of Design, 1946-47; New York University, B. S., 1948; University of Wisconsin, M. S. , 1950. *Principal occupation:* Museum director. *Home address:* 3001 Monta Vista, Olympia, Wash. 98502. *Affiliations:* Art director, University of Wisconsin; curator, Wisconsin State Historical Society; art director, Old Sturbridge Village; curator, Buffalo Historical Society; special representative, Bethlehem Steel Company; director-curator, National Geographic Society; director, State Capitol Museum, Olympia, Wash. , 1964-. *Military service:* U. S. Army, 1943-46. *Memberships:* American Association of Museums; American Association for State and Local History; Society of American Archivists; Canal Society of New York State; Early American Industries Association.

HORSMAN, REGINALD 1931-
   (professor)

Born October 24, 1931, Leeds (Yorkshire), England. *Education:* University of Birmingham (England), B. A. , 1952, M. A. , 1955; Indiana University, Ph. D. , 1958. *Principal occupation:* Professor of history. *Address:* Department of History, University of Wisconsin - Milwaukee, Milwaukee, Wis. 53211. *Affiliations:* Instructor, University of Wisconsin - Milwaukee, 1958-59; assistant professor, University of Wisconsin - Milwaukee, 1959-62; associate professor, University of Wisconsin - Milwaukee, 1962-64; professor, University of Wisconsin - Milwaukee, 1964-. *Memberships:* American Historical Association; Mississippi Valley Historical Association; American Association of University Professors. *Awards, honors:* William H. Kiekhofer Award (University of Wisconsin) for Excellence in Teaching, 1961; Guggenheim Fellowship, 1965-66. *Interests:* Work in British-American relations; history of American westward expansion; American-Indian relations; opera; art; sports. *Published works: The Causes of the War of 1812* (University of Pennsylvania Press, 1962); *Matthew Elliott, British Indian Agent* (Wayne State University Press, 1964); *Expansion and American Indian Policy, 1783-1812* (Michigan State University Press, 1966).

HOSMER, JERALYN PRUGH 1934-
   (museum curator)

Born October 2, 1934, Dayton, Ohio. *Education:* Diploma, Goffstown High School, 1951; B.A., Principia College, 1955; M.A., Teachers College, Columbia, New York, 1958. *Principal occupation:* Museum curator. *Address:* c/o School of Nations Museum, Principia College, Elsah, Ill. *Other professional posts:* Teacher, Oyster Bay and Locust Valley, Long Island, N. Y. *Community activities:* Church committees; P. T. A. ; local garden club; Faculty-Staff Club. *Memberships:* American Association of Museums; American Friends of Attingham. *Awards, honors:* Scholarship, National Trust Summer School, Attingham Park, England. *Interests:* Travel along East Coast of United States, England, France, Spain.

HOUSER, ALLAN (Apache) 1914-
   (artist, art instructor)

Born June 30, 1914, Okla. *Education:* Private study; Utah State University. *Principal occupation:* Artist, art instructor. *Home address:* 1020 Camino Carlos Rey, Santa Fe, N. M. 87501. *Affiliations:* Instructor in sculpture and advanced painting, Institute of American Indian Arts, Santa Fe, N. M. *Community activities:* Southwestern Association on Indian Affairs (board of directors). *Awards, honors:* Guggenheim Scholarship; Palmes Academiques (France); four Grand Purchase Prizes, Philbrook Art Center, Tulsa, Okla. *Interests:* Sculpture, painting, book illustration, lecturing; writing; outdoor painting and sketching; recording stories. Travels to the Navajo Reservation, New York City, Mexico City. *Biographical sources: Indians of Today* (Indian Council Fire, 1960). *Published works:* Mr. Houser's illustrations have appeared in eight books.

HOWARD, HELEN ADDISON 1904-
   (journalist, historical writer)

Born August 4, 1904, Missoula, Mont. *Education:* University of Montana, B. A., 1927; University of Southern California, M. A., 1933. *Principal occupation:* Journalist, historical writer. *Home address:* 410 S. Lamer St. , Burbank, Calif. *Affiliations:* Reporter and feature writer, *Daily Missoulian,* Missoula, Mont. , 1923-29; radio-TV monitor-editor, Radio Reports, Inc., 1943-1956; confidential survey work, U. S. Department of Agriculture, Los Angeles,

Calif., 1943; Los Angeles Police Department (Records and Identification Division). *Military service:* Cavalry Unit, Women's Ambulance and Defense Corps. *Community activities:* California Rangers, youth cavalry organization (Captain, "C" Troop, 1954-56). *Memberships:* Alumni Association, University of Montana, 1927; General Alumni Association, University of Southern California, 1933; Equestrian Trails, Inc. (Corral 15), 1951; Montana Historical Society, 1955-. *Awards:* Army Citation of Merit, for highest grade in Basic Chemical Welfare Course, 1943; *War Chief Joseph* dramatized for radio in commemoration of American Indian Day, over KFI-NBC network, 1949; subject of biographical sketch over radio station KGVO, 1952, entitled "Writers of Montana." *Interests:* History of American Pacific Northwest; riding Arabian horses; travel. *Published works: War Chief Joseph* (Caxton Printers, Ltd., 1941; University of Nebraska Press, 1964); contributing editor, *Frontier Omnibus* (Montana State University Press, 1962); *Northwest Trail Blazers* (Caxton Printers, Ltd., 1963); *Saga of Chief Joseph* (Caxton Printers, Ltd., 1965).

HOWARD, RICHARD FOSTER 1902-
(museum director)

Born July 26, 1902, Plainfield, N.J. *Education:* Harvard University, B.S., 1924; Pennsylvania Medical School; Cornell University. *Principal occupation:* Museum director. *Home address:* 4183 Cliff Rd., Birmingham, Ala. *Affiliations:* Secondary school teaching, The Hill School, Chestnut Hill Academy, 1924-28; staff psychologist, Pennsylvania Museum of Art, 1932-35; director, Dallas Museum of Fine Arts, 1935-42; military government, Germany, 1946-49; director, Des Moines Art Center, 1949-50; director, Birmingham Museum of Art, 1951-. *Military service:* U.S. Army Reserve, 1920-59 (E.T.O. Medal for three campaigns; Bronze Star; Stella Della Solidarieta d'Italia; Order of White Lion of Bohemia). *Memberships:* Renaissance Society; American Federation of Arts; American Museums Association; Numismatic Society of America; Southern Art Museum Directors. *Published works: Museum Security* (American Museum Association, 1959).

HOWARD, WILLIAM C. 1920- (educator)

Born June 1, 1920, Hettinger, N.D. *Education:* Eastern Montana College, B.A., 1950; Colorado State College, M.A., 1954. *Principal occupation:* Educator. *Home address:* 2403 Houser Blvd., Helena, Mont. 59601. *Affiliations:* Director of school lunch programs, Department of Public Instruction, Mont., 1957-60; director of Indian education, Department of Public Instruction, Mont., 1960-. *Military service:* U.S. Naval Reserve, active and inactive. *Memberships:* National Education Association; American School Food Service Association.

HOWE, OSCAR (Sioux) 1915- (artist, teacher)

Born May 13, 1915, Joe Creek, S.D. *Education:* Dakota Wesleyan University, B.A., 1952; University of Oklahoma, M.F.A., 1954. *Principal occupation:* Artist and teacher. *Home address:* 128 Walker, Vermillion, S.D. *Affiliations:* Artist in residence, Dakota Wesleyan University, 1948-52; director of art, Pierre High School, Pierre, S.D., 1953-57; artist in residence, assistant professor of creative arts, University of South Dakota, 1957-. *Military service:* U.S. Army, 1942-45. *Memberships:* Delta Phi Delta; International Institute of Arts and Letters (Fellow, 1960). *Awards, honors:* Subject, *This is Your Life* television program, 1960; Grand Purchase Award, Philbrook Art Center, Tulsa, Okla., 1947; Second Award, Philbrook Art Center, 1949; Second Award, Philbrook Art Center, 1950; First Prize, Philbrook Art Center, 1951; Second and Third Prize, Philbrook Art Center, 1952; Dorothy Field Award, Denver Art Museum, 1952; Second Award and Honorable Mention, Philbrook Art Center, 1953; Purchase Award, Denver Art Museum, 1953; Grand Purchase Prize, Philbrook Art Center, 1954; First Prize and Honorable Mention, Philbrook Art Center, 1954; Santa Fe Railroad Award, Denver Art Museum, 1954; Second Prize, Philbrook Art Center, 1956; Purchase Award, Museum of New Mexico, 1956; Mary Benjamin Rogers Award, Museum of New Mexico, 1958; Grand Prize and Grand Purchase Prize, Philbrook Art Center, 1959; Second Prize, Philbrook Art Center, 1960; First Award and Third Award, Philbrook Art Center, 1961; Grand Purchase Prize and

Honorable Mention, Philbrook Art Center, 1962; Grand Prize and Honorable Mention, Philbrook Art Center, 1963; First Award, Philbrook Art Center, 1965. Numerous one-man shows in the United States; paintings on permanent exhibit in several U.S. museums. *Books illustrated: Legends of the Mighty Sioux* (Albert Whitman, 1941); *The Little Lost Sioux* (Albert Whitman, 1942); *Bringer of the Mystery Dog* (Haskell Institute Printing Dept., 1943); *North American Indian Costumes* (C. Szwedzicki, Nice, France, 1952).

HOWE, STANLEY 1935- (museum curator)

Born August 11, 1935, Gobles, Mich. *Education:* Daytona Beach Junior College. *Principal occupation:* Museum curator. *Home address:* Route 1, Box 487-D, Ormond Beach, Fla. 32074. *Affiliations:* Manager, Museum of Speed, 1961-64; curator, Museum of Arts and Sciences, Daytona Beach, Fla. *Community activities:* Tomoka Gem and Mineral Society (editor, *Tomoka Coquine*); assistant curator, local historical society; Boy Scouts of America (explorer). *Memberships:* Florida Historical Society; Halifax Historical Society. *Interests:* Private collection of local Indian artifacts; work on Florida history in progress.

HOWELL, JAMES PAYER (Cherokee) 1921- (B.I.A. agency superintendent)

Born April 1, 1921, Fort Gibson, Okla. *Education:* Haskell Institute, 1938-40; University of Kansas; George Washington University; Everett Junior College. *Principal occupation:* B.I.A. agency superintendent. *Home address:* Box 285, Tuba City, Ariz. 86045. *Affiliations:* Assistant clerk, Potawatomi Agency, Horton, Kan., 1940-49; chief clerk, Haskell Institute, 1949-56; various positions at Western Washington Agency, Everett, Wash., and Fort Belknap Agency, Harlem, Mont., 1956-61; assistant personnel officer, Aberdeen Area Office, Bureau of Indian Affairs, Aberdeen, S.D., 1961-63; superintendent, Fort Berthold Agency, New Town, N.D., 1963-66; superintendent Tuba City Agency, Tuba City, Ariz. *Military service:* U.S. Army Air Force, 1942-46 (Air Medal with Oak Leaf cluster; 330th Bomb Group Unit Citation).

Community activities: Kiwanis Club, Lawrence, Kan., and New Town, N.D.; Lions Club, Harlem, Mont. (president, 1960).

HOWELLS, WILLIAM WHITE 1908- (professor of anthropology)

Born November 27, 1908, New York, N.Y. *Education:* St. Paul's School, 1926; Harvard University, S.B., 1930; Ph.D., 1934. *Principal occupation:* Professor of anthropology. *Home address:* Kittery Point, Me. 03905. *Affiliations:* Teaching fellow in anthropology, Harvard University, 1930; research associate in physical anthropology, American Museum of Natural History, 1932-43; assistant professor of anthropology, University of Wisconsin, 1939-46 (associate professor, 1946-48; professor, 1948-54; professor of integrated liberal studies, 1948-54; chairman, Department of Sociology and Anthropology, 1953-54; curator of somatology, faculty, Peabody Museum, 1955-; professor of anthropology, Harvard University, 1954- (chairman of department, 1960-); associate, Lowell House, 1955. *Military service:* U.S. Navy Reserve, 1943-46. *Memberships:* American Academy of Arts and Sciences (Fellow); American Anthropological Association (president, 1951); American Association for the Advancement of Science; American Association of Physical Anthropologists; Society of American Archaeology; American Society of Human Genetics; American Society of Naturalists; American Eugenics Society; American Institute of Human Paleontology; Geographical Society of Lisbon; Anthropological Society of Paris; Anthropological Society of Vienna; Taven Club; Badminton and Tennis Clubs of Boston; Century Club; River Club; Harvard Faculty Club. *Awards, honors:* Viking Fund Medal in physical anthropology, 1954. *Expeditions:* Excavation of Gallen Priory, Harvard Irish Survey, 1935. *Published works: Mankind So Far* (1944); *The Heathens* (1948); editor, *Early Man in the Far East* (1949); *Back of History* (1954); *Mankind in the Making* (1959); editor, *Ideas on Human Evolution* (1962); editor, *American Journal of Physical Anthropology* 1949-54; associate editor, *Human Biology* 1955-; articles in various scientific publications.

HOYT, ELIZABETH E. 1893- (professor)

Born January 27, 1893, Augusta, Me. *Education:* Boston University, B.A., 1913; Radcliffe College, Ph.D., 1925. *Principal occupation:* Professor. *Home address:* Ames, Iowa. *Affiliations:* Professor, Department of Economics, Iowa State University. *Memberships:* American Economic Review; American Association of University Professors, 1925-. *Awards, honors:* Fulbright for study of cultural change, 1950-51; Ford Foundation Fellowship, 1957-58. *Interests:* Choice-making as seen in psychology, anthropology, and economics; travels to Japan, Korea, China, Soviet Union, Europe, Africa. *Published works: Primitive Trade* (Kegan Paul, 1926); *Consumption of Wealth* (Macmillan, 1928); *Consumption in Our Society* (McGraw-Hill, 1938); *The Income of Society* (Ronald, 1950); *American Income and Its Use* (Harper, 1954); *Tama: An American Conflict* (Iowa State University, 1964).

HRUSKA, ROBERT J.   1930- (museum curator)

Born August 8, 1930, Calumet, Mich. *Principal occupation:* Museum curator. *Home address:* 1242 High St., Oshkosh, Wis. 54901. *Affiliations:* Assistant director and curator of anthropology, Oshkosh Public Museum. *Military service:* U.S. Merchant Marine. *Memberships:* Wisconsin Archaeological Survey; Wisconsin Archaeological Society (president). *Interests:* Great Lakes archaeology; study of Old Copper Culture, Riverside Site, Menominee County, Mich.; digs at Riverside Site, Peshtigo, Wis., South Dakota (Arikara Indians).

HUGHES, CHARLES CAMPBELL   1929- (professor)

Born January 26, 1929, Salmon, Idaho. *Education:* Harvard University, B.A., 1951; Cornell University, M.A., 1953, Ph.D., 1957. *Principal occupation:* Professor of

anthropology. *Home address:* 1036 Wildwood Drive, East Lansing, Mich. 48823. *Affiliations:* Senior research associate, Cornell University, 1956-62; Fellow, Center for Advanced Study in the Behavioral Sciences, 1961-62; director, African Studies Center, Michigan State University, 1962-. *Military service:* U.S. Army Reserve, 1951-57. *Memberships:* American Anthropological Association; American Ethnological Society; Arctic Institute of North America; American Association for the Advancement of Science; Society for Applied Anthropology (member, executive board); International African Institute; African Studies Association. *Awards, honors:* Phi Beta Kappa, Harvard College, 1951; Phi Kappa Phi, Cornell University, 1956; Sigma Xi, Cornell University, 1958. *Published works: An Eskimo Village in the Modern World* (Cornell University Press, 1960); *People of Cove and Woodlot: Communities from the Viewpoint of Social Psychiatry* (Basic Books, 1960); *Psychiatric Disorder Among the Yoruba* (Cornell University Press, 1963).

HUMPHREY, DONALD G.   1920- (museum director)

Born May 3, 1920, Hutchinson, Kan. *Education:* University of Kansas, B.F.S., 1948; State University of Iowa, M.F.A., 1950; Ph.D., 1958. *Principal occupation:* Museum director. *Home address:* 4621 S. Quaker St., Tulsa, Okla. 74105. *Affiliations:* Instructor, State University of Iowa, 1950-51, 1957-58; assistant professor, University of Oklahoma, 1952-57; director, Philbrook Art Center, Tulsa, Okla., 1959-. *Military service:* U.S. Army, 1942-46. *Community activities:* Tulsa Arts Festival, 1961-66 (visual arts chairman); Governor's Council on Arts and Humanities (visual arts chairman). *Memberships:* American Association of Museums; Mountain-Plains Conference; Oklahoma Museum Association. *Interests:* Travels and tours in Europe; photography. *Published works: Albert Bloch: A Retrospective of His Work* (Philbrook Art Center, 1961); articles in various magazines.

HUNT, W. BEN 1888- (commercial artist)

Born March 13, 1888, Milwaukee, Wis. *Education:* South District High School; Academy of Fine Arts, Chicago, Ill. *Principal occupation:* Commercial artist. *Home address:* 11221 W. Jamesville Blvd., Hales Corners, Wis. 53130. *Affiliations:* Western Printing and Litho Co.; Times-Union News; Bosch Hunt General Store; Hunt Brothers Advertising Artists. *Other professional posts:* Teacher, Milwaukee Vocational School. *Community activities:* Hales Corners Village Board (trustee). *Awards, honors:* Silver Beaver and Silver Antelope, Boy Scouts of America; honorary curator, Milwaukee Public Museum; Distinguished Service Award, Whithall Area Education Association. *Interests:* Litho engraving; commercial art; woodworking; archery; wrought iron work; pewter; whittling; Indian lore and crafts; travel throughout United States, in Canada, South Pacific, New Zealand, Australia, Mexico. *Published works: American Indian Beadwork,* with B. Bursheare (Bruce); *Indian and Camp Handicraft* (Bruce); *Indiancraft* (Bruce); *Indian Silversmithing* (Bruce); *The Flat Bow,* with John Metz (Bruce); *Building a Log Cabin* (Bruce); *Rustic Construction* (Bruce); *101 Alphabets,* with Ed. D. Hunt (Bruce); *Whittling With Ben Hunt* (Bruce); *Let's Whittle* (Bruce); *Kachina Dolls* (Milwaukee Public Museum); *Golden Book of Indian Crafts and Lore* (Golden Press); *Golden Book of Crafts and Hobbies* (Golden Press); *Contemporary Carving and Whittling* (in progress -- expected publication by Bruce).

Home address: R. D. 5, Mechanicsburg, Penna. *Affiliations:* Secondary school teacher, Sharpsville, Penna., 1936-45; production clerk, Westinghouse Electric and Manufacturing Co., Sharon, Penna., 1944-46; assistant historian, Pennsylvania Historical and Museum Commission, Harrisburg, Penna., 1946-48 (senior archivist, 1948-56, associate historian, 1956-61, chief, Division of Research and Publications, 1961-). *Community activities:* School director. Memberships: Society of American Archivists; American Indian Ethnohistoric Conference; Pennsylvania Historical Association; Society for Pennsylvania Archaeology; Historical Society of Western Pennsylvania; Cumberland County Historical Society (director, 1962). *Awards, honors:* Phi Beta Kappa (Allegheny College, 1933); Award of Merit, American Association for State and Local History, 1961. *Interests:* Colonial and frontier history, especially of Pennsylvania; archaeology; linguistics; travels in United States, Canada, and Mexico. *Published works: The Provincial Fort at Carlisle* (Hamilton Library and Historical Association, 1956); contributor, Witthoft, John and W. Fred Kinsey, *Susquehannock Miscellany* (Pennsylvania Historical and Museum Commission, 1959); *Forts on the Pennsylvania Frontier, 1753-1758* (Pennsylvania Historical and Museum Commission, 1960); *Archibald Loudon, Pioneer Historian* (Cumberland County Historical Society, 1964).

HUNTER, WILLIAM A(LBERT) 1908- (writer)

Born September 24, 1908, Kinsman, Ohio. *Education:* Allegheny College, B.A., 1933; University of California, M.A., 1935. *Principal occupation:* Writer, historian.

HYDE, DOUGLAS (Nez Perce) 1946- (artist)

Born July 28, 1946, in "Nez Perce country," Idaho. *Education:* Institute of American Indian Arts. *Principal occupation:* Artist. *Home address:* 1222 Bryden, Lewiston, Idaho. *Awards, honors:* First Place, Sculpture, Scottsdale (Ariz.), 1965; Honorable Mention, Philbrook Art Center Indian Annual, Tulsa (Okla.), 1965.

I

IGLAUER, EDITH (writer)

Born Cleveland, Ohio. *Education:* Wellesley College, B. A. ; Graduate School of Journalism, Columbia University, M. S. *Principal occupation:* Free lance writer. *Home address:* 1435 Lexington Avenue, New York, N. Y. *Affiliations:* Writer, reporter, Office of War Information, Washington, D. C. , 1941-43, with special attention to Mrs. Roosevelt; accredited war correspondent, *Cleveland News*, 1945; free lance writer, *Cleveland News*, *Harper's*, 1945-; free lance writer, *The New Yorker*, *Maclean's* (Canadian), 1958-. *Memberships:* Authors' League; Arctic Institute. *Awards, honors:* Commencement Award, Wellesley College; Woodrow Wilson Award in modern politics. *Interests:* Extensive travel; family. *Published works: The New People: The Eskimo's Journey into Our Time* (Doubleday & Co., 1966; published in Great Britain by Jonathan Cape).

IRWIN, CONSTANCE (FRICK) 1913- (teacher, writer)

Born May 11, 1913, Evansville, Ind. *Education:* Indiana University, B. A. , 1934, M. A. , 1941; Columbia University, B. S. , 1947. *Principal occupation:* Instructor in library science, writer, librarian. *Home address:* 246 Marietta Ave. , Iowa City, Iowa. *Affiliations:* High school librarian, Evansville, Ind. , 1937-42, 1946-54; librarian, Evansville College, 1946; editor, Columbia University Press, 1947-50. *Military service:* U. S. Naval Reserve (active duty, Naval Intelligence). *Awards:* Phi Beta Kappa. *Interests:* Travel in Europe; archaeology; history and prehistory; sports; English and American literature; crafts. *Published works: Fair Gods and Stone Faces* (St. Martin's); *Tourney Team* (Harcourt, Brace & World, 1954); *Five Against the Gods* (Harcourt, Brace & World, 1955); *Patch* (Harcourt, Brace & World, 1957); *Jonathan D.* (Lothrop, Lee & Shepard, 1959); *The Comeback Guy* (Harcourt, Brace & World, 1961).

ISRAEL, MARION 1882- (writer)

Born December 7, 1882, Peabody, Mass. *Education:* University of California. *Principal occupation:* Writer. *Home address:*

5182 Scottwood Rd., Paradise, Calif. 95969. *Affiliations:* Secretary, 1914-20, assistant to director of visual education division, 1920-29, director, division of visual education, 1929-40, division of elementary curriculum, 1940-47, Office of Superintendent of Schools, Los Angeles County, Calif. *Other occupations:* Research assistance and manuscript editing. *Memberships:* Butte County Historical Society, 1960-. *Interests:* History, anthropology, mythology, literature, drama, social criticism, the American Indian; member, editorial board, *Tales of the Paradise Ridge* (Paradise Fact and Folklore, 1961-). *Published works: Apaches* (Melmont, 1959); *Dakotas* (Melmont, 1959); *Cherokees* (Melmont, 1961); *Ojibway* (Melmont, 1962).

IVEY, ZELDA C. 1884- (museum director, historian)

Born July 8, 1884, Fort Atkinson, Wis. *Education:* Minnesota School of Business. *Principal occupation:* Museum director, historian. *Home address:* 400 Madison Ave. , Fort Atkinson, Wis. 53538. *Affiliations:* Director and historian, Hoard Museum, Fort Atkinson, Wis. *Military service:* Co-chairman, War Work, World War II; service on ration boards, welfare boards, and recruiting board for Nurse Reserve. *Memberships:* Wisconsin Historical Society; Lake Mills-Aztalan Historical Society; Watertown, Rock County and Fort Atkinson historical societies. *Awards, honors:* Founder, Dwight Foster Museum (Hoard Museum). *Published works:* Historical works, privately published.

J

JACKSON, DONALD 1919- (editor)

Born June 19, 1919, Glenwood, Iowa. *Education:* Iowa State University, B. S. , 1942; State University of Iowa, Ph. D. , 1948. *Principal occupation:* Editor. *Home address:* 1508 Dawson Dr. , Champaign, Ill. 60822. *Affiliations:* Editor, University of Illinois Press. *Military service:* U. S. Naval Reserve, 1943-46. *Memberships:* American Historical Association; Society of American Historians; Western History Association; Missouri Historical Society; State Historical Society of Iowa; Illinois

State Historical Society. *Awards, honors:* Regional History Award, Missouri Historical Society, 1965, for *Letters of the Lewis and Clark Expedition. Interests:* Trans-Mississippi history; history of America; exploration; the American Indian. *Published works: Archer Pilgrim* (Dodd, Mead, 1942); *Black Hawk: An Autobiography* (University of Illinois Press, 1955); *Letters of the Lewis and Clark Expedition* (University of Illinois Press, 1962); *The Journals of Zebulon Montgomery Pike: With Letters and Related Documents* (University of Oklahoma Press, 1966).

JACKSON, GRACE 1911- (librarian, writer)

Born September 8, 1911, Chicago, Ill. *Education:* University of California at Los Angeles, B. A., 1934, M. L. S., 1935, M. A., 1950. *Principal occupation:* Librarian, writer. *Home address:* 304 E. Fredericks, Barstow, Calif. 92311. *Affiliations:* Librarian, Compton College, 1936-39; librarian, Westmont College, 1940; librarian, McMurray College, Abilene, Texas, 1960-63. *Military service:* U. S. Army Air Force librarian. *Memberships:* American Library Association; Catholic Library Association; Council for Technological Advancement; National Education Association. *Published works: Cynthia Ann Parker* (Naylor, 1959); *Quanah Parker, Last Chief of the Comanches* (Exposition, 1963).

JACOBS, MELVILLE 1902- (professor of anthropology and linguistics)

Born July 3, 1902, New York, N. Y. *Education:* City College of New York, B. A., 1922; Columbia University, M. A., 1923, Ph. D., 1931. *Principal occupation:* Professor of anthropology and linguistics. *Home address:* 2016 N.E. Ravenna Blvd., Seattle, Wash. 98105. *Affiliations:* Professor of anthropology and linguistics, University of Washington, 1928-. *Other professional posts:* Visiting professor, University of Wisconsin, 1961-62. *Memberships:* American Anthropological Association; American Ethnological Society; Linguistic Society of America; Sigma Xi; American Association of University Professors; American Folklore Society (president, 1963-64). *Interests:* Field researches on languages, folklores, and ethnographies of various American Indian groups in Oregon and Washington. *Published works: Northwest Sahaptin Grammar* (University of Washington Press, 1931); *Northern Sahaptin Texts* (Columbia University, two volumes, 1934, 1937); *Coos Texts* (University of Washington Press, two volumes, 1939, 1940); *Kalapuya Texts* (University of Washington Press, 1945); *General Anthropology,* with B. J. Stern (Barnes and Noble, 1947); *Clackamas Chinook Texts* (Indiana University Press, two volumes, 1958, 1959); *Nehalem Tillamook Tales,* with E. D. Jacobs (University of Oregon Press, 1959); *The People Are Coming Soon* (University of Washington Press, 1960); *The Content and Style of an Oral Literature* (University of Chicago Press, 1959); *Pattern in Cultural Anthropology* (Dorsey Press, 1964).

JAMES, HARRY C. 1896- (educator, conservationist, writer)

Born April 25, 1896, Ottawa, Ontario, Can. *Education:* Collegiate Institute; University of California. *Principal occupation:* Educator, conservationist, writer. *Addresses:* Lolomi Lodge, San Jacinto Mts., Calif. (home); P. O. Box 716, Banning, Calif. 92220 (mailing). *Affiliations:* Founder and president, The Trailfinders; founder, Desert Protective Council, Inc. *Other professional posts:* Headmaster, Trailfinders School for Boys. *Military service:* Canadian Signal Corps. *Community activities:* Indian Welfare League. *Memberships:* American/Austrian and Swiss Alpine Clubs; Federation of Western Outdoor Clubs. *Awards, honors:* Adopted Hopi; American Motors Conservation Award, 1962; Award of Merit, The Desert Protective Council, Inc., 1964. *Interests:* Mountain climbing, music, Indian lore. *Published works: Treasure of the Hopitu* (Young and McAllister, 1927); *Haliksai Hopi Folk Tales* (Desert Printing Co.); *The Hopi Indians* (Caxton, 1956); *A Day with Honau, A Hopi Indian Boy* (Children's Press, 1957); *A Day with Poli, A Hopi Indian Girl* (Children's Press, 1957); *Red Man - White Man* (Naylor, 1958); *The Hopi Indian Butterfly Dance* (Children's Press, 1959); *A Day in Oraibi, A Hopi Indian Village* (Children's Press, 1959); *The Cahuilla Indians* (Westernlore Press, 1960); *Grizzly Adams* (Children's Press, 1963).

JAMES, OVERTON (Chickasaw) 1925- (educator)

Born July 21, 1925, Bromide, Okla. *Education:* Southeastern State College, B.A., 1949, M.A., 1955. *Principal occupation:* Educator. *Home address:* 6033 Glencove Place, Oklahoma City, Okla. *Affiliations:* Teacher and athletic coach, 1949-59; sales manager, *Compton's Pictured Encyclopedia,* 1960-65; governor, Chickasaw Nation of Oklahoma, 1963-; field representative, State Department of Education, Indian Division, Oklahoma City, Okla., 1965-. *Military service:* U.S. Navy, 1943-46. *Community activities:* Choctaw-Chickasaw Confederation (president); Inter-Tribal Council of Five Civilized Tribes (vice president); Oklahomans for Indian Opportunity (treasurer and education chairman); Five Civilized Tribes Museum (board of directors). *Memberships:* National Education Association; Oklahoma Education Association; National Congress of American Indians; Red Red Rose; Masons; Veterans of Foreign Wars; American Legion. *Awards:* In October of 1963 Mr. James became the twenty-seventh governor of the Chickasaw Nation and the youngest ever to serve as governor. *Interests:* College baseball and track; played professional baseball with the Ardmore, Oklahoma team in the Sooner State League, 1949-59; hunting and fishing; golf.

JANE, MARY C.   1909-   (teacher, writer)

Born September 18, 1909, Needham, Mass. *Education:* State Teachers College, Bridgewater, Mass., B.S., 1931. *Principal occupation:* Teacher, writer. *Home address:* Pump St., Newcastle, Me. *Affiliations:* Teacher, Needham, Mass., two years; Chester, Mass., three years; New Castle, Me., two years. *Community activities:* Library trustee. *Memberships:* Poetry Fellowship of Maine (president, 1947-48). *Interests:* "As a former teacher, was much interested in the school on Indian Island at Old Town, Maine (and in) the children there." *Published works: Eleven Mysteries for Children* (J.B. Lippincott Co.); *Mystery in Old Quebec* (J.B. Lippincott Co., 1955); *Mystery in Longfellow Square* (J.B. Lippincott Co., 1964); *Indian Island Mystery* (1965); and eight others.

JEMISON, EDMUND L.   (Seneca)   1913-
(social worker)

Born July 8, 1913, Basom, N.Y. *Education:* University of Buffalo, B.A., 1951,

certificate of social work. *Principal occupation:* Social worker. *Home address:* 776 Bloomingdale Rd., Basom, N.Y. 14013. *Affiliation:* Social worker, Department of Social Welfare, Buffalo Area Office. *Military service:* U.S. Army Air Corps, 1940-46. *Community activities:* Akron Masonic Lodge; Order of Eastern Star (patron-elect, 1966). *Memberships:* Indian Bowling Association.

JENKINS, MILDRED M.   1906-   (writer, secretary, librarian)

Born March 15, 1906, Sedro-Woolley, Wash. *Education:* Bellingham Business College. *Principal occupation(s):* Writer, secretary, librarian. *Home address:* 851 Lake Whatcom Blvd., Bellingham, Wash. 98225. *Affiliations:* Librarian, Bellingham Public Library. *Other professional posts:* Secretary to editor, Bellingham *Herald.* *Community activities:* Cub Scouts (den mother); 4-H Club. *Interests:* Northwest historical research, with emphasis on the cultures of the coastal Indians prior to the coming of the white man. *Published works: Before the White Man Came* (Binfords and Mort).

JENKINS, MYRA ELLEN   1916-
(archivist, historian)

Born September 26, 1916, Elizabeth, Colo. *Education:* University of Colorado, B.A., 1937, M.A., 1938; University of New Mexico, Ph.D., 1953. *Principal occupation:* Archivist, historian. *Home address:* 1022 Don Cubero, Santa Fe, N.M. 87501. *Affiliations:* "Educational positions," 1939-50; free lance historical research, 1953-59; historical expert witness, U.S. Indian Claims Commission, for pueblos of Laguna, Taos and Nambe, 1957-62; archivist, Museum of New Mexico, 1959-60; archivist-historian, State of New Mexico Records Center, 1960-. *Community activities:* Old Santa Fe Historical Foundation (research committee); historiographer of the Episcopal Diocese of New Mexico and Southwest Texas. *Memberships:* Society of American Archivist, 1960-; Historical Society of New Mexico, 1959-; Western History Association, 1961-. *Interests:* United States and Latin American history, particularly of the Southwest and northern Mexico, with emphasis on archival and primary documentation; preservation of historic buildings and sites; travel to and study of Indian pueblos of Acoma, Laguna and Taos. *Published works: The Baltasar Baca Grant, History of an Encroachment* (Museum of New Mexico, 1961); articles and reviews in professional journals.

JOHN, ANGELO MARVIN (Navajo) 1946- (artist)

Born February 5, 1946, Holbrook, Ariz. *Education:* Institute of American Indian Arts, 1962-65; Arizona State University, 1965-. *Principal occupation:* Artist, student. *Home address:* 29 Clark Homes, Flagstaff, Ariz. 86001. *Community activities:* Navaho Youth Conference (president, 1965); Institute of American Indian Arts (student body president, 1965). *Awards, honors:* Track Trophy, Varsity Track Team, Arizona State University; awards received from Institute of American Indian Arts, Scottsdale Exhibition, Philbrook Art Center. *Interests:* Mr. John writes, "I am interested in track (the two-mile run); Indian art; reading (recent history)."

JOHNS, GLENN DAVID (Skokomish) 1947- (artist)

Born December 15, 1947, Shelton, Wash. *Education:* Institute of American Indian Arts; Stewart Indian School. *Principal occupation:* Artist. *Home address:* Star Route 1, Box 165-A, Shelton, Wash. *Awards, honors:* Second Place, 1965 Scottsdale National Indian Arts Exhibition. *Exhibits:* Second Annual Exhibition of American Indian Painting (U. S. Department of the Interior Art Gallery); Young American Indian Artists (Riverside Museum).

JOHNSON, DONALD M. 1907- (museum director)

Born February 12, 1907, Detroit, Mich. *Education:* Pratt Institute, Diploma, 1929; Art Students League; New York School of Industrial Art. *Principal occupation:* Museum director. *Home address:* 1219 Moreland Ave. , Jefferson City, Mo. 65102. *Affiliations:* First preparator, Museum of the City of New York; visual information specialist, National Park Service, Museum Section; head preparator, Illinois State Museum; director, Missouri State Museum. *Community activities:* Boy Scouts of America (merit badge counselor). *Memberships:* Midwest Museums Conference (vice president); Cole County Historical Museum (board of directors); American Association of Museums (committee on personnel placement). *Interests:* Travel in United States and Canada; photography; electro-mechanical devices; technomation, etc. *Published works: Missouri Museum* (Resources and Development Commission, 1957); *The Key to Organizing the Community Museum* (Resources and Development Commission, 1960).

JOHNSON, FREDERICK 1904- (curator, archaeologist)

Born January 16, 1904, Everett, Mass. *Education:* Tufts College, degree, 1929; Harvard University, graduate work. *Principal occupation:* Curator, archaeologist. *Home address:* 1 Woodland Rd. , Andover, Mass. 10801. *Affiliations:* Curator, R. S. Peabody Foundation, Andover, Mass., 1936-. *Memberships:* Society for American Archaeology (president; treasurer); American Anthropological Association (executive secretary); Geological Society of America (Fellow). *Interests:* Archaeology of North and Central America. *Published works: The May and Their Neighbors* (University of Utah Press, 1962); *Radiocrabon Dating* (University of Chicago Press, 1965); articles in various scientific and popular journals.

JOHNSON, KATHRYN S. 1913- (teacher, writer)

Born October 12, 1913, Magnolia, Miss. *Education:* Northwestern State College, Natchitoches, La. , B. A. , 1952; Louisiana State College, B. S. , 1959. *Principal occupation:* Teacher, writer. *Home address:* Reeves, La. 70658. *Memberships:* Delta Kappa Gamma, 1964-; Louisiana Teachers Association. *Interests:* "Each summer my husband and I travel, spending several weeks in Montana, where he fishes and I collect rocks. Another of my interests is oil painting." *Published works: Patteran* (The Naylor Co. , 1964).

JOHNSON, KENNETH M.   1903-
(attorney)

Born August 25, 1903. *Education:* Stanford University, B. A. , 1926; Stanford Law School, LL. D. , 1928. *Principal occupation:* Attorney. *Home address:* 35 Montalvo Ave. , San Francisco, Calif. 94116. *Affiliations:* Vice president and counsel, Bank of America, San Francisco, 1936-. *Memberships:* California State Bar; San Francisco and American Bar Associations; California Historical Society; Historical Society of Southern California; American Society for Local History. *Interests:* California history, with emphasis on legal and political matters. *Published works: Aerial California* (Dawson's Book Shop, 1961); *Limantour vs. the United States* (Dawson's Book Shop, 1961); *The Pious Fund* (Dawson's Book Shop, 1963); *The Fair Will Case* (Dawson's Book Shop, 1964); *Champagne and Shoes* (Peregrine Press, 1962); *The New Almaden Mines* (Talisman Press, 1963); *San Francisco As It Is* (Talisman Press, 1964); *K-344, or the Indians of California vs. the United States* (Dawson's Book Shop, 1965).

JOHNSON, MERL L.   1919-   (excavator, museum curator)

Born May 2, 1919, Loupe City, Neb. *Education:* High school. *Principal occupation:* Excavator, museum curator. *Home address:* Route 4, Box 84, Kearney, Neb. *Affiliations:* Curator, Fort Kearney Museum, Kearney, Neb. *Military service:* U. S. Army, 1942-46.

JOHNSTON, CHARLES M.   1926-
(associate professor of history)

Born April 1, 1926, Hamilton, Ontario, Can. *Education:* McMaster University, B. A. , 1949; University of Pennsylvania, M. A. , 1950, Ph. D. , 1954. *Principal occupation:* Associate professor of history. *Address:* Department of History, McMaster University, Hamilton, Ontario, Can. *Affiliations:* Associate professor of history, McMaster University. *Other professional posts:* Consultant, Ontario Centennial Centre of Science and Technology. *Community activities:* Ontario Archaeological and Historic Sites Advisory Board; Documentary Research Committee, City of Hamilton,

Ont. ; local school board. *Memberships:* Canadian Historical Association; Ontario Historical Society. *Awards, honors:* Canada Council Research Fellowship for study in the United Kingdom, 1963-64. *Interests:* Canadian and regional history; British Imperial history of the 19th century. Travel to the United Kingdom and Europe, 1963-64. *Published works: The Head of the Lake* (Duncan and Co. , 1958); *The Valley of the Six Nations* (University of Toronto Press, 1964); presently completing a regional history of southwestern Ontario.

JONES, ROBERT HUHN   1927-
(associate professor of history)

Born July 30, 1927, Chicago, Ill. *Education:* University of Illinois, B. A. , 1950, M. A. , 1951, Ph. D. , 1957. *Principal occupation:* Associate professor of history. *Home address:* 3967 Darrow Rd. , Stow, Ohio 44224. *Affiliations:* Associate professor of history, Kent State University, 1957-65; associate professor of history, Western Reserve University, 1965-. *Military service:* U. S. Army Signal Corps, 1945-47. *Memberships:* Phi Alpha Theta, 1951-; American Historical Association, 1955-; Organization of American Historians, 1957-; Western History Association (charter member, 1963-); American Association of University Professors, 1957-. *Awards, honors:* Visiting research professor of economic history, Lilly Foundation Grant, University of Illinois, 1962-63; Postdoctoral Fellow, Lilly Foundation Grant, University of Illinois, 1964; Kent State University Faculty Summer Research Grant, 1960. *Interests:* U. S. Civil War history; westward movement; travel throughout the United States and Canada. *Published works: The Civil War in the Northwest* (University of Oklahoma Press, 1960); co-author, *Ohio Civil War Leaders* (Ohio State University, 1966).

JONES, WEYMAN   1928-
(communications director)

Born February 6, 1928, Lima, Ohio. *Education:* Harvard University, A. B. (cum laude), 1950. *Principal occupation:* Communications director. *Home address:* 3211

Rolling Rd., Chevy Chase, Md. 20015. *Affiliation:* Director of communications, I.B.M. Federal Systems Division. *Travels:* U. S. S. R., Brookings Institution Public Affairs Fellowship, 1964. *Military service:* U. S. Navy, 1950-55.

JOSEPHY, ALVIN M., Jr.   1915-
(writer, editor)

Born May 18, 1915, Woodmere, N. Y. *Education:* Harvard University, 1932-34. *Principal occupation:* Writer, editor. *Home address:* Kinsman Lane, Bruce Park, Greenwich, Conn. *Affiliations:* Associate editor, *Time* magazine, 1951-60; writer and editor, *American Heritage,* 1960- ; consultant to Secretary of the Interior Udall, 1963. *Military service:* U.S. Marine Corps, 1943-45 (Bronze Star). *Community activities:* Democratic State Central Committee, 1956-60; candidate for Connecticut Legislature, Democratic Party, 1958, 1960. *Memberships:* National Congress of American Indians (consultant); Association on American Indian Affairs (board member); Advisory Board on Indians, Episcopal Church; Third Marine Division Association; conservation and historical associations. *Awards, honors:* Western Heritage Award, National Cowboy Hall of Fame, 1962; Eagle Feather Award, National Congress of American Indians, 1964. *Interests:* History, culture and concerns of the American Indians; western American history; conservation; extensive western travel. *Published works:* Co-author, *The U. S. Marines on Iwo Jima* (Dial Press, Penguin, 1945); *The Long and the Short and the Tall* (Knopf, 1946); co-author, *My Greatest War Story* (Whittlesey House, 1946); co-author, *Uncommon Valor* (Duell, Sloan and Pearce, 1946); co-author, *American Heritage Book of the Pioneer Spirit* (Simon and Schuster, 1959); editor, *American Heritage Book of Indians* (Simon and Schuster, 1961); editor, *American Heritage History of Flight* (Simon and Schuster, 1962); *The Patriot Chiefs* (Viking, 1961); editor, *American Heritage Book of Natural Wonders* (Simon and Schuster, 1963); editor, *American Heritage History of World War I* (Simon and Schuster, 1964); editor, *American Heritage Encyclopedic Guide to the United States* (Dell, 1965); editor, *The American Heritage History of the Great West* (Simon and Schuster, 1965); *The Nez Perce Indians and the Opening of the Northwest* (Yale University Press, 1965).

JUNALUSKA, ARTHUR SMITH   (Cherokee)
1918-   (writer, director, producer, lecturer, choreographer)

Born November 30, 1918, Cherokee Nation, Cherokee, N. C. *Education:* Cherokee Indian School; Haskell Institute; Okmulgee Junior College; Eckels College of Embalming; Lister Institute of Medical Research, London School of Medicine. *Principal occupation:* Executive and artistic director, American Indian Society of Creative Arts, Inc., New York City. *Other professional posts:* Writer of plays for radio, television and stage; performer; founder, American Indian Drama Company; director of drama, South Dakota Wesleyan University, 1958; creator, writer and producer of "Dance of the Twelve Moons," an American Indian Dance Company production; director and coordinator, Indian Village, Freedomland (a New York City amusement park), 1960-61; consultant and technical advisor for motion pictures and plays; director of performing arts, Indian Festival of Arts, La-Grande, Ore. *Military service:* U.S. Army, World War II.

K

KAHN, FRANKLIN   (Navajo)   1934-
(artist)

Born May 25, 1934, Pine Springs, Ariz. *Education:* Stewart Indian School. *Principal occupation:* Artist. *Home address:* 3315 N. Steues Blvd., Flagstaff, Ariz. 86001. *Affiliations:* Sketch artist and sign painter, Federal Sign and Signal Corp., Flagstaff, Ariz. *Community activities:* Parent-Teachers' Association (chairman, 1962-63). *Memberships:* American Bowling Association; Good Fellowship; American Indian Service Committee, Bahai's. *Awards, honors:* Second prize, Scottsdale International Art Exhibit. *Interests:* Watercolor and oil painting; Indian designs and symbols. *Published works:* Illustrator, *Going Away to School* (Bureau of Indian Affairs, 1951).

KATEXAC, BERNARD   (Eskimo)   1922-
(student in vocational arts)

Born May 2, 1922, King Island, Alaska. *Education:* University of Alaska. *Principal occupation:* Student in vocational arts.

Home address: Box 488, Nome, Alaska 99762. *Military service:* S. F. C. National Guard (Armed Forces Medal). *Interests:* Arts and crafts; woodcuts; etching; jewelry; wood sculpture.

KEELER, W. W. (Cherokee) 1908-
(industrial executive)

Born April 5, 1908, Dalhart, Texas. *Education:* Kansas University. *Principal occupation:* Industrial executive. *Home address:* 1118 S. Dewey, Bartlesville, Okla. 74004. *Affiliations:* Chairman, Executive Committee, Phillips Petroleum Co. *Other professional posts:* Director of refining, Petroleum Administration for War; chairman, Military Petroleum Advisory Board. *Community activities:* White House Youth Conference; Bartlesville Kiwanis Club (president and director); Bartlesville Chamber of Commerce (director); National Council, Committee on Inter-Racial Service, Boy Scouts of America (member-at-large); Cherokee Area Council (vice president); Boys' Club of Bartlesville Y.M.C.A. (chairman); United Community Fund of Bartlesville (president); Dwight Presbyterian Mission (director); Crippled Children's Fund Committee (chairman); Gilcrease Museum (board of directors); First National Bank, Bartlesville, Okla. (director); Southwest Regional Office, Institute of International Education (former advisor); National Advisory Committee on the War on Poverty Program; Governor's Committee for Eastern Oklahoma Economic Development; National Petroleum Refiners Association (trustee); National Petroleum Council; American Petroleum Institute; Mid-Continent Oil and Gas Association; Independent Petroleum Association on America; Military-Industrial Conference Committee; National Association of Manufacturers (director); National Petroleum Council Committee; Cherokee Foundation (founder and trustee); Cherokee Nation (principal chief); Commission on the Rights, Liberties and Responsibilities of the American Indian; group to study operation of the Bureau of Indian Affairs in Alaska (chairman). *Memberships:* Sigma Chi; Sigma Tau; York Rite; Scottish Rite Mason; Shriners; Royal Jesters. *Awards, honors:* All-American Indian Award, 1957, 1961; Honorary LL. D., Distinguished Service Citation, University of Kansas Alumni Association.

KEEN, RALPH F. (Cherokee) 1934-
(educator)

Born August 31, 1934, Hominy, Okla. *Education:* Northeastern State College, B. A. (Education), 1951; Kansas State College of Pittsburg; Kansas State University. *Principal occupation:* Educator. *Address:* 817 Aitken St., Reno, Nev. *Affiliations:* Training instructor in printing, Haskell Institute, Lawrence, Kan. *Military service:* U. S. Air Force, 1958-61. *Memberships:* Kansas Education Association; National Education Association; American Congress of Parents and Teachers.

KEITH, C. HOBART *(Blue Horse)*
(Oglala Sioux) 1922- (artist and sculptor)

Born March 8, 1922, Pine Ridge, S.D. *Education:* Colorado Springs Fine Arts Center, 1938-41. *Principal occupation:* Artist and sculptor. *Home address:* P. O. Box 444, Pine Ridge, S. D. 57770. *Military service:* U. S. Navy, 1942-46. *Biographical sources: Der Missionar,* a Swiss publication (November, 1946). *Published works:* Mr. Keith has authored several newspaper articles on Indian affairs.

KEITH, HAROLD 1903- (sports information director, writer)

Born April 8, 1903, Lambert, Okla. territory. *Education:* Northwestern State Teachers College, 1921-22, 1923-25; University of Oklahoma, B. A. (History), 1929, M. A. (History), 1938. *Principal occupation:* Sports information director, writer. *Home address:* 2318 Ravenwood Lane, Rt. 4, Hall Park, Norman, Okla. 73069. *Affiliations:* Sports information director, University of Oklahoma. *Community activities:* Kiwanis Club (board of directors). *Memberships:* College Sports Information Directors of America (president, 1964-1965); National Collegiate Athletic Association (public relations committee); National Football Hall of Fame Nominating Committee. *Published works: Boys' Life of Will Rogers* (Crowell, 1936); *Sports and Games* (Crowell, 1940); *Shotgun Shaw* (Corwell); *A Pair of Captains* (Crowell); *Oklahoma Kickoff* (privately printed); *Rifles for Watie* (Crowell, 1957); *Komantcia* (Crowell, 1965).

KELLAWAY, WILLIAM 1926- (librarian)

Born March 9, 1926, Melbourne, Australia. *Education:* Oxford University, B.A., 1949, M.A., 1955. *Principal occupation:* Librarian. *Home address:* 2 Grove Terrace, London, N.W. 5, England. *Affiliations:* Library assistant, Guildhall Library, 1950-60; librarian, Institute of Historical Research, University of London, 1960-. *Other professional posts:* Honorary general editor, London Record Society. *Memberships:* F.R. Historical Society. *Interests:* History of London. *Published works: New England Company, 1649-1776* (Longmans, Green; Barnes and Noble, 1961).

KELLY, ISABEL 1906- (anthropologist)

Born January 5, 1906, Santa Cruz, Calif. *Education:* University of California, B.A., 1926, M.A., 1927, Ph.D., 1932. *Principal occupation:* Anthropologist (private research, 1961-). *Home address:* Domicilio conocido, Tepepan (z. 23), D.F. Mexico. *Affiliations:* Research associate, University of California, 1932-37, 1939, 1940; research associate, Gila Pueblo Archaeological Foundation, 1937, 1938; Guggenheim Foundation, Mexico (Fellow, 1941, 1943); anthropologist, Institute for Social Anthropology, Smithsonian Institution, Mexico, 1946-50; analyst, International Cooperation Administration, Mexico, Bolivia, Pakistan, 1951-60. *Memberships:* American Anthropological Association; American Ethnological Association; Society for American Archaeology; Society for Applied Anthropology; Sociedad Mexicana de Antropologia. *Interests:* Ethnographic field work among the Coast Miwok and Chemehuevi Indians of California, the Northern and Southern Paiute of the Great Basin, and the Lowland and Highland Totonac of eastern Mexico; archaeological survey and excavation in west Mexico; studies in applied anthropology including public health, community development, housing, nutrition. *Published works: Southern Paiute Ethnography* (Anthropological Papers No. 69, Glen Canyon Series 21, University of Utah Press, 1964); *Folk Practices in North Mexico* (Institute of Latin American Studies, University of Texas, 1965); various monographs and articles.

KENNEDY, MICHAEL STEPHEN 1912-
(museum director)

Born July 21, 1912, Belt, Mont. *Education:* University of Montana, B.A. (Journalism), 1933; Northwestern University, M.S. (Journalism), 1952. *Principal occupation:* Museum director. *Home address:* 622 Harrison Ave., Helena, Mont. *Affiliations:* Newspaper reporting and editing, California, Illinois, Montana; free lance writing; photography; public relations; director, Federal Writers' Program for Montana, 1937-42; administrative assistant, editor, *Montana, The Magazine of Western History,* assistant director and director, The Historical Society of Montana, 1952-. *Other professional posts:* Consultant, Western Heritage Center and Cowboy Hall of Fame, Oklahoma City, Okla.; consultant, Museum of the Great Plains, Lawton, Okla. *Military service:* U.S. Army (three Bronze Battle Stars). *Memberships:* National Writers' Club; Sons and Daughters of Montana Pioneers; American Association for State and Local History; The Westerners; American Historical Association; American Association of Museums; Sigma Delta Chi (life member). *Interests:* "Photography; rare book and art collecting; skiing; dry fly fishing; trail riding; travel; five children; book design and layout." *Published works: Land of Nakota* (State Publishing Co., 1942); *The Assiniboines* (University of Oklahoma Press, 1961); *Cowboys and Cattlemen* (Hastings House, 1964); *Red Man's West* (Hastings House, 1965).

KENNY, HAMILL THOMAS 1901-
(teacher)

Born May 4, 1901, Piedmont, W. Va. *Education:* Columbia University, B.A., 1924; Teachers College, Columbia University, M.A., 1925; University of Maryland, Ph.D., 1951. *Principal occupation:* Teacher. *Home address:* P.O. Box 31, Mt. Rainier, Md. 20822. *Affiliations:* Assistant in English, Columbia University, 1927-28; teacher of English, Potomac State College, 1926; teacher of English, California Preparatory School, Covina, Calif., 1928-29; teacher of English, Allegheny County, Md., 1935-45; lecturer in English, University College, University of Maryland. *Memberships:* American Name Society; Maryland Historical Society; English Graduate Union (Columbia University); Columbia University Alumni Association; Maryland University Alumni Association; Delta Phi Alpha (1934); Phi

Kappa Phi (honorary scholarship), University of Maryland (1950). *Interests:* "Teaching of English language and literature; writing and research in the fields of Algonquian linguistics, Algonquian and American place-names (Maryland place-names, specifically)." Travels to Canada, Alaska, Brazil, Argentina, Chile, Peru, Colombia, Ecuador, Ireland, England, Hungary, Scandinavia, Germany, Greece, Italy, Spain, Cairo, Malaya, India, Burma, Thailand. *Published works: West Virginia Place Names, Their Origin and Meaning* (Place Names Press, 1945); *Origin and Meaning of the Indian Place Names of Maryland* (Waverly Press, 1961); numerous articles in scholarly journals.

KENT, KATE PECK   1914-
(anthropologist)

Born May 10, 1914, Washington, D.C. *Education:* University of Denver, B.A., 1935; Columbia University, 1935-37; University of Arizona, M.A., 1950. *Principal occupation:* Anthropologist. *Address:* Department of Anthropology, University of Denver, Denver, Colo. *Affiliations:* Curator, Indian Art, Denver Art Museum, 1937-38 (curator, Native Arts, 1943-45); instructor in anthropology, University of Denver, Denver, Colo., 1950-64 (adjunct assistant professor of anthropology, 1964-). *Memberships:* Sigma Xi, 1947; American Anthropological Association, 1938; African Studies Association, 1965. *Interests:* "Ethnohistory of the North American Indian; Pacific and African primitive religion; history of anthropological theory; special interest in art and technology of primitive peoples -- especially weaving." *Published works: Cultivation and Weaving of Cotton in the Prehistoric Southwest* (American Philosophical Society, 1957); *Story of Navajo Weaving* (Heard Museum, 1961); *Montezuma Castle Archaeology, Part II - Textiles* (Southwestern Monuments Association, 1962).

KIDD, KENNETH E.   1906-   (teacher, researcher)

Born 1906, Barrie, Ontario, Can. *Education:* University of Toronto; University of Chicago. *Principal occupation:* Teacher, researcher. *Home address:* 266 Burnham St., Peterborough, Ontario, Can. *Affiliations:* Associate professor of anthropology, Trent University, Peterborough,

Ontario, Canada. *Memberships:* American Anthropological Association (Fellow, 1950-); Society for American Archaeology, 1945-; Ontario Historical Society. *Awards, honors:* Guggenheim Fellowship, 1951-52. *Interests:* Archaeology of Ontario, especially historical archaeology; Iroquois Indians of Ontario and New York State; Blackfoot Indians of Alberta and Montana. *Published works: The Excavation of Ste. Marie Island* (University of Toronto Press, 1949); *Canadians of Long Ago* (Longmans, 1949); *Indian Rock Paintings of the Great Lakes,* with S. Dewdney (University of Toronto Press for the Quetico Foundation, 1962).

KILMAN, EDWARD   1896-   (editor)

Born November 27, 1896, Ennis, Texas. *Education:* Sam Houston Normal Institute, 1916-18. *Principal occupation:* Editor. *Home address:* 3906 Fernwood Dr., Houston, Texas 77021. *Affiliations:* Reporter, feature writer; state capitol and political correspondent, 1925-42; editorial page editor, Houston *Post*, 1942-65. *Military service:* U.S. Army; Texas National Guard, 1918. *Community activities:* Houston Kiwanis Club (president, 1948); Boy Scouts of America (board member). *Memberships:* Philosophical Society of Texas; Southwestern Historical Association; Harris County Historical Society (president, 1960); Sigma Delta Chi; Texas Historical Board, 1935; Sons of Republic of Texas, 1946-; Texas Centennial of Statehood, 1945 (commissioner); Texas State Parks Board, 1955-63. *Awards, honors:* Prize for editorial writing, Associated Press, Managing Editors Association of Texas, 1948; Associated Press award for editorial on death of Governor Ross Sterling, 1949; Kiwanis International Certificate of Appreciation, 1948. *Interests:* Newspaper work; sailboating; Texas history. *Published works: Texas Musketeers* (Johnson, 1935); *The Battle of San Jacinto and the San Jacinto Campaign* (Webb Printing Co., 1947); *Hugh Roy Cullen, Biography* (Prentice-Hall, 1954); *Cannibal Coast* (Naylor, 1959).

KILPATRICK, ANNA GRITTS (Oklahoma Cherokee)   1917-   (teacher, writer)

Born March 7, 1917, Echota, Okla. *Education:* Southern Methodist University, B.S.,

1958. *Principal occupation:* Teacher, writer. *Home address:* 5350 Montrose Dr., Dallas, Texas. *Affiliations:* Teacher, Dallas, Texas, public schools. *Published works: Friends of Thunder* (S.M.U. Press), *Walk in Your Soul* (S.M.U. Press), *The Shadow of Sequoyah* (University of Oklahoma Press), all with Jack Frederick Kilpatrick.

KILPATRICK, JACK FREDERICK
  (Oklahoma Cherokee) 1915-
  (professor of music)

Born September 23, 1915, Stillwell, Okla. *Education:* Bacone College, 1933-35; Northeastern State College of Oklahoma, 1935; University of Redlands, Mus. B., 1938; Catholic University of America, Mus. M., 1946; University of Redlands, Mus. D., 1950. *Principal occupation:* Professor of music. *Home address:* 5350 Montrose Dr., Dallas, Texas. *Affiliations:* Professor of music, School of the Arts, Southern Methodist University. *Military service:* Instructor, U.S. Navy School of Music, 1943-45. *Memberships:* Phi Beta Kappa; American Anthropological Association; Society for Ethnomusicology; American Composers Alliance; Pi Kappa Lambda. *Awards:* National Science Foundation Grant; Danforth Foundation Fellowship; American Philosophical Society Grant; Carnegie Foundation Grant; Tobin Foundation Grant; achievement awards, Cherokee Nation, National Federation of Music Clubs. *Published works: Friends of Thunder* (Southern Methodist University Press, 1964), *Walk in Your Soul* (Southern Methodist University Press, 1965), *The Shadow of Sequoyah* (University of Oklahoma Press, 1965), all co-authored with Anna Gritts Kilpatrick; *Sequoyah: Of Earth and Intellect* (Encino Press, 1965).

KING, CLARENCE E., Sr. 1909-
  (principal chief, Ottawa Tribe of
  Oklahoma)

Born January 1, 1909, Miami, Okla. *Education:* High school. *Principal occupation:* Principal chief, Ottawa Tribe of Oklahoma; self-employed electrician. *Home address:* R.R. 1, Miami, Okla. 74354. *Military service:* U.S. Navy, 1944-46 (Asiatic and Pacific Medals, World War II Medal).

KINIETZ, W. VERNON 1907- (teacher)

Born May 6, 1907, Lapeer, Mich *Education:* University of Michigan, B.A., 1928; University of Chicago, M.A., 1933. *Principal occupation:* Teacher. *Home address:* 124 W. Union, Apt. 5, Fullerton, Calif. 92632. *Affiliations:* Archaeologist, University of Illinois, 1930-32; ethnohistorian, University of Michigan, 1935-42; metallurgist, Chrysler Corp., Highland Park, Mich., 1942-44. *Community activities:* Sky Valley Chamber of Commerce (president). *Interests:* Indians of the Great Lakes area; archaeology of the Southwest and of Central and South America. Travels to Peru, Mexico, Haiti, Puerto Rico, Europe from North Cape to Madrid. *Biographical sources: American Men of Science* (1942); *Published works:* Editor, *Meearmeear Traditions* (University of Michigan Press, 1938); co-editor, *Shawnese Traditions* (University of Michigan Press, 1939); *Indians of the Western Great Lakes* (University of Michigan Press, 1940, 1965); *John Mix Stanley and His Indian Paintings* (University of Michigan Press, 1942); *Delaware Culture Chronology* (Indiana Historical Society, 1946); *Chippewa Village* (Cranbrook Institute of Science, 1947).

KINLEY, HARRY EVAN 1882-
  (museum curator)

Born August 16, 1882, Sandusky, Ohio. *Education:* High School. *Principal occupation:* Museum curator. *Affiliations:* Curator, Wyandotte Museum, Upper Sandusky, Ohio. *Other occupations:* Salesman, 1930-63. *Community activities:* County Centennial, 1845 (general chairman); Upper Sandusky Centennial, 1848 (general chairman). *Memberships:* Wyandotte County Historical Society; Wyandotte Museum. *Work in progress: Indian Life in Ohio.*

KINNEY, JAY P. 1875- (attorney)

Born September 18, 1875, Snowdon, N.Y. *Education:* Cornell University, B.A., 1902, M.F. (Agriculture and Forestry), 1913; National University, LL.B., 1908. *Principal occupation:* Attorney. *Home address:* Hartwick, Otsego County, N.Y. *Affiliations:* High school principal, Milford and Cooperstown, N.Y., 1903-06; examiner, U.S. Patent Office, 1906-10; forester, U.S.

Indian Service, 1910-33; general supervisor of construction, U. S. Indian Service, 1933-42; forester, Office of Utilization, U. S. Department of the Interior, 1942-45; specialist in forestry, U. S. Department of Justice, 1945-54; attorney and research specialist, U. S. Department of Justice, 1959-65. *Community activities:* Washington Section, Society of American Foresters (chairman, 1932-34). *Memberships:* Society of American Foresters, 1912-65; American Forestry Association, 1911-65. *Published works: Forest Law in America Prior to 1789* (Cornell University, 1914); *Essentials of American Timber Law* (John Wiley and Sons, 1916); *Development of Forest Law in America* (John Wiley and Sons, 1917); *A Continent Lost - A Civilization Won* (Johns Hopkins Press, 1937); *Indian Forest and Range* (Forestry Enterprises, 1953).

KINSEY, W. FRED 1929- (museum director)

Born July 2, 1929, York, Penna. *Education:* Columbia University, B. A. , 1951. M. A. , 1953. *Principal occupation:* Museum director. *Home address:* 524 Saratoga Rd. , Lancaster, Penna. 17603. *Affiliations:* Curator of anthropology, Pennsylvania Historical and Museum Commission, 1955-60; chief curator, Pennsylvania Historical and Museum Commission, 1960-63; director, North Museum, Franklin and Marshall College, 1963-. *Military service:* U. S. Army, 1953-55. *Memberships:* Society for American Archaeology; American Anthropological Association; Society for Pennsylvania Archaeology; American Association of Museums; Eastern States Archaeological Federation (secretary). *Awards, honors:* National Science Foundation Grant; National Park Service Grant; Franklin and Marshall Faculty Research Grant. *Published works:* Editor, *Susquehannock Miscellany* (Pennsylvania Historical and Museum Commission).

KITTLE, JAMES R. 1934- (state park director)

Born October 19, 1934, Sidney, Neb. *Education:* North Dakota State University, B.S., 1958, M. S. , 1965. *Principal occupation:* State park director. *Address:* c/o Fort Lincoln State Park, Mandan, N. D. 58501. *Affiliations:* Director, Fort Lincoln State

Park, Mandan, N. D. *Military service:* U. S. Army, 1958-62. *Memberships:* American Institute of Park Executives; The Nature Conservancy; Wilderness Society; National Campers and Hikers Association; Yellowstone-Missouri Fort Union Commission (advisor). *Interests:* Protection and preservation of natural and scenic areas.

KLEIN, BERNARD 1921- (editor, publisher)

Born September 20, 1921, Bronx, N. Y. *Education:* City College of New York, B.A., 1942. *Principal occupation:* Editor, publisher. *Addresses:* 17 Pine Brook Drive, White Plains, N. Y. (home); 104 Fifth Ave. , New York, N.Y. 10011 (office). *Affiliations:* President, U. S. List Co. , Inc. , 1946-; president and chief editor, B. Klein and Co. , 1953-. *Military service:* U. S. Army, 1943-45 (sergeant). *Community activities:* Masons; B'nai B'rith. *Memberships:* Direct Mail Advertising Association. *Interests:* "The research and development of useful and marketable reference books. " *Biographical sources: Who's Who in the East; Who's Who in Commerce and Industry; Contemporary Authors. Published works:* Editor, *Guide to American Directories,* six editions (B. Klein and Co., 1954, 1956, 1958, 1960; Prentice-Hall, 1962; McGraw-Hill, 1965); editor, *Guide to American Educational Directories,* two editions (B. Klein and Co. , 1962; McGraw-Hill, 1965); editor, with Daniel Icolari, *Reference Encyclopedia of the American Indian* (B. Klein and Co. , 1967); several periodical business publications.

KLUCKHOHN, FLORENCE ROCKWOOD 1905- (lecturer)

Born January 14, 1905, Ill. *Education:* University of Wisconsin, B. A., 1927; Radcliffe College, Ph. D., 1941. *Principal occupation:* Lecturer in social relations. *Home address:* 50 Fresh Pond Pkwy., Cambridge, Mass. 02138. *Affiliations:* Lecturer, Wellesley College, 1940-47; lecturer in sociology and research associate in Laboratory of Social Relations, Harvard University, 1947-. *Other posts:* Trustee, The Age Center of New England, Inc.; research analyst, Far Eastern Division, Office of War Information and the Foreign Analysis Division, Military Intelligence Services,

1944-45. *Memberships:* Phi Beta Kappa; American Sociological Association; American Academy of Political and Social Science; Group for the Advancement of Psychiatry (consultant, 1950-); American Anthropological Association; Society for Applied Anthropology. *Published works: The American Family: Past and Present* and *America's Women* (Delphian Society, 1952); *Variations in Value Orientations*, with Fred L. Strodtbeck (Harper & Row, 1961); *The Problems and Promise of American Democracy, Unit 1: Man, Society and Social Order*, edited by Donald H. Riddle (McGraw-Hill, 1964).

KNIGHT, OLIVER 1919- (associate professor)

Born June 16, 1919, Brownwood, Texas. *Education:* University of Oklahoma, B. A., 1953, M. A., 1954; University of Wisconsin, Ph. D., 1959. *Principal occupation:* Associate professor of journalism. *Home address:* 1727 Van Hise Ave., Madison, Wis. 53705. *Affiliations:* Newspaperman--Washington correspondent, reporter, copyreader, city editor; college public relations official, 1938-58; assistant professor of journalism, Indiana University. *Military service:* U. S. Army, 1943-46; U. S. Army Reserve. *Memberships:* Organization of American Historians; Western History Association; American Historical Association; Association for Education in Journalism. *Published works: Following the Indian Wars* (University of Oklahoma Press, 1960); "Introduction," Finerty, John F., *War-Path and Bivouac* (University of Oklahoma Press, 1961); "Foreword," Gillette, James, *Six Years with the Texas Rangers* (University of Oklahoma Press, 1963); *I Protest: Selected Disquisitions of E. W. Scripps* (University of Wisconsin Press, 1966).

KOLB, DELMAR M. 1912- (museum director)

Born January 14, 1912, Chicago, Ill. *Education:* University of Chicago, Ph. D., 1933, J. D., 1936. *Principal occupation:* Museum director. *Home address:* 1305 Malaga La., Santa Fe, N. M. 87501. *Affiliations:* Director, Museum of International Folk Art, Museum of New Mexico. *Other professional posts:* Director, Pensacola Art Center, Florida; curator, St. Paul Art

Center. *Military service:* U. S. Army, 1942-46 (Good Conduct Medal). *Memberships:* American Association of Museums.

KRACHER, ANTHONY B. 1933- (teacher)

Born January 15, 1933, Chewelah, Wash. *Education:* Eastern Washington State College, B. A. (Education), 1962. *Principal occupation:* Teacher. *Home address:* New Stuyahok, Alaska 99636. *Affiliation:* Principal-teacher, Anchorage, Alaska, Bureau of Indian Affairs.

KROPP, AMALIA M. 1894- (teacher-museum curator)

Born June 16, 1894, Leelanau County, Mich. *Education:* Art Institute of Chicago, Certificate, 1917; University of Chicago, B. A. E., 1932; Wayne State University, M. A. E., 1941. *Principal occupation:* Teacher, museum curator. *Home address:* Cedar, Mich. 49621. *Affiliations:* Art teacher, Detroit public schools; director, Leelanau Historical Museum, Leland, Mich. *Community activities:* Alumni, art, civic, church, poverty, and others. *Memberships:* Artists and Craftsmen (president); American Craftsmen's Council, local crafts groups; League of Women Extension; Farm Bureau. *Published works: Diary of G. N. Smith, 1949-1957* (in progress).

KUKA, KING D. 1946- (artist, rancher)

Born August 13, 1946, Browning, Mont. *Education:* Institute of American Indian Arts, Diploma, 1965. *Principal occupation:* Artist, rancher. *Home address:* Box 62, Valier, Mont. 59486. *Military service:* U. S. Army (Basic Combat Training), 1965-. *Awards, honors:* Most Valuable Basketball Player, Institute of American Indian Arts, 1964-65; Second Prize (Short Story), Third Prize (Poetry), Vincent Price Awards in Creative Writing, 1964; First Prize (Legend), Scottsdale National Indian Arts Exhibition, 1965; Short Story Award, High School Creative Writing Awards, New Mexico State University, 1964. Painting and sculpture exhibits at Riverside Museum, New York, N. Y.; San Francisco; Philbrook Art Center, Tulsa, Okla. ; Gallery of Indian Arts, Washington, D. C. *Interests:* Mr.

Kuka's main interest is Fine Arts, which he plans to make his major subject in college. He is currently preparing the outline for a book on Indian culture.

KURATH, GERTRUDE PROKOSCH 1903-
(dance ethnologist and musicologist)

Born August 19, 1903, Chicago, Ill. *Education:* University of Texas, University of Chicago, 1917-20; Bryn Mawr College, B.A., 1922, M.A., 1928; Yale School of Drama, 1929-30. *Principal occupation:* Dance ethnologist and musicologist. *Home address:* 1125 Spring St., Ann Arbor, Mich. 48103. *Affiliations:* Pageant director, Rhode Island School of Design, 1932-45; teacher of dance, Brown University Extension, 1936-45; director, Creative Dance Guild, 1937-46; dance critic, Ann Arbor *News,* 1961-. *Other professional posts:* Field employee, New York State Museum, 1952; dance consultant, *Webster's International Dictionary,* third edition; field employee, National Museum of Canada, 1962-. *Community activities:* Community Music School, Providence, R.I. (dance director, 1935-40); Ann Arbor Dance Theater (ethnic dance consultant, 1965). *Memberships:* American Folklore Society (council, 1946-); Michigan Folklore Society, 1947- (president, treasurer, editor); Michigan Academy of Science, 1952-; Sociedad Mexicana de Antropologia, 1951-; Society for Ethnomusicology, 1953- (dance editor, council); Archaeological Society of New Mexico, 1957-; Dance Research Center (director, 1963-). *Awards, honors:* Adopted Chippewa and Onondaga Indian; research grants from Viking Fund, 1949, Wenner-Gren Foundation for Anthropological Research, 1960-61, 1963-65, American Philosophical Society, 1951-52, 1954-55, 1957, Michigan Academy of Science, 1953-56 (these grants for Amerindian field work, reports, recordings, films, publications). *Interests:* Dance ethnology, musicology; esthetics of modern creative dance; dance composition; outdoor sports -- especially swimming and skating. *Travels:* Mexico, New Mexico, Wisconsin, Ontario, New York State, on field studies of American Indian ceremonies. *Published works: The Iroquois Eagle Dance,* with W.N. Fenton (Bureau of American Ethnology Bulletin, 1953); *Songs of the Wigwam* (Cooperative Recreation Service, 1955); *Songs and Dances of the Great Lakes Indians,* recording (Folkways Records, 1956);

Dances of Anahuac, with S. Marti (Aldine and Viking Fund Publication No. 38, 1964); *Dance and Song Rituals of Six Nations Reserve, Ontario* (National Museum of Canada, 1966); *Dance and Music in Tewa Plaza Ceremonies, New Mexico* (Museum of New Mexico Press, 1966).

L

LA BARRE, WESTON 1911-
(professor of anthropology)

Born December 13, 1911, Uniontown, Penna. *Education:* Princeton University, B.A., summa cum laude, 1933; Yale University, Ph.D. (with honors), 1937. *Principal occupation:* Professor of anthropology. *Home address:* GM Duke Station, Durham, N.C. 27706. *Affiliations:* Professor of anthropology, Duke University, 1946-; visiting clinical professor, University of North Carolina Medical School, 1955-. *Other professional posts:* General editor, *Landmarks in Anthropology. Military service:* U.S. Naval Reserve. *Memberships:* American Anthropological Association (Fellow); Current Anthropology (Fellow); Phi Beta Kappa; Sigma Xi; Group for the Advancement of Psychiatry, 1959-. *Awards, honors:* Sterling Fellow, Yale University; Social Science Research Council Fellow; Guggenheim Fellow; National Science Foundation Fellow; Roheim Memorial Award, 1958. *Interests:* Psychological anthropology; Americanist studies; primitive religion; music and art; human biology; crisis cults. *Published works: The Aymara Indians of the Lake Titicaca Plateau* (American Anthropological Association, 1948); *L'Animal Humaine* (Payot, 1956); *They Shall Take Up Serpents: Psychology of the Southern Snake-Handling Cult* (University of Minnesota Press, 1962); *The Peyote Cult* (Yale University Publications in Anthropology, 1938; Shoe String Press, 1964); *The Human Animal* (University of Chicago Press, 1954, 1965).

LA BRECHE, P.T. (Blackfoot) 1915-
(B.I.A. agency superintendent)

Born November 22, 1915, East Glacier, Mont. *Education:* Capital College, B.A.,

1938; LaSalle Institute, LL.B., 1956. *Principal occupation:* B.I.A. agency superintendent. *Home address:* Star Route, Dixon, Mont. *Affiliation:* Superintendent, Flathead Agency, Bureau of Indian Affairs. *Other professional posts:* Program officer; credit officer; industrial development specialist. *Military service:* 1942-46 (American Theatre Ribbon; Victory Medal). *Community activities:* Lions Club (president); Boy Scouts of America. *Awards:* Meritorious Group Award, U.S. Department of the Interior, 1955.

LA CLAIR, LEO JOHN (Muckleshoot)
    1941- (teacher)

Born February 15, 1941, Auburn, Wash. *Education:* Central Washington State College, B.A., 1964; University of Colorado; University of Utah. *Principal occupation:* Teacher. *Home address:* Star Route, Box 681, Marysville, Wash. *Affiliation:* Program assistant, Indian Program, American Friends Service Committee, Seattle, Wash. *Community activities:* Committee on Educational Opportunities for American Indians and Alaska Natives (Council on Indian Affairs). *Memberships:* National Association of Intergroup Relations Officials; National Indian Youth Council. *Awards:* United Scholarship Service and American Indian Development, Inc. scholarships; Eleanor Roosevelt Foundation Grant.

LAMB, E. WENDELL 1896- (teacher)

Born February 2, 1896, Amboy, Ind. *Education:* Earlham College, B.Sc., 1921. *Principal occupation:* Teacher. *Home address:* Box 25, Amboy, Ind. *Interests:* "Have collected much Indian material"; travel to Europe and Africa, 1917-19. *Published works: Indian Lore* (Shultz, 1964).

LAMPMAN, EVELYN SIBLEY 1907-
    (writer)

Born April 18, 1907, Dallas, Ore. *Education:* Oregon State University, B.S., 1929. *Principal occupation:* Writer of children's books. *Home address:* 6810 S.E. Yamhill St., Portland, Ore. 97215. *Interests:* "History, particularly the Western U.S. and Mexico. I have lived in the West all my life and have traveled in Mexico." *Published*

works: Navajo Sister (Doubleday, 1956); *Witch Doctor's Son* (Doubleday, 1954); *Temple of the Sun* (Doubleday, 1964).

LAROM, HENRY V. 1903- (teacher,
    writer)

Born July 9, 1903, Saranac Lake, N.Y. *Education:* University of Virginia, 1922-25; University of Montana, B.A., 1931, M.A., 1951. *Principal occupation:* Teacher, writer. *Home address:* 8 Zabriskie Terrace, Monsey, N.Y. 10952. *Affiliations:* Copy chief, Batten, Barton, Durstine & Osborn, 1933-45; assistant professor, University of Montana, 1952-59; dean, Rockland Community College, 1959-63 (chairman, English Department, 1963-). *Other professional posts:* Director, Regional Arts Roundup (Rockefeller Fund), University of Montana, 1952-54; director, Montana State University Writers' Conference, 1952-59. *Community activities:* Saranac Lake Free Library (director); Montana Institute of the Arts (director); Rockland County Mental Health Association (director). *Memberships:* National Council of Teachers of English; American Association of University Professors. *Awards, honors:* Boys Club of America Award for *Mountain Pony and the Pinto Colt,* 1949. *Interests:* Mr. Larom writes, "I have always been interested in the West. In 1924, I hitchhiked to the Valley Ranch (Valley, Wyo.). Here for a number of years I was a 'dude wrangler' and learned to love horses, fishing, and 'the big sky country.' Here also I learned about western horses from oldtimers. My interest in Indians came only when I attended and worked on several Indian Institutes at the University of Montana. Out of this experience came the book, *Ride Like an Indian.* I wanted to show young people a way to break down prejudice. Above all, I like teaching, and writing for young people." *Published works: Mountain Pony* (McGraw-Hill, 1946); *Mountain Pony and the Pinto Colt* (McGraw-Hill, 1948); *Mountain Pony and the Rodeo Mystery* (McGraw-Hill, 1949); *Mountain Pony and the Elkhorn Mystery* (McGraw-Hill, 1950); *Bronco Charlie, Rider for the Pony Express* (McGraw-Hill, 1951); *Ride Like an Indian* (McGraw-Hill, 1958); reprints of many of these titles by Grosset & Dunlap, Teen-Age Book Club, Children's Weekly Reader Book Club, Hachette (French); one German translation.

LATHEM, ANDREW W.   1918-   (B. I. A. agency superintendent)

Born December 4, 1918, Sebastopol, Miss. *Education:* East Central Junior College, 1938-40; Mississippi State College, B. S. (Agricultural Education), 1942. *Principal occupation:* B. I. A. agency superintendent. *Home address:* Box 188, Hoopa, Calif. 95546. *Affiliations:* Superintendent, Hoopa Agency, Hoopa, Calif. *Military service:* U. S. Army, 1943-46. *Community activities:* Kiwanis Club (vice president, president); American Legion (service officer); Chamber of Commerce (board of directors).

LAUBIN, GLADYS W.   (lecturer, entertainer)

Home address: Grand Teton National Park, Moose, Wyo. 83012. *Principal occupation:* Lecturer and entertainer (presentation of Indian dances on the concert stage). *Memberships:* Association on American Indian Affairs; National Congress of American Indians; Chicago Indian Center; Jackson Hole Fine Arts Foundation. *Awards, honors:* Adopted member of Sioux Tribe; dance prizes, Standing Rock and Crow reservations. *Interests:* Research among Sioux, Crow, Blackfeet, Cherokee, Kiowa and other American Indian tribes related to dance, customs, Indian lore, music; photography; painting; costume making; woodcraft; camping. *Published works:* Co-author, *The Indian Tipi* (University of Oklahoma Press, 1957). Documentary art films, produced with Reginald Laubin: *Old Chiefs Dance, Talking Hands, War Dance, Indian Musical Instruments, Ceremonial Pipes and Tipi How* (University of Oklahoma, 1951-58).

LAUBIN, REGINALD   (lecturer, entertainer)

Home address: Grand Teton National Park, Moose, Wyo. 83012. *Education:* Hartford Art School; Norwich Art School. *Principal occupation:* Lecturer and entertainer (presentation of American Indian dances and lore on the concert stage). *Memberships:* Association on American Indian Affairs; National Congress of American Indians; Chicago Indian Center; Jackson Hole Fine Arts Foundation. *Awards, honors:* Guggenheim Fellowship, 1951; adopted son of Chief One Bull, nephew of Sitting Bull; dance prizes,

Standing Rock and Crow Reservations. *Interests:* Research among Sioux, Crow, Blackfeet, Cherokee, Kiowa and other tribes on dance, custom, lore, music and general anthropology; archery; manufacture of tackle; photography; horsemanship; duplication of Indian craft techniques; primitive camping and cooking; woodcraft. *Published works:* The Indian Tipi (University of Oklahoma, 1957); series in *Boy's Life* on Indian crafts; six documentary films on Indian dance and culture, produced with Gertrude Laubin (University of Oklahoma).

LAURITZEN, JONREED   1902-   (novelist)

Born July 22, 1902, Richfield, Utah. *Education:* "Educated by schoolteacher parents and self, on northern Arizona ranch." *Principal occupation:* Novelist. *Home address:* 1635 Kent Place, Thousand Oaks, Calif. *Posts:* Former field secretary to Secretary Ickes, U. S. Department of the Interior. *Memberships:* Writers Guild of America. *Awards, honors:* Award for *The Ordeal of the Young Hunter*, Child Study Association, 1954; award for *The Legend of Billy Bluesage*, Southern California Council on Children's Literature, 1962; Gold Medal Award for *The Everlasting Fire*, Commonwealth Club of California, 1962. *Interests:* World travel; Western exploration; gardening. Mr. Lauritzen writes: "Explored many out-of-the-way places of the canyon country. Was first into source of Tapeats Creek of Thunder River in Grand Canyon. Studied Navajo traditions and transitional ways and traveled the Navajo country extensively before the paved roads came." *Published works:* *Arrows into the Sun* (Knopf, 1942); *Song Before Sunrise* (Doubleday, 1945); *The Rose and the Flame* (Doubleday, 1947); *The Ordeal of the Young Hunter* (Little, Brown, 1954); *The Young Mustangers* (Little, Brown, 1957); *Treasure of the High Country* (Little, Brown, 1959); *The Glitter-Eyed Wouser* (Little, Brown, 1960); *The Legend of Billy Bluesage* (Little, Brown, 1961); and others.

LA VIOLETTE, FORREST E.   1904- (professor)

Born January 9, 1904, North Dakota. *Education:* University of Washington, B. A. , 1933; University of Chicago, M. A. , 1934,

Ph. D. , 1946. *Principal occupation:* Professor. *Addresses:* 1307 Pine, New Orleans, La. 70118 (home); Department of Sociology and Anthropology, Tulane University, New Orleans, La. 70118 (business). *Affiliations:* Instructor, University of Washington, 1936-40; associate professor, McGill University, 1940-49; professor, Tulane University, 1949-. *Other professional posts:* Instructor, radiophysics, Royal Canadian Air Force, 1941-43. *Military service:* U. S. Naval Reserve, 1923-27. *Memberships:* American Sociological Association; Southern Sociological Society. *Interests:* Dr. LaViolette writes, "Race relations; migration in Colombia -- at the present time I spend summers at the International Center for Medical Research and Training at the Universidad del Valle, Cali, Colombia. There I direct research in cultural ecology and have a staff for the study of migration and urbanization in the Cauca Valley, an Andean valley of basic significance in the national development of Colombia. I am also engaged in some work in the Rain Forest area of Colombia. Various Tulane students doing their doctoral dissertations used our Center as a base for their field work. This work is an established program of our department. " *Published works: The American Japanese* (Canadian Institute of International Affairs, 1946); *Canadian Japanese and World War II* (University of Toronto Press, 1948); *The Struggle for Survival* (University of Toronto Press, 1961); *Community Structure, Organizational Structure and Citizen Participation in Communitywide Activities,* with T. Ktsanes and John Rohrer (Urban Life Research Institute, Tulane University, 1956); thirty-two book reviews and twenty-three articles in various journals.

LAWSHE, FRED E. 1884- (teacher, museum curator)

Born November 22, 1884, Bruce, S. D. *Education:* South Dakota State College, D. C. ; Bliss Electrical School; Minnesota University; Dunwoody Institute; Mankato Teachers' College; Hewitt School of Chiropractic; Stout State College. *Principal occupation:* Teacher, museum curator. *Home address:* 1063 Dwane St. , South St. Paul, Minn. 55075. *Affiliations:* Teacher, South St. Paul, 1918-58. *Other professional posts:* Doctor of chiropractic, 1917; curator, Dakota County Historical Museum, 1958-. *Community activities:* Church elder;

Kiwanis Club; Dakota County Historical Society (president); Minnesota Historical Society; Territorial Pioneers. *Memberships:* Minnesota Archaeological Society. *Awards, honors:* Outstanding Senior Citizen of Minnesota, 1964; Governor's Council on Aging; Outstanding Male Senior Citizen of Minnesota, 1965. *Interests:* Industrial arts; printing; electricity; metal work; carpentry; plastics; archaeological expeditions in Minnesota, Wisconsin, North and South Dakota. *Published works: Adventures in Puzzledom* (Graphic Quiz, 1952); *Health, Happiness, Success Through a Hobby* (Graphic Quiz, 1958).

LEAVITT, JEROME E. 1916- (professor of education)

Born August 1, 1916, Verona, N. J. *Education:* Newark State College, B. S. , 1938; Teachers College, Columbia University, 1938-39; School of Education, New York University, M. A. , 1942; University of Colorado, 1949-50; Northwestern University, Ed. D. , 1952; visiting scholar, University of Arizona, 1958-59, 1965. *Principal occupation:* Professor of education. *Home address:* 9444 S.E. Salmon St., Portland, Ore. 97216. *Affiliations:* Elementary teacher, Roslyn Heights, N. Y. 1932-42; instructor, Sperry Gyroscope Co., 1942-45; elementary principal, Los Alamos, N. M. , 1945-49; instructor in education, Northwestern University, 1950-52; associate professor of education, Oregon State System of Higher Education, 1952-58; professor of education, School of Education, Portland State College, 1952-. *Other professional posts:* American specialist in education, U. S. State Department, Cyprus, 1961; member of teams conducting surveys of public school systems in United States; chairman, Evaluating Committee, Oregon State Department of Education, Marylhurst College; research associate, Evaluation of the Arkansas Experiment in Teacher Education; coordinator, preparation of self-study reports in liberal arts and teacher education, Portland State College; research consultant, Oregon State Department of Education, 1963-; owner, Jerome E. Leavitt Publishing Services, 1964-; editor, Social Science Series, G. P. Putnam's Sons, 1965-. *Memberships:* Oregon Education Association; National Education Association; Association for Childhood Education International; Phi Delta Kappa; American Association of University Professors; Association for Supervision and Curriculum Development; National Society for the Study of Education; American Educational Research Association; National Society of College Teachers of Education. *Published works:* Editor, *Nursery-Kindergarten Education* (McGraw-Hill, 1958); editor, *Readings in Elementary Education,* (Wm. C. Brown, 1961); *Terrariums and Aquariums* (Children's Press, 1961); *America and Its Indians* (Children's Press, 1961; Grosset and Dunlap); *The Beginning Kindergarten Teacher* (Burgess Publishing Co., 1965); *Creative Teaching in the Elementary School* (Burgess Publishing Co., 1965); *The American Indian and the Buffaloes* (Holt, Rinehart & Winston, 1966); various magazine articles.

LECKIE, WILLIAM H. 1915- (professor of history)

Born October 18, 1915, Runge, Texas. *Education:* Texas College of Arts and Industries, B.A., 1947, M.A., 1948; University of Oklahoma, Ph.D., 1954. *Principal occupation:* Professor of history. *Affiliations:* Professor, Texas College of Arts and Industries, 1947-63; professor of history, executive officer, College of Arts and Sciences, University of Toledo, 1963-. *Military service:* U.S. Army Air Corps, 1942-46 (two commendations for meritorious work). *Memberships:* American Association of University Professors; American Historical Association; Mississippi Valley Historical Association; Western History Association; Phi Kappa Phi. *Awards, honors:* University Scholar, University of Oklahoma. *Interests:* Teaching and research; fishing; golf. Extensive travel in western United States, Canada and Mexico. *Published works: Military Conquest of the Southern Plains* (University of Oklahoma Press, 1963).

LEE, ROBERT H. (Bob) 1920- (newspaper editor)

Born May 28, 1920, Minneapolis, Minn. *Education:* High school. *Principal occupation:* Editor. *Home address:* Boulder Canyon Route, Sturgis, S.D. 57785. *Affiliations:* Wire, state and Sunday editor, consecutively, for Rapid City *Daily Journal,* Rapid City, S.D., nine years; reporter,

Minneapolis *Tribune; Rocky Mountain News,* Denver, Colo.; political columnist, *Daily Plainsman,* Huron, S.D.; political columnist, *Public Opinion,* Watertown, S.D.; political columnist, *American News,* Aberdeen, S.D.; vice president and editor, Black Hills Publishers, Sturgis, S.D. *Military service:* U.S. Army, S.D.N.G., 1940-45, 1947-64; Bronze Star. *Community activities:* Executive secretary to Governor Foss, S.D., 1954-59; director, Sturgis Rotary Club; founder, Sturgis Chamber of Commerce; Black Hills Corral of The Westerners. *Memberships:* South Dakota Historical Society, 1947- (director, 1964-); Crazy Horse Memorial Commission (director). *Awards, honors:* Award for reporting of 1949 South Dakota blizzard, Associated Press; award for coverage of theft of Chief Sitting Bull's body from North Dakota grave and reburial in South Dakota, Associated Press. *Published works: Dakota Panorama* (Midwest-Bear Printing Co., 1961); *Last Grass Frontier* (Black Hills Publishers, Inc., 1964).

LEEKLY, THOMAS B. 1910- (magazine production manager)

Born March 9, 1910, Parker, S.D. *Education:* Dakota Wesleyan University, B.A., 1931; University of South Dakota, M.A., 1935; University of Colorado; University of Pennsylvania. *Principal occupation:* Magazine production manager. *Home address:* Route 1, Waynesville, Ohio. *Affiliations:* Instructor in English, University of Pennsylvania; East Coast operations manager, *Time,* Inc.; production manager, *Newsweek* magazine, Dayton, Ohio. *Interests:* Mr. Leekly writes, "Both my boyhood in Dakota and considerable travel in Canada have contributed to my interest in Indian customs and folklore. From the Canadian and northern Minnesota trips have come my recent collection of Chippewa folktales, *The World of Manabozho.* I am currently working on a similar collection of Sioux materials. The Indian studies have really been a part of a larger interest in the Canadian-American frontier. During the past fifteen years I have traveled many of the old canoe routes which took the fur traders out to Indian country." *Published works: King Herla's Quest* (Vanguard, 1956); *The Riddle of the Black Knight* (Vanguard, 1957); *Rescue for Brownie* (Vanguard, 1959); *The World of Manabozho* (Vanguard, 1965).

LEIGHTON, DOROTHEA C.   1908-
(mental health researcher)

Born September 2, 1908, Lunenburg, Mass.
Education: Bryn Mawr College, B. A., 1930.
Principal occupation: Mental health researcher. *Home address:* 221A Vance St.,
Chapel Hill, N. C. 27514. *Affiliations:*
Special physician, U. S. Office of Indian Affairs, 1942-45; research associate, Cornell
University, 1949-65; mental health researcher, School of Public Health, University of North Carolina, 1965-. *Community
activities:* Parent-Teachers Association
(president, vice president); Community
Council of Trumansburg, N. Y. ; women's
church organization. *Memberships:* American Psychiatric Association; American
Anthropological Association; American Association for the Advancement of Science;
American Association of University Professors; American Sociological Association. *Awards, honors:* S. S. R. C. Postdoctoral Research Training Fellowship, 1939-
40; John Simon Guggenheim Fellowship,
1946-47. *Interests:* Indian education research; mental health and its relationship
to environmental factors. *Published works:*
The Navaho Door, with A. H. Leighton (Harvard University Press, 1944); *The Navaho*,
with Clyde Kluckhohn (Harvard University
Press, 1946); *Children of the People*, with
Clyde Kluckhohn (Harvard University Press,
1947); *People of the Middle Place*, with John
Adair (Yale University Press); *The Character of Danger*, with others (Basic Books,
1963); *Psychiatric Disorder Among the Yoruba*, with others (Cornell Press, 1963).

LENSKI, LOIS   1893-   (writer, illustrator)

Born October 14, 1893, Springfield, Ohio.
Education: Ohio State University, B.S. (Education), 1915; Art Students League, 1915-
19; Westminster School of Art, London,
1919-20. *Principal occupation:* Writer, illustrator. *Home address:* Lutean Shores,
Tarpon Springs, Fla. 33589. *Awards, honors:* Hon. Litt.D., Wartburg College, 1959;
University of North Carolina, D. H. L.; Ohi-
oana Medal for *Bayou Suzette*, 1944; Child
Study Association Award for *Judy's Journey;*
Newberry Medal, American Library Association, 1946. *Interests:* History, gardening,
painting. *Published works: The Little Auto*
(Walck, 1934); *Phebe Fairchild* (Lippincott,
1936); *Indian Captive* (Lippincott, 1941);

Puritan Adventure (Lippincott, 1944); *The
Little Fire Engine* (Walck, 1946); *Straw-
berry Girl* (Lippincott, 1945); *Cotton in My
Sack* (Lippincott, 1949); *Papa Small* (Walck,
1951); *We Live in the South* (Lippincott,
1952); *Little Sioux Girl* (Lippincott, 1958);
the *Davy* books; the *Read-and-Sing* Books
(Walck).

LEVIN, NORMAN BALFOUR   1922-
(educator)

Born January 14, 1922, New York, N. Y.
Education: University of Texas, B.S., 1946,
M. A., 1955; University of Pennsylvania,
Ph. D., 1960. *Principal occupation:* Edu-
cator. *Home address:* 815 Delaware Ave.,
S. W., Washington, D. C. *Affiliations:* Vi-
siting lecturer, University of Pennsylvania;
assistant professor, University of North Dakota; visiting lecturer, Georgetown University; assistant professor, Howard University. *Other professional posts:* Visiting
lecturer, American University; director,
N. D. E. A. ; associate director, Howard
University. *Military service:* U. S. Army.
Community activities Corcoran Gallery,
Smithsonian Institution; National Gallery of
Fine Art. *Memberships:* Linguistic Society
of Great Britain, Linguistic Society of America; Modern Language Association; American Association of University Professors; American Association of Teachers of
Spanish and Portuguese; Canadian Linguistics Society; Washington Linguistics Society; Linguistic Society of Manitoba and North
Dakota. *Awards, honors:* Carnegie, American specialist C. U. ; state Fulbright;
Merit Award, Howard University. *Interests:*
American Indian languages; structural linguistics; romance, Slavic linguistics; travel
in South America, Africa, Europe. *Published works: The Assiniboine Language*
(Indiana University Research Center in Anthropology, Folklore, and Linguistics, Part
II, International Journal of American Linguistics, Vol. 30, No. 3, 1964); *Problems
in the Linguistic Description of Nakota* (Proceedings of the 36th International Congress
of Americanists, Madrid); *Contrived Speech
Forms, the Core of the H. U. Sociolect*
(Howard University, 1965); *A Phonemic
Sketch of Bubibatate Dialect* (Homenaje A.
Mendez Pidal, Madrid); *Typology, Three
Syntactic Types, Fact or Reality?* (Lin-
guistica, Mouton, The Hague, 1965).

LEWIS, ART(HUR)   *(Neetha Loosa)*
(Choctaw)   1914-   (silversmith)

Born June 4, 1914, Marlow, Okla. *Education:* Elementary school. *Principal occupation:* Silversmith. *Home address:* P.O. Box 113, El Prado, N.M. 87529. *Awards, honors:* First Prize for bolo tie, Gallup Inter-Tribal Ceremonial, 1938. *Interests:* Silversmithing and cutting turquoise.

LINK, MARTIN A.   1934-   (museum director)

Born September 26, 1934, Madison, Wis. *Education:* University of Arizona, B.A. (Anthropology), 1958. *Principal occupation:* Museum director. *Address:* P.O. Box 54, Window Rock, Ariz. 86515. *Affiliations:* Director, Navajo Tribal Museum, Window Rock, Ariz. ; Councillor, Arizona Academy of Science (treasurer, 1964-); Gallup Museum of Arts and Crafts, Gallup, N.M. *Military service:* U.S. Army, 1960-62. *Community activities:* Knights of Columbus; Gallup Junior Chamber of Commerce; Plateau Sciences Society. *Memberships:* Arizona Academy of Science; New Mexico Archaeological Society; Western Museum League.

LISITZKY, GENE (Mrs. David Zablodowsky)   1899-   (writer)

Born September 23, 1899, Highland, Kan. *Education:* University of Arizona, 1918-20; Columbia School of Journalism, B.Litt., 1923. *Principal occupation:* Writer. *Published works: Thomas Jefferson* (Viking Press, 1933); *Four Ways of Being Human* (Viking Press, 1956).

LISTER, ROBERT H.   1915-   (professor of anthropology)

Born August 7, 1915, Las Vegas, N.M. *Education:* University of New Mexico, B.A., 1937, M.A. , 1938; Harvard University, Ph.D. , 1950. *Principal occupation:* Professor of anthropology. *Address:* Department of Anthropology, University of Colorado, Boulder, Colo. 80304. *Affiliations:* Professor of anthropology, University of Colorado. *Military service:* U.S. Army,

1941-45. *Memberships:* Society for American Archaeology; American Anthropological Association. *Interests:* Archaeological expeditions to Southwestern United States, Mexico, Republic of the Sudan. *Published works: Excavations at Cojumatlan, Michoacan, Mexico* (University of New Mexico, 1949); *Excavations at Hells Midden, Dinosaur National Monument* (University of Colorado, 1951); *Present Status of Archaeology of Western Mexico* (University of Colorado, 1955); *Archaeological Investigations on Uncompahgre Plateau, West Central Colorado* (Denver Museum of Natural History, 1956); *Archaeological Investigations in the Northern Sierra Madre Occidental, Chihuahua and Sonora, Mexico* (University of Colorado, 1958); *The Coombs Site* (University of Utah, 1961); *Contributions to Mesa Verde Archaeology, I, Site 499, Mesa Verde National Park, Colorado* (1965); *Contributions to Mesa Verde Archaeology, II, Site 875, Mesa Verde National Park, Colorado* (1965).

LOMAHAFTEWA, LINDA   (Hopi)   1947-   (artist)

Born July 3, 1947, Phoenix, Ariz. *Education:* San Francisco Art Institute. *Principal occupation:* Artist. *Home address:* Shungopavi Village, Second Mesa, Ariz. *Awards:* Honorable Mention, Exhibit of Contemporary Indian Artists, Museum of New Mexico.

LONE DOG, LOUISE   (Mohawk-Delaware)   1928-   (writer)

Born January 11, 1928, Chillicothe, Ohio. *Education:* High school. *Principal occupation:* Writer. *Home address:* 350 W. 56th St. , New York, N.Y. 10019. *Awards, honors:* College scholarship. *Interests:* "Writing -- a cookbook (using) herbal seasonings, derived from ancient knowledge; a book of poems for adults and children, many (taken) from 'automatic' writings; painting cards in watercolors. " *Published works: Strange Journey* (Naturegraph Co. , 1964).

LONGACRE, ROBERT E.   1922-   (teacher of linguistics)

Born August 13, 1922, Akron, Ohio. *Education:* Houghton College, B. A., 1943; University of Pennsylvania, Ph. D., 1955. *Principal occupation:* Teacher of linguistics. *Home address:* #22067, Mexico 22, DF (Mexico). *Affiliations:* Summer Institute of Linguistics; professor of grammar, University of Oklahoma; lecturer, University of Michigan. *Memberships:* Linguistic Society of America. *Interests:* Trique (Indian) language of Oaxaca, Mexico; genetic affinities of Mexican Indian languages; translator of *New Testament* into Trique language. *Published works. Preto Mixtecan* (Indiana University Press); *Grammar Discovery Procedures* (Mouton and Co.).

LOVELESS, ANDREW MICHAEL 1934-
(historian)

Born March 16, 1934, Chicago, Ill. *Education:* Jacksonville University, B. A., 1960. *Principal occupation:* Historian. *Address:* Custer Battlefield National Monument, P. O. Box 416, Crow Agency, Mont. 59022. *Affiliations:* Park historian, National Park Service, Department of the Interior, 1960-. *Military service:* U. S. Marines, 1952-55 (Good Conduct Medal; Korean Service Medal; United Nations Medal; National Defense Medal). *Memberships:* Custer Battlefield Association (executive secretary; member, board of directors, 1963). *Interests:* Cave exploration; archaeology (investigation of several Colonial and Indian sites in north Florida).

LURIE, NANCY OESTREICH 1924-
(associate professor of anthropology)

Born January 24, 1924, Milwaukee, Wis. *Education:* University of Wisconsin, B. A., 1945; University of Chicago, M. A., 1947; Northwestern University, Ph. D., 1952. *Principal occupation:* Associate professor of anthropology. *Home address:* 4045 N. Downer Ave., Milwaukee, Wis. 53211. *Affiliations:* Instructor, anthropology and sociology, University of Wisconsin - Milwaukee, 1947-49; substitute instructor, University of Colorado, 1950; instructor, anthropology and sociology, University of Wisconsin - Milwaukee, 1951-53; research associate, North American ethnology, Peabody Museum, Harvard University, 1954-56; consultant and expert witness for law firms representing tribal clients before U. S. Indian Claims Commission, 1954-; lecturer in anthropology, Rackham School of Graduate Studies Extension Service, University of Michigan, 1956-61; lecturer in anthropology, School of Public Health, University of Michigan, 1959-61; part-time faculty, Department of Anthropology, Wayne State University, 1960; assistant coordinator, American Indian Chicago Conference, University of Chicago, 1960-61; assistant professor of anthropology, University of Wisconsin - Milwaukee, 1963-. *Memberships:* American Anthropological Association (Fellow); Central States Anthropological Society (secretary-treasurer, 1953; program chairman, 1964; first vice president and president-elect, 1964-65); American Ethnological Society; Sigma Xi; Society for Applied Anthropology; American Indian Ethnohistoric Conference; Wisconsin Archaeological Society. *Awards, honors:* Award of Merit for *Mountain Wolf Woman*, American Society for State and Local History, 1962. *Interests:* Dr. Lurie writes, "The North American Indian, with field studies among the Winnebago of Nebraska and Wisconsin, the Dogrib Indians of the Canadian Northwest Territories; (am) co-director of Research Project in Community Development undertaken by the Wisconsin Winnebago, with funds from the Social Security Administration of the Department of Health, Education and Welfare (1962-), with Winnebago co-directors Helen Miner Miller and Nadine Day Sieber. Other general interests are the problems of cultural change and persistence; applied anthropology. Current Fulbright appointment (lectureship, University of Aarhus, Denmark) involves teaching a course on the American Indian and a course on applied anthropology." *Published works: Mountain Wolf Woman, Sister of Crashing Thunder* (University of Michigan Press, 1961; reissued as paperback, 1966); *The Subsistence Economy of the Dogrib Indians of Lac La Martre, Canadian Northwest Territories*, with June Helm (Northern Research and Coordination Centre, Ottawa, Canada, 1961); editor, with Stuart Levine, "An American Indian Renascence?", special issue, *Midcontinent American Studies Journal* (University of Kansas, Lawrence, 1965); numerous articles in professional journals and other publications.

LYMAN, STANLEY D. 1913- (B. I. A. agency superintendent)

Born October 7, 1913, Helena, Mont. *Education:* Yankton College, B.A., 1936; Colorado State College, M.A., 1943. *Principal occupation:* B. I. A. agency superintendent. *Home address:* #1131, Poplar, Mont. 59255. *Affiliations:* Superintendent, Fort Peck Agency, Bureau of Indian Affairs, Poplar, Montana; field employment assistance officer; relocation officer. *Community activities:* Lions Club (board of directors); Masonic Lodge.

MC

McALLESTER, DAVID P.   1916-
(professor of anthropology)

Born August 6, 1916, Everett, Mass. *Education:* Harvard College, B.A., 1938; Columbia University, Ph.D., 1949. *Principal occupation:* Professor of anthropology. *Home address:* 62 Prospect St., Portland, Conn. *Other professional posts:* Board of directors, Verde Valley School, Sedona, Ariz.; board of directors, Museum of Navaho Art, Santa Fe, Ariz., 1964-. *Community activities:* Boys Committee, Y. M. C. A.; clerk, Middletown Friends Meeting; Verde Valley School, Sedona, Ariz. (board of directors); Museum of Navajo Art. *Memberships:* American Anthropological Association (Fellow); Society for Ethnomusicology (president, 1963-65). *Awards, honors:* Social Science Research Council Grant, 1950; Guggenheim Fellowship, 1957; National Science Foundation Grant, 1963, 1964, 1965. *Interests:* American Indian ethnography, arts, literature, music; field work with Hopi, Navajo, Apache, Comanche, Penobscot, Passamaquoddy; Navajo ceremonials; Polynesian music. *Published works: Peyote Music* (Wenner-Gren Foundation, 1949); *Myth of the Great Star Chant* (Museum of Navajo Ceremonial Art, 1956); *Enemy Way Music* (Peabody Museum, 1954); *Indian Music in the Southwest* (Taylor Museum, 1961).

McCARTHY, RICHARD L.   (business manager, writer)

Education: University of Buffalo. *Principal occupation:* Business manager and clerk, Board of Education. *Home address:*

40 Grant St., Lockport, N. Y. 14094. *Community activities:* Kiwanis Club (past president); Niagara County Historical Society (past president). *Awards, honors:* Silver Beaver Award, Boy Scouts of America; Honorary Curator of Archaeology, Buffalo and Erie County Historical Society; Fellow, New York State Archaeological Association; adopted Seneca. *Interests:* Archaeology, geology, botany; school business affairs. *Published works: The Portage Site* (Buffalo and Erie County Historical Society); *The Iroquois,* with Harrison Newman (Buffalo and Erie County Historical Society); *Prehistoric People of Western New York*, with Harrison Newman (Buffalo and Erie County Historical Society); *Joncaire's Post Located* (Buffalo and Erie County Historical Society); *British Regiments at the Lewiston Portage Site* (Buffalo and Erie County Historical Society).

McCARY, BEN C.   1901-   (associate professor of modern languages)

Born February 19, 1901, Alberene, Va. *Education:* University of Richmond, B. A., 1923; Universite de Toulouse (France), Doctorat d'Universite, 1928. *Principal occupation:* Associate professor. *Home address:* Box 123, Williamsburg, Va. 23185. *Affiliations:* Associate professor of modern languages, College of William and Mary, 1930-. *Community activities:* Williamsburg (Va.) School Board (member); Selective Service Board, Williamsburg (chairman). *Memberships:* American Association of University Professors; American Association of Teachers of French; Virginia Historical Society; Association for the Preservation of Virginia Antiquities; Archaeological Society of Virginia (president). *Interests:* The history and literature of 17th- and 18th-century France; Indians of Virginia -- prehistoric and historic. *Published works: La France d'aujourd'hui et d'hier* (American Book Co., 1939); editor and translator, *Travels in the Interior of the United States,* etc. (Edwards Bros, 1950); editor and translator, *Memoirs, or a Quick Glance at My Various Travels,* etc. (Continental Book Co., 1959); *Indians in Seventeenth-Century Virginia* (Garrett and Massie, 1957); *John Smith's Map of Virginia* (Garrett and Massie, 1957).

McCOMBS, SOLOMON   (Creek)   1913-
(artist, lecturer)

Born May 17, 1913, Eufaula, Okla. *Education:* Bacone College, 1931-38; Tulsa University Downtown College, 1943. *Principal occupation:* Artist, lecturer. *Addresses:* 4501 Arlington Blvd. , Arlington, Va. 22203 (home); U. S. Department of State, Washington, D. C. (business). *Affiliation:* Illustrator, U. S. Department of State, 1956-. *Memberships:* Society of Federal Artists and Designers (auditor and treasurer, 1956-57); American Indian and Eskimo Cultural Foundation (president, 1963-); National Congress of American Indians, 1965; Council of American Indians, 1965. *Awards:* Waite Phillips Special Indian Artists Award, 1965; designer, Five Civilized Tribes Museum Seal; winner, Annual Scottsdale National Indian Arts Exhibition Poster Contest, 1962, 1964; Second Prize, Indian Art Exhibit, Museum of New Mexico, 1963; All American Indian Days, Sheridan, Wyo. , 1964, 1965; Annual American Indian Artist Exhibition, Philbrook Art Center, Tulsa, Okla. *Interests:* Graphics; architectural drafting; designing; American Indian art. *Tour:* Painting; exhibits and lectures throughout Middle East, Africa, India, Burma, sponsored by the U. S. Department of State.

McCRACKEN, H. L. (Delaware - Cherokee) 1900- (accountant)

Born October 24, 1900, Rogers County, Okla. *Education:* University of Oklahoma. *Principal occupation:* Accountant. *Home address:* 1347 Osage, Bartlesville, Okla. 74003. *Affiliations:* Manager, Tax Division, Comptroller's Department, Phillips Petroleum Co., Bartlesville, Okla. , 1925-65 (now retired). *Memberships:* Mid-Continent Oil & Gas Association (tax committee); Independent Petroleum Association of America (tax study committee); Michigan Petroleum Industries Committee (advisory committee); Mid-Continent Oil & Gas Association Committee on State Taxation of Interstate Commerce and on Taxation Committee of the Texas Manufacturers Association (Phillips Petroleum Co. representative); Delaware Indian Business Committee (chairman, 1951-); Oklahomans for Indian Opportunity (board member). *Interests:* "Taxes -- principally Federal and state income taxes. I am interested in all matters involving the American Indian. "

McCURDY, R. D. 1889- (rancher, museum curator)

Born August 15, 1889, Dickens, Iowa. *Principal occupation:* Rancher, museum curator. *Home address:* Box 46, Broadus, Mont. 59317. *Affiliations:* Rancher; officer, Powder River County; curator, Museum of Natural History, Broadus, Mont. ; teacher in rural schools of Iowa, North Dakota, Minnesota and Montana. *Community activities:* Eastern Montana Congregational Church (registrar); Red Cross; Boy Scouts of America. *Memberships:* Wyoming Archaeological Society; Archaeological Society of Montana.

McDANIEL, ED WAHOO (Choctaw-Chickasaw) 1938- (professional football player)

Born June 19, 1938, Burniece, La. *Education:* University of Oklahoma, B.S. *Principal occupation:* Professional football player. *Home address:* 4325 Harvard, Midland, Texas 79702. *Awards, honors:* Voted Outstanding North American Indian Athlete by Micmac Indians. *Biographical sources:* *Four Thousand-Dollar Quarterback* (book).

McDERMOTT, JOHN FRANCIS 1902- (cultural historian)

Born April 18, 1902, St. Louis, Mo. *Education:* Washington University, B. A., 1923, M. A., 1924. *Principal occupation:* Cultural historian. *Home address:* 6345 Westminster Pl. , St. Louis, Mo. 63130. *Affiliations:* Instructor in English, 1924-36, assistant professor of English, 1936-49, associate professor of English, 1949-61, associate professor of American cultural history, 1961- (currently on leave), Washington University, St. Louis, Mo.; research professor of humanities, Southern Illinois University, 1963-. *Other professional posts:* Chairman, Conference on France in the Mississippi Valley, Washington University, 1956, 1964; chairman, Conference on Research Opportunities in American Cultural History, Washington University, 1959; advisory board, *Papers on Language and Literature,* 1965-; general editor, *Travels on the Western Waters* series, Southern Illinois University Press, 1965-. *Military service:* U.S. Army Air Force, 1942-45 (captain). *Memberships:* Modern Language Association; Modern Humanities Research Association (life member); Bibliographical Society of America; American Antiquarian Society; Institut Francais de Washington (trustee, 1958-); Academie de Macon (associe member perpetuel); Society of American Historians; American Name Society; American Studies Association; American Folklore Society; American Association of University Professors; National Folk Festival Association; Mississippi Valley Historical Association; American Historical Association; State Historical Society of Missouri; Illinois State Historical Society; Indiana Historical Society; Kansas Historical Society; Minnesota Historical Society; New York Historical Society; Missouri Historical Society; William Clark Society; St. Louis Westerners; Henry Shaw Memorial Association; St. Louis Historical Documents Foundation (president and editor, 1948-). *Awards, honors:* Newberry Library Fellow, Midwestern Studies, 1947-48; Guggenheim Memorial Fellow, 1954-. Research grants from Washington University, 1950, 1957, 1960, American Philosophical Society, 1939, 1940, 1944, 1947, 1958-59, 1963, 1964, Michigan State University, 1950-51, American Council of Learned Societies, 1960, Pro-Helvetia Foundation, Zurich, 1961, Henry E. Huntington Library and Art Gallery, 1965, Southern Illinois University, 1963, 1964, 1965, Palmes Academiques, 1966. *Published works:* Editor, *The Collected Verse of Lewis Carroll* (Dutton, 1929); editor, with K. B. Taft and D. O. Jensen, *Contemporary Thought* (Houghton Mifflin, 1929); *The Techniques of Composition,* with K. B. Taft and D. O. Jensen (Richard R. Smith, 1931; fifth edition, Rinehart, 1960); editor, *Modern Plays* (Harcourt, 1932); editor, with K. B. Taft and D. O. Jensen, *Contemporary Opinion* (Houghton Mifflin, 1933); editor, *The Russian Journal and Other Selections from the Work of Lewis Carroll* (Dutton, 1935); *Private Libraries in Creole Saint Louis* (Johns Hopkins Press, 1938); editor, *Tixier's Travels on the Osage Prairies* (University of Oklahoma Press, 1940); *A Glossary of Mississippi Valley French, 1673-1850* (Washington University Press, 1941); *English Communication,* with K. B. Taft, D. O. Jensen and W. H. Yeager (Farrar & Rinehart, 1943); editor, *The Western Journals of Washington Irving* (University of Oklahoma Press, 1944); editor, with

J. P. Donnelly, R. J. Boylan, B. R. Gieseker, C. van Ravenswaay, and I. Dillard, *Old Cahokia: A Narrative and Documents Illustrating the First Century of Its History* (St. Louis Historical Documents Foundation, 1949); editor, *Travels in Search of the Elephant: The Wanderings of Alfred S. Waugh, Artist, 1845-46* (Missouri Historical Society, 1951); editor, *Up the Missouri with Audobon: The Journal of Edward Harris* (University of Oklahoma Press, 1951); editor, *The Early Histories of St. Louis* (St. Louis Historical Documents Foundation, 1952); editor, *Journal of an Expedition to the Mauvaises Terres and the Upper Missouri in 1850,* by Thaddeus A. Culbertson (Smithsonian Institution, 1952); editor, *Indian Sketches Taken During an Expedition to the Pawnee Tribes, 1833, by John Treat Irving, Jr.* (University of Oklahoma Press, 1955); editor, *A Tour on the Prairies by Washington Irving* (University of Oklahoma Press, 1956); editor, *Memoir, or a Cursory Glance at My Different Travels and My Sojourn in the Creek Nation,* by Louis LeClerc de Milford (Lakeside Press, 1956); editor, *Prairie and Mountain Sketches* (University of Oklahoma Press, 1957); *The Lost Panoramas of the Mississippi* (University of Chicago Press, 1958); *The Art of Seth Eastman* (Smithsonian Institution, 1959); *George Caleb Bingham, River Portraitist* (University of Oklahoma Press, 1959); *Seth Eastman, Pictorial Historian of the Indian* (University of Oklahoma Press, 1961); editor, *Research Opportunities in American Cultural History* (University of Kentucky Press, 1961); editor, *Streaks of Squatter Life,* by John S. Robb (Scholars' Facsimilies, 1962); editor, *The Western Journals of Dr. George Hunter, 1795-1894* (American Philosophical Society, 1963); editor, *Audobon in the West* (University of Oklahoma Press, 1965); editor, *The World of Washington Irving* (Dell, 1965); editor, *The French in the Mississippi Valley* (University of Illinois Press, 1965); editor, *The Frontier Re-examined* (in press); editor, *A Panoramist on the Overland Trail in 1849: The Diary and Sketches of F. Wilkins* (in press); numerous articles and reviews.

McDONALD, GERALD DOAN 1905-
(librarian)

Born June 5, 1905, Wilmington, Ohio. *Education:* Wilmington College, B.A., 1927; Haverford College, M.A., 1928; Columbia

University, School of Library Service, B. S. (Library Service), 1930. *Principal occupation:* Librarian. *Home address:* 36 W. 10th St., New York, N. Y. 10011. *Affiliations:* Cleveland Public Library, 1928-29; Chief, American and Genealogy Division, New York Public Library. *Military service:* U. S. Army, 1942-45. *Memberships:* American Antiquarian Society; American Historical Association. *Awards, honors:* L. H. D., Wilmington College, 1953. *Published works: Educational Motion Pictures and Libraries* (American Library Association, 1942); *A Way of Knowing* (Thomas Y. Crowell Co., 1958).

McDONALD, WALTER W. (Salish and Kootenai) 1910- (tribal officer)

Born February 16, 1910, St. Ignatius, Mont. *Education:* Haskell Institute; varied business and vocational training. *Principal occupation:* Tribal officer. *Address:* St. Ignatius, Mont. *Memberships:* Surgeon General's Committee; Montana Correctional Association; Lake County Rural Development Committee; Advisory Board on Indian Affairs, University of Montana (chairman); Affiliated Tribes of Northwest Indians (past president); Montana Inter-Tribal Policy Board (past president); Confederated Salish and Kootenai Tribes. *Awards:* Recipient of plaque awarded jointly by Confederated Salish and Kootenai Tribal Council and the Bureau of Indian Affairs for twenty years of service to American Indians, December, 1964.

McGAVRAN, GRACE W. (free lance writer)

Born Damoh, C. P., India. *Education:* Butler University, B. A., 1919; Boston University, M. A., 1924. *Principal occupation:* Free lance writer. *Home address:* c/o Mrs. E. B. Seelye, 516 Beloit Avenue, Berkeley 8, Calif. *Affiliations:* Teacher, high school, 1919-21; librarian, College of Missions, 1921-23; director of Christian education, 1924-25; Missionary Education Department, United Christian Missionary Society, 1925-35; editor, *Children's Work,* Presbyterian Board of Christian Education, 1942-47. *Interests:* Extensive travels include England, Mexico, Belgian Congo, and many home mission fields. *Published works: We Gather Together* (Friendship Press, 1951); *Yakima Boy* (Friendship Press, 1952); *All Through the Year* (Bethany Press, 1958); *Stories of the Book of Books* (Friendship Press, 1960); *Boy of the Congo Forest* (Bethany Press, 1961); *The Thunder Egg* (Friendship Press, 1961); *Men Who Dared in Bible Times* (Bethany Press, 1962); *The Golden Coin* (Friendship Press, 1963).

McGAW, JESSIE BREWER (teacher)

Born Montgomery County, Tennessee. *Education:* Duke University, B. A., Peabody College, M. A. *Principal occupation:* Teacher. *Affiliations:* Teacher of Latin and English, University of Houston. *Published works: Little Elk Hunts Buffalo* (Nelson); *Painted Pony Runs Away* (Nelson); *How Medicine Man Cured Paleface Woman* (W. R. Scott)

McGREGOR, JOHN C. 1905- (professor of anthropology, archaeologist)

Born November 10, 1905. *Education:* University of Arizona, B. A., 1931, M. A., 1932; University of Chicago, Ph. D., 1946. *Principal occupation:* Professor of anthropology, archaeologist. *Affiliations:* Instructor, 1931-38, assistant professor, 1938-42, museum director, 1938-42, Arizona State College; curator, 1931-38, archaeologist and field director, 1939-42, Museum of Northern Arizona; acting chief, 1942-45, administrative assistant, 1945-48, Illinois State Museum; associate professor, 1942-52, professor of anthropology, University of Illinois, 1952-. *Memberships:* Sigma Xi; American Association for the Advancement of Science (Fellow); Society for American Archaeology; American Anthropological Association; Illinois Archaeological Survey (president, 1956-60, 1962-65); Tree Ring Society, 1958-. *Expeditions:* University of Arizona Expeditions, 1926-31; Museum of Northern Arizona expeditions, 1931-40; director, Museum of Northern Arizona expedition to Bonito Terrace, Ariz., 1935; director, Museum of Northern Arizona and State College expedition to Ridge Ruin, Ariz., 1938-39; director, Illinois State Museum and University of Chicago expedition to Starved Rock, Ill.,

1947-48; director, University of Illinois expeditions to Red Butte, Ariz., 1949, the Pool Site, Ill., 1950, Mount Floyd, Ariz., 1951, the Irving Site, 1952, the Pollock Site, Ariz., 1953, the Illinois River, Ill., 1954, the Pollock Site, Ariz., 1955, the Hull Site, Ill., 1956, Rock Island, Ill., 1959, the Pershing Site, Ariz., 1960, the Two Kivas Site, Ariz., 1962, 1964. *Published works: Culture of Sites Which Were Occupied Shortly Before the Eruption of Sunset Crater* (Bulletin 9, Museum of Northern Arizona, 1936); *Winona Village* (Bulletin 12, Museum of Northern Arizona, 1937); *How Some Important Northern Arizona Pottery Types Were Dated* (Bulletin 13, Museum of Northern Arizona, 1938); *Winona and Ridge Ruin* (Bulletin 18, Museum of Northern Arizona, 1941); *Southwestern Archaeology* (University of Chicago Press, 1941); *Archaeology and Social Change* (Illinois Academy of Science, Transactions, Volume 40, 1947); *The Cohonina Culture of Northwestern Arizona* (University of Illinois Press, 1951); *The Pool and Irving Villages* (University of Illinois Press, 1958); *Southwestern Archaeology* (second edition, University of Illinois Press, 1965); various books, bulletins, articles and reviews.

McINTOSH, W. E. "DODE" (Muskogee or Creek) 1893- (principal chief, Creek Indian Nation)

Born January 26, 1893, Carthage, Tenn. *Education:* Normal School (Teachers), First Grade Certificate. *Principal occupation:* Principal chief, Creek Indian Nation. *Home address:* 11 E. Independence, Tulsa, Okla. 74106. *Affiliations:* Former real estate broker. *Military service:* U.S. Army, 1918. *Community activities:* County assessor, county treasurer. *Memberships:* Oklahoma Historical Society (chairman, historical sites); Tulsa County Historical Society (former president; chairman, board of directors); North Tulsa Chamber of Commerce (board member). *Awards, honors:* Official Western Heritage Award, 1965; Outstanding Indian, National Cowboy Hall of Fame. *Interests:* "Education for every Creek Indian boy and girl; sanitation in every home, among other interests. (I have) traveled the Highlands of Scotland (August, 1964); attended gathering of McIntosh Clan; visited thirty states. (I am a) rare book collector (and) musician."

McKEOWN, MARTHA FERGUSON 1903- (teacher, writer)

Born September 13, 1903, Astoria, Ore. *Education:* Willamette University, B.A., 1923; University of Oregon, M.A., 1937; University of Washington. *Principal occupation:* Teacher, writer. *Home address:* 15727 S.E. Dana Rd., Portland, Ore. 97222. *Affiliations:* Teacher, dean of girls, Mosier High School, 1923-24; teacher, dean of girls, Odell High School, 1927-34; teacher, dean of girls, Sherwood High School, 1935-36; teacher, dean of girls, Tigard High School, 1935-36; dean of women, teacher of English, Multnomah College, 1939-43; director, Oregon Older Girls Conference, 1943-47; English teacher and counselor, Wy-east High School, 1947-61; teacher of English, counselor, Oregon Senior High School. *Community activities:* Sons and Daughters of Oregon Pioneers; Daughters of the American Revolution; Oregon State Regent, 1948-50; Honorary State Regent; Delta Gamma; Delta Kappa Gamma. *Memberships:* Oregon Historical Association; National Education Association; Oregon Education Association; Theta Sigma Phi. *Awards, honors:* Adopted member, Wy'am Tribe, Celilo Falls; Woman of the Year, Portland Women's Forum; Woman of Achievement, Theta Sigma Phi, 1958; Anselm Forum Award for Dedicated Service in Human Relations, 1959; Award for Racial Understanding, National Council of Christians and Jews. *Interests:* Writing; teaching; travel through United States, Canada, Alaska, Mexico. *Published works: The Trail Led North* (Macmillan, 1948); *Alaska Silver* (Macmillan, 1951); *Them Was the Days* (Macmillan, 1950); *Linda's Indian Home* (Binfords and Mort, 1956); *Come to Our Salmon Feast* (Binfords and Mort, 1959); *Mountains Ahead* (Putnam, 1961).

McLEAN, ROBERT ELDON (teacher)

Education: University of Utah, B.S., 1960, M.S. (Educational Administration and Recreation), 1961. *Principal occupation:* Teacher. *Affiliations:* Salt Lake Board of Education, Salt Lake City, Utah; playground director; supervisor, Salt Lake County Recreation. *Military service:* U.S. Army, 1948-52 (Good Conduct Medal; Captain's Citation for Inchon Invasion, Korea). *Memberships:* Inter-Tribal Indian Group, Salt

Lake City; Tribe of Many Feathers, Brigham Young University; Katchina Indian Dancers; Utah State Archaeological Society; National Education Association. *Awards, honors:* Individual Service Award, Inter-Tribal Indian Group; First Place Award, Magna Parade Committee; Special Award, Kearns Parade Committee; awards, Days of '47 Parade Committee; First Place Awards, Appaloosa Horse Clubs and Ponies of America; first place award in Indian dancing, Salt Lake County Fair. *Interests:* Indian dancing and lore; danced for various films, fairs, and pageants; presentation of Indian programs for K.U. E. D., educational television, University of Utah; travel and research on Hopi, Navajo, Apache and other reservations. *Published works: American Indian Dances*, with John Squires (Ronald Press); *Recreational Program of the Hopi Indians*, thesis (University of Utah).

McMONAGLE, JOHN WILLIAM 1937-
(guidance counselor, museum director)

Born July 18, 1937, Albany, N. Y. *Education:* St. Lawrence University, B. A.; Colgate University. *Principal occupation:* Guidance counselor, museum director. *Home address:* 714 Highland Ave., Rome, N. Y. 13440. *Affiliations:* Guidance counselor, Holland Patent Central School; assistant director, director, Fort Stanwix Museum, Rome, N. Y.; science teacher, Rome Free Academy. *Memberships:* Rome Teachers Association; New York State Teachers Association; Holland Parent Teachers Association; New York State Counselors Association; Rome Historical Society; First Presbyterian Church. *Interests:* Youth guidance; art and history, particularly local New York State history.

McNEER, MAY (writer)

Born in Tampa, Florida. *Education:* University of Georgia; Pulitzer School of Journalism, Columbia University, B. Litt., 1926. *Principal occupation:* Free lance writer. *Home address:* Lambs Lane, Cresskill, N. J. *Memberships:* P. E. N. International. *Interests:* "Children's books; have lived in Mexico, traveled in Europe, etc. Summers spent in Ontario, Canada, off in the bush." *Published works: Prince*

Bantam (Macmillan, 1929); *Waif Maid* (Macmillan, 1930); *Stop Tim* (Farrar & Rinehart, 1930); *Tales from the Crescent Moon,* with Charlotte Lederer (Farrar & Rinehart, 1931); *Tinka, Minka, Linka,* with Charlotte Lederer (Farrar & Rinehart, 1931); *The Story of the Great Plains* (Harper, 1943); *The Gold Rush* (Grosset, 1944); *The Covered Wagon* (Grosset, 1944); *The Story of California* (Harper, 1944); *The Story of the Southern Highlands* (Harper, 1945); *The Golden Flash* (Viking,1947); *The Story of Florida* (Harper, 1947); *The Story of the Southwest* (Harper, 1948); *The California Gold Rush* (Landmark Books, 1950); *John Wesley* (Abingdon, 1951); *Up a Crooked River* (Viking, 1952); *Martin Luther* (Abingdon, 1953); *The Mexican Story* (Farrar, Straus, 1953); *War Chief of the Seminoles* (Landmark Books, 1954); *Little Baptiste* (Houghton, 1954); *America's Abraham Lincoln* (Houghton Mifflin, 1957); *The Canadian Story* (Farrar, Straus, 1958); *Armed with Courage* (Abingdon, 1958); *My Friend Mac* (Houghton Mifflin, 1960); *The Alaska Gold Rush* (Landmark Books, 1960); *America's Mark Twain* (Houghton Mifflin, 1962); *The Hudson River* (Garrard, 1962); *The American Indian Story* (Farrar, Straus, 1963); *Give Me Freedom* (Abingdon); *Profile of American History* (Hammond); editor, *Children of the New Forest* (Macmillan); contributor to numerous anthologies; short stories in various periodicals. Many of Miss McNeer's books have been illustrated by her husband, Lynd Ward.

McNICKLE, D'ARCY (Salish and Kootenai) 1904- (organization executive, writer)

Born January 18, 1904, St. Ignatius, Mont. *Education:* University of Montana; Oxford University; University of Grenoble. *Principal occupation:* Organization executive, writer. *Home address:* 133 Davidson Crescent, Regina, Sask., Can. *Affiliation:* Executive director, American Indian Development, Inc. *Memberships:* American Anthropological Association (Fellow); Society for Applied Anthropology; Current Anthropology. *Awards:* Guggenheim Fellowship, 1963-64. *Interest:* American Indian affairs -- co-founder, National Congress of American Indians. *Published works: The Surrounded* (Dodd, Mead, 1936); *They Came Here First* (Lippincott, 1949); *Runner in the Sun* (Winston, 1954); *Indians and Other Americans*, with Harold E. Fey (Harper and Row, 1959); *The Indian Tribes of the United States -- Ethnic and Cultural Survival* (Oxford University Press, 1962); *North American Indians (Encyclopaedia Britannica*, current edition).

McREYNOLDS, EDWIN C.   1890-
(teacher)

Born April 30, 1890, Springfield, Mo. *Education:* University of Oklahoma, B. A., 1922, M. A., 1924, Ph. D., 1945. *Principal occupation:* Teacher. *Home address:* 1501 S. Lincoln, Norman, Okla. 73069. *Affiliations:* High school teacher, Oklahoma City, Okla., 1922-26; associate professor, Central State College, 1926-29; dean and instructor, Coffeyville Junior College, 1930-38; instructor and director of summer sessions, Joplin Junior College, 1938-43; assistant professor, professor, 1943-60; professor of history, summer session, Southwest Missouri State College, 1963; professor of history, Cottey College, 1960-. *Military service:* U. S. Army, 344th Infantry, 1917-1919. *Memberships:* American Historical Association; Mississippi Valley Historical Association; St. Louis Corral of the Westerners; State Historical Society of Missouri; Oklahoma Historical Society; Arkansas Historical Association; Phi Beta Kappa, 1922. *Awards, honors:* Outstanding Teaching Award, University of Oklahoma; Distinguished Service Citation, University of Oklahoma Association, 1960. *Interests:* "Extensive travel (through) the United States. (From) 1957 to 1958, (I) work(ed) on Indian land claims in Oklahoma, and served as an expert witness before the Indian commissioners when arguments were presented by a Chicago law firm. Intensive research in the archives of the U. S. Library of Congress and in the states of Oklahoma, Missouri, Florida, and Arkansas. *Published works: Oklahoma: A History of the Sooner State* (University of Oklahoma, 1954); *The Seminoles* (University of Oklahoma Press, 1957); *Oklahoma: The Story of Its Past and Present*, with Alice Marriott and Estelle Faulconer (University of Oklahoma Press, 1961); *Missouri: A History of the Crossroad State* (University of Oklahoma Press, 1962); *Historical Atlas of Oklahoma*, with John Morris (University of Oklahoma Press, 1965).

M

MacGREGOR, GORDON   1902-
(professor, anthropologist)

Born July 5, 1902, Haverhill, Mass. *Education:* Yale College, B. A., 1925; Harvard University, Ph. D., 1935. *Principal occupation:* Professor of anthropology, applied anthropologist. *Home address:* 6353 Cross Woods Drive, Falls Church, Va. 22044. *Affiliations:* Professor, American University; deputy associate commissioner, Bureau of Indian Affairs. *Memberships:* American Anthropological Association(Fellow); Society for Applied Anthropology (Fellow; president); Anthropological Society of Washington (president). *Expeditions:* Archaeologist, Harvard University - University of Pennsylvania, Czechoslovakia, 1931, anthropologist, Bishop Museum (Honolulu) expeditions to Samoa, Tonga, Rotuma, Fiji, Tokelau, Solomon Islands, 1931-34; archaeologist; Harvard University expedition to Ireland, 1935; archaeologist, Egyptian Exploration Society expedition to Egypt, 1936; applied anthropologist, Tudor Engineering Co. expedition to Afghanistan, 1936. *Published works:* Co-author, *The Walapai Indians* (American Anthropologist Memoir, 1935); co-author, *The Changing Indian* (University of Oklahoma Press, 1942); *Warriors Without Weapons* (University of Chicago Press, 1946); *Anthropology To-Day* (University of Chicago Press, 1953); *Applied Anthropology in Government*, with Edward Kennard (University of Chicago Press, 1953).

MADSEN, BRIGHAM D.   1914-
(university administrator)

Born October 21, 1914, Magna, Utah. *Education:* Idaho State University, Certificate, 1934; University of Utah, B. A., 1938; University of California, Berkeley, M. A., 1940, Ph. D., 1948. *Principal occupation:* University administrator. *Home address:* 2181 Lincoln Lane, Salt Lake City, Utah 84117. *Affiliations:* Chairman, History Department, Brigham Young University, 1953-54; president, Madsen Bros. Construction Co., Inc., 1954-61; assistant director of training, Peace Corps, Washington, D. C., 1964-65; director of training, VISTA, Office of Economic Opportunity, Washington, D. C., 1965; dean, Division of Continuing Education, University of Utah, 1965-. *Military service:* U. S. Army Infantry, 1943-46. *Memberships:* Phi Kappa Phi; Phi Alpha Theta. *Published works: The Bannock of Idaho* (Caxton Printers, Ltd., 1958).

MAHOOD, RUTH I. 1908- (museum curator)

Born March 9, 1908, Buckingham, Ill. *Education:* Central State College, B. A. (History), 1933; Colorado University, M. A. (History), 1942. *Principal occupation:* Museum curator. *Home address:* 816 Victor Ave., Inglewood, Calif. 90302. *Affiliations:* Teacher, Junior High School, Buckingham, Ill.; teacher of history, Verden, Okla., 1938-42; teacher, Los Angeles city and county schools, 1942-46; instructor in history, Los Angeles County Museum, 1954-57; chief curator of history, Los Angeles County Museum. *Community activities:* Governor Brown's California History Commission, 1963-; Governor Brown's California Civil War Centennial Committee, 1961-; Governor Brown's California Heritage Preservation Commission, 1963; Los Angeles County Landmarks Committee, 1954-. *Memberships:* American Association of Museums; Pilot Club of Los Angeles (president, 1963-64); Western Museums League (president, 1961-62); Kappa Delta Pi; Delta Kappa Gamma; Historical Society of Southern California; National Trust for Historic Preservation; Science and History Alliance of Los Angeles County Museum of Natural History; Committee to Preserve the History of Los Angeles; Film Council of Los Angeles; Conference of California Historical Society (regional vice president, 1959-); Junior Historical Museum (chairman, 1964). *Awards, honors:* Award of Merit for work in California history, California Historical Society, 1964; Award of Achievement, Civil War Centennial Commission, 1965. *Published works:* Editor, *The Twenty-One Dioramas of California History* (Los Angeles County Museum of Natural History, 1965); articles in various journals.

MALONE, HENRY THOMPSON 1916- (professor of history)

Born July 4, 1916, Albany, Ga. *Education:* Clemson University, B. S., 1937; Emory

University, M. A., 1949, Ph. D., 1952; Shrivenham Army University, England, 1945. *Principal occupation:* Professor of history. *Home address:* 1146 Oxford Rd., N. E., Atlanta, Ga. 30306. *Affiliations:* Student-teacher, Emory University, 1948-52; director of development and professor of history, Georgia State College, 1952-. *Other professional posts:* Assistant circulation manager, *The Stars and Stripes,* European edition (Germany). *Military service:* U. S. Army, 1943-46 (Bronze Star Medal). *Community activities:* Kiwanis (president, lieutenant governor, district secretary-treasurer, district governor-elect); Georgia Leadership Institute; Georgia Mental Health Association (chairman, education committee); Heart Fund (section chairman); United Appeal; Cerebral Palsey Fund. *Memberships:* Southern Historical Association, 1948-; American Alumni Council, 1955-; American College Public Relations Association, 1961-. *Awards, honors:* Literary Achievement Award, Georgia Writers Association, 1957; McClung Award, East Tennessee Historical Society, for article on Cherokees; M. L. Brittan Service Award as student at Emory University; Georgia State College yearbook honoree, 1955. *Interests:* Research consultant on Cherokee history; alumni work, Georgia State College. *Published works: Cherokees of the Old South* (University of Georgia Press, 1956); *The Episcopal Church in Georgia: A History* (Diocese of Atlanta, 1960).

MALONE, P. V. 1913- (public school teacher)

Born July 16, 1913, San Augustine, Texas. *Education:* Texas College, B. A.; Texas Southern University, M. A. *Principal occupation:* Public school teacher. *Home address:* 2000 N. Main St., Jasper, Texas 75951. *Affiliations:* Principal, J. H. Rowe Elementary School, Jasper, Texas. *Military service:* U. S. Navy, 1942-45. *Community activities:* Jasper's Lone Star Youth Council (founder and first president). *Memberships:* Jasper County Teachers Association (president, 1952-59; T.S.A.T., 1948-; Texas Principals' Association, 1948-; National Association of Elementary Principals, 1948-. *Awards:* Certificate of Honor, Texas College. *Interests:* Teaching. *Published works: Sam Houston's Indians* (Naylor, 1961).

MANAKEE, HAROLD RANDALL 1908-
(historical society director)

Born April 17, 1908, Baltimore, Md. *Education:* Johns Hopkins University, B. S., 1941. *Principal occupation:* Historical society director. *Affiliations:* Teacher and administrator, Baltimore Public Schools, 1927-42; director, World War II Records Division, Maryland Historical Society, 1946-59; assistant director, Maryland Historical Society; director, Maryland Historical Society, 1962-. *Military service:* U. S. Naval Reserve. *Memberships:* Rotary Club of Baltimore; Baltimore Bibliophiles; Johns Hopkins Club; Edgar Allan Poe Society. *Awards, honors:* Phi Delta Kappa, Johns Hopkins University; honorary member, Phi Alpha Theta, Georgetown University. *Interests:* American history -- particularly Maryland. *Published works:* Co-author, *My Maryland* (Ginn and Co., 1934; Maryland Historical Society, 1955); co-author, *Active Citizenship* (Winston, 1951); editor, *Maryland in World War II*, four vols. (Maryland Historical Society, 1949-1958); *Indians of Early Maryland* (Maryland Historical Society, 1959); *Maryland in the Civil War* (Maryland Historical Society, 1961).

MANATOWA, ELMER, Jr.   (Sac and Fox)
1933-   (tribal officer)

Born February 6, 1933, Pawnee, Okla. *Education:* Oklahoma State University, 1951-52; Central State College, B. S. (Education), 1958. *Principal occupation:* Tribal officer. *Home address:* 1337 E. Cherry, Cushing, Okla. 74023. *Affiliations:* Sales and traffic manager, Midland Cooperatives, Inc., Cushing, Okla. *Military service:* U. S. Army. *Community activities:* Cushing Jaycees (president); Cushing Youth and Community Center (president); Sac and Fox of Oklahoma (principal chief). *Memberships:* American Petroleum Institute. *Awards, honors:* Jaycee of the Year, 1963, 1964.

MANNING, PHYLLIS (ANNE) (Mrs. F. J.)
1903-   (free-lance writer)

Born June 2, 1903, Chippewa Falls, Wis. *Education:* Eau Claire State Normal College, Teacher Certification, 1922; LaSalle Business Institute. *Principal occupation:* Free-lance writer. *Home address:* Route 1, Box 876, Flagstaff, Ariz. 86001. *Affiliations:* Secretary, Director of Finance, Miami, Fla. ; administrative assistant to dean of men, University of Miami, 1946-47; secretary to head, Department of English, Yale University, 1945-46; administrative assistant to dean of instruction and director of Graduate School, Northern Arizona University, 1947-60. *Other posts:* Lecturer to high school and college journalism and creative writing classes. *Community activities:* Pilot Club International (district lieutenant governor, governor, director, international executive committee); Doney Park Improvement Association (secretary-treasurer, 1948-49); Political Central Committee (secretary-treasurer, 1954-58); Symphony Guild; Community Concerts Association (board member); Rocking Charioteers (secretary, 1961-); Humane Society (state executive committee); Chamber of Commerce, Flagstaff, Ariz., (chamber maid); Goodwill Industries (board of directors); Kachina Dolls Toastmistress Club. *Memberships:* National Writers Club; National Federation of Press Women (executive committee); Flagstaff Writers Club (chairman, 1951-53, 1960); Arizona Press Women (president). *Awards, honors:* 4-H Leader Meritorious Service Award; First Place, Arizona Press Women Writing Contest for book, *Spirit Rocks and Silver Magic,* 1963; Senior Citizen Creative Achievement Award for *Spirit Rocks and Silver Magic,* Arizona State Fair Association, 1964; honored at Arizona State University as author of children's stories, 1963. *Interests:* Mrs. Manning writes, "I taught elementary (school) in Wisconsin for three years; took secretarial training and did executive and administrative secretarial work in schools of higher learning until retirement in 1960. Reading, oil painting, homemaking and travel are my avocations. In 1951 I started to write. I have toured the United States and Canada extensively -- in 1963 I went to Hawaii and toured the Islands; in 1964 I cruised six weeks to Hawaii, Japan, Okinawa, Taiwan, the Philippines and Guam. I have driven into Mexico, but briefly. I have studied the natives of the countries I have visited to compare (them) with Indian cultures. In Wisconsin where I was born I lived near the Chippewa Indians; in Miami, Florida, near the Seminoles; (now) in Arizona I live within twenty-five miles of the Navajo Reservation and less than one hundred miles from the Hopi Reservation. I have become fast friends with members of both tribes. Have been 'surrounded' by Indians all my life, and thus the intense interest." *Published works: Spirit Rocks and Silver Magic* (Caxton Printers, Ltd., 1962).

MARCHAND, THELMA (Colville) 1932-
(tribal officer)

Born April 17, 1932, Okanogan County, Wash. *Education* Wenatchee Junior College. *Principal occupation:* Tribal officer. *Home address:* 320 Columbia St., Omak, Wash. *Affiliations:* Secretary, Colville Business (Tribal) Council.

MARCHIANDO, PATRICIA 1939-
(archaeologist)

Born January 6, 1939, Greensburg, Penna. *Education:* University of Oregon, M.A., 1965. *Principal occupation:* Archaeologist. *Home address:* 2030 Riverside Dr., Trenton, N.J. *Affiliations:* Assistant curator of archaeology, New Jersey State Museum. *Interests:* New World archaeology, physical anthropology; field experience in Columbia River region, eastern Oregon, Bay of Dundy, New Brunswick, Upper Delaware Valley, Upper Umpqua Valley. *Published works: A Technological and Statistical Analysis of Upper Umpqua River Artifacts* (University of Oregon, 1965).

MARCHMAN, WATT P. 1911-
(museum, library and foundation director)

Born September 1, 1911, Eatonton, Ga. *Education:* Rollins College, B.A., 1933, M.A. 1937; Duke University, 1936. *Principal occupation:* Museum, library and foundation director. *Addresses:* 1500 Buckland Ave., Fremont, Ohio 43420 (home); Rutherford B. Hayes Library and Museum, 1337 Hayes Ave., Fremont, Ohio 43420 (business). *Principal affiliations:* Director, The Rutherford B. Hayes Library; director of research, The Rutherford B. Hayes Foundation; manager, The Rutherford B. Hayes State Memorial. *Military service:* U.S. Army, E.T.O., 1943-1946; Signal Corps, special troops. *Community activities:* Rotary Club of Fremont (past president); The Birchard Public Library, Fremont, Ohio (trustee, secretary of board, 1953-). *Memberships:* American Historical Association; American Association for State and Local History; Society of American Archivists; Ohio Library Association; The Manuscript Society (former vice president and trustee); Historical Association of Southern Florida; Florida Historical Society; Ohio Historical Society. *Vocational interests:* American history, 1865-1900; Ohio and Florida history; The Hayes Administration in foreign affairs. *Travels:* U.S. and Canada; Europe during military service. *Published works: The Rutherford B. Hayes State Memorial* (Ohio Historical Society, 1962).

MARRIOTT, ALICE LEE 1910-
(writer, anthropologist)

Born January 8, 1910. *Education:* Oklahoma City University, B.A., 1930; University of Oklahoma, B.A., 1935. *Principal occupations:* Writer, anthropologist. *Affiliations:* Associate, Southwest Research Associates; library field representative, curator of ethnology, visiting instructor in anthropology, University of Oklahoma. *Other professional posts:* Field representative, Indian Arts and Crafts Board, U.S. Department of the Interior; research associates, Beloit College-Logan Museum. *Community activities:* American Red Cross (general field, 1942-46); Oklahoma Indian Council, Inc. (anthropological consultant); Oklahoma City Y.W.C.A. (anthropological consultant). *Memberships:* American Anthropological Association (Fellow); Phi Beta Kappa; Sigma Xi. *Awards, honors:* University of Oklahoma Achievement Award; Oklahoma Hall of Fame; Woman of the Year, Theta Sigma Phi, University of Oklahoma Chapter; Cowboy Hall of Fame Recognition Award; Guggenheim, Rockefeller and Bollingen Fellowships; Neosho Fellowship; University of Oklahoma Field Research Fellowship. *Interests:* Field research among the Kiowas of western Oklahoma, 1934-; Tewa Pueblos, 1946-65; Hopi Second Mesa Villages, 1954-65; acculturated urban tribes, 1934-; representative, Cherokee; Oklahoma and Montana Cheyenne; Oklahoma Arapaho; Comanche; ethnohistory, ethnography and archaeology. *Published works: Ten Grandmothers* (University of Oklahoma Press, 1945); *Maria, the Potter of San Ildefonso* (University of Oklahoma Press, 1948); *The Valley Below* (University of Oklahoma Press, 1950); *Hell on Horses and Women* (University of Oklahoma Press, 1953); *The First Comers* (Longmans - McKay, 1960);

Oklahoma: Its Past and Its Present, with
Edwin McReynolds and Estelle Faulconer
(Longmans - McKay, 1962); *Greener Fields*
(Doubleday, 1962); *Saynday's People* (University of Nebraska, 1963); *Indian Annie*
(Longmans - McKay, 1965).

MARTIN, FRAN   1906-   (writer)

Born October 23, 1906, Montclair, N. J.
Education: Barnard College, B.A., 1962;
Old Dominion College. *Principal occupation:* Writer. *Home address:* Cloncurry
Rd., Norfolk, Va. 23505. *Community activities:* Norfolk Children's Theatre (board
member); Norfolk Symphony (board member); Irene Leaehe Society, Norfolk Museum
(board member). *Awards, honors;* Award
for poetry and prose, Irene Leaehe Association of Norfolk Society of Arts, 1940-63;
Outstanding Achievement, Department of
English, Old Dominion College, 1962. *Interests:* Miss Martin writes, "My chief interest at present is getting a Master of Arts
degree in English. I do a great deal of volunteer writing for civic clubs, etc., and I
soon hope to finish work on another children's book." Travels to Europe and to the
Northwest Coast of the U.S. *Published
works: Knuckles Down!* (Harper); *Sea Room*
(Harper); *No School Friday* (Harper); *Nine
Tales of Raven* (Harper); *Nine Tales of Coyote* (Harper); *Pirate Island* (Harper).

MASON, PHILIP P.   1927-
(historian-archivist)

Born April 28, 1927, Salem, Mass. *Education:* Boston University, B.A., 1950; University of Michigan, M.A., 1951, Ph.D.
1956. *Principal occupation:* Historian, archivist. *Affiliations:* Professor of history,
university archivist, director, Labor History Archives, Wayne State University.
Military service: U.S. Naval Reserve,
1945-46. *Memberships:* Society of American Archivists, 1954- (executive secretary,
1963-); Mississippi Valley Historical Association, 1951-; Michigan Historical Society (trustee, vice president, president);
Detroit Historical Society, 1958- (trustee,
historian); Michigan Archaeology Society,
1955-. *Awards, honors:* Fellow, Society
of American Archivists; A.H. Bach Fellow, Boston University, 1948-51. *Interests:*

Ethnohistory; American history; history of
exploration and travels; American labor
history. *Published works: Schoolcraft's
Expedition to Lake Itasca: The Discovery
of the Source of the Mississippi* (Michigan
State University Press, 1958); *Schoolcraft
-- The Literary Voyager or Muzzeniegun*
(Michigan State University Press, 1962);
co-author, *Harper of Detroit* (Wayne State
University Press, 1964); *The Origin and
Growth of a Great Metropolitan Hospital*
(Wayne State University Press, 1964); *Detroit, Fort Lernolult, and the American
Revolution* (Wayne State University Press,
1964).

MASSEY, EDNA H. (Mrs. Fred H.)
(Oklahoma Cherokee) 1913- (artist,
designer, teacher)

Born July 11, 1913, Stilwell, Okla. *Education:* Haskell Institute; George Washington University. *Principal occupation:* Artist, designer, teacher. *Home address:*
2231 Bancroft Pl., N.W., Washington, D.C.
20008. *Affiliations:* Artist, art teacher,
textile designer; interior designer, arts
and crafts specialist, Bureau of Indian Affairs, U.S. Department of the Interior.
Memberships: Creative Crafts Council,
Smithsonian Institution; Cherry Tree Textile Designers; Craft House (sponsor);
American Craftsmens Council (craftsman
member). *Awards, honors:* First Prize,
Textile Design, Creative Crafts Biennial,
1960; Second Prize, Textile Design, Creative Crafts Biennial, 1962.

MATHEWS, JOHN JOSEPH   (Osage)
1894(5)-   (rancher, author)

Born November 16, 1894(5), in what is now
Pawhuska, Okla. *Education:* University of
Oklahoma, B.A., 1920; Oxford University
(England), B.A. Oxon, 1923. *Principal occupation:* Rancher, author. *Home address:*
The Blackjacks, P.O. Box 1247, Pawkuska,
Okla. 74056. *Military service:* U.S. Air
Force, 1917-18. *Community activities:*
Oklahoma State Board of Education, 1935;
Osage Indian (Business) Council, 1934-42;
American Legion. *Memberships:* Phi Beta
Kappa; The Order of Daedalians (a society
of airplane pilots of the Armed Forces of
the U.S., prior to the Armistice of 1918).

Awards, honors: Book-of-the-Month-Club Award for *Wah'Kon-Tah,* 1932; Award of Merit, American Association for State and Local History for *The Osages: Children of the Middle Waters;* Distinguished Service Citation, University of Oklahoma; Guggenheim Fellowship (Mexico), 1939-40. *Interests:* Mr. Mathews writes, "If writing is my vocation, my chief interest in man and in life in general is the effect of the 'third force' on man. Force No. 1: Self-preservation. Force No. 2: Reproduction. Force No. 3: Man's profound urge to understand and come to terms with a super-being. *Avocation:* Wildlife photography; hunting; ornithology. " *Published works: Wah'Kon-Tah* (University of Oklahoma Press, 1932); *Sundown* (Longmans, Green and Co., 1934); *Talking to the Moon* (University of Chicago Press, 1945); *Life and Death of an Oilman* (University of Oklahoma Press, 1951); *The Osages: Children of the Middle Waters* (University of Oklahoma Press, 1961).

MAULDIN, JANE McCARTY   (Choctaw)
   1936-   (commercial artist)

Born January 19, 1936, Tulsa, Okla. *Education:* High school. *Principal occupation:* Commercial artist. *Home address:* 1549 N. Marion, Tulsa, Okla. 74115. *Affiliations:* Commercial artist, Floyd Gates Studio (thirteen years). *Memberships:* American Art Exchange, 1965-. *Shows:* Oklahoma Annual Exhibit, 1964, 1966; Philbrook Indian Art Annual Exhibit, 1965, 1966; U. S. Department of the Interior Annual Indian Art Exhibition. *Interests:* Mrs. Mauldin writes, "I like to paint when I can, but with the family it's pretty hard; like to travel -- have been to California and New York this year (1966). I've only been entering art exhibitions for the past three years along with my sister Valjean (McCarty) Hessing. My hobbies are painting and photography; when the children get a little older I can have more time to develop my ability. "

MAULE, STUART H.   1931-
   (national monument administrator)

Born July 8, 1931, Los Angeles, Calif. *Education:* University of California, B. A., 1956. *Principal occupation:* National monument administrator. *Affiliations:* Administrator, superintendent and archaeologist,

Effigy Mounds National Monument, Davenport, Iowa (National Park Service), 1956-. *Military service:* U. S. Army, 1952-54. *Memberships:* Northern Arizona Society for Science and Art; Society for American Archaeology; Anthropological Society of Washington. *Published works: Corn Growing at Wupatki National Monument* (Museum of Northern Arizona, 1962).

MAYHALL, MILDRED P.   1902-
   (teacher)

Born December 20, 1902, Austin, Texas. *Education:* University of Texas, B.A., 1924, M. A., 1926, Ph. D., 1939; University of Chicago. *Principal occupation:* Teacher. *Home address:* 1906 Raleigh Ave., Austin, Texas 78703. *Affiliations:* Tutor in anthropology, University of Texas, 1925-27; instructor in anthropology, University of Texas, 1927-45; teacher of history and sociology, Stephen F. Austin High School, Austin, Texas, 1956-64. *Community activities:* Methodist Church; Parent-Teachers' Association; Violet Crown Garden Club; Austin Rose Society. *Memberships:* Daughters of the American Revolution, 1923-; Daughters of the Republic of Texas, 1924-; American Anthropological Association, 1927-50; Texas Historical Association, 1927-; National Geographic Society, 1922-; American Rose Society, 1949- (consulting rosarian, 1952-); Phi Beta Kappa; Chi Upsilon; Pi Lambda Theta; Kappa Delta Pi; Sigma Xi. *Awards, honors:* Award of Merit Citation for Junior Historian work, Stephen F. Austin High School, from American Heritage; award for film, *The Indians of Texas,* 1960; Certificate of Commendation, Texas State Historical Association, 1964. *Interests:* Anthropology, ethnology and history of Indians of Texas and North America; Texas history; photography; horses; roses. *Published works: The Kiowas* (University of Oklahoma, 1962); editor, *This is Austin -- Capital of Texas* (Junior Historians and Distributive Education Chapters of the Austin High Schools, 1964); *Indian Wars of Texas* (Texian Press, 1965).

MEADOWCROFT, ENID LA MONTE   1898-
   (writer and editor of children's books)

Born March 31, 1898, New York, N. Y. *Education:* Lesley Normal School, 1918.

Principal occupation: Writer and editor of children's books. *Home address:* Lakeview Ave., Lakeville, Conn. *Affiliations:* Teacher, The Bergen School, New Jersey 1919-23; teacher, The Catling School, Ore., 1925-28; teacher, The Browning School, New York, 1928-41. *Other professional posts:* Supervising editor, Signature Books, Grosset & Dunlap, 1952-64; supervising editor, How They Lived Books, Garrard Publishing Co. *Interests:* Writing, reading; travel; music. *Published works: The Adventures of Peter Whiffen* (Thomas Y. Crowell, 1936); *The Gift of the River* (Thomas Y. Crowell, 1937); *The First Year* (Thomas Y. Crowell, 1937); *By Wagon and Flatboat* (Thomas Y. Crowell, 1938); *Aren't We Lucky* (Thomas Y. Crowell, 1939); *Along the Erie Towpath* (Thomas Y. Crowell, 1940); *Benjamin Franklin* (Thomas Y. Crowell, 1941); *Abraham Lincoln* (Thomas Y. Crowell, 1942); *Shipboy with Columbus* (Thomas Y. Crowell, 1942); *Silver for General Washington* (Thomas Y. Crowell, 1944); *On Indian Trails with Daniel Boone* (Thomas Y. Crowell, 1947); *China's Story* (Thomas Y. Crowell, 1946); *By Secret Railway* (Thomas Y. Crowell, 1948); *Texas Star* (Thomas Y. Crowell, 1950); *The Story of George Washington* (Grosset & Dunlap, 1952); *The Story of Benjamin Franklin* (Grosset & Dunlap, 1952); *The Story of Thomas Alva Edison* (Grosset & Dunlap, 1952); *The Story of Davy Crockett* (Grosset & Dunlap, 1953); *The Story of Crazy Horse* (Grosset & Dunlap, 1954); *We Were There at the Opening of the Erie Canal* (Grosset & Dunlap, 1958); *Holding the Fort with Daniel Boone* (Thomas Y. Crowell, 1958); *Land of the Free* (Thomas Y. Crowell, 1961); *Scarab for Luck* (Thomas Y. Crowell, 1964); *Crazy Horse - Sioux Warrior* (Garrard, 1965).

MEINHOLTZ, ROLLAND R. (Cherokee) 1937- (drama instructor)

Born August 20, 1937, Oklahoma City, Okla. *Education:* Northwestern University, B.S., 1959; University of Washington, M.A. (drama), 1964. *Principal occupation:* Drama instructor. *Home address:* 2023 Hopi Rd., Santa Fe, N.M. *Affiliations:* Teacher, public schools of Washington and California; instructor in drama, Institute of American Indian Arts, Santa Fe, N.M. *Interests:* Acting; direction and adaptation of plays;

travels throughout the United States in connection with the Festival of Indian Performing Arts, Washington, D.C.

MENARD, NELLIE (STAR BOY) (Rosebud Sioux) 1910- (arts and crafts specialist)

Born June 3, 1910, Rosebud, S.D. *Education:* High school. *Principal occupation:* Arts and crafts specialist. *Home address:* Box 1165, Rapid City, S.D. 57701. *Affiliations:* Teacher of native Indian crafts, Bureau of Indian Affairs In-Service Summer School for Teachers, 1939; manager, Rosebud Arts & Crafts, 1937-42; manager, Northern Plains Arts & Crafts, 1943-46; arts and crafts specialist, Sioux Indian Museum and Crafts Center, Rapid City, S.D., 1953-. *Community activities:* Rosebud Reservation delegate to Museum of Modern Art and Museum of the American Indian; attended Indian Arts and Crafts Conference, Central Office, Bureau of Indian Affairs, Washington, D.C. *Awards, honors:* Pendelton Robe, for submitted blanket design, Pendleton Mills, 1929; Superior Performance Award, Indian Arts and Crafts Board, U.S. Department of the Interior; numerous awards bestowed by the Sioux people. *Interests:* Sioux culture.

MERRY, EDWARD S. 1911- (newspaper editor, association executive)

Born September 21, 1911, Ogdensburg, N.Y. *Education:* Albany State Teachers College, 1928-29; Alfred University, 1930-31; Ohio University, 1931-33. *Principal occupation:* Newspaper editor; association executive. *Home address:* 604 S. Woodrow, Gallup, N.M. 87301. *Affiliations:* Newspaper editor, Massena, N.Y., 1940-45; newspaper editor, St. Albans, Vt., 1946-51; newspaper editor, Burlington, Vt., 1951-52; newspaper manager, Gallup, N.M., 1952-53; secretary-manager, Inter-Tribal Indian Ceremonial Association, Gallup, N.M.; secretary, United Indian Traders Association, Gallup, N.M. *Military service:* U.S. Marine Corps, 1943-46.

MILES, CHARLES 1894- (writer)

Born June 27, 1894, Claquato, Wash. *Education:* University of California, B.A., 1920;

graduate work, 1930-31. *Principal occupation:* Writer. *Home address:* 5070 Cochrane Ave., Oakland, Calif. 94618. *Affiliations:* Reporter, San Francisco *Chronicle*; teacher, Oakland Board of Education; co-editor, *Building a State,* Washington State Historical Society, 1938; editorial staff, *Hobbies* Magazine, 1960-66. *Military service:* U. S. Army, World War I. *Community activities:* American Legion (adjutant, Post 5). *Memberships:* Society for American Archaeology; Oregon Archaeological Society; Washington State Historical Society; Western Historical Association; National Education Association. *Interests:* Mr. Miles writes, "My chief vocation is writing or teaching of writing -- newspaper, magazine, publicity, and book. Chief interest is in historical topics, specifically of the Pacific Northwest, and in the material culture side of native life in North America. These accompanied by an extensive collection which was used as the pictorial material in the book, *Indian and Eskimo Artifacts of North America.* The latter interest is reflected in several years of monthly articles on Indian matters in *Hobbies* Magazine. The historical writing began with a newspaper column out of which came an engagement to organize the fifty-year anniversary book of the Washington State Historical Society, *Building a State,* in which I did some of the writing and editing. This historical research and writing has been resumed after retirement. Six months of 1963 were spent in research in Washington, D. C., and London, England. This was a third residence in Europe; others -- 1910-11 and 1922-23, the former as a student in London, the latter studying painting in Paris. (I have) some art interest; some commercial art work; art editor and artist for the University of California magazine, *The Pelican.* Magazine articles on Hiroshige prints and on Oriental rugs based on collections of both. Nearly all of the photography in *Indian and Eskimo Artifacts of North America* is my work, also most of the illustrative material in the *Hobbies* Magazine Indian articles. I was born of pioneer parents in an historic pioneer community when Indians were still 'about,' and puncheon, broadaxes and even canoes likewise; pioneer history and surroundings are familiar ground, and Indians are neighbors rather than oddities." *Published works: Building a State* (Washington State Historical Society, 1939); *Indian and Eskimo Artifacts of North America* (Henry Regnery Co., 1963).

MILLER, ARVID E. (Stockbridge-Munsee) 1908- (tribal council president)

Born October 10, 1908, Shawano County, Wis. *Education:* University of Wisconsin. *Principal occupation:* Tribal council president. *Home address:* Route 1, Stockbridge-Munsee Community, Bowler, Wis. *Affiliations:* Chief, Tribal Council, Stockbridge-Munsee Band of Mohicans; president, Great Lakes Inter-Tribal Council of Wisconsin. *Community activities:* Town Board (member); Indian Security Foundation of Wisconsin (president); Governor's Commission on Human Rights; Bowler Small Business Administration (president); Public Housing Authority. *Membership*: National Congress of American Indians (regional vice president).

MILLER, ELMO 1914- (B. I. A. agency superintendent)

Born September 23, 1914, Nephi, Utah. *Education:* Utah State University, B. S., (Agriculture), 1939. *Principal occupation:* B. I. A. agency superintendent. *Home address:* P. O. Box 193, Coulee Dam, Wash. 99116. *Affiliations:* Superintendent, Colville Agency, Bureau of Indian Affairs, Colville, Wash. *Community activities:* Coulee Dam Rotary Club (past president). *Award:* Citation for Superior Performance, U. S. Government. *Interests:* Administrative management.

MILLER, ROBERT L. (Seminole-Creek) 1908- (educator)

Born November 11, 1908, Wewoka, Okla. *Education:* Oklahoma A & M., B. A. (Journalism), 1953; Drake University; East Central State University. *Principal occupation:* Educator. *Home address:* 512 Dee Anne, Norman, Okla. 73069. *Affiliation:* Coordinator, Indian Education Program, Human Relations Center, University of Oklahoma. *Other professional posts:* Editor, *Indian Education Newsletter.* *Military service:* 1942-43.

MILLER, ROLAND E.   (Stockbridge-
Munsee) 1918-   (B. I. A. officer)

Born April 21, 1918, Gresham, Wis. *Education:* Haskell Institute, 1932-37. *Principal occupation:* B.I.A. officer. *Affiliations:* Various administrative positions with the Bureau of Indian Affairs, 1937-; chief budget officer, Bureau of Indian Affairs, 1966-. *Military service:* U. S. Army, 1940-45, 1950-52. *Community activities:* Lutheran Church.

MILLS, EARL H.   (Mashpee Wampanoag)
1929-   (teacher, tribal officer)

Born March 30, 1929, Mashpee, Mass. *Education:* Arnold College, B.S., 1952; Bridgewater State, M.A., 1959. *Principal occupation:* Teacher, tribal officer. *Home address:* 229 Jones Rd., Falmouth, Mass. 02540. *Affiliations:* Director of physical education and athletics, Lawrence High School, Falmouth, Mass. *Military service:* U.S. Army, 1946-48. *Community activities:* Tales of Cape Cod (director); Old Indian Meeting House Authority, Inc. (president); Community Action Program of Barnstable County (director); Mashpee Wampanoag Tribe (tribal executive). *Memberships:* Massachusetts Coaches Association; Track Association; Athletic Directors Association; Cape Cod Coaches Association; Falmouth Teachers Organization; Barnstable County Teachers Organization; Massachusetts Teachers Organization. *Awards, honors:* John Antal Award, Outstanding Football Player. *Interests:* Physical education and athletics; remedial education; biology.

MINER, MARCELLA HIGH BEAR
(Cheyenne River Sioux) 1935-
(tribal officer)

Born July 31, 1935, Cheyenne Agency, S. D. *Education:* Cheyenne River Board School, Diploma, 1954; Aberdeen School of Commerce, Diploma, 1957. *Principal occupation:* Tribal officer. *Home address:* Eagle Butte, S.D. 57625. *Affiliations:* Tribal treasurer, Cheyenne River Sioux Tribal Council, Eagle Butte, S. D., 1962-66. *Community activities:* Cheyenne River Mission, Episcopal Church (treasurer).

MINTON, CHARLES E.   1898-
(Indian affairs director, State of New Mexico)

Born July 1, 1898, St. Louis, Mo. *Education:* St. Louis University, LL. B., 1923, LL. M., 1924. *Principal occupation:* Indian affairs director, State of New Mexico. *Home address:* 227 Washington Ave., Santa Fe, N. M. 87501. *Affiliations:* Headmaster, Santa Fe Country Day School, 1931-35; state director, New Mexico Writers' Project; founder and director, New Mexico Boys' Ranch, 1943-50; founder and director, Indian Youth Council, 1954-61; executive director, New Mexico Commission on Indian Affairs. *Other professional posts:* Editor and publisher, *Indian News*, Newsletter of the New Mexico Association of Indian Affairs. *Military service:* U. S. Army, 1918-19. *Memberships:* Kiwanis Club, 1943-; Old Santa Fe Association; Historic Santa Fe Foundation. *Awards:* Plaque from "the Indian youth of the Southwest," 1963; Optimist of the Year, 1948, Albuquerque Optimist Club. *Interests:* Indian affairs and history. *Published works: New Mexico: A Guide to the Colorful State* (Hastings House, Works Projects Administration, 1940); consultant to numerous anthropologists and authors of books in the field of Indian affairs.

MOFSIE, LOUIS   (Hopi-Winnebago) 1936-
(art educator)

Born May 3, 1936, New York, N.Y. *Education:* State University of New York, Buffalo, B.S., 1958; Pratt Institute. *Principal occupation:* Art educator. *Home address:* 323 Schermerhorn St., Brooklyn, N.Y. 11217. *Affiliations:* Art instructor, East Meadow (L. I., N. Y.) Board of Education. *Community activities:* Thunderbird American Indian Dancers of New York (director); Indian League of the Americas of New York (president, 1961-63). *Memberships:* New York State Art Teachers Association; National Art Education Association; Long Island Art Teachers Association; Classroom Teachers Association. *Awards, honors:* Association of Southwestern Indians Award for painting submitted to the Annual Indian Artists Exhibition, Santa Fe Art Museum. *Interests:* Art instruction; Indian dance; travels across United States, into Mexico and Canada.

MOLLOY, ANNE STEARNS 1907-
  (writer)

Born October 4, 1907, Boston, Mass. *Education:* Mt. Holyoke College. *Principal
occupation:* Writer of books for children.
Home address: Newmarket Rd. , Exeter,
N. H. 03833. *Community activities:* Exeter
Public Library (trustee). *Interests:* Indian
life in South America, the United States and
Canada; travel to Peru and Chile. *Published
works: Captain Waymouth's Indians* (Hastings House, 1956) among twenty-odd others.

MOMADAY, AL (Kiowa) 1913-
  (artist, educator)

Born July 2, 1913, Mountain View, Okla.
Education: University of New Mexico; Uni-
versity of California, Los Angeles; Famous
Artists Schools. *Principal occupation:* Ar-
tist, educator. *Home address:* Box 67,
Jemez Pueblo, N. M. 87024. *Affiliations:*
Principal, Jemez Day School. *Memberships:* National Congress of American Indians; Artists' Equity Association; National
Education Association; New Mexico Indian
Arts Committee. *Awards:* New Mexico
State Fair Grand Award, 1962; Grand Award,
Indian Painting, All American Indian Days,
Sheridan, Wyo. , 1955; Grand Award Indian Painting, American Indian Exposition;
bronze plaque (awarded jointly to Mr. Momaday and his wife, Natachee Scott Momaday, also an artist), African Women Educators, 1962; Outstanding Southwestern Indian Artists Award, Dallas Exchange Club,
1956; First Prize, Indian Painting, Philbrook Art Center, Tulsa, Okla., 1956; First
Prize, Indian Painting, Scottsdale National
Indian Art Exhibition, Scottsdale, Ariz. ,
1964.

MOMADAY, NATACHEE SCOTT (North
  Carolina Cherokee) 1913- (artist,
  writer, teacher)

Born February 13, 1913, Fairview, Ky.
Education: Haskell Institute; Crescent Col-
lege, B. A. , 1933. *Principal occupation:*
Artist, writer, teacher. *Home address:*
Jemez Pueblo, N. M. *Affiliations:* Civil
service teacher, Albuquerque, Shiprock,
Chinle, Navajo Service, Ariz. *Other pro-
fessional posts:* Personnel director,

H. A. A. F. , Hobbs, N. M. ; former newspaper reporter. *Community activities:* Committee, State Library Association. *Memberships:* Delta Kappa Gamma; National
League of American Pen Women; United
Daughters of the Confederacy; Daughters of
the American Revolution. *Awards:* Campfire Girls of Detroit; Boy Scouts of America; Arts and Crafts Fair, Albuquerque,
N. M. ; Inter-Tribal Indian Ceremonial Association. *Published works: Owl in the
Cedar Tree* (Ginn and Co., 1965); *Woodland
Princess,* a book of twenty-four poems (Mc
Hughes Co., 1931); co-author, *Velvet Ribbons* (privately printed, 1942).

MONTGOMERY, ELIZABETH RIDER
  (writer)

Born Peru, South America. *Education:*
Western Washington College, 1924-25; Uni-
versity of California, Los Angeles, 1927-
28. *Principal occupation:* Writer. *Home
address:* 4801 Beach Dr. , S. W. , Seattle,
Wash. 98116. *Affiliations:* Public school
teacher, Wash., Calif.; staff writer, Scott,
Foresman and Co. *Community activities:*
Youth Symphony (former president); Girl
Scouts; Cub Scouts; Alki Congregational
Church; Seattle Friends of the Library.
Memberships: Seattle Free Lances, 1946-
(president, 1955-56); National League of
American Penwomen; National Press Women. *Awards, honors:* Play prizes; Press
Women and Penwomen Awards; Matrix Table, Seattle, 1953; Parent-Teachers' Association, 1954; and others. *Interests:*
Children's and young adult fiction and plays;
adult fiction; watercolor painting; stamp
collecting; music; rug making. *Published
works: We Look and See* (Scott, Foresman,
1940); *We Work and Play* (Scott, Foresman,
1940); *We Come and Go* (Scott, Foresman,
1940); *Sally Does It* (Appleton-Century,
1940); *Good Times with Our Friends* (Scott,
Foresman, 1941); *Bonnie's Baby Brother*
(Lippincott, 1942); *Story Behind Great In-
ventions* (Dodd, Mead, 1944); *Three Friends*
(Scott, Foresman, 1944); *Story Behind Great
Medical Discoveries* (Dodd, Mead, 1945);
Keys to Nature's Secrets (Dodd, Mead, 1946);
Story Behind Great Books (Dodd, Mead,
1946); *Five in the Family* (Scott, Foresman,
1945); *The Girl Next Door* (Scott, Fores-
man, 1946); *Story Behind Great Stories*
(Dodd, Mead, 1947); *Happy Days with Our*

Friends (Scott, Foresman, 1948); *You* (Scott, Foresman, 1948); *Story Behind Modern Books* (Dodd, Mead, 1949); *All Kinds of People* (Row, Peterson, 1950); *Three Miles an Hour* (Dodd, Mead, 1952); *Story Behind Musical Instruments* (Dodd, Mead, 1953); *Half-Pint Fisherman* (Dodd, Mead, 1959); *Just Like Me* (Scott, Foresman, 1957); *Being Six* (Scott, Foresman, 1957); *Seven or So* (Scott, Foresman, 1957); *Eight to Nine* (Scott, Foresman, 1957); *Going on Ten* (Scott, Foresman, 1958); *Story Behind Popular Songs* (Dodd, Mead, 1958); *Second Fiddle Sandra* (Dodd, Mead, 1958); *About Yourself* (Scott, Foresman, 1959); *Till Time Be Conquered* (Alki Church, 1959); *Susan and the Storm* (T. Nelson, 1960); *Mystery of Edison Brown* (Scott, Foresman, 1960); *Alexander Graham Bell* (Garrard, 1963); *The Klep* (Pub Pioneer Drama, 1963); *Tide Treasure Camper* (Ives-Washburn, 1963); *Hernando De Soto* (Garrard, 1964); *Lewis and Clark* (Garrard, 1966); *Two Kinds of Courage* (Ives-Washburn, 1966); *Chief Seattle* (Garrard, 1966).

MONTOYA, GERONIMA CRUZ (Pueblo) 1915- (artist, teacher)

Born September 22, 1915, San Juan Pueblo, N. M. *Education:* St. Joseph's College, B.S., 1958; University of New Mexico; Claremont College. *Principal occupation:* Art teacher, Santa Fe, N. M. *Home address:* 1008 Calle de Suenos, Santa Fe, N. M. *Community activities:* Community Concert Association (captain); San Juan Pueblo Choir (secretary-treasurer). *Awards:* School of American Research Purchase Award; Museum of New Mexico Special Category Prize, Inter-Tribal Indian Ceremonial, Gallup, N. M. ; Special Prize, Scottsdale National Indian Art Exhibition, Scottsdale, Ariz. ; Special Prize, Philbrook Art Center, Tulsa, Okla. ; DeYoung Museum Purchase Prize; honorarium for prize-winning student.

MOORE, WILLIAM J. 1938- (museum director)

Born August 4, 1938, Asheboro, N.C. *Education:* High Point College, B.S. , 1960. *Principal occupation:* Museum director. *Home address:* 1217 Pamlico Drive,

Greensboro, N.C. 27408. *Affiliations:* Director, Greensboro Historical Museum. *Other professional post:* Assistant to archaeologist, Town Creek Indian Mound, Mt. Gilead, N.C., 1959. *Memberships:* Rotary International; Archaeological Society of North Carolina; American Association for State and Local History; North Carolina Literary and Historical Association; Civil War Roundtable. *Interests:* Archaeology and American history.

MORRIS, LOVERNE L.   1896-   (writer)

Born September 23, 1896, Lyon County, Kan. *Education:* Emporia State Teachers College, Diploma, 1916. *Principal occupation:* Writer. *Home address:* 1664 Thunderbird Dr., Apt. 17D, Seal Beach, Calif. 90740. *Affiliations:* Editor, Temple City *Times*, 1942-45; reporter and feature writer, *Daily News*, Whittier, Calif. , 1946-62; editor, El Monte *Independent*. *Community activities:* Temple City Chamber of Commerce. *Memberships:* Writers Club of Whittier (charter member and founding president); La Puente Historical Society; Governor Pio Pico Mansion Society. *Awards, honors:* Temple City Chamber of Commerce; Associated Coordinating Councils of Whittier Area; Theta Sigma Chi Play Award, 1940; local awards, Whittier Friends of the Library, for history and research. *Interests:* Indian culture, nature study, social history, politics, economics. *Published works:* The American Indian as Farmer (Melmont Publishers, Inc., 1963); *Whittier Area History* (Historical Publishers, 1963).

MORRIS, RICHARD B.   1904- (professor and historian)

Born July 24, 1904, New York, N. Y. *Education:* City College of New York, B. A. , (cum laude), 1924; Columbia University, M. A. , Ph. D. *Principal occupation:* Professor and historian. *Home address:* 151 Ridgeway St. , Mount Vernon, N. Y. 10552. *Affiliations:* Gouverneur Morris professor of history, Columbia University, 1949-. *Other professional posts:* Visiting professor, Princeton University, 1947-48. *Memberships:* American Historical Association; Phi Beta Kappa, and others. *Awards, honors:* Joint Award ($1,000), Colonial Dames of America and National Society of Colonial

Dames, for best book in colonial history, 1930. *Published works: Studies in the History of American Law* (1930); *Government and Labor in Early America* (Columbia University Press, 1946); *The American Revolution: A Brief History* (Van Nostrand); editor, *Encyclopedia of American History* (Harper & Row); *Fair Trial* (Knopf, 1952); *First Book of the Revolution* (Franklin Watts); *First Book of the Constitution* (Franklin Watts); *First Book of the Indian Wars* (Franklin Watts); *First Book of the War of 1812* (Franklin Watts); *The Peacemakers* (Harper & Row, 1965).

MORRISON, BUFORD 1919-
(B. I. A. area field representative)

Born November 24, 1919, Lenna, Okla. *Education:* Haskell Institute. *Principal occupation:* B. I. A. area field representative. *Affiliations:* Area field representative, Horton Agency, Bureau of Indian Affairs, Horton, Kan. *Military service:* U. S. Army, 1942-45 (four campaign stars). *Community activities:* Kiwanis Club (board of directors, 1966); Chamber of Commerce.

MORRISON, GEORGE (Chippewa) 1919-
(artist and teacher of art)

Born September 30, 1919, Grand Marais, Minn. *Education:* Minneapolis School of Art, Certificate, 1943; Art Students League, 1943-46. *Principal occupation:* Artist and teacher of art. *Home address:* 132 Transit St. , Providence, R. I. 02906. *Affiliations:* Art instructor, Cape Ann Art School, Rockport, Mass. , 1947; art instructor, Rockport Art School, Rockport, Mass. , 1948; private art classes, New York, 1948-51; art instructor, Camp Robinson Crusoe, 1949; art therapist, Wiltwyck School for Boys, 1957; visiting artist, Minneapolis School of Art, 1959; visiting artist, State College of Iowa, 1961; visiting critic, Cornell University, 1962; visiting artist, Pennsylvania State University, 1963; assistant professor of art, Rhode Island School of Design, 1963-. *Memberships:* Pyramid Group 1945-49; Grand Central Moderns Gallery, 1948-62; Audobon Artists, 1955-; Federation of Modern Painters and Sculptors, 1955-; Museum

of Modern Art Lending Service (representation), 1955-61; Karlis Gallery (associate), 1958-60; J. Thomas Gallery, 1964-; Museum of Rhode Island School of Design, 1963-; Walker Art Center Rental Gallery (representation) 1954-61; Kilbride-Bradley Gallery (associate), 1959-61; Lincoln Art Association (representation), 1954-58; Baltimore Museum Lending Gallery (representation), 1959-62; Dayton Art Institute Circulating Library (representation), 1956-58, 1960-62; Columbus Museum Circulating Gallery (representation), 1954-55. *Exhibitions:* Numerous one-, two- and three-man shows, invitational exhibitions and group shows in the United States, France, the Netherlands, South America, Japan. Mr. Morrison's work is a part of many private, corporate and museum collections in the United States and abroad. *Awards, honors:* Lucy Gilbert Award, Minneapolis School of Art, 1941; Woman's Club Scholarship, Minneapolis School of Art, 1942; Vanderlip Traveling Scholarship, Minneapolis School of Art, 1943; Bernays Scholarship, Art Students League, 1943; scholarship grants, Consolidated Chippewa Agency, 1941-42; Fulbright Scholarship (France), 1952-53; John Hay Whitney Fellowship, 1953-54.

MORTON, RICHARD LEE 1889-
(professor of history)

Born September 20, 1889, Prince Edward County, Va. *Education:* Hampden Sydney College, B. A., 1910; University of Virginia, M. A. , 1915, Ph. D., 1918; Harvard University, M. A. , 1917. *Principal occupation:* Professor of history. *Home address:* 116 Chandler Court, Williamsburg, Va. 23185. *Affiliations:* Principal, high school, Spring Garden, Va. , 1910-12; instructor, Martinsburg, W. Va. , 1912-13; camp library work and acting librarian, Camp Lee, Va. , 1919, associate professor of history and political science and acting head of department, College of William and Mary, 1919-21; professor of history and head, Department of History, College of William and Mary, 1921-59; chairman, Division of the Social Sciences, College of William and Mary, 1944-47; chancellor professor of history, 1959-. *Other professional posts:* Member, summer school faculty, University of Virginia, 1940; editor, William and Mary

Quarterly, 1944-47 (editorial board, 1954, 1956-60). *Military service:* Psychological Co., No. 1, Camp Greenleaf, Ga., 1918; Psychological Examining Board, Camp Meade, Md., 1918. *Community activities:* Bruton Parish Episcopal Church (vestryman and junior warden); Williamsburg Club, Rotary International (president, 1955-56); Williamsburg Community Council (vice-president, 1955-56); Historians of Colonial Williamsburg (advisory committee of historians, 1939-43); Institute of Early American History and Culture (council of historians, 1943-46, 1947-50, 1952-55, 1955-59); member, state commissions. *Memberships:* American Historical Association (honorary member, 1965-); American Association of University Professors (twice president of local chapter); Southern Historical Association (honorary member, 1962-); Virginia Historical Society; Virginia Social Science Association (president, 1931); Association for the Preservation of Virginia Antiquities. *Awards, honors:* Raven Society, University of Virginia; Phi Beta Kappa; Omicron Delta Kappa; Sigma Upsilon; Tau Kappa Alpha; Sigma Pi; Litt. D., Hampden-Sydney College, 1926; LL. D., College of William and Mary, 1965; Annual Distinguished Service Award, Virginia Social Science Association, 1964; Research Grant, Social Science Research Council, 1931; Grant, General Education Board, 1942-43; Richard Lee Morton Scholarship, College of William and Mary, founded in 1959 by students, faculty and others; awards for *Colonial Virginia. Published works: The Negro in Virginia Politics, 1865-1902* (Phelps-Stokes Fellowship Papers, No. 4, University of Virginia, 1919); *Virginia Since 1861,* Vol. III, *History of Virginia,* three vols., with P. A. Bruce and L. G. Tyler (University of Chicago Press, 1924); editor, *Present State of Virginia* by Hugh Jones (University of North Carolina Press, 1956); *Colonial Virginia,* two vols. (University of North Carolina Press, 1960); supervising editor, *Virginia Lives, the Old Dominion Who's Who* (Hopkinsville, 1964); *Revolutionary Virginia* (in progress).

MOWAT, FARLEY McGILL   1921-
    (writer)

Born May 12, 1921, Belleveille, Ont, Can. *Education:* University of Toronto, B. A., 1949. *Principal occupation:* Writer. *Home*

address: Burgeo, Newfoundland, Can. *Affiliations:* Canada Department of Northern Affairs, 1949-50. *Military service:* Canadian Army, 1939-45. *Awards, honors:* Anisfield Wolfe Award; Governor General's Medal. *Interests:* Canadian North; field work in Keewatin territory, 1949-50 (Ihalmiut tribe); Beothuk Indians of Newfoundland. *Published works: People of the Deer* (Little, Brown, 1952); *Lost in the Barrens* (Little, Brown, 1952); *The Regiment* (McClelland and Stewart, 1953); *Grey Seas Under* (Little, Brown, 1958); *Coppermine Journey* (Little, Brown, 1958); *The Desperate People* (Little, Brown, 1959); *Ordeal By Ice* (Little, Brown, 1961); *Owls in the Family* (Little, Brown, 1962); *The Serpent's Coil* (Little, Brown, 1962); *The Black Joke* (Little, Brown, 1963); *Never Cry Wolf* (Little, Brown, 1963); *Westviking* (Little, Brown, 1965); *Riddle of the Viking Grave* (Little, Brown, 1966).

MOYER, JOHN WILLIAM   1905-
    (staff member, Chicago Natural History Museum)

Born June 13, 1905, Georgetown, Ohio. *Education:* University of Cincinnati, 1923-26; Chicago Art Institute, 1927-29. *Principal occupation:* Staff member, Chicago Natural History Museum, 1929-. *Home address:* 307 Groveland Trail, Michiana Shores, Michigan City, Ind. 46361. *Other posts:* Consul of the United States of America to India, 1951-55. *Military service:* U. S. Navy, 1942-45. *Memberships:* Adventurer's Club; Shikar-Safari Club. *Interests:* "Various expeditions, trips, etc., to nearly all parts of the globe. (Interested in) production of motion picture travelogue programs -- people, places and wildlife." *Published works: Practical Taxidermy* (The Ronald Press, Inc., 1953); *Famous Indian Chiefs* (M.A. Donohue & Co., 1957); *Trophy Heads* (The Ronald Press, Inc., 1962).

MURDOCK, GEORGE PETER   1897-
    (professor of anthropology)

Born May 14, 1897, Meriden, Conn. *Education:* Yale College, B. A., 1919; Harvard Law School, 1919-20; Yale University Graduate School, Ph. D., 1925. *Principal occupation:* Professor of anthropology. *Home address:* 4150 Bigelow Blvd., Pittsburgh,

Penna. 15213. *Affiliations:* Assistant professor, associate professor, professor, Yale University, 1928-60; Mellon professor of anthropology, University of Pittsburgh, 1960-. *Other professional posts:* Division of Behavioral Sciences, National Research Council (chairman, 1964-66). *Military service:* U.S. Army, 1918; U.S. Naval Reserve, 1943-46. *Memberships:* American Anthropological Association (president, 1955); American Ethnological Society (president, 1952-53); American Geographical Society; American Sociological Association; Society for Applied Anthropology (president, 1947). *Awards, honors:* Viking Fund Medal in general anthropology, 1949; member, National Academy of Sciences. *Interests:* "Ethnological field work among the Haida Indians of British Columbia (1932), among the Tenino Indians of Oregon (1934, 1935), and among the Trukese of the Central Pacific (1947)." *Travels:* "Four trips around the world, plus separate trips to Great Britain, France, Germany, the Soviet Union, Guam, New Zealand, Japan, and the Philippines." *Published works: Our Primitive Contemporaries* (Macmillan, 1934); editor, *Studies in the Science of Society* (Yale University Press, 1937); *Ethnographic Bibliography of North America* (1941; Human Relations Area Files Press, 1960); *Social Structure* (Macmillan, 1949); *Africa* (McGraw-Hill, 1959); *Culture and Society* (University of Pittsburgh Press, 1965).

MURPHY, C. L. (Charlotte Murphy)
1924- (writer)

Born November 15, 1924, New York, N. Y. *Education:* Green Mountain College for Women, 1943-44. *Principal occupation:* Writer. *Home address:* 30 Mercedes Rd, Brockton, Mass. 02401. *Published works: Buffalo Grass* (Dial Press, 1966).

MURPHY, C. L. (Lawrence A. Murphy)
1924- (teacher, writer)

Born May 17, 1924, Brockton, Mass. *Education:* Massachusetts Maritime Academy, B. S., 1944; Boston University, B. S., 1950;

M. A., 1951. *Principal occupation:* Teacher, writer. *Home address:* 30 Mercedes Rd., Brockton, Mass. 02401. *Military service:* Merchant Marine; U.S. Navy 1942-47. *Published works: Buffalo Grass* (Dial Press, 1966).

MURRAY, KEITH A.   1910-
(professor of history)

Born October 31, 1910, Nez Perce, Idaho. *Education:* Whitworth College, B. A., 1935; University of Washington, M. A., 1940, Ph. D., 1946. *Principal occupation:* Professor of history. *Address:* Department of History, Western Washington State College, Bellingham, Wash. 98225. *Affiliations:* Admissions director, Whitworth College, 1936-39; history teacher, public schools of Richland, Coupeville, and Kent, Wash., 1940-45; professor and chairman, Department of History, Western Washington State College, Bellingham, Wash., 1946-. *Other professional posts:* Historian-ranger, Lava Beds National Monument, National Park Service, summers of 1954, 1956, 1958. *Community activities:* Washington State Parks and Recreation Commission (chairman, historic sites advisory board); Washington Department of Public Instruction (chairman, committee on Washington State history examination); Bellingham Rotary Club (president). *Memberships:* Washington State Historical Society, 1947-; Pacific Northwest History Conference, 1947- (conference chairman, 1964); Western History Association, 1964- (member, conference program committee, 1966); American History Association, 1965-. *Awards, honors:* Award of Merit, "Excellence in Teaching and Writing," Pacific Northwest History Conference, 1965. *Interests:* "Western and Pacific Northwestern history. Field research includes work at Lava Beds National Monument; travels through Rocky Mountain West, 1955 and 1957, photographing historic sites; to Alaska in 1962 to visit and photograph gold rush of 1898 locations. *Avocational interest:* "Music. For twenty-two years I have been the director of an oratorio society in northwestern Washington; for nine years a member of a male quartet." *Published works: The Modocs and Their War* (University of Oklahoma Press, 1959).

N

NASH, PHILLEO 1909- (former Commissioner, Bureau of Indian Affairs)

Born October 25, 1909, Wisconsin Rapids, Wis. *Education:* University of Wisconsin, B.A., 1932; University of Chicago, Ph.D., 1937. *Principal occupation:* Former commissioner, Bureau of Indian Affairs (1960-65). *Home address:* 800 - 4th St., S.W., Washington, D.C. 20024. *Affiliations:* Vice president and director, Biron Cranberry Co., 1929-46; president, Biron Cranberry Co., 1946-. *Other professional posts:* Lecturer in anthropology, University of Toronto, 1937-41; special lecturer in anthropology, University of Wisconsin, 1941-42; special assistant to the director, Domestic Operations, Office of War Information, 1942-45; special assistant, The White House, 1946-52; administrative assistant to the President of the United States, 1952-53; lieutenant governor, Wisconsin, 1959-61. *Military service:* Special consultant to the secretary of war, 1943. *Community activities:* Georgetown Day School, Washington, D.C. (president, 1945-52); Menominee Tribal Trust (vice chairman, 1961); Wisconsin Governor's Refugee Committee (chairman, 1959-61); Association on American Indian Affairs (board member, 1942-61); Democratic Party of Wisconsin (chairman, 1955-57); Wisconsin Cranberry Growers Association (president, 1960). *Memberships:* Theta Delta Chi; Cosmos Club; American Anthropological Association; Washington Anthropological Society; National Capital Democratic Club; Society for Applied Anthropology. *Awards, honors:* Sigma Xi (honorary science society); Honorary Curator, Milwaukee Public Museum. *Interests:* Applied anthropology. *Published works:* Editor, *Spanish Speaking Americans and the War* (Office of Inter-American Affairs, 1944); *Enemy Japan* (O.W.I. pamphlet, 1945); *The Command of Negro Troops* (Training Division, U.S. Army, 1945); *Final Report of the President's Committee on Fair Employment Practices* (U.S. Government Printing Office, 1946); *Report to the Secretary of the Interior by the Task Force on Indian Affairs* (Department of the Interior, 1961); numerous speeches published by the Department of the Interior; magazine and newspaper articles.

NEIHARDT, JOHN G. 1881- (writer, poet, critic, professor)

Born January 8, 1881, Sharpsburg, Ill. *Education:* Wayne State College, B.S., 1897. *Principal occupation(s):* Writer, poet, critic, professor. *Home address:* Skyrim Farm, Route 7, Columbia, Mo. 65201. *Affiliations:* Literary editor, Minneapolis *Journal*, 1912-22; literary editor, St. Louis *Post-Dispatch*, 1926-38; director of information, Bureau of Indian Affairs, 1943-46; lecturer in English, University of Missouri, 1949-. *Awards, honors:* Hon. Litt.D., University of Nebraska, 1917; Hon. LL.D., Creighton University, 1927; Hon. Litt.D., University of Missouri, 1946. *Memberships:* National Institute of Arts and Letters; International Institute of Arts and Letters; Academy of American Poets. *Biographical sources: Webster's Biographical Dictionary; International Who's Who; Oxford Companion to American Literature; Who's Who in America. Published works: Black Elk Speaks* (University of Nebraska Press); *When the Tree Flowered; Indian Tales and Others; The Song of the Indian Wars; The Song of the Messiah,* among others.

NEVIN, EVELYN C. 1910- (writer)

Born February 22, 1910, Council Bluffs, Iowa. *Education:* Washington State University, 1929-33; New York University. *Principal occupation:* Writer; teacher of creative writing. *Home address:* Rainier, Ore. 97048. *Affiliations:* Associate editor, *Jack and Jill* magazine, Curtis Publishing Co.; editor, *Trailblazer and Stories,* Westminster Press. *Memberships:* National Press Women. *Awards, honors:* Miss Nevin's book, *Underground Escape,* chosen for James Weldon Johnson Collection, New York City Library, as outstanding book on Negro history and culture. *Published works: The Lost Children of the Shoshones* (Westminster Press, 1946; appeared as a serial in *Jack and Jill* magazine); *Sign of the Anchor* (Westminster Press, 1947; also published in Holland); *Underground Escape* (Westminster Press, 1949; also published in Norway); *Captive of the Delawares* (Abingdon-Cokesbury, 1952; also appeared as a serial in *Jack and Jill* magazine); *The River Spirit and the Mountain Demons* (D. Van Nostrand, 1965).

NEW, LLOYD H. (professional name, *Lloyd Kiva*) (Cherokee) 1916- (artist, craftsman)

Born February 18, 1916, Fairland, Okla. *Education:* Oklahoma State University, 1933-34; Art Institute of Chicago, 1934-35; University of New Mexico, 1937; University of Chicago, B.A.E., 1938; Laboratory of Anthropology (Santa Fe, N.M.), 1939. *Principal occupation:* Artist, craftsman. *Address:* Institute of American Indian Arts, Cerrillos Rd., Santa Fe, N.M. 87501. *Affiliations:* Director, Indian Exhibit, Arizona State Fair, 1939-50; instructor in arts and crafts, U.S. Indian School, Phoenix, Ariz., 1939-41; conducted arts and crafts survey in Mexico, summer, 1941; established Lloyd Kiva Studios, Scottsdale, Ariz., 1945; instructor in art education, U.S. Indian summer schools for teachers -- Carson City, Nev., 1949, Santa Fe, N.M. and Salem, Ore., 1950, Brigham City, Utah, 1951; designer of handwoven Oklahoma Cherokee tweeds for suits, coats, and casuals, 1949; co-director, Southwest Indian Arts Project (sponsored by the Rockefeller Foundation), University of Arizona, 1959-61; art director, Institute of American Indian Arts, 1962-. *Other professional posts:* Founding member, Arizona Craftsmen's Council, Scottsdale, Ariz., 1953; founding president, Designer-Craftsman Chapter, American Craftsmen's Council, 1958; second vice president, Heard Museum of Anthropology and Primitive Art; commissioner, Indian Arts and Crafts Board, U.S. Department of the Interior, 1961. *Community activities:* "Founded, in partnership with Wes Segner, Fifth Avenue as a new street in Scottsdale (Ariz.), 1950. . . (By 1955), Scottsdale had been established as a general craft-centered community and was known as a center for arts and crafts activities. (I) built the Kiva Craft Center, an attractive architectural compound of buildings containing twenty-five arts and crafts and related themes on a pool-centered patio, containing silver and goldsmiths, leather workers, fabric designers and printers, ceramists, glassworkers, fashion designers, architects and interior decorators. The Center still holds its place as a cultural center in a rapidly expanding commercial community"; Scottsdale Chamber of Commerce (director, 1956). *Awards, honors:* Invited to First International Fashion Design Show (Atlantic City, N.J.), Philadelphia Museum of Art, 1951; Second International Design Show, 1952; associate member, American Institute of Decorators; Merit Award for Textile Design, Museum of

Modern Art (New York City), 1956; International Design Award for Textile Designs by Indian Students, The American Institute of Interior Designers, 1962. *Interests:* Mr. New writes, referring to the period during which he established the Lloyd Kiva Studios in Scottsdale, Arizona, "During this period (I) was devoted to the problem: Can Indian craftsmen produce contemporary craft items for general use, enabling the craftsmen to earn a living, pursuing their crafts in a general society? This implies some understanding of design inspiration from Indian tradition, careful craftsmanship, and fashion, and marketing. (My) 'Kiva Bags' (a craft item Mr. New created) have been marketed by outstanding fashion stores throughout the country: Elizabeth Arden, Lord & Taylor, Nieman-Marcus, L.S. Ayres, Neustater's and Goldwater's. Top fashion publications have featured (these) and other Kiva fashions from time to time. Some are: *Harper's Bazaar, Town and Country, The New Yorker, Life, Holiday, London Herald, National News Weekly,* and *Cosmopolitan.*" Mr. New has attended various conferences relating to indigenous arts and crafts forms in the United States and Mexico. *Published works: Using Cultural Difference as a Basis for Creative Expression* (Institute of American Indian Arts, U.S. Department of the Interior, 1964).

NEWCOMB, FRANC JOHNSON 1887-
   (teacher, writer)

Born March 31, 1887, Greenfield, Wis. *Education:* Teacher's College, LaCrosse, Wis., Diploma. *Principal occupation:* Teacher, writer. *Home address:* 1123 Las Lomas Rd., N.E., Albuquerque, N.M. 87106. *Affiliations:* Teacher, Ft. Defiance Navajo School, 1912-13; writer, lecturer, trader, Navajo Reservation. *Community activities:* Woman's Club; Visiting Nursing Auxiliary; Social Service; Senior Citizens of Albuquerque. *Memberships:* State Folklore Society, 1938-; Museum of Navajo Arts, 1937-; Western Indian Welfare Society, 1953-. *Awards, honors:* Wendall T. Bush Fund Award for research, Columbia University, 1928; Smithsonian Research Fund, 1925, 1926. *Interests:* Navajo religion and folktales; sandpaintings and sacred fetishes; research on the Navajo Reservation. *Published works: Origin Legend of the Eagle Chant (American Folklore Magazine,* 1937);

Navajo Omens and Taboos (Rydal Press, 1940); *A Study of Navajo Symbolism* (Peabody Museum, 1958); *Hosteen Klah: Navajo Medicine Man and Sandpainter* (University of Oklahoma Press, 1964); *Navajo Folk Tales* (Museum of New Mexico, 1966).

NEWCOMB, WILLIAM W., Jr. 1921- (museum director, professor of anthropology)

Born October 30, 1921, Detroit, Mich. *Education:* Albion College, 1939-41; University of Michigan, B.A., M.A., Ph.D., 1953. *Principal occupation:* Museum director, professor of anthropology. *Home address:* 6206 Shoal Creek Blvd., Austin, Texas 78757. *Affiliations:* Instructor, University of Texas, 1947-50, 1951-52; curator of anthropology, Texas Memorial Museum, 1954-57; assistant professor, Colgate University; director, Texas Memorial Museum. *Military service:* U.S. Army, World War II. *Memberships:* American Anthropological Association (Fellow); American Association of Museums; Texas Academy of Science; Texas Institute of Letters; Texas Archeological Society. *Awards, honors:* Awards for *Indians of Texas*, Texas Institute of Letters, Dallas Public Library. *Interests:* American Indian ethnology, particularly Plains and Texas; culture change; primitive art; ethnographic field work with Delaware Indians; archaeological field work in Arkansas and Texas; rock art of the Texas Indians; ethnohistory of Wichita. *Published works: The Culture and Acculturation of the Delaware Indians* (University of Michigan Press, 1956); *The Indians of Texas* (University of Texas Press, 1961); *The Rock Art of Texas* (University of Texas Press -- in press).

NEWHALL, BEAUMONT 1908- (museum director, writer)

Born June 22, 1908, Lynn, Mass. *Education:* Harvard College, B.A., 1930; Harvard University, M.A., 1931. *Principal occupation:* Museum director, writer. *Home address:* 7 Rundel Park, Rochester, N.Y. 14607. *Affiliations:* Librarian and curator of photography, Museum of Modern Art, 1935-42, 1945-46; curator, George Eastman House, 1948-58; director, George Eastman House, 1958-. *Other professional posts:* Lecturer, Rochester Institute of Technology, 1956-; member, faculty, Salzburg Seminar in American Studies, Austria, 1958, 1959. *Military service:* U.S. Army Air Force, 1942-45. *Community activities:* Rochester Civic Music Association (director, 1964-). *Memberships:* Photographic Society of America; Royal Photographic Society; American Museum Association; College Art Association. *Awards, honors:* Guggenheim Fellowship, 1947; Progress Medal, Photographic Society of America, 1965; Bertram Cos lecturer, Royal Photographic Society; honorary member, Professional Photographers Association; Deutsche Photographische Gesellschaft. *Published works:* Co-author, *Masters of Photography* (Braziller, 1958); *The Daguerrotype in America* (Duell, Sloan and Pearce, 1961); *The History of Photography* (Museum of Modern Art, 1964).

NEWMAN, HARRISON 1912- (writer)

Born April 17, 1912, Newark, Ohio. *Education:* Centre College, B.A., 1933. *Principal occupation:* Writer. *Home address:* 296 Pine St., Lockport, N.Y. 14094. *Awards, honors:* Honorary adoption into Turtle Clan, Tonawanda Band of Seneca Indians, 1963. *Interests:* American Indians; archaeology. *Published works: Primitive Peoples of Western New York,* with Richard L. McCarthy (Buffalo and Erie County Historical Society); *The Iroquois,* with Richard L. McCarthy (Buffalo and Erie County Historical Society).

NICHOLSON, MARY EILEEN (Colville) 1924- (tribal officer)

Born March 1, 1924, Okanogan County, Wash. *Education:* St. Mary's Mission. *Principal occupation:* Farmer, tribal officer. *Home address:* Route 1, Box 90, Tonasket, Wash. 98855. *Affiliations:* Member, Colville Business (Tribal) Council. *Community activities:* Western Farmers Association; Agricultural Stabilization Conservation Service (committee member).

NICHOLSON, NARCISSE, Jr. (Colville) 1925- (tribal officer)

Born February 5, 1925, Tonasket, Wash. *Education:* High school. *Principal occupation:* Tribal officer. *Home address:* 618

S. Index, Omak, Wash. *Affiliations:* Chairman, Colville Business Council. *Other professional posts:* Recreation Development Committee, Grand Coulee and Coulee Dam Chambers of Commerce (executive committee). *Military service:* U.S. Army, 1943-46 (European-African-Middle Eastern Service Medal; American Theater Service Medal; Good Conduct Medal; Victory Medal).

NITZ, HENRY C.   1893-   (pastor)

Born January 29, 1893, Dallas, Wis. *Education:* Dr. Martin Luther College; Northwestern College, B.A., 1915; Evangelical Lutheran Seminary, 1919. *Principal occupation:* Pastor. *Home address:* General Delivery, Eitzen, Minn. *Affiliations:* Pastor and missionary, Apache Reservation, Ariz.; pastor, Rockford, Minn.; pastor, Waterloo, Wis.; district president, Seminary Board of Control; editorial writer. *Interests:* Languages, word origins; spent six weeks exploring Puerto Rico for World Missions of the Wisconsin Evangelical Lutheran Synod. *Published works:* Translator, *Jaalahn,* by Gustav Harders (1954); *Trophies of Grace* (Northwestern Publishing House, 1962).

NORBECK, EDWARD   1915-   (professor of anthropology)

Born March 18, 1915, Prince Albert, Sask., Can. *Education:* University of Michigan, B.A., 1948, M.A., 1949, Ph.D., 1952. *Principal occupation:* Professor of anthropology. *Home address:* 2420 Locke Lane, Houston, Texas. *Affiliations:* Associate professor of anthropology, Rice University, 1960-62; professor of anthropology, Rice University, 1962-. *Other professional posts:* Editor, *Rice University Studies,* 1962-; director, Symposium of Prehistoric Man in the New World, Rice University, 1962. *Military service:* Military Intelligence, U.S. Army, 1943-47. *Memberships:* American Anthropological Association; American Ethnological Society; Association for Asian Studies; Houston Archaeological Society; Japanese Society for Ethnology; Society for the Scientific Study of Religion. *Awards, honors:* Phi Beta Kappa, Phi Kappa Phi; Sigma Xi; various fellowships, including Senior Postdoctoral Fellowship, National Science Foundation. *Interests:* Ethnological theory; kinship and social structure;

cultural change and evolution; religion; anthropological study of culturally elaborate societies. *Field research:* Japan, 1964-65 -- research in Tokyo, and in rural northeastern Japan, on postwar economic and social changes; Hawaii, 1956 -- study of technological and social change in a pineapple plantation community; Japan, 1950-51 -- study of a fishing community, with special emphasis on the effects of Western culture upon distinctively Japanese ways of life, Ontario, Canada, summer, 1949 -- member of archaeological expedition on American Indian archaeology. *Published works: Takashima, a Japanese Fishing Community* (University of Utah Press, 1954); *Pineapple Town -- Hawaii* (University of California Press, 1959); *Religion in Primitive Society* (Harper, 1961); co-editor, *Prehistoric Man in the New World* (University of Chicago Press, 1964); *Changing Japan, Case Studies in Anthropology* (Holt, Rinehart & Winston, 1965).

NOYES, PHYLLIS   (Colville)   1947- (artist)

Born November 2, 1947, Inchelium, Wash. *Education:* Institute of American Indian Arts. *Principal occupation:* Artist. *Home address:* Route 1, Box 420, Sumner, Wash. *Awards, honors:* First Prize, Scottsdale Indian Exhibition, 1963.

NYE, WILBUR S.   1898-   (colonel, U.S. Army, retired)

Born October 12, 1898, Canton, Ohio. *Education:* U.S. Military Academy, West Point, B.S., 1920; University of Pennsylvania, M.S., 1931. *Principal occupation:* Colonel, U.S. Army, retired; writer, editor. *Home address:* Pennsboro Manor, Wormleysburg, Penna. *Affiliations:* Associate editor, Stackpole Co.; editor, *F.A. Journal,* 1939-42; chief historian, U.S. Army, Europe, 1950-54; editor, *Civil War Times Illustrated. Military service:* U.S. Army, 1917-54 (Legion of Merit, Bronze Star, Army Commendation Medal, Croix de Guerre with Palm; numerous campaign ribbons and stars). *Community activities:* West Shore School System, Cumberland County, Penna. (school director). *Memberships:* Harrisburg Civil War Round Table; Panhandle-Plains Historical Society; Cumberland County Historical Society; North Carolina Historical Society; Oklahoma Historical Society. *Interests:* History, travel. *Published works: Carbine and Lance* (University of Oklahoma Press, 1937); *Battle Gettysburg, a Guided Tour* (Stackpole, 1959); *I Fought with Geronimo* (Stackpole, 1960); *Bad Medicine and Good: Tales of the Kiowas* (University of Oklahoma Press, 1962); *Here Come the Rebels* (Louisiana State University Press, 1965); editor of over forty books published by The Stackpole Co.

O

OAKES, MAUD (writer, anthropologist, artist)

Principal occupation: Artist, writer, anthropologist. *Home address:* Partington Ridge, Big Sur, Calif. 93920. *Interests:* North American Indians; Central American Indians; comparative religion; symbolism. *Published works: Where the Two Came to Their Father* (1943); *The Two Crosses of Todos Santos* (Pantheon, 1951); *Beyond the Windy Place* (Farrar, Straus & Young, 1951); *Beautyway: A Navajo Ceremonial* (Bollingen Series, 1957); *The Wisdom of the Serpent* (Braziller, 1963).

OFFICER, JAMES E. 1924- (associate commissioner, Bureau of Indian Affairs)

Born July 28, 1924, Boulder, Colo. *Education:* University of Kansas, B.A., 1950; University of Arizona, Ph.D., 1964. *Principal occupation:* Associate commissioner, Bureau of Indian Affairs. *Home address:* 320 N St., S.W., Washington, D.C. 20024. *Affiliations:* Information officer, Department of State, 1950-53; instructor, University of Arizona, 1957-60; associate commissioner, Bureau of Indian Affairs, Department of the Interior. *Other occupations:* Radio announcer, writer, program director, various stations in Kansas and Arizona, 1942-44, 1946-50, 1953-56. *Military service:* U.S. Army, 1945-46. *Community activities:* Democratic Party (precinct commissioner). *Memberships:* American Anthropological Association (Fellow, 1953-); American Sociological Society 1958-; Society for Applied Anthropology (Fellow, 1962-); Phi Beta Kappa; Phi Kappa Phi; Sigma Xi; Alpha Delta Kappa. *Awards, honors:* Quill and Scroll National Journalism

Scholarship, 1942. *Interests:* Indian affairs; photography; writing; travel. *Published works: Indians in School* (University of Arizona Press, 1956).

O'KANE, WALTER COLLINS 1877- (writer)

Born November 10, 1877, Columbus, Ohio. *Education:* Ohio State University, B.A., 1897, M.A., 1909. *Principal occupation:* Writer. *Home address:* P.O. Box 25, Wonalancet, N.H. 03897. *Affiliations:* Professor, University of New Hampshire, 1909-50. *Other professional posts:* Entomologist, State of New Hampshire. *Military service:* Tenth O.V.I., Spanish-American War. *Memberships:* American Association for the Advancement of Science (Hon. Fellow); American Association of Economic Entomologists (president); Entomological Society of America (honorary member). *Awards, honors:* Sc.D. (Hon.), Ohio State University, 1932. *Interests:* Travels in the Hopi Reservation at various times over a twenty-five-year period. *Published works: Jim and Peggy at Meadowbrook Farm* (Macmillan); *Jim and Peggy at Appletop Farm* (Macmillan); *Trails and Summits of the White Mountains* (Houghton Mifflin); *Trails and Summits of the Green Mountains* (Houghton Mifflin); *Trails and Summits of the Adirondacks* (Houghton Mifflin); *Injurious Insects* (Macmillan); *Sun in the Sky* (University of Oklahoma Press); *The Hopis: Portrait of a Desert People* (University of Oklahoma Press).

OLD COYOTE, BARNEY (Crow) 1923- (government official)

Born April 10, 1923, St. Xavier, Mont. *Education:* Morningside College, 1945-47. *Principal occupation:* Government official. *Home address:* 12409 Stirrup Lane, Bowie, Md. 20715. *Affiliations:* National Park Service, Crow Agency, Mont.; Bureau of Indian Affairs, Fort Yates, N.D.; Bureau of Indian Affairs, Crow Agency, Mont.; Bureau of Indian Affairs, Aberdeen, S.D.; Bureau of Indian Affairs, Rocky Boys, Mont. Bureau of Indian Affairs, Rosebud, S.D.; special assistant to secretary, U.S. Department of the Interior, 1964-. *Military service:* U.S. Army Air Corps, 1941-45. *Community activities:* American Legion (post commander); Knights of Columbus (grand knight); Parent-Teachers' Association (president); National Federation of Federal Employees (president, credit union; chairman, board of directors). *Awards, honors:* Special Achievement Award and Management Training Intern, Bureau of Indian Affairs. *Interests:* Mr. Old Coyote writes, "General interest is in the welfare of Indians and youth of all races, particularly in the education and general participation in the American way of life of all citizens during formative years; conservation of natural and human resources and the genuine appreciation of the esthetic values of the American way of life."

OLDS, FOREST D. (Miami Tribe of Oklahoma) 1911- (farmer, stockman)

Born March 5, 1911, Miami, Okla. *Education:* Elementary school. *Principal occupation:* Farmer, stockman. *Home address:* Route 2, Miami, Okla. *Affiliations:* Chief, Miami Tribe of Oklahoma; clerk, North Fairview School Board. *Community activities:* Ottawa County Farm Bureau (director); Ottawa County Soil and Water Conservation District (director). *Memberships:* Oklahomans for Indian Opportunity (board of directors); Miami Co-op Association, Inc. (vice president); Metropolitan Area Planning Commission at Miami. *Awards, honors:* Goodyear Tire and Rubber Co. Award for outstanding accomplishment in soil conservation, 1964. *Interests:* Conservation; research into history of Miami Tribe; travel to former homesites of the Miami Tribe in Indiana, Kansas, and Ohio; trip to Washington, D.C., to testify before Congressional committees as a representative of the Miami Tribe; serves as a resource contact for Dr. Bert Anson, Ball State University, in compiling a history of the Miami Tribe.

O'LEARY, THOMAS V. 1910- (industrial executive)

Born March 24, 1910, Elmira, N.Y. *Education:* Canisius College, B.A.; University of Scranton, B.A. *Principal occupation:* Industrial executive. *Home address:* 1722 Martins Lane, Gladwyne, Penna. 19035. *Affiliations:* Lecturer in journalism, University of Scranton, Marywood College, Scranton, Penna., 1946-53; news editor, Scranton *Times,* 1940-53; managing editor,

Main Line Times, 1953-59; lecturer, St. Joseph's College, 1956-; vice president, Philadelphia Suburban Water Co. *Community activities:* Easter Seal Society of Southeast Pennsylvania (vice president, director); Keystone-AAA Club (director); Penjerdel (director). *Memberships:* Public Relations Society of America; Poor Richard Club; Pen and Pencil Club. *Awards, honors:* George Washington Medal, Freedoms Foundation. *Interests:* Historical research, particularly of the Colonial period. *Published works: Mark of the Turtle* (Chilton Books, 1962).

OLSON, CLYDE B., Sr. 1912- (archaeologist, museum director)

Born February 15, 1912, Cooperstown, N.Y. *Education:* High school. *Principal occupation:* Archaeologist, museum director. *Home address:* R.D. 2, Cooperstown, N.Y. 13326. *Affiliations:* Archaeologist and director, Cooperstown Indian Museum, Cooperstown, N.Y. *Memberships:* New York State Archaeological Association; Eastern States Federation; North East Museums Association; Pennsylvania Archaeological Association; New Jersey Society for Archaeology; Missouri Archaeological Society. *Interests:* Archaeology -- expeditions in and near New York State.

OLSON, JAMES C. 1917- (historian, administrator)

Born January 23, 1917, Bradgate, Ohio. *Education:* Morningside College, B.A., 1938; University of Nebraska, M.A., 1939, Ph.D., 1942. *Principal occupation:* Historian and administrator. *Home address:* 3415 S. 37th St., Lincoln, Neb. *Affiliations:* Director, Nebraska State Historical Society, 1946-56; professor of history and chairman, Department of History, University of Nebraska, 1956-. *Military service:* U.S. Army Air Force, 1942-46. *Memberships:* American Historical Association; American Association for State and Local History (president, 1962-64; executive board). *Published works: J. Sterling Morton* (University of Nebraska Press, 1942); *History of Nebraska* (University of Nebraska Press, 1955); *Red Cloud and the Sioux Problem* (University of Nebraska Press, 1965).

OPLER, MORRIS EDWARD   1907-
(professor of anthropology)

Born May 16, 1907, Buffalo, N. Y. *Education:* University of Buffalo, B. A. (Sociology), 1929, M. A. (Anthropology), 1930; University of Chicago, Ph. D. (Anthropology), 1933. *Principal occupation:* Professor of anthropology. *Affiliations:* Fellow, Laboratory of Anthropology, Santa Fe, N. M., 1931; Fellow, Social Science Research Council, 1932-33; research assistant and associate, Department of Anthropology, University of Chicago, 1933-35; Fellow, General Education Board, 1935-36; assistant anthropologist, Bureau of Indian Affairs, 1936-37; visiting lecturer, Department of Sociology, Reed College, 1937-38; assistant professor of anthropology, Claremont College, 1938-42; lecturer, Department of Sociology and Anthropology, University of Wisconsin, 1941; social science analyst, War Relocation Authority, 1943-44; social science analyst, Office of War Information, 1944-45; deputy chief and chief, Foreign Morale Analysis Division, Office of War Information, 1945; visiting and assistant professor, Howard University, 1945-48; professor of anthropology and Asian studies, Cornell University, 1948-; director, Cornell University Indian Program, 1948-; visiting professor, Lucknow University, India, 1949-50; Fellow, Center for Advanced Study in the Behavioral Sciences, 1956-57. *Other professional posts:* Advisory board, *Journal of Asian Studies*, 1955-58; associate editor, *Journal of American Folklore*, 1959-. *Memberships:* Sigma Xi; Phi Beta Kappa; Alpha Kappa Delta; Phi Delta Kappa; Research Club, Cornell University; American Association of University Professors; American Sociological Society; American Anthropological Association (Fellow; executive board, 1949-52; president-elect, 1961-62; president, 1962-63); Society for Applied Anthropology; Association for Asian Studies; American Ethnological Society; American Folklore Society (Fellow; first vice president, 1946-47; executive committee, 1950; council member, 1957-60). *Published works: The Ethnobiology of the Chiricahua and Mescalero Apache*, with Edward F. Castetter (University of New Mexico Bulletin, Ethnobiological Studies in the American Southwest, No. III, University of New Mexico Press, 1936); *Dirty Boy: A Jicarilla Tale of Raid and War* (American Anthropological Association, Memoirs, No. 52, 1938); *Myths and Tales of the Jacarilla*

Apache Indians (Stechert, 1938); *Myths and Legends of the Lipan Apache Indians* (J. J. Augustin, 1940); *An Apache Life-Way: The Economic, Social, and Religious Institutions of the Chiricahua Indians* (University of Chicago Press, 1941; University Microfilms, Inc.; Cooper Square Publishers, 1966); *Myths and Tales of the Chiricahua Apache Indians* (Banta Publishing Co., 1942); *The Character and Derivation of the Jicarilla Holiness Rite* (University of New Mexico, 1943); *Childhood and Youth in Jicarilla Apache Society* (The Southwest Museum, 1946).

ORR, CAROL   (Mrs. J. A. Maas)
(Colville)   1943-   (artist)

Born August 21, 1943, Republic, Wash. *Education:* University of Washington, B. A., 1965. *Principal occupation:* Free lance artist (portraits, murals, Indian theme paintings). *Home address:* 1304 N. E. 42, Seattle, Wash. *Community activities:* Participant in Seattle Indian Days celebration -- exhibit of works, 1966. *Memberships:* University of Washington Alumni Association; Lambda Rho Art Honorary, University of Washington, 1964-; University of Washington Honors Program. *Awards:* Four-year scholarship, Colville Tribe; University of Washington Tuition Scholarship; Federal Scholarship for four years (art studies, University of Washington); Award, Philbrook Art Exhibit; Second Prize, Indian Show, La Grande, Ore., 1965. *Interests:* Miss Orr plans to continue her studies and her art -- portraits on commission, book jackets and illustrations, feature illustrations, mural commissions on any theme, etc. Miss Orr's works appear in the following museums and collections: U. S. Department of the Interior, Portland, Ore., and Coulee Dam, Wash.; Mrs. Jesse Casey, Spokane, Wash.; permanent collection, Fort Okanogan Museum; Willis Carey Museum; Peltier Gallery, Spokane, Wash.; School of Art, University of Washington; Philleo Nash, Washington, D. C.; Dr. Charles Benson, Omak, Wash.; Mr. and Mrs. Harold Maas, Wenatchee, Wash. *Mural commissions:* U. W. Balmer Hall (business mosaic), Seattle, Wash.

ORR, HOWELL M.   (Chickasaw)
(artist, teacher)

Born Washington, Okla. *Education:* Bacone College; North Eastern State, B. F. A.; University of Tulsa; University of Gto San Miguel, M. F. A.; University of the Americas; University of Nevada. *Principal occupation:* Art teacher, Valley High School, Las Vegas, Nev. *Military service:* U.S. Army, 1952-54. *Community activities:* Democratic Central Committee (trustee); League of Young Democrats; National Guard; Central Labor Council, A. F. L. -C. I. O. (trustee). *Memberships:* American Federation of Teachers (treasurer); Committee on Political Education; Great Book Club. Awards, honors: First Place, Contemporary Indian Art, Santa Fe, N. M. *Interests:* American Indian history and lore; Mexican culture and history; Mexican mural painting. *Exhibits:* El Instituto Mexican Norteamericano; San Miguel National Show; National Mexican Show; National Indian Show; American Mexican Culture Center; Bassarted National, Mexico; Oklahoma State Show; Oklahoma Indian Show; Arts and Crafts Board, U.S. Department of the Interior; Department of State Traveling Show; Department of the Interior European Traveling Show; Contemporary Indian Art, Santa Fe, N. M.; Inter-Tribal Indian Ceremonials, Gallup, N. M.; National Art Roundup. Las Vegas, Nev.; American Indian Show, Anadarko, Okla.; Scottsdale (Ariz.) Contemporary Show; Las Vegas Art League; Heard Museum of Anthropology and Primitive Art, Phoenix, Ariz.

OSBORN, GEORGE COLEMAN 1904-
(professor of history and social sciences)

Born May 15, 1904, Learned, Miss. *Education:* Mississippi College, B.A., 1927; Indiana University, M.A., 1932, Ph.D., 1938. *Principal occupation:* Professor of history and social sciences. *Home address:* 1714 N.W. 7th Ave., Gainesville, Fla. 32601. *Affiliations:* Chairman, Division of Social Sciences, Berry College, 1935-46; associate professor of history and co-director, U.S. Army A.S.T.P. program, University of Mississippi, 1942-44; chairman, Division of Social Sciences, Memphis State University, 1944-47; associate professor of history and social sciences, University of Florida, 1947-55; professor of history and social sciences, University of Florida, 1955-. *Community activities:* Masonic Order; Kiwanis Club; Sigma Pi; Alpha Phi Omega; Phi Alpha Theta. *Memberships:* American Historical Society, 1935-; American Academy of Social and Political Sci-

ence, 1935-; Southern Historical Association, 1935-; Mississippi Valley Historical Society, 1935-; American Association of University Professors. *Awards, honors:* Grants bestowed by the American Philosophical Society, the Woodrow Wilson Foundation, and the University of Florida. *Interests:* Recent United States history; social science; travel to Europe, Canada, United States. *Published works: John Sharp Williams: Planter-Statesman of the Deep South* (Louisiana State University Press, 1963); contributor to *Encyclopaedia Britannica* and various journals.

OSBORN, RACHEL A. 1909- (minister)

Born April 8, 1909, Muncie, Ind. *Education:* Friends University, B.A., 1939; Hartford Theological Seminary, 1946-47; Woodbrooke Friends School, England, 1958. *Principal occupation:* Minister. *Home address:* Kickapoo Friends Center, R.R. 2, McLoud, Okla. 74851. *Affiliations:* Minister and pastor, Kickapoo Friends Center, Indian mission. *Other professional posts:* Representative, Friends World Committee; minister in Detroit, Mich., Denver, Colo., Gonie, N.H., and South Glens Falls, N.Y. *Memberships:* Friends World Committee. *Awards, honors:* Quaker Leadership Grant, 1958. *Interests:* Social and economic conditions of underprivileged and minority groups; delinquency and crime.

OSBORNE, CHESTER G. 1915-
(teacher, writer)

Born September 18, 1915, Portsmouth, N.H. *Education:* New England Conservatory, Diploma and Mus.B., 1937; Northwestern University, Mus.M. *Principal occupation:* Music teacher. *Home address:* Box 517, Center Moriches, L.I., N.Y. 11934. *Affiliations:* Music teacher, Center Moriches public schools. *Other professional posts:* Curator of manuscripts, Museum, Manor of St. George. *Military service:* U.S. Army, 1942-46 (Meritorious Service Award). *Community activities:* Center Moriches Music Award Committee; New York State School Music Association (adjudicator). *Memberships:* Music Educators National Conference (life member); New York State Teachers Association. *Awards, honors:* Junior Book Award, Boys' Clubs of America, for *The First Lake Dwel-*

lers, 1957. *Interests:* Children's literature; regional history (contributing editor, *Long Island Forum*); archaeology. *Published works: The First Bow and Arrow* (Follett, 1951); *The First Puppy* (Follett, 1953); *The First Lake Dwellers* (Follett, 1956); *The First Wheel* (Follett, 1959); *The Wind and the Fire* (Prentice-Hall, 1959).

OSGOOD, ERNEST STAPLES   1888-
(professor)

Born October 29, 1888, Lynn, Mass. *Education:* Dartmouth College, B.A., 1912; University of Wisconsin, Ph.D., 1927. *Principal occupation:* Professor. *Home address:* 360 1/2 E. Bowman St., Wooster, Ohio 44691. *Affiliations:* Instructor, Helena High School, 1914-24; teaching assistant, University of Wisconsin, 1924-27; professor, University of Minnesota, 1927-57; professor, College of Wooster, 1958-. *Memberships:* American Historical Association; Mississippi Valley Historical Association; 1927-. *Awards, honors:* Pickering Prize in history, Dartmouth College, 1911; Herbert Baxter Adams Fellowship, University of Wisconsin; Guggenheim Fellowship. *Interests:* American history; history of the frontier. *Published works: Day of the Cattleman* (University of Minnesota Press, 1929; University of Chicago Press, 1956); editor, *Field Notes of William Clark* (Yale University Press, 1964).

OWENS, M. LILLIANA   1898-   (writer, teacher)

Born May 13, 1898, St. Louis, Mo. *Education:* Loretto Heights College, B.A., 1924; St. Louis University, M.A., 1928, Ph.D., 1935. *Principal occupation:* Writer, teacher. *Home address:* 3407 Lafayette Ave., St. Louis, Mo. 63104. *Community activities:* Committee on Social Studies, Archdiocese of Denver, Colo. (chairman and president, 1942-43); Sandoval County Teachers Association, State of New Mexico (president, 1944-45); 37th Annual Conference, Catholic Library Association (chairman, 1961). *Memberships:* Gallery of Living Catholic Authors, Inc.; American Catholic Historical Society; Catholic Library Association. *Awards, honors:* Colorado Press Women Award, 1949; Library Certificates of Approval, State of Texas, 1955. *Interests:* American and Western

history; travel throughout the United States. *Published works: Women Tell the Story of the Southwest* (Naylor, 1939); *History of St. Patrick Parish* (Acme Publishing Co., 1943); *Jesuit Beginnings in New Mexico, 1867-1882* (Revista Catolica Press, 1950); *Carlos M. Pinto, S.J.* (Revista Catolica Press, 1951); *Most Reverend Anthony J. Schuler, J.J., D.D.* (Revista Catolica Press, 1958); *Loretto in Missouri* (B. Herder Book Co., 1964); *Loretto on the Old Frontier* (Khoury Bros., Inc., 1965); historical comic strips; monographs; newspaper and magazine articles.

OWHI, HARRY   (Colville)   1928-
(tribal officer)

Born November 14, 1928, Nespelem, Wash. *Education:* North Idaho College of Education; Kinman Business University; University of New Mexico. *Principal occupation:* Tribal officer. *Home address:* P.O. Box 324, Nespelem, Wash. *Affiliations:* Executive secretary, Colville Business (Tribal) Council. *Military service:* U.S. Army, 1946-47.

P

PAGEL, JOSEPH T.   1916-
(museum curator)

Born January 17, 1916, Holton, Kan. *Education:* Washburn University; Clark College. *Principal occupation:* Museum curator. *Home address:* 17707 N.W. 50th Ave., Vancouver, Wash. *Affiliations:* Curator, Clark County Historical Museum, Vancouver, Wash. *Military service:* U.S. Army, 1943-45. *Memberships:* Fort Vancouver Historical Society; Oregon Archaeological Society.

PAHSETOPAH, PAUL   (Osage-Cherokee)
1932-   (artist)

Born September 10, 1932, Pawhuska, Okla. *Education:* High school. *Principal occupation:* Artist (Indian art -- paintings and crafts). *Home address:* 1400 E. 34th, Tulsa, Okla. *Affiliations:* Electrician, Burtek Inc. *Military service:* U.S. Army, 1952-54 (Korean Service Medal, Bronze Star, United Nations Medal, National Defense Medal, R.O.K. Unit Citation, Good Conduct Medal).

Memberships: Osage Nation Organization (councilman). *Awards, honors:* Indian Art (painting) Awards, Philbrook Art Center, Tulsa, Okla., 1963, 1965. *Interests:* Traveled mainly in Oklahoma and the Southwest; sings for an all-Indian dance troupe.

PAINTER, LEVINUS KING 1889-
(minister)

Born July 12, 1889, Spiceland, Ind. *Education:* Earlham College, B.A., 1913; Hartford Theological Seminary, B.D., 1916. *Principal occupation:* Minister. *Home address:* Bagdad Rd., Collins, N.Y. 14034. *Affiliations:* "Religious work," Thomas Indian School, Iroquois, N.Y., twelve years; chaplain, Gowanda State Mental Hospital, Helmuth, N.Y., three years; field staff, American Friends Service Committee, western Penna., 1936-39; Federal relief program, Penna., 1939-41 (state field supervisor, National Youth Administration); United National Relief for Palestine Refugees, 1949; delegate, Friends World Conference, England, 1952. *Community activities:* School board, Collins, N.Y.; Town of Collins (historian). *Memberships:* Friends Associated Executive Committee on Indian Affairs (chairman); Indian Committee, National Council of Churches; American Friends Board of Missions; American Academy of Political and Social Science; Parent-Teachers' Association (honorary life member). *Awards, honors:* Silver Beaver Award, Boy Scouts of America. *Interests:* Travel to East Africa, Middle East, Central Africa, Madagascar, Greece, Austria, Switzerland, England, Japan, Taiwan, Thailand, India, Belgian Congo. *Published works:* The Collins Story (Niagara Frontier Press, 1962); The Hill of Vision (Nairobi, Kenya, 1966); magazine articles.

PAPPAN, JOHN L. 1927- (B.I.A.
agency superintendent)

Born March 8, 1927, Newkirk, Okla. *Education:* Oklahoma State University, B.S., 1950. *Principal occupation:* B.I.A. agency superintendent. *Home address:* P.O. Box 1, Fort Hall, Idaho. *Affiliations:* Superintendent, Fort Hall Agency, Bureau of Indian Affairs; soil conservationist, loan examiner, program officer, tribal operations officer for various Bureau of Indian Affairs agencies. *Military service:* U.S. Navy,

1945-46. *Community activities:* Lions Club (secretary, 1955). *Memberships:* Masonic Order, 1954. *Awards, honors:* Superior Performance Award, Bureau of Indian Affairs.

PARISH, PEGGY 1927- (writer, teacher)

Born July 14, 1927, Manning, S.C. *Education:* University of South Carolina, B.A., 1948. *Principal occupation:* Teacher, writer. *Home address:* 160 E. 89th St., New York, N.Y. 10028. *Affiliations:* Texhoma Schools, Okla.; Dalton Schools, Inc., New York, N.Y. *Memberships:* Authors' Guild. *Interests:* Creative and educational materials for children. *Published works: Littlest Raccoon* (Golden, 1961); *Manners* (Golden, 1962); *Let's Be Indians* (Harper, 1962); *Good Hunting, Little Indian* (Wm. R. Scott, 1962); *Willy Is My Brother* (Wm. R. Scott, 1963); *Amelia Bedelia* (Harper & Row, 1963); *Thank You, Amelia Bedelia* (Harper & Row, 1964); *The Story of Grains* (Grosset & Dunlap, 1965).

PARKER, DONALD DEAN 1899-
(professor)

Born October 3, 1899, Street, Harfort County, Md. *Education:* Park College, B.A., 1922; University of Washington, M.A., 1932; University of Chicago, B.D., 1936, Ph.D., 1936. *Principal occupation:* Professor of history (retired). *Home address:* Plaza del Monte, Box 1888, Santa Fe, N.M. 87501. *Affiliations:* Director of library and instructor of English, Shantung Christian University, Tsinanfu, China, 1922-24; instructor, Y.M.C.A. School, north China, 1924, 1925; library staff, University of Chicago, 1926-27; library staff, Seattle Public Library, 1927-28; teacher, Camarines Sur High School, Philippines, 1929-30; manager, College Men's Dormitory, Manila, Philippines; librarian, Union Theological Seminary, Manila, Philippines, 1930-31; principal, teacher, Union High School of Manila, 1930-35; instructor in English, Silliman University, Philippines, summers, 1933-34; librarian, Lake Forest College, 1936-37; professor of history, Park College, 1937-40; assistant state supervisor, State of Missouri, Historical Records Survey, 1940-42; professor of history and head, Department of History and Political Science, South Dakota State University, 1943-65. *Other professional posts:* Editor, *Union Voice and Union Echo* (Manila, Philippines), 1931-35; president, South Dakota Heritages, Inc., 1955-. *Memberships:* South Dakota Historical Society. *Interests:* Local and regional history writing. *Travels:* Europe, 1925-26, summers, 1960, 1963. Lived in China (1922-25), the Philippines (1929-35), and Europe (1925-26). *Published works: Local History, How to Gather It, Write It, and Publish It* (Social Science Research Council, 1944); *Early Explorations and Fur Trading in South Dakota* (South Dakota Historical Society, 1950); *Recollections of Philander Prescott: Frontiersman of the Old Northwest, 1819-1862* (University of Nebraska Press, 1966); several other local, regional and family histories, privately printed.

PARKER, E.M. 1902- (museum curator)

Born April 19, 1902, Hopkins, Penna. *Principal occupation:* Museum curator. *Home address:* R.D. 1, Brookville, Penna. 15825. *Affiliations:* Sign writer, 1924-; curator, E.M. Parker Museum. *Community activities:* School director; Brookville and Franklin chambers of commerce. *Memberships:* International Sign Association; Pennsylvania Archaeological Society; Ohio Archaeological Society; gun collecting societies. *Interests:* Signs of all types; history of the American Indian, particularly the Iroquois; early American furniture; American arms. *Published works:* Articles in local newspapers.

PARKER, MACK 1896- (writer, farmer)

Born November 7, 1896, near Ogeeche, Okla. *Education:* Privately educated (Teachers Certificate, 1916). *Principal occupation:* Writer, farmer. *Home address:* R.R. 4, Box 194, Joplin, Mo. 64803. *Other professional posts:* Teacher, salesman. *Military service:* U.S. Army, 1918-19; Marine Corps, 1942 (Good Conduct Medal). *Community activities:* Speakers Bureau, Department of Americanism, Veterans of Foreign Wars (past commander). *Memberships:* Missouri Writers Guild; Masonic Lodge; Nevada Masonic Order (past master); Letter Carriers Association, 1925-45. *Awards, honors:* Award, Veterans of Foreign Wars, for patriotic program and lectures on Americanism. *Interests:* American way of life; youth programs; Indian welfare; travel throughout the United States. *Published works: The Amazing Red Man* (Naylor, 1960).

PARKHILL, FORBES 1892- (writer)

Born December 31, 1892, Denver, Colo. *Education:* University of Colorado, 1910-11. *Principal occupation:* Writer. *Home address:* 1510 E. 9th Ave., Apt. 203, Denver, Colo. 80218. *Memberships:* Western Writers of America; Colorado Authors League; Denver Press Club; The Westerners; Western History Association. *Published works: Troopers West* (Farrar & Rinehart, 1945); *Last of the Indian Wars* (Crowell, Collier, 1962).

PARSONS, NEIL (Blackfoot) 1938- (art instructor)

Born March 2, 1938, Browning, Mont. *Education:* Montana State University, B.S. (Art), 1961, M.S. (Applied Art), 1964. *Principal occupation:* Art instructor. *Home address:* 513 Salazar, Santa Fe, N.M. 87502. *Affiliations:* Graphic illustrator, Boeing Aircraft Co.; art instructor, Institute of American Indian Arts. *Military service:* U.S. Air Force Reserve, 1961-64. *Memberships:* Pi Kappa Alpha; Delta Phi Delta; Montana Institute of Arts. *Awards:* Joseph Kinsey Howard Memorial Fellowship, 1963. *Exhibitions:* Contemporary American Indian Artists, Museum of New Mexico; New Mexico Biannual, Museum of New Mexico; Bureau of Indian Affairs Indian Invitational, Department of the Interior, Washington, D.C.; Southwest Print and Drawing, Dallas Museum; Own Your Own Invitational, Denver Museum; Intermountain Painting and Sculpture, Salt Lake City Art Center; Intermountain Printmakers, Salt Lake City Art Center; Northwest Annual Painting, Seattle Art Museum; Northwest Printmakers, Henry Gallery, University of Washington; Montana Institute of Arts State Festival; Sixteenth Mid-America Annual Exhibition, Atkins Museum, Kansas City, Mo., 1966; and others. Work featured in collections of Dr. Verne Dusenberry, Lloyd Kiva New, Museum of the Plains Indian.

PATTERSON, PATRICK *(Kemoha)* (Apache-Seneca) 1914- (museum director, artist)

Born December 29, 1914, Centralia, Ill. *Education:* University of Oklahoma, B.F.A. *Principal occupation:* Museum director, artist. *Home address:* 912 Osage, Bartlesville, Okla. 74003. *Affiliation:* Director, Woolaroc Museum, Bartlesville, Okla. *Other occupation:* Artist. *Memberships:* Sequoyah Club; Boy Scouts of America; Girl Scouts. *Interests:* Anthropology and ethnology of the American Indian. *Published works: Woolaroc Museum* (Frank Phillips Foundation, Inc.).

PAUAHTY, LINN D. *(How-Aun-T ahgyah)* (Kiowa) 1905- (minister)

Born July 14, 1905, Carnegie, Okla. *Education:* Cameron Agricultural and Mechanical College, B.S., 1936; Oklahoma A. & M., B.S., 1939; Southern Methodist University, B.D., 1943. *Principal occupation:* Minister. *Home address:* 1415 Carlson Drive, Klamath Falls, Ore. 97601. *Affiliations:* Minister, National Board of Missions of the Methodist Church. *Other professional posts:* Oregon Annual Conference on Indian Mission Work (Paiute and Modoc tribes); member, board of directors, Indian Festival of Arts, LaGrande, Ore. *Community activities:* Indian Council Fire. *Memberships:* Governor's Commission on Human Rights, 1958-61; Indian Festival of Arts (board of directors); National Congress of American Indians; Society for Ethnomusicology. *Awards, honors:* Leadership Achievement, Methodist Historical Society; Who's Who in Methodism; Outstanding Indian Leadership of Today, Indian Council Fire, 1960. *Interests:* Anthropology; native religions and ceremonies of the southern and Plains tribes; medicine man's cult and practices; Kiowa history; research and study of the songs and music of the southern and northern Plains tribes.

PAYNE, DORIS A. 1906- (chaplain's assistant, writer)

Born August 17, 1906, Santa Monica, Calif. *Education:* University of California, B.A., 1931. *Principal occupation:* Chaplain's assistant, writer. *Home address:* Route 2, Box 918, Sonora, Calif. 95370. *Affiliations:* Assistant to chaplain, Sonora Community Hospital, 1963-. *Military service:* W.A.C., 1944-45. *Interests:* Collection of Indian artifacts, chiefly Klamath and Modoc,

now housed in the Wi-ne-ma Hotel, Klamath Falls, Ore. *Published works: Captain Jack, Modoc Renegade* (Binfords and Mort, 1938).

PAYNE, MARVIN LEWIS (Cherokee) 1927- (animal inspector)

Born April 7, 1927, Pittsburgh, Penna. *Principal occupation:* Animal inspector. *Home address:* Four Winds Farm, R.D. 3, Coraopolis, Penna. 15108. *Affiliations:* Animal inspector, West Pennsylvania Humane Society; breeder and trainer of Appaloosa horses. *Military service:* U.S. Navy. *Community activities:* Greater Pittsburgh Horse Shows Association (president); Pennsylvania Appaloosa Association (president). *Memberships:* Masonic Order; American Horse Shows Association. *Awards, honors:* Champion, Indian Costume Division, Horse Shows Association, three consecutive years. *Interests:* Television and rodeo appearances; 4-H Club lecturer.

PAYTON, KENNETH L. (Cherokee) 1926- (B.I.A. agency superintendent)

Born August 3, 1926, Picher, Okla. *Education:* Oklahoma State University, B.S., 1949. *Principal occupation:* B.I.A. agency superintendent. *Home address:* 3508 Alaska Pl., N.E., Albuquerque, N.M. 87111. *Affiliations:* Superintendent, Mescalero Agency, Bureau of Indian Affairs, Mescalero, N.M. *Military service:* U.S. Navy, 1944-46. *Community activities:* Lions International; Benevolent and Protective Order of Elks. *Memberships:* Soil Conservation Society of America.

PEACOCK, KENNETH 1922- (musicologist)

Born April 7, 1922, Toronto, Can. *Education:* Royal Conservatory of Music, A.R.C.T., 1938; University of Toronto, Mus.B., 1943. *Principal occupation:* Musicologist. *Home address:* 540 Brierwood Ave., Ottawa, Can. *Affiliations:* Musicologist, National Museum of Canada. *Memberships:* Canadian Folk Music Society (vice president); Canadian Authors Association. *Awards, honors:* McGill Chamber Music Award for String Quartet. *Interests:* Musicological research among Indian tribes of Ontario, Manitoba, Saskatchewan, Alberta, and British Columbia; research in New-foundland and Cape Breton among English, French and Gaelic groups; research among Canada's smaller ethnic minorities; collection of musical artifacts and instruments; musical composition; photography. *Published works: Favorite Songs of Newfoundland,* with Alan Mills (B.M.I. Canada, Ltd., 1958); *The Native Songs of Newfoundland* (Queen's Printer, 1960); *Survey of Ethnic Folkmusic Across Western Canada* (Queen's Printer, 1963); *Songs of the Newfoundland Outports,* three vols. (Queen's Printer, 1965); *Twenty Ethnic Songs from Western Canada* (Queen's Printer, 1965); *Bridal Suite,* piano solo (B.M.I. Canada, Ltd., 1948); *Music of the Doukhobors* (Queen's Printer, 1966).

PECKHAM, HOWARD HENRY   1910-
(library director)

Born July 13, 1910, Ann Arbor, Mich. *Education:* Olivet College, 1927-29; University of Michigan, B.A., 1931, M.A., 1933. *Principal occupation:* Library director. *Affiliations:* Director, William L. Clements Library, South University St., Ann Arbor, Mich. *Community activities:* Rotary Club. *Memberships:* American Association for State and Local History (president, 1954-56); American Historical Association; Society of American Archivists; Organization of American Historians; American Antiquarian Society; Bibliographical Society of America. *Published works: Captured by Indians* (Rutgers University Press, 1954); *Pontiac and the Indian Uprising* (University of Chicago Press, 1961).

PECKHAM, STEWART L.   1927-
(archaeologist)

Born March 3, 1927, Albany, N.Y. *Education:* Syracuse University, 1947-49; University of New Mexico, B.A., 1952. *Principal occupation:* Archaeologist. *Home address:* Tano Rd., Santa Fe, N.M. *Affiliations:* Associate curator, Museum of New Mexico. *Military service:* U.S. Army, 1945-47. *Memberships:* Society for American Archaeology. *Published works:* Editor, *Highway Salvage Archaeology,* Vols. 3 and 4 (Museum of New Mexico, 1957, 1963); *An Archaeological Survey of the Chuska Valley and the Chaco Plateau,* with John P. Wilson (Museum of New Mexico, 1966).

PEGUES, CLARENCE EUGENE   1932-
(teacher)

Born February 13, 1932, Texarkana, Texas. *Education:* Huston-Tillotson College, B.S., 1953; Prairie View A. & M., M.Ed., 1961. *Principal occupation:* Teacher. *Home address:* Nenahnezad Boarding School, Fruitland, N.M. 87416. *Affiliations:* Teacher, Nenahnezad Boarding School, 1955-. *Military service:* A.M.E.D.S., 1953-55 (Good Conduct Medal, European Campaign Medal). *Community activities:* Veterans of Foreign Wars (former quartermaster).

PEITHMANN, IRVIN M.   1904-
(researcher, writer)

Born October 11, 1904. *Principal occupation:* Researcher, writer. *Home address:* 201 S. Dixon, Carbondale, Ill. 62901. *Affiliations:* Research assistant (American Indian), Southern Illinois University. *Memberships:* Oklahoma Historical Society; Indian Hall of Fame (charter member). *Awards, honors:* Gold Award, Illinois State Archaeological Society, 1940; Distinguished Service Award, Navy Club of U.S., 1958. *Interests:* Florida Seminoles; travel to Canada, Alaska, southeast U.S., Cuba. *Published works: Echoes of the Red Man* (Exposition Press, 1954); *Unconquered Seminole Indians* (Great Outdoors Publishing Co., 1957); *The Choctaw Indians of Mississippi* (Southern Illinois University Press, 1961); *Red Men of Fire* (Charles C. Thomas, 1964); *Indians of Southern Illinois* (Charles C. Thomas, 1964); *Broken Peace Pipes* (Charles C. Thomas, 1964).

PENTEWA, RICHARD SITKO   (Hopi)
1927-   (artist)

Born April 12, 1927, Oraibi, Ariz. *Education:* Oklahoma A. & M. College, School of Technical Training, 1957. *Principal occupation:* Artist (painting and sculpture). *Home address:* P.O. Box 145, Oraibi, Ariz. *Military service:* U.S. Army, 1952-54 (Good Conduct Medal, Korean Service Medal, Combat Infantry Badge, U.N. Service Medal, National Defense Service Medal). *Memberships:* Hopi Tribal Council. *Awards, honors:* First Premium, Open Lot Indian Art, Arizona State Fair, 1947; First Prizes, Museum of Northern Arizona; First Prizes, Inter-Tribal Indian

Ceremonial, Gallup, N.M. *Interests:* Art; travel to Korea and Japan while serving in U.S. Army.

PERKINS, ALAN W.   1937-   (museum director)

Born January 2, 1937. *Education:* Northwestern University, B.A. (History), 1959; Clark University, 1959-64. *Principal occupation:* Museum director. *Affiliations:* Director, Wyoming Historical and Geological Society Museum; editor, *Wyoming Review*, publication of the Wyoming Historical and Geological Society. *Memberships:* Historical Association of Northeastern Pennsylvania (secretary-treasurer, 1964-65); American Association of Museums; American Association for State and Local History; American Historical Association. *Interests:* Art; history; photography; "outdoor living"; archaeology; writing.

PERRY, FRANCES R.   1897-
(librarian, curator)

Born January 5, 1897, Black River Falls, Wis. *Education:* Teachers College, Oshkosh, Wis., 1918-21; Teachers College, Columbia University, B.S., 1931. *Principal occupation:* Librarian, curator. *Home address:* 386 Main, Black River Falls, Wis. 54615. *Affiliations:* Teacher, 1915-31; librarian, Public Library, Black River Falls, Wis.; curator, Jackson County Historical Society. *Memberships:* Jackson County Historical Society; Historical Society of Wisconsin; councils of local historical societies. *Interests:* Local history, particularly of the Winnebago Indians.

PERRY, T.J.   1919-   (B.I.A. agency superintendent)

Born May 10, 1919, Paoli, Okla. *Education:* Cameron State College, 1951-52; Oklahoma State University, B.S., 1955. *Principal occupation:* B.I.A. agency superintendent. *Home address:* 219 Miami Blvd., Miami, Okla. 74354. *Affiliations:* Assistant county agent, Okmulgee, Okla., 1955-57; soil conservationist, Bureau of Indian Affairs, 1957-61; superintendent, Miami Agency, Bureau of Indian Affairs, Miami, Okla. *Military service:* U.S. Army Air Force, 1942-45 (Asiatic Pacific Award;

American Campaign Medal; Presidential Unit Citation; Good Conduct Medal; four bronze service stars).

PETERSON, HAROLD L.   1922-
(historian, museum curator)

Born May 22, 1922, Peekskill, N.Y. *Education:* Drew University, B.A., 1945; University of Wisconsin, M.A., 1947. *Principal occupation:* Historian, museum curator. *Home address:* 5113 - 8th Rd., N., Arlington, Va. 22205. *Affiliations:* Military advisor, Plimoth Plantation. 1949-; military advisor, Colonial Williamsburg, 1949-50; weapons consultant, Henry Ford Museum, 1953-; historian and museum curator, National Park Service, Washington, D.C. *Military service:* U.S. Army, 1942-43. *Memberships:* Company of Military Historians (founder, past president, governor); National Rifle Association (director); International Association of Museums of Arms and Military History (executive council); other professional associations. *Awards, honors:* Distinguished Service Medal, U.S. Department of the Interior; Order of St. Barbara, U.S. Artillery and Guided Missiles Center, Fort Sill; Ancient Order of the Artillerist, U.S. Artillery and Guided Missiles Center. *Interests:* History of the development of all forms of arms and armor; military history; travels in the United States, Canada, and Europe. *Published works: The American Sword* (Riling, 1954, 1965); *American Knives* (Scribner's, 1958); *Notes on Ordnance of the American Civil War* (American Ordnance Association, 1959); *A History of Firearms* (Scribner's, 1961); *The Treasury of the Gun* (Golden Press, 1962); *Forts in America* (Scribner's, 1964); *Encyclopedia of Firearms* (Dutton, 1964); *American Indian Tomahawks* (Museum of the American Indian, Heye Foundation, 1965).

PETERSON, JOHN   1919-   (hotel manager)

Born November 5, 1919, Bismarck, N.D. *Education:* North Dakota State University, 1937-40. *Principal occupation:* Hotel manager. *Addresses:* 225 Tower Ave., Bismarck, N.D. (home); Grand Pacific Hotel, Bismarck, N.D. (business). *Affiliations:* Manager, Grand Pacific Hotel, 1940-. *Community activities:* Bismarck Chamber of Commerce (director); Bismarck-Mandan

Community Theatre (president); Bismarck Rotary Club (director). *Memberships:* Bismarck Zoological Society (director); Foundation of North American Indian Culture (president); North Dakota Hotel-Motel Association (president).

PHILLIPS, DONALD E.   1903-   (historical (society director)

Born March 18, 1903. *Education:* De Pauw University, 1921-23; University of Arizona, B.A.; Oklahoma University, M.A. *Principal occupation:* Historical society director. *Address:* 949 E. 2nd St., Tucson, Ariz. 85719. *Affiliations:* Reporter-editor, *Arizona Daily Star;* manager, Press Bureau, University of Arizona; executive secretary, State Bar of Arizona; administrative director, Arizona Pioneers' Historical Society. *Memberships:* Public Relations Society of Phoenix (president, board of directors); Arizona Chapter, Public Relations Society of America (treasurer, board of directors). *Awards, honors:* Phi Delta Epsilon Medal of Merit; Helms Foundation Award for excellence in college publicity.

PICKUP, JIM   (Cherokee)   1885- (minister)

Born January 8, 1885, in "Cherokee Indian territory." *Education:* Elementary school. *Principal occupation:* Minister. *Home address:* City Route D, Tahlequah, Okla. *Affiliations:* Minister, Cherokee County; chief, Keetoowah Band of the Cherokee Tribe. *Community activities:* Instrumental in organization of the Keetoowah Band of the Cherokee Tribe, 1949; Economic Opportunity Ozark Work-Study Project. *Memberships:* Adair Indian Credit Association (board of directors). *Interests:* Mr. Pickup has traveled through eighteen states on visits to U.S. Indian missions.

PIETROFORTE, ALFRED   1925-   (speech instructor)

Born March 25, 1925, Philadelphia, Penna. *Education:* College of the Sequoias, A.A., 1952; Fresno State College, B.A., 1954, M.A., 1961. *Principal occupation:* Speech instructor. *Home address:* 2113 S. Church St., Visalia, Calif. *Affiliations:* Instructor in speech and general semantics, College of the Sequoias. *Community activities:* Visalia Optimist Club (secretary). *Memberships:* California Federation of Teachers, 1963-65. *Interests:* English; public speaking; general semantics; music -- church and community choirs and productions; American folk music -- especially the music of the California Indians. Mr. Pietroforte writes, "My publication, *Songs of the Yokuts and Paiutes,* took two years to complete. This meant extensive travel to a number of Indian reservations and rancherias as well as visiting informants who have left the reservations and have made their homes in the cities and towns of California." *Published works: Songs of the Yokuts and Paiutes* (Naturegraph Co., 1965).

PITTS, PAUL WARREN   (Osage)   1904- (principal chief, Osage Tribe of Indians)

Born November 1, 1904, Osage Reservation, Indian Territory, Okla. *Education:* Missouri Military Academy. *Principal occupation:* Farmer, rancher; principal chief, Osage Tribe of Indians. *Home address:* Pawhuska Indian Village, Pawhuska, Okla. 74056. *Community activities:* Rotary Club. *Memberships:* National Congress of American Indians (executive board). *Interests:* Mr. Pitts writes, "I have been actively engaged in Osage tribal affairs since 1938, first serving as secretary of the Osage Tribal Council (the governing body of the Osage Tribe), and later as principal chief, (the office) I currently hold. The principal chief's office is an elective office by a majority vote of the Tribe. Also, (I was) the Osage Tribe's official delegate to the Brussels World's Fair in 1957."

POE, CHARLSIE   1909-   (writer)

Born May 28, 1909, Jones County, Texas. *Education:* Hardin-Simmons University. *Principal occupation:* Writer. *Home address:* 207 W. Truett, Winters, Texas 79567. *Affiliations:* Teacher, Winters, Texas, 1942-49; free lance reporter, Abilene *Reporter-News,* 1955-; free lance reporter, Winters *Enterprise,* 1955-. *Community activities:* Band Mothers Club (past president); Parent-Teachers' Association; Diversity Club. *Memberships:* Runnels County History Survey Committee (secretary, 1963-); National Federation of Press

Women, Inc., 1965-; Texas Press Women, Inc., 1965-. *Interests:* Travel in the United States -- visits to Indian reservations. *Published works: Angel to the Papagos* (Naylor, 1964).

POLELONEMA, OTIS (Hopi) 1902-
(artist, weaver)

Born February 12, 1902, Shongopovy, Ariz. *Education:* High school. *Principal occupation:* Artist, weaver. *Home address:* Second Mesa, P.O. Box 758, Shongopovy, Ariz. *Affiliations:* "Hopi Indian religious business in Shongopovy Village, Arizona, (for) forty years." *Awards, honors:* Mr. Polelonema has received various awards at the Inter-Tribal Indian Ceremonial, Gallup, N.M., at the Northern Museum, at exhibitions in Flagstaff and Scottsdale, Arizona, and at the Phoenix State Fair and the Santa Fe Museum. *Interests:* Textile weaving; exhibitions.

POPOVI DA (Tewa Pueblo) 1922-
(craftsman)

Born April 10, 1922, Santa Fe, N.M. *Education:* Canyon School of Art. *Principal occupation:* Craftsman; operator, Indian crafts studio. *Home address:* San Ildefonso Pueblo, Santa Fe, N.M. 87501. *Military service:* 1943-46 (Good Conduct Medal; special recognition for service under the Manhattan Engineers). *Community activities:* San Ildefonso Pueblo (governor); All-Pueblo Council (chairman); New Mexico State Art Commission (board member); New Mexico Association on Indian Affairs (board member). *Awards, honors:* National Indian Arts Council, Scottsdale, Ariz.; Gallup Inter-Tribal Ceremonial; New Mexico State Fair; New Mexico Craft Fair; Philbrook Museum, Tulsa, Okla.; Museum Fur Volkerkunde, West Germany. *Interests:* Preservation of the traditional Indian art and culture of the Pueblos.

POSTON, BENJAMIN RALPH 1917-
(agrologist)

Born November 27, 1917, Manitoba, Can. *Education:* University of Manitoba, B.Sc.A., 1950; Colorado State University, M.E., 1964. *Principal occupation:* Agrologist. *Home address:* 109-595 River Ave.,

Winnipeg, 13, Man., Can. *Affiliations:* Agrologist, Manitoba Department of Agriculture and Conservation (formerly agricultural representative, 1950-62). *Military service:* Royal Canadian Air Force, 1940-45. *Community activities:* Indian and Eskimo Association. *Memberships:* M.I.A., C.S.R.E., A.I.C. *Interests:* Agriculture; welfare of Canadian Indians; music. *Published works: The People of Indian Ancestry in Manitoba* (Manitoba Department of Agriculture and Immigration, 1959); *Factors Influencing Tenure of Select Senior 4-H Members in Manitoba, Canada* (Colorado State University, 1964).

POUND, MERRITT BLOODWORTH 1898-
(professor of history and political science)

Born December 17, 1898, Barnesville, Ga. *Education:* University of Georgia, B.A., M.A., 1924; University of North Carolina, Ph.D., 1939. *Principal occupation:* Professor of history and political science. *Home address:* 652 Milledge Circle, Athens, Ga. 30601. *Affiliations:* Assistant and associate professor of history, University of Georgia, 1926-41; professor of political science and head of department, University of Georgia, 1941-64. *Military service:* U.S. Air Force, 1918, 1942-45. *Community activities:* Council of Athens, Ga., 1949-55. *Memberships:* Southern Political Science Association, 1931- (president, 1950; secretary). *Awards, honors:* Phi Beta Kappa; Phi Kappa Phi; Pi Sigma Alpha. *Interests:* Travel to India, South America, Africa, Europe. *Published works: Georgia Citizenship* (Johnson Publishing Co., 1939); *Principles of American Government*, with A.B. Saye and J.F. Allums (Prentice-Hall, 1950); *Benjamin Hawkins - Indian Agent* (University of Georgia Press, 1951).

POWERS, WILLIAM K. 1934-
(journalist)

Born July 31, 1934, St. Louis, Mo. *Principal occupation:* Journalist. *Home address:* 15 Aldrich Rd., Kendall Park N., N.J. *Affiliations:* Editor and publisher, *Powwow Trails. Memberships:* Society of American Indian Tradition (director, 1960-62); Monroe Powwow Committee (chairman, 1966-67); United Association of the American Indian, Two Bears Longhouse; Society for Ethnomusicology, 1965-. *Interests:* American Indian music, linguistics, dance, religion; translation of Indian songs and texts; music diffusion; contemporary Indian culture; travel to Indian reservations. *Published works: Indian Dancing* (G. P. Putnam's Sons, 1966); numerous articles in professional journals. *Works in preparation: Contemporary Music and Dance of the Western Sioux; A Lakota Dictionary.*

PRAUS, ALEXIS A. 1913- (museum director)

Born March 24, 1913, New York, N.Y. *Education:* New York University, B.S., 1939; Yale University, M.A., 1941. *Principal occupation:* Museum director. *Home address:* 1709 Dover Rd., Kalamazoo, Mich. 49001. *Military service:* World War II, 1943-45. *Community activities:* Governor's Cultural Commission; Kalamazoo Historical Commission. *Memberships:* Rotary Club; Midwest Museum Conference; American Association of Museums. *Interests:* Pioneer techniques and American history of the 19th century; Indian archaeology and ethnology; Nebraska Archaeological Expeditions, 1937-38. *Published works: Bibliography of Michigan Archaeology* (Anthropological Papers, Museum of Anthropology, University of Michigan, Vol. 22, 1964); numerous articles in scholarly journals.

PRINGLE, WILMA REED (Choctaw-Chickasaw) 1928- (artist)

Born December 6, 1928, Wilburton, Okla. *Education:* Haskell Institute, 1945-47; St. Joseph's Academy, Dallas, Texas, 1947-48; Los Angeles City College, 1956-58. *Principal occupation:* Artist, part-time secretary. *Home address:* 1026 Sanborn Ave., Apt. 206, Hollywood, Calif. 90029. *Memberships:* United Nations Association; Dallas Council on World Affairs; Poetry Society of Texas; Chaparral Poetry Society of Los Angeles; Westwood Art Association. *Awards, honors:* Honor Mention, Painting, Indian Art Annual, Philbrook Art Center, Tulsa, Okla., 1963; Honor Mention, Poetry, Scottsdale Indian Art Exhibition, Scottsdale, Ariz., 1965; Honor Mention, Painting, Indian Art Annual, Philbrook Art Center, 1966. *Exhibitions:* Museum of Contemporary Art, Dallas, Texas, 1962; Philbrook Art Center, 1963; Museum of New Mexico, Santa Fe, N.M., 1963; Inter-Tribal Indian

Ceremonial, Gallip, N.M., 1963; Dallas Osteopathic Hospital, 1963; Art Gallery, U.S. Department of the Interior, Washington, D.C., 1964; American Indian Art Exhibition, Charlotte, N.C., 1964; Westwood Art Association Gallery, Los Angeles, Calif., 1965; Art Gallery, U.S. Department of the Interior, 1965; Philbrook Art Center, 1966.

PROCTER, GIL(BERT) 1893- (museum director)

Born September 18, 1893, Santa Monica, Calif. *Education:* Throop Polytechnic Institute; University of Southern California. *Principal occupation:* Museum director. *Address:* U.S. Highway 90, Nogales, Ariz. *Affiliations:* Professor of military science and tactics; military attache, U.S. Embassy, Quito, Ecuador; chief of counterintelligence, U.S.A.S.F., Washington, D.C., and 1st U.S. Army group, London, U.K.; U.S. Army intelligence officer, Arizona and western Mexico; chief of staff, U.S. Army Advance Section, Bonn, Germany; director, Pete Kitchen Museum, Nogales, Ariz. *Military service:* Regular Army, 1917-46 -- retired as Colonel, Infantry. *Awards, honors:* Legion of Merit, Star of Abdon Calderon, Ecuador. *Community activities:* Chamber of Commerce, Santa Cruz County (president); Pimeria Alta Historical Society (president). *Memberships:* American Association of Museums. *Interests:* Indians; Spanish priests in the Southwest; the pioneer in the Southwest; travels to Mexico, Ecuador, France, England, Germany, and Belgium. *Published works: Tucson, Tubac, Tumacacori, Tohell* (Arizona Silhouettes, 1956); *People of the Moonlight* (Pete Kitchen Museum, 1958); *Panchita* (Naylor Co., 1960); *Saddle Creaks of a Cowpoke* (Pete Kitchen Museum, 1963); *The Trails of Pete Kitchen* (Dale Stuart King, 1964).

PRUCHA, FRANCIS PAUL 1921- (associate professor of history)

Born January 4, 1921, River Falls, Wis. *Education:* River Falls State College, B.S., 1941; University of Minnesota, M.A., 1947; Harvard University, Ph.D., 1950; St. Louis University, 1952-54; St. Mary's College, S.T.L., 1958. *Principal occupation:* Associate professor of history. *Address:* Marquette University, Milwaukee, Wis.

53233. *Affiliations:* Associate professor of history, Marquette University, 1960-. *Military service:* U.S. Army Air Force, 1942-46. *Memberships:* American Historical Association, 1949; Organization of American Historians, 1954-; State Historical Society of Wisconsin, 1960-; American Catholic Historical Association, 1960- (executive committee, 1962-65); Milwaukee County Historical Society (board of directors, 1964-). *Published works: Broadax and Bayonet* (State Historical Society of Wisconsin, 1953); *Army Life on the Western Frontier* (University of Oklahoma Press, 1958); *American Indian Policy in the Formative Years* (Harvard University Press, 1962); *Guide to the Military Posts of the United States, 1789-1895* (State Historical Society of Wisconsin, 1964).

Q

QUIMBY, GEORGE I. 1913- (museum curator, professor of anthropology)

Born May 4, 1913, Grand Rapids, Mich. *Education:* University of Michigan, B.A., M.A., 1938; University of Chicago, 1938-39. *Principal occupation:* Museum curator, professor of anthropology. *Affiliations:* Archaeologist, Muskegon Centennial Association, 1937; supervisor, Works Projects Administration Laboratory of Parthian Archaeology, University of Michigan, 1938; chief supervisor, Works Projects Administration Archaeological Survey of Louisiana, Louisiana State University, 1939-41; director, Muskegon Museum, 1941-42; curator, Chicago Natural History Museum, 1942-65; lecturer in anthropology, Northwestern University, 1947-53; lecturer in new world archaeology, University of Chicago, 1947-; lecturer, University of Oslo, 1952; curator, Thomas Burke Memorial Washington State Museum, University of Washington, 1965-. *Memberships:* American Anthropological Association (Fellow); Arctic Institute of North America (associate); Society for American Archaeology (secretary, 1948-52; vice president, 1953-54; president, 1957-58); Central States Anthropological Society (president, 1948-49); American Indian Ethnohistoric Conference; American Association for the Advancement of Science (Fellow); Current Anthropology (associate); Southeastern Archaeological Conference; Sigma Xi; Kennicott Club. *Awards, honors:* Horace Rackham Fellow, University of Michigan, 1937-38; Wenner-Gren Foundation Grant for study of European museums, 1952;

American Council of Learned Societies Grant for research in Great Lakes archaeology, 1961-62. *Interests:* North American archaeology and ethnology; Eskimos and Indians; cultural ecology; underwater archaeology; culture history; field work in archaeology in New Mexico, Mississippi, Louisiana, Michigan, Wisconsin, Ontario, and Hudson's Bay. *Published works: Aleutian Islanders, Eskimos of the North Pacific* (Chicago Natural History Museum, Anthropology Leaflet No. 35, 1944); *The Tehefuncte Culture, An Early Occupation of the Lower Mississippi Valley* (Memoirs of the Society for American Archaeology, No. 2, 1945); *Indians Before Columbus,* with Paul S. Martin and Donald Collier (Chicago, 1947); *The Medora Site, West Baton Rouge Parish, Louisiana* (Field Museum Anthropological Series, Vol. 24, No. 2, Chicago, 1951); *Indians of the Western Frontier, Paintings of George Catlin* (Chicago Natural History Museum Handbook, 1954); *The Bayou Goula Site, Iberville Parish, Louisiana* (Fieldiana Anthropology, Vol. 47, No. 2, Chicago, 1957); *Indian Life in the Upper Great Lakes, 11,000 B.C. to A.D. 1800* (University of Chicago Press, 1960); articles and reviews in various professional journals.

R

RACHLIS, EUGENE 1920- (writer, editor)

Born February 5, 1920, Boston, Mass. *Education:* Boston University, B.S., 1941. *Principal occupation:* Writer, editor. *Home address:* 1158 Fifth Ave., New York, N.Y. 10029. *Affiliations:* Editor, Lewis Harris and Associates, New York, N.Y.; free lance writing. *Military service:* U.S. Army, World War II. *Memberships:* National Press Club. *Published works: Peter Stuyvesant and His New York* (Random House); *They Came to Kill* (Random House); *The Land Lords* (Random House); *Story of the U.S. Coast Guard* (Random House); *The Low Countries* (Time-Life Books); *Indians of the Plains* (American Heritage); *The Voyages of Henry Hudson* (Random House).

RAVE, AUSTIN GERALD (Cheyenne River Sioux) 1946- (artist)

Born August 5, 1946, Dewey County, S.D. *Education:* Institute of American Indian Arts. *Principal occupation:* Artist, student. *Home address:* Box 463, Eagle Butte, S.D. *Memberships:* Minneconjou Cultural Society, 1964-. *Awards, honors:* Second Prize, Special Student Competition, Indian Art Exhibition, Scottsdale, Ariz., 1966. *Exhibits:* Washington, D.C.; The Riverside Museum, New York, N.Y.; Pensacola, Fla.; Santa Fe, N.M.; Scottsdale, Ariz., Tulsa, Okla.; Scotland.

RAWLING, GERALD STUART 1923-
(bank submanager)

Born January 17, 1923, Mitcham, Surrey, England. *Education:* Ratcliffe College, Leicester, England. *Principal occupation:* Bank submanager. *Home address:* Abinger, Weston Lane, Bath County, Somerset, England. *Affiliations:* Submanager, Westminster Bank, Bath County, Somerset, England. *Military service:* Royal Marines, 1941-46. *Interests:* "History of the American fur trade in the Far West." *Published works: The Pathfinders* (Macmillan, 1964).

RAY, DOROTHY JEAN 1919-
(anthropologist)

Born October 10, 1919, Cedar Falls, Iowa. *Education:* State College of Iowa, B.A., 1941; Radcliffe College; University of Washington. *Principal occupation:* Anthropologist, writer. *Home address:* 18905 - 73rd Ave., N.E., Bothell, Wash. 98011. *Community activities:* Local library groups. *Awards, honors:* Merchant Scholarship, State College of Iowa; Arctic Institute of North America Research Grant. *Interests:* Primitive art; primitive political organization; arctic and subarctic culture change; ethnohistory and ethnology; history and geography; social anthropology; Mexican ethnology and social anthropology. Field work in Alaska, 1950, 1955; Seward Peninsula and Kobuk River, 1961, 1964; museum studies in Eskimo art; field work in Mexico, 1957, 1958, 1962, 1963, Noatak River, Alaska, 1947, northern Europe, 1960, Labrador, 1960. *Published works: Artists of the Tundra and the Sea* (University of Washington Press, 1961); *Eskimo Masks and Ceremonialism* (University of Washington Press, 1966).

RAY, VERNE F. 1905- (professor of anthropology)

Born March 13, 1905, Enfield, Ill. *Education:* University of Washington, B.A.,

M.A.; University of California (Berkeley), Jr. Cert.; Yale University, Ph.D. *Principal occupation:* Professor of anthropology. *Home address:* 18905 - 73rd Ave., N.E., Bothell, Wash. 98011. *Affiliations:* Associate dean, Graduate School, University of Washington; research director, Human Relations Area Files; professor of anthropology, University of Washington. *Military service:* U.S. Coast Guard Reserve. *Memberships:* American Ethnological Society (former president; former editor), and many others. *Interests:* "North American ethnology and social anthropology, with emphasis on the Arctic, the Plateau, and Mesoamerica." *Biographical sources: American Men of Science. Published works: The Sanpoil and Nespelem: Salishan Peoples of Northeastern Washington* (University of Washington Press); *Cultural Relations in the Plateau of Northwestern America* (Southwest Museum); *Lower Chinook Ethnographic Notes* (University of Washington Press); *Primitive Pragmatists: The Modoc Indians of Northern California* (American Ethnological Society Publications); and others.

READ, CHARLOTTE M. (historian, museum curator)

Born Batavia, N.Y. *Education:* Private instruction specializing in psychology, history, museum directorship, languages, and writing. *Principal occupation:* Historian, museum curator. *Home address:* 8900 Read Rd., East Pembroke, N.Y. 14056. *Affiliations:* Historian, Genesee County Department of History; director, Holland Land Office Museum, 1956-. *Community activities:* East Pembroke First Baptist Church; Genesee Chapter, American Cancer Society (director); Genesee County Chapter, American Red Cross (director, secretary of board); Genesee County Women's Republican Club (past president, treasurer, executive board); election inspector; Civil Defense. *Memberships:* Batavia-Genesee Zonta Club; Batavia Business and Professional Women; Daughters of the American Revolution (state historian); Holland Purchase Historical Society; American Association for State and Local History; American Association of Museums; New York State Historical Association; Central New York Genealogical Society; Cobblestone Society; LeRoy Historical Society; Landmarks Preservation Society (Genesee, Western New York, National Trust); Folklore Society. *Interests:*

Genealogical research; ceramics; music; writing. *Published works:* Articles dealing with local history.

READING, ROBERT S.   1892-
   (engineer, writer)

Born July 17, 1892, Richmond, Texas. *Education:* Texas A. & M., B.S. (Engineering and Electrical Engineering), 1910. *Principal occupation:* Engineer, writer. *Home address:* 1312 Ficklin Ave., Corsicana, Texas. *Affiliations:* District manager, Southern Cities Distributing Co., 1922-29; district manager, Lone Star Gas Co., El Paso, Texas, 1929-40; district manager, Lone Star Gas Co., Corsicana, Texas, 1940-54. *Community activities:* City commissioner, Corsicana, Texas, 1957-58; mayor of Corsicana, Texas, 1959-64; Community Chest (president); Army Board (chairman). *Memberships:* Salvation Army (life member); United States Conference of Mayors; Kentucky Colonel; Rotary Club; Masons; Corsicana Chamber of Commerce; Zeta Omicron; Phi Theta Kappa. *Awards, honors:* Distinguished Citizenship Award, Veterans of Foreign Wars; Silver Beaver Award, Boy Scouts of America. *Published works: Arrows Over Texas* (Naylor, 1960); *Indian Civilizations* (Naylor, 1961).

RED CORN, CHARLES H.   (Osage)   1936-
   (textile and leather craftsman)

Born June 21, 1936, Pawhuska, Okla. *Education:* University of Oklahoma. *Principal occupation:* Textile and leather craftsman. *Home address:* Indian Village, Pawhuska, Okla. 74056. *Military service:* U.S. Army, 1959-61. *Community activities:* Pawhuska Indian Village and Community Association (board of directors). *Interests:* Mr. Red Corn writes, "(I am interested in) new uses of Plains Indian artistic principles in textitles and silver jewelry. I am still, after four years, in an experimental and study stage, although I have to sell what I produce. (However), I am getting closer to the look I want."

RED ELK, HERMAN   (Sioux)   1918-
   (artist)

Born March 27, 1918, Poplar, Mont. *Education:* High school. *Principal occupation:*
Artist. *Home address:* Box 571, Rapid City, S.D. 57701. *Affiliations:* Art work demonstrator, Tipi Shop, Inc., Rapid City, S.D.; skin painter, Sioux Indian Museum, Rapid City, S.D. *Military service:* U.S. Army, 1940-45. *Awards, honors:* First Place, Oil Painting, Scenery, Charcoal Sketching, Watercolor Portrait Skin Painting, Ink Sketching, Pennington County Fair, 1965. *Interests:* "General art -- cassein, watercolors, pencil, oil."

REID, DOROTHY MARION   1906-
   (children's librarian)

Born November 7, 1906, Edinburgh, Scotland. *Education:* Weyburn Collegiate, Weyburn, Sask., Can.; Regina Teachers' College, Regina, Sask., Can.; library course, Ontario Department of Education. *Principal occupation:* Children's librarian. *Home address:* R.R. 3, Riverdale Rd., Fort William, Ont., Can. *Affiliations:* Head, Children's Department, Main Library, Fort William, Ont., Can. *Memberships:* Ontario Library Association, 1946- (publicity committee in children's work). *Awards, honors:* Book of the Year Award, Children's Literature in English, for *Tales of Nanabozho,* Canadian Association of Children's Librarians, 1964. *Interests:* Mrs. Reid writes, "A great love and admiration (for) Canada, particularly this beautiful and rugged Lakehead area, which has been the source of much poetry, published in various periodicals, as well as the source of the atmosphere for *Tales of Nanabozho.* Vocational interests include a desire to promote increased efficiency in library operations, to permit more time to devote to the public's interests and needs. Travels? Visited many parts of the world in my childhood -- Australia, India, Europe, as well as much of Canada and the northern United States. Am now content to wander in our native woods and gather impressions of tranquility. My chief interests -- my husband, children and grandchildren, and growing old gracefully!" *Published works: Tales of Nanabozho* (Oxford University Press, Canada, 1963; Henry Z. Walck, United States, 1963).

REIFEL, BEN   (Rosebud Sioux)   1906-
   (member of Congress)

Born September 19, 1906, Parmelee, S.D. *Education:* South Dakota State University, B.S., 1932; Harvard University, D.P.A.,

1952, M.P.A., 1956. *Principal occupation:* Member of Congress, 1960-. *Home address:* 800 - 4th St., S.W., Washington, D.C. *Affiliations:* Former area director, Bureau of Indian Affairs. *Military service:* U.S. Army, 1942-46. *Community activities:* Boy Scouts of America (council president; member, regional board of directors); Episcopal Church (committee on racial minorities); Episcopal Men of South Dakota; Elks; American Legion; Tuberculosis and Health Association (state leader); Parent-Teachers' Association; National Conference of Indian Workers (president, triennial conference); University of South Dakota Development Committee. *Memberships:* Arrow, Inc., 1955- (president). *Awards:* Outstanding American Indian Award, Sheridan, Wyo., 1956.

RENO, THOMAS R.   1939- (educator)

Born November 16, 1939, Canton, Ohio. *Education:* Ohio University, 1958-60; Arizona State University, B.A. (Education), 1961, M.A. (Education), 1965. *Principal occupation:* Educator. *Address:* c/o Lukachukai School, Lukachukai, Ariz. 86507. *Affiliations:* Volunteer, Peace Corps, Iran, 1962-64; research in Indian education, Arizona State University; assistant director, Navajo Demonstration School Project, Lukachukai School, Lukachukai, Ariz.

RESSLER, THEODORE WHITSON   1926- (organization secretary, writer)

Born June 14, 1926, Brooklyn, N.Y. *Education:* Brooklyn College, B.A., 1951. *Principal occupation:* Organization secretary, writer. *Home address:* 99 Galant Drive, Warwick, R.I. 02886. *Affiliations:* Camp worker, Y.M.C.A., Providence, R.I.; youth worker, Y.M.C.A., Perth Amboy, N.J.; community worker, Y.M.C.A., Bergen County, N.J.; youth worker, Y.M.C.A., Brooklyn, N.Y. *Community activities:* Boy Scouts of America (scoutmaster); Rotary Club (youth committee chairman); Academy Players of East Greenwich, R.I. (actor); Greater Providence Chamber of Commerce (recreation committee); Y.M.C.A. Camp Directors Association (president). *Memberships:* Association of Secretaries, Y.M.C.A. (executive committee, New England Area). *Awards, honors:* Bronze Arrowhead for long experi-

ence in scouting and achievement in the field of training, National Scout Office, Region 2, Boy Scouts of America. *Interests:* Mr. Ressler writes, "Major interest lies in my work in the Y.M.C.A. with youth and especially in camping. Other than that, I do a little bowling, play some golf and am involved in my local church in teaching, and with the local Boy Scout troop. I enjoy travel but do not get much of a chance to do any, although my wife and I will travel to Lima, Peru, for a month, where I will be engaged in training Peruvian Y.M.C.A. camp leaders." *Published works: Treasury of American Indian Tales* (Association Press, 1956).

REUTTER, WINIFRED   1909- (writer)

Born March 10, 1909, near Stanton, Iowa. *Education:* Rural schools of Mellette County, S.D., 1923. *Principal occupation:* Writer. *Home address:* Route 1, White River, S.D. 57579. *Affiliations:* Columnist, "Beef Notes by a CowBelle," *American Hereford Journal*, 1959-; news correspondent, Rapid City *Journal*, Rapid City, S.D., 1965-; stringer service for Associated Press and Keloland (K.P.L.O.-TV), 1963-. *Community activities:* School board; Mellette County Cow-Belles (secretary and publicity); Sunday school teacher, 1956-. *Memberships:* National, state and local CowBelles; South Dakota Historical Society; Mellette County Art Club; South Dakota Press Women; National Press Women; South Dakota Poetry Society (patron, member); Rosebud Geological Society (liaison officer, 1965-66); Badlands Sandhills Earth Science Club, 1964- (director, 1966-); Lutheran Church; Midwest Federation. *Awards, honors:* Honor Award, National Federation of Presswomen, 1962; Annual Honor Award (First Place), National Federation of Presswomen, 1963; Writers Honor Award (Second Place), National Federation of Presswomen, 1964. *Interests:* Local history; photography; writing; poetry; maintains large collection of Indian artifacts and crafts. *Published works: Prairie Poetry* (Scott, 1928); *Mellette County Memories* (Argus Printers, 1961); *Early Dakota Days* (Argus Printers, 1962).

RHODES, WILLARD   1901- (ethnomusicologist, educator)

Born May 12, 1901, Deshler, Ohio. *Edu-*

cation: Heidelberg College, B.A., B.Mus., 1922; Columbia University, M.A., 1925; Ecole Normale de Musique, 1925-27. *Principal occupation:* Ethnomusicologist, educator. *Home address:* 15 Claremont Ave., New York, N.Y. 10027. *Affiliations:* Assistant conductor and chorus master, American Opera Company, 1927-30; assistant conductor, Cincinnati Summer Opera Company, 1928-33; director, Rhodes Chamber Opera Company, 1930-35; director of music, Bronxville Public Schools, 1935-37; professor of music, Columbia University, 1937-; education specialist, U.S. Bureau of Indian Affairs, 1937-50; consultant, Library of Congress, 1951. *Memberships:* Society for Ethnomusicology (founding member and first president); Society for Asian Music (president); International Folk Music Council (chairman, executive board); African Studies Association (founding Fellow); International Institute for Comparative Music Studies (scientific board). *Interests:* Research and recording of North American Indian music, 1938-51; recording of African music, 1958-59; research and study of Carnatic music in Madras, India, 1965-66. *Published works:* Ten long-playing records of North American Indian music with notes (Library of Congress); two records of North American Indian music and one record of Mormon folk songs (Folkways Records); articles in scholarly journals.

RICHESIN, M. LESTER 1930- (teacher)

Born October 10, 1930, Omaha, Ark. *Education:* Harding College, B.A., 1953; McNeese State College, 1958; Drury College, M.A., 1964. *Principal occupation:* Teacher. *Address:* Bureau of Indian Affairs, Selawik, Alaska 99770. *Affiliations:* Clerk, U.S. Post Office, 1954-56; teacher, Reorganized District 3, Republic, Mo., 1957-65; principal, Selawik Day School, Bureau of Indian Affairs, Selawik, Alaska, 1965-. *Community activities:* Cub Scouts, Republic, Mo. (cubmaster); Little League (manager). *Memberships:* National Education Association, 1965. *Awards, honors:* Order of Merit Award, Boy Scouts of America. *Interests:* Counseling; travel to Alaska, Canada, and the Arctic.

RICKEY, DON, Jr. 1925- (park planner)

Born August 3, 1925, Chicago, Ill. *Education:* Northern Montana College, 1946-47; University of Kentucky, B.A., 1950; Okla-

homa State University, M.A., 1951; University of Oklahoma, Ph.D., 1960. *Principal occupation:* Park planner. *Home address:* 4716 N. 22nd St., Omaha, Neb. *Affiliations:* Chief research historian, Jefferson National Expansion Memorial; historian, Custer Battlefield National Monument. *Other professional posts:* Librarian and historian, Phillips Collection, University of Oklahoma Library. *Military service:* U.S. Navy, 1943-46, 1951. *Memberships:* United Indian War Veterans; Western History Association; Company of Military Historians. *Published works: Forty Miles a Day on Beans and Hay* (University of Oklahoma Press, 1963).

RIDDLES, LEONARD *(Black Moon)* (Comanche) 1919- (artist)

Born June 28, 1919, Walters, Okla. *Education:* High school. *Principal occupation:* Artist, farmer and rancher. *Home address:* R. 1, Walters, Okla. *Military service:* U.S. Army, 1941-45 (Sharp Shooter Carbine, Service Ribbon, two bronze stars, 8P Service Ribbon, American Defense Ribbon). *Community activities:* Comanche Tribal Council (former officer); Masons. *Memberships:* American Indian Artists Association. *Awards, honors:* First Prize, Plains Division, Philbrook Art Center, 1963; Second Prize, Bismarck, N.D. Art Exhibit, 1963; First Prize and Grand Award, American Indian Exposition, 1964; Third Prize, Inter-Tribal Indian Ceremonial, Gallup, N.M., 1964; Mrs. Thomas B. Curtin Award, Museum of New Mexico, Santa Fe, N.M., 1964; Honor Mention, Philbrook Art Center, 1965. *Exhibitions* (in addition to those listed under *Awards, honors*): U.S. Department of the Interior Gallery, 1965. Interests: Mr. Riddles writes, "(I am) interested in the history of the American Indian and in any phase of archaeological study. We do research on the Comanche Tribe, so (I) find all expeditions of real interest. Museums are also of great interest to me." Mr. Riddles illustrated the jacket for *Buried Colts* by Harley Smith. *Published works:* Mr. Riddles writes, "I'm working on a book about the Comanche people . . . a non-fiction (work) on Comanche life and culture."

RIDLE, JULIA BROWN 1923- (writer)

Born May 29, 1923, Doris, Calif. *Education:* Oregon State University. *Principal occupation:* Writer. *Home address:* P.O. Box 194, Ennis, Mont. 59729. *Memberships:* The Authors' Guild, Inc., 1964-; The National League of American Penwomen, 1964-. *Published works: Hog Wild!* (Harper & Row, 1961); *Mohawk Gamble* (Harper & Row, 1963).

RIGG, ROD C. 1926- (instructor, museum director)

Born August 19, 1926, Stockton, Calif. *Education:* College of the Pacific, B.A., 1958; University of the Pacific, M.A., 1963. *Principal occupation:* Instructor, museum director. *Home address:* 1305 Occidental Ave., Stockton, Calif. 95203. *Affiliations:* Instructor, University of the Pacific, 1959-; president and director, San Joaquin County Junior Museum Association, 1963-. *Community activities:* Delta Amateur Radio Club (president, 1962). *Memberships:* Phi Delta Kappa, 1961-; Alpha Epsilon Rho, 1953-. *Interests:* Educational radio and television; science education; junior museum movement; electronics; photography. *Published works:* Articles in various magazines.

RIRABAYASHI, GORDON L. (professor of sociology)

Education: University of Washington, B.A., 1946, M.A., 1949, Ph.D., 1952. *Principal occupation:* Professor of sociology. *Affiliations:* Instructor in sociology, University of Washington, 1947-51; research sociologist, Doukhobor Research Committee, University of British Columbia, 1951; assistant to associate professor of sociology and chairman, Department of Sociology, American University of Beirut, 1952-55; associate professor and assistant director, Social Research Centre, American University of Cairo, Egypt, 1955-59; professor of sociology and head, Department of Sociology, University of Alberta, 1959-. *Published works: Industrialization in Alexandria* (American University Press, 1959); *The Problem of Assisting Aboriginal Canadians to Urban Adjustment* (Indian-Eskimo Association of Canada, 1962); *The Metis in Alberta Society,* with B.Y. Card (University of Alberta, 1963).

ROBBINS, LYNN A. 1935- (archaeologist)

Born December 28, 1935, Ogden, Utah. *Education:* University of Utah, B.A., 1959. *Principal occupation:* Archaeologist. *Home address:* P.O. Box 156, Bloomfield, N.M. 87413. *Affiliations:* Archaeologist, Chaco Canyon National Monument, Bloomfield, N.M. (National Park Service), 1962-. *Memberships:* Society for American Archaeology; Current Anthropology; Society for New Mexico Archaeology; San Juan Archaeological Society. *Interests:* Anasazi prehistory; member, Glen Canyon Archaeological Salvage Expedition, University of Utah, 1958.

ROBERSON, HAROLD D. 1927- (B.I.A. agency superintendent)

Born December 10, 1927, Goldthwaite, Texas. *Education:* Howard Payne College; Texas A. & M. University, B.S., 1949. *Principal occupation:* B.I.A. agency superintendent. *Home address:* Fort Belknap Agency, Bureau of Indian Affairs, Harlem, Mont. 59526. *Affiliations:* Soil Conservation Service, U.S. Department of Agriculture; range conservationist, Bureau of Indian Affairs; projects development officer, Lame Deer, Mont.; ranch manager, Goldthwaite, Texas; superintendent, Fort Belknap Agency, Bureau of Indian Affairs. *Community activities:* Lions Club; Junior Chamber of Commerce; Affiliated Men's Club; Baptist Church. *Interests:* Management and administration.

ROBERTS, JOHN M(ILTON) 1916- (professor of anthropology)

Born December 8, 1916, Omaha, Neb. *Education:* University of Nebraska, B.A., 1937; University of Chicago, 1937-39; Yale University, Ph.D., 1947. *Principal occupation:* Professor of anthropology. *Home address:* 348 Warren Rd., Ithaca, N.Y. 14850. *Affiliations:* Assistant professor, University of Minnesota, 1947-48; assistant professor, Harvard University, 1948-53; associate professor and professor, University of Nebraska, 1953-58; professor of anthropology, Cornell University, 1958-. *Other posts:* Center for Advanced Study in the Behavioral Sciences (Fellow, 1956-57). Military service: U.S. Army, 1942-45 (Silver Star, Bronze Star). *Memberships:*

American Anthropological Association; American Ethnological Society (president, 1960); Northeast Anthropological Association (president-elect); Society for American Archaeology; Society for Applied Anthropology; Linguistic Society of America; Royal Anthropological Institute (Fellow); American Sociological Association; American Association for the Advancement of Science (Fellow). *Interests:* Anthropology -- special interest in North American ethnology, psychological anthropology, and anthropological theory. *Published works: Three Navaho Households: A Comparative Study in Small Group Culture* (Harvard University, 1951); *Zuni Law: A Field of Values* (Harvard University, 1954); *Zuni Daily Life* (University of Nebraska Press, 1956; Human Relations Area Files Press, 1965); *The Language of Experience: A Study in Methodology* (Indiana University Press, 1956); *Zuni Kin Terms* (University of Nebraska Press, 1956).

ROBINSON, DOROTHY F.   1895-
(teacher, librarian)

Born April 5, 1895, Phoenix, Ariz. *Education:* University of Southern California, B.A., 1924, M.A. (History), 1927; Stanford University, 1947, 1953. *Principal occupation:* Teacher, librarian (retired, 1965). *Home address:* 1921 Cavalier Drive, Tempe, Ariz. 85281. *Affiliations:* Teacher, Campus Laboratory School, Arizona State University, 1927-53; librarian, Campus Laboratory School, Arizona State University, 1953-65. *Community activities:* 4-H Club; Garden Club; Junior Red Cross; Parent-Teachers' Association (life member). *Memberships:* National Education Association; American Library Association; Delta Kappa Gamma, 1941-; Kappa Delta Pi, 1965-; American Association for Supervision and Curriculum Development. *Interests:* "Better teaching in the grades; gardening; sewing; writing; Arizona and Indian history; travel." *Published works: Arizona for Boys and Girls* (Tyler Printing Co., 1959; revised 1966); *Making of Arizona* (Tyler Printing Co., 1961; revised 1963); *Geographical Background of Arizona* (Tyler Printing Co., 1965); *Navajo Indians Today* (Naylor, 1966).

ROCK, HOWARD (Eskimo) 1911-
(editor)

Born August 10, 1911, Point Hope, Alaska. *Education:* University of Washington, 1938-40. *Principal occupation:* Editor. *Home address:* Box 1287, Fairbanks, Alaska 99701. *Affiliations:* Editor, *Tundra Times* (periodical), Fairbanks, Alaska. *Military service:* U.S. Army Airways Communication System (Air Force), 1942-44. *Community activities:* Inupiat Paitot, an Eskimo organization of northern Alaska (executive secretary). *Interests:* Painting and designing Alaska scenes on ivory.

ROE, FRANK GILBERT   1878- (writer, locomotive engineer)

Born August 2, 1878, Sheffield, Yorkshire, England. *Education:* Elementary public schools in England. *Principal occupation:* Writer (formerly a locomotive engineer). *Home address:* 2547 Killarney Rd., Cadboro Bay, Victoria, B.C., Can. *Affiliations:* Locomotive engineer, Canadian National Railways, Locomotive Service, 1909-43. *Memberships:* English Place-Name Society, 1924; Canadian Historical Association, 1936; University of Alberta, 1951; Royal Society of Canada, 1960. *Awards, honors:* Honorary LL.D., University of Alberta, 1951; Fellow, Royal Society of Canada, 1960. *Interests:* "American-Canadian history of the Indians from 1492 onward, most particularly in relation to the discovery and eventual extermination of the buffalo; English history (in general), very particularly the study of English place-names and surnames; very fond of biography. Have traveled very considerably over the world, but only for pleasure." *Published works: The North American Buffalo* (University of Toronto Press, 1951); *The Indian and the Horse* (University of Oklahoma Press, 1955).

ROELFS, ED F.   1890- (museum curator)

Born April 14, 1890, Hallam, Neb. *Education:* York Business College. *Principal occupation:* Museum curator. *Home address:* 323 E. Montezuma Ave., Cortez, Colo. 81321. *Affiliations:* Curator, Four Corners Museum, Cortez, Colo. *Military service:* U.S. Air Force.

ROGERS, GEORGE WILLIAM   1917-
(economist)

Born April 15, 1917, San Francisco, Calif. *Education:* University of California, Berkeley, B.A., 1942, M.A., 1943; Harvard University, M.P.A., 1948, Ph.D., 1950. *Principal occupation:* Economist. *Home address:* 1790 Evergreen Ave., Juneau, Alaska 99801. *Affiliations:* Economist, U.S. Department of the Interior, 1946-56; social scientist, Arctic Institute of North America, 1956-60; research professor, University of Alaska, 1960-. *Other professional posts:* Editorial staff, *Inter-Nord,* Centre d'Etudes Arctigne et Finno-Scandinaves, Sorbonne, Paris, France. *Community activities:* City councilman, 1956-58; city charter committee, 1959. *Memberships:* American Economic Association, 1945-; American Geographical Society, 1960-; Regional Science Association, 1955-; Arctic Institute of North America, 1954-; American Association for the Advancement of Science, 1964-. *Awards, honors:* "Best Alaska Book, 1960," Golden North Press Association. *Interests:* Regional and natural resources; human geography; study of Alaska's aboriginal peoples; travel and study in Canada and Japan. *Published works: Alaska in Transition* (Johns Hopkins Press, 1960); *The Future of Alaska* (Johns Hopkins Press, 1962); *Alaska's Population of Economy, 1950-1980,* two vols. (University of Alaska, 1963).

ROGERS, WILL, Jr. (Cherokee) 1911- (actor, speaker)

Born October 20, 1911, New York, N.Y. *Education:* Stanford University, B.A., 1935. *Principal occupation:* Actor, speaker. *Home address:* 9538 Brighton Way, Beverly Hills, Calif. 90210. *Affiliations:* Publisher, *The Beverly Hills Citizen* (newspaper), 1935-53. *Military service:* U.S. Army (Bronze Star). *Community activities:* Member of Congress, 16th District, California. *Memberships:* Arrow, Inc. (honorary president); National Congress of American Indians.

ROSS, EDWARD HUNTER 1906- (museum curator)

Born May 31, 1906, Fort Screven, Ga. *Education:* Union College, B.A., 1927. *Principal occupation:* Museum curator. *Affiliations:* Museum curator, National Park Service, 1947-53; cataloguer, Colonial Williamsburg, 1953-56; curator of ethnology,

The Newark Museum, Newark, N.J. *Military service:* U.S. Army, 1943-47. *Memberships:* Archeological Society of New Jersey (vice president, 1965-). *Interests:* Ethnological and archaeological material from the Americas, Africa, the Pacific Islands, Australia; museum methods and techniques; archaeology of U.S. historic sites; archaeology of Britain; culture contacts; design forms; travel in Europe.

ROSS, LILLIE M. 1919- (writer)

Born January 6, 1919, Washington, Okla. *Principal occupation:* Writer. *Home address:* 8404 Montal St., Lamont, Calif. 93241. *Community activities:* Lamont Women's Club; Parent-Teachers' Association; Lamont Veterans of Foreign Wars Auxiliary (president). *Awards, honors:* Five Year Pin, Veterans of Foreign Wars Auxiliary; award, Parent-Teachers' Association. *Interests:* History and monuments. *Published works: Life of an Indian Captive* (Dorrance, 1965).

ROUCEK, JOSEPH S. 1902- (professor of sociology)

Born 1902, Prague, Czechoslovakia. *Education:* Prague Commercial Academy; University of Prague; Occidental College, B.A., 1925; New York University, M.A., 1927, Ph.D., 1937. *Principal occupation:* Professor of sociology. *Home address:* 395 Lakeside Drive, Bridgeport, Conn. 06606. *Affiliations:* Professor of social sciences, Centenary Junior College, 1929-33; Pennsylvania State University, 1933-35; New York University, 1935-39; Hofstra College, 1939-48; Kent State University, 1940; San Francisco State College, 1941-42, 1944-46; Reed College, 1941; College of the Pacific, 1942; consultant, Inter-American Workshop, New Mexico Highlands University, 1943; University of Wyoming, 1944; San Diego State College, 1945; Occidental College, 1945, 1948, 1949; professor and chairman, Departments of Sociology and Political Science, University of Bridgeport, 1948-; University of British Columbia, 1951; University of Puerto Rico, 1952; Portland Summer School, 1954. *Other occupations:* Concert pianist; lecturer; motion picture actor; vaudeville performer. *Memberships:* Instituto de Estudios Politicos, Madrid, Spain (honorary member). *Awards, honors:* Order of Knighthood of the Star of Romania, Romanian Government; Knighthood of the Crown of Yugoslavia, Yugoslavian Government; lecturer at various European universities. *Published works: The Working of the Minorities System Under the League of Nations* (Orbis, 1928); *Contemporary Roumania and Her Problems* (Stanford University, 1932); *The Poles in the United States of America* (Baltic Institute, 1937); *Our Racial and National Minorities,* with Francis J. Brown (Prentice-Hall, 1937, 1939); *Politics of the Balkans* (McGraw-Hill, 1939); *Contemporary World Politics,* with Francis J. Brown and Charles Hodges (John Wiley, 1939, 1940); *Introduction to Politics,* with Roy V. Peel (Thomas Y. Crowell Co., 1941); *Contemporary Europe* (D. Van Nostrand Co., 1941, 1947); editor, *Sociological Foundations of Education* (Thomas Y. Crowell Co., 1942); *One America,* with Francis J. Brown (Prentice-Hall, 1945, 1948, 1952); editor, *Central Eastern Europe: Crucible of World Wars* (Prentice-Hall, 1946); editor, *Twentieth Century Political Thought* (Philosophical Library, 1946); editor, *Governments and Politics Abroad* (Funk and Wagnalls, 1947); *Balkan Politics* (Stanford University, 1948); editor, *Social Control* (D. Van Nostrand Co., 1947, 1956); editor, *Slavonic Encyclopedia* (Philosophical Library, 1949); *Introduction to Political Science,* with George B. deHuszar (Thomas Y. Crowell Co., 1950); *Sociology: An Introduction,* with Roland L. Warren (Littlefield, Adams, 1951); co-editor, with others, *Contemporary Social Science,* two vols. (Stackpole Co., 1953, 1954); *The Development of Educational Sociology: School, Society and Sociology* (University of Bridgeport, 1956); editor, *Juvenile Delinquency* (Philosophical Library, 1958); editor, *Contemporary Sociology* (Philosophical Library, 1958); editor, with Howard B. Jacobsen, *Automation and Society* (Philosophical Library, 1959); editor, *The Challenge to Science Education* (Philosophical Library, 1949); editor, *Contemporary Political Ideologies* (Philosophical Library, 1960); editor, *Sociology of Crime* (Philosophical Library, 1960); collaborator and co-author, *The Heritage of American Education* (Allyn and Bacon, 1962); contributing editor, *A Mass Communications Dictionary* (Philosophical Library, 1962); *Behind the Iron Curtain,* with Kenneth V. Lottich (Caxton Printers, Ltd., 1964); editor, *The Difficult Child* (Philosophical Library, 1964); editor, *The Exceptional Child* (Philosophical Library, 1964); contributor to various encyclopedias and journals.

ROUEN, DAVID L. 1939- (educator)

Born February 9, 1939, Erie, Penna. *Education:* Slippery Rock State Teachers College, B.S., 1961; Northern Arizona University, M.A., 1965. *Principal occupation:* Educator. *Address:* Round Rock Day School, Bureau of Indian Affairs, Chinle, Ariz. *Affiliations:* Principal, Round Rock Day School, Bureau of Indian Affairs. *Military service:* U.S. Army. *Community activities:* Lions Club. *Memberships:* National Education Association; American Education Association; Council for Technological Advancement. *Awards, honors:* Most Valuable Player Award, Basketball (all-star team). *Interests:* Navajo Indians; hunting; basketball. *Published works: Locating the Achievement Decline of the Navaho Student in the Chinle Schools* (A.S.C., 1965).

ROUGEAU, MONROE 1930- (educator)

Born August 13, 1930, Boyce, La. *Education:* University of Southwestern Louisiana, B.S., 1952; University of Arkansas, M.Ed., 1955; University of Utah, Ph.D., 1963. *Principal occupation:* Educator. *Home address:* Sleetmute Day School, Bureau of Indian Affairs, Sleetmute, Alaska 99668. *Affiliations:* Principal-teacher, Sleetmute Day School, Bureau of Indian Affairs, Sleetmute, Alaska. *Other professional posts:* Former teacher, principal, superintendent. *Military service:* U.S. Army, 1952-54. *Community activities:* Village advisor in all affairs. *Memberships:* National Education Association. *Interests:* School administration; Alaskan natives.

ROVIN, CHARLES B. 1912- (social work administrator)

Born April 2, 1912, St. Louis, Mo. *Education:* University of Missouri, B.A., 1932; University of Chicago, M.A. (Social Service Administration), 1938. *Principal occupation:* Social work administrator. *Home address:* 5701 N. 18th Rd., Arlington, Va. 22205. *Affiliations:* Social worker and social work supervisor, Chicago Relief Administration, 1935-36; public assistance analyst, Bureau of Public Assistance, Social Security Board, Washington, D.C., 1938-42; worked with refugees and displaced persons, Germany and Switzerland, U.S. Army, 1942-46; area relocation officer, Muskogee Area Office, Bureau of Indian Affairs, 1950; assistant chief, Branch of Relocation, Bureau of Indian Affairs, 1951-55; chief, Branch of Welfare, Bureau of Indian Affairs, 1956-. *Military service:* U.S. Army, 1942-46. *Community activities:* Arlington Economic Opportunity Committee (board of directors). *Memberships:* American Public Welfare Association; National Association of Social Workers. *Interests:* "Make maximum contribution to helping Indian people develop their potential and cope with the serious problems facing them."

RUBY, ROBERT H.   1921-   (physician, surgeon)

Born April 23, 1921, Mabton, Wash. *Education:* Whitworth College, B.S., 1942; Washington University, M.D., 1945. *Principal occupation:* Physician, surgeon. *Home address:* 426 W. Northshore Drive, Moses Lake, Wash. *Military service:* U.S. Army, 1946-47; U.S. Public Health Service, 1953-54. *Community activities:* Moses Lake Library Board (chairman); Moses Lake Museum Board (chairman); Grant County Historical Society (director); Washington State Library Trustees (vice chairman). *Memberships:* American Medical Association; Washington State Medical Association; Grant County Medical Association. *Published works:* Oglala Sioux (Vantage Press, 1955); *Half-Sun on the Columbia* (University of Oklahoma Press, 1965).

RUNS ABOVE, MARVIN K.   (Rosebud Sioux) 1925-   (artist, leather craftsman)

Born May 19, 1925, Rosebud, S.D. *Education:* Elementary school. *Home address:* General Delivery, Parmelee, S.D. 57566. *Community activities:* Tribal police officer; Alcoholics Anonymous, Rosebud Reservation. *Interests:* Mr. Runs Above writes, "Leather craft is my primary vocational interest; welding and ranching are avocational interests -- also bareback and bronc riding in rodeos."

RUSH, ERNEST, Sr.   (Cherokee)   1901- (teacher)

Born August 24, 1901, Mt. Calm, Hill County, Texas. *Education:* Highlands University, B.A., 1955. *Principal occupation:* Teacher. *Address:* Tuntutuliak, Alaska 99680. *Affiliations:* Principal-teacher, Tuntutuliak Day School, Bureau of Indian Affairs, Tuntutuliak, Alaska. *Military service:* U.S. Army Air Force, civilian training administrator, Fort Sumner Air Field, 1943-45. *Community activities:* Boy Scouts of America (former scoutmaster).

RUSHMORE, HELEN   1898-   (teacher, writer)

Born January 19, 1898, Independence, Kan. *Education:* University of Tulsa, B.A., M.A. *Principal occupation:* Teacher. *Home address:* 1537 S. Delaware, Tulsa, Okla. 74104. *Memberships:* National Education Association; Oklahoma Education Association; Order of the Eastern Star; Oklahoma Historical Society; National League of American Penwomen. *Interests:* Writing for children; fishing; Indian silverwork; travel throughout the United States, Canada, and Mexico. *Published works:* The Shadow of Robbers Roost (World, 1960); *The Dancing Horses of Acoma* (World, 1963); *Chief Takes Over* (Harcourt, Brace & World).

RUSKIN, GERTRUDE McDARIS   (Cherokee) (author)

Born Swannanoa, N.C. *Education:* Normal school. *Principal occupation:* "Keeping before the public the true history and traditions of the Cherokee people." *Home address:* Tall Timbers, 2663 Fair Oaks Rd., Decatur, Ga. 30031. *Community activities:* Mrs. Ruskin has held membership in various women's organizations and has served variously as the drama chairman, pageantry chairman and Indian affairs chairman of several of these. In addition, she is the official ambassador of the Cherokee Nation. *Memberships:* Standingdeer Tribe (scribe). *Awards, honors:* Honorary chief of the Cherokees (honorary name, Princess Chewani). *Interests:* Mrs. Ruskin is very much interested in the history and traditions of the Cherokee people. She has been active in many related historic preservation movements, has written and published several books on the Cherokees, and maintains an extensive collection of Cherokee artifacts. *Published works: Chief Standing Deer* (privately printed, 1956); *John Ross, Chief of an Eagle Race* (privately printed, 1963); is now arranging publication of drama on Sequoyah and is writing a major work based on research conducted over a thirty-year period.

RUSSELL, FRANCIS 1910- (writer)

Born December 10, 1910, Boston, Mass. *Education:* University of Breslau, 1931-32; Harvard University, M.A., 1937. *Principal occupation:* Writer. *Home address:* 24 Cunningham Rd., Wellesley Hills, Mass. 02181. *Military service:* Canadian Army, 1941-46. *Memberships:* Authors' Guild; Black Watch Association; Goethe Society. *Awards, honors:* Guggenheim Fellow, 1964, 1965; award, Mystery Writers of America, 1962. *Interests:* History; German; ornithology; travel throughout Europe. *Published works: Three Studies in Twentieth Century Obscurity* (Hunt and Flowes, 1954); *Tragedy in Nedhorn* (1962); *American Heritage Book of the Pioneer Spirit* (1959); *The Great Interlude* (McGraw-Hill, 1964).

RUSSELL, SOLVEIG PAULSON (Mrs. E.C.) 1904- (writer)

Born March 28, 1904, Salt Lake City, Utah. *Education:* University of Oregon, B.S., 1936. *Principal occupation:* Writer of children's books and magazine material. *Home address:* 1635 State St., Salem, Ore. 97301. *Memberships:* Authors' Guild of America; National Writers Club. *Interests:* Craftwork -- weaving, woodcarving, etc.; photography; summer camping trips into British Columbia. *Published works: Trees for Tomorrow, Wildlife for Tomorrow, Fruits, Nuts, Navaho Land, Yesterday and Today* (Melmont Publishers, Inc.); *A Is for Apple and Why, Sugaring Time* (Abingdon Press); *All Kinds of Legs, What Good Is a Tail?, Sound, Indian Big and Indian Little* (Bobbs-Merrill); *From Rocks to Rockets, From Barter to Gold, Wonderful Stuff, the Story of Clay* (Rand McNally); *This Home for Me* (Broadman Press); *Lines and Shapes* (Henry Z. Walck); *Study of Trees Made Simple* (Ken Publishing Co.); 1,697 verses, stories and articles in various children's magazines; four additional titles in progress, expected publication in 1966.

RYAN, J.C. 1889- (writer)

Born October 25, 1889, Muscatine, Iowa. *Education:* Cornell College, B.A., 1915. *Principal occupation:* Industrial executive (retired), writer. *Home address:* 5221 Nina Drive, Tucson, Ariz. 85704. *Affiliations:* Sales manager, Paper and Zinc Departments, Ball Brothers Co., Muncie, Ind., 1922-44; executive vice president for operations, Ray-O-Vac Co., Madison, Wis., 1944-57. *Community activities:* Salvation Army (chairman, advisory board); Tucson Fund-Raising Review Board (chairman); Red Cross (chairman, blood bank committee). *Awards, honors:* Cornell College Alumni Achievement Award, 1958; Tucson Man of the Year, 1961; Spur Award for writing of the American West, Western Writers of America, 1964-65. *Published works: A Skeptic Dude in Arizona* (Naylor, 1962); *Revolt Along the Rio Grande* (Naylor, 1965); *Uncle Jack Saw Custer Fall* (in press).

S

SAINTE-MARIE, BUFFY (Cree) 1942- (folksinger, poet)

Born February 20, 1942, Craven, Sask., Can. *Education:* University of Massachusetts, B.A. (Philosophy), 1963. *Principal occupation:* Folksinger, poet. *Address:* c/o Herbert S. Gart, 161 W. 54th St., New York, N.Y. 10019. *Affiliations:* Recording artist, Vanguard Recording Society. *Other occupations:* Free-lance writer on Indian culture and affairs; associate editor, *The Native Voice* (Vancouver, B.C., Can.). *Interests:* Lecturing on Indian affairs; composing; singing. Miss Sainte-Marie writes, "I am best known for songs and poems directly related to past and present American Indian affairs. (I have contributed) to *The Native Voice, Thunderbird, American Indian Horizons, and Boston Broadside* in the fields of North American Indian music and Indian affairs. Have lived on and visited reserves (reservations) in fifteen states and four provinces; have traveled, lectured and sung in England, France, Canada, Italy, and Mexico, and have given performances in concert and on television internationally and in all major American cities."

SAUBEL, KATHERINE SIVA (Cahuilla) 1920- (museum trustee)

Born March 7, 1920, Los Coyotes Reservation, Calif. *Principal occupation:* Museum trustee. *Education:* University of Colorado. *Home address:* Box 373, Banning, Calif. 92220. *Affiliations:* Trustee, Malki Museum, Banning, Calif.; Los Coyotes Tribal Council. *Community activities:* Veterans of Foreign Wars (historian). *Awards, honors:* Scholarship, Indian Leadership Training Program, University of Colorado. *Published works: Economic Botany of the Cahuilla Indian,* with Lowell John Bear (Riverside County Museum, 1966).

SAUL, C. TERRY (Tobaksi)   (Choctaw-
    Chickasaw) 1921- (artist)

Born April 2, 1921, Sardis, Okla. *Education:* Bacone Junior College, 1940; University of Oklahoma, B.F.A., 1948, M.F.A., 1949; Art Students' League, New York, N.Y., 1951-52. *Principal occupation:* Commercial artist. *Home address:* 1536 Maple Ave., Bartlesville, Okla. 74003. *Affiliations:* Owner and operator, Village Arts Studio, 1950; technical illustrator and staff artist, Curtis-Wright, Garfield, N.J.; commercial artist, Phillips Petroleum Co., Bartlesville, Okla., 1955-; "I have a studio in my home and paint for various Indian shows and exhibits and commissioned murals and paintings." *Military service:* U.S. Army, 45th and 65th Infantry Divs., 1940-45 (Purple Heart, Bronze Star, American Defense Service Ribbon, Good Conduct Medal). *Memberships:* Art Students' League, New York, N.Y. (life member). *Awards, honors:* Numerous awards received from American Indian Exposition, Anadarko, Okla.; National Indian Art Show, Bismarck, N.D.; Denver Art Museum; Gilcrease Museum, Tulsa, Okla.; Inter-Tribal Indian Ceremonial, Gallup, N.M.; Philbrook Art Center, Tulsa, Okla.; American Indian Exposition, Charlotte, N.C.; Museum of New Mexico, Santa Fe, N.M.; National Indian Arts Exhibitions, Scottsdale, Ariz.; All-American Indian Days, Sheridan, Wyo. Numerous one-man and group shows, traveling exhibitions, etc. Represented in many museums, and in private and public collections throughout the United States and in Denmark, Austria, The Netherlands, Germany, and in several foreign embassies.

SCHAAFSMA, POLLY DIX   1935-
    (research writer)

Born October 24, 1935, Springfield, Vt. *Education:* Mount Holyoke College, B.A., 1957; University of Colorado, M.A., 1962. *Principal occupation:* Research writer. *Home address:* Box 776, Arroyo Hondo, N.M. 87513. *Affiliations:* Non-staff research archaeologist, Museum of New Mexico; research writer, Museum of Navajo Ceremonial Art, Santa Fe, N.M. *Memberships:* Society for American Archaeology, 1961-. *Interests:* Prehistoric Indian rock art, particularly of the Navajo and Pueblo cultures of the Southwest; evolution and stylistic development of art forms; Indian religion; primitive art; travels to Mexico. *Published works: Rock Art of the Navajo Reservoir District* (Museum of New Mexico, 1963); *Southwest Indian Pictographs and Petroglyphs* (Museum of New Mexico, 1965).

SCHEELE, WILLIAM E.   1920-
    (museum director)

Born 1920, Cleveland, Ohio. *Education:* Cleveland School of Art; Western Reserve University. *Principal occupation:* Museum director. *Affiliations:* Director, Cleveland Museum of Natural History. *Military service:* U.S. Army, 1942-46. *Interests:* Painting subjects of natural history; gem cutting; fossil hunting. *Published works: The Mound Builders* (World, 1960); *The Earliest Americans* (World, 1963).

SCHELL, ROLFE F.   1917- (writer,
    engineer)

Born November 27, 1917, Keeseville, N.Y. *Education:* Cornell University, B.S., 1940. *Principal occupation:* Writer, engineer. *Memberships:* Cornell Society of Engineers. *Interests:* Photography; Yucatan. *Biographical sources: Who's Who in Florida,* 1965. *Published works: A Yank in Yucatan* (1963), *One Thousand Years on Mound Key* (1963), *Florida's Fascinating Everglades* (1963), all published by Island Press.

SCHILDT, GARY (Blackfeet)   1938-
    (artist, sculptor)

Born June 5, 1938, Helena, Mont. *Education:* City College of San Francisco, A.A., 1962. *Principal occupation:* Artist, sculptor. *Home address:* P.O. Box 43, Browning, Mont. 59417. *Awards, honors:* Scholastic scholarship to San Francisco Academy of Fine Arts awarded by the City College of San Francisco; numerous first place awards in amateur and professional art shows. Mr. Schildt writes, "I have shown my work in . . . Washington, D.C.; Cooper Gallery, Helena, Mont.; Russell Gallery, Great Falls, Mont.; Art in the Park, Great Falls, Mont.; First Annual Art Exhibit, East Glacier Park, Mont.; and several local art exhibits. I have permanent showings in the Saddle Back Inn, Los Angeles, Calif.; Flathead Lake Galleries, Big Fork, Mont.; Galleria del Monte, Santa Barbara, Calif.; Trailside Galleries, Jackson Hole, Wyo.; and am represented in many private collections." Mr. Schildt's illustrations appear in *The Big North* (Tasher Association, 1966).

SCHNEIDER, DAVID M.   1918-
   (anthropologist)

Born November 11, 1918, New York, N.Y. *Education:* Cornell University, B.S., 1940; Harvard University, Ph.D., 1949 *Principal occupation:* Anthropologist. *Home address:* 5518 S. Harper Ave., Chicago, Ill. 60637. *Memberships:* American Anthropological Association (Fellow); Royal Anthropological Institute (Fellow); Association of Social Anthropologists (Fellow).

SCHOENWETTER, JAMES   1935-
   (archaeological palynologist)

Born January 2, 1935, Chicago, Ill. *Education:* University of Arizona, M.S., 1960; Southern Illinois University, Ph.D., 1966. *Principal occupation:* Archaeological palynologist. *Home address:* 1924 Hopi Rd., Santa Fe, N.M. *Affiliations:* Curator, Museum of New Mexico. *Memberships:* Society for American Archaeology, 1956-. *Interests:* Anthropological theory; cultural ecology; archaeology; general botany; ecology and paleoecology; paleoclimatology; field work in the American Southwest, Great Lakes area, Mississippi Valley, and northern and central Mexico. *Published works: Alluvial and Palynological Reconstruction of Environments* (University of New Mexico, 1964); *The Reconstruction of Past Environments* (Fort Burgwin Press, 1964).

SCHOLDER, FRITZ   (Mission)   1937-
   (artist)

Born October 6, 1937, Breckenridge, Minn. *Education:* Sacramento State College, B.A., 1960; University of Arizona, M.F.A., 1964. *Principal occupation:* Artist. *Home address:* Box 4712, Santa Fe, N.M. 87501. *Affiliations:* Instructor of advanced painting, Institute of American Indian Arts, Santa Fe, N.M. *Memberships:* National Board of Academic Development of the World University Roundtable. *Awards, honors:* Tucson Festival Award, Tenth Southwestern Painters' Festival Show, Tucson Art Center, 1960; First Prize (oils), First California Spring Festival Exhibition, Sacramento, Calif., 1961; Ford Foundation Purchase Award, "The Southwest: Painting and Sculpture," Houston Museum of Fine Arts, 1962; Edwin B. Hopkins Purchase Award in Drawing, Thirteenth Southwestern Drawing and Print Show, Dallas Museum of Fine Arts, 1963; First Prize for Painting by an American Artist, West Virginia Centennial Exhibition of Painting and Sculpture, Huntington Galleries, 1963; Hallmark Purchase Award, Tenth Mid-America Annual Exhibition, Nelson Gallery of Art, Kansas City, Mo. Numerous exhibitions throughout the United States; exhibition at the Palacio de la Virreina, Barcelona, Spain.

SCHOLES, WALTER V.   1916-
   (professor)

Born July 26, 1916, Bradford, Ill. *Education:* University of Michigan, Ph.D., 1944. *Principal occupation:* Professor. *Home address:* 1515 Ross, Columbia, Mo. *Affiliations:* Professor, University of Missouri, 1944-. *Memberships:* American Historical Society; Mississippi Valley Historical Association; Conference on Latin American Diplomacy. *Published works: Diego Ramirez Visita* (University of Missouri Press, 1946); editor, *Mexico During the War with the U.S.* (University of Missouri Press, 1950); *Mexican Politics During the Juarez Regime* (University of Missouri Press, 1957).

SCHULZ, PAUL E.   1910-   (naturalist, interpreter)

Born September 24, 1910, Bremen, Germany. *Education:* University of California, B.A., 1933. *Principal occupation:* Naturalist, interpreter. *Home address:* 4850 Read Rd., New Orleans, La. 70127. *Af-*

filiations: Regional naturalist, Southeast Regional Office, National Park Service; park naturalist, Lassen Volcanic and Grand Canyon National Parks; geologist, Hawaii National Park. *Military service:* U.S. Army. *Interests:* Natural history; geology and ecology. Travels in Europe and the United States, "backjacking on the Appalachian Trail." *Published works: Lassen's Place Names* (Loomis Museum Association); *Geology of Lassen's Landscapes* (Loomis Museum Association); *Indians of the Lassen Volcano National Park Vicinity* (Loomis Museum Association).

SCHUNK, HAROLD W.   (Yankton Sioux)
   1907-   (B.I.A. agency superintendent)

Born July 25, 1907, Philip, S.D. *Education:* Southern State College, B.S., 1931; graduate work, South Dakota State University, 1951, 1952, 1953. *Principal occupation:* B.I.A. agency superintendent. *Home address:* Rosebud, S.D. 57570. *Affiliations:* Public school teacher, 1931-33; manager, Civilian Conservation Camp, Bureau of Indian Affairs; head teacher, Cherry Creek, S.D., Day School, Bureau of Indian Affairs; teacher, Cheyenne River Boarding School, Bureau of Indian Affairs; superintendent, Sisseton Agency, Bureau of Indian Affairs, 1952-54; superintendent, Turtle Mountain Consolidated Agency, Bureau of Indian Affairs, 1954-57; superintendent, Fort Yates Agency, Bureau of Indian Affairs, 1957-59; superintendent, Rosebud Agency, Bureau of Indian Affairs, 1959-. *Military service:* U.S. Army, 1943-46. *Community activities:* Veterans of Foreign Wars (commander, 1949-50; district commander, 1951); Kiwanis Club (director, 1956); Todd County Lions Club (president, 1964); Boy Scouts of America; Episcopal Church (lay reader); Masons; Scottish Rite and Shrine, Aberdeen, S.D.; York Rite, Sisseton, S.D. *Memberships:* South Dakota Historical Society (member, executive board; president, 1963-). *Awards, honors:* Citation, Rosebud Tribal Council; Twenty-five Year Pin, Boy Scouts of America, for many offices and positions held. *Interests:* "Public relations for the Indian people." Mr. Schunk maintains an extensive library on Indians, Indian affairs, and related subjects.

SCHWARTZ, MELVIN L.   1919-   (B.I.A. agency superintendent)

Born October 13, 1919, McClusky, N.D. *Principal occupation:* B.I.A. agency superintendent. *Home address:* P.O. Box 85, Fort Duchesne, Utah 84026. *Affiliations:* Superintendent, Uintah and Ouray Agency, Bureau of Indian Affairs, Fort Duchesne, Utah. *Military service:* U.S. Army.

SCUDDER, RALPH EDWIN   1901-
   (teacher, educational administrator)

Born February 4, 1901, Vevay, Ind. *Education:* State Teachers College, B.A., 1926; Montana University, M.A., 1940. *Principal occupation:* Teacher, educational administrator. *Home address:* 632 W. Pilger, Roseburg, Ore. 97470. *Affiliations:* Superintendent of schools, Argos, Ind., 1928-30; principal, high school, Valley City, N.D., 1932; public school teacher, Glendive, Mont., 1933-35; school superintendent, Montana, 1937-41, 1945-58. *Community activities:* Rotary Club (president, 1939). *Memberships:* Oregon Education Association; Roseburg Education Association; Montana Education Association (president, 1940). *Interests:* Color photography; travel in the United States. *Published works: Custer Country* (Binfords and Mort, 1963).

SCULL, FLORENCE DOUGHTY   1905-
   (school administrator)

Born June 16, 1905, Somers Point, N.J. *Education:* State Normal School, N.J., Diploma, 1924; Teachers College, Columbia University, B.S., 1931, M.A., 1934; University of California, Berkeley, 1937; Rutgers University. *Principal occupation:* School administrator. *Home address:* 41 E. Meyran Ave., Somers Point, N.J. 08244. *Affiliations:* Elementary teacher, New Jersey, 1924-30; superintendent of schools, Somers Point, N.J., 1934-46; principal, Lincoln Elementary School, N.J., 1946-64 (retired). *Community activities:* Somers Point Public Library (librarian); New Brunswick Branch, Zonta International (president); American Association of University Women (corresponding secretary, program chairman); Daughters of the American Revolution. *Memberships:* Atlantic County Historical Society; New Jersey Education Association, 1924-; National Education Association, 1924-; New Jersey Parent-Teachers' Association, 1924- (life member); Somers Point Parent-Teachers' Association (president, 1934-36); National Retired Teachers Association, 1964-; principals' associations. *Interests:* Elementary school supervision and administration; writing for children; travel to Europe, Canada, Bermuda, Nassau, and throughout the United States. *Published works: Bear Teeth for Courage* (Van Nostrand, 1964).

SEABOURN, BERT D.   (Cherokee)
1931-   (artist)

Born July 9, 1931, Iraan, Texas. *Education:* Oklahoma City University. *Principal occupation:* Artist. *Home address:* 3123 S.W. 63rd St., Oklahoma City, Okla. 73159. *Affiliations:* Oklahoma Gas and Electric Co. *Military service:* U.S. Navy, 1951-55. *Community activities:* Yukon Chamber of Commerce. *Memberships:* Oklahoma City Art Directors Club (editor, *Mosaic,* Club's monthly publication); Oklahoma City Art Guild. *Awards, honors:* Favorite Painting Award, Oklahoma City Festival of the Arts, 1960; Third Place, Oklahoma City Art Show, 1960; Third Award, Plains Division, Inter-Tribal Indian Ceremonial, 1965.

SEARS, WILLIAM H.   1920-
(archaeologist)

Born December 17, 1920, Valley Stream, N.Y. *Education:* University of Chicago, M.A., 1947; University of Michigan, Ph.D., 1951. *Principal occupation:* Archaeologist. *Home address:* 771 N.E. 32nd St., Boca Raton, Fla. *Affiliations:* Assistant professor, University of Georgia, 1948-55; assistant curator, curator, professor, Florida State Museum, 1955-64; professor, Florida Atlantic University, 1964-. *Other professional posts:* Archaeologist, Georgia Department of State Parks, 1948-54. *Military service:* U.S. Marine Corps, 1942-45. *Memberships:* Society for American Archaeology (vice president); American Archaeological Association, 1948- (Fellow). *Interests:* The prehistory of the southeastern United States; field research and excavations. *Published works: Excavations at Kolomoki: Final Report* (University of Georgia Press, 1956); many technical reports in journals, 1948-.

SEELEY, ELIZABETH STERLING
(museum curator)

Born Bridgeport, Conn. *Education:* Miss Fanny Smith School; Masters School. *Principal occupation:* Museum curator. *Home address:* 63 Brooklawn Ave., Bridgeport, Conn. *Affiliations:* Office worker, Bullard Co., Bridgeport, Conn., 1942-46; curator, The Barnum Museum, 1950-. *Community activities:* Daughters of the American Revolution (public relations chairman). *Memberships:* Bridgeport Historical Society (founder, director, vice president); Antiquarian and Landmarks Society of Connecticut; National Trust for Historic Preservation; Stratford Historical Society; Fairfield Historical Society; Monroe Historical Society; Circus Historical Society; Circus Fans of America; P. T. Barnum Top (treasurer); Junior League of Bridgeport; The Somers Circus Museum (advisory board); American Association of Museums. *Interests:* Genealogical research; history of Connecticut and the United States; visiting historic spots; collecting circus material; lecturing.

SELLS, RANDY L.   1935-   (education specialist)

Born October 10, 1935, Carnegie, Okla. *Education:* Southwestern State College, Weatherford, Okla., B.S., 1960, M.S., 1965. *Principal occupation:* Education specialist. *Home address:* 1009 Old Mescalero Rd., Tularosa, N.M. 88352. *Affiliations:* Education specialist (adult education), Bureau of Indian Affairs, Tularosa, N.M. *Military service:* U.S. Marine Corps, 1954-57 (Good Conduct Medal). *Community activities:* Boy Scouts of America; 4-H Club. *Interests:* Education and psychology; anthropology and sociology.

SENECA, MARTIN   (Seneca)   1912-
(tribal officer)

Born August 8, 1912, Erie County, N.Y. *Education:* Bacone Junior College. *Principal occupation:* Tribal officer. *Home address:* Box 177, Versailles, N.Y. 14168. *Affiliations:* Machinist and supervisor, Gowanda State Hospital; president, Seneca Nation of Indians. *Military service:* U.S. Army Air Corps, 1942-43. *Community activities:* Executive director, Public Housing, Gowanda, N.Y.; Masons.

SETON, JULIA M.   (Julia M. Buttree)
1889- (writer, lecturer)

Born May 15, 1889, New York, N.Y. *Education:* Hunter College, B.A., 1909. *Principal occupation:* Writer, lecturer. *Home address:* Seton Village, Santa Fe, N.M. 87502. *Affiliations:* Co-founder, Seton Village, Santa Fe, N.M. *Community activities:* Community theater. *Memberships:* American Museum of Natural History. *Interests:* Lecturing throughout Europe and America. *Published works: Rhythm of the Redman,* as Julia M. Buttree; *Pulse of the Pueblo; Indian Creation Stories; Trail and Campfire Stories; American Indian Art; Indian Costume Book; Gospel of the Redman,* with Ernest Thompson Seton; *Sing, Sing, What Shall I Sing;* various magazine articles and stories.

SHABAGLIAN, SARAH K.   1919-
(historical society director)

Born September 19, 1919, New Britain, Penna. *Education:* University of Pennsylvania, B.A. (Art Education), 1940; Teachers College, Columbia University, M.A. (Education). *Principal occupation:* Historical society director. *Affiliations:* Director, Huntington Historical Society. *Military service:* American Red Cross, Italy, Okinawa, 1945-48. *Memberships:* Long Island Historical Society.

SHANNON, TERRY (writer)

Born Bellingham, Wash. *Education:* Washington State College, 1924-27, 1940-41; University of Washington, 1945; University of California, Los Angeles, 1956. *Principal occupation:* Writer. *Home address:* 605 Jasmine Ave., Corona del Mar, Calif. 92625. *Awards, honors:* Junior Literary Guild Awards for *. . and Juan; Kidlik's Kayak; Running Fox, the Eagle Hunter.* Boys' Clubs of America Junior Book Awards for *About Caves* (1961); *A Trip to Mexico* (1962). *Interests:* American Indian cultures (especially Southwest and the Northwest Coast); archaeology and oceanography. *Travels:* Europe, Canada, and Mexico. *Published works:* Miss Shannon writes, "Please note that I am only half the team -- I work with artist Charles Payzant -- together we form the author-artist team of Shannon-Payzant." *Today is Story Day,*

Wheels Across America (Aladdin, 1954); *A Trip to Paris* (1959), *A Trip to Mexico* (1961), *A Trip to Quebec* (1963), *Children's Press; Trail of the Wheel* (1962), *Red is for Luck* (1963), *Around the World with Gogo* (1964), *Saucer in the Sea* (1965), *Man in the Sea* (1966), *Golden Gate Junior Books; Jumper, Santa's Little Reindeer,* (Jolly Books, Avon Publishing Co., 1952); *About Caves* (1960), *About Ready-to-Wear Clothes* (1961), *About Food and Where It Comes From* (1961), *About Land, the Rain, and Us* (1963), *A Dog Team for Ongluk* (1962), *A Playmate for Puna* (1963), Melmont Publishers, Inc.; *Among the Rocks* (1956), *At Water's Edge* (1955), Sterling Publishing Co.; *Little Wolf, the Rain Dancer* (1954), *Tyee's Totem Pole* (1955), *Come Summer, Come Winter* (1956), *Running Fox, the Eagle Hunter* (1957), *Desert Dwellers* (1958), *Where Animals Live* (1958), *Kidlik's Kayak* (1959), *The Wonderland of Plants* (1960), *. . .and Juan* (1961), *Stones, Bones and Arrowheads* (1962), *Wakapoo and the Flying Arrows* (1963), Albert Whitman & Co.

SHAPP, MARTHA   1910- (educator)

Born January 16, 1910, New York, N.Y. *Education:* Barnard College, B.A., 1929; Teachers College, Columbia University, M.A., 1940. *Principal occupation:* Educator. *Home address:* 166 E. 61st St., New York, N.Y. 10021. *Affiliations:* Educational research, National Council, Y.M.C.A., 1930-33; elementary school teacher, New York City public schools, 1933-49; curriculum research, Bureau of Curriculum Research, New York City Board of Education, 1949-53; curriculum coordinator, New York City elementary schools, 1953-60; editor-in-chief, *Book of Knowledge,* 1960-. *Other professional posts:* Member, Clinton (N.Y.) Youth Commission, 1947-49. *Memberships:* Association for Supervision and Curriculum Development; New York State Association for Supervision and Curriculum Development; Association for Childhood Education International; National Council for Geographic Education; National Council on Social Studies; National Council of Administrative Women in Education; New York State English Council; International Reading Association; New York Society for Experimental Study in Education; Women's City Club. *Published works: Let's Find Out Books,* with Charles Schapp; numerous educational filmstrips.

SHARP, EDITH LAMBERT 1917-
(writer)

Born March 7, 1917, Brandon, Man., Can.
Principal occupation: Writer. *Home address:* 445 Martin St., Penticton, British Columbia, Can. *Community activities:* Okanagan Summer School of the Arts (director). *Memberships:* Conservative Association; Community Arts Council; Penticton Chamber of Commerce; Business and Professional Women's Club (honorary member); Penticton Writers' Group (honorary member). *Awards, honors:* Little, Brown of Canada Award; Canadian Governor General's Medal for juvenile novel; Hans Christian Andersen Diploma of Merit (Luxembourg). *Published works: Nkwala* (Little, Brown of Canada, 1958); *The Little People of Crazy Mountain* (T. Nelson & Sons, 1963).

SHAVER, RALPH K. 1906- (monument
superintendent)

Born December 25, 1906, Rowan County, N.C. *Education:* Catawba College, B.A., 1931; University of Idaho, M.S. *Principal occupation:* Monument superintendent. *Home address:* Pipestone National Monument, Pipestone, Minn. 56164. *Affiliations:* Division of Resource Management and Visitor Protection, Pipestone National Monument (National Park Service). *Military service:* U.S. Air Force (Good Conduct Medal, Battle Star, Pacific Theater Medal). *Community activities:* Lions Club; United Commercial Travelers. *Memberships:* National Wildlife Federation; National Geographic Society.

SHELTON, DONALD 1923- (teacher)

Born February 28, 1923. *Education:* University of Maryland; Union College, B.A., 1962. *Principal occupation:* Teacher. *Address:* Canyon Village, Alaska. *Affiliations:* Teacher, Canyon Village Instructional Aid School, Bureau of Indian Affairs, Canyon Village, Alaska. *Military service:* U.S. Marine Corps, 1942-46; U.S. Air Force, 1955-59.

SHERWOOD, MORGAN B. 1929-
(assistant professor of history)

Born October 22, 1929, Anchorage, Alaska.
Education: San Diego State College, B.A., 1953; University of California, Berkeley, Ph.D., 1962. *Principal occupation:* Assistant professor of history. *Affiliations:* Assistant professor, University of Cincinnati, 1964-65; assistant professor of history, University of California at Davis, 1965-. *Military service:* U.S. Army, 1953-54. *Memberships:* American Historical Association; Organization of American Historians; Western History Association. *Interests:* Alaskan history; history of the American West; history of science in America. *Published works: Exploration of Alaska, 1865-1900.* (Yale University Press, 1965); co-editor, *The Politics of American Science* (Rand McNally, 1965).

SHIRK, GEORGE H. 1913- (attorney)

Born May 1, 1913, Oklahoma City, Okla. *Education:* University of Oklahoma, B.A., 1935, LL.B., 1936. *Principal occupation:* Attorney. *Affiliations:* Attorney, Bar of the Supreme Court of the United States. *Military service:* U.S. Army (Legion of Merit, Bronze Star, Croix de Guerre, Chevalier, French Legion of Honor). *Memberships:* Phi Delta Phi; Phi Delta Theta; Oklahoma Historical Society, 1959- (president); Greater Oklahoma City Safety Council (president, 1959-63); Oklahoma Civil War Centennial Commission. *Awards, honors:* Elected to Oklahoma Alpha Chapter, Phi Beta Kappa, 1965. *Published works: A Rambler in Oklahoma* (Harlow, 1953); co-editor, *Oklahoma Place Names* (University of Oklahoma, 1965).

SIDES, DOROTHY S. 1902- (technical
illustrator)

Born July 4, 1902, Rochester, N.Y. *Education:* University of Rochester, Bevier Art School, B.A., 1919; Accademia di Belle Arti, Florence, Italy; Ecole de Colarossi, Paris, France, 1924. *Principal occupation:* Technical illustrator. *Affiliations:* Draftsman, Food Machinery Corp., Riverside, Calif., 1944-47; design instructor, Riverside Junior College, 1944-47; assistant chief engineer, Vacu-Blast Corp., Belmont, Calif., 1950-59. *Awards, honors:* U.S. Government "E" Award, "Water Buffalo" design, 1946; First Prize, Copenhagen Institute of Indian Ceramic Design, 1936; Leading Women of America Award for

Decorative Art of the Southwest Indians,
1939. *Interests:* Technical illustration;
industrial design; book illustration; archi-
tecture; inter-American relationships; tra-
vel throughout the United States, the South
Seas, Brazil, Europe, and the Middle East.
*Published works: Decorative Art of the
Southwest Indians* (Fine Arts Press, 1936;
Dover Publications, 1961; Peter Smith);
California Missions (Fine Arts Press,
1937); *Seven Questions of Tihur* (Fine Arts
Press, 1938).

SILVERBERG, ROBERT (Walter Drummond, Ivar Jorgensen, Calvin M. Knox,
David Osborne, Robert Randall)
(writer)

Born New York, N.Y. *Education:* Columbia University, B.A., 1956. *Principal occupation:* Writer. *Home address:* 5020
Goodridge Ave., New York, N.Y. *Interests:*
Mr. Silverberg sold a science fiction novel
while a sophomore in college and has been
writing ever since. His major interests
center on archaeological, anthropological
and historical subjects. He has traveled
widely in the United States and abroad.
*Published works: Treasures Beneath the
Sea* (Whitman, 1960); *Lost Cities and Vanished Civilizations* (Chilton, 1962); *Empires
in the Dust* (Chilton, 1963); *Home of the Red
Man: Indian North America Before Columbus* (New York Graphic Society, 1963); *The
Old Ones: Indians of the American Southwest*
(New York Graphic Society, 1965); and many
others.

SLATE, GORDON R.   1936- (teacher)

Born October 31, 1936, Burns, Ore. *Education:* Central Oregon College, Certificate, 1957; University of Oregon, B.S.,
1960. *Principal occupation:* Teacher. *Address:* c/o Mt. Village Day School, Bureau
of Indian Affairs, Mt. Village, Alaska 99632.
Affiliations: Teacher, Eureka City Schools,
Eureka, Calif., 1959-63; teacher, Hooper
Bay School, Bureau of Indian Affairs, Hooper Bay, Alaska, 1963-64; teacher-princi-
pal, Mt. Village Day School, Bureau of Indian Affairs, Mt. Village, Alaska, 1964-.

Military service: Army National Guard,
1958-65.

SMITH, CARLYLE S.   1915- (professor
of anthropology, museum curator)

Born March 8, 1915, Great Neck, N.Y.
Education: Columbia University, B.A.,
1938, Ph.D., 1949. *Principal occupation:*
Professor of anthropology, museum curator. *Affiliations:* Field unit supervisor,
Archaeological Survey of Nebraska, 1939;
assistant, Hudson Valley Archaeological
Survey, 1940; laboratory supervisor, Archaeological Survey of Louisiana, 1940-41;
archaeologist, Norwegian Archaeological
Expedition to Easter Island, 1955-56; professor of anthropology, University of Kansas, 1960-; curator of anthropology, Museum of Natural History, University of Kansas, Lawrence, Kan., 1960-. *Military service:* U.S. Army Air Force, 1943-46.
Memberships: American Anthropological
Association, 1938-; American Ethnological
Society, 1938-; Society for American Archaeology, 1938-; Sigma Xi. *Awards, honors:* Member, National Research Council,
1961-64; National Science Foundation
Grants, 1963-65; American Philosophical
Society Grants, 1960, 1964; travel grants;
Fellow, Company of Military Historians,
1964. *Interests:* Expeditions and field work
in New York, 1932-46; North Dakota, 1938;
Nebraska, 1939; Louisiana, 1940-41; Kansas, 1947-; South Dakota, 1950-53, 1955,
1959; Easter Island and the East Pacific,
1955-56; France, 1960; Hiva Oa, French
Polynesia, 1963; Italy, 1964. *Published
works: The Archaeology of Coastal New
York* (American Museum of Natural History, Anthropological Publications, Vol.
43, 1950); *The Spain Site, a Winter Village
in Fort Randall Reservoir, South Dakota,*
with Roger Grange, Jr. (Smithsonian Institution, Bureau of American Ethnology, Bulletin No. 169, 1958); co-author, *Archaeology of Easter Island* (Reports of the Norwegian Archaeological Expedition to Easter
Island and the East Pacific, 1961).

SMITH, DELBERT J.   1933- (educator)

Born October 5, 1933, Beelick Knob, W.
Va. *Education:* Ohio State University,
B.S., 1959. *Principal occupation:* Educa-
tor. Address: c/o Nunapitchuk Day School,
Bureau of Indian Affairs, Nunapitchuk,

Alaska. *Affiliations:* Principal-teacher, Nunapitchuk Day School, Bureau of Indian Affairs, Nunapitchuk, Alaska. Military service: U.S. Marine Corps, 1952-55. *Memberships:* American Physical Therapy Association; Photographic Society of America.

SMITH, DON LELOOSKA (Cherokee) 1933- (woodcarver)

Born August 31, 1933, Sonona, Calif. *Education:* High school. *Principal occupation:* Woodcarver. *Home address:* Ariel, Wash. *Affiliations:* Lecturer, dance programmer, Oregon Museum of Science and Industry. *Awards, honors:* Award, Inter-Tribal Indian Ceremonial, Gallup, N.M., 1966. *Interests:* Woodcarving, Northwest Coast styles; Indian dance and drama; Indian music; various forms of Indian arts and crafts.

SMITH, HORACE N. (engineer, farmer)

Born Hagerstown, Ind. *Education:* Cleveland Institute of Radio Electronics. *Principal occupation:* Engineer, farmer. *Home address:* R.R. 2, Hagerstown, Ind. 47346. *Community activities:* Hagerstown Volunteer Fire Department; Civil Defense director, county communications; Optimist Club; local school board. *Memberships:* American Friends Board of Missions (executive committee); Whites Institute, Wabash, Ind. (board member); Associated Executive Committee of Friends on Indian Affairs (vice chairman); Association of Public Safety Communications Officers; American Radio Relay League (local club officer); American Farm Bureau (past president).

SMITH, KEELY (of Indian descent; tribe not known) 1935- (entertainer)

Born March 9, 1935, Norfolk, Va. *Address:* Keely Smith Enterprises, Inc., 2419 Las Vegas Blvd., Las Vegas, Nev. *Affiliations:* Appeared on Joe Brown Radio Gang, Norfolk, Va., 1946-49; appeared with Saxie Dowell Navy Band, 1949-50; appeared with Louis Prima's Orchestra, 1950-54; co-starred with Louis Prima as entertainer-singer in nightclubs, 1955-61; television appearances, including Dinah Shore Show, Frank Sinatra and Dean Martin shows; co-starred with Robert Mitchum in motion pic-

ture, "Thunder Road," 1957; recordings for Capitol Records, Dot Records; president, Enterprise Music Corp. *Memberships:* A.S.C.A.P.; American Indian Center. *Awards, honors:* Disc Jockeys Favorite Female Award, 1958; Most Promising TV Performer Award, National Academy of Musical Arts, 1958; Grammy Award, National Academy of Recording Arts and Sciences, 1958; Number One Female Vocalist Award, Billboard and Variety magazines, 1958, 1959; Playboy Jazz Award, 1959; Top Variety Entertainer Award, Diners' Club, 1959; Joey Award for Best Variety Act, 1960. *Published works:* Coauthor, *Half Child-Half Woman.*

SMITS, EDWARD J. 1933- (museum curator)

Born December 11, 1933, Freeport, N.Y. *Education:* Hofstra College, B.A. (History); New York University, M.A., Ph.D. (candidate). *Principal occupation:* Museum curator. *Home address:* 14 Wavy Lane, Wantagh, N.Y. *Affiliations:* Curator, Nassau County Historical Museum. *Military service:* U.S. Army Reserve. *Community activities:* Levittown Public Library (trustee). *Memberships:* Roslyn Landmark Society (trustee); Freeport Historical Society (trustee); Nassau County Historical Society (trustee); Valley Stream Museum (trustee); Friends of Nassau County Historical Museum (trustee); Long Island Historical Society (trustee). *Awards, honors:* Fulbright Study Grant, Scandinavian museums, 1965. *Published works:* *Creation of Nassau County* (County of Nassau, 1962); articles for professional museum and historical periodicals.

SNODGRASS, JEANNE O. 1927- (museum curator, commercial artist)

Born September 12, 1927, Muskogee, Okla. *Education:* Northeastern State College; University of Oklahoma. *Principal occupation:* Museum curator, commercial artist. *Home address:* 119 E. 34th St., Tulsa, Okla. 74105. *Affiliations:* Curator of Indian art and assistant to director, Philbrook Art Center, Tulsa, Okla., 1956-. *Community activities:* Association on American Indian Affairs, Inc. (arts and crafts committee); Oklahoma Museums Association (past secretary, charter member). *Memberships:*

Tulsa Historical Society (charter member). *Awards, honors:* Honorary Indian princess, 1965. *Interests:* American Indian art; American Indian history. *Published works: American Indian Paintings* (Philbrook Art Center, 1964); editor, *The Art and Romance of Indian Basketry* (Philbrook Art Center, 1964); *Dictionary of American Indian Artists* (Museum of the American Indian, Heye Foundation, 1965); articles in various periodicals.

SONNE, CONWAY B. 1917- (credit executive, writer)

Born December 28, 1917, Logan, Utah. *Education:* Utah State University, B.S., 1940; Harvard Graduate School of Business Administration, M.B.A., 1946. *Principal occupation:* Credit executive, writer. *Home address:* 3348 St. Michael Drive, Palo Alto, Calif. *Affiliations:* Assistant general credit manager, Standard Oil Company of California. *Military service:* U.S. Army (Army Commendation Ribbon). *Memberships:* Utah State Historical Society; American Petroleum Credit Association (vice president, director); Credit Managers Association of Northern and Central California (vice president, director). *Awards, honors:* Executive Award, Graduate School of Credit and Financial Management, Stanford University, 1956; Balfour Award, Utah Province, Sigma Chi, 1940. *Interests:* Credit and financial management; American Indian history and anthropology; Utah and California history; Mormon history; Western colonization by Mormons. *Published works: Knight of the Kingdom* (Deseret Book Co., 1949); *What Would You Write?* (Standard Oil Company of California, 1956); *World of Wakara* (The Naylor Co., 1962).

SONNICHSEN, C. L. 1901- (teacher, administrator, writer)

Born September 20, 1901, Fonda, Iowa. *Education:* University of Minnesota, B.A., 1924; Harvard University, M.A., 1927, Ph.D., 1931. *Principal occupation:* Teacher, administrator, writer. *Home address:* 4151 N. Stanton St., El Paso, Texas. *Affiliations:* Instructor, Carnegie Institute of Technology, 1927-29; associate professor, Texas Western College, 1931-33; professor, chairman, Department of English, Texas Western College, 1933-60; dean,

Graduate Division, Texas Western University, 1960-. *Memberships:* Society of American Historians; Texas State Historical Association (Fellow); Texas Folklore Society; New Mexico Folklore Society; New Mexico Historical Association; Panhandle-Plains Historical Association; Western History Association; Denver Corral of the Westerners; English Westerners; Texas Institute of Letters. *Awards, honors:* Bowdoin Prize, Harvard University, 1931; Rockefeller Fellow (University of Oklahoma, 1949); Theta Sigma Phi honoree, 1958, 1960; Harry Yandell Benedict Professorship of English, Texas Western College, 1964-. *Interests:* Western frontier history and folklore. *Published works: Billy King's Tombstone* (Caxton, 1942); *Roy Bean* (Macmillan, 1943; Devin-Adair, 1958; Hillman, 1959); *Cowboys and Cattle Kings* (University of Oklahoma Press, 1950); *I'll Die Before I'll Run* (Harper, 1951; Devin-Adair, 1962); *Alias Billy the Kid,* with William V. Morrison (University of New Mexico Press, 1955); *Ten Texas Feuds* (University of New Mexico Press, 1957); *The Mescalero Apaches* (University of Oklahoma Press, 1958); *Tularosa* (Devin-Adair, 1960); *The El Paso Salt War* (Carl Hertzog, 1961); *The Southwest in Life and Literature* (Devin-Adair, 1962); *Outlaw* (Alan Swallow, 1965).

SOSIN, JACK M. 1928- (professor of history)

Born April 17, 1928, Hartford, Conn. *Education:* University of Connecticut, B.A., 1950, M.A., 1951; Indiana University, Ph.D., 1958. *Principal occupation:* Professor of history. *Home address:* 2526 A St., Lincoln, Neb. *Affiliations:* Instructor, assistant professor, associate professor, professor, University of Nebraska, 1958-. *Military service:* U.S. Army, 1952-54. *Memberships:* Association of American Historians; American Historical Association. *Published works: Whitehall and the Wilderness* (University of Nebraska Press, 1961); *Agents and Merchants* (University of Nebraska Press, 1965).

SOUTHERN, PEGGY FREEMAN (Sac and Fox) 1923- (tribal officer)

Born August 7, 1923, Sayre, Okla. *Education:* Haskell Institute; Hills Business College. *Principal occupation:* Tribal officer.

Home address: 1508 N. Harvard, Oklahoma City, Okla. 73127. *Affiliations:* Office manager, Macdonald Oil Corp. *Community activities:* Sac and Fox Tribe of Oklahoma (secretary-treasurer, 1958-); Desk and Derrick Club of Oklahoma City.

SPACE, RALPH (Delaware) 1902-
(farmer)

Born July 7, 1902, Sussex, N.J. *Principal occupation:* Fur farmer, dairy farmer. *Home address:* Beemerville Road, Sussex, N.J. 07461. *Affiliations:* Owner, Space Farms, Sussex, N.J.

SPICER, EDWARD H. 1906-
(professor of anthropology)

Born November 29, 1906, Cheltenham, Penna. *Education:* University of Arizona, B.A., 1932, M.A., 1933; University of Chicago, Ph.D., 1939. *Principal occupation:* Professor of anthropology. *Home address:* 5344 E. Fort Lowell Road, Tucson, Ariz. *Affiliations:* Instructor, Dillard University, 1938-39; head, community analysis section, War Relocation Authority, Washington, D.C., 1942-46; professor of anthropology, University of Arizona, 1946-. *Other professional posts:* Visiting professor, Cornell University, 1948-50; visiting professor, University of California, Santa Barbara, 1958. *Memberships:* American Anthropological Association (editor, executive board); Society for Applied Anthropology (vice president); American Association for the Advancement of Science. *Awards, honors:* John Simon Guggenheim Foundation Fellow, 1941-42, 1955-56; Southwestern Library Association Award for best book on the Southwest, 1964; National Science Foundation Senior Postdoctoral Fellowship, 1963-64. *Interests:* Acculturation; the southwestern United States; northwestern New Mexico; research in Mexico, 1941-42, 1947, 1955-56, 1963-64; research in Peru, 1964. *Published works: A Yaqui Village in Arizona* (University of Chicago Press, 1940); *Potam, A Yaqui Village in Sonora* (American Anthropological Association, 1954); editor, *Human Problems in Technological Change* (Russell Sage, 1952; John Wiley, 1965); editor, *Perspectives in American Indian Culture Change* (University of Chicago Press, 1962); *Cycles of Conquest: The Impact of Spain, Mexico, and the U.S. on the Indians of the Southwest, 1533-1960* (University of Arizona Press, 1963).

SPRING, MAY R. (Tonawanda) 1899-
(community worker)

Born May 17, 1899, Tonawanda Indian Reservation, N.Y. *Education:* High school. *Principal occupation:* Community worker. *Home address:* 986 Bloomingdale Road, Basom, N.Y. 14013. *Affiliations:* Custodian, Tonawanda Indian Community House, Akron, N.Y.; former employee, New York State Department of Social Welfare. *Community activities:* Tonawanda Indian Baptist Church. *Memberships:* Local History Club, Batavia, N.Y.; Tonawanda Indian Community House (board of directors; past president; past secretary).

SPRUCE, BERYL BLUE (San Juan-Laguna Pueblo) 1934- (obstetrician)

Born November 24, 1934, Santa Fe, N.M. *Education:* Stanford University, B.S., 1960; University of Southern California, M.D., 1964. *Principal occupation:* Obstetrician. *Home address:* 6000 N. 9th St., Philadelphia, Penna. 19141. *Community activities:* Indian Rights Association, American Friends Service Committee (board of directors); National Indian Youth Council. *Memberships:* American College of Obstetrics and Gynecology (Junior Fellow); Phi Rho Sigma. *Awards, honors:* John Hay Whitney Fellow, 1961-62.

SQUIRES, CEDRIC P. 1924- (state park superintendent)

Born May 1, 1924, Wake Forest, N.C. *Education:* Wake Forest College, 1941-42, 1946-48. *Principal occupation:* State park superintendent. *Address:* Morrow Mountain State Park, Route 2, Albemarle, N.C. 28001. *Affiliations:* Superintendent, Morrow Mountain State Park, Albemarle, N.C. *Other professional posts:* North Carolina Department of Revenue. *Military service:* U.S. Navy, 1942-46.

SQUIRES, JOHN L. 1906- (professor of health, physical education and recreation)

Born January 20, 1906, Brigham City, Utah. *Education:* University of Utah, B.S., 1930, M.S., 1943, Ph.D., 1952. *Principal occupation:* Professor of health, physical education and recreation. *Home address:* 3254 Joyce Drive, Salt Lake City, Utah 84109. *Affiliations:* Professor of health, physical education and recreation, University of Utah, 1955- (chairman, recreation section, Department of Health, Physical Education and Recreation, 1949-64). *Other professional posts:* Director, Salt Lake County Recreation Department, Spruces Summer Camp for Boys and Girls, 1955-57; coordinator and supervisor, Salt Lake County Recreation Department, Boys' Clubs of America, 1958-64; researcher, Patton State Hospital, 1958; director, Ute Tribe Summer Recreation and Education Camp, 1959; consultant, Bountiful Junior Chamber of Commerce Recreation Committee, 1958-59; recreation consultant, Green River, Wyo., Chemical Co., 1960; research and planning, University of Utah Community Development Department, 1960-64; community planning, Clearfield, Utah, 1961; community planning, Community Development Department, for American Fork, Draper, North Salt Lake, Bountiful, North Clearfield, Utah, 1960-64; research and planning, Bureau of Economic and Business Research, University of Utah College of Business, 1963-. *Memberships:* American Association for Health, Physical Education and Recreation; Utah Recreation and Parks Association; Utah Education Association; Utah Interagency for Recreation; Phi Delta Kappa; Salt Lake County Community Welfare Council. *Awards, honors:* Good Citizenship Award, 1941, 1942; Outstanding Service Award, Rotary Club of Salt Lake City. *Published works: American Indian Dances,* with Robert E. McLean (Ronald Press, 1963); *Fun Crafts for Children* (Prentice-Hall, 1964).

STEELE, WILLIAM OWEN   1917-
(author)

Born December 22, 1917, Franklin, Tenn. *Education:* Cumberland University, B.A., 1940; University of Chattanooga, 1951-52. *Principal occupation:* Author. *Home address:* 808 Fairmount Ave., Signal Mt., Tenn. *Awards, honors:* New York *Herald-Tribune* Spring Festival Award for *Winter Danger,* 1954; Jane Addam Children's Book Award for *The Perilous Road,* 1958; run-

ner-up for Newberry Medal, American Library Association Notable Book; William Allen White Children's Book Award for *Flaming Arrows,* 1960; Thomas A. Edison Award for *Westward Adventure: The True Stories of Six Pioneers,* 1962. *Interests:* History and anthropology; hiking; nature study. *Published works: The Golden Root* (Aladdin, 1951); *The Buffalo Knife* (Harcourt, 1952); *Over-Mountain Boy* (Aladdin, 1952); *John Sevier, Pioneer Boy* (Bobbs-Merrill, 1953); *The Story of Daniel Boone* (Grosset & Dunlap, 1953); *Wilderness Journey* (Harcourt, 1953); *Story of Lief Ericson* (Grosset & Dunlap, 1954); *Winter Danger* (Harcourt, 1954); *Frances Marion, Young Swamp Fox* (Bobbs-Merrill, 1954); *Tomahawks and Trouble* (Harcourt, 1955); *We Were There on the Oregon Trail* (Grosset & Dunlap, 1955); *De Soto, Child of the Sun* (Aladdin, 1956); *Davy Crockett's Earthquake* (Harcourt, 1956); *The Lone Hunt* (Harcourt, 1956); *We Were There With the Pony Express* (Grosset & Dunlap, 1956); *Flaming Arrows* (1957), *Daniel Boone's Echo* (1957), *Perilous Road* (1958), *Andy Jackson's Water Well* (1959), *The Far Frontier* (1959), *The Spooky Thing* (1960), *Westward Adventure: The True Stories of Six Pioneers* (1962), all published by Harcourt, Brace & World; *Wayah of the Real People* (Colonial Williamsburg, 1964).

STEFFEN, JOHN W.   1928-   (school administrator)

Born June 15, 1928, Halliday, N.D. *Education:* Dickinson State College, B.A., 1955; University of North Dakota, 1959; Black Hills State College, 1962, 1965. *Principal occupation:* School administrator. *Address:* c/o Twin Buttes School, Bureau of Indian Affairs, Halliday, N.D. 58636. *Affiliations:* Teacher, Corcoran Elementary School, Calif., 1955-56; teacher, Pierre Boarding School, 1956-60; principal-teacher, Iron Lightning Day School, 1960-63; principal-teacher, Twin Buttes School, Bureau of Indian Affairs, Halliday, N.D. *Military service:* U.S. Army, 1951-52. *Community activities:* Parent-Teachers' Association; Community Development; Elks; American Legion; Boy Scouts of America. *Memberships:* North Dakota Education Association; Dickinson State College Alumni Association; Assumption Abbey Alumni Association. *Interests:* Special education;

remedial education; library development; space exploration and astronomy; general science.

STEPHENSON, MARION BAILEY 1898- (teacher)

Born September 22, 1898, Masonville, N.Y. *Education:* George Peabody College, B.A., 1943. *Principal occupation:* Teacher. *Home address:* East River Road, Bainbridge, N.Y. *Affiliations:* Teacher, Onondaga Indian Reservation, South Syracuse, N.Y.; teacher, Ridgefield Park, N.J., 1923-24; teacher, Friends' Academy, Locust Valley, N.Y., 1924-26; teacher, Flushing Progressive School, 1947-48; teacher, Tuxedo Park Private School, 1953-54. *Interests:* Reading and writing; golf; travels to Cuba, Nassau, Europe, 1960-61. *Published works: Nyah's Quest* (Vantage, 1958); *Miracle of the Mohawks* (Pageant, 1964).

STEPHENSON, ROBERT L. 1919- (anthropologist)

Born February 18, 1919, Portland, Ore. *Education:* University of Oregon, B.A. (Anthropology), 1940, M.A. (Anthropology), 1942; University of Michigan, Ph.D. (Anthropology), 1956; U.S. Department of Agriculture Management Development School, Certificate, 1962. *Principal occupation:* Anthropologist. *Home address:* 9205 Santayana Drive, Fairfax, Va. 22030. *Affiliations:* Laboratory supervisor, University of Texas, Works Projects Administration, 1940-41; assistant professor, Washington and Jefferson College, 1941; assistant curator, Museum of Natural History, University of Oregon; owner and operator, 1st Street Food Store, 1946-47; salesman of rock-wool insulation, 1947; field director, Texas River Basin Surveys, Smithsonian Institution, 1947-51; chief, Missouri Basin Project, River Basin Surveys, 1953-63; assistant professor, University of Nebraska, 1960-61; acting director, River Basin Surveys, Smithsonian Institution, Washington, D.C., 1963. *Other professional posts:* Assistant editor, *American Antiquity,* 1960-63; associate editor, editor, *Plains Anthropologist,* 1960-63. *Military service:* U.S. Marine Corps Reserve, 1942-63. *Memberships:* Condon Club, University of Oregon; Sigma Xi; Society for American Archaeol-

ogy; American Anthropological Association (Fellow); American Association for the Advancement of Science (Fellow); Society for Applied Anthropology (Fellow); Society of Vertebrate Paleontology; Anthropological Society of Washington; archaeological societies of Texas, Oregon, Missouri, Oklahoma and Maryland; Nebraska Academy of Science (past chairman, anthropology section); Nebraska State Historical Society; Oregon Historical Society; Toastmasters International (past club president and district officer). *Interests:* Expeditions and field work -- excavations of Catlow Cave and Roaring Springs Cave, Oregon, 1937, 1938; archaeological survey of Warner Valley, 1938; excavation of Ft. Rock Cave, 1939; archaeological salvage in area flooded by Grand Coulee Dam, Wash., 1939; excavation of sites in northern California and south-central Oregon, University of Oregon, 1940; excavation of Pueblo Pardo, 1941; analysis of specimens from Accokeek Creek Site, Md., 1952. Travels to Canada, Mexico, Brazil, British Guiana, Trinidad, British West Indies, Puerto Rico, Hawaii, Alaska, and throughout the United States. *Published works: Excavations at Pueblo Pardo* (Museum of New Mexico, 1960); *The Accokeek Creek Site* (University of Michigan, 1963); *Quaternary Human Occupation of the Plains* (Princeton University, 1965); numerous reviews, articles, and monographs.

STEVENS, JOHN W. (Passamaquoddy) 1933- (tribal chief)

Born August 11, 1933, Washington County, Me. *Education:* High school. *Principal occupation:* Tribal chief. *Home address:* Peter Dana Point, Indian Township Reservation, Washington County, Me. *Affiliations:* Chief, Passamaquoddy Tribe, 1955-. *Military service:* U.S. Marines, 1951-54 (Presidential Unit Citation, Korean Presidential Unit Citation, Good Conduct Medal, United Nations Medal). *Memberships:* Local 26, International Brotherhood of Firemen and Oilers, A.F.L.-C.I.O. *Interests:* Mr. Stevens writes, "Being the chief of an Indian tribe of about a thousand members who are struggling in court and on all fronts to overcome local discrimination and poverty and to have our reservation treaty rights respected by the State of Maine is enough of a task, and doesn't leave much time for anything else."

STEVENSON, AUGUSTA 1890- (teacher, writer)

Born 1890, Patriot, Ind. *Education:*Butler University, B.A. *Principal occupation:* Teacher, writer. *Home address:* 410 N. Meridian St., Indianapolis, Ind. *Affiliations:* Teacher, Indianapolis public schools. *Memberships:* Indiana Pioneer Society; Women's Press Club; Pen Women of America; Indianapolis Propylaeum. *Published works: Children's Classics in Dramatic Form* (Houghton Mifflin); *Dramatized Series from American History* (Houghton Mifflin); *Childhood of Famous Americans Series* (Bobbs-Merrill).

STEWARD, RAY F. 1933- (teacher, administrator)

Born January 3, 1933, Salem, Ore. *Education:* Simpson Bible College, 1951-53; Cascade College, 1953; Seattle Pacific College, B.A. (Education), 1959. *Principal occupation:* Teacher, administrator. *Address:* c/o Kipnuk Day School, Bureau of Indian Affairs, Kipnuk, Alaska. *Affiliations:* Teacher, Crystal Springs Elementary School, 1958-61; teacher, Kotzebue Day School, Bureau of Indian Affairs, 1961-63; principal-teacher, Kipnuk Day School, Bureau of Indian Affairs, Kipnuk, Alaska. *Military service:* U.S. Army, 1953-55 *Community activities:* Crystal Springs Parent-Teachers' Association (vice president); Kotzebue Aero Club (vice president). *Memberships:* Kipnuk Parent-Teachers' Association (advisor, 1963-); Kipnuk Citizens' Band Radio Club.

STEWART, OMER C. 1908- (professor of anthropology)

Born August 17, 1908, Provo, Utah. *Education:* University of Utah, B.A., 1933; University of California, Berkeley, Ph.D., 1939; University of Minnesota, 1940. *Principal occupation:* Professor of anthropology. *Affiliations:* Teaching assistant in anthropology, University of California, 1935-37; instructor in anthropology, University of Texas, 1939; instructor in anthropology, University of Minnesota, 1941-42; assistant professor of anthropology, University of Colorado, 1945-49; associate professor of anthropology, University of Colorado, 1949-54; chairman, Department of Social Scien-

ces, University of Colorado, 1952-54; professor of anthropology and chairman, Div. of Anthropology, Dept. of Social Sciences, University of Colorado, 1954-56; chairman, Dept. of Anthropology, University of Colorado, 1957-59; director, Tri-Ethnic Research Project, University of Colorado, 1959-64. *Military service:* Liaison officer to Ethnographic Board, Office of Chief of Staff, War Dept., Washington, D.C., 1942-43. *Memberships:* American Anthropological Association (Fellow; executive committee, Western States Branch, 1950-52); Society for American Archaeology; Society for Applied Anthropology (Fellow; vice president, 1960; board of directors, 1960-64); Colorado Archaeological Society (executive secretary, 1949-52; editor, *Southwestern Lore,* 1949-53); American Association for the Advancement of Science (Fellow); Colorado-Wyoming Academy of Science; American Ecological Association. *Awards, honors:* Social Science Research Council Postdoctoral Fellowship, 1940-41; University of Colorado Faculty Research Fellowships, 1951, 1956; Sigma Xi; Phi Beta Kappa; Phi Sigma; Social Science Research Council Conference on Political Behavior, University of Michigan, 1949; International Symposium on Man's Role in Changing the Face of the Earth, 1955; Tall Timbers Fire Ecology Conference, 1963; lecturer, University of Utah School of Alcohol Studies, 1963. *Interests:* Expeditions and field work -- archaeology of Utah and northern Arizona, 1931-33; ethnogeography of Pomo Indians, northern California; culture element distribution of Northern Paiute and Washo Indians of Nevada, Oregon and California, and Ute and Southern Paiute of Utah, Arizona, Colorado; study of peyote cult of Washo and Northern Paiute of Nevada and eastern California, University of California, 1935-38; study of primitive child development, Zuni, N.M., and community study of Mormon village of Alpine, Ariz., Social Science Research Council, 1940-41; community analysis, Ignacio, Colorado, University of Colorado, 1948-50; ethnohistory of Pit River, Washo, Northern Paiute, Shoshone, Southern Paiute, Ute, Chippewa, and Ottawa, 1953-58; values and behavior on the Ute Reservation, U.S. Department of Health, Education and Welfare, 1959-63. *Published works: Ute Peyotism* (Series in Anthropology, No. 1, University of Colorado, 1948); *Navaho and Ute Peyotism: A Chronological and Distributional Study,* with David F. Aberle (University of Colorado Series in Anthropology,

No. 6, 1957); numerous monographs, articles and book reviews in professional journals.

STILES, MARTHA BENNETT 1933-
(writer)

Born March 30, 1933, Manila, Philippine Islands. *Education:* College of William and Mary; University of Michigan, B.S., 1954. *Principal occupation:* Writer. *Home address:* 2580 Newport Road, Ann Arbor, Mich. *Memberships:* Authors' Guild. *Awards, honors:* Phi Beta Kappa; Avery Hopwood awards. *Published works: One Among the Indians* (Dial Press, 1962) *The Strange House at Newburyport* (Dial Press, 1963); *The Sixth Hour* (Dial Press, 1966).

STIRLING, MATTHEW W. 1896-
(anthropologist)

Born August 28, 1896, Salinas, Calif. *Education:* University of California, B.A., 1920; George Washington University, M.A., 1922. *Principal occupation:* Anthropologist. *Affiliations:* Director, Bureau of American Ethnology, Smithsonian Institution, 1927-57. *Military service:* U.S. Navy, 1917-18. *Memberships:* American Anthropological Association; Washington Academy of Medicine. *Awards, honors:* Franklin Burr Award, 1939, 1941, 1958; honorary D.Sc., Tampa University. *Interests:* Archaeological and ethnological expeditions in the United States, Europe, Africa, Mexico, Central America, South America, East Indies, New Guinea. *Published works: Origin Myth of Acoma* (Smithsonian Institution, 1942); *Stone Monuments of Southern Mexico* (Smithsonian Institution, 1943); *Indians of the Americas* (National Geographic Society, 1955).

STONE, WILLARD (Cherokee) 1916-
(artist, wood sculptor)

Born February 26, 1916, Oktaha, Okla. *Education:* High school. *Principal occupation:* Artist, wood sculptor. *Home address:* Star Route East, Locust Grove, Okla. *Other occupations:* Die finisher, designer, pattern-maker, inventor. *Community activities:* Kiwanis Club; Masons. *Memberships:* Five Civilized Tribes Museum, Muskogee, Okla.; Gilcrease Museum, Tulsa, Okla.; National Cowboy Hall of Fame, Okla-

homa City, Okla.; Philbrook Art Center, Tulsa, Okla. *Awards, honors:* National Competition, Sculpture, Philbrook Art Center, Tulsa, Okla. -- First Place, 1959, Second Place, 1960, Second Place, 1961, Honorable Mention, 1962, First Place, 1963, Second Place, 1964, Second Place, 1965; Muskogee Annual Art Competition -- First Place, 1961, 1962; Special Award, Indian Arts and Crafts Board, Bureau of Indian Affairs, 1966. *Interests:* Sculpture, painting, sketching. Mr. Stone is an official representative of the Cherokee Tribe.

STRONG, EMORY 1903- (engineer, writer)

Born December 17, 1903, Vancouver, Wash. *Education:* Oregon State University, B.S., 1932. *Principal occupation:* Engineer, writer. *Home address:* 2753 N.E. Wiberg Lane, Portland, Ore. *Affiliations:* Mechanical engineer, Bonneville Power Administration. *Memberships:* Oregon Archaeological Society, 1952- (editor). *Interests:* The Columbia River -- Mr. Strong has explored the major United States portion by boat on numerous occasions, has photographed most of the petroglyphs on the river, and has located most village sites and Lewis and Clark campsites on the Columbia below the Snake River. He has traveled on the Snake, Colorado, Green, Yampa and San Juan Rivers. *Published works: Stone Age on the Columbia River* (Binfords and Mort, 1959); *Wakemap Mound Report* (Oregon Archaeological Society, 1959); editor, *Indian Trade Goods* (Oregon Archaeological Society, 1965).

STURTEVANT, WILLIAM C. 1926-
(anthropologist)

Born 1926, New Jersey. *Education:* University of California, B.A., 1949; Yale University, Ph.D., 1955. *Principal occupation:* Anthropologist. *Affiliations:* General anthropologist and curator, Office of Anthropology, Smithsonian Institution. *Military service:* U.S. Naval Reserve, 1945-46. *Memberships:* American Anthropological Association, and others. *Interests:* Ethnology of eastern North American Indians.

SULLIVAN, MARIE   1901-   (writer)

Born February 22, 1901, Union Parish, La. *Education:* High school. *Principal occupation:* Writer. *Home address:* 121 E. Adams St., Falfurrias, Texas 78355. *Community activities:* State Garden Club of Texas (past member and secretary); Circle Two, Presbyterian Women of the Church (past chairman). *Awards, honors:* Garden Club Citizen of the Year, 1958-59, State Garden Club of Texas. *Published works: Truthful Hatchet* (The Naylor Co., 1966).

SUNDOWN, ARNOLD   (Iroquois)   1914-
   (silversmith)

Born August 4, 1914. *Education:* High school. *Principal occupation:* Silversmith. *Home address:* 7066 Meadville Road, Basom, N.Y. 14013. *Affiliations:* Silversmith, Rochester Museum of Arts and Sciences, Rochester, N.Y., 1931-39.

SWADESH, MORRIS   1909-   (teacher)

Born January 22, 1909, Holyoke, Mass. *Education:* University of Chicago, Ph.D., 1930, M.A., 1931; Yale University, Ph.D., 1933. *Principal occupation:* Teacher. *Home address:* Arquitectura 45, Mexico 20, D.F., Mexico. *Affiliations:* Professor, Universidad Nacional Autonoma de Mexico, 1955-. *Military service:* U.S. Army, 1942-46. *Memberships:* Linguistic Society of America, 1932-; American Anthropological Association, 1946-; Linguistic Circle of New York, 1943- (editor, *Word*, 1946-50); Sociedad Mexicana de Antropologia e Historia, 1939-; Academia de la Investigacion Cientifica, 1959-. *Interests:* The American Indian; word linguistics. *Published works: Nootka Texts,* with Edward Sapir, (Linguistic Society of America, 1938); *Chinese in Your Pocket* (Henry Holt, 1947); *Native Accounts of Nootka Ethnography,* with Edward Sapir (International Journals of American Linguistics, 1955); *Songs of the Nootka Indians of Western Vancouver Island* (American Philosophical Society).

SWEAZEY, RAY WILLIAM   1914-
   (organization executive)

Born December 15, 1914, Newark, N.J.

Education: Coleman College, 1933-36; National Training School for Professional Leaders in Scouting, 1941. *Principal occupation:* Organization executive. *Home address:* R.D. 1, Box 205-C, Jamesburg, N.J. 08831. *Affiliations:* District scout executive, 1941-43, assistant scout executive, 1943-47, scout executive, 1947-50, deputy regional scout executive, 1950-54, national director of interracial relations, 1954-61, national director, American Indian relationships and urban relationships, National Council, Boy Scouts of America, 1961-. *Community activities:* Rotary Club, 1948-50; Presbyterian Council; Arrow, Inc. (board of directors). *Memberships:* American Society of Planning Officials, 1962-; Zeta Psi Alumni Association, 1959-; Alpha Phi Omega, 1942-; National Association of Housing and Redevelopment Officials, 1962-; National Association of Intergroup Relations Officials, 1958-; National Congress of American Indians, 1955-. *Awards, honors:* Honorary member, Blackfeet Tribe; Fellowship Degree, Boy Scouts of America, 1961. *Interests:* Field work in Indian and Eskimo areas; recruiting and training leadership; model railroading. Has written articles for various publications.

T

TANTAQUIDGEON, GLADYS   (Mohegan)
   1899-   (museum curator)

Born June 15, 1899, New London, Conn. *Education:* University of Pennsylvania. *Principal occupation:* Museum curator. *Home address:* 1819 Norwich, New London Tpke., Uncasville, Conn. 06382. *Affiliations:* Curator, Tantaquidgeon Indian Museum, Uncasville, Conn. *Memberships:* Connecticut Archaeological Society. Has written articles published in ethnological and anthropological journals.

TANTAQUIDGEON, HAROLD   (Mohegan)
   1904-   (museum curator, lecturer)

Born June 18, 1904, Montville, Conn. *Education:* Elementary school. *Principal occupation:* Museum curator, lecturer. *Home address:* 1819 Norwich, New London Tpke., Uncasville, Conn. 06382. *Affiliations:* Curator, Tantaquidgeon Indian Museum, Uncasville, Conn. *Other occupations:* Lecturer and instructor in history and ethnology of Mohegan and neighboring tribes. *Military service:* U.S. Army Air Corps, 1943-45; U.S. Army, 1950-53 (Purple Heart, Air Medal). *Community activities:* Boy Scouts of America; 4-H Club. *Biographical source: Mohegan Chief: The Story of Harold Tantaquidgeon* (Funk and Wagnalls, 1965).

TAULBEE, DANIEL J.   (Comanche)
    1924-   (artist)

Born April 7, 1924, Montana. *Education:* Famous Artists School, Westport, Conn. *Principal occupation:* Artist. *Home address:* 2712 Nettie, Butte, Mont. *Affiliations:* Illustrator, Anaconda Co.; proprietor, Heritage American Art Gallery. *Military service:* U.S. Army. *Awards, honors:* Gold Medal, Burr Gallery, New York, N.Y. *Interests:* One-man exhibits of oil paintings, watercolors, pen and ink drawings throughout the United States; depicts "authentic Indian and Western life as I saw and lived them." *Permanent collections:* Farnsworth Museum, Maine; Peabody Museum, Cambridge, Mass.; Philbrook Art Center, Tulsa, Okla.; Russell Museum, Montana; Statesville Museum, North Carolina; Whitney Museum, Cody, Wyo.

TAX, SOL   1907-   (professor of
    anthropology)

Born October 30, 1907, Chicago, Ill. *Education:* University of Wisconsin, Ph.B., 1931; University of Chicago, Ph.D., 1935. *Principal occupation:* Professor of anthropology. *Home address:* 5537 S. Woodlawn Ave., Chicago, Ill. 60637. *Affiliations:* Professor of anthropology, University of Chicago, 1948- (dean, University Extension, 1963-). *Other professional posts:* Research associate, Wenner-Gren Foundation for Anthropological Research, 1958-; editor, *Current Anthropology* and Viking Fund Publications in Anthropology, 1959-; consultant, U.S. Office of Education, 1955-. *Community activities:* U.S. National Commission for UNESCO (executive committee, 1963-65); Illinois State Museum Board (secretary, 1954). *Memberships:* American Anthropological Association (Fellow; president, 1958-59); National Research Council; American Association for the Advancement of Science; Society for Applied Anthropology; American Folklore Society. *Awards, hon-*

ors: Viking Fund Medal in Anthropology, 1961; honorary member, Royal Anthropological Institute of Great Britain and Ireland; honorary member, Chilean Anthropological Society; honorary member, Czechoslovakian Anthropological Society. *Interests:* Social anthropology of North and Middle American Indians; originator of concept of "action" anthropology. *Published works: Heritage of Conquest* (Free Press, 1952); editor, *Indian Tribes of Aboriginal America* (University of Chicago, 1952); editor, *Acculturation in the Americas* (University of Chicago, 1952); *Penny Capitalism: A Guatemalan Indian Economy* (Smithsonian Institution, 1953, 1963); editor, *Appraisal of Anthropology Today* (University of Chicago, 1953); editor, *Evolution After Darwin*, three vols. (University of Chicago, 1960); editor, *Horizons of Anthropology* (Aldine, 1963).

TAYLOR, JOHN LEWIS   1910-
    (geographer)

Born November 25, 1910, Oriska, N.D. *Education:* State Teachers College, B.A. (Education), 1935; Clark University, M.A. (Geography), 1940; Columbia University, M.A. (Political Science), 1944; Clark University, Ph.D. (Geography), 1953. *Principal occupation:* Geographer. *Home address:* 7101 Bridle Path Lane, Rosemary Terrace, Hyattsville, Md. *Affiliations:* Director of education, Trust Territory of the Pacific Islands, 1950-53; consultant on territorial and Indian affairs, Committee on Interior and Insular Affairs, House of Representatives, Washington, D.C., 1953-. *Military service:* U.S. Navy, 1942-47, 1950-51. *Community activities:* Methodist Church; Parent-Teachers' Association; Masons. *Memberships:* Association of American Geographers; National Council on Geographic Education; American Polar Society; Antarctican Society; National Geographic Society. *Interests:* Expeditions and visitations to Antarctica, South Pole, 1959, 1964; Pacific Islands; Malaysia, 1940-42. *Published works:* Articles and book reviews on island and Indian affairs.

TAYLOR, VIRGINIA   (Cherokee)   1922-
    (commercial artist)

Born September 15, 1922, Los Angeles, Calif. *Education:* Art Center School, Los

Angeles, Calif. *Principal occupation:* Commercial artist; illustrator; art teacher. *Home address:* Route 4, Box 411, Albany, Ore. 97321. *Affiliations:* Cartoonist and humorous greeting card designer, Buzza-Cardoza Greeting Card Co., Los Angeles, Calif., 1945-49; assistant art director, Buzza-Cardoza Greeting Card Co., 1949; free-lance commercial artist, 1950-57; staff artist, Publications Office, Oregon State University, 1957-; art coordinator and designer, Oregon State University Press, 1960-; assistant professor of art, Oregon State University, 1964-; graphic designer and assistant to museum coordinator, Marine Science Laboratory, Department of Oceanography, Oregon State University, 1965. *Awards, honors:* First Award, Indian Festival of Arts, La Grande, Ore., 1965; Third Award, Oregon State Fair, Salem, Ore., 1965; Honor Mention, Twenty-one American Indian Art Exhibition, Philbrook Art Center, Tulsa, Okla., 1966. *Interests:* Miss Taylor writes, "American Indian history; painting and drawing the American Indian today as well as events in Indian history. Over the past twenty-five years I've worked around various tribes of Indians in different parts of the United States, trying to paint and draw them as they are and were. I have worked with Indian groups, especially children, giving drawing lessons. While this avocation (painting) has been with me most of my life, it is only recently that I have submitted my work to shows. When sending work to group shows, such as our faculty invitational group showings, my work is always of an 'Indian' nature -- to promote interest in Indian art by showing work where it might not otherwise be seen."

TEBBEL, JOHN (Ojibwa) 1912-
(teacher, writer)

Born November 16, 1912, Boyne City, Mich. *Education:* Central Michigan University, B.A., 1935, Litt.D., 1948; School of Journalism, Columbia University, M.S., 1937. *Principal occupation:* Teacher, writer. *Home address:* 32 Washington Square West, New York, N.Y. 10011. *Affiliations:* Professor of journalism, New York University. *Awards, honors:* First honorary member, National Association of Book Editors, 1965; Columbia University School of Journalism Alumni Medal, 1964. *Interests:* Writing; travels to British Isles and Europe. *Pub-*

lished works: An American Dynasty (1947); *The Marshall Fields* (1947); *George Horace Lorimer and the Saturday Evening Post* (1948); *Battle for North America* (1948); *Your Body* (1951); *The Conqueror* (1951); *Touched With Fire* (1952); *The Life and Good Times of William Randolph Hearst* (1952); *George Washington's America* (1954); *A Voice in the Street* (1954); *The Magic of Balanced Living* (1956); *The American Indian Wars* (Harper, 1960); *The Inheritors* (Putnam, 1962); *The Epicure's Companion* (1962); *The Middle West* (1963); *From Rags to Riches* (Macmillan, 1963); *Compact History of the American Newspaper* (Hawthorn Books); contributor to *Saturday Review* and other magazines.

TEICHER, MORTON IRVING 1920-
(professor)

Born March 10, 1920, New York, N.Y. *Education:* City College of New York, B.S.S., 1940; University of Pennsylvania, M.S.W., 1942; University of Toronto, Ph.D. (Philosophy), 1956. *Principal occupation:* Professor. *Home address:* 138 Thornbury Rd., Scarsdale, N.Y. 10585. *Affiliations:* Chief social worker, Veterans Administration, Boston, Mass., 1946-48; chief psychiatric social worker, Toronto (Can.) Psychiatric Hospital, 1948-56; assistant professor, University of Toronto, 1948-56; director, Department of Social Work, Yeshiva University, New York, N.Y., 1956-57; director, dean, Yeshiva University School of Social Work, 1957-. *Other professional posts:* Consultant, Oppenheimer College of Social Service, Lukasa, Northern Rhodesia, 1962-63; book review editor, *Journal of Jewish Communal Service. Military service:* U.S. Army, 1942-46. *Community activities:* New York State Democratic Committee (public affairs committee); Democratic Party Research Advisory Council, New Rochelle, N.Y. (chairman); has served as Democratic district leader of the 21st District, 3rd Ward, New Rochelle, N.Y. *Memberships:* National Association of Social Workers (chairman, Westchester County Chapter, 1960); American Anthropological Association; Society for Applied Anthropology (editorial board, *Human Organization*). *Travels:* Assam, 1943-46; Southampton Island, Northwest Territories, 1951-52; Northern Rhodesia, Africa, 1962-63; Europe (study tour), summer, 1964; Zambia, Africa, 1965; Israel, summer, 1965. *Published works: Windigo Psychosis: A Study of a Relationship Between Belief and Behavior Among the Indians of Northeastern Canada* (University of Washington Press for the American Ethnological Society, 1960); *Essays on Creativity in the Sciences* (New York University Press, 1963); articles in scholarly journals in the fields of psychology, psychiatry, social work, and anthropology.

TEMPLE, WAYNE C.   1924- (historian, editor, archivist)

Born February 5, 1924, Richwood, Ohio. *Education:* University of Illinois, B.A., cum laude (History), 1949, M.A., 1951, Ph.D., 1956; Lincoln Memorial University, Lincoln Diploma of Honor, 1963. *Principal occupation:* Historian, editor, archivist. *Home address:* 821 1/2 S. 5th St., Springfield, Ill. 62703. *Affiliations:* Assistant professor of history, University of Illinois, 1949-54; curator of ethnohistory, Illinois State Museum, 1954-58; professor of history, Lincoln Memorial University, 1958-64; editor-in-chief, *Lincoln Herald*, 1958-; archivist, Illinois State Archives, 1964-. *Military service:* U.S. Army, 1943-46 (two citations). *Community activities:* Abraham Lincoln Council, Boy Scouts of America (troop committee chairman, explorer advisor, assistant district commissioner); First Presbyterian Church (deacon; steering committee). *Memberships:* Royal Society of Arts (life Fellow, 1962); Lincoln Sesquicentennial Commission (honorary member, 1959); U.S. Civil War Centennial Commission (advisory council, 1960-66); Order of the Arrow; Phi Delta Theta; Chi Gamma Iota; Delta Sigma Rho; Tau Kappa Alpha; Alpha Psi Omega; Sigma Tau Delta; Kappa Delta Pi; Sigma Pi Beta; Lincoln Academy of Illinois (government faculty); Lincoln Group of D.C. (honorary member). *Awards, honors:* Scouter's Award, National Council, Boy Scouts of America; Lincoln Medallion, Lincoln Sesquicentennial Commission; Honor Key for writing, Sigma Tau Delta; Major, Civil War Press Corps. *Interests:* Lincolniana; Civil War history; Indians of Illinois; Boy Scouts of America; guns; historical research; drama and poetry; travels in Scotland, England, France, Germany, Switzerland. *Published works: Indian Villages of the Illinois Country: Historic Tribes* (Illinois State Museum, 1958; revised edition, 1966); *Lincoln the Rail-splitter* (Willow Press, 1961); editor, *Campaigning with Grant* (Indiana University Press, 1961); editor, *The Civil War Letters of Henry C. Bear* (Lincoln Memorial University Press, 1961); editor, *Lincoln As Seen by C.C. Brown* (Crabgrass Press, 1963).

THOMPSON, ENID T.   1919- (librarian)

Born December 24, 1919, Idaho Falls, Idaho. *Education:* Montana State University, B.A., 1941; University of Denver, M.A., 1959. *Principal occupation:* Librarian. *Home address:* 3730 Allison Court, Wheatridge, Colo. 80033. *Affiliations:* Librarian, Butte Free Public Library, 1940-43; librarian, Denver Public Library, 1956-62; librarian, State Historical Society of Colorado, 1962. *Memberships:* Colorado Library Association; Special Libraries Association.

THOMPSON, HILDEGARD   1901- (educator)

Born January 13, 1901, De Pauw, Ind. *Education:* Indiana State Teachers College, 1927; University of Louisville, B.S., 1930. *Principal occupation:* Educator. *Home address:* 510 - 21st St., N.W., Washington, D.C. 20006. *Affiliations:* Teacher, Harrison County public schools, 1922-31; teacher and textbook writer, Bureau of Education, Philippine Islands, 1931-36; educational supervisor, Bureau of Indian Affairs, U.S. Department of the Interior, 1937-49; educational director, Bureau of Indian Affairs, U.S. Department of the Interior, 1949-65. *Other professional posts:* Editor, *Indian Education,* periodical, 1952-65. *Memberships:* National Education Association; Adult Education Association; Council of Administrative Women; Society for International Development; Academy of Political and Social Science. *Awards, honors:* Award, Navajo Tribe, for furthering Navajo education. *Interests:* Writing and lecturing on Indian affairs; bilingual education; travel to the Orient, Europe, and Mexico. *Published works: Navajo Life Readers* (Bureau of Indian Affairs, 1945); *Getting to Know American Indians Today* (Coward-McCann, 1965); *Education for Cross-Cultural Enrichment* (Bureau of Indian Affairs, 1965); articles for various magazines.

THOMPSON, J. ERIC S.   1898-
  (archaeologist)

Born December 31, 1898, London, England.
Education: Winchester College; Cambridge
University. *Principal occupation:* Archae-
ologist. *Home address:* Harvard, Ashdon,
Saffron Walden, Essex, England. *Affilia-
tions:* Assistant curator, Chicago Museum
of Natural History, 1926-34; archaeologist,
Carnegie Institution of Washington, 1935-58;
investigador, Seminario de Cultura Maya,
University of Mexico, 1958-. *Military ser-
vice:* British Army, 1918. *Memberships:*
Society for American Archaeology; Royal
Anthropological Institute. *Awards, honors:*
Viking Fund Medal for Anthropology, Wenner-Gren Foundation; Encomienda de Isabel
la Catolica, Spanish government; Orden del
Aguila Azteca, Mexican government; Drexel
Wharton Medal, University of Pennsylvania.
Interests: Maya civilization, particularly
hieroglyphic writing; field trips to Mexico,
Guatemala, British Honduras. *Published
works: Mexico Before Cortez* (Scribner's,
1933); *Maya Hieroglyphic Writing: Introduction* (Carnegie Institution of Washington,
1950); *The Rise and Fall of Maya Civilization* (University of Oklahoma Press, 1958);
Maya Archaeologist (University of Oklahoma Press, 1963).

THOMPSON, RAYMOND H.   1924- (museum director, professor of anthropology)

Born May 10, 1924, Portland, Me. *Education:* Tufts University, B.S., summa
cum laude, 1947; Harvard University,
M.A., 1950, Ph.D., 1955. *Principal occupation:* Museum director, professor of
anthropology. *Affiliations:* Fellow, Division of Historical Research, Carnegie Institution of Washington, 1949-51; assistant
professor and director, Museum of Anthropology, University of Kentucky, Lexington,
Ky., 1952-56; head, Department of Anthropology, University of Arizona, 1964-; director, Arizona State Museum, University of
Arizona, Tucson, Ariz., 1964-. *Military
service:* U.S. Navy Construction Battalion.
Memberships: American Association for
the Advancement of Science (Fellow); American Anthropological Association (Fellow); American Ethnological Society; American Indian Ethnohistoric Conference; Arizona Archaeological and Historical Society;
Northern Arizona Society for Science and
Art; Society for American Archaeology;
Tree Ring Society; Sociedad Mexicana de

Antropologia; Arizona Academy of Sciences;
Seminario de Cultura Maya; Current Anthropology (associate). *Interests:* Anthropological theory; Southwestern and Mesoamerican
archaeology. Expeditions: Upper Gila Archaeological Expedition, New Mexico, Peabody Museum, Harvard University, 1949;
expedition to Yucatan, Carnegie Institution
of Washington, 1949-50. *Published works:
Modern Yucatecan Maya Pottery* (Memoirs
of the Society for American Archaeology,
No. 15, 1958).

THRAPP, DAN L.   1913- (journalist)

Born June 26, 1913, West Chicago, Ill.
Education: University of Wisconsin, 1930-
31; University of Illinois, 1935-37; Univer-
sity of Missouri, B.S. (Journalism), 1938.
Principal occupation: Journalist. *Home
address:* 11529 Starlight Ave., Whittier,
Calif. *Affiliations:* Religion editor, Los
Angeles *Times,* 1950-. *Military service:*
U.S. Army, 1943-46 (four Battle Stars;
C.B.I. Theater; Chinese decoration).
Memberships: Religious Newswriters As-
sociation, 1955-. *Awards, honors:* Reli-
gious newswriting awards. *Interests:*
American frontier; Indian wars; early cat-
tle days; frontier characters; Apache wars
and culture. *Published works: Al Sieber,
Chief of Scouts* (University of Oklahoma
Press, 1964).

TIMMONS, ALICE M.   (Cherokee)
  1914- (librarian)

Born August 10, 1914, Vinita, Okla. *Edu-
cation:* Chilocco Indian School; Northeastern
State University. *Principal occupation:*
Librarian. *Home address:* 2725 Walnut Rd.,
Norman, Okla. 73069. *Affiliations:* Librar-
ian, University of Oklahoma, Norman, Okla.
Community activities: Cancer Fund Com-
mittee, Big One Fund; Parent-Teachers'
Association; Campfire Girls. *Awards, hon-
ors:* Norman Garden Clubs Flower Show.
Memberships: Sequoyah Club; Norman Sor-
osis Club; Gaillardia Garden Club; Indian
Welfare Christmas Project.

TIMMONS, BOYCE D.   (Cherokee)   1911-
  (administrator)

Born February 6, 1911, Pawhuska, Okla.
Education: Oklahoma State University,
B.S., 1932; University of Oklahoma,

LL.B., 1937. *Principal occupation:* Administrator. *Home address:* 2725 Walnut Rd., Norman, Okla. 73069. *Affiliations:* Director of registration, University of Oklahoma. *Other professional posts:* Consultant on Indian affairs, Southwest Center on Human Relations. *Community activities:* Junior Chamber of Commerce; Boy Scouts of America; Church Congregation (president). *Memberships:* Oklahoma Association of Collegiate Registrars and Admissions Officers (former president); Oklahoma Bar Association. *Awards, honors:* Achievement Plaque, National Independent Students Association, Outstanding Citizen, Junior Chamber of Commerce. *Interests:* Indian students' faculty advisor; sponsor, weekly radio program, "Indians for Indians"; sponsor, Sequoyah Club, University of Oklahoma; member, University Scholarship Committee; former editor, *Oklahoma Indian Newsletter.*

TITIEV, MISCHA 1901- (professor of anthropology)

Born September 11, 1901, Russia. *Education:* Harvard College, B.A., 1923; Harvard University, Ph.D., 1935. *Principal occupation:* Professor of anthropology. *Home address:* 910 Heather Way, Ann Arbor, Mich. 48104. *Affiliations:* Professor of anthropology, University of Michigan, 1936-. *Military service:* Office of Strategic Services. *Memberships:* American Anthropological Association; American Ethnological Society; American Association for the Advancement of Science; Royal Anthropological Institute of Great Britain and Ireland; Chi Kappa Phi; Sigma Xi. *Awards, honors:* Fellow in ethnology, Laboratory of Anthropology, 1932; Grant-in-Aid to Japan, 1951; Fulbright Grant to Australia, 1954; Ford Fellowship in Behavioral Sciences, 1961. *Interests:* General anthropology; Hopi culture and culture change; travel to India, Assam, Burma, China, Japan, Australia, Tasmania, New Zealand, New Guinea, Hawaii, United States. *Published works:* *The Science of Man* (Holt, Rinehart & Winston, 1954, 1963); *Introduction to Cultural Anthropology* (Holt, Rinehart & Winston, 1959).

TOMMANEY, THOMAS (Creek) 1913- (school superintendent)

Born June 12, 1913, Eufala, Okla. *Education:* University of Kansas, B.A., 1938; Oklahoma State University, M.S., 1950. *Principal occupation:* School superintendent. *Address:* Haskell Institute, Lawrence, Kan. 66044. *Affiliations:* Superintendent, Intermountain School, Bureau of Indian Affairs, Brigham City, Utah; director of schools, Navajo Agency, Window Rock, Ariz.; assistant general superintendent (community services), Navajo Agency; superintendent, Haskell Institute, Lawrence, Kan. -- employed twenty-seven years with the Branch of Education of the Bureau of Indian Affairs. *Military service:* U.S. Army Air Force, 1944-45. *Community activities:* Rotary International; Lawrence Chamber of Commerce. *Memberships:* American Association of School Administrators; Phi Delta Kappa, 1952-. *Interests:* "Major interest of my career has been to assist Indian youth in (acquiring) an education and preparing for productive adult lives. Have traveled extensively in western United States. Enjoy opportunity of speaking to non-Indian groups about our Indian people, so they are better informed!"

TONG, MARVIN E., Jr. 1922- (museum director)

Born June 26, 1922, Springfield, Mo. *Education:* Southwest Missouri State College, 1940-43; University of Arkansas, 1944. *Principal occupation:* Museum director. *Home address:* 207 N. 8th St., Lawton, Okla. 73502. *Affiliations:* Director, Great Plains Historical Association, 1961-; director, Museum of the Great Plains, 1960-. *Military service:* U.S. Army Air Force, 1943-46. *Community activities:* Missouri State Park Board (advisory council); School of Forestry, University of Missouri (advisory council); 19th Plains Anthropological Conference (chairman); 11th Mountain-Plains Museums Conference (chairman). *Memberships:* Society for American Archaeology; Plains Anthropological Conference; Oklahoma Museums Association (president); Oklahoma Anthropological Society; Missouri Archaeological Society (trustee, 1955-61). *Awards, honors:* Achievement Award, Missouri Archaeological Society. *Interests:* Paleo-Indian of the Plains; Plains archaic complexes; excavations at Molly Cave, Tater Hole Cave, Garrison Cave; archaeological surveys of Norfolk Reservoir, Bull Shoals Reservoir, Table Rock Reservoir, Pomme de Terre Reservoir; co-leader, 1st International Expedition, Southern Methodist University and Museum of the Great Plains. *Published works: Christian Century: Its First 100 Years* (Standard Printing Co., 1954).

TOPPAH, HERMAN (Kiowa) 1923-
(artist)

Born August 17, 1923, Carnegie, Okla. *Education:* High school. *Principal occupation:* Artist. *Home address:* General Delivery, Carnegie, Okla. *Military service:* U.S. Army, 1943. *Memberships:* American Indian Artists Association, Lawton, Okla. *Awards, honors:* Second Award (special category), 18th Annual American Indian Artists Exhibition, Philbrook Art Center, Tulsa, Okla., 1963.

TRAYLOR, HERBERT LEE 1907-
(teacher)

Born July 10, 1907, Moro, Texas. *Education:* New Mexico Western University, B.S., 1942; New Mexico State University, M.S., 1955. *Principal occupation:* Teacher. *Home address:* Box 416, Capitan, N.M. *Affiliations:* Teacher, Bureau of Indian Affairs, Mescalero, N.M. *Community activities:* Elks; Lions International; Kiwanis Club; Otero County Teachers Organization (president, 1946-47); Ruidoso Teachers Organization (president, 1955). *Memberships:* New Mexico Teachers' Association. *Published works: Early Mining in Lincoln County* (in progress).

TREADWELL, ERWIN (Red Fox)
(Unkechaug) 1918- (tribal chief)

Born January 17, 1918, Roslyn Heights, L.I., N.Y. *Education:* High school. *Principal occupation:* Tribal chief. *Home address:* 201 Poosepatuck Lane, Poosepatuck Reservation, Mastic, L.I., N.Y. 11950. *Community activities:* Unkechaug Indian Tribe (chief); A.F.L.-C.I.O. (committeeman); Boy Scouts of America. *Awards, honors:* Award for aircraft work, Grumman Aircraft Co. *Interests:* Lecturing on Long Island Indian tribes; Indian dance group. Mr. Treadwell is working on a history of the Long Island tribes.

TRELEASE, ALLEN WILLIAM 1928-
(professor of history)

Born January 31, 1928, Boulder, Colo. *Education:* University of Illinois, B.A., 1950, M.A., 1951; Harvard University, Ph.D., 1955. *Principal occupation:* Professor of history. *Home address:* Aurora, N.Y. *Affiliations:* Professor of history, Wells College, Aurora, N.Y. *Memberships:* American Indian Ethnohistoric Conference; American Historical Association; Organization of American Historians. *Interests:* The reconstruction period after the Civil War. *Published works: Indian Affairs in Colonial New York: The Seventeenth Century* (Cornell University Press, 1960).

TRENHOLM, VIRGINIA COLE 1902-
(historical writer and researcher)

Born March 12, 1902, Columbia, Mo. *Education:* University of Missouri, B.A., M.A. *Principal occupation:* Historical writer and researcher. *Home address:* Box 503, Wheatland, Wyo. *Affiliations:* Faculty member, Stephens College, Columbia, Mo.; faculty member, Park College, Parkville, Mo. *Community activities:* Wyoming Mayflower Society (governor). *Memberships:* Wyoming Pioneer Association (president); Wyoming State Historical Society; American Association for State and Local History; Theta Sigma Phi; Wyoming Press Women; Western Writers of America. *Awards, honors:* Historical Award for *The Shoshonis: Sentinels of the Rockies,* Wyoming State Historical Society, 1965. *Interests:* Ethnohistory of the Indians of the West; "extensive travel in America and abroad, but have found my most rewarding experiences exploring my locale, visiting historic sites, and learning to know the people about whom I write." *Published works: Footprints on the Frontier* (Douglas Enterprise, 1945); co-author, *Wyoming Pageant* (Bailey School Supply, 1958); co-author, *The Shoshonis: Sentinels of the Rockies* (University of Oklahoma Press, 1964).

TSABETSAYE, ROGER JOHN (Zuni Pueblo) 1941- (artist, jewelry and silver craftsman)

Born October 29, 1941, Zuni, N.M. *Education:* Institute of American Indian Arts; School for American Craftsmen, Rochester

Institute of Technology. *Principal occupation:* Artist, jewelry and silver craftsman. *Home address:* Box 254, Zuni, N.M. *Affiliations:* Mr. Tsabetsaye produces and markets his own craft items. *Community activities:* Traveled with the Zuni Performing Dance Group in 1965, acting as the official representative of the governor of Zuni Pueblo. *Awards, honors:* Grand Award (Student Division), Special Award, Museum of New Mexico, 1957; First Award, New Mexico State Fair, 1958; First and Second Awards, New Mexico State Fair, 1959; "Student with the Greatest Promise" Award, Governor Paul Fanin Trophy, Second Award, Scottsdale Arts and Crafts Exhibition, 1960; First Award (painting, Pueblo Division), Indian Arts Exhibition, Tulsa, Okla., 1960; First Award (Professional Division), Special Award, Museum of New Mexico, 1960; Honorable Mention, Indian Arts Exhibition, Tulsa, Okla., 1961. Commissioned by President and Mrs. Johnson to design a silver necklace which was presented to the wife of a Costa Rican official. *Interests:* Art. *Biographical sources: Dictionary of American Indian Artists* by Jeanne Snodgrass (Museum of the American Indian, Heye Foundation, 1966).

TSA-TOKE, LEE MONETT (Kiowa) 1929- (artist, guide)

Born March 21, 1929, Lawton, Okla. *Education:* High school. *Principal occupation:* Artist and guide. *Home address:* 114 W. Texas St., Anadarko, Okla. *Affiliations:* Guide, Indian City, U.S.A. *Memberships:* American Indian Artists Association, Lawton, Okla., 1965-. *Awards, honors:* Second Prize, Philbrook Art Center, Tulsa, Okla., 1958; Third Prize, All Plains Indian, 1959; First Prize, Indian Exposition, Anadarko, Okla., 1960; First Prize, Inter-Tribal Indian Ceremonial, Gallup, N.M., 1954; Special Award, Kirkwood, Mo. *Interests:* Traveled with the Kiowa Dance Troupe, performing in Hershey, Penna. (American Indian drumbeats); painting; performs at various tribal affairs.

TSINAJINNIE, ANDY (Navajo) 1919- (artist)

Born November 16, 1919, Chinle, Ariz. *Education:* College of Arts and Crafts, Oakland, Calif. *Principal occupation:*

Artist. *Home address:* Box 542, Scottsdale, Ariz. *Military service:* U.S. Army Air Force, 1940-45. *Awards, honors:* Grand Award, Philbrook Art Center, 1951; National Textile Design Award, American Institute of Interior Design; French Medal Award, Paul Coze, Paris, France. *Published works (as illustrator): Spirit Rocks and Silver Magic* (Caxton Printers, Ltd.); *Peetie the Pack Rat and Other Desert Stories* (Caxton Printers, Ltd.); *Who Wants to Be a Prairie Dog?* (Haskell Institute); and others.

TUMLIN, L.H., Jr. (state park superintendent)

Education: Daughans Business College. *Principal occupation:* State park superintendent. *Address:* c/o Etowah Indian Mounds, Cartersville, Ga. *Affiliations:* Superintendent, Etowah Indian Mounds (park and museum), Cartersville, Ga. *Military service:* U.S. Air Force, 1941-45. *Community activities:* Cartersville Kiwanis Club (support of churches committee); Cartersville Chamber of Commerce (board of directors); American Legion post (commander); Men's Brotherhood, First Baptist Church (president, 1964-65). *Awards, honors:* Award for Outstanding Work, Support of Churches Committee, Kiwanis Club, 1964.

TUNIS, EDWIN 1897- (artist and designer, advertising illustrator)

Born December 8, 1897, Cold Spring Harbor, N.Y. *Education:* Baltimore City College; Maryland Institute of Art and Design. *Principal occupation:* Artist and designer, advertising illustrator. *Home address:* R.F.D. 1, Reistertown, Md. *Military service:* U.S. Army Air Force, 1917. *Awards, honors:* Notable Children's Book Award for *Frontier Living*, American Library Association, 1961; runner-up for Newberry Medal for *Frontier Living*, 1961; Honor Book Award, Children's Spring Book Festival, New York *Herald Tribune* for *Colonial Craftsmen*, 1965. *Interests:* Painting and reading. *Published works: Indians* (1959), *Frontier Living* (1961), *Colonial Craftsmen* (1965), all published by The World Publishing Co.

TURNER, KATHERINE C.   (teacher)

Born March 11, 1910. *Principal occupation:* Teacher. *Home address:* 1210 Mill St., Tempe, Ariz. *Published works: Red Men Calling on the Great White Father* (University of Oklahoma Press, 1951).

U

UDALL, STEWART LEE   1920-
   (Secretary of the Interior)

Born January 31, 1920, St. Johns, Ariz. *Education:* University of Arizona, LL. B., 1948. *Principal occupation:* Secretary of the Interior, U.S. Department of the Interior, Washington, D.C. 20242. *Affiliations:* Admitted to Arizona bar, 1948; member, 84th and 86th Congresses, 2nd Dist., Ariz.; Secretary of the Interior, 1961-. *Military service:* U.S.A.A.F., 1944. *Memberships:* American Bar Association. *Published works: The Quiet Crisis* (1963).

UNDERHILL, RUTH MURRAY   1884-
   (anthropologist, writer)

Born August 22, 1884, Ossining, N.Y. *Education:* Vassar College, B.A., 1905; London School of Economics, 1907-08; Columbia University, Ph.D., 1934. *Principal occupation:* Anthropologist, writer. *Home address:* 2623 S. Clayton St., Denver, Colo. 80210. *Affiliations:* Investigator in social work, Boston, Mass., New York, N.Y., 1909-17; anthropological study and writing, Bureau of Indian Affairs, U.S. Department of the Interior, 1937-49; professor of anthropology, University of Denver, 1949-52; professor of anthropology, New York State Teachers College, 1954-55; series on Indians, KRMA-TV, Denver, Colo., 1957-58; seminars in anthropology, Colorado Women's College, University of Colorado. *Community activities:* International House (board of directors, 1959-65; honorary vice president, 1965-66). *Memberships:* American Anthropological Association, 1930- (council member); American Ethnological Society, 1931- (president, 1960-61); American Association for the Advancement of Science. *Awards, honors:* LL.D., Uni-

versity of Denver, 1962; D.Sc., University of Colorado, 1965; citation for service, Colorado Women's College, 1963; citation for promotion of intercultural relations, Downtown Community School, New York, N.Y., 1962. *Interests:* American Indians (reservation and living conditions; education); travel throughout the United States, India, Australia, New Zealand, Europe; attended anthropological conferences in England, Brazil, and Austria. *Published works: Ethnology of the Papago Indians,* with Edward Castetter (University of New Mexico Bulletin, No. 275, 1935); *Autobiography of a Papago Woman* (American Anthropological Association, 1936); *A Papago Calendar Record* (University of New Mexico Bulletin, No. 322, 1938); *Singing for Power: The Song Magic of the Papago Indians* (University of California, 1938); *First Penthouse Dwellers of America* (J.J. Augustin, 1938; Laboratory of Anthropology); *Social Organization of the Papago Indians* (Columbia University, 1939); *Hawk Over Whirlpools* (J.J. Augustin, 1940); *U.S. Indian Service Series on Indian Life and Customs -- The Northern Paiute Indians, Indians of Southern California, Pueblo Crafts, Workaday Life of the Pueblos, Indians of the Pacific Northwest, Here Come the Navaho!, The Papago Indians and Their Relatives, the Pima, People of the Crimson Evening* (Bureau of Indian Affairs, Haskell Institute); *Papago Indian Religion* (Columbia University, 1946); *Ceremonial Patterns in the Greater Southwest* (American Ethnological Society, Monograph No. 13, 1948); articles on Indians and anthropology for children's encyclopedias -- *World Book, Collier's Encyclopedia, Children's Encyclopedia, Grolier Society,* 1948; *Red Man's America: A History of Indians in the United States* (University of Chicago Press, 1953); *The Navajos* (University of Oklahoma Press, 1956); *Beaverbird* (Coward-McCann, 1958); *First Came the Family* (William Morrow, 1958); *Antelope Singer* (Coward-McCann, 1961); *Red Man's Religion* (University of Chicago Press, 1965); articles for various publications.

URELL, CATHERINE   (teacher,
   research associate)

Born Tioga, Penna. *Education:* City College of New York, B.S., 1928, M.S. (Education), 1930; New York University, Ph.D. (Education), 1935. *Principal occupation:* Teacher, research associate. *Home ad-*

dress: 141 Joralemon St., Brooklyn, N.Y. 11201. *Affiliations:* Teacher, Scarsdale, N.Y., public schools, 1929-44; researcher, Curriculum and Editorial Research Bureaus, 1944-64; Follett Publishing Co. *Community activities:* Brooklyn Mental Health Association (board); Arthritis and Rheumatism Association (board). *Memberships:* National Council for the Social Studies. *Interests:* Travel to Europe, Mexico, southeast Asia, southern Asia, the Middle East, Egypt, Tunisia, Morocco. *Published works:* Senior author, *Big City Series*, nine books (1953-58), senior author, *Indians, Settlers and Pioneers* (1955), senior author, *Living in New York* (1962), all published by Follett Publishing Co.

UTLEY, ROBERT M.   1929-   (historian)

Born October 31, 1929, Bauxite, Ark. *Education:* Purdue University, B.S., 1951; Indiana University, M.A., 1952. *Principal occupation:* Historian. *Home address:* 6529 Hitt Rd., McLean, Va. *Affiliations:* Seasonal historian, Department of the Interior, National Park Service, Custer Battlefield National Monument, Mont., 1947-52; historian, Department of Defense, Washington, D.C., 1954-57; regional historian, Department of the Interior, National Park Service, Southwest Region, Santa Fe, N.M., 1957-64; chief historian, Department of Defense, Washington, D.C., 1965-. *Military service:* U.S. Army, 1952-56. *Memberships:* American Historical Association; Organization of American Historians; Western History Association (executive council, 1962-; editorial board); Historical Society of New Mexico; Washington and Santa Fe Corrals of the Westerners. *Interests:* Historic sites conservation; American Indians; the American frontier. *Published works:* *Custer and the Great Controversy* (Westernlore Press, 1962); *The Last Days of the Sioux Nation* (Yale University Press, 1963); editor, *Battlefield and Classroom* (Yale University Press, 1964).

V

VAIL, ROY   1902-   (museum curator)

Born November 9, 1902, Orange County, N.Y. *Education:* New York State College, Morrisville, N.Y. *Principal occupation:* Museum curator. *Home address:* Route 1, Warwick, N.Y. *Affiliations:* Curator, Warwick Valley Museum. *Military service:* U.S. Naval Reserve. *Community activities:* Warwick Central School Board (president); Orange and Ulster Cooperative School Board (president). *Memberships:* Sons of the American Revolution; National Recreation Association; Historical Society, Town of Warwick (president, 1960-). *Interests:* Hunting (African safari, 1963); guns; antiques. *Published works:* Articles for various magazines.

VAN EVERY, DALE   1896-   (writer)

Born July 23, 1896, Lovering, Mich. *Education:* Stanford University, B.A., 1920. *Principal occupation:* Writer. *Home address:* 750 El Bosque Rd., Santa Barbara, Calif. *Affiliations:* Correspondent and editor, United Press, 1920-28; writer and producer of motion pictures, 1928-42. *Military service:* U.S. Army A.S., 1917-19. *Interests:* Mr. Van Every writes, "Since 1942 (my) writing has been concentrated on novels and works of history dealing with (the) early American frontier." *Published works:* *The A.E.F. in Battle* (Appleton, 1928); *Westward the River* (Putnam, 1945); *The Shining Mountains* (Messner, 1948); *Bridal Journey* (Messner, 1950); *The Captive Witch* (Messner, 1951); *The Trembling Earth* (Messner, 1953); *Men of the Western Waters* (Houghton Mifflin, 1956); *The Voyagers* (Holt, 1957); *Our Country Then* (Holt, 1958); *The Scarlet Feather* (Holt, 1959); *Forth to the Wilderness* (Morrow, 1961); *A Company of Heroes* (Morrow, 1962); *Ark of Empire* (Morrow, 1963); *The Final Challenge* (Morrow, 1964).

VAN RIPER, GUERNSEY, Jr.   1909-
(author)

Born July 5, 1909, Indianapolis, Ind. *Education:* De Pauw University, B.A.; Harvard University, M.B.A. *Principal occupation:* Author. *Home address:* 1142 W. 38th St., Indianapolis, Ind. *Memberships:* Phi Kappa Psi; Sigma Delta Chi; Phi Beta Kappa. *Awards, honors:* Phi Beta Kappa. *Published works:* *Babe Ruth: Baseball Boy* (1959), *Knute Rockne: Young Athlete* (1959), *Lou Gehrig: Boy of the Sandlots* (1959), *Jim Thorpe: Indian Athlete* (1961), *Richard Byrd: Boy of the South Pole* (1962), *Will Rogers: Young Cowboy* (1962), all published by The Bobbs-Merrill Co.

VAUGHAN, ALDEN T. 1929- (assistant professor of history)

Born January 23, 1929, Providence, R.I. *Education:* Amherst College, B.A., 1950; Columbia University, M.A., 1956, M.A., 1958, Ph.D., 1964. *Principal occupation:* Assistant professor of history. *Home address:* 395 Riverside Drive, New York, N.Y. 10027. *Affiliations:* Assistant professor of history, Columbia University, 1961-. *Military service:* U.S. Navy, 1951-55 (active); 1950-51, 1955- (inactive). *Memberships:* Society of American Historians (secretary-treasurer); American Historical Association, 1958-; Organization of American Historians, 1962-; American Association of University Professors, 1963-; Reserve Officers of America, 1963-. *Interests:* American colonial and revolutionary history; American historiography. *Published works: New England Frontier: Puritans and Indians, 1620-1675* (Little, Brown, 1965); *Chronicles of the American Revolution* (Grosset & Dunlap, 1965).

VAUGHN, J.W. 1903- (attorney, writer)

Born March 4, 1903, Dadeville, Mo. *Education:* University of Missouri, B.A., 1925; University of Denver Law School, LL.B., 1929. *Principal occupation:* Attorney, writer. *Home address:* 521 W. Main St., Windsor, Colo. *Affiliations:* Town attorney, Windsor, Colo., 1930-. *Community activities:* Methodist Church; Windsor Lodge. *Memberships:* Phi Alpha Delta; Company of Military Historians (Fellow); Wyoming Pioneer Association (patron); Custer Battlefield Historical and Museum Association. *Interests:* Indian wars of 1865-76 in Wyoming and Montana. *Published works: With Crook at the Rosebud* (Stackpole, 1956); *Reynolds Campaign on Powder River* (University of Oklahoma Press, 1961); *The Battle of Platte Bridge* (University of Oklahoma Press, 1964).

VICTOR, WILMA L. (Choctaw) 1919- (school superintendent)

Born November 5, 1919, Idabel, Okla. *Education:* University of Kansas, 1937-39; Wisconsin State College, B.S., 1941; University of Oklahoma, M.Ed., 1953. *Principal occupation:* School superintendent. *Home address:* Cottage 330, Intermountain

School, Brigham City, Utah 84302. *Affiliations:* Public secondary school teacher, Idabel, Okla., two years; secondary teacher, Bureau of Indian Affairs, Shiprock, N.M., one and one-half years; academic department head, Bureau of Indian Affairs, Brigham City, Utah, ten years; supervisory educational specialist, Bureau of Indian Affairs, Brigham City, Utah, one and one-half years; school principal, Bureau of Indian Affairs, Santa Fe, N.M., two and one-half years; school superintendent, Intermountain School, Bureau of Indian Affairs, Brigham City, Utah, 1964-. *Military service:* Women's Army Corps, 1943-46. *Memberships:* American Association of School Administrators; Northern Utah Chapter, Council for Exceptional Children; Governor's Committee on Indian Affairs in Utah; Utah State Conference on Social Welfare; Kappa Delta Pi. *Awards, honors:* Superior Performance Award, Bureau of Indian Affairs. *Interests:* "Have traveled to Europe with an alumni group from the University of Oklahoma." *Biographical sources: Indians of Today* (Indian Council Fire, 1960).

VIGIL, MARTIN (Tesuque Pueblo) 1896- (tribal officer)

Born January 25, 1896, Tesuque Pueblo, N.M. *Education:* St. Catherine's Indian School. *Principal occupation:* Tribal officer. *Home address:* Tesuque Pueblo, Route 1, Box 59, Santa Fe, N.M. 87501. *Affiliations:* Chairman, All Pueblo Council. *Other professional posts:* Spokesman and interpreter. *Community activities:* Santa Fe County Commission; Governor's staff (honorary colonel); Tesuque Pueblo (former governor). *Memberships:* New Mexico Commission on Indian Affairs.

VIZENOR, GERALD ROBERT (Chippewa) 1934- (guidance director, poet)

Born October 22, 1934, Minneapolis, Minn. *Education:* University of Minnesota, B.A., 1960; University of Minnesota, M.A. candidate, 1964. *Principal occupation:* Guidance director, poet. *Home address:* 101 Seymour, S.E., Minneapolis, Minn. 55414. *Affiliations:* Guidance director, Department of Corrections, Minneapolis, Minn. *Military service:* U.S. Army, 1952-55. *Memberships:* Delta Phi Lambda (honorary writers' fraternity). *Published works: Sum-*

mer in the Spring, Ojibway Lyric Poems (Nodin Press, 1965); *Seventeen Chirps* (Nodin Press, 1964); *Raising the Moon Vines* (Callimachus Publishing Co., 1964).

VOGET, FRED W. 1913- (professor of anthropology)

Born February 12, 1913, Salem, Ore. *Education:* University of Oregon, B.A., 1936; Yale University, Ph.D., 1948. *Principal occupation:* Professor of anthropology. *Home address:* 133 W. Lake Drive, Edwardsville, Ill. *Affiliations:* Assistant professor, McGill University; professor, University of Arkansas; associate professor, professor, University of Toronto; professor of anthropology, University of Southern Illinois, 1965-. *Military service:* U.S. Army, 1942-46. *Memberships:* American Anthropological Association (Fellow); American Ethnological Society; Society for Applied Anthropology; American Association of University Professors. *Interests*: Ethnology of Plains and North American Indians; acculturation; history of ethnological theory; ethnology of Africa. *Published works:* Articles in the field of anthropology.

VOGT, EVON ZARTMAN, Jr. 1918- (professor of anthropology)

Born August 20, 1918, Gallup, N.M. *Education:* University of Chicago, B.A., 1941, M.A., 1946, Ph.D., 1948. *Principal occupation:* Professor of anthropology. *Home address:* 79 Spruce Hill Road, Weston, Mass. *Affiliations:* Instructor, 1948-50, assistant professor, 1950-55, associate professor, 1955-59, professor of anthropology, 1959-, Harvard University. *Other professional posts:* Assistant curator of American ethnology, 1950-59, curator of middle American ethnology, 1960-, Peabody Museum; member, Division of Anthropology and Psychology, National Research Council, 1955-57. *Military service:* U.S. Naval Reserve, 1942-46. *Memberships:* Center for Advanced Study in the Behavioral Sciences (Fellow, 1956-57); American Academy of Arts and Sciences (Fellow); American Anthropological Association (Fellow; executive board, 1958-60); Society for American Archaeology; Royal Anthropological Institute of Great Britain and Ireland; American Folklore Society. *Published works: Navaho Veterans* (1951); *Modern Homesteaders*

(1955); *Reader in Comparative Religion*, with W.A. Lessa (1958); *Water Witching U.S.A.*, with Ray Hyman (1959).

VOIGHT, VIRGINIA FRANCES 1909- (writer)

Born March 30, 1909, New Britain, Conn. *Education:* Yale School of Fine Arts; Austin School of Commercial Art. *Principal occupation:* Writer. *Home address:* 74 Marne St., Hamden, Conn. 06514. *Interests:* Miss Voight writes, "My chief interest in connection with my work lies in the field of nature study, and in research in American history, especially in the history, culture, and woodlore of the American Indian. My hobbies are herb gardening, nature study, bird-watching, reading, and collecting books for my library. When I have time, I plan to return to my lost hobby of sketching and painting watercolors." *Published works: Apple Tree Cottage* (Holiday House, 1949); *The House in Robin Lane* (Holiday House, 1951); *Zeke and the Fisher Cat* (Holiday House, 1953); *Lions in the Barn* (Holiday House, 1956); *Mystery at Deer Hill* (Funk and Wagnalls, 1958); *Black Elephant* (Prentice-Hall, 1959); *The Missing $10,111 Bill* (Funk and Wagnalls, 1960); *The Girl from Johnnycake Hill* (Prentice-Hall, 1961); *Treasure of Hemlock Mountain* (Funk and Wagnalls, 1961); *A Book for Abe* (Prentice-Hall, 1963); *Uncas: Sachem of the Wolf People* (Funk and Wagnalls, 1963); *Picta, the Painted Turtle* (Putnam, 1963); *Mystery in the Museum* (Funk and Wagnalls, 1964); *Nathan Hale* (Putnam, 1965); *Patch, the Baby Mink* (Putnam, 1965); *Mohegan Chief: The Story of Harold Tantaquidgeon* (Funk and Wagnalls, 1965); *Sacajawea, Guide to Lewis and Clark* (Putnam, 1966).

VON MUELLER, KARL (Dean Miller) 1915- (writer, historian)

Born February 3, 1915, Minden, Neb. *Education:* University of Nebraska, 1933-35; Creighton University, 1936-37; Chicago Technical College, 1945; Santa Monica City College, 1957-59; University of California, Los Angeles, 1955-56. *Principal occupation:* Author, historian, "adventurer." *Affiliations:* Manager, Exanimo Press; editor, Gazette Publishing Co.; general manager, Goldenrich Press. *Other professional posts:* Technical consultant to industry on publishing. *Memberships:* Western Writers of America, 1963-; Associated Geographers of America, 1957- (national president, 1957-59); American Radio Relay League, 1959-; Association for State and Local History, 1962-. *Interests:* Ghost towns and historic sites pertaining to the development of the West; collection of photographs pertaining to historic sites in the western United States, historic Indians and descendants of famous Indians, graves of famous Indians and other Indian sites. *Published works: African Violet Manual* (Goldenrich Press, 1948); *Photographers Manual* (Goldenrich Press, 1948); *Models Manual* (Goldenrich Press, 1949); *Facets of Indian Culture Along the Oregon and Mormon Trails* (Adventure Press, 1957); *Historical Sites in Arizona* (Adventure Press, 1957); *Ghosttown Directory* (Associated Geographers of America, 1957); *Historical Sites in Nebraska* (Adventure Press, 1958); *Historical Sites in Wyoming* (Adventure Press, 1958); *Historical Sites in Montana* (Adventure Press, 1958); *Historical Sites in New Mexico* (Adventure Press, 1958); *Treasure Hunter's Manual* (Audobon, 1959, 1960; KvonM, 1961).

W

WADLEY, MARIE LUCILLE (Cherokee-Shawnee) 1906- (B.I.A. official)

Born December 16, 1906, Pensacola, Okla. *Education:* Draughon's Business College, Muskogee, Okla., 1923-25; Muskogee Junior College, 1952-55. *Principal occupation:* B.I.A. official. *Home address:* 2417 Arline St., Muskogee, Okla. 74401. *Affiliations:* Tribal operations officer, Muskogee Area Office, Bureau of Indian Affairs, 1925-. *Community activities:* St. Paul Methodist Church; Wesleyan Service Guild, St. Paul Methodist Church (president; secretary; chairman, various committees); Soroptimist Club of Muskogee; Five Civilized Tribes Museum (board of directors; first president; executive secretary); Daco-Tah Indian Club (various offices); National Hall of Fame for Famous Indians (advisory board); Muskogee Community Council (board of directors); The Louie LaFlore Scholarship Fund, Inc. (board of directors; registered agent; executive secretary); The Five Civilized Tribes Foundation, Inc. (board of directors; registered agent; execu-

tive secretary); Murrow Indian Children's Home (board of directors); The Grant Foreman Centennial Scholarship Fund (board of directors; executive secretary); The Inter-Tribal Council of the Five Civilized Tribes (executive secretary, 1950-); Cherokee Nation or Tribe of Oklahoma (executive secretary, 1948-); The Cherokee National Historical Society, Inc. (board of directors); The Cherokee Foundation, Inc. (board of directors); Beta Sigma Chapter, Beta Sigma Phi (sponsor); Human Relations Institute, Muskogee, Okla. (chairman); Governor's Committee to Further Employment of Handicapped; Oklahoma Semi-Centennial Commission (planning committee); Oklahoma Federation of Federal Employees (state secretary); Parent-Teachers' Association (state group relations committee). *Awards, honors:* Distinguished Service Award for services beyond the call of duty, Cherokee Nation or Tribe of Oklahoma, 1954; Certificate of Special Recognition for Outstanding Service, Cherokee Nation or Tribe of Oklahoma, 1964; Cash Award and Citation for Superior Performance, Bureau of Indian Affairs, 1965; Distinguished Service Award, U.S. Department of the Interior, 1966; Order of the Rose Degree for Outstanding Service to Beta Sigma Phi, International, 1966; Life Membership Pin, Wesleyan Service Guild, St. Paul Methodist Church; Citation for Community Services, Muskogee Elks Club; Certificate of Merit, Thomas Gilcrease Institute of American History and Art. *Interests:* "Home, music, travel, people, writing and speaking." *Published works: The Five Civilized Tribes. . . Their Contribution to Our Civilization* (Postmaster's Gazette, 1962); *A Biographical Sketch of Houston Benge Tehee* (Chronicles of Oklahoma, Oklahoma Historical Society, 1959); *We Must Have a Goal* (Cazequanica, 1959).

WAINWRIGHT, NICHOLAS B.   1914- (director, editor)

Born July 12, 1914, Saraunac, N.Y. *Education:* Princeton University, B.A., 1936; University of Pennsylvania, M.A., 1951. *Principal occupation:* Director, editor. *Home address:* R.D. 1, Ambler, Penna. *Affiliations:* Editor, director, Historical Society of Pennsylvania, 1952-. *Military service:* U.S. Army, 1941-46. *Community activities:* Library Company of Philadelphia (president). *Memberships:* Walpole Society; American Antiquarian Society. *Awards, honors:* Athenaeum Award of Philadelphia for literary achievement. *Published works: George Groghan* (University of North Carolina Press, 1959); *Colonial Grandeur in Philadelphia: The House and Furniture of General John Cadwalader* (Historical Society of Pennsylvania, 1964); *Irvine Story* (Historical Society of Pennsylvania, 1964).

WAKEFIELD, ALFRED S.   1920-
  (minister, museum curator)

Born April 15, 1920, River Forest, Ill. *Education:* Illinois College; Roosevelt University, B.A., 1943; McCormick Theological Seminary, 1943-46; Garrett Biblical Institute, 1947; University of Illinois, 1947-49. *Principal occupation:* Minister, Presbyterian Church; museum curator. *Affiliations:* Curator, Highland Iowa-Sac Indian Museum, Highland, Kan. *Military service:* U.S. Army (civilian chaplain). *Community activities:* County Ministerial Association (president); Topeka-Highland Presbytery (council member); County Mental Health Clinic (board of governors); Radio-TV Committee, Kansas City Area (chairman); Boy Scouts of America; County Economic Opportunity Committee (chairman); high school coach; Kiwanis Club. *Memberships:* Kansas Mental Health Association; Ministerial Association. *Awards, honors:* Distinguished Citizen Award, Kankakee, Ill. *Interests:* Radio and television; early American and Indian history; mental health; travel to Alaska and throughout the United States.

WAKEMAN, RICHARD K.   (Flandreau Santee Sioux) 1923- (tribal officer)

Born February 9, 1923, Flandreau, S.D. *Education:* Haskell Institute, Lawrence, Kan. *Principal occupation:* Tribal officer. *Home address:* R.R. 1, Flandreau, S.D. 57028. *Affiliations:* President, Flandreau Santee Sioux (Tribal) Council. *Military service:* U.S. Marine Corps, 1942-45; U.S. Army, 1951-53 (Presidential Unit Citation; Commendation; Asiatic Pacific Award). *Community activities:* South Dakota Indian Commission; South Dakota Letter Carriers (president); Dakota Presbytery (moderator); Masonic Lodge. *Interests:* Tribal history.

WALKER, LOUISE JEAN   1891-
  (associate professor of English)

Born February 10, 1891, Jackson, Mich. *Education:* Albion College, B.A., 1917; Columbia University, M.A., 1924; University of Colorado, 1936; University of Michigan, 1943. *Principal occupation:* Associate professor of English. *Home address:* 907 W. Lowell St., Kalamazoo, Mich. *Affiliations:* English teacher, high schools in Midland, Cadillac, and Battle Creek, Mich., 1917-23; Department of English, Western Michigan University, 1924-61; professor of English, Highlands University, Las Vegas, N.M., 1951, 1953; associate professor of English, Western Michigan University, 1961-. *Community activities:* Young Women's Christian Association; Daughters of the American Revolution (speaker); Parent-Teachers' Association; teachers' and church organizations. *Memberships:* American Association of University Women; Faculty Women's Organization (secretary); National Folklore Society; National Council of English Teachers; Michigan Academy of Arts and Sciences; Michigan Historical Society; Michigan Library Association; First Methodist Church; Michigan Education Association. *Awards, honors:* Bookland and Her People, No. 18, a national contest offered by Teachers College for lesson unit series, sponsored by Dr. William A. McCall. *Interests:* Travel and study of the British Isles and the European Continent, the United States, Canada, Mexico, and Nassau. Other interests include antiques and classical music. *Published works: Legends of Green Sky Hill* (Wm. B. Eerdmans Publishing Co., 1959); *Red Indian Legends* (Odhams Press, London, 1961); *Woodland Wigwams* (Hillsdale Educational, 1963); *Beneath the Singing Pines* (Hillsdale Educational, 1965).

WALLACE, AMOS LEWIS   (Eskimo)
  1920- (craftsman)

Born November 28, 1920, Juneau, Alaska. *Education:* High school. *Principal occupation:* Craftsman. *Home address:* 837 W. 7th St., Juneau, Alaska 99801. *Military service:* U.S. Army. *Community activities:* Alaska Native Brotherhood, Camp 2, 1958- (financial secretary; president); Centennial Committee. *Memberships:* Toastmasters. Mr. Wallace's work is displayed at the Brooklyn Children's Museum, the Museum of Natural History, the Indian Village at Disneyland, the University of Alaska, and at the Boston Children's Museum -- all hand-carved totems.

WALLACE, ANTHONY F.C.   1923-
(professor of anthropology)

Born April 15, 1923, Toronto, Can. *Education:* University of Pennsylvania, B.A., 1947, M.A., 1949, Ph.D., 1950. *Principal occupation:* Professor of anthropology. *Home address:* 614 Convent Rd., Chester, Penna. *Affiliations:* Chairman and professor, Department of Anthropology, University of Pennsylvania, 1961-; medical research scientist, Eastern Pennsylvania Psychiatric Institute, 1961-. *Other professional posts:* Member, National Research Council, Division of Behavioral Sciences; U.S. Office of Education, Research Advisory Committee; member, Behavioral Science Study Section, National Institute of Mental Health. *Military service:* U.S. Army, 1942-45. *Memberships:* American Anthropological Association (Fellow); American Association for the Advancement of Science (Fellow; chairman, Section H); American Sociological Association (Fellow); Sigma Xi; Philadelphia Anthropological Society (president, 1957-58; council member). *Awards, honors:* Harrison Fellow, University of Pennsylvania; Faculty Research Fellow, Social Science Research Council; Research Grant, Penrose Fund, American Philosophical Society; Auxiliary Research Grant, Social Science Research Council; principal investigator, M883 and M1166, National Institute of Mental Health. *Published works: The Modal Personality Structure of the Tuscarora Indians, as Revealed by the Rorschach Test* (Bureau of American Ethnology, Bulletin 150, 1952); *Housing and Social Structure: A Preliminary Survey, with Special Reference to Multi-Storey, Low-Rent Public Housing Projects* (Philadelphia Housing Authority, 1952); *Human Behavior in Extreme Situations: A Survey of the Literature and Suggestions for Further Research* (National Academy of Sciences - National Research Council, Disaster Study No. 1, 1956); *Emergency Medical Care in Disasters: A Summary of Recorded Experience,* with John Raker and Jeannette Rayner (National Academy of Sciences - National Research Council, Disaster Study No. 6, 1956); editor, *Men and Cultures: Selected Papers of the Fifth International Congress of Anthropological and Ethnological Sciences* (University of Pennsylvania Press, 1960); "The Meaning of Kinship Terms," with John Atkins *(American Anthropologist,* No. 62, 1950, pp. 58-80; reprinted by The Bobbs-Merrill Co.); *Culture and Personal-*

ity (Random House, 1961); editor and author of Introduction, *The Ghost-Dance Religion and the Sioux Outbreak of 1890* (University of Chicago Press, 1965); *The Concept of Culture: A Resource Unit in World Cultures* (Department of Public Instruction, Commonwealth of Pennsylvania, 1965); numerous articles in professional journals.

WALLACE, ERNEST   1906-   (professor of history)

Born June 6, 1906, Daingerfield, Texas. *Education:* East Texas State University, B.S. (Education), 1932; Texas Technological College, M.A., 1935; Texas University, Ph.D., 1942; Harvard University, 1952-53. *Principal occupation:* Professor of history. *Address:* Department of History, Texas Technological College, Lubbock, Texas. *Affiliations:* Teacher, coach, principal, Texas public schools, 1925-36; instructor, University of Texas, 1937, 1938, 1942; instructor, 1936-41, assistant professor of history, 1941-43, associate professor of history, 1943-45, professor of history, 1945-, assistant dean, arts and sciences, 1954-55, Texas Technological College. *Memberships:* American Historical Association; Mississippi Valley Historical Association; Southern History Association; Western History Association; Texas State History Association (executive council); West Texas History Association (president, 1952; assistant editor, 1960-); Panhandle-Plains Historical Association; Texas Archaeological Society (secretary-treasurer; assistant editor, 1948-53). *Awards, honors:* Ford Foundation Fellowship, 1952-53; best example for book-length studies of social sciences in the South, for studies on the Comanche Indians, Southern Regional Educational Board, 1959. *Interests:* Land cases concerning the Comanche, Kiowa, Kiowa-Apache, and Apache Indians. *Published works: Charles DeMorse, Pioneer Editor and Statesman* (Texas Technological Press, 1943); *The Comanches: Lords of the South Plains,* with E. Adamson Hoebel (University of Oklahoma Press, 1952); *Documents of Texas History* with D.M. Vigness (Steck Co., 1963); *Ranald S. Mackenzie on the Texas Frontier* (Texas Technological Museum, 1965); *Texas in Turmoil, 1849-1876* (Vaughn-Steck Co., 1965); articles in various journals; contributions to *Builders of the Southwest, Handbook of Texas, Encyclopaedia Britannica.*

WALLACE, PAUL A.W.   1891-
(professor of English)

Born October 31, 1891, Cobourg, Can. *Education:* University of Toronto, B.A., 1915, M.A., 1923, Ph.D., 1925. *Principal occupation:* Professor of English. *Home address:* 1027 Drexel Hills Blvd., New Cumberland, Penna. 17070. *Affiliations:* Lecturer, University of Alberta, 1920-22; instructor, University of Toronto, 1923-25; professor, Lebanon Valley College, 1925-49; associate historian, Pennsylvania Historical and Museum Commission, 1949-65; professor of English, fellow in the humanities, Lebanon Valley College, 1965-. *Other professional posts:* Editor, *Pennsylvania History*, 1951-57. *Military service:* Canadian Expeditionary Force, 1916-18. *Memberships:* Modern Language Association, 1925-49; American Historical Association, 1949-; Pennsylvania Historical Association, 1935-; Association of the American Indian, 1950-. *Awards, honors:* Litt.D. (hon.), Muhlenberg College, 1950; L.H.D. (hon.), Moravian College, for *Thirty Thousand Miles with John Heckewelder. Interests:* Research and writing on historical subjects. *Published works: Conrad Weiser, Friend of Colonist and Mohawk* (University of Pennsylvania, 1945); *The White Roots of Peace* (University of Pennsylvania, 1946); *The Muhlenbergs of Pennsylvania* (University of Pennsylvania, 1950); *Thirty Thousand Miles with John Heckewelder* (University of Pittsburgh, 1958); *Indians in Pennsylvania* (Pennsylvania Historical and Museum Commission, 1961); *Pennsylvania, Seed of a Nation* (Harper & Row, 1962); *Indian Paths of Pennsylvania* (Pennsylvania Historical and Museum Commission -- forthcoming).

WALLIS, RUTH SAWTELL   1895-
(anthropologist, author, educator)

Born March 15, 1895, Springfield, Mass. *Education:* Radcliffe College, B.A., 1919, M.A., 1923; Columbia University, Ph.D., 1929; Vassar College; Ecole d'Anthropologie; University of Munich. *Principal occupation:* Anthropologist, author, educator. *Home address:* Box 66, South Woodstock, Conn. 06267. *Affiliations:* Editor, research assistant, Peabody Museum, Harvard University, 1920-23; Columbia University, 1926; anthropologist, Bureau Educational Exper., New York, N.Y., 1926-30; assistant professor, State University of Iowa,

1930-31; assistant professor, Hamline University, 1931-36; anthropometrist, Bureau of Home Economics, U.S. Bureau of Agriculture, 1937-38; labor market analyst, War Manpower Commission, 1942-43; professor of anthropology and sociology, Annhurst College, 1956-. *Memberships:* Minnesota Historical Society. *Awards, honors:* Phi Beta Kappa; Sigma Xi. *Interests:* Social anthropology of Canadian (Eastern or Santee) Dakota and Micmac. Field expeditions to French Pyrenees (prehistoric archaeology), 1924; Maritime Provinces, 1950, 1953; Manitoba, 1951, 1952 -- ethnography; writing murder mystery novels. *Published works: Primitive Hearths in the Pyrenees,* with Ida Treat (Appleton, 1927); *Too Many Bones* (Dodd, Mead, 1943; Dell); *No Bones About It* (Dodd, Mead, 1944; Bantam); *Blood from a Stone* (Dodd, Mead, 1945; Bantam); *Dold Bed in the Clay* (Dodd, Mead, 1947); *Forget My Fate* (Dodd, Mead, 1950); *The Micmac Indians of Eastern Canada, with Wilson D. Wallis* (University of Minnesota Press, 1955); *The Malicete Indians, with Wilson D. Wallis* (National Museum of Canada, 1957); has also written several monographs on prehistoric archaeology and the growth of children.

WALLIS, WILSON D(ALLAM)   1886-
(teacher)

Born March 7, 1886, Forest Hill, Md. *Education:* Dickinson College, B.A., 1907, M.A., 1910; Oxford University, B.S.C., Diploma in Anthropology, 1910; University of Pennsylvania, Ph.D., 1915. *Principal occupation:* Teacher. *Home address:* Box 66, South Woodstock, Conn. 06267. *Affiliations:* Instructor, University of Pennsylvania, 1911-15; instructor, University of California, Berkeley, 1915-16; assistant professor, Reed College, 1921-23; associate professor, professor, University of Minnesota, 1923-54. *Military service:* U.S. Army. *Memberships:* American Anthropological Association; American Ethnological Society; American Association of University Professors. *Interests:* Ethnographic field work among the Micmac in the Canadian Maritime Provinces, 1911, 1912, 1950, 1953; among the Dakota in Manitoba, 1914, 1951, 1952. *Published works: Messiahs: Christian and Pagan* (R.G. Badger, 1918); *Introduction to Anthropology* (Harper, 1926); *Introduction to Sociology* (Crofts, 1927); *Culture and Progress* (McGraw-Hill,

1930); *Religion in Primitive Society* (Crofts, 1939); *Readings in Sociology* (Crofts, 1940); *The Micmac Indians of Eastern Canada,* with Ruth Sawtell Wallis (University of Minnesota Press, 1955); *The Malicete Indians,* with Ruth Sawtell Wallis (National Museum of Canada, 1957); *Culture Patterns in Christianity* (Coronado Press, 1964); *Messiahs: Their Role in Civilization* (American Council on Public Affairs, 1964).

WALLOWER, LUCILLE (author, illustrator)

Born Waynesboro, Penna. *Education:* Pennsylvania Museum School of Art; Traphagen School of Fashion. *Principal occupation:* Author, illustrator. *Home address:* 54 W. Tulpehocken St., Philadelphia, Penna. *Affiliations:* Librarian, Harrisburg Public Library, 1943-44; director, Harrisburg Art Association Studio, 1943-48; assistant children's librarian, Harrisburg Public Library, 1944-46; fashion artist, Pomeroy's, Inc., Harrisburg, Penna., 1946-49; children's librarian, Abington Library, Jenkintown, Penna., 1959-. *Memberships:* Pennsylvania Library Association. *Published works: A Conch Shell for Molly* (David McKay, 1940); *Chooky* (David McKay, 1942); *The Roll of Drums* (Albert Whitman, 1945); editorial consultant, *The Pennsylvania Story* (Pennsylvania Valley Publishers, 1950); *Your Pennsylvania* (Pennsylvania Valley Publishers, 1953); *Pennsylvania Primer* (Pennsylvania Valley Publishers, 1954); *Old Satan* (David McKay, 1955); *Indians of Pennsylvania* (Pennsylvania Valley Publishers, 1956); *The Hippity Hopper* (David McKay, 1957); *The Morning Star* (David McKay, 1957); *All About Pennsylvania* (Pennsylvania Valley Publishers, 1958); *They Came to Pennsylvania* (Pennsylvania Valley Publishers, 1960); *The Lost Prince* (David McKay, 1963); *Your State* (Pennsylvania Valley Publishers, 1963); *Pennsylvania A B C* (Pennsylvania Valley Publishers, 1964).

WALTRIP, LELA 1904- (teacher)

Born February 2, 1904, Coleman County, Texas. *Education:* Highlands University, B.A., 1935; Eastern New Mexico University, M.A., 1955. *Principal occupation:* Teacher. *Home address:* 811 S. 4th St., Artesia, N.M. *Affiliations:* Teacher, New Mexico public schools. *Memberships:* Delta Kappa Gamma; American Association of University Women; Business and Professional Women's Association; New Mexico Education Association; National Education Association; local education association. *Awards, honors:* First Prize for children's book, Texas Writers' Conference, 1958. *Interests:* Teaching; music; writing; travel; research. *Published works: White Harvest* (1960), *Quiet Boy* (1961), *Purple Hills* (1962), *Indian Women* (1964), all co-authored with Rufus Waltrip and published by David McKay Co.

WALTRIP, RUFUS 1898- (teacher, writer)

Born September 26, 1898, Rosenburg, Texas. *Education:* Highlands University, B.A., 1936; University of New Mexico, M.A., 1947. *Principal occupation:* Teacher, writer. *Home address:* 811 S. 4th St., Artesia, N.M. *Affiliations:* English teacher, principal, director of guidance and testing, New Mexico public schools. *Community activities:* Rotary International; local writers' workshop (co-sponsor); Boy Scouts of America. *Memberships:* National Education Association (life member); New Mexico Education Association (organizer, former chairman, creative writing section). *Awards, honors:* First Prize for children's book, Texas Writers' Conference, 1958. *Interests:* Teaching; research; writing; travel. *Published works: White Harvest* (1960), *Quiet Boy* (1961), *Purple Hills* (1962), *Indian Women* (1964), all co-authored with Lela Waltrip and published by David McKay Co.

WALZ, ERMA HICKS (Cherokee) 1915- (B.I.A. officer)

Born October 10, 1915, Hulbert, Okla. *Education:* Haskell Institute; Northwestern University. *Principal occupation:* B.I.A. officer. *Home address:* 4113 N. 27th Rd., Arlington, Va. 22207. *Affiliations:* Chief tribal operations officer, Bureau of Indian Affairs, Washington, D.C. *Interests:* Sewing; gardening; skating.

WAMMACK, THEDA 1910- (museum director)

Born November 18, 1910, Okmulgee, Okla. *Education:* High school. *Principal occupation:* Museum director. *Home address:* 420 N. Central Ave., Okmulgee, Okla. 74447. *Affiliations:* Director, Creek Council House and Museum, Okmulgee, Okla. *Community activities:* Creek Indian Memorial Association (secretary, 1957); Okmulgee Community Center (agent, 1964-65); Okmulgee Business and Professional Women (corresponding secretary, 1962-65). *Memberships:* American Association of Museums, 1960-; Oklahoma Historical Society, 1957-; Gilcrease Institute of American History and Art, 1958-; Oklahoma Museums Association, 1957-; Okmulgee County Art Guild, 1964-. *Interests:* Writing and painting; writes weekly column, "Cimascope," pertaining to Creek Council House history and Creek culture, published in Okmulgee County newspaper.

WARD, BENJAMIN PARKER   1921-
(educator)

Born January 26, 1921, Little River, S.C. *Education:* Ulingate Junior College, A.A., 1948; University of South Carolina, B.S., 1950; A.S.T.C., M.A., 1954; Montana State College, 1958; Utah State University, Ed.S., 1964. *Principal occupation:* Educator. *Home address:* R.F.D., Faith, S.D. 57626. *Affiliations:* Principal, Red Scaffold Day School, Bureau of Indian Affairs, Faith, S.D. *Military service:* U.S. Naval Reserve, 1942-45 (South Pacific Medal; American Defense Medal; Good Conduct Medal); National Guard, 1950-52. *Community activities:* Boy Scouts of America, Belcourt, N.D. (advisor). *Memberships:* South Dakota Education Association; National Education Association; Beta Club, 1936-39. *Awards, honors:* Only non-Indian to attend Red Scaffold tribal ceremony, Cheyenne River, S.D.

WARREN, HELENE   1921- (geologist)

Born September 12, 1921, New Jersey. *Education:* University of New Mexico, B.S., 1946. *Principal occupation:* Geologist. *Home address:* 209 Sombrio, Santa Fe, N.M. *Affiliations:* Curator of geology, Research Division, Museum of New Mexico, 1964-. *Memberships:* New Mexico Geological Society; International Association

for Quaternary Research. *Interests:* Microscopic petrography; geomorphology; archaeology.

WARREN, PEARL ERNA KALLAPPA
(Makah) 1911- (organization executive)

Born August 13, 1911, Neah Bay, Wash. *Education:* High school. *Principal occupation:* Organization executive. *Home address:* 3419 Densmore Ave., N., Seattle, Wash. 98103. *Affiliations:* Executive director, Seattle Indian Center, Seattle, Wash. *Community activities:* American Indian Women's Service League (president, 1958-61); Western Washington Intertribal Council; American Indian Associates; Foqueleetsa Fellowship; Economic Opportunity Board, Seattle and King County, Wash. (board member); Catholic Interracial Council (board member); Totem Club, Queen Anne High School. *Awards, honors:* Civic Unity, American Women's Service League; Matrix Table, Seattle, Wash., honors winner; Woman of Achievement Award, Theta Sigma Phi. *Interests:* Lecturing on Indian affairs.

WATERS, FRANK   1902- (writer)

Born July 25, 1902, Colorado Springs, Colo. *Education:* Colorado College. *Principal occupation:* Writer. *Home address:* Taos, N.M. *Military service:* U.S. Army, 1942-43; propaganda analyses, Office of Inter-American Affairs. *Community activities:* New Mexico Arts Commission (vice chairman). *Memberships:* International Institute of Arts and Letters, Switzerland, 1962-. *Awards, honors:* Silver Medal Award for *The Man Who Killed the Deer*, Commonwealth Club, 1942. *Interests:* Archaeology, ethnology, psychology; pack trips through the Sierra Madre Mountains; research among the Tarahumara Indians. *Published works: The Wild Earth's Nobility* (Liveright, 1935); *Below Grass Roots* (Liveright, 1937); *Midas of the Rockies* (Covici-Friede, 1937); *Dust Within the Rock* (Liveright, 1940); *People of the Valley* (Farrar & Rinehart, 1941; Alan Swallow, 1962); *River Lady*, with Houston Branch (Farrar & Rinehart, 1941; English and French editions; motion picture, 1949); *The Man Who Killed the Deer* (Farrar & Rinehart, 1942; University of Denver, 1951; Alan Swallow, 1954; German, English and French editions);

The Colorado (Rivers of America Series, Farrar & Rinehart, 1946; Rinehart & Co., 1959); *The Yogi of Cockroach Court* (Rinehart & Co., 1947); *Masked Gods: Navajo and Pueblo Ceremonialism* (University of New Mexico, 1950; Alan Swallow, 1962); *The Earp Brothers of Tombstone* (C.N. Potter, 1960; British editions); *Book of the Hopi* (Viking, 1963); *Leon Gaspard* (Northland Press, 1964).

WEAVER, OTTO K.   1918-   (B.I.A. agency superintendent)

Born September 24, 1918, Sayre, Okla. *Education:* Utah State University, B.S. (Watershed Development and Public Administration), 1950. *Principal occupation:* B.I.A. agency superintendent. *Address:* Crow Agency, Mont. 59022. *Affiliations:* Soil conservationist, Navajo and Hopi Agency, Bureau of Indian Affairs, 1950-57; land operations officer, Uintah and Ouray Agency, Bureau of Indian Affairs, 1957-61; superintendent, Crow Agency, Bureau of Indian Affairs, Crow Agency, Mont., 1961-. *Military service:* U.S. Army, 1941-45 (Special Efficiency Award for mine planning; Good Conduct Medal; special services awards; theatre awards). *Community activities:* American Legion; Lions Club; Kiwanis Club; Elks; charitable activities. *Memberships:* Range Management Society of America, 1951-; Soil Conservation Society of America, 1951-. *Interests:* Public administration; tourist and recreation development; development of natural resources; travel to Canada, through the United States, and Mexico.

WEBB, NANCY McIVOR   1926-   (sculptor)

Born December 27, 1926, Concord, N.H. *Education:* Smith College, 1944-47. *Principal occupation:* Sculptor. *Home address:* Wellfleet, Me. 02667. *Affiliations:* Art director, Noonday Press, 1956-58. *Awards, honors:* Grand Prize, Cambridge Art Association, 1966. *Published works: Aguk of Alaska* (Prentice-Hall, 1963); *Makima of the Rain Forest* (Prentice-Hall, 1964).

WEDEL, WALDO R.   1908-   (museum curator, anthropologist, writer)

Born September 10, 1908, Newton, Kan. *Education:* University of Arizona, B.A., 1930; University of Nebraska, M.A., 1931; University of California, Ph.D., 1936. *Principal occupation:* Museum curator, anthropologist, writer. *Home address:* 5432 - 30th Place, N.W., Washington, D.C. 20015. *Affiliations:* Assistant curator, Department of Anthropology, U.S. National Museum, Smithsonian Institution, Washington, D.C., 1936-. *Other professional posts:* Field director, Missouri River Basin Surveys, Smithsonian Institution, 1946-50. *Memberships:* American Association for the Advancement of Science; American Anthropological Association; Society for American Archaeology (president, 1948-49); Anthropological Society of Washington; Kansas Academy of Sciences; Kansas Anthropological Association. *Awards, honors:* Award, Biological Sciences, for distinguished service in investigations of prehistoric human ecology in the Great Plains, Washington Academy of Sciences, 1947; elected to membership in National Academy of Sciences, 1965. *Interests:* Prehistory and aboriginal human ecology of the Great Plains of North America; archaeology and ethnology of western North America; ethnohistory of the Midwest and the Great Plains. *Published works: Archeological Investigations at Buena Vista Lake, Kern County, California* (Bureau of American Ethnology, Smithsonian Institution, 1941); *Archeological Investigations in Platte and Clay Counties, Missouri* (U.S. National Museum, Smithsonian Institution, 1943); *An Introduction to Kansas Archeology* (Bureau of American Ethnology, Smithsonian Institution, 1959); *Prehistoric Man on the Great Plains* (University of Oklahoma Press, 1961).

WELCH, LAWRENCE B.   1922-   (school administrator)

Born October 18, 1922, Franklin, N.C. *Education:* Brevard Junior College, 1940-42; Oklahoma City University, 1943; Western Carolina Teachers College, M.A. (Elementary Education), 1961. *Principal occupation:* School administrator. *Address:* c/o Barrow Day School, Bureau of Indian Affairs, Barrow, Alaska 99723. *Affiliations:* Administrator, Barrow Day School, Bureau of Indian Affairs, Barrow, Alaska. *Military service:* U.S. Air Force, 1943-45 (E.T.O. Ribbon, with five bronze stars;

Air Medal; three oak leaf clusters; Certificate of Valor). *Community activities:* Masons; Veterans of Foreign Wars.

WELTFISH, GENE 1902- (associate professor of anthropology)

Born August 7, 1902, New York, N.Y. *Education:* Barnard College, B.A., 1925; Columbia University, Ph.D., 1950. *Principal occupation:* Associate professor of anthropology. *Address:* P.O. Box 1713, Grand Central Post Office, New York, N.Y. 10017. *Affiliations:* Associate professor of anthropology, Fairleigh Dickinson University. *Memberships:* American Anthropological Association (Fellow); American Association for the Advancement of Science (Fellow); Society for Applied Anthropology (Fellow); American Indian Ethnohistoric Conference; Society for Ethnomusicology. *Interests:* Field work among the Indians of Oklahoma, New Mexico, Arizona, North Dakota, Louisiana, Nebraska, and Iowa. *Published works: Caddoan Texts* (American Ethnological Society, 1937); *The Origins of Art* (Bobbs-Merrill, 1953); *The Lost Universe* (Basic Books, 1965).

WESLEY, CLARENCE (San Carlos Apache) 1912- (cattleman)

Born December 27, 1912, Bylas, Ariz. *Education:* High school. *Principal occupation:* Cattleman. *Home address:* P.O. Box 43, Valentine, Ariz. *Community activities:* Rotary Club, Miami, Ariz. (president). *Memberships:* National Congress of American Indians, 1959-61; Arrow, Inc. (vice president). *Interests:* Mr. Wesley writes, "I am interested in travel and in work among all tribes of Indians in the United States."

WEST, WALTER RICHARD (DICK) *(Wah-pah-nah-yah)* (Cheyenne) 1912- (artist)

Born September 8, 1912, Darlington, Okla. *Education:* Haskell Institute; Bacone Junior College; University of Oklahoma, B.F.A., 1941, M.F.A., 1950; graduate work, Redlands University, Tulsa University. *Principal occupation:* Artist. *Address:* Bacone College, Muskogee, Okla. 74420. *Affiliations:* Art instructor, Phoenix Indian School, 1941-42, 1946-47; director, Art Depart-

ment, Bacone College, 1947-. *Military service:* U.S. Navy, 1942-46. *Community activities:* Muskogee Rotary Club; Bacone Scout Committee (institutional representative, chairman); Oklahoma Tuberculosis Association (honorary state chairman, Christmas Seal Tuberculosis Fund Drive, 1960-61). *Memberships:* Delta Phi Delta; Muskogee Art Guild; Southwestern Art Association; Bacone College Education Association (president); Oklahoma Education Association (chairman, art section, district). *Awards, honors:* Awards, Philbrook Art Center, Tulsa, Okla. -- First Prize, Third Prize, 1946, Grand Prize, 1946, 1949, First Prize (oils), 1950, Oklahoma State Competition, First Prize (sculpture), 1960, Oklahoma State Competition, Second Prize (sculpture), 1963, Oklahoma State Competition, Honorable Mention (sculpture), 1964, Oklahoma State Competition. *Other awards:* Winner, National Post Office Mural Contest, Okemah, Okla., 1941; Citation, Indian Arts and Crafts Board, U.S. Department of the Interior, 1960; Waite Phillips Award (and trophy) for contributions over a period of years, Philbrook Art Center, 1964. Numerous exhibitions and one-man shows throughout the United States. Illustrations appear in *The Thankful People* (Caxton Printers, Ltd., 1950); *Tales of the Cheyennes* (Houghton Mifflin, 1953); *Indian Legends* (Lyons and Carnahan, 1963).

WHEELER, SESSIONS S. 1911- (teacher)

Born April 27, 1911, Fernley, Nev. *Education:* University of Nevada, B.S., 1934, M.S., 1935. *Principal occupation:* Teacher. *Home address:* 25 Moore Lane, Reno, Nev. *Affiliations:* Biology instructor and chairman, Science Department, Reno High School, Reno, Nev., 1936-; assistant professor of conservation education, University of Nevada, summers, 1955-; visiting professor of conservation education, University of Southern California, summer, 1961. *Other professional posts:* Executive director, Nevada State Fish and Game Commission, 1947-50; trustee, Max C. Fleischmann Foundation of Nevada, 1952-; trustee, Nevada State Museum, 1955-60. *Community activities:* Nevada State Indian Affairs Commission. *Memberships:* Mr. Wheeler is a member of various teachers' and sportsmen's associations. *Awards, honors:* Nash Conservation Certificate of Merit, 1953; Outstanding Biology Teacher Award, National Association of Biology Teachers, 1962; Distinguished Nevadan Award, University of Nevada, 1963; Conservation Education Award, National Wildlife Federation and Sears, Roebuck Foundation, 1965; Smokey Bear Award, United States Forest Service, 1965. *Interests:* "The outdoors, Indians, and Nevada history." Mr. Wheeler has camped and fished in many of the primitive areas of the western United States, Canada, and Alaska. *Published works:* Co-author, *Conservation and Nevada* (Nevada Department of Education, 1949); co-author, *Nevada Conservation Adventure* (Nevada Department of Education, 1954, 1959); *Paiute* (Caxton Printers, Ltd., 1965).

WHEELOCK, LEWIS F.   1924- (museum and archives director)

Born February 7, 1924, Des Moines, Iowa. *Education:* Harvard College, B.A., 1949; State University of Iowa, Ph.D., 1956. *Principal occupation:* Museum and archives director. *Affiliations:* Professor of history, Parsons College, 1952-60; visiting lecturer in history, University of Kansas, 1961-63; director, Museum and Archives, Menninger Foundation, Topeka, Kan., 1963-. *Military service:* U.S. Army, 1942-45. *Community activities:* Episcopal Church. *Memberships:* American Historical Association; Kansas Historical Society; Mississippi Valley Historical Association; American Association of Museums. *Interests:* Travel in the Philippines, Europe, Greece.

WHITE, JOHN R.   1912- (B.I.A. agency superintendent)

Born November 28, 1912, Spencer, Ind. *Education:* University of Wyoming. *Principal occupation:* B.I.A. agency superintendent. *Address:* c/o Rocky Boy's Agency, Bureau of Indian Affairs, Box Elder, Mont. 59521. *Affiliations:* Industrial development specialist, Billings Area Office, Bureau of Indian Affairs; information officer, Southern Ute Tribe, 1954-; assistant to superintendent, Consolidated Ute Agency, Bureau of Indian Affairs, 1961; superintendent, Rocky Boy's Agency, Bureau of Indian Affairs. *Other professional posts:* Newspaper writer and editor. *Published works:* Story of the *Southern Utes* (Southern Ute Tribe, 1955); *The Blackfeet Flood* (Billings Area Office,

Bureau of Indian Affairs, 1964); editor, *The Montana-Wyoming Indian* (Billings Area Office, Bureau of Indian Affairs, 1965).

WHITE, LESLIE A.   1900- (anthropologist)

Born January 19, 1900, Salida, Colo. *Education:* Columbia University, B.A., 1923, M.A., 1924; University of Chicago, Ph.D., 1927. *Principal occupation:* Anthropologist. *Home address:* 819 Avon Rd., Ann Arbor, Mich. 48104. *Affiliations:* Instructor, assistant professor, University of Buffalo, 1927-30; curator of anthropology, Buffalo Museum of Science, 1927-30; assistant professor, associate professor, professor, University of Michigan, 1930-. *Other professional posts:* Visiting professor, University of Chicago, summer, 1931; visiting professor, Yale University, 1947; visiting professor, Columbia University, 1948; visiting professor, Harvard University, 1949; visiting professor, University of California, 1957. *Military service:* U.S. Navy, 1918-19. *Memberships:* American Anthropological Association (president, 1963-64); American Association for the Advancement of Science, 1932- (vice president, chairman, Section H, 1959); American Folklore Society (former treasurer); American Association of University Professors. *Awards, honors:* Distinguished Faculty Achievement Award, University of Michigan, 1957; Viking Medal for Cultural Anthropology, Wenner-Gren Foundation for Anthropological Research, 1959; Sc.D. (hon.), University of Buffalo, 1962. *Interests:* Anthropology, culturology, ethnological theory, history of anthropology. Field work among Pueblo Indians (Arizona, New Mexico), 1926-57; anthropological tours to U.S.S.R. and Caucasus mountains, 1929; to Mexico on various occasions; to the Far East and Indonesia, 1936. *Published works:* The Pueblo of Santa Ana, New Mexico (American Anthropological Association, 1942); *The Science of Culture* (Farrar, Straus & Co., 1949); *The Evolution of Culture* (McGraw-Hill, 1959).

WHITE, RUTH M.   (Sac and Fox)   1908- (artist, art instructor)

Born October 14, 1908, Tulsa, Okla. *Education:* Northwestern State College; Bacone College; Northeastern State College; Utah State College; University of Oklahoma;

Fine Arts Academy; and others. *Private instructors:* Henry Clayton Staples, Elliott O'Hara, Frederick Taubes. *Principal occupation:* Artist, art instructor. *Home address:* 1043 - 9th St., Alva, Okla. 73717. *Affiliations:* Northwestern State College; Connors A. & M. College. *Other occupation:* Private art instructor. *Memberships:* National Association of Women Artists of New York; Methodist Church; Texas Watercolor Society; Association of Oklahoma Artists; Southwestern Art Association; Philbrook Art Center; Muskogee Art Guild; Oklahoma Education Association; Wagoner Archery Club (lifetime honorary member); International Arts and Letters of Switzerland (life Fellow); Conservative Art Group of Eastern Oklahoma (president, 1963). *Awards, honors:* Allied Artists of West Virginia; Oklahoma Artists; Witte Museum; two hundred awards received at various state fairs; Grand Prize, Muskogee Art Show; National Indian Show, Scottsdale, Ariz.; Award, Wyoming Fair, 1964-65; Citation for community service, K.B.I.X.-TV (Muskogee, Okla.), 1950; Outstanding Service Award, Muskogee Elks Club, 1962; Fellow, International Arts and Letters of Switzerland. *Interests:* Originator of "spoon" painting, 1952; initiator, Art Loan Library, Connors College, 1955, and Art Slide Library, 1963. *Exhibits:* Germany, Switzerland, France, England, Canada, Japan, United States; Indian museums -- Santa Fe, N.M.; Southwest Indian Museum; North American Indian Museum (Marathon, Fla.); state fairs. *One-man shows:* New York, New Orleans, Tulsa (Philbrook Art Center), Colorado, Texas, Iowa. *Published works: Do's and Don'ts of Art, Timely Tips on Drawing* (privately printed).

WHITEFORD, ANDREW HUNTER   1913-
(professor of anthropology, museum director)

Born September 1, 1913, Winnipeg, Can. *Education:* Beloit College, B.A., 1937; University of Chicago, M.A., 1943, Ph.D., 1950. *Principal occupation:* Professor of anthropology, museum curator. *Home address:* 2550 Hawthorne Drive, Beloit, Wis. 53511. *Affiliations:* Professor and chairman, Department of Anthropology, Beloit College; director, Logan Museum of Anthropology, Beloit, Wis. *Memberships:* American Anthropological Association (Fellow); Current Anthropology (Fellow); Central

States Anthropological Society (president, 1964); Wisconsin Archaeological Survey (Fellow); Sigma Xi; Phi Beta Kappa; Omicron Delta Kappa; Pi Epsilon Delta. *Published works: Two Cities of Latin America: A Comparative Description of Social Classes* (Logan Museum of Anthropology; Anchor Series, Doubleday & Co., 1960); *Teaching Anthropology* (Logan Museum of Anthropology, 1960).

WHITEHORSE, ROLAND (Kiowa)   1920-
(illustrator, artist, graphics supervisor)

Born April 6, 1920, Carnegie, Okla. *Education:* Bacone College, 1947-48; Dallas Art Institute, 1951-52. *Principal occupation:* Illustrator, artist, graphics supervisor. *Home address:* Box 265, Algin, Okla. *Affiliations:* Supervisor, illustrator, 4th U.S. Army, north Texas, Oklahoma, and Arkansas; civil service instructor, supervisor. *Other professional posts:* Art director, American Indian Exposition, Anadarko, Okla.; art director, Underwood's Cafeteria and Frontier Center. *Military service:* U.S. Army, European Theatre, 9th Infantry Division, 1941-45. *Memberships:* Southwestern Artists Association, Dallas, Texas, 1956-57; American Indian Artists Association (chairman); Thomas Gilcrease Institute, 1965-66; Art Council of Lawton, Okla., 1966; Great Plains Historical Association, Lawton, Okla. *Interests:* Painting, art instruction. Mr. Whitehorse's illustrations appear in *Winter Telling Stories*, by Alice Marriott, and in *Heap Big Laugh*, by Dan M. Madrano.

WHITING, ALFRED FRANK   1912-
(museum curator)

Born May 22, 1912, Burlington, Vt. *Education:* University of Vermont, B.S., 1933; University of Michigan, M.A., 1934; University of Chicago, 1936-43. *Principal occupation:* Museum curator. *Home address:* 20 West St., Hanover, N.H. 03755. *Affiliations:* Curator of anthropology, Dartmouth College Museum, Hanover, N.H., 1955-; research associate, Museum of Northern Arizona, Flagstaff, Ariz., 1954-. *Memberships:* American Anthropological Association. *Interests:* Ethnobotany; field trips to Mexico, Arizona, New Mexico. *Published works: Ethnobotany of the Hopi* (Museum of Northern Arizona Bulletin, No. 15, 1939).

WILCOX, R. TURNER 1888- (artist,
author)

Born April 29, 1888, New York, N.Y. *Education:* Public schooling, private tutoring,
and art study in Paris, France, and Munich,
Germany. *Principal occupation:* Artist,
author. *Home address:* 24 Ravine Rd.,
Tenafly, N.J. 07670. *Affiliations:* Fashion
editor, *Women's Wear Daily* (Fairchild Publications); spent several years in the commercial illustration field, then concentrated
on historic costumes, writing and illustrating the subject. *Published works: The Mode
in Costume* (Scribner's, 1942, 1948, 1958);
The Mode in Hats and Headdress (Scribner's,
1945, 1959); *The Mode in Footwear* (Scribner's, 1948); *The Mode in Furs* (Scribner's,
1951); *Five Centuries of American Costume*
(Scribner's, 1965); *Folk and Festival Costume of the World* (Scribner's, 1965); *Dictionary of World Costume* (in preparation).

WILLCOX, JACQUELIN H.   1926-
(museum curator)

Born September 26, 1926, Petersburg, Va.
Education: Mary Washington College, B.S.,
1948. *Principal occupation:* Museum curator. *Home address:* 4508 Hanover Ave.,
Richmond, Va. *Affiliations:* Curator of
school services, The Valentine Museum,
Richmond, Va. *Community activities:* Local Parent-Teachers' Association; The Virginia Bankers Association; Sunday school,
St. Paul's Episcopal Church; gives talks
utilizing museum artifacts and slides at local public schools. *Memberships:* The
Twenty Three Hundred Club, sponsored by
the Historic Richmond Foundation; Association for Preservation of Virginia Antiquities;
English Speaking Union; Virginia Archaeologists Society. *Interests:* City planning;
personal visual aids for school children.
Mrs. Willcox believes in the adage, "Learn
from what you see," and applies this concept
in her museum tours and school talks.

WILLIAMS, DAVID, Sr.   (Thlinket)
1905- (totem carver)

Born May 9, 1905, Douglas, Alaska. *Education:* Elementary school. *Principal occupation:* Totem carver. *Home address:*
9 Front St., Hoonah, Alaska 99829. *Com-*

munity activities: Presbyterian Church
(deacon, six years; elder, eight years; trustee, four years).

WILLIAMS, DAVID EMMETT   *(Tos-que)*
(Kiowa-Apache-Tonkawa)   1933-
(artist)

Born August 20, 1933, Redstone, Okla. *Education:* Bacone College. *Principal occupation:* Artist. *Home address:* 4221 Verdugo Rd., Los Angeles, Calif. 90065. *Memberships:* American Tribal Dancers and
Singers Club, 1963- (head drummer and
singer). *Awards, honors:* First Place,
American Indian Arts Exposition, Charlotte,
N.C.; Second Award, Tulsa, Okla.; Third
Award, Bismarck, N.D.; Third Place, Tulsa, Okla.; honorable mentions. Numerous
one-man shows; work represented in permanent collections of several museums.

WILLOYA, EMMA   (Eskimo)   1898-
(association officer)

Born July 15, 1898, Fort Barrow, Alaska.
Education: Brevig Mission School, Teller,
Alaska. *Principal occupation:* Association
officer. *Home address:* P.O. Box 484,
Nome, Alaska 99762. *Affiliations:* Manager, Nome Skin Sewers Association, 1945-
60. *Community activities:* Office of Price
Administration, Nome, Alaska (agent); Women's Group, Lutheran Church (officer);
Sunday school, Lutheran Church (teacher,
translator); Native School Board; supervisor
of skin-sewing of symbolic plaques for Air
Force Chapel, Fairbanks, Alaska, and for
Our Savior's Lutheran Church, Nome, Alaska. *Memberships:* Nome Skin Sewers Association; Our Savior's Lutheran Church.
Awards, honors: Citations received from
Presidents Roosevelt and Truman for work
done for Office of Price Administration.
Interests: Mrs. Willoya writes, "My major
interest has been in helping my people . . .
by helping the women make and sell their
own hand-made products. Whenever possible, I have served on boards and committees where our needs could be presented."
In 1950, Mrs. Willoya represented the Eskimos in the Nome area at the invitation of
the Legislative Reference Service of the
Library of Congress; in 1951, she was invited to attend the annual Arts and Crafts
Board Conference; in 1961, she assisted

Dorothy Jean Ray in the research for her book, *Artists of the Tundra and the Sea* (University of Washington Press).

WILSON, JOHN P. 1935- (archaeologist)

Born December 24, 1935, Knoxville, Ill. *Education:* University of Illinois, B.S. (Mechanical Engineering), 1958, M.A. (Anthropology), 1961; doctoral candidate, Harvard University, 1959-63. *Principal occupation:* Archaeologist. *Home address:* 233 Johnson St., Apt. 6, Santa Fe, N.M. 87501. *Affiliations:* Historic sites archaeologist, Museum of New Mexico, Santa Fe, N.M. *Memberships:* Sigma Xi, 1959-; Society for American Archaeology, 1958-; local archaeological societies. *Interests:* Southwestern and midwestern archaeology; southwestern ethnohistory; ceramic analysis; antique automobiles; field work at Altar de Sacrificios, Guatemala; survey work in Illinois; historic site excavations at Rock Island, Ill.; surveys and archaeological salvage projects in Arizona. *Published works: Archaeological Survey of the Chuska Valley and the Chaco Plateau,* with Stewart L. Peckham (Museum of New Mexico).

WINTHER, OSCAR OSBURN 1903- (professor)

Born December 22, 1903, Weeping Water, Neb. *Education:* University of Oregon, B.A., 1925; Harvard University, M.A., 1928; University of California, Berkeley, 1929; Stanford University, Ph.D., 1934. *Principal occupation:* Professor. *Home address:* 1310 Maxwell Lane, Bloomington, Ind. 47403. *Affiliations:* Instructor, Stanford University, 1929-36; professor, Indiana University, 1937-. *Other professional posts:* Visiting professor, University of Oregon, Brigham Young University, University of New Mexico, Johns Hopkins University, Stanford University, California Institute of Technology; managing editor, *Mississippi Valley Historical Review, Journal of American History,* 1936-. *Memberships:* American Historical Association (former president); Organization of American Historians; Western History Association (president, 1964-65); Royal Historical Society, England (Fellow); Society of American Historians (Fellow). *Awards, honors:* Fulbright Scholar, England, 1952-53; Guggenheim Fellowship, 1959; senior research as-

sociate, Huntington Library, 1960; Distinguished Visiting Professor, University of Birmingham, England, 1966. *Interests:* American history; travels to Canada, Mexico, Europe, and through the United States. *Published works: Via Western Express and Stagecoach* (Stanford University, 1945); *The Great Northwest* (Knopf, 1948); *The Old Oregon Country* (Stanford University, 1950); *The Transportation Frontier* (Holt, Rinehart & Winston, 1964); articles on the American West in professional journals.

WISE, ANTHONY 1921- (recreational industrialist)

Born March 15, 1921, Hayward, Wis. *Education:* Ohio State University, B.A., 1942; Harvard University, M.B.A., 1947. *Principal occupation:* Recreational industrialist. *Home address:* Hayward, Wis. 54843. *Affiliations:* Owner, Mount Telemark Ski Area; owner, Historyland, Inc.; owner, Wise Bros. Land Co. *Military service:* U.S. Army, 1942-46 (Silver Star, Bronze Star). *Community activities:* Mayor, City of Hayward; Wisconsin State Historical Society (board of curators). *Interests:* Chippewa Indians; lumbering and fur trade industries.

WITTHOFT, JOHN 1921- (archaeologist)

Born October 4, 1921, Oneonta, N.Y. *Education:* New York State Teachers College, B.A., 1944; University of Pennsylvania, M.A., 1946; University of Michigan, 1946-48. *Principal occupation:* Archaeologist. *Home address:* 1316 N. 2nd St., Harrisburg, Penna. 17108. *Affiliations:* Teaching fellow, University of Michigan, 1946-48; state anthropologist, Harrisburg, Penna., 1948-. *Published works: Green Corn Ceremonialism in the Eastern Woodlands* (University of Michigan, 1949); editor, with W. Fred Kinsey, *Susquehannock Miscellany* (Pennsylvania Historical and Museum Commission, 1959); *Prehistory of Pennsylvania* (Pennsylvania Historical and Museum Commission, 1965).

WITTLAKE, EUGENE B. 1912- (professor of botany, museum director)

Born August 14, 1912, Sheridan, Wyo. *Education:* Augustana College, B.A., 1936;

University of Iowa, M.S., 1938; University of Kansas, Ph.D., 1954. *Principal occupation:* Professor of botany, museum director. *Address:* Drawer HH, State College, Ark. 72467. *Affiliations:* Undergraduate assistant, Augustana College, Rock Island, Ill.; botanical technician, Ohio State University, Columbus, Ohio; instructor of botany, University of Arkansas, Fayetteville, Ark.; graduate assistant, University of Kansas, Lawrence, Kan.; assistant professor of biology, Iowa State Teachers College, Cedar Falls, Iowa; assistant professor (1956-59) and professor of botany, Arkansas State College, State College, Ark., 1960-; director, Arkansas State Museum, Arkansas State College, 1960-. *Other professional posts:* Curator, Jonesboro Centennial Museum. *Military service:* U.S. Army Medical Corps, 1943-46. *Community activities:* Cub Scouts of America; Community Concerts Association (board member); Craighead County Historical Society (president; vice president). *Memberships:* Arkansas Academy of Science, 1946-; Arkansas Archaeological Society, 1960-; Southeast Museum Conference; Oklahoma Historical Society; Sigma Xi. *Interests:* "Major interest in paleobotany and plant morphology; field expeditions with groups of graduate and undergraduate students to build the collection of Arkansas flora and fauna maintained in the Arkansas State Museum exhibits; excavation of local Indian mounds with students." *Published works:* Research on botanical subjects, 1938-60.

WOLF, RAYMOND R.   1935- (teacher, administrator)

Born August 23, 1935, Zeeland, N.D. *Education:* Ellendale State College, B.S. (Education), 1960. *Principal occupation:* Teacher, administrator. *Home address:* R.R. 2, Tama, Iowa 52339. *Affiliations:* Administrator, South Tama County School District, Bureau of Indian Affairs, Tama, Iowa. *Military service:* U.S. Navy. *Memberships:* North Dakota Education Association, 1960-. *Interests:* Mr. Wolf writes, "Administration in the Bureau of Indian Affairs -- to be able to assist the American Indian in any way I am able; work (toward) the redevelopment of needy and poverty-stricken areas."

WOLLE, MURIEL SIBELL   1898- (art teacher)

Born April 3, 1898, Brooklyn, N.Y. *Education:* Parsons School of Design, Diploma (Costume Design and Advertising), 1920; New York University, B.S. (Art Education), 1928; University of Colorado, M.A. (English Literature), 1930. *Principal occupation:* Art teacher. *Affiliations:* Instructor in fine arts, State College for Women, Denton, Texas, 1920-23; instructor in advertising, Parsons School of Design, New York, N.Y., 1923-26; professor, Fine Arts Department, University of Colorado, 1926- (head of department, 1928-47). *Community activities:* Delta Phi Delta; Soroptimist Club (president, 1956-57); Visiting Nurse Association (board of directors). *Memberships:* Colorado Mountain Club, 1938-; Colorado Authors' League, 1964-; Denver Women's Press Club, 1965-; National Association of Women Artists, 1930-50; The Westerners (corresponding member, 1944-). *Awards, honors:* Eloise Egan Prize, National Association of Women Artists, 1935; Purchase Prize, Springfield Museum, 1943; Annual Faculty Research Lecturer, University of Colorado, 1947; Woman of the Month, The American Soroptimist, 1956; Norlin Medal for Distinguished Achievement in One's Field, University of Colorado, 1957; Laureate Member, Delta Phi Delta, 1958. *Interests:* "Extensive study of Southwest Indian arts and crafts -- Pueblo, Navajo, Apache. I have developed and teach a course in Southwest Indian Art at the University of Colorado; have made an intensive pictorial and historic study of the old mining camps of the West, and have over 1,500 sketches of the old camps found in twelve western states and the slides made from those sketches. I have traveled widely throughout the western part of the United States, studying and sketching Indians and mining sites and towns." *Published works: Ghost Cities of Colorado* (Muriel Sibell, 1933); *Cloud Cities of Colorado* (Muriel Sibell, 1934); *Stampede to Timberline, the Ghost Mining Camps of Colorado* (Muriel S. Wolle, 1949); *The Bonanza Trail* (Indiana University Press, 1953); *Montana Pay Dirt* (Alan Swallow, Sage Books, 1963).

WOOD, GERALD L.   1932- (archaeologist)

Born March 30, 1932, Eugene, Ore. *Education:* Arizona State University, 1956-57; San Diego State College, B.A. (Anthropology), 1960. *Principal occupation:* Archaeologist. *Address:* c/o Aztec Ruins National Monument, Route 1, Box 101, Aztec, N.M. 87410. *Affiliations:* Archaeologist, National Park Service, 1960-62; archaeologist, Museum of New Mexico, 1962; park archaeologist, Aztec Ruins National Monument, Aztec, N.M., 1963-. *Other professional posts:* Curator of geology, San Juan County Museum. *Interests:* Southwestern archaeology; photography; geology.

WOODENLEGS, JOHN (Northern
 Cheyenne) 1912- (tribal officer)

Born October 10, 1912, Lame Deer, Mont. *Education:* High school. *Principal occupation:* Tribal officer. *Home address:* Lame Deer, Mont. *Affiliations:* President, Northern Cheyenne Tribal Council, 1955- (member, 1949-55). *Other posts:* Manager, Northern Cheyenne Steer Enterprise. *Memberships:* Montana Intertribal Policy Board; Northern Cheyenne Native American Church (president, 1950-). *Awards, honors:* Northern Cheyenne Tribal Council Achievement Award, 1965. *Interests:* "One of my main objectives has been to use the help of any source -- Federal, state, or private organizations -- to help the Northern Cheyennes." Travels in the United States and Europe. Mr. Woodenlegs appeared as one of the principal actors in the Warner Bros. short, "Forgotten Cheyennes."

WOODWARD, GRACE S. 1898- (writer)

Born September 14, 1898, Joplin, Mo. *Education:* Missouri University, 1917-18; Oklahoma University, 1918-19; Columbia University, 1919-20. *Principal occupation:* Writer. *Home address:* 321 Pan American Bldg., Tulsa, Okla. 74103. *Community activities:* Cerebral Palsy Association. *Memberships:* Daughters of American Colonists; Association for the Preservation of Virginia Antiquities; Thomas Gilcrease Institute of American History and Art; Daughters of the American Revolution (inactive); Tuesday Writers. *Interests:* "Travel (is) coincidental with research for the books I write. I always visit the places I write about. Have just returned from a trip to England -- research at the British Museum and the Oxford and Cambridge archives for a forthcoming historical book on Pocahontas." *Published works:* The Man Who Conquered Pain (Beacon Press, 1962); *The Cherokees* (Univer-

sity of Oklahoma Press, 1963); contributor to *Parents Magazine* (1937-40) and to *The Mothers Encyclopedia* (1942) under pen name of Marion S. Doan; authored "The Forecast" (1933-38) and other magazine and newspaper feature articles.

WORCESTER, DONALD E. 1915-
 (professor of history)

Born April 29, 1915, Tempe, Ariz. *Education:* Bard College, B.A., 1939; University of California, Berkeley, M.A., 1940, Ph.D., 1947. *Principal occupation:* Professor of history. *Home address:* 5800 Wedgworth Rd., Fort Worth, Texas 76133. *Affiliations:* Lecturer, University of California, Davis, fall, 1946; lecturer, University of California, Berkeley, spring, 1947; assistant professor, professor, and head, Department of History, University of Florida, 1947-63; professor of history and head, Department of History, Texas Christian University, 1963-. *Other professional posts:* Visiting professor, University of Madrid, 1956-57; managing editor, *Hispanic American Historical Review*, 1960-65. *Military service:* U.S. Naval Reserve (active duty, 1941-45). *Community activities:* Fort Worth Country Day School (advisory council, 1965-). *Memberships:* Phi Alpha Theta (president, 1961, 1962); American Historical Association; New Mexico Historical Society; Western Writers of America; Western History Association. *Awards, honors:* Smith-Mundt Visiting Professor, University of Madrid, 1956-57. *Interests:* Research on the Plains Indians, Navajos and Apaches; the spread of the Spanish horse; Latin America. Travels to Europe and all Latin American countries. *Published works:* The Interior Provinces of New Spain (Quivara Society, 1951); *The Growth and Culture of Latin America*, with Wendell Schaeffer (Oxford, 1956); *Lone Hunter's Gray Pony* (Walck, 1956); *Lone Hunter and the Cheyennes* (Hale, Walck, 1957); *Lone Hunter's First Buffalo Hunt* (Hale, Walck, 1958); *Lone Hunter and the Wild Horses* (Walck, 1959); *Kit Carson: Mountain Scout* (Houghton Mifflin, 1959); *John Paul Jones: Soldier of the Sea* (Houghton Mifflin, 1961); *War Pony* (Walck, 1960); *Sea Power and Chilean Independence* (University of Florida Press, 1962); *The Three Worlds of Latin America* (Dutton, 1963); editor, *Fifty Years on the Trail* (University of Oklahoma Press, 1963); *Ameri-*

can Civilization with Maurice Boyd (Allyn and Bacon, 1964); *Man and Civilization*, with Kent and Robert Forster (Lyons and Carnahan, 1965).

WORMINGTON, HANNAH MARIE   1914-
(archaeologist)

Born September 5, 1914, Denver, Colo. *Education:* University of Denver, 1931-35; Radcliffe College, M.A., 1950, Ph.D., 1954. *Principal occupation:* Archaeologist. *Home address:* 4600 E. 17th Ave., Denver, Colo. 80220. *Affiliations:* Curator of archaeology, Denver Museum of Natural History, 1937-; assistant professor, University of Denver, 1947-49; visiting lecturer, University of Colorado, 1950-53. *Memberships:* American Anthropological Association; American Association of Physical Anthropologists; Society for American Archaeology (vice president, 1940-41, 1955-56). *Awards, honors:* Alumni Award, University of Denver, 1952. *Interests:* Early cultures of the New World; excavations in the United States, Canada, and Mexico; sites and museums visited in Algeria, Austria, Belgium, Brazil, Czechoslovakia, Cuba, England, Germany, Hungary, Italy, the Netherlands, Poland, Spain, Switzerland, the U.S.S.R. (including Siberia). *Published works: Prehistoric Indians of the Southwest* (Denver Museum of Natural History, 1947); *A Reappraisal of the Fremont Culture* (Denver Museum of Natural History, 1955); *Archaeological Investigations of the Uncompahgre Plateau*, with Robert Lister (Denver Museum of Natural History, 1956); *Ancient Man in North America* (Denver Museum of Natural History, 1957); *An Introduction to the Archaeology of Alberta, Canada*, with R.G. Forbis (Denver Museum of Natural History, 1965).

WORTHYLAKE, MARY MOORE   1904-
(educator)

Born February 17, 1904, Wakonda, S.D. *Education:* University of Oregon, 1920-22; Western Washington College of Education, B.A., 1941, M.Ed., 1954; University of California, Berkeley, 1958-60. *Principal occupation:* Educator. *Home address:* Route 1, Box 518, Cresswell, Ore. *Affiliations:* Primary school teacher, Oregon, Washington, and California; assistant professor, Western Washington College, 1960-

62; research associate, Teachers College, Columbia University, 1963-65. *Community activities:* Ashland Teachers Association (vice president, president, 1948-50); Orinda Teachers Association (secretary, 1958). *Memberships:* Delta Kappa Gamma; Phi Lambda Theta; Kappa Delta Pi; National Education Association; Association of Student Teaching; Association for Higher Education. *Awards, honors:* "Friend of the Lummis," Ferndale, Wash.; award flight to Washington, D.C., for 50th Anniversary of Powered Flight, 1953. *Interests:* Teaching; work with accelerated students; writing travel articles and books for children. *Published works: Nika Illahee* (Melmont, 1962); *Moolack, Young Salmon Fisherman* (Melmont, 1963); *Children of the Seed Gatherers* (Melmont, 1964).

WYMAN, LELAND C.   1897-
(teacher and researcher)

Born February 20, 1897, Livermore Falls, Me. *Education:* Bowdoin College, B.A., 1918; Harvard University, Ph.D., 1922. *Principal occupation:* Teacher and researcher. *Home address:* 5 Furnival Rd., Jamaica Plain, Mass. 02130. *Affiliations:* Professor (professor emeritus, 1962-), Boston University, 1945-. *Other professional posts:* Curator of archives, Museum of Northern Arizona, Flagstaff, Ariz. *Military service:* U.S. Army Medical Corps (bacteriologist, Walter Reed General Hospital), 1918-19. *Memberships:* American Physiological Society; American Anthropological Association; American Academy of Arts and Sciences. *Awards, honors:* Phi Beta Kappa, 1917; University Lecturer, Boston University, 1958-59. *Interests:* Physiology (endocrinology); American Indian art; art of India and Persia; numismatics; mineralogy; travel to Europe, Asia, the Middle East, Egypt, Iran, India, Pakistan. *Published works: The Windways of the Navaho* (Taylor Museum, 1962); *The Red Antway of the Navaho* (Museum of Navajo Ceremonial Art, 1965); *Blessingway* (University of Arizona); numerous papers, monographs and books in the fields of physiology, anthropology, and art.

Y

YOUNG, JOHN V.   1909- (public relations officer)

Born January 25, 1909, Fruitvale, Calif. *Education:* San Jose State College, 1927-31. *Principal occupation:* Public relations officer. *Home address:* 767 - 42nd St., Los Alamos, N.M. 87544. *Affiliations:* Reporter and editor, 1930-42; personnel director and public relations manager, Eitel-McCullough, Inc., 1942-45; personnel director, Los Alamos Scientific Laboratory, Los Alamos, N.M., 1945-59; public relations officer, Los Alamos Scientific Laboratory, 1959-. *Community activities:* Los Alamos Board of Educational Trustees; Mesa Library Board; Town Planning Board; Los Alamos Building and Loan Association (board of directors); Los Alamos National Bank (board of founders); Mesa Parent-Teachers'•Association. *Memberships:* Sierra Club of California, 1932-; American Newspaper Guild, 1937-42. *Interests:* Free lance writing and photography; conservation and wildlife; natural history. *Published works: Contemporary Pueblo Indian Pottery,* with Frank H. Harlow (Museum of New Mexico, 1966); numerous magazine and newspaper articles.

Z

ZEITNER, C.A.   1903-   (museum director)

Born June 12, 1903, Avon, S.D. *Education:* Northwestern College. *Principal occupation:* Museum director. *Address:* Mission, S.D. 57555. *Affiliations:* Proprietor, Zeitner Geological Museum, Mission, S.D. *Community activities:* Former mayor, Mission, S.D.; County School Board (treasurer); Lions Club. *Memberships:* Society of Vertebrate Paleontology, 1950-; American Geological Institute; Rosebud Geological Society; Western Fairburn Geological Society; Des Moines Lapidary Society; Tri County Gem and Mineral Society. *Awards, honors:* First Honorary Member, Midwest Federation of Mineralogical Societies. *Interests:* Local Indian artifact collection; visits to Indian cultural sites in United States, Canada, Mexico. Has written articles for various journals.

ZEITNER, JUNE CULP   1916-   (museum director)

Born February 7, 1916, Bay City, Mich.

Education: Northern State College, B.S., 1936. *Principal occupation:* Museum director. *Address:* Mission, S.D. 57555. *Affiliations:* Proprietor, Zeitner Geological Museum, Mission, S.D. *Other professional posts:* Contributing editor, *Earth Science* magazine. *Community activities:* Former high school superintendent. *Memberships:* Society of Vertebrate Paleontology, 1950-; American Federation of Mineralogical Societies (nomenclature committee); Midwest Federation of Mineralogical Societies (regional vice president and public relations director); American Geological Institute; Badlands Sandhill Earth Science Club (president and chairman of board); Rosebud Geological Society; Western Fairburn Geological Society; Des Moines Lapidary Society; Tri County Gem and Mineral Society. *Awards, honors:* First Honorary Member, Midwest Federation of Mineralogical Societies. *Interests:* Local Indian artifact collection; visits to Indian cultural sites in the United States, Canada, Mexico. *Published works: Midwest Gem Trails* (GEMAC); co-author, *Agates of North America (Lapidary Journal);* articles in various journals.

ZINER, FEENIE   1921-   (writer)

Born March 22, 1921, Brooklyn, N.Y. *Education:* Brooklyn College, B.A., 1941; New York School of Social Work, M.A. (Social Service), 1944. *Principal occupation:* Writer. *Home address:* 85 Myrtle Ave., Dobbs Ferry, N.Y. 10522. *Affiliations:* Social worker, Veterans Administration, Chicago, Ill.; social worker, Institute for Juvenile Research, Chicago, Ill.; social worker, Park Ridge School for Girls, Park Ridge, Ill. *Interests:* Miss Ziner writes, "I am the mother of five children, the wife of an artist, and the general manager of a large and lively household. I have been writing, primarily for children and young people, for the past fifteen years. In my spare time, I enjoy playing the piano and carving in stone. I am the most un-traveled of women, but find life absorbing in my own microcosmic sector of it." *Published works: True Book of Time* (Children's Press, 1956); *Little Sailor's Big Pet* (Parnassus Press, 1958); *Wonderful Wheels* (Melmont, 1959); *Counting Carnival* (Coward-McCann, 1960); *Hiding* (Golden Gate Junior Books, 1961); *The Pilgrims and Plymouth Colony* (American Heritage Junior Library, 1961); *Dark Pilgrim* (Chilton, 1965).

ZUNI, JOSE A.   (Isleta Pueblo)   1921-
(B.I.A. agency superintendent)

Born April 26, 1921, Isleta Pueblo, N.M.
Education: University of New Mexico, B.A.,
1949. *Principal occupation:* B.I.A. agency
superintendent. *Home address:* P.O. Box
67, Stewart, Nev. 89437. *Affiliations:* Superintendent, Nevada Agency, Bureau of Indian Affairs, Stewart, Nev. *Military service:* U.S. Army Air Force, 1943-45 (Air
Medal; four Oak Leaf Clusters). *Community activities:* Isleta Pueblo (lieutenant
governor; tribal judge); Isleta Tribal Council (member). *Interests:* Public administration.